BARNES & NOBLE

Italian Dictionary

English-Italiano
Italian-Inglese

Peter F. Ross

BARNES
& NOBLE
B O O K S
NEW YORK

Copyright © 1982 by Laurence Urdang Associates
Glossary of menu terms and special American usage entries
copyright © 1983 by Hippocrene Books
All rights reserved.

This edition published by Marboro Books Corp.,
a division of Barnes & Noble, Inc.,
by arrangement with Hippocrene books.

1992 Barnes & Noble Books

ISBN 0-88029-937-1

Printed and bound in the United States of America

M 9 8 7 6 5 4

Abbreviations/Abbreviazioni

adj adjective
admin administration
adv adverb
aero aeronautics
agg aggettivo
agric agriculture, agricoltura
anat anatomy, anatomia
arch architecture, architettura
art article, articolo
astrol astrology, astrologia
astron astronomy, astronomia
auto automobilismo
aux auxiliary
avv avverbio
biol biology, biologia
bot botany, botanica
chem chemistry
chim chimica
coll colloquial
comm commerce, commercio
cong congiunzione
conj conjunction
derog derogatory
dir diritto
econ economics, economia
elec electricity
elett elettricità
f feminine, femminile
fam familiar, familiare
ferr ferrovia
fig figurato
filos filosofia
fis fisica
foto fotografia
gastr gastronomia
geog geography, geografia

geol geology, geologia
geom geometry, geometria
gramm grammar, grammatica
impol impolite
inter interiezione
interj interjection
invar invariable, invariabile
m masculine, maschile
mar marina
mat matematica
math mathematics
mec mechanical, meccanica
med medicine, medicina
mil military, militare
n noun
naut nautical
phone telephone
phot photography
pl plural, plurale
pol politics, politica
prep preposition, preposizione
pron pronoun, pronome
psic psicologia, psichiatria
psych psychology, psychiatry
rail railways
rel religion, religione
s sostantivo
sing singular, singolare
spreg spregiativo
tec tecnologia
tech technical
TV television, televisione
v verb, verbo
V vide (see, vedi)
volg volgare
zool zoology, zoologia

Italian pronunciation

As wide variations exist between pronunciations in different parts of
Italy, we have favoured the standard accepted in the north as this is
rapidly gaining general acceptance.

a sano ['sano]

ɛ bene ['bɛne]

e festa ['festa]

i tinto ['tinto]

ɔ brodo ['brɔdo]

o mondo ['mondo]

u fune ['fune]

b bene ['bɛne]

d dito ['dito]

f fine ['fine]

g gallo ['gallo]

j lezione [le'tsjone]

k capo ['kapo]

l legge ['leddʒe]

m mago ['mago]

n nitido ['nitido]

p pulce ['pultʃe]

r rete ['rete]

s sabbia ['sabbja]

t tanto ['tanto]

v via ['via]

w quando ['kwando]

z viso ['vizo]

dz zucchero ['dzukkero]

ts anzi ['antsi]

ʃ sciame ['ʃame]

tʃ cibo ['tʃibo]

dʒ gentile [dʒen'tile]

ʎ figlio ['fiʎo]

ɲ ragno ['raɲo]

ŋ smoking ['zmɔkiŋ]

The symbol ' indicates that the following syllable should be stressed.

Pronuncia inglese

a hat [hat]
e bell [bell]
i big [big]
o dot [dot]
ʌ bun [bʌn]
u book [buk]
ə alone [ə'loun]
a: card [ka:d]
ə: word [wə:d]
i: team [ti:m]
o: torn [to:n]
u: spoon [spu:n]
ai die [dai]
ei ray [rei]
oi toy [toi]
au how [hau]
ou road [roud]
eə lair [leə]
iə fear [fiə]
uə poor [puə]
b back [bak]
d dull [dʌl]
f find [faind]

g gaze [geiz]
h hop [hop]
j yell [jel]
k cat [kat]
l life [laif]
m mouse [maus]
n night [nait]
p pick [pik]
r rose [rouz]
s sit [sit]
t toe [tou]
v vest [vest]
w week [wi:k]
z zoo [zu:]
θ think [θiŋk]
ð those [ðouz]
ʃ shoe [ʃu:]
ʒ treasure ['treʒə]
tʃ chalk [tʃo:k]
dʒ jump [dʒʌmp]
ŋ sing [siŋ]

Il simbolo ' precede la sillaba che ha l'accento tonico principale.
Il simbolo , precede la sillaba che ha l'accento tonico secondario.

Guide to the dictionary

Irregular plural forms are shown at the headword and in the text. The following categories of Italian plural forms are considered regular:

albero	alberi
viale	viali
chiesa	chiese
amica	amiche
lunga	lunghe
città	città
tesi	tesi

In addition, masculine Italian words ending in **-a** are considered regular if they form their plural in **-i**. Masculine words ending in **-co** and **-go** form their plurals in **-chi** and **-ghi** unless the word is of more than two syllables and the **-co** or **-go** preceded by a vowel, in which case the plural is formed in **-ci** and **-gi**. Exceptions to this rule are considered irregular.

Irregular verbs listed in the verb tables are marked with an asterisk in the headword list. Compounds are not listed in the verb tables.

Adverbs are shown only if their formation is irregular. English adverbs are considered regular if they are formed by adding *-ly* or *-ally* to the adjective. Italian adverbs are considered regular if they are formed by adding *-mente* to the feminine form of the adjective.

Guida all'uso del vocabolario

I plurali irregolari dei sostantivi sono indicati sia sotto la voce di partenza sia nel testo stesso. Le seguenti categorie vengono considerate di formazione regolare in inglese:

cat	cats
glass	glasses
fly	flies
half	halves
wife	wives

I verbi irregolari nell'apposita tavola sono contraddistinti con un asterisco nella lista delle voci di partenza. Non sono compresi nella tavola i verbi composti.

Gli avverbi sono indicati con voci proprie solo quando si tratta di formazioni irregolari. Vengono considerati regolari in inglese gli avverbi formati con l'aggiunta di *-ly* o di *-ally* all'aggettivo. Vengono considerati regolari in italiano gli avverbi formati mediante l'aggiunta di *-mente* al femminile dell'aggettivo.

Italian irregular verbs

Infinitive	Present	Past Absolute	Future	Past Participle
addurre	adduco	addussi	addurrò	addotto
affiggere	affiggo	affissi	affiggerò	affisso
affliggere	affliggo	afflissi	affliggerò	afflitto
alludere	alludo	allusi	alluderò	alluso
andare	vado	andai	andrò	andato
annettere	annetto	annessi	annetterò	annesso
apparire	appaio	apparvi	apparirò	apparso
appendere	appendo	appesi	appenderò	appeso
aprire	apro	aprii	aprirò	aperto
ardere	ardo	arsi	ardirò	arso
assistere	assisto	assistetti	assisterò	assistito
assolvere	assolvo	assolsi	assolverò	assolto
assumere	assumo	assunsi	assumerò	assunto
avere	ho	ebbi	avrò	avuto
bere	bevo	bevvi	berrò	bevuto
cadere	cado	caddi	cadrò	caduto
cogliere	colgo	colsi	coglierò	colto
comprimere	comprimo	compressi	comprimerò	compresso
concedere	concedo	concedetti	concederò	concesso
conoscere	conosco	conobbi	conoscerò	conosciuto
correre	corro	corsi	correrò	corso
crescere	cresco	crebbi	crescerò	cresciuto
cuocere	cuocio	cossi	cuocerò	cotto
dare	do	diedi	darò	dato
dire	dico	dissi	dirò	detto
dirigere	dirigo	diressi	dirigerò	diretto
discutere	discuto	discussi	discuterò	discusso
dissuadere	dissuado	dissuasi	dissuaderò	dissuaso
distinguere	distinguo	distinsi	distinguerò	distinto
dolere	dolgo	dolsi	dorrò	doluto
dovere	debbo	dovetti	dovrò	dovuto
emergere	emergo	emersi	emergerò	emerso
erigere	erigo	eressi	erigerò	eretto
esigere	esigo	esigetti	esigerò	esatto
espellere	espello	espulsi	espellerò	espulso
esplodere	esplodo	esplosi	esploderò	esploso

Infinitive	Present	Past Absolute	Future	Past Participle
estinguere	estinguo	estinsi	estinguerò	estinto
evadere	evado	evasi	evaderò	evaso
fare	faccio	feci	farò	fatto
flettere	fletto	flessi	fletterò	flesso
fondere	fondo	fusi	fonderò	fuso
friggere	friggo	frissi	friggerò	fritto
giacere	giaccio	giacqui	giacerò	giaciuto
godere	godo	godetti	godrò	goduto
incutere	incuto	incussi	incuterò	incusso
infliggere	infliggo	inflissi	infliggerò	inflitto
invadere	invado	invasi	invaderò	invaso
leggere	leggo	lessi	leggerò	letto
mettere	metto	misi	metterò	messo
mordere	mordo	morsi	morderò	morso
morire	muoio	morii	morirò	morto
muovere	muovo	mossi	muoverò	mosso
nascere	nasco	nacqui	nascerò	nato
nascondere	nascondo	nascosi	nasconderò	nascosto
nuocere	nuoccio	nocqui	nuocerò	nociuto
offrire	offro	offersi	offrirò	offerto
parere	paio	parvi	parrò	parso
perdere	perdo	perdetti	perderò	perso
persuadere	persuado	persuasi	persuaderò	persuaso
piacere	piaccio	piacque	piacerò	piaciuto
porgere	porgo	porsi	porgerò	porto
porre	pongo	posi	porrò	posto
potere	posso	potei	potrò	potuto
proteggere	proteggo	protessi	proteggerò	protetto
redimere	redimo	redensi	redimerò	redento
redigere	redigo	redassi	redigerò	redatto
reggere	reggo	ressi	reggerò	retto
rifulgere	rifulgo	rifulsi	rifulgerò	rifulso
rimanere	rimango	rimasi	rimarrò	rimasto
rispondere	rispondo	risposi	risponderò	risposto
rodere	rodo	rosi	roderò	roso
rompere	rompo	ruppi	romperò	rotto
sapere	so	seppi	saprò	saputo
scegliere	scelgo	scelsi	sceglierò	scelto
scindere	scindo	scissi	scinderò	scisso

Infinitive	Present	Past Absolute	Future	Past Participle
sciogliere	sciolgo	sciolsi	scioglierò	sciolto
scoprire	scopro	scoprii	scoprirò	scoperto
scorgere	scorgo	scorsi	scorgerò	scorto
scrivere	scrivo	scrissi	scriverò	scritto
scuotere	scuoto	scossi	scuoterò	scosso
sedere	siedo	sedetti	sederò	seduto
solere	soglio	solei	solerò	solito
sommergere	sommergo	sommersi	sommergerò	sommerso
sorgere	sorgo	sorsi	sorgerò	sorto
spandere	spando	spansi	spanderò	spanto
spargere	spargo	sparsi	spargerò	sparso
spegnere	spengo	spensi	spegnerò	spento
stare	sto	stetti	starò	stato
stringere	stringo	strinsi	stringerò	stretto
struggere	struggo	strussi	struggerò	strutto
svellere	svello	svelsi	svellerò	svelto
tacere	taccio	tacqui	tacerò	taciuto
tenere	tengo	tenni	terrò	tenuto
togliere	tolgo	tolsi	toglierò	tolto
torcere	torco	torsi	torcerò	torto
trarre	traggo	trassi	trarrò	tratto
udire	odo	udii	udirò	udito
ungere	ungo	unsi	ungerò	unto
uscire	esco	uscii	uscirò	uscito
valere	valgo	valsi	varrò	valso
vedere	vedo	vidi	vedrò	visto
venire	vengo	venni	verrò	venuto
vincere	vinco	vinsi	vincerò	vinto
vivere	vivo	vissi	vivrò	vissuto
volere	voglio	volli	vorrò	voluto
volgere	volgo	volsi	volgerò	volto

For verbs ending in:

-**cedere** see **concedere**
-**durre** see **addurre**
-**endere** see **appendere**
-**figgere** see **affiggere**
-**idere** or -**udere** see **alludere**

-**nettere** see **annettere**
-**ngere** (except **stringere**) see **ungere**
-**parire** see **apparire**
-**primere** see **comprimere**
-**sistere** see **assistere**

Verbi inglesi irregolari

Infinito	Preterito	Participo Passato	Infinito	Preterito	Participo Passato
abide	abode	abode	**deal**	dealt	dealt
arise	arose	arisen	**dig**	dug	dug
awake	awoke	awoken	**do**	did	done
be	was	been	**draw**	drew	drawn
bear	bore	borne	**dream**	dreamed	dreamed
		or born		or dreamt	or dreamt
beat	beat	beaten	**drink**	drank	drunk
become	became	become	**drive**	drove	driven
begin	began	begun	**dwell**	dwelt	dwelt
behold	beheld	beheld	**eat**	ate	eaten
bend	bent	bent	**fall**	fell	fallen
bet	bet	bet	**feed**	fed	fed
beware			**feel**	felt	felt
bid	bid	bidden	**fight**	fought	fought
		or bid	**find**	found	found
bind	bound	bound	**flee**	fled	fled
bite	bit	bitten	**fling**	flung	flung
bleed	bled	bled	**fly**	flew	flown
blow	blew	blown	**forbid**	forbade	forbidden
break	broke	broken	**forget**	forgot	forgotten
breed	bred	bred	**forgive**	forgave	forgiven
bring	brought	brought	**forsake**	forsook	forsaken
build	built	built	**freeze**	froze	frozen
burn	burnt	burnt	**get**	got	got
	or burned	or burned	**give**	gave	given
burst	burst	burst	**go**	went	gone
buy	bought	bought	**grind**	ground	ground
can	could		**grow**	grew	grown
cast	cast	cast	**hang**	hung	hung
catch	caught	caught		or hanged	or hanged
choose	chose	chosen	**have**	had	had
cling	clung	clung	**hear**	heard	heard
come	came	come	**hide**	hid	hidden
cost	cost	cost	**hit**	hit	hit
creep	crept	crept	**hold**	held	held
cut	cut	cut	**hurt**	hurt	hurt

Infinito	Preterito	Participio Passato	Infinito	Preterito	Participio Passato
keep	kept	kept	say	said	said
kneel	knelt	knelt	see	saw	seen
knit	knitted	knitted	seek	sought	sought
	or knit	or knit	sell	sold	sold
know	knew	known	send	sent	sent
lay	laid	laid	set	set	set
lead	led	led	sew	sewed	sewn
lean	leant	leant			or sewed
	or leaned	or leaned	shake	shook	shaken
leap	leapt	leapt	shear	sheared	sheared
	or leaped	or leaped			or shorn
learn	learnt	learnt	shed	shed	shed
	or learned	or learned	shine	shone	shone
leave	left	left	shoe	shod	shod
lend	lent	lent	shoot	shot	shot
let	let	let	show	showed	shown
lie	lay	lain	shrink	shrank	shrunk
light	lit	lit	shut	shut	shut
	or lighted	or lighted	sing	sang	sung
lose	lost	lost	sink	sank	sunk
make	made	made	sit	sat	sat
may	might		sleep	slept	slept
mean	meant	meant	slide	slid	slid
meet	met	met	sling	slung	slung
mow	mowed	mown	slink	slunk	slunk
must			slit	slit	slit
ought			smell	smelt	smelt
pay	paid	paid		or smelled	or smelled
put	put	put	sow	sowed	sown
quit	quitted	quitted			or sowed
	or quit	or quit	speak	spoke	spoken
read	read	read	speed	sped	sped
rid	rid	rid			or speeded or speeded
ride	rode	ridden	spell	spelt	spelt
ring	rang	rung		or spelled	or spelled
rise	rose	risen	spend	spent	spent
run	ran	run	spill	spilt	spilt
saw	sawed	sawn		or spilled	or spilled
		or sawed	spin	spun	spun

Infinito	Preterito	Participo Passato	Infinito	Preterito	Participo Passato
spit	spat	spat	swim	swam	swum
split	split	split	swing	swung	swung
spread	spread	spread	take	took	taken
spring	sprang	sprung	teach	taught	taught
stand	stood	stood	tear	tore	torn
steal	stole	stolen	tell	told	told
stick	stuck	stuck	think	thought	thought
sting	stung	stung	throw	threw	thrown
stink	stank or stunk	stunk	thrust	thrust	thrust
			tread	trod	trodden
stride	strode	stridden	wake	woke	woken
strike	struck	struck	wear	wore	worn
string	strung	strung	weave	wove	woven
strive	strove	striven	weep	wept	wept
swear	swore	sworn	win	won	won
sweep	swept	swept	wind	wound	wound
swell	swelled	swollen or swelled	wring	wrung	wrung
			write	wrote	written

Glossary of menu terms

Italy is a happy place to eat. Waiters, food store owners, hostesses all urge you to have something good to eat. Italian cuisine is based on the food that is available locally, and it is, therefore, seasonal. A good look at a market will give you an idea of what is most abundant and freshest.

There are three main meals and any number of informal snacks in Italy. **Prima colazione** (breakfast) is usually only coffee and bread for Italians. If you want a more substantial meal, try a café at midmorning, or better yet, shop in a food store or open market the night before. **Colazione** (or **pranzo**) is lunch and **cena** is dinner. These two meals are much alike; choose to have your major meal at whichever time is convenient. (If you plan to have two large meals, include some vigorous sightseeing or sports; you will have consumed a lot of food.)

Traditionally each of the regions of Italy (Tuscany, Latium, Venezia, Apulia, etc.) had its own distinctive cuisine, employing its own particular crops, cheeses, and wines, quite different from that of other regions. Modern standardization is having its effects here as elsewhere, but you will still find dishes on local menus which are not found any place else. Only some of the more famous of these regional specialties could be included here.

The title **ristorante** is used for the larger, more elegant — and more expensive — eating establishments. For every **ristorante**, there are many **trattorie** (singular: **trattoria**), where one might eat in plainer surroundings, and much more cheaply, food at least as good as that in a **ristorante**. In recent years **trattorie** have been disappearing, but a good one is still worth looking for.

Italian eating establishments usually list all or most of the following categories on their menus: **antipasta** (hors d'oeuvre), **minestre** (soups), **pasta** (spaghetti, etc.), **pesce** (seafood), **carne** (meats), **contorni** (vegetables), **insalata** (salads), **uova** (egg dishes), **formaggi** (cheeses), **frutta** (fruits), **dolci** (desserts). A very special Italian meal might include an item from every category, but the waiter (**cameriere**) of today knows that the tourist is not so ambitious.

Most Italian restaurants offer a fixed-price meal (**prezzo fisso**, abbreviation p.f.), a full-course dinner, no substitutions allowed. If you order from the full menu, you may find some dishes marked **piatti del giorno** or **pronti**. These are ready to serve. Others will be **piatti da farsi**, dishes which have to be made up. This may take a far amount of time.

You must ask for the check (**conto**); it is not brought automatically. Law now requires that you be given a legible itemized bill. There will be a fixed percentage added for service (**servizio**), but your waiter will still expect a modest tip in addition.

Antipasti (Hors d'Oeuvre)

Italian hors d'oeuvre may range from a single dish to a wide selection of appetizers. A typical antipasto might include cold cuts: **salami** there are a number of regional varieties, Genovese, Milanese, etc; **prosciutto** thin sliced uncooked ham; **mortadella** similar to U.S. bologna but with more fat; **coppa** pork sausage

fish: **acciughe** anchovies; **tonno** tuna; **sardine** sardines

vegetables done as salads: **fagioli** beans; **carciofi** artichokes; **peperoni** peppers (sweet); **peperoncini** small pickled peppers

pickles: **funghi sott'olio** pickled mushrooms; **caponata** eggplant in sweet and sour sauce

hardcooked eggs: **uova sode coi tonno** eggs stuffed with tuna; **uova sode coi spinachi** eggs stuffed with spinach

Dishes which may be served separately or as part of an antipasto:

prosciutto e melone sliced ham with honeydew melon

prosciutto e fichi sliced ham with figs

crostini di acciughe anchovies on toast

crostini alla napoletana toast with anchovies, cheese, and tomatoes

crostini alla fiorentina chicken livers on toast

mozzarella in carozza fried cheese sandwiches

Minestre (Soups)

Soups are as important a part of the Italian menu as pasta (and the two are never taken at the same meal; generally lunch is accompanied by some form of pasta, dinner by soup). Most soups are either **brodo**, broth of chicken, meat, fish, or vegetables, either plain or with pasta **(pastina in brodo)**; or **minestrone** (literally "big soup," combinations of several fresh and dried vegetables). All are served with generous helpings of grated cheese **(parmigiana, romana)**. Every region has its own particular version of **minestrone**, e.g. **minestrone alla Genovese, alla Milanese**, etc.; and the vegetables used will vary according to what is in season. Other famous soups:

zuppa di pesce Italian equivalent of bouillabaisse, a stew of mixed fish and shellfish (the combination varies according to the area)

zuppa di cozze mussel soup

minestra di pasta e fagioli bean and pasta soup

stracciatella broth with egg strands

zuppa pavese poached egg in broth with toast

Pasta

Pasta is a mainstay of the Italian menu but **not** the principal dish Americans often make of it. Nor is it just spaghetti and macaroni; there are literally hundreds of different sizes and shapes of dried pasta made of the semolina flour in common use in Italy. For example, **vermicelli** (finer than spaghetti); **rigatoni** (ridged tubes); **ziti** (smaller tubes); **linguine** (flat narrow strips); **tagliatelle** (broader than **linguine**); **lasagne** (very broad); **farfalle** (butterfly-shaped bows, used in soups); and many, many more. Also, the same pasta is often called by another name in different regions: what is called **tagliatelle** in Bologna is **fettucine** in Rome. In general, **pasta asciutte** ("dry pasta," even when served swimming in sauce) is distinguished from **pasta in brodo**, soup with some variety of pasta in it.

Pasta with sauces:

al burro dressed with butter

aglio e olio with olive oil and lightly fried garlic

alla Bolognese with rich meat sauce

alle cozze with mussels

alla carbonara with a sauce of bacon and lightly cooked egg

al pesto (Genovese) with a sauce of fresh basil, pine nuts, and cheese pounded to paste (a specialty of Genoa)

Pasta stuffed and baked (usually served as main dishes):

cannelloni tubes of pasta stuffed with meat or cheese and baked in sauce

lasagne layers of flat pasta baked with cheese and tomato sauce

lasagne verde lasagne made with spinach kneaded into the dough giving it a pale green color

gnocchi dumplings made of semolina, potato, or corn meal baked with butter, cheese, or other sauce

ravioli pasta dumplings stuffed with meat, cheese, or various vegetables, served plain or with sauce

Riso (Rice)

Northern Italy is rice country, and there the distinctive rise dish, **risotto**, may take the place of the pasta course on the menu.

risotto alla Milanese rice cooked in chicken stock and wine sauce with a touch of saffron

risotto alla Piemontese rice in a meat sauce with cheese

risotto alla marinara rice cooked in fish stock with shrimp and mussels

risi e bisi risotto with green peas (a specialty of Venice)

arancini "oranges": rice balls stuffed with meat, cheese, and tomato sauce and deep-fried (a specialty of Sicily)

Polenta

Italians don't eat corn on the cob, but they are fond of this corn-meal dish. To call it "corn-meal mush" may discourage those unfamiliar with what the Italian do with it. Every region has its own special way of cooking **polenta**, and it is served with a variety of sauces, meats, and cheeses. Be sure to try it.

Pesce (Fish)

Italian waters are rich in fish, but it is difficult to give the tourist an idea of what is available, for the varieties are so different and even types of fish vary from region to region. For example, **cozze** is a common word for mussel, but in Genoa mussels are called **muscoli**; in Venice they are called **peoci**, etc. Some common names are:

acciughe anchovies; **anguille** eels (small); **calamare** squid; **calamaretti** baby squid; **capitone** eels (large); **cozze** mussels; **merluzzo** cod; **sardine** sardines; **scampi** shrimp; **scungilli** conch; **spigola** bream; **tonno** tunny; **triglie** mullet; **trote** trout

Fish is usually cooked by grilling (**alla griglia**), frying (**fritti**) or roasting (**arrosto**), whole (including the head), or in slices.

Some common fish sauces:

alla marinara sailor style with tomato and herbs

alla pizzaiola tomato sauce

alla Napoletana lemon juice, oil, and herbs

alla Siciliana capers, olives, and herbs

Baccalà is a popular stew of dried cod with tomatoes and herbs.

Carni e Pollame (Meats and Fowl)

Meat, in Italy, almost invariably means veal (**vitello**) — so much so that menus normally carry the seemingly contradictory item **bistecca di vitello** — literally, "veal beefsteak." Some areas offer excellent dishes of lamb (**agnello**) and pork (**maiale**).

Similarly, fowl mainly means chicken (**pollo**); but turkey (**tachino**) is quite common, and game birds like pheasant (**fagiano**) are excellent when avialable.

Veal is very commonly served in the form of **scallope** (or **scaloppini**), thin slices fried with various sauces: **scallope al Marsala**, wine sauce; **alla piccata**, lemon juice; **alla Bolognese**, topped with cheese.

saltimbocca a Roman specialty, is veal scallops topped with thin slices of ham and cheese, and cooked with sage

costolette breaded veal cutlets; **alla Milanese**, lightly fried and served with lemon wedges; **alla Modenese**, baked in wine and tomato sauce; **alla Parmeggiana**, baked with tomatoes and cheese

arrosto di vitello veal roast

vitello tonnato pot roast of veal in tuna sauce

arista florentina pork roast Florentine style

bistecca alla florentina grilled steak (usually cooked well done on the outside and rare on the inside)

bistecca alla pizzaiola fried steak with sauce of tomato and herbs

costoletto di agnello piccante lamb chops fried with herbs and dressed with lemon juice

abbacchio al forno roast leg of lamb

ossobucchi alla Milanese veal shanks with marrow cooked in wine

stufato rich beef stew (meat may vary) with wine and herbs

fritto misto deep-fried pieces of organ meats (liver, heart, brains, etc)

fegato alla Veneziana liver and onions

rognoni trifolati kidneys cooked with anchovies and lemon juice

cervelli fritti calf brains sliced, breaded, and fried

regalo cocks' combs in wine sauce

pollo alla cacciatore chicken stewed with wine, tomatoes, mushrooms, and herbs

pollo alla diavola chicken covered with red pepper flakes and cooked in a light wine sauce

pollo alla Romana chicken stewed with tomatoes, peppers, wine, and herbs

petti di pollo alla Bolognese chicken breasts topped with ham and cheese

petti di pollo al Marsala chicken breasts cooked in wine

fegato di pollo alla salvia chicken livers cooked with sage

Contorni (di verdure) (Vegetables)

In Italian restaurants, while some vegetables may be served with the meat, it is common for vegetables to be eaten as a separate course, often before the main dish. Cooking is usually simple: green vegetables are blanched or steamed briefly and served with olive oil and lemon. Eggplant, tomatoes, and peppers are often stuffed with meat or vegetable mixtures and various spices.

carciofi artichokes (Italian artichokes are usually smaller and tenderer than the American kind and eaten whole)

melanzane eggplant

zucchine zucchini

peperoni sweet peppers

finocchi fennel (rather like celery with an anise flavor)

piselli peas

spinaci spinach

pomidori tomatoes

patate potatoes; **patate fritte** — "French-fried" potatoes

funghi mushrooms

cavalfiore cauliflower

legumi beans

sedani celery

cipolle onions

broccoli broccoli

asparago asparagus

carota carrots

Insalate (Salads)

Salads are an important part of the Italian meal, and may appear as part of the antipasto, as an accompaniment to the main dish, or as a separate course after the meat. Most are very simple with vinegar (or lemon juice) and oil dressing. Restaurants usually set the table with cruets of vinegar and oil so that the diner may make his own dressing. Many of the vegetables listed as hot dishes under **contorni** may also be served cold as salad.

insalata verde green salad, lettuce and other available greens

insalata de pomidori tomato salad

insalata di broccoli broccoli salad (fresh or cooked)

insalata di melanzane eggplant salad

insalata di finocchi fennel salad

fagiolini al tonno salad of green beans and tuna

insalata Nizzarda salad Nicoise: lettuce, tomatoes, green beans, peppers, olives, and anchovies in vinegar and oil.

Uova (Egg Dishes)

Eggs are never served for breakfast in Italy (though a homesick tourist may sometimes coax a dish of scrambled eggs from a sympathetic cook with the phrase **uova strapazzate**). But they are often fare for lunch or a light supper.

uova al tegamino fried eggs served in the cooking pan

frittata the Italian omelet; unlike the French variety, it is turned and browned on both sides, cooked right through; often served with chopped meats, vegetables, fish, as : **frittata coi carcioff** artichoke omelet; **frittata con tonno** omelet with tuna; **frittata con zucchine** omelet with zucchini; **frittata con spinachi** spinach omelet; **uova al piatto coi pomidori** eggs poached in tomato sauce; **uova al piatto coi fegatini** eggs with chicken livers.

Formaggi (Cheeses)

Italy produces many excellent cheeses, and they are an indispensable element in the Italian cuisine. Many are also delicious for eating and form a separate course in the Italian dinner, between the main dish and dessert. Some common eating cheeses:

gorgonzola a blue veined cheese, similar to Roquefort but richer and stronger flavored

bel paese a mild, smooth cheese, excellent for eating and cooking

Parmigiano Parmesan, always served grated with pasta and main dishes, also served for eating

pecorino sheeps' milk cheese, widely used for eating fresh; for grating when aged

provolone a sweet eating cheese when fresh; acquires a sharp flavor when aged and is used for cooking

mozzarella a fresh cheese, rather like cottage cheese; used for cooking and eating

ricotta a creamy fresh cheese eaten and used in desserts

Frutte (Fruits)

It is not unusual for an Italian meal to end with cheese and fruit rather than a formal dessert. Fruits are usually served raw and peeled at the table (an Italian never touches his fruit except with knife and fork; this seems difficult to the un-initiate but can be learned).

mele apples
Arancie oranges
pesche peaches
banane bananas
fragole strawberries
ciliege cherries
pera pears
fichi figs
melone melon
macedonia de frutta mixed fruit salad

Dolci (Desserts)

zabaglione (or zabaione) custard-flavored with Marsala wine
montebianco puréed chestnuts flavored with Marsala and topped with whipped cream
cassata rich cheese cake flavored with liqueurs (a specialty of Sicily)
dolce al rhum rum cake
pan di spagna sponge cake
budino di ricotta ricotta cheese pudding
gelata, spumone ice cream
granite fruit ices

Bevande (Drinks)

Italian restaurants do not usually serve cocktails; the Italian preference is for an aperitif (**aperitivo**), of which there are many. **Vermouth bianco** is probably the most popular. With the meal, it is usually a safe bet to take one of the local wines — every region has its own vintages, and they often have a remarkable affinity for the local dishes. Some wines which are available country-wide are:

Asti spumante the Italian champagne
Bardo a robust full-bodied red (**rosso**)
Valpolicella a light red
Soave one of the best whites (bianco)

Chianti real Chianti is a revelation if you have encountered only imitations
Orvieto a superb white: either dry **(secco)** or semi-sweet **(abboccato)**
Est! Est! Est! a white famous since the Middle Ages
Frascati the classic white wine of Rome
Capri and **Ischia** the Neapolitan islands produce good dry reds and whites
Lacrima Christi the famous dessert wine from Mount Vesuvius
Marsala (dolce) the dessert wine of Sicily

Coffee. Most Italians like to end their meal with the strong sweet **espresso. Cappuccino** is strong coffee with milk. **Caffelatte** is coffee and milk half-and-half.
Tea **(te)** is usually available. Nowadays, you can usually order milk with your meal **(bicchiere di latte)** without causing a major sensation. Italians often drink bottled mineral water **(acqua minerale)** with their meal in preference to wine. Many varieties are available nationally.

English—Italiano

A

a, an [ə, ən] *art* un, uno *m*; una *f*.

aback [ə'bæk] *adv* be taken aback essere colto di sorpresa.

abandon [ə'bændən] *v* abbandonare. *n* abbandono *m*.

abashed [ə'baʃt] *adj* confuso.

abate [ə'beit] *v* diminuire. **abatement** *n* diminuzione *f*.

abattoir ['abətwaɪ] *n* macello *m*.

abbey ['abi] *n* abbazia *f*. **abbess** *n* badessa *f*. **abbot** *n* abate *m*.

abbreviate [ə'briːvieit] *v* abbreviare. **abbreviation** *n* abbreviazione *f*.

abdicate ['abdikeit] *v* abdicare. **abdication** *n* abdicazione *f*.

abdomen ['abdəmən] *n* addome *m*. **abdominal** *adj* addominale.

abduct [əb'dʌkt] *v* rapire. **abduction** *n* rapimento *m*.

aberration [abə'reiʃən] *n* aberrazione *f*. **aberrant** *adj* aberrante.

abet [ə'bet] *v* favoreggiare. **aid and abet** farsi complice di.

abeyance [ə'beiəns] *n* sospensione *f*. **in abeyance** in sospeso.

abhor [əb'hoɪ] *v* aborrire. **abhorrence** *n* aborrimento *m*. **abhorrent** *adj* aborrevole, odioso.

*****abide** [ə'baid] *v* (*wait*) aspettare; (*tolerate*) soffrire. **abide by** sostenere, restar fedele a.

ability [ə'biləti] *n* abilità *f*. **to the best of one's ability** come meglio potrà.

abject [,abdʒekt] *adj* abietto.

ablaze [ə'bleiz] *adj* in fiamme, risplendente.

able ['eibl] *adj* capace; (*talented*) abile. **able-bodied** *adj* robusto. **be able** potere, essere in grado di.

abnormal [ab'noɪml] *adj* anormale. **abnormality** *n* anormalità *f*.

aboard [ə'boɪd] *adv*, *prep* a bordo (di). **all aboard!** tutti a bordo! **go aboard** imbarcarsi.

abode [ə'boud] *V* abide. *n* dimora *f*.

abolish [ə'boliʃ] *v* abolire. **abolition** *n* abolizione *f*.

abominable [ə'bominəbl] *adj* abominevole. **abominate** *v* detestare. **abomination** *n* abominazione *f*.

aborigine [abə'ridʒini] *n* indigeno *m*.

abortion [ə'boɪʃən] *n* aborto *m*. **abort** *v* abortire.

abound [ə'baund] *v* abbondare.

about [ə'baut] *adv* (*around*) intorno; (*nearly*) verso, presso, circa; (*concerning*) su. *prep* di, su; intorno a. **be about to** stare per.

above [ə'bʌv] *adv* in alto, di sopra. *prep* sopra, al di sopra di; (*number*) più di; (*rank*) superiore a. **above all** soprattutto. **above-mentioned** *adj* suddetto. **from above** dall'alto.

abrasion [ə'breiʒən] *n* abrasione *f*. **abrasive** *adj* abrasivo.

abreast [ə'brest] *adv* **keep abreast of** or **with** tenersi al corrente di. **two abreast** due per due.

abridge [ə'bridʒ] *v* abbreviare. **abridgement** *n* abbreviazione *f*.

abroad [ə'broɪd] *adv* all'estero.

abrupt [ə'brʌpt] *adj* brusco.

abscess ['abses] *n* ascesso *m*.

abscond [ab'skond] *v* rendersi latitante.

absent ['absənt] *adj* assente. **absent-minded** *adj* distratto. *v* **absent oneself** assentarsi. **absence** *n* assenza *f*. **absentee** *n* assente *m*. **absenteeism** *n* assenteismo *m*.

absolute ['absoluɪt] *adj* assoluto. **absolutely** *adv* assolutamente, perfettamente. **absolutism** *n* assolutismo *m*.

absolve [əb'zolv] v assolvere. **absolution** n assoluzione f.

absorb [əb'zotb] v assorbire. **be absorbed in** essere concentrato in. **absorbent** adj assorbente. **absorbing** adj (coll) molto interessante. **absorption** n assorbimento m.

abstain [əb'stein] v astenersi. **abstention** n astensione f.

abstemious [əb'stiːmiəs] adj astemio.

abstinence ['abstinəns] n astinenza f.

abstract ['abstrakt; v ab'strakt] adj astratto. v astrarre. **abstractedly** adv distrattamente. **abstraction** n astrazione f.

absurd [əb'səːd] adj assurdo, ridicolo. **absurdity** n assurdità f.

abundance [ə'bʌndəns] n abbondanza f. **abundant** adj abbondante.

abuse [ə'bjus; v ə'bjuzz] n abuso m; insulto m. v abusare di, maltrattare; insultare, oltraggiare. **abusive** adj offensivo; abusivo.

abyss [ə'bis] n abisso m. **abysmal** adj abissale; profondo.

academy [ə'kadəmi] n accademia f. **academic** n, adj accademico, -a.

accede [ak'siːd] v accedere.

accelerate [ak'seləreit] v accelerare. **acceleration** n accelerazione f. **accelerator** n acceleratore m.

accent ['aksənt] n accento m. v accentuare; (gramm) accentare.

accept [ak'sept] v accettare, accogliere. **acceptable** adj (agreeable) gradevole; accettabile. **acceptance** n accettazione f.

access ['akses] n accesso m. **accessible** adj accessibile.

accessory [ak'sesəri] n accessorio m; (law) complice m, f. adj accessorio.

accident ['aksidənt] n accidente m, infortunio m. **by accident** per caso. **accidental** adj fortuito.

acclaim [ə'kleim] v acclamare. n also **acclamation** acclamazione f.

acclimatize [ə'klaimətaiz] v acclimatare.

accolade ['akəleid] n abbraccio m.

accommodate [ə'komədeit] v accomodare; (lodge) ospitare; (provide) provvedere (di). **accommodating** adj cortese, conciliante. **accommodation** n (housing) alloggio m; (hotel) posto m.

accompany [ə'kʌmpəni] v accompagnare. **accompaniment** n accompagnamento m. **accompanist** n accompagnatore, -trice m, f.

accomplice [ə'kʌmplis] n complice m, f.

accomplish [ə'kʌmplif] v compiere, realizzare. **accomplished** adj (talented) compito. **accomplishment** n effettuazione f; talento m.

accord [ə'koːd] v concedere, accordare. n accordo m. **of one's own accord** spontaneamente. **in accordance with** in conformità con. **accordingly** adv pertanto, quindi, di conseguenza. **according to** secondo.

accordion [ə'koːdiən] n fisarmonica f.

accost [ə'kost] v rivolgersi a.

account [ə'kaunt] n (report) relazione f, versione f; (status) importanza f; (bank) conto m. **by all accounts** a quanto si dice. **on no account** a nessuna condizione. **on one's own account** per propria iniziativa. v **account for** spiegare la ragione di, giustificare. **accountant** n contabile m, f, ragioniere m.

accrue [ə'kruː] v accrescere.

accumulate [ə'kjumjuleit] v accumulare. **accumulation** n ammasso m, accumulamento m.

accurate ['akjurət] adj accurato, preciso. **accuracy** n accuratezza f, precisione f.

accuse [ə'kjuzz] v accusare, incolpare. **the accused** n l'imputato, -a m, f. **accusation** n accusa f.

accustom [ə'kʌstəm] v abituare.

ace [eis] n asso m. **within an ace of** a un dito di.

ache [eik] n dolore m. v far male, dolere.

achieve [ə'tʃiːv] v concludere, ottenere, compiere. **achievement** n compimento m, successo m.

acid ['asid] n, adj acido.

acknowledge [ək'nolidʒ] v riconoscere, ammettere. **acknowledge receipt of** accusare ricevuta di. **acknowledgement** n riconoscimento m; ricevuta f.

acne ['akni] n acne m.

acorn ['eikoɪn] n ghianda f.

acoustic [ə'kustik] adj acustico. **acoustics** pl n acustica f sing.

acquaint [ə'kweint] v avvertire, mettere al corrente. **acquaintance** n (knowledge) conoscenza f; (person) conoscente m, f. **become acquainted with** (person) fare la conoscenza di; (thing) informarsi su.

acquiesce [akwi'es] v acconsentire tacitamente. **acquiescence** n acquiescenza f. **acquiescent** adj acquiescente.

acquire [ə'kwaiə] v acquisire, acquistare.

acquisition [akwi'ziʃən] n acquisto m; acquisizione f. **acquisitive** adj avido di guadagno.

acquit [ə'kwit] v esonerare. **acquit oneself** comportarsi. **acquittal** n (law) assoluzione f.

acrid ['akrid] adj acre, pungente.

acrimony ['akriməni] n acrimonia f. **acrimonious** adj acrimonioso, astioso.

acrobat ['akrəbat] n acrobata m, f. **acrobatic** adj acrobatico. **acrobatics** pl n acrobazie f pl.

across [ə'kros] adv per traverso; (crossword) orizzontali. prep al di là di, attraverso.

acrylic [ə'krilik] adj acrilico.

act [akt] v agire; (theatre) recitare; (behave) comportarsi. **act as** fungere da. **act for** agire per conto di. n (deed) azione f; (theatre) atto m; (law) decreto m. **actor** n attore m. **actress** n attrice f.

action ['akʃən] n azione f; (law) processo m; (mil) combattimento m. **out of action** fuori uso.

active ['aktiv] adj attivo, energico. **activate** v attivare. **activist** n attivista m. **activity** n attività f.

actual ['aktʃuəl] adj effettivo, reale. **actually** adv effettivamente.

actuate ['aktjueit] v mettere in atto or moto.

acupuncture ['akjupʌŋktʃə] n acupuntura f.

acute [ə'kjuːt] adj acuto, perspicace.

adamant ['adəmənt] adj inflessibile.

Adam's apple [adəm'zapl] n pomo d'Adamo m.

adapt [ə'dapt] v adattare, modificare. **adaptability** n adattibilità f. **adaptable** adj adattabile. **adaptation** n adattamento m. **adapter** n (theatre) riduttore m; (elec) raccordo m.

add [ad] v aggiungere. **add to** aumentare. **add up** fare la somma di, sommare. **addition** n addizione f. **additional** adj supplementare.

addendum [ə'dendəm] n aggiunta f.

adder ['adə] n vipera f.

addict ['adikt; v ə'dikt] n (drug) drogato, -a m, f; tossicomane m, f. **be addicted to** essere abituato or dedito a. **addiction** n dedizione f; tossicomania f.

additive ['aditiv] n aggiunta f.

address [ə'dres] v (letter) indirizzare; (meeting, etc.) rivolgere la parola a, fare un discorso a. **address oneself to** mettersi a. n (speech) discorso m; (letter) indirizzo m, recapito m. **addressee** n destinatario m.

adenoids ['adənoidz] pl n adenoidi f pl.

adept [ə'dept] nm, adj esperto.

adequate ['adikwət] adj sufficiente, adeguato.

adhere [ə'hiə] v aderire, attaccarsi. **adhesion** n adesione f. **adhesive** nm, adj adesivo.

adherent [ə'hiərənt] n partigiano m, seguace m.

adjacent [ə'dʒeisənt] adj adiacente, contiguo.

adjective ['adʒiktiv] n aggettivo m.

adjoin [ə'dʒoin] v confinare (con). **adjoining** adj adiacente.

adjourn [ə'dʒəːn] v aggiornare, rinviare. **adjournment** n rinvio m.

adjudicate [ə'dʒuːdikeit] v aggiudicare. **adjudicator** n arbitro m.

adjust [ə'dʒʌst] v regolare, mettere a punto. **adjustment** n adattamento m, rettifica f.

ad-lib ['ad'lib] v improvvisare.

administer [əd'ministə] v amministrare; (med) somministrare. **administration** n amministrazione f. **administrative** adj amministrativo. **administrator** n amministratore, -trice m, f.

admiral ['admərəl] n ammiraglio m.

admire [əd'maiə] v ammirare. **admirable** adj ammirevole. **admiration** n ammirazione f. **admiringly** adv con meraviglia.

admit [əd'mit] v ammettere; concedere; confessare. **admissible** adj ammissibile. **admission** n ammissione f. **admittance** n ingresso m, entrata f.

adolescence [adə'lesns] n adolescenza f. **adolescent** n(m+f), adj adolescente.

adopt [ə'dopt] v adattare. **adopted** adj (child) adottivo. **adoption** n adozione f.

adore [ə'doi] v adorare. **adoration** n adorazione f.

adorn [ə'doin] v abbellire, guarnire. **adornment** n ornamento m.

adrenaline [ə'drenəlin] n adrenalina f.

adrift [ə'drift] adv alla deriva.

adroit [ə'droit] adj abile, destro.

adulation [adju'leiʃən] n adulazione f.

adult ['adʌlt] n, adj adulto, -a.

adulterate [ə'dʌltəreit] *v* adulterare; (*wine*) sofisticare.

adultery [ə'dʌltəri] *n* adulterio *m*. **adulterer** *n* adultero, -a *m, f*.

advance [əd'vɑːns] *v* avanzare, progredire, anticipare. *n* avanzamento *m*; (*mil*) marcia in avanti *f*; (*cash*) anticipo *m*. **book in advance** prenotare.

advantage [əd'vɑːntidʒ] *n* vantaggio *m*, beneficio *m*. **take advantage of** approfittare di. **advantageous** *adj* vantaggioso.

advent ['ædvənt] *n* avvento *m*.

adventure [əd'ventʃə] *n* avventura *f*, impresa rischiosa *f*. **adventurer** *n* avventuriero *m*. **adventurous** *adj* avventuroso.

adverb ['ædvəːb] *n* avverbio *m*.

adversary ['ædvəsəri] *n* avversario, -a *m, f*.

adverse ['ædvəːs] *adj* avverso. **adversity** *n* avversità *f*.

advertise ['ædvətaiz] *v* annunziare, fare pubblicità a. **advertisement** *n* annunzio *m*, inserzione *f*. **advertising** *n* pubblicità *f*.

advise [əd'vaiz] *v* consigliare, raccomandare. **ill-advised** *adj* imprudente, inopportuno. **well-advised** *adj* saggio. **advice** *n* consiglio *m*, suggerimento *m*. **advisable** *adj* opportuno, consigliabile. **adviser** *n* consulente *m, f*. **advisory** *adj* consultivo.

advocate ['ædvəkeit] *v* sostenere.

aerial ['eəriəl] *adj* aereo. *n* antenna *f*.

aerodynamics [eərədai'næmiks] *n* aerodinamica *f*.

aeronautics [eərə'nɔːtiks] *n* aeronautica *f*.

aeroplane ['eərəplein] *n* aereo *m*.

aerosol ['eərəsɔl] *n* aerosol *m*.

aesthetic [iːs'θetik] *adj* estetico. **aesthetics** *n* estetica *f*.

affair [ə'feə] *n* affare *m*. **have an affair** avere una relazione intima.

affect[1] [ə'fekt] *v* (*influence*) colpire, toccare.

affect[2] [ə'fekt] *v* (*pretend*) fingere, simulare.

affection [ə'fekʃən] *n* affetto *m*, affezione *f*. **affectionate** *adj* affezionato.

affiliate [ə'filieit] *v* affiliare. **affiliation** *n* affiliazione *f*.

affinity [ə'finəti] *n* affinità *f*.

affirm [ə'fəːm] *v* affermare, confermare. **affirmation** *n* affermazione *f*, conferma *f*. **affirmative** *adj* affermativo.

affix [ə'fiks] *v* affiggere.

afflict [ə'flikt] *v* affliggere, angosciare. **affliction** *n* afflizione *f*, dolore *m*.

affluent ['æfluənt] *adj* ricco, opulento. **affluence** *n* affluenza *f*, ricchezza *f*.

afford [ə'fɔːd] *v* avere i mezzi per; (*produce*) dare, offrire; (*allow oneself to*) permettersi di.

affront [ə'frʌnt] *n* affronto *m*, offesa *f*. *v* insultare, offendere.

afloat [ə'flout] *adv* a galla.

afoot [ə'fut] *adv* a piedi; (*fig*) in atto.

aforesaid [ə'fɔːsed] *adj* suddetto, sopranominato.

afraid [ə'freid] *adj* impaurito, pauroso, spaventato. **be afraid of** temere, aver paura di.

afresh [ə'freʃ] *adv* da capo, nuovamente.

Africa ['æfrikə] *n* Africa *f*. **African** *n, adj* africano, -a.

aft [ɑːft] *adv* a poppa.

after ['ɑːftə] *prep* dopo, in seguito a. *adv* dopo, poi. *conj* dopo che. **after all** dopo tutto, insomma. **afterwards** *adv* dopo, poi.

afternoon [ˌɑːftə'nuːn] *n* pomeriggio *m*, dopo pranzo *m*. **good afternoon!** buona sera!

aftershave ['ɑːftəʃeiv] *n* dopobarba *m* invar.

again [ə'gen] *adv* di nuovo, ancora. **again and again** ripetutamente. **never again** mai più.

against [ə'genst] *prep* contro, in opposizione a.

age [eidʒ] *n* età *f*; era *f*. **of age** maggiorenne. **old age** vecchiaia *f*. **under age** minorenne. *v* invecchiare. **aged** *adj* vecchio; (*seasoned*) invecchiato.

agency ['eidʒənsi] *n* agenzia *f*, rappresentanza *f*.

agenda [ə'dʒendə] *n* ordine del giorno *m*.

agent ['eidʒənt] *n* agente *m, f*; rappresentante *m, f*.

aggravate ['ægrəveit] *v* aggravare; (*coll*) irritare. **aggravation** *n* aggravamento *m*; (*coll*) irritazione *f*.

aggregate ['ægrigət] *nm, adj* aggregato.

aggression [ə'greʃən] *n* aggressione *f*. **aggressive** *adj* aggressivo. **aggressor** *n* aggressore *m*.

aghast [ə'gɑːst] *adj* stupefatto, atterrito.

agile ['ædʒail] *adj* agile. **agility** *n* agilità *f*.

agitate ['ædʒiteit] *v* agitare, turbare. **agitation** *n* agitazione *f*. **agitator** *n* agitatore, -trice *m, f*.

agnostic [ag'nostik] *n, adj* agnostico, -a. **agnosticism** *n* agnosticismo *m*.

ago [ə'gou] *adv* fa.

agog [ə'gog] *adj* bramoso.

agony ['agəni] *n* agonia *f*, angoscia *f*. **be in agony** soffrire dolori atroci.

agree [ə'griː] *v* essere *or* andare d'accordo, convenire, accordarsi. **agreeable** *adj* piacevole, simpatico. **agreement** *n* accordo *m*, patto *m*, contratto *m*.

agriculture ['agrikʌltʃə] *n* agricoltura *f*. **agricultural** *adj* agricolo.

aground [ə'graund] *adv* arenato. **run aground** incagliarsi.

ahead [ə'hed] *adv* (in) avanti.

aid [eid] *v* aiutare, sovvenire, soccorrere. *n* aiuto *m*, sussidio *m*. **first aid** pronto soccorso *m*. **in aid of** a favore di.

aim [eim] *v* puntare, prendere di mira; aspirare. *n* mira *f*; (*purpose*) scopo *m*, proposito *m*.

air [eə] *n* aria *f*; (*bearing*) aspetto *m*, contegno *m*. *v* ventilare.

airbed ['eəbed] *n* materassino pneumatico *m*.

airborne ['eəbɔːn] *adj* aerotrasportato.

air-conditioned *adj* ad aria condizionata.

aircraft ['eəkraift] *n* aereo *m*. **aircraft-carrier** *n* portaerei *m invar*.

airfield ['eəfiːld] *n* campo d'aviazione *m*.

air force *n* aviazione *f*.

air-hostess *n* assistente di volo *f*, hostess *f invar*.

air lift *n* ponte aereo *m*.

airline ['eəlain] *n* linea aerea *f*.

airmail ['eəmeil] *n* posta aerea *f*.

airport ['eəpɔːt] *n* aeroporto *m*.

air-raid *n* incursione aerea *f*. **air-raid shelter** rifugio antiaereo *m*.

airtight ['eətait] *adj* ermetico, impenetrabile all'aria.

airy ['eəri] *adj* arioso, ben ventilato.

aisle [ail] *n* navata *f*.

ajar [ə'dʒaː] *adj* socchiuso.

akin [ə'kin] *adj* simile, parente.

alabaster ['alabaistə] *n* alabastro *m*.

alarm [ə'laim] *n* allarme *m*. **alarm clock** sveglia *f*. *v* allarmare.

alas [ə'las] *interj* purtroppo!

Albania [al'beinjə] *n* Albania *f*. **Albanian** *n*(*m*+*f*), *adj* albanese.

albatross ['albatros] *n* albatro *m*.

albino [al'biːnou] *n, adj* albino -a.

album ['albəm] *n* album *m*.

alchemy ['alkəmi] *n* alchimia *f*. **alchemist** *n* alchimista *m, f*.

alcohol ['alkəhol] *n* alcool *m*.

alcoholic [alkə'holik] *adj* alcoolico. *n* alcoolizzato, -a *m, f*. **alcoholism** *n* alcoolismo *m*.

alcove ['alkouv] *n* nicchia *f*.

alderman ['ɔːldəmən] *n* assessore municipale *m*.

ale [eil] *n* birra *f*.

alert [ə'ləːt] *adj* vigilante. *v* avvertire. **be on the alert** stare all'erta.

algebra ['aldʒibrə] *n* algebra *f*.

alias ['eiliəs] *adv* altrimenti detto.

alibi ['alibai] *n* alibi *m invar*.

alien ['eiliən] *n, adj* straniero, -a, forestiero, -a. **alienate** *v* alienare. **alienation** *n* alienazione *f*.

alight¹ [ə'lait] *v* scendere, smontare.

alight² [ə'lait] *adj* acceso, illuminato.

align [ə'lain] *v* allineare.

alike [ə'laik] *adj* simile, somigliante. *adv* ugualmente. **be alike** assomigliarsi.

alimentary canal [ali'mentəri] *adj* alimentare.

alimony ['alimoni] *n* alimenti *m pl*.

alive [ə'laiv] *adj* vivo, vivente. **alive to** sensibile a.

alkaline ['alkəlain] *adj* alcalino.

all [ɔːl] *adj* tutto. *adv* completamente. *n* tutti *m pl*, tutte *f pl*. **all right!** va bene! **All Saints' Day** Ognissanti *m*. **All Souls' Day** giorno dei morti *m*. **all the same** con tutto ciò. **not at all** niente affatto.

allay [ə'lei] *v* calmare.

allege [ə'ledʒ] *v* allegare, asserire. **alleged** *adj* sedicente.

allegiance [ə'liːdʒəns] *n* obbedienza *f*, fedeltà *f*.

allegory ['aligəri] *n* allegoria *f*.

allergy ['alədʒi] *n* allergia *f*. **allergic** *adj* allergico.

alleviate [ə'liːvieit] *v* alleviare, attenuare.

alley ['ali] *n* vicolo *m*.

alliance [ə'laiəns] *n* alleanza *f*, patto *m*.

alligator ['aligeitə] *n* alligatore *m*.

alliteration [əlitə'reiʃən] *n* allitterazione *f*.

allocate ['aləkeit] *v* assegnare, collocare. **allocation** *n* assegnamento *m*.

allot [ə'lot] *v* assegnare. **allotment** *n* (*land*) lotto *m*, pezzo di terreno *m*; (*portion*) parte assegnata *f*.

allow [ə'lau] *v* permettere, concedere. **allow for** tener conto di. **allow me!**

permetta! **allowance** ʰ (*grant*) assegno *m*; (*reduction*) sconto *m*.

alloy ['aloi; *v* ə'loi] *n* lega *f*. *v* legare, amalgamare.

allude [ə'luːd] *v* riferirsi (a), alludere (a). **allusion** *n* allusione *f*, riferimento *m*.

allure [ə'ljuə] *n* fascino *m*. *v* affascinare. **alluring** *adj* seducente.

ally ['alai; *v* ə'lai] *n* alleato, -a *m*, *f*. *v* alleare.

almanac ['oːlmənak] *n* almanacco *m*.

almighty [oːl'maiti] *adj* onnipotente. **the Almighty** *n* il Padreterno *m*.

almond ['aːmənd] *n* (*nut*) mandorla *f*; (*tree*) mandorlo *m*.

almost ['oːlmoust] *adv* quasi.

alms [aːmz] *pl n* elemosina *f* *sing*. **give alms** fare l'elemosina. **almshouse** *n* ospizio dei poveri *m*.

aloft [ə'loft] *adv* in alto.

alone [ə'loun] *adj* solo. *adv* solo, da solo; (*only*) solamente. **leave alone** lasciar stare.

along [ə'loŋ] *prep* lungo. **along with** insieme a. **come along!** su! avanti! **alongside** *prep* accanto a.

aloof [ə'luːf] *adj* riservato, freddo. *adv* a distanza.

aloud [ə'laud] *adv* ad alta voce.

alphabet ['alfəbit] *n* alfabeto *m*.

Alps [alps] *pl n* **the Alps** le Alpi *f pl*. **alpine** *adj* alpino.

already [oːl'redi] *adv* già.

also ['oːlsou] *adv* anche, pure, inoltre.

altar ['oːltə] *n* altare *m*. **altarpiece** *n* pala d'altare *f*. **high altar** altare maggiore *m*.

alter ['oːltə] *v* alterare, cambiare, alterarsi. **alteration** *n* cambiamento *m*, mutamento *m*.

alternate ['oːltəneit; *adj* oːl'təːnət] *v* alternare, alternarsi, ·succedersi. *adj* alterno. **alternation** *n* alternazione *f*, successione reciproca *f*.

alternative [oːl'təːnətiv] *adj* alternativo. *n* alternativa *f*.

although [oːl'ðou] *conj* sebbene, benché.

altitude ['altitjuːd] *n* altezza *f*, altitudine *f*; (*aircraft*) quota *f*.

altogether [oːltə'geðə] *adv* complessivamente, nell'insieme.

altruistic [altru'istik] *adj* altruistico. **altruism** *n* altruismo *m*. **altruist** *n* altruista *m*, *f*.

aluminium [alju'miniəm] *n* alluminio *m*.

always ['oːlweiz] *adv* sempre.

am [am] *V* be.

amalgamate [ə'malgəmeit] *v* amalgamare. **amalgam** *n* amalgama *m*.

amass [ə'mas] *v* accumulare.

amateur ['amətə] *n* dilettante *m*, *f*. **amateurish** *adj* da dilettante.

amaze [ə'meiz] *v* stupire, meravigliare. **amazement** *n* stupore *m*, meraviglia *f*. **amazing** *adj* straordinario, stupendo.

ambassador [am'basədə] *n* ambasciatore, -trice *m*, *f*.

amber ['ambə] *n* ambra *f*.

ambidextrous [ambi'dekstrəs] *adj* ambidestro.

ambiguous [am'bigjuəs] *adj* ambiguo.

ambition [am'biʃən] *n* ambizione *f*. **ambitious** *adj* ambizioso.

ambivalent [am'bivələnt] *adj* ambivalente. **amble** ['ambl] *v* camminare lentamente.

ambulance ['ambjuləns] *n* ambulanza *f*.

ambush ['ambuʃ] *n* imboscata *f*, agguato *m*. *v* tendere un agguato.

ameliorate [ə'miːliəreit] *v* migliorare.

amenable [ə'miːnəbl] *adj* trattabile, suscettibile.

amend [ə'mend] *v* emendare, correggere. **amendment** *n* emendamento *m*, correzione *f*. **make amends** fare ammenda.

amenity [ə'miːnəti] *n* amenità *f*. **amenities** *pl n* comodità *f pl*.

America [ə'merikə] *n* America *f*. **American** *n*, *adj* americano, -a.

amethyst ['amiθist] *n* ametista *f*.

amiable ['eimiəbl] *adj* gentile, amabile.

amicable ['amikəbl] *adj* amichevole.

amid [ə'mid] *prep* fra, tra, in mezzo a.

amiss [ə'mis] *adv* **take amiss** aversene a male.

ammonia [ə'mouniə] *n* ammoniaca *f*.

ammunition [amju'niʃən] *n* munizioni *f pl*.

amnesia [am'niːziə] *n* amnesia *f*.

amnesty ['amnəsti] *n* amnistia *f*.

amoeba [ə'miːbə] *n* ameba *f*.

among [ə'mʌŋ] *prep* fra, tra, in mezzo a.

amoral [ei'morəl] *adj* amorale.

amorous ['amərəs] *adj* amoroso.

amorphous [ə'moːfəs] *adj* amorfo.

amount [ə'maunt] *n* quantità *f*, importo *m*, somma *f*. *v* ammontare, equivalere.

ampere ['ampeə] *n* ampere *m invar*.

amphetamine [am'fetəmiːn] *n* amfetamina *f*, anfetamina *f*.

amphibian [amˈfibiən] *nm, adj* anfibio.
amphitheatre [ˈamfiθiətə] *n* anfiteatro *m*.
ample [ampl] *adj* ampio, abbondante.
amplify [ˈamplifai] *v* amplificare, ampliare. **amplification** *n* amplificazione *f*. **amplifier** *n* amplificatore *m*.
amputate [ˈampjuteit] *v* amputare. **amputation** *n* amputazione *f*.
amuse [əˈmjuːz] *v* divertire, dilettare. **amusement** *n* divertimento *m*, svago *m*. **amusing** *adj* divertente, buffo.
anachronism [əˈnakrənizəm] *n* anacronismo *m*.
anaemia [əˈniːmiə] *n* anemia *f*. **anaemic** *adj* anemico.
anaesthetic [anəsˈθetik] *nm, adj* anestetico. **anaesthesia** *n* anestesia *f*. **anaesthetist** *n* anestesista *m, f*. **anaesthetize** *v* anestetizzare.
anagram [ˈanəgram] *n* anagramma *m*.
anal [einl] *adj* anale.
analogy [əˈnalədʒi] *n* analogia *f*. **analogous** *adj* analogo (*m pl* -ghi).
analysis [ənˈaləsis] *n, pl* -**ses** analisi *f*. **analyse** *v* analizzare. **analyst** *n* analista *m, f*. **analytical** *adj* analitico.
anarchy [ˈanəki] *n* anarchia *f*. **anarchic** *adj* anarchico. **anarchist** *n* anarchico, -a *m, f*.
anathema [əˈnaθəmə] *n* anatema *f*.
anatomy [əˈnatəmi] *n* anatomia *f*. **anatomical** *adj* anatomico. **anatomist** *n* anatomista *m, f*.
ancestor [ˈansestə] *n* antenato *m*. **ancestral** *adj* avito. **ancestry** *n* stirpe *f*, lignaggio *m*.
anchor [ˈaŋkə] *n* ancora *f*. *v* ancorare.
anchovy [ˈantʃəvi] *n* acciuga *f*.
ancient [ˈeinʃənt] *adj* antico (*m pl* -chi), anziano.
ancillary [anˈsiləri] *adj* ausiliario, sussidiario.
and [and] *conj* e, ed.
anecdote [ˈanikdout] *n* aneddoto *m*.
anemone [əˈneməni] *n* anemone *f*.
anew [əˈnjuː] *adv* da capo, di nuovo.
angel [ˈeindʒəl] *n* angelo *m*. **angelic** *adj* angelico.
anger [ˈaŋgə] *n* rabbia *f*, stizza *f*, ira *f*. *v* far arrabbiare.
angina [anˈdʒainə] *n* (*med*) angina *f*.
angle [ˈaŋgl] *n* (*corner*) angolo *m*; (*viewpoint*) punto di vista *m*.
angling [ˈaŋgliŋ] *n* pesca all'amo *f*. **angler** *n* pescatore *m*.

angry [ˈaŋgri] *adj* arrabbiato, stizzito.
anguish [ˈaŋgwiʃ] *n* angoscia *f*, tormento *m*. *v* angosciare, tormentare.
angular [ˈaŋgjulə] *adj* angolare.
animal [ˈaniməl] *n* animale *m*, bestia *f*. *adj* animale.
animate [ˈanimət; *v* ˈanimeit] *adj* animato, vivente. *v* animare. **animated** *adj* vivace. **animation** *n* animazione *f*.
animosity [aniˈmosəti] *n* animosità *f*.
aniseed [ˈanisiːd] *n* anice *m*.
ankle [ˈaŋkl] *n* caviglia *f*.
annals [ˈanlz] *pl n* annali *m pl*.
annex [əˈneks; *n* ˈaneks] *v* annettere. *n* annesso *m*; (*hotel*) dipendenza *f*. **annexation** *n* annessione *f*.
annihilate [əˈnaiəleit] *v* annientare. **annihilation** *n* annientamento *m*.
anniversary [aniˈvəːsəri] *nm, adj* anniversario.
annotate [ˈanəteit] *v* annotare.
announce [əˈnauns] *v* annunciare, rendere noto. **announcement** *n* annuncio *m*. **announcer** *n* annunciatore, -trice *m, f*.
annoy [əˈnoi] *v* dar noia a, disturbare, seccare. **annoyance** *n* fastidio *m*, noia *f*. **annoying** *adj* seccante, fastidioso.
annual [ˈanjuəl] *adj* annuale, annuo. *n* (*book*) annuario *m*; (*plant*) pianta annuale *f*. **annually** *adv* annualmente.
annuity [əˈnjuːiti] *n* annualità *f*. **life annuity** *n* vitalizio *m*.
annul [əˈnʌl] *v* annullare. **annulment** *n* annullamento *m*.
Annunciation [ənʌnsiˈeiʃn] *n* (*rel*) Annunziazione *f*.
anode [ˈanoud] *n* anodo *m*.
anomaly [əˈnoməli] *n* anomalia *f*. **anomalous** *adj* anomalo, irregolare.
anonymous [əˈnoniməs] *adj* anonimo.
anorak [ˈanərak] *n* giacca a vento *f*.
another [əˈnʌðə] *adj, pron* un altro. **one another** l'un l'altro.
answer [ˈansə] *v* rispondere (a). **answer for** rispondere di. *n* risposta *f*.
ant [ant] *n* formica *f*. **ant-hill** *n* formicaio *m*.
antagonize [anˈtagənaiz] *v* provocare l'ostilità (di). **antagonism** *n* antagonismo *m*. **antagonist** *n* antagonista *m, f*.
antecedent [antiˈsiːdənt] *adj* antecedente. **antecedents** *pl n* i precedenti *m pl*; (*forbears*) antenati *m pl*.

antelope ['æntəloup] n antilope f.

antenatal [ænti'neitl] adj prenatale.

antenna [æn'tenə] n antenna f.

anthem ['ænθəm] n inno m.

anthology [æn'θolədʒi] n antologia f.

anthropology [ænθrə'polədʒi] n antropologia f. **anthropologist** n antropologo, -a m, f.

anti-aircraft [ænti'eəkraift] adj contraereo.

antibiotic [antibai'otik] nm, adj antibiotico.

antibody ['ænti,bodi] n anticorpo m.

anticipate [æn'tisipeit] v anticipare, prevenire. **in anticipation** in anticipo.

anticlimax [ænti'klaimæks] n conclusione banale f.

anticlockwise [ænti'klokwaiz] adj, adv in senso antiorario.

antics ['æntiks] pl n buffoneria f sing.

anticyclone [ænti'saikloun] n anticiclone m.

antidote ['æntidout] n antidoto m.

antifreeze ['æntifriiz] n antigelo m.

antipathy [æn'tipəθi] n antipatia f.

antique [æn'tiik] adj antico (m pl -chi). n oggetto antico m. **antique dealer** n antiquario m. **antiquity** n antichità f.

anti-Semitic [ænti'æntisə'mitik] n antisemita m, f. **anti-Semitism** n antisemitismo m.

antiseptic [ænti'septik] nm, adj antisettico.

antisocial [ænti'souʃəl] adj antisociale.

anti-tank [ænti'tæŋk] adj anticarro.

antithesis [æn'tiθəsis] n, pl -ses antitesi f.

antler ['æntlə] n corno m.

antonym ['æntənim] n antonimo m.

anus ['einəs] n ano m.

anvil ['ænvil] n incudine f.

anxious ['æŋkʃəs] adj ansioso, preoccupato. **anxiety** n ansia f, ansietà f.

any ['eni] adj del, della, etc.; qualche invar; alcuno. pron alcuno, nessuno, ne. **anybody** or **anyone** pron qualcuno, alcuno; chiunque. **anyhow** or **anyway** adv in ogni caso, tuttavia; ad ogni modo. **anything** pron qualcosa, qualche cosa; (everything) qualunque cosa. **anywhere** adv in qualunque luogo, in alcun luogo; (everywhere) dovunque.

apart [ə'paːt] adv a parte, in disparte. **come apart** disfarsi. **tell apart** distinguere l'uno dall'altro.

apartment [ə'paːtmənt] n appartamento m, alloggio m.

apathy ['æpəθi] n apatia f. **apathetic** adj apatico.

ape [eip] n scimmia f. v scimmiottare, imitare.

aperitif [əperi'tiːf] n aperitivo m.

aperture ['æpətjuə] n apertura f.

apex ['eipeks] n vertice m, apice m.

aphid ['eifid] n afide m.

aphrodisiac [æfrə'diziak] n afrodisiaco m.

apiece [ə'piːs] adv a testa, per ciascuno, per uno.

apology [ə'polədʒi] n scusa f, giustificazione f. **apologetic** adj apologetico. **apologize** v chiedere scusa, scusarsi.

apoplexy ['æpəpleksi] n apoplessia f. **apoplectic** adj apoplettico. **apoplectic fit** colpo apoplettico m.

apostle [ə'posl] n apostolo m.

apostrophe [ə'postrəfi] n (punctuation) apostrofo m; (speech) apostrofe f.

appal [ə'poil] v inorridire, sgomentare. **appalling** adj terribile, spaventoso.

apparatus [æpə'reitəs] n apparecchio m, apparato m.

apparent [ə'pærənt] adj apparente, evidente, manifesto.

apparition [æpə'riʃən] n visione f, fantasma m.

appeal [ə'piil] n appello m. v appellarsi, fare appello; (law) ricorrere in appello. **appealing** adj attraente, commovente.

appear [ə'piə] v apparire, sembrare, parere. **appearance** n apparenza f, aspetto m. **put in an appearance** fare atto di presenza.

appease [ə'piiz] v calmare, pacificare. **appeasement** n pacificazione f.

appendix [ə'pendiks] n appendice m. **appendicitis** n appendicite f.

appetite ['æpitait] n appetito m. **appetizing** adj gustoso, succolento.

applaud [ə'ploid] v applaudire. **applause** n applauso m.

apple [æpl] n (fruit) mela f; (tree) melo m.

apply [ə'plai] v rivolgersi, fare domanda; (refer) riferirsi; (use) applicare. **apply oneself** v dedicarsi a. **appliance** n apparecchio m, strumento m. **applicable** adj applicabile, idoneo. **applicant** n candidato m. **application** n domanda f, richiesta f. **application form** modulo di richiesta m.

appoint [ə'point] v nominare; (arrange) fissare. **appointment** n (engagement) appuntamento m; (post) nomina f.

apportion [əˈpɔːʃən] v distribuire.
appraisal [əˈpreizl] n valutazione f. **appraise** v stimare, valutare.
appreciate [əˈpriːʃieit] v (esteem) apprezzare, stimare; (be aware of) rendersi conto di; (increase in value) aumentare di valore. **appreciable** adj apprezzabile, sensibile. **appreciation** n apprezzamento m, stima f.
apprehend [apriˈhend] v cogliere, arrestare. **apprehension** n arresto m; (worry) timore m. **apprehensive** adj timoroso, preoccupato.
apprentice [əˈprentis] n apprendista m, f. **apprenticeship** n tirocinio m, apprendistato m.
approach [əˈproutʃ] v avvicinare; (come near) avvicinarsi (a). n avvicinamento m, accesso m.
appropriate [əˈprouprieit] v ə'prouprieit] adj adatto, opportuno. v impadronirsi di.
approve [əˈpruːv] v approvare, dare il benestare. **approval** n approvazione f, benestare m. **on approval** in visione, in esame. **approved** adj approvato, convalidato, riconosciuto.
approximate [əˈprɔksimeit] adj ə'prɔksimət] v approssimare. adj approssimativo. **approximately** adv approssimativamente, all'incirca, su per giù.
apricot ['eiprikɔt] n (fruit) albicocca f; (tree) albicocco m.
April ['eiprəl] n aprile m.
apron ['eiprən] n grembiule m, grembiale m.
apt [apt] adj atto, adatto.
aptitude ['aptitjuːd] n abilità f, attitudine f.
aqualung ['akwəlʌŋ] n autorespiratore m.
aquarium [əˈkweəriəm] n acquario m.
Aquarius [əˈkweəriəs] n Acquario m.
aquatic [əˈkwatik] adj acquatico.
aqueduct ['akwidʌkt] n acquedotto m.
Arab ['arəb] n, adj arabo, -a. **Arabia** n Arabia f. **Arabic** n (language) arabo m.
arable ['arəbl] adj arabile.
arbitrary ['aːbitrəri] adj arbitrario.
arbitrate ['aːbitreit] v arbitrare. **arbitration** n arbitraggio m.
arc [aːk] n arco m. **arc lamp** lampada ad arco f.
arcade [aːˈkeid] n portico m, galleria f.
arch¹ [aːtʃ] n arco m, volta f. v curvare, arcuare.

arch² [aːtʃ] adj (chief) arci-.
archaeology [aːkiˈɔlədʒi] n archeologia f. **archaeologist** n archeologo, -a m, f.
archaic [aːˈkeiik] adj arcaico.
archbishop [aːtʃˈbiʃəp] n arcivescovo m.
archduke [aːtʃˈdjuːk] n arciduca m.
archery ['aːtʃəri] n tiro all'arco m. **archer** n arciere m.
archetype ['aːkitaip] n archetipo m.
archipelago [aːkiˈpeləgou] n arcipelago (pl -ghi) m.
architect ['aːkitekt] n architetto, -a m, f. **architecture** n architettura f.
archives ['aːkaivz] pl n archivio m sing.
arctic ['aːktik] adj artico.
ardent ['aːdənt] adj ardente, appassionato.
ardour ['aːdə] n ardore m, fervore m.
arduous ['aːdjuəs] adj arduo, difficile.
are [aː] V be.
area ['eəriə] n area f, superficie f, zona f.
arena [əˈriːnə] n arena f.
argue ['aːgjuː] v argomentare, discutere, disputare. **arguable** adj discutibile. **argument** n argomento m, discussione f. **argumentative** adj polemico.
arid ['arid] adj arido.
Aries ['eəriːz] n Ariete m.
*****arise** [əˈraiz] v alzarsi, sorgere.
arisen [əˈrizn] V arise.
aristocracy [ariˈstɔkrəsi] n aristocrazia f. **aristocrat** n aristocratico, -a m, f. **aristocratic** adj aristocratico.
arithmetic [əˈriθmətik] n aritmetica f.
ark [aːk] n arca f. **Noah's Ark** arca di Noè f.
arm¹ [aːm] n (limb) braccio m (pl -a f). **armchair** n poltrona f. **arm in arm** a braccetto. **armpit** n ascella f. **within arm's reach** a portata di mano.
arm² [aːm] n (weapon) arma (pl -i) f. **bear arms** essere sotto le armi. **be up in arms against** essere in rivolta contro. **coat of arms** stemma m. v armare.
armistice [ˈaːmistis] n armistizio m.
armour ['aːmə] n armatura f, corazza f. **armourer** n armiere m. **armour-plated** adj corazzato. **armoury** n arsenale m.
army ['aːmi] n esercito m, armata f.
aroma [əˈroumə] n aroma m.
arose [əˈrouz] V arise.
around [əˈraund] prep attorno a, intorno a. adv intorno. **all around** tutto intorno.
arouse [əˈrauz] v destare, eccitare.

arrange [əˈreindʒ] v accomodare, ordinare; (*music*) adattare; (*meeting, etc.*) organizzare; (*put in order*) sistemare. **arrangement** n combinazione f; accomodamento m; adattamento m. **come to an arrangement** mettersi d'accordo.

array [əˈrei] n schieramento m; mostra imponente f. v ornare, schierare.

arrears [əˈriəz] pl n arretrati m pl. **be in arrears** avere degli arretrati.

arrest [əˈrest] n arresto. **under arrest** in stato d'arresto. v arrestare, sospendere.

arrive [əˈraiv] v arrivare, giungere. **arrival** n arrivo m; (*person*) arrivato, -a m, f.

arrogant [ˈærəgənt] adj arrogante. **arrogance** n arroganza f.

arrow [ˈarou] n freccia f.

arse [ais] n (*vulgar*) culo m.

arsenal [ˈaisənl] n arsenale m.

arsenic [ˈaisnik] n arsenico m.

arson [ˈaisn] n incendio doloso m.

art [ait] n arte f. **art gallery** galleria d'arte f, pinacoteca f. **artful** adj astuto.

artefact [ˈaitifakt] n artefatto m.

artery [ˈaitəri] n arteria f.

arthritis [aiˈθraitis] n artrite f.

artichoke [ˈaititʃouk] n carciofo m.

article [ˈaitikl] n articolo m; oggetto m.

articulate [aiˈtikjuleit; adj aiˈtikjulət] v articolare. adj articolato, distinto.

artifice [ˈaitifis] n artifizio m, astuzia f.

artificial [aitiˈfiʃəl] adj artificiale, finto. **artificiality** n artificiosità f.

artillery [aiˈtiləri] n artiglieria f.

artisan [aitiˈzan] n artigiano, -a m, f.

artist [ˈaitist] n artista m, f. **artistic** adj artistico.

as [az] adv come, quanto. conj come; (*while*) mentre; (*because*) poiché, siccome. as ... as cosí ... come, tanto ... quanto. prep da. **as far as** (*distance*) sino a. **as for** or **to** per quanto riguarda. **as if** come se. **as long as** finché, purché. **as much** altrettanto. **as soon as** (non) appena. **as well** anche. **as well as** (*in addition to*) oltre a.

asbestos [azˈbestos] n asbesto m, amianto m.

ascend [əˈsend] v salire, ascendere. **ascendancy** n ascendente m. **ascension** n ascensione f. **ascent** n ascesa f, salita f.

ascertain [asəˈtein] v accertarsi di, verificare.

ascetic [əˈsetik] adj ascetico. n asceta m, f.

ash[1] [aʃ] n (*cinder*) cenere f. **ashen** adj cinereo. **ashtray** n portacenere m.

ash[2] [aʃ] n (*tree*) frassino m.

ashamed [əˈʃeimd] adj vergognoso. **be ashamed of** vergognarsi di.

ashore [əˈʃoi] adv a terra, sulla riva.

Ash Wednesday n mercoledì delle Ceneri m.

Asia [ˈeiʃə] n Asia f. **Asian** n, adj asiatico, -a.

aside [əˈsaid] adv da parte, a parte, in disparte. n (*theatre*) parole dette a parte f pl.

ask [aisk] v domandare, chiedere. **ask about** informarsi di or su. **ask after** chiedere notizie di.

askew [əˈskjui] adv di traverso.

asleep [əˈsliip] adj addormentato. **fall asleep** addormentarsi.

asparagus [əˈsparəgəs] n asparago m.

aspect [ˈaspekt] n aspetto m, apparenza f.

asphalt [ˈasfalt] n asfalto m.

asphyxiate [əsˈfiksieit] v asfissiare.

aspire [əˈspaiə] v ambire. **aspiration** n ambizione f.

aspirin [ˈaspərin] n aspirina f.

ass [as] n asino m, somaro m.

assail [əˈseil] v assalire, aggredire. **assailant** n aggressore m.

assassinate [əˈsasineit] v assassinare. **assassin** n assassino, -a m, f. **assassination** n assassinio m.

assault [əˈsoilt] n assalto m, attacco m. v assalire, attaccare.

assemble [əˈsembl] v riunire, riunirsi; (*put together*) montare. **assembly** n assemblea f, riunione f. **assembly line** catena di montaggio f.

assent [əˈsent] v assentire, approvare. n assenso m, consenso m.

assert [əˈsoit] v asserire, sostenere. **assert oneself** farsi valere, imporsi. **assertion** n asserzione f, rivendicazione f.

assess [əˈses] v valutare, stimare. **assessment** n valutazione f, imposizione di tassa f. **assessor** n assessore m, agente del fisco m.

asset [ˈaset] n bene m. **assets** pl n attività f pl.

assiduous [əˈsidjuəs] adj assiduo.

assign [əˈsain] v assegnare; (*law*) delegare. **assignee** n mandatario m. **assignment** n assegnazione f, attribuzione f.

assimilate [ə'simileit] v assimilare. **assimilation** n assimilazione f.

assist [ə'sist] v assistere, aiutare. **assistance** n assistenza f, soccorso m. **assistant** n assistente m, f, aiutante m, f; (shop) commesso, -a m, f.

associate [ə'sousieit; v ə'sousiət] v associare, associarsi. **associate with** frequentare. n socio, -a m, f, collega m, f. **association** n associazione f, società f; (club) circolo m.

assorted [ə'sottid] adj assortito. **assortment** n assortimento m.

assume [ə'sjuim] v assumere; presumere. **assumption** n assunzione f, supposizione f. **assuming that** supposto che.

assure [ə'ʃuə] v assicurare. **assurance** n assicurazione f, certezza f, promessa f.

asterisk [ˈastərisk] n asterisco m.

asthma [ˈasmə] n asma m.

astonish [ə'stoniʃ] v stupire, meravigliare. **astonishing** adj sbalorditivo, sorprendente. **astonishment** n sorpresa f, stupore m.

astound [ə'staund] v stupefare, stupire. **astounding** adj stupefacente, sbalorditivo.

astray [ə'strei] adv fuori strada. **go astray** smarrirsi. **lead astray** sviare, traviare.

astride [ə'straid] adv a cavalcioni.

astringent [ə'strindʒənt] adj astringente.

astrology [ə'strolədʒi] n astrologia f. **astrologer** n astrologo, -a m, f.

astronaut [ˈastrənott] n astronauta m, f.

astronomy [ə'stronəmi] n astronomia f. **astronomer** n astronomo, -a m, f. **astronomic(al)** adj astronomico.

astute [ə'stjurt] adj astuto, furbo.

asunder [ə'sandə] adv a pezzi.

asylum [ə'sailəm] n ricovero m, rifugio m; (for the insane) manicomio m.

at [at] prep a, in, da.

ate [et] V eat.

atheism [ˈeiθiizəm] n ateismo m. **atheist** n ateo, -a m, f.

Athens [ˈaθinz] n Atene f. **Athenian** n(m+f), adj ateniese.

athlete [ˈaθliit] n atleta m, f. **athletic** adj atletico. **athletics** n atletica f.

Atlantic [ət'lantik] nm, adj atlantico.

atlas [ˈatləs] n atlante m.

atmosphere [ˈatməsfiə] n atmosfera f; ambiente m. **atmospheric** adj atmosferico. **atmospherics** pl n disturbi atmosferici m pl.

atom [ˈatəm] n atomo m. **atomic** adj atomico.

atone [ə'toun] v espiare, fare ammenda. **atonement** n espiazione f.

atrocious [ə'trouʃəs] adj atroce, terribile. **atrocity** n atrocità f.

attach [ə'tatʃ] v attaccare, attribuire. **become attached to** affezionarsi a. **attachment** n (friendship) affezione f; (law) sequestro m; (tech) accessorio m.

attaché [ə'taʃei] n addetto m. **attaché case** n valigetta rigida f, borsa per documenti f.

attack [ə'tak] v attaccare, assalire. n attacco m; offensiva f; (med) accesso m. **attacker** n aggressore m.

attain [ə'tein] v ottenere, raggiungere. **attainment** n raggiungimento m, conseguimento m. **attainments** pl n coltura f sing.

attempt [ə'tempt] v tentare, provare. n tentativo m, prova f; (crime) attentato m.

attend [ə'tend] v (wait on) servire, accompagnare; (listen) prestar attenzione; (be present at) assistere. **attendance** n presenza f; servizio m. **attendant** n inserviente m, f; sorvegliante m, f, assistente m, f.

attention [ə'tenʃən] n attenzione f, cura f. **pay attention** far attenzione, stare attento. **attentive** adj attento, sollecito, premuroso.

attic [ˈatik] n attico m, soffitta f.

attire [ə'taiə] n abbigliamento m. v vestire.

attitude [ˈatitjud] n atteggiamento m, posa f.

attorney [ə'təmi] n procuratore m. **power of attorney** procura f.

attract [ə'trakt] v attrarre, attirare; affascinare. **attraction** n attrazione f; fascino m. **attractive** adj attraente; affascinante.

attribute [ˈatribjut; v ə'tribjut] n attributo m, qualità f. v attribuire, ascrivere. **attribution** n attribuzione f.

attrition [ə'triʃən] n attrito m.

atypical [ei'tipikl] adj atipico.

aubergine [ˈoubəʒim] n melanzana f.

auburn [ˈotbən] adj invar color rame.

auction [ˈoikʃən] n asta f. v vendere all'asta. **auctioneer** n venditore all'asta m, banditore m.

audacious [or'deiʃəs] adj audace, intrepido. **audacity** n temerità f.

audible ['ɔɪdəbl] *adj* udibile. **audibility** *n* udibilità *f*.

audience ['ɔɪdjəns] *n* pubblico *m*; *(assembly of spectators)* uditorio *m*; *(formal interview)* udienza *f*.

audiovisual [ɔɪdiou'viʒuəl] *adj* audiovisivo.

audit ['ɔɪdit] *n* controllo *m*, verifica dei conti *f*, revisione *f*. *v* rivedere, verificare i conti. **auditor** *n* revisore di conti *m*; sindaco *m*.

audition [ɔɪ'diʃən] *n* audizione *f*. *v* ascoltare in audizione.

auditorium [ɔɪdi'tɔɪriəm] *n* sala per concerti *f*, auditorio *m*.

augment [ɔɪg'ment] *v* aumentare, crescere.

August ['ɔɪgəst] *n* agosto *m*.

aunt [aɪnt] *n* zia *f*.

au pair [ou 'peə] *n* ragazza alla pari *f*.

aura ['ɔɪrə] *n* aura *f*.

auspicious [ɔɪ'spiʃəs] *adj* propizio, di buon augurio.

austere [ɔɪ'stiə] *adj* austero. **austerity** *n* austerità *f*.

Australia [o'streiljə] *n* Australia *f*. **Australian** *n, adj* australiano, -a.

Austria ['ɔstriə] *n* Austria *f*. **Austrian** *n, adj* austriaco, -a.

authentic [ɔɪ'θentik] *adj* autentico. **authenticate** *v* convalidare. **authenticity** *n* autenticità *f*.

author ['ɔɪθə] *n* autore, -trice *m, f*.

authority [ɔɪ'θɔrəti] *n* autorità *f*; *(influence)* ascendente *m*; *(accepted source)* fonte autorevole *f*. **on good authority** da fonte autorevole. **authoritative** *adj* autorevole. **authoritarian** *adj* autoritario.

authorize ['ɔɪθəraiz] *v* autorizzare. **authorization** *n* autorizzazione *f*.

autobiography [ɔttoubai'ɔgrəfi] *n* autobiografia *f*. **autobiographical** *adj* autobiografico.

autocratic [ɔttou'kratik] *adj* autocratico.

autograph ['ɔttəgrɑɪf] *n* autografo *m*. *v* autografare.

automatic [ɔttə'matik] *adj* automatico. **automation** *n* automazione *f*.

automobile ['ɔttəmbiul] *n* automobile *f*; *(fam)* macchina *f*.

autonomous [ɔt'tɔnəməs] *adj* autonomo.

autopsy ['ɔttopsi] *n* autopsia *f*.

autumn ['ɔttəm] *n* autunno *m*. **autumnal** *adj* autunnale.

auxiliary [ɔɪg'ziljəri] *n, adj* ausiliario, -a.

avail [ə'veil] *v* servire, giovare a. **avail oneself of** servirsi di. *n* vantaggio *m*. **be of no avail** non servire a nulla.

available [ə'veiləbl] *adj* disponibile, libero; *(to hand)* sotto mano. **availability** *n* disponibilità *f*.

avalanche [ə'avalɑɪnʃ] *n* valanga *f*.

avarice ['avəris] *n* avarizia *f*. **avaricious** *adj* avaro.

avenge [ə'vendʒ] *v* vendicare, vendicarsi. **avenger** *n* vendicatore, -trice *m, f*.

avenue ['avinjuɪ] *n* viale *m*.

average ['avəridʒ] *n* media *f*. **on average** in media. *adj* medio. *v* fare la media.

aversion [ə'vɔɪʃən] *n* avversione *f*, antipatia *f*. **not be averse to** non aver nulla in contrario a.

avert [ə'vɔɪt] *n* *(turn away)* distogliere; *(ward off)* allontanare; *(prevent)* prevenire.

aviary ['eiviəri] *n* uccelliera *f*.

aviation [eivi'eiʃən] *n* aviazione *f*.

avid ['avid] *adj* avido.

avocado [ə'vɑɪkaidou] *n* pera avocado *f*.

avoid [ə'void] *v* evitare, schivare. **avoidance** *n* fuga *f*. **avoid** *n* evitare *m*.

await [ə'weit] *v* aspettare, attendere.

*awake** [ə'weik] *adj* sveglio. *v* svegliare, svegliarsi. **awaken** *v* risvegliare, risvegliarsi. **awakening** *n* risveglio *m*.

award [ə'wɔɪd] *n* premio *m*; *(honour)* onorificenza *f*. *v* aggiudicare, premiare, conferire.

aware [ə'weə] *adj* consapevole, conscio. **be aware of** sapere, rendersi conto di. **awareness** *n* consapevolezza *f*, sensibilità *f*.

away [ə'wei] *adv* lontano, via; *(absent)* fuori.

awe [ɔt] *n* timore reverenziale *m*. **awe-struck** *adj* in preda a timore. **awe-inspiring** *adj* che incute rispetto.

awful ['ɔtful] *adj* terribile, spaventoso. **awfully** *adv* terribilmente; *(coll)* molto.

awkward ['ɔtkwəd] *adj* goffo, sgraziato.

awl [ɔtl] *n* lesina *f*.

awning ['ɔmin] *n* tenda *f*.

awoke [ə'wouk] *V* **awake**.

awoken [ə'woukn] *V* **awake**.

axe [aks] *n* ascia *f*, scure *f*.

axiom ['aksiəm] *n* assioma *m*.

axis ['aksis] *n* asse *m*.

axle ['aksl] *n* asse *m*; perno *m*.

B

babble ['babl] v balbettare, ciarlare. n balbettio m.

baby ['beibi] n bimbo, -a m, f, bebè m. **babysitter** n babysitter m, f invar. **babyish** adj bambinesco.

bachelor ['batʃələ] n scapolo m. **Bachelor of Arts/Science** n laureato, -a in lettere/scienze m, f.

back [bak] n (anat) dorso m, schiena f; (chair) schienale m; (reverse) rovescio m. **back to front** a rovescio. adv dietro, indietro, di ritorno. v appoggiare, sostenere; (bet on) scommettere su, puntare su. **back out** ritirarsi.

*****backbite** ['bakbait] v calunniare, sparlare di.

backbone ['bakboun] n spina dorsale f.

backdate [ˌbakˈdeit] v retrodatare.

backfire [ˌbakˈfaiə] v far ritorno di fiamma; (coll) andare all'aria.

background ['bakgraund] n sfondo m; (milieu) ambiente m.

backhand ['bakhand] n rovescio m.

backlash ['baklaʃ] n contraccolpo m.

backlog ['baklog] n arretrati m pl.

back pay n arretrati di paga m pl.

backside [baksaid] n sedere m.

*****backslide** ['bakslaid] v ricadere nell'errore.

backstage [bakˈsteidʒ] adv dietro le quinte.

backstroke ['bakstrouk] n nuoto sul dorso m.

backward ['bakwəd] adj tardivo, arretrato.

backwards ['bakwədz] adv indietro, all'indietro.

backwater ['bakwoːtə] n (pool) acqua stagnante f; (place) posto dove non succede mai nulla m.

bacon ['beikən] n pancetta f.

bacteria [bak'tiəriə] pl n batteri m pl.

bad [bad] adj cattivo, malvagio, dannoso, brutto; (serious) grave. **bad language** parolacce f pl. **feel bad** sentirsi male. **go bad** andare a male. **badly** adv male, malamente; (seriously) gravemente.

badge [badʒ] n distintivo m, emblema m.

badger ['badʒə] n tasso m. v molestare.

baffle ['bafl] v sconcertare, confondere. **baffling** adj sconcertante.

bag [bag] n sacco m, borsa f, borsetta f. v insaccare; (coll) impadronirsi di, prendere.

bail¹ [beil] n (law) cauzione f, garanzia f. **grant bail** concedere libertà provvisoria (su cauzione). **stand bail for** rendersi garante per. v dar garanzia per, prestar cauzione a. **bail out** ottenere libertà provvisoria (su cauzione) per.

bail² or **bale** [beil] v **bail out** (flooded boat) aggottare; (from aircraft) lanciarsi.

bailiff ['beilif] n (law) funzionario incaricato a fare sequestri m; (of estate) fattore m.

bait [beit] n (fishing) esca f; (lure) lusinga f. v adescare; (annoy) tormentare.

bake [beik] v cuocere al forno. **baker** n fornaio panettiere m. **bakery** n panificio m. **baking powder** lievito minerale m, bicarbonato m. **baking tin** teglia f.

balance ['baləns] n equilibrio m, armonia f; (scales) bilancia f; (comm) bilancio m. **balance of payments** bilancia dei pagamenti f. v bilanciare, equilibrare; (comm) fare il bilancio.

balcony ['balkəni] n balcone m; (theatre) balconata f.

bald [boːld] adj calvo; (naked) nudo, disadorno. **baldness** n calvizie f invar.

bale¹ [beil] n balla f. v imballare.

bale² V **bail²**.

baleful ['beilful] adj maligno, distruttivo.

ball¹ [boːl] n palla f; (inflatable) pallone m; (sphere) sfera f. **ball-bearings** pl n cuscinetti a sfere m pl. **ball-point pen** penna a sfera f.

ball² [boːl] n (dance) ballo m. **ballroom** n sala da ballo f.

ballad ['baləd] n ballata f; (music) canzone popolare f.

ballast ['baləst] n zavorra f. v zavorrare.

ballet ['balei] n balletto m. **ballet dancer** ballerino, -a m, f.

ballistic [bə'listik] adj balistico. **ballistic missile** proiettile balistico m.

balloon [bə'luːn] n pallone m, aerostato m; (toy) palloncino m. **balloonist** n aeronauta m.

ballot ['balət] n votazione f, scrutinio m; (paper) scheda f. v ballottare, votare segretamente. **ballot-box** n urna elettorale f.

bamboo [bam'bu:] n bambù m.

ban [ban] n proibizione f, bando m, interdizione f. v proibire, interdire.

banal [bə'naːl] adj banale.

banana [bə'naːnə] n (fruit) banana f; (tree) banano m.

band¹ [band] n (troop) banda f, schiera f; (music) banda f, orchestrina f. **bandstand** n palco per banda m. v **band together** legare insieme.

band² [band] n (strip) striscia f, fascia f.

bandage ['bandidʒ] n benda f, fascia f. v bendare, fasciare.

bandit ['bandit] n bandito m.

bandy ['bandi] adj storto, curvo. **bandy-legged** adj a gambe storte. v **bandy words** scambiare parole.

bang [baŋ] n colpo m, botta f. v sbattere.

bangle ['baŋgl] n braccialetto m.

banish ['baniʃ] v bandire, esiliare. **banishment** n bando m, esilio m.

banister ['banistə] n ringhiera f.

banjo ['bandʒou] n banjo m invar.

bank¹ [baŋk] n (edge) sponda f; (river) riva f. v arginare.

bank² [baŋk] n banca f, banco m. **bank account** conto in banca m. **bank holiday** festa legale f. **bank manager** direttore di banca m. v depositare in banca. **bank on** contare su.

bankrupt ['baŋkrʌpt] adj fallito. v far fallire. **bankruptcy** n fallimento m.

banner ['banə] n stendardo m, insegna f.

banquet ['baŋkwit] n banchetto m.

banter ['bantə] v canzonare, prendere in giro. n presa in giro f.

baptize [bap'taiz] v battezzare. **baptism** n battesimo m. **baptismal** adj battesimale. **Baptist** n battista m.

bar [baː] n (metal) sbarra f, stanga f; (line) striscia f; (chocolate) tavoletta f; (law) ordine degli avvocati m; barriera f; (drinks) bar m invar; (music) battuta f. **barmaid** n cameriera al banco f, barista f. **barman** n barista m. v proibire, impedire, escludere. prep eccetto, tranne.

barbarian [baː'beəriən] n, adj barbaro, -a.

barbecue ['baːbikjuː] n arrosto all'aperto m. v arrostire all'aperto.

barb [baːb] n spina f. **barbed** adj pungente. **barbed wire** filo spinato m.

barber ['baːbə] n barbiere m, parrucchiere m.

barbiturate [baː'bitjurət] n barbiturato m.

bare [beə] adj (without covering) scoperto; (simple) semplice; (naked, unadorned) nudo; (just sufficient) appena sufficiente. v denudare, rivelare. **barefoot** adj, adv scalzo, a piedi scalzi. **barely** adv appena.

bargain ['baːgin] n (transaction) affare m; (offer) occasione f. **into the bargain** per giunta, in più. v contrattare, mercanteggiare.

barge [baːdʒ] n barcone m, chiatta f. v **barge in** intervenire a sproposito, irrompere. **barge into** imbattersi per caso.

baritone ['baːritoun] n baritono m.

bark¹ [baːk] n (dog) latrato m. v abbaiare, latrare.

bark² [baːk] n (tree) scorza f, corteccia f.

barley ['baːli] n orzo m. **barley sugar** zucchero d'orzo m. **barley water** tisana d'orzo f.

barn [baːn] n granaio m.

barometer [bə'romitə] n barometro m.

baron ['barən] n barone m. **baroness** n baronessa f. **baronet** n baronetto m.

baroque [bə'rok] nm, adj barocco.

barracks ['barəks] pl n caserma f sing.

barrage [bararʒ] n sbarramento m.

barrel ['barəl] n (cask) barile m, botte f; (gun, etc.) canna f. **barrel organ** organetto m.

barren ['barən] adj sterile, infecondo.

barricade [bari'keid] n barricata f. v barricare.

barrier ['bariə] n barriera f.

barrister ['baristə] n avvocato m.

barrow ['barou] n carretta f; (archaeol) tumulo m.

barter ['baːtə] v barattare. n baratto m.

base¹ [beis] v fondare, basare. n base f, fondamento m. **baseless** adj infondato.

base² [beis] adj vile, basso. **baseness** n bassezza f.

basement ['beismənt] n sottosuolo m.

bash [baʃ] n colpo violento m. v colpire violentemente.

bashful ['baʃful] adj timido, vergognoso.

basic ['beisik] adj fondamentale; (chem) basico.

basil ['bazl] n basilico m.

basin ['beisin] n bacino m, catino m; (wash-basin) lavabo m.

basis ['beisis] n, pl -ses base f, fondamento m.

bask [baːsk] v crogiolarsi.

basket ['baːskit] *n* cesto *m*, paniere *m*.
basketball *n* pallacanestro *f*.
Basle [baːl] *n* Basilea *f*.
bas-relief ['basriˌliːf] *n* bassorilievo *m*.
bass¹ [beis] *n* basso *m*.
bass² [bas] *n* (*sea*) branzino *m*, spigola *f*; (*freshwater*) pesce persico *m*.
bassoon [bə'suːn] *n* fagotto *m*.
bastard ['bastəd] *n*, *adj* bastardo, -a.
baste [beist] *v* (*cookery*) arrosolare; (*sewing*) imbastire; (*beat*) bastonare.
bastion ['bastjən] *n* bastione *m*.
bat¹ [bat] *n* (*cricket, baseball*) mazza *f*; (*table tennis*) racchetta *f*. *v* battere.
bat² [bat] *n* (*zool*) pipistrello *m*. **blind as a bat** cieco come una talpa.
batch [batʃ] *n* lotto *m*, partita *f*; (*bread*) infornata *f*.
bath [baːθ] *n* bagno *m*. *v* fare un bagno; lavare. **bathchair** *n* carrozzella per invalidi *f*. **bathmat** *n* stuoia da bagno *f*. **bathrobe** *n* accappatoio *m*. **bathroom** *n* stanza da bagno *f*.
bathe [beið] *v* bagnare, fare un *or* il bagno. **bather** *n* bagnante *m*, *f*. **bathing cap** cuffia da bagno *f*. **bathing costume** costume da bagno *m*. **bathing trunks** calzoncini da bagno *m pl*.
baton ['batn] *n* (*mil*) bastone *m*; (*music*) bacchetta *f*.
battalion [bə'taljən] *n* battaglione *m*.
batter¹ ['batə] *v* percuotere, colpire con violenza. **battering ram** (*mil*) ariete *m*.
batter² ['batə] *n* (*cookery*) pastella *f*.
battery ['batəri] *n* batteria *f*, pila *f*.
battle ['batl] *n* battaglia *f*, combattimento *m*. **battlefield** *n* campo di battaglia *m*. **battleship** *n* nave da battaglia *f*. *v* combattere, lottare.
bawdy ['boːdi] *adj* licenzioso.
bawl [boːl] *v* urlare, gridare.
bay¹ [bei] *n* (*geog*) baia *f*, golfo *m*, insenatura *f*.
bay² [bei] *v* (*cry*) abbaiare. *n* latrato *m*. **at bay** a bada.
bay³ [bei] *n* (*tree*) lauro *m*.
bayonet ['beiənit] *n* baionetta *f*.
bay window *n* finestra sporgente *f*.
***be** [biː] *v* essere, esistere; (*remain*) stare.
beach [biːtʃ] *n* spiaggia *f*, lido *m*.
beacon ['biːkən] *n* faro *m*; (*fire*) falò *m*.
bead [biːd] *n* grano *m*; (*liquid*) goccia *f*.
beagle ['biːgl] *n* cane da caccia *m*.
beak [biːk] *n* becco *m*, rostro *m*.
beaker ['biːkə] *n* coppa *f*.

beam [biːm] *n* (*wood*) trave *f*; (*light*) raggio *m*; (*radio*) segnale *m*; (*smile*) sorriso *m*. *v* irradiare; (*smile*) sorridere.
bean [biːn] *n* fava *f*, fagiolo *m*; (*coffee*) chicco *m*. **French bean** fagiolino *m*. **full of beans** energico.
***bear¹** [beə] *v* (*carry*) portare; (*support weight*) reggere; (*tolerate*) soffrire, sopportare; (*give birth to*) dare alla luce. **bear oneself** comportarsi. **bear with** aver pazienza con. **bearable** *adj* sopportabile.
bearer *n* portatore, -trice *m*, *f*.
bear² [beə] *n* orso, -a *m*, *f*.
beard [biəd] *n* barba *f*. *v* sfidare. **bearded** *adj* barbuto. **beardless** *adj* imberbe.
bearing ['beəriŋ] *n* condotta *f*, contegno *m*; (*aircraft*) rilevamento *m*; (*mech*) cuscinetto *m*. **bearings** *pl n* orientamento *n sing*, senso di direzione *m sing*. **lose one's bearings** disorientarsi.
beast [biːst] *n* bestia *f*, animale *m*. **beastly** *adj* bestiale; (*coll*) veramente cattivo.
***beat** [biːt] *v* battere; (*hit*) bastonare; (*heart*) palpitare; (*defeat*) sconfiggere; (*eggs, etc.*) sbattere. *n* battito *m*, palpito *m*; (*music*) battuta *f*; (*police*) ronda *f*. **beating** *n* bastonata *f*, sconfitta *f*.
beaten ['biːtn] *V* beat.
beauty ['bjuːti] *n* bellezza *f*. **beautiful** *adj* bello. **beautify** *v* abbellire.
beaver ['biːvə] *n* castoro *m*.
became [bi'keim] *V* become.
because [bi'koz] *conj* perché, poiché. **because of** a causa di.
beckon ['bekən] *v* chiamare con un cenno.
***become** [bi'kʌm] *v* diventare, divenire. **becoming** *adj* che sta bene; (*suitable*) conveniente.
bed [bed] *n* letto *m*; (*sea*) fondo *m*; (*coal*) giacimento *m*; (*flowers*) aiuola *f*. **bedbug** *n* cimice *m*. **bedroom** *n* camera da letto *f*. **bedside** *n* capezzale *m*. **bedsitter** *n* camera studio *f*. **bedspread** *n* copriletto *m*. **double bed** letto matrimoniale *m*. **go to bed** andare a letto. **twin beds** letti gemelli *m pl*. **bedding** *n* (*sheets*) lenzuola *f pl*; (*covers*) coperte *f pl*.
bedevil [bi'devl] *v* vessare.
bedlam ['bedləm] *n* confusione *f*.
bedraggled [bi'dragld] *adj* fradicio, inzaccherato.
bee [biː] *n* ape *f*. **beehive** *n* alveare *m*. **bee-keeper** *n* apicoltore *m*.

beech [biːtʃ] n faggio m.

beef [biːf] n manzo m. **beefsteak** n bistecca f.

been [biːn] V be.

beer [biə] n birra f.

beetle ['biːtl] n scarabeo m. **black beetle** scarafaggio m.

beetroot ['biːtruːt] n barbabietola f.

before [bi'foː] adv prima, già. prep prima di, davanti a. conj prima che. **beforehand** adv in anticipo.

befriend [bi'frend] v sostenere, mostrarsi amico a.

beg [beg] v implorare, pregare; (for alms) chiedere l'elemosina. **beggar** n mendicante m, f.

began [bi'gan] V begin.

***begin** [bi'gin] v cominciare, iniziare. **to begin with** anzitutto. **beginner** n principiante m, f. **beginning** n principio m, inizio m.

begrudge [bi'grʌdʒ] v invidiare.

begun [bi'gʌn] V begin.

behalf [bi'haːf] n **on behalf of** a nome di.

behave [bi'heiv] v comportarsi. **behaviour** n condotta f, comportamento m.

behead [bi'hed] v decapitare.

beheld [bi'held] V behold.

behind [bi'haind] adv dietro, indietro; (late) in ritardo. prep dietro a or di, dopo. **behindhand** adv in arretrato, in ritardo. n (coll) sedere m.

***behold** [bi'hould] v vedere. **beholder** n osservatore, -trice m, f.

beige [beiʒ] adj beige invar.

being [biːiŋ] n essere m, creatura f. **for the time being** per il momento.

belated [bi'leitid] adj tardivo.

belch [beltʃ] v ruttare. n rutto m.

belfry ['belfri] n campanile m.

Belgium ['beldʒəm] n Belgio m. **Belgian** n(m+f), adj belga (m pl -gi).

believe [bi'liːv] v credere, pensare, aver fede in. **make believe** v far finta. **belief** n, pl -s fede f, credenza f, opinione f. **believable** adj credibile. **believer** n credente m, f, fedele m, f.

bell [bel] n campana f; (door) campanello m. **bellringer** n campanaro m. **bell-tower** n campanile m.

belligerent [bi'lidʒərənt] adj belligerente.

bellow [belou] v urlare, muggire.

bellows ['belouz] pl n soffietto m sing, mantice m sing.

belly ['beli] n pancia f, ventre m.

belong [bi'loŋ] v appartenere, spettare, far parte (di). **belongings** pl n roba f sing, effetti personali m pl.

beloved [bi'lʌvid] n, adj amato, -a.

below [bi'lou] adv sotto, di sotto, giù. prep sotto, al di sotto di, inferiore a.

belt [belt] n cintura f; (mech) cinghia f; (zone) fascia f. v (coll: hit) picchiare; (coll: rush) precipitarsi.

bench [bentʃ] n (workshop) banco m; (long seat) panchina f, panca f; (law) magistratura f.

***bend** [bend] v piegare, curvare. n curva f, svolta f.

beneath [bi'niːθ] adv giù, abbasso. prep sotto, al di sotto di.

benefactor ['benəfaktə] n benefattore, -trice m, f. **benefaction** n beneficenza f.

benefit ['benəfit] n beneficio m, vantaggio m, utilità f. v giovare a, far bene a, approfittare. **beneficial** adj vantaggioso, utile. **beneficiary** n, adj beneficiario, -a.

benevolent [bi'nevələnt] adj benevolo, caritatevole. **benevolence** n benevolenza f.

benign [bi'nain] adj benevolo; (med) benigno.

bent [bent] V bend. adj curvato; (determined) risoluto; (dishonest) corrotto. n tendenza f.

bequeath [bi'kwiːð] v lasciare per testamento. **bequest** n lascito m.

bereaved [bi'riːvd] **be bereaved** essere in lutto. **bereavement** n lutto m.

beret ['berei] n beretto m.

berry ['beri] n bacca f, chicco m.

berserk [bə'səːk] adv **go berserk** montare su tutte le furie.

berth [bəːθ] n (sleeping) cuccetta f; (naut) posto d'ormeggio m. **give a wide berth to** evitare. v ancorare.

beside [bi'said] prep accanto a, presso, vicino a. **be beside oneself** essere fuori di sè. **besides** adv d'altronde, inoltre, per di più.

besiege [bi'siːdʒ] v assediare.

best [best] adj il migliore. adv meglio. **as best one can** come meglio si può. **the best possible** il meglio possibile. **come off best** avere la meglio. **do one's best** fare del proprio meglio. **the best** il meglio. **to the best of my knowledge** per quanto ne sappia.

bestial ['bestjəl] adj bestiale.

bestow [bi'stou] *v* conferire, dare.

bet [bet] *n* scommessa *f*. *v* scommettere.

betray [bi'trei] *v* tradire, svelare. **betrayal** *n* tradimento *m*.

better ['betə] *adj* meglio, migliore. *adv* meglio, in modo migliore. *v* migliorare. **all the better** tanto meglio. **be** *or* **feel better** star meglio. **get the better of** aver la meglio su.

between [bi'twiin] *adv* in mezzo. *prep* tra, fra, in mezzo a.

beverage ['bevəridʒ] *n* bevanda *f*, bibita *f*.

*beware [bi'weə] *v* guardarsi da, stare attento a. **beware of the dog!** attenti al cane!

bewilder [bi'wildə] *v* sconcertare, confondere. **bewildered** *adj* sconcertato, perplesso. **bewildering** *adj* sconcertante. **bewilderment** *n* disorientamento *m*.

beyond [bi'jond] *adv* oltre, più in là. *prep* oltre, al di là di.

bias ['baiəs] *n* inclinazione *f*, pregiudizio *m*, preconcetto *m*. **on the bias** *(tailoring)* per sbieco. **biased** *adj* prevenuto.

bib [bib] *n* bavaglino *m*.

Bible ['baibl] *n* bibbia *f*. **biblical** *adj* biblico.

bibliography [bibli'ogrəfi] *n* bibliografia *f*. **bibliographer** *n* bibliografo, -a *m*, *f*. **bibliographical** *adj* bibliografico.

biceps ['baiseps] *n* bicipite *m*.

bicker ['bikə] *v* litigare, bisticciare. **bickering** *n* bisticciare *m invar*.

bicycle ['baisikl] *n* bicicletta *f*.

*bid [bid] *n* offerta *f*; *(cards)* dichiarazione *f*. *v* *(order)* comandare; *(auction)* offrire; *(cards)* dichiarare. **bidder** *n* offerente *m*, *f*; dichiaratore, -trice *m*, *f*. **bidding** *n* ordine *m*; dichiarazione *f*.

bide [baid] *v* **bide one's time** aspettare il momento propizio.

bidet ['bidei] *n* bidè *m*.

biennial [bai'eniəl] *adj* biennale.

bifocals [bai'foukəlz] *pl n* lenti bifocali *f pl*.

big [big] *adj* grande, grosso, importante.

bigamy ['bigəmi] *n* bigamia *f*. **bigamist** *n* bigamo *m*. **bigamous** *adj* bigamo.

bigot ['bigət] *n* bigotto *m*, fanatico, -a *m*, *f*. **bigoted** *adj* bigotto, fanatico. **bigotry** *n* bigotteria *f*, fanatismo *m*.

bikini [bi'kiini] *n* bikini *m invar*.

bilateral [bai'latərəl] *adj* bilaterale.

bilingual [bai'liŋgwəl] *adj* bilingue.

bilious ['biljəs] *adj* *(med)* biliare; *(irritable)* collerico; *(sickly)* nauseante. **bile** *n* bile *f*. **biliousness** *n* travaso di bile *m*.

bill¹ [bil] *n* *(hotel, restaurant)* conto *m*; *(shop, invoice)* fattura *f*; *(pol)* progetto di legge *m*, atto *m*; *(poster)* affisso *m*; *(theatre)* cartellone *m*. **bill of fare** menù *m*. *v* fatturare; *(poster)* affiggere; *(theatre)* mettere in programma.

bill² [bil] *n* *(beak)* becco *m*, rostro *m*.

billiards ['biljədz] *n* biliardo *m*.

billion ['biljən] *n* *(10¹²)* bilione *m*, mille miliardi *m pl*; *(10⁹)* miliardo *m*.

billow ['bilou] *n* onda *f*; *(smoke)* ondata *f*. *v* *(sail)* gonfiarsi; *(smoke)* emanare.

bin [bin] *n* recipiente *m*; *(dustbin)* pattumiera *f*.

binary ['bainəri] *adj* binario.

*bind [baind] *v* legare, attaccare; *(book)* rilegare; *(force)* costringere. *n* *(slang)* scocciatura *f*.

binding ['baindiŋ] *n* legatura *f*, legame *m*; *(book)* rilegatura *f*. *adj* impegnativo, obbligatorio.

binoculars [bi'nokjuləz] *pl n* binocolo *m sing*.

biography [bai'ogrəfi] *n* biografia *f*. **biographer** *n* biografo, -a *m*, *f*. **biographical** *adj* biografico.

biology [bai'olədʒi] *n* biologia *f*. **biological** *adj* biologico. **biologist** *n* biologo, -a *m*, *f*.

birch [bəːtʃ] *n* betulla *f*.

bird [bəːd] *n* uccello *m*. **bird's-eye view** veduta a volo d'uccello *f*.

birth [bəːθ] *n* nascita *f*; origine *f*; discendenza *f*. **birth certificate** atto di nascita *m*. **birth control** controllo delle nascite *m*. **birthday** *n* compleanno *m*. **birthmark** *n* voglia *f*. **birthplace** *n* luogo di nascita *m*. **birth rate** natalità *f*, indice demografico *m*. **give birth to** mettere al mondo, dare alla luce.

biscuit ['biskit] *n* biscotto *m*.

bishop ['biʃəp] *n* *(church)* vescovo *m*; *(chess)* alfiere *m*.

bison ['baisən] *n* bisonte *m*.

bit¹ [bit] *V* **bite**. *n* *(horse)* morso *m*; *(drill)* punta *f*, morsa *f*.

bit² [bit] *n* *(morsel)* boccone *m*; *(small piece)* pezzo *m*, pezzetto *m*. **bit by bit** poco a poco. **do one's bit** fare la propria parte. **wait a bit!** aspetta un po'!

bitch [bitʃ] *n* cagna *f*; *(slang)* antipatica *f*. **bitchy** *adj* malvagio.

*bite [bait] *n* morso *m*; (*insect*) puntura *f*; (*fish*) l'abboccare *m*; (*food*) boccone *m*. *v* mordere, addentare. **biting** *adj* pungente, mordente.

bitten ['bitn] *V* **bite**.

bitter ['bitə] *adj* amaro, aspro, accanito. **bitter-sweet** *adj* agrodolce. **to the bitter end** ad oltranza. **bitterness** *n* amarezza *f*, rancore *m*.

bizarre [bi'zɑː] *adj* bizzarro, strano.

black ['blak] *adj* nero. **things look black** le cose si mettono male. *n* (*colour*) nero *m*; (*person*) negro, -a *m*, *f*. **blacken** *v* annerire.

blackberry ['blakbəri] *n* (*fruit*) mora *f*; (*bush*) rovo *m*.

blackbird ['blakbəid] *n* merlo *m*.

blackboard ['blakbɔid] *n* lavagna *f*.

blackcurrant [,blak'kʌrənt] *n* ribes nero *m* *invar*.

blackhead ['blakhed] *n* comedone *m*.

blackleg ['blakleg] *n* crumiro *m*.

blackmail ['blakmeil] *n* ricatto *m*. *v* ricattare. **blackmailer** *n* ricattatore, -trice *m*, *f*.

black market *n* borsa nera *f*.

blackout ['blakaut] *n* oscuramento *m*; (*med*) svenimento *m*.

blacksmith ['blaksmiθ] *n* fabbro *m*.

blackshirt ['blak'ʃɔit] *n* camicia nera *f*.

bladder ['bladə] *n* vescica *f*.

blade [bleid] *n* lama *f*; (*oar, propeller*) pala *f*; (*grass*) filo d'erba *m*.

blame [bleim] *n* biasimo *m*, responsabilità *f*. *v* biasimare, incolpare, rimproverare. **blameless** *adj* innocente.

blanch [blɑintʃ] *v* (*cookery*) sbollentare; (*go pale*) impallidire.

bland [bland] *adj* blando.

blank [blaŋk] *adj* vuoto, in bianco; (*puzzled*) perplesso. *n* spazio vuoto *m*; (*cartridge*) cartuccia a salve *f*. **point blank** a bruciapelo.

blanket ['blaŋkit] *n* coperta *f*. *v* ricoprire.

blare [bleə] *v* squillare, sonare con tutta forza. *n* (*trumpet*) squillo *m*; (*loud noise*) chiasso *m*.

blaspheme [blas'fiim] *v* bestemmiare. **blasphemous** [*adj*] blasfemo, empio. **blasphemy** *n* bestemmia *f*.

blast [blɑist] *n* (*wind*) raffica *f*; esplosione *f*. *v* far esplodere, far saltare. **blast-furnace** *n* altoforno (*pl* altiforni) *m*.

blatant ['bleitənt] *adj* vistoso, evidente.

blaze [bleiz] *n* (*flame*) fiamma *f*; (*sudden outburst of fire*) vampata *f*. *v* ardere, divampare. **blazer** *n* giacca sportiva *f*.

bleach [bliitʃ] *v* scolorire, candeggiare. *n* candeggina *f*.

bleak [bliik] *adj* (*desolate*) triste; (*dreary*) squallido; (*depressing*) deprimente.

bleat [bliit] *v* belare.

bled [bled] *V* **bleed**.

*bleed [bliid] *v* sanguinare, perder sangue. **bleeding** *n* emorragia *f*, perdita di sangue *f*.

blemish ['blemiʃ] *n* difetto *m*, imperfezione *f*. *v* sfigurare, macchiare.

blend [blend] *v* mescolare, combinare. *n* miscela intima *f*.

bless [bles] *v* benedire. **be blessed with** godere di, essere dotato di. **bless you!** salute! **blessing** *n* benedizione *f*.

blew [bluu] *V* **blow²**.

blind [blaind] *adj* cieco. **blind drunk** ubriaco fradicio. **blind spot** punto cieco *m*. **turn a blind eye** to chiudere gli occhi davanti a. **blindness** *n* cecità *f*. *v* accecare, ingannare. *n* (*window*) tendina *f*, persiana *f*; (*pretence*) finzione *f*.

blindfold ['blaindfould] *n* benda (agli occhi) *f*. *v* bendare gli occhi.

blink [bliŋk] *v* battere le palpebre; (*wink*) ammiccare.

bliss [blis] *n* beatitudine *f*. **blissful** *adj* beato.

blister ['blistə] *n* bolla *f*, vescica *f*. *v* far venire vesciche; coprirsi di vesciche.

blizzard ['blizəd] *n* tormenta *f*, bufera *f*.

blob [blob] *n* macchia *f*.

bloc [blok] *n* blocco *m*.

block [blok] *v* bloccare, sbarrare. *n* blocco *m*, ceppo *m*; (*large building*) palazzo *m*; (*obstacle*) ostacolo *m*. **block letter** stampatello *m*; (*capital*) maiuscola *f*.

blockade [blo'keid] *n* blocco *m*, assedio *m*. *v* bloccare.

bloke [blouk] *n* (*coll*) tipo *m*.

blond [blond] *adj* biondo. **blonde** *n* bionda *f*.

blood [blʌd] *n* sangue *m*; (*descent*) stirpe *f*. **blood clot** coagulo di sangue *m*. **blood-curdling** *adj* raccapricciante. **blood group** gruppo sanguigno *m*. **bloodhound** *n* segugio *m*. **blood poisoning** setticemia *f*. **blood pressure** pressione sanguigna *f*. **bloodshed** *n* carneficina *f*. **bloodshot** *adj* arrossato. **bloodthirsty** *adj* assetato di sangue. **bloody** *adj* macchiato di sangue; (*slang*) maledetto.

bloom [bluːm] v fiorire. n fiore m, fioritura f.

blot [blɒt] n macchia f, sgorbio m. v macchiare. **blot out** cancellare. **blotting paper** carta assorbente f.

blouse [blauz] n blusa f, camicetta f.

blow[1] [blou] n colpo m; (fist) pugno m; (stick) bastonata f. **come to blows** venire alle mani.

***blow**[2] [blou] v soffiare; (trumpet, etc.) suonare. **blow away** spazzar via. **blow one's nose** soffiarsi il naso. **blow out** spegnere. **blow up** (explode) far saltare; (inflate) gonfiare.

blown [bloun] V **blow**[2].

blubber ['blʌbə] n (whale) grasso di balene m. v (weep) piangere singhiozzando.

blue [bluː] nm, adj azzurro; (pale) celeste; (dark) blu. **bluebell** n giacinto selvatico m. **blueprint** n progetto m.

bluff [blʌf] v ingannare; (cards) bluffare. n vanteria infondata f; (poker) bluff m invar.

blunder [blʌndə] n errore m, papera f. v commettere un errore.

blunt [blʌnt] adj (not sharp) ottuso, spuntato; (frank) brusco. v smussare, ottundere.

blur [bləː] v rendere confuso, oscurare. n offuscamento m, macchia f.

blush [blʌʃ] v arrossire. n rossore m.

boar [boː] n cinghiale m.

board [boːd] v (ship, etc.) abbordare, imbarcarsi. n (wood) asse m, tavola f; (food) vitto m; (examiners) commissione f. **board of directors** consiglio d'amministrazione m. **full board** pensione completa f. **half board** mezza pensione f. **on board** a bordo. **boarding house** pensione f. **boarding school** collegio m.

boast [boust] n vanto m. v vantare. **boastful** adj millantatore, vanaglorioso.

boat [bout] n barca f, battello m. **boat race** gara di canottaggio f. **boating** n canottaggio m.

bob [bɒb] v **bob up** (come to surface) venire a galla. **bob up and down** muoversi in su e in giù.

bobbin [bobin] n bobina f.

bodice ['bodis] n busto m, liseuse f.

body ['bodi] n corpo m; entità f; gruppo m; (corpse) cadavere m; (organization) ente m. **bodyguard** n guardia del corpo f.

bog [bog] n palude f, pantano m.

bogus ['bougəs] adj falso.

bohemian [ou'hiːmiən] adj da artista.

boil[1] [boil] v bollire, far bollire, lessare. **boiler** n caldaia f. **boiler suit** tuta f. **boiling point** punto d'ebollizione m.

boil[2] [boil] n (swelling) foruncolo m.

boisterous ['boistərəs] adj chiassoso, impetuoso.

bold [bould] adj audace, ardito, sfacciato. **boldness** n audacia f, coraggio m.

bolster ['boulstə] n capezzale m, cuscino m. v **bolster up** sostenere.

bolt [boult] n (for nut) bullone m; (door) catenaccio m; (arrow) freccia f. v (bar) sprangare; (run away) scappare. **a bolt from the blue** un fulmine a ciel sereno. **bolt upright** diritto come un fuso.

bomb [bom] n bomba f. v bombardare. **bombing** n bombardamento m.

bond [bond] n (tie) legame m, vincolo m; (agreement) impegno m; (comm) titolo m; (law) cauzione f. **bonded warehouse** magazzino doganale m. **bondage** n schiavitù f.

bone [boun] n osso m (pl -a f). v dissossare. **bony** adj ossuto.

bonfire ['bonfaiə] n falò m.

bonnet ['bonit] n (hat) cappellino m; (car) cofano m.

bonus ['bounəs] n gratifica f, premio m.

booby trap ['buːbi] n mina nascosta f, trappola esplosiva f; (pitfall) trabocchetto m.

book [buk] n libro m. v (reserve) prenotare.

bookcase ['bukkeis] n scaffale m.

booking ['bukiŋ] n prenotazione f.

bookkeeping ['bukkiːpiŋ] n contabilità f. **bookkeeper** n contabile m, f.

booklet ['buklit] n opuscolo m.

bookmaker ['bukmeikə] n bookmaker m invar, allibratore m.

bookmark ['bukmaːk] n segnalibro m.

bookseller ['bukselə] n libraio m.

bookshop ['bukʃop] n libreria f.

bookstall ['bukstoːl] n edicola f.

boom [buːm] n (noise) rimbombare, tuonare; (econ) essere in gran voga. n rimbombo m, tuono m; (econ) boom m invar.

boorish ['buəriʃ] adj grossolano.

boost [buːst] n pressione f, spinta f. v aumentare, spingere.

boot [buːt] n (*shoe*) stivale m; (*car*) portabagagli m.

booth [buːð] n baracca f, cabina f.

booze [buːz] (*coll*) n bevanda alcoolica f. v ubriacarsi, sbronzarsi.

border ['bɔːdə] n orlo m, limite m, frontiera f. v (*embroidery*) orlare; (*geog*) confinare (con). **borderline case** caso limite m.

bore¹ [bɔː] n (*hole*) buco m, foro m; (*gun*) calibro m. v forare, trapanare; (*mech*) alesare.

bore² [bɔː] v (*weary*) seccare, annoiare. n (*person*) seccatore, -trice m, f; (*matter*) seccatura f; noia f.

bore³ [bɔː] V **bear¹**.

born [bɔːn] adj nato. **be born** nascere.

borne [bɔːn] V **bear¹**.

borough ['bʌrə] n comune m, borgo m.

borrow ['borou] v prendere a prestito, farsi prestare.

bosom ['buzəm] n petto m, seno m.

boss [bos] n capo m, direttore m. v comandare. **bossy** adj prepotente.

botany ['botəni] n botanica f. **botanical** adj botanico. **botanist** n botanico, -a m.

both [bouθ] adj, pron ambedue, entrambi, tutti e due.

bother ['boðə] n seccatura f, noia f. v seccare, preoccuparsi.

bottle ['botl] n bottiglia f. v imbottigliare. **bottleneck** n ingorgo m. **bottle-opener** n apribottiglie m invar.

bottom ['botəm] n fondo m. adj ultimo, inferiore. **bottomless** adj senza fondo.

bough [bau] n ramo m.

bought [bɔːt] V **buy**.

boulder ['bouldə] n macigno m, masso roccioso m.

bounce [bauns] v (*far*) rimbalzare. n balzo m, rimbalzo m.

bound¹ [baund] v saltare, rimbalzare. n salto m, balzo m. **by leaps and bounds** a passi da gigante.

bound² [baund] n confine m, restrizione f. v porre limiti a, confinare. **boundary** n limite m, frontiera f. **boundless** adj illimitato.

bound³ [baund] adj **bound for** diretto per, con destinazione per.

bound⁴ [baund] V **bind**.

bouquet [buːkei] n mazzo m.

bourgeois ['buəʒwai] n(m+f), adj borghese.

bout [baut] n periodo d'attività m; (*illness*) attacco m; (*match*) ripresa f.

bow¹ [bau] n (*greeting*) saluto m; (*bend*) inchino m. v inchinarsi, salutare, chinare.

bow² [bou] n (*archery*) arco m; (*violin*, *etc.*) archetto m; (*ribbon*) fiocco m. **bow-legged** adj dalle gambe storte. **bow-tie** n cravatta a farfalla f.

bow³ [bau] n (*naut*) prua f, prora f.

bowels ['bauəlz] pl n viscere f pl.

bowl¹ [boul] n (*basin*) scodella f, bacino m.

bowl² [boul] n (*ball*) boccia f. v far rotolare, servire la palla. **bowls** n gioco delle bocce m. **bowler** n (*hat*) bombetta f.

box¹ [boks] n scatola f, cassetta f; (*theatre*) palco m. **box number** casella postale f. **box office** botteghino m.

box² [boks] v fare a pugni, fare del pugilato, fare la boxe. **boxing** n pugilato m, boxe f.

Boxing Day n giorno di San Stefano m.

boy [boi] n ragazzo m. **boyhood** n fanciullezza f. **boyish** adj da ragazzo.

boycott ['boikot] n boicottaggio m. v boicottare.

bra [braː] n reggipetto m, reggiseno m.

brace [breis] v fortificare, rinvigorire. n sostegno; (*tool*) trapano m; (*pair*) coppia f. **braces** pl n bretelle f pl.

bracelet ['breislit] n braccialetto m.

bracken ['brakən] n felce f.

bracket ['brakit] n mensola f, braccio m; (*printing*) parentesi f invar. **put in brackets** mettere fra parentesi. **bracket together** accoppiare.

brag [brag] v vantarsi. **braggart** n fanfarone m.

brain [brein] n cervello m. **brainwashing** n lavaggio del cervello m. **brainwave** n idea geniale f. **brainy** adj intelligente.

braise [breiz] v brasare, cuocere a stufato.

brake [breik] n freno m. v frenare, serrare il freno.

bramble ['brambl] n (*bush*) rovo m; (*fruit*) mora f.

bran [bran] n crusca f.

branch [braːntʃ] n ramo m; (*office*) succursale f. **branch off** biforcarsi. **branch out** estendersi.

brand [brand] n (*trademark*) marchio m; (*grade*, *make*) marca f; (*marking*) marchio m, stigma m; (*burning wood*) tizzone m. **brand-new** adj nuovo di zecca.

nuovo fiammante. *v* marchiare, stigmatizzare.

brandish ['brandiʃ] *v* brandire.

brandy ['brandi] *n* cognac *m*, acquavite *f*.

brass [brɑːs] *n* ottone *m*. **brassy** *adj* d'ottone; (*impudent*) sfacciato.

brassiere ['brasiə] *V* **bra**.

brave [breiv] *adj* prode, coraggioso, ardito. *v* sfidare, affrontare. **bravery** *n* audacia *f*, coraggio *m*.

brawl [brɔːl] *n* rissa *f*, zuffa *f*. *v* rissare, azzuffarsi.

brawn [brɔːn] *n* (*strength*) forza muscolare *f*; (*meat*) testina *f*.

brazen ['breizn] *adj* sfacciato, impudente; (*brass*) di ottone.

breach [briːtʃ] *n* violazione *f*, rottura *f*; (*mil*) breccia *f*. *v* far una breccia in, rompere.

bread [bred] *n* pane *m*. **breadcrumbs** *pl n* briciole di pane *f pl*.

breadth [bredθ] *n* larghezza *f*, ampiezza *f*; (*cloth*) altezza *f*.

*****break** [breik] *n* rottura *f*, frattura *f*; interruzione *f*, pausa *f*; (*chance*) opportunità *f*. *v* rompere, spezzare, infrangere; (*record*) battere. **at breakneck speed** a rompicollo. **break away** fuggire, distaccarsi. **break off** mandare a monte. **break out** (*war*) scoppiare. **breakthrough** *n* scoperta *f*, innovazione *f*. **breakable** *adj* fragile. **breakage** *n* rottura *f*.

breakdown ['breikdaun] *n* crollo *m*; (*car*) panna *f*; (*nerves*) esaurimento nervoso *m*. *v* **break down** demolire; analizzare; (*car*) avere una panna; (*nerves*) avere un esaurimento nervoso.

breakfast ['brekfəst] *n* prima colazione *f*.

breast [brest] *n* petto *m*, seno *m*. **breast-bone** *n* sterno *m*. **breast-stroke** *n* nuoto a rana *m*.

breath [breθ] *n* respiro *m*, fiato *m*, soffio *m*. **breathless** *adj* ansimante. **breathtaking** *adj* sorprendente.

breathalyser ['breθəlaizə] *n* analizzatore del fiato *m*.

breathe [briːð] *v* respirare, prender fiato; (*sigh*) sospirare. **breathing** *n* respirazione *f*.

bred [bred] *V* **breed**.

*****breed** [briːd] *v* generare, allevare. *n* razza *f*, stirpe *f*. **breeding** *n* (*animals*) allevamento *m*; (*manners*) educazione *f*.

breeze [briːz] *n* brezza *f*. **breezily** *adv* con disinvoltura.

brew [bruː] *v* (*beer*) far fermentare; (*tea*) preparare; (*storm*) essere nell'aria. *n* miscela *f*. **brewer** *n* birraio *m*. **brewery** *n* birreria *f*.

bribe [braib] *v* corrompere, allettare. *n* dono a scopo di corruzione *m*; (*coll*) bustarella *f*. **bribery** *n* corruzione *f*.

brick [brik] *n* mattone *m*. **bricklayer** *n* muratore *m*. **drop a brick** fare una gaffe.

bride [braid] *n* sposa *f*, sposina *f*. **bridal** *adj* nuziale. **bridegroom** *n* sposo *m*. **bridesmaid** *n* damigella d'onore della sposa *f*.

bridge[1] [bridʒ] *n* ponte *m*. *v* congiungere. **bridge a gap** colmare una lacuna.

bridge[2] [bridʒ] *n* (*cards*) bridge *m*.

bridle ['braidl] *n* briglia *f*, freno *m*. *v* risentirsi. **bridle-path** *n* sentiero percorribile a cavallo *m*.

brief [briːf] *adj* breve. *n* riassunto *m*; istruzioni *m pl*; lettera *f*. *v* riassumere per sommi capi; (*law*) affidare una causa. **brief-case** *n* borsa *f*.

brigade [bri'geid] *n* brigata *f*.

bright [brait] *adj* lucido, risplendente; (*lively*) vivace; (*clever*) intelligente. **brighten** *v* rendere più brillante, illuminare. **brightness** *n* luminosità *f*, splendore *m*.

brilliant ['briljənt] *adj* brillante.

brim [brim] *n* orlo *m*, bordo *m*; (*hat*) falda *f*. **brimful** *adj* colmo.

brine [brain] *n* acqua salata *f*.

*****bring** [briŋ] *v* portare, condurre. **bring about** causare. **bring back** riportare; restituire. **bring up** educare; vomitare.

brink [briŋk] *n* orlo *m*.

brisk [brisk] *adj* vivace, arzillo.

bristle ['brisl] *n* (*human*) pelo duro *m*; (*animal*) setola *f*. *v* rizzarsi.

Britain ['britn] *n* Gran Bretagna *f*. **British** *adj* britannico. **Briton** *n* britannico, -a *m*, *f*.

brittle ['britl] *adj* fragile.

broach [broutʃ] *v* (*subject*) intavolare un discorso su.

broad [brɔːd] *adj* (*wide*) largo, ampio; (*overall*) generale. **broad bean** fava *f*. **broad-minded** *adj* di larghe vedute. **broaden** *v* allargare.

*****broadcast** ['brɔːdkɑːst] *v* trasmettere alla radio. *adj* radiodiffuso. *n* trasmissione radio *f*.

broccoli ['brokəli] n broccolo m.
brochure ['brouʃuə] n opuscolo m.
broke [brouk] V **break**. adj (coll) al verde, rovinato.
broken ['broukən] V **break**.
broker ['broukə] n agente m, commissionario m, sensale m.
bronchitis [broŋ'kaitis] n bronchite f.
bronze [bronz] n bronzo m. v abbronzare.
brooch [broutʃ] n spilla f.
brood [bruːd] n covata f, figliolanza f. v covare; (think) meditare.
brook [bruk] n ruscello m. v ammettere.
broom [bruːm] n (brush) scopa f; (plant) ginestra f.
broth [broθ] n brodo m.
brothel ['broθl] n bordello m.
brother ['brʌðə] n fratello m. **brother-in-law** n cognato m. **brotherhood** n fratellanza f, fraternità f. **brotherly** adj fraterno.
brought [broːt] V **bring**.
brow [brau] n fronte f; (hill) cima f. **browbeat** v intimidire.
brown [braun] nm, adj bruno, marrone, castano. v abbrunire, abbronzare; (cooking) rosolare.
browse [brauz] v brucare, scartabellare.
bruise [bruːz] v ammaccare, intaccare. n livido m, contusione f. **bruised** adj (person) contuso; (fruit) ammaccato.
brunette [bruː'net] nf, adj bruna, brunetta.
brush [brʌʃ] n spazzola f; spazzolino m; (paint) pennello m; (encounter) scontro m. v spazzolare. **brush against** sfiorare. **brush aside** ignorare. **brush up** (revise) ripassare.
brusque [brusk] adj brusco.
Brussels ['brʌsəlz] n Brusselle f. **Brussels sprouts** cavoli di Brusselle m pl.
brute [bruːt] nm, adj bruto. **brutal** adj brutale.
bubble ['bʌbl] n bolla f. v formar bolle, gorgogliare.
buck [bʌk] n maschio m; (deer) daino m. **buck-tooth** n dente sporgente m. **pass the buck** scaricare la responsabilità. v **buck up** (rear up) impennarsi; (coll: cheer up) rallegrarsi.
bucket ['bʌkit] n secchio m, secchia f.
buckle ['bʌkl] n fibbia f, fermaglio m. v affibbiare.
bud [bʌd] n bocciolo m, gemma f. v

germogliare, sbocciare. **nip in the bud** troncare sul nascere.
budge [bʌdʒ] v scostarsi.
budget ['bʌdʒit] n bilancio preventivo m. v fare un bilancio preventivo.
buffalo ['bʌfəlou] n bufalo, -a m, f.
buffer ['bʌfə] n (trains) respingente m. **buffer state** stato cuscinetto m.
buffet[1] ['bʌfit] v (hit) schiaffeggiare. n schiaffo m.
buffet[2] ['bufei] n (cafeteria) buffet m, caffè ristoratore m; (sideboard) credenza f. **cold buffet** cibi freddi m pl.
bug [bʌg] n cimice f; (coll) piccolo insetto m.
bugger ['bʌgə] (impol) n sodomita m; (fellow) tizio m; (derog) brutto ceffo m. v inculare. **bugger off** svignarsela. **bugger off!** va a quel paese! va al diavolo! **buggery** n sodomia f, pederastia f.
bugle ['bjuːgl] n tromba f.
*****build** [bild] v costruire, fabbricare. n corporatura f. **building** n edificio m, costruzione f. **building society** n società immobiliare f, credito edilizio m.
built [bilt] V **build**.
bulb [bʌlb] n (plant) bulbo m; (light) lampadina f.
Bulgaria [bʌl'geəriə] n Bulgaria f. **Bulgarian** n, adj bulgaro, -a.
bulge [bʌldʒ] n protuberanza f, gonfiore m. v gonfiarsi, sporgere.
bulk [bʌlk] n massa f, volume m. **the bulk** la maggior parte f. **bulky** adj massiccio, voluminoso.
bull [bul] n toro m; (papal) bolla f. **bulldog** n mastino m. **bulldozer** n livellatrice f. **bullfight** n corrida f. **bull's eye** centro (del bersaglio m).
bullet ['bulit] n pallottola f. **bullet-proof** adj blindato, corazzato.
bulletin ['bulətin] n bollettino m.
bullion ['buliən] n lingotto (di metallo prezioso) m.
bully ['buli] n prepotente m. v tiranneggiare, maltrattare.
bum [bʌm] (coll) n sedere m. adj scadente. v **bum around** vagabondare.
bump [bʌmp] v urtare. n protuberanza f, bernoccolo m. **bump into** (collide) andare a sbattere contro; (meet) incontrare per caso. **bumpy** adj irregolare.
bumper ['bʌmpə] n (mot) paraurti m. adj abbondante.

bun [bʌn] n (cake) focaccia f; (hair) crocchia f.

bunch [bʌntʃ] n fascio m, mazzo m, gruppo m; (grapes) grappolo d'uva m. v riunire, raggruppare.

bundle ['bʌndl] n fagotto m, involto m. v mettere insieme alla rinfusa, fare un involto di, affastellare.

bungalow ['bʌŋgəlou] n bungalow m, villino ad un piano m.

bungle ['bʌŋgl] v sciupare, lavorar male. n lavoro malfatto m. **bungler** n confusionario m, guastamestieri m.

bunion ['bʌnjən] n protuberanza callosa f.

bunk [bʌŋk] n cuccetta f.

bunker ['bʌŋkə] n (coal) carbonaia f; (mil) ricovero militare seminterrato m; (golf) ostacolo m.

buoy [boi] n gavitello m, boa f. **buoyancy** n galleggiabilità f. **buoyant** adj galleggiante.

burden ['bəidn] n peso m, onere m. v caricare, tassare.

bureau ['bjuərou] n (desk) scrittoio m; (office) ufficio m.

bureaucracy [bju'rokrəsi] n burocrazia f. **bureaucrat** n burocrate m, f. **bureaucratic** adj burocratico.

burglar ['bəiglə] n scassinatore m, ladro m. **burgle** v scassinare, svaligiare.

*****burn** [bəin] v bruciare, scottare, risplendere. **burn down** incendiare. n ustione f, scottatura f. **burner** n bruciatore m, becco a gas m.

burnt [bəint] V burn.

burrow ['bʌrou] n tana f, covo m. v farsi una tana, scavare.

*****burst** [bəist] n scoppio m, raffica f. v scoppiare, esplodere.

bury ['beri] v seppellire, sotterrare. **burial** n sepoltura f.

bus [bʌs] n autobus m invar. **bus station** capolinea (pl capilinea) m. **bus stop** fermata dell'autobus f.

bush [buʃ] n (shrub) cespuglio m; (woodland) macchia f. **bushy** adj folto.

business ['biznis] n affare m, mestiere m. **business-like** adj metodico. **businessman** n uomo d'affari m.

bust¹ [bʌst] n (anat) busto m, petto m.

bust² [bʌst] adj (coll: bankrupt) rovinato. v rovinare.

bustle ['bʌsl] n trambusto m, agitazione f. v agitarsi, affaccendarsi.

busy ['bizi] adj occupato, attivo, indaffarato. **busybody** n ficcanaso m. v **busy oneself with** occuparsi di.

but [bʌt] conj ma. adv (only) solo, soltanto. prep (except) eccetto, tranne.

butane ['bjuitein] n butano m.

butcher ['butʃə] n macellaio m. **butcher's shop** macelleria f. v macellare, massacrare. **butchery** n strage f, massacro m.

butler ['bʌtlə] n maggiordomo m.

butt¹ [bʌt] n (gun) calcio m, impugnatura f; (cigarette) mozzicone m.

butt² [bʌt] n (laughing-stock) bersaglio m, zimbello m.

butt³ [bʌt] n (hit) cornata f, cozzo m. v cozzare, urtare con la testa. **butt in** interrompere, intromettersi.

butter ['bʌtə] n burro m. v imburrare.

buttercup ['bʌtəkʌp] n ranuncolo m.

butterfly ['bʌtəflai] n farfalla f.

buttocks ['bʌtəks] pl n natiche f pl.

button ['bʌtn] n bottone m. **buttonhole** n occhiello m, asola f. v attaccare un bottone. **button up** abbottonare.

buttress ['bʌtris] n sostegno m, sperone m. v sostenere.

*****buy** [bai] v acquistare, comprare. n acquisto m. **buyer** n compratore m.

buzz [bʌz] n ronzio m; (phone) telefonata f. v ronzare; telefonare.

by [bai] adv vicino. prep da, con, a, di, per, entro, fra. **by and large** generalmente parlando. **by the way** a proposito. **by-law** n legge locale f. **bypass** n circonvallazione f; deviazione stradale f. **by-product** n prodotto secondario m. **bystander** n astante m, f. **byword** n detto m.

C

cab [kab] n tassì m.

cabaret ['kabərei] n caffè concerto m, cabaret m invar.

cabbage ['kabidʒ] n cavolo m.

cabin ['kabin] n cabina f, capanna f.

cabinet ['kabinit] n (furniture) armadietto m; (pol) gabinetto m; (cocktails) bar m invar. **cabinet-maker** n ebanista m.

cable ['keibl] n cavo m; telegramma m. v telegrafare. **cable-car** n funivia f.

cackle ['kakl] v (hens) schiamazzare; (people) chiacchierare. n schiamazzo m, chiacchiera f.

cactus ['kaktəs] n cactus m.
caddie ['kadi] n (golf) caddie m.
cadence ['keidəns] n cadenza f.
cadet [kə'det] n cadetto m.
café ['kafei] n caffè m.
cafeteria [kafə'tiəriə] n bar-ristorante m.
caffeine ['kafim] n caffeina f.
cage [keidʒ] n gabbia f. v ingabbiare. cagey adj cauto.
cake [keik] n (sweet) torta f, focaccia f, dolce m; (soap) saponetta f, pezzo di sapone m. v incrostare.
calamine ['kaləmain] n calamina f.
calamity [kə'laməti] n calamità f, disgrazia f.
calcium ['kalsiəm] n calcio m.
calculate ['kalkjuleit] v calcolare. calculation n calcolo m. calculator n calcolatore m, macchina calcolatrice f.
calendar ['kaləndə] n calendario m.
calf¹ [kaf] n (animal) vitello, -a m, f.
calf² [kaf] n (leg) polpaccio m.
calibre ['kalibə] n calibro m, qualità f.
call [kɔːl] n chiamata f, appello m, grido m, visita f. call-box n cabina telefonica f. call-girl n ragazza squillo f. v chiamare. call off annullare. call on visitare. call up telefonare; (mil) richiamare sotto le armi. calling n vocazione f.
callous ['kaləs] adj insensibile. n insensibilità f.
calm [kaːm] adj calmo. v calmare. calm down calmarsi. n calma f.
calorie ['kaləri] n caloria f.
came [keim] V come.
camel ['kaməl] n cammello m.
camera ['kamərə] n macchina fotografica f. (film/television) cameraman n operatore (cinematografico/televisivo) m.
camouflage ['kaməflaʒ] v mimetizzazione f, mascheramento m. v mimetizzare, mascherare.
camp [kamp] n campo m, accampamento m. camp-bed n branda f. campsite n campeggio m. v accamparsi, campeggiare.
campaign [kam'pein] n campagna f. v fare una campagna.
campus ['kampəs] n campo universitario m.
camshaft ['kamʃaft] n albero a camme or eccentrici m.
*can¹ [kan] v (be able) potere, essere in grado di; (know how) sapere.

can² [kan] n scatola f, recipiente m. can-opener n apriscatole m invar. v mettere in scatola.
Canada ['kanədə] n Canadà m. Canadian n(m+f), adj canadese.
canal [kə'nal] n canale m.
canary [kə'neəri] n canarino m.
cancel ['kansəl] v annullare, disdire. cancellation n annullamento m.
cancer ['kansə] n cancro m. Cancer n Cancro m.
candid ['kandid] adj candido, sincero.
candidate ['kandidət] n candidato, -a m, f.
candle ['kandl] n candela f; (church) cero m. candlelight n lume di candela m. candlestick n candeliere m.
candour ['kandə] n franchezza f.
candy ['kandi] n (US) caramella f. candied adj candito.
cane [kein] n canna f, bastone m; (school) verga f. v bastonare.
canine ['keinain] adj canino.
canister ['kanistə] n latta f.
cannabis ['kanəbis] n hascisc m.
cannibal ['kanibəl] n cannibale m. cannibalism n cannibalismo m.
cannon ['kanən] n cannone m. cannonball n palla di cannone f.
canoe [kə'nuː] n canoa f.
canon ['kanən] n canone m, criterio m; (church dignitary) canonico m. canonical adj canonico. canonize v canonizzare.
canopy ['kanəpi] n baldacchino m.
canteen [kan'tiːn] n (dining place) mensa f; (cutlery) posateria f.
canter ['kantə] n piccolo galoppo m. v andare al piccolo galoppo.
canvas ['kanvəs] n tela f; (sails) velatura f.
canvass ['kanvəs] v (orders, votes) sollecitare. canvasser n sollecitatore, -trice m, f.
canyon ['kanjən] n burrone m.
cap [kap] n (hat) berretto m; (bathing) cuffia f; (mech) coperchio m, cappello m. v coprire; sorpassare.
capable ['keipəbl] adj capace. capability n capacità f.
capacity [kə'pasəti] n capacità f, abilità f. in the capacity of nella qualità di.
cape¹ [keip] n (cloak) mantellina f.
cape² [keip] n (geog) capo m, promontorio m.

caper[1] ['keipə] n (bot) cappero m.

caper[2] ['keipə] n capriola f.

capillary [kə'piləri] adj capillare. n vaso capillare m.

capital ['kapitl] n capitale f; (arch) capitello m; (letter) maiuscola f; adj capitale. capitalism n capitalismo m. capitalist n(m+f), adj capitalista. capitalize v capitalizzare.

Capitol ['kapitl] n Campidoglio m.

capitulate [kə'pitjuleit] v capitolare. capitulation n resa f.

capricious [kə'prifəs] adj capriccioso.

Capricorn ['kaprikoin] n Capricorno m.

capsicum ['kapsikəm] n peperone m.

capsize [kap'saiz] v capovolgere, capovolgersi.

capsule ['kapsjuil] n capsula f.

captain ['kaptin] n (chief) capo m; (army, team) capitano m; (navy) capitano di vascello m; comandante m. v comandare.

caption ['kapfən] n didascalia f.

captive ['kaptiv] n, adj prigioniero, -a; schiavo, -a. captivate v cattivare. captivity n cattività f, prigionia f.

capture ['kaptfə] v catturare. n cattura f. captor n catturatore m.

car [kai] n macchina f, automobile f. car park parcheggio m. go by car andare in macchina.

carafe [kə'raf] n caraffa f.

carat ['karət] n carato m.

caravan ['karəvan] n (vehicle) roulotte (pl -s) f, (travelling group) carovana f.

caraway ['karəwei] n cumino m.

carbohydrate [kaibə'haidreit] n carboidrato m.

carbon ['kaibən] n carbonio m. carbon paper carta carbone f.

carbuncle ['kaibʌŋkl] n carbonchio m, pustola f.

carburettor ['kaibjuretə] n carburatore m.

carcass ['kaikəs] n carcassa f.

card [kaid] n carta f; (greetings, etc.) cartolina f; (playing) carta da gioco; (visiting) biglietto da visita m; (index) scheda f.

cardboard ['kaidboid] n cartone m, cartoncino m.

cardiac ['kaidiak] adj cardiaco. cardiac arrest arresto cardiaco m.

cardigan ['kaidigən] n golf m, giacca f.

cardinal ['kaidənl] nm, adj cardinale.

care [keə] v curare; preoccuparsi; interessarsi. n cura f, premura f; ansietà f; responsabilità f. carefree adj spensierato. care of presso. caretaker n custode m, f. care-worn adj preoccupato. careful adj attento; (thorough) curato. careless adj disattento, trascurato. carelessness n trascuratezza f.

career [kə'riə] n carriera f.

caress [kə'res] n carezza f. v accarezzare.

cargo ['kaigou] n carico (pl -chi) m.

caricature ['karikətjuə] n caricatura f. v mettere in caricatura. caricaturist n caricaturista m, f.

carnage ['kainid3] n strage f.

carnal ['kainl] adj carnale, sensuale.

carnation [kai'neifən] n garofano m.

carnival ['kainivəl] n carnevale m.

carnivorous [kai'nivərəs] adj carnivoro. carnivore n carnivoro m.

carol ['karəl] n cantico m. Christmas carol cantico di Natale m.

carpenter ['kaipəntə] n falegname m. carpentry n falegnameria f, ebanisteria f.

carpet ['kaipit] n tappeto m, moquette f.

carriage ['karid3] n (vehicle) carrozza f, vettura f; (bearing) portamento m; (railway) vagone m.

carrier ['kariə] n portatore, -trice m, f; (comm) trasportatore m; (med) vettore m. carrier bag sacchetto per acquisti m. carrier pigeon piccione viaggiatore m.

carrot ['karət] n carota f.

carry ['kari] v portare, trasportare. carrycot n culla portabile f. carry on proseguire, gestire. carry out eseguire, realizzare. carry over riportare.

cart [kait] n carro m, carretta f. cartload n carrettata f. turn cartwheels fare la ruota. v cart off portar via.

cartilage ['kaitilid3] n cartilagine f.

cartography [kai'togrəfi] n cartografia f. cartographer n cartografo, -a m, f.

carton ['kaitən] n scatola di cartone f; (cigarettes) stecca f.

cartoon [kai'tuin] n (drawing) cartone m; (film) cartone animato m; (caricatura f. cartoonist n disegnatore, -trice m, f; caricaturista m, f.

cartridge ['kaitrid3] n cartuccia f.

carve [kaiv] v (meat) tagliare, trinciare; (art) scolpire, intagliare. carving n intaglio m. carving knife trinciante m.

cascade [kas'keid] n cascata f. v scrosciare.

case¹ [keis] n (*matter*) caso m, fatto m, questione f; cosa f; (*law*) causa f, processo m. **in any case** ad ogni modo. **in case** qualora. **in most cases** in genere. **in that case** allora.

case² [keis] n (*box*) scatola f; (*luggage*) valigia f; (*glasses, pens*) astuccio f.

cash [kaʃ] v incassare, riscuotere. n denaro m; contanti m pl. **cash desk** cassa f. **cash payment** pagamento in contanti m. **petty cash** spese varie f pl.

cashier¹ [kaˈʃiə] n cassiere, -a m, f.

cashier² [kaˈʃiə] v destituire.

cashmere [kaʃˈmiə] n cachemire m invar.

casing [ˈkeisiŋ] n copertura f, rivestimento m.

casino [kəˈsiinou] n casinò m.

casket [ˈkaiskit] n cofanetto m; (*coffin*) cassa da morto f.

casserole [ˈkasəroul] n casseruola f. v cucinare in umido.

cassette [kəˈset] n cassetta f.

cassock [ˈkasək] n tonaca f.

*cast [kaist] n (*throw*) lancio m, getto m; (*mould*) forma f, calco m; (*metal*) fusione f; (*theatre*) complesso m, insieme degli attori m; (*plaster*) ingessatura f. v lanciare, gettare; (*metal*) fondere; (*theatre*) dare la parte. **cast away** gettar via. **cast iron** ghisa f. **cast-off** adj abbandonato.

caste [kaist] n casta f.

castle [ˈkaisl] n castello m.

castor [ˈkaistə] n (*furniture*) rotella al piede di mobili f; (*condiments*) ampolliera f. **castor oil** olio di ricino m. **castor sugar** zucchero semolato m.

castrate [kəˈstreit] v castrare. **castration** f castratura f.

casual [ˈkaʒuəl] adj casuale, fortuito, disinvolto.

casualty [ˈkaʒuəlti] n vittima f; (*accident*) incidente m; (*hospital*) pronto soccorso m.

cat [kat] n gatto, -a m, f. **cat's eye** catarifrangente m. **catty** adj malevolo.

catalogue [ˈkatəlog] n catalogo (pl -ghi) m, elenco m. v elencare.

catalyst [ˈkatəlist] n catalizzatore f. **catalysis** n, pl -ses catalisi f.

catamaran [katəməˈran] n catamarano m.

catapult [ˈkatəpʌlt] n catapulta f, fionda f. v scagliare.

cataract [ˈkatərakt] n cateratta f.

catarrh [kəˈtaɪ] n catarro m.

catastrophe [kəˈtastrəfi] n catastrofe f. **catastrophic** adj catastrofico.

*catch [katʃ] n preda f, cattura f; (*door*) spranga f; (*fish*) retata f. v prendere, acchiappare; (*fish*) pescare. **catch-phrase** n frase fatta f. **catch up with** raggiungere. **catchword** n slogan m. **catching** adj (*med*) contagioso, infettivo.

category [ˈkatəgəri] n categoria f. **categorical** adj categorico.

cater [ˈkeitə] v provvedere cibo. **cater for** provvedere a. **caterer** n approvvigionatore, -trice m, f. **catering** n approvvigionamento m.

caterpillar [ˈkatəpilə] n bruco m.

cathedral [kəˈθiidrəl] n cattedrale f.

catheter [ˈkaθətə] n catetere m.

cathode [ˈkaθoud] n catodo m.

catholic [ˈkaθəlik] n, adj cattolico, -a. **catholicism** n cattolicesimo m.

catkin [ˈkatkin] n gattino m.

cattle [ˈkatl] n bestiame m.

caught [kɔit] V **catch**.

cauliflower [ˈkɔliflauə] n cavolfiore m.

cause [kɔiz] n causa f, ragione f, motivo m. v causare, provocare, suscitare.

causeway [ˈkɔizwei] n strada rialzata f; (*main highway*) strada maestra f.

caustic [ˈkɔistik] adj caustico.

caution [ˈkɔiʃən] n cautela f, circospezione f; (*law*) diffida f, ammonimento m. v ammonire, mettere in guardia. **cautious** adj cauto, prudente.

cavalry [ˈkavəlri] n cavalleria f.

cave [keiv] n caverna f, grotta f.

caviar [ˈkaviaɪ] n caviale m.

cavity [ˈkavəti] n cavità f, buco m.

cease [siis] v cessare, smettere. **cease-fire** n tregua f, cessate il fuoco m invar. **ceaseless** adj continuo, incessante.

cedar [ˈsiidə] n cedro m.

ceiling [ˈsiiliŋ] n soffitto m.

celebrate [ˈseləbreit] v celebrare, festeggiare, far festa. **celebration** n festa f, commemorazione f. **celebrity** n celebrità f.

celery [ˈseləri] n sedano m.

celestial [səˈlestiəl] adj celestiale, celeste.

celibate [ˈselibət] n, adj celibe m. **celibacy** n celibato m.

cell [sel] n (*room*) cella f; (*biol*) cellula f; (*elec*) pila f.

cellar [ˈselə] n cantina f, sottosuolo m.

cello ['tʃelou] n violoncello m. **cellist** n violoncellista m, f.

cellular ['seljulə] adj cellulare.

cement [sə'ment] n cemento m. v cementare, consolidare.

cemetery ['semətri] n cimitero m, camposanto m.

censor ['sensə] n censore m. v censurare. **censorious** adj ipercritico. **censorship** n censura f.

censure ['senʃə] n censura f.

census ['sensəs] n censimento m.

cent [sent] n centesimo m, soldo m.

centenary [sen'tinəri] nm, adj centenario.

centigrade ['sentigreid] adj centigrado.

centimetre ['sentimi:tə] n centimetro m.

centipede ['sentipi:d] n millepiedi m invar.

centre ['sentə] n centro m. v centrare, accentrare. **central** adj centrale. **central heating** riscaldamento centrale m. **centralization** n centralizzazione f. **centralize** v centralizzare.

centrifugal [sen'trifjugəl] adj centrifugo (m pl -ghi). **centrifuge** n centrifuga f.

century ['sentʃuri] n secolo m.

ceramic [sə'ramik] adj ceramico. **ceramics** n ceramica f.

cereal ['siəriəl] nm, adj cereale.

cerebral ['serəbrəl] adj cerebrale.

ceremony ['serəməni] n cerimonia f, funzione f. **stand on ceremony** far complimenti. **ceremonial** adj solenne, rituale. **ceremonious** adj formalista, cerimonioso.

certain ['sə:tn] adj certo, sicuro. **certainly** adv certo, certamente, senza dubbio. **certainty** n certezza f, sicurezza f.

certificate [sə'tifikət] n certificato m, atto m, diploma m. **certify** v certificare, attestare, vidimare; (declare insane) classificare come pazzo.

cervix ['sə:viks] n cervice f.

cesspool ['sespu:l] n cloaca f.

chafe [tʃeif] v irritarsi.

chaffinch ['tʃafintʃ] n fringuello m.

chain [tʃein] n catena f. **chain-smoke** v fumare ininterrottamente. **chain store** magazzino a catena m. v incatenare.

chair [tʃeə] n sedia f, seggio m; (university) cattedra f. **chairlift** n seggiovia f. **chairman** n presidente m. v presiedere.

chalk [tʃɔ:k] n gesso m. **chalky** adj gessoso; pallido.

challenge ['tʃalindʒ] n sfida f, provocazione f. v sfidare, opporsi a, provocare. **challenging** adj stimolante, provocatorio.

chamber ['tʃeimbə] n camera f. **chambermaid** n cameriera f. **chamber music** musica da camera f.

chameleon [kə'mi:liən] n camaleonte m.

chamois ['ʃamwa:] n camoscio m; (leather) pelle di camoscio f.

champagne [ʃam'pein] n champagne m.

champion ['tʃampiən] n campione, -essa m, f. **championship** n campionato m. v difendere, sostenere.

chance [tʃa:ns] n caso m, fortuna f, opportunità f, rischio m. **by chance** per caso. v (risk) arrischiare; (happen) capitare. adj fortuito.

chancellor ['tʃa:nsələ] n cancelliere m; (university) rettore titolare m.

chandelier [ʃandə'liə] n lampadario m.

change [tʃeindʒ] n cambio m, mutamento m; (money) resto m, spiccioli m pl. v cambiare, mutare, cambiarsi. **changeable** adj variabile, mutevole. **changeability** n variabilità f. **changeless** adj immutevole, costante.

channel ['tʃanl] n canale m. **English Channel** Manica f. v incanalare.

chant [tʃa:nt] n canto m, salmodia f. v cantare, salmodiare.

chaos ['keios] n caos m.

chap¹ [tʃap] v screpolare, screpolarsi. n fessura f.

chap² [tʃap] n (fellow) tipo m, tizio m.

chapel ['tʃapəl] n cappella f.

chaperon ['ʃapəroun] n chaperon f. v accompagnare.

chaplain ['tʃaplin] n cappellano m.

chapter ['tʃaptə] n capitolo m.

char¹ [tʃa:] v carbonizzare, bruciare.

char² [tʃa:] v fare i lavori di casa. **charwoman** n donna di servizio f, donna a mezzo servizio f.

character ['karəktə] n carattere m, indole f, qualità f; (acting) personaggio m. **characterization** n caratterizzazione f. **characterize** v caratterizzare.

characteristic [karəktə'ristik] adj caratteristico. n caratteristica f.

charcoal ['tʃa:koul] n carbone di legna m.

charge [tʃa:dʒ] n spesa f, costo m; cura f, custodia f; (law) accusa f; (mil) carica f. **free of charge** gratis, gratuito. **in charge**

addetto, incaricato. **take charge of** incaricarsi di. v addebitare; caricare. **chargeable** adj addebitabile.

charity ['tʃærəti] n carità f, elemosina f. **charitable** adj caritatevole.

charm [tʃɑːm] n fascino m, incantesimo m; (trinket) portafortuna m invar. v affascinare, incantare. **charming** adj incantevole, affascinante.

chart [tʃɑːt] n mappa f, diagramma m, grafico m, quadro m. v tracciare un diagramma or grafico di.

charter [tʃɑːtə] n carta f, documento m; (flight) volo charter m. v (document) istituire; (hire) noleggiare. **chartered accountant** ragioniere diplomato m.

chase [tʃeis] n caccia f, inseguimento m. v cacciare, inseguire; (jewellery) incastonare; (metal) cesellare.

chasm ['kæzəm] n abisso m.

chassis ['ʃæsi] n telaio m.

chaste [tʃeist] adj casto, austero. **chastity** n castità f, purezza f.

chastise [tʃæs'taiz] v castigare, punire. **chastisement** n castigo (pl -ghi) m, punizione f.

chat [tʃæt] n chiacchiera f, chiacchierata f. v chiacchierare.

chatter ['tʃætə] v chiacchierare; (teeth) battere. n chiacchiera f.

chauffeur ['ʃoufə] n autista m, f.

chauvinism ['ʃouvinizəm] n sciovinismo m. **chauvinist** (m+f), adj sciovinista.

cheap [tʃiːp] adj economico, a buon mercato, poco caro; (derog) spregevole. **cheapen** v abbassare il prezzo di, screditare.

cheat [tʃiːt] n imbroglione, -a m, f, truffatore, -trice m, f; (cards) baro, -a m, f. v imbrogliare, truffare; barare. **cheating** n imbroglio m, truffa f.

check [tʃek] n controllo m, pausa f, ostacolo m; (chess) scacco m. v controllare, verificare, fermare; (chess) dare scacco. **check in** registrare all'arrivo. **check up on** informarsi su.

check [tʃek] n assegno m. **check book** n. libretto di ... gni m.

cheek [tʃiːk] n guancia f; (insolence) faccia tosta f. **cheeky** adj sfacciato, sfrontato.

cheer [tʃiə] n (shout) applauso m; (mood) allegria f, buonumore m. **cheerio!** interj ciao! arrivederci! v applaudire. **cheer up**

rallegrare, rallegrarsi. **cheerful** adj allegro, di buonumore. **cheerless** adj triste.

cheese [tʃiːz] n formaggio m. **cheesecloth** n garza f. **cheese-paring** adj tirchio.

chef [ʃef] n capocuoco (pl -chi) m.

chemical ['kemikl] n prodotto chimico m. adj chimico.

chemistry ['kemistri] n chimica f. **chemist** n chimico, -a m, f, farmacista m, f. **chemist's shop** farmacia f.

cherish ['tʃeriʃ] v tener caro, nutrire, amare.

cherry ['tʃeri] n (fruit) ciliegia f; (tree) ciliegio m.

chess [tʃes] n scacchi m pl. **chessboard** n scacchiera f.

chest [tʃest] n cassa f; (anat) petto m, torace m. **chest of drawers** cassettone m.

chestnut ['tʃesnʌt] n (fruit) castagna f; (tree) castagno m. adj castano.

chew [tʃuː] v masticare. **chew over** meditare. **chewing-gum** n chewing gum m invar, gomma da masticare f.

chicken ['tʃikin] n pollo m; (chick) pulcino m. **chicken-coop** n pollaio m. **chickenpox** n varicella f.

chicory ['tʃikəri] n cicoria f, indivia f.

chick-pea ['tʃikpiː] n cece m.

chide [tʃaid] v sgridare.

chief [tʃiːf] nm, pl -s, adj capo, principale.

chilblain ['tʃilblein] n gelone m.

child [tʃaild] n, pl children bambino, -a m, f; ragazzo, -a m, f; (offspring) figlio, -a m, f. **childbirth** n parto m. **childhood** n infanzia f. **childish** adj puerile, infantile. **childlike** adj da bambino, semplice, innocente.

chill [tʃil] v raffreddare, agghiacciare. adj freddo, gelido. n freddo m, brivido m; (illness) raffreddore m. **catch a chill** buscarsi un raffreddore. **take the chill off** intiepidire. **chilly** adj freddo, fresco, freddoloso.

chilli ['tʃili] n peperone m, pepe rosso m.

chime [tʃaim] v suonare, scampanare. n scampanio m, rintocco m.

chimney ['tʃimni] n camino m, caminetto m. **chimney-pot** n ciminiera f, fumaiolo m. **chimney-sweep** n spazzacamino m.

chimpanzee [tʃimpən'ziː] n scimpanzè m.

chin [tʃin] n mento m. **chin-strap** n sottogola m invar.

china ['tʃainə] n porcellana f, ceramica f. **china clay** caolino m.

China ['tʃainə] n Cina f. **Chinese** n(m+f), adj cinese.

chink¹ [tʃiŋk] n (fissure) fessura f, crepa f.

chink² [tʃiŋk] n (sound) tintinnio m. v tintinnare.

chip [tʃip] n scheggia f, frammento m, truciolo m; (gambling) cip (pl -s) m, gettone m. **chips** pl n (cookery) patatine fritte f pl. v scheggiare. **chip in** intervenire; (contribute money) contribuire.

chiropodist [ki'ropədist] n pedicure m, f invar.

chirp [tʃəːp] v cinguettare, pigolare. n cinguettio m, pigolio m. **chirpy** adj allegro.

chisel ['tʃizl] n cesello m, bulino m. v cesellare.

chivalry ['ʃivəlri] n galanteria f. **chivalrous** adj galante.

chive [tʃaiv] n erba cipollina f.

chlorine ['kloːriːn] n cloro m.

chlorophyll ['klorəfil] n clorofilla f.

chocolate ['tʃokələt] n cioccolato m, cioccolatino m; (drink) cioccolata f. adj cioccolato invar.

choice [tʃois] n scelta f, assortimento m. adj scelto, di prima qualità.

choir ['kwaiə] n coro m.

choke [tʃouk] v soffocare, strozzare. n (motor) valvola dell'aria f, diffusore m.

cholera [kolərə] n colera m.

*choose [tʃuːz] v scegliere, eleggere, preferire.

chop¹ [tʃop] n (meat) braciola f; (blow) colpo m. v (split) spaccare; (mince) tagliuzzare, tritare. **chop down** abbattere. **chopper** n accetta f. **chopping-block** n tagliere m. **choppy** adj mareggiato.

chop² [tʃop] v **chop and change** fare e disfare. **chop logic** cavillare.

chops [tʃops] pl n mascelle f pl. **lick one's chops** leccarsi i baffi.

chord [koːd] n corda f, accordo m.

chore [tʃoː] n (task) lavoro m, compito m. **household chores** lavori domestici m pl.

choreography [kori'ogrəfi] n coreografia f. **choreographer** n coreografo, -a m, f.

chorus ['koːrəs] n coro m. **choral** adj corale. **chorister** n corista m, f.

chose [tʃouz] V **choose**.

chosen ['tʃouzn] V **choose**.

Christ [kraist] n Cristo m.

christen ['krisn] v battezzare; (name) chiamare. **christening** n battesimo m.

Christian ['kristʃən] n, adj cristiano, -a. **Christian Democrat** democriziano, -a m, f. **Christian name** nome di battesimo m. **Christendom** n cristianesimo m. **Christianity** n cristianità f.

Christmas ['krisməs] n Natale m. adj di Natale; natalizio.

chromatic [krə'matik] adj cromatico.

chromium ['kroumiəm] n cromo m. **chromium-plate** v cromare. **chromium-plating** n cromatura f.

chromosome   ['krouməsoum]   n cromosoma m.

chronic ['kronik] adj cronico.

chronicle ['kronikl] n cronaca f. v narrare, fare la cronaca di.

chronological [kronə'lodʒikəl] adj cronologico.

chrysalis ['krisəlis] n crisalide f.

chrysanthemum   [kri'sanθəməm]   n crisantemo m.

chubby ['tʃʌbi] adj paffuto, grassoccio.

chuck [tʃʌk] v gettare, buttare. **chuck out** buttar fuori.

chuckle ['tʃʌkl] v ridacchiare, ridere di soppiatto.

chunk [tʃʌŋk] n grosso pezzo m; (food) fetta f.

church [tʃəːtʃ] n chiesa f. **church-goer** n praticante m, f. **churchyard** n cimitero m, camposanto m.

churlish ['tʃəːliʃ] adj burbero.

churn [tʃəːn] n zangola f. v agitare, sbattere.

chute [ʃuːt] n (slide) scivolo m; (waterfall) cascata f.

cider ['saidə] n sidro m.

cigar [si'gaː] n sigaro m.

cigarette [sigə'ret] n sigaretta f. **cigarette-end** n mozzicone m. **cigarette-lighter** n accendino m.

cinder ['sində] n tizzone m, cenere f. **burnt to a cinder** carbonizzato.

cine camera ['sini] n macchina da presa f.

cinema ['sinəmə] n cinema m.

cinnamon ['sinəmən] n cannella f.

circle ['səːkl] n cerchio m, circolo m; (theatre) galleria f; (environment) ambiente m. v girare attorno a, accerchiare; (aeroplane) volteggiare. **circular** adj circolare. n volantino m. **circulate** v circolare, mettere in circolazione, girare. **circulation** n (movement) circolazione f; (distribution) tiratura f.

circuit ['səːkit] *n* circuito *m*, giro *m*.
circumcise ['səːkəmsaiz] *v* circoncidere.
circumcision *n* circoncisione *f*.
circumference [sə'kʌmfərəns] *n* circonferenza *f*.
circumscribe ['səːkəmskraib] *v* circoscrivere.
circumstance ['səːkəmstəns] *n* circostanza *f*, condizione *f*. circumstantial *adj* particolareggiato. circumstantial evidence prove indiziarie indirette *f pl*.
circus ['səːkəs] *n* circo *m*; (*convergence of streets*) largo *m*.
cistern ['sistən] *n* cisterna *f*, serbatoio *m*.
cite [sait] *v* citare. citation *n* citazione *f*; (*mil*) encomio *m*.
citizen ['sitizn] *n* cittadino, -a *m, f*. citizenship *n* cittadinanza *f*.
citrus fruits ['sitrəs] *pl n* agrumi *m pl*.
city ['siti] *n* città *f*; (*business centre*) centro degli affari *m*. city hall municipio *m*.
civic ['sivik] *adj* civico, municipale.
civil ['sivl] *adj* civile; (*polite*) cortese, educato. civil engineer ingegnere civile *m*. civil engineering ingegneria civile *f*. civil servant funzionario, -a statale *m, f*. Civil Service amministrazione dello Stato *m*. civil war guerra civile *f*.
civilian [sə'viljən] *n(m+f), adj* civile, borghese. in civilian clothes in borghese.
civilization [,sivilai'zeiʃən] *n* civiltà *f*, civilizzazione *f*. civilize *v* civilizzare, incivilire. civilized *adj* civilizzato.
clad [klad] *adj* vestito.
claim [kleim] *n* (*right*) diritto *m*; (*title*) titolo *m*; (*complaint*) reclamo *m*; (*insurance*) rivendicazione *f*; asserzione *f*. *v* chiedere, esigere; rivendicare; asserire.
clairvoyant [kleə'voiənt] *n* chiaroveggente *m, f*.
clam [klam] *n* vongola *f*.
clamber ['klambə] *v* arrampicarsi.
clammy ['klami] *adj* viscido.
clamour ['klamə] *n* clamore *m*, schiamazzo *m*. *v* strepitare, vociferare. clamorous *adj* clamoroso, strepitoso.
clamp [klamp] *n* morsa *f*, morsetto *m*. *v* tener fermo, stringere. clamp down on far smettere.
clan [klan] *n* tribù *f*, famiglia *f*. clannish *adj* imbevuto di spirito di parte.
clandestine [klan'destin] *adj* clandestino.
clang [klaŋ] *n* suono metallico *m*, strepito *m*. *v* strepitare.

clap [klap] *n* (*blow, noise*) colpo *m*, scoppio *m*; applauso *m*, battimano *m*. *v* applaudire. clap hands battere le mani. clap into prison sbattere in prigione. clapper *n* (*bell*) battaglio *m*. claptrap *n* sproloquio *m*.
claret ['klarət] *n* chiaretto *m*.
clarify ['klarəfai] *v* chiarire, raffinare.
clarinet [klarə'net] *n* clarinetto *m*. clarinettist *n* clarinettista *m, f*.
clash [klaʃ] *n* (*noise*) strepito *m*; (*collision*) urto *m*; (*conflict*) scontro *m*, contrasto *m*; (*colours, sounds*) stonatura *f*. *v* urtare, urtarsi; scontrarsi; stonare.
clasp [klaːsp] *n* (*device*) fermaglio *m*; (*grasp*) stretta *f*; (*embrace*) abbraccio *m*. clasp-knife *n* coltello a serramanico *m*. *v* agganciare, stringere, abbracciare.
class [klaːs] *n* classe *f*, categoria *f*, qualità *f*. class-mate *n* compagno, -a di classe *m, f*. classroom *n* aula *f*. *v* also classify classificare. classy *adj* di classe.
classic ['klasik] *nm, adj* classico.
clatter ['klatə] *n* fracasso *m*. *v* far fracasso.
clause [klɔːz] *n* clausola *f*, proposizione *f*, articolo *m*.
claustrophobia [klɔːstrə'foubiə] *n* claustrofobia *f*. claustrophobic *adj* claustrofobico.
claw [klɔː] *n* artiglio *m*; (*tool*) raffio *m*. *v* (*seize*) aggraffare; (*scratch*) graffiare.
clay [klei] *n* argilla *f*, creta *f*.
clean [kliːn] *adj* pulito, nitido. clean-shaven *adj* sbarbato. make a clean breast confessare tutto. *v* pulire; (*remove stains*) smacchiare. cleanliness *n* pulizia *f*, nettezza *f*.
cleanse [klenz] *v* pulire, depurare.
clear [kliə] *adj* chiaro, limpido; ovvio; libero. keep clear of tenersi lontano da. *v* chiarire, chiarificare; (*empty*) vuotare; (*overcome*) superare; (*law*) assolvere; (*comm*) sdoganare. clear away portar via; (*table*) sparecchiare. clear off andarsene. clear up chiarire, mettere in chiaro; (*weather*) rasserenarsi; (*tidy*) rassettare. clearance *n* (*customs*) sdoganamento *m*; (*sale*) liquidazione *f*; (*distance*) gioco *m*. clearing *n* (*land*) radura *f*; (*bank*) clearing *m*; (*emptying*) sgombro *m*.
clef [klef] *n* chiave *f*.
clench [klentʃ] *v* stringere. with clenched fists a pugni stretti.

clergy ['klɔːdʒi] n clero m. **clergyman** n ecclesiastico m, pastore m, prete m.

clerical ['klerikəl] adj (church) clericale; (office) d'ufficio, impiegatizio. **clerical error** n errore materiale m, errore di trascrizione m.

clerk [klaːk] n impiegato, -a m, f; commesso, -a m, f.

clever ['klevə] adj abile, ingegnoso, bravo. **cleverness** n abilità f, ingegnosità f, intelligenza f.

cliché ['kliːʃei] n espressione stereotipata f, frase fatta f.

click [klik] n scatto m, schiocco m. v scattare, schioccare.

client ['klaiənt] n cliente m, f.

cliff [klif] n scoglio m.

climate ['klaimət] n clima m.

climax ['klaimaks] n apice m, apogeo m.

climb [klaim] v scalare, salire, arrampicarsi. n scalata f, salita f. **climb down** scendere; (withdraw) tirarsi indietro. **climb over** scavalcare.

****cling** [kliŋ] v aggrapparsi, aderire.

clinic ['klinik] n clinica f, ambulatorio m. **clinical** adj clinico.

clip¹ [klip] n (cut) taglio m; (slap) scappellotto m. v tagliare, tosare. **clip the wings of** tarpare le ali a.

clip² [klip] n (fastener) fermaglio m, graffa f.

clipper ['klipə] n (boat) clipper m, goletta f.

clitoris ['klitəris] n clitoride f.

cloak [klouk] n (garment) mantello m, cappa f; (mask) maschera f; (pretext) pretesto m, scusa f. v (conceal) celare. **cloak and dagger** cappa e spada. **cloakroom** n guardaroba m.

clock [klɔk] n orologio m. **clockmaker** n orologiaio m. **clockwork** n meccanismo d'orologeria m. **clockwise** adv in senso orario.

clog [klɔg] n (shoe) zoccolo m. v intasare.

cloister ['klɔistə] n chiostro m. v rinchiudere in convento.

close¹ [klouz] v chiudere, concludere. **close down** (shop) chiudere bottega. **close ranks** serrare le file. n (end) fine f.

close² [klous] n (place) recinto m. adj vicino, stretto; (intimate) intimo. **close by** vicino.

closet ['klɔzit] n gabinetto m, studio m. v rinchiudere.

clot [klɔt] n grumo m, coagulo m; (coll) scemo, -a m, f. v raggrumare, coagulare,

coagularsi, rapprendersi. **clotted cream** panna rappresa f.

cloth [klɔθ] n panno m, stoffa f, tessuto m; (for dishes) strofinaccio m.

clothe [klouð] v vestire, abbigliare; (dress) vestirsi. **clothes** pl n vestiti m pl, abiti m pl, indumenti m pl. **clothes line** corda per il bucato f. **clothes peg** molletta f. **clothing** n vestiario m, abbigliamento m.

cloud [klaud] n nuvola f. **cloudburst** n acquazzone m. v annuvolare; (obscure) offuscare. **cloud over** annuvolarsi. **cloudy** adj nuvoloso; (liquid) torbido.

clove¹ [klouv] n (plant) garofano m; (spice) chiodo di garofano m.

clove² [klouv] n (part of bulb) spicchio m.

clover ['klouvə] n trifoglio m.

clown [klaun] n pagliaccio m, buffone, -a m, f. v fare il pagliaccio. **clownery** n pagliacciata f. **clownish** adj pagliaccesco.

club [klʌb] n (stick) mazza f, randello m; (golf) bastone da golf m; (social) circolo m, club m; (cards) fiore m. v picchiare, bastonare. **club together** associarsi, riunirsi.

clue [kluː] n indizio m, chiave f.

clump [klʌmp] n gruppo m, cespo m.

clumsy ['klʌmzi] adj maldestro, goffo. **clumsiness** n goffaggine f, malaccortezza f.

clung [klʌŋ] V **cling**.

cluster ['klʌstə] n gruppo m; (bunch) grappolo m.

clutch [klʌtʃ] n presa f; (mot) frizione f. **fall into the clutches of** cadere nelle grinfie di. v afferrare, aggrapparsi a.

clutter ['klʌtə] n ingombro m, confusione f. v ingombrare.

coach [koutʃ] n carrozza f; (bus) corriera f, torpedone m; (tutor) ripetitore, -trice m, f; (sport) allenatore, -trice m, f. **coachbuilder** n carrozziere m. **coachwork** n carrozzeria f. v (teach) dare lezioni private; (sport) allenare.

coagulate [kou'agjuleit] v coagulare, coagularsi, accagliarsi. **coagulant** n coagulante m.

coal [koul] n carbone m. **coal-tar** n catrame m. **coalmine** n miniera di carbone f.

coalition [kouə'liʃən] n coalizione f.

coarse [kɔːs] adj (rude) grossolano, rozzo; (rough) ruvido. **coarseness** n volgarità f, ruvidezza f.

coast [koust] *n* costa *f*, litorale *m*. *v* (*cycling*) scendere a ruota libera; (*motoring*) andare in folle. **coastal** *adj* costiero.

coat [kout] *n* soprabito *m*, cappotto *m*; (*jacket*) giacca *f*; (*animal*) pelame *m*, pelliccia *f*; (*paint*) mano *f*. **coat-hanger** *n* attaccapanni *m*. **coat-of-arms** *n* stemma *m*. **coating** *n* rivestimento *m*. *v* coprire, rivestire.

coax [kouks] *v* blandire, lusingare.

cobbler ['koblə] *n* ciabattino *m*, calzolaio *m*.

cobra ['koubrə] *n* cobra *m*.

cobweb ['kobweb] *n* ragnatela *f*.

cocaine [kə'kein] *n* cocaina *f*.

cock[1] [kok] *n* (*male bird*) uccello maschio *m*; (*chicken*) gallo *m*; (*tap*) rubinetto *m*; (*gun*) cane *m*; (*vulgar*) cazzo *m*. **cocky** *adj* impertinente, pieno di sè.

cock[2] [kok] *v* (*gun*) armare; (*ears*) drizzare. **cock a snook** fare maramco.

cockle ['kokl] *n* cardio *m*, cockle-shell *n* conchiglia *f*.

cockpit ['kokpit] *n* (*plane*) carlinga *f*, cabina di guida *f*; (*naval*) cassero *m*.

cockroach ['kokroutʃ] *n* scarafaggio *m*.

cocktail ['kokteil] *n* cocktail *m*.

cocoa ['koukou] *n* cacao *m*.

coconut ['koukənʌt] *n* noce di cocco *f*.

cocoon [kə'kuːn] *n* bozzolo *m*.

cod [kod] *n* merluzzo *m*. **cod-liver oil** olio di fegato di merluzzo *m*.

code [koud] *n* cifrario *m*, codice *m*.

codeine ['koudiːn] *n* codeina *f*.

coeducation [kouedjuˈkeiʃən] *n* scuola mista *f*.

coerce [kouˈəːs] *v* costringere, forzare.

coexist [kouigˈzist] *v* coesistere. **coexistence** *n* coesistenza *f*.

coffee ['kofi] *n* caffè *m*. **coffee bean** chicco di caffè *m*. **coffee pot** caffettiera *f*.

coffin ['kofin] *n* cassa da morto *f*, bara *f*, feretro *m*.

cog [kog] *n* dente *m*.

cohabit [kouˈhabit] *v* coabitare.

coherent [kouˈhiərənt] *adj* coerente. **cohesion** *n* coesione *f*.

coil [koil] *n* rotolo *m*, bobina *f*. *v* avvolgere, attorcigliare, ravvolgere.

coin [koin] *n* moneta *f*.

coincide [kouinˈsaid] *v* coincidere. **coincidence** *n* coincidenza *f*.

colander ['koləndə] *n* colabrodo *m*, colino *m*.

cold [kould] *adj* freddo, gelido; (*unfriendly*) riservato. **be cold** (*person*) aver freddo; (*weather*) far freddo. *n* freddo *m*; (*illness*) raffreddore *m*. **catch a cold** prendere un raffreddore, raffreddarsi. **have a cold** essere raffreddato.

colic ['kolik] *n* colica *f*.

collaborate [kəˈlabəreit] *v* collaborare. **collaboration** *n* collaborazione *f*. **collaborator** *n* collaboratore, -trice *m*, *f*.

collapse [kəˈlaps] *v* crollare, afflosciarsi. *n* crollo *m*, collasso *m*, rovina *f*.

collar ['kolə] *n* colletto *m*, bavero *m*; (*animal*) collare *m*; (*mech*) manicotto *m*. *v* afferrare per il collo; (*take possession*) appropriarsi di.

colleague ['koliːg] *n* collega *m pl* -ghi) *m*, *f*.

collect [kəˈlekt] *v* raccogliere, riunire; (*take delivery*) prendere in consegna, ricuperare; (*make collection of*) far collezione di; (*meet*) radunarsi. **collect call** *n* (*US*) chiamata rovesciata *f*. **collected** *adj* calmo, padrone di sè. **collection** *n* collezione *f*, raccolta *f*; (*charity*) colletta *f*. **collective** *adj* collettivo. **collector** *n* collezionista *m*, *f*.

college [ˈkolidʒ] *n* collegio *m*, istituto *m*, università *f*.

collide [kəˈlaid] *v* scontrarsi, investire. **collision** *n* urto *m*, scontro *m*, investimento *m*.

colloid ['koloid] *n* colloide *m*.

colloquial [kəˈloukwiəl] *adj* familiare. **colloquialism** *n* espressione familiare *f*.

colon ['koulon] *n* (*biol*) colon *m invar*; (*gramm*) due punti.

colonel ['kəːnl] *n* colonnello *m*.

colonnade [kolə'neid] *n* colonnata *f*, portico *m*.

colony ['koloni] *n* colonia *f*. **colonial** *n*, *adj* coloniale. **colonize** *v* colonizzare.

colossal [kə'losəl] *adj* colossale, enorme.

colour ['kʌlə] *n* colore *m*, tinta *f*. **colour bar** discriminazione razziale *f*. **colourblind** *adj* daltonico. *v* colorare, tingere, colorire. **coloured** *adj* colorato, colorito, a colori; (*person*) di colore. **colourful** *adj* pittoresco, a tinte vivaci. **colouring** *n* colorito *m*.

colt [koult] *n* puledro *m*.

column ['koləm] *n* colonna *f*; (*newspaper*) rubrica *f*, cronaca *f*. **columnist** *n* cronista *m*, *f*, giornalista *m*, *f*.

coma ['koumə] n coma m invar.

comb [koum] n pettine m; (horse) striglia f; (birds) cresta f. v pettinare, strigliare. comb one's hair pettinarsi.

combat ['kombat] n combattimento m, lotta f. v combattere, lottare. combatant n combattente m, f.

combine [kəm'bain] n 'kombain] v combinare, unire, abbinare, combinarsi. n associazione f, consorzio m. combine-harvester n mietitrebbiatrice f. combination n combinazione f.

combustion [kəm'bʌstʃən] n combustione f. internal combustion engine motore a combustione interna m.

*come [kʌm] v venire, arrivare, giungere. come about accadere. come across incontrare per caso, trovare per caso. come in entrare. come into force entrare in vigore. come off (succeed) riuscire. come to blows venire alle mani. come to light venire alla luce. come up salire; (to the surface) venire a galla.

comedy ['komədi] n commedia f. comedian n commediante m, f, comico, -a m, f.

comet ['komit] n cometa f.

comfort ['kʌmfət] n agio m, conforto m, consolazione f, agiatezza f. v consolare, confortare.

comic ['komik] n comico, -a m, f; (periodical) giornaletto a fumetti m. adj comico. comic opera opera buffa f. comic strip fumetto m. comical adj comico.

comma ['komə] n virgola f. in inverted commas fra virgolette.

command [kə'maind] n comando m, ordine m. v comandare; (mil) ordinare, avere il comando di. commander n comandante m, capo m. commanding position posizione dominante f. commandment n comandamento m, precetto m.

commandeer [komən'diə] v requisire.

commando [kə'maindou] n truppe d'assalto f pl, commando m invar.

commemorate [kə'meməreit] v commemorare. commemoration n commemorazione f.

commence [kə'mens] v cominciare, iniziare. commencement n inizio m, principio m.

commend [kə'mend] v raccomandare, lodare. commendable adj lodevole, encomiabile. commendation n lode f, encomio m.

comment ['koment] n commento m, osservazione f, rilievo m. v commentare, fare delle osservazioni. commentary n commentario m, cronaca f. commentator n commentatore, -trice m, f; cronista m, f; radiocronista m, f.

commerce ['komɔis] n commercio m, scambi m pl. commercial adj commerciale.

commiserate [kə'mizəreit] v commiserare, compiangere.

commission [kə'miʃən] n commissione f, delegazione f; (authority) incarico m; (comm) provvigione f; (mil) brevetto da ufficiale m. v incaricare, dare una carica; nominare ufficiale; (ship) armare. commissionaire n portiere m. commissioned officer ufficiale m. non-commissioned officer sottufficiale m. commissioner n commissario m.

commit [kə'mit] v commettere; affidare, rimettere. commit oneself impegnarsi. commit to memory imparare a memoria. commitment n impegno m. committed adj impegnato.

committee [kə'miti] n comitato m, commissione f.

commodity [kə'modəti] n merce f, derrata f.

common ['komən] adj comune, ordinario, volgare. n parco demaniale m. commonplace adj ordinario, banale. common sense buonsenso m.

commotion [kə'mouʃən] n agitazione f, confusione f.

commune[1] [kə'mjuin] v intrattenersi, discutere.

commune[2] ['komjuin] n comune m, comunità f. communal adj comunale, in comune.

communicate [kə'mjumikeit] v comunicare, informare, trasmettere. communicate with essere in comunicazione con. communication n comunicazione f, informazione f, rapporto m.

communion [kə'mjuinjən] n comunione f.

communism ['komjunizəm] n comunismo m. communist n(m+f), adj comunista.

community [kə'mjuinəti] n comunità f.

commute [kə'mjuit] v commutare; (travel) fare il pendolare. commuter n pendolare m, f.

compact[1] [kəm'pakt; n 'kompakt] adj compatto, serrato. n (powder) portacipria m invar.

compact[2] [ˈkɒmpakt] n (agreement) patto m, accordo m.

companion [kəmˈpanjən] n compagno, -a m, f. companionship n compagnia f, cameratismo m, amicizia f.

company [ˈkʌmpəni] n compagnia f, comitiva f; (comm) ditta f, società f; (ship) equipaggio m. in the company of accompagnato da. part company with separarsi da.

compare [kəmˈpeə] v paragonare, confrontare, essere paragonabile a. comparable adj paragonabile, comparabile. comparative adj comparativo, relativo. compared with rispetto a, di fronte a. comparison n confronto m, paragone m.

compartment [kəmˈpɑːtmənt] n compartimento m, casella f; (railway) scompartimento m.

compass [ˈkʌmpəs] n bussola f. compasses pl n compasso m sing. v cingere, circondare.

compassion [kəmˈpaʃən] n compassione f, pietà f, misericordia f. compassionate adj misericordioso, pieno di compassione.

compatible [kəmˈpatəbl] adj compatibile. compatibility n compatibilità f.

compel [kəmˈpel] v costringere, obbligare, forzare. compel respect farsi rispettare. compelling adj irresistibile.

compensate [ˈkɒmpənseit] v compensare, ricompensare, indennizzare. compensation n compenso m, ricompensa f; (comm) compensazione f.

compete [kəmˈpiːt] v concorrere, fare concorrenza a, gareggiare. competition n (contest) gara f; (rivalry) concorrenza f; (exam) concorso m. competitive adj competitivo. competitor n concorrente m, f; rivale m, f.

competent [ˈkɒmpətənt] adj competente, capace. competence n competenza f, capacità f.

compile [kəmˈpail] v compilare. compilation n compilazione f.

complacent [kəmˈpleisnt] adj soddisfatto di sè.

complain [kəmˈplein] v lamentarsi, lagnarsi. complaint n (discontent) lamentela f; (merchandise) reclamo m; (illness) malattia f.

complement [ˈkɒmpləmənt] n complemento m. v completare, fare da complemento a. complementary adj complementare.

complete [kəmˈpliːt] adj completo, intero. v completare, finire. completion n fine f, compimento m.

complex [ˈkɒmpleks] nm, adj complesso.

complexion [kəmˈplekʃən] n (skin) colorito m; (nature) aspetto m.

complicate [ˈkɒmplikeit] v complicare. complicated adj complicato, complesso. complication n difficoltà f.

complicity [kəmˈplisəti] n complicità f.

compliment [ˈkɒmpləmənt] n complimento m. v congratularsi con. complimentary adj (flattering) lusinghiero; (free) di favore.

comply [kəmˈplai] v ubbidire, acconsentire. in compliance with conforme a.

component [kəmˈpounənt] nm, adj componente.

compose [kəmˈpouz] v comporre. composed adj calmo. composer n compositore, -trice m, f. composite adj composto, misto. composition n composizione f.

compost [ˈkɒmpost] n concime m.

composure [kəmˈpouʒə] n compostezza f, calma f.

compound[1] [kəmˈpaund] v (compose) comporre; (mix) mescolare; (settle) regolare. n composto m, miscela f. adj composto.

compound[2] [ˈkɒmpaund] n (enclosure) campo m, accampamento m.

comprehend [kɒmpriˈhend] v comprendere, capire. comprehensible adj comprensibile. comprehension n comprensione f. comprehensive adj comprensivo, esauriente.

compress [kəmˈpres; n ˈkɒmpres] v comprimere. n compressa f. compression n compressione f.

comprise [kəmˈpraiz] v includere.

compromise [ˈkɒmprəmaiz] n compromesso m. v giungere a un compromesso; (endanger) compromettere. compromising adj compromettente, imbarazzante.

compulsion [kəmˈpʌlʃən] n costrizione f, obbligo m. compulsive adj coercitivo. compulsory adj obbligatorio.

compunction [kəmˈpʌŋkʃən] n rimorso m.

computer [kəmˈpjuːtə] n computer (pl -s) m, elaboratore elettronico m.

comrade [ˈkɒmrid] n compagno, -a m, f; camerata m, f. comradeship n cameratismo m.

concave [konˈkeiv] adj concavo.

conceal [kənˈsiːl] v celare, nascondere.

concede [kənˈsiːd] v concedere, ammettere, riconoscere.

conceit [kənˈsiːt] n vanità f, presunzione f. **conceited** adj vanitoso, presuntuoso.

conceive [kənˈsiːv] v concepire; immaginare. **conceivable** adj concepibile, immaginabile.

concentrate [ˈkonsəntreit] v concentrare. n concentrato m. **concentration** n concentrazione f. **concentration camp** campo di concentramento m.

concentric [kənˈsentrik] adj concentrico.

concept [ˈkonsept] n concetto m, nozione f.

conception [kənˈsepʃən] n concezione f, idea f.

concern [kənˈsɜːn] n (care) sollecitudine f, preoccupazione f; (business) affare m, faccenda f; interesse m; (firm) azienda f, ditta f. v riguardare, toccare. **concerned** adj in questione; (anxious) preoccupato. **concerning** prep riguardo a, in merito a, inerente a.

concert [ˈkonsət] n concerto m. **concerted** adj predisposto, stabilito d'accordo con altri.

concertina [konsəˈtiːnə] n fisarmonica f.

concerto [kənˈtʃɜːtou] n concerto m.

concession [kənˈseʃən] n concessione f.

conciliate [kənˈsilieit] v conciliare. **conciliation** n conciliazione f. **conciliatory** adj conciliatorio.

concise [kənˈsais] adj conciso, breve.

conclude [kənˈkluːd] v concludere, dedurre. **conclusion** n conclusione f, fine f. **in conclusion** adv in fine, insomma. **conclusive** adj conclusivo.

concoct [kənˈkokt] v (contrive) inventare. **concoction** n intruglio m, pasticcio m.

concrete [ˈkonkriːt] adj concreto. n calcestruzzo m, cemento m. **concrete mixer** betoniera f. **reinforced concrete** cemento armato m. v cementare, rivestire di calcestruzzo.

concussion [kənˈkʌʃən] n commozione cerebrale f.

condemn [kənˈdem] v condannare. **condemnation** n condanna f.

condense [kənˈdens] v condensare. **condensation** n condensazione f.

condescend [kondiˈsend] v degnarsi. **condescending** adj condiscendente. **condescension** n condiscendenza f.

condition [kənˈdiʃən] n condizione f. v condizionare. **conditional** adj condizionale.

condolence [kənˈdoulens] n condoglianza f. **express condolences** fare le condoglianze.

condom [ˈkondom] n preservativo m.

condone [kənˈdoun] v perdonare.

conducive [kənˈdjuːsiv] adj contribuente.

conduct [kənˈdʌkt; n ˈkondʌkt] v condurre; (music) dirigere. **conduct oneself** comportarsi. n condotta f, comportamento m.

conductor [kənˈdʌktə] n (transport) biglettario, -a m, f; (music) direttore d'orchestra m; (physics) conduttore m.

cone [koun] n cono m; (fir) pigna f.

confectioner [kənˈfekʃənə] n pasticciere, -a m, f. **confectioner's shop** n pasticceria f.

confederate [kənˈfedərət] adj confederato, alleato. v confederarsi, allearsi.

confer [kənˈfɜː] v conferire, consultarsi. **conference** n conferenza f. **conferment** n conferimento m.

confess [kənˈfes] v confessare, ammettere; (rel) confessarsi. **confession** n confessione f, professione f. **confessor** n confessore m.

confetti [kənˈfeti] n coriandoli m pl.

confide [kənˈfaid] v confidare. **confidant**, -e n confidente m, f. **confidence** n fiducia f; sicurezza di sè f. **have confidence in** aver fiducia in. **in confidence** in confidenza. **confident** adj fiducioso, sicuro. **confidential** adj riservato.

confine [kənˈfain] n confine m. v relegare; (to barracks) consegnare. **be confined** (childbirth) partorire. **confinement** n imprigionamento m, segregazione f; (childbirth) parto m.

confirm [kənˈfɜːm] v confermare; (statement) ribadire; (rel) cresimare; (law) omologare. **confirmation** n conferma f; (law) ratifica f; (rel) confermazione f, cresima f. **confirmed** adj confermato; (belief) convinto, impenitente.

confiscate [ˈkonfiskeit] v confiscare.

conflict [ˈkonflikt; v kənˈflikt] n conflitto m, lotta f, contrasto m. v conflict with essere in disaccordo or contrasto con. **conflicting** adj (evidence) contraddittorio; (interests) contrastante.

conform [kən'fɔːm] v conformare, adattarsi. **conformist** n conformista m, f. **conformity** n conformità f. **in conformity with** conforme a, conformemente a.

confound [kən'faund] v sconcertare, sconvolgere.

confront [kən'frʌnt] v affrontare; (law) mettere a confronto. **confrontation** n confronto m.

confuse [kən'fjuːz] v confondere, sconcertare, disorientare, scambiare. **confusing** adj sconcertante, che rende perplesso. **confusion** n confusione f, disordine m.

congeal [kən'dʒiːl] v (freeze) congelare, congelarsi; coagulare, coagularsi.

congenial [kən'dʒiːniəl] adj congeniale.

congenital [kən'dʒenitl] adj congenito, innato.

congested [kən'dʒestid] adj congestionato. **congestion** n congestione f.

conglomeration [kənˌglɒmə'reiʃən] n conglomerazione f.

congratulate [kən'grætjuleit] v congratularsi con, felicitare, felicitarsi con. **congratulation** n felicitazione f. **congratulations!** interj auguri!

congregate ['kɒŋgrigeit] v congregare, riunirsi. **congregation** n (rel) comunità f, adunanza dei fedeli f.

congress ['kɒŋgres] n congresso m.

conical ['kɒnikəl] adj conico.

conifer ['kɒnifə] n conifera f.

conjecture [kən'dʒektʃə] v supporre. n supposizione f.

conjugal ['kɒndʒugəl] adj coniugale.

conjugate ['kɒndʒugeit] v coniugare. **conjugation** n coniugazione f.

conjunction [kən'dʒʌŋkʃən] n congiunzione f.

conjunctivitis [kənˌdʒʌŋkti'vaitis] n congiuntivite f.

conjure [kʌndʒə; (invoke) kən'dʒuə] v fare giochi di prestigio; (invoke) scongiurare. **conjure up** evocare. **conjurer** n prestigiatore, -trice m, f. **conjuring trick** gioco di prestigio m.

connect [kə'nekt] v connettere, congiungere; associare; (trains) far coincidenza. **connection** n connessione f, rapporto m; coincidenza f. **in connection with** in merito a.

connoisseur [kɒnə'səː] n intenditore, -trice m, f.

connotation [kɒnə'teiʃən] n significato implicito m.

conquer ['kɒŋkə] v conquistare, vincere. **conqueror** n conquistatore, -trice m, f; vincitore, -trice m, f. **conquest** n conquista f, vittoria f.

conscience ['kɒnʃəns] n coscienza f.

conscientious [kɒnʃi'enʃəs] adj coscienzioso, diligente. **conscientious objector** obiettore di coscienza m.

conscious ['kɒnʃəs] adj conscio, cosciente; (deliberate) intenzionale. **consciousness** n coscienza f.

conscript ['kɒnskript] v chiamare alle armi, arruolare. n soldato di leva m. **conscription** n leva f.

consecrate ['kɒnsikreit] v consacrare. **consecration** n consacrazione f.

consecutive [kən'sekjutiv] adj consecutivo.

consensus [kən'sensəs] n consenso m, assenso m.

consent [kən'sent] v consentire, acconsentire. n consenso m, benestare m, accordo m.

consequence ['kɒnsikwəns] n conseguenza f, effetto m, importanza f. **consequently** adv di conseguenza, quindi, perciò.

conserve [kən'səːv] v conservare, preservare. n conserva f. **conservation** n preservazione f. **conservative** adj conservativo, cauto; (pol) conservatore. **conservatoire** n (music) conservatorio m. **conservatory** n serra f.

consider [kən'sidə] v considerare, giudicare, ritenere, pensare. **considerable** adj notevole. **considerate** adj sollecito, riguardoso. **consideration** n considerazione f, riflessione f; (feeling, regard) riguardo m, sollecitudine f, delicatezza f.

consign [kən'sain] v consegnare, affidare. **consignee** n destinatario, -a m, f. **consignor** n mittente m, f. **consignment** n spedizione f, invio m; (goods) partita di merce f.

consist [kən'sist] v consistere (in), essere composto. **consistency** n consistenza f. **consistent** adj regolare, costante, coerente.

console[1] [kən'soul] v confortare. **consolation** n consolazione f, conforto m.

console[2] ['kɒnsoul] n (arch) mensola f; (furniture) mobile m; (tech) quadro di comando m.

consolidate [kən'sɔlideit] v consolidare. **consolidation** n consolidazione f.

consommé [kən'sɔmei] n brodo m.

consonant ['kɔnsənənt] n consonante f.

consortium [kən'sɔttiəm] n consorzio m.

conspicuous [kən'spikjuəs] adj cospicuo, evidente.

conspire [kən'spaiə] v complottare. **conspiracy** n complotto m, congiura f.

constable ['kʌnstəbl] n vigile m, poliziotto m.

constant ['kɔnstənt] adj costante, invariabile. n costante f.

constellation [kɔnstə'leiʃən] n costellazione f.

constipation [kɔnsti'peiʃən] n stitichezza f. **constipated** adj stitico.

constitute ['kɔnstitjuːt] v costituire, creare. **constituent** nf, adj costituente. **constituency** n collegio elettorale m. **constitution** n costituzione f; statuto m; (health) salute f.

constraint [kən'streint] n (restriction) costrizione f; (embarrassment) imbarazzo m.

constrict [kən'strikt] v stringere, restringere, comprimere. **constriction** n restringimento m; (tight feeling) oppressione f.

construct [kən'strʌkt] v costruire. **construction** n costruzione f; (building) edificio m; (meaning) senso m. **constructive** adj costruttivo, positivo.

consul ['kɔnsəl] n console. **consulate** n consolato m.

consult [kən'sʌlt] v consultare; (consider) tener conto di. **consultant** n consulente m, f, esperto, -a m, f. **consultation** n consultazione f; (med) consulta f. **consulting room** (med) studio m.

consume [kən'sjuːm] v consumare. **consumer** n consumatore, -trice m, f. **consumer goods** generi di consumo m pl.

contact ['kɔntakt] n contatto m; (acquaintance) conoscenza f. v mettere in contatto con, mettersi in contatto. **contact lens** n lente a contatto f.

contagious [kən'teidʒəs] adj contagioso.

contain [kən'tein] v contenere, includere. **container** n recipiente m.

contaminate [kən'tamineit] v contaminare, inquinare. **contamination** n contaminazione f, inquinamento m.

contemplate ['kɔntəmpleit] v contemplare, meditare; (intend to) proporsi,

aver intenzione di. **contemplation** n contemplazione f.

contemporary [kən'tempərəri] n, adj contemporaneo, -a; coetaneo, -a.

contempt [kən'tempt] n disprezzo m. **contempt of court** oltraggio alla corte m. **contemptible** adj spregevole. **contemptuous** adj sprezzante, altezzoso.

contend [kən'tend] v contendere, sostenere, affermare. **bone of contention** pomo della discordia m.

content¹ [kən'tent] n contenuto m.

content² [kən'tent] adj contento, soddisfatto. v accontentare.

contest ['kɔntest; v kən'test] n gara f, lotta f. v contestare, impugnare.

context ['kɔntekst] n contesto m.

continent ['kɔntinənt] nm, adj continente. **continental** adj continentale.

contingency [kən'tindʒənsi] n contingenza f.

continue [kən'tinjuː] v continuare, proseguire. **continual** or **continuous** adj continuo, ininterrotto. **continuation** n seguito m. **continuity** n continuità f; (film) sceneggiatura f.

contort [kən'tɔtt] v contorcere. **contortion** n contorcimento m. **contortionist** n contorsionista m, f.

contour ['kɔntuə] n contorno m. **contour map/line** carta/curva ipsometrica f.

contraband ['kɔntrəband] n contrabbando m.

contraception [kɔntrə'sepʃən] n pratiche antifecondative f pl. **contraceptive** nm, adj anticoncezionale, anticoncettivo, antifecondativo.

contract ['kɔntrakt; v kən'trakt] n patto m, accordo m, contratto m. v (draw together) contrarre, restringere; (acquire, take on) contrarre; (enter into) contrattare. **contraction** n contrazione f.

contradict [kɔntrə'dikt] v contraddire, smentire. **contradiction** n contraddizione f, smentita f.

contralto [kən'traltou] n contralto m.

contraption [kən'trapʃən] n congegno m, aggeggio m.

contrary ['kɔntrəri] nm, adj contrario, opposto. **contrary to** contrariamente a. **on the contrary** al contrario, anzi.

contrast ['kɔntraist; v kən'traist] n contrasto m, antitesi f invar. v contrastare, confrontare, mettere in contrasto.

contravene [kɔntrə'viːn] v contravvenire a.

contribute [kən'tribjut] v contribuire. **contributor** n contributore, -trice m, f; (writer) collaboratore, -trice m, f. **contribution** n contributo m; (writing) articolo m.

contrive [kən'traiv] v riuscire a, escogitare.

control [kən'troul] v controllare, dominare. n controllo m, autorità f. **controls** pl n comandi pl m. **remote control** controllo a distanza m, telecontrollo m.

controversy [kən'trɔvəsi] n controversia f. **controversial** adj controverso.

convalesce [kɔnvə'les] v rimettersi in salute. **convalescence** n convalescenza f. **convalescent home** convalescenziario m.

convector [kən'vektə] nm, adj convettore.

convenience [kən'viːnjəns] n comodo m, comodità f, convenienza f. **at the earliest convenience** alla prima occasione. **public convenience** gabinetto pubblico m. **convenient** adj conveniente, comodo.

convent ['kɔnvənt] n convento m.

convention [kən'venʃən] n convenzione f; (meeting) adunata f; (agreement) accordo m. **convene** v convocare, adunare. **conventional** adj convenzionale.

converge [kən'vɔːdʒ] v convergere.

converse [kən'vɔːs; n, adj 'kɔnvɔːs] v versare. nm, adj contrario, opposto. **conversation** n conversazione f.

convert [kən'vɔːt; n 'kɔnvɔːt] v convertire, trasformare. n convertito, -a m, f. **convertible** n (car) auto decapottabile f.

convex [kɔn'veks] adj convesso.

convey [kən'vei] v trasportare; (impart) esprimere. **conveyance** n mezzo di trasporto m; (law) atto di cessione m. **conveyor belt** nastro trasportatore m.

convict [kən'vikt; n 'kɔnvikt] v condannare. n carcerato, -a m, f; prigioniero, -a m, f.

conviction [kən'vikʃən] n (sentence) condanna f; persuasione f, convinzione f.

convince [kən'vins] v convincere, persuadere.

convivial [kən'viviəl] adj allegro.

convoy [kən'vɔi] n convoglio m, scorta f. v convogliare, scortare.

convulsion [kən'vʌlʃən] n convulsione f. v **be convulsed (with laughter)** contorcersi (dalle risa).

cook [kuk] n cuoco, -a m, f. v cuocere,

cucinare, far la cucina. **cook the books** falsificare i registri. **cooker** n fornello m. **cookery** or **cooking** n cucina f, arte culinaria f.

cool [kuːl] adj fresco, calmo. v rinfrescare, raffreddare. **cooler** n refrigerante m; (slang) gattabuia f.

coop [kuːp] n stia f. v **coop up** stipare, pigiarsi.

cooperate [kou'ɔpəreit] v cooperare. **cooperation** n cooperazione f, collaborazione f. **cooperative** adj cooperativo. **cooperator** n collaboratore, -trice m, f.

coordinate [kou'ɔːdineit] v coordinare. n coordinata f. adj coordinato. **coordination** n coordinazione f.

cop [kɔp] n (slang) poliziotto m. v pescare. **cop it** prenderle.

cope¹ [koup] v riuscire. **cope with** far fronte a.

cope² [koup] n cappa f.

Copenhagen [koupən'heigən] n Copenhagen f.

copious ['koupiəs] adj abbondante.

copper¹ ['kɔpə] n rame m. adj color rame.

copper² ['kɔpə] n (slang) poliziotto m.

copulate ['kɔpjuleit] v accoppiarsi. **copulation** n accoppiamento m, copulazione f.

copy ['kɔpi] v copiare; ricopiare, riprodurre; imitare. n copia f, trascrizione f, imitazione f; (book) esemplare m. **copyright** n diritti d'autore m pl.

coral ['kɔrəl] n corallo m.

cord [kɔːd] n corda f; (string) spago m; (elec) filo m, cavo m.

cordial ['kɔːdiəl] adj cordiale, caloroso.

cordon ['kɔːdn] n cordone m. **cordon off** fare cordone intorno a, isolare.

corduroy ['kɔːdərɔi] n fustagno m.

core [kɔː] n centro m; (fruit) torsolo m; (mech) anima f.

cork [kɔːk] n (bark) sughero m; (stopper) tappo m, turacciolo m. **corkscrew** n cavatappi m invar. v turare. **corked** adj (wine) che sa di turacciolo.

corn¹ [kɔːn] n (grain) grano m; (wheat) frumento m; (maize) mais m invar, granturco m. **cornflour** n farina finissima di granturco f. **corny** adj banale.

corn² [kɔːn] n (toe) callo m.

corner ['kɔːnə] n angolo m; (football) corner m invar, calcio d'angolo m. v (prevent escape) mettere alle strette; (stock) accaparrare; (drive) fare una curva.

cornet ['kɔɪnit] *n* (*music*) cornetta *f*; (*ice-cream*) cono *m*.

coronary ['kɔrənəri] *adj* coronario. **coronary thrombosis** trombosi coronaria *f*.

coronation [kɔrə'neiʃən] *n* incoronazione *f*.

corporal¹ ['kɔɪpərəl] *adj* (*bodily*) corporale; (*material*) corporeo.

corporal² ['kɔɪpərəl] *n* caporale, -a *m*, *f*.

corporation [‚kɔɪpə'reiʃən] *n* corporazione *f*, ente *m*.

corps [kɔɪ] *n* corpo *m*.

corpse [kɔɪps] *n* cadavere *m*.

correct [kə'rekt] *v* correggere. *adj* corretto, giusto, esatto. **correction** *n* correzione *f*, rettifica *f*.

correlate ['kɔrəleit] *v* mettere in correlazione. **correlated** *adj* correlativo. **correlation** *n* correlazione *f*.

correspond [kɔrə'spond] *v* corrispondere, equivalere; (*letters*) essere in corrispondenza, scambiare lettere. **correspondence** *n* corrispondenza *f*, scambio di lettere *m*. **correspondent** *n* corrispondente *m*, *f*. **corresponding** *adj* corrispondente.

corridor ['kɔridɔɪ] *n* corridoio *m*.

corrode [kə'roud] *v* corrodere, corrodersi. **corrosion** *n* corrosione *f*. **corrosive** *adj* corrosivo.

corrupt [kə'rʌpt] *v* corrompere. *adj* corrotto. **corruption** *n* corruzione *f*.

corset ['kɔɪsit] *n* busto *m*; (*orthopaedic*) corsetto *m*.

Corsica ['kɔɪsikə] *n* Corsica *f*. **Corsican** *n*, *adj* corso, -a.

cosh [kɔʃ] *n* randello *m*.

cosmetic [koz'metik] *nm*, *adj* cosmetico. **cosmetics** *pl n* prodotti di bellezza *m pl*.

cosmic ['kozmik] *adj* cosmico. **cosmonaut** *n* cosmonauta *m*, *f*.

cosmopolitan [kozmə'politən] *nm*, *adj* cosmopolitano.

*****cost** [kost] *n* costo *m*, prezzo *m*. *v* costare. **costly** *adj* costoso, caro.

costume ['kostjuɪm] *n* costume *m*, abito *m*; (*suit*) tailleur *m*.

cosy ['kouzi] *adj* comodo, intimo, accogliente.

cot [kot] *n* lettino *m*, culla *f*.

cottage ['kotidʒ] *n* villino *m*, casetta *f*.

cotton ['kotn] *n* cotone *m*. **cotton-wool** *n* bambagia *f*, ovatta *f*; (*med*) cotone idrofilo *m*.

couch [kautʃ] *n* divano *m*, canapè *m*.

cough [kof] *n* tosse *f*. **cough mixture** sciroppo per la tosse *m*. *v* tossire.

could [kud] *V* **can¹**

council ['kaunsəl] *n* consiglio *m*; (*rel*) concilio *m*. **councillor** *n* consigliere *m*, membro del consiglio *m*.

counsel ['kaunsəl] *n* (*advice*) consiglio *m*; (*lawyer*) avvocato *m*. *v* raccomandare, consigliare. **counsellor** *n* consigliere, -a *m*, *f*; (*consultant*) consulente *m*, *f*.

count¹ [kaunt] *v* contare, includere. **count on** contare su, fare affidamento su. *n* conto *m*, calcolo *m*; (*law*) capo d'accusa *m*.

count² [kaunt] *n* conte *m*. **countess** *n* contessa *f*.

countenance ['kauntinəns] *n* espressione *f*. *v* tollerare.

counter¹ ['kauntə] *n* (*token*) gettone *m*; (*table top*) banco *m*; (*device*) calcolatore *m*.

counter² ['kauntə] *v* opporsi a, controbattere. *adj* contrario, opposto.

counteract [kauntə'rakt] *v* neutralizzare, invalidare, mandare a vuoto.

counter-attack *n* contrattacco *m*. *v* contrattaccare.

counterfeit ['kauntəfit] *adj* falsificato, falso. *v* falsificare.

counterfoil ['kauntəfoil] *n* matrice *f*, figlia *f*.

counterpart ['kauntəpaɪt] *n* contropartita *f*, complemento *m*.

country ['kʌntri] *n* (*countryside*) campagna *f*; (*state*) paese *m*; (*homeland*) patria *f*.

county ['kaunti] *n* provincia *f*, regione *f*.

coup [kuɪ] *n* **coup de grace** colpo di grazia *m*. **coup d'état** colpo di stato *m*.

couple ['kʌpl] *n* coppia *f*, paio *m* (*pl* -a *f*). *v* accoppiare, abbinare.

coupon ['kuɪpon] *n* tagliando *m*, scontrino *m*.

courage ['kʌridʒ] *n* coraggio *m*. **courageous** *adj* coraggioso.

courgette [kuə'ʒet] *n* zucchina *f*, zucchino *m*.

courier ['kuriə] *n* accompagnatore, -trice *m*, *f*; messaggero, -a *m*, *f*.

course [kɔɪs] *n* corso *m*, percorso *m*, linea *f*; (*food*) piatto *m*; (*aircraft*) rotta *f*. **in due course** a tempo debito. **in the course of** durante, nel corso di. **of course** naturalmente, beninteso.

court [kɔːt] n corte f; (law) tribunale m; (tennis) campo m. **court-martial** n corte marziale f. **courtyard** n cortile m. v corteggiare, far la corte a.

courteous ['kɔːtiəs] adj cortese, gentile. **courtesy** n cortesia f, gentilezza f.

cousin ['kʌzn] n cugino, -a m, f.

cove [kouv] n insenatura f.

cover ['kʌvə] n coperta f, copertura f; (shelter) riparo m; (book) copertina f. v coprire, ricoprire; (travel) percorrere; (journalism) riferire. **covering** n copertura f. **covering letter** lettera d'accompagnamento f.

cow [kau] n vacca f, mucca f. v intimidire.

coward ['kauəd] n vigliacco, -a m, f; vile m, f. **cowardly** adj vigliacco, vile. **cowardice** n vigliaccheria f.

cower ['kauə] v accovacciarsi, rannicchiarsi.

cowl [kaul] n (chimney) comignolo m; (hood) cappa f; (car) cofano m.

coy [koi] adj ritroso, timido.

crab [krab] n granchio m.

crack [krak] n (opening) screpolatura f, fessura f; (whip) schiocco m; (rifle) scoppio m; (noise) schianto m. **have a crack at** provare a fare. v spaccare, schioccare, screpolare.

cracker ['krakə] n (biscuit) cracker (pl -s) m, gallettina f; (firework) mortaretto m.

crackle ['krakl] v crepitare, scricchiolare. n crepitio m, scricchiolio m.

cradle ['kreidl] n culla f. v cullare.

craft [kraːft] n mestiere m, professione f; (cunning) astuzia f; (boat) imbarcazione f. **crafty** adj astuto.

cram [kram] v ficcare, cacciare.

cramp [kramp] n (med) crampo m. v paralizzare, bloccare.

cranberry ['kranbəri] n mirtillo rosso m.

crane [krein] n gru f invar. v crane one's neck allungare il collo.

crank [krank] n (mech) gomito m, manovella f; eccentrico, -a m, f. v **crank up** avviare.

crap [krap] n (vulgar) merda f; (impol: nonsense) scemenze f pl, stupidaggini f pl. v (vulgar) cacare.

crash [kraʃ] n (collision) scontro m; (noise) fracasso m; (collapse) crollo m; (aircraft) caduta f. **crash-helmet** n casco paraurti m. **crash-landing** n atterraggio di fortuna m. v (clash) scontrarsi; fracassare; crollare; precipitare.

crate [kreit] n cassa f. v imballare.

crater ['kreitə] n cratere m.

crave [kreiv] v ambire, bramare. **craving** n smania f, brama f.

crawl [krɔːl] v trascinarsi, strisciare. n (swimming) crawl m invar.

crayfish ['kreifiʃ] n gambero (di fiume) m.

crayon ['kreiən] n pastello m, matita colorata f.

craze [kreiz] n mania f, pazzia f. **crazy** adj pazzo, matto. **drive crazy** far impazzire.

creak [kriːk] v cigolare, scricchiolare. n cigolio m, scricchiolio m.

cream [kriːm] n panna f, crema f. v scremare. **creamy** adj cremoso; (soft) morbido.

crease [kriːs] n piega f, grinza f. v sgualcirsi, raggrinzarsi. **creased** adj raggrinzato; (clothes) sgualcito.

create [kri'eit] v creare, provocare. **creation** n creazione f. **creative** adj creativo, originale. **creativity** n potenza creativa f, originalità f. **creator** n creatore, -trice m, f. **creature** n creatura f.

credentials [kri'denʃəlz] pl n credenziali f pl.

credible ['kredəbl] adj credibile. **credibility** n credibilità f.

credit ['kredit] n credito m; (trustworthyness) fiducia f; considerazione f; (bank) attivo m. **credit balance** saldo attivo m. **credit card** carta di credito f. v (comm) accreditare; (have faith in) credere, prestar fede a; (ascribe) attribuire. **creditable** adj degno di lode, che fa onore. **creditor** n creditore, -trice m, f.

credulous ['kredjuləs] adj credulo, ingenuo.

creed [kriːd] n credo m, professione di fede f.

*****creep** [kriːp] v strisciare, insinuarsi; (plants) arrampicarsi. **creeper** n (plant) pianta rampicante f. **creepy** adj che dà i brividi.

cremate [kri'meit] v cremare. **cremation** n cremazione f. **crematorium** n crematorio m.

crept [krept] V creep.

crescent ['kresnt] n mezzaluna f.

cress [kres] n crescione m. **mustard and cress** crescione inglese m, agretto m. **watercress** n crescione d'acqua m.

crest [krest] n cresta f, ciuffo m; (heraldry, helmet) cimiero m. crestfallen adj mortificato.

crevice ['krevis] n crepa f, fessura f.

crew [kru] n equipaggio m, squadra f.

crib [krib] n (rel) presepio m; (bed) lettino m; (manger) mangiatoia f; (coll) bigino m. v plagiare.

cricket[1] ['krikit] n (insect) grillo m.

cricket[2] ['krikit] n (sport) cricket m.

crime [kraim] n delitto m, reato m. criminal n(m+f), adj criminale.

crimson ['krimzn] adj cremisi.

cringe [krindʒ] v comportarsi in modo servile.

crinkle ['kriŋkl] n grinza f. v raggrinzire.

cripple ['kripl] n storpio, -a m, f; invalido, -a m, f. v storpiare, mutilare, paralizzare.

crisis ['kraisis] n, pl -ses crisi f invar.

crisp [krisp] adj (lively) nitido; (bracing) invigorante; (firm, fresh) fresco; (brittle) croccante; (crinkled) crespo. crisps pl n patatine fritte croccanti f pl.

criterion [krai'tiəriən] n, pl -ria criterio m.

criticize ['kritisaiz] v criticare, esprimere un giudizio su. critic n critico m. critical adj critico. criticism n critica f; (philosophy) criticismo m. critique n saggio critico m.

croak [krouk] v gracchiare, gracidare; (grumble) brontolare. n gracchiare m, gracchio m, gracidio m.

crochet ['krouʃei] v lavorare all'uncinetto.

crockery ['krokəri] n vasellame m, stoviglie f pl.

crocodile ['krokədail] n coccodrillo m.

crocus ['kroukəs] n croco m.

crook [kruk] n (hook) uncino m; (bishop's) pastorale m; (shepherd's) bastone da pastore m; (criminal) truffatore, -trice m, f. v piegare, curvare.

crooked ['krukid] adj (bent) piegato, storto; disonesto.

crop [krop] n (produce) raccolto m; (riding) frusta f; (gullet) gozzo m. v (clip hair) tagliar corto; (trees) mozzare; (cut grain, etc.) mietere. come a cropper far fiasco.

croquet ['kroukei] n croquet m invar.

cross [kros] n croce f. adj arrabbiato. be cross arrabbiarsi. v incrociare; (street, etc.) attraversare; (threshold) varcare; (cheque) sbarrare; (annoy) ostacolare. cross oneself segnarsi. cross one's mind

venire in mente a uno. cross out cancellare. cross-examine v sottoporre a interrogatorio. cross-examination n interrogatorio m. cross-eyed adj strabico. crossfire n fuoco incrociato m cross-legged adj a gambe accavallate. cross-reference n richiamo m, crossroads n crocevia m, incrocio m. crossword n cruciverba m invar, parole incrociate f pl. crossing n traversata f.

crotchet ['krotʃit] n (music) semiminima f; (hook) uncinetto m. crotchety adj irritabile.

crouch [krautʃ] v rannicchiarsi.

crow[1] [krou] n (bird) corvo m, cornacchia f. as the crow flies in linea diretta. crow's nest coffa f. crow's foot ruga f, zampa di gallina f.

crow[2] [krou] v cantare, esultare; (boast) vantarsi, trionfare.

crowd [kraud] n folla f, massa f, compagnia f. v affollare, ammassare. crowded adj affollato, stipato, pieno zeppo.

crown [kraun] n corona f; (hat) cocuzzolo m; (head) calotta f; (road) colmo m. crown-prince n principe ereditario m. v incoronare; (reward) ricompensare; (tooth) mettere una corona a. to crown it all come se non bastasse.

crucial ['kruʃəl] adj decisivo, critico.

crucify ['krusifai] v crocifiggere, mettere in croce; tormentare, mortificare. crucifix n crocifisso m. crucifixion n crocifissione f.

crude [kruud] adj (rough, vulgar) grossolano, rozzo, volgare; (unrefined) grezzo.

cruel ['kruəl] adj crudele. be cruel to maltrattare. cruelty n crudeltà f.

cruise [kruz] n crociera f. go on a cruise fare una crociera.

crumb [krʌm] n briciola f.

crumble ['krʌmbl] v sgretolare; (collapse) crollare. crumbly adj friabile.

crumple ['krʌmpl] v sgualcire, sgualcirsi; (collapse) sfasciarsi, accasciarsi.

crunch [krʌntʃ] v sgretolare, sgranocchiare. n scricchiolio m; (critical point) momento di crisi m.

crusade [kru'seid] n crociata f. crusader n crociato m.

crush [krʌʃ] v schiacciare, frantumare; (destroy) annientare. n calca f, ressa f. have a crush on prendersi una cotta per. crusher n frantoio m.

crust [krʌst] n crosta f, corteccia f. **crusty** adj crostoso; (surly) burbero.

crutch [krʌtʃ] n gruccia f, stampella f.

crux [krʌks] n **the crux of the matter** il nodo della questione m.

cry [krai] n urlo m, strillo m, lamento m. v urlare, gridare; (weep) piangere.

crypt [kript] n cripta f. **cryptic** adj ambiguo, misterioso.

crystal ['kristl] n cristallo m. **crystallization** n cristallizzazione f. **crystallize** v cristallizzare.

cub [kʌb] n cucciolo m.

cube [kjuːb] n cubo m. v elevare al cubo. **cubic** adj cubico.

cubicle ['kjuːbikl] n stanzino m; (changing-room) spogliatoio m.

cuckold ['kʌkould] n cornuto m. v fare le corna a.

cuckoo ['kukuː] n cuculo m, cucù m.

cucumber [kjuːˈkʌmbə] n cetriolo m.

cuddle ['kʌdl] v coccolare, abbracciare teneramente. n abbraccio tenero m.

cue[1] [kjuː] n (theatre) battuta d'entrata f; (hint) spunto m.

cue[2] [kjuː] n (billiards) stecca f.

cuff[1] [kʌf] n (shirt) polsino m. **cuff-links** pl n gemelli m pl.

cuff[2] [kʌf] n (hit) schiaffo m, sberla f. v schiaffeggiare.

culinary ['kʌlinəri] adj culinario, gastronomico.

culminate ['kʌlmineit] v concludersi. **culmination** n culmine m.

culprit ['kʌlprit] n colpevole m, f.

cult [kʌlt] n culto m.

cultivate ['kʌltiveit] v coltivare. **cultivation** n coltivazione f, coltura f.

culture ['kʌltʃə] n cultura f; (land, plants) coltura f. **cultural** adj culturale. **cultured** adj colto.

cumbersome ['kʌmbəsəm] adj ingombrante.

cunning ['kʌnin] adj scaltro, astuto. n astuzia f, scaltrezza f.

cup [kʌp] n tazza f; (sport) coppa f.

cupboard ['kʌbəd] n armadio m, credenza f. **cupboard love** amore interessato m.

curate ['kjuərət] n curato m, parroco m.

curator [kjuəˈreitə] n direttore, -trice di museo m, f; curatore, -trice m, f.

curb [kəːb] v frenare.

curdle ['kəːdl] v cagliare, cagliarsi; (blood) gelare.

cure [kjuə] n cura f, rimedio m. v sanare,

guarire; (food) conservare; (salt) salare; (smoke) affumicare.

curfew ['kəːfjuː] n coprifuoco m.

curious ['kjuəriəs] adj (odd) strano, curioso, insolito; (inquisitive) curioso.

curl [kəːl] n ricciolo m. v arricciare, arrotolare; (lip) torcere. **curl up** rannicchiarsi; (animal) accucciarsi. **curler** n bigodino m.

currant ['kʌrənt] n ribes m invar; (dried) uva passa f, uvetta f.

currency ['kʌrənsi] n decorrenza f; (money) valuta f, moneta legale f.

current ['kʌrənt] n corrente f. adj corrente, comune.

curry ['kʌri] n curry m invar. v **curry favour** ingraziarsi.

curse [kəːs] n (oath) bestemmia f; (evil) maledizione f. v bestemmiare, maledire. **be cursed with** essere afflitto da.

curt [kəːt] adj brusco.

curtail [kəːˈteil] v limitare, ridurre.

curtain ['kəːtn] n cortina f; (cloth) tenda f, tendina f; (theatre) sipario m.

curtsy ['kəːtsi] n inchino m. v inchinarsi.

curve [kəːv] n curva f, svolta f. v curvare, svoltare.

cushion ['kuʃən] n cuscino m; (billiards) sponda f. v smorzare, assorbire.

custody ['kʌstədi] n custodia f, guardia f. **take into custody** arrestare. **custodian** n guardiano m, custode m, f.

custom ['kʌstəm] n costume m, usanza f, abitudine f. **customs** n dogana f. **customs officer** doganiere, -a m, f. **customary** adj abituale, solito. **customer** n cliente m, f.

****cut** [kʌt] n taglio m, incisione f; (wound) ferita f. v tagliare, incidere; (wound) ferire; (cards) alzare le carte. **cut down** ridurre; (fell) abbattere. **cut off** tagliar via; (suspend) sospendere. **cut out** ritagliare; omettere; (elec) interrompere. **cut it out!** piantala! **cut price** prezzo ridotto m. **cut-throat** adj spietato.

cute [kjuːt] adj grazioso, ingegnoso.

cutlery ['kʌtləri] n posate f pl, posateria f; (knives) coltelleria f.

cutlet ['kʌtlit] n costoletta f, cotoletta f.

cutting ['kʌtin] adj tagliente. n (newspaper) ritaglio m; (plant) margotta f; (railway) trincea f.

cycle ['saikl] n ciclo m, periodo m; (bicycle) bicicletta f. v andare in bicicletta. **cyclic** adj ciclico. **cycling** n ciclismo m. **cyclist** n ciclista m, f.

cyclone ['saikloun] n ciclone m.

cylinder ['silində] n cilindro m; (revolver) tamburo m; (printing) rullo m; (gas) bombola f.

cymbal ['simbəl] n cembalo m.

cynic ['sinik] n cinico, -a m, f. **cynical** adj cinico. **cynicism** n cinismo m.

cypress ['saiprəs] n cipresso m.

Cyprus ['saiprəs] n Cipro m. **Cypriot** n(m+f), adj cipriota.

cyst [sist] n cisti f.

Czechoslovakia [,tʃekəslə'vakiə] n Cecoslovacchia f. **Czech** n, adj ceco, -a, cecoslovacco, -a.

D

dab [dab] v toccare leggermente; applicare. n (small quantity) tocco m; (light blow) colpetto m.

dabble ['dabl] v (dip, paddle) guazzare. **dabble in** dilettarsi a; fare da dilettante.

dad [dad] n babbo m, papà m.

daffodil ['dafədil] n narciso m.

daft [daːft] adj scemo, sciocco.

dagger ['dagə] n pugnale m, stiletto m. **be at daggers drawn** essere ai ferri corti.

daily ['deili] adj giornaliero, quotidiano. n giornale m; (maid) domestica a giornata f. adv ogni giorno, quotidianamente.

dainty ['deinti] adj delicato, squisito.

dairy ['deəri] n latteria f. **dairy produce** latticini m pl.

daisy ['deizi] n margherita f.

dam [dam] n diga f, argine m. v sbarrare, arginare.

damage ['damidʒ] n danno m, guasto m; (law) indennizzo m. v danneggiare, guastare, nuocere. **damaging** adj dannoso.

damn [dam] v dannare, maledire. interj maledizione! n (negligible amount) bel niente m.

damp [damp] adj umido, madido. n umido m. v also **dampen** (moisten) inumidire; (dull) smorzare, deprimere. **damper** n (furnace) valvola di tiraggio f; (elec) smorzatore m; (music) sordina f.

damson ['damzən] n (fruit) susina selvatica f; (tree) susino selvatico m.

dance [daːns] n danza f, ballo m. v danzare, ballare. **dancer** n danzatore, -trice m, f; ballerino -a m, f.

dandelion ['dandi,laiən] n dente di leone m.

dandruff ['dandrəf] n forfora f.

danger ['deindʒə] n pericolo m. **dangerous** adj pericoloso.

dangle ['daŋgl] v (far) ciondolare or dondolare.

Danish ['deiniʃ] nm, adj danese. **Dane** n danese m, f.

dare [deə] v (be bold) osare; (challenge) sfidare. **I dare say** suppongo; probabilmente; (not deny) non nego.

daring ['deəriŋ] adj audace. n audacia f.

dark [daːk] n also **darkness** buio m, oscurità f. adj buio, oscuro, cupo. **darken** v scurire, offuscare, rabbuiarsi.

darling ['daːliŋ] n tesoro m, gioia f, favorito, -a m, f. adj carissimo, amatissimo.

darn [daːn] v rammendare. n rammendo m, rammendatura f.

dart [daːt] n dardo m, freccia f. v (move swiftly) balzare, slanciarsi, precipitarsi; (throw) lanciare.

dash [daʃ] v buttare, urtare; (spoil) frustrare; (rush) scappare. n spruzzo m; (rush) slancio m; (drink) goccio m; (pinch) pizzico m; (printing) lineetta f. **dashboard** n cruscotto m.

data ['deitə] pl n dati m pl, elementi m pl. **data processing** elaborazione di dati f.

date[1] [deit] n (calendar) data f; (appointment) appuntamento m. v datare, fare appuntamento con. **date from** risalire a. **out of date** fuori moda, antiquato. **up to date** aggiornato.

date[2] [deit] n (fruit) dattero m.

daughter ['dɔːtə] n figlia f, figliola f. **daughter-in-law** n nuora f.

daunt [dɔːnt] v intimidire.

dawdle ['dɔːdl] v sprecar tempo, bighellonare. **dawdler** n fannullone, -a m, f; bighellone, -a m, f.

dawn [dɔːn] n alba f, aurora f; (beginning) inizio m. v albeggiare; (appear) apparire, manifestarsi.

day [dei] n giorno m, giornata f. **by day** di giorno. **daybreak** n alba f, spuntar del giorno m. **daylight** n luce del giorno f. **every other day** un giorno sì e uno no. **the day before yesterday** ieri l'altro. **the day after tomorrow** dopodomani.

daydream ['deidriːm] v sognare ad occhi aperti; fantasticare. n sogno ad occhi aperti m, fantasticheria f.

daze [deiz] *v* stordire, sbalordire. *n* stupore *m*.

dazzle [ˈdæzl] *v* abbagliare.

dead [ded] *adj* morto, defunto; *(coll: absolute)* assoluto, completo. **dead drunk** ubriaco fradicio. **deadline** *n* scadenza *f*. **deadlock** *n* punto morto *m*; incaglio *m*. **dead slow** a passo d'uomo. **deaden** *v* attutire. **deadly** *adj* mortale.

deaf [def] *adj* sordo. **turn a deaf ear** fare orecchi da mercante. **deaf-mute** *n* sordomuto, -a *m, f*. **deafen** *v* rendere sordo, intontire. **deafness** *n* sordità *f*.

***deal** [diːl] *v* (*cards*) dare le carte. **deal in** commerciare in. **deal with** occuparsi di; (*things*) trattare di; (*people*) avere rapporti con. *n* (*business*) affare *m*; (*agreement*) accordo *m*; (*amount*) quantità *f*. **dealer** *n* commerciante *m, f*; (*retail*) dettagliante *m, f*; (*wholesale*) grossista *m, f*.

dealt [delt] *V* deal.

dean [diːn] *n* (*university*) preside di facoltà *m, f*; (*rel*) decano *m*.

dear [diə] *adj* caro. **oh dear!** ahimè! Dio mio!

death [deθ] *n* morte *f*. **death certificate** certificato di morte *m*. **death duties** tassa di successione *f sing*. **death warrant** sentenza di morte *f*. **deathly** *adj, adv* mortale; cadaverico.

debase [diˈbeis] *v* degradare, svalutare.

debate [diˈbeit] *v* dibattere, discutere. *n* dibattito *m*, discussione *f*.

debit [ˈdebit] *n* debito *m*; (*accounts*) dare *m*. *v* addebitare.

debris [ˈdeibriː] *n* detrito *m*, macerie *f pl*.

debt [det] *n* debito *m*; (*obligation*) obbligo *m*. **debt collector** *n* esattore, -trice *m, f*. **debtor** *n* debitore, -trice *m, f*.

decade [ˈdekeid] *n* decennio *m*.

decadent [ˈdekədənt] *adj* decadente.

decant [diˈkænt] *v* travasare. **decanter** *n* caraffa *f*.

decay [diˈkei] *v* deperire, putrefare, putrefarsi, andare in rovina; (*teeth*) cariare. *n* sfacelo *m*, rovina *f*, deperimento *m*.

deceased [diˈsiːst] *n, adj* defunto, -a. **decease** *n* decesso *m*.

deceit [diˈsiːt] *n* inganno *m*, truffa *f*. **deceitful** *adj* falso, perfido.

deceive [diˈsiːv] *v* ingannare, imbrogliare, illudersi.

December [diˈsembə] *n* dicembre *m*.

decent [ˈdiːsənt] *adj* (*proper*) decente; (*fitting*) decoroso; (*fair*) discreto; (*respectable*) bravo. **decency** *n* decenza *f*, decoro *m*.

deceptive [diˈseptiv] *adj* ingannevole, illusorio. **deception** *n* inganno *m*, imbroglio *m*.

decibel [ˈdesiˌbel] *n* decibel *m invar*.

decide [diˈsaid] *v* decidere, decidersi. **decided** *adj* deciso, risoluto.

deciduous [diˈsidjuəs] *adj* deciduo.

decimal [ˈdesiməl] *nm, adj* decimale.

decipher [diˈsaifə] *v* decifrare.

decision [diˈsiʒən] *n* decisione *f*. **decisive** *adj* decisivo.

deck [dek] *n* (*naut*) ponte *m*, coperta *f*; (*cards*) mazzo *m*. *v* ornare. **deck-chair** *n* sedia a sdraio *f*.

declare [diˈkleə] *v* dichiarare, proclamare. **declaration** *n* dichiarazione *f*, proclama *m*.

decline [diˈklain] *v* (*refuse*) rifiutare; (*gramm*) declinare; (*deteriorate*) deperire. *n* (*gradual loss*) declino *m*; deterioramento *m*; decadenza *f*.

decompose [ˌdiːkəmˈpouz] *v* decomporre. **decomposition** *n* decomposizione *f*, putrefazione *f*.

decorate [ˈdekəˌreit] *v* decorare, ornare; (*house*) verniciare. **decoration** *n* decorazione *f*, ornamento *m*. **decorator** *n* (*interior*) arredatore, -trice *m, f*; (*building*) decoratore, -trice *m, f*, pittore, -trice *m, f*. **decorous** *adj* decoroso. **decorum** *n* decoro *m*.

decoy [diːˈkoi] *n* richiamo *m*, uccello da richiamo *m*, esca *f*; (*person*) adescatore, -trice *m, f*.

decrease [diˈkriːs] *n* diminuire. *n* diminuzione *f*, ribasso *m*.

decree [diˈkriː] *n* decreto *m*, ordinanza *f*. *v* decretare.

decrepit [diˈkrepit] *adj* decrepito.

dedicate [ˈdediˌkeit] *v* dedicare. **dedication** *n* dedicazione *f*; (*book*) dedica *f*.

deduce [diˈdjuːs] *v* dedurre, inferire. **deduction** *n* (*inference*) deduzione *f*.

deduct [diˈdʌkt] *v* dedurre, sottrarre. **deduction** *n* (*subtraction*) sottrazione *f*.

deed [diːd] *n* fatto *m*, azione *f*; (*law*) atto notarile, strumento *m*; (*undertaking*) impresa *f*. **good deed** buona azione *f*.

deep [diːp] *adj* profondo, alto; *(colour)* scuro, cupo. **deep-rooted** or **deep-seated** *adj* radicato. **deepen** *v* approfondire.

deep-freeze *v* surgelare. *n* congelatore *m*, freezer *m* invar.

deer [diə] *n (roe)* capriolo *m; (fallow)* daino *m*.

deface [di'feis] *v* sfregiare, mutilare.

defamatory [di'famətəri] *adj* diffamatorio. **defamation** *n* diffamazione *f*, calunnia *f*.

default [di'fɔlt] *v* rendersi contumace. *n* **by default** in contumacia. **in default of** in difetto di.

defeat [di'fiːt] *n* sconfitta *f*, disfatta *f*. *v* sconfiggere. **defeatism** *n* disfattismo *m*. **defeatist** *n* disfattista *m, f*.

defect[1] [diːfekt] *n* difetto *m*, mancanza *f*. **defective** *adj* difettoso, imperfetto; *(gramm)* difettivo.

defect[2] [di'fekt] *v* disertare. **defection** *n* diserzione *f*, defezione *f*.

defend [di'fend] *v* difendere, proteggere. **defence** *n* difesa *f*. **defenceless** *adj* indifeso, senza difesa. **defendant** *n* imputato, -a *m, f*. **defender** *n* difensore *m*.

defensive [di'fensiv] *adj* difensivo. *n* difensiva *f*. **be on the defensive** stare sulla difesa.

defer[1] [di'fə] *v (put off)* rimandare, rinviare.

defer[2] [di'fə] *v (yield to)* sottoporsi. **deferential** *adj* rispettoso, deferente.

deficient [di'fiʃənt] *adj* deficiente, incompleto, insufficiente. **deficiency** *n* deficienza *f*, mancanza *f*, carenza *f*.

deficit ['defisit] *n* deficit *m* invar, disavanzo *m*.

define [di'fain] *v* definire, precisare. **definition** *n* definizione *f*.

definite ['definit] *adj* definito, determinato, preciso.

deflate [di'fleit] *v* sgonfiare; *(comm)* deflazionare. **deflation** *n* sgonfiamento *m*, deflazione *f*.

deflect [di'flekt] *v* deviare. **deflection** *n* deviazione *f*.

deform [di'fɔm] *v* deformare. **deformity** or **deformation** *n* deformazione *f*.

defraud [di'frɔd] *v* frodare, defraudare.

defray [di'frei] *v* **defray expenses** rimborsare le spese.

defrost [diː'frost] *v* scongelare.

deft [deft] *adj* destro, lesto. **deftness** *n* destrezza *f*, agilità *f*.

defunct [di'fʌŋkt] *adj* defunto.

defy [di'fai] *v* sfidare, provocare. **defiance** *n (resistance)* sfida *f;* dispetto *m*. **in defiance of** a dispetto di. **defiant** *adj* ribelle, ricalcitrante.

degenerate [di'dʒenərit; *v* di'dʒenəreit] *adj* degenerato, perverso. *v* degenerare. **degeneracy** or **degeneration** *n* degenerazione *f*.

degrade [di'greid] *v* degradare. **degrading** *adj* degradante.

degree [di'griː] *n* grado *m; (diploma)* titolo di studio *m*, laurea *f*.

dehydrate [diː'haidreit] *v* disidratare. **dehydration** *n* disidratazione *f*.

de-icer [diː'aisə] *n* dispositivo antighiaccio *m*.

deign [dein] *v* degnarsi.

deity ['diːiti] *n* divinità *f*, deità *f*.

dejected [di'dʒektid] *adj* avvilito, abbattuto.

delay [di'lei] *n* ritardo *m*, indugio *m*. *v* ritardare, differire.

delegate ['deləgit; *v* 'deləgeit] *n* delegato, -a *m, f*. *v* delegare, autorizzare. **delegation** *n* delegazione *f*.

delete [di'liːt] *v* espungere. **deletion** *n* cancellatura *f*, espunzione *f*.

deliberate [di'libərət; *v* di'libəreit] *adj (intentional)* voluto; *(unhurried)* misurato; *(carefully considered)* ponderato. *v* deliberare, riflettere. **deliberation** *n* riflessione *f*, deliberazione *f*.

delicate ['delikət] *adj* delicato, fine; *(sensitive)* sensibile. **delicacy** *n* delicatezza *f;* sensibilità *f; (food)* leccornia *f*.

delicious [di'liʃəs] *adj* delizioso; *(food)* squisito.

delight [di'lait] *n* delizia *f*, diletto *m*. *v* dilettare. **delight in** rallegrarsi di. **delighted** *adj* ben lieto. **delightful** *adj* delizioso, incantevole, simpaticissimo.

delinquency [di'liŋkwənsi] *n* delinquenza *f*. **delinquent** *n(m+f), adj* delinquente.

delirious [di'liriəs] *adj (feverish)* delirante; *(wildly excited)* ebbro.

deliver [di'livə] *v (hand over)* recapitare, consegnare; *(set free)* liberare; *(save)* salvare; *(speech)* pronunciare. **deliverance** *n* liberazione *f*. **delivery** *n* consegna *f; (birth)* parto *m; (diction)* dizione *f*.

delta ['deltə] *n* delta *m*.

delude [di'luːd] *v* deludere, deludersi. **delusion** *n* delusione *f*.

deluge ['deljud3] *n* diluvio *m. v* diluviare.

delve [delv] *v* (*dig*) scavare; (*research*) far ricerche.

demand [di'maɪnd] *v* esigere, pretendere. *n* pretesa *f*, richiesta *f*. **in demand** ricercato. **on demand** su richiesta. **demanding** *adj* esigente.

demented [di'mentid] *adj* demente, impazzito.

democracy [di'mokrəsi] *n* democrazia *f*. **democrat** *n* democratico, -a *m, f*. **democratic** *adj* democratico.

demolish [di'molif] *v* demolire, abbattere. **demolition** *n* demolizione *f*.

demon ['diɪmən] *n* demonio *m*, diavolo *m*.

demonstrate ['demənstreit] *v* dimostrare. **demonstrable** *adj* dimostrabile. **demonstration** *n* dimostrazione *f*; (*proof*) prova *f*; (*meeting*) manifestazione *f*. **demonstrative** *adj* dimostrativo; (*feeling*) espansivo.

demoralize [di'morəˌlaiz] *v* demoralizzare, scoraggiare.

demure [di'mjuə] *adj* modesto, schivo.

den [den] *n* tana *f*.

denial [di'naiəl] *n* (*contradiction*) smentita *f*; (*negation*) diniego *m*; (*refusal*) rifiuto *m*.

denim ['denim] *n* tela pesante *f*.

Denmark ['denmaːk] *n* Danimarca *f*.

denomination [diˌnomi'neifən] *n* denominazione *f*; (*belief*) setta *f*, religione *f*; (*money*) taglio *m*. **denominator** *n* denominatore *m*.

denote [di'nout] *v* denotare, indicare.

denounce [di'nauns] *v* denunciare; (*openly accuse*) inveire contro.

dense [dens] *adj* denso, fitto. **density** *n* densità *f*.

dent [dent] *n* tacca *f*, ammaccatura *f. v* intaccare, ammaccare.

dental ['dentl] *adj* dentale; (*of dentistry*) dentistico.

dentist ['dentist] *n* dentista *m, f*. **dentistry** *n* odontoiatria *f*.

denture ['dentʃə] *n* dentiera *f*.

denude [di'njuɪd] *v* denudare, privare.

denunciation [dinʌnsi'eifən] *n* denuncia *f*.

deny [di'nai] *v* negare, smentire. **deny oneself** privarsi di, fare a meno di.

deodorant [diɪ'oudərənt] *nm, adj* deodorante.

depart [di'paːt] *v* (*leave*) partire; (*diverge*) deviare. **departure** *n* partenza *f*, deviazione *f*.

department [di'paːtmənt] *n* reparto *m*. **department store** grande magazzino *m*.

depend [di'pend] *v* dipendere, fare assegnamento. **depend on** dipendere da, fare assegnamento su. **dependable** *adj* fidato. **dependence** *n* dipendenza *f*. **dependent** *n*(*m*+*f*), *adj* dipendente.

depict [di'pikt] *v* rappresentare, descrivere.

deplete [di'pliːt] *v* esaurire, vuotare.

deplore [di'ploː] *v* biasimare, disapprovare. **deplorable** *adj* riprensibile, biasimevole.

deport [di'poːt] *v* deportare, espellere. **deportation** *n* deportazione *f*, espulsione *f*.

depose [di'pouz] *v* (*dismiss*) deporre; (*witness*) testimoniare. **deposition** *n* deposizione *f*, testimonianza *f*.

deposit [di'pozit] *v* depositare, posare. *n* deposito *m*; (*security*) cauzione *f*, pegno *m*. **deposit account** conto vincolato *m*.

depot ['depou] *n* deposito *m*, magazzino *m*, parco *m*.

deprave [di'preiv] *v* corrompere, depravare.

depreciate [di'priːfiˌeit] *v* deprezzare; (*money*) svalutare; (*belittle*) screditare, denigrare. **depreciation** *n* deprezzamento *m*, svalutazione *f*; discredito *m*, denigrazione *f*.

depress [di'pres] *v* deprimere. **depressed** *adj* depresso, abbattuto; (*market*) basso. **depressing** *adj* deprimente, triste. **depression** *n* depressione *f*; (*comm*) crisi *f invar*.

deprive [di'praiv] *v* privare. **deprivation** *n* privazione *f*.

depth [depθ] *n* profondità *f*, altezza *f*. **be out of one's depth** non essere all'altezza.

deputy ['depjuti] *n* delegato *m*, deputato *m*. **deputation** *n* deputazione *f*.

derail [di'reil] *v* uscire dalle rotaie, deragliare. **derailment** *n* deragliamento *m*.

derelict ['derilikt] *adj* derelitto, abbandonato.

deride [di'raid] *v* deridere, schernire. **derision** *n* derisione *f*, scherno *m*. **derisive** or **derisory** *adj* irrisorio, derisivo.

derive [di'raiv] *v* derivare, provenire. **derivation** *n* derivazione *f*, provenienza *f*, origine *f*.

derogatory [di'rogətəri] *adj* sprezzante, diffamante.

descend [di'send] v scendere; (*come from*) derivare, discendere. **descent** n discesa f; (*ancestry*) discendenza f, lignaggio m. **descendant** n discendente m, f.

describe [di'skraib] v descrivere. **description** n descrizione f.

desert¹ ['dezət] n deserto m.

desert² [di'zəːt] v disertare, abbandonare. **deserter** n disertore m. **desertion** n diserzione f, abbandono m.

desert³ [di'zəːt] n **get one's just deserts** ricevere quel che si merita.

deserve [di'zəːv] v meritare, essere degno di.

design [di'zain] v (*plan*) progettare; (*intend*) destinare. n disegno m, progetto m; (*intention*) proposito m. **have designs on** avere delle mire su. **designer** n progettista m, f, modellista m, f.

designate ['dezigneit] v designare. adj designato.

desire [di'zaiə] v desiderare, bramare. n (*wish*) desiderio m; (*craving*) brama f, passione f. **desirable** adj desiderabile.

desk [desk] n scrivania f; (*school*) banco m; (*cash*) cassa f.

desolate ['desələt] adj desolato; (*barren*) deserto; (*lonely*) solitario; (*sad*) afflitto, rattristato.

despair [di'speə] n disperazione f. v disperare.

desperate ['despərət] adj disperato; (*hopeless*) senza speranza. **desperation** n disperazione f.

despise [di'spaiz] v disprezzare.

despite [di'spait] prep malgrado.

despondent [di'spondənt] adj accasciato, depresso.

despot ['despot] n despota m, f.

dessert [di'zəːt] n dessert m invar.

destine ['destin] v destinare. **destination** n destinazione f, recapito m. **destiny** n destino m, sorte f.

destitute ['destitjuːt] adj indigente.

destroy [di'stroi] v distruggere. **destruction** n distruzione f.

detach [di'tatʃ] v staccare, distaccare. **detached** adj staccato; (*house*) isolato; (*aloof*) distaccato; (*objective*) obiettivo. **detachment** n distacco m; (*army*) distaccamento m; indifferenza f; obiettività f.

detail ['diːteil] n particolare m, dettaglio m. v dettagliare, descrivere minutamente.

detain [di'tein] v detenere; (*delay*) trattenere. **detainee** n detenuto, -a m, f; carcerato, -a m, f.

detect [di'tekt] v scoprire, individuare. **detection** n scoperta f. **detective** n detective m invar, investigatore, -trice m, f. **detective novel** romanzo poliziesco m, romanzo giallo m.

détente [dei'tɑ̃nt] n distensione f.

detention [di'tenʃən] n detenzione f.

deter [di'təː] v dissuadere, scoraggiare. **deterrent** n deterrente m.

detergent [di'təːdʒənt] nm, adj detergente, detersivo.

deteriorate [di'tiəriəreit] v deteriorare, peggiorare. **deterioration** n deterioramento m, peggioramento m.

determine [di'təːmin] v determinare, stabilire; decidere. **determination** n determinazione f, risolutezza f. **determined** adj determinato, risoluto.

detest [di'test] v detestare, odiare. **detestable** adj detestabile, odioso.

detonate ['detəneit] v detonare, esplodere. **detonation** n detonazione f, esplosione f. **detonator** n detonatore m.

detour ['diːtuə] n deviazione f.

detract [di'trakt] v detrarre.

detriment ['detrimənt] n **to the detriment of** a scapito di.

deuce [djuːs] n (*cards*) due m; (*tennis*) quaranta pari.

devalue [diː'valjuː] v svalutare. **devaluation** n svalutazione f.

devastate ['devəsteit] v devastare, rovinare. **devastating** adj devastatore; (*highly effective*) schiacciante.

develop [di'veləp] v sviluppare; elaborare; (*land*) usare come terreno da costruzione. **develop into** diventare. **developer** n (*phot*) sviluppatore m; (*land*) persona che apporta migliorie f. **development** n sviluppo m; evoluzione f; (*land*) valorizzazione di terreno f.

deviate ['diːvi,eit] v deviare. **deviation** n deviazione f.

device [di'vais] n (*contrivance*) congegno m; (*crafty scheme*) schema m, espediente m; (*heraldry*) motto m, divisa f.

devil ['devl] n diavolo m, demonio m. **devilish** adj diabolico, infernale.

devious ['diːviəs] adj indiretto, tortuoso.

devise [di'vaiz] v escogitare, progettare.

devoid [di'void] adj privo.

devolution [diːvə'luːʃən] n devoluzione f.

devote [di'vout] v dedicare, consacrare. **devoted** adj devoto, affezionato. **devotion** n devozione f; (prayer) preghiere f pl.

devour [di'vauə] v divorare.

devout [di'vaut] adj devoto, pio, fervente.

dew [dju:] n rugiada f.

dextrous ['dekstrəs] adj destro, abile. **dexterity** n destrezza f.

diabetes [,diəə'bi:ti:z] n diabete m. **diabetic** nm, adj diabetico.

diagnose [,diəəg'nouz] v fare la diagnosi. **diagnosis** n, pl -ses diagnosi f. **diagnostic** adj diagnostico.

diagonal [dai'agənəl] nf, adj diagonale.

diagram ['daiə,gram] n diagramma m.

dial ['daiəl] n (watch) quadrante m; (telephone) disco combinatore m. v (number) comporre.

dialect ['daiəlekt] n dialetto m.

dialogue ['daiəlog] n dialogo (pl -ghi) m.

diameter [dai'amitə] n diametro m.

diamond ['daiəmənd] n diamante m. **diamonds** pl n (cards) quadri m pl.

diaper ['daipə] n (US) pannolino (per neonati) m.

diaphragm ['daiə,fram] n diaframma m.

diarrhoea [,daiə'riə] n diarrea f.

diary ['daiəri] n diario m, agenda f.

dice [dais] n dado m.

dictate [dik'teit] v dettare, imporre. n (order) comando m; (rule) regola f. **dictation** n dettato m. **dictator** n dittatore m. **dictatorial** adj dittatorio, dittatoriale. **dictatorship** n dittatura f.

dictionary ['dikʃənəri] n dizionario m, vocabolario m.

did [did] V **do**.

die [dai] v morire. **die away** scomparire. **die down** spegnersi lentamente.

diehard ['daihad] n(m+f), adj tradizionalista, intransigente.

diesel ['di:zəl] n **diesel engine** motore diesel m. **diesel oil** gasolio m, nafta f.

diet ['daiət] n dieta f; (food) alimentazione f, vitto m. **be on a diet** stare a dieta, stare or essere a regime. **dietary** adj dietetico.

differ ['difə] v essere diverso, differire; (disagree) dissentire. **difference** n differenza f. **different** adj differente, diverso.

difficult ['difikʌlt] adj difficile; (troublesome, tricky) difficoltoso. **difficulty** n difficoltà f.

diffident ['difidənt] adj timido.

*dig [dig] v scavare; (agric) vangare. n (archaeol) scavi m pl.

digest [dai'dʒest; n 'daidʒest] v digerire, assimilare. n sommario m, selezione f. **digestible** adj digeribile. **digestion** n digestione f.

digit ['didʒit] n (figure) numero semplice m, cifra f; (finger, toe) dito m. **digital** adj digitale.

dignified ['digni,faid] adj dignitoso, nobile.

dignity ['digniti] n dignità f.

digress [dai'gres] v digredire, deviare. **digression** n digressione f.

digs [digz] pl n alloggio m sing.

dilapidated [di'lapi,deitid] adj decrepito.

dilate [dai'leit] v dilatare.

dilemma [di'lemə] n dilemma m.

diligent ['dilidʒent] adj diligente, assiduo.

dilute [dai'lu:t] v diluire, allungare. adj diluito.

dim [dim] v attenuare, affievolire. adj fioco, tenue; (stupid) poco intelligente.

dimension [di'menʃən] n dimensione f.

diminish [di'miniʃ] v diminuire, ridurre.

diminutive [di'minjutiv] adj diminutivo, minuscolo.

dimple ['dimpl] n fossetta f.

din [din] n fracasso m, baccano m.

dine [dain] v pranzare. **dining car** vagone ristorante m. **dining room** sala da pranzo f.

dinghy ['dingi] n barca f.

dingy ['dindʒi] adj squallido.

dinner ['dinə] n pranzo m, cena f.

dinosaur ['dainə,sot] n dinosauro m.

diocese ['daiəsis] n diocesi f invar.

dip [dip] v abbassare, tuffare, immergere. n immersione f; (swim) nuotata f; inclinazione f.

diphthong ['difθoŋ] n dittongo m.

diploma [di'ploumə] n diploma m.

diplomacy [di'plouməsi] n diplomazia f. **diplomat** n diplomatico m. **diplomatic** adj diplomatico.

dipstick ['dipstik] n asta di livello f.

dire [daiə] adj **dire need** bisogno urgente m. **dire straits** miseria, tuffare, squallida f sing.

direct [di'rekt] adj diretto, immediato; sincero. v dirigere, amministrare. **direction** n direzione f; (management) amministrazione f; (address) indirizzo m; (stage) didascalia f. **director** n (comm) amministratore, -trice m, f; (theatre)

regista m, f. **directory** n annuario m, guida f; (phone) elenco telefonico m.

dirt [dəːt] n sporcizia f. **dirty** adj sporco, sudicio. **dirty word** parolaccia f.

disability [disə'biləti] n incapacità f, inabilità f. **disabled** nm, adj invalido, mutilato.

disadvantage [disəd'vaintidʒ] n svantaggio m.

disagree [disə'griː] v non andar d'accordo, non essere d'accordo. **disagree with** (food) far male a. **disagreeable** adj sgradevole, antipatico. **disagreement** n disaccordo m, dissenso m.

disappear [disə'piə] v sparire, scomparire. **disappearance** n scomparsa f.

disappoint [disə'point] v deludere. **disappointed** adj deluso, scontento. **disappointment** n delusione f.

disapprove [disə'pruːv] v disapprovare, riprovare. **disapproval** n disapprovazione f.

disarm [dis'aːm] v disarmare. **disarmament** n disarmo m.

disaster [di'zaːstə] n disastro m, disgrazia f; calamità f. **disastrous** adj disastroso.

disband [dis'band] v sbandare, sciogliere, congedare.

disc or US **disk** [disk] n disco m.

discard [dis'kaːd] v scartare.

discern [di'səːn] v discernere, scorgere. **discerning** adj avveduto, accorto. **discernment** n discernimento m, giudizio m.

discharge [dis'tʃaːdʒ] v scaricare; (dismiss) licenziare; (law) assolvere; (radiation) emettere; (med) suppurare; (a duty) adempiere; (a debt) saldare. n scarico m; licenziamento m; assoluzione f; emissione f; suppurazione f; (elec) scarica f.

disciple [di'saipl] n discepolo, -a m, f.

discipline ['disiplin] n disciplina f. v disciplinare. **disciplinary** adj disciplinare.

disclaim [dis'kleim] v ripudiare, confessare, smentire. **disclaimer** n ripudio m, smentita f; denunzia di un contratto f.

disclose [dis'klouz] v svelare, rivelare. **disclosure** n rivelazione f.

discolour [dis'kʌlə] v scolorire, sbiadire.

discomfort [dis'kʌmfət] n disagio m. v mettere a disagio.

disconcert [diskən'səːt] v sconcertare. **disconcerting** adj sconcertante.

disconnect [diskə'nekt] v sconnettere; (mech) disinnestare.

disconsolate [dis'kɔnsələt] adj sconsolato, desolato.

discontinue [diskən'tinjuː] v sospendere, interrompere, terminare.

discord ['diskɔid] n discordia f, dissenso m; (music) dissonanza f, disarmonia f. **discordant** adj discorde; (noise) discordante; dissonante.

discotheque [diskətek] n discoteca f.

discount ['diskaunt] v (disregard) non badare a. n sconto m, ribasso m.

discourage [dis'kʌridʒ] v scoraggiare. **discouragement** n scoraggiamento m. **discouraging** adj scoraggiante.

discover [dis'kʌvə] v scoprire. **discovery** n scoperta f.

discredit [dis'kredit] v screditare, mettere in dubbio.

discreet [di'skriːt] adj discreto, riservato. **discretion** n discrezione f; prudenza f; (judgment) giudizio m. **discretionary** adj discrezionale.

discrepancy [di'skrepənsi] n divario m, disaccordo m.

discrete [di'skriːt] adj separato, distinto, discreto.

discriminate [di'skrimi,neit] v discriminare, differenziare. **discriminating** adj penetrante, giudizioso. **discrimination** n discriminazione f, distinzione f.

discus ['diskəs] n disco m.

discuss [di'skʌs] v discutere, dibattere. **discussion** n discussione f, dibattimento m.

disease [di'ziːz] n malattia f. **diseased** adj malato, ammalato.

disembark [disim'baːk] v sbarcare.

disengage [disin'geidʒ] v disimpegnare, liberare; (mech) disinnestare. **disengaged** adj libero.

disfigure [dis'figə] v sfigurare, deturpare.

disgrace [dis'greis] n disonore m, vergogna f, scandalo m, ignominia f. v disonorare, screditare. **disgraceful** adj vergognoso.

disgruntled [dis'grʌntld] adj di cattivo umore, scontento.

disguise [dis'gaiz] v camuffare, mascherare. n maschera f, travestimento m.

disgust [dis'gʌust] n disgusto m, ribrezzo m, schifo m. v disgustare, far schifo, nauseare. **disgusting** adj disgustoso, schifoso.

dish [diʃ] n piatto m. **dishcloth** n

strofinaccio per i piatti *m*. **dishwasher** *n* lavapiatti *m*.

dishearten [dis'hɑːtn] *v* scoraggiare.

dishevelled [di'ʃevəld] *adj* scapigliato, arruffato.

dishonest [dis'ɒnist] *adj* disonesto. **dishonesty** *n* disonestà *f*.

dishonour [dis'ɒnə] *v* disonorare. *n* disonore *m*, infamia *f*. **dishonourable** *adj* disonorevole.

disillusion [disi'luːʒən] *v* disilludere, disingannare. *n* disillusione *f*, disinganno *m*.

disinfect [disin'fekt] *v* disinfettare. **disinfectant** *nm*, *adj* disinfettante.

disinherit [disin'herit] *v* diseredare.

disintegrate [dis'intigreit] *v* disintegrare, disgregare, disfare, disfarsi. **disintegration** *n* disfacimento *m*, sfacelo *m*, disintegrazione *f*.

disinterested [dis'intristid] *adj* disinteressato.

disjointed [dis'dʒɔintid] *adj* sconnesso, incoerente.

dislike [dis'laik] *v* detestare, sentire antipatia per. *n* antipatia *f*, avversione *f*.

dislocate [dis'ləkeit] *v* dislocare; (*joint*) lussare. **dislocation** *n* dislocazione *f*; lussazione *f*.

dislodge [dis'lɒdʒ] *v* sloggiare, scacciare.

disloyal [dis'lɔiəl] *adj* sleale, infedele. **disloyalty** *n* slealtà *f*, infedeltà *f*.

dismal [dizməl] *adj* triste, lugubre, malinconico.

dismantle [dis'mantl] *v* smantellare.

dismay [dis'mei] *v* costernare, sgomentare. *n* costernazione *f*, sgomento *m*.

dismiss [dis'mis] *v* (*send away*) respingere; (*discard*) scartare; (*discharge*) licenziare. **dismissal** *n* licenziamento *m*.

dismount [dis'maunt] *v* smontare.

disobey [disə'bei] *v* disubbidire, disobbedire. **disobedience** *n* disubbidienza *f*. **disobedient** *adj* disubbidiente.

disorder [dis'ɔːdə] *n* disordine *m*, confusione *f*; (*med*) disturbo *m*. **disorderly** *adj* disordinato.

disorganized [dis'ɔːgənaizd] *adj* disorganizzato. **disorganization** *n* disorganizzazione *f*.

disown [dis'oun] *v* ripudiare, rinnegare.

disparage [di'sparidʒ] *v* denigrare, screditare.

disparity [dis'pariti] *n* disparità *f*.

dispassionate [dis'paʃənit] *adj* spassionato, obiettivo.

dispatch [di'spatʃ] *v* spedire, inviare; (*settle*) sbrigare; (*kill*) spacciare. *n* spedizione *f*; (*mil*) dispaccio *m*; (*speed*) prontezza *f*, sollecitudine *f*.

dispel [di'spel] *v* dissipare, scacciare.

dispense [di'spens] *v* dispensare, distribuire; (*justice*) amministrare. **dispense with** fare a meno di. **dispensary** *n* dispensario *m*, farmacia *f*.

disperse [di'spɜːs] *v* disperdere, sparpagliare, dileguarsi. **dispersion** *n* dispersione *f*, diffusione *f*.

displace [dis'pleis] *v* spostare; (*take place of*) soppiantare. **displaced person** profugo (*pl* -ghi) *m*, -a *f*. **displacement** *n* spostamento *m*.

display [di'splei] *v* mostrare, esibire, ostentare, manifestare. *n* mostra *f*, manifestazione *f*, esposizione *f*.

displease [dis'pliːz] *v* spiacere, dispiacere, scontentare. **displeasure** *n* dispiacere *m*, ira *f*.

dispose [di'spouz] *v* disporre, sistemare. **dispose of** sbarazzarsi di, eliminare. **disposal** *n* (*control*) disposizione *f*; (*act of disposing*) sistemazione *f*. **disposed** *adj* disposto, intenzionato. **disposition** *n* disposizione *f*, tendenza *f*; (*character*) indole *f*.

disprove [dis'pruːv] *v* confutare.

dispute [di'spjuːt] *n* disputa *f*, vertenza *f*; (*quarrel*) lite *f*. *v* contestare.

disqualify [dis'kwɒlifai] *v* (*sport*) squalificare; (*render unfit*) incapacitare; (*law*) interdire. **disqualification** *n* squalifica *f*, incapacità *f*, interdizione *f*.

disregard [disrə'gɑːd] *v* non far caso a, ignorare. *n* noncuranza *f*, inosservanza *f*.

disreputable [dis'repjutəbl] *adj* malfamato, vergognoso.

disrespect [disrə'spekt] *n* mancanza di rispetto *f*, irriverenza *f*. **disrespectful** *adj* poco rispettoso, che non mostra rispetto.

disrupt [dis'rʌpt] *v* scompigliare, mettere in confusione. **disruption** *n* scompiglio *m*.

dissatisfy [di'satisfai] *v* scontentare. **dissatisfaction** *n* insoddisfazione *f*.

dissect [di'sekt] *v* sezionare; (*corpse*) secare; (*analyse*) analizzare. **dissection** *n* sezionamento *m*; dissezione *f*; analisi *f*.

dissent [di'sent] *n* dissenso *m*. *v* dissentire.

dissident ['disidənt] *n*(*m+f*), *adj* dissidente.

dissimilar [di'similə] *adj* dissimile.

dissipated ['disipeitid] *adj* dissoluto.

dissociate [di'sousieit] *v* dissociare, sdoppiare. **dissociation** *n* dissociazione *f*, sdoppiamento *m*.

dissolve [di'zolv] *v* sciogliere, sciogliersi, dissolvere. **dissolute** *adj* dissoluto, licenzioso.

dissuade [di'sweid] *v* dissuadere, distogliere. **dissuasion** *n* dissuasione *f*, distoglimento *m*.

distance ['distəns] *n* distanza *f*, lontananza *f*; (*reserve*) riserbo *m*. **distant** *adj* distante, lontano, remoto; riservato.

distaste [dis'teist] *n* avversione *f*. **distasteful** *adj* sgradevole.

distemper [di'stempə] *n* (*paint*) intonaco *m*; (*canine*) cimurro *m*. *v* intonacare.

distended [di'stendid] *adj* dilatato.

distil [di'stil] *v* distillare. **distillation** *n* distillazione *f*. **distillery** *n* distilleria *f*.

distinct [di'stiŋkt] *adj* differente, diverso; distinto; (*clear*) chiaro. **distinction** *n* distinzione *f*, differenza *f*. **distinctive** *adj* caratteristico, distintivo.

distinguish [di'stiŋgwiʃ] *v* distinguere, differenziare, individuare. **distinguish oneself** farsi notare. **distinguishable** *adj* distinguibile. **distinguished** *adj* distinto, insigne.

distort [di'stoɪt] *v* deformare, alterare. **distortion** *n* deformazione *f*, alterazione *f*.

distract [di'strakt] *v* distrarre; (*disturb*) turbare. **distraction** *n* distrazione *f*.

distraught [di'stroɪt] *adj* turbato.

distress [di'stres] *n* (*anxiety*) angoscia *f*; (*poverty*) miseria *f*; (*ship*) pericolo *m*; (*worry*) preoccupazione *f*. *v* angosciare, affliggere, preoccupare. **distressed** *adj* dolente, angosciato. **distressing** *adj* penoso, doloroso.

distribute [di'stribjut] *v* distribuire. **distribution** *n* distribuzione *f*. **distributor** *n* distributore *m*.

district ['distrikt] *n* distretto *m*, quartiere *m*, zona *f*.

distrust [dis'trʌst] *v* diffidare di, sospettare, non aver fiducia in. *n* sospetto *m*, sfiducia *f*, diffidenza *f*.

disturb [di'stɜɪb] *v* disturbare, incomodare. **disturbance** *n* disturbo *m*; (*breach of peace*) sommossa *f*.

ditch [ditʃ] *n* fossa *f*, fossato *m*. *v* (*abandon*) piantare.

ditto ['ditou] *adv* idem.

divan [di'van] *n* divano *m*.

dive [daiv] *v* tuffarsi, fare un tuffo, sommergersi. *n* (*plunge*) tuffo *m*; (*coll*) taverna *f*, bettola *f*. **diver** *n* palombaro *m*. **diving board** trampolino *m*. **diving suit** scafandro *m*.

diverge [dai'vɜɪdʒ] *v* divergere.

diversify [dai'vɜɪsifai] *v* diversificare, differenziare.

divert [dai'vɜɪt] *v* deviare; distrarre; (*amuse*) divertire. **diversion** *n* (*distraction*) diversivo *m*, distrazione *f*; (*mil*) diversione *f*; deviazione *f*.

divide [di'vaid] *v* dividere, separare. **divided** *adj* diviso. **dividers** *pl n* compasso *m sing*. **division** *n* divisione *f*.

dividend ['dividend] *n* dividendo *m*.

divine [di'vain] *adj* divino, sacro. *n* teologo *m*, sacerdote *m*. *v* scoprire, indovinare; (*prophesy*) pronosticare. **diviner** *n* (*soothsayer*) indovino, -a *m*, *f*; (*user of divining rod*) rabdomante *m*. **divinity** *n* divinità *f*.

divorce [di'vois] *n* divorzio *m*. *v* divorziare, divorziarsi.

divulge [dai'vʌldʒ] *v* divulgare, diffondere.

dizzy ['dizi] *adj* vertiginoso. **feel dizzy** avere il capogiro; sentirsi girare la testa. **dizziness** *n* capogiro *m*, vertigine *f*.

*do [du] *v* fare; (*suffice*) bastare; (*achieve*) compiere; (*carry out*) eseguire. **do away with** abolire; (*kill*) uccidere. **do-it-yourself** *adj* da fare da soli. **do out of** deprivare di. **do up** (*clothes, etc.*) abbottonare. **do without** fare a meno di. **how do you do?** come stai? (*polite*) come stai? **make do** arrangiarsi.

docile ['dousail] *adj* docile, mansueto.

dock¹ [dok] *n* (*wharf*) banchina *f*; (*waterway*) bacino *m*; (*port area*) zona portuale *f*. *v* attraccare. **docker** *n* portuale *m*. **dockyard** *n* cantiere navale *m*.

dock² [dok] *v* mozzare, troncare.

dock³ [dok] *n* (*law*) banco degli imputati *m*.

docket ['dokit] *n* bolletta *f*.

doctor ['doktə] *n* dottore, -essa *m*, *f*; (*med*) medico, -chessa *m*, *f*. **doctorate** *n* dottorato *m*.

doctrine ['doktrin] *n* dottrina *f*. **doctrinal** *adj* dottrinale.

document ['dokjumənt] *n* documento *m*. *v* documentare. **documentary** *n* documentario *m*. **documentation** *n* documentazione *f*.

dodge [dɔdʒ] v schivare, scansare. n sotterfugio m, stratagemma f.

doe [dou] n selvaggina femmina f; (deer) daina f; (rabbit) femmina del coniglio f; (hare) lepre femmina f.

dog [dɔg] n cane m. **dog-eared** adj accartocciato, con le orecchie. **dogrose** n rosa canina f. **dog-tired** adj stanco morto. **dogtooth** n dente canino m. v pedinare. **be dogged by** essere perseguitato da. **dogged** adj ostinato, accanito.

doge [doudʒ] n doge m.

dogma ['dɔgmə] n dogma m. **dogmatic** adj dogmatico.

dole [doul] n sussidio di disoccupazione m. v **dole out** distribuire.

doll [dɔl] n bambola f, pupa f. v **doll up** agghindarsi, abbellirsi.

dollar ['dɔlə] n dollaro m.

dolphin ['dɔlfin] n delfino m.

domain [də'mein] n (land) proprietà f; (law) demanio m; (control, sphere of activity) dominio m.

dome [doum] n cupola f.

domestic [də'mestik] adj domestico; (not foreign) nazionale. n domestico, -a m, f. **domesticate** v addomesticare. **domesticity** n domesticità f.

domicile ['dɔmisail] n domicilio m.

dominate ['dɔmi,neit] v dominare. **dominant** adj dominante.

domineer [dɔmi'niə] v signoreggiare. **domineering** adj imperioso; (overbearing) prepotente.

dominion [də'minjən] n dominio m; autorità f.

domino ['dɔminou] n domino m.

don[1] [dɔn] v vestire, indossare.

don[2] [dɔn] n (Spanish title) don m invar; (scholar) docente universitario, -a m, f.

donate [də'neit] v donare. **donation** n dono m, donazione f. **donor** n donatore, -trice m, f.

done [dʌn] V **do**.

donkey ['dɔŋki] n asino, -a m, f; somaro, -a m, f.

doom [dum] n destino m, sorte f; (ruin) rovina f. v destinare, condannare. **doomed** adj condannato. **doomsday** n giorno del giudizio m.

door [dɔ:] n porta f, uscio m. **doorbell** n campanello m. **door-handle** n maniglia f. **door-keeper** n portiere, -a m, f, portinaio, -a m, f. **door-knocker** n battiporta m,

batacchio m. **doormat** n zerbino m, stoino m. **doorstep** n soglia f. **doorway** n entrata f, portone m.

dope [doup] n (slang: drug) stupefacente m, droga f; (slang: information) notizie f pl. v drogare. **dopey** adj inebetito.

dormant ['dɔmənt] adj addormentato, latente.

dormitory ['dɔmitəri] n dormitorio m.

dormouse ['dɔ,maus] n ghiro m.

dose [dous] n dose f. v dosare.

dot [dɔt] n punto m. v punteggiare. **on the dot** in orario. **dotty** adj (coll) picchiatello.

dote [dout] v **dote on** essere infatuato di.

double ['dʌbl] v raddoppiare. **double up** piegare or piegarsi in due; contorcersi. adj doppio. n doppio m; (person) sosia m invar. **at the double** a passo di corsa. **double-barrelled** adj a doppia canna. **double bass** contrabbasso m. **double bed** letto matrimoniale m. **double-breasted** adj a doppio petto. **double-cross** v fare il doppio gioco, tradire.

doubt [daut] n dubbio m, incertezza f. v dubitare, mettere in dubbio. **doubtful** adj dubbio, incerto, problematico. **doubtless** adv senza dubbio.

dough [dou] n pasta f; (slang) quattrini m pl. **doughnut** n ciambella f, krapfen m invar.

dove [dʌv] n colomba f. **dovecot** n colombaia f. **dovetail** n (carpentry) incastrare a coda di rondine; (fit exactly) combaciare, far combaciare.

dowdy ['daudi] adj sciatto, trasandato.

down[1] [daun] adv giù, di sotto, per terra. adj depresso, abbattuto. **down and out** ridotto in miseria. v **down tools** abbandonare il lavoro.

down[2] [daun] n (plumage) piumino m, lanugine f; (soft hair) peluria f.

downcast ['daun,ka:st] adj abbattuto, depresso.

downfall ['daun,fɔl] n rovina f, caduta f. **downhearted** [daun'ha:tid] adj depresso, scoraggiato.

downhill [daun'hil] adv in discesa.

downpour ['daun,pɔ:] n acquazzone m.

downright ['daun,rait] adv categoricamente, nettamente.

downstairs [daun'steəz] adv da basso, al piano inferiore. **go downstairs** scendere le scale.

drip

downstream [ˌdaun'striːm] adv a valle, seguendo la corrente.

downtrodden ['daunˌtrɒdn] adj oppresso.

downward ['daunwəd] adj discendente.

downwards ['daunwədz] adv in giù, verso il basso.

dowry ['dauəri] n dote f.

doze [douz] v sonnecchiare, fare un pisolino. **doze off** assopirsi. **dozy** adj sonnolento.

dozen ['dʌzn] n dozzina f.

drab [dræb] adj squallido, scialbo.

draft [drɑːft] n (sketch) abbozzo m; (preliminary copy) brutta copia f; (conscription) leva f; (written order) tratta f, cambiale f; (bank) assegno circolare m. v abbozzare, delineare; (conscript) chiamare sotto le armi, arruolare.

drag [dræg] v trascinare; (search) dragare; (extract) strappare. n trazione f. **in drag** vestito da donna.

dragon ['dragən] n drago m; (woman) megera f. **dragon-fly** n libellula f.

drain [drein] n fogna f, tubo di scarico m. v (draw off) scolare, prosciugare; (med) drenare; (exhaust) esaurire; (drink up) bere fino all'ultimo. **drainage** n scarico m, fognatura f, drenaggio m. **draining board** scolatoio m. **drainpipe** n grondaia f.

drama ['drɑːmə] n dramma m. **dramatic** adj drammatico, impressionante. **dramatist** n drammaturgo, -a m, f. **dramatize** v drammatizzare.

drank [dræŋk] V **drink**.

drape [dreip] v drappeggiare.

draper ['dreipə] n negoziante di tessuti m, f. **drapery** n tessuti m pl; tendaggio m.

drastic ['dræstik] adj drastico.

draught or US **draft** [drɑːft] n (air current) corrente d'aria f; (drink) sorso m; (pull) tiro m; (fishing) retata f. **draughts** n gioco della dama m. **draughtsman** n disegnatore, -trice m, f, progettista m, f; (of documents) compilatore, -trice m, f. **it's draughty** c'è una corrente d'aria.

draw [drɔː] v (pull) tirare; (attract) attirare, attrarre; (picture) disegnare; (sport) pareggiare; (extract) estrarre. **draw back** ritirarsi. **drawback** n inconveniente m. **drawbridge** n ponte levatoio m. **draw near** avvicinarsi. **draw on** (funds) attingere (a). n (sport) pareggio m. **drawing** n disegno m. **drawing-board** n tavola

da disegno f. **drawing-pin** n puntina da disegno f. **drawing-room** n salotto m.

drawer ['drɔːə] n cassetto m. **chest of drawers** cassettone m. **drawers** pl n (underclothes) mutandine f pl.

drawl [drɔːl] v strascicare le parole.

drawn [drɔːn] V **draw**.

dread [dred] v aver paura di. n timore m, paura f, fobia f. **dreadful** adj spaventoso.

***dream** [driːm] n sogno m; visione f. v sognare; immaginare. **dreamer** n sognatore, -trice m, f; visionario, -a m, f. **dreamy** adj (vague) vago.

dreamt [dremt] V **dream**.

dreary ['driəri] adj triste; (boring) noioso. **dreariness** n tristezza f.

dredge [dredʒ] v dragare.

dregs [dregz] pl n feccia f sing; (coffee) fondo m sing.

drench [drentʃ] v inzuppare, bagnare.

dress [dres] v (clothe) vestire; (salad, etc.) condire; (wounds) bendare. n abito m, vestito m. **dress circle** prima galleria f. **dressmaker** n sarta f. **dressmaking** n confezione di abiti da donna f. **dress rehearsal** prova generale f. **dressing** n condimento m; benda f. **dressing down** rimprovero m. **dressing-gown** n vestaglia f. **dressing-room** n camerino m. **dressing-table** n toilette (pl -s) f.

dresser[1] ['dresə] n (furniture) credenza f.

dresser[2] ['dresə] n (theatre) vestiarista m, f; (med) assistente medico, -a m, f.

drew [druː] V **draw**.

dribble ['dribl] v sbavare; (trickle) gocciolare; (ball) palleggiare. n bava f; gocciolamento m; palleggio m.

drier ['draiə] n (clothes) asciugatrice f; (hair) asciugacapelli m.

drift [drift] n andare alla deriva; (wander aimlessly) lasciarsi andare. **drift apart** perdersi di vista. n tendenza f, direzione f; (movement) deriva f; (current) corrente f.

drill[1] [dril] n trivella f, sonda f, trapano m. v trapanare, sondare.

drill[2] [dril] n esercitazioni f pl, addestramento m. v esercitare, fare esercitazioni, addestrare.

***drink** [driŋk] v bere. n bibita f, bevanda f. **drinkable** adj bevibile, potabile. **drinking fountain** n fontanella f. **drinking water** acqua potabile f.

drip [drip] v gocciolare. n gocciolio m, gocciolatura f; (slang) persona insulsa f.

dripping n stillicidio m; (fat) grasso colato m.

•drive [draiv] v condurre; (car) guidare; (push) spingere. **drive away** scacciare. n (road) viale m; (trip) corsa f, giro m; energia f, iniziativa f; (golf) colpo forte m. **driver** n guidatore, -trice m, f. **driving-licence** n patente di guida f. **driving-test** n esame di guida m.

drivel ['drivl] n (nonsense) sciocchezze f pl. v dir sciocchezze.

driven ['drivn] V **drive**.

drizzle ['drizl] v piovigginare. n pioggerella f.

drone [droun] n (bee) fuco m, pecchione m; (idler) fannullone m; (hum) ronzio m. v (hum) ronzare. **droning** adj ronzante, monotono.

droop [druːp] v afflosciarsi, accasciarsi. n accasciamento m. **drooping** adj piegato in giù, floscio.

drop [drop] n goccia f; (fall) caduta f. v (fall) cadere; (let fall) far cadere; (lower) calare; diminuire, abbassarsi. **dropper** n contagocce m. **droppings** pl n sterco m sing.

dropout ['dropaut] n emarginato, -a m, f. v **drop out** ritirarsi, rinunciare.

drought [draut] n siccità f.

drove [drouv] V **drive**.

drown [draun] v annegare, affogare.

drowsy ['drauzi] adj sonnolento, assopito.

drudge [drʌdʒ] v sfacchinare, sgobbare. n sgobbone, -a m, f. **drudgery** n sfacchinata f.

drug [drʌg] n medicinale m, droga f, stupefacente m. **drug-addict** n drogato, -a m, f, tossicomane m, f. v narcotizzare, drogare.

drum [drʌm] n tamburo m, timpano m; (cylinder) cilindro m, rullo m. **drumstick** n bacchetta da tamburo f; (chicken) coscia di pollo f. v suonare il tamburo; (beat) tamburellare. **drummer** n tamburo m.

drunk [drʌŋk] V **drink**. adj ubriaco (m pl -chi), sbronzo. **get drunk** ubriacarsi. **drunkard** n ubriacone, -a m, f; sbronzo, -a m, f. **drunkenness** n ubriachezza f.

dry [drai] adj asciutto, secco; (uninteresting) monotono; (caustic) mordace. v asciugare, seccare. **dry-clean** v lavare a secco. **dry-cleaning** n lavaggio a secco m. **dry rot** carie del legno f.

dual ['djuəl] adj doppio, duplice.

dubbed ['dʌbd] adj (film) doppiato; (name) qualificato.

dubious ['djuːbiəs] adj dubbio, equivoco, incerto. **dubiousness** n incertezza f.

duchess ['dʌtʃis] n duchessa f.

duck[1] [dʌk] n (zool) anitra f. **duckling** n anatroccolo m.

duck[2] [dʌk] v (plunge) tuffare, immergere; (dodge) schivare; (lower the head) chinarsi di colpo.

dud [dʌd] adj inutile. n (explosive) proiettile che non esplode m.

due [djuː] adj (owing) da pagarsi; (rightful, proper) debito; (attributable) dovuto; (expected) atteso, in arrivo. adv direttamente. **due to** a causa di. **dues** pl n dazio m sing, diritti m pl.

duel ['djuəl] n duello m, lotta f.

duet [dju'et] n duetto m.

duffel bag ['dʌfəl] n sacca da viaggio f.

duffel coat ['dʌfəl] n montgomery m invar.

dug [dʌg] V **dig**.

duke [djuːk] n duca m.

dull [dʌl] adj (unintelligent) ottuso; (boring) noioso; (slow) lento; monotono; (not sharp) non tagliente; (weather) grigio. v attutire, attenuare, intorpidire. **dullness** n lentezza f; noia f.

duly ['djuːli] adv debitamente.

dumb [dʌm] adj muto, reticente; (slang: foolish) scemo. **dumbfound** v sbalordire, stupire.

dummy ['dʌmi] adj falso, finto. n (man of straw) uomo di paglia m; (cards) morto m; (baby's) biberon m invar, poppatoio m; (model) manichino m.

dump [dʌmp] n (tip) luogo di scarico m; (coll) posto triste m. v (get rid of) scartare, disfarsi di; (unload) scaricare.

dunce [dʌns] n ignorante m, f.

dune [djuːn] n duna f.

dung [dʌŋ] n letame m, sterco m.

dungarees [dʌŋgə'riːz] pl n (overalls) tuta f sing.

dungeon ['dʌndʒən] n segreta f, cella sotterranea f.

duplicate v 'djuːplikət] n v 'djuːplikeit] adj duplice, doppio. n duplicato m, duplice copia f, doppione m. v duplicare.

durable ['djuərəbl] adj durevole, duraturo.

duration [dju'reiʃən] n durata f.

during ['djuriŋ] *prep* durante, nel corso di.

dusk [dʌsk] *n* crepuscolo *m*.

dust [dʌst] *n* polvere *f*. *v* (*clean*) spolverare; (*sprinkle*) cospargere. **dustbin** *n* pattumiera *f*. **dustman** *n* spazzino *m*. **dustpan** *n* paletta per la spazzatura *f*. **duster** *n* spolverino *m*, strofinaccio *m*. **dusty** *adj* polveroso.

Dutch [dʌtʃ] *adj* olandese. **Dutch person** olandese *m*, *f*. **go Dutch** fare *or* pagare alla romana.

duty ['djuti] *n* dovere *m*; (*customs*) dogana *f*.

duvet ['duvei] *n* piumino *m*.

dwarf [dwoːf] *n* nano *m*. *v* (*make appear small*) far sembrare piccolo; (*render insignificant*) sminuire.

*** dwell** [dwel] *v* (*reside*) dimorare. **dwell on** soffermarsi su. **dwelling** *n* dimora *f*, abitazione *f*.

dwelt [dwelt] *V* **dwell**.

dwindle ['dwindl] *v* diminuire; (*decline*) deperire.

dye [dai] *n* colorante *m*, tintura *f*. *v* colorare, tingere. **dyed in the wool** inveterato, radicato. **dyer** *n* tintore *m*.

dyke [daik] *n* diga *f*, argine *m*.

dynamic [dai'namik] *adj* dinamico. **dynamics** *n* dinamica *f*.

dynamite ['dainəmait] *n* dinamite *f*.

dynamo ['dainə,mou] *n* dinamo *f invar*.

dynasty ['dinasti] *n* dinastia *f*.

dysentery ['disəntri] *n* dissenteria *f*.

dyslexia [dis'leksiə] *n* dislessia *f*.

dyspepsia [dis'pepsiə] *n* dispepsia *f*.

E

each [iːtʃ] *adj* ogni, ciascuno. *pron* ognuno. *adv* (*apiece*) l'uno, l'una. **each other** l'un l'altro.

eager ['iːgə] *adj* avido, premuroso; impaziente. **eagerness** *n* impazienza *f*; zelo *m*; brama *f*.

eagle ['iːgl] *n* aquila *f*.

ear[1] [iə] *n* orecchio *m*. **be up to one's ears in ...** aver ... fin sopra i capelli. **earache** *n* mal d'orecchi *m*. **eardrum** *n* timpano *m*. **earmark** *v* contrassegnare; (*set aside*) mettere da parte; (*money*) stanziare. **ear-plug** *n* tappo per orecchi *m*. **ear-ring** *n* orecchino *m*. **ear-splitting**

adj assordante. **within earshot** a portata d'orecchio.

ear[2] [iə] *n* spiga *f*.

earl [əːl] *n* conte *m*.

early ['əːli] *adv* presto, di buon'ora. *adj* primo; (*morning*) mattiniero, mattutino; (*before time*) prematuro; (*ancient*) antico (*m pl* -chi).

earn [əːn] *v* guadagnare, meritare. **earnings** *pl n* guadagni *m pl*, stipendio *m*.

earnest ['əːnist] *adj* serio, coscienzioso. **be in earnest** fare sul serio. **earnestness** *n* serietà *f*.

earth [əːθ] *n* terra *f*; (*world*) mondo *m*; (*soil*) terreno *m*. **earthquake** *n* terremoto *m*. *v* (*elec*) mettere a terra. **earthenware** *n* terraglia *f*. **earthly** *adj* terrestre. **earthy** *adj* (*coarse*) grossolano; robusto.

earwig ['iəwig] *n* forbicina *f*.

ease [iːz] *n* agio *m*, comodo *m*. **at ease** tranquillo. **ill at ease** a disagio. *v* agevolare, alleggerire.

easel ['iːzl] *n* cavalletto *m*.

east [iːst] *adj* orientale, dell'est. *n* oriente *m*, est *m*. **Middle/Near/Far East** medio/prossimo/estremo oriente *m*. **eastward** *adv*, *adj* verso est, ad est, verso oriente.

Easter ['iːstə] *n* Pasqua *f*.

easy ['iːzi] *adj* facile, semplice; (*informal*) disinvolto; (*compliant*) accomodante. **easy chair** poltrona *f*. **easy-going** *adj* (*placid*) bonaccione, pacione; indolente; tollerante.

*** eat** [iːt] *v* mangiare. **eatable** *adj* mangiabile, mangereccio.

eaten ['iːtn] *V* **eat**.

eavesdrop ['iːvzdrop] *v* origliare.

ebb [eb] *n* riflusso *m*; declino *m*. *v* rifluire; declinare.

eccentric [ik'sentrik] *nm*, *adj* eccentrico. **eccentricity** *n* eccentricità *f*.

ecclesiastical [iklizi'astikl] *adj* ecclesiastico.

echo ['ekou] *v* echeggiare, far eco a. *n* eco *f*, *m* (*pl* -i *m*).

eclair [ei'kleə] *n* bignè *m invar*.

eclipse [i'klips] *n* eclissi *f*. *v* eclissare.

ecology [i'kolədʒi] *n* ecologia *f*.

economy [i'konəmi] *n* economia *f*. **economical** *or* **economic** *adj* economico, a buon prezzo; (*thrifty*) frugale. **economics** *n* economia *f*, scienze economiche *f pl*. **economist** *n* economista *m*, *f*. **economize** *v* economizzare, fare economia.

ecstasy ['ekstəsi] *n* estasi *f*. **ecstatic** *adj* estatico.

eczema ['eksimə] *n* eczema *m*.

edge [edʒ] *n* orlo *m*, margine *m*; *(blade)* filo *m*; *(road)* ciglio *m*; *(river)* sponda *f*. **be on edge** avere i nervi. *v* orlare.

edible ['edəbl] *adj* mangereccio, mangiabile.

Edinburgh ['edinbərə] *n* Edimburgo *f*.

edit ['edit] *v* curare, redigere, dirigere. **editor** *n* redattore, -trice *m, f*; *(newspaper)* direttore, -trice *m, f*. **editorial** *n* articolo di fondo *m*. **edition** *n* edizione *f*.

educate ['edju,keit] *v* educare, istruire. **educated** *adj* colto, istruito. **education** *n* educazione *f*, istruzione *f*; *(teaching)* insegnamento *m*, pedagogia *f*.

eel [iil] *n* anguilla *f*.

eerie ['iəri] *adj* *(strange)* misterioso; *(causing fear)* pauroso.

effect [i'fekt] *n* effetto *m*; conseguenza *f*, risultato *m*; impressione *f*. **take effect** entrare in vigore. **with effect from** a partire da. *v* effettuare, realizzare. **effective** *adj* efficace, efficiente.

effeminate [i'feminət] *adj* effeminato.

effervescent [,efə'vesənt] *adj* effervescente.

efficient [i'fiʃənt] *adj* efficiente, capace. **efficiency** *n* efficienza *f*, capacità *f*; *(machine)* rendimento *m*.

effigy ['efidʒi] *n* effigie *f*.

effort ['efət] *n* sforzo *m*, fatica *f*. **make an effort** sforzarsi, fare di tutto. **effortless** *adj* senza sforzo.

egg [eg] *n* uovo *m* *(pl -a f)*. **egg-cup** *n* portauovo *m*. **egg-shaped** *adj* ovale. **eggshell** *n* guscio d'uovo *m*. **egg-whisk** *n* frullino *m*. **egg on** aizzare.

ego ['iigou] *n* ego *m*. **egocentric** *adj* egocentrico. **egoism** *n* egoismo *m*. **egoist** *n* egoista *m, f*. **egoistic(al)** *adj* egoista, egoistico. **egotism** *n* egotismo *m*. **egotist** *n* egotista *m, f*. **egotistic(al)** *adj* egotista.

Egypt ['iidʒipt] *n* Egitto *m*. **Egyptian** *n, adj* egiziano, -a; *(ancient)* egizio, -a.

eiderdown ['aidədaun] *n* piumino *m*.

eight [eit] *nm, adj* otto. **eighth** *nm, adj* ottavo.

eighteen [ei'tiin] *nm, adj* diciotto. **eighteenth** *nm, adj* diciottesimo.

eighty ['eiti] *nm, adj* ottanta. **eightieth** *nm, adj* ottantesimo.

either ['aiðə] *pron, adj* l'uno o l'altro; *(each)* ciascuno dei due, tutti e due. *adv* nemmeno, neppure, neanche. *conj* **either** ... **or** ... o ... o ..., **sia ... che ...**, sia ... sia ...

ejaculate [i'dʒakjuleit] *v* eiaculare; esclamare. **ejaculation** *n* eiaculazione *f*, esclamazione *f*.

eject [i'dʒekt] *v* espellere, gettar fuori. **ejector seat** sedile eiettabile *m*.

eke [iik] *v* **eke out** supplire. **eke out a living** sbarcare il lunario.

elaborate [i'labərit; *adj* i'labərət] *v* elaborare, sviluppare. *adj* elaborato, minuzioso.

elapse [i'laps] *v* passare, decorrere.

elastic [i'lastik] *nm, adj* elastico.

elated [i'leitid] *adj* giubilante, euforico.

elbow ['elbou] *n* gomito *m*. **elbow-room** *n* libertà di movimento *f*. *v* *(jostle)* dar gomitate.

elder[1] ['eldə] *adj* più vecchio, maggiore. *n* anziano, -a *m, f*. **elderly** *adj* di una certa età, anziano.

elder[2] ['eldə] *n* sambuco *(pl -chi)* *m*. **elderberry** *n* bacca di sambuco *f*.

eldest ['eldist] *adj* più vecchio, maggiore, primogenito.

elect [i'lekt] *v* eleggere, scegliere. *adj* eletto, scelto. **election** *n* elezione *f*. **electioneering** *n* campagna elettorale *f*. **electorate** *n* elettorato *m*. **elector** *n* elettore, -trice *m, f*.

electricity [elek'trisəti] *n* elettricità *f*. **electric** *adj* elettrico. **electric appliances** elettrodomestici *m pl*. **electrician** *n* elettricista *m*. **electrify** *v* elettrificare. **electrocution** *n* elettroesecuzione *f*. **electrode** *n* elettrodo *m*. **electrolysis** *n* elettrolisi *f*. **electron** *n* elettrone *m*. **electronic** *adj* elettronico. **electronics** *n* elettronica *f*.

elegant ['eligənt] *adj* elegante, fine. **elegance** *n* eleganza *f*, finezza *f*.

elegy ['elidʒi] *n* elegia *f*. **elegiac** *adj* elegiaco.

element ['eləmənt] *n* elemento *m*, fattore *m*. **elemental** *adj* fondamentale. **elementary** *adj* elementare.

elephant ['elifənt] *n* elefante *m*. **elephantine** *adj* elefantesco.

elevate ['eliveit] *v* elevare, innalzare; *(exalt)* esaltare. **elevated** *adj* alto, eminente. **elevation** *n* *(altitude)* altezza *f*; *(drawing)* proiezione ortogonale *f*; *(grandeur)* elevatezza *f*. **elevator** *n* *(lift)* ascensore *m*.

eleven [i'levn] *nm, adj* undici. **eleventh** *nm, adj* undicesimo.

elf [elf] *n* elfo *m*, folletto *m*.

eligible ['elidʒəbl] *adj* eleggibile; desiderabile.

eliminate [i'limineit] *v* eliminare, scartare. **elimination** *n* eliminazione *f*.

elite [ei'li:t] *n* élite (*pl* -s) *f*, fior fiore *m invar*.

ellipse [i'lips] *n* ellisse *f*.

elm [elm] *n* olmo *m*.

elocution [elə'kju:ʃən] *n* elocuzione *f*.

elope [i'loup] *v* fuggire. **elopement** *n* fuga *f*.

eloquent ['eləkwənt] *adj* eloquente, rettorico. **eloquence** *n* eloquenza *f*, rettorica *f*.

else [els] *adv, pron* altro, altrimenti. **elsewhere** *adv* altrove.

elucidate [i'lu:sideit] *v* chiarire, spiegare.

elude [i'lu:d] *v* eludere, evitare. **elusive** *adj* evasivo, elusivo.

emaciated [i'meisieitid] *adj* scarno, emaciato.

emanate ['eməneit] *v* emanare, emettere, scaturire. **emanation** *n* emanazione *f*, emissione *f*.

emancipate [i'mansipeit] *v* emancipare. **emancipation** *n* emancipazione *f*.

embalm [im'ba:m] *v* imbalsamare.

embankment [im'baŋkmənt] *n* argine *m*, lungofiume *m*.

embargo [im'ba:gou] *n* embargo *m*, sanzioni *f pl*, proibizione *f*.

embark [im'ba:k] *v* imbarcare. **embark on** intraprendere.

embarrass [im'barəs] *v* mettere in imbarazzo. **embarrassment** *n* imbarazzo *m*.

embassy ['embəsi] *n* ambasciata *f*.

embellish [im'beliʃ] *v* abbellire, ornare. **embellishment** *n* abbellimento *m*.

ember ['embə] *n* tizzone *m*. **embers** *pl n* brace *f pl*.

embezzle [im'bezl] *v* appropriarsi indebitamente. **embezzlement** *n* appropriazione indebita *f*, malversazione *f*. **embezzler** *n* malversatore, -trice *m, f*.

embitter [im'bitə] *v* rendere amaro, amareggiare.

emblem ['embləm] *n* emblema *m*, simbolo *m*.

embody [im'bodi] *v* incorporare; (*comprise*) comprendere; incarnare; concretare.

emboss [im'bos] *v* sbalzare, fare in rilievo, scolpire in rilievo.

embrace [im'breis] *v* abbracciare. *n* abbraccio *m*.

embroider [im'broidə] *v* ricamare; (*embellish*) abbellire. **embroidery** *n* ricamo *m*.

embryo ['embriou] *n* embrione *m*. **embryonic** *adj* embrionale.

emerald ['emərəld] *n* smeraldo *m*.

emerge [i'mə:dʒ] *v* emergere.

emergency [i'mə:dʒənsi] *n* emergenza *f*, caso imprevisto *m*. **emergency exit** uscita di sicurezza *f*. **in case of emergency** in caso di urgenza.

emigrate ['emigreit] *v* emigrare. **emigration** *n* emigrazione *f*.

eminent ['eminənt] *adj* eminente, distinto.

emit [i'mit] *v* emettere, emanare. **emission** *n* emissione *f*.

emotion [i'mouʃən] *n* emozione *f*, sentimento *m*, commozione *f*. **emotional** emotivo; impressionabile.

empathy ['empəθi] *n* empatia *f*, immedesimazione *f*.

emphasis ['emfəsis] *n, pl* -ses enfasi *f*, veemenza *f*, rilievo *m*. **emphasize** *v* dare rilievo a, mettere in evidenza. **emphatic** *adj* enfatico, risoluto, intenso.

empire ['empaiə] *n* impero *m*. **emperor** *n* imperatore *m*. **empress** *n* imperatrice *f*.

empirical [im'pirikəl] *adj* empirico.

employ [im'ploi] *v* impiegare; (*use*) adoperare, usare. **employee** *n* impiegato, -a *m, f*. **employer** *n* padrone, -a *m, f*; datore, -trice di lavoro *m, f*. **employment** *n* impiego (*pl* -ghi) *m*, lavoro *m*. **employment agency** ufficio di collocamento *m*.

empower [im'pauə] *v* autorizzare.

empty ['empti] *adj* vuoto. *v* vuotare, scaricare. **empty-handed** *adj* a mani vuote.

emulate ['emjuleit] *v* emulare. **emulation** *n* emulazione *f*.

emulsion [i'mʌlʃən] *n* emulsione *f*.

enable [i'neibl] *v* mettere in grado di, permettere; (*law*) abilitare.

enact [i'nakt] *v* (*ordain*) ordinare; (*decree*) decretare; (*put into operation*) promulgare; (*theatre*) recitare.

enamel [i'naməl] *n* smalto *m*. *v* smaltare.

enamoured [i'naməd] *adj* innamorato.

enchant [in'tʃa:nt] *v* incantare, affascinare, ammaliare. **enchanting** *adj* incantevole. **enchantment** *n* incanto *m*, incantesimo *m*, fascino *m*.

encircle [in'səːkl] v cingere, accerchiare. **encirclement** n accerchiamento m.

enclose [in'klouz] v rinchiudere; (letter) allegare. **enclosure** n recinto m; (letter) allegato m; (rel) clausura f.

encore ['oŋkoi] nm, interj bis.

encounter [in'kauntə] v incontrare, affrontare. n incontro m; (battle) lotta f.

encourage [in'kʌridʒ] v incoraggiare, favorire, stimolare. **encouragement** n incitamento m, stimolo m.

encroach [in'kroutʃ] v **encroach on** abusare di; (intrude on) invadere.

encumber [in'kʌmbə] v ingombrare, impacciare; (burden) sopraffare. **encumbrance** n (hindrance) impaccio m; (burden) carico (pl -chi) m.

encyclopedia [insaiklə'piːdiə] n enciclopedia f.

end [end] n fine f, termine m; (purpose) scopo m; (result) conclusione f. **in the end** infine. **make ends meet** sbarcare il lunario. v finire, concludere, terminare. **endless** adj interminabile, senza fine.

endanger [in'deindʒə] v mettere in pericolo, compromettere.

endear [in'diə] v rendere caro. **endearing** adj simpatico, amabile.

endeavour [in'devə] v cercare, tentare. n sforzo m, tentativo m.

endemic [en'demik] n endemico.

endive ['endiv] n indivia f, cicoria f.

endorse [in'dois] v approvare; (sign) vistare; (cheque) girare; (record infringement) annotare le infrazioni commesse. **endorsement** n visto m, girata f, annotazione delle infrazioni commesse f.

endow [in'dau] v dotare, fornire. **endowment** n dotazione f, donazione f.

endure [in'djuə] v tollerare, sopportare; (last) durare; resistere. **endurance** n resistenza f.

enema ['enəmə] n clistere m, enteroclisma m.

enemy ['enəmi] n nemico, -a m, f; avversario, -a m, f.

energy ['enədʒi] n energia f. **energetic** adj energico.

enfold [in'fould] v avvolgere.

enforce [in'fois] v imporre, far valere, far rispettare. **enforced** adj obbligatorio, imposto. **enforcement** n imposizione f, applicazione f.

engage [in'geidʒ] v (employ) assumere, impiegare; (occupy) impegnare,

occupare; (mil) attaccare; (interlock) ingranare, innestare; (reserve) prenotare. **engaged** adj (busy) occupato; (betrothed) fidanzato. **get engaged** fidanzarsi. **engagement** n fidanzamento m; (employment) impiego (pl -ghi) m; (obligation) impegno m; (appointment) appuntamento m.

engine ['endʒin] n motore m, macchina f; (rail) locomotiva f.

engineer [endʒi'niə] n ingegnere, -a m, f; meccanico, -a m, f; tecnico, -a m, f; (mil) geniere m. v (construct) costruire; (contrive) macchinare, tramare. **engineering** n costruzione f; (study, science) ingegneria f.

England ['ingländ] n Inghilterra f. **English** n (m+f), adj inglese.

engrave [in'greiv] v incidere, intagliare; (printing) imprimere. **engraver** n incisore m. **engraving** n incisione f.

engrossed [in'groust] adj preso (da), immerso.

engulf [in'gʌlf] v ingolfare.

enhance [in'hɑns] v intensificare, aumentare, migliorare.

enigma [i'nigmə] n enigma m. **enigmatic** adj enigmatico, misterioso.

enjoy [in'dʒoi] v godere, apprezzare. **enjoy oneself** divertirsi. **enjoyable** adj divertente, piacevole. **enjoyment** n piacere m, godimento m, gioia f, divertimento m.

enlarge [in'lɑdʒ] v ingrandire. **enlarge on** dilungarsi su. **enlargement** n ingrandimento m; (med) ipertrofia f.

enlighten [in'laitn] v illuminare, chiarire. **enlightenment** n schiarimento m, delucidazione f; (history) illuminismo m.

enlist [in'list] v arruolare; (obtain) ottenere. **enlistment** n arruolamento m.

enliven [in'laivn] v animare, ravvivare.

enmity ['enməti] n ostilità f.

enormous [i'noiməs] adj enorme, immenso.

enough [i'nʌf] adv abbastanza, sufficientemente. adj sufficiente, abbastanza, bastante. **be enough** bastare. interj basta!

enquire [in'kwaiə] V **inquire**.

enrage [in'reidʒ] v far arrabbiare. **enraged** adj arrabbiato, furioso.

enrich [in'ritʃ] v arricchire, abbellire.

enrol [in'roul] v (mil) arruolare; (college, etc.) iscrivere. **enrolment** n arruolamento m; iscrizione f.

enslave [in'sleiv] v far schiavo, assoggettare. **enslavement** n schiavitù f.

ensue [in'sjuː] v seguire, risultare.

ensure [in'ʃuə] v assicurare, garantire.

entail [in'teil] v comportare, implicare.

entangle [in'taŋgl] v impigliare, aggroviliare; (involve) coinvolgere. **entanglement** n impiccio m, imbroglio m.

enter ['entə] v entrare (in); penetrare; (join) iscriversi a; (record) notare.

enterprise ['entə praiz] n impresa f, iniziativa f. **enterprising** adj intraprendente, pieno d'iniziativa.

entertain [entə'tein] v (amuse) divertire; (receive guests) ricevere ospitare; (consider) concepire, prendere in considerazione. **entertainer** n (actor) attore, -trice m, f; (singer) cantante m, f. **entertaining** adj divertente, piacevole. **entertainment** n divertimento m, spettacolo m.

enthral [in'θrɔːl] v affascinare.

enthusiasm [in'θjuːzi azəm] n entusiasmo m. **enthusiast** n entusiasta m, f; (fam) tifoso, -a m, f. **enthusiastic** adj entusiastico, appassionato.

entice [in'tais] v sedurre, allettare. **enticement** n seduzione f, allettamento m.

entire [in'taiə] adj intero, completo, assoluto. **in its entirety** nel suo insieme.

entitle [in'taitl] v dar diritto a, qualificare, autorizzare; (name) intitolare. **entitlement** n diritto m, titolo m.

entity ['entəti] n entità f.

entrails ['entreilz] pl n viscere f pl.

entrance[1] ['entrəns] n entrata f, ingresso m, ammissione f.

entrance[2] [in'trains] v incantare, estasiare.

entrant ['entrənt] n candidato, -a m, f; concorrente m, f.

entreat [in'triːt] v supplicare, implorare. **entreaty** n supplica f, preghiera f.

entrée ['ontrei] n (main course) piatto principale m, secondo piatto m; (first course) primo piatto m.

entrench [in'trentʃ] v trincerare, rafforzare. **entrenched** adj (set) radicato.

entrepreneur [ontrəprə'nɜː] n imprenditore, -trice m, f.

entrust [in'trʌst] v affidare.

entry ['entri] n entrata f; (book-keeping) partita f; annotazione f.

entwine [in'twain] v intrecciare.

enumerate [i'njuːməreit] v annoverare, elencare.

enunciate [i'nʌnsi eit] v enunciare; articolare.

envelop [in'veləp] v avvolgere.

envelope ['envə loup] n busta f.

environment [in'vaiərənmənt] n ambiente m.

envisage [in'vizidʒ] v contemplare, immaginare.

envoy ['envoi] n inviato, -a m, f.

envy ['envi] n invidia f. v invidiare. **envious** adj invidioso.

enzyme ['enzaim] n enzima m.

ephemeral [i'femərəl] adj effimero, passeggero.

epic ['epik] adj epico. n epopea f.

epicure ['epikjuə] n epicureo m; (gourmet) buongustaio, -a m, f.

epidemic [epi'demik] n epidemia f. adj epidemico.

epilepsy ['epilepsi] n epilessi f. **epileptic** nm, adj epilettico.

epilogue ['epilog] n epilogo (pl -ghi) m.

Epiphany [i'pifəni] n Epifania f.

episcopal [i'piskəpəl] adj vescovile.

episode ['episoud] n episodio m, incidente m.

epitaph ['epi taɪf] n epitaffio m.

epitome [i'pitəmi] n epitome f, compendio m.

epoch ['iːpok] n epoca f.

equable ['ekwəbl] adj equanime, sereno, uniforme.

equal ['iːkwəl] adj eguale, uguale, pari. v uguagliare; (in calculations) fare. **equality** n uguaglianza f, parità f. **equalize** v ragguagliare; (sport) pareggiare.

equanimity [ekwə'nimiti] n equanimità f, serenità f.

equate [i'kweit] v uguagliare, paragonare. **equation** n equazione f.

equator [i'kweitə] n equatore m.

equestrian [i'kwestriən] adj equestre.

equilateral [iːkwi'lætərəl] adj equilatero.

equilibrium [iːkwi'libriəm] n equilibrio m. **equilibrate** v equilibrare, bilanciare.

equinox ['iːkwinɔks] n equinozio m.

equip [i'kwip] v (array) allestire; (furnish) attrezzare, fornire (di); dotare (di). **equipment** n equipaggiamento m, attrezzatura f.

equity ['ekwəti] n giustizia f; imparzialità f; (property) valore netto m; (securities) azioni ordinarie f pl.

equivalent [i'kwivələnt] nm, adj equivalente.

era ['iərə] n era f, epoca f.
eradicate [i'radi,keit] v sradicare, estirpare.
erase [i'reiz] v cancellare.
erect [i'rekt] v erigere, costruire. adj eretto, dritto. **erection** n erezione f.
ermine ['əmin] n ermellino m.
erode [i'roud] v erodere. **erosion** n erosione f.
erotic [i'rotik] adj erotico.
err [əː] v errare; (make mistakes) sbagliare; (sin) peccare.
errand ['erənd] n commissione f. **errand-boy** n fattorino m.
erratic [i'ratik] adj erratico.
error ['erə] n errore m, sbaglio m, torto m. **erroneous** adj erroneo.
erudite ['erudait] adj erudito, dotto. **erudition** n erudizione f.
erupt [i'rupt] v (volcano) eruttare; (burst out) erompere. **eruption** n eruzione f.
escalate ['eskə,leit] v intensificare. **escalation** n intensificazione f. **escalator** n scala mobile f.
escalope ['eskə,lop] n scaloppina f.
escape [is'keip] v fuggire, sfuggire; (avoid) evitare. n fuga f, evasione f. **escapism** n evasione dalla realtà f.
escort ['eskort; v i'skort] n scorta f. v scortare.
esoteric [esə'terik] adj esoterico.
especial [i'spefəl] adj notevole, particolare. **especially** adv specie, specialmente.
espionage ['espiə,narʒ] n spionaggio m.
esplanade [esplə'neid] n spianata f, lungomare m.
essay ['esei] n saggio m, tema m.
essence ['esns] n essenza f; (gist) nocciolo m.
essential [i'senfəl] adj essenziale, indispensabile.
establish [i'stablif] v stabilire, fondare; (ascertain) constatare; (set up) istituire, instaurare; (fix) determinare. **established** adj (set) radicato; (beyond question) indubbio. **establishment** n costituzione f, fondazione f; (house) casa f; (organization) personale effettivo m.
estate [i'steit] n (property) tenuta f; (possessions) beni m pl, patrimonio m. **estate agent** agente immobiliare m. **estate car** giardinietta f. **housing estate** quartiere residenziale m.
esteem [i'stim] n stima f, considerazione f. v stimare, apprezzare.

estimate ['esti,meit; n 'estimət] v (value) valutare; (judge) stimare; (assess cost) preventivare. n preventivo m; valutazione f. **estimation** n valutazione f; considerazione f.
estrange [i'streindʒ] v alienare. **estrangement** n alienazione f; allontanamento m.
estuary ['estjuəri] n estuario m.
eternal [i'təml] adj eterno. **eternity** n eternità f.
ether ['iθə] n etere m.
ethereal [i'θiəriəl] adj etereo, evanescente.
ethical ['eθikl] adj etico, morale. **ethics** pl n etica f sing, morale f sing.
ethnic ['eθnik] adj etnico. **ethnology** n etnologia f.
etiquette ['eti,ket] n etichetta f, comportamento m, cerimoniale m.
etymology [,eti'molədʒi] n etimologia f. **etymological** adj etimologico.
Eucharist ['juːkərist] n eucaristia f.
eunuch ['juːnək] n eunuco (pl -chi) m.
euphemism ['juːfə,mizəm] n eufemismo m. **euphemistic** adj eufemistico.
euphoria [juː'foːriə] n euforia f. **euphoric** adj euforico.
Europe ['juərəp] n Europa f. **European** n, adj europeo, -a. **European Economic Community** Comunità Economica Europea f.
euthanasia [,juːθə'neiziə] n eutanasia f.
evacuate [i'vakju,eit] v evacuare, sfollare. **evacuation** n evacuazione f, sfollamento m.
evade [i'veid] v evadere, evitare, eludere. **evasion** n evasione f. **evasive** adj evasivo, elusivo.
evaluate [i'valju,eit] v valutare. **evaluation** n valutazione f.
evangelical [,iːvan'dʒelikəl] adj evangelico. **evangelist** n evangelista m.
evaporate [i'vapə,reit] v evaporare, far evaporare. **evaporation** n evaporazione f.
eve [iːv] n vigilia f.
even ['iːvən] adj (flat) piano, piatto; (regular) uniforme, regolare; (not odd) pari. adv (still) ancora; (indeed) perfino. **even if** benché, sebbene, quantunque. v livellare, uguagliare.
evening ['iːvniŋ] n sera f, serata f. **evening class** classe or scuola serale f. **evening dress** abito da sera m.
evensong ['iːvən,soŋ] n vespro m.

event [i'vent] n avvenimento m, evento m; (*outcome*) eventualità f; (*sport*) gara f.
eventful adj ricco di vicende, memorabile. **eventual** adj finale, contingente. **eventually** adv alla fine, ultimamente.

ever ['evə] adv sempre, mai. **ever since** da quando, da allora. **evergreen** nm, adj sempreverde. **everlasting** adj eterno, perpetuo, perenne. **hardly ever** quasi mai.

every ['evri] adj ogni, ognuno, ciascuno. **everybody** or **everyone** pron ognuno, tutti pl. **everyday** adj quotidiano, normale. **every now and then** di tanto in tanto. **every other day** un giorno sì un giorno no. **everything** pron tutto, ogni cosa. **everywhere** adv dovunque, dappertutto.

evict [i'vikt] v sfrattare. **eviction** n sfratto m.

evidence ['evidəns] n prova f, evidenza f; (*law*) testimonianza f, deposizione f. **give evidence** (*law*) deporre, testimoniare. **evident** adj evidente, manifesto, ovvio.

evil ['iːvl] adj cattivo, malvagio. n male m, peccato m. **evil-doer** malfattore, -trice m, f. **evil eye** malocchio m. **evil-looking** adj losco. **evil-minded** adj malintenzionato.

evoke [i'vouk] v evocare.

evolve [i'volv] v evolvere, sviluppare. **evolution** n evoluzione f.

ewe [juː] n pecora (femmina) f.

exacerbate [ig'zasəbeit] v esacerbare, inasprire, irritare.

exact [ig'zakt] adj esatto, preciso. v esigere, richiedere. **exacting** adj esigente, impegnativo. **exactitude** n esattezza f, precisione f.

exaggerate [ig'zadʒəreit] v esagerare. **exaggeration** n esagerazione f.

exalt [ig'zolt] v esaltare. (*praise*) vantare, lodare. **exaltation** n esaltazione f.

examine [ig'zamin] v esaminare; verificare; (*med*) visitare; (*law*) interrogare. **examination** n esame m; verifica f; visita medica f; (*law*) interrogatorio m. **examiner** n ispettore, -trice m, f.

example [ig'zaːmpl] n esempio m; (*specimen*) esemplare m. **for example** per esempio.

exasperate [ig'zaːspəreit] v esasperare; esacerbare; irritare. **exasperating** adj esasperante. **exasperation** n esasperazione f.

excavate ['ekskəveit] v scavare. **excavation** n scavo m.

exceed [ik'siːd] v eccedere, superare. **exceedingly** adv estremamente.

excel [ik'sel] v eccellere.

excellent ['eksələnt] adj eccellente, ottimo. **excellence** n eccellenza f, superiorità f. **Excellency** n Eccellenza f.

except [ik'sept] prep eccetto, salvo, tranne, all'infuori di. v escludere, eccettuare.

excerpt ['eksəːpt] n estratto m, brano m.

excess [ik'ses] n eccesso m, sovrabbondanza f. **excess baggage** eccedenza di bagaglio f. **excess weight** soprappeso m. **excessive** adj eccessivo, smoderato.

exchange [iks'tʃeindʒ] n cambio m, scambio m; (*phone*) centralino m. **rate of exchange** cambio m. v cambiare, scambiare.

exchequer [iks'tʃekə] n tesoro m, erario m.

excise ['eksaiz] n imposta di consumo f. v recidere, tagliar via.

excite [ik'sait] v eccitare, stimolare, provocare. **excitable** adj eccitabile, impressionabile. **excitement** n eccitamento m, agitazione f, emozione f.

exclaim [ik'skleim] v esclamare. **exclamation** n esclamazione f. **exclamation mark** punto esclamativo m.

exclude [ik'skluːd] v escludere. **excluding** prep escluso, eccetto. **exclusion** n esclusione f. **exclusive** adj esclusivo. **exclusivity** n esclusiva f.

excommunicate [ekskə'mjuːnikeit] v scomunicare. **excommunication** n scomunica f.

excrement ['ekskrəmənt] n sterco m, feci f pl. **excrete** v defecare. **excretion** n escrezione f.

excruciating [ik'skruːʃieitiŋ] adj atroce.

excursion [ik'skəːʃən] n escursione f, gita f.

excuse [ik'skjuːz] n scusa f, pretesto m. **make excuses** scusarsi. v scusare, perdonare; giustificare. **excuse from** esonerare da. **excuse me!** scusi!

execute ['eksikjuːt] v eseguire, mettere in esecuzione, effettuare; (*kill*) giustiziare. **execution** n esecuzione f; (*death*) esecuzione capitale f. **executioner** n boia m invar.

executive [ig'zekjutiv] adj esecutivo. n (*body*) esecutivo m; (*person*) funzionario,

-a m, f. **executor** n esecutore, -trice m, f. testamentario, -a m, f.

exemplify [ig'zempli,fai] v esemplificare, illustrare.

exempt [ig'zempt] v esentare, esonerare. adj esente. **exemption** n esenzione f, dispensa f.

exercise ['eksə,saiz] n esercizio m, uso m; (task) compito m; (mil) manovra f. v esercitare, usare. **exercise-book** , quaderno m.

exert [ig'zə:t] v esercitare. **exert oneself** sforzarsi. **exertion** n sforzo m.

exhale [eks'heil] v emanare; (breathe out) esalare.

exhaust [ig'zɔːst] v stancare, esaurire, estenuare. n scarico (pl -chi) m, scappamento m. **exhausted** adj sfinito, esausto. **exhausting** adj faticoso, estenuante. **exhaustion** n esaurimento m.

exhibit [ig'zibit] v esibire, esporre. n oggetto per mostra m; (law) oggetto di appoggio m. **exhibition** n mostra f, esposizione f. **exhibitionism** n esibizionismo m. **exhibitionist** n esibizionista m, f. **exhibitor** n esibitore, -trice m, f.

exhilarating [ig'zilə,reitiŋ] adj esilarante, rallegrante.

exigency [ig'zidʒənsi] n esigenza f, necessità f.

exile ['eksail] n (expulsion) esilio m; (person) esule m, f, esiliato, -a m, f. v esiliare, mettere al bando.

exist [ig'zist] v esistere, vivere. **existence** n esistenza f, vita f. **existentialism** n esistenzialismo m. **existing** adj esistente, attuale.

exit ['egzit] n uscita f. v uscire.

exodus ['eksədəs] n esodo m.

exonerate [ig'zonə,reit] v esonerare, assolvere.

exorbitant [ig'zɔːbitənt] adj esorbitante, esagerato.

exorcize ['eksɔːsaiz] v esorcizzare. **exorcism** n esorcismo m. **exorcist** n esorcista m, f.

exotic [ig'zotik] adj esotico; (strange) strano.

expand [ik'spand] v espandere, estendere. **expansion** n espansione f.

expanse [ik'spans] n spazio m, distesa f.

expatriate [eks'peitrieit; n, adj eks'peitriət] v espatriare, emigrare. n, adj espatriato, -a.

expect [ik'spekt] v (await) aspettare; anticipare; (believe) credere. **expectant** adj in attesa. **expectation** n aspettativa f, attesa f, prospettiva f.

expedient [ik'spiːdiənt] n espediente m, accorgimento m. adj opportuno, conveniente.

expedition [,ekspi'diʃən] n spedizione f. **expeditious** adj sbrigativo.

expel [ik'spel] v espellere, scacciare.

expenditure [ik'spenditʃə] n spesa f, consumo m.

expense [ik'spens] n spesa f. **expense account** conto spese m. **expensive** adj caro, costoso.

experience [ik'spiəriəns] v provare, subire. n esperienza f; incidente m, avventura f.

experiment [ik'sperimənt] n esperimento m, prova f. v sperimentare, provare, fare esperimenti. **experimental** adj sperimentale.

expert ['ekspəːt] adj esperto, perito, competente. n esperto, -a m, f, perito, -a m, f; conoscitore, -trice m, f.

expertise [,ekspəː'tiːz] n perizia f, maestria f.

expire [ik'spaiə] v scadere, terminare; (die) morire. **expiry** n termine m, scadenza f.

explain [ik'splein] v spiegare, chiarire. **explanation** n spiegazione f, chiarimento m. **explanatory** adj esplicativo.

expletive [ek'spliːtiv] n (profanity) bestemmia f.

explicit [ik'splisit] adj esplicito, chiaro.

explode [ik'sploud] v esplodere, far saltare, scoppiare; (discredit) screditare. **explosion** n esplosione f.

exploit[1] [ik'sploit] n impresa f. **exploits** pl n gesta f pl.

exploit[2] [ik'sploit] v sfruttare, valorizzare. **exploitation** n sfruttamento m, valorizzazione f.

explore [ik'splɔː] v esplorare; studiare. **exploration** n esplorazione f; studio m. **exploratory** adj esploratorio.

exponent [ik'spounənt] n esponente m, f; (representative) interprete m, f, rappresentante m, f. **exponential** adj esponenziale.

export [ik'spɔːt; v ik'spɔːt] n esportazione f. v esportare.

expose [ik'spouz] v esporre, mostrare; (reveal) svelare; (unmask) smascherare. **exposition** n spiegazione f; mostra f.

exposure n esposizione f; smascheramento m; rivelazione f; (phot) posa f.

express [ik'spres] adj espresso, esplicito. **express train** direttissimo m, rapido m. v esprimere. **expression** n espressione f; manifestazione f; (phrase) modo di dire m. **expressionless** adj impassibile. **expressway** (mot) n autostrada

expulsion [ik'spʌlʃən] n espulsione f.

expurgate ['ekspəgeit] v espurgare.

exquisite ['ekswizit] adj squisito; (intense) vivo, acuto.

extend [ik'stend] v estendere, prolungare. **extension** n estensione f; (time) proroga f; (phone) telefono interno m. **extensive** adj esteso, vasto.

extent [ik'stent] n estensione f; limite m.

extenuating [ik'stenjueitiŋ] adj attenuante.

exterior [ik'stiəriə] nm, adj esterno.

exterminate [ik'stə:mi,neit] v sterminare, annientare. **extermination** n sterminio m, annientamento m.

external [ik'stə:nl] adj esterno.

extinct [ik'stiŋkt] adj estinto.

extinguish [ik'stiŋgwiʃ] v estinguere, spegnere. **fire extinguisher** estintore m.

extol [ik'stoul] v esaltare, lodare.

extort [ik'stɔ:t] v estorcere, strappare. **extortion** n estorsione f. **extortionate** adj esorbitante, esagerato.

extra ['ekstrə] adj extra invar, straordinario, supplementare, in più. n (theatre) comparsa f; (additional charge) spesa extra f. adv in più.

extract [ik'strakt] v estrarre; (tooth) cavare. **extraction** n estrazione f; origine f.

extradite ['ekstrə,dait] v estradare. **extraditable** adj passibile di estradizione. **extradition** n estradizione f.

extramural [,ekstrə'mjuərəl] adj fuori le mura; (university) al di fuori dell'università. **extramural course** corso libero m.

extraneous [ik'streiniəs] adj estraneo.

extraordinary [ik'strɔ:dənəri] adj straordinario, eccezionale, fenomenale.

extravagant [ik'stravəgənt] adj stravagante; (wasteful) prodigo, spendereccio; (exaggerated) esagerato. **extravagance** n stravaganza f, prodigalità f.

extreme [ik'stri:m] adj estremo, ultimo. n estremo m. **extremist** n estremista m, f. **extremity** n estremità f.

extricate ['ekstri,keit] v **extricate oneself** districarsi, tirarsi d'impaccio, liberarsi.

extrovert ['ekstrəvə:t] nm, adj estroverso.

exuberant [ig'zju:bərənt] adj esuberante. **exuberance** n esuberanza f.

exude [ig'zju:d] v emanare.

exult [ig'zʌlt] v esultare. **exultant** adj esultante, trionfante, festante. **exultation** n esultazione f, trionfo m.

eye [ai] n occhio m; (needle) cruna f. **see eye to eye (with)** vederla allo stesso modo (di). v adocchiare, osservare.

eyeball ['aibɔ:l] n bulbo oculare m.

eyebrow ['aibrau] n sopracciglio m.

eyelash ['ailaʃ] n ciglio m (pl -a f).

eyelet ['ailit] n occhiello m.

eyelid ['ailid] n palpebra f.

eye-opener n fatto rivelatore m.

eye shadow n bistro m, ombretto m.

eyesight ['aisait] n vista f, visione f.

eyesore ['aisɔ:] n pugno in un occhio m.

eyewitness ['ai,witnis] n testimonio oculare m.

F

fable ['feibl] n favola f.

fabric ['fabrik] n (cloth) tessuto m, stoffa f; (structure) struttura f.

fabricate ['fabrikeit] v (make up) inventare; (fake) falsificare; (construct) fabbricare. **fabrication** n costruzione f, invenzione f.

fabulous ['fabjuləs] adj favoloso.

façade [fə'sɑ:d] n facciata f.

face [feis] n faccia f, volto m, viso m; (clock) quadrante m; (type) carattere m. v (look towards) fronteggiare; (confront) affrontare; (cover) rivestire. **face-cloth** n pezzuola per lavarsi f. **face-lift** n plastica facciale f; (restyling) restauro m. **face-pack** n maschera di bellezza f. **face value** valore nominale m. **lose face** perdere prestigio.

facet ['fasit] n (small plane) faccetta f; (aspect) aspetto m.

facetious [fə'si:ʃəs] adj arguto, spiritoso.

facial ['feiʃəl] adj facciale.

facile ['fasail] adj (glib) superficiale, pronto; (easy) facile.

facilitate [fə'sili,teit] v facilitare, agevolare.

facility [fə'siləti] n facilità f; (help) facilitazione f, agevolazione f; opportunità f. **facilities** pl n servizi m pl.

facing ['feisiŋ] n (covering) rivestimento m; (dress) risvolto m.

facsimile [fak'simǝli] n facsimile m invar.

fact [fakt] n fatto m, verità f. **as a matter of fact** in effetti. **fact-finding** adj di inchiesta. **in fact** infatti. **factual** adj effettivo.

faction ['fakʃǝn] n fazione f, dissenso m. **factious** adj fazioso, partigiano.

factor ['faktǝ] n fattore m; agente m, f.

factory ['faktǝri] n fabbrica f, stabilimento m.

faculty ['fakǝlti] n facoltà f.

fad [fad] n capriccio m; (fashion) moda f.

fade [feid] v (colour) sbiadire; (lose freshness) appassire; (disappear) svanire. **fade away** affievolirsi.

fag [fag] v sfacchinare. n (hard work) sgobbata f; (slang) sigaretta f. **fag-end** n cicca f. **fagged out** stanco morto.

fail [feil] v fallire; (fall short) mancare; (not pass) bocciare, essere respinto. **without fail** senza fallo. **failure** n insuccesso m, mancanza f.

failing ['feiliŋ] n debole m, difetto m. adj debile. prep salvo.

faint [feint] v svenire. adj fiacco, tenue, appena percettibile. **feel faint** sentirsi venir meno. **not have the faintest idea** non avere la più pallida idea.

fair¹ [feǝ] adj (colouring) biondo, chiaro; (unbiased) giusto, imparziale; (moderately good) discreto. **fair copy** bella copia f. **fair play** comportamento leale m. adv secondo le regole. **fairly** adv (moderately) abbastanza; (properly) giustamente. **in all fairness** in tutta franchezza.

fair² [feǝ] n fiera f, mercato m.

fairy ['feǝri] n fata f. **fairy-tale** n fiaba f.

faith [feiθ] n (belief) fede f; (confidence) fiducia f. **faith-healer** n guaritore, -trice per suggestione m, f. **faithful** adj fedele. **faithless** adj che non ha fede, sleale.

fake [feik] v contraffare, fingere. n (object) contraffazione f; (person) impostore, -a m, f.

falcon ['fɔ:lkǝn] n falco m, falcone m.

*****fall** [fɔ:l] v cadere, cascare; (collapse) crollare; (lower) abbassarsi. **fall asleep** addormentarsi. **fall back on** ricorrere a. **fall behind** rimanere indietro; (fig) essere in arretrato. **fall ill** ammalarsi. **fall-out** n pioggia radioattiva f. **fall through** fallire.

n caduta f; crollo m, rovina f; abbassamento m; (autumn) autunno m.

fallacy ['falǝsi] n falsità f. **fallacious** adj fallace, falso.

fallen ['fɔ:lǝn] V **fall.**

fallible ['falǝbl] adj fallibile. **fallibility** n fallibilità f.

fallow ['falou] adj a maggese.

false [fɔ:ls] adj falso, artificiale, finto. **false alarm** falso allarme m. **false pretences** (law) millantato credito m. **false teeth** denti artificiali m pl. **falsehood** n menzogna f. **falseness** n perfidia f. **falsify** v falsificare.

falsetto [fɔ:l'setou] n falsetto m.

falter ['fɔ:ltǝ] v (waver) vacillare, titubare; (speak hesitatingly) balbettare. **faltering** adj titubante.

fame [feim] n fama f, rinomanza f. **famed** adj rinomato.

familiar [fǝ'miljǝ] adj familiare; intimo; (impudent) sfacciato; (well-known) noto. **be on familiar terms with** aver dimestichezza con. **familiarity** n familiarità f; intimità f; (impertinence) sfacciataggine f.

family ['famǝli] n famiglia f. **family allowance** assegni familiari m pl. **family tree** albero genealogico m.

famine ['famin] n carestia f.

famished ['famiʃt] adj affamato.

famous ['feimǝs] adj famoso, celebre.

fan¹ [fan] n ventaglio m; (mechanical) ventilatore m. **fan-belt** n cinghia per ventilatore f. v (flames) soffiare su; (excite) aizzare. **fan oneself** farsi vento.

fan² [fan] n (admirer) tifoso, -a m, f.

fanatic [fǝ'natik] n, adj fanatico, -a; (sport) tifoso, -a. **fanaticism** n fanatismo m; tifo m.

fancy ['fansi] adj elaborato, raffinato, di fantasia. **fancy-dress** n costume m. **fancy-dress ball** ballo in maschera m. n immaginazione f, fantasia f, capriccio m. v desiderare, immaginare. **fanciful** adj fantasioso, capriccioso.

fanfare ['fanfeǝ] n fanfara f.

fang [faŋ] n zanna f.

fantastic [fan'tastik] adj fantastico, strano.

fantasy ['fantǝsi] n fantasia f, capriccio m.

far [fa:] adv, adj lontano, distante; (much) molto. **as far as** (place) fino a. **as far as I know** a quanto sappia. **far-fetched** adj improbabile, forzato. **far-reaching** adj di gran portata. **far-sighted** *adj* (*prudent*) previdente. **so far** (*up to this point*) fin qui.

farce [faɪs] *n* farsa *f*.

fare [feə] *n* tariffa *f*, prezzo del biglietto *m*; (*person*) viaggiatore, -trice *m*, *f*; (*food*) vitto *m*. *v* vivere, trovarsi.

farewell [feə'wel] *n* addio *m*, congedo *m*. *interj* addio!

farm [faɪm] *n* fattoria *f*, podere *m*. **farm-house** *n* casa colonica *f*. *v* coltivare, fare l'agricoltore. **farm out** dare in appalto. **farmer** *n* agricoltore, contadino, -a *m*, *f*. **farming** *n* agricoltura *f*, coltivazione *f*.

fart [faɪt] (*vulgar*) *n* scoreggia *f*. *v* fare scoregge.

farther ['faɪðə] *adj, adv* più lontano; ulteriore. **farthest** *adj* il più lontano.

fascinate ['fasi,neit] *v* affascinare, incantare. **fascinating** *adj* affascinante, avvincente. **fascination** *n* fascino *m*, attrattiva *f*.

fascism ['faʃizəm] *n* fascismo *m*. **fascist** *n*(*m+f*), *adj* fascista.

fashion ['faʃən] *n* (*manner*) modo *m*, maniera *f*; (*dress*) moda *f*; (*style*) stile *m*; (*vogue*) voga *f*. **after a fashion** in un certo modo. **in fashion** alla moda. **out of fashion** fuori moda. *v* foggiare, modellare. **fashionable** *adj* elegante, di moda.

fast¹ [faɪst] *adj* rapido, veloce; (*firmly held*) fisso, saldo; (*colour*) solido. *adv* presto, rapidamente. **the clock is ... fast** l'orologio va avanti di ....

fast² [faɪst] *n* digiuno *m*. *v* digiunare.

fasten ['faɪsn] *v* legare, fissare, agganciare, attaccare. **fastener** or **fastening** *n* chiusura *f*, fermaglio *m*.

fastidious [fa'stidiəs] *adj* meticoloso, schifiltoso.

fat [fat] *adj, nm* grasso. **fatten** *v* ingrassare. **fatty** *adj* grasso, untuoso.

fatal ['feitl] *adj* fatale, ineluttabile. **fatalism** *n* fatalismo *m*. **fatalist** *n* fatalista *m*, *f*. **fatality** *n* fatalità *f*.

fate [feit] *n* fato *m*, destino *m*. **fated** *adj* destinato. **fateful** *adj* decisivo.

father ['faɪðə] *n* padre *m*; (*coll*) babbo *m*. *v* procreare, originare. **fatherhood** *n* paternità *f*. **father-in-law** *n* suocero *m*. **fatherland** *n* patria *f*. **fatherly** *adj* paterno.

fathom ['faðəm] *v* (*understand*) indovinare, penetrare; (*depth*) sondare. *n* braccio *m*.

fatigue [fə'tiːg] *n* stanchezza *f*, esaurimento *m*. *v* stancare.

fatuous ['fatjuəs] *adj* fatuo, frivolo, vuoto.

fault [foɪlt] *n* (*flaw*) difetto *m*, imperfezione *f*; errore *m*; (*cause for blame*) colpa *f*; (*geol*) faglia *f*; (*tennis*) fallo *m*. **be at fault** essere colpevole. **find fault with** criticare, biasimare. **faultless** *adj* senza colpa. **faulty** *adj* difettoso.

favour ['feivə] *n* favore *m*, piacere *m*. *v* favorire, favoreggiare, preferire. **favourable** *adj* favorevole, vantaggioso.

favourite ['feivrit] *adj* preferito. *n* favorito, -a *m*, *f*.

fawn¹ [foɪn] *n* (*zool*) daino *m*, cerbiatto *m*. *adj* (*colour*) fulvo.

fawn² [foɪn] *v* **fawn on** adulare.

fear [fiə] *v* temere, aver paura di. *n* timore *m*, paura *f*. **fearful** *adj* terribile, spaventoso. **fearless** *adj* intrepido.

feasible ['fiːzəbl] *adj* fattibile, realizzabile. **feasibility** *n* praticabilità *f*.

feast [fiːst] *n* festa *f*, banchetto *m*.

feat [fiːt] *n* impresa *f*, azione *f*.

feather ['feðə] *n* penna *f*, piuma *f*. **feather-bed** *n* letto di piume *m*. **feathered** *adj* pennuto.

feature ['fiːtʃə] *n* caratteristica *f*, tratto distintivo *m*; (*newspaper*) elzeviro *m*; (*geog*) configurazione *f*. **features** *pl n* (*anat*) lineamenti *m pl*. *v* dar rilievo a; (*theatre*) presentare. **featureless** *adj* scialbo.

February ['februəri] *n* febbraio *m*.

fed [fed] *V* **feed**.

federal ['fedərəl] *adj* federale. **federation** *n* federazione *f*.

fee [fiː] *n* onorario *m*, parcella *f*; (*school*) retta *f*; (*entrance fee*) tassa d'iscrizione *f*.

feeble ['fiːbl] *adj* debole, fiacco. **feebleminded** *adj* cretino, debole di mente. **feebleness** *n* debolezza *f*.

***feed** [fiːd] *v* nutrire; (*supply*) alimentare; (*eat*) mangiare, nutrirsi. *n* mangime *m*, nutrimento *m*; (*baby*) poppata *f*. **feed-back** *n* retroreazione *f*, feedback *m invar*; (*response*) reazione. **fed up** (*coll*) stufo.

***feel** [fiːl] *v* (*touch*) tastare, toccare; (*emotion*) sentire. **feel like** sentirsi disposto a. **feeler** *n* tentacolo *m*; (*proposal*) sondaggio *m*. **feeling** *n* (*physical*) senso *m*, sensazione *f*; (*emotion*) sensibilità *f*, suscettibilità *f*; (*affection*) affetto *m*.

feet [fiːt] V foot.

feign [fein] v fingere, simulare, far finta.

feline ['fiːlain] adj felino.

fell¹ [fel] V fall.

fell² [fel] v (cut down) abbattere; (strike down) atterrare.

fellow ['felou] n individuo m, tipo m; (companion) compagno m, collega m, f; (member) membro m, socio m. **fellow-countryman** n compatriota m, f. **fellowship** n (companionship) cameratismo m; (rel) comunità f; (allowance) borsa di studio f.

felony ['feləni] n crimine m. **felon** n delinquente m, f.

felt¹ [felt] V feel.

felt² [felt] n feltro m.

female ['fiːmeil] n femmina f. adj also **feminine** femminile.

feminism ['feminizəm] n femminismo m. **feminist** n femminista m, f.

fence [fens] n (barrier) steccato m, palizzata f; (receiver of stolen goods) ricettatore, -trice m, f; (sport) tirar di scherma. **fence in** recintare. **fencing** n recinto m; (sport) scherma f.

fend [fend] v **fend for oneself** provvedere a sè stesso, arrangiarsi. **fend off** parare, schivare.

fender ['fendə] n paracenere m invar; (US) paraurti m.

fennel ['fenl] n finocchio m.

ferment ['fəːment; v fə'ment] n fermento m. v fermentare. **fermentation** n fermentazione f.

fern [fəːn] n felce f.

ferocious [fə'rouʃəs] adj feroce. **ferocity** n ferocia f.

ferret ['ferit] n furetto m. v **ferret out** scovare.

ferry ['feri] n traghetto m. v traghettare.

fertile ['fəːtail] adj fertile, fecondo. **fertility** n fertilità f, fecondità f. **fertilize** v (enrich) fertilizzare; fecondare. **fertilizer** n fertilizzante m, concime m.

fervent ['fəːvənt] adj fervente, fervido. **fervour** n fervore m, ardore m.

fester ['festə] v suppurare; (rankle) bruciare.

festival ['festəvəl] n festival m invar, festa f.

festoon [fə'stuːn] v decorare con festoni. n festone m.

fetch [fetʃ] v andare a prendere; (call)

chiamare; (a price) realizzare. **fetching** adj attraente.

fête [feit] n festa f. v festeggiare.

fetid ['fiːtid] adj fetido, puzzolente.

fetish ['fetiʃ] n feticcio m, idolo m.

fetter ['fetə] n catena f. v incatenare.

feud [fjuːd] n lite f. v essere in lotta.

feudal ['fjuːdl] adj feudale. **feudalism** n feudalesimo m.

fever ['fiːvə] n febbre f. **feverish** adj febbricitante; (restless) febbrile.

few [fjuː] pron, adj pochi, -e. **a few** alcuni, -e. **quite a few** parecchi, parecchie. **fewer** adj meno invar. **fewest** adj meno invar.

fiancé [fi'onsei] n fidanzato m. **fiancée** n fidanzata f.

fiasco [fi'askou] n fiasco m.

fib [fib] (coll) n frottola f. v raccontar frottole.

fibre ['faibə] n fibra f. **fibreglass** n fibra di vetro f. **fibrous** adj fibroso.

fickle ['fikl] adj volubile. **fickleness** n volubilità f.

fiction ['fikʃən] n (invention) finzione f; (novels, etc.) novellistica f, narrativa f. **fictional** or **fictitious** adj fittizio, immaginario.

fiddle ['fidl] n violino m; (coll: fraud) imbroglio m, truffa f. v suonare il violino; (coll: cheat) truffare, imbrogliare. **fit as a fiddle** sano come un pesce.

fidelity [fi'deləti] n fedeltà f.

fidget ['fidʒit] v muoversi irrequietamente, dimenarsi. **fidgety** adj irrequieto, nervoso.

field [fiːld] n campo m; (of knowledge, etc.) settore m. **field glasses** binocolo m sing. **field marshal** maresciallo m.

fiend [fiːnd] n demonio m. **fiendish** adj infernale, diabolico.

fierce [fiəs] adj feroce, intenso.

fiery ['faiəri] adj focoso, ardente.

fifteen [fif'tiːn] nm, adj quindici. **fifteenth** nm, adj quindicesimo.

fifth [fifθ] nm, adj quinto.

fifty ['fifti] nm, adj cinquanta. **fiftieth** nm, adj cinquantesimo.

fig [fig] n fico m.

*fight [fait] v lottare, combattere. n lotta f, combattimento m; (scuffle) zuffa f.

figment ['figmənt] n **figment of the imagination** finzione f.

figure ['figə] n (numeral) cifra f; (shape) forma f; (pictorial) figura f; (character) personaggio m; (bodily form) linea f.

figurehead n (naut) polena f; (derog) uomo di paglia m. **figure of speech** modo di dire m. v (appear) apparire. **figure out** calcolare.

filament ['filəmənt] n filamento m.

file¹ [fail] n (dossier) pratica f; archivio m; (for papers) cartella f; (card with details) scheda f; (row) fila f. v archiviare, mettere in ordine, registrare. **filing** n schedare m. **filing cabinet** schedario m. **single file** fila indiana f.

file² [fail] n (tool) lima f. v limare, levigare.

filial ['filiəl] adj filiale.

fill [fil] v riempire; (tooth) otturare. **fill in** completare, inserire. **fill up** (mot) fare il pieno. **filling** n (cookery) ripieno m; (tooth) otturazione f. **filling station** stazione di rifornimento f.

fillet ['filit] n (meat) filetto m. v disossare.

film [film] n pellicola f; (phot, cinema) film m invar. **film star** divo, -a del cinema m, f. v girare un film.

filter ['filtə] n filtro m. **filter-tip** n filtro m. v filtrare.

filth [filθ] n sudiciume m, sporcizia f; oscenità f. **filthy** adj sudicio, sporco; lurido, osceno.

fin [fin] n pinna f.

final ['fainl] adj finale, ultimo. n finale f. **finalist** n finalista m, f. **finally** adv infine.

finance [fai'nans] n finanza f. v finanziare. **financial** adj finanziario. **financier** n finanziere m, finanziatore m.

finch [fintʃ] n fringuello m.

***find** [faind] v scoprire, trovare. **find out** scoprire.

fine¹ [fain] adj (high quality) pregiato, raffinato; (minute) fine; (accomplished) bravo; (beautiful) bello. adv bene.

fine² [fain] n (penalty) multa f. v multare.

finesse [fi'nes] n finezza f.

finger ['fiŋgə] n dito m (pl dita f). **cross one's fingers** toccar ferro. **finger bowl** lavadita m invar. **finger-mark** n ditata f. **fingernail** n unghia f. **fingerprint** n impronta digitale f. **fingertip** n punta delle dita f. v (touch) palpare.

finish ['finiʃ] v finire, concludere. n fine f, conclusione f; (surface) finitura f; (textile) appretto m.

finite ['fainait] adj limitato, circoscritto; (math) finito.

Finland ['finlənd] n Finlandia f. **Finn** n

finlandese m, f. **Finnish** nm, adj finlandese.

fir [fə:] n abete m.

fire ['faiə] n fuoco m; (conflagration) incendio m; (heater) stufa f. **catch fire** prender fuoco. **hang fire** indugiare. **set fire to** appiccare il fuoco a, incendiare. v (shoot) sparare; (dismiss) licenziare, silurare; (inflame) eccitare, infiammare; (inspire) ispirare.

fire alarm n allarme d'incendio m.

firearm ['faiə,a:m] n arma da fuoco f.

fire brigade n corpo dei vigili del fuoco m.

fire door n esercitazione antincendio f.

fire drill n pompa antincendio f.

fire engine n uscita di sicurezza f.

fire escape n uscita di sicurezza f.

fire extinguisher n estintore m.

firefly ['faiəflai] n lucciola f.

fire-guard n parafuoco m, paracenere m invar.

fireman ['faiəmən] n pompiere m, vigile del fuoco m.

fireplace ['faiə,pleis] n focolare m, camino m, caminetto m.

fireproof ['faiə,pru:f] adj incombustibile, resistente al fuoco.

fireside ['faiə,said] n focolare m.

fire station n caserma dei pompieri f.

firewood ['faiə,wud] n legna da ardere f.

fireworks ['faiə,wə:ks] pl n fuochi d'artifizio pl.

firing squad n plotone d'esecuzione m.

firm¹ [fə:m] adj fermo; (steady) saldo; (steadfast) risoluto; solido; stabile. **stand firm** tener duro. **firmness** n fermezza f; saldezza f; risolutezza f.

firm² [fə:m] n (comm) ditta f, azienda f.

first [fə:st] adj primo. adv prima; in primo luogo; anzitutto. **first aid** pronto soccorso m. **first-class** adj ottimo, di prima qualità, eccellente; (rail, etc.) di prima classe. **first floor** primo piano m. **first-hand** adj di prima mano. **first name** nome di battesimo m.

fiscal ['fiskəl] adj fiscale.

fish [fiʃ] n pesce m. v pescare. **fishy** adj (coll) losco.

fishbone ['fiʃ,boun] n lisca f.

fisherman ['fiʃəmən] n pescatore m.

fish fingers pl n bastoncini di pesce m pl.

fishing ['fiʃiŋ] n pesca f. **fishing boat** peschereccio m. **fishing rod** canna da pesca f.

fishmonger ['fiʃ,mʌŋgə] n pescivendolo, -a m, f.

fishpond ['fiʃ,pond] n vivaio m.

fission ['fiʃən] n fissione f.

fissure ['fiʃə] n fessura f.

fist [fist] n pugno m.

fit¹ [fit] adj (suitable) adatto; competente; (healthy) sano. **keep fit** mantenersi sano, mantenersi in forma. **in misura** f. v (clothes, etc.) star bene; (suit) adeguare, convenire. **fit in** incastrare. **fitting** adj conveniente, adatto. **fittings** pl n suppellettili m pl, arredi m pl.

fit² [fit] n accesso m, attacco m. **fitful** adj intermittente.

five [faiv] n, adj cinque.

fix [fiks] v fissare, stabilire. **fix up** sistemare, mettere a posto. n (coll) difficoltà f, guaio m. **fixation** n fissazione f. **fixed** adj fisso, stabile. **fixture** n (accessory) attrezzatura f; (sport) avvenimento sportivo m.

fizz [fiz] v frizzare. n spumante m. **fizzy** adj effervescente, frizzante.

fizzle ['fizl] v **fizzle out** far cilecca.

flabbergast ['flæbəgɑ:st] v sbalordire.

flabby ['flæbi] adj floscio, flaccido.

flag¹ [flæg] n (banner) bandiera f. **flag-pole** n asta di bandiera f. **flagship** n nave ammiraglia f. v **flag down** intimare di fermarsi.

flag² [flæg] v (tire) indebolirsi, accasciarsi.

flag³ [flæg] n (stone) lastra (di pietra) f.

flagon ['flægən] n bottiglione m.

flagrant ['fleigrənt] adj flagrante.

flair [fleə] n intuito m, inclinazione f.

flake [fleik] v sfaldare, sfaldarsi. n falda f, scaglia f. **flaky** adj a scaglie. **flaky pastry** sfoglia f.

flamboyant [flæm'bɔiənt] adj sgargiante.

flame [fleim] n fiamma f. v fiammeggiare, risplendere. **burst into flames** divampare. **flaming** adj fiammeggiante, violento.

flamingo [flə'miŋgou] n fiammingo m.

flan [flæn] n sformato m, torta f.

flank [flæŋk] v fiancheggiere. n fianco m, lato m.

flannel ['flænl] n (fabric) flanella f; (facecloth) pezzuola per lavarsi f. v (slang) abbindolare con le chiacchiere.

flap [flæp] v agitare; (wings) battere; (coll) agitarsi. n lembo m; (wings) colpo m; panico m.

flare [fleə] n fiammata f, bagliore m; (rocket) razzo m. v brillare; (clothes)

svasare. **flare up** divampare; (anger, etc.) arrabbiarsi.

flash [flæʃ] n baleno m, lampo m. v balenare. **flashback** n scena retrospettiva f, flashback m invar. **flash bulb** lampadina flash f. **flashlight** n fotolampo m, flash m invar.

flask [flɑ:sk] n flacone m, borraccia f.

flat¹ [flæt] adj piatto, piano; (tyre) a terra; (net) netto; (stale) svanito, insipido. f (music) bemolle m. **flat-footed** adj con i piedi piatti. **flat out** a briglia sciolta. f (music) bemolle m. **flatten** v appiattire, livellare.

flat² [flæt] n appartamento m.

flatter ['flætə] v adulare, lusingare. **flatterer** n adulatore, -trice m, f. **flattering** adj lusinghiero. **flattery** n lusinghe f pl, adulazione f.

flatulence ['flætjuləns] n flatulenza f. **flatulent** adj flatulento.

flaunt [flɔ:nt] v ostentare, pavoneggiarsi.

flautist ['flɔ:tist] n flautista m, f.

flavour ['fleivə] n sapore m, gusto m. v condire. **flavouring** n condimento m.

flaw [flɔ:] n tacca f, difetto m. **flawed** adj difettoso. **flawless** adj perfetto.

flax [flæks] n lino m. **flaxen** adj di lino; (colour) biondissimo.

flea [fli:] n pulce f.

fleck [flek] n chiazza f, macchia f. v chiazzare, macchiare.

fled [fled] V **flee**.

*flee [fli:] v fuggire, scappare.

fleece [fli:s] n vello m. v (coll) pelare, derubare.

fleet [fli:t] n flotta f; (of cars) parco m.

fleeting ['fli:tiŋ] adj fugace, transitorio.

Flemish ['flemiʃ] nm, adj fiammingo.

flesh [fleʃ] n carne f; (fruit) polpa f.

flew [flu:] V **fly¹**.

flex [fleks] v flettere. n filo or cavo elettrico m. **flexible** adj flessibile. **flexibility** n flessibilità f.

flick [flik] n colpetto m. v dare un colpetto a.

flicker ['flikə] v tremolare. n tremolio m.

flight¹ [flait] n (flying) volo m; (steps) rampa f. **flighty** adj frivolo.

flight² [flait] n (fleeing) fuga f.

flimsy ['flimzi] adj tenue, fragile; (inadequate) insufficiente.

flinch [flintʃ] v (wince) sussultare; (shrink from) sottrarsi a. **without flinching** senza batter ciglio.

*fling [fliŋ] v lanciare, scagliare, buttare. n **have one's fling** godersela.

flint [flint] n selce f; (lighter) pietrina f.

flip [flip] n colpetto m. v dare un colpetto a. **flip a coin** fare testa e croce. **flip through** sfogliare, dare una scorsa a.

flippant ['flipənt] adj poco serio, frivolo. **flippancy** n mancanza di serietà f.

flirt [fləːt] v flirtare. n dongiovanni m; civetta f.

flit [flit] v svolazzare; (disappear) squagliarsela.

float [flout] v galleggiare, stare a galla. n galleggiante m; (angling) sughero m; (procession) carro m.

flock¹ [flok] n (animals) branco m; (birds) stormo m; (sheep) gregge m; (crowd) folla f. v accorrere in massa, affluire. **flock together** radunarsi.

flock² [flok] n fiocco m; (mattress filling) borra f.

flog [flog] v bastonare, frustare; (sell) spacciare.

flood [flʌd] v inondare, allagare. n inondazione f, alluvione f, diluvio m; (outpouring) torrente m, ondata f. **flood-light** n riflettore m. **floodlit** adj illuminato a giorno.

floor [flɔː] n pavimento m; (storey) piano m. **floorboard** n tavola di pavimento f. **take the floor** (speak) prendere la parola; (dance) ballare. v pavimentare; (knock down) atterrare.

flop [flop] n tonfo m; (coll) fiasco m. v cader di schianto; (coll) fallire.

Florence ['florəns] n Firenze f. **Florentine** n, adj fiorentino, -a.

florist ['florist] n fioraio, -a m, f; fiorista m, f.

flotsam ['flotsəm] n relitti m pl. **flotsam and jetsam** (people) relitti umani m pl.

flounce¹ [flauns] v dimenare.

flounce² [flauns] n balza f.

flounder ['flaundə] v dibattersi, dimenarsi; (speech) impappinarsi. n passera di mare f.

flour [flauə] n farina f. **floury** adj farinoso.

flourish ['flʌriʃ] v (prosper) fiorire; (brandish) brandire. n (fanfare) squillo di tromba m; (writing) ghirigoro m; (speech) fioretta tura f; (gesture) largo gesto m.

flout [flaut] v sprezzare, schernire.

flow [flou] n corrente f, flusso m. v scorrere, circolare.

flower ['flauə] n fiore m. **flower-bed** n aiuola f. **flower-pot** n vaso da fiori m. v fiorire, essere in fiore. **flowering** adj in fiore. **flowery** adj fiorito.

flown [floun] V **fly¹**.

flu [fluː] n influenza f.

fluctuate ['flʌktjuˌeit] v fluttuare. **fluctuation** n fluttuazione f.

flue [fluː] n gola del camino f.

fluent ['fluənt] adj corrente, scorrevole. **speak fluently** parlare correntemente.

fluff [flʌf] n lanugine f, peluria f.

fluid ['fluid] nm, adj fluido, liquido.

fluke [fluːk] n (lucky chance) colpo fortunato m.

flung [flʌŋ] V **fling**.

fluorescent [fluə'resnt] adj fluorescente. **fluoride** ['fluəraid] n fluoruro m. **fluoridation** n fluorizzazione f.

flush¹ [flʌʃ] n (colouring) rossore m; (rush of liquid) flusso m; (blushing) vampa f; (poker) flush m invar. v (wash out) pulire con un getto d'acqua; (lavatory) vuotare; (redden) arrossire, avvampare.

flush² [flʌʃ] adj (level) a livello, rasente; (slang: rich) ben fornito.

fluster ['flʌstə] v turbare, confondere.

flute [fluːt] n flauto m.

flutter ['flʌtə] v battere; agitare, confondere; (fly) svolazzare. n battito m, agitazione f; (bet) scommessa f.

flux [flʌks] n flusso m.

*fly¹ [flai] v volare; (flutter) svolazzare; (flag) sventolare; (flee) fuggire, scappare. **fly away** or **off** volar via. **flyleaf** n risguardo m. **flyover** n cavalcavia m invar. **flysheet** n volantino m. **flywheel** n volano m. **flying squad** squadra mobile f.

fly² [flai] n (insect) mosca f.

foal [foul] n puledro m.

foam [foum] n schiuma f. **foam rubber** gomma piuma f. v spumeggiare.

focus ['foukəs] n fuoco m, centro m. v concentrare; (bring into focus) mettere a fuoco. **focal** adj focale.

fodder ['fodə] n mangime m, foraggio m.

foe [fou] n nemico, -a m, f; avversario, -a m, f.

foetus ['fiːtəs] n feto m.

fog [fog] n nebbia f. **fog-bound** adj fermo per la nebbia. **fog-horn** n sirena f nella nebbia f. **foggy** adj nebbioso.

foible ['foibl] n debole m.

foil¹ [foil] v frustrare, sventare.

foil² [foil] n lamina (di metallo) f; (tinfoil) stagnola f; (contrast) contrappeso m.

foist [foist] v rifilare, affibbiare.

fold¹ [fould] v piegare; (envelop) avvolgere. **fold one's arms** incrociare le braccia. **fold (up)** (collapse) chiudere, cessare l'esercizio. n piega f, ripiegatura f. **folder** n cartella f. **folding** adj pieghevole.

fold² [fould] n (enclosure) ovile m.

foliage ['fouliidʒ] n fogliame m.

folk [fouk] n gente f, popolo m. **folk dance** danza rustica f. **folklore** n folclore m. **folk song** canto popolare m.

follicle ['folikl] n follicolo m.

follow ['folou] v seguire, succedere; (understand) capire; (result) risultare, conseguire. **follower** n seguace m, f. **following** adj seguente, successivo.

folly ['foli] n follia f.

fond [fond] adj affettuoso, affezionato. **become fond of** affezionarsi a. **be fond of** voler bene a; (person) amare.

fondle ['fondl] v accarezzare, coccolare.

font [font] n fonte battesimale f.

food [fuid] n cibo m, vitto m; (foodstuffs) generi alimentari m pl.

fool [full] n sciocco, -a m, f; cretino, -a m, f; (jester) buffone, -a m, f, pagliaccio m. **foolhardy** adj temerario. **foolproof** adj sicurissimo. v (deceive) ingannare. **foolish** adj sciocco, insensato. **foolishness** n sciocchezza f.

foolscap ['fuilskap] n carta protocollo f.

foot [fut] n, pl **feet** piede m; (birds, animals) zampa f. v **foot the bill** saldare il conto. **on foot** a piedi. **put one's foot down** farsi valere. **put one's foot in it** fare una gaffe.

football ['fut,boil] n football m invar, pallone m. **footballer** n calciatore m.

foot-bridge ['fut,bridʒ] n passerella f.

foothold ['fut,hould] n punto d'appoggio m.

footing ['futiŋ] n (foundation) base f; (mutual standing) relazioni f pl.

footlights ['fut,laits] pl n luci della ribalta f pl.

footnote ['fut,nout] n postilla f, nota in calce f.

footpath ['fut,paθ] n sentiero m.

footprint ['fut,print] n orma f.

footstep ['fut,step] n passo m.

footwear ['fut,weə] n calzatura f.

for [fol] prep per, a favore di, a, di, da. conj poiché.

forage ['foridʒ] v foraggiare. n foraggio m.

forbade [fol'bad] V **forbid.**

*****forbear** [fol'beə] v astenersi da, pazientare.

*****forbid** [fol'bid] v proibire, vietare. **forbidding** adj austero, formidabile.

forbidden [fol'bidn] V **forbid.**

force [fols] n forza f. **in force** in vigore. v forzare; (compel) costringere. **forceful** adj energico.

forceps ['folseps] pl n forcipe m sing.

ford [foid] n guado m. v guadare.

fore [fol] adj anteriore. **come to the fore** venire alla ribalta.

forearm ['folraim] n avambraccio m.

forebear ['folbeə] n antenato, -a m, f.

foreboding [fol'boudiŋ] n presagio m.

*****forecast** ['folkaist] n previsione f, pronostico m. v prevedere.

forecourt ['folkoit] n cortile m.

forefather ['folfaiðə] n antenato m, avo m.

forefinger ['folfiŋgə] n indice m.

forefront ['folfrʌnt] n prima linea f.

foreground ['folgraund] n primo piano m.

forehand ['folhand] nm, adj (tennis) diritto.

forehead ['forid] n fronte f.

foreign ['forən] adj straniero, forestiero; (trade, etc.) estero; (not belonging) estraneo. **foreigner** n straniero, -a m, f; forestiero, -a m, f.

foreleg ['folleg] n zampa anteriore f.

foreman ['folmən] n caposquadra (pl capisquadra) m, capo operaio m; (jury) presidente m.

foremost ['folmoust] adj principale, primo. adv in primo luogo. **first and foremost** anzitutto.

forename ['folneim] n nome di battesimo m.

forensic [fə'rensik] adj forense. **forensic medicine** medicina legale f.

forerunner ['folrʌnə] n precursore m.

*****foresee** [fol'sii] v prevedere. **foreseeable** adj prevedibile.

foreshadow ['fol'fadou] v adombrare.

foreshorten [fol'foitn] v scorciare. **foreshortened** adj di scorcio.

foresight ['folsait] n (prevision) preveggenza f; (care for future) previdenza f.

foreskin ['fɔːskin] *n* prepuzio *m*.

forest ['fɔrist] *n* foresta *f*. **forester** *n* guardia forestale *f*. **forestry** *n* selvicoltura *f*.

forestall [fɔː'stɔːl] *v* anticipare, prevenire.

foretaste ['fɔːteist] *n* pregustazione *f*.

***foretell** [fɔː'tel] *v* predire, pronosticare.

forethought ['fɔːθɔːt] *n* premeditazione *f*, previdenza *f*.

forever [fɔ'revə] *adv* per sempre.

foreword ['fɔːwɜːd] *n* prefazione *f*.

forfeit ['fɔːfit] *n* (*pawn*) pegno *m*; (*fine*) multa *f*. *v* (*give up*) dover abbandonare; pagare il fio.

forgave [fə'geiv] *V* **forgive.**

forge[1] [fɔːdʒ] *v* (*counterfeit*) falsificare, contraffare; (*metal*) forgiare. *n* fucina *f*. **forger** *n* falsario, -a *m*, *f*. **forgery** *n* contraffazione *f*, falso *m*.

forge[2] [fɔːdʒ] *v* avanzare. **forge ahead** farsi strada; (*take lead*) distanziarsi, staccarsi.

***forget** [fə'get] *v* dimenticare, scordare, non ricordarsi di. **forget-me-not** *n* nontiscordardimè *m*. **forget oneself** lasciarsi andare. **forgetful** *adj* smemorato.

***forgive** [fə'giv] *v* perdonare, rimettere. **forgiveness** *n* perdono *m*, indulgenza *f*. **forgiving** *adj* clemente, indulgente.

forgiven [fə'givn] *V* **forgive.**

***forgo** [fɔ'gou] *v* rinunciare a.

forgot [fə'gɔt] *V* **forget.**

forgotten [fə'gɔtn] *V* **forget.**

fork [fɔːk] *n* (*cutlery*) forchetta *f*; (*agriculture*) forca *f*, forcone *m*; (*road*) bivio *m*; (*branching*) biforcazione *f*. *v* forcare; biforcarsi. **fork out** (*slang: pay*) metter mano alla borsa.

forlorn [fə'lɔːn] *adj* disperato, desolato.

form [fɔːm] *n* forma *f*; (*document*) modulo *m*; (*bench*) banco *m*; (*school*) classe *f*. *v* formare. **formation** *n* formazione *f*. **formative** *adj* formativo.

formal ['fɔːməl] *adj* formale, esplicito. **formality** *n* formalità *f*, cerimonia *f*.

format ['fɔːmat] *n* formato *m*.

former ['fɔːmə] *adj* precedente, anteriore. **the former** il primo. **formerly** *adv* in passato, già, in altri tempi.

formidable ['fɔːmidəbl] *adj* formidabile, spaventoso, terribile.

formula ['fɔːmjulə] *n, pl* -ae formula *f*.

formulate ['fɔːmjuleit] *v* formulare. **formulation** *n* formulazione *f*.

***forsake** [fə'seik] *v* abbandonare.

forsaken [fə'seikn] *V* **forsake.**

forsook [fə'suk] *V* **forsake.**

fort [fɔːt] *n* fortezza *f*, forte *m*.

forth [fɔːθ] *adv* avanti; (*out of concealment*) fuori. **and so forth** e così via. **forthcoming** *adj* imminente, prossimo. **forthright** *adj* franco, schietto. **forthwith** *adv* immediatamente.

fortify ['fɔːtifai] *v* fortificare, rafforzare, dar forza a; (*wine*) alcolizzare. **fortification** *n* fortificazione *f*.

fortitude ['fɔːtitjuːd] *n* forza d'animo *f*; (*virtue*) fortezza *f*.

fortnight ['fɔːtnait] *n* quindicina *f*, due settimane *f pl*. **fortnightly** *nm, adj* quindicinale, bimensile.

fortress ['fɔːtris] *n* fortezza *f*.

fortuitous [fɔː'tjuːitəs] *adj* fortuito.

fortune ['fɔːtʃən] *n* fortuna *f*; (*riches*) ricchezza *f*; futuro *m*. **fortune-teller** *n* chiromante *m*, *f*. **fortune-telling** *n* chiromanzia *f*. **fortunate** *adj* fortunato.

forty ['fɔːti] *nm, adj* quaranta. **fortieth** *nm, adj* quarantesimo.

forum ['fɔːrəm] *n* foro *m*; (*court*) tribuna *f*.

forward ['fɔːwəd] *adj* avanzato; presuntuoso. *adv also* **forwards** avanti, in avanti. **look forward to** anticipare con piacere. **put forward** proporre. *v* spedire, inoltrare; (*mail*) rispedire.

fossil ['fɔsl] *n* fossile *m*. **fossilized** *adj* fossilizzato.

foster ['fɔstə] *v* (*child*) allevare; incoraggiare; nutrire, alimentare. **foster-child** *n* figlio adottivo *m*. **foster-parents** *pl n* genitori adottivi *m pl*.

fought [fɔːt] *V* **fight.**

foul [faul] *adj* lurido, schifoso; (*weather*) pessimo. **foul play** (*crime*) delitto *m*; (*sport*) gioco falloso *m*.

found[1] [faund] *V* **find.**

found[2] [faund] *v* fondare, istituire, basare. **foundation** *n* fondazione *f*; istituto *m*; (*base*) fondamento *m*, base *f*. **founder** *n* fondatore, -trice *m*, *f*.

founder ['faundə] *v* (*sink*) colare a picco.

foundry ['faundri] *n* fonderia *f*.

fountain ['fauntin] *n* fontana *f*. **fountain pen** penna stilografica *f*.

four [fɔː] *nm, adj* quattro. **foursome** *n* quattro *m*. **on all fours** (a) carponi. **fourth** *nm, adj* quarto.

fourteen [fo'tim] *nm, adj* quattordici. **fourteenth** *nm, adj* quattordicesimo.

fowl [faul] *n* pollame *m*; (*chicken*) pollo *m*.

fox [foks] *n* volpe *f*; (*sly person*) furbacchione *m*, furbo, -a *m, f*. **foxglove** *n* digitale *f*. **fox-hound** *n* bracco *m*. **v** (*coll*) ingannare. **foxed** *adj* perplesso.

foyer ['foiei] *n* ridotto *m*.

fraction ['frakʃən] *n* frazione *f*.

fracture [fraktʃə] *n* frattura *f*, rottura *f*. *v* rompere, fratturare.

fragile ['fradʒail] *adj* fragile; (*delicate*) gracile.

fragment ['fragmənt] *n* frammento *m*.

fragrant ['freigrənt] *adj* fragrante, profumato. **fragrance** *n* profumo *m*.

frail [freil] *adj* fragile, gracile.

frame [freim] *n* struttura *f*; (*skeleton*) ossatura *f*; (*picture*) cornice *f*; (*machine*) telaio *m*. **frame of mind** disposizione d'animo *f*, umore *m*. **framework** *n* (*mech*) intelaiatura *f*; (*outline*) abbozzo *m*. *v* incorniciare, costruire; (*compose*) redigere; (*fabricate evidence*) calunniare.

France [frams] *n* Francia *f*.

franchise ['frantʃaiz] *n* (*privilege*) franchigia *f*; (*comm*) concessione *f*.

frank [fraŋk] *adj* sincero, schietto. **frankness** *n* sincerità *f*, schiettezza *f*.

frantic ['frantik] *adj* frenetico.

fraternal [frə'təml] *adj* fraterno. **fraternity** *n* fratellanza *f*; (*friendship*) fraternità *f*. **fraternize** *v* fraternizzare.

fraud [frod] *n* (*deceit*) frode *f*, inganno *m*; (*deceiver*) impostore, -a *m, f*, truffatore, -trice *m, f*. **fraudulent** *adj* fraudolento, doloso.

fraught [frot] *adj* (*tense*) nervoso. **fraught with** pieno *or* denso di.

fray¹ [frei] *v* (*unravel*) logorare, consumare. **frayed** *adj* (*clothes, etc.*) logoro dall'uso, liso. **frayed nerves** nervi scoperti *m pl*.

fray² [frei] *n* (*brawl*) mischia *f*.

freak [frik] *n* fenomeno *m*; figura grottesca *f*, mostro *m*.

freckle ['frekl] *n* lentiggine *f*. **freckled** *adj* lentigginoso.

free [fri] *adj* libero; (*without payment*) gratis, gratuito; (*unconstrained*) disinvolto, sciolto; (*lavish*) generoso. **free from** esente da. **freehold** *n* proprietà fondiaria assoluta *f*. **freelance** *adj* indipendente. **Freemason** *n* massone *m*.

free speech libertà di parola *f*. **free trade** libero scambio *m*. **free will** libero arbitrio *m*. *v* liberare. **freedom** *n* libertà *f*.

freesia ['frizɪə] *n* fresia *f*.

*freeze [friz] *v* gelare, congelare; (*block*) bloccare. *n* gelo *m*. **freezer** *n* congelatore *m*, freezer *m invar*. **freezing** *adj* gelido. **below freezing** sotto zero. **freezing point** punto di congelamento *m*.

freight [freit] *n* (*cargo*) carico *m*; (*charge*) nolo *m*; (*conveyance*) trasporto *m*. **freight train** treno merci *m*. *v* trasportare. **freighter** *n* nave da carico *f*.

French [frentʃ] *nm, adj* francese. **French bean** *n* fagiolino verde *m*, cornetto *m*. **French horn** corno (a pistoni) *m*. **Frenchman/woman** *n* francese *m, f*. **french fries** *pl n* patatine fritte *f pl*

frenzy ['frenzi] *n* frenesia *f*. **frenzied** *adj* frenetico.

frequent ['frikwənt; *v* fri'kwent] *adj* frequente. *v* frequentare. **frequency** *n* frequenza *f*.

fresco ['freskou] *n* affresco *m*.

fresh [freʃ] *adj* fresco; (*water*) dolce; (*brisk*) vigoroso; (*cheeky*) insolente. **fresh from** appena venuto da. **freshman** *n* matricola *f*. **freshen** *v* rinfrescare, rinnovare. **freshness** *n* freschezza *f*, vigore *m*.

fret¹ [fret] *v* inquietarsi. **fretful** *adj* irritabile.

fret² [fret] *n* (*pattern*) fregio *m*. *v* ornare con fregi, traforare. **fretwork** *n* lavoro di traforo *m*.

friar ['fraiə] *n* frate *m*. **friary** *n* convento di frati *m*.

friction ['frikʃən] *n* attrito *m*; (*conflict*) dissenso *m*.

Friday ['fraidei] *n* venerdì *m*.

fridge [fridʒ] *n* (*coll*) frigorifero *m*.

fried [fraid] *adj* fritto.

friend [frend] *n* amico, -a *m, f*. **make friends** fare amicizia. **friendless** *adj* senza amici. **friendliness** *n* amichevolezza *f*, cordialità *f*. **friendly** *adj* amichevole, cordiale, gentile. **be friendly with** essere amico di. **friendship** *n* amicizia *f*.

frieze [friz] *n* fregio *m*.

frigate ['frigit] *n* fregata *f*.

fright [frait] *n* spavento *m*. **frighten** *v* spaventare, allarmare. **be frightened** aver paura. **frightening** *adj* spaventevole, terribile. **frightful** *adj* terribile.

frigid ['fridʒid] *adj* freddo; (*woman*) frigido. **frigidity** *n* freddezza *f*; frigidità *f*.

frill [fril] *n* fronzolo *m*. **frilly** *adj* carico di fronzoli.

fringe [frindʒ] *n* (*border*) orlo *m*; limite *m*; (*ornamental border, hair*) frangia *f*; periferia *f*. *v* ornare di frange.

frisk [frisk] *v* saltellare; (*search*) perquisire. **frisky** *adj* vivace.

fritter[1] ['fritə] *v* **fritter away** sprecare.

fritter[2] ['fritə] *n* (*cookery*) frittella *f*.

frivolity [fri'voliti] *n* frivolezza *f*. **frivolous** *adj* superficiale, frivolo.

frizz [friz] *v* arricciare. *n* ricciolo *m*. **frizzy** *adj* ricciuto.

fro [frou] *adv* **to and fro** avanti e indietro.

frock [frok] *n* vestito *m*.

frog [frog] *n* rana *f*. **frogman** *n* uomo rana *m*.

frolic ['frolik] *v* trastullarsi, scherzare. *n* scherzo *m*.

from [from] *prep* da, per, da parte di.

front [frʌnt] *n* parte anteriore *f*; (*mil, pol*) fronte *m*; (*arch*) facciata *f*; (*seaside*) lungomare *m*. *adj* primo, anteriore. **front door** portone *m*. **in front of** davanti a.

frontier [frʌntiə] *n* frontiera *f*, confine *m*.

frost [frost] *n* gelo *m*. **frost-bite** *n* gelone *m*. *v* brinare; (*cookery*) glassare. **frosted glass** vetro smerigliato *m*. **frosty** *adj* (*weather*) gelido; (*manner*) freddo.

froth [froθ] *n* schiuma *f*. *v* spumare, schiumare.

frown [fraun] *v* aggrottare le ciglia, corrugare la fronte. **frown at** guardare in cagnesco. *n* cipiglio *m*, viso arcigno *m*.

froze [frouz] *V* **freeze**.

frozen ['frouzn] *V* **freeze**. *adj* gelato, congelato; bloccato.

frugal ['frugəl] *adj* frugale, sobrio.

fruit [fruit] *n* frutto *m*; (*collectively*) frutta *f*; (*result*) risultato *m*. **fruit salad** macedonia di frutta *f*. *v* (*bear fruit*) fruttare. **fruiterer** *n* fruttivendolo, -a *m*, *f*. **fruitful** *adj* fecondo; (*profitable*) redditizio. **fruition** *n* realizzazione *f*. **fruitless** *adj* infruttuoso; inutile. **fruity** *adj* saporito; di frutta; (*wine*) dal gusto d'uva.

frustrate [frʌ'streit] *v* frustrare. **frustration** *n* frustrazione *f*.

fry [frai] *v* friggere. **frying pan** padella *f*.

fuchsia ['fjuːʃə] *n* fucsia *f*.

fuck [fʌk] *v* (*vulgar*) fottere, chiavare.

fuel ['fjuəl] *n* combustibile *m*; (*mot*) carburante *m*. **fuel oil** gasolio *m*, nafta *f*. *v* alimentare.

fugitive ['fjuːdʒitiv] *adj* (*runaway*) fuggitivo, fuggiasco; (*fleeting*) effimero, fugace. *n* fuggiasco, -a *m*, *f*; profugo, -a *m*, *f*.

fugue [fjuːg] *n* fuga *f*.

fulcrum ['fʌlkrəm] *n* fulcro *m*.

fulfil [ful'fil] *v* adempiere, compiere, soddisfare. **fulfilment** *n* adempimento *m*, realizzazione *f*.

full [ful] *adj* pieno; completo; intero. **full-length** *adj* di lunghezza normale; (*portrait*) in piedi. **full moon** luna piena *f*. **full-sized** *adj* di grandezza naturale. **full stop** punto *m*. **full-time** *adj, adv* a tempo intero, a orario completo. **fully** *adv* completamente.

fumble ['fʌmbl] *v* brancolare.

fume [fjuːm] *v* emettere fumo; (*coll: rage*) arrabbiarsi, imperversare. *n* fumo *m*, esalazione *f*.

fumigate ['fjuːmigeit] *v* suffumicare.

fun [fʌn] *n* spasso *m*, divertimento *m*, scherzo *m*. **funfair** *n* luna park *m invar*. **in fun** per ridere. **make fun of** prendere in giro.

function ['fʌŋkʃən] *n* funzione *f*; (*purpose*) scopo *m*; (*duty*) mansione *f*; (*ceremony*) cerimonia *f*. *v* funzionare. **functional** *adj* funzionale.

fund [fʌnd] *n* fondo *m*, riserva *f*, capitale *m*. **funds** *pl n* soldi *m pl*.

fundamental [fʌndə'mentl] *adj* fondamentale, basilare.

funeral ['fjuːnərəl] *n* funerale *m*. *adj* funebre. **funereal** *adj* funereo.

fungus ['fʌŋgəs] *n*, *pl* -gi fungo *m*. **fungicide** *n* anticrittogamico *m*.

funnel ['fʌnl] *n* imbuto *m*; (*ship*) ciminiera *f*.

funny ['fʌni] *adj* divertente, comico; (*odd*) strano. **funny story** barzelletta *f*. **the funny thing is** il bello è.

fur [fəː] *n* (*skin*) pelo *m*; pelliccia *f*. *v* incrostarsi. **furrier** *n* pellicciaio *m*. **furry** *adj* peloso.

furious ['fjuəriəs] *adj* furibondo, arrabiatissimo.

furnace ['fəːnis] *n* fornace *f*.

furnish ['fəːniʃ] *v* (*supply*) fornire, dotare; (*house, etc.*) arredare, ammobiliare.

furniture ['fəːnitʃə] *n* mobilio *m*, mobili *m pl*; (*fittings*) attrezzatura *f*.

furrow ['fʌrəu] n solco m; (brow) ruga f, grinza f.

further ['fəːðə] adj ulteriore, più lontano. adv più lontano, oltre. **furthermore** adv inoltre. **further on** più avanti. **further up** più in su. v favorire, promuovere.

furthest ['fəːðist] adj in più lontano, estremo.

furtive ['fəːtiv] adj furtivo, di soppiatto.

fury ['fjuəri] n furia f.

fuse[1] [fjuːz] n (elec) valvola f, fusibile m. **blow a fuse** saltare la corrente. v (melt) fondere; (blend) amalgamare, unire. **fusion** n fusione f.

fuse[2] [fjuːz] n (bomb) detonatore m.

fuselage ['fjuːzəˌlaːʒ] n fusoliera f.

fuss [fʌs] v lamentarsi, agitarsi. **fuss over** affaccendarsi attorno a. n scalpore m, trambusto m. **make a fuss** fare un gran chiasso. **fussy** adj pignolo, meticoloso.

futile ['fjuːtail] adj vano, inutile. **futility** n inutilità f.

future ['fjuːtʃə] n futuro m, avvenire m. adj futuro.

fuzz [fʌz] n lanugine f, peluria f. **fuzzy** adj peloso; (unclear) sfocato.

G

gabble ['gabl] v borbottare. n borbottio m.

gaberdine [gabə'diːn] n gabardina f.

gable ['geibl] n pigna f, frontone m.

gadget ['gadʒit] n congegno m, dispositivo m.

gag[1] [gag] n bavaglio m. v imbavagliare.

gag[2] [gag] n (joke) battuta f.

gaiety ['geiəti] n allegria f.

gaily ['geili] adv allegramente.

gain [gein] n guadagno m, profitto m. v guadagnare; (obtain) ottenere.

gait [geit] n andatura f, passo m.

gala ['gaːlə] n festa f.

galaxy ['galəksi] n galassia f.

gale [geil] n bufera f, burrasca f.

gallant ['galənt] adj (courageous) prode; (courtly) galante. n cavaliere m. **gallantry** n valore m, coraggio m; galanteria f.

gall-bladder ['gɔːlˌbladə] n cistifellea f, vescica biliare f.

galleon ['galiən] n galeone m.

gallery ['galəri] n galleria f; (theatre) loggione m.

galley ['gali] n (naut) galea f; (kitchen) cambusa f.

gallop ['galəp] n galoppo m; galoppata f. v galoppare, andare al galoppo.

gallows ['galouz] n patibolo m.

gallstone ['gɔːlstoun] n calcolo biliare m.

galore [gə'lɔː] adv in quantità.

galvanize ['galvənaiz] v galvanizzare. **galvanometer** n galvanometro m.

gambit ['gambit] n gambetto m.

gamble ['gambl] v (risk) rischiare, arrischiare; (game) giocare. n impresa rischiosa f, speculazione f. **gambler** n giocatore, -trice m, f. **gambling** n gioco d'azzardo m.

game [geim] n gioco m; (match) partita f; (hunting) selvaggina f. **gamekeeper** n guardacaccia m. adj (plucky) che ha del fegato.

gammon ['gamən] n prosciutto m.

gander ['gandə] n papero m.

gang [gan] n squadra f, gruppo m; (youths, thieves, etc.) banda f. v **gang up** allearsi. **gangster** n gangster m invar, bandito m.

gangling ['ganglin] adj allampanato.

gangrene ['gangriːn] n cancrena f.

gangway ['ganwei] n passaggio m, corsia f; (naut) barcarizzo m.

gaol V **jail**.

gap [gap] n (breach) breccia f; (opening) apertura f; (hole) buco m; (vacant space) vuoto m; intervallo m; (divergence) distacco m.

gape [geip] v stare a bocca aperta; (open wide) spalancare.

garage ['garaːʒ] n garage m invar; (repairs) autorimessa f.

garbage ['gaːbidʒ] (US) n rifiuti m pl. **garbage can** bidone della spazzatura m.

garble ['gaːbl] v mutilare.

garden ['gaːdn] n giardino m. v fare del giardinaggio. **gardener** n giardiniere, -a m, f. **gardening** n giardinaggio m.

gargle ['gaːgl] v gargarizzare. n gargarismo m.

garish ['geəriʃ] adj vistoso.

garland ['gaːlənd] n ghirlanda f. v inghirlandare.

garlic ['gaːlik] n aglio m.

garment ['gaːmənt] n indumento m, capo di vestiario m.

garnish ['gaːniʃ] v guarnire, adornare. n ornamento m, guarnizione f.

garret ['gærət] n soffitta f.

garrison ['gærisn] n guarnigione f, presidio m. v presidiare.

garrulous ['gærələs] adj loquace.

garter ['gɑːtə] n giarrettiera f.

gas [gæs] n gas m invar; (US: petrol) benzina f. **gas cooker** fornello a gas m. **gas fire** stufa a gas f. **gas mask** maschera antigas f. v asfissiare.

gash [gæʃ] n sfregio m, squarcio m. v sfregiare, squarciare.

gasket ['gæskit] n guarnizione f.

gasoline ['gæsə,liin] n (US) benzina f.

gasp [gɑːsp] v boccheggiare, ansimare. n rantolo m.

gastric ['gæstrik] adj gastrico.

gastronomy [gɑ'stronəmi] n gastronomia f. **gastronomic** adj gastronomico.

gate [geit] n cancello m, porta f. **gatecrash** v fare il portoghese, entrare senza invito or pagare. **gatepost** n montante del cancello m. **gateway** n entrata f, portone m.

gateau ['gætou] n pasticcino m, gateau m.

gather ['gæðə] v cogliere; (bring together) raccogliere; (infer) dedurre; (assemble) radunarsi. **gathering** n riunione f, adunata f.

gaudy ['gɔːdi] adj vistoso.

gauge [geidʒ] n (measure) misura f; (instrument) calibro m; (rail) scartamento m. v misurare, calibrare.

gaunt [gɔːnt] adj emaciato, desolato.

gauze [gɔːz] n garza f.

gave [geiv] V give.

gay [gei] adj vivace, allegro; (slang) omosessuale.

gaze [geiz] v mirare, guardare fissamente. n fissare. n sguardo fisso m.

gazelle [gə'zel] n gazzella f.

gazette [gə'zet] n gazzetta ufficiale f.

gazetteer [gæzə'tiə] n dizionario geografico m.

gear [giə] n (mot) marcia f, velocità f; (equipment, tools) arnesi m pl, attrezzatura f; (belongings) roba f. **change gear** cambiare velocità. **gearbox** n scatola del cambio f. **gear lever** leva del cambio f. v preparare, adattare.

gelatine ['dʒelə,tiin] n gelatina f.

gelignite ['dʒelig,nait] n gelatina esplosiva f.

gem [dʒem] n gemma f.

Gemini ['dʒemini] n Gemelli m pl.

gender ['dʒendə] n genere m, sesso m.

gene [dʒiin] n gene m.

genealogy [dʒiini,alədʒi] n genealogia f. **genealogical** adj genealogico.

general ['dʒenərəl] nm, adj generale. **general practitioner** medico generico m. **generalization** n generalizzazione f. **generalize** v generalizzare.

generate ['dʒenəreit] v generare, produrre. **generation** n generazione f. **generator** n generatore m.

generic [dʒi'nerik] adj generico.

generous ['dʒenərəs] adj generoso. **generosity** n generosità f.

genetic [dʒi'netik] adj genetico. **geneticist** n genetista m, f. **genetics** n genetica f.

Geneva [dʒi'niivə] n Ginevra f.

genial ['dʒiiniəl] adj gioviale, simpatico.

genital ['dʒenitl] adj genitale. **genitals** pl n organi genitali m pl.

genius ['dʒiiniəs] n genio m.

Genoa ['dʒenouə] n Genova f. **Genoese** n(m+f), adj genovese.

genteel [dʒen'tiil] adj signorile. **gentility** n signorilità f.

gentle ['dʒentl] adj tenero; (mild) mite; (not steep) dolce. **gentleman** n signore m; (of good breeding, etc.) gentiluomo m. **gentlemanly** adj signorile. **gentleness** n dolcezza f, gentilezza f. **gently** adv dolcemente; adagio, piano.

gentry ['dʒentri] n piccola nobiltà f.

gents [dʒents] n (sign) uomini, signori.

genuine ['dʒenjuin] adj genuino, autentico; sincero. **genuinely** adv (really) veramente.

genus ['dʒiinəs] n genere m.

geography [dʒi'ogrəfi] n geografia f. **geographer** n geografo, -a m, f. **geographical** adj geografico.

geology [dʒi'olədʒi] n geologia f. **geological** adj geologico. **geologist** n geologo, -a m, f.

geometry [dʒi'omətri] n geometria f. **geometric** adj geometrico.

geranium [dʒə'reiniəm] n geranio m.

geriatric [dʒeri'atrik] adj geriatrico. **geriatrics** n geriatria f.

germ [dʒəːm] n germe m.

Germany ['dʒəːməni] n Germania f. **German** n, adj tedesco, -a. **German measles** rosolia f, rubeola f.

germinate ['dʒəːmineit] v germinare. **germination** n germinazione f.

gerund ['dʒerənd] n gerundio m.

gesticulate [dʒe'stikju,leit] v gesticolare. **gesticulation** n gesticolazione f.

gesture ['dʒestʃə] n gesto m. v gesticolare, fare gesti.

****get** [get] v (obtain) ottenere, procurare; (fetch) andare a prendere; (receive) ricevere; (understand) capire; (become) diventare; (reach) arrivare. **get across** attraversare; (make understand) far capire. **get along with** andare d'accordo con. **get at** (reach) raggiungere; (hint) alludere. **getaway** n fuga f. **get off** scendere. **get out** uscire. **get up** alzarsi.

geyser ['giːzə] n (geog) geyser m; (waterheater) scaldabagno m.

ghastly ['gɑːstli] adj orrendo; (pale) spettrale.

gherkin ['gɜːkin] n cetriolino m.

ghetto ['getou] n ghetto m.

ghost [goust] n fantasma m, spettro m. **ghostly** adj spettrale.

giant ['dʒaiənt] n gigante, -essa m, f. adj gigantesco, gigante.

gibberish ['dʒibəriʃ] n discorso incomprensibile m.

gibe [dʒaib] n beffa f; scherno m. v gibe at beffarsi di, beffare.

giblets ['dʒiblits] pl n rigaglie f pl, frattaglie f pl.

giddy ['gidi] adj (flighty) incostante, volubile; (dizzy) preso da vertigini; (height) vertiginoso. **feel giddy** avere il capogiro. **giddiness** n capogiro m, vertigini f pl.

gift [gift] n dono m, regalo m. **gifted** adj dotato.

gigantic [dʒai'gantik] adj gigantesco.

giggle ['gigl] v ridere scioccamente. n risatina sciocca f. **have the giggles** avere la ridarella.

gill [gil] n (fish) branchia f; (mushroom) lamella f.

gilt [gilt] n doratura f. adj dorato.

gimmick ['gimik] n (coll: device) congegno m; stratagemma m.

gin [dʒin] n gin m invar.

ginger ['dʒindʒə] n zenzero m. adj fulvo. **gingerly** ['dʒindʒəli] adj cauto.

gipsy ['dʒipsi] n zingaro, -a m, f.

giraffe [dʒi'rɑːf] n giraffa f.

girder ['gɜːdə] n trave maestra f, putrella f.

girdle ['gɜːdl] n busto m, cintura f. v cingere.

girl [gɜːl] n ragazza f. **girlfriend** n amica f. **girlish** adj da ragazza.

giro ['dʒairou] n giroconto m, postagiro m.

girth [gɜːθ] n circonferenza f.

gist [dʒist] n nocciolo m.

****give** [giv] v dare; (present) regalare; (relinquish) cedere. **give away** regalare; (betray) tradire; (secret) rivelare. **give back** restituire. **give in** cedere. **give oneself up** costituirsi. **give out** distribuire. **give rise to** risultare in. **give up** abbandonare; (cease) smettere. n elasticità f.

given ['givn] V give.

glacier ['glasiə] n ghiacciaio m.

glad [glad] adj lieto, contento. **gladden** v rallegrare. **gladly** adv con piacere.

glamour ['glamə] n fascino m. **glamorous** adj affascinante.

glance [glɑːns] n sguardo m. **at a glance** a prima vista. v dare un'occhiata.

gland [gland] n ghiandola f. **glandular** adj ghiandolare.

glare [gleə] n (light) bagliore m; (fierce look) sguardo torvo m. v **glare at** guardare con cipiglio, guardare con occhio torvo.

glass [glɑːs] n vetro m; (container) bicchiere m. **glasses** pl n occhiali m pl. **glassy** adj vitreo.

glaze [gleiz] n smalto m, patina f. v smaltare, verniciare; (fit with glass) fornire di vetri.

gleam [gliːm] v luccicare. n barlume m, lucicchio m.

glean [gliːn] v racimolare.

glee [gliː] n gioia f. **gleeful** adj pieno di gioia.

glib [glib] adj facondo.

glide [glaid] v scivolare, scorrere; (aero) planare. **glider** n aliante m. **gliding** n volo a vela m.

glimmer ['glimə] v luccicare; (of dawn) albeggiare. n barlume m, lucicchio m.

glimpse [glimps] n occhiata f, visione f. v intravedere.

glint [glint] n lucicchio m. v luccicare, scintillare.

glisten ['glisn] v luccicare, brillare.

glitter ['glitə] v brillare, scintillare. n lucentezza f.

gloat [glout] v gongolare (malignamente).

globe [gloub] n globo m. **global** adj globale.

gloom [gluːm] n (darkness) oscurità f; (depression) malinconia f, tristezza f. **gloomy** adj malinconico, triste.

glory ['glɔːri] n gloria f, splendore m. **glorify** v glorificare. **glorious** adj illustre, splendido.

gloss¹ [glos] n (lustre) lucentezza f; (appearance) apparenza f. **glossy** adj lucido.

gloss² [glos] n (explanation) chiosa f. v chiosare, commentare.

glossary ['glosəri] n lessico m.

glove [glʌv] n guanto m.

glow [glou] v risplendere; ardere. n rossore m; (colour) luminosità f. **glowing** adj acceso, ardente; fervente.

glucose ['gluːkous] n glucosio m.

glue [gluː] n colla f. v incollare.

glum [glʌm] adj tetro, cupo.

glut [glʌt] n sovrabbondanza f. v saturare.

glutton ['glʌtən] n ghiottone, -a m, f; goloso, -a m, f. **gluttonous** adj ghiotto, goloso. **gluttony** n golosità f.

gnarled [naːld] adj nodoso.

gnash [naʃ] v **gnash one's teeth** digrignare i denti.

gnat [nat] n zanzara f.

gnaw [nɔː] v rodere, rosicchiare. **gnawing** adj rosicante.

gnome [noum] n gnomo m.

*go [gou] v andare; (become) diventare. **go away** andarsene. **go back** ritornare. **go-between** n intermediario m. **go by** passare; (be guided by) regolarsi su. **go down** scendere; (sink) affondare. **go in** entrare. **go off** esplodere; (spoil) guastarsi; (leave) andarsene. **go on** continuare. **go out** uscire. **go up** salire. **go without** fare a meno di. n energia f; (try) colpo m. **on the go** molto attivo.

goad [goud] n pungolo m. v incitare.

goal [goul] n (aim) meta f; (sport) porta f, rete f. **goalkeeper** n portiere m. **goal-post** n palo della porta m.

goat [gout] n capra f.

gobble ['gobl] v inghiottire.

goblin ['goblin] n folletto m.

god [god] n dio (pl dei) m. **goddaughter** n figlioccia f. **godfather** n padrino m. **godmother** n madrina f. **godson** n figlioccio m. **goddess** n dea f.

goggles ['goglz] pl n occhiali di protezione m pl.

gold [gould] n oro m. **goldfinch** n cardellino m. **goldfish** n pesce dorato or rosso m. **gold mine** miniera d'oro f. **goldsmith** n orefice m. **golden** adj d'oro; (colour) aureo. **golden rule** regola d'oro f.

golf [golf] n golf m. **golf course** campo di golf m. **golfer** n giocatore, -trice di golf m, f.

gondola ['gondələ] n gondola f.

gone [gon] V go.

gong [goŋ] n gong m invar.

gonorrhoea [gonə'riə] n gonorrea f.

good [gud] adj buono; valido; (well-behaved, clever) bravo. **good afternoon** buon giorno; (later) buona sera. **goodbye** interj addio; arrivederci; (coll) ciao. **good-for-nothing** n buono a nulla m. **good-looking** adj bello. **good morning** buon giorno. **goodnight** interj buona notte. **goodwill** n benevolenza f; (comm) avviamento m. **n bene m**, vantaggio m. **be no good** non servire. **for good** per sempre. **goodness** n bontà f, gentilezza f, virtù f.

Good Friday n Venerdì Santo m.

goods [gudz] pl n merce f pl, beni m pl. **goods train** treno merci m.

goose [guːs] n, pl **geese** oca f.

gooseberry ['guzbəri] n uva spina f.

gore [gɔː] v trafiggere.

gorge [gɔːdʒ] n (geol) gola f. v rimpinzarsi (di).

gorgeous ['gɔːdʒəs] adj splendido.

gorilla [gə'rilə] n gorilla m invar.

gorse [gɔːs] n ginestrone m.

gory ['gɔːri] adj cruento.

gosling ['gozliŋ] n papero, -a m, f.

gospel ['gospəl] n vangelo m; (coll: truth) verità implicita f.

gossip ['gosip] n ciarla f, pettegolezzo m; (person) ciarlone, -a m, f, chiacchierone, -a m, f. v ciarlare, chiacchierare.

got [got] V get.

Gothic ['goθik] adj gotico.

gourd [guəd] n zucca f.

gourmet ['guəmei] n buongustaio, -a m, f.

gout [gaut] n gotta f.

govern ['gʌvən] v governare f; (gramm) reggere. **governess** n governante f. **government** n governo m. **governor** n governatore m; (coll: boss) capo m.

gown [gaun] n (dress) veste f; (robe) toga f.

grab [græb] v arraffare. n strappo m.

grace [greis] n grazia f, eleganza f. v adornare. **graceful** adj grazioso. **gracious** adj benigno.

grade [greid] n grado m; (level) livello m; classe f. v classificare.

gradient ['greidiənt] n gradiente m; (slope) pendio m.

gradual ['grædjuəl] adj graduale. **gradually** adv poco a poco.

graduate ['grædjuət; v 'grædjueit] n laureato, -a m, f. v laurearsi.

graft[1] [græft] n (bot) innesto m; (med) trapianto m; (hard work) sgobbata f. v innestare; trapiantare; sgobbare.

graft[2] [græft] n (bribery) corruzione f. v corrompere.

grain [grein] n (seed) chicco m, granello m; (wheat) grano m; (wood) venatura f; (leather) grana f. **against the grain** contro pelo.

gram [græm] n grammo m.

grammar ['græmə] n grammatica f. **grammatical** adj grammaticale.

gramophone ['græməfoun] n grammofono m.

granary ['grænəri] n granaio m.

grand [grænd] adj (imposing) grandioso; (first rate) splendido. **grandchild** n nipote m, f; nipotino, -a m, f. **grandfather** n nonno m. **grandmother** n nonna f. **grand piano** pianoforte a coda m. **grandstand** n tribuna coperta f. **grand total** somma f. **grandeur** n grandiosità f.

granite ['grænit] n granito m.

grant [grænt] v (confer) concedere, accordare; (give) dare; (admit) ammettere. **take for granted** ritenere per certo. n (student) borsa di studio f; concessione f.

granule ['grænjuːl] n granello m.

grape [greip] n acino m, chicco d'uva m. **grapes** pl n uva f sing. **grapevine** n vite f; (coll) canali confidenziali m pl.

grapefruit ['greipfruːt] n pompelmo m.

graph [græf] n (math) grafico m; diagramma m. **graphic** adj grafico. **graph paper** carta millimetrata f.

grapple ['græpl] v **grapple with** venire alle prese con.

grasp [graːsp] v afferrare; (understand) capire. n stretta f. **grasping** adj avaro.

grass [graːs] n erba f; (lawn) prato m. **grasshopper** n cavalletta f. **grassy** adj erboso.

grate[1] [greit] n graticola f. **grating** n inferriata f.

grate[2] [greit] v grattugiare; (sound harshly) stridere; (irritate) dare sui nervi.

grateful ['greitful] adj riconoscente, grato.

gratify ['grætifai] v appagare.

gratitude ['grætitjuːd] n gratitudine f.

gratuitous [grə'tjuitəs] adj (free) gratuito; (without cause) ingiustificato.

gratuity [grə'tjuəti] n (tip) mancia f; (unsolicited gift) gratifica f.

grave[1] [greiv] n tomba f, sepolcro m. **gravedigger** n becchino m. **gravestone** n lapide funeraria f. **graveyard** n cimitero m.

grave[2] [greiv] adj grave.

gravel ['grævəl] n ghiaia f.

gravity ['grævəti] n gravità f. **gravitate** v gravitare.

gravy ['greivi] n sugo di carne m; salsa f.

graze[1] [greiz] v (touch) sfiorare; (scrape) scalfire. n scalfitura f, lesione superficiale f.

graze[2] [greiz] v (animal) pascolare.

grease [griːs] n grasso m, unto m. **greaseproof paper** carta oleata f. v ungere, ingrassare. **greasy** adj grasso, unto; (slippery) scivoloso.

great [greit] adj grande; (very good) magnifico; (very large) grandissimo. **Great Britain** Gran Bretagna f. **greatly** adv molto. **greatness** n grandezza f.

Greece [griːs] n Grecia f. **Greek** n, adj greco (pl -ci), -a.

greed [griːd] n ingordigia f. **greedy** adj ingordo.

green [griːn] adj verde. n verde m; (land) prato m; (golf) green m. **greenfly** n afide m. **greengage** n prugna verde f. **greengrocer** n erbivendolo, -a m, f, fruttivendolo, -a m, f. **greenhouse** n serra f. **green light** luce verde f. **greens** pl n verdura f sing.

Greenland ['griːnlənd] n Groenlandia f. **Greenlander** n groenlandese m, f.

greet [griːt] v salutare. **greeting** n saluto m.

gregarious [gri'geəriəs] adj gregario, socievole.

grenade [grə'neid] n granata f.

grew [gruː] V grow.

grey [grei] adj grigio.

grid [grid] n (network) rete f; (map) reticolo m; (grating) grata f.

grief [griːf] n dolore m, afflizione f. **come to grief** far fiasco or cilecca.

grieve [griːv] v (upset) affliggere, addolorare; (sorrow) affliggersi. **grievance** n (injustice) ingiustizia f; (complaint) lamentela f. **grievous** adj doloroso, atroce.

grill [gril] n (cookery) graticola f, gratella f; (grilled meat) carne ai ferri f. v (cookery) cucinare ai ferri; (question severely) sottoporre a un interrogatorio severo.

grille [gril] n inferriata f, grata f.

grim [grim] adj (unrelenting) inesorabile; (fierce) feroce; (forbidding) arcigno. **grimly** adv con severità.

grimace [gri'meis] n smorfia f. v fare smorfie.

grime [graim] n sudiciume m. **grimy** adj sudicio.

grin [grin] v fare un largo sorriso. n largo sorriso m.

*__grind__ [graind] v (pulverize) macinare; (sharpen) affilare; (teeth) digrignare. n (coll: hard work) sgobbata f.

grip [grip] v stringere; (hold interest) avvincere; (take firm hold) far presa. n presa f, stretta f; (control) padronanza f. **come to grips with** venire alle prese con.

gripe [graip] n colica f. v (coll) lagnarsi.

grisly ['grizli] adj orribile, macabro.

gristle ['grisl] n cartilagine f. **gristly** adj cartilaginoso.

grit [grit] n (sand) sabbia f; (mech) graniglia f; (coll: courage) fegato m. v (teeth) digrignare. **gritty** adj sabbioso.

groan [groun] v gemito m, lamento m. v gemere, lamentarsi.

grocer ['grousə] n droghiere, -a m, f. **grocer's** n (shop) drogheria f. **groceries** pl n generi coloniali m pl.

groin [groin] n inguine m.

groom [grum] n stalliere m; (bridegroom) sposo m. v preparare; (horse) strigliare.

groove [gruːv] n solco m. v scanalare.

grope [group] v brancolare. **grope for** cercare a tentoni, brancolare in cerca di.

gross [grous] adj grossolano, volgare; (not net) lordo. v (income) avere un introito lordo di. n grossa f.

grotesque [grə'tesk] adj fantastico; (incongruous) grottesco.

grotto ['grotou] n grotta f.

ground[1] [graund] V **grind**.

ground[2] [graund] n (soil) terreno m;

(earth, floor) terra f; (sport) campo m; (reason) motivo m; (bottom) fondo m. **ground floor** pianterreno m. **grounds** pl n (sediment) deposito m sing; (dregs) fondi m pl. v (base) fondare; (teach) insegnare i primi elementi; (aircraft) impedire di volare. **grounding** n base f. **groundless** adj infondato.

group [gruːp] n gruppo m. v raggruppare, disporre.

grouse[1] [graus] n (bird) urogallo m.

grouse[2] [graus] (coll) v brontolare, lamentarsi. n lagnanza f.

grove [grouv] n boschetto m.

grovel ['grovl] v umiliarsi; (cringe) striciare.

*__grow__ [grou] v crescere; (thrive) prosperare; (become) diventare. **grown-up** n, adj adulto, -a. **grow on** piacere sempre più. **grow up** crescere, sorgere. **grower** n coltivatore, -trice m, f. **growth** n crescita f, progresso m; (med) escrescenza f, tumore m.

growl [graul] v ringhiare; (rumble) brontolare. n ringhio m; brontolio m.

grown [groun] V **grow**.

grub [grʌb] n (insect) larva f, bruco m; (coll) roba da mangiare f. v ripulire; (uproot) sradicare.

grubby ['grʌbi] adj (dirty) sudicio; (contemptible) abietto.

grudge [grʌdʒ] n rancore m. **bear a grudge against** nutrire rancore verso. v (give reluctantly) dare malvolentieri; (resent) invidiare. **grudgingly** adv malvolentieri.

gruelling ['gruːliŋ] adj faticoso.

gruesome ['gruːsəm] adj raccapricciante.

gruff [grʌf] adj (surly) burbero; (hoarse) rauco; (harsh) aspro.

grumble ['grʌmbl] v (complain) lagnarsi; (growl) brontolare. n lagnanza f, brontolio m.

grumpy ['grʌmpi] adj scontroso.

grunt [grʌnt] v grugnire. n grugnito m.

guarantee [garən'tiː] v garantire, rispondere di. n garanzia f.

guard [gaːd] v (keep safe) custodire; (watch over) sorvegliare; (keep watch) stare in guardia. **guard against** badare a. n guardia m, f; (appliance) protezione f; (railway) capotreno m. **guarded** adj cauto. **guardian** n custode m; (legal) tutore m.

guerrilla [gə'rilə] *n* guerrigliero *m*. **guerrilla warfare** guerriglia *f*.

guess [ges] *n* congettura *f*, supposizione *f*. **at a rough guess** a occhio e croce. *v* indovinare.

guest [gest] *n* ospite *m*, *f*; (*of hotel*) cliente *m*, *f*. **guest-house** *n* pensione *f*.

guide [gaid] *n* guida *f*; (*of tourists*) cicerone *m*. **guidebook** *n* guida *f*. *v* guidare; (*advise*) consigliare; (*direct*) dirigere. **be guided by** seguire il consiglio di. **guidance** *n* (*leadership*) guida *f*; (*instruction*) norma *f*.

guild [gild] *n* corporazione *f*.

guile [gail] *n* astuzia *f*. **guileless** *adj* ingenuo.

guillotine ['gilətiːn] *n* ghigliottina *f*.

guilt [gilt] *n* colpa *f*. **guiltless** *adj* innocente. **guilty** *adj* colpevole. **have a guilty conscience** avere la coscienza sporca *or* cattiva.

guinea-pig ['ginipig] *n* cavia *f*.

guitar [gi'taː] *n* chitarra *f*. **guitarist** *n* chitarrista *m*, *f*.

gulf [gʌlf] *n* (*geog*) golfo *m*; (*wide separation*) abisso *m*.

gull [gʌl] *n* gabbiano *m*.

gullet ['gʌlit] *n* (*throat*) gola *f*; (*oesophagus*) esofago *m*.

gullible ['gʌləbl] *adj* credulo. **gullibility** *n* credulità *f*.

gully ['gʌli] *n* (*canyon*) burrone *m*; (*ditch*) cunetta *f*.

gulp [gʌlp] *n* (*food*) boccone *m*; (*drink*) sorso *m*. *v* (*food*) ingoiare; (*drink*) tracannare; (*choke*) soffocare.

gum¹ [gʌm] *n* (*secretion*) gomma *f*; (*glue*) colla *f*. *v* ingommare; incollare.

gum² [gʌm] *n* (*mouth*) gengiva *f*.

gun [gʌn] *n* fucile *m*; cannone *m*. **gunfire** *n* sparatoria *f*. **gunman** *n* bandito armato *m*. **gunner** *n* artigliere *m*. **gunpowder** *n* polvere da sparo *f*. **gunshot** *n* colpo di fucile *m*.

gurgle ['gəːgl] *v* gorgogliare. *n* gorgoglio *m*.

gush [gʌʃ] *n* sgorgo *m*; (*language*) torrente *m*. *v* (*liquid*) scaturire; (*speech*) parlare con effusione.

gust [gʌst] *n* raffica *f*.

gusto ['gʌstou] *n* fervore *m*.

gut [gʌt] *n* budello *m* (*pl* -a *f*). **guts** *pl n* (*coll*) fegato *m sing*. *v* sbudellare.

gutter ['gʌtə] *n* (*house*) grondaia *f*; (*street*)

cunetta *f*; (*conduit*) condotto *m*. **guttersnipe** *n* scugnizzo *m*.

guy¹ [gai] *n* tipo *m*, individuo *m*.

guy² [gai] *n* (*rope*) tirante *m*.

gymnasium [dʒim'neiziəm] *n* palestra *f*. **gymnast** *n* ginnasta *m*, *f*. **gymnastics** *n* ginnastica *f*.

gynaecology [gainə'kolədʒi] *n* ginecologia *f*. **gynaecological** *adj* ginecologico. **gynaecologist** *n* ginecologo, -a *m*, *f*.

gypsum ['dʒipsəm] *n* gesso *m*.

gyrate [dʒai'reit] *v* girare, roteare.

gyroscope ['dʒairəˌskoup] *n* giroscopio *m*.

H

haberdasher ['habədaʃə] *n* merciaio, -a *m*, *f*. **haberdashery** *n* merceria *f*.

habit ['habit] *n* abitudine *f*; (*dress*) tonaca *f*. **habitual** *adj* abituale. **habitually** *adv* di solito.

habitable ['habitəbl] *adj* abitabile.

habitat ['habitat] *n* ambiente *m*.

hack¹ [hak] *v* tagliare, troncare. **hacksaw** *n* seghetto *m*.

hack² [hak] *n* (*horse*) ronzino *m*; (*writer*) scribacchino *m*.

hackneyed ['haknid] *adj* trito, comune.

had [had] *V* have.

haddock ['hadək] *n* eglefino *m*.

haemorrhage ['hemoridʒ] *n* emorragia *f*.

haemorrhoids ['hemərəidz] *pl n* emorroidi *f pl*.

hag [hag] *n* vecchiaccia *f*, strega *f*.

haggard ['hagəd] *adj* smunto, scarno.

haggle ['hagl] *v* mercanteggiare.

Hague [heig] *n* l'Aia *f*.

hail¹ [heil] *n* grandine *f*. **hailstone** *n* chicco di grandine *m*. *v* grandinare.

hail² [heil] *v* salutare; (*call*) chiamare. **hail from** essere oriundo di. *interj* salve! *n* saluto *m*.

hair [heə] *n* capelli *m pl*; (*single strand*) capello *m*; (*of animals*) pelo *m*. **split hairs** cercare il pelo nell'uovo. **hairy** *adj* capelluto; peloso.

hairbrush ['heəbrʌʃ] *n* spazzola per capelli *f*.

haircut ['heəkʌt] *n* taglio dei capelli *m*. **have a haircut** farsi tagliare i capelli.

hairdresser ['heəˌdresə] *n* parrucchiere, -a *m*, *f*.

hair-dryer ['heə‚draiə] n asciugacapelli m invar.

hairpin ['heəpin] n forcina f.

hair-raising ['heə‚reiziŋ] adj raccapricciante.

hake [heik] n nasello m.

half [haif] adj mezzo. n mezzo m, metà f; (sport: period) tempo m. **in half** in due.

half-and-half adj, adv metà e metà.

half-back ['haifbak] n mediano m.

half-baked [‚haifbeikt] adj (coll) inesperto, immaturo.

half-breed ['haifbriid] nm, adj ibrido.

half-brother ['haifbrʌðə] n fratellastro m.

half-hearted [‚haif'haitid] adj esitante, poco entusiasta.

half-hour [‚haif'auə] n mezz'ora f.

half-mast [‚haif'maist] n **at half-mast** a mezz'asta.

half-moon [‚haif'muin] n mezzaluna f.

half-sister ['haifsistə] n sorellastra f.

half-time [‚haif'taim] n intervallo m.

half-tone ['haiftoun] n mezzatinta f, fotoriproduzione f.

halfway [‚haif'wei] adj, adv a metà strada. **meet halfway** giungere a un compromesso.

half-witted [‚haif'witid] adj scemo, deficiente.

halibut ['halibət] n halibut m invar, ippoglosso m.

hall [hoil] n (entrance) entrata f; (room) sala f, salone m; (building) villa f, casa signorile f.

hallmark ['hoilmaik] n marchio d'autenticità m; elemento caratteristico m. v marcare.

hallowed ['haloud] adj venerato.

hallucination [hə‚luisi'neiʃən] n allucinazione f.

halo ['heilou] n aureola f; (astron) alone m.

halt [hoilt] n fermata f; (temporary) sosta f. v sostare, fermare, fermarsi. interj alt!

halter ['hoiltə] n capestro m; cavezza f.

halve [haiv] v dimezzare, ridurre della or alla metà.

ham [ham] n prosciutto m.

hamburger ['hambəigə] n hamburger m invar.

hammer ['hamə] n martello m. v martellare.

hammock ['hamək] n amaca f.

hamper¹ ['hampə] v intralciare, ostacolare.

hamper² ['hampə] n paniere m.

hamster ['hamstə] n criceto m.

hand [hand] n mano (pl -i) f; (clock) lancetta f; (worker) operaio, -a m, f. **at hand** a portata di mano. **by hand** a mano. **hands down** completamente, con facilità. **hands off!** via le mani! **hands up!** alto le mani! **in hand** (under control) sotto controllo; (available) a disposizione; (being dealt with) in corso. **on hand** presente; (available) disponibile. **on the other hand** d'altra parte. v (give) dare, porgere. **hand down** trasmettere, tramandare. **hand in** or **over** consegnare. **hand out** distribuire. **handful** n manata f; piccolo gruppo m.

handbag ['handbag] n borsetta f.

handbill ['handbil] n volantino m.

handbook ['handbuk] n manuale m.

handbrake ['handbreik] n freno a mano m.

handcuff ['handkʌf] n manetta f. v ammanettare.

handicap ['handikap] n svantaggio m, impedimento m; (sport) handicap m invar. v impedire.

handicraft ['handikraift] n artigianato m; (trade) mestiere m.

handiwork ['handiwəik] n (personal work) opera f.

handkerchief ['haŋkətʃif] n fazzoletto m.

handle ['handl] n manico m; (door) maniglia f; (crank) manovella f. v (manipulate) maneggiare; (deal with) trattare. **handlebar** n manubrio m.

handmade [‚hand'meid] adj fatto a mano.

hand-out ['handaut] n comunicato m, campione pubblicitario m.

hand-pick [‚hand'pik] v scegliere a mano.

handrail ['handreil] n ringhiera f.

handshake ['handʃeik] n stretta di mano f.

handsome ['hansəm] adj bello; generoso, considerevole.

handstand ['hand‚stand] n posata verticale sulle mani f.

hand-towel ['hand‚tauəl] n asciugamano m.

handwriting ['hand‚raitiŋ] n calligrafia f.

handy ['handi] adj (accessible) a portata di mano; (deft) destro, abile; (convenient) comodo.

*hang [haŋ] v pendere, appendere, sospendere; (execute) impiccare. **hang around** bazzicare. **hanger** n (clothes) attaccapanni *m invar.* **hanger-on** *n* scroccone *m.* **hangman** *n* boia *m invar.* **hang on** persistere, indugiare; (*phone*) restare in linea. **hangover** *n* postumi di una sbornia *m pl.*

hangar ['haŋə] *n* hangar *m invar*; aviorimessa *f.*

hanker ['haŋkə] *v* (*take place*) **hanker after** bramare. **hankering** *n* forte desiderio *m*, brama *f.*

haphazard [ˌhapˈhazəd] *adj* casuale.

happen ['hapən] *v* (*take place*) accadere, succedere. **as it happens** per caso. **happening** *n* avvenimento *m.*

happy ['hapi:] *adj* felice, contento, lieto; (*in greetings*) buono. **happy-go-lucky** *adj* spensierato. **happiness** *n* felicità *f*, contentezza *f.*

harass ['harəs] *v* molestare, tormentare, irritare. **harassment** *n* tormento *m*, molestia *f.*

harbour ['haibə] *n* porto *m. v* (*shelter*) dare asilo a.

hard [haid] *adj* duro; difficile; severo. *adv* molto; (*solidly*) sodo. **hard and fast** immutabile. **hard-boiled** *adj* (*egg*) sodo; (*person*) duro. **hard core** nucleo *m.* **hard-headed** *adj* accorto, pratico. **hard-hearted** *adj* insensibile. **hard up** al corto di quattrini. **hardware** *n* ferramenta *f pl*; (*computer*) meccanismo *m.* **hard-wearing** *adj* duraturo, durevole. **hard work** lavoro faticoso *m.* **try hard** provare assiduamente. **work hard** lavorar sodo. **hardness** *n* durezza *f.* **hardship** *n* privazione *f.*

hardly ['haidli] *adv* (*not exactly*) non esattamente; (*barely, almost not*) quasi, appena; (*with difficulty*) a stento.

hardy ['haidi] *adj* robusto, resistente; (*courageous*) coraggioso.

hare [heə] lepre *f.* **hare-brained** *adj* scervellato.

harm [haim] *n* male *m*, danno *m. v* nuocere a, far male a. **harmful** *adj* nocivo, dannoso. **harmless** *adj* innocuo, inoffensivo.

harmony ['haiməni] *n* armonia *f*, accordo *m.* **harmonic** *adj* armonico, armonioso. **harmonize** *v* armonizzare.

harness ['hainis] *n* briglia *f. v* imbrigliare.

harp [haip] *n* arpa *f.* **harpist** *n* arpista *m*, *f.*

harpoon [haiˈpuin] *n* rampone *m. v* ramponare.

harpsichord ['haipsiˌkoid] *n* clavicembalo *m.*

harrowing ['harouiŋ] *adj* straziante.

harsh [haiʃ] *adj* aspro, duro. **harshness** *n* asprezza *f*, durezza *f.*

harvest ['haivist] *n* raccolto *m. v* raccogliere, mietere.

has [haz] *V* **have**.

hash [haʃ] *n* carne tritata *f*; (*coll: mess*) confusione *f*, pasticcio *m.* **make a hash of** sciupare, mandare a rotoli.

hashish ['haʃiːʃ] *n* (h)ascisc *m invar.*

haste [heist] *n* fretta *f.* **hasten** *v* precipitare, affrettarsi. **hasty** *adj* frettoloso.

hat [hat] *n* cappello *m.*

hatch¹ [hatʃ] *v* (*bring forth*) covare; (*contrive*) tramare.

hatch² [hatʃ] *n* (*naut*) boccaporto *m*; (*opening*) portello *m*, sportello *m.*

hatchet ['hatʃit] *n* accetta *f.*

hate [heit] *v* odiare. *n also* **hatred** odio *m.* **hateful** *adj* odioso.

haughty ['hoiti] *adj* altezzoso, arrogante.

haul [hoil] *n* tiro *m*; (*fish*) retata *f*; (*coll: booty*) bottino *m. v* tirare.

haunch [hointʃ] *n* anca *f.*

haunt [hoint] *v* perseguitare, ossessionare. *n* ritrovo *m.* **haunting** *adj* ossessionante.

*****have** [hav] *v* avere. **have to** avere da, dovere. **have it in for** avercela con. **have on** (*wear*) portare; (*have planned*) aver intenzione di fare, aver da fare; (*coll: tease*) prendere in giro.

haven ['heivn] *n* (*harbour*) porto *m*; (*shelter*) rifugio *m.*

haversack ['havəsak] *n* bisaccia *f.*

havoc ['havək] *n* **play havoc with** rovinare, far strage di.

hawk¹ [hoik] *n* falco *m*, falcone *m.*

hawk² [hoik] *v* spacciare; fare il venditore ambulante.

hawthorn ['hoiθoin] *n* biancospino *m.*

hay [hei] *n* fieno *m.* **go haywire** perdere le staffe. **hay fever** raffreddore del fieno *m.* **haystack** *n* fienile *m.*

hazard ['hazəd] *n* (*danger*) pericolo *m*; (*risk*) rischio *m. v* azzardare. **hazardous** *adj* pericoloso, rischioso.

haze [heiz] *n* foschia *f.* **hazy** *adj* nebuloso, indistinto.

hazel ['heizl] *n* (*tree*) nocciolo *m.* **hazelnut** *n* nocciola *f.* *adj* color nocciola *invar.*

he [hit] *pron* egli, lui. **he who** colui che.

head [hed] *n* testa *f*; (*leader*) capo *m. v* (*lead*) essere a capo di; (*direct*) dirigere.

headache ['hedeik] n mal di testa m; (coll) preoccupazione f.

headdress ['heddres] n copricapo m.

heading n (title) intestazione f; (topic) voce f.

headlamp ['hedlamp] n also **headlight** (mot) faro m, fanale m.

headland ['hedlənd] n promontorio m.

headline ['hedlain] n titolo m. **headlines** pl n (news) sommario m sing.

headlong ['hedlɔŋ] adv a capofitto.

headmaster [,hed'maistə] n preside m.

headphones ['hedfounz] pl n cuffia f sing.

headquarters [,hed'kwɔːtəz] n (mil) quartiere generale m; (office) sede f, direzione f.

headrest ['hedrest] n appoggiatesta m invar.

headscarf ['hedskaːf] n foulard m invar.

headstrong ['hedstrɔŋ] adj testardo, cocciuto.

headway ['hedwei] n progresso m. **make headway** fare strada.

heady ['hedi] adj impetuoso; (intoxicating) che dà alla testa.

heal [hiːl] v guarire, sanare.

health [helθ] n salute f. **healthy** adj (person) sano; (climate, etc.) salubre.

heap [hiːp] n mucchio m. v ammucchiare.

*hear [hiə] v udire, sentire; (be informed of) venire a sapere. **hear about** aver notizie di. **hear from** aver notizie da. **hearing** n udito m; (audience) udienza f. **hearsay** n voce f.

heard [həːd] V **hear**.

hearse [həːs] n carro funebre.

heart [haːt] n cuore m; (feeling) animo m; (essential part) parte centrale f, centro m. **by heart** a memoria. **hearts** pl n (cards) cuori m pl. **take to heart** prendersi a cuore.

heart attack n attacco cardiaco m.

heartbeat ['haːtbiːt] n battito del cuore m.

heart-breaking ['haːtbreikiŋ] adj straziante. **heart-broken** adj accorato, affranto.

heartburn ['haːtbəːn] n bruciore di stomaco m.

heartening ['haːtniŋ] adj incoraggiante.

heartfelt ['haːtfelt] adj sincero.

hearth [haːθ] n focolare m.

heartless ['haːtləs] adj spietato, insensibile.

hearty ['haːti] adj (warm-hearted) caloroso; sincero; vigoroso.

heat [hiːt] n calore m, caldo m; (sport) batteria f; (oestrum) estro m. **heat wave** calura f. v scaldare, riscaldare. **heated** adj animato. **heater** n riscaldatore m; stufa elettrica f. **heating** n riscaldamento m.

heath [hiːθ] n brughiera f.

heathen ['hiːðn] n, adj pagano, -a.

heather ['heðə] n erica f.

heave [hiːv] v sollevare; (retch) avere i conati di vomito. **heave a sigh** tirare un sospiro. n sollevamento m.

heaven ['hevn] n cielo m, paradiso m. **for heaven's sake!** per l'amor del cielo! **good heavens!** santo cielo! **heavenly** adj divino, delizioso.

heavy ['hevi] adj pesante, forte. **heavy-weight** n peso massimo m.

Hebrew ['hiːbruː] n (language) ebraico m; (person) ebreo, -a m, f. adj ebraico; ebreo.

heckle ['hekl] v interrompere con domande imbarazzanti.

hectare ['hektaː] n ettaro m.

hectic ['hektik] adj febbrile.

hedge [hedʒ] n siepe f; (bet) copertura f. v (bet) coprire dai rischi. **as a hedge against** per mettersi al riparo contro.

hedgehog ['hedʒhɔg] n riccio m.

heed [hiːd] v badare a, dar retta a. **heedless** adj noncurante.

heel [hiːl] n (anat) calcagno m; (shoe) tacco m. **Achilles' heel** tallone d'Achille m.

hefty ['hefti] adj robusto.

heifer ['hefə] n giovenca f.

height [hait] n altezza f; (hill) collina f; (highest degree) colmo m; (highest point) culmine m. **heighten** v intensificare.

heir [eə] n erede m, f.

held [held] V **hold**.

helicopter ['helikɔptə] n elicottero m.

hell [hel] n inferno m. **hellish** adj infernale.

hello [hə'lou] interj (on meeting) ciao! (phone) pronto!

helm [helm] n timone m.

helmet ['helmit] n elmo m, elmetto m; (motorcyclist, airman) casco m.

help [help] n aiuto m, assistenza f; (remedy) rimedio m. v aiutare, assistere. **helpful** adj utile, vantaggioso. **helping** n porzione f. **helpless** adj impotente, indifeso.

hem [hem] n orlo m. v orlare. **hem in** rinchiudere, accerchiare.

hemisphere ['hemi,sfiə] n emisfera f.

hemp [hemp] n canapa f.

hen [hen] n gallina f.

hence [hens] adv quindi.

henna ['henə] n tintura di henna f.

her [hɜː] pron (direct object) la; (indirect object) le; (after prep) lei. adj (il) suo, (la) sua; (pl) (i) suoi, (le) sue.

herald ['herəld] n araldo m, messaggero m.

heraldry ['herəldri] n araldica f.

herbs [hɜːbz] pl n erbe aromatiche f pl.

herd [hɜːd] n gregge m, mandria f; (people) massa f. **herd together** raggruppare, radunare.

here [hiə] adv qui, qua; (emphasizing) ecco. **here I am!** eccomi qua!

hereabouts ['hiərə,bauts] adv qui vicino.

hereafter [,hiər'aːftə] adv d'ora innanzi, in futuro. n **the hereafter** l'al di là m.

hereby [,hiə'bai] adv così, con questo.

hereditary [hi'reditri] adj ereditario.

heredity [hi'redəti] n eredità f.

heresy ['herəsi] n eresia f. **heretic** n eretico, -a m, f. **heretical** adj eretico.

herewith [,hiə'wiθ] adv con questo; (correspondence) con la presente.

heritage ['heritidʒ] n patrimonio m.

hermit ['hɜːmit] n eremita m.

hernia ['hɜːniə] n ernia f.

hero ['hiərou] n eroe m; (principal character) protagonista m. **heroic** adj eroico. **heroine** n eroina f; protagonista f.

heroin ['herouin] n eroina f.

heron ['herən] n airone m.

herring ['heriŋ] n aringa f. **herring-bone** adj a lisca di pesce.

hers [hɜːz] pron il suo, la sua; (pl) i suoi, le sue.

herself [hɜː'self] pron lei stessa; (after prep) sè (stessa); (reflexive) si; (emphatic) proprio lei.

hesitate ['heziteit] v esitare. **hesitant** adj esitante. **hesitation** n esitazione f. **without hesitation** decisamente.

heterogeneous [hetərə'dʒiːniəs] adj eterogeneo.

heterosexual [hetərə'seksuəl] adj eterosessuale.

hexagon ['heksəgən] n esagono m. **hexagonal** adj esagonale.

heyday ['heidei] n (prime) fiore m; più bel periodo m; (splendour) fulgore m.

hiatus [hai'eitəs] n interruzione f; (med) iato m.

hibernate ['haibəneit] v svernare; (of animals) ibernare.

hiccup ['hikʌp] n singhiozzo m. v singhiozzare. **have hiccups** avere il singhiozzo.

hid [hid] V **hide¹**.

hidden [hidn] V **hide¹**.

*hide¹ [haid] v nascondere, nascondersi. **hide-out** n nascondiglio m.

hide² [haid] n (raw) pelle f; (dressed) cuoio m. **hidebound** adj gretto, di mentalità ristretta.

hideous ['hidiəs] adj orrendo, ripugnante.

hiding¹ ['haidiŋ] n **be in hiding** essere o tenersi nascosto. **go into hiding** nascondersi, darsi alla macchia.

hiding² ['haidiŋ] n (beating) batosta f.

hierarchy ['haiəraːki] n gerarchia f.

high [hai] adj alto, elevato; (of meat) andato a male. **it's high time** è ora. **leave high and dry** piantare in asso. adv in alto. n culmine f; (weather) anticiclone m. **highness** n altezza f.

highbrow ['haibrau] n(m+f), adj intellettuale.

high chair n seggiolina f.

high-fidelity adj ad alta fedeltà.

high frequency adj ad alta frequenza.

high jump n salto in alto m.

highlight ['hailait] v mettere in rilievo. n clou m invar, culmine m.

high-pitched [,hai'pitʃd] adj acuto.

high point n culmine m.

high-powered adj potente, dinamico.

high pressure n alta pressione f. **high-pressure** adj ad alta pressione; (coll) aggressivo.

high-rise block adj a molti piani.

high-spirited [,hai'spiritid] adj vivace. **high spirits** pl n buonumore m sing.

high street n corso m.

highway ['haiwei] n strada maestra f. **highway code** codice della strada m.

hijack ['haidʒak] v (goods) rubare in transito; (aero) dirottare. **hijacker** n dirottatore m, pirata dell'aria m. **hijacking** n dirottamento m.

hike [haik] n gita a piedi f. v fare una gita o escursione a piedi.

hilarious [hi'leəriəs] adj divertente, allegro.

hill [hil] n colle m, collina f; (slope) salita f.

him [him] pron (direct object) lo; (indirect object) gli; (after prep) lui.

himself [him'self] *pron* lui stesso; *(after prep)* sè (stesso); *(reflexive)* si; *(emphatic)* proprio lui.

hinder ['hində] *v (make difficult)* intralciare; *(make impossible)* impedire.

Hindu [hin'du] *n(m+f)*, *adj* indù *invar*. **Hinduism** *n* induismo *m*.

hinge [hindʒ] *n* cardine *m*, perno *m*. *v (depend)* dipendere (da).

hint [hint] *n* cenno *m*, allusione *f*; *(clue)* suggerimento *m*; *(slight amount)* traccia *f*. *v* far capire, accennare, alludere.

hip [hip] *n* fianco *m*, anca *f*.

hippopotamus [hipə'potəməs] *n* ippopotamo *m*.

hire [haiə] *v* prendere a nolo, noleggiare. **hire out** dare a nolo, noleggiare. *n* nolo *m*, noleggio *m*. **hire purchase** vendita a rate *f*.

his [hiz] *adj* (il) suo, (la) sua; *(pl)* (i) suoi, (le) sue. *pron* il suo, la sua; *(pl)* i suoi, le sue.

hiss [his] *v* sibilare. *n* sibilo *m*. **hissing** *adj* sibilante.

history ['histəri] *n* storia *f*; *(past)* passato *m*. **historian** *n* storico *m*. **historic** *adj* storico; memorabile.

*hit [hit] *n* colpo *m*, botta *f*; successo *m*. *v* colpire, battere. **hit on** scoprire. **hit-or-miss** *adv* alla buona.

hitch [hitʃ] *v* attaccare. **hitch-hike** *v* fare l'autostop. **hitch up** tirar su. *n (obstacle)* intoppo *m*; *(knot)* nodo *m*.

hitherto [,hiðə'tu:] *adv* finora.

hive [haiv] *n* alveare *m*.

hoard [hɔːd] *n* scorta *f*, mucchio *m*. *v* ammucchiare.

hoarding ['hɔːdiŋ] *n (billboard)* tabellone *m*.

hoarse [hɔːs] *adj* rauco. **hoarseness** *n* raucedine *f*.

hoax [houks] *n* beffa *f*.

hobble ['hobl] *v* zoppicare.

hobby ['hobi] *n* passatempo *m*, hobby *m invar*.

hock¹ [hok] *n (joint)* garretto *m*.

hock² [hok] *n (wine)* vino bianco del Reno *m*.

hockey ['hoki] *n* hockey *m invar*.

hoe [hou] *n* zappa *f*. *v* zappare.

hog [hog] *n* maiale *m*, porco *m*. *v (coll)* monopolizzare.

hoist [hoist] *n* montacarichi *m invar*. *v* sollevare.

*hold¹ [hould] *n* presa *f*, stretta *f*; *(dominating influence)* ascendente *m*. **get hold of** *(grasp)* afferrare; *(obtain)* ottenere. *v* tenere; contenere; esser valido. **hold back** trattenere. **hold out** resistere. **hold up** *(delay)* ostacolare; *(stop by force)* fermare per derubare; *(exhibit)* esibire. **hold-up** *n* intoppo *m*; *(robbery)* rapina a mano armata *f*. **holder** *n* supporto *m*; detentore *m*. **holding** *n (land)* tenuta *f*; *(shares)* pacchetto (di azioni) *m*.

hold² [hould] *n (naut)* stiva *f*.

hole [houl] *n* buco *m*; *(in the ground)* buca *f*; *(burrow)* tana *f*; *(predicament)* guaio *m*.

holiday ['holədi] *n (day)* giorno festivo *m*, festa *f*; *(period)* vacanza *f*. **go on holiday** andare in vacanza *or* villeggiatura. **holiday-maker** *n* villeggiante *m*, *f*.

Holland ['holənd] *n* Olanda *f*.

hollow ['holou] *adj* cavo; concavo; *(not solid)* vuoto; *(of sound)* cupo; falso. *n* buca *f*, cavità *f*; *(anat)* cavo *m*.

holly ['holi] *n* agrifoglio *m*.

holster ['houlstə] *n* fondina *f*.

holy ['houli] *adj* santo, sacro.

homage ['homidʒ] *n* omaggio *m*. **pay homage to** rendere omaggio a.

home [houm] *n (house)* casa *f*, domicilio *m*; *(land)* patria *f*; *(institution)* ricovero *m*, rifugio *m*; *(habitat)* ambiente naturale *m*. **at home** a casa. **feel at home** sentirsi a proprio agio. **leave home** lasciare la casa paterna. *adj* domestico, casalingo. *adv* a casa; in patria; *(all the way)* a fondo. **strike home** colpire nel vivo.

homecoming ['houm,kʌmiŋ] *n* ritorno in casa *or* patria *m*.

home-grown [houm'groun] *adj* nostrano.

homeless ['houmləs] *adj* senza tetto.

homely ['houmli] *adj* semplice, senza pretese; *(unattractive)* brutto.

home-made [,houm'meid] *adj* fatto in casa.

homesick ['houmsik] *adj* nostalgico.

homework ['houmwək] *n* compiti di casa *m pl*.

homicide ['homisaid] *n (crime)* omicidio *m*; *(murderer)* omicida *m*, *f*. **homicidal** *adj* micidiale.

homogeneous [homə'dʒiːniəs] *adj* omogeneo.

homosexual [homə'seksuəl] *n(m+f)*, *adj* omosessuale.

honest ['onist] adj onesto. **honestly!** interj davvero! **honesty** n onestà f.

honey ['hʌni] n miele m. **honeycomb** n favo m. **honeymoon** n luna di miele f.

honeysuckle ['hʌnisʌkl] n caprifoglio m.

honour ['onə] n onore m; (respect) stima f. v onorare; (comm) far onore a. **honours** pl n (titles) onorificenza f sing. **honorary** adj onorario. **honourable** adj onorevole, stimato, probo.

hood [hud] n cappuccio m; (mot) cappotta f.

hoof [huf] n zoccolo m.

hook [huk] n gancio m; (fishing) amo m. v agganciare.

hooligan ['huːligən] n teppista m.

hoop [huːp] n cerchio m.

hoot [huːt] v (car) suonare il clacson; (shriek) stridere; (hiss) fischiare. **hooter** n sirena f; (car) clacson m invar.

hop¹ [hop] v saltellare. n salterello m.

hop² [hop] n (bot) luppolo m.

hope [houp] n speranza f. v sperare. **hopeful** adj pieno di speranza, fiducioso; (promising) promettente. **hopeless** adj senza speranza, disperato; (not resolvable) irrimediabile.

horde [hoːd] n banda f.

horizon [hə'raizn] n orizzonte m. **horizontal** adj orizzontale.

hormone ['hoːmoun] n ormone m.

horn [hoːn] n corno (pl -a) m; (mot) clacson m invar.

hornet ['hoːnit] n calabrone m.

horoscope ['horəskoup] n oroscopo m.

horrible ['horibl] adj also **horrid** orribile, orrendo.

horrify ['horifai] v inorridire, raccapricciare. **horrifying** adj raccapricciante.

horror ['horə] n orrore m, spavento m.

hors d'oeuvre [oː'dəːvr] n antipasto m.

horse [hoːs] n cavallo m.

horseback ['hoːsbak] n **on horseback** a cavallo.

horse-chestnut n ippocastano m.

horse-fly n tafano m.

horseman ['hoːsmən] n cavaliere m.

horsepower ['hoːs,pauə] n cavallo vapore m.

horse-race n corsa ippica f.

horseradish ['hoːs,radiʃ] n cren m invar; (plant) barbaforte m.

horseshoe ['hoːʃʃuː] n ferro di cavallo m.

horsewoman ['hoːs,wumən] n cavallerizza f.

horticulture ['hoːtikʌltʃə] n orticultura f.

hose [houz] n (stocking) calza f, calzino m; (pipe) tubo flessibile m, manichetta f. v **hose (down)** dare una lavata a, annaffiare.

hosiery ['houziəri] n calzetteria f.

hospitable [ho'spitəbl] adj ospitale.

hospital ['hospitl] n ospedale m. **hospitalize** far ricoverare in ospedale.

hospitality [,hospi'taliti] n ospitalità f.

host¹ [houst] n oste m, ospite m. **hostess** n ospite f, ostessa f.

host² [houst] n moltitudine f, gran numero m.

host³ [houst] n (rel) ostia f.

hostage ['hostidʒ] n ostaggio m.

hostel ['hostl] n ostello m, alloggio m.

hostile ['hostail] adj ostile. **hostility** n antagonismo m. **hostilities** pl n ostilità f pl.

hot [hot] adj caldo; ardente, impetuoso; (pungent, peppery) forte, piccante. **be hot** aver caldo. **hot-blooded** adj dal sangue caldo. **hot-headed** adj impetuoso. **hot-house** n serra f. **hotplate** n scaldavivande m invar; (hob) fornello m. **hot-tempered** adj irascibile.

hotel [hou'tel] n albergo m. **hotel-keeper** n albergatore, -trice m, f.

hound [haund] n bracco m.

hour ['auə] n ora f. **hours** pl n (time spent) orario m sing. **kilometres/miles per hour** chilometri/miglia all'ora.

hourly ['auəli] adj orario. adv (every hour) ogni ora; (hour by hour) d'ora in ora, continuamente.

house [haus; v hauz] n casa f; (theatre attendance) sala f; (audience) pubblico m; (dynasty) dinastia f, famiglia f; (comm) ditta f. v (shelter) alloggiare; (put in safe place) mettere al sicuro.

houseboat ['hausbout] n casa galleggiante f, houseboat f invar.

housebound ['hausbaund] adj costretto a stare a casa.

housebreaking ['haus,breikiŋ] n scasso m.

household ['haushould] n famiglia f, casa f. adj casalingo, domestico.

housekeeper ['haus,kiːpə] n massaia f, governante f. **housekeeping** n economia domestica f.

housemaid ['hausmeid] n domestica f, cameriera f.

house-to-house adj di porta in porta.

housewife ['hauswaif] n massaia f, casalinga f.

housework ['hauswək] n lavori di casa m pl.

housing ['hauziŋ] n alloggio m. **housing estate** quartiere residenziale m.

hovel ['hovəl] n tugurio m.

hover ['hovə] v librarsi. **hovercraft** n hovercraft m invar.

how [hau] adv come, in che modo; (to what extent) quanto. **how are you?** come sta? **how do you do** (after introduction) piacere; buon giorno. **how much** quanto. **how many** quanti. **how often** quante volte. conj che.

however [hau'evə] adv comunque, tuttavia. conj nonostante, tuttavia.

howl [haul] v ululare, lamentarsi. n ululato m, lamento m.

hub [hʌb] n parte centrale f; (of wheel) mozzo m. **hub cap** coppa f.

hubbub ['hʌbʌb] n baccano m.

huddle ['hʌdl] v **huddle together** affollarsi, accalcarsi.

hue [hju:] n colore m, tinta f.

huff [hʌf] n stizza f, risentimento m. **in a huff** offeso.

hug [hʌg] v abbracciare. n abbraccio m.

huge [hju:dʒ] adj enorme, immenso.

hulk [hʌlk] n carcassa f. **hulking** adj goffo.

hull [hʌl] n (shell) guscio m; (husk) buccia f; (of nuts) mallo m; (pod) baccello m; (naut) scafo m.

hum [hʌm] v ronzare; cantare a bocca chiusa, canterellare. n ronzio m.

human ['hju:mən] adj umano. **human being** essere umano m.

humane [hju:'mein] adj umanitario, umano, compassionevole.

humanism ['hju:mənizəm] n umanesimo m. **humanist** n umanista m, f.

humanitarian [hju:mæni'teəriən] adj filantropico. n filantropo, -a m, f.

humanity [hju:'mænəti] n umanità f; compassione f.

humble ['hʌmbl] adj umile, modesto. v umiliare.

humdrum ['hʌmdrʌm] adj monotono, noioso.

humid ['hju:mid] adj umido. **humidity** n umidità f.

humiliate [hju:'milieit] v umiliare.

humility [hju:'miləti] n umiltà f.

humour ['hju:mə] n (mood) umore m; stato d'animo m, disposizione f; (comic quality) comicità f. v compiacere, accontentare. **humorist** n umorista m, f. **humorous** adj divertente, spiritoso.

hump [hʌmp] n gobba f; (hill) cresta f.

hunch [hʌntʃ] n gobba f. **have a hunch** (coll) avere un sospetto. **hunchback** n gobbo m. **hunchbacked** adj gobbo.

hundred ['hʌndrəd] nm, adj cento. **hundredth** nm, adj centesimo.

hung [hʌŋ] V hang.

Hungary ['hʌŋgəri] n Ungheria f. **Hungarian** n(m+f), adj ungherese.

hunger ['hʌŋgə] n fame f, appetito m. **hungry** adj affamato. **be hungry** aver fame.

hunt [hʌnt] n caccia f; (pursuit) inseguimento m; (search) ricerca affannosa f. v andare a caccia di; inseguire; cercare affannosamente. **hunter** n cacciatore m.

hurdle ['hə:dl] n ostacolo m. v fare la corsa a ostacoli.

hurl [hə:l] v scagliare, scaraventare.

hurrah [hu'ra:] interj evviva!

hurricane ['hʌrikən] n uragano m. **hurricane lamp** lanterna controvento f.

hurry ['hʌri] n fretta f. **be in a hurry** aver fretta. v affrettare. **hurry up** sbrigarsi.

*hurt [hə:t] v far male a, nuocere a; (wound) ferire; (feel painful) dolere. n dolore m, male m; ferita f; offesa f. **feel hurt** rimanere offeso.

husband ['hʌzbənd] n marito m.

hush [hʌʃ] n silenzio m. interj zitto! v far tacere. **hush-hush** adj (coll) segretissimo. **hush up** nascondere, dissimulare; (suppress) soffocare.

husk [hʌsk] n guscio m, baccello m.

husky ['hʌski] adj (of voice) rauco, fioco; (burly) grande e grosso.

hustle ['hʌsl] n spintone m. v spingere, sbrigarsi.

hut [hʌt] n capanna f, baracca f.

hutch [hʌtʃ] n conigliera f.

hyacinth ['haiəsinθ] n giacinto m.

hybrid ['haibrid] nm, adj ibrido.

hydrant ['haidrənt] n idrante m.

hydraulic [hai'drolik] adj idraulico.

hydrocarbon [,haidrou'ka:bən] n idrocarburo m.

hydro-electric [,haidroui'lektrik] adj idroelettrico.

hydrofoil ['haidroufoil] n aliscafo m.

hydrogen ['haidrədʒən] *n* idrogeno *m*.

hyena [hai'inə] *n* iena *f*.

hygiene ['haidʒim] *n* igiene *f*. **hygienic** *adj* igienico.

hymn [him] *n* inno *m*, canto sacro *m*.

hyphen ['haifən] *n* lineetta *f*.

hypnosis [hip'nousis] *n* ipnosi *f*. **hypnotic** *adj* ipnotico. **hypnotism** *n* ipnotismo *m*, ipnosi *f*. **hypnotist** *n* ipnotizzatore, -trice *m*, *f*.

hypochondria [haipə'kondriə] *n* ipocondria *f*. **hypochondriac** *n*, *adj* ipocondriaco, -a.

hypocrisy [hi'pokrəsi] *n* ipocrisia *f*. **hypocrite** *n* ipocrita *m*, *f*. **hypocritical** *adj* ipocrita.

hypodermic [haipə'dəːmik] *adj* ipodermico.

hypotenuse [hai'potənjuːz] *n* ipotenusa *f*.

hypothesis [hai'poθəsis] *n*, *pl* -ses ipotesi *f*. **hypothetical** *adj* ipotetico.

hysterectomy [histə'rektəmi] *n* isterectomia *f*.

hysteria [his'tiəriə] *n* isterismo *m*. **hysterical** *adj* isterico. **hysterics** *pl n* crisi isterica *f sing*.

I

I [ai] *pron* io.

ice [ais] *n* ghiaccio *m*. **iceberg** *n* iceberg *m invar*. **ice-cold** *adj* freddo come il ghiaccio, glaciale, gelido. **ice cream** gelato *m*. **ice lolly** ghiacciolo *m*. **ice rink** pista di pattinaggio *f*. *v* (*cookery*) glassare; (*cover with ice*) ghiacciare. **icing** *n* glassa *f*. **icy** *adj* glaciale, gelido.

Iceland ['aislənd] *n* Islanda *f*. **Icelander** *n* islandese *m*, *f*. **Icelandic** *adj* islandese.

icicle ['aisikl] *n* ghiacciolo *m*.

icon ['aikon] *n* icona *f*. **iconoclast** *n* iconoclasta *m*, *f*.

idea [ai'diə] *n* idea *f*, concetto *m*, impressione *f*.

ideal [ai'diəl] *nm*, *adj* ideale. **idealist** *n* idealista *m*, *f*. **idealistic** *adj* idealistico. **idealize** *v* idealizzare.

identical [ai'dentikəl] *adj* identico.

identify [ai'dentifai] *v* identificare. **identification** *n* identificazione *f*.

identity [ai'dentiti] *n* identità *f*. **identity card** carta d'identità *f*. **identity parade**

confronto all'americana *m*. **mistaken identity** errore di persona *m*.

ideology [aidi'olədʒi] *n* ideologia *f*. **ideological** *adj* ideologico.

idiom ['idiəm] *n* (*expression*) frase idiomatica *f*; (*language*) idioma *m*. **idiosyncrasy** [idiə'siŋkrəsi] *n* idiosincrasia *f*.

idiot ['idiət] *n* idiota *m*, *f*; cretino, -a *m*, *f*. **idiotic** *adj* idiota, cretino, imbecille.

idle ['aidl] *adj* (*lazy*) pigro; (*doing nothing*) disoccupato; (*machine*) fermo; (*worthless*) vano. *v* stare senza far nulla; (*machine*) girare a folle. **idler** *n* fannullone, -a *m*, *f*.

idol ['aidl] *n* idolo *m*. **idolatry** *n* idolatria *f*. **idolize** *v* idoleggiare.

idyllic [i'dilik] *adj* idillico.

if [if] *conj* se. **as if** come se. **if not** se no. **if you please** per piacere.

ignite [ig'nait] *v* accendere, dar fuoco a; (*catch fire*) prender fuoco.

ignition [ig'niʃən] *n* accensione *f*. **ignition key** interruttore dell'accensione *m*.

ignorant ['ignərənt] *adj* ignorante. **be ignorant of** ignorare. **ignorance** *n* ignoranza *f*.

ignore [ig'noː] *v* (*disregard*) non badare a, trascurare; (*refrain from seeing/recognizing/hearing*) fingere di non vedere/riconoscere/sentire.

ill [il] *adj* (*sick*) malato; (*bad*) cattivo. *nm*, *adv* male. **ill-advised** *adj* malavveduto. **ill-bred** *or* **ill-mannered** *adj* maleducato. **ill-treat** *v* maltrattare. **illness** *n* malattia *f*.

illegal [i'liːgəl] *adj* illegale.

illegible [i'ledʒəbl] *adj* illeggibile.

illegitimate [ili'dʒitimit] *adj* illegittimo.

illicit [i'lisit] *adj* illecito.

illiterate [i'litərit] *n*(*m+f*), *adj* analfabeta.

illogical [i'lodʒikəl] *adj* illogico.

illuminate [i'luminei̯t] *v* illuminare, rischiarare. **illuminating** *adj* illuminante. **illumination** *n* illuminazione *f*.

illusion [i'luːʒən] *n* illusione *f*.

illustrate ['iləstreit] *v* illustrare. **illustration** *n* illustrazione *f*.

illustrious [i'lʌstriəs] *adj* illustre, celebre.

image ['imidʒ] *n* immagine *f*, ritratto *m*. **imagery** *n* immagini *f pl*.

imagine [i'mædʒin] *v* farsi un'idea di, immaginarsi; (*suppose*) supporre; (*believe*) credere. **imaginary** *adj* immaginario. **imagination** *n* immaginazione *f*, fantasia *f*.

imbalance [im'bæləns] n squilibrio m.
imbecile ['imbə,si:l] n(m+f), adj imbecille.
imitate ['imi,teit] v imitare, contraffare. **imitation** n imitazione f, copia f, contraffattura f.
immaculate [i'mækjulit] adj immacolato.
immaterial [,imə'tiəriəl] adj (unimportant) di nessuna importanza.
immature [imə'tjuə] adj immaturo. **immaturity** n immaturità f.
immediate [i'mi:diət] adj immediato. **immediately** adv immediatamente, subito.
immense [i'mens] adj immenso.
immerse [i'mə:s] v immergere. **immersion** n immersione f. **immersion heater** riscaldatore a immersione m.
immigrate ['imi,greit] v immigrare. **immigrant** n(m+f), adj immigrante. **immigration** n immigrazione f.
imminent ['iminənt] adj imminente.
immobile [i'moubail] adj immobile, fermo. **immobilize** v immobilizzare.
immoral [i'mɔrəl] adj immorale. **immorality** n immoralità f.
immortal [i'mɔ:tl] adj immortale. **immortality** n immortalità f. **immortalize** v immortalare.
immovable [i'mu:vəbl] adj inamovibile, fisso.
immune [i'mju:n] adj immune. **immunity** n immunità f. **immunization** n immunizzazione f. **immunize** v immunizzare.
imp [imp] n folletto m.
impact ['impækt] n urto m, scontro m; (effect) impressione f.
impair [im'pεə] v danneggiare, menomare.
impale [im'peil] v impalare.
impart [im'pɑ:t] v impartire.
impartial [im'pɑ:ʃəl] adj imparziale. **impartiality** n imparzialità f.
impasse [am'pɑːs] n impasse m, intoppo m.
impatient [im'peiʃənt] adj impaziente. **get impatient** impazientirsi. **impatience** n impazienza f.
impeach [im'pi:tʃ] v accusare; (call in question) mettere in dubbio, imputare.
impeccable [im'pekəbl] adj impeccabile.
impede [im'pi:d] v ostacolare, impedire.
impediment [im'pedimənt] n impedimento m, ostacolo m. **speech impediment** difetto or impedimento di lingua m.
impel [im'pel] v spingere, impellere.

impending [im'pendiŋ] adj imminente.
imperative [im'perətiv] nm, adj imperativo.
imperfect [im'pə:fikt] nm, adj imperfetto.
imperial [im'piəriəl] adj imperiale. **imperialism** n imperialismo m.
imperil [im'peril] v mettere in pericolo, compromettere.
impersonal [im'pə:sənl] adj impersonale, comune.
impersonate [im'pə:sə,neit] v impersonare; (theatre) interpretare.
impertinent [im'pə:tinənt] adj impertinente. **impertinence** n impertinenza f.
impervious [im'pə:viəs] adj impervio; impermeabile; (fig) sordo.
impetuous [im'petjuəs] adj impetuoso.
impetus ['impətəs] n impeto m, slancio m.
impinge [im'pindʒ] v **impinge on** colpire.
implement ['implimənt; v 'impliment] n attrezzo m, utensile m. v adempiere. **implementation** n adempimento m.
implicate ['implikeit] v implicare, coinvolgere. **implication** n implicazione f.
implicit [im'plisit] adj implicito.
implore [im'plɔ:] v supplicare.
imply [im'plai] v (mean) significare; (suggest) far pensare a.
impolite [impə'lait] adj scortese, sgarbato.
import [im'pɔ:t] v importare. n (comm) importazione f; importanza f. **importer** n importatore m.
importance [im'pɔ:təns] n importanza f. **important** adj importante.
impose [im'pouz] v imporre. **impose on** abusare di. **imposing** adj imponente. **imposition** n imposizione f.
impossible [im'posəbl] adj impossibile. **impossibility** n impossibilità f.
impostor [im'postə] n impostore m.
impotent ['impotənt] adj impotente. **impotence** n impotenza f.
impound [im'paund] v confiscare.
impoverish [im'povəriʃ] v impoverire.
impractical [im'præktikəl] adj (person) privo di senso pratico; (thing) inservibile, non pratico.
impregnate ['impreg,neit] v impregnare. **impregnation** n impregnazione f.
impress [im'pres] v colpire, fare impressione su; (urge) raccomandare; (print) imprimere, stampare. **impression** n impressione f; (print) stampa f, ristampa f. **impressive** adj impressionante.

imprint ['imprint] n impronta f.

imprison [im'prizn] v carcerare. **imprisonment** n carcerazione f.

improbable [im'probəbl] adj improbabile. **improbability** n improbabilità f.

impromptu [im'promptju:] adj improvvisato. adv all'improvviso.

improper [im'propə] adj (inappropriate) improprio; (unseemly) indecente, indecoroso.

improve [im'pru:v] v migliorare; (increase value) valorizzare; (get better) star meglio. **improve on** perfezionare. **improvement** n miglioramento m; (making more valuable) miglioria f.

improvise ['imprəvaiz] v improvvisare. **improvisation** n improvvisazione f.

impudent ['impjudənt] adj sfacciato. **impudence** n sfacciataggine f.

impulse ['impʌls] n impulso m, stimolo m. **impulsive** adj impulsivo.

impure [im'pjuə] adj impuro. **impurity** n impurità f.

in [in] prep in; (within) tra, entro. adv dentro, a casa, in sede.

inability [,inə'biləti] n incapacità f.

inaccessible [,inak'sesəbl] adj inaccessibile.

inaccurate [in'akjurit] adj inesatto. **inaccuracy** n inesattezza f.

inactive [in'aktiv] adj inattivo, passivo.

inadequate [in'adikwit] adj inadeguato, insufficiente, inetto. **inadequacy** n inadeguatezza f.

inadmissible [inəd'misəbl] adj inammissibile.

inadvertent [,inəd'vəːtənt] adj involontario.

inane [in'ein] adj insensato, futile.

inanimate [in'animit] adj (not animate) inanimato; (lifeless) esanime.

inarticulate [,inaː'tikjulit] adj (person) che non sa esprimersi; inarticolato.

inasmuch [,inəz'mʌtʃ] conj dacchè, poichè.

inaudible [in'ordəbl] adj inaudibile.

inaugurate [i'nɔːgjuˌreit] v inaugurare. **inaugural** adj inaugurale. **inauguration** n inaugurazione f.

inauspicious [inoː'spiʃəs] adj infausto.

inbred [,in'bred] adj (inborn) innato; (resulting from. inbreeding) endogamo. **inbreeding** n endogamia f.

incalculable [in'kalkjuləbl] adj incalcolabile, imprevedibile.

incapable [in'keipəbl] adj incapace, inetto.

incendiary [in'sendiəri] adj incendiario.

incense¹ ['insens] n incenso m.

incense² [in'sens] v irritare, provocare.

incentive [in'sentiv] n incentivo m.

incessant [in'sesənt] adj continuo.

incest ['insest] n incesto m. **incestuous** adj incestuoso.

inch [intʃ] n pollice m. **inch by inch** gradatamente. v **inch forward** avanzare poco alla volta.

incident ['insidənt] n caso m, episodio m; (event with serious consequences) incidente f. **incidental** adj incidentale. **incidentally** adv tra parentesi, a proposito.

incinerator [in'sinəˌreitə] n inceneritore m. **incinerate** v incenerire.

incisive [in'saisiv] adj acuto.

incite [in'sait] v incitare, spronare. **incitement** n incitamento m.

incline [in'klain] v inclinare, chinare. **be inclined to** essere propenso or disposto a. n piano inclinato m, pendio m. **inclination** n inclinazione f; propensione f.

include [in'klu:d] v includere. **inclusion** n inclusione f. **inclusive** adj compreso.

incoherent [inkə'hiərənt] adj incoerente.

income ['inkʌm] n entrata f, reddito m. **income tax** imposta sull'entrata f. **incoming** adj in arrivo.

incompatible [inkəm'patəbl] adj incompatibile. **incompatibility** n incompatibilità f.

incompetent [in'kompitənt] adj incompetente. **incompetence** n incompetenza f.

incomplete [,inkəm'pliːt] adj incompleto.

incomprehensible [in,kompri'hensəbl] adj incomprensibile.

inconceivable [inkən'siːvəbl] adj inconcepibile.

inconclusive [inkən'kluːsiv] adj inconcludente.

incongruous [in'kongruəs] adj incongruo.

inconsiderate [,inkən'sidərit] adj sconsiderato; (person) che manca di riguardo.

inconsistent [,inkən'sistənt] adj inconsistente. **inconsistency** n inconsistenza f.

incontinence [in'kontinəns] n incontinenza f. **incontinent** adj incontinente.

inconvenience [inkən'viːnjəns] n sconvenienza f. v sconvenire, disturbare. **inconvenient** adj sconveniente, scomodo.

incorporate [in'kɔːpəˌreit] v incorporare.

incorrect [inkə'rekt] adj scorretto.

increase [in'kriːs] v aumentare, ingrandirsi, crescere. n aumento m. **increasingly** adv sempre più.

incredible [in'kredəbl] adj incredibile.

incredulous [in'kredjuləs] adj incredulo.

increment ['iŋkrəmənt] n incremento m, aumento m.

incriminate [in'krimineit] v incolpare.

incubate ['iŋkjuˌbeit] v incubare. **incubation** n incubazione f. **incubator** n incubatrice f.

incumbent [in'kʌmbənt] adj be incumbent on spettare a.

incur [in'kəː] v incorrere in.

incurable [in'kjuərəbl] adj incurabile.

indebted [in'detid] adj (owing money) indebitato; (under obligation) riconoscente.

indecent [in'diːsnt] adj indecente. **indecency** n indecenza f; (law) oltraggio al pudore m.

indeed [in'diːd] adv infatti, effettivamente, proprio. interj davvero!

indefatigable [indi'fatigəbl] adj indefesso.

indefinite [in'definit] adj indefinito, vago, illimitato.

indelible [in'deləbl] adj indelebile; (memory) indimenticabile.

indemnity [in'demnəti] n indennità f; (sum paid) indennizzo m. **indemnify** v indennizzare.

indent [in'dent] v (notch) dentellare; (make recess) incavare. **indentation** n incavo m, dentellatura f, rientranza f; (printing) capoverso m.

independent [ˌindi'pendənt] adj indipendente. **independence** n indipendenza f.

index ['indeks] n indice m. **index card** scheda f. **index finger** indice m.

India ['indjə] n India f. **India rubber** gomma f. **Indian** n, adj indiano, -a. **Indian ink** inchiostro di china m.

indicate ['indikeit] v indicare.

indict [in'dait] v accusare. **indictment** n accusa f; (law) atto d'accusa m.

indifferent [in'difrənt] adj indifferente. **indifference** n indifferenza f.

indigenous [in'didʒinəs] adj indigeno.

indigestion [ˌindi'dʒestʃən] n indigestione f.

indignant [in'dignənt] adj sdegnato. **feel indignant** indignarsi, sdegnarsi (contro).

indignity [in'dignəti] n indegnità f.

indirect [ˌindi'rekt] adj indiretto.

indiscreet [ˌindi'skriːt] adj indiscreto. **indiscretion** n indiscrezione f.

indiscriminate [ˌindi'skriminit] adj indiscriminato.

indispensable [ˌindi'spensəbl] adj indispensabile.

indisposed [ˌindi'spouzd] adj indisposto.

individual [ˌindi'vidjuəl] n individuo m. adj individuale, particolare.

indoctrinate [in'doktriˌneit] v indottrinare. **indoctrination** n indottrinamento m.

indolent ['indələnt] adj indolente. **indolence** n indolenza f.

indoor ['indɔː] adj di or da casa. **indoors** adv in casa, all'interno, dentro.

induce [in'djuːs] v indurre.

indulge [in'dʌldʒ] v (gratify) appagare, soddisfare; essere indulgente verso. **indulge in** abbandonarsi a, dedicarsi a. **indulgence** n indulgenza f. **indulgent** adj indulgente.

industry ['indəstri] n industria f; diligenza f, zelo m. **industrial** adj industriale. **industrialize** v industrializzare. **industrious** adj diligente, operoso.

inebriated [i'niːbrieitid] adj ubriaco.

inedible [in'edibl] adj immangiabile.

inefficient [ini'fiʃnt] adj inefficiente. **inefficiency** n inefficienza f.

inept [i'nept] adj inetto, incapace.

inequality [ini'kwɔləti] n ineguaglianza f.

inert [i'nəːt] adj inerte. **inertia** n inerzia f.

inevitable [in'evitəbl] adj inevitabile.

inexcusable [inik'skjuːzəbl] adj imperdonabile, ingiustificabile.

inexhaustible [inig'zɔːstəbl] adj inesauribile.

inexpensive [ˌinik'spensiv] adj a buon mercato, poco caro.

inexperienced [ˌinik'spiəriənst] adj inesperto.

inexplicable [inik'splikəbl] adj inspiegabile.

infallible [in'faləbl] adj infallibile. **infallibility** n infallibilità f.

infamous ['infəməs] adj infame. **infamy** n infamia f.

infancy ['infənsi] n infanzia f.

infant ['infənt] n infante m, bambino, -a m, f. **infantile** adj infantile, puerile. **infant prodigy** bambino prodigio m.

infantry ['infəntri] *n* fanteria *f*.

infatuated [in'fætjueitid] *adj* infatuato. **be infatuated** prendere una cotta.

infect [in'fekt] *v* infettare. **infection** *n* infezione *f*. **infectious** *adj* infettivo.

infer [in'fəi] *v* dedurre, desumere. **inferable** *adj* deducibile. **inference** *n* inferenza *f*, deduzione *f*.

inferior [in'fiəriə] *n(m+f)*, *adj* inferiore. **inferiority** *n* inferiorità *f*.

infernal [in'fəːnl] *adj* infernale.

infest [in'fest] *v* infestare.

infidelity [,infi'deliti] *n* infedeltà *f*.

infiltrate ['infil,treit] *v* infiltrare. **infiltration** *n* infiltrazione *f*.

infinite ['infinit] *nm*, *adj* infinito. **infinity** *n* infinità *f*, infinito m.

infinitive [in'finitiv] *nm*, *adj* infinito.

infirm [in'fəːm] *adj* infermo. **infirmity** *n* infermità *f*.

inflame [in'fleim] *v* infiammare. **inflammable** *adj* infiammabile. **inflammation** *n* infiammazione *f*.

inflate [in'fleit] *v* gonfiare. **inflation** *n* inflazione *f*.

inflection [in'flekʃən] *n* inflessione *f*.

inflexible [in'fleksəbl] *adj* inflessibile.

inflict [in'flikt] *v* infliggere.

influence ['influəns] *n* influenza *f*, ascendente m. *v* influire su, influenzare. **influential** *adj* autorevole, importante.

influenza [,influ'enzə] *n* influenza *f*.

influx ['inflʌks] *n* afflusso m, affluenza *f*.

inform [in'fɔːm] *v* informare, far sapere a. **inform against** *or* **on** (*denounce*) denunziare. **informant** *n* informatore, -trice m, *f*. **informer** *n* spia *f*, delatore, -trice m, *f*.

informal [in'fɔːml] *adj* alla buona, senza cerimonia, non ufficiale. **informality** *n* mancanza di formalità *f*.

information [,infə'meiʃən] *n* informazioni *f pl*, notizie *f pl*. **for your information** a titolo di informazione.

infra-red [infrə'red] *adj* infrarosso.

infrequent [in'friːkwənt] *adj* raro.

infringe [in'frindʒ] *v* violare, trasgredire. **infringement** *n* violazione *f*.

infuriate [in'fjuəri,eit] *v* fare arrabbiare. **be infuriated** essere furibondo *or* arrabbiatissimo.

ingenious [in'dʒiːnjəs] *adj* ingegnoso. **ingenuity** *n* ingegnosità *f*.

ingot ['iŋgət] *n* lingotto m.

ingredient [in'griːdjənt] *n* ingrediente m.

inhabit [in'habit] *v* abitare, vivere, dimorare. **inhabitant** *n* abitante m, *f*.

inhale [in'heil] *v* inalare.

inherent [in'hiərənt] *adj* inerente.

inherit [in'herit] *v* ereditare. **inheritance** *n* eredità *f*.

inhibit [in'hibit] *v* inibire. **inhibition** *n* inibizione *f*.

inhuman [in'hjuːmən] *adj* inumano. **inhumanity** *n* inumanità *f*.

iniquity [i'nikwəti] *n* iniquità *f*. **iniquitous** *adj* iniquo.

initial [i'niʃl] *nf*, *adj* iniziale. *v* siglare.

initiate [i'niʃi,eit] *v* iniziare, istituire. **initiation** *n* iniziazione *f*, inizio m.

initiative [i'niʃiətiv] *n* iniziativa *f*.

inject [in'dʒekt] *v* iniettare; (*introduce*) immettere. **injection** *n* iniezione *f*.

injure ['indʒə] *v* (*damage*) danneggiare; (*hurt*) far male a; (*wound*) ferire; (*law*) ledere. **injurious** *adj* dannoso, nocivo. **injury** *n* male m; danno m; torto m; ferita *f*.

injustice [in'dʒʌstis] *n* ingiustizia *f*.

ink [iŋk] *n* inchiostro m. **ink-well** *n* calamaio m.

inkling ['iŋkliŋ] *n* sospetto m, sentore m.

inland ['inlənd; *adv* in'lænd] *adj* interno. *adv* all' *or* nell'interno.

in-laws ['in,lɔːs] *pl n* (*coll*) parenti acquisiti *m pl*.

*inlay [in'lei] *v* intarsiare. *n* intarsio m.

inlet ['inlet] *n* (*geog*) insenatura *f*.

inmate ['inmeit] *n* (*of hospital, etc.*) ricoverato, -a m, *f*; (*of prison*) carcerato, -a m, *f*.

inn [in] *n* locanda *f*, osteria *f*, albergo m. **innkeeper** *n* locandiere, -a m, *f*; oste, -essa m, *f*; albergatore, -trice m, *f*.

innate [i'neit] *adj* innato.

inner ['inə] *adj* interno, interiore; (*thoughts, etc.*) intimo. **inner tube** camera d'aria *f*.

innocent ['inəsnt] *n(m+f)*, *adj* innocente. **innocence** *n* innocenza *f*.

innocuous [i'nokjuəs] *adj* innocuo.

innovation [inə'veiʃən] *n* innovazione *f*, novità *f*. **innovate** *v* innovare. **innovator** *n* innovatore, -trice m, *f*.

innuendo [,inju'endou] *n* insinuazione *f*.

innumerable [i'njumərəbl] *adj* innumerevole.

inoculate [i'nokju,leit] *v* inoculare. **inoculation** *n* inoculazione *f*.

inorganic [,inoːˈɡanik] *adj* inorganico.

input [ˈinput] *n* (*elec*) alimentazione *f*; (*computer*) input *m invar*.

inquest [ˈinkwest] *n* inchiesta *f*, istruttoria *f*.

inquire [inˈkwaiə] *v* chiedere, domandare. **inquiry** *n* domanda *f*, informazione *f*, inchiesta *f*.

inquisition [,inkwiˈziʃən] *n* inquisizione *f*, inchiesta *f*.

inquisitive [inˈkwizətiv] *adj* curioso.

insane [inˈsein] *adj* pazzo, matto. **insanity** *n* pazzia *f*, follia *f*.

insatiable [inˈseiʃəbl] *adj* insaziabile.

inscribe [inˈskraib] *v* (*enrol*) inscrivere; (*engrave*) incidere. **inscription** *n* iscrizione *f*, dedica *f*.

insect [ˈinsekt] *n* insetto *m*. **insecticide** *n* insetticida *m*.

insecure [,insiˈkjuə] *adj* malsicuro, instabile. **insecurity** *n* incertezza *f*, instabilità *f*.

inseminate [inˈsemineit] *v* inseminare. **insemination** *n* inseminazione *f*.

insensible [inˈsensəbl] *adj* insensibile; (*unconscious*) privo di sensi.

insensitive [inˈsensətiv] *adj* insensibile, indifferente.

inseparable [inˈsepərəbl] *adj* inseparabile.

insert [inˈsəːt; *n* ˈinsəːt] *v* inserire. *n also* **insertion** inserzione *f*.

inshore [,inˈʃoː] *adj* costiero. *adv* verso la riva.

inside [inˈsaid] *adv* dentro, internamente. *prep* dentro, all'interno. *adj* interno, interiore; (*confidential*) riservato. *n* interno *m*; (*soccer*) mezzala *f*. **inside out** a rovescio.

insidious [inˈsidiəs] *adj* insidioso, perfido.

insight [ˈinsait] *n* discernimento *m*, intuito *m*.

insignificant [,insigˈnifikənt] *adj* insignificante.

insincere [,insinˈsiə] *adj* insincero.

insinuate [inˈsinjueit] *v* insinuare, dare ad intendere. **insinuation** *n* insinuazione *f*.

insipid [inˈsipid] *adj* insipido.

insist [inˈsist] *v* insistere. **insistence** *n* insistenza *f*. **insistent** *adj* insistente.

insolent [ˈinsələnt] *adj* impertinente. **insolence** *n* impertinenza *f*.

insoluble [inˈsoljubl] *adj* insolubile; (*not solvable*) insolvibile.

insomnia [inˈsomniə] *n* insonnia *f*. **insomniac** *n* insonne *m*, *f*.

inspect [inˈspekt] *v* ispezionare, verificare; (*troops*) passare in rivista. **inspection** *n* ispezione *f*, verifica *f*; rivista *f*. **inspector** *n* ispettore, -trice *m*, *f*; (*bus*, *train*) controllore, -a *m*, *f*; (*police*) commissario *m*.

inspire [inˈspaiə] *v* ispirare, infondere. **inspiration** *n* ispirazione *f*.

instability [,instəˈbiləti] *n* instabilità *f*.

install [inˈstoːl] *v* installare. **installation** *n* installazione *f*.

instalment [inˈstoːlmənt] *n* (*comm*) rata *f*; (*serial*) puntata *f*.

instance [ˈinstəns] *n* esempio *m*. **for instance** per esempio.

instant [ˈinstənt] *adj* immediato; urgente; (*comm*) corrente; (*of food*) istantaneo. *n* istante *m*, momento *m*. **instantaneous** *adj* istantaneo.

instead [inˈsted] *adv* invece.

instep [ˈinstep] *n* (*anat*) collo del piede *m*; (*shoe*) collo della scarpa *m*.

instigate [ˈinstigeit] *v* istigare. **instigation** *n* istigazione *f*.

instil [inˈstil] *v* instillare, infondere.

instinct [ˈinstiŋkt] *n* istinto *m*. **instinctive** *adj* istintivo.

institute [ˈinstitjuːt] *n* istituto *m*. *v* istituire, iniziare. **institution** *n* istituzione *f*.

instruct [inˈstrʌkt] *v* (*teach*) istruire; (*direct*) dare istruzioni *or* disposizioni a. **instruction** *n* istruzione *f*, disposizioni *f pl*. **instructive** *adj* istruttivo. **instructor** *n* istruttore, -trice *m*, *f*, insegnante *m*, *f*.

instrument [ˈinstrəmənt] *n* strumento *m*; (*tool*) arnese *m*; (*law*) titolo *m*, atto *m*. **instrumental** *adj* strumentale. **be instrumental in** essere utile a.

insubordinate [,insəˈboːdənət] *adj* insubordinato. **insubordination** *n* insubordinazione *f*.

insufficient [,insəˈfiʃənt] *adj* insufficiente.

insular [ˈinsjulə] *adj* insulare; (*outlook*) gretto.

insulate [ˈinsjuleit] *v* isolare. **insulating tape** nastro isolante *m*. **insulation** *n* isolamento *m*.

insulin [ˈinsjulin] *n* insulina *f*.

insult [inˈsʌlt; *n* ˈinsʌlt] *v* insultare, offendere. *n* insulto *m*, offesa *f*.

insure [inˈʃuə] *v* assicurare. **insurance** *n* assicurazione *f*.

intact [inˈtakt] *adj* intatto.

intake ['inteik] n (*consumption*) consumo m; (*employment*) assunzione f; (*people newly taken on*) reclute f pl.
intangible [in'tandʒəbl] adj intangibile.
integral ['intigrəl] adj integrale.
integrate ['intigreit] v integrare. **integration** n integrazione f.
integrity [in'tegrəti] n integrità f.
intellect ['intilekt] n intelletto m. **intellectual** n(m+f), adj intellettuale.
intelligent [in'telidʒənt] adj intelligente. **intelligence** n intelligenza f; informazioni f pl. **intelligentsia** n intellighenzia f.
intelligible [in'telidʒəbl] adj intelligibile.
intend [in'tend] v intendere, aver l'intenzione di. **intended** adj premeditato, voluto.
intense [in'tens] adj intenso, profondo.
intent¹ [in'tent] n intento, proposito m, intenzione f. **to all intents and purposes** a tutti gli effetti.
intent² [in'tent] adj intento, assorto. **intent on** deciso a.
intention [in'tenʃən] n intenzione f, proposito m. **intentional** adj intenzionale.
inter [in'təː] v seppellire. **interment** n sepoltura f.
interact [intər'akt] v esercitare un'azione reciproca, interagire. **interaction** n azione reciproca f.
intercede [intə'siːd] v intercedere.
intercept [intə'sept] v intercettare. **interception** n intercettazione f.
interchange [intə'tʃaindʒ] v scambiare. **interchangeable** adj intercambiabile, scambievole.
intercom ['intəkom] n citofono m.
intercourse ['intəkoːs] n rapporti m pl.
interest ['intrist] v interessare. **be interested in** interessarsi di. n interesse m. **interesting** adj interessante.
interfere [intə'fiə] v interferire, immischiarsi. **interference** n interferenza f.
interim ['intərim] n interim m. adj provvisorio, temporaneo.
interior [in'tiəriə] nm, adj interno. **interior decorator** arredatore, -trice m, f.
interjection [intə'dʒekʃən] n interiezione f.
interlude ['intəluːd] n interludio m.
intermediary [intə'miːdiəri] n intermediario m.
intermediate [intə'miːdiət] adj intermedio.

interminable [in'təːminəbl] adj senza fine.
intermission [intə'miʃən] n interruzione f.
intermittent [intə'mitənt] adj intermittente.
intern [in'təːn] v internare. **internment** n internamento m.
internal [in'təːnl] adj interno, interiore.
international [intə'naʃənl] adj internazionale.
interpose [intə'pouz] v frapporre.
interpret [in'təːprit] v interpretare. **interpretation** n interpretazione f. **interpreter** n interprete m, f.
interrogate [in'terəgeit] v interrogare. **interrogation** n interrogazione f. **interrogative** adj, nm interrogativo.
interrupt [intə'rʌpt] v interrompere. **interruption** n interruzione f.
intersect [intə'sekt] v intersecare. **intersection** n intersezione f.
intersperse [intə'spəːs] v cospargere.
interval ['intəvəl] n intervallo m.
intervene [intə'viːm] v intervenire. **intervention** n intervento m.
interview ['intəvjuː] n intervista f, colloquio m. v intervistare.
intestine [in'testin] n intestino m. **intestinal** adj intestinale.
intimate¹ ['intimət] adj intimo, familiare. **intimacy** n intimità f.
intimate² ['intimeit] v intimare, suggerire. **intimation** n intimazione f.
intimidate [in'timideit] v intimidire, intimorire. **intimidation** n intimidazione f.
into ['intu] prep in, dentro.
intolerable [in'tolərəbl] adj insopportabile, intollerabile.
intolerant [in'tolərənt] adj intollerante. **intolerance** n intolleranza f.
intonation [intə'neiʃən] n intonazione f.
intoxicate [in'toksikeit] v intossicare; (*with drink*) ubriacare; (*excite*) esaltare. **intoxicated** adj ubriaco, eccitato.
intransigent [in'transidʒənt] adj intransigente.
intransitive [in'transitiv] adj intransitivo.
intravenous [intrə'viːnəs] adj endovenoso.
intrepid [in'trepid] adj intrepido.
intricate ['intriket] adj complicato, complesso. **intricacy** n complicazione f.
intrigue ['intriːg; v in'triːg] n intrigo (pl

-ghi) *m.* *v* (*plot*) intrigare; (*excite curiosity*) incuriosire. **intriguing** *adj* interessante, affascinante.

intrinsic [in'trinsik] *adj* intrinseco.

introduce [,intrə'djus] *v* introdurre; (*people*) presentare. **introduction** *n* introduzione *f*, presentazione *f*. **introductory** *adj* introduttivo, introduttivo.

introspective [,intrə'spektiv] *adj* introspettivo. **introspection** *n* introspezione *f*.

introvert ['intrəvə:t] *n*, introverso, -a.

intrude [in'trud] *v* intrudere. **intrusion** *n* intrusione *f*.

intuition [,intju'iʃən] *n* intuito *m*; (*psychol, etc.*) intuizione *f*. **intuitive** *adj* intuitivo.

inundate ['inʌndeit] *v* inondare, allagare. **inundation** *n* allagamento *m*.

invade [in'veid] *v* invadere. **invader** *n* invasore *m*. **invasion** *n* invasione *f*.

invalid¹ [in'vælid] *n*, *adj* invalido, -a; malato, -a.

invalid² [in'vælid] *adj* (*not valid*) invalido, senza validità, nullo. **invalidate** *v* invalidare, annullare.

invaluable [in'væljuəbl] *adj* inestimabile, incalcolabile.

invariable [in'veəriəbl] *adj* invariabile, costante.

invective [in'vektiv] *n* invettiva *f*.

invent [in'vent] *v* inventare. **invention** *n* invenzione *f*.

inventory ['invəntri] *n* inventario *m*.

invert [in'və:t] *v* invertire; (*inside out*) rovesciare; (*upside down*) capovolgere. **inverted commas** virgolette *f pl*. **inversion** *n* inversione *f*, rovesciamento *m*.

invertebrate [in'və:tibrət] *nm*, *adj* invertebrato.

invest [in'vest] *v* investire. **investment** *n* investimento *m*.

investigate [in'vestigeit] *v* investigare, svolgere indagini. **investigation** *n* indagine *f*.

invigorating [in'vigəreitin] *adj* che invigorisce, fortificante.

invincible [in'vinsəbl] *adj* invincibile.

invisible [in'vizəbl] *adj* invisibile. **invisibility** *n* invisibilità *f*.

invite [in'vait] *v* invitare; provocare; (*lay oneself open to*) esporsi a. **invitation** *n* invito *m*. **inviting** *adj* attraente, seducente.

invoice ['invois] *n* fattura *f*. *v* fatturare.

invoke [in'vouk] *v* invocare. **invocation** *n* invocazione *f*.

involuntary [in'voləntəri] *adj* involontario.

involve [in'volv] *v* (*imply*) implicare; (*implicate*) coinvolgere; (*entail*) comportare. **involvement** *n* implicazione *f*.

inward [in'wəd] *adj* interno, intimo. **inwardly** *adv* interiormente. **inwards** *adv* verso il centro.

iodine ['aiədin] *n* iodio *m*.

ion ['aiən] *n* ione *m*.

irate [ai'reit] *adj* arrabbiato.

Ireland ['aiələnd] *n* Irlanda *f*. **Irish** *n*(*m*+*f*), *adj* irlandese.

iris ['aiəris] *n* (*anat*) iride *f*; (*bot*) giaggiolo *m*.

irk [ə:k] *v* infastidire, dar noia a. **irksome** *adj* seccante, noioso.

iron ['aiən] *n* ferro *m*; (*for pressing*) ferro da stiro *m*. **iron curtain** cortina di ferro *f*. **ironmonger's** *n* ferramenta *f*. *v* stirare. **ironing board** tavola da stiro *f*.

irony ['aiərəni] *n* ironia *f*. **ironic** *adj* ironico.

irrational [i'ræʃənl] *adj* irrazionale.

irregular [i'regjulə] *adj* irregolare. **irregularity** *n* irregolarità *f*.

irrelevant [i'reləvənt] *adj* non pertinente.

irreparable [i'repərəbl] *adj* irreparabile.

irresistible [,iri'zistəbl] *adj* irresistibile.

irrespective [,iri'spektiv] *adj* **irrespective of** senza riguardo a, senza tener conto di.

irresponsible [,iri'sponsəbl] *adj* irresponsabile. **irresponsibility** *n* irresponsabilità *f*.

irrevocable [i'revəkəbl] *adj* irrevocabile.

irrigate ['irigeit] *v* irrigare. **irrigation** *n* irrigazione *f*.

irritate ['iriteit] *v* irritare. **irritating** *adj* irritante. **irritation** *n* irritazione *f*.

Islam ['izlaːm] *n* Islam *m*. **Islamic** *adj* islamico.

island ['ailənd] *n* isola *f*.

isolate ['aisəleit] *v* isolare. **isolation** *n* isolamento *m*.

issue ['iʃu] *n* questione *f*, problema *m*; (*outcome*) conclusione *f*; edizione *f*; (*shares, etc.*) emissione *f*. *v* pubblicare; emettere; uscire.

isthmus ['isməs] *n* istmo *m*.

it [it] *pron* (*subject*) esso, -a; (*direct object*) lo, la; (*indirect object*) gli, le.

italic [i'tælik] *adj* (*handwriting*) italico;

(*printing*) corsivo. **in italics** in (carattere) corsivo.

Italy ['itɔli] *n* Italia *f*. **Italian** *n, adj* italiano, -a; (*language*) italiano *m*.

itch [itʃ] *n* (*sensation*) prurito *m*; (*desire*) gran voglia *f*. *v* sentire prurito.

item ['aitəm] *n* voce *f*, capo *m*, pezzo *m*.

itinerary [ai'tinərəri] *n* itinerario *m*.

its [its] *adj* (il) suo, (la) sua; (*pl*) (i) suoi, (le) sue.

itself [it'self] *pron* (*reflexive*) si; (*after prep*) sè; (*emphatic*) se esso, -a, se stesso, -a.

ivory ['aivəri] *n* avorio *m*.

ivy ['aivi] *n* edera *f*.

J

jab [dʒab] *n* puntura *f*. *v* pungere, punzecchiare.

jack [dʒak] *n* (*car*) cricco *m*; (*cards*) fante *m*; (*bowls*) boccino *m*. *v* **jack up** alzare.

jackdaw ['dʒakdɔɪ] *n* taccola *f*.

jacket ['dʒakit] *n* giacca *f*; (*of book*) copertina *f*; (*boiler, etc.*) rivestimento *m*. **jacket potato** patata in camicia *m*.

jack-knife ['dʒaknaif] *n* coltello a serramanico *m*.

jackpot ['dʒakpot] *n* posta intera *f*, monte premi *m*. **hit the jackpot** avere un colpo di fortuna.

jade [dʒeid] *n* giada *f*.

jaded ['dʒeidid] *adj* stracco, spossato.

jagged ['dʒagid] *adj* scabro, intaccato, dentellato.

jaguar ['dʒagjuə] *n* giaguaro *m*.

jail *or* **gaol** [dʒeil] *n* prigione *f*, carcere *m*. *v* incarcerare, mettere in prigione.

jam¹ [dʒam] *v* (*block*) bloccare; (*cause to stop functioning*) intralciare; (*squeeze*) pigiare; (*radio*) disturbare; (*traffic*) intasare. **jam on the brakes** bloccare i freni. *n* (*traffic*) intasamento *m*. **get into a jam** mettersi nei pasticci.

jam² [dʒam] *n* marmellata *f*, conserva di frutta *f*.

janitor ['dʒanitə] *n* portinaio, -a *m, f*.

January ['dʒanjuəri] *n* gennaio *m*.

Japan [dʒə'pan] *n* Giappone *m*. **Japanese** *n* (*m+f*), *adj* giapponese.

jar¹ [dʒaɪ] *n* (*vessel*) brocca *f*; (*usually with lid*) barattolo *m*.

jar² [dʒaɪ] *v* vibrare; produrre un suono aspro. **jarring** *adj* discorde.

jargon ['dʒaɪgən] *n* gergo *m*.

jasmine ['dʒazmin] *n* gelsomino *m*.

jaundice ['dʒɔmdis] *n* itterizia *f*. **jaundiced** *adj* distorto, invelenito.

jaunt [dʒɔmt] *n* gita *f*.

jaunty ['dʒɔmti] *adj* vivace, disinvolto.

javelin ['dʒavəlin] *n* giavellotto *m*.

jaw [dʒɔɪ] *n* (*upper*) mascella *f*; (*lower*) mandibola *f*.

jay [dʒei] *n* ghiandaia *f*.

jazz [dʒaz] *n* jazz *m invar*.

jealous ['dʒeləs] *adj* geloso. **become jealous** ingelosirsi. **make jealous** ingelosire. **jealousy** *n* gelosia *f*.

jeans [dʒins] *pl n* jeans *m pl*.

jeep [dʒiɪp] *n* jeep *f invar*.

jeer [dʒiə] *v* schernire, canzonare. *n* derisione *f*, scherno *m*.

jelly ['dʒeli] *n* gelatina *f*, budino di gelatina *m*.

jeopardize ['dʒepədaiz] *v* mettere a repentaglio, arrischiare. **jeopardy** *n* repentaglio *m*.

jerk [dʒəɪk] *n* (*shock*) scossa *f*; (*pull*) strappo *m*; (*sudden start*) scatto *m*. *v* scuotere; dare uno strappao; scattare.

jersey ['dʒəɪzi] *n* (*fabric*) jersey *m invar*; (*garment*) maglione *m*.

jest [dʒest] *n* scherzo *m*, burla *f*. *v* scherzare. **jester** *n* buffone *m*.

Jesuit ['dʒezjuit] *adj, nm* gesuita. **Jesuitical** *adj* gesuitico.

Jesus ['dʒiɪzəs] *n* Gesù *m*. **Jesus Christ** Gesù Cristo.

jet [dʒet] *n* getto *m*, zampillo *m*; (*spout*) becco *m*; (*aero*) aviogetto *m*, aeroplano a reazione *m*. **jet-black** *adj* (*nero*) ebano *invar*. **jet engine** motore a reazione *m*.

jettison ['dʒetisn] *v* buttar via, disfarsi di.

jetty ['dʒeti] *n* molo *m*, banchina *f*.

Jew [dʒuɪ] *n* ebreo, -a *m, f*. **Jewish** *adj* (*person*) ebreo; (*thing*) ebraico.

jewel ['dʒuəl] *n* gioiello *m*; (*watch*) rubino *m*; (*treasure*) tesoro *m*. **jeweller** *n* gioielliere *m*. **jewellery** *n* gioielleria *f*.

jib¹ [dʒib] *n* (*sail*) fiocco *m*; (*crane*) braccio *m*.

jib² [dʒib] *v* **jib at** essere restio *or* ritroso a.

jig¹ [dʒig] *n* (*machine tool*) maschera di montaggio *f*. *v* lavorare con maschere.

jig² *n* (*dance*) giga *f*. *v* ballare la giga. **jig up and down** salterellare su e giù.

jiggle ['dʒɪgl] v dondolare, muoversi in qua e in là.

jigsaw ['dʒɪgsɔt] n sega da traforo f. **jigsaw puzzle** puzzle m.

jilt [dʒɪlt] v piantare in asso.

jingle ['dʒɪŋgl] n (sound) tintinnio m; (song) ritornello m, cantilena f. v tintinnare.

jinx [dʒɪŋks] n malocchio m.

job [dʒɔb] n impiego (pl -ghi) m, lavoro m; (coll) affare m, mestiere m.

jockey ['dʒɔki] n fantino m. v maneggiare.

jocular ['dʒɔkjulə] adj faceto.

jodhpurs ['dʒɔdpəz] pl n calzoni da equitazione m pl.

jog [dʒɔg] v (sport) fare il footing; (horse) andare al piccolo trotto. **jog the memory** richiamare alla memoria. **jog** (push) spinta f; (nudge) colpetto m; (elbowing) gomitata f; (trot) piccolo trotto m.

join [dʒɔin] n giuntura f. v unire, congiungere, unirsi a; (become member) iscriversi a, entrare. **join in** entrare a far parte di.

joiner ['dʒɔinə] n falegname m.

joint [dʒɔint] n (join) giuntura f; articolazione f; (plant) nodo m; (meat) taglio (di carne) m; (coll: bar, etc.) bettola f. adj comune, collettivo.

joist [dʒɔist] n trave f, travicello m.

joke [dʒɔuk] n scherzo m, barzelletta f. **no joke** un affare serio m. v scherzare.

joker n burlone m; (cards) jolly m invar, matta f.

jolly ['dʒɔli] adj divertente, ameno, gaio. adv molto.

jolt [dʒɔult] v scuotere, far sobbalzare. n scossa f, sobbalzo m.

jostle ['dʒɔsl] n (push) spinta f; (elbowing) gomitata f. v fare a gomitate, spingersi avanti.

journal ['dʒəɪnl] n periodico m; (daily record) diario m, giornale m; (day-book) brogliaccio m. **journalism** n giornalismo m. **journalist** n giornalista m, f.

journey ['dʒəɪni] n viaggio m. v viaggiare. **go on a journey** andare or mettersi in viaggio.

jovial ['dʒɔuviəl] adj gioviale, lieto.

jowl ['dʒaul] n (jaw) mascella f; (flesh) gota f.

joy [dʒɔi] n gioia f, allegrezza f, allegria f. **joyful** or **joyous** adj gioioso.

jubilant ['dʒuːbilənt] adj giubilante.

jubilee ['dʒuːbiliː] n giubileo m.

Judaism ['dʒuːdeiizəm] n giudaismo m.

judge [dʒʌdʒ] n giudice m; (of competition) arbitro m; (expert) intenditore, -trice m, f. v giudicare, considerare. **judgment** n giudizio m; (law) sentenza f; (opinion) parere m. **Last Judgment** giudizio universale m.

judicial [dʒuːˈdiʃəl] adj giudiziario; legale.

judiciary [dʒuːˈdiʃiəri] n magistratura f.

judicious [dʒuːˈdiʃəs] adj giudizioso, prudente.

judo ['dʒuːdou] n judo m invar, giudò m.

jug [dʒʌg] n brocca f, caraffa f.

juggernaut ['dʒʌgənɔtt] n (lorry) grosso autotreno m.

juggle ['dʒʌgl] v giocolare, prestigiare; (trick) truffare. **juggle with** svisare, travisare. **juggler** n giocoliere, -a m, f; prestigiatore, -trice m, f.

jugular ['dʒʌgjulə] adj giugulare.

juice [dʒuːs] n succo m, sugo m. **juicy** adj sugoso, succolento.

jukebox ['dʒuːkbɔks] n jukebox m invar.

July [dʒuˈlai] n luglio m.

jumble ['dʒʌmbl] n miscuglio m, confusione f. **jumble sale** bazar di beneficenza m invar.

jump [dʒʌmp] n salto m; (sudden rise) balzo m; (nervous) sussulto m. **long/high jump** salto in lungo/alto m. v saltare, fare un salto; sussultare; (of prices) rincarare. **jump at** accettare con entusiasmo. **jump off** lanciarsi da. **jump over** scavalcare.

jumper ['dʒʌmpə] n (pullover) maglione m, pullover m invar; (jacket) casacca f; (person) saltatore, -trice m, f.

junction ['dʒʌŋktʃən] n congiunzione f; (rail) nodo ferroviario m.

juncture ['dʒʌŋkʃə] n frangente m, momento (critico) m.

June [dʒuːn] n giugno m.

jungle ['dʒʌŋgl] n giungla f.

junior ['dʒuːnjə] adj minore, più giovane.

juniper ['dʒuːnipə] n ginepro m.

junk[1] [dʒʌŋk] n (rubbish) roba vecchia f, robaccia f, rifiuti m pl.

junk[2] [dʒʌŋk] n (boat) giunca f.

junta ['dʒʌntə] n giunta f.

jurisdiction [dʒuərisˈdikʃən] n giurisdizione f.

jury ['dʒuəri] n giuria f. **juror** n giurato, -a m, f.

just [dʒʌst] *adj* giusto, preciso. *adv* giusto, per l'appunto, proprio; *(barely)* appena; *(not more than)* soltanto.

justice ['dʒʌstis] *n* giustizia *f*; *(judge)* giudice *m*, magistrato *m*. **do justice to** *(show appreciation)* far onore a; *(concede what is due)* apprezzare, stimare.

justify ['dʒʌstifai] *v* giustificare, scusare. **justifiable** *adj* giustificabile, scusabile, legittimo. **justification** *n* giustificazione *f*, scusa *f*.

jut [dʒʌt] *v* sporgere, protendere (in fuori).

jute [dʒuːt] *n* giuta *f*.

juvenile ['dʒuːvənail] *adj* giovanile, per ragazzi, minorenne.

juxtapose [,dʒʌkstə'pouz] *v* giustapporre. **juxtaposition** *n* giustapposizione *f*.

K

kaleidoscope [kə'laidəskoup] *n* caleidoscopio *m*.

kangaroo [kaŋɡə'ruː] *n* canguro *m*.

karate [kə'rɑːti] *n* karatè *m invar*.

keel [kiːl] *n* chiglia *f*. **v keel over** capovolgersi.

keen [kiːn] *adj (cutting)* tagliente; *(sharp)* aguzzo; *(perceptive)* vivo, perspicace; *(biting)* mordace; *(eager)* appassionato, entusiasta. **keenness** *n* passione *f*, entusiasmo *m*, intensità *f*; *(eagerness)* ardore *m*.

*****keep** [kiːp] *v* tenere; mantenere; conservare; *(hold in custody)* custodire; *(manage)* gestire; *(observe)* osservare, rispettare. **keep at** persistere, continuare a fare. **keep back** *(stay behind)* stare indietro; *(withhold)* trattenere. **keep down** reprimere. **keep good time** *(watch)* funzionare bene. **keep in with** mantenersi in buoni rapporti con. **keep on** continuare. **keep out** non lasciar entrare; restar fuori. **keep to** aderire a. *n* **earn one's keep** mantenersi. **for keeps** per sempre. **keeper** *n* guardiano, -a *m*, *f*; custode *m*, *f*.

keeping ['kiːpiŋ] *n* custodia *f*. **in keeping with** conforme o consono a.

keepsake ['kiːpseik] *n* ricordo *m*.

keg [keɡ] *n* barilotto *m*.

kennel ['kenl] *n* canile *m*.

kept [kept] *V* keep.

kerb [kəːb] *n* banchina *f*.

kernel ['kəːnl] *n* nocciolo *m*, nucleo *m*.

kerosene ['kerəsiːn] *n* cherosene *m*.

kettle ['ketl] *n* bollitore *m*, pentola *f*.

kettledrum ['ketldrʌm] *n* timpano *m*.

key [kiː] *n* chiave *f*; *(part of keyboard)* tasto *m*. **keyboard** *n* tastiera *f*. **keyhole** *n* buco della chiave *m*. **keynote** *n* nota determinante *f*.

khaki ['kɑːki] *adj* cachi.

kick [kik] *v* dare un calcio a, dare una pedata a; protestare. **kick off** iniziare. **kick out** buttar fuori. **kick up** scatenare, provocare. *n* calcio *m*, pedata *f*; *(force)* forza *f*.

kid[1] [kid] *n (child)* bimbo, -a *m*, *f*; *(goat)* capretto *m*. **handle with kid gloves** trattare coi guanti.

kid[2] [kid] *v (coll)* prendere in giro.

kidnap ['kidnap] *v* rapire. **kidnapper** *n* rapitore, -trice *m*, *f*.

kidney ['kidni] *n (organ)* rene *m*; *(food)* rognone *m*. **kidney bean** fagiolo *m*.

kill [kil] *v* uccidere, ammazzare. **killer** *n* assassino, -a *m*, *f*.

kiln [kiln] *n* forno *m*.

kilo ['kiːlou] *n* chilo *m*. **kilogram** *n* chilogrammo *m*.

kilometre ['kiləmitrə] *n* chilometro *m*.

kilt [kilt] *n* gonnellino scozzese *m*.

kin [kin] *n* parenti *m pl*; *(kinship)* parentela *f*. **kinsman** *n* parente *m*. **next of kin** parente prossimo *m*.

kind[1] [kaind] *adj* gentile, cortese, buono; *(well-meant)* cordiale. **kind-hearted** *adj* benevolo. **kindly** *adv* gentilmente; *(please)* per cortesia, per favore. **kindness** *n* gentilezza *f*, cortesia *f*.

kind[2] [kaind] *n* genere *m*, specie *f*, razza *f*.

kindergarten ['kindəɡaːtn] *n* giardino d'infanzia *m*, asilo (infantile) *m*.

kindle ['kindl] *v* accendere; *(excite)* eccitare.

kindred ['kindrid] *n* parentela *f*. *adj* affine, simile. **kindred spirit** anima gemella *f*.

kinetic [kin'etik] *adj* chinetico.

king [kiŋ] *n* re *m invar*. **kingdom** *n* regno *m*.

kingfisher ['kiŋ,fiʃə] *n* martin pescatore *m*.

kink [kiŋk] *n* attorcigliamento *m*, piega *f*; *(whim)* ghiribizzo *m*. **kinky** *adj (odd)* strambo; *(coll)* pervertito.

kiosk ['kiɔsk] n chiosco m; (newsagent) edicola f.

kipper ['kipə] n aringa affumicata f.

kiss [kis] n bacio m. v baciare.

kit [kit] n (tools) attrezzi m pl, utensili m pl; (outfit) corredo m. v attrezzare. **kit out** equipaggiare.

kitchen ['kitʃin] n cucina f.

kite [kait] n aquilone m; (bird) nibbio m.

kitten ['kitn] n micio m, gattino m.

kitty ['kiti] n (joint pool) fondo comune m; (cards) posta f.

kleptomania [kleptə'meiniə] n cleptomania f. **kleptomaniac** n cleptomane m, f.

knack [nak] n destrezza f, bernoccolo m.

knapsack ['napsak] n zaino m.

knave [neiv] n furfante m; (cards) fante m.

knead [niːd] v impastare.

knee [niː] n ginocchio m (pl -a f). **kneecap** n rotula f, patella f. **knee-deep** adj che arriva fino al ginocchio; (submerged) sommerso.

*****kneel** [niːl] v inginocchiarsi, mettersi in ginocchio.

knelt [nelt] V kneel.

knew [njuː] V know.

knickers ['nikəz] pl n mutandine f pl.

knife [naif] n coltello m. v accoltellare.

knight [nait] n cavaliere m.

*****knit** [nit] v lavorare a maglia, fare la calza; (join together) unire. **knit one's brows** aggrottare le ciglia. **knitting needle** ferro da calza m. **knitwear** n maglieria f.

knob [nɔb] n pomo m, manopola f; (protuberance) bitorzolo m. **knobbly** adj bitorzoluto, nodoso.

knock [nɔk] v (at door) bussare; (hit) colpire, battere; (of motor engine) battere in testa. **knock about** (mistreat) malmenare; (wander aimlessly) fare vita randagia. **knock down** (strike) abbattere; demolire; (lower) abbassare. **knock-kneed** adj dalle gambe a X. **knock off** (stop work) tralasciare, smettere; (deduct) dedurre; (coll: steal) far man bassa, portar via; (complete hurriedly) buttar giù. **knock out** (stun) far perdere i sensi a; (put out of action) mettere fuori combattimento. **knock together** (make hurriedly) acciabattare. **knock up** (wake) svegliare; (tennis) bussata f; (blow) batosta f. **knocker** n battiporta m invar, picchiotto m.

knot [nɔt] n nodo m. v annodare. **knotted** adj nodoso, annodato, pieno di nodi. **knotty** adj pieno di nodi; difficile, complesso.

*****know** [nou] v (facts) sapere; (be acquainted with) conoscere; (understand) capire; (recognize) riconoscere. **as far as is known** per quanto si sappia. **know about** essere informato su, essere al corrente di. **know how to** sapere. **n in the know** (coll) al corrente. **knowing** adj accorto, intelligente. **known** adj noto, conosciuto. **make known** far sapere or conoscere, divulgare, render noto.

knowledge ['nɔlidʒ] n cognizione f, conoscenze f pl.

known [noun] V know.

knuckle ['nʌkl] n nocca f. **knuckle down** applicarsi. **knuckle under** sottomettersi, piegarsi.

kosher ['kouʃə] adj kasher, cascer.

L

label ['leibl] n etichetta f; (strip of paper) cartellino m; definizione f. v etichettare, qualificare.

laboratory [lə'bɔrətəri] n laboratorio m.

labour ['leibə] n (toil) lavoro m; (hard work, task) fatica f; (effort) sforzo m; (workforce) manodopera f; (childbirth) doglie del parto f pl, travaglio del parto m. **Labour Party** partito laburista m. **labour-saving** adj che risparmia fatica. v faticare, lavorare. **labour under** essere vittima di. **laborious** adj laborioso, faticoso.

laburnum [lə'bəːnəm] n laburno m.

labyrinth ['labərinθ] n labirinto m.

lace [leis] n pizzo m, merletto m, brina f; (string, cord) laccio m; (braid) gallone m. v (fasten) allacciare; (trim with lace) ornare di pizzi; (add to drink) correggere. **lacemaker** n trinaia f.

lacerate ['lasəreit] v lacerare.

lack [lak] n mancanza f, insufficienza f. v mancare (di).

lackadaisical [lakə'deizikəl] adj svogliato, infingardo.

lacquer ['lakə] n lacca f. v laccare.

lad [lad] n ragazzo m, giovanotto m.

ladder ['ladə] n scala f; (stocking) smagliatura. v smagliarsi. **ladder-proof** adj indemagliabile.

laden ['leidn] adj carico (m pl -chi).

ladle ['leidl] n (dish-shaped) mestolo m; (cup-shaped) ramaiuolo m, cucchiaione m. v scodellare.

lady ['leidi] n signora f. **lady of the house** padrona di casa f.

ladybird ['leidibəːd] n coccinella f.

lag¹ [lag] v avanzare lentamente. **lag behind** rimanere indietro. n ritardo m, intervallo m.

lag² [lag] v (cover) rivestire di materiale isolante, isolare. **lagging** n rivestimento isolante m.

lager ['laːgə] n birra (chiara) f.

lagoon [lə'guːn] n laguna f.

laid [leid] V **lay¹**.

lain [lein] V **lie¹**.

lair [leə] n tana f.

laity ['leiəti] n **the laity** i laici m pl.

lake [leik] n lago m.

lamb [lam] n agnello m.

lame [leim] adj zoppo, storpio; (poor) debole, insufficiente. **lame duck** fallito m.

lament [lə'ment] n lamento m. v lamentare, compiangere. **lamented** adj compianto.

laminate ['lamineit] v laminare.

lamp [lamp] n lampada f, lume m; (of car, ship) fanale m. **lamp-holder** n portalampada m. **lamp-post** n lampione m. **lampshade** n paralume m.

lance [laːns] n lancia f. v incidere col bisturi. **lancet** n bisturi m invar.

land [land] n terra f; (country) paese m; (agricultural area) campagna f; (site, soil) terreno m. v (put on shore) sbarcare, approdare; (from the air) atterrare; (obtain) ottenere. **landing** n sbarco m; atterraggio m; (of stairs) pianerottolo m. **landlady** ['landleidi] n padrona di casa f, proprietaria f.

landlord ['landloːd] n padrone di casa m, proprietario m; (of inn) oste m.

landmark ['landmaːk] n punto di riferimento m.

landscape ['landskeip] n paesaggio m.

landslide ['landslaid] n frana f.

lane [lein] n (between houses) vicolo m; (track) sentiero m; (part of road, sports track) corsia f.

language ['langwidʒ] n (of a nation) lingua f; (means of expression) linguaggio m.

languish ['langwiʃ] v languire.

lanky ['lanki] adj alto e magro.

lantern ['lantən] n lanterna f.

lap¹ [lap] n (anat) grembo m; (loose fold) falda f, piega f; (circuit) giro m; (part of journey) tappa f.

lap² [lap] v lambire. **lap up** lappare; (coll) ascoltare or accettare con avidità.

lapel [lə'pel] n risvolto m.

Lapland ['lapland] n Lapponia f. **Lapp** m(m+f), adj lappone.

lapse [laps] n svista f, errore m; (time) corso m, periodo m; (law) scadenza f; decadenza f. v (become void) scadere; (decline) decadere; (time) trascorrere. **lapsed** adj (law) decaduto; (rel) apostata.

larceny ['laːsəni] n furto m.

larch [laːtʃ] n larice m.

lard [laːd] n strutto m.

larder ['laːdə] n dispensa f.

large [laːdʒ] adj grande, ampio. **at large** in libertà; (in general) in complesso.

lark¹ [laːk] n (bird) allodola f.

lark² [laːk] n (coll) burla f. v **lark about** divertirsi.

larva ['laːvə] n, pl **larvae** larva f.

larynx ['lariŋks] n laringe f. **laryngitis** n laringite f.

laser ['leizə] n laser m invar.

lash [laʃ] n sferzata f; (eye) ciglio m (pl -a f). v (whip) sferzare; (tie) legare. **lash out** menar colpi; (coll: money) non badare a spese. **lash out at** inveire contro.

lass [las] n fanciulla f, giovane f.

lassitude ['lasitjuːd] n stanchezza f.

lasso [la'suː] n lasso m, laccio m. v catturare al lasso or laccio.

last¹ [laːst] adj finale, ultimo; (past) scorso, passato. **last but one** penultimo. **last night** ieri sera. adv (after all others) per ultimo; (most recently) l'ultima volta; finalmente. **at last** alla fine, finalmente.

last² [laːst] v durare. **lasting** adj durevole.

latch [latʃ] n saliscendi m invar, chiavistello m. v chiudere con saliscendi. **latch on to** afferrare.

late [leit] adj tardo; recente; (former) precedente; (dead) defunto, fu. adv (not on time) in ritardo; (not early) tardi. **lately** adv recentemente. **lateness** n ritardo *m.* **later** *adv* più tardi, dopo. **see you later!** a più tardi! **latest** *adj* ultimo; recentissimo. **at the latest** al più tardi.

latent ['leitənt] *adj* latente.

lateral ['latərəl] *adj* laterale.

lathe [leið] *n* tornio *m.*

lather ['laiðə] *n* schiuma *f. v (of soap)* far schiuma.

Latin ['latin] *nm, adj* latino.

latitude ['latitjud] *n* latitudine *f.*

latrine [lə'trim] *n* latrina *f.*

latter ['latə] *adj* secondo, ultimo. **the latter** il secondo, questo.

lattice ['latis] *n* traliccio *m,* grata *f.*

laugh [laif] *v* ridere. **laugh at** ridere per or di. *n* risata *f;* (*coll*) spasso *m.* **have a laugh** fare una risata. **laughable** *adj* ridicolo, risibile. **laughing stock** zimbello *m.* **laughter** *n* riso *m* (*pl* -a *f*), risata *f.*

launch¹ ['lomtʃ] *v* varare; (*give a start*) lanciare; (*attack*) sferrare.

launch² ['lomtʃ] *n* (*naut*) lancia *f.*

launder ['lomdə] *v* fare il bucato, lavare e stirare. **launderette** *n* lavanderia automatica *f,* lavanderia a gettoni *f.* **laundry** *n* (*place*) lavanderia *f;* (*clothes, etc.*) bucato *m.*

laurel ['lorəl] *n* alloro *m,* lauro *m.*

lava ['lɑvə] *n* lava *f.*

lavatory ['lavətəri] *n* gabinetto *m,* ritirata *f.*

lavender ['lavində] *n* lavanda *f.*

lavish ['laviʃ] *adj* prodigo, generoso. *v* dispensare or spendere largamente.

law [loi] *n* legge *f;* (*profession*) diritto *m;* (*rule*) norma *f,* regola *f.* **law-abiding** *adj* ligio alla legge. **lawsuit** *n* causa *f,* processo *m.* **lawful** *adj* legittimo, lecito. **lawyer** *n* avvocato, -essa *m, f.*

lawn [loin] *n* prato rasato *m.* **lawn-mower** *n* falciatrice *or* tosatrice per prati *f.*

lax [laks] *adj* rilassato; negligente.

laxative ['laksətiv] *nm, adj* lassativo.

*****lay**¹ [lei] *v* posare, mettere; (*eggs*) deporre; (*table*) apparecchiare. **lay-by** *n* area or piazzola di sosta or parcheggio *f.* **lay down** posare per terra; stabilire. **lay off** (*workers*) sospendere. **lay on** disporre, installare. **layout** *n* disposizione *f;* (*sketch*) tracciato *m,* pianta *f.* **lay out** (*spread*) stendere; (*coll: spend*) sborsare. **be laid up** essere costretto di rimanere a letto.

lay² [lei] *adj* laico; non professionale. **layman** *n* laico, -a *m, f;* profano, -a *m, f.*

lay³ [lei] *V* **lie**¹.

layer ['leiə] *n* strato *m.*

lazy ['leizi] *adj* pigro, indolente. **laziness** *n* pigrizia *f.*

*****lead**¹ [liid] *v* condurre; influenzare; (*bring*) portare; (*be at head of*) essere in testa di, essere al comando di; (*act as guide*) guidare; (*make go*) indurre. *n* direzione *f,* comando *m;* (*for dog*) guinzaglio *m;* (*theatre*) primo attore, prima attrice *m, f.* **be in the lead** essere in testa. **take the lead** (*sport*) passare in testa. **leader** *n* capo *m,* dirigente *m, f;* (*newspaper*) articolo di fondo *m.* **leadership** *n* direzione *f,* comando *m.* **leading** *adj* principale, primo.

lead² [led] *n* piombo *m.* **leaden** *adj* di piombo.

leaf [liif] *n* (*plant*) foglia *f;* (*paper*) foglio *m;* (*table*) asse *f. v* **leaf through** sfogliare. **leaflet** *n* volantino *m,* manifestino *m.*

league [liig] *n* lega *f;* classe *f.*

leak [liik] *n* (*escape*) fuga *f;* (*crack*) fessura *f;* (*boat*) falla *f;* (*news*) trapelamento *m. v* trapelare; (*boat*) far acqua; trapelare.

*****lean**¹ [liin] *v* appoggiare, inclinare, pendere. **lean against** appoggiarsi a. **lean out** sporgersi. **lean towards** tendere verso. **leaning** *n* inclinazione *f,* propensione *f.*

lean² [liin] *adj* magro, scarno; (*poor*) povero.

leant [lent] *V* **lean**¹.

*****leap** [liip] *n* salto *m,* balzo *m.* **by leaps and bounds** a passi da gigante. *v* saltare, balzare. **leap-frog** *n* cavallina *f.* **leap year** anno bisestile *m.*

leapt [lept] *V* **leap.**

*****learn** [ləin] *v* imparare, studiare; (*become informed*) sentire, apprendere. **learned** *adj* dotto, erudito, colto. **learner** *n* (*beginner*) principiante *m, f;* allievo, -a *m, f;* apprendista *m, f.* **learning** *n* cultura *f,* erudizione *f.*

learnt [ləint] *V* **learn.**

lease [liis] *n* affitto *m,* contratto d'affitto *m. v* affittare.

leash [liiʃ] *n* guinzaglio *m.*

least [liist] *adj* minimo. *pron, adv* (il) meno. **at least** almeno, almeno. **not in the least** per nulla, affatto.

leather ['leðə] *n* cuoio *m,* pelle *f.* **leather goods** pelletteria *f sing.*

*****leave**¹ [liiv] *v* lasciare; abbandonare; (*go out from*) uscire da; (*depart*) partire. **leave alone** lasciar stare, lasciare in pace.

leave home andar via. leave out omettere. be left rimanere. be left over avanzare.

leave² [liiv] n permesso m; (holiday) licenza f, congedo m.

lecherous ['letʃərəs] adj lussurioso, lascivo. lecher n libertino m. lechery n lascivia f.

lectern ['lektən] n leggio m.

lecture ['lektʃə] n lezione f, conferenza f; (reprimand) ramanzina f, sgridata f. v tenere una conferenza; dare un corso di lezioni; (rebuke) predicare, fare una paternale a. lecturer n conferenziere, -a m, f; (university) docente m, f.

led [led] V lead¹.

ledge [ledʒ] n (window) davanzale m; (projecting part) sporgenza f.

ledger ['ledʒə] n (libro) mastro m.

lee [lii] n (shelter) riparo m; (naut) sottovento m. leeward adj, adv sottovento.

leech [liitʃ] n sanguisuga f.

leek [liik] n porro m.

leer [liə] v guardare di sbieco. n sguardo sbieco m.

leeway ['liiwei] n (naut) deriva f. make up leeway recuperare lo svantaggio.

left¹ [left] V leave¹.

left² [left] adj sinistro. n sinistra f. the Left (pol) la Sinistra. adv a sinistra, verso sinistra, sulla sinistra. left-hand adj sinistro. left-handed adj mancino.

leg [leg] n gamba f; (furniture) piede m; (lap) tappa f; (poultry) coscia f; (meat) cosciotto m.

legacy ['legəsi] n lascito m, eredità f.

legal ['liigəl] adj lecito, legittimo, legale. legality n legalità f. legalize v legalizzare, legittimare.

legend ['ledʒənd] n leggenda f. legendary adj leggendario.

Leghorn ['leg'hoin] n Livorno m.

legible ['ledʒəbl] adj leggibile. legibility n leggibilità f.

legion ['liidʒən] n legione f.

legislate ['ledʒisleit] v promulgare leggi. legislation n legislazione f.

legitimate [lə'dʒitimət] adj legittimo, lecito. v legittimare. legitimacy n legittimità f.

leisure ['leʒə] n agio m, tempo libero m. leisurely adj fatto con comodo.

lemon ['lemən] n limone m. adj color limone invar. lemonade n limonata f. lemon juice succo di limone m.

*lend [lend] v prestare, dare in prestito.

length [leŋθ] n lunghezza f; (time) durata f; (cloth) taglio m. at length per disteso. lengthen v allungare. lengthy adj lungo.

lenient ['liiniənt] adj benigno, indulgente. leniency n indulgenza f.

lens [lenz] n lente f; (camera) obiettivo m.

lent [lent] V lend.

Lent [lent] n quaresima f.

lentil ['lentil] n lenticchia f.

Leo ['liiou] n Leone m.

leopard ['lepəd] n leopardo m.

leotard ['liiətaid] n calzamaglia (pl calzemaglie) f.

leper ['lepə] n lebbroso, -a m, f. leprosy n lebbra f.

lesbian ['lezbiən] n lesbica f.

less [les] adj minore, meno. nm, adv, prep meno. lessen v diminuire. lesser adj minore, inferiore.

lesson ['lesn] n lezione f.

lest [lest] conj per paura che.

*let [let] v lasciare, permettere; (rent) affittare. let down (lower) calare; (hair) sciogliere; (disappoint) deludere; (dress) allungare. let in fare entrare. let know far sapere. let out far uscire, liberare; (dress) allargare; (secret) lasciar sfuggire; (emit) fare.

lethal ['liiθəl] adj letale.

lethargy ['leθədʒi] n letargia f. lethargic adj letargico.

letter ['letə] n lettera f; (character) carattere m. letter-box n buca delle lettere f. lettering n iscrizione f.

lettuce ['letis] n lattuga f.

leukaemia [lur'kiimiə] n leucemia f.

level ['levl] n livello m, piano m; (height, position) altezza f. v livellare, spianare. adj piano, uniforme; (equal) pari. be level with essere a livello di. level crossing passaggio a livello m. level-headed adj equilibrato.

lever ['liivə] n leva f. leverage n leva f, stimolo m.

levy ['levi] n imposta f, contributo m. v imporre, esigere.

lewd [luid] adj lascivo, osceno.

liable ['laiəbl] adj responsabile. liable to soggetto a, passibile di. liability n obbligo m, responsabilità f; (comm) passività f, deficit m invar.

liaison [liˈeizon] *n* legame *m*; (*sexual*) relazione amorosa *f.*

liar [ˈlaiə] *n* bugiardo, -a *m, f.*

libel [ˈlaibəl] *n* diffamazione *f*, calunnia *f. v* diffamare, calunniare. **libellous** *adj* diffamatorio, calunnioso.

liberal [ˈlibərəl] *adj* liberale, generoso. *n* liberale *m, f.* **liberalism** *n* liberalismo *m.*

liberate [ˈlibəreit] *v* liberare, mettere in libertà. **liberation** *n* liberazione *f.*

liberty [ˈlibəti] *n* libertà *f.*

Libra [ˈliːbrə] *n* Libra *f.*

library [ˈlaibrəri] *n* biblioteca *f.* **librarian** *n* bibliotecario, -a *m, f.*

libretto [liˈbretou] *n* libretto *m.*

lice [lais] *V* **louse**.

licence [ˈlaisəns] *n* licenza *f*, permesso *m*; (*driving*) patente (di guida) *f*; (*arms*) porto d'armi *m.* **license** *v* autorizzare. **licensee** *n* gestore autorizzato *m*, concessionario *m.*

lichen [ˈlaikən] *n* lichene *m.*

lick [lik] *v* leccare. *n* leccata *f.*

lid [lid] *n* coperchio *m.*

*lie¹ [lai] *v* giacere, stare sdraiato. **lie down** coricarsi, sdraiarsi. **lie in** (*stay in bed*) restare a letto; (*consist of*) consistere di. **lie with** spettare a.

lie² [lai] *n* (*untruth*) bugia *f*, menzogna *f. v* mentire, dire una bugia.

lieu [luː] *n* **in lieu of** invece di.

lieutenant [lefˈtenənt] *n* tenente *m.*

life [laif] *n* vita *f.* **lifeless** *adj* esanime.

lifebelt [ˈlaifbelt] *n* salvagente *m.*

lifeboat [ˈlaifbout] *n* scialuppa di salvataggio *f.*

life insurance *n* assicurazione sulla vita *f.*

life-jacket *n* cintura di salvataggio *f.*

lifeline [ˈlaiflain] *n* linea di communicazione vitale *f.*

lifelong [ˈlaiflɔŋ] *adj* di tutta la vita.

lifetime [ˈlaiftaim] *n* vita *f*, durata della vita *f.*

lift [lift] *n* ascensore *m*; (*coll: ride*) autostop *m. v* sollevare, alzare.

*light¹ [lait] *n* luce *f*, lume *m*; illuminazione *f.* **switch on/off the light** accendere/spegnere la luce. *adj* chiaro. **light bulb** ampolla *f.* **lighthouse** *n* faro *m.* **light-year** *n* anno luce *m. v* accendere. **lighten** *v* illuminare, illuminarе. **lighter** *n* (*for cigarette*) accendino *m.* **lighting** *n* illuminazione *f.*

light² [lait] *adj* leggero. **light-headed** *adj*

frivolo; (*giddy*) preso da vertigini. **light-hearted** *adj* gaio. **lighten** *v* alleggerire, alleviare. **lightness** *n* leggerezza *f.*

*light³ [lait] *v* **light upon** imbattersi in.

lightning [ˈlaitniŋ] *n* fulmine *m*, lampo *m.* **lightning conductor** *n* parafulmine *m.*

like¹ [laik] *adj* simile, uguale. *prep* come. **be or look like** rassomigliare a. **liken** *v* paragonare. **likeness** *n* somiglianza *f*; (*portrait*) ritratto *m.* **likewise** *adv* parimenti, altrettanto.

like² [laik] *v* gradire; (*want*) volere. **I like . . .** mi piace . . . **likeable** *adj* simpatico. **liking** *n* simpatia *f*, gusto *m.* **have a liking for** trovar simpatico *or* gradevole.

likely [ˈlaikli] *adj* probabile, verosimile. *adv* probabilmente. **likelihood** *n* probabilità *f.*

lilac [ˈlailək] *nm, adj* lilla *invar.*

lily [ˈlili] *n* giglio *m.* **lily-of-the-valley** *n* mughetto *m.*

limb [lim] *n* arto *m*, membro *m* (*pl* -a *f*).

limbo [ˈlimbou] *n* limbo *m.*

lime¹ [laim] *n* calce *f.* **limestone** *n* calcare *m.*

lime² [laim] *n* (*fruit*) limetta *f*; (*linden*) tiglio *m.*

limelight [ˈlaimˌlait] *n* luci della ribalta *f pl.* **be in the limelight** essere alla ribalta.

limit [ˈlimit] *n* limite *m*, ambito *m. v* limitare. **limitation** *n* limitazione *f.* **limitless** *adj* illimitato.

limousine [ˈliməˌziːn] *n* berlina *f*, limousine *f invar.*

limp¹ [limp] *v* zoppicare. *n* zoppicamento *m.*

limp² [limp] *adj* floscio; (*weak*) debole.

limpet [ˈlimpit] *n* patella *f.*

line [lain] *n* linea *f*; (*row*) fila *f*; (*string*) corda *f*; (*wrinkle*) ruga *f*; (*of letters*) riga *f. v* rigare; (*clothes*) foderare; (*border*) fiancheggiare. **line up** allineare. **linear** *adj* lineare.

linen [ˈlinin] *n* lino *m*; (*sheets, etc.*) biancheria *f. adj* di lino.

liner [ˈlainə] *n* (*naut*) transatlantico *m*; (*aero*) aereo di linea *m.*

linger [ˈliŋgə] *v* indugiare, soffermarsi. **lingering** *adj* protratto.

lingerie [ˈlãʒəri] *n* biancheria per signora *f.*

linguist [ˈliŋgwist] *n* linguista *m, f*; poliglotta *m, f.* **linguistic** *adj* linguistico. **linguistics** *n* linguistica *f.*

lining ['lainiŋ] n (clothes) fodera f; rivestimento interno m.

link [liŋk] n (of chain) anello m; (bond) legame m; (mech) collegamento m. v collegare, congiungere.

linoleum [li'nouliəm] n linoleum m invar.

linseed ['linsi:d] n semi di lino m pl. **linseed oil** olio di semi di lino m.

lint [lint] n filaccia (di lino) f.

lion ['laiən] n leone m. **lioness** n leonessa f.

lip [lip] n labbro m (pl -a f). **lip-read** v capire dal movimento delle labbra. **lipstick** n rossetto m.

liqueur [li'kjuə] n liquore m.

liquid ['likwid] nm, adj liquido. **liquidate** v liquidare; eliminare. **liquidation** n liquidazione f.

liquor ['likə] n bevanda alcoolica f.

liquorice ['likəris] n liquirizia f.

lisp [lisp] v essere o parlar bleso. n blesità f.

list¹ [list] n lista f, elenco m. v elencare, registrare.

list² [list] v (naut) sbandare. n sbandamento m.

listen ['lisn] v ascoltare; (heed) badare. **listener** n ascoltatore, -trice f.

listless ['listlis] adj languido, svogliato.

lit [lit] V **light**.

litany ['litəni] n litania f.

literal ['litərəl] adj letterale. **literally** adv alla lettera, letteralmente.

literary ['litərəri] adj (writing) letterario; (people) letterato.

literate ['litərət] adj che sa leggere e scrivere. **literacy** n il saper leggere e scrivere m.

literature ['litrətʃə] n letteratura f.

litigation [liti'geiʃən] n lite f, causa f. **litigate** v essere in causa.

litre ['li:tə] n litro m.

litter ['litə] n rifiuti m pl, immondizia f; (zool) figliata f; (bed, etc.) lettiga f. v sparpagliare, lasciare in disordine.

little ['litl] adj piccolo, piccino; (not much) un po' di, poco; (short) breve. nm, adv poco. **little by little** a poco a poco.

liturgy ['litədʒi] n liturgia f.

live¹ [liv] v vivere; (reside) abitare, stare. **live by** or **on** vivere di. **live down** far dimenticare. **live up to** mettere in pratica, giustificare.

live² [laiv] adj vivo; (broadcast) dal vivo, in ripresa diretta; (coal, etc.) ardente; (wire) sotto tensione.

livelihood ['laivlihud] n vita f.

lively ['laivli] adj vivace, animato. **liveliness** n vivacità f.

liven ['laivn] v **liven up** animare.

liver ['livə] n fegato m.

livestock ['laivstok] n bestiame m.

livid ['livid] adj livido.

living ['liviŋ] adj vivente, vivo. n vita f. **living room** stanza di soggiorno f.

lizard ['lizəd] n lucertola f.

load [loud] n carico m; (weight) peso m; (quantity carried) portata f; (elec) carica f. v caricare. **loaded** adj caricato, carico; (question) insidioso; (slang) ricco.

loaf¹ [louf] n pane m.

loaf² [louf] v oziare, girellare, stare con le mani in mano. **loafer** n bighellone, -a m, f; fannullone, -a m, f.

loan [loun] n prestito m. v prestare, dare in prestito.

loathe [louð] v aborrire, detestare. **loathing** n disgusto m. **loathsome** adj disgustoso.

lob [lob] (sport) n pallonetto m. v fare un pallonetto.

lobby ['lobi] n atrio m, anticamera f; (theatre) ridotto m. v influenzare con manovre di anticamera.

lobe [loub] n (anat) lobo m.

lobster ['lobstə] n aragosta f.

local ['loukəl] adj locale, del luogo. **locality** n località f. **localize** v circoscrivere, delimitare.

locate [lə'keit] v individuare; determinare la posizione di; situare. **location** n posizione f, sito m; (cinema) set m invar.

lock¹ [lok] n serratura f; (canal) conca f. **locksmith** n magnano m. **lock, stock, and barrel** barca e barattini. **under lock and key** sotto chiave. v serrare, chiudere a chiave; (mech) bloccare. **lock away** mettere al sicuro. **lock in** rinchiudere. **lock out** chiudere fuori; (workers) fare una serrata. **lock up** chiudere a chiave, mettere sotto chiave.

lock² [lok] n (of hair) ciocca f, ricciolo m.

locker ['lokə] n armadietto m.

locket ['lokit] n medaglione m.

locomotive [loukə'moutiv] n locomotiva f.

locust ['loukəst] n cavalletta f.

lodge [lodʒ] n capanna f; (porter's) portineria f. v alloggiare; (put in place, deposit) deporre, collocare; (report) presentare. **lodge a complaint** sporgere querela. **lodger** n pensionante m, f. **lodging** n alloggio m.

loft [loft] n solaio m, soffitta f. **lofty** adj alto; (style) nobile.

log [log] n ceppo m, tronco m. **logbook** n registro m; (naut) giornale di bordo m; (mot) libretto di circolazione m. v registrare.

logarithm ['logariðm] n logaritmo m.

loggerheads ['logəhedz] n **be at loggerheads** prendersi per i capelli, essere ai ferri corti.

logic ['lodʒik] n logica f. **logical** adj logico.

loin [loin] n (cookery) lombata f. **gird up one's loins** apprestarsi.

loiter ['loitə] v bighellonare, passare oziando.

lollipop ['lolipop] n lecca lecca m invar.

London ['lʌndən] n Londra f.

lonely ['lounli] adj solitario, solo. **loneliness** n solitudine f.

long¹ [lon] adj lungo. adv a lungo. **as long as** finquanto. **long-distance** adj a lunga distanza; (phone) interurbano. **long-playing record** disco microsolco m. **long-range** adj (distance) a lunga portata; (time) a lunga scadenza. **long-sighted** adj presbite; (having foresight) previdente. **long-standing** adj di vecchia data. **long-wave** adj (radio) a onde lunghe. **long-winded** adj prolisso.

long² [lon] v bramare, aver gran desiderio (di). **longing** n brama f, desiderio ardente m.

longevity [lon'dʒevəti] n longevità f.

longitude ['londʒitjud] n longitudine f.

loo [lu] n (coll) gabinetto m.

look [luk] n sguardo m, occhiata f; (appearance) aspetto m; espressione f. v guardare; (appear, seem) sembrare, parere. **look after** (care for) occuparsi di, badare a. **look at** guardare, considerare. **look down on** guardare con disprezzo. **look for** cercare. **look forward to** aspettare con impazienza. **look out** guardar fuori, affacciarsi; (be on guard) stare attento. **look over** ripassare, riesaminare.

loom¹ [lum] v apparire (indistintamente), intravedere; (be imminent) incombere.

loom² [lum] n telaio m.

loop [lup] n cappio m, laccio m, anello m. v fare un cappio or laccio, allacciare.

loophole ['luphoul] n scappatoia f.

loose [lus] adj sciolto, libero; (tooth) caduco. **come** or **get loose** allentarsi. **let loose** liberare. **loose-fitting** adj ampio. **loose-leaf** adj a fogli staccati. **loosely** adv scioltamente; in senso lato. **loosen** v sciogliere, allentare.

loot [lut] n bottino m. v far man bassa, saccheggiare. **looting** n saccheggio m.

lop [lop] v potare. **lop off** mozzare.

lopsided [,lop'saidid] adj sbilenco, asimmetrico.

lord [lotd] n signore m; (English title) lord m invar. **lordship** n signoria f.

lorry ['lori] n autocarro m, camion m invar. **lorry-driver** n camionista m.

*lose [luz] v perdere, smarrire; (clock) ritardare. **lose interest** non interessarsi più. **lose one's temper** arrabbiarsi.

loss [los] n perdita f, danno m. **be at a loss** non sapere cosa fare, essere disorientato.

lost [lost] V **lose**. adj perso, smarrito. **lost cause** causa persa f. **lost property** oggetti smarriti m pl.

lot [lot] n (destiny) sorte f; (of land) lotto m; (method of decision) sorteggio m; (comm) partita f; (coll: large amount) grande quantità f; **a lot of** molto. **lots of** tanti. **the whole lot** tutto quanto. **what a lot of** quanto.

lotion ['louʃən] n lozione f.

lottery ['lotəri] n lotteria f.

lotus ['loutəs] n loto m.

loud [laud] adj forte, alto; (gaudy) vistoso. adv forte. **loud-mouthed** adj sguaiato. **loudspeaker** n altoparlante m. **loudness** n forza f, altezza di voce f.

lounge [laundʒ] n salotto m; sala di ritrovo f. v oziare, dondolarsi.

louse [laus] n, pl **lice** pidocchio m. **lousy** adj pidocchioso; (slang: bad) schifoso.

love [lʌv] n amore m; (tennis) zero m. **fall in love (with)** innamorarsi (di). **love affair** relazione amorosa f. **make love (to)** fare all'amore (con). **with love** (in letter) affettuosamente. v amare, voler bene a. **lovable** adj amabile, simpatico. **lovely** adj bello, grazioso, incantevole. **lover** n amante m, f; (enthusiast) appassionato, -a m, f. **loving** adj affettuoso.

low [lou] adj basso; (coll) depresso; volgare. adv basso, in basso. **lowbrow** adj incolto, popolare. **low-lying** adj situato in pianura. **low-necked** adj scollato. **lowly** adj umile, dimesso.

lower ['louə] adj più basso, inferiore. v abbassare, ridurre; (flag) ammainare; degradare.

loyal ['loiəl] adj fedele, devoto, leale. **loyalty** n fedeltà f, devozione f, lealtà f.

lozenge ['lozindʒ] n pastiglia f, pasticca f.

lubricate ['luːbrikeit] v lubrificare. **lubricant** nm, adj lubrificante. **lubrication** n lubrificazione f.

lucid ['luːsid] adj (easily understood) chiaro; (clear) limpido; (bright) lucido.

luck [lʌk] n fortuna f; (chance) sorte f. **bad luck** sfortuna f. **be in/out of luck** essere fortunato/sfortunato. **good luck** buona fortuna f. **lucky** adj fortunato.

lucrative ['luːkrətiv] adj lucroso, redditizio.

ludicrous ['luːdikrəs] adj ridicolo, irrisorio.

lug [lʌg] v tirare, trascinare.

luggage ['lʌgidʒ] n bagaglio m. **hand luggage** bagaglio a mano m. **left luggage** deposito bagagli m. **luggage rack** n (rail) rete portabagagli f.

lukewarm ['luːkwoːm] adj tiepido.

lull [lʌl] n momento di calma m; (truce) tregua f. v (put to sleep) far addormentare; calmare.

lumbago [lʌm'beigou] n lombaggine f.

lumber[1] ['lʌmbə] n legname m; (useless articles) cianfrusaglie f pl. v (encumber) ingombrare, accatastare. **lumberjack** n boscaiolo m.

lumber[2] ['lʌmbə] v (move clumsily) muoversi pesantemente or goffamente.

luminous ['luːminəs] adj luminoso.

lump [lʌmp] n massa f; (swelling) gonfiore m. **lump sum** somma globale f. **lump together** mettere insieme. **lumpy** adj grumoso.

lunacy ['luːnəsi] n pazzia f.

lunar ['luːnə] adj lunare.

lunatic ['luːnətik] n, adj pazzo, -a, matto, -a. **lunatic asylum** manicomio m.

lunch [lʌntʃ] n colazione f, pranzo m. v far colazione, pranzare.

lung [lʌŋ] n polmone m.

lunge [lʌndʒ] v scagliarsi. n rapido movimento in avanti m.

lurch[1] [ləːtʃ] v barcollare, sbandare. n barcollamento m, sbandamento m.

lurch[2] [ləːtʃ] n **leave in the lurch** piantare in asso.

lure [luə] n (bait) esca f; (fascination) fascino m. v adescare, attirare, affascinare.

lurid ['luərid] adj raccapricciante.

lurk [ləːk] v (be in hiding) nascondersi; (lie in wait) stare in agguato.

luscious ['lʌʃəs] adj succulento.

lush [lʌʃ] adj lussureggiante.

lust [lʌst] n brama f; (sexual) libidine f; concupiscenza f. v **lust after** aver brama or sete di.

lustre ['lʌstə] n splendore m.

lute [luːt] n liuto m.

Luxembourg ['lʌksəm,bəːg] n Lussemburgo m.

luxury ['lʌkʃəri] n lusso m. **luxuriant** adj lussureggiante, rigoglioso. **luxurious** adj lussuoso, di lusso.

lynch [lintʃ] v linciare.

lynx [links] n lince f.

lyre [laiə] n lira f.

lyrical ['lirikəl] adj lirico.

lyrics ['liriks] pl n parole (di una canzone) f pl.

M

mac [mak] n (coll) impermeabile m.

macabre [mə'kaːbr] adj macabro.

macaroni [makə'rouni] n maccheroni m pl.

mace[1] [meis] n (club) mazza f.

mace[2] [meis] n (spice) macis f invar.

machine [mə'ʃiːn] n macchina f. **machinegun** n mitragliatrice f. **machine tool** macchina utensile f. v lavorare a macchina. **machinery** n macchinario m; (system) organizzazione f. **machinist** n macchinista m, f.

mackerel ['makrəl] n sgombro m.

mackintosh ['makin,toʃ] n impermeabile m.

mad [mad] adj matto, pazzo; furioso. **drive mad** far impazzire. **go mad** impazzire. **madden** v far impazzire. **madness** n pazzia f.

madam ['madəm] n signora f.

made [meid] V **make**.

magazine [magə'ziːn] n (publication) rivista f, periodico m; (phot) magazzino m; (rifle) caricatore m.

maggot ['magət] n larva f.

magic ['madʒik] adj magico. n magia f, incanto m. **magician** n mago m, stregone m; (conjurer) illusionista m.

magistrate ['madʒistreit] n magistrato m, pretore m. **magistrature** n magistratura f, pretura f.

magnanimous [mag'nanimǝs] adj magnanimo. **magnanimity** n magnanimità f.

magnate ['magneit] n magnate m.

magnet ['magnǝt] n magnete m, calamita f. **magnetic** adj magnetico. **magnetism** n magnetismo m. **magnetize** v magnetizzare.

magnificent [mag'nifisnt] adj magnifico, splendido. **magnificence** n magnificenza f.

magnify ['magnifai] v magnificare, ingrandire. **magnifying glass** lente d'ingrandimento f. **magnification** n ingrandimento m.

magnitude ['magnitjud] n grandezza f.

magnolia [mag'noulia] n magnolia f.

magpie ['magpai] n gazza f.

mahogany [mǝ'hogǝni] n mogano m.

maid [meid] n domestica f, donna di servizio f. **old maid** vecchia zitella f.

maiden ['meidǝn] n fanciulla f. adj primo; (journey) inaugurale. **maiden lady** signorina f. **maiden name** nome da ragazza m.

mail¹ [meil] n posta f. **mail order** vendita per catalogo f. v imbucare, mandare per posta.

mail² [meil] n (armour) maglia di ferro f. **mailed fist** pugno di ferro m.

maim [meim] v mutilare, storpiare.

main [mein] adj principale, essenziale. **mainland** n terra ferma f. **mainspring** n (of watch) molla principale f; (impelling cause) movente principale f. **mainstay** n (chief support) sostegno m, braccio destro m. **mainstream** n tendenza dominante f. n (gas, water, etc.) conduttura principale f. **in the main** nel complesso, in genere. **mainly** adv soprattutto; in genere.

maintain [mein'tein] v mantenere; (support) sostenere; (assert) affermare. **maintenance** n mantenimento m; (machinery, etc.) manutenzione f; (alimony) alimenti m pl.

maisonette [meizǝ'net] n casetta f.

maize [meiz] n mais m invar, granturco m invar.

majesty ['madʒǝsti] n maestà f. **majestic** adj maestoso.

major ['meidʒǝ] nm, adj maggiore. **majority** n maggioranza f; (age) maggiore età f.

*make [meik] v fare; produrre. **make**

believe dare da intendere, far finta di. **make-believe** n finzione f, illusione f. **make do** arrangiarsi. **make out** preparare; decifrare; (understand) capire. **make up** costituire, costruire; inventare; compensare; (cosmetics) truccare. **make-up** n trucco m, truccatura f; composizione f; costituzione f. **maker** n creatore, -trice m, f; fabbricante m, f.

makeshift ['meikʃift] adj di fortuna, improvvisato. n espediente m.

maladjusted [malǝ'dʒʌstid] adj disadattato.

malaise [ma'leiz] n malessere m.

malaria [mǝ'leǝriǝ] n malaria f.

male [meil] n maschio m. adj maschio, maschile.

malevolent [mǝ'levǝlǝnt] adj malevolo. **malevolence** n malevolenza f.

malfunction [mal'fʌŋkʃǝn] n funzionamento difettoso m.

malice ['malis] n malizia f, malignità f. **with malice aforethought** con premeditazione maliziosa. **malicious** adj malizioso, maligno.

malignant [mǝ'lignǝnt] adj maligno. **malignancy** n malignità f.

malinger [mǝ'lingǝ] v darsi malato, scansar fatiche. **malingerer** n scansafatiche, f invar.

mallet ['malit] n maglio m, martello (di legno) m. **malleable** adj malleabile.

malnutrition [malnju'triʃǝn] n malnutrizione f.

malt [moilt] n malto m.

Malta ['moiltǝ] n Malta f. **Maltese** n(m+f), adj maltese.

maltreat [mal'trit] v maltrattare. **maltreatment** n maltrattamento m.

mammal ['mamǝl] n mammifero m.

mammoth ['mamǝθ] n mammut m. adj enorme, mastodontico.

man [man] n, pl men uomo (pl uomini) m. v equipaggiare, presidiare. **manly** adj virile.

manage ['manidʒ] v dirigere, amministrare; (cope) farcela. **manage to** riuscire a, fare in modo da. **manage without** fare a meno di. **manageable** adj (people) trattabile, docile; (things) maneggevole. **management** n amministrazione f, direzione f. **manager** n direttore m. **manageress** n direttrice f. **managing director** consigliere delegato m.

mandarin ['mandərin] *n* mandarino *m*.

mandate ['mandeit] *n* mandato *m*. **mandatory** *adj* mandatario.

mandolin ['mandəlin] *n* mandolino *m*.

mane [mein] *n* criniera *f*.

mange [meindʒ] *n* rogna *f*. **mangy** *adj* rognoso.

mangle¹ ['maŋgl] *v* (*disfigure*) deformare, mutilare.

mangle² ['maŋgl] *n* (*wringer*) mangano *m*. *v* manganare.

manhandle [man'handl] *v* manovrare a mano; (*treat harshly*) malmenare.

manhole ['manhoul] *n* botola *f*. **manhole cover** tombino *m*.

mania ['meiniə] *n* mania *f*. **maniac** *n* maniaco, -a *m, f*. **maniacal** *adj* maniaco.

manicure ['manikjuə] *n* manicure *f invar*.

manifest ['manifest] *adj* evidente, palese. *v* manifestare, dimostrare. *n* (*comm*) manifesto (di bordo) *m*, nota di carico *f*.

manifesto [mani'festou] *n* manifesto *m*, proclama *m*.

manifold ['manifould] *adj* molteplice, vario. *n* (*tech*) collettore *m*.

manipulate [mə'nipjuleit] *v* maneggiare. **manipulation** *n* maneggio *m*. **manipulative** *adj* manipolatore.

mankind [man'kaind] *n* umanità *f*, genere umano *m*.

man-made [man'meid] *adj* artificiale, sintetico.

manner ['manə] *n* modo *m*, maniera *f*; stile *m*; sorta *f*, specie *f*. **manners** *pl n* maniere *f pl*, educazione *f sing*. **mannerism** *n* affettazione *f*, manierismo *m*.

manoeuvre [mə'nuːvə] *n* manovra *f*. *v* manovrare, maneggiare.

manor ['manə] *n* castello *m*, maniero *m*.

manpower ['man,pauə] *n* manodopera *f*; forze di lavoro *f pl*; capacità lavorativa *f*.

mansion ['manʃən] *n* palazzo *m*, casa signorile *f*.

mantelpiece ['mantlpiːs] *n* mensola (del caminetto) *f*.

manual ['manjuəl] *nm, adj* manuale. **manually** *adv* a mano.

manufacture [manju'faktʃə] *n* manifattura *f*, fabbricazione *f*, confezione *f*. *v* fabbricare. **manufacturer** *n* fabbricante *m*.

manure [mə'njuə] *n* concime *f*, fertilizzante *m*.

manuscript ['manjuskript] *nm, adj* manoscritto.

many ['meni] *adj, pron* molti, -e. **as many** altrettanti, -e. **how many** quanti, -e. **so many** tanti, -e. **too many** troppi, -e.

map [map] *n* mappa *f*, carta geografica *f*; (*of town*) pianta *f*. **off the map** remoto. *v* **map out** tracciare.

maple ['meipl] *n* acero *m*.

mar [maː] *v* guastare, rovinare.

marathon ['marəθən] *n* maratona *f*.

marble ['maːbl] *n* marmo *m*; (*glass ball*) bilia *f*. *adj* di marmo, marmoreo.

march [maːtʃ] *n* marcia *f*. *v* marciare. **march-past** *n* sfilata *f*.

March [maːtʃ] *n* marzo *m*.

marchioness [maːʃə'nes] *n* marchesa *f*.

mare [meə] *n* cavalla *f*.

margarine [maːdʒə'riːn] *n* margarina *f*.

margin ['maːdʒin] *n* margine *m*. **marginal** *adj* marginale.

marguerite [maːgə'riːt] *n* margherita *f*.

marigold ['marigould] *n* calendola *f*.

marijuana [mari'waːnə] *n* marijuana *f invar*, canapa indiana *f*.

marina [mə'riːnə] *n* porticciuolo *m*.

marinade [mari'neid] *n* marinata *f*. *v* marinare.

marine [mə'riːn] *adj* marino, marittimo. *n* (*fleet*) marina *f*; (*soldier*) soldato di marina *m*.

marital ['maritl] *adj* coniugale.

maritime ['maritaim] *adj* marittimo.

marjoram ['maːdʒərəm] *n* maggiorana *f*.

mark¹ [maːk] *n* segno *m*; (*brand*) marchio *m*; (*rating*) voto *m*; (*trace*) traccia *f*. **marksman** *n* tiratore scelto *m*. *v* segnare; notare; osservare; (*correct, grade*) dare i voti a. **mark off** delimitare. **mark out** tracciare. **marking** *n* marchio *m*. **markings** *pl n* segni caratteristici *m pl*.

mark² [maːk] *n* (*money*) marco *m*.

market ['maːkit] *n* mercato *m*. **market garden** orto *m*. **market research** ricerca di mercato *f*. *v* mettere in vendita. **marketing** *n* marketing *m invar*.

marmalade ['maːməleid] *n* marmellata *f*.

maroon¹ [mə'ruːm] *nm, adj* (*colour*) marrone rossastro.

maroon² [mə'ruːm] *v* abbandonare.

marquee [maː'kiː] *n* grande tenda *f*; padiglione *m*.

marquess ['maːkwis] *n* marchese *m*.

marriage ['maridʒ] *n* matrimonio *m*. **marriage licence** dispensa di matrimonio *f*.

marrow ['marou] *n* zucca *f*.

marry ['mari] *v* sposare. **married** *adj* sposato. **get married** sposarsi.

Mars [maːz] *n* Marte *m*. **Martian** *n*, *adj* marziano, -a.

marsh [maʃ] *n* palude *f*. **marshy** *adj* paludoso.

marshal ['maːʃəl] *v* disporre; (*mil*) schierare. *n* maresciallo *m*.

martial ['maːʃəl] *adj* marziale.

martin ['maːtin] *n* balestruccio *m*.

martyr ['maːtə] *n* martire *m, f. v* martirizzare. **martyrdom** *n* martirio *m*.

marvel ['maːvəl] *n* meraviglia *f. v* meravigliarsi. **marvel at** stupirsi di, ammirare.

marvellous ['maːvələs] *adj* meraviglioso.

marzipan [maːziˈpan] *n* marzapane *m*.

mascara [maˈskaːrə] *n* mascara *m invar*.

mascot ['maskət] *n* portafortuna *m invar*, mascotte *f*.

masculine ['maskjulin] *adj* maschile, virile. **masculinity** *n* mascolinità *f*, virilità *f*.

mash [maʃ] *v* ridurre in polpa, schiacciare; (*cookery*) fare un purè di. *n* (*cookery*) passata *f*, purè *m*.

mask [maːsk] *n* maschera *f. v* mascherare; (*hide*) nascondere.

masochist ['masəkist] *n* masochista *m, f. adj* masochistico. **masochism** *n* masochismo *m*.

mason ['meisn] *n* muratore *m*; (*freemason*) massone *m*. **masonic** *adj* massonico. **masonry** *n* muratura *f*.

masquerade [maskəˈreid] *n* mascherata *f. v* **masquerade as** mascherarsi da, farsi passare per.

mass¹ [mas] *n* massa *f*; (*bulk*) mole *f*; (*great number*) gran numero *m*; (*large amount*) grande quantità *f*. **masses** *pl n* (*coll*) mucchio *m sing*. **mass meeting** adunata popolare *f*. **mass-produced** *adj* prodotto in serie. **mass-production** *n* produzione in serie *or* massa *f*.

mass² [mas] *n* (*rel*) messa *f*.

massacre ['masəkə] *n* massacro *m*, strage *f. v* massacrare, far strage di.

massage ['masaːʒ] *n* massaggio *m. v* massaggiare. **masseur** *n* massaggiatore *m*. **masseuse** *n* massaggiatrice *f*.

massive ['masiv] *adj* massiccio, solido.

mast [maːst] *n* albero *m*.

mastectomy [maˈstektəmi] *n* mastectomia *f*.

master ['maːstə] *n* padrone *m*, signore *m*; (*of ship*) capitano *m*; (*school*) professore *m*. **masterpiece** *n* capolavoro *m. v* dominare, impadronirsi di; (*learn*) conoscere a perfezione. **masterly** *adj* magistrale.

masturbate ['mastəbeit] *v* masturbarsi. **masturbation** *n* masturbazione *f*.

mat [mat] *n* (*covering*) tappeto *m*; (*for floor*) stuoia *f*; (*at door*) zerbino *m*; (*on table*) sottopiatto *m*.

match¹ [matʃ] *n* (*light*) fiammifero *m*. **matchbox** *n* scatola da fiammiferi *f*.

match² [matʃ] *v* (*clothes, colours, etc.*) andare bene insieme; corrispondere; (*oppose*) opporre; (*equal*) uguagliare. *n* (*equal*) uguale *m, f*, pari *m, f*; (*contest, partner*) partita *f*. **matchmaker** *n* sensale di matrimoni. **meet one's match** trovare un degno avversario.

mate [meit] *n* compagno, -a *m, f*; (*help*) aiuto *m*, assistente *m, f*; (*naut*) secondo *m*.

material [məˈtiəriəl] *n* (*substance*) sostanza *f*, materia *f*; materiale *m*; (*fabric*) stoffa *f. adj* materiale, essenziale. **materialize** *v* realizzarsi, prender corpo.

maternal [məˈtəːnl] *adj* materno. **maternity** *n* maternità *f*.

mathematics [maθəˈmatiks] *n* matematica *f*. **mathematical** *adj* matematico. **mathematician** *n* matematico, -a *m, f*.

matinee ['matinei] *n* rappresentazione diurna *f*.

matins ['matinz] *n* mattutino *m*.

matriarch ['meitriaːk] *n* matrona *f*. **matriarchal** *adj* matriarcale.

matrimony ['matriməni] *n* matrimonio *m*. **matrimonial** *adj* matrimoniale.

matrix ['meitriks] *n* matrice *f*.

matron ['meitrən] *n* (*hospital*) capoinfermiera *f*; (*institution*) direttrice *f*.

matt [mat] *adj* matto, opaco.

matter ['matə] *v* importare. *n* materia *f*; (*thing, affair*) cosa *f*, affare *m*; (*of book, etc.*) argomento *m*, questione *f*. **as a matter of fact** in realtà, fatto sta che. **matter-of-fact** *adj* pratico. **what's the matter?** cosa c'è?

mattress ['matris] *n* materasso *m*.

mature [məˈtjuə] *v* maturare; (*become due*) scadere. **maturity** *n* maturità *f*.

maudlin ['moːdlin] *adj* lamentevole, querulo.

maul [mɔːl] v dilaniare.
mausoleum [ˌmɔːsɔ'liːm] n mausoleo m.
mauve [mouv] adj (color) malva invar.
maxim ['maksim] n massima f.
maximum ['maksiməm] nm, adj massimo.
***may** [mei] v potere. **maybe** può darsi, forse.
May [mei] n maggio m.
mayonnaise [ˌmeiɔ'neiz] n maionese f.
mayor [mɛə] n sindaco m.
maze [meiz] n labirinto m.
me [miː] pron mi; (after prep) me. **it's me** sono io.
meadow ['medou] n prato m.
meagre ['miːgə] adj scarso.
meal¹ [miːl] n (food) pasto m.
meal² [miːl] n (grain) farina f.
***mean¹** [miːn] v significare, voler dire; intendere; destinare.
mean² [miːn] adj gretto; (miserly) avaro; (shabby) meschino; (low) basso. **meanness** n grettezza f; avarizia f.
mean³ [miːn] n (average) media f. adj medio.
meander [mi'andə] v divagare.
meaning ['miːniŋ] n significato m, senso m. adj significativo.
means [miːnz] n mezzi m pl. **by means of** per mezzo di. **by no means** niente affatto. **by some means or other** in qualche modo.
meant [ment] V **mean¹**.
meanwhile ['miːnwail] adv also **in the meantime** nel frattempo, intanto.
measles ['miːzlz] n morbillo m. **German measles** n rosolia f, rubeola f. **measly** adj (wretched) miserabile.
measure ['meʒə] n misura f; (action) provvedimento m. **made to measure** fatto su misura. v misurare; (estimate) valutare. **measurement** n misura f. **measurements** pl n dimensioni f pl.
meat [miːt] n carne f. **meaty** adj sostanzioso.
mechanic [mi'kanik] n meccanico m. **mechanical** adj meccanico. **mechanism** n meccanismo m. **mechanized** adj meccanizzato.
medal ['medl] n medaglia f.
meddle ['medl] v immischiarsi, intromettersi. **meddler** n ficcanaso m invar.
media ['miːdiə] pl n mezzi di comunicazione m pl.
median ['miːdiən] adj mediano. n mediana f.

mediate ['miːdieit] v fare da mediatore or intermediario. **mediation** n mediazione f. **mediator** n mediatore, -trice m, f.
medical ['medikəl] adj medico. n (examination) esame medico m. **medication** n medicazione f. **medicinal** adj medicinale.
medicine n (science) medicina f; (substance) medicinale m, farmaco m.
medieval [medi'iːvəl] adj medievale.
mediocre [miːdi'oukə] adj mediocre. **mediocrity** n mediocrità f.
meditate ['mediteit] v meditare. **meditation** n meditazione f.
Mediterranean [ˌmeditə'reiniən] n Mediterraneo m. adj mediterraneo.
medium ['miːdiəm] n (spiritualist) medium m, f invar; (biology) brodo (di coltura) m; (agency) mezzo m. **happy medium** giusto mezzo m. adj medio.
medley ['medli] n miscuglio m, pasticcio m.
meek [miːk] adj mansueto, mite. **meekness** n mansuetudine f.
***meet** [miːt] v incontrare; (by arrangement) trovare; (gather) riunirsi. **meeting** n incontro m, riunione f.
megaphone ['megəfoun] n megafono m.
melancholy ['melənkəli] n malinconia f. adj also **melancholic** malinconico.
mellow ['melou] adj maturo; (wine) amabile; (soft) morbido. v maturare; (person) intenerirsi.
melodrama ['melədramə] n melodramma m. **melodramatic** adj melodrammatico.
melody ['melədi] n melodia f. **melodious** adj melodioso.
melon ['melən] n melone m.
melt [melt] v fondere, sciogliere; (feeling) intenerire. **melt down** fondere. **melting point** punto di fusione m. **melting pot** crogiuolo m.
member ['membə] n membro m; (of society, club, etc.) socio, -a m, f; (of parliament) deputato, -a m, f. **membership** n (number) numero dei soci m; (condition) l'essere socio m.
membrane ['membrein] n membrana f.
memento [mə'mentou] n ricordo m.
memo ['memou] n appunto m.
memoirs ['memwaːz] pl n memorie f pl.
memorandum [memə'randəm] n appunto m, promemoria m invar; (document) memorandum m invar.

memorial [mi'motriəl] *n* monumento *m*. *adj* commemorativo.

memory ['meməri] *n (faculty)* memoria *f*; *(recollection)* ricordo *m*. **memorable** *adj* memorabile. **memorize** *v* imparare a memoria.

men [men] *V* **man**.

menace ['menis] *n* minaccia *f*. *v* minacciare. **menacing** *adj* minaccioso.

menagerie [mi'nadʒəri] *n* serraglio *m*.

mend [mend] *v* riparare, aggiustare; *(get better)* migliorare. **mend one's ways** ravvedersi. *n* **be on the mend** stare rimettendosi. **mending** *n* rammendo *m*.

menial ['miniəl] *adj* servile, umile.

meningitis [menin'dʒaitis] *n* meningite *f*.

menopause ['menəpoːz] *n* menopausa *f*.

menstrual ['menstruəl] *adj* mestruale. **menstruate** *v* mestruare. **menstruation** *n* mestruazione *f*.

mental ['mentl] *adj* mentale; *(home, hospital)* psichiatrico. **mentality** *n* mentalità *f*.

menthol ['menθɒl] *n* mentolo *m*.

mention ['menʃən] *v* accennare a, parlare di, citare. **don't mention it!** prego! il **mention** *n* menzione *f*, cenno *m*; citazione *f*.

menu ['menjuː] *n* menu *m invar*, lista dei cibi *f*.

mercantile ['məːkəntail] *adj* mercantile.

mercenary ['məːsinəri] *nm*, *adj* mercenario.

merchandise ['məːtʃəndaiz] *n* merce *f*.

merchant ['məːtʃənt] *n* commerciante *m*, *f*. **merchant navy** marina mercantile *f*.

mercury ['məːkjuri] *n* mercurio *m*.

mercy ['məːsi] *n* pietà *f*, carità *f*. **at the mercy of** alla mercè di. **merciful** *adj* pietoso, caritatevole.

mere [miə] *adj* puro, mero.

merge [məːdʒ] *v* fondere, amalgamare. **merger** *n* fusione *f*.

meridian [mə'ridiən] *n* meridiano *m*.

meringue [mə'raŋ] *n* meringa *f*.

merit ['merit] *n* merito *m*, valore *m*. *v* meritare.

mermaid ['məːmeid] *n* sirena *f*.

merry ['meri] *adj* allegro; *(coll)* brillo. **merry-go-round** *n* carosello *m*. **merry-making** *n* festa *f*.

mesh [meʃ] *n* maglia *f*; *(net)* rete *f*. **in mesh** ingranato.

mesmerize ['mezməraiz] *v* ipnotizzare; affascinare.

mess [mes] *n* confusione *f*, pasticcio *m*; *(eating place)* mensa *f*. **be in a mess** *(of things)* essere in disordine; *(of people)* trovarsi nei guai. **make a mess of** rovinare. *v* **mess about** perdersi in cose inutili; *(inconvenience)* disturbare. **mess up** rovinare. **messy** *adj* confuso, disordinato; *(dirty)* sporco.

message ['mesidʒ] *n* messaggio *m*. **messenger** *n* messaggero *m*; *(errand boy)* fattorino *m*.

met [met] *V* **meet**.

metabolism [mi'tabəlizm] *n* metabolismo *m*. **metabolic** *adj* metabolico.

metal ['metl] *n* metallo *m*. **metallic** *adj* metallico. **metallurgy** *n* metallurgia *f*.

metamorphosis [metə'mɔːfəsis] *n* metamorfosi *f invar*.

metaphor ['metəfə] *n* metafora *f*. **metaphoric(al)** *adj* metaforico.

metaphysics [metə'fiziks] *n* metafisica *f*. **metaphysical** *adj* metafisico.

meteor ['miːtiə] *n* meteora *f*. **meteoric** *adj* meteorico; rapidissimo.

meteorology [miːtiə'rolədʒi] *n* meteorologia *f*. **meteorological** *adj* meteorologico. **meteorologist** *n* meteorologo, -a *m*, *f*.

meter ['miːtə] *n* contatore *m*; *(parking)* parchimetro *m*. *v* misurare.

methane ['miːθein] *n* metano *m*.

method ['meθəd] *n* metodo *m*, modo *m*. **methodical** *adj* metodico, sistematico.

methylated spirits ['meθileitid] *n* alcool denaturato *m*.

meticulous [mi'tikjuləs] *adj* meticoloso.

metre ['miːtə] *n* metro *m*. **metric** *adj* metrico.

metronome ['metrənoum] *n* metronomo *m*.

metropolis [mə'trɒpəlis] *n* metropoli *f*. **metropolitan** *adj* metropolitano.

mettle ['metl] *n* **put someone on his mettle** mettere qualcuno alla prova.

mews [mjuːz] *n* vicolo *m*.

miaow [miːˈau] *v* miagolare.

mice [mais] *V* **mouse**.

microbe ['maikroub] *n* microbo *m*.

microfilm ['maikrəfilm] *n* microfilm *m invar*.

microphone ['maikrəfoun] *n* microfono *m*.

microscope ['maikrəskoup] *n* microscopio *m*. **microscopic** *adj* microscopico. **microscopy** *n* microscopia *f*.

mid [mid] *adj* **in mid** ... a metà ... , in mezzo a ... , in pieno .... **midday** *n* mezzogiorno *m*. **midnight** *n* mezzanotte *f*. **mid-ocean** *n* alto mare *m*. **midsummer** *n* mezza estate *f*. **midway** *adv* a metà strada.

middle [midl] *n* mezzo *m*, centro *m*. *adj* medio. **middle-aged** *adj* di mezza età. **Middle Ages** Medio Evo *m sing*. **middle-class** *adj* borghese. **middle man** *n* intermediario *m*.

midge [midʒ] *n* zanzara *f*.

midget [midʒit] *n* nano *m*.

midst [midst] *n* mezzo *m*, centro *m*. **in the midst of** nel mezzo di, in mezzo a, fra.

midwife [midwaif] *n* levatrice *f*. **midwifery** *n* ostetricia *f*.

might[1] [mait] *V* **may**.

might[2] [mait] *n* (*power*) forza *f*, potenza *f*. **mighty** [maiti] *adj* forte, potente. *adv* (*coll*) estremamente.

migraine [miːgrein] *n* emicrania *f*.

migrate [maigreit] *v* migrare. **migrant** *n*, *adj* migratore, -trice. **migration** *n* migrazione *f*. **migratory** *adj* migratorio.

Milan [miˈlan] *n* Milano *f*. **Milanese** *n*(*m*+*f*), *adj* milanese.

mild [maild] *adj* mite. **mildness** *n* mitezza *f*.

mildew [mildjuː] *n* muffa *f*. **mildewy** *adj* ammuffito.

mile [mail] *n* miglio *m* (*pl* -a *f*). **mileage** *n* distanza percorsa in miglia *f*, chilometraggio *m*. **mileometer** *n* contachilometri *m invar*.

militant [militənt] *n*(*m*+*f*), *adj* militante, attivista.

military [militəri] *adj* militare. **militarism** *n* militarismo *m*. **militate** *v* militare. **militia** *n* milizia *f*.

milk [milk] *n* latte *m*. **milkman** *n* lattaio *m*. *v* mungere; (*exploit*) sfruttare.

mill [mil] *n* (*flour*) mulino *m*; (*textiles*) stabilimento *m*; (*tech*) fresa *f*; (*coffee*) macinino *m*. **millstone** *n* macina *f*; (*burden*) macigno *m*. *v* macinare; (*metal*) laminare; (*crowd*) circolare. **milling** *n* (*corn*) macinatura *f*; (*metal*) laminazione *f*; (*tech*) fresatura *f*; (*coins*) zigrinatura *f*.

millennium [miˈleniəm] *n* millennio *m*.

millet [milit] *n* miglio *m*.

milligram [miligram] *n* milligrammo *m*.

millilitre [miliˌliːtə] *n* millilitro *m*.

millimetre [miliˌmiːtə] *n* millimetro *m*.

milliner [milinə] *n* modista *f*.

million [miljən] *n* milione *m*. **millionaire** *n* milionario, -a *m*, *f*. **millionth** *nm*, *adj* milionesimo.

mime [maim] *n* (*art*) mimica *f*; (*artist*) mimo, -a *m*, *f*. *v* mimare.

mimic [mimik] *v* contraffare; (*ape*) scimmiottare. *n* imitatore, -trice *m*, *f*; contraffattore, -trice *m*, *f*. **mimicry** *n* mimica *f*; (*zool*) mimetismo *m*.

mimosa [miˈmouzə] *n* mimosa *f*.

minaret [minəˈret] *n* minareto *m*.

mince [mins] *v* tritare, tagliuzzare. **not mince one's words** parlare apertamente. *n* (*meat*) carne tritata *f*. **make mincemeat of** (*coll*) demolire. **mincer** *n* tritatutto *m invar*.

mind [maind] *n* mente *f*, intelletto *m*, spirito *m*; (*reason*) ragione *f*; (*opinion*) parere *m*. **bear in mind** tenere a mente. **make up one's mind** decidersi. **peace of mind** serenità *f*. **piece of one's mind** (*reprimand*) rimprovero *m*. **speak one's mind** parlar chiaro. **state of mind** stato d'animo *m*. *v* badare a, occuparsi di; (*watch out*) far attenzione. **do you mind if ... ?** ti dispiace se ... ? **never mind!** non importa! **mindful** *adj* attento. **mindless** *adj* (*heedless*) sbadato; (*senseless*) insensato.

mine[1] [main] *pron* il mio, la mia; (*pl*) i miei, le mie.

mine[2] [main] *n* miniera *f*; (*explosive*) mina *f*. *v* (*dig*) scavare; (*extract*) estrarre; (*mil*) minare. **mine-detector** *n* rilevatore di mine *m*. **minefield** *n* campo minato *m*. **minesweeper** *n* dragamine *m invar*. **miner** *n* minatore *m*.

mineral [minərəl] *nm*, *adj* minerale.

mingle [mingl] *v* mescolare, mischiarsi.

miniature [minitʃə] *n* miniatura *f*. *adj* in miniatura.

minim [minim] *n* (*music*) minima *f*.

minimum [miniməm] *n* minimo *m*. **minimal** *adj* minimo. **minimize** *v* minimizzare.

mining [mainin] *n* estrazione *f*, scavo *m*; (*mil*) posa di mine *f*. *adj* minerario.

minister [ministə] *n* (*pol*) ministro, -a *m*, *f*; (*rel*) sacerdote *m*; (*diplomat*) incaricato, -a *m*, *f*. *v* **minister to** soccorrere. **minister to the needs of** provvedere ai bisogni di. **ministerial** *adj* ministeriale. **ministry** *n* ministero *m*; (*clergy*) clero *m*.

mink [mink] *n* visone *m*.

minor ['mainə] *adj* minore, più piccolo, meno importante. *n* minorenne *m, f.*

minority *n* minoranza *f;* (*age*) minorità *f,* età minore *f.*

minstrel ['minstrəl] *n* menestrello *m,* cantante *m.*

mint[1] [mint] *n* (*bot*) menta *f.*

mint[2] [mint] *n* zecca *f.* **be in mint condition** essere nuovo di zecca. **have a mint of money** avere un mucchio di soldi. *v* coniare.

minuet [minju'et] *n* minuetto *m.*

minus ['mainəs] *prep* meno.

minute[1] ['minit] *n* minuto *m;* momento *m.* **minutes** *pl n* (*of meeting*) verbale *m* sing. *v* (*record*) prendere nota; (*enter in minutes*) mettere agli atti.

minute[2] [mai'njut] *adj* minuto; (*detailed*) minuzioso.

minx [minks] *n* (*coll*) civetta *f.*

miracle ['mirəkl] *n* miracolo *m.* **miraculous** *adj* miracoloso.

mirage ['mira3] *n* miraggio *m.*

mirror ['mirə] *n* specchio *m. v* riflettere, rispecchiare.

mirth [mə:θ] *n* ilarità *f,* allegria *f.*

misadventure [misəd'ventʃə] *n* infortunio *m,* disavventura *f.*

misanthropist [miz'anθrəpist] *n* misantropo, -a *m, f.* **misanthropic** *adj* misantropico. **misanthropy** *n* misantropia *f.*

misapprehension [misapri'henʃən] *n* equivoco *m,* malinteso *m.* **misapprehend** *v* fraintendere.

misbehave [misbi'heiv] *v* comportarsi male. **misbehaviour** *n* cattiva condotta *f.*

miscalculate [mis'kalkjuleit] *v* calcolar male. **miscalculation** *n* calcolo errato *m.*

miscarriage [mis'karid3] *n* (*med*) aborto *m.* **miscarry** *v* abortire.

miscellaneous [misə'leiniəs] *adj* miscellaneo.

mischance [mis'tʃans] *n* sventura *f.*

mischief ['mistʃif] *n* (*harm*) danno *m;* (*of child, etc.*) fastidi *m pl;* (*teasing*) malizia *f.* **be up to mischief** combinare un brutto tiro. **make mischief** creare discordia. **mischief-maker** *n* attaccabrighe *m invar.* **mischievous** *adj* malizioso; (*of child*) birichino.

misconception [miskən'sepʃən] *n* malinteso *m.*

misconduct [mis'kondʌkt] *n* cattiva condotta *f.*

misdeed [mis'di:d] *n* misfatto *m,* delitto *m.*

misdemeanour [misdi'mi:nə] *n* (*misbehaviour*) cattiva condotta *f;* (*crime*) delitto *m.*

miser ['maizə] *n* avaro, -a *m, f.* **miserly** *adj* avaro.

miserable ['mizərəbl] *adj* (*unhappy*) infelice, triste; (*pitiful*) pietoso; (*painful*) penoso; depresso.

misery ['mizəri] *n* miseria *f;* sofferenze *f pl.*

misfire [mis'faiə] *v* fare cilecca *or* fiasco.

misfit [misfit] *n* (*person*) spostato, -a *m, f.*

misfortune [mis'fɔːtʃən] *n* sfortuna *f,* disgrazia *f.*

misgiving [mis'givin] *n* dubbio *m.*

misguided [mis'gaidid] *adj* fuori posto, sviato.

mishap ['mishap] *n* disgrazia *f,* contrattempo *m.*

misjudge [mis'dʒʌdʒ] *v* farsi un'idea sbagliata di, giudicare male.

*mislay [mis'lei] *v* smarrire.

*mislead [mis'li:d] *v* ingannare. **misleading** *adj* ingannevole.

misnomer [mis'noumə] *n* termine improprio *m.*

misplace [mis'pleis] *v* mettere fuori posto.

misprint ['misprint] *n* errore tipografico *m.*

miss[1] [mis] *n* colpo mancato *m. v* mancare (a); (*not catch*) perdere; (*skip*) saltare; (*not find*) non trovare; (*regret absence of*) sentire la mancanza di. **miss out** omettere. **be missing** mancare.

miss[2] [mis] *n* signorina *f.*

missile ['misail] *n* missile *m.*

mission ['miʃən] *n* missione *f.* **missionary** *n, adj* missionario, -a.

mist [mist] *n* caligine *f,* foschia *f. v* offuscare. **misty** *adj* caliginoso, fosco.

*mistake [mi'steik] *n* errore *m,* sbaglio *m.* **by mistake** per errore. **make a mistake** sbagliare, fare un errore. *v* (*confuse*) confondere, scambiare. **mistaken** *adj* sbagliato, falso.

mistletoe ['misltou] *n* vischio *m.*

mistress ['mistris] *n* padrona *f;* (*school*) insegnante *f;* (*lover*) amante *f.*

mistrust [mis'trʌst] *v* diffidare di, non aver fiducia in. *n* diffidenza *f,* sfiducia *f.* **mistrustful** *adj* diffidente.

*misunderstand [misʌndə'stand] *v*

fraintendere, capir male. **misunderstanding** n malinteso m, equivoco m. **misunderstood** adj incompreso.

misuse [mis'juzs; v mis'juzz] n abuso m; uso incorretto m. v abusare; (ill-treat) maltrattare; (use badly) adoperare male.

mitigate ['mitigeit] v mitigare; (law) attenuare. **mitigation** n (law) attenuante f.

mitre ['maitə] n (rel) mitra f; (carpentry) ugnatura f. v ugnare.

mitten ['mitn] n mezzo quanto m, muffola f.

mix [miks] v mescolare, mischiare; combinare. **mix up** confondere. **mix-up** n confusione f. **mixed** adj misto. **mixer** n (tech) agitatore m. **be a good mixer** essere socievole. **mixture** n miscela f; miscuglio m.

moan [moun] n (complaint) lamento m; (groan) gemito m. v lamentarsi; gemere.

moat [mout] n fosso m, fossato m.

mob [mob] n folla f, marmaglia f, plebaglia f. v molestare, assalire.

mobile ['moubail] adj mobile. **mobility** n mobilità f. **mobilization** n mobilitazione f. **mobilize** v mobilitare.

moccasin ['mokəsin] n mocassino m.

mock [mok] v deridere, canzonare. adj finto, falso. **mockery** n presa in giro f, derisione f. **mocking** adj beffardo. **mocking-bird** n mimo m.

mode [moud] n modo m, maniera f.

model ['modl] n modello m; (art) modello, -a m, f; (fashion) indossatore, -trice m, f. adj modello, esemplare. v modellare, fare l'indossatore.

moderate ['modərət; v 'modəreit] adj misurato, moderato; (price) modico. v moderare. **moderation** n misura f, moderazione f. **in moderation** moderatamente.

modern ['modən] adj moderno. **modernization** n rimodernamento m. **modernize** v rimodernare.

modest ['modist] adj modesto. **modesty** n modestia f.

modify ['modifai] v modificare. **modification** n modifica f.

modulate ['modjuleit] v modulare. **modulation** n modulazione f.

module ['modjuːl] n modulo m.

mohair ['mouheə] n mohair m invar.

moist [moist] adj umido. **moisten** v inumidire; (surface) umettare. **moisture** n umidità f. **moisturize** v umidificare.

molar ['moulə] nm, adj molare.

molasses [mə'lasiz] n melassa f.

mold (US) V **mould.**

mole[1] [moul] n (on skin) neo m.

mole[2] [moul] n (zool) talpa f.

molecule ['molikjuːl] n molecola f. **molecular** adj molecolare.

molest [mə'lest] v molestare.

mollify ['molifai] v placare.

mollusc ['moləsk] n mollusco m.

mollycoddle ['molikodl] v coccolare.

molt (US) V **moult.**

molten ['moultən] adj fuso.

moment ['moumənt] n momento m, istante m. **at the moment** attualmente. **momentary** adj momentaneo. **momentous** adj grave, importante. **momentum** n impeto m, slancio m.

Monaco ['monəkou] n Monaco f.

monarch ['monək] n monarca m, f. **monarchist** n, adj monarchico, -a. **monarchy** n monarchia f.

monastery ['monəstəri] n monastero m. **monastic** adj monastico.

Monday ['mʌndi] n lunedì m.

money ['mʌni] n denaro m, soldi m pl. **money-box** n salvadanaio m. **money-lender** n usuraio m. **money order** vaglia m invar. **monetary** adj monetario.

mongol ['mongəl] adj mongolo; (med) mongoloide. **Mongolia** n Mongolia f.

mongrel ['mʌngrəl] nm, adj bastardo.

monitor ['monitə] n (radio) ascoltatore m; (tech) monitor m invar. v (radio) ascoltare; controllare. **monitoring service** servizio d'ascolto m.

monk [mʌnk] n monaco m, frate m.

monkey ['mʌnki] n scimmia f.

monogamy [mə'nogami] n monogamia f. **monogamous** adj monogamo.

monogram ['monəgram] n monogramma m.

monograph ['monəgraːf] n monografia f.

monolithic [,monə'liθik] adj monolitico.

monologue ['monəlog] n monologo (pl -ghi) m.

monopolize [mə'nopəlaiz] v monopolizzare. **monopoly** n monopolio m.

monosyllable ['monəsiləbl] n monosillabo m. **monosyllabic** adj monosillabico, monosillabo.

monotony [mə'notəni] n monotonia f. **monotone** n tono uniforme m. **monotonous** adj monotono.

monsoon [mon'sum] *n* monsone *m*.

monster ['monstə] *n* mostro *m*. **monstrosity** *n* mostruosità *f*. **monstrous** *adj* mostruoso.

month [mʌnθ] *n* mese *m*.

monthly ['mʌnθli] *n* (*periodical*) rivista mensile *f*. *adj* mensile. *adv* al mese, mensilmente.

monument ['monjument] *n* monumento *m*. **monumental** *adj* monumentale.

mood[1] [mud] *n* umore *m*, stato d'animo *m*. **feel in the mood to** sentirsi disposto a, aver voglia di. **moodiness** *n* malumore *m*; volubilità *f*. **moody** *adj* capriccioso; (*sulky*) di malumore.

mood[2] [mud] *n* (*gramm*) modo *m*.

moon [mum] *n* luna *f*. **moonlight** *n* chiaro di luna *m*.

moor[1] [muə] *n* brughiera *f*. **moorhen** *n* gallinella d'acqua *f*.

moor[2] [muə] *v* ormeggiare, ancorare. **mooring** *n* ormeggio *m*, ancoraggio *m*.

moose [mus] *n* alce *m*.

moot [mut] *adj* discutibile.

mop [mop] *n* scopa di cotone per lavaggio *f*; (*of hair*) zazzera *f*. *v* **mop one's brow** asciugarsi la fronte. **mop up** asciugare; rastrellare.

mope [moup] *v* fare il broncio, immusonirsi.

moped ['mouped] *n* ciclomotore *m*.

moral ['morəl] *nf*, *adj* morale. **morals** *pl n* morale *f sing*. **morale** *n* morale *m*. **moralist** *n* moralista *m*, *f*. **morality** *n* moralità *f*, buon costume *m*.

morbid ['mɔːbid] *adj* morboso, patologico.

more [mɔi] *adv* più, di più; (*again*) ancora. *nm*, *adj* più. **more and more** sempre più. **more than** più di *or* che.

moreover [mɔːˈrouvə] *adv* inoltre, per di più.

morgue [mɔig] *n* obitorio *m*.

morning ['mɔɪniŋ] *n* mattina *m*, mattinata *f*. **this morning** stamane. **tomorrow morning** domattina. *adj* del mattino, mattutino.

moron ['mɔɪron] *n* deficiente *m*, *f*. **moronic** *adj* deficiente, scemo.

morose [mə'rous] *adj* scontroso.

morphine ['mɔːfiːn] *n* morfina *f*.

Morse code [mɔis] *n* alfabeto Morse *m*.

morsel ['mɔisəl] *n* boccone *m*.

mortal ['mɔitl] *n*(*m*+*f*), *adj* mortale. **mortality** *n* mortalità *f*.

mortar ['mɔitə] *n* (*vessel, arms*) mortaio *m*; (*building*) malta *f*.

mortgage ['mɔigidʒ] *n* ipoteca *f*. *v* ipotecare, impegnare.

mortify ['mɔitifai] *v* mortificare. **mortification** *n* mortificazione *f*.

mortuary ['mɔitjuəri] *n* camera ardente *or* mortuaria *f*.

mosaic [mə'zeiik] *n* mosaico *m*.

Moscow ['moskou] *n* Mosca *f*.

mosque [mosk] *n* moschea *f*.

mosquito [mə'skiitou] *n* zanzara *f*.

moss [mos] *n* muschio (*m*), musco *m*. **mossy** *adj* muscoso.

most [moust] *adj* (*majority*) la maggior parte di, il più di; (*greatest*) il più grande, il maggiore. *n* il più *m*; (*greatest part*) la maggior parte *f*; (*majority*) la maggioranza *f*, i più *m pl*. *adv* il più; (*very*) molto, assai.

motel [mou'tel] *n* motel *m invar*, autostello *m*.

moth [moθ] *n* lepidottero *m*. **clothes moth** tarma *f*. **mothball** *n* pallina antitarmica *f*.

mother ['mʌðə] *n* madre *f*; (*coll*) mamma *f*. *v* aver cura di come una madre. **mother-in-law** *n* suocera *f*. **mother-of-pearl** *n* madreperla *f*. **mother tongue** madrelingua *f*. **motherly** *adj* materno.

motion ['mouʃən] *n* moto *m*, movimento *m*; (*proposal*) mozione *f*; (*law*) istanza *f*. **go through the motions** far finta. **set in motion** avviare, mettere in moto. *v* accennare a, far cenno a. **motionless** *adj* immobile.

motivate ['moutiveit] *v* motivare, spingere. **motivation** *n* spinta *f*, stimolo *m*.

motive ['moutiv] *n* motivo *m*, ragione *f*.

motor ['moutə] *nm*, *adj* motore. **motorboat** *n* motoscafo *m*. **motor car** automobile *f*, macchina *f*. **motorcycle** *n* motocicletta *f*. **motorcyclist** *n* motociclista *m*, *f*. **motorway** *n* autostrada *f*. *v* andare in macchina. **motoring** *n* automobilismo *m*. **motorist** *n* automobilista *m*, *f*. **motorize** *v* motorizzare.

mottled ['motld] *adj* chiazzato.

motto ['motou] *n* motto *m*, massima *f*.

mould[1] *or US* **mold** [mould] *n* stampo *m*, forma *f*. *v* formare, foggiare, modellare.

mould[2] *or US* **mold** [mould] *n* muffa *f*. **mouldy** *adj* ammuffito. **go mouldy** ammuffire.

moult or US **molt** [moult] v mutare, fare la muta.

mound [maund] n tumulo m; (heap) mucchio m.

mount[1] [maunt] v montare. n (setting) montatura f.

mount[2] [maunt] n monte m.

mountain ['mauntən] n montagna f. **mountaineer** n alpinista m, f. **mountaineering** n alpinismo m. **mountainous** adj montuoso, alpestre.

mourn [mɔːn] v rimpiangere, essere in lutto per. **mourning** n lutto m, cordoglio m. **mournful** adj triste; lugubre.

mouse [maus] n, pl **mice** topo m. **mousetrap** n trappola (per topi) f. **mousy** adj (colour) grigio topo; timido.

mousse [muːs] n mousse f, spuma f.

moustache [məˈstɑːʃ] n baffi m pl.

mouth [mauθ] n bocca f; (of river) foce f. **mouth organ** armonica f. **mouthpiece** n (spokesman) portavoce m invar; (of pipe) bocchino m. v declamare. **mouthful** n boccone m.

move [muːv] v muovere, spostare; (house) traslocare; (arouse feelings) commuovere; (propose) proporre. **move away** or **off** allontanare; (depart) partire. **move back** indietreggiare; (return) tornare. **move forward** avanzare. **move in** occupare. **move out** uscire, sgombrare. **move up** (raise) salire; (get closer) avvicinarsi. n mossa f, passo m; (house) trasloco m. **movable** adj movibile. **movement** n movimento m; (sign) cenno m; (tech) meccanismo m. **moving** adj commovente; (in motion) in moto.

movie ['muːvi] n (US) film m invar.

***mow** [mou] v falciare.

mown [moun] V **mow**.

Mr ['mistə] n signor m.

Mrs ['misiz] n signora f.

much [mʌtʃ] pron, adj molto. adv molto, assai. **as much as** (tanto) quanto. **how much** quanto. **so much** tanto. **too much** troppo.

muck [mʌk] n letame m; (coll: filth) porcheria f. v **muck about** (coll) bighellonare. **muck up** (coll) rovinare.

mucus ['mjuːkəs] n muco m. **mucous membrane** mucosa f.

mud [mʌd] n fango m. **mudguard** n parafango m. **mudslinger** n maldicente m, f. **muddy** adj fangoso, inzaccherato.

muddle ['mʌdl] n confusione f, pasticcio m. v **muddle through** arrabattarsi. **muddle up** confondere. **muddler** n confusionario, -a m, f.

muff [mʌf] n manicotto m. v mancare, sbagliare.

muffle ['mʌfl] v smorzare, attutire.

mug [mʌg] n (cup) tazza f; (coll: face) muso m, ceffo m; (slang: fool) gonzo m. v assalire.

mulberry ['mʌlbəri] n (fruit) mora di gelso f; (tree) gelso m.

mule[1] [mjuːl] n (zool) mulo m. **mulish** adj (stubborn) duro.

mule[2] [mjuːl] n (slipper) ciabatta f, pianela f.

mullet ['mʌlit] n (grey) muggine m; (red, triglia f.

multicoloured [ˌmʌltiˈkʌləd] adj multicolore.

multimillionaire [ˌmʌltimiljəˈneə] n multimilionario, -a m, f.

multiple ['mʌltipl] adj multiplo, molteplice. n multiplo m.

multiply ['mʌltiplai] v moltiplicare. **multiplication** n moltiplicazione f. **multiplicity** n varietà f.

multiracial [ˌmʌltiˈreiʃəl] adj multirazziale.

multitude ['mʌltitjuːd] n moltitudine f, massa f.

mum [mʌm] adj **keep mum** star zitto.

mumble ['mʌmbl] v borbottare.

mummy[1] ['mʌmi] n (corpse) mummia f. **mummify** v mummificare.

mummy[2] ['mʌmi] n (coll: mother) mamma f, mammina f.

mumps [mʌmps] n orecchioni m pl.

munch [mʌntʃ] v sgranocchiare.

mundane [mʌnˈdein] adj mondano.

municipal [mjuːˈnisipəl] adj municipale. **municipality** n comune m.

mural ['mjuərəl] n pittura murale f.

murder ['mɔːdə] n assassinio m. v assassinare, ammazzare; (coll) massacrare. **murderer** n assassino m. **murderess** n assassina f. **murderous** adj micidiale.

murmur ['mɔːmə] n mormorio m. v mormorare.

muscle ['mʌsl] n muscolo m.

muse[1] [mjuːz] n musa f.

muse[2] [mjuːz] v meditare, riflettere.

museum [mjuːˈziəm] n museo m.

mushroom ['mʌʃrum] n fungo m. v (gather) raccogliere funghi; (spread) dilagare, svilupparsi rapidamente.

music ['mjuːzik] n musica f. **musician** n musicista m, f.

musical ['mjuːzikl] adj musicale; (gifted) dotato per la musica. n musical m invar.

musk [mʌsk] n (zool) muschio m.

musket ['mʌskit] n moschetto m.

Muslim ['mʌzlim] n, adj musulmano, -a.

muslin ['mʌzlin] n mussola f.

mussel ['mʌsl] n mitilo m, cozza f.

must [mʌst] v dovere. n (coll) cosa essenziale f.

must² [mʌst] n (wine) mosto m.

mustard ['mʌstəd] n senape f, mostarda f.

muster ['mʌstə] v radunare. **muster up courage** farsi coraggio. n **pass muster** essere accettabile.

mute [mjuːt] adj muto, taciturno. n muto, -a m, f; (music) sordina f.

mutilate ['mjuːtileit] v mutilare, mozzare. **mutilation** n mutilazione f.

mutiny ['mjuːtini] n ammutinamento m, ribellione f. v ammutinarsi, ribellarsi. **mutinous** adj ammutinato, ribelle.

mutter ['mʌtə] v brontolare, borbottare.

mutton ['mʌtn] n carne ovina f, castrato m. **dead as mutton** morto stecchito.

mutual ['mjuːtʃuəl] adj mutuo, reciproco; comune.

muzzle ['mʌzl] n (gun) imboccatura f; (animal) muso m; (device) museruola f. v mettere la museruola a; (silence) far tacere.

my [mai] adj (il) mio, (la) mia; (pl) (i) miei, (le) mie.

myself [mai'self] pron io stesso; (after prep) me stesso; (reflexive) mi.

myopia [mai'oupiə] n miopia f. **myopic** adj miope.

mystery ['mistəri] n mistero m, segreto m. **mysterious** adj misterioso, strano.

mystic ['mistik] n mistico, -a m, f. **mystical** adj mistico, misterioso. **mysticism** n misticismo m, mistica f.

mystify ['mistifai] v mistificare, disorientare.

mystique [mi'stiːk] n mistica f.

myth [miθ] n mito m. **mythical** adj mitico. **mythological** adj mitologico. **mythology** n mitologia f.

N

nag¹ [nag] v rimbrottare, brontolare. **nagging** adj bisbetico.

nag² [nag] n ronzino m.

nail [neil] n (anat) unghia f; (metal) chiodo m. **nail-brush** n spazzolino per le unghie m. **nail-file** n lima per le unghie f. **nail polish** smalto per le unghie m. **nail-scissors** pl n forbici per le unghie f pl.

naive [nai'iːv] adj ingenuo. **naivety** n ingenuità f.

naked ['neikid] adj nudo, scoperto. **strip naked** spogliare. **nakedness** n nudità f.

name [neim] v chiamare. n nome m. **go by the name of** chiamarsi. **my name is ...** mi chiamo .... **namesake** n omonimo m. **nameless** adj anonimo. **namely** adv cioè.

nanny ['nani] n bambinaia f.

nap¹ [nap] n (doze) pisolino m. v fare or schiacciare un pisolino.

nap² [nap] n (cloth) pelo m.

nape [neip] n nuca f.

napkin ['napkin] n tovagliolo m.

nappy ['napi] n pannolino m.

narcotic [naːˈkotik] n, adj narcotico.

narrate [nəˈreit] v narrare, raccontare. **narration** n racconto m. **narrative** n narrativa f. **narrator** n narratore, -trice m, f.

narrow ['narou] adj stretto; limitato; (person, mind, etc.) ristretto. **narrow-gauge** adj (railway) a scartamento ridotto. **narrow-minded** adj gretto, di mente ristretta. v restringere, limitare. **narrowly** adv per un pelo, a stento.

nasal ['neizəl] adj nasale.

nasturtium [nəˈstəːtʃəm] n nasturzio m.

nasty ['naːsti] adj (filthy) disgustoso; (offensive) ripugnante; (unpleasant) cattivo, sgradevole. **nastiness** n cattiveria f.

nation ['neiʃən] n nazione f. **national** adj nazionale. **national insurance** assicurazione sociale f. **nationalism** n nazionalismo m. **nationalist** n(m+f), adj nazionalista. **nationality** n nazionalità f. **nationalization** n nazionalizzazione f. **nationalize** v nazionalizzare.

native ['neitiv] adj (original inhabitant) indigeno, -a; (of town, etc.) nativo, -a, oriundo, -a.

nativity [nəˈtivəti] n natività f.

natural ['natʃərəl] adj naturale; normale;

istintivo. **naturalization** n naturalizzazione f. **naturalize** v naturalizzare.

nature ['neitʃə] n natura f; (condition) indole f; disposizione f.

naught [nɔːt] n nulla m. **come to naught** ridurre a zero.

naughty ['nɔːti] adj cattivo; (mischievous) birichino; indecente, spinto.

nausea ['nɔːziə] n nausea f; fastidio m. **nauseous** adj nauseabondo, disgustoso.

nautical ['nɔːtikəl] adj nautico.

naval ['neivəl] adj navale, marittimo.

nave[1] [neiv] n (of church) navata f.

nave[2] [neiv] n (hub) mozzo m.

navel ['neivəl] n ombelico m.

navigate ['navigeit] v navigare, pilotare. **navigable** adj navigabile. **navigation** n navigazione f. **navigator** n navigatore m; (officer) ufficiale di rotta m.

navy ['neivi] n marina militare f. **navy blue** adj blu marino.

near [niə] adj vicino. prep vicino a, accanto a. adv vicino. v avvicinare. **near at hand** a portata di mano. **near-sighted** adj miope. **nearby** adj, adv, prep vicino (a). **nearly** adv quasi.

neat [niːt] adj (orderly) ordinato, accurato; elegante; (undiluted) liscio. **neatness** n ordine m; eleganza f.

nebulous ['nebjuləs] adj vago, nebuloso.

necessary ['nesisəri] adj necessario, indispensabile. **necessity** n necessità f, bisogno m.

neck [nek] n (anat) collo m; (of dress) scollatura f. **have a stiff neck** avere il torcicollo. **neck and neck** testa a testa. **necklace** n collana f. **necktie** n cravatta f.

nectar ['nektə] n nettare m. **nectarine** n pesca noce f.

née [nei] adj nata.

need [niːd] n bisogno m, necessità f; (poverty) miseria f. **if need be** caso mai, se c'è bisogno. v aver bisogno di; (require) richiedere. **needed** adj necessario. **needless** adj inutile, superfluo. **needy** adj indigente, bisognoso.

needle ['niːdl] n ago m; (knitting) ferro m; (gramophone) puntina f. **needlework** n (sewing) cucitura f; (embroidery) ricamo m. v (coll) punzecchiare.

negative ['negativ] adj negativo. n negativa f. **answer in the negative** rispondere di no.

neglect [ni'glekt] n negligenza f, trascuratezza f. v trascurare. **neglect to** mancare di. **negligent** adj negligente. **negligible** adj trascurabile.

negligée ['negliʒei] n negligé m invar, vestaglia f.

negotiate [ni'gouʃieit] v trattare, negoziare; (obstacle, etc.) superare. **negotiable** adj negoziabile. **negotiation** n trattativa f, negoziato m.

Negro ['niːgrou] nm, adj negro. **Negress** n negra f.

neigh [nei] v nitrire. n nitrito m.

neighbour ['neibə] n vicino, -a m, f. **next-door neighbour** vicino di casa m. **neighbourhood** n vicinanza f, paraggi m pl. **neighbouring** adj adiacente, vicino. **neighbourly** adj socievole, da buon vicino.

neither ['naiðə] adj nè l'uno nè l'altro. adv **neither ... nor ...** nè ... nè .... pron nessuno, nè l'uno nè l'altro.

neon ['niːon] n neon m.

nephew ['nefjuː] n nipote m.

nepotism ['nepotizəm] n nepotismo m.

nerve [nɔːv] n nervo m; coraggio m; (coll: cheek) sfacciataggine f, faccia tosta f. **get on the nerves of** dare sui nervi a. **nerve-racking** adj snervante. **nervous** adj nervoso; apprensivo. **get nervous** inquietarsi. **nervous breakdown** esaurimento nervoso m.

nest [nest] n nido m. **nest egg** gruzzolo m. v annidarsi.

nestle ['nesl] v annidarsi, accoccolarsi.

net[1] [net] n rete f. **network** n rete f. v (enclose) cintare con reti; (catch) prendere con reti; (ball) mandare in rete. **netting** n reticolato m.

net[2] [net] adj netto.

Netherlands ['neðələndz] pl n Paesi Bassi m pl.

nettle ['netl] n ortica f. **nettle-rash** n orticaria f. v irritare.

neurosis [nju'rousis] n nevrosi f. **neurotic** n, adj nevrotico, -a.

neuter ['njuːtə] adj neutro. v castrare.

neutral ['njuːtrəl] adj neutrale; (tech) neutro. n neutrale m, f. **neutrality** n neutralità f. **neutralize** v neutralizzare. **neutron** n neutrone m.

never ['nevə] adv (non ...) mai. **never-ending** adj interminabile.

nevertheless [nevəðə'les] adv, conj ciononostante, tuttavia.

new [njuː] *adj* nuovo. **new-born** *adj* neonato. **newcomer** *n* nuovo venuto, nuova venuta *m, f.*

news [njuːz] *n* novità *f pl*, notizie *f pl*, informazioni *f pl.* **news agency** agenzia d'informazioni *f.* **newsagent** *n* giornalaio *m.* **news bulletin** notiziario *m; (radio)* giornale radio *m.* **news item** notizia *f.* **newspaper** *n* giornale *m.* **newsprint** *n* carta da giornale *f.* **newsreel** *n* cinegiornale *m.*

newt [njuːt] *n* tritone *m.*

New Year *n* Anno nuovo *m.* **Happy New Year!** Buon Anno! **New Year's Day** il Capodanno *m.* **New Zealand** *n* Nuova Zelanda *f.* **New Zealander** neozelandese *m, f.*

next [nekst] *adj* prossimo; *(nearest)* più vicino; *(following)* successivo, seguente. *adv (after)* dopo, poi; *(later)* in seguito. **next-of-kin** *n* parente prossimo *m, f.*

nib [nib] *n* pennino *m.*

nibble ['nibl] *n (morsel)* bocconcino *m.* v rosicchiare.

nice [nais] *adj* bello; piacevole, simpatico; *(subtle)* sottile; delicato; *(refined)* elegante, fine. **nicely** *adv* proprio bene. **nicety** *n* esattezza *f.* **niceties** *pl n* finezze *f pl,* sfumature *f pl.*

niche [nitʃ] *n* nicchia *f.*

nick [nik] *v* intaccare; *(slang: steal)* arraffare; *(slang: catch)* acchiappare. *n* tacca *f.* **in the nick of time** all'ultimo momento.

nickel ['nikl] *n* nichel *m; (US: coin)* nichelino *m.*

nickname ['nikneim] *n* nomignolo *m,* soprannome *m. v* soprannominare.

nicotine ['nikətiːn] *n* nicotina *f.*

niece [niːs] *n* nipote *f.*

niggling ['nigliŋ] *adj* insignificante.

night [nait] *n* notte *f; (evening)* sera *f.* **have a good/bad night** dormir bene/male. **night-club** *n* night *m invar.* **nightdress** *n* camicia da notte *f.* **nightfall** *n* tramonto *m.* **nightmare** *n* incubo *m.* **nightmarish** *adj* opprimente, spaventoso. **stay the night** pernottare.

nightingale ['naitiŋgeil] *n* usignolo *m.*

nightly ['naitli] *adj* notturno; *(every night)* di tutte le sere. *adv* ogni notte *or* sera.

nil [nil] *n* nulla *m,* niente *m,* zero *m.*

nimble ['nimbl] *adj* agile, svelto. **nimbleness** *n* agilità *f.*

nine [nain] *nm, adj* nove. **ninepins** *n* birilli *m pl.* **ninth** *nm, adj* nono.

nineteen [nain'tiːn] *nm, adj* diciannove. **nineteenth** *nm, adj* diciannovesimo.

ninety ['nainti] *nm, adj* novanta. **ninetieth** *nm, adj* novantesimo.

nip¹ [nip] *v* pizzicare; *(bite)* morsicare. **nip in** intromettersi, entrare lestamente. **nip in the bud** stroncare sul nascere. **nip out** fare un salto. *n (frost)* gelo *m; (bite)* morso *m.* **nippy** *adj (speedy)* svelto; *(cold)* frizzante.

nip² [nip] *n (drop)* bicchierino *m,* sorso *m.*

nipple ['nipl] *n* capezzolo *m; (tech)* rubinetto *m.*

nit [nit] *n* lendine *m; (coll)* stupido, -a *m, f.*

nitrogen ['naitrədʒən] *n* azoto *m.*

no [nou] *adj* nessuno, neppure uno; *(forbidden)* vietato. *adv* no; *(with comparative)* non. *n* no *m invar.*

noble ['noubl] *n(m+f), adj* nobile. **nobility** *n* nobiltà *f.*

nobody ['noubodi] *pron* nessuno. *n* zero *m,* sconosciuto, -a *m, f.*

nocturnal [nok'təːnl] *adj* notturno.

nod [nod] *n* cenno col capo *m. v* fare un cenno col capo; *(doze)* sonnecchiare; *(assent)* annuire; *(greet)* salutare. **nodding acquaintance** conoscenza superficiale *f.*

noise [noiz] *n* rumore *m; (loud)* baccano *m.* **background noise** rumori di fondo *m pl.* **big noise** *(coll)* pezzo grosso *m.* **noiseless** *adj* silenzioso. **noisy** *adj* rumoroso, chiassoso.

nomad ['noumad] *n(m+f), adj* nomade.

nominal ['nominl] *adj* nominale; simbolico.

nominate ['nomineit] *v* nominare; *(propose)* proporre. **nomination** *n* nomina *f.*

nominative ['nominətiv] *nm, adj* nominativo.

nonchalant ['nonʃələnt] *adj* indifferente, noncurante. **nonchalance** *n* indifferenza *f,* noncuranza *f.*

nonconformist [nonkən'foːmist] *n(m+f), adj* dissidente, anti-conformista.

nondescript ['nondiskript] *adj* inclassificabile, qualunque.

none [nʌn] *pron* nessuno, nulla, niente. *adv* affatto, punto. **none other than** nientedimeno che.

nonentity [non'entəti] n nullità f, zero m.
nonetheless [ˌnʌnðə'les] adv ciononostante, tuttavia.
nonsense ['nonsəns] n nonsenso m, assurdo m; (coll) sciocchezze f pl. **nonsensical** adj assurdo, sciocco. **talk nonsense** dire sciocchezze.
non-stop [non'stop] adj continuo, ininterrotto.
noodles ['nuːdlz] pl n tagliatelle f pl, taglierini m pl.
nook [nuk] n cantuccio m, angolo m.
noon [nuːn] n mezzogiorno m.
no-one ['nəuwʌn] pron nessuno.
noose [nuːs] n nodo scorsoio m, laccio m.
nor [noː] conj nè, neppure, nemmeno.
norm [noːm] n norma f, modello m. **normal** adj normale, regolare. **normally** adv di solito.
north [noːθ] n nord m, settentrione m. adj also **northern** del nord, settentrionale. **northerly** adj di nordo; da nordo; a nordo. **north-east** n nordest m. **north-eastern** del nordest. **north-west** n nordovest m. **north-western** del nordovest.
Norway ['noːweɪ] n Norvegia f. **Norwegian** n(m+f), adj norvegese.
nose [nəuz] n naso m; (of animal, aeroplane, etc.) muso m. v fiutare. **nose around** esplorare. **nosy** adj (coll) curioso.
nostalgia [no'stældʒə] n nostalgia f, rimpianto m. **nostalgic** adj nostalgico.
nostril ['nostrəl] n narice f.
not [not] adv non. **not at all** niente affatto. **not even** neppure, neanche.
notable ['nəutəbl] adj notevole, degno di nota.
notary ['nəutəri] n notaio m.
notch [notʃ] n tacca f, intaglio m. v intaccare.
note [nəut] n nota f, appunto m, commento m; (money) biglietto m. **note-book** n taccuino m. **notepaper** n carta da lettere or scrivere. **noteworthy** adj degno di nota, notevole. **take note of** prendere atto di. **take notes** prendere appunti. **notation** n notazione f. v notare; osservare. **noted** adj noto, rinomato.
nothing ['nʌθiŋ] n niente m, zero m. adv per nulla, niente (affatto). **next to nothing** quasi nulla. **nothing but** null'altro che. **nothing less than** semplicemente.
notice ['nəutis] n avviso m, annuncio m;

(advance warning) preavviso m; (criticism) recensione f. **give notice** (dismiss) licenziare. **notice-board** n tabellone m. **take notice of** fare attenzione a. v notare, rilevare. **noticeable** adj apparente, percettibile.
notify ['nəutifaɪ] v notificare, avvertire. **notification** n notifica f.
notion ['nəuʃən] n nozione f, idea f.
notorious [nəu'toːriəs] adj notorio, famigerato. **notoriety** n notorietà f.
notwithstanding [notwið'stændiŋ] prep nonostante, malgrado. adv ciononostante, con tutto ciò.
nougat ['nuːgaː] n torrone m.
nought [noːt] n zero m.
noun [naun] n nome m, sostantivo m.
nourish ['nʌriʃ] v nutrire, alimentare. **nourishing** adj nutriente. **nourishment** n cibo m, alimento m.
novel[1] ['novəl] n romanzo m. **novelist** n romanziere, -a m, f.
novel[2] ['novəl] adj nuovo, originale; (unusual) insolito. **novelty** n novità f.
November [nə'vembə] n novembre m.
novice ['novis] n novizio, -a m, f.
now [nau] adv ora, adesso. **from now on** d'ora in poi. **just now** or ora. **nowadays** adv oggigiorno, al giorno d'oggi. **now and again** ogni tanto, di quando in quando. **until now** finora.
nowhere ['nəuweə] adv in nessun luogo.
noxious ['nokʃəs] adj nocivo, malefico.
nozzle ['nozl] n (spout) becco m; (tech) ugello m.
nuance ['njuːãs] n sfumatura f.
nuclear ['njuːkliə] adj nucleare.
nucleus ['njuːkliəs] n nucleo m.
nude ['njuːd] n, adj nudo, -a. **nudism** n nudismo m. **nudist** n nudista m, f. **nudity** n nudità f.
nudge [nʌdʒ] n colpetto m. v dare un colpetto a.
nugget ['nʌgit] n pepita f.
nuisance ['njuːsns] n fastidio m, seccatura f; (law) infrazione f. **make a nuisance of oneself** seccare tutti.
null [nʌl] adj nullo. **null and void** senza validità legale.
numb [nʌm] adj intorpidito; (stunned) intontito. v intorpidire, paralizzare. **numbness** n torpore m.
number ['nʌmbə] n numero m; (numeral) cifra f; quantità f. **number plate** targa f. v

numerare, contare. **numberless** adj innumerevole.

numeral ['njuːmərəl] n cifra f.

numerical [njuːˈmerikl] adj numerico.

numerous ['njuːmərəs] adj numeroso.

nun [nʌn] n monaca f, suora f. **become a nun** prendere il velo. **nunnery** n convento m.

nurse [nəːs] v curare, fare l'infermiere; (suckle) allattare; (hope, grievance, etc.) nutrire, covare. n infermiere, -a m, f; (children's) balia f, bambinaia f. **nursing** n professione d'infermiera f. **nursing home** casa di cura f, clinica f.

nursery ['nəːsəri] n (children's) camera dei bambini f; (plants, etc.) vivaio m, serra f. **day nursery** asilo infantile m. **nursery rhyme** filastrocca f. **nursery school** giardino d'infanzia m.

nurture ['nəːtʃə] v (feed) nutrire; (rear) allevare. n nutrimento m; allevamento m.

nut [nʌt] n noce f; (tech) dado m; (coll: head) zucca f. **be nuts** (coll) essere matto. **in a nutshell** in poche parole. **nutcrackers** pl n schiaccianoci m invar. **nutmeg** n noce moscata f. **nut-tree** n noce m.

nutrient ['njuːtriənt] adj nutriente. n nutrimento m.

nutrition [njuːˈtriʃən] n alimentazione f. **nutritious** adj nutriente.

nuzzle ['nʌzl] v accucciolarsi, rannicchiarsi.

nylon ['nailon] n nailon m.

nymph [nimf] n ninfa f. **nymphomaniac** n ninfomane f.

O

oak [ouk] n quercia f.

oar [oː] n remo m.

oasis [ouˈeisis] n, pl -ses oasi f invar.

oath [ouθ] n (promise) giuramento m; (profanity) bestemmia f.

oats [outs] pl n avena f sing. **oatmeal** n farina d'avena f.

obedient [əˈbiːdiənt] adj ubbidiente, obbediente. **obedience** n ubbidienza f, obbedienza f.

obese [əˈbiːs] adj obeso. **obesity** n obesità f.

obey [əˈbei] v ubbidire, obbedire.

obituary [əˈbitjuəri] n necrologia f.

object ['obʒikt; v əbˈʒekt] n oggetto m; (aim) scopo m. v obiettare, protestare. **objection** n obiezione f, protesta f. **have no objection to** aver nulla in contrario a. **objectionable** adj offensivo, sgradevole, riprensibile. **objective** nm, adj obiettivo.

oblige [əˈblaidʒ] v costringere, obbligare; fare un favore a. **be obliged to** (have to) dovere; (be grateful to) essere riconoscente a. **obligation** n (law) obbligazione f; (binding promise) obbligo (pl -ghi) m; (duty) dovere m. **obligatory** adj obbligatorio. **obliging** adj cortese, accomodante.

oblique [əˈbliːk] adj obliquo; indiretto.

obliterate [əˈblitəreit] v obliterare, cancellare; (destroy) distruggere. **obliteration** n distruzione f.

oblivion [əˈbliviən] n oblio m. **oblivious** adj dimentico (m pl -chi).

oblong ['oblon] adj bislungo.

obnoxious [əbˈnokʃəs] adj odioso, offensivo.

oboe ['oubou] n oboe m. **oboist** n oboista m, f.

obscene [əbˈsiːn] adj osceno. **obscenity** n oscenità f.

obscure [əbˈskjuə] adj (not clear) ambiguo, oscuro; (inconspicuous) vago. v offuscare, velare. **obscurity** n oscurità f.

observe [əbˈzəːv] v (see) osservare; notare, rilevare; (rel) praticare. **observance** n osservanza f. **observant** adj osservante. **observation** n osservazione f, attenzione f. **keep under observation** tenere in osservazione. **observatory** n osservatorio m. **observer** n osservatore, -trice m, f.

obsess [əbˈses] v ossessionare. **obsession** n ossessione f.

obsolescent [obsəˈlesnt] adj che sta cadendo in disuso.

obsolete ['obsəliːt] adj caduto in disuso; antiquato.

obstacle ['obstəkl] n ostacolo m.

obstetrics [obˈstetriks] n ostetricia f. **obstetrician** n ostetrico, -a m, f.

obstinate ['obstinət] adj ostinato. **obstinacy** n ostinatezza f.

obstreperous [əbˈstrepərəs] adj ribelle.

obstruct [əbˈstrakt] v impacciare, ostacolare. **obstruction** n impaccio m, ostacolo m.

obtain [əbˈtein] v ottenere, procurare. **obtainable** adj ottenibile, raggiungibile.

obtrusive [əb'truːsiv] *adj* importuno; invadente. **obtrusion** *n* invadenza *f*.

obtuse [əb'tjuːs] *adj* ottuso.

obverse ['ɒbvəːs] *n* faccia *f*, diritto *m*; (*counterpart*) inverso *m*.

obvious ['ɒbviəs] *adj* ovvio, evidente.

occasion [ə'keiʒən] *v* causare. *n* (*time*) occasione *f*, volta *f*; (*cause*) motivo *m*, ragione *f*. **rise to the occasion** mostrarsi all'altezza. **occasional** *adj* saltuario, sporadico. **occasionally** *adv* ogni tanto.

occult ['ɒkʌlt] *adj* occulto. *n* forze occulte *f pl*.

occupy ['ɒkjupai] *v* occupare. **occupant** *or* **occupier** *n* occupante *m, f*. **occupation** *n* occupazione *f*; (*trade*) mestiere *m*, professione *f*. **occupational** *adj* del lavoro, professionale.

occur [ə'kəː] *v* succedere, capitare; (*come to mind*) venire in mente. **occurrence** *n* avvenimento *m*, caso *m*.

ocean ['ouʃən] *n* oceano *m*.

ochre ['oukə] *n* ocra *f*. *adj* (*color*) ocra.

o'clock [ə'klɒk] *adv* **one o'clock** l'una. **two/three/etc. o'clock** le due/tre/etc.

octagon ['ɒktəgən] *n* ottagono *m*. **octagonal** *adj* ottagonale.

octane ['oktein] *n* ottano *m*.

octave ['ɒktiv] *n* ottava *f*.

October [ɒk'toubə] *n* ottobre *m*.

octopus ['ɒktəpəs] *n* polpo *m*.

oculist ['ɒkjulist] *n* oculista *m, f*.

odd [ɒd] *adj* (*not even*) dispari; (*not paired*) scompagnato; (*strange*) strano, bizzarro; (*casual*) casuale; (*approximately*) circa. **oddity** *n* stranezza *f*; (*person*) eccentrico, -a *m, f*. **oddments** *pl n* rimasugli *m pl*, scampoli *m pl*.

odds [ɒdz] *pl n* probabilità *f pl*, differenza *f sing*; (*betting*) posta *f sing*. **be at odds with** essere in disaccordo con. **lay odds** scommettere. **odds and ends** cosette varie *f pl*, rimasugli *m pl*.

ode [oud] *n* ode *f*.

odious ['oudiəs] *adj* odioso.

odour ['oudə] *n* odore *m*. **odourless** *adj* inodoro.

oesophagus [iː'sɒfəgəs] *n* esofago *m*.

of [ɒv] *prep* di.

off [ɒf] *adv* via, distante. *prep* lontano da, fuori (di). *adj* (*holiday*) libero; (*food*) marcio, non buono. **be off** (*cancelled*) non aver luogo.

offal ['ɒfəl] *n* frattaglie *f pl*.

offend [ə'fend] *v* offendere. **offence** *n* offesa *f*; (*law*) infrazione alla legge *f*. **take offence** offendersi. **offender** *n* colpevole *m, f*; trasgreditore, -trice *m, f*.

offensive [ə'fensiv] *adj* offensivo; (*disagreeable*) sgradevole; insolente. *n* offensiva *f*.

offer ['ɒfə] *v* offrire, presentare, dare. *n* offerta *f*, proposta *f*.

offhand [ɒf'hand] *adj* noncurante. *adv* all'improvviso.

office ['ɒfis] *n* (*place*) ufficio *m*; (*post, function*) carica *f*. **head office** *n* sede (centrale) *f*. **officer** *n* funzionario, -a *m, f*; (*mil, etc.*) ufficiale *m*.

official [ə'fiʃəl] *adj* ufficiale. *n* funzionario, -a *m, f*.

officious [ə'fiʃəs] *adj* inframmettente, invadente.

offing ['ɒfiŋ] *n* **in the offing** in vista.

off-load [ɒf'loud] *v* scaricare.

off-peak [ɒf'piːk] *adj* non di punta.

off-putting ['ɒf,putiŋ] *adj* sconcertante, che lascia perplesso.

off-season [ɒf'siːzn] *adj* fuori stagione.

offset [ɒf'set; *n* 'ɒfset] *v* compensare, controbilanciare. *n* (*print*) offset *m invar*.

offshoot [ɒf'ʃuːt] *n* ramo *m*.

offshore [ɒf'ʃɔː] *adv* al largo. *adj* di terra.

offside [ɒf'said] *adj, adv* fuori gioco.

offspring ['ɒfspriŋ] *n* prole *f*; frutto *m*.

offstage [ɒf'steidʒ] *adv, adj* fuori scena.

often ['ɒfn] *adv* spesso, sovente, molte volte. **how often** quante volte. **too often** troppe volte.

ogre ['ougə] *n* orco *m*.

oil [ɔil] *n* olio *m*; petrolio *m*; gasolio *m*. **oilfield** *n* giacimento petrolifero *m*. **oil-fired** *adj* a gasolio *or* nafta. **oil-painting** *n* pittura a olio *f*. **oilskin** *n* tela impermeabile *f*. **oil-well** *n* pozzo petrolifero *m*. *v* ungere, lubrificare. **oily** *adj* oleoso, untuoso.

ointment ['ɔintmənt] *n* unguento *m*.

old [ould] *adj* vecchio, antico (*m pl* -chi); (*not new*) usato. **old age** vecchiaia *f*. **old-fashioned** *adj* fuori moda. **old man** vecchio *m*. **old people** vecchi *m pl*. **old woman** vecchia *f*. **oldish** *adj* vecchiotto.

olive ['ɒliv] *n* oliva *f*. **olive green** *adj* verde oliva. **olive grove** oliveto *m*. **olive oil** olio d'oliva *m*. **olive-tree** *n* olivo *m*.

Olympic [ə'limpik] *adj* olimpico. **Olympic Games** olimpiadi *f pl*.

omelette ['omlit] n frittata f.

omen ['oumən] n presagio m, segno m.

ominous ['ominəs] adj sinistro, minaccioso.

omit [ou'mit] v omettere, tralasciare. **omission** n omissione f.

omnipotent [om'nipətənt] adj onnipotente. **omnipotence** n onnipotenza f.

on [on] prep su, sopra; a. adv su. adj (gas, elec, etc.) acceso; (tap) aperto.

once [wʌns] adv una volta. **all at once** ad un tratto. **at once** subito.

one [wʌn] n, adj uno, -a. pron uno; (impersonal) si. **oneself** pron sè (stesso); (reflexive) si. **one by one** a uno a uno. **one-sided** adj unilaterale; parziale; ineguale. **one-way street** senso unico m. **the one** quello, -a. **which one?** quale?

onion ['ʌnjən] n cipolla f.

onlooker ['onlukə] n spettatore, -trice m, f.

only ['ounli] adj solo, unico. conj ma. adv solo, soltanto. **only just** appena.

onset ['onset] n inizio m.

onshore ['onʃoɪ] adv a terra.

onslaught ['onslɔɪt] n attacco m, assalto m.

onus ['ounəs] n onere m, obbligo (pl -ghi) m.

onward ['onwəd] adj che progredisce or avanza. **onwards** adv (in) avanti.

onyx ['oniks] n onice m.

ooze [uɪz] v colare, trasudare.

opal ['oupəl] n opale m.

opaque [ə'paik] adj opaco (m pl -chi). **opacity** n opacità f.

open ['oupən] v aprire; iniziare; inaugurare. **open wide** spalancare. nm, adj aperto. **lay oneself open** to esporsi a. **open-handed** adj generoso. **open-hearted** adj sincero. **open-minded** adj spregiudicato, libero da preconcetti. **open-mouthed** adj, adv a bocca aperta.

opening ['oupəniŋ] adj introduttivo, inaugurale. n apertura f; inaugurazione f.

opera ['opərə] n opera f. **opera glasses** binocoli da teatro m pl. **opera house** teatro dell'opera m. **opera singer** cantante lirico, -a m, f. **operetta** n operetta f.

operate ['opəreit] v operare. **operation** n operazione f; (activity) attività f; (surgical) intervento (chirurgico) m. **come into operation** entrare in vigore. **operative** adj

operativo; attivo; (surgical) operatorio. **operator** n operatore, -trice m, f; (phone) telefonista m, f.

ophthalmic [of'θælmik] adj oftalmico.

opinion [ə'pinjən] n opinione f, parere m, giudizio m. **in the opinion of** secondo. **opinionated** adj dogmatico, intransigente.

opium ['oupiəm] n oppio m.

opponent [ə'pounənt] n avversario, -a m, f.

opportune [opə'tjuɪn] adj opportuno, giusto.

opportunity [opə'tjuɪnəti] n occasione f.

oppose [ə'pouz] v opporre, combattere; contrastare. **opposed** adj opposto, contrario. **opposition** n opposizione f.

opposite ['opəzit] nm, adj opposto, contrario. prep di fronte a, dirimpetto a.

oppress [ə'pres] v opprimere. **oppression** n oppressione f. **oppressive** adj oppressivo, opprimente. **oppressor** n oppressore m.

opt [opt] v optare. **opt out** decidere di non partecipare.

optical ['optikl] adj ottico. **optician** n ottico m. **optics** n ottica f.

optimism ['optimizəm] n ottimismo m. **optimist** n ottimista m, f. **optimistic** adj ottimistico.

optimum ['optiməm] n optimum m, meglio m. adj migliore.

option ['opʃən] n opzione f, scelta f. **optional** adj facoltativo.

opulent ['opjulənt] adj opulento. **opulence** n opulenza f.

or [oɪ] conj o, oppure. **either . . . or . . .** o . . . o . . . . **or else** altrimenti.

oracle ['orəkl] n oracolo m.

oral ['orəl] adj orale.

orange ['orindʒ] n (fruit) arancia f; (tree, colour) arancio m. adj (colour) arancio, arancione. **orange juice** succo d'arancio m; (drink) spremuta d'arancio f. **orange squash** aranciata f.

orator ['orətə] n oratore, -trice m, f. **oration** n orazione f.

orbit ['oɪbit] n orbita f.

orchard ['oɪtʃəd] n frutteto m.

orchestra ['oɪkəstrə] n orchestra f. **orchestral** adj orchestrale. **orchestrate** v orchestrare. **orchestration** n orchestrazione f.

orchid ['oɪkid] n orchidea f.

ordain [oɪ'dein] v ordinare.

ordeal [oɪ'diɪl] n dura prova f, travaglio m.

order ['ɔːdə] n ordine m; comando m; classe f, grado m; (*commission*) ordinazione f. in order that affinché, perché. in order to per, allo scopo di. out of order guasto. v ordinare. order about mandar qua e là.

orderly ['ɔːdəli] adj ordinato, regolare. n attendente m, inserviente m.

ordinal ['ɔːdinl] adj ordinale.

ordinary ['ɔːdənəri] nm, adj ordinario, solito, comune.

ore [ɔː] n minerale m.

oregano [ori'gɑːnou] n origano m.

organ ['ɔːgən] n organo m. organ-pipe n canna d'organo f. organic adj organico.
organist n organista m, f.

organism ['ɔːgənizəm] n organismo m.

organize ['ɔːgənaiz] v organizzare. organization n organizzazione f. organizer n organizzatore, -trice m, f.

orgasm ['ɔːgæzm] n orgasmo m.

orgy ['ɔːdʒi] n orgia f.

orient ['ɔːriənt] n oriente m. v orientare.
oriental adj orientale.

orientate ['ɔːriənteit] v orientare. orientation n orientamento m.

origin ['ɔridʒin] n origine f. originate v originare. originate from derivare or provenire da. originator n creatore, -trice m, f; originatore, -trice m, f.

original [ə'ridʒinl] adj originale; (*authentic, primitive*) originario. n originale m. originality n originalità f. originally adv in origine.

ornament ['ɔːnəmənt] n ornamento m; (*music*) abbellimento m; (*object, fitting*) suppellittile f. v abbellire. ornamentation n abbellimento m.

ornate [ɔː'neit] adj ornato.

ornithology [ɔːni'θɔlədʒi] n ornitologia f.
ornithologist n ornitologo, -a m, f.

orphan ['ɔːfən] n orfano, -a m, f. v rendere orfano. be orphaned rimanere orfano. orphanage n orfanotrofio m.

orthodox ['ɔːθədɔks] adj ortodosso.
orthodoxy n ortodossia f.

orthopaedic [ɔːθə'piːdik] adj ortopedico.
orthopaedics n ortopedia f. orthopaedist n ortopedico, -a m, f.

oscillate ['ɔsileit] v (far) oscillare; (*fluctuate*) vacillare. oscillation n oscillazione f.

ostensible [ɔ'stensəbl] adj ostensibile.

ostentatious [ɔsten'teiʃəs] adj ostentato, ostentoso.

osteopath ['ɔstiəpæθ] n osteologo, -a m, f.

ostracize ['ɔstrəsaiz] v osteggiare, mettere al bando.

ostrich ['ɔstritʃ] n struzzo m.

other ['ʌðə] adj altro, diverso. on the other hand d'altra parte. other people gli altri. pron altro. each other l'un l'altro.
otherwise ['ʌðəwaiz] adv altrimenti.

otter ['ɔtə] n lontra f.

*ought ['ɔːt] v dovere.

our [auə] adj (il) nostro, (la) nostra; (*pl*) (i) nostri, (le) nostre.

ours [auəz] pron il nostro, la nostra; (*pl*) i nostri, le nostre.

ourselves [auə'selvz] pron noi (stessi); (*reflexive*) ci.

oust [aust] v espellere, soppiantare.

out [aut] adj (*not alight*) spetto. adv via, fuori; (*to the end*) alla fine. feel out of it sentirsi a disagio. out of (*without*) senza. out of action fuori servizio, guasto. out of date antiquato; (*ticket, etc.*) scaduto. out of doors all'aperto. out of place inopportuno. out of pocket in perdita. out of print esaurito, fuori stampa. out of time stonato. out of work disoccupato.

outboard ['autbɔːd] adj fuoribordo.

outbreak ['autbreik] n scoppio m; (*riot*) sommossa; eruzione f; epidemia f.

outbuilding ['autbildiŋ] n edificio annesso m, dipendenza f.

outburst ['autbəːst] n scoppio m; (*invective*) tirata f.

outcast ['autkɑːst] n, adj proscritto, -a, reietto, -a.

outcome ['autkʌm] n esito m, risultato m.

outcry ['autkrai] n grido m, scalpore m.

*outdo [aut'duː] v sorpassare.

outdoor ['autdɔː] adj all'aperto.

outer ['autə] adj esterno, esteriore.

outfit ['autfit] n corredo m, equipaggiamento m; (*coll*) compagnia f.

outgoing ['autgouiŋ] adj uscente, in partenza; (*person*) estroverso, espansivo.
outgoings pl n spese f pl.

*outgrow [aut'grou] v (*grow taller than*) sorpassare in altezza; (*clothes*) diventare troppo grande per.

outhouse ['authaus] n fabbricato annesso m.

outing ['autiŋ] n gita f, scampagnata f.

outlandish [aut'landiʃ] adj esotico.

outlast [aut'lɑːst] v durare più a lungo di, sopravvivere a.

outlaw ['autlɔɪ] n fuorilegge m, f invar. v mettere al bando, proscrivere.

outlay ['autlei] n spesa f, dispendio m.

outlet ['autlit] n sfogo m, sbocco m.

outline ['autlain] v delineare; (draft) abbozzare. n contorno m; (general sketch) abbozzo m. **outlines** pl n elementi m pl.

outlive [aut'liv] v sopravvivere a.

outlook ['autluk] n (view) veduta f; (future prospect) prospettiva f; (mental view) modo di vedere m, vedute f pl.

outlying ['autlaiiŋ] adj periferico, lontano.

outnumber [aut'nʌmbə] v superare in numero.

outpatient ['autpeiʃənt] n paziente esterno or ambulatoriale m, f.

outpost ['autpoust] n avamposto m.

output ['autput] n produzione f; (yield) rendimento m.

outrage ['autreidʒ] n oltraggio m. v oltraggiare.

outrageous [aut'reidʒəs] adj (disgraceful) vergognoso; offensivo; (excessive) esagerato.

outright ['autrait; adj aut'rait] adj completo, categorico. adv (at once) subito; (entirely) completamente; (openly) apertamente.

outset ['autset] n **at the outset** al principio.

outside [aut'said; adj 'autsaid] adj esterno, esteriore; (extraneous) estraneo. adv fuori, all'aperto. prep fuori di; (except) all'infuori di. n esterno m. **at the outside** (coll) tutt'al più. **outsider** n estraneo m; (sport) outsider m invar.

outsize ['autsaiz] adj di taglia forte, fuori misura.

outskirts ['autskɔːts] pl n dintorni m pl, periferia f sing.

outspoken [aut'spoukən] adj franco, esplicito, schietto.

outstanding [aut'standiŋ] adj (striking) eminente, notevole; (unpaid) in sospeso, arretrato.

outstrip [aut'strip] v distanziare.

outward ['autwəd] adj esterno, esteriore, superficiale; (journey) d'andata. **outwardly** adv in apparenza.

outweigh [aut'wei] v superare in importanza.

outwit [aut'wit] v superare in astuzia.

oval ['ouvəl] nm, adj ovale.

ovary ['ouvəri] n ovaia f.

ovation [ou'veiʃən] n ovazione f.

oven ['ʌvn] n forno m.

over ['ouvə] adv oltre, al di sopra; (in excess) in più; (finished) finito. prep su, sopra; (across) al di là di; (more than) più di. **over here** qui, da questa parte. **over there** là, laggiù.

overall ['ouvərɔːl] adj globale, completo. n (workman's) tuta f; (scientist's) camice m; (woman's) grembiulone m. adv in complesso.

overbalance [ouvə'baləns] v sbilanciare, perdere l'equilibrio.

overbearing [ouvə'beəriŋ] adj prepotente, altezzoso.

overboard ['ouvəbɔːd] adv in mare or acqua.

overcast [ouvə'kaːst] adj coperto, nuvoloso.

overcharge [ouvə'tʃaːdʒ] v far pagare troppo.

overcoat ['ouvəkout] n cappotto m, soprabito m.

overcome [ouvə'kʌm] v superare. adj sopraffatto, commosso.

overcrowded [ouvə'kraudid] adj sovraffollato. **overcrowding** n sovraffollamento m.

*overdo [ouvə'duː] v esagerare; (overcook) stracuocere.

overdose ['ouvədous] n dose eccessiva f.

overdraft ['ouvədraːft] n scoperto (di conto) m.

*overdraw [ouvə'drɔː] v andare allo scoperto.

overdrive ['ouvədraiv] n marcia sovramoltiplicata f.

overdue [ouvə'djuː] adj in ritardo, tardivo; (bill) scaduto.

overestimate [ouvə'estimeit] v sopravvalutare.

overexpose [ouvəik'spouz] v sovraesporre. **overexposure** n sovraesposizione f.

overflow [ouvə'flou; n 'ouvəflou] v (flood) inondare; (river) straripare; (vessel) traboccare. n (outlet) troppopieno m. **overflow pipe** scarico del troppopieno m.

overgrown [ouvə'groun] adj ricoperto di vegetazione.

*overhang [ouvə'haŋ; n 'ouvəhaŋ] v sporgere sopra; (impend) incombere su, minacciare. n aggetto m; (mountaineering) strapiombo m.

overhaul [ouvə'hɔɪl] v (*investigate*) esaminare; (*repair*) ripassare, riparare. n esame minuzioso m.

overhead [ouvə'hed] adv in alto, di sopra. adj di sopra, aereo. **overheads** pl n spese generali f pl.

*****overhear** [ouvə'hiə] v udire per caso; (*eavesdrop*) origliare.

overheat [ouvə'hiɪt] v surriscaldare.

overjoyed [ouvə'dʒɔid] adj felicissimo, colmo di gioia.

overland [ouvə'land] adj, adv per terra.

overlap [ouvə'lap] v sovrapporre, accavallare; coincidere or corrispondere in parte con.

overlay ['ouvəlei; v ouvə'lei] n copertura f. v ricoprire; incrostare.

overleaf [ouvə'liɪf] adv see **overleaf** vedi retro.

overload [ouvə'loud; n 'ouvəloud] v sovraccaricare. n sovraccarico m.

overlook [ouvə'luk] v (*miss*) lasciarsi sfuggire, non rilevare; condonare; (*ignore*) non tener conto di, trascurare; (*house, etc.*) dare su.

overnight [ouvə'nait] adv di notte; (*suddenly*) d'un tratto. **stay overnight** pernottare.

overpower [ouvə'pauə] v sopraffare, dominare. **overpowering** adj irresistibile.

overrate [ouvə'reit] v sopravvalutare.

overreach [ouvə'riɪtʃ] v **overreach oneself** sopravvalutare le proprie forze.

overriding [ouvə'raidiŋ] adj di primaria importanza.

overrule [ouvə'ruɪl] v (*decision*) annullare; (*plea*) respingere.

*****overrun** [ouvə'rʌn] v invadere, infestare.

overseas [ouvə'siɪz] adv oltremare. adj d'oltremare, straniero.

overseer [ouvə'siə] n ispettore, -trice m, f, sorvegliante m, f.

overshadow [ouvə'ʃadou] v oscurare; (*render insignificant*) eclissare.

*****overshoot** [ouvə'ʃuɪt] v (*miss*) fallire; (*go beyond*) oltrepassare. **overshoot the mark** passare il segno. **overshoot the runway** atterrare lungo.

oversight ['ouvəsait] n svista f, inavvertenza f.

*****oversleep** [ouvə'sliɪp] v dormire troppo a lungo, dormire oltre all'ora stabilita.

overspill ['ouvəspil] n sovrappiù m.

overt [ou'vɔɪt] adj manifesto, palese.

*****overtake** [ouvə'teik] v sorpassare.

*****overthrow** [ouvə'θrou; n 'ouvəθrou] v rovesciare, sconfiggere. n rovesciamento m.

overtime ['ouvətaim] n ore straordinarie f pl.

overtone ['ouvətoun] n (*implication*) sfumatura f.

overture ['ouvətjuə] n (*music*) ouverture f, preludio m; (*proposal*) proposta f; (*political*) apertura f.

overturn [ouvə'tən] v rovesciare, capovolgere.

overweight [ouvə'weit] adj **be overweight** pesare troppo.

overwhelm [ouvə'welm] v (*defeat*) sopraffare; (*crush*) schiacciare; (*with kindness, etc.*) colmare. **overwhelmingly** adv in modo schiacciante.

overwork [ouvə'wəɪk] v (far) lavorar troppo. n eccesso di lavoro m.

overwrought [ouvə'rɔɪt] adj teso, turbato, agitato.

ovulate ['ovjuleit] v ovulare. **ovulation** n ovulazione f.

owe [ou] v dovere. **owing** adj dovuto. **owing to** dovuto a, grazie a.

owl [aul] n gufo m, civetta f.

own [oun] adj proprio. **get one's own back** rendere pan per focaccia. **on one's own** da solo. v possedere; (*recognize*) riconoscere; confessare. **owner** n proprietario, -a m, f. **ownership** n proprietà f, possesso m.

ox [oks] n, pl **oxen** bue (pl buoi) m. **oxtail** n coda di bue f.

oxygen ['oksidʒən] n ossigeno m.

oyster ['oistə] n ostrica f.

ozone ['ouzoun] n ozono m.

P

pace [peis] n passo m; (*speed*) velocità f. **keep pace with** (*walking*) camminare di pari passo con; (*keep up to date*) tenersi al corrente di. v **pace off** misurare a passi. **pace up and down** andare su e giù.

Pacific [pə'sifik] nm, adj pacifico.

pacifism ['pasifizəm] n pacifismo m. **pacifist** n pacifista m, f.

pacify ['pasifai] v pacificare.

pack [pak] n (*parcel, package*) pacco m; (*of animals*) imballo m; (*rucksack*) zaino m; (*cards*) mazzo m; (*thieves*) banda f;

(*hounds*) muta *f*. **pack of lies** tessuto di bugie *m*. *v* imballare; (*suitcases*) fare (le valige); (*cram*) pigiare. **packed** *adj* (*full*) pieno zeppo. **packing** *n* confezione *f*, imballaggio *m*; (*tech*) guarnizione *f*. **do one's packing** fare le valige, fare i bagagli.

package ['pækidʒ] *n* pacco *m*. *adj* (*deal, etc*.) comprensivo.

packet ['pækit] *n* pacchetto *m*.

pact [pækt] *n* patto *m*.

pad¹ [pæd] *n* (*cushion*) cuscinetto *m*, tampone *m*; (*notepaper*) taccuino *m*; (*paw*) zampa *f*. *v* imbottire. **pad out** (*speech, essay, etc*.) infarcire. **padding** *n* imbottitura *f*; infarcimento *m*.

pad² [pæd] *v* camminare a passo felpato.

paddle¹ ['pædl] *n* (*of boat*) pagaia *f*; (*tech*) spatola *f*; (*zool*) pinna *f*. **paddle-boat** *n* piroscafo a ruote *m*. *v* remare piano.

paddle² ['pædl] *v* sguazzare (nell'acqua). **paddling pool** piscina per bambini *f*.

paddock ['pædək] *n* recinto *m*; (*racing*) paddock *m invar*.

paddy-field ['pædifiːld] *n* risaia *f*.

padlock ['pædlok] *n* lucchetto *m*. *v* chiudere col lucchetto.

paediatric [piːdi'ætrik] *adj* pediatrico. **paediatrician** *n* pediatra *m*, *f*. **paediatrics** *n* pediatria *f*.

pagan ['peigən] *n*, *adj* pagano, -a.

page¹ [peidʒ] *n* (*book*) pagina *f*.

page² [peidʒ] *n also* **page-boy** paggio *m*; (*hotel*) piccolo *m*. *v* (*coll*) chiamare.

pageant ['pædʒənt] *n* corteo storico *m*. **pageantry** *n* fasto *m*.

paid [peid] *V* **pay**.

pain [pein] *n* dolore *m*, sofferenza *f*. **be at pains to** sforzarsi di. **on pain of** sotto pena di. **painkiller** *n* analgesico *m*, antidolorifico *m*. **painstaking** *adj* laborioso. *v* addolorare, far male a. **painful** *adj* doloroso. **painless** *adj* indolore.

paint [peint] *v* dipingere, pitturare; (*decorate*) verniciare. *n* colore *m*, vernice *f*. **paint-box** *n* scatola di colori *f*. **paintbrush** *n* pennello *m*. **painter** *n* pittore, -trice *m*, *f*; decoratore *m*. **painting** *n* quadro *m*, pittura *f*.

pair [peə] *n* paio *m* (*pl* -a *f*), coppia *f*. *v* accoppiare.

pal [pæl] *n* (*coll*) compagno, -a *m*, *f*.

palace ['pæləs] *n* palazzo *m*. **palatial** *adj* sontuoso.

palate ['pælit] *n* palato *m*. **palatable** *adj* saporito.

pale¹ [peil] *adj* pallido. *v* impallidire. **paleness** *n* pallore *m*.

pale² [peil] *n* (*stake*) palo *m*. **beyond the pale** *adj* (*coll*) impossibile.

palette ['pælit] *n* tavolozza *f*. **palette knife** spatola *f*.

pall¹ [pɔːl] *v* smettere *or* cessare di interessare; (*weary*) stancare.

pall² [pɔːl] *n* drappo funebre *m*.

palm¹ [pɑːm] *n* (*of hand*) palmo *m*. **v palm off** affibbiare. **palmist** *n* chiromante *m*, *f*. **palmistry** *n* chiromanzia *f*.

palm² [pɑːm] *n* (*tree*) palma *f*. **Palm Sunday** Domenica delle Palme *f*.

palpitation [ˌpælpi'teiʃən] *n* palpitazione *f*.

pamper ['pæmpə] *v* viziare.

pamphlet ['pæmflit] *n* opuscolo *m*; (*polemical*) libello *m*.

pan [pæn] *n* pentola *f*, casseruola *f*, padella *f*. **pancake** *n* frittela *f*. **Pancake Tuesday** martedì grasso *m*.

pancreas ['pæŋkriəs] *n* pancreas *m invar*. **pancreatic** *adj* pancreatico.

panda ['pændə] *n* panda *m invar*.

pander ['pændə] *v* **pander to** favorire, andare incontro a.

pane [pein] *n* vetro *m*.

panel ['pænl] *n* pannello *m*; (*jury*) lista *f*; (*instruments*) cruscotto *m*. **panelling** *n* rivestimento a pannelli *m*.

pang [pæŋ] *n* dolore acuto *m*, spasimo *m*.

panic ['pænik] *n* panico *m*, allarme *m*. **panic-stricken** *adj* colto dal panico. *v* essere in preda al panico. **panicky** *adj* apprensivo.

panorama [ˌpænə'rɑːmə] *n* panorama *m*.

pansy ['pænzi] *n* (*flower*) viola del pensiero *f*; (*coll: homosexual*) finocchio *m*.

pant [pænt] *v* anelare, sbuffare.

panther ['pænθə] *n* pantera *f*.

pantomime ['pæntəmaim] *n* pantomina *f*; (*Christmas*) spettacolo di Natale *m*.

pantry ['pæntri] *n* dispensa *f*.

pants [pænts] *pl n* mutande *f pl*.

papal ['peipl] *adj* papale. **papacy** *n* papato *m*.

paper ['peipə] *n* carta *f*; documento *m*; (*treatise*) discorso *m*; (*news*) giornale *m*. **paperback** *n* edizione economica *f*. **paper-clip** *n* fermaglio *m*, agrafe *f*. **paper-mill** *n* cartiera *f*. **paperweight** *n* fermacarte *m invar*. **paperwork** *n* lavoro d'ufficio *m*; documenti *m pl.* *v* tappezzare.

paprika ['paprikə] *n* paprica *f.*

par [paɪ] *n* **above/below par** sopra/sotto la pari. **feel below par** sentirsi (un po') giù. **on a par with** alla pari con.

parable ['parəbl] *n* parabola *f.*

parabola [pə'rabələ] *n* parabola *f.*

parachute ['parəʃuɪt] *n* paracadute *m invar.* *v* scendere col paracadute. **parachutist** *n* paracadutista *m, f.*

parade [pə'reid] *n (display)* sfoggio *m*; *(mil)* sfilata *f*; *(sea-front)* lungomare *m. v* ostentare, sfoggiare; sfilare.

paradise ['parədais] *n* paradiso *m.*

paradox ['parədoks] *n* paradosso *m.* **paradoxical** *adj* paradossale.

paraffin ['parəfin] *n* paraffina liquida *f*; *(oil)* cherosene *m*, petrolio da illuminazione *m.*

paragraph ['parəgraɪf] *n* paragrafo *m*; *(news item)* trafiletto *m.*

parallel ['parəlel] *adj* parallelo. **parallel line** parallela *f. n* parallelo *m*; *(comparison)* paragone *m.*

paralyse ['parəlaiz] *v* paralizzare. **paralysis** *n, pl* **-ses** paralisi *f.* **paralytic** *n, adj* paralitico, -a.

parameter [pə'ramitə] *n* parametro *m.*

paramilitary [,parə'militəri] *adj* paramilitare.

paramount ['parəmaunt] *adj* sommo, supremo.

paranoia [,parə'noiə] *n* paranoia *f.* **paranoiac** *or* **paranoid** *n, adj* paranoico, -a.

parapet ['parəpit] *n* parapetto *m.*

paraphernalia [,parəfə'neiliə] *n* oggetti vari *m pl*, cianfrusaglie *f pl.*

paraphrase ['parəfreiz] *n* parafrasi *f. v* parafrasare.

paraplegic [,parə'pliːdʒik] *n, adj* paraplegico, -a. **paraplegia** *n* paraplegia *f.*

parasite ['parəsait] *n* parassita *m, f.* **parasitic** *adj* parassita, parassitico.

parasol ['parəsol] *n* parasole *m.*

paratrooper ['parə,truːpə] *n (soldato)* paracadutista *m.*

parcel ['paɪsl] *n* pacco *m*, pacchetto *m.* **by parcel post** a mezzo pacco postale. **part and parcel of** parte integrale di. *v* **parcel up** impacchettare.

parched [paɪtʃt] *adj* riarso. **be parched with thirst** morire dalla sete.

parchment ['paɪtʃmənt] *n* pergamena *f*,

cartapecora *f.* **parchment paper** carta pergamenata *f.*

pardon ['paɪdn] *n* perdono *m*; *(law)* grazia *f*; *(for minor fault)* scusa *f.* **I beg your pardon** mi scusi. *v* scusare; perdonare; graziare. *interj* prego? **pardonable** *adj* perdonabile.

pare [peə] *v* sbucciare, pelare. **pare down** ridurre.

parent ['peərənt] *n* padre, madre *m, f.* **parents** *pl n* genitori *m pl.* **parental** *adj* dei genitori. **parenthood** *n* l'essere genitori *m.*

parenthesis [pə'renθəsis] *n, pl* **-ses** parentesi *f.*

pariah [pə'raiə] *n* paria *m invar.*

Paris ['paris] *n* Parigi *f.* **Parisian** *n, adj* parigino, -a.

parish ['pariʃ] *n* parrocchia *f*; *(civil)* comune *m.* **parish priest** parroco *m* (*pl* -chi) *m.* **parishioner** *n* parrocchiano, -a *m, f.*

parity ['pariti] *n* parità *f.*

park [paɪk] *n* parco *m. v* parcheggiare, posteggiare. **parking** *n* posteggio *m*, parcheggio *m.* **parking meter** parchimetro *m.*

parliament ['paɪləmənt] *n* parlamento *m.* **member of parliament** deputato *m.* **parliamentary** *adj* parlamentare.

parlour ['paɪlə] *n* salotto *m.* **parlour game** gioco di società *m.*

Parmesan [,paɪmi'zan] *n (cheese)* (formaggio) parmigiano *m*, grana *m invar.*

parochial [pə'roukiəl] *adj* provinciale.

parody ['parədi] *n* parodia *f. v* parodiare.

parole [pə'roul] *v* rilasciare sulla parola. *n* rilascio sulla parola *m.*

paroxysm ['parəksizəm] *n* parossismo *m*, accesso *m.*

parrot ['parət] *n* pappagallo *m.*

parsley ['paɪsli] *n* prezzemolo *m.*

parsnip ['paɪsnip] *n* pastinaca *f.*

parson ['paɪsn] *n* prete *m*, parroco *m.* **parsonage** *n* casa parrocchiale *f*, presbiterio *m.*

part [paɪt] *n* parte *f*; *(theatre)* ruolo *m*; *(district)* quartiere *f.* **part-time** *adv, adj* a mezzo tempo. **spare part** pezzo di ricambio *m.* **take part** prender parte. *v* separare, spartire; *(hair)* dividere. **part with** rinunciare a. **parting** *n* separazione *f*, addio *m*; *(hair)* divisa dei capelli *f*, riga *f.*

*partake [paɪteik] *v* **partake of** consumare.

partial ['pɑːʃəl] adj parziale. **be partial to** avere un debole per. **partiality** n preferenza f. **partially** adv in parte.

participate [pɑːˈtisipeit] v partecipare. **participant** n partecipante m, f. **participation** n partecipazione f.

participle ['pɑːtisipl] n participio m.

particle ['pɑːtikl] n particella f.

particular [pəˈtikjulə] adj particolare, speciale; (exacting) esigente. **in particolare** m, dettaglio m. **particularly** adv in particolare, specie.

partisan [pɑːtiˈzan] n, adj partigiano, -a.

partition [pɑːˈtiʃən] n spartizione f; (of room) tramezzo m. v spartire; tramezzare.

partly ['pɑːtli] adv in parte.

partner ['pɑːtnə] n (comm) socio m; compagno, -a m, f, partner (pl -s) m, f. v far da compagno a, associarsi a. **partnership** n società f, associazione f.

partridge ['pɑːtridʒ] n pernice f.

party ['pɑːti] n (group) compagnia f, gruppo m; (entertainment) festa f, trattenimento m; (pol) partito m; (law) parte f. **third party** terzi m pl.

pass [pɑːs] n (mountain) passo m, valico (pl -chi) m; (permit) permesso m; (mil) libera uscita f; (school) promozione f; (sport) allungo m. v passare, superare; promuovere; allungare. **pass by** (disregard) non curarsi di; (in front of) passare davanti a. **pass off** far passare (per). **pass on** trasmettere; (die) morire. **pass out** (faint) svenire.

passage ['pɑːsidʒ] n passaggio m; (in book) brano m.

passenger ['pɑːsindʒə] n viaggiatore, -trice m, f. **passenger train** treno viaggiatori m.

passer-by ['pɑːsəˈbai] n passante m, f.

passing ['pɑːsiŋ] adj passeggero, transitorio; casuale. **in passing** (in passage or sfuggita); (by the way) tra parentesi.

passion ['pɑːʃən] n passione f, entusiasmo m. **passionate** adj appassionato, ardente.

passive ['pasiv] nm, adj passivo. **passivity** n passività f.

Passover ['pɑːsouvə] n Pasqua degli ebrei f.

passport ['pɑːspɔːt] n passaporto m.

password ['pɑːswɔːd] n parola d'ordine f.

past [pɑːst] prep al di là di, oltre; (after) dopo. **five past six** le sei e cinque. adj passato, scorso; (former) ex. adv davanti, oltre. n passato m.

pasta ['pɑːstə] n pasta f, pastasciutta f.

paste [peist] n pasta f; (adhesive) colla f. v incollare.

pastel ['pɑːstəl] n pastello m.

pasteurize ['pɑːstʃəraiz] v pastorizzare. **pasteurization** n pastorizzazione f.

pastime ['pɑːstaim] n passatempo m.

pastoral ['pɑːstərəl] adj pastorale.

pastry ['peistri] n pasta f. **pastry-cook** n pasticciere, -a m, f.

pasture ['pɑːstʃə] n pascolo m, pastura f. v pascolare.

pasty¹ ['peisti] adj pallido; (consistency) pastoso.

pasty² ['pasti] n (pie) pasticcio m.

pat¹ [pat] adj pronto, apposito. adv (aptly) a proposito; (exactly) precisamente.

pat² [pat] n (light blow) colpetto m; (of butter) pezzetto m. v dare un colpetto a.

patch [patʃ] n (material) pezza f, toppa f; (land) pezzo m. **go through a bad patch** attraversare un momento brutto. v rattoppare. **patch up** rattoppare, accomodare; (quarrel) comporre. **patchy** adj rattoppato; (not uniform) irregolare.

pâté ['patei] n pasticcio m, pâté m invar.

patent ['peitənt] adj manifesto, ovvio. **patent leather** pelle verniciata f. **patent medicine** specialità medicinale f. n brevetto m. v brevettare.

paternal [pəˈtəːnl] adj paterno. **paternity** n paternità f.

path [pɑːθ] n sentiero m; (course, way) via f, strada f.

pathetic [pəˈθetik] adj patetico, commovente.

pathology [pəˈθolədʒi] n anatomia patologica f. **pathological** adj patologico. **pathologist** n anatomo patologo, anatoma patologa m, f.

patient ['peiʃənt] adj paziente. n paziente m, f, malato, -a m, f. **be patient** pazientare, aver pazienza. **patience** n pazienza f.

patio ['patiou] n patio m invar.

patriarchal ['peitriɑːkəl] adj patriarcale. **patriarch** n patriarca m.

patriot ['patriət] n patriota m, f. **patriotic** adj patriottico. **patriotism** n patriottismo m.

patrol [pəˈtroul] n pattuglia f. v andare in pattuglia, ispezionare.

patron ['peitrən] n patrono m, protettore m; (customer) cliente abituale m, f, avventore, -a *m, f.* **patronage** *n* protezione *f*, auspici *m pl.* **patronize** *v* favorire, proteggere; frequentare. **patronizing** *adj* condiscendente.

patter¹ ['patə] *v* (*sound*) picchiettare. **n** picchiettio *m.*

patter² ['patə] *n* (*speech*) cicalata *f*, ciancia *f. v* cicalare, cianciare.

pattern ['patən] *n* modello *m*, tipo *m*; disegno *m. v* modellare.

paunch [pointʃ] *n* pancia *f.* **paunchy** *adj* panciuto.

pauper ['pɔːpə] *n* povero, -a *m, f*; mendicante *m, f.* **pauperize** *v* impoverire.

pause [pɔːz] *n* pausa *f*; esitazione *f. v* fare una pausa; esitare.

pave [peiv] *v* pavimentare. **pave the way** preparare il terreno. **pavement** *n* marciapiede *m.* **paving stone** lastra da selciato *f.*

pavilion [pə'viljən] *n* padiglione *m.*

paw [pɔː] *n* zampa *f. v* (*ground*) scalpitare; (*handle*) palpeggiare.

pawn¹ [pɔːn] *n* (*deposit*) pegno *m.* **pawnbroker** *n* prestatore su pegno *m.* **pawnshop** *n* monte di pietà *m. v* pignorare, dare in pegno.

pawn² [pɔːn] *n* (*chess*) pedina *f.*

***pay** [pei] *n* paga *f*, stipendio *m.* **in the pay of** al servizio di. **pay-roll** *n* organico *m. v* pagare; (*settle*) saldare; (*profit*) rendere; (*attention, etc.*) fare. **pay back** rimborsare, restituire. **pay in** versare. **pay off** liquidare. **payable** *adj* pagabile. **payee** *n* beneficiario, -a *m, f.* **payment** *n* pagamento *m*, versamento *m.*

pea [piː] *n* pisello *m.*

peace [piːs] *n* pace *f*; tranquillità *f.* **breach of the peace** violazione dell'ordine pubblico *f.* **peace-loving** *adj* pacifico. **peace offering** dono propiziotorio *m.* **peace-time** *n* tempo di pace *m.* **peaceful** *adj* pacifico.

peach [piːtʃ] *n* (*fruit*) pesca *f*; (*tree*) pesco *m.*

peacock ['piːkɒk] *n* pavone *m.* **peacock blue** *nm, adj.* blu pavone. **peahen** *n* pavona *f.*

peak [piːk] *n* cima *f*, vetta *f*; (*highest point*) massimo *m*; (*on cap*) visiera *f.* **peak hours** ore di punta *f pl.* **peak load** carico massimo *m. v* raggiungere il massimo.

peal [piːl] *n* (*bells*) scampanio *m*; (*thunder, laughter*) scoppio *m*, scroscio *m. v* scampanare; (*thunder*) rimbombare.

peanut ['piːnʌt] *n* arachide *f.*

pear [peə] *n* (*fruit*) pera *f*; (*tree*) pero *m.*

pearl [pɜːl] *n* perla *f.* **pearly** *adj* (*like pearl*) perlaceo; (*adorned with pearls*) perlato.

peasant ['pezənt] *n* contadino, -a *m, f.*

peat [piːt] *n* torba *f.*

pebble ['pebl] *n* ciottolo *m.* **pebbly** *adj* ciottoloso.

peck [pek] *v* beccare; (*food*) mangiucchiare; (*kiss*) dare un bacetto a, baciucchiare. **n** beccata *f*; baciucchio *m.*

peckish ['pekiʃ] *adj* **feel peckish** sentirsi vuoto *ov* affamato.

peculiar [pi'kjuːljə] *adj* strano, particolare. **peculiarity** *n* particolarità *f*, stranezza *f.*

pedal ['pedl] *n* pedale *m. v* pedalare.

pedantic [pi'dantik] *adj* pedante. **pedant** *n* pedante *m, f.* **pedantry** *n* pedanteria *f.*

peddle ['pedl] *v* spacciare.

pedestal ['pedistl] *n* piedistallo *m.*

pedestrian [pi'destriən] *adj* pedonale; (*commonplace*) pedestre. **n** pedone *m.* **pedestrian precinct** zona pedonale *f.*

pedigree ['pedigriː] *n* genealogia *f*; (*of animals*) pedigree *m invar. adj* di razza.

pedlar ['pedlə] *n* (*salesman*) venditore ambulante *m.*

peel [piːl] *n* buccia *f. v* sbucciare; (*paint, skin*) staccarsi. **peeler** *n* sbucciatore *m.* **peelings** *pl n* bucce *f pl.*

peep [piːp] *n* occhiata (furtiva) *f*, sguardo furtivo *m. v* dare un'occhiatina, spiare. **peep-hole** *n* spiraglio *m.* **peep out** mostrarsi appena.

peer¹ [piə] *v* **peer at** scrutare, guardare da presso.

peer² [piə] *n* pari *m.* **peerage** *n* nobiltà *f.*

peevish ['piːviʃ] *adj* permaloso, scontroso.

peg [peg] *n* piolo *m*; (*violin, etc.*) bischero *m*; (*washing*) molletta *f.* **off the peg** *adj* pronto. *v* (*prices*) stabilire. **peg out** (*coll: die*) crepare.

pejorative [pə'dʒɒrətiv] *adj* peggiorativo.

Peking [piː'kiŋ] *n* Pechino *f.* **Pekingese** *n* (*dog*) (*cane*) pechinese *m.*

pelican ['pelikən] *n* pellicano *m.*

pellet ['pelit] *n* pallottola *f*, pallina *f*; (*pill*) pillola *f.*

pelmet ['pelmit] *n* mantovana *f.*

pelt¹ [pelt] *v* scagliare; (*rain*) piovere

dirottamente, diluviare. *n* **at full pelt** a piena velocità.

pelt² [pelt] *n* pelliccia *f.*

pelvis ['pelvis] *n* pelvi *f;* bacino *m.* **pelvic** *adj* pelvico.

pen¹ [pen] *n (for writing)* penna *f. v* scrivere.

pen² [pen] *n* recinto *m; (for sheep)* ovile *m; (for pigs)* porcile *m.* v **pen in** rinchiudere.

penal ['piːnl] *adj* penale. **penalize** *v* punire. **penalty** *n* pena *f; (fine)* multa *f.* **penalty kick** *(sport)* calcio di rigore *m.*

penance ['penəns] *n* penitenza *f.*

pencil ['pensl] *n* matita *f.* **pencil-sharpener** *n* temperamatite *m invar.*

pendant ['pendənt] *n* ciondolo *m.*

pending ['pendiŋ] *adj* in sospeso. *prep* in attesa di.

pendulum ['pendjuləm] *n* pendolo *m.* **pendulum clock** orologio a pendolo *m.*

penetrate ['penitreit] *v* penetrare. **penetration** *n* penetrazione *f.*

pen-friend *n* amico. **-a** per corrispondenza *m, f.*

penguin ['pengwin] *n* pinguino *m.*

penicillin [peni'silin] *n* penicillina *f.*

peninsula [pə'ninjulə] *n* penisola *f.* **peninsular** *adj* peninsulare.

penis ['piːnis] *n* pene *m.*

penitent ['penitənt] *n(m + f), adj* penitente. **penitence** *n* penitenza *f,* pentimento *m.* **penitentiary** *n (prison)* penitenziario *m; (church dignitary)* penitenziere *m.*

penknife ['pennaif] *n* temperino *m.*

pen-name *n* pseudonimo *m.*

pennant ['penənt] *n* pennello *m.*

penniless ['peniləs] *adj* al verde, senza un soldo.

pension ['penʃən] *n* pensione *f. v* **pension off** mettere a riposo, mettere in pensione. **pensioner** *n* pensionato, **-a** *m, f.*

pensive ['pensiv] *adj* pensoso, pensieroso, preoccupato.

pentagon ['pentəgən] *n* pentagono *m.* **pentagonal** *adj* pentagonale.

penthouse ['penthaus] *n* attico *m.*

pent-up [,pent'ʌp] *adj* represso.

penultimate [pi'nʌltimit] *adj* penultimo.

people ['piːpl] *n* popolo *m,* nazione *f. pl n* gente *f sing; (coll: family)* i suoi *m pl. v* popolare.

pepper ['pepə] *n* pepe *m.* **peppercorn** *n* grano di pepe *m.* **pepper-mill** *n* macinapepe *m invar.* **peppermint** *n (herb)* menta piperita *f; (sweet)* mentina *f.* **pepper-pot** *n* pepaiola *f.* v *(season)* pepare; *(dot)* cospargere; *(hit)* tempestare.

per [pəː] *prep* a. **as per** secondo. **per cent** percento. **percentage** *n* percentuale *f.*

perceive [pə'siːv] *v* rilevare, scorgere, accorgersi di.

perceptible [pə'septibl] *adj* percettibile; visibile. **perceptibility** *n* percettibilità *f;* visibilità *f.*

perception [pə'sepʃən] *n* percezione *f.* **perceptive** *adj* percettivo, sensibile.

perch¹ [pəːtʃ] *n* posatoio *m. v* posarsi.

perch² [pəːtʃ] *n (fish)* pesce persico *m.* ·

percolate ['pəːkəleit] *v* filtrare. **percolator** *n* percolatore *m.*

percussion [pə'kʌʃən] *n* percussione *f.*

perennial [pə'reniəl] *adj* perenne; perpetuo. *v* pianta perenne *f.*

perfect ['pəːfikt; *v* pə'fekt] *adj* perfetto, ideale; *(real)* vero. *v* perfezionare. **perfection** *n* perfezione *f.*

perforate ['pəːfəreit] *v* perforare. **perforation** *n* perforazione *f.*

perform [pə'fɔːm] *v* eseguire, compire; *(music, theatre)* recitare. **performance** *n* esecuzione *f;* recita *f; (show)* spettacolo *m.* **performer** *n* artista *m, f.*

perfume ['pəːfjuːm] *n* profumo *m.* v profumare. **perfumery** *n* profumeria *f.*

perfunctory [pə'fʌŋktəri] *adj* fatto alla buona, meccanico, indifferente.

perhaps [pə'haps] *adv* forse, magari.

peril ['peril] *n* rischio *m.* **perilous** *adj* rischioso, pericoloso.

perimeter [pə'rimitə] *n* perimetro *m.*

period ['piəriəd] *n* periodo *m; (full stop)* punto fermo *m; (med)* mestruazione *f. adj* antico *(m pl -chi),* storico. **periodic** *adj* periodico. **periodical** *nm, adj* periodico.

peripheral [pə'rifərəl] *adj* periferico. **periphery** *n* periferia *f.*

periscope ['periskoup] *n* periscopio *m.*

perish ['periʃ] *v* perire; *(food, etc.)* guastarsi, deperire. **perishable** *adj* deperibile.

perjure ['pəːdʒə] *v* spergiurare. **perjurer** *n* spergiuro *m.* **perjury** *n* spergiuro *m,* giuramento falso *m.*

perk [pəːk] *v* **perk up** rianimarsi, ravvivarsi. **perky** *adj* vispo.

perm [pəːm] *n* permanente *f.* **have a perm** farsi fare la permanente.

permanent ['pəmənənt] adj permanente.

permeate ['pəːmieit] v permeare.

permit ['pəːmit; v pə'mit] n permesso m, licenza f. v permettere. **permissible** adj permissibile. **permission** n permesso m. **permissive** adj permissivo.

permutation [,pəːmjuˈteiʃən] n permutazione f.

pernicious [pəˈniʃəs] adj pernicioso.

pernickety [pəˈnikəti] adj pignolo.

perpendicular [,pəipənˈdikjulə] nf, adj perpendicolare.

perpetrate ['pəːpitreit] v commettere. **perpetration** n perpetrazione f. **perpetrator** n perpetratore, -trice m, f.

perpetual [pəˈpetʃuəl] adj perpetuo.

perpetuate [pəˈpetʃueit] v perpetuare. **perpetuation** n perpetuazione f. **in perpetuity** in perpetuo.

perplex [pəˈpleks] v confondere, rendere perplesso. **perplexed** adj perplesso, confuso. **perplexing** adj imbarazzante. **perplexity** n perplessità f, imbarazzo m.

persecute ['pəːsikjuːt] v perseguitare. **persecution** n persecuzione f.

persevere [,pəisiˈviə] v perseverare. **perseverance** n perseveranza f, assiduità f. **persevering** adj perseverante, assiduo.

persist [pəˈsist] v persistere, ostinarsi, perseverare. **persistence** n perseveranza f, persistenza f, ostinazione f. **persistent** adj ostinato, persistente.

person ['pəisn] n persona f, individuo m. **personage** n personaggio m. **personal** adj personale; (disparaging) offensivo, di carattere personale. **personality** n personalità f; carattere m; celebrità f. **personify** [pəˈsonifai] v personificare. **personification** n personificazione f.

personnel [,pəisəˈnel] n personale m, impiegati m pl.

perspective [pəˈspektiv] n prospettiva f.

perspire [pəˈspaiə] v sudare. **perspiration** n sudore m.

persuade [pəˈsweid] v persuadere. **persuasion** n persuasione f. **persuasive** adj persuasivo.

pert [pəːt] adj (lively) vispo; impudente, insolente.

pertain [pəˈtein] v **pertain to** riguardare, appartenere a. **pertinent** adj pertinente, a proposito. **pertinence** n pertinenza f.

perturb [pəˈtəːb] v turbare, sconcertare.

peruse [pəˈruːz] v leggere attentamente.

pervade [pəˈveid] v pervadere. **pervasive** adj penetrante.

perverse [pəˈvəːs] adj perverso. **perversity** n perversità f.

pervert ['pəːvəːt; v pəˈvəːt] n pervertito, -a m, f. v pervertire. **perversion** n perversione f, pervertimento f.

pessimism ['pesimizəm] n pessimismo m. **pessimist** n pessimista m, f. **pessimistic** adj pessimista, pessimistico.

pest [pest] n animale or parassita nocivo m; (coll: nuisance) seccatore m. **pest control** disinfestazione f. **pesticide** n pesticida m.

pester ['pestə] v seccare.

pet [pet] n animale favorito m; (favourite) cocco, -a m, f. adj prediletto. **pet aversion** avversione spiccata f. **pet name** nomignolo m. v coccolare. **petting** n (slang) carezze amorose f pl.

petal ['petl] n petalo m.

petition [pəˈtiʃən] n petizione f, supplica f. v presentare una petizione or supplica.

petrify ['petrifai] v pietrificare, paralizzare. **petrified** adj allibito, pietrificato.

petrol ['petrəl] n benzina f. **petrol-tank** n serbatoio m.

petroleum [pəˈtrouliəm] n petrolio m.

petticoat ['petikout] n sottana f.

petty ['peti] adj insignificante; (mean) meschino. **petty cash** piccola cassa f, fondo per le piccole spese m. **petty officer** capo m. **pettiness** n piccolezza f, meschinità f.

petulant ['petjulənt] adj scontroso, irritabile. **petulance** n scontrosità f, irritabilità f.

pew [pjuː] n banco (di chiesa) m.

pewter ['pjuːtə] n peltro m.

phantom ['fantəm] n fantasma m.

pharmacy ['faːməsi] n farmacia f. **pharmaceutical** adj farmaceutico. **pharmacist** n farmacista m, f.

pharynx ['fariŋks] n faringe f.

phase [feiz] n fase f.

pheasant ['feznt] n fagiano m.

phenomenon [fəˈnomənən] n, pl -ena fenomeno m. **phenomenal** adj fenomenale.

phial ['faiəl] n fiala f.

philanthropy [fiˈlanθrəpi] n filantropia f. **philanthropic** adj filantropico. **philanthropist** n filantropo, -a m, f.

philately [fiˈlatəli] n filatelia f. **philatelist** n filatelico, -a m, f.

philosophy [fi'losəfi] n filosofia f. **philosopher** n filosofo, -a m, f. **philosophical** adj filosofico.

phlegm [flem] n (mucus) muco m; (sluggishness) flemma f.

phlegmatic [fleg'matik] adj flemmatico.

phobia ['foubiə] n fobia f.

phone [foun] n (coll) telefono m. v telefonare (a).

phonetic [fə'netik] adj fonetico. **phonetics** n fonetica f.

phoney ['founi] (coll) adj falso, fasullo. n ipocrita m, f; impostore m.

phosphate ['fosfeit] n fosfato m.

phosphorescence [fosfə'resəns] n fosforescenza f. **phosphorescent** adj fosforescente.

phosphorus ['fosfərəs] n fosforo m.

photo ['foutou] n (coll) foto f.

photocopy ['foutou,kopi] n fotocopia f. v fotocopiare.

photogenic [,foutou'dʒenik] adj fotogenico.

photograph ['foutəgraif] n fotografia f. v fotografare. **photographer** n fotografo m. **photographic** adj fotografico. **photography** n fotografia f.

phrase [freiz] n frase f, modo di dire m. v esprimere, formulare.

physical ['fizikəl] adj fisico.

physician [fi'ziʃən] n medico m.

physics ['fiziks] n fisica f. **physicist** n fisico, -a m, f.

physiology [,fizi'olədʒi] n fisiologia f. **physiological** adj fisiologico. **physiologist** n fisiologo, -a m, f.

physiotherapy [,fiziou'θerəpi] n fisioterapia f. **physiotherapist** n fisioterapista m, f.

physique [fi'ziːk] n fisico m.

piano [pi'anou] n pianoforte m. **pianist** n pianista m, f.

pick¹ [pik] v (choose) scegliere; (pluck) cogliere. **pick out** scegliere. **pickpocket** n borsaiolo m. **pick up** raccogliere; (recover) star meglio; (passenger) far salire; (learn) imparare. **pick-up** n pick-up. m. (choice) scelta f; (best) fior fiore m.

pick² [pik] n piccone m.

picket ['pikit] n picchetto m. v picchettare.

pickle ['pikl] v marinare; (in vinegar) mettere sott'aceto. n (coll: predicament) pasticcio m. **pickles** pl n sottaceti m pl. **pickled** adj sottaceto.

picnic ['piknik] n picnic m invar, colazione all'aperto f.

pictorial [pik'tɔːriəl] adj illustrato.

picture ['piktʃə] v immaginare, figurare. n (painting) quadro m; foto f; (image) immagine f; film m. **be in the picture** essere informato. **pictures** n (coll) cinema m. **put in the picture** mettere al corrente.

picturesque [,piktʃə'resk] adj pittoresco.

pidgin ['pidʒən] n linguaggio bastardo or maccheronico m.

pie [pai] n pasticcio m; (sweet) crostata f.

piece [piːs] n pezzo m. **piecemeal** adv gradualmente, un po' alla volta. **piecework** n lavoro a cottimo m. v rappezzare. **piece together** aggiustare, mettere assieme.

Piedmont ['piːdmɒnt] n Piemonte m.

pier [piə] n molo m, banchina f.

pierce [piəs] v forare, penetrare. **piercing** adj acuto, penetrante; (wind) pungente.

piety ['paiəti] n devozione religiosa f.

pig [pig] n maiale m, porco (pl -ci) m. **pigheaded** adj ostinato, testardo. **pigheadedness** n testardaggine f. **pig-iron** n ghisa f. **piglet** n porcellino m. **pigskin** adj cinghiale. **pigsty** n porcile m. **pigtail** n codino m.

pigeon ['pidʒən] n piccione m. **carrier pigeon** piccione viaggiatore m. **clay pigeon** piattello m.

pigeon-hole n casella f. v incasellare.

pigment ['pigmənt] n pigmento m.

pike [paik] n (fish) luccio m.

pilchard ['piltʃəd] n sardina f, sarda f.

pile¹ [pail] n (heap) mucchio m; (building) fabbricato m. v accumulare. **pile on** (coll) esagerare. **pile up** accatastare.

pile² [pail] n (post) palo m. **pile-driver** n battipalo m.

pile³ [pail] n (of carpet, etc.) pelo m.

piles [pailz] pl n (med) emorroidi f pl.

pilfer ['pilfə] v rubacchiare. **pilferer** n ladruncolo m.

pilgrim ['pilgrim] n pellegrino m. **pilgrimage** n pellegrinaggio m.

pill [pil] n pillola f. **pillbox** n scatoletta per pillole f; (mil) casamatta f.

pillage ['pilidʒ] n saccheggio m. v saccheggiare.

pillar ['pilə] n pilastro m, colonna f. **pillar-box** n buca delle lettere f.

pillion ['piljən] n sella posteriore f, sedile posteriore m. **ride pillion** viaggiare sul sedile posteriore.

pillow ['pilou] n guanciale m. **pillowslip** n federa f.

pilot ['pailət] n pilota m, f. v pilotare.

pimento [pi'mentou] n (allspice) pimento m; (capsicum) peperone m.

pimp [pimp] n ruffiano m.

pimple ['pimpl] n pustoletta f, foruncolo m.

pin [pin] n spillo m; (brooch) spilla f. **pincushion** n portaspilli m invar. **pinpoint** v determinare con precisione. **pinprick** n (annoyance) seccatura f. v puntare. **pin down** inchiodare. **pin-up** n (girl) ragazza da copertina f, pin-up f invar.

pinafore ['pinəfoɪ] n grembiulino m.

pincers ['pinsəz] pl n pinza f sing, tenaglia f sing.

pinch [pintʃ] v pizzicare; (hurt) far male a; (coll: steal) rubare; (coll: catch) acchiappare. n (nip) pizzicotto m; (small quantity) pizzico (pl -chi) m. **at a pinch** caso mai.

pine¹ [pain] n (tree) pino m. **pine-cone** n pigna f.

pine² [pain] v languire. **pine for** desiderare ardentemente.

pineapple ['painapl] n ananas m.

pinion¹ ['pinjən] n (tech) pignone m.

pinion² ['pinjən] v (shackle) legare.

pink [piŋk] adj rosa invar. n (colour) rosa m invar; (flower) garofano m. **in the pink of condition** in ottima forma.

pinnacle ['pinəkl] n cima f, colmo m; (arch) pinnacolo m.

pioneer [paiə'niə] n pioniere, -a m, f. v aprire la strada a.

pious ['paiəs] adj pio, devoto.

pip¹ [pip] n (seed) seme m, granello m.

pip² [pip] n (phone) segnale acustico m.

pipe [paip] n tubo m, condotto m; (for smoking) pipa f. **pipe-cleaner** n nettapipe m invar. **pipedream** n illusione f. **pipeline** n oleodotto m; linea di comunicazione f. **pipe down!** sta zitto! **pipe up** farsi sentire. **piping** n (sewing) cordonetto m. **piping hot** caldo bollente.

piquant ['piːkənt] adj piccante, mordace.

pique [piːk] n dispetto m. v **feel piqued** risentirsi.

pirate ['paiərət] n pirata m. **pirate radio** radiopirata m. v (radio) servirsi abusivamente di; (book) plagiare. **piracy** n pirateria f.

pirouette [piru'et] n piroetta f. v piroettare.

Pisces ['paisiz] n Pesci m pl.

piss [pis] (vulgar) n piscia f. v pisciare. **pissed** adj sbronzo.

pistachio [pi'staːʃiou] n pistacchio m.

pistol ['pistl] n pistola f.

piston ['pistən] n pistone m.

pit [pit] n fossa f; (theatre) platea f; (scar) buttero m. v **pit against** opporre.

pitch¹ [pitʃ] n lancio m; (degree) grado m; (music) tono m, registro m; (sport) campo m, terreno m. v lanciare; (tent) piantare; (fix) fissare; (ship) beccheggiare. **pitchfork** n forcone m.

pitch² [pitʃ] n pece f. **pitch-dark** adj buio pesto.

pitfall ['pitfoɪl] n trappola f, tranello m.

pith [piθ] n midollo m. **pithy** adj succinto.

pittance ['pitəns] n somma irrisoria f.

pituitary [pi'tjuitəri] n ipofisi f, glandola pituitaria f.

pity ['piti] n pietà f, compassione f; (shame) peccato m. **what a pity!** che peccato! v avere pietà di, compatire. **pitiful** adj (wretched) pietoso; (contemptible) miserabile. **pitiless** adj spietato.

pivot ['pivət] n perno m, fulcro m. v imperniare.

placard ['plakaɪd] n cartellone m.

placate [plə'keit] v placare, conciliare.

place [pleis] n luogo m, posto m. **out of place** inopportuno. **put in one's place** umiliare. **take place** aver luogo, accadere. v mettere, posare, porre; (order) piazzare.

placenta [plə'sentə] n placenta f.

placid ['plasid] adj placido.

plagiarize ['pleidʒəraiz] v plagiare. **plagiarism** n plagio m. **plagiarist** n plagiario, -a m, f.

plague [pleig] n (disease) peste f; (calamity) piaga f. v tormentare, affliggere.

plaice [pleis] n passera di mare f.

plaid [plad] n plaid m invar.

plain [plein] adj chiaro; (simple) semplice; (frank) schietto; (not patterned) a tinta unita; (unattractive) brutto. **in plain clothes** in borghese. **plain cooking** cucina semplice or casalinga f. n pianura f.

plaintiff ['pleintif] n querelante m, f; attore, -trice m, f.

plaintive ['pleintiv] adj querulo, lamentoso.

plait [plat] n (braid) treccia f; (pleat) piega f. v intrecciare; piegare.

plan [plan] n piano m, progetto m; intenzione f; (drawing) disegno m; (map) pianta f. v progettare; intendere; (econ) pianificare.

plane[1] [plein] n (flat surface) piano m, livello m; (coll) aereo m. adj piano.

plane[2] [plein] n (tool) pialla f. v piallare.

plane[3] [plein] n (tree) platano m.

planet ['planit] n pianeta m. **planetarium** n planetario m. **planetary** adj planetario.

plank [plaŋk] n asse f, tavola f.

plankton ['plaŋktən] n plancton m invar.

plant [plaint] n (bot) pianta f; (manufacturing) impianto m, stabilimento m. v piantare. **plantation** n piantagione f.

plaque [plaik] n placca f.

plasma ['plazmə] n plasma m.

plaster ['plaistə] n intonaco m; (med) impiastro m; (for wound) cerotto m. **plaster of Paris** gesso m. v intonacare; impiastrare; ingessare.

plastic ['plastik] adj plastico. n plastica f.

plate [pleit] n (dish) piatto m; (of metal) lamiera, lastra f; (denture) dentiera f; (metallic ware) argenteria f; (in book) tavola f, illustrazione f. **plate-glass** n cristallo m. v galvanizzare; (silver) argentare.

plateau ['platou] n altipiano m.

platform ['platform] n piattaforma f; (rail) binario m.

platinum ['platinəm] n platino m.

platonic [plə'tonik] adj platonico.

platoon [plə'tuin] n plotone m.

plausible ['plo:zəbl] adj ammissibile, credibile.

play [plei] v giocare; (musical instrument) suonare; (act) recitare. **play down** minimizzare. **play fair** comportarsi lealmente. **play truant** marinare la scuola. n gioco m, divertimento m; (theatre) spettacolo m. **playboy** n playboy m, buontempone m. **playground** n cortile di scuola m, campo m. **playmate** n compagno, -a di gioco m, f. **play-pen** n recinto per bambini m, box m invar. **play-school** n asilo m. **playwright** n commediografo, -a m, f; drammaturgo, -a m, f. **player** n giocatore, -trice m, f; (music) suonatore, -trice m, f; (theatre) attore, -trice m, f. **playful** adj

scherzoso, giocoso. **playing card** carta da gioco f. **playing field** campo sportivo m.

plea [pliː] n difesa f, supplica f; (excuse) scusa f.

plead [pliid] v implorare; perorare. **plead guilty/innocent** dichiararsi colpevole/innocente. **plead with** intercedere presso. **pleading** n perorazione f.

please [pliz] v piacere (a), contentare, soddisfare. **please oneself** fare il proprio comodo. adv per favore, per cortesia. **pleased** adj contento, lieto, soddisfatto. **pleasing** adj piacevole, gradevole. **pleasure** n piacere m, favore m.

pleat [pliit] n piega f. v pieghettare.

pledge [pledʒ] n promessa solenne f; (undertaking) impegno m. v impegnare, garantire; promettere solennemente.

plenty ['plenti] n abbondanza f. **in plenty** in abbondanza. **plenty of** abbastanza. **plentiful** adj abbondante.

pleurisy ['pluərisi] n pleurite f.

pliable ['plaiəbl] adj flessibile. **pliability** n flessibilità f.

pliers ['plaiəz] pl n pinza f sing, tenaglia f sing.

plight [plait] n stato m.

plimsoll ['plimsəl] n scarpa da tennis f.

plod [plod] v **plod along** tirare avanti. **plodder** n sgobbone, -a m, f.

plonk [ploŋk] n (coll) vino comune m.

plot[1] [plot] n (story) trama f, intreccio m; (secret plan) congiura f, complotto m. v tramare, complottare; (trace) tracciare. **plotter** n cospiratore, -trice m, f.

plot[2] [plot] n (land) lotto or pezzo di terreno m.

plough [plau] n aratro m. v arare; (coll: fail exam) trombare. **plough back** riinvestire. **plough through** (book, etc.) leggere con fatica.

pluck [plʌk] v cogliere; (feathers) spennare; (tug at) strappare. **pluck up courage** farsi coraggio. n (courage) fegato m. **be plucky** aver fegato.

plug [plʌg] n tappo m; (elec) spina f; (mot) candela f. v tappare.

plum [plʌm] n (fruit) prugna f, susina f; (tree) prugno m, susino m. adj (colour) prugna.

plumage ['pluimidʒ] n piumaggio m.

plumb [plʌm] adj verticale. adv **a** piombo; (absolutely) proprio. n piombo *m*, scandaglio *m*. v sondare; (*naut*) scandagliare. **plumber** *n* idraulico *m*.

plume [plum] *n* penna *f*, piuma *f*; (*on helmet*) pennacchio *m*.

plummet ['plʌmit] *v* piombare.

plump[1] [plʌmp] *adj* (*fat*) grassoccio, paffuto.

plump[2] [plʌmp] v **plump for** scegliere.

plunder ['plʌndə] *n* bottino *m*. v spogliare, depredare.

plunge [plʌndʒ] *n* tuffo *m*. v tuffare; immergere; (*rush*) lanciarsi. **plunger** *n* (*tech*) stantuffo *m*.

pluperfect [plu'pəfikt] *n* trapassato remoto *m*.

plural ['pluərəl] *nm*, *adj* plurale. **in the plural** al plurale.

plus [plʌs] *adj* addizionale. *prep* più.

plush [plʌʃ] *n* felpa *f*. *adj* lussuoso.

plutocrat ['pluttəkrat] *n* plutocrate *m*, *f*.

ply[1] [plai] *v* (*travel*) viaggiare regolarmente; (*trade*) esercitare.

ply[2] [plai] *n* (*layer*) strato *m*; (*wool*) filo *m*. **plywood** *n* legno compensato *m*.

pneumatic [nju'matik] *adj* pneumatico.

pneumonia [nju'mouniə] *n* polmonite *f*.

poach[1] [poutʃ] *v* (*game*) cacciare di frodo; (*fish*) pescare di frodo; (*encroach upon*) usurpare. **poacher** *n* bracconiere *m*.

poach[2] [poutʃ] *v* (*cookery*) lessare. **poached egg** uovo affogato *m*, uovo in camicia *m*.

pocket ['pokit] *n* tasca *f*, taschino *m*; (*billiards*) buca *f*. **be out of pocket** rimetterci. v intascare. *adj* tascabile. **pocketbook** *n* taccuino *m*. **pocket-knife** *n* temperino *m*. **pocket-money** *n* soldi per le piccole spese *m pl*.

pod [pod] *n* baccello *m*.

podgy ['podʒi] *adj* grassotto, paffuto.

poem ['pouim] *n* poesia *f*.

poet ['pouit] *n* poeta *m*. **poetess** *n* poetessa *f*. **poetic** *adj* poetico. **poetry** *n* poesia *f*.

poignant ['poinjənt] *adj* intenso, vivo, commovente.

point [point] *n* punto *m*; (*sharp end*) punta *f*; (*elec*) presa *f*. **be on the point of** stare per. **make a point of** insistere su. **point-blank** *adv* a bruciapelo; (*coll*) di punto in bianco. v indicare, addittare; (*aim*) puntare; (*brickwork*) affilettare. **pointed** *adj* acuto. **pointer** *n* (*hint*) indicazione *f*; (*dog*) pointer *m*. **pointing** *n* affilettatura *f*. **pointless** *adj* inutile.

poise [poiz] *n* equilibrio *m*, compostezza *f*, portamento *m*. v equilibrare, essere in equilibrio.

poison ['poizən] *n* veleno *m*. v avvelenare. **poisonous** *adj* velenoso.

poke [pouk] *n* spinta *f*, gomitata *f*. v (*stick into*) ficcare; (*thrust*) cacciare; (*fire*) attizzare. **poke about** frugare. **poke fun at** beffarsi di. **poker** *n* attizzatoio *m*. **poky** *adj* meschino, piccolo.

poker[2] [pouka] *n* (*cards*) poker *m*. **poker-faced** *adj* impassibile.

Poland ['poulənd] *n* Polonia *f*. **Pole** *n* polacco, -a *m*, *f*. **Polish** *nm*, *adj* polacco.

polar ['poulə] *adj* polare. **polar bear** orso bianco *m*. **polarize** v polarizzare. **polarity** *n* polarità *f*.

pole[1] [poul] *n* (*post*) palo *m*, asta *f*. **pole-vault** *n* salto all'asta *m*.

pole[2] [poul] *n* (*geog*) polo *m*.

police [pə'liːs] *n* polizia *f*. **policeman** *n* carabiniere *m*, poliziotto *m*, vigile *m*. **police station** questura *f*. v mantenere l'ordine, sorvegliare, vigilare.

policy[1] ['poləsi] *n* politica *f*, linea di condotta *f*.

policy[2] ['poləsi] *n* (*insurance*) polizza *f*.

polio ['pouliou] *n* poliomielite *f*.

polish ['poliʃ] *n* (*for shoes, etc.*) lucido *m*; (*for nails*) smalto *m*; raffinatezza *f*. v lucidare, lustrare. **polish off** (*dispose of quickly*) sbrigare; liquidare. **polish up** ripassare.

polite [pə'lait] *adj* cortese, garbato. **politeness** *n* cortesia *f*, garbo *m*.

politics ['politiks] *n* politica *f*. **politic** *adj* espediente. **political** *adj* politico. **politician** *n* uomo politico *m*.

polka ['polkə] *n* polca *f*.

poll [poul] *n* elezione *f*; (*casting of votes*) votazione *f*; (*votes cast*) voti *m pl*. **opinion poll** sondaggio d'opinioni *m*. v ottenere voti. **polling booth** cabina elettorale *f*.

pollen ['polən] *n* polline *m*. **pollinate** v impollinare. **pollination** *n* impollinazione *f*.

pollute [pə'luːt] *v* inquinare. **pollution** *n* inquinamento *m*.

polo ['poulou] *n* polo *m*. **polo-neck** *n* collo ciclista *m*. **polo-neck sweater** ciclista *f*.

polygamy [pə'ligəmi] *n* poligamia *f*. **polygamist** *n* poligamo *m*. **polygamous** *adj* poligamo.

polygon ['pɒligən] n poligono m. **polygonal** adj poligonale.

polytechnic [ˌpɒli'teknik] n politecnico m.

polythene ['pɒliθin] n politene m.

pomegranate ['pɒmigranit] n melagrana f.

pomp [pɒmp] n pompa f, sfarzo m. **pompous** adj pomposo, ampolloso.

pond [pɒnd] n stagno m.

ponder ['pɒndə] v ponderare; valutare. **ponderous** adj ponderoso, pesante.

pontiff ['pɒntif] n pontefice m, papa m. **pontifical** adj pontificio. **pontificate** v pontificare.

pontoon [pɒn'tuɪn] n pontone m; (cards) ventuno m.

pony ['pouni] n pony m.

poodle ['puɪdl] n cane barbone m.

poof [puf] n (derog) finocchio m.

pool¹ [puɪl] n (pond) stagno m; (puddle) pozzanghera f; (swimming) piscina f.

pool² [puɪl] v mettere in comune. n fondo comune m; (football) totocalcio m.

poor [puə] adj povero; mediocre; (meagre) magro; (not good) cattivo. **poorly** ['puəli] adj malaticcio. adv male. feel poorly non sentirsi troppo bene.

pop¹ [pɒp] v schioccare, saltare. **pop in** fare una breve visita. **pop out** saltar fuori. **pop up** apparire. n schiocco m; (drink) bibita gassata f.

pop² [pɒp] adj popolare. **pop-art** n pop-art f. **pop music** musica pop f.

pope [poup] n papa m.

poplar ['pɒplə] n pioppo m.

poppy ['pɒpi] n papavero m.

popular ['pɒpjulə] adj popolare; (favourite) ben visto. **popularity** n popolarità f. **popularize** v divulgare.

population [ˌpɒpju'leiʃən] n popolazione f. **populate** v popolare.

porcelain ['pɔɪslin] n porcellana f.

porch [pɔɪtʃ] n portico m.

porcupine ['pɔɪkjupain] n porcospino m.

pore¹ [pɔɪ] n (opening) poro m.

pore² [pɔɪ] v **pore over** meditare su, essere assorto in.

pork [pɔɪk] n carne suina f, carne di maiale f.

pornography [pɔɪ'nɒgrəfi] n pornografia f. **pornographic** adj pornografico.

porous ['pɔɪrəs] adj poroso.

porpoise ['pɔɪpəs] n focena f.

porridge ['pɒridʒ] n pappa di fiocchi d'avena f.

port¹ [pɔɪt] n (harbour) porto m.

port² [pɔɪt] n (naut: left) sinistra f, babordo m.

port³ [pɔɪt] n (wine) porto m invar.

portable ['pɔɪtəbl] adj portatile.

portent ['pɔɪtent] n (omen) presagio m; (marvel) portento m. **portentous** adj prodigioso, portentoso; grave.

porter ['pɔɪtə] n (janitor) portinaio, -a m, f; (carrier) facchino m.

portfolio [pɔɪt'fouliou] n (pol) portafoglio m; (case) cartella f.

porthole ['pɔɪthoul] n oblò m.

portion ['pɔɪʃən] n porzione f. v ripartire.

portrait ['pɔɪtrət] n ritratto m. **portrait-painter** n ritrattista m, f.

portray [pɔɪ'trei] v rappresentare.

Portugal ['pɔɪtjugl] n Portogallo m. **Portuguese** n(m+f), adj portoghese.

pose [pouz] n posa f; (posture) atteggiamento m. v posare, atteggiarsi (a); (propound) porre.

posh [pɒʃ] adj elegante.

position [pə'ziʃən] n posizione f, situazione f; (employment) posto m. v collocare, piazzare.

positive ['pɒzətiv] adj positivo; (certain) sicuro. n (phot) positiva f; (gramm) positivo m.

possess [pə'zes] v possedere, avere. **possessed** adj ossesso, frenetico. **possession** n possesso m. **possessions** pl n (goods) beni personali pl m. **possessive** nm, adj possessivo. **possessor** n possessore m, possessore f.

possible ['pɒsəbl] adj possibile. **possibility** n possibilità f. **possibly** adv (perhaps) forse, può darsi; (if possible) possibilmente.

post¹ [poust] n (pole) palo m. v affiggere.

post² [poust] n (job) posto m. v collocare.

post³ [poust] n (mail) posta f. **post-box** n buca da lettere f. **postcard** n cartolina f. **postman** n postino m. **postmark** n timbro postale m. **postmarked** adj timbrato. **post office** posta f, ufficio postale m. **post office box** casella postale f. v imbucare; (book-keeping) registrare. **keep posted** tenere al corrente. **postage** n tariffa postale f. **postage stamp** francobollo m. **postal** adj postale. **postal order** vaglia postale m invar.

poste restante [poust'restãt] adv fermo posta.

poster ['pousta] n cartellone m, manifesto m, avviso pubblicitario m.

posterior [po'stiaria] adj posteriore.

posterity [po'steriti] n posterità f.

postgraduate [poust'grædjuit] adj di perfezionamento or specializzazione. n laureato, -a che continua gli studi universitari m, f.

posthumous ['postjumas] adj postumo.

post-mortem [poust'mɔːtəm] n autopsia f.

postpone [pous'poun] v posporre, rinviare. **postponement** n rinvio m.

postscript [pousskript] n poscritto m.

postulate ['postjuleit; n 'postjulət] v postulare. n postulato m.

posture ['postʃə] n posizione f; (attitude) atteggiamento m. v assumere una posa.

pot [pot] n vaso m; (pan) pentola f; (container) recipiente m. v (plant) piantare in vaso; (billiards) mandare in buca. **pot-belly** n pancione m. **pot-bellied** adj panciuto. **take pot luck** mangiare alla buona.

potassium [pə'tasjəm] n potassio m. **potash** n potassa f.

potato [pə'teitou] n patata f.

potent ['poutant] adj potente, forte. **potency** n potenza f.

potential [pə'tenʃəl] adj, nm potenziale.

pot-hole ['pothoul] n (cave) spelonca f; (in road) buca f. **pot-holer** n speleologo, -a m, f. **pot-holing** n speleologia f.

potion ['pouʃən] n pozione f.

potter[1] ['potə] v **potter about** lavoricchiare.

potter[2] ['potə] n ceramista m, f, vasaio, -a m, f.

pottery ['potəri] n (ware) ceramica f; (workshop) laboratorio di ceramiche m.

potty[1] ['poti] adj (coll) matto.

potty[2] ['poti] n (coll) vaso da notte m, pitale m.

pouch [pautʃ] n borsa f, tasca f, sacchetto m.

poultice ['poultis] n cataplasma m.

poultry ['poultri] n pollame m. **poulterer** n pollivendolo, -a m, f.

pounce [pauns] n sbalzo m. v balzare. **pounce on** piombare su, saltare addosso a.

pound[1] [paund] v (hit) pestare, battere. n colpo m.

pound[2] [paund] n (weight) libbra f; (sterling) lira sterlina f.

pound[3] [paund] n (enclosure) recinto m.

pour [pɔː] v versare, riversarsi; (rain) scrosciare.

pout [paut] v fare il broncio. n broncio m.

poverty ['povəti] n povertà f, miseria f. **poverty-stricken** adj bisognoso, indigente.

powder ['paudə] n polvere f; (cosmetic) cipria f. **powder compact** portacipria m invar. **powder puff** piumino per la cipria m. v polverizzare, incipriare. **powdery** adj polveroso.

power ['pauə] n potere m; (pol, phys, etc.) potenza f; (tech) energia f, forza f. **powers** pl n facoltà f pl. **power station** centrale elettrica f. **powerful** adj potente. **powerless** adj impotente, incapace.

practicable ['praktikəbl] adj fattibile.

practical ['praktikəl] adj pratico. **for practical purposes** in pratica. **practical joke** beffa f. **practically** adv in effetto, quasi.

practice ['praktis] n pratica f; esercizio m; (sport) allenamento m; clientela f; (rel) praticante. **normal practice** regola f. **out of practice** fuori esercizio.

practise ['praktis] v praticare, esercitare; (music) esercitarsi; (sport) allenarsi. **practised** adj esperto, pratico. **practising** adj (rel) praticante.

practitioner [prak'tiʃənə] n **general practitioner** medico generico m.

pragmatic [prag'matik] adj prammatico; (officious) inframmettente; dogmatico. **pragmatism** n pragmatismo m; dogmatismo m.

Prague [praːg] n Praga f.

prairie ['preəri] n prateria f.

praise [preiz] n lode f, elogio m. v lodare, elogiare. **praiseworthy** adj lodevole.

pram [pram] n carrozzella f.

prance [prams] v pavoneggiarsi; (child) saltellare; (horse) impennarsi.

prank [prank] n burla f, tiro m. **play a prank on** fare un tiro a.

prattle ['pratl] v cianciare, ciarlare.

prawn [prɔːn] n gambero m, palemone m.

pray [prei] v pregare. **prayer** n preghiera f. **prayer-book** n libro di preghiere m; (missal) messale m.

preach [priːtʃ] v predicare. **preach a sermon** fare una predica. **preacher** n predicatore m.

preamble [priː'ambl] n preambolo m.

prearrange [priːə'reindʒ] v predisporre.

precarious [pri'keəriəs] *adj* precario, incerto.

precaution [pri'kɔːʃən] *n* precauzione *f*.

precede [pri'siːd] *v* precedere. **precedence** *n* precedenza *f*. **precedent** *n* precedente *m*.

precinct ['priːsiŋkt] *n (area)* zona *f*; ambito *m*.

precious ['preʃəs] *adj* prezioso.

precipice ['presipis] *n* precipizio *m*.

precipitate [pri'sipiteit; *adj* pri'sipitət] *v* precipitare; *(hurry up)* affrettare. *n* precipitato *m*. *adj* precipitoso.

précis ['preisi] *n* sunto *m*.

precise [pri'sais] *adj* preciso, esatto; *(strict)* puntiglioso. **precision** *n* precisione *f*, esattezza *f*.

preclude [pri'kluːd] *v* precludere.

precocious [pri'kouʃəs] *adj* precoce. **precociousness** *n* precocità *f*.

preconceive [ˌpriːkən'siːv] *v* avere preconcetti su. **preconception** *n* preconcetto *m*.

precursor [pri'kəːsə] *n* precursore *m*.

predatory ['predətəri] *adj* predatore, rapace.

predecessor ['priːdisesə] *n* predecessore *m*.

predestine [pri'destin] *v* predestinare. **predestination** *n* predestinazione *f*.

predicament [pri'dikəmənt] *n* situazione imbarazzante *f*, pasticcio *m*.

predicate ['predikət] *n* predicato *m*.

predict [pri'dikt] *v* predire, pronosticare. **predictable** *adj* prevedibile. **prediction** *n* predizione *f*.

predispose [ˌpriːdi'spouz] *v* predisporre. **predisposition** *n* predisposizione *f*.

predominate [pri'domineit] *v* predominare, prevalere. **predominance** *n* predominio *m*, ascendente *f*.

pre-eminent [priː'eminənt] *adj* preminente, per eccellenza. **pre-eminence** *n* preminenza *f*.

preen [priːn] *v* **preen oneself** *(bird)* lisciarsi le penne; *(person)* agghindarsi.

prefabricate [priː'fabrikeit] *v* prefabbricare. **prefab** *n (coll)* casa prefabbricata *f*.

preface ['prefis] *n* prefazione *f*. *v* premettere.

prefect ['priːfekt] *n* prefetto *m*; *(school)* capoclasse *m*.

prefer [pri'fəː] *v* preferire. **preferable** *adj* preferibile. **preference** *n* preferenza *f*. **preference shares** azioni privilegiate *f pl*. **preferential** *adj* preferenziale, di favore.

prefix ['priːfiks] *n* prefisso *m*. *v* prefiggere.

pregnant ['pregnənt] *adj* incinta; *(animal)* gravida. **pregnancy** *n* gravidanza *f*.

prehistoric [ˌpriːhi'storik] *adj* preistorico. **prehistory** *n* preistoria *f*.

prejudice ['predʒədis] *n* pregiudizio *m*, prevenzione *f*. **have a prejudice against** esser prevenuto contro. *v* pregiudicare, compromettere. **prejudiced** *adj* prevenuto.

preliminary [pri'liminəri] *nm, adj* preliminare.

prelude ['preljuːd] *n* preludio *m*.

premarital [priː'maritl] *adj* prematrimoniale.

premature [premə'tʃuə] *adj* prematuro.

premeditate [priː'mediteit] *v* premeditare. **premeditation** *n* premeditazione *f*.

premier ['premiə] *adj* primo, primario. *n* primo ministro *m*.

premiere ['premieə] *n* prima (rappresentazione) *f*.

premise ['premis] *n* premessa *f*. **premises** *n* locali *m pl*. **off the premises** fuori. **on the premises** sul posto.

premium ['priːmiəm] *n* premio *m*; *(finance)* aggio *m*. **at a premium** *(econ)* sopra la pari.

premonition [ˌpremə'niʃən] *n* premonizione *f*.

preoccupied [priː'okjupaid] *adj* preoccupato. **preoccupation** *n* preoccupazione *f*.

prepare [pri'peə] *v* preparare. **preparation** *n* preparazione *f*. **preparatory** *adj* preparatorio.

preposition [ˌprepə'ziʃən] *n* preposizione *f*.

preposterous [pri'postərəs] *adj* assurdo.

prerequisite [priː'rekwizit] *n* requisito (principale) *m*.

prerogative [pri'rogətiv] *n* prerogativa *f*.

prescribe [pri'skraib] *v* prescrivere. **prescription** *n* prescrizione *f*; *(med)* ricetta medica *f*.

presence ['prezns] *n* presenza *f*; *(appearance)* aspetto *m*.

present¹ ['preznt] *adj* presente, attuale. *n (time)* presente *m*. **at present** attualmente. **for the present** per ora. **presently** *adv* quanto prima.

present² [pri'zent; *n* 'preznt] *v* presentare, offrire. *n (gift)* regalo *m*. **presentable** *adj* presentabile. **presentation** *n* presentazione *f*.

preserve [pri'zɜːv] v conservare, preservare; (*appearances*) salvare. n (*food*) conserva f; (*reserve*) riserva f. **preservation** n preservazione f. **preservative** nm, adj preservativo.

preside [pri'zaid] v **preside over** presiedere a.

president ['prezidənt] n presidente m. **presidency** n presidenza f. **presidential** adj presidenziale.

press [pres] v premere; (*squeeze*) comprimere, schiacciare; far pressione su; insistere su; (*iron*) stirare. **press-button** n pulsante m. **press-stud** n bottone automatico m. n (*newspapers*) stampa f; (*printing*) macchina da stampa f; (*publishing house*) casa editrice f; (*tech*) torchio m. **press cutting** ritaglio (di giornale) m. **pressing** adj urgente.

pressure ['preʃə] n pressione m. **pressure-cooker** n pentola a pressione f. **pressurize** v pressurizzare; (*force*) far pressione su.

prestige [pre'stiːʒ] n prestigio m.

presume [pri'zjuːm] v presumere, supporre. **presumption** n presunzione f, supposizione f; arroganza f. **presumptuous** adj presuntuoso. **presumptive** adj presunto.

pretend [pri'tend] v pretendere; (*feign*) fingere, far finta. **pretence** n pretesa f; (*pretext*) pretesto m. **pretension** n pretensione f. **pretentious** adj pretenzioso, pieno di pretese.

pretext ['priːtekst] n pretesto m.

pretty ['priti] adj carino, simpatico. adv (*quite*) piuttosto, abbastanza; (*moderately*) quasi.

prevail [pri'veil] v prevalere. **prevail upon** persuadere, indurre. **prevalent** adj prevalente.

prevent [pri'vent] v impedire. **prevention** n prevenzione f; (*med*) profilassi f.

preview ['priːvjuː] n anteprima f.

previous ['priːviəs] adj precedente, anteriore. **previously** adv prima.

prey [prei] n preda f. **be/fall a prey to** essere/cadere in preda a. v **prey on** predare; (*fear, etc.*) rodere.

price [prais] n prezzo m. **price-list** n listino dei prezzi m. v valutare, fare il prezzo di. **priceless** adj impagabile; (*very amusing*) divertentissimo.

prick [prik] v pungere, punzecchiare.

prick up one's ears drizzare le orecchie. n puntura f.

prickle ['prikl] n spina f. **prickly** adj spinoso; (*sensitive*) difficile. **prickly pear** fico d'India m.

pride [praid] n orgoglio m, amor proprio m; (*best part*) fiore m. v **pride oneself on** essere orgoglioso di.

priest [priːst] n prete m, sacerdote m. **priesthood** n sacerdozio m.

prig [prig] n borioso, -a m, f. **priggish** adj borioso.

prim [prim] adj affettato, compassato; (*formal*) cerimonioso.

primary ['praiməri] adj primario, fondamentale, primo. **primary school** scuola elementare f.

primate ['praimət] n primate m. **primacy** n primato m.

prime [praim] adj primo; di prima qualità. n fiore m, primavera f. v (*arms*) innescare; (*paint*) mesticare; (*information*) mettere al corrente; (*pump*) adescare. **primer** n (*book*) testo elementare m; (*paint*) mestica f.

primitive ['primitiv] adj primitivo.

primrose ['primrouz] n primula f.

primus stove ['praiməs] n fornello a petrolio m.

prince [prins] n principe m. **princess** n principessa f.

principal ['prinsəpəl] adj principale, primo. n (*of business*) principale m, f; (*of school*) direttore, -trice m, f; (*comm*) capitale m.

principle ['prinsəpəl] n principio m.

print [print] v stampare, imprimere; (*handwriting*) scrivere a stampatello. n stampa f; impressione f; (*phot*) copia f. **out of print** esaurito. **printer** n tipografo m. **printing** n tipografia f; (*edition*) tiratura f.

prior[1] ['praiə] adj precedente, anteriore. **prior to** prima di. **priority** n precedenza f.

prior[2] ['praiə] n priore m. **prioress** n priora f. **priory** n convento m, monastero m.

prise [praiz] v far leva su. **prise open** forzare.

prism ['prizm] n prismo m.

prison ['prizn] n prigione f. **prisoner** n prigioniero, -a m, f. **take prisoner** far prigioniero.

private ['praivət] adj privato, personale. n soldato semplice m. **privacy** n intimità f.

privet ['privət] n ligustro m.

privilege ['privəlidʒ] n privilegio m.

privy ['privi] adj privato. **be privy to** essere a conoscenza di.

prize [praiz] n (reward) premio m. **prize-fighter** n pugile m. **prize-giving** n distribuzione dei premi f. **prizewinner** n vincitore, -trice m, f. v apprezzare, valutare.

probable ['probəbl] adj probabile. **probability** n probabilità f.

probation [prə'beiʃən] n (law) libertà condizionata f; (for job, etc.) periodo di prova m. **probationary** adj di prova.

probe [proub] v esplorare, sondare. n (investigation) sondaggio m, inchiesta f; (instrument) sonda f.

problem ['probləm] n problema m. **problematic** adj problematico.

proceed [prə'siid] v procedere, proseguire. **proceeds** pl n ricavo m sing, incasso m sing. **procedure** n procedura f; (proceeding) procedimento m.

process ['prouses] n processo m, andamento m; (procedure) procedimento m. v trattare, trasformare. **processed cheese** formaggio fuso m.

procession [prə'seʃən] n processione f, sfilata f.

proclaim [prə'kleim] v proclamare. **proclamation** n proclama m.

procrastinate [prə'krastineit] v procrastinare.

procreate ['proukrieit] v procreare. **procreation** n procreazione f.

procure [prə'kjuə] v procurare. **procurement** n approvvigionamento m.

prod [prod] v (incite) sollecitare; (push) spingere.

prodigy ['prodidʒi] n prodigio m.

produce [prə'djuːs; n 'prodjuːs] v produrre; (pull out) tirar fuori; (theatre) mettere in scena. n prodotti or generi agricoli m pl. **producer** n produttore, -trice m, f; (theatre, etc.) regista m, f. **product** n prodotto m, frutto m. **production** n produzione f; messa in scena f. **productive** adj produttivo; fertile. **productivity** n produttività f.

profane [prə'fein] adj profano. **profanity** n profanità f; (language) bestemmia f.

profess [prə'fes] v professare, manifestare; (practise) esercitare; (imply) pretendere di. **professed** adj (avowed)

dichiarato. **profession** n professione f; dichiarazione f.

professional [prə'feʃənl] n professionista m, f. adj professionale. **professionalism** n professionismo m.

professor [prə'fesə] n professore, -essa m, f.

proficient [prə'fiʃənt] adj competente, provetto. **proficiency** n perizia f, competenza f.

profile ['proufail] n profilo m.

profit ['profit] n profitto m, guadagno m. v (be of benefit to) giovare a, essere utile a. **profit from** approfittare di, trarre profitto da. **profitable** adj vantaggioso; lucroso.

profound [prə'faund] adj profondo.

profuse [prə'fjuːs] adj abbondante, prodigo. **apologize profusely** profondersi in scuse. **profusion** n abbondanza f.

prognosis [prog'nousis] n prognosi f.

programme ['prougram] n programma m. v programmare.

progress ['prougres] v progredire, avanzare. n progresso m, andamento m. **progression** n progressione f. **progressive** adj progressivo.

prohibit [prə'hibit] v proibire, vietare. **prohibition** n proibizione f, divieto m; (of alcohol) proibizionismo m.

project ['prodʒekt] n progetto m, disegno m. v (plan) progettare; (math, screen) proiettare; (protrude) sporgere. **projectile** n proiettile m. **projection** n proiezione f; sporgenza f. **projector** n proiettore m.

proletariat [proulə'teəriət] n proletariato m. **proletarian** n, adj proletario, -a.

proliferate [prə'lifəreit] v proliferare.

prolific [prə'lifik] adj prolifico.

prologue ['proulog] n prologo (pl -ghi) m.

prolong [prə'loŋ] v prolungare.

promenade [promə'naid] v fare una passeggiata. n passeggiata f; (sea-front) lungomare m.

prominent ['prominənt] adj prominente; eminente, importante. **prominence** n prominenza; eminenza f. **give prominence to** dar risalto a.

promiscuous [prə'miskjuəs] adj indiscriminato. **promiscuity** n promiscuità f.

promise ['promis] v promettere, assicurare. n promessa f, assicurazione f. **promising** adj che promette bene.

promontory ['promantari] *n* promontorio *m*.

promote [pra'mout] *v* promuovere; *(comm)* lanciare. **promotion** *n* promozione *f*; lancio *m*.

prompt [prompt] *adj* pronto, sollecito. *v* ispirare, suggerire.

prone [proun] *adv* bocconi. **be prone to** essere disposto *or* propenso a.

prong [proŋ] *n* rebbio *m. v* infilzare.

pronoun ['prounaun] *n* pronome *m*.

pronounce [pra'nauns] *v* pronunciare; dichiarare. **pronounced** *adj* pronunciato, spiccato. **pronouncement** *n* dichiarazione *f*. **pronunciation** *n* pronuncia *f*.

proof [pruːf] *n* prova *f*; *(printing)* bozza *f*. *adj* impenetrabile, resistente (a). *v* impermeabilizzare.

prop¹ [prop] *n* appoggio *m*, sostegno *m*; *(building)* puntello *m. v* **prop up** sorreggere, appoggiare; puntellare.

prop² [prop] *n (coll)* oggetto teatrale *m*.

propaganda [propa'ganda] *n* propaganda *f*.

propagate ['propageit] *v* propagare. **propagation** *n* propagazione *f*.

propel [pra'pel] *v* spingere avanti, azionare. **propellant** *n* propellente *m*. **propeller** *n* elica *f*.

proper ['propa] *adj* proprio; *(right)* particolare; *(good)* buono. **properly** *adv* come si deve; correttamente; *(well)* bene.

property ['propati] *n* proprietà *f*; possesso *m*, beni *m pl*.

prophecy ['profasi] *n* profezia *f*. **prophesy** *v* fare il profeta, predire.

prophet ['profit] *n* profeta *m*. **prophetess** *n* profetessa *f*. **prophetic** *adj* profetico.

propitious [pra'piʃas] *adj* propizio, favorevole.

proportion [pra'poːʃan] *n* proporzione *f*. **out of proportion** sproporzionato, smisurato. **proportional** *adj* proporzionale.

propose [pra'pouz] *v* proporre, intendere; fare una proposta di matrimonio. **proposal** *n* proposta *f*; offerta di matrimonio *f*. **proposition** *n* proposta *f*; *(gramm)* proposizione *f*.

proprietor [pra'praiata] *n* proprietario *m*, padrone *m*. **proprietress** *n* proprietaria *f*, padrona *f*.

propriety [pra'praiati] *n* decoro *m*, decenza *f*.

propulsion [pra'pʌlʃan] *n* propulsione *f*.

prose [prouz] *n* prosa *f*. **prosaic** *adj* prosaico, banale.

prosecute ['prosikjuːt] *v* citare in giudizio, processare. **prosecution** *n* processo *m*. **prosecutor** *n* procuratore *m*, pubblico ministero *m*.

prospect ['prospekt; *v* pra'spekt] *n* prospettiva *f*, aspettativa *f*; *(view)* prospetto *m. v* esplorare. **prospective** *adj* futuro.

prospectus [pra'spektas] *n* prospetto *m*.

prosper [pra'spa] *v* prosperare. **prosperity** *n* prosperità *f*. **prosperous** *adj* prospero, benestante.

prostitute ['prostitjuːt] *v* prostituire. *n* prostituta *f*, puttana *f*. **prostitution** *n* prostituzione *f*.

prostrate [pro'streit; *adj* 'prostreit] *v* prostrare, prosternare. *adj* abbattuto.

protagonist [prou'tagonist] *n* protagonista *m, f*.

protect [pra'tekt] *v* proteggere. **protection** *n* protezione *f*. **protective** *adj* protettivo. **protector** *n* protettore, -trice *m, f*. **protectorate** *n* protettorato *m*.

protégé [protaʒei] *n* protetto, -a *m, f*.

protein ['proutiːn] *n* proteina *f*.

protest [pra'test; *n* 'proutest] *v* protestare. *n* protesta *f*; *(comm)* protesto *m*; *(pol)* contestazione *f*. **under protest** protestando.

Protestant ['protistant] *n(m+f)*, *adj* protestante. **Protestantism** *n* protestantesimo *m*.

protocol ['proutakol] *n* protocollo *m*.

proton ['prouton] *n* protone *m*.

protoplasm ['proutaplazam] *n* protoplasma *m*.

prototype ['proutataip] *n* prototipo *m*.

protract [pra'trakt] *v* protrarre, prolungare.

protractor [pra'trakta] *n* goniometro *m*.

protrude [pra'truːd] *v* sporgere.

proud [praud] *adj* orgoglioso, fiero.

prove [pruːv] *v* dimostrare, confermare.

proverb ['provaːb] *n* proverbio *m*.

provide [pra'vaid] *v* provvedere, fornire. **provide against** premunirsi contro. **provided that** purché. **providence** *n* provvidenza *f*.

province ['provins] *n* provincia *f*. **provincial** *adj* provinciale.

provision [pra'viʒan] *n* provvedimento *m*. **provisions** *pl n* viveri *m pl*, provviste *f pl*. **provisional** *adj* provvisorio.

proviso [pra'vaizou] *n* stipulazione *f*, condizione *f*.

provoke [prə'vouk] v provocare, irritare. **provocation** n provocazione f. **provocative** adj provocativo.

prow [prau] n prua f, prora f.

prowess ['prauis] n (ability) bravura f; (bravery) prodezza f, valore m.

prowl [praul] v girare furtivamente, vagare.

proximity [prok'simiti] n prossimità f.

proxy ['proksi] n (agency, authorization) procura f; (person) procuratore, -trice m, f.

prude [pruid] n persona che affetta pudore, puritano, -a m, f. **prudish** adj che affetta pudore, puritano.

prudent ['pruidənt] adj prudente, cauto. **prudence** n prudenza f, avvedutezza f.

prune¹ [pruin] v sfrondare; (tree) potare.

prune² [pruin] n prugna secca f.

pry [prai] v curiosare, ficcare il naso (in).

psalm [saim] n salmo m.

pseudonym ['sjuidənim] n pseudonimo m.

psychedelic [,saikə'delik] adj psichedelico.

psychiatry [sai'kaiətri] n psichiatria f. **psychiatric** adj psichiatrico. **psychiatrist** n psichiatra m, f.

psychic ['saikik] adj psichico.

psychoanalysis [,saikouə'nalisis] n psicanalisi f. **psychoanalyse** v psicanalizzare. **psychoanalyst** n psicanalista m, f. **psychoanalytic** adj psicanalitico.

psychology [sai'kolədʒi] n psicologia f. **psychological** adj psicologico. **psychologist** n psicologo, -a m, f.

psychopath ['saikəpaθ] n psicopatico, -a m, f.

psychosis [sai'kousis] n psicosi f. **psychotic** n, adj psicotico, -a.

psychosomatic [,saikəsə'matik] adj psicosomatico.

psychotherapy [,saikə'θerəpi] n psicoterapia f. **psychotherapist** n psicoterapista m, f.

pub [pʌb] n bar m invar.

puberty ['pjuibəti] n pubertà f.

pubic ['pjuibik] adj pubico.

public ['pʌblik] nm, adj pubblico. **public holiday** festa civile f. **public library** biblioteca comunale f. **public school** collegio privato m. **public-spirited** adj dotato di senso civico. **publican** n proprietario del bar m, oste m.

publication [,pʌbli'keifən] n pubblicazione f.

publicity [pʌb'lisəti] n pubblicità f. **publicist** n pubblicista m, f.

publicize ['pʌblisaiz] v divulgare; (advertise) fare la pubblicità a.

publish ['pʌblif] v pubblicare. **publisher** n (person) editore m; (firm) casa editrice f.

pucker ['pʌkə] v corrugare, raggrinzare.

pudding ['pudiŋ] n budino m, dolce m.

puddle ['pʌdl] n pozzanghera f.

puerile ['pjuərail] adj puerile.

puff [pʌf] n (of wind) soffio m; (of smoke) buffata f; (of breath) alito m; (powder) piumino m; (pipe, cigarette) boccata f. **puff pastry** pasta sfoglia f. v sbuffare.

pull [pul] n tirata f, strappo m; (influence) ascendente m. v tirare; (haul) trascinare. **pull back** tirare indietro, trattenere. **pull down** tirar giù; demolire. **pull in** (train) entrare in stazione. **pull oneself together** riprendere animo. **pull up** tirar su; (plant, etc.) strappare; (stop) fermarsi.

pulley ['puli] n puleggia f.

pullover ['pul,ouvə] n pullover m invar.

pulp [pʌlp] n polpa f. v ridurre in polpa.

pulpit ['pulpit] n pulpito m.

pulsate [pʌl'seit] v palpitare, pulsare. **pulsation** n pulsazione f.

pulse¹ [pʌls] n (beat) polso m; (elec) impulso m; vitalità f. v pulsare.

pulse² [pʌls] n (vegetables) legumi m pl.

pulverize ['pʌlvəraiz] v polverizzare.

pump [pʌmp] n pompa f. **petrol pump** distributore di benzina m. v pompare; (bullets) scaricare.

pumpkin ['pʌmpkin] n zucca f.

pun [pʌn] n gioco di parole m. v fare giochi di parole.

punch¹ [pʌntf] v (hit) picchiare, dare un pugno e cazzotto a. n pugno m; (coll) cazzotto m; (energy) forza f. **punch-drunk** adj stordito.

punch² [pʌntf] n (drink) ponce m.

punch³ [pʌntf] n (tool) punzone m. v (tickets) forare; (tech) punzonare; (stamp) imprimere.

punctual ['pʌŋktfuəl] adj puntuale. **punctuality** n puntualità f.

punctuate ['pʌŋktfueit] v interrompere ripetutamente; (sentence) mettere la punteggiatura. **punctuation** n punteggiatura f.

puncture ['pʌŋktfə] n puntura f; (tyre) foratura f. **have a puncture** avere una gomma a terra. v forare, bucare.

pungent ['pʌndʒənt] adj pungente, aspro; caustico.

punish ['pʌniʃ] v punire, castigare. **punishment** n punizione f, castigo (pl -ghi) m. **punitive** adj punitivo.

punt¹ [pʌnt] n (boat) barchino m.

punt² [pʌnt] v (bet) puntare. **punter** n giocatore d'azzardo m, scommettitore m.

puny ['pjuːni] adj sparuto, debole.

pupil¹ ['pjuːpl] n (school) allievo, -a m, f, alunno, -a m, f.

pupil² ['pjuːpl] n (anat) pupilla f.

puppet ['pʌpit] n burattino m.

puppy ['pʌpi] n cagnolino m.

purchase ['pɜːtʃəs] v acquistare, comprare. n acquisto m; (tech) presa f. **purchaser** n compratore, -trice m, f.

pure ['pjuə] adj puro. **purify** v purificare, depurare. **purity** n purezza f.

purée ['pjuəreɪ] n purè m.

purgatory ['pɜːgətəri] n purgatorio m.

purge [pɜːdʒ] v (purify) purgare; (pol) epurare. n purga f, epurazione f.

puritan ['pjuəritən] n, adj puritano, -a. **puritanism** n puritanesimo m.

purl [pɜːl] v (knitting) lavorare a punto rovescio; (edge) smerlare. n punto rovescio m; punto smerlo m.

purple ['pɜːpl] n porpora f. adj purpureo; (of face) paonazzo.

purpose ['pɜːpəs] n scopo m, proposito m. **on purpose** apposta.

purr [pɜː] n fusa f pl. v far le fusa.

purse [pɜːs] n borsa f; (for money) borsellino m. v contrarre.

purser ['pɜːsə] n commissario di bordo m.

pursue [pə'sjuː] v (seek to attain) perseguire; (follow closely) perseguitare; (continue) seguire, proseguire. **pursuit** n (quest) ricerca f; (chase) inseguimento m; (activity) impiego m (pl -ghi) m.

pus [pʌs] n pus m, materia f.

push [puʃ] n spinta f; (effort) sforzo m, energia f; (initiative) iniziativa f. **push-chair** n carozzina f. v spingere; (urge) spronare; (product) lanciare. **push away** allontanare. **push back** respingere. **push-over** n vittima facile f. **pushing** adj energico, aggressivo.

***put** [put] v mettere, porre; (question) rivolgere; (idea) esprimere. **put about** (rumour) diffondere. **put across** (explain) spiegare. **put aside** or by mettere da parte, risparmiare. **put down** (suppress) sopprimere; (land) atterrare; (ascribe) attribuire. **put forward** proporre, nominare. **put off** rinviare; (get rid of) sbarazzarsi di; (cause to dislike) ripugnare. **put out** (extinguish) spegnere; (inconvenience) disturbare. **put up** (lodge) offrire alloggio a; (stay) prendere alloggio; (raise) alzare; (notice, etc.) affiggere. **put up with** sopportare.

putrid ['pjuːtrid] adj putrido.

putt [pʌt] v colpire leggermente, fare il putting. n colpo leggero m, putting m invar.

putty ['pʌti] n stucco m. v stuccare.

puzzle ['pʌzl] n indovinello m; enigma m. v confondere, rendere perplesso. **puzzled** adj perplesso.

pygmy ['pigmi] n, adj pigmeo, -a.

pyjamas [pə'dʒɑːməz] pl n pigiama m sing.

pylon ['pailən] n pilone m.

pyramid ['pirəmid] n piramide f.

python ['paiθən] n pitone m.

Q

quack¹ [kwak] v (duck) schiamazzare.

quack² [kwak] n (med) ciarlatano m, medicastro m.

quadrangle ['kwɒdræŋgl] n (math) quadrangolo m; (arch) corte quadrangolare f.

quadrant ['kwɒdrənt] n quadrante m.

quadrilateral [kwɒdrə'lætərəl] nm, adj quadrilatero.

quadruped ['kwɒdruped] n quadrupede m.

quadruple [kwɒd'ruːpl] adj quadruplo.

quagmire ['kwægmaiə] n pantano m.

quail¹ [kweil] n (bird) quaglia f.

quail² [kweil] v aver paura, sgomentarsi.

quaint [kweint] adj interessante or pittoresco in un modo insolito.

quake [kweik] v tremare; (person) fremere. n (coll: earthquake) terremoto m.

Quaker ['kweikə] n quacchero, -a m, f.

qualify ['kwɒlifai] v qualificare; (define) precisare. **qualification** n qualifica f; (limitation) riserva f. **qualified** adj qualificato, idoneo; (limited) condizionato.

quality ['kwɒləti] n qualità f.

qualm [kwɑɪm] n scrupolo m, apprensione f.

quandary ['kwondəri] n situazione difficile f, imbarazzo m.

quantify ['kwontifai] v quantificare.

quantity ['kwontəti] n quantità f.

quantum ['kwontəm] n quanto m.

quarantine ['kworəntiɪn] n quarantena f. v mettere in quarantena.

quarrel ['kworəl] n lite f, bisticcio m. **pick a quarrel** attaccar briga. v litigare, bisticciare. **quarrelsome** adj litigioso.

quarry[1] ['kwori] n (prey) preda f.

quarry[2] ['kwori] n (mining) cava f. v scavare.

quarter ['kworɪə] n quarto m; (three months) trimestre m; (district, mercy) quartiere m. **at close quarters** da vicino. **quarters** pl n (mil) accantonamento m sing. v dividere in quattro; (mil) acquartierare. **quarterly** nm, adj trimestrale.

quartet [kwor'tet] n quartetto m.

quartz [kwots] n quarzo m.

quash [kwoʃ] v sopprimere; (law) annullare, cassare.

quaver ['kweivə] n (music) croma f; (shaky voice) tremolio m. v tremolare.

quay [kiɪ] n banchina f.

queasy ['kwiɪzi] adj che sente nausea.

queen [kwiɪn] n regina f.

queer [kwiə] adj strambo, bizzarro. **feel queer** sentirsi male. n (coll: homosexual) finocchio m.

quell [kwel] v reprimere, sopprimere.

quench [kwentʃ] v spegnere. **quench one's' thirst** dissetarsi.

query ['kwiəri] n domanda f, quesito m. v chiedersi; (raise doubt) mettere in dubbio.

quest [kwest] n ricerca f.

question ['kwestʃən] n questione f, domanda f; (gramm) interrogazione f; problema m. **question mark** punto interrogativo m. v interrogare; (query) mettere in dubbio.

queue [kjuɪ] n coda f. v fare la coda, mettersi in coda.

quibble ['kwibl] n cavillo m. v cavillare.

quick [kwik] adj rapido, veloce; (lively) vivace. **quicksand** n sabbia mobile f. **quicksilver** n argento vivo m. **quick-tempered** adj impulsivo. **quick-witted** adj sveglio. adv presto. n **cut to the quick**

toccare sul vivo. **quicken** v affrettare, accelerare.

quid [kwid] n (coll) sterlina f.

quiet ['kwaiət] adj tranquillo, quieto. **keep quiet** tacere, star zitto. n quiete f, tranquillità f, silenzio m. **on the quiet** di nascosto. **quieten** v calmare, acquietare.

quill [kwil] n penna f.

quilt [kwilt] n trapuntare. n trapunta f; (duvet) piumino m.

quince [kwins] n cotogna f.

quinine [kwi'niɪn] n chinino m.

quinsy ['kwinzi] n angina f.

quintet [kwin'tet] n quintetto m.

quirk [kwɜɪk] n tic chio m, vezzo m.

****quit** [kwit] v lasciare, abbandonare; (depart) partire.

quite [kwait] adv perfettamente, bene, affatto, proprio; (somewhat) abbastanza.

quits [kwits] adj pari. **call it quits** far pari e patta. **double or quits** lascia o raddoppia.

quiver[1] ['kwivə] v fremere; (voice) tremolare. n fremito m; tremolio m.

quiver[2] ['kwivə] n (arrows) faretra f.

quiz [kwiz] n quiz m invar. v interrogare. **quizzical** adj (odd) curioso; (ridiculing) beffardo.

quota ['kwoutə] n quota f, rata f; (trade) contingente m.

quotation n citazione f. **quotation marks** virgolette f pl.

quote [kwout] v citare; (price) quotare.

quotient ['kwouʃnt] n quoziente m.

R

rabbi ['rabai] n rabbino m.

rabbit ['rabit] m coniglio m.

rabble ['rabl] n plebaglia f.

rabies ['reibiz] n rabbia f. **rabid** adj (med) idrofobo; furioso; fanatico.

race[1] [reis] n (sport) corsa f, gara f. **race-course** n ippodromo m. **racehorse** n cavallo da corsa m. **race-track** n pista f. v correre; (compete) gareggiare con. **racing** adj da corsa. **racy** adj vivace, piccante.

race[2] [reis] n razza f. **racial** adj razziale. **racialism** or **racism** n razzismo m. **racialist** or **racist** n(m+f), adj razzista.

rack[1] [rak] n rastrelliera f; (for plates) scolapiatti m invar; (tech) cremagliera f;

(*for luggage*) rete *f.* v **rack one's brains** scervellarsi, lambiccarsi il cervello.

rack¹ [rak] *n* **go to rack and ruin** andare in malora.

racket¹ ['rakit] *n* (*bat*) racchetta *f.*

racket² ['rakit] *n* (*noise*) baccano *m*, chiasso *m*; (*dishonest scheme*) truffa *f.*

radar ['reidə] *n* radar *m.*

radial ['reidiəl] *adj* radiale.

radiant ['reidiənt] *adj* raggiante; splendido; (*joyful*) esultante; (*phys, tech*) radiante. **radiance** *n* splendore *m.*

radiate ['reidieit] *v* irradiare, raggiare. **radiation** *n* irradiazione *f*; (*phys*) radiazione *f.* **radiator** *n* (*car*) radiatore *m*; (*central heating*) termosifone *m.*

radical ['radikl] *n*(*m*+*f*), *adj* radicale.

radio ['reidiou] *nf invar, adj* radio.

radioactive [reidiou'aktiv] *adj* radioattivo. **radioactivity** *n* radioattività *f.*

radiography [reidi'ogrəfi] *n* radiografia *f.*

radiology [reidi'olədʒi] *n* radiologia *f.* **radiologist** *n* radiologo, -a *m, f.*

radish ['radiʃ] *n* ravanello *m.*

radium ['reidiəm] *n* radio *m.*

radius ['reidiəs] *n* raggio *m.*

raffia ['rafiə] *n* rafia *f.*

raffle ['rafl] *n* riffa *f.*

raft [rɑːft] *n* zattera *f.*

rafter ['rɑːftə] *n* trave *f.*

rag¹ [rag] *n* (*cloth*) straccio *m*, cencio *m*; (*derog: newspaper*) giornalaccio *m.* **ragged** *adj* lacero, cencioso.

rag² [rag] (*coll*) *v* prendere in giro. *n* baldoria *f.*

rage [reidʒ] *n* rabbia *f*, collera *f*; (*enthusiasm*) passione *f*, moda *f.* **be in a rage** essere furioso or arrabbiato. **fly into a rage** infuriarsi. *v* montare su tutte le furie, infuriarsi; (*storm, etc.*) imperversare. **rage against** inveire contro. **raging** *adj* furioso, violento.

raid [reid] *n* incursione *f*, razzia *f.* *v* fare un'incursione in, razziare, invadere. **raider** *n* razziatore *m.*

rail [reil] *n* (*bar*) sbarra *f*; (*barrier*) ringhiera *f*; (*handrail*) corrimano *m invar*; (*for train*) rotaia *f*, binario *m.* **by rail** col treno. **go off the rails** perdere le staffe. **railway** *n* ferrovia *f.*

railings ['reiliŋz] *pl n* cancellata *f sing*, inferriata *f sing.*

rain [rein] *n* pioggia *f.* **rainbow** *n* arcobaleno *m.* **raincoat** *n* impermeabile *m.* **raindrop** *n* goccia di pioggia *f.* *v*

piovere. **rain cats and dogs** piovere a catinelle. **rainy** *adj* piovoso.

raise [reiz] *v* (*lift up*) alzare; (*rear*) allevare; (*bring up*) sollevare; (*increase*) aumentare; (*cause*) suscitare.

raisin ['reizən] *n* uva secca *f.*

rake [reik] *n* (*tool*) rastrello *m.* *v* rastrellare. **rake up the past** rivangare il passato.

rally ['rali] *n* (*meeting*) raduno *m*; (*mot*) rally *m invar*; (*recovery*) ricupero di forze *m*, ripresa *f*; (*tennis, etc.*) scambio di colpi *m.* *v* radunare; riprendersi.

ram [ram] *n* montone *m.* *v* ficcare; (*of ships*) speronare.

ramble ['rambl] *n* gita *f*, giro *m.* *v* vagare, girovagare; (*speech*) divagare; (*mind*) delirare. **rambling** *adj* (*unconnected*) sconnesso, sconclusionato. **rambling rose** rosa rampicante *f.*

ramp [ramp] *n* rampa *f.*

rampage [ram'peidʒ] *n* **go on the rampage** andare su tutte le furie.

rampant ['rampənt] *adj* (*unchecked*) sfrenato; (*heraldry*) rampante.

rampart ['rampɑːt] *n* bastione *m.*

ramshackle ['ramʃakl] *adj* cadente.

ran [ran] *V* **run.**

ranch [rɑːntʃ] *n* fattoria (per l'allevamento di bestiame) *f*, ranch *m invar.*

rancid ['ransid] *adj* rancido.

rancour ['raŋkə] *n* amarezza *f*, rancore *m.*

random ['randəm] *adj* casuale, fortuito. **at random** a casaccio.

randy ['randi] *adj* lascivo.

rang [raŋ] *V* **ring².**

range [reindʒ] *n* (*assortment*) gamma *f*; (*mountains*) catena *f*; (*scope*) portata *f*; (*for shooting*) campo di tiro *m*; (*of voice*) estensione *f*; (*stove*) fornello *m.* **out of range** fuori tiro. **range-finder** *n* telemetro *m.* **within range** a portata; (*of gun*) a tiro. *v* (*arrange*) disporre; (*set in order*) schierare; (*between limits*) estendersi, variare.

rank¹ [raŋk] *n* (*class*) grado *m*; (*row*) fila *f.* **ranks** *pl n* truppe *f pl.* *v* (*arrange*) schierare; classificare; considerare.

rank² [raŋk] *adj* (*excessive*) rigoglioso; (*utter*) assoluto; (*smell*) puzzolente.

rankle ['raŋkl] *v* bruciare; (*cause bitterness*) amareggiare.

ransack ['ransak] *v* mettere sossopra, rovistare.

ransom ['rænsəm] n riscatto m. v riscattare.

rap [ræp] v picchiare, colpire. **rap over the knuckles** rimproverare. n colpetto m. **take the rap** accollarsi il biasimo.

rape [reip] n stupro m, violenza carnale f; (abduction) rapimento m. v violentare, stuprare; rapire.

rapid ['ræpid] adj rapido, veloce. **rapidity** n rapidità f.

rapier ['reipiə] n spada f, stocco m.

rapture ['ræptʃə] n estasi f. **rapturous** adj estatico.

rare¹ ['reə] adj (scarce) raro. **rarity** n rarità f.

rare² ['reə] adj (meat) al sangue.

rascal ['rɑːskəl] n briccone m, mascalzone m.

rash¹ [ræʃ] adj avventato, sconsiderato. **rashness** n avventatezza f, imprudenza f.

rash² [ræʃ] n (med) eruzione f.

rasher ['ræʃə] n fetta (di prosciutto) f.

raspberry ['rɑːzbəri] n lampone m. **blow a raspberry** (coll) fare una pernacchia.

rat [ræt] n ratto m; (coll: traitor) traditore m. **smell a rat** (coll) avere dei sospetti.

rate [reit] n (charge) tasso m; (speed) velocità f, passo m; (degree) grado m. **at any rate** comunque. **at this rate** così, a questo passo. **ratepayer** n contribuente m, f. **rates** n imposta f sing. v stimare, valutare, considerare.

rather ['rɑːðə] adv piuttosto, anzi. interj certo! altro che! **I would rather . . .** preferirei . . . .

ratify ['rætifai] v ratificare. **ratification** n ratifica f.

ratio ['reiʃiou] n rapporto m, proporzione f.

ration ['ræʃən] n razione f. **rations** pl n viveri m pl. v razionare.

rational ['ræʃənl] adj razionale.

rattle ['rætl] v sbatacchiare; (disconcert) sconcertare. n sbatacchio m; (toy, instrument) raganella f; (in throat) rantolo m.

raucous ['rɔːkəs] adj rauco.

ravage ['rævidʒ] v devastare. n devastazione f.

rave [reiv] v delirare. **rave about** andar pazzo di.

raven ['reivən] n corvo m.

ravenous ['rævənəs] adj vorace. **be ravenous** avere una fame da lupo.

ravine [rə'viːn] n burrone m.

ravish ['ræviʃ] v (delight) incantare; (rape) violentare. **ravishing** adj incantevole.

raw [rɔː] adj (not cooked) crudo; (not refined) greggio; (untrained) inesperto. **raw material** materia prima f. **touch on the raw** toccare sul vivo.

ray¹ [rei] n raggio m.

ray² [rei] n (fish) razza f.

rayon ['reion] n raion m.

razor ['reizə] n rasoio m. **razor blade** lametta f.

reach [riːtʃ] n portata f; (continuous stretch) tratto m. **out of reach** fuori mano. **within reach** a portata di mano. v (get to) raggiungere; (hand) porgere.

react [ri'ækt] v reagire. **reaction** n reazione f. **reactionary** n, adj reazionario, -a. **reactor** n reattore m.

***read** [riːd] v leggere; studiare. **well-read** adj istruito. **readable** adj leggibile. **reader** n lettore, -trice m, f. **readership** n lettori m pl. **reading** n lettura f; interpretazione f.

readjust [riːə'dʒʌst] v raggiustare.

ready ['redi] adj pronto, preparato; (willing) disposto. **get ready** preparare, prepararsi. **ready-made** adj confezionato. **ready money** contanti m pl.

real [riəl] adj reale, effettivo, genuino. **real estate** beni immobili m pl. **realism** n realismo m. **realist** n realista m, f. **realistic** adj realistico. **reality** n realtà f.

realize ['riəlaiz] v realizzare. **realization** n realizzazione f.

really ['riəli] adv effettivamente, (before adj) proprio. interj davvero.

realm [relm] n dominio m; (special field) campo m.

reap [riːp] v mietere; (profit, etc.) raccogliere.

reappear [riːə'piə] v riapparire. **reappearance** n ricomparsa f.

rear¹ [riə] n (back) dietro m, parte posteriore f; (mil) retroguardia f. **at the rear of** dietro a. **rear-view mirror** retrovisore m. **stay in the rear** restare per ultimo. adj posteriore.

rear² [riə] v (raise) allevare; (horse, etc.) impennarsi; (elevate) innalzare.

rearm [ri'ɑːm] v riarmare. **rearmament** n riarmo m.

rearrange [riːə'reindʒ] v riordinare. **rearrangement** n riordinamento m.

reason ['rizn] n ragione f, causa f; (judgment) ragionevolezza f. **it stands to reason** è evidente. v ragionare. **reasonable** adj ragionevole, giusto. **reasoning** n modo di ragionare m.

reassure [riə'ʃuə] v rassicurare. **reassurance** n rassicurazione f.

rebate ['riːbeit] n sconto m.

rebel ['rebl] v ribellarsi. n ribelle m, f. **rebellion** n ribellione f. **rebellious** adj ribelle.

rebound [ri'baund; n 'riːbaund] v rimbalzare. n rimbalzo m.

rebuff [ri'bʌf] v respingere, rifiutare. n scacco m, rifiuto m.

*rebuild [riː'bild] v ricostruire. **rebuilding** n ricostruzione f.

rebuke [ri'bjuːk] n rimprovero m. v rimproverare.

recall [ri'koːl] v richiamare; (remember) rievocare, ricordare. n richiamo m, memoria f. **past recall** irrevocabile.

recap ['riːkap] (coll) v ricapitolare. n ricapitolazione f.

recede [ri'siːd] v recedere, inclinarsi all'indietro.

receipt [ri'siːt] v quietanzare. n ricevuta f. **receipts** pl n incasso m sing, entrate f pl.

receive [ri'siːv] v ricevere; (sustain) sostenere, riportare; (stolen goods) ricettare. **receiver** n ricettatore, -trice m, f; (bankruptcy) curatore fallimentare m; (phone) ricevitore m.

recent ['riːsnt] adv recente. **recently** adv di recente, poco fa.

receptacle [rə'septəkl] n recipiente m; (bot) ricettacolo m.

reception [rə'sepʃən] n ricevimento m; (radio) ricezione f. **receptionist** n segretaria f, receptionist f invar. **receptive** adj ricettivo.

recess [ri'ses] n nicchia f, pausa f; (holiday) vacanza f. **recesses** pl n (of mind, etc.) recessi m pl.

recession [rə'seʃən] n recessione f.

recharge [riː'tʃɑːdʒ] v ricaricare.

recipe ['resəpi] n ricetta f.

recipient [rə'sipiənt] n destinatario, -a m, f. adj ricevente.

reciprocate [rə'siprəkeit] v contraccambiare, reciprocare; (tech) alternarsi. **reciprocal** adj reciproco. **reciprocity** n reciprocità f.

recite [rə'sait] v recitare. **recital** n (narrative) racconto m; (entertainment) recital m invar. **recitation** n recitazione f.

reckless ['rekləs] adj imprudente, avventato. **recklessness** n avventatezza f.

reckon ['rekən] v contare; (consider) giudicare. **reckon on** contare su. **reckon with** prendere in considerazione. **reckoning** n (bill) resa dei conti f.

reclaim [ri'kleim] v redimere; (land) bonificare; (material) ricuperare. **reclamation** n bonifica f.

recline [rə'klain] v appoggiarsi.

recluse [rə'kluːs] n eremita m.

recognize ['rekəgnaiz] v riconoscere. **recognition** n riconoscimento m. **recognizable** adj riconoscibile.

recoil [rə'koil] v rinculare. **recoil from** rifuggire da. n rinculo m.

recollect [rekə'lekt] v rammentarsi di. **recollection** n memoria f, ricordo m.

recommence [riːkə'mens] v ricominciare.

recommend [rekə'mend] v raccomandare, consigliare. **recommendation** n raccomandazione f.

recompense ['rekəmpens] v compensare, risarcire. n indennizzo m, risarcimento m.

reconcile ['rekənsail] v mettere d'accordo, riconciliare. **reconcile oneself to** rassegnarsi a. **reconciliation** n rappacificazione f.

reconnoitre [rekə'noitə] v fare un sopralluogo; (mil) fare una ricognizione. **reconnaissance** n esplorazione f, sopralluogo (pl -ghi) m; (mil) ricognizione f.

reconstruct [riːkən'strʌkt] v ricostruire. **reconstruction** n ricostruzione f.

record [rə'koːd; v 'rekoːd] v registrare; notare; (as document) mettere a verbale. n tale registro m; (court report) verbale m; (sport) record m invar; disco m; (dossier) stato di servizio m. **keep a record of** prendere nota di. **off the record** ufficiosamente. **record-player** n giradischi m invar. **recorder** n (music) flautino m. **recording** n registrazione f.

recount [ri'kaunt] v riferire, raccontare.

recoup [ri'kuːp] v rifarsi di, compensare.

recourse [ri'koːs] n **have recourse to** ricorrere a. **without recourse** senza rivalsa.

recover [rə'kʌvə] v (get back) riprendere, ricuperare; (regain health) rimettersi.

recovery n ricupero m; (health) guarigione f.

recreation [rekri'eiʃən] n ricreazione f, passatempo m, svago m.

recrimination [rəkrimi'neiʃən] n recriminazione f.

recruit [rə'kruːt] n recluta f. v arruolare. **recruitment** n reclutamento m.

rectangle ['rektangl] n rettangolo m. **rectangular** adj rettangolare.

rectify ['rektifai] v rettificare; (elec) raddrizzare.

rectum ['rektəm] n retto m.

recuperate [rə'kjuːpəreit] v ricuperare; (get well again) rimettersi. **recuperation** n ricupero m.

recur [ri'kəː] v ricorrere, ritornare. **recurrence** n ricorrenza f; (of illness) ricaduta f. **recurrent** adj ricorrente.

red [red] adj rosso. **go red** (person) arrossire; (thing) diventar rosso. **redcurrant** n ribes m invar. **red-handed** adj in flagrante. **red herring** diversivo m. **red-hot** adj rovente. **Red Indian** n pellerossa (pl pellirosse) m, f. **n in the red** scoperto. **reddish** adj rossastro.

redeem [rə'diːm] v redimere, estinguere, svincolare. **redeeming feature** particolare che salva m. **redeemable** adj redimibile. **redemption** n redenzione f; salvezza f; liberazione f.

redress [rə'dres] n riparazione f, soddisfazione f. v soddisfare, correggere.

reduce [rə'djuːs] v ridurre. **reduced** adj ridotto. **reduction** n riduzione f.

redundant [rə'dʌndənt] adj superfluo. **make redundant** (employee) mettere in cassa di integrazione.

reed [riːd] n canna f; (of musical instrument) linguetta f.

reef [riːf] n scogliera f.

reek [riːk] v puzzare. n puzzo m.

reel[1] [riːl] n rocchetto m; (fishing) mulinello m; (film) rotolo m. v arrotolare. **reel off** rifilare.

reel[2] [riːl] v (sway) barcollare; (of head) girare.

refectory [rə'fektəri] n refettorio m.

refer [rə'fəː] v (report, ascribe) riferire; (consult) ricorrere, rivolgersi; (send back) rimandare. **referring to** con riferimento a. **reference** n riferimento m; (testimonial) referenza f, attestato m.

referee [refə'riː] n arbitro m. v arbitrare.

referendum [refə'rendəm] n referendum m.

refill ['riːfil] n refill m invar, pezzo di ricambio m.

refine [rə'fain] v raffinare. **refined** adj raffinato, squisito. **refinement** n (tech) raffinazione f; (manners) raffinatezza f. **refinery** n raffineria f.

reflation [rə'fleiʃn] n reflazione f.

reflect [rə'flekt] v riflettere; (manifest) rispecchiare. **reflection** n riflessione f. **on reflection** a pensarci su. **reflector** n riflettore m; (of vehicle) catarifrangente m.

reflex ['riːfleks] nm, adj riflesso. **reflexive** adj riflessivo.

reform [rə'foːm] n riforma f. v riformare, correggere. **reformation** n riforma f. **reformatory** n riformatorio m. **reformer** n riformatore, -trice m, f.

refract [rə'frakt] v rifrangere. **refraction** n rifrazione f.

refractory [rə'fraktəri] adj refrattario; (stubborn) ostinato.

refrain[1] [rə'frein] v astenersi, trattenersi.

refrain[2] [rə'frein] n ritornello m, ripresa f.

refresh [rə'freʃ] v rinfrescare, ristorare. **refresher course** corso di aggiornamento m. **refreshments** pl n rinfreschi m pl.

refrigerator [ri'fridʒəreitə] n frigorifero m.

refuel [ri'fjuəl] v rifornirsi di carburante.

refuge ['refjuːdʒ] n rifugio m. **take refuge** rifugiarsi. **refugee** n profugo, -a m, f.

refund [ri'fʌnd; n 'riːfʌnd] v rimborsare. n rimborso m.

refuse[1] [rə'fjuːz] v rifiutare, dire di no; (deny) negare, respingere; (prohibit) vietare. **refusal** n rifiuto m; (option) diritto di opzione m.

refuse[2] ['refjuːs] n rifiuti m pl, immondizia f.

refute [ri'fjuːt] v confutare.

regain [ri'gein] v riacquistare, riprendere. **regain consciousness** riprendere i sensi, rianimarsi.

regal ['riːgəl] adj regale.

regard [ri'gaːd] v (consider) stimare; (concern) riguardare. n riguardo m; rispetto m; considerazione f; deferenza f. **with regard to** riguardo a, per quanto riguarda. **regardless of** senza badare or riguardo a.

regatta [rə'gatə] n regata f.

regent ['riːdʒənt] n reggente m. **regency** n reggenza f.

regime [rei'ʒiim] n regime m.

regiment ['redʒimənt] n reggimento m. v irreggimentare. **regimental** adj reggimentale. **regimentation** n irreggimentazione f.

region ['riidʒən] n regione f, zona f. **regional** adj regionale.

register ['redʒistə] n registro m; (voting) lista elettorale f; (professional) albo m. v registrare; (show) indicare; (enter formally) iscriversi. **registered letter** (lettera) raccomandata f. **registered office** sede legale f. **registrar** n segretario m; ufficiale di stato civile m. **registration** registrazione f; iscrizione f. **registry office** ufficio di stato civile m.

regress [ri'gres] v regredire. **regression** n regressione f. **regressive** adj regressivo.

regret [rə'gret] n dispiacere m, rammarico m. **regrets** pl n (sorrow) rimorsi m pl; (excuses) scuse f pl. v rimpiangere, rammicarsi di. **regretful** adj spiacente. **regrettable** adj spiacevole.

regular ['regjulə] adj regolare. **regularity** n regolarità f.

regulate ['regjuleit] v regolare. **regulation** n regolamento m; (rule) regola f.

rehabilitate [riihə'biliteit] v riabilitare. **rehabilitation** n riabilitazione f.

rehearse [rə'həːs] v (theatre) provare; (enumerate) ripetere, recitare. **rehearsal** n prova f. **dress rehearsal** prova generale f.

reign [rein] n regno m. v regnare; prevalere.

reimburse [riiim'bəːs] v rimborsare. **reimbursement** n rimborso m.

rein [rein] n redine f, briglia f. **give free rein to** dare libero sfogo a. v **rein in** frenare.

reincarnation [riiinkaː'neiʃən] n reincarnazione f.

reindeer ['reindiə] n renna f.

reinforce [riiin'foːs] v rinforzare. **reinforced concrete** cemento armato m. **reinforcement** n rinforzo m.

reinstate [riiin'steit] v reintegrare. **reinstatement** n reintegrazione f.

reinvest [riiin'vest] v rinvestire.

reissue [ri'iʃuː] n nuova emissione f, ristampa f. v emettere di nuovo, ristampare.

reject [rə'dʒekt; n 'riidʒekt] v rifiutare, respingere; (discard) scartare. n scarto m. **rejection** n rifiuto m.

rejoice [rə'dʒois] v rallegrarsi, gioire. **rejoicing** n allegrezza f, allegria f.

rejoin [rə'dʒoin] v (join again) ricongiungere; (come back to) tornare a; (answer) rispondere; (law) replicare. **rejoinder** n risposta f, replica f.

rejuvenate [rə'dʒuːvəneit] v ringiovanire. **rejuvenation** n ringiovanimento m.

relapse [rə'laps] v ricadere; (med) riammalarsi. n ricaduta f.

relate [rə'leit] v (tell) narrare; (refer) riferire, riguardare; (be connected) aver rapporto. **related** adj associato, congiunto; (family) parente.

relation [rə'leiʃn] n (family) parente m, f; (connection) rapporto m; (narration) racconto m. **relationship** n parentela f, rapporto m.

relative ['relətiv] adj relativo. **relative to** (concerning) riguardante. n parente m, f. **relativity** n relatività f.

relax [rə'laks] v rilassare, allentare; (rest) riposarsi. **relaxation** n distensione f, riposo m; (entertainment) svago m.

relay ['riːlei; v ri'lei] n (shift) turno m; (elec) relè m invar, soccorritore m; (radio) trasmissione f. **relay race** (corsa a staffetta f. v trasmettere.

release [rə'liːs] v liberare, rimettere in libertà; (launch) lanciare; (let go) mollare; (publication) mettere in circolazione. n liberazione f; lancio m; (press) comunicato stampa m.

relent [rə'lent] v placarsi, cedere. **relentless** adj inesorabile, spietato.

relevant ['reləvənt] adj pertinente, a proposito. **relevance** n pertinenza f.

reliable [ri'laiəbl] adj fidato; sicuro; (information) attendibile. **reliability** n sicurezza f; (person) fidatezza f; attendibilità f.

relic ['relik] n reliquia f.

relief [rə'liif] n (alleviation) sollievo m; (help) soccorso m; (prominence) rilievo m. **relief map** n plastico m, levata topografica f.

relieve [rə'liːv] v alleviare; (help) soccorrere. **feel relieved** sentirsi sollevato.

religion [rə'lidʒən] n religione f. **religious** adj religioso, devoto.

relinquish [rə'liŋkwiʃ] v abbandonare, rinunziare a.

relish ['reliʃ] v apprezzare, godere. n piacere m, godimento m.

reluctant [rə'lʌktənt] *adj* restio, riluttante. **reluctance** *n* riluttanza *f*. **reluctantly** *adv* di malavoglia, a malincuore.

rely [rə'lai] *v* contare, fare assegnamento, fidarsi (di).

remain [rə'mein] *v* rimanere, restare. **remainder** *n* resto *m*, avanzo *m*. **remains** *pl n* resti *m pl*; (*mortal*) spoglie *f pl*.

remand [rə'maind] *v* rinviare. *n* rinvio *m*.

remark [rə'maːk] *n* nota *f*, osservazione *f*, commento *m*. *v* notare, osservare. **remarkable** *adj* notevole.

remarry [riː'mari] *v* risposarsi.

remedy ['remədi] *n* rimedio *m*. *v* rimediare, correggere; (*heal*) curare. **remedial** *adj* (*school*) correttivo; (*law*) riparatore.

remember [ri'membə] *v* ricordare, ricordarsi (di), rammentare. **remembrance** *n* memoria *f*, ricordo *m*.

remind [rə'maind] *v* ricordare, rammentare, richiamare alla mente. **reminder** *n* promemoria *m invar*, ricordo *m*.

reminiscence [remə'nisens] *n* reminiscenza *f*. **reminiscent** *adj* che rammenta.

remiss [rə'mis] *adj* negligente, disattento.

remit [rə'mit] *v* (*transmit*) rimettere; (*abate*) mitigare; (*send back*) rinviare; perdonare. **remittance** *n* rimessa *f*.

remnant ['remnənt] *n* scampolo *m*, resto *m*.

remorse [rə'mois] *n* rimorso *m*. **remorseful** *adj* preso *or* tormentato dal rimorso. **remorseless** *adj* spietato.

remote [rə'mout] *adj* remoto, lontano; (*faint*) pallido. **remote control** telecomando *m*.

remove [rə'muːv] *v* (*take off*) togliere; (*do away with*) eliminare; (*withdraw*) ritirare; (*move house*) traslocare. **removal** *n* (*house*) trasloco *m*; (*med*) ablazione *f*; (*act of removing*) rimozione *f*.

remunerate [rə'mjunəreit] *v* ricompensare. **remuneration** *n* ricompensa *f*, rimunerazione *f*. **remunerative** *adj* rimunerativo.

renaissance [rə'neisəns] *n* rinascimento *m*.

rename [riː'neim] *v* rinominare.

render ['rendə] *v* rendere; rappresentare; (*give back*) restituire; (*cookery*) struggere; (*building*) incalcinare.

rendezvous ['rondivuː] *n* appuntamento *m*, convegno *m*.

renegade ['renigeid] *n*, *adj* rinnegato, -a.

renew [rə'njuː] *v* rinnovare. **renewal** *n* rinnovamento *m*.

renounce [ri'nauns] *v* rinunciare a, ripudiare. **renouncement** *or* **renunciation** *n* rinunzia *f*.

renovate ['renəveit] *v* rinnovare, ripristinare; (*buildings*) restaurare. **renovation** *n* ripristinamento *m*; restauro *m*.

renown [rə'naun] *n* fama *f*. **renowned** *adj* rinomato, famoso, celebre.

rent[1] [rent] *v* affittare; (*take, occupy*) prendere in affitto; (*let out*) dare in affitto. *n* affitto *m*.

rent[2] [rent] *n* (*tear*) strappo *m*, rottura *f*.

reopen [riː'oupən] *v* riaprire. **reopening** *n* riapertura *f*.

reorganize [riː'oɪgənaiz] *v* riorganizzare. **reorganization** *n* riorganizzazione *f*.

rep[1] [rep] *n* (*coll*) teatro stabile, compagnia stabile *f*.

rep[2] [rep] *n* (*coll*) rappresentante *m*, *f*.

repair [ri'peə] *v* riparare, aggiustare. *n* riparazione *f*. **beyond repair** irreparabile. **in good/bad repair** in buono/cattivo stato. **repairer** *n* riparatore, -trice *m*, *f*.

repartee [repaɪ'tiɪ] *n* battuta di spirito *f*.

repatriate [riɪ'patrieit] *v* rimpatriare. **repatriation** *n* rimpatrio *m*.

*****repay** [ri'pei] *v* ripagare; (*refund*) rimborsare. **repayment** *n* rimborso *m*; ricompensa *f*.

repeal [ri'piɪl] *v* revocare, annullare. *n* revoca *f*, annullamento *m*.

repeat [rə'piɪt] *v* ripetere; (*food*) tornare a gola. *n* ripetizione *f*; (*music*) ripresa *f*.

repel [rə'pel] *v* respingere. **repellent** *adj* repellente.

repent [rə'pent] *v* pentirsi. **repentance** *n* penitenza *f*; (*regret*) pentimento *m*.

repercussion [riɪpə'kʌʃən] *n* ripercussione *f*.

repertoire ['repətwaɪ] *n* repertorio *m*.

repertory ['repətəri] *n* teatro stabile *m*. **repertory company** compagnia stabile *f*.

repetition [repə'tiʃn] *n* ripetizione *f*. **repetitive** *adj* che si ripete.

replace [rə'pleis] *v* rimpiazzare; (*put back*) rimettere a posto; sostituire. **replaceable** *adj* sostituibile. **replacement** *n* sostituzione *f*.

replay ['riːplei; *v* riː'plei] *n* rivincita *f*. *v* fare la rivincita.

replenish [rə'pleniʃ] *v* rifornire. **replenishment** *n* rifornimento *m*.

replica ['replikə] n facsimile m invar, copia f.

reply [rə'plai] n risposta f. v rispondere.

report [rə'pɔːt] n rapporto m, relazione f; (school) pagella f; (rumour) voce f; (noise) scoppio m. v (relate) riferire, fare un rapporto; denunciare; presentarsi. **reporter** n cronista m, f; reporter m invar.

repose [rə'pouz] n riposo m. v riposarsi.

reprehensible [repri'hensəbl] adj biasimevole, riprensibile.

represent [repri'zent] v rappresentare; (depict) raffigurare. **representation** n rappresentazione f. **representative** [repri'zentətiv] adj rappresentativo, caratteristico. n rappresentante m, f; (pol) deputato, -a m, f.

repress [rə'pres] v reprimere. **repressed** adj represso. **repression** n repressione f. **repressive** adj repressivo.

reprieve [rə'priːv] v graziare. n grazia f.

reprimand ['reprimaːnd] v rimproverare, sgridare. n rimprovero m, predica f.

reprint [riː'print] n; n 'riːprint] v ristampare. n ristampa f.

reprisal [rə'praizəl] n rappresaglia f.

reproach [rə'prout∫] v rimproverare, biasimare. n rimprovero m, biasimo m.

reproduce [riːprə'djuːs] v riprodurre. **reproduction** n riproduzione f. **reproductive** adj riproduttivo.

reprove [rə'pruːv] v rimproverare, sgridare. **reproof** n rimprovero m.

reptile ['reptail] n rettile m.

republic [rə'pʌblik] n repubblica f. **republican**, n adj repubblicano, -a.

repudiate [rə'pjuːdieit] v ripudiare; (disown) disconoscere; (reject) respingere. **repudiation** n ripudio m.

repugnant [rə'pʌgnənt] adj ripugnante. **repugnance** n ripugnanza f.

repulsion [rə'pʌl∫n] n ripulsione f, ripugnanza f. **repulsive** adj ributtante, schifoso.

repute [rə'pjuːt] v reputare, stimare. n also **reputation** reputazione f, fama f. **reputable** adj rispettabile, stimabile, onorevole. **reputedly** adv presumibilmente.

request [ri'kwest] n richiesta f, domanda f. v richiedere, domandare, sollecitare.

requiem ['rekwiəm] n requiem m invar.

require [rə'kwaiə] v richiedere; (demand)

esigere, pretendere; rendere necessario. **requirement** n esigenza f, bisogno m.

requisite ['rekwizit] adj necessario, indispensabile. n requisito m.

requisition [rekwi'zi∫ən] v requisire. n (mil) requisizione f, ordine m.

re-route [riː'ruːt] v deviare.

resale [riː'seil] n rivendita f.

rescue ['reskjuː] n salvataggio m, soccorso m. v liberare; soccorrere. **rescuer** n liberatore, -trice m, f; soccorritore, -trice m, f.

research [ri'sɔːt∫] n ricerca f, indagine f. v fare or compiere ricerche, indagare. **researcher** n ricercatore, -trice m, f.

resemble [rə'zembl] v somigliare, rassomigliare. **resemblance** n somiglianza f, rassomiglianza f.

resent [ri'zent] v risentirsi di, offendersi or sdegnarsi per. **resentful** adj offeso, sdegnoso. **resentment** n risentimento m, sdegno m, rancore m.

reserve [rə'zɔːv] v riservare. n riserva f; (manner) riserbo m; (circumspection) riservatezza f. **reservation** n riserva f; (booking) prenotazione f.

reservoir ['rezəvwaː] n cisterna f, serbatoio m; (artificial lake) lago artificiale m, bacino di riserva m.

reside [rə'zaid] v dimorare, risiedere. **residence** n residenza f, dimora f. **residence permit** permesso di soggiorno m. **resident** n(m+f), adj residente. **residential** adj residenziale.

residue ['rezidjuː] n residuo m. **residual** adj residuo, rimanente.

resign [rə'zain] v dimettersi, rassegnare le dimissioni; (surrender) rinunciare a. **resign oneself to** rassegnarsi a. **resignation** n dimissioni f pl, rassegnazione f. **resigned** adj rassegnato.

resilient [rə'ziliənt] adj flessibile. **be resilient** (person) aver capacità di recupero. **resilience** n flessibilità f, resilienza f; capacità di recupero f.

resin ['rezin] n resina f. **resinous** adj resinoso.

resist [rə'zist] v resistere (a). **resistance** n resistenza f. **resistant** adj resistente.

***resit** [riː'sit] v ripetere.

resolute ['rezəluːt] adj deciso, risoluto. **resolution** n risoluzione f; (determination) risolutezza f; decisione f.

resolve [rə'zolv] v risolvere; decidere; (clear up) chiarire. n decisione f.

resonant ['rezənənt] *adj* risonante. **resonance** *n* risonanza *f*.

resort [rə'zɔːt] *v* resort to ricorrere a. *n* (*recourse*) ricorso *m*; (*expedient*) risorsa *f*; (*holiday*, *etc.*) luogo di soggiorno *m*, stazione di villeggiatura *f*.

resound [rə'zaund] *v* risonare, echeggiare.

resource [rə'zɔːs] *n* risorsa *f*. **resourceful** *adj* pieno di risorse, ingegnoso.

respect [rə'spekt] *v* rispettare, aver riguardo per. *n* rispetto *m*; (*esteem*) stima *f*, riguardo *m*; (*detail*) aspetto *m*. **pay one's respects to** rendere omaggio a. **with due respect** coi debiti riguardi. **with respect to** riguardo a, quanto a. **respectable** *adj* rispettabile; onesto; considerevole. **respectful** *adj* rispettoso. **respectively** *adv* rispettivamente.

respiration [respə'reiʃn] *n* respirazione *f*. **respirator** *n* (*med*) respiratore *m*; (*gas mask*) maschera antigas *f*. **respiratory** *adj* respiratorio.

respite ['respait] *n* tregua *f*, proroga *f*.

respond [rə'spond] *v* rispondere; reagire. **respondent** *n* (*law*) imputato, -a *m, f*. **response** *n* risposta *f*; reazione *f*; (*church*) responsorio *m*. **responsive** *adj* sensibile.

responsible [rə'sponsəbl] *adj* responsabile. **responsibility** *n* responsabilità *f*.

rest¹ [rest] *v* riposarsi; (*place*) posare; (*stay*) stare, fermarsi. *n* riposo *m*; (*support*) appoggio *m*. **restful** *adj* riposante, tranquillo. **restive** *adj* restio. **restless** *adj* inquieto, irrequieto.

rest² [rest] *n* resto *m*.

restaurant ['restront] *n* ristorante *m*, trattoria *f*. **restaurant car** vagone ristorante *m*.

restore [rə'stɔː] *v* ristabilire; (*building*, *etc.*) restaurare. **restoration** *n* ristabilimento *m*; restauro *m*; (*history*) restaurazione *f*.

restrain [rə'strein] *v* trattenere, reprimere, frenare. **restraint** *n* freno *m*, ritegno *m*; limitazione *f*.

restrict [rə'strikt] *v* restringere, limitare. **restriction** *n* restrizione *f*, limitazione *f*. **restrictive** *adj* restrittivo.

result [rə'zʌlt] *v* risultare, derivare. *n* risultato *m*, esito *m*. *v* risultare, derivare. **resultant** *adj* risultante.

resume [rə'zjuːm] *v* riprendere; riassumere. **resumption** *n* ripresa *f*.

résumé ['reizumei] *n* riassunto *m*.

resurgence [ri'sɜːdʒəns] *n* risurrezione *f*, rinascita *f*.

resurrect [rezə'rekt] *v* risuscitare. **resurrection** *n* risurrezione *f*.

resuscitate [rə'sʌsiteit] *v* risuscitare.

retail ['riːteil] *n* vendita al dettaglio *or* minuto *f*. *v* (*sell*) vendere al dettaglio *or* minuto; (*tell*) raccontare, dettagliare. *adv, adj* al dettaglio *or* minuto. **retailer** *n* dettagliante *m*.

retain [rə'tein] *v* ritenere, mantenere. **retainer** *n* (*law*) caparra *f*.

retaliate [rə'talieit] *v* contraccambiare, rendere la pariglia. **retaliation** *n* contraccambio *m*, rappresaglia *f*.

retard [rə'taɪd] *v* ritardare, ostacolare. **retarded** *adj* tardivo.

retch [retʃ] *v* aver conati di vomito.

reticent ['retisənt] *adj* reticente, riservato, taciturno. **reticence** *n* reticenza *f*, riservatezza *f*, taciturnità *f*.

retina ['retinə] *n* retina *f*.

retinue ['retinjuː] *n* seguito *m*.

retire [rə'taiə] *v* ritirarsi; (*go to bed*) andare a letto; (*give up work*) andare in pensione. **retired** *adj* in pensione, a riposo; (*withdrawn*) ritirato, appartato. **retirement** *n* ritirata *f*; riposo *m*.

retort¹ [rə'tɔːt] *v* ribattere, rimbeccare. *n* (*reply*) ritorsione *f*, rimbecco *m*.

retort² [rə'tɔːt] *n* (*chem*) storta *f*.

retrace [rə'treis] *v* (*follow up*) rintracciare; (*go back over*) ripercorrere; risalire alle origini di.

retract [rə'trakt] *v* (*withdraw*) ritirare, far rientrare; (*disown*) disdire.

retreat [rə'triːt] *n* ritiro *m*; rifugio *m*, asilo *m*; (*mil*) ritirata *f*. *v* ritirarsi, indietreggiare.

retrieve [rə'triːv] *v* ricuperare; riparare; rimediare. **retrieval** *n* ricupero *m*. **retriever** *n* (*dog*) cane da riporto *m*.

retrograde ['retrəgreid] *adj* retrogrado.

retrospect ['retrəspekt] *n* **in retrospect** guardando indietro. **retrospective** *adj* retrospettivo.

return [rə'tɜːn] *v* tornare, ritornare; (*put back*) rimettere; (*reciprocate*) contraccambiare; (*give back*) restituire; (*send back*) rinviare. *n* ritorno *m*; restituzione *f*; rinvio *m*; (*profit*) utile *m*; (*report*) relazione *f*, rapporto *m*; (*statement*) rendiconto *m*. **by return of post** a giro di posta. **in return for** in cambio di. **return**

match rivincita *f*. **return ticket** biglietto di andata e ritorno *m*.

reunite [rijuː'nait] *v* riunire. **reunion** *n* riunione *f*.

rev [rev] *v* (*mot*) n giro *m*. **rev counter** contagiri *m invar*.

reveal [rə'viːl] *v* rivelare, manifestare. **revelation** *n* rivelazione *f*.

revel ['revl] *v* (*take pleasure*) trovar diletto; (*make merry*) far baldoria. *n* also **revelry** baldoria *f*.

revenge [rə'vendʒ] *n* vendetta *f*. *v* vendicare.

revenue ['revinjuː] *n* (*income*) rendita *f*; (*yield*) reddito *m*; (*of state*) erario *m*; (*department*) fisco *m*.

reverberate [rə'vəːbəreit] *v* (*sound*) risonare, riecheggiare; (*heat, light*) riverberare. **reverberation** *n* riverberazione *f*.

reverence ['revərəns] *n* riverenza *f*, venerazione *f*. **reverend** *nm, adj* reverendo. **reverent** *adj* riverente. **reverential** *adj* reverenziale.

reverse [rə'vəːs] *v* rovesciare; (*inside out*) rivoltare; (*mot*) far marcia indietro. **reverse the charges** addebitare al destinatario. *adj* contrario, rovescio, inverso. *n* contrario *m*, rovescio *m*, inverso *m*; (*mot*) retromarcia *f*. **reversal** *n* rovesciamento *m*; (*law*) revoca *f*. **reversible** *adj* reversibile; (*law*) revocabile; (*fabric*) a due diritti.

revert [rə'vəːt] *v* ritornare.

review [rə'vjuː] *n* (*survey*) rassegna *f*, esame *m*; critica *f*, recensione *f*; (*mil, periodical*) rivista *f*. *v* riesaminare; fare la critica di; passare in rivista. **reviewer** *n* critico *m*.

revise [rə'vaiz] *v* rivedere, correggere. **revision** *n* revisione *f*.

revive [rə'vaiv] *v* rianimare, risvegliare; (*restore to use*) ripristinare. **revival** *n* risveglio *m*; ripristino *m*; (*theatre*) ripresa *f*.

revoke [rə'vouk] *v* revocare.

revolt [rə'voult] *v* ribellarsi; (*feel disgust*) provare orrore; (*cause disgust*) disgustare. **revolting** *adj* rivoltante, disgustoso; (*rebellious*) ribelle.

revolution [revə'luːʃən] *n* rivoluzione *f*; (*turn*) giro *m*. **revolutionary** *n, adj* revoluzionario, -a.

revolve [rə'volv] *v* (*turn*) girare; (*depend*) basarsi (su), dipendere (da). **revolver** *n*

rivoltella *f*. **revolving** *adj* (*door*) girevole; (*credit*) rotativo.

revue [rə'vjuː] *n* rivista *f*.

revulsion [rə'vʌlʃən] *n* ripugnanza *f*, disgusto *m*; (*med*) revulsione *f*.

reward [rə'woːd] *n* ricompensa *f*, compenso *m*. *v* ricompensare, rimunerare. **rewarding** *adj* rimunerativo.

rhetoric ['retərik] *n* retorica *f*. **rhetorical** *adj* retorico.

rheumatism ['ruːmətizəm] *n* reumatismo *m*. **rheumatic** *adj* reumatico.

Rhine [rain] *n* Reno *m*.

rhinoceros [rai'nosərəs] *n* rinoceronte *m*.

rhododendron [roudə'dendrən] *n* rododendro *m*.

rhombus ['rombəs] *n* rombo *m*.

rhubarb ['ruːbaːb] *n* rabarbaro *m*.

rhyme [raim] *n* rima *f*. *v* rimare, far rima.

rhythm ['riðəm] *n* ritmo *m*. **rhythmic** *adj* ritmico.

rib [rib] *n* costola *f*. **ribbed** *adj* a coste, scanalato.

ribbon ['ribən] *n* nastro *m*. **torn to ribbons** ridotto a brandelli.

rice [rais] *n* riso *m*.

rich [ritʃ] *adj* ricco; (*full*) pieno, abbondante; (*food*) pesante; (*colour*) intenso. **riches** *pl n* ricchezza *f sing*. **richness** *n* ricchezza *f*.

rickety ['rikəti] *adj* traballante, instabile; (*med*) rachitico.

****rid** [rid] *v* liberare, sbarazzare. **get rid of** sbarazzarsi di. **good riddance!** che liberazione!

ridden ['ridn] *V* **ride**.

riddle[1] ['ridl] *n* indovinello *m*, enigma *m*. **speak in riddles** parlare per enigmi.

riddle[2] ['ridl] *v* crivellare.

****ride** [raid] *n* (*on horseback*) passeggiata a cavallo *f*; (*on bicycle*) passeggiata in bicicletta *f*; (*in vehicle*) corsa *f*, giro *m*. **take for a ride** (*make fun of*) prendere in giro; (*deceive*) imbrogliare. *v* cavalcare, andare a cavallo. **rider** *n* (*horse*) cavallerizzo, -a *m*, *f*; ciclista *m*, *f*; motociclista *m*, *f*; (*additional clause*) clausola aggiunta *f*, codicillo *m*. **riding school** maneggio *m*.

ridge [ridʒ] *n* (*geog*) cresta *f*; (*raised strip*) costa *f*; (*roof*) colmo *m*; (*meteorology*) espansione di alta pressione *f*. *v* corrugare, incresparsi.

ridicule ['ridikjuːl] *v* mettere in ridicolo, canzonare. *n* ridicolo *m*. **be an object of**

ridicule esser posto in ridicolo. **ridiculous** *adj* ridicolo, assurdo.

rife [raif] *adj* diffuso, corrente.

rifle¹ ['raifl] *n* fucile *m*. **rifle-range** *n* poligono di tiro *m*.

rifle² ['raifl] *v* svaligiare. **rifle through** rovistare *or* frugare in.

rift [rift] *n* crepa *f*, spacco *m*; (*in relations*) disaccordo *m*, screzio *m*; (*geol*) falda *f*.

rig [rig] *n* (*naut*) attrezzatura *f*; (*industry*) impianto *m*; (*fraudulent dealing*) broglio *m*, manipolazione *f*. *v* attrezzare; (*equip*) montare; manipolare, manovrare.

right [rait] *adj* corretto, giusto; (*geom*) retto; (*not left*) destro. **be right** aver ragione. **right-angled** *adj* ad angolo retto. **right-hand man** braccio destro *m*. **right wing** (*pol*) destra *f*. **right-winger** *n* persona di destra *f*. *n* bene *m*, giusto *m*; (*law*) diritto *m*; (*not left*) destra *f*. **right of way** (*vehicles*) precedenza *f*; (*law*) servitù di passaggio *f*; (*path*) passaggio pubblico *m*. *adv* bene; (*exactly*) proprio; direttamente; completamente; (*direction*) a destra. **right away** subito. *v* (*restore to position*) raddrizzare; (*correct*) aggiustare, accomodare, metere a posto; (*redress*) riparare. **rightful** *adj* legittimo. **rightly** *adv* giustamente.

righteous ['raitʃəs] *adj* retto, giusto. **righteousness** *n* rettitudine *f*.

rigid ['ridʒid] *adj* rigido, inflessibile, rigoroso. **rigidity** *n* rigidezza *f*; (*stiffness*) rigidità *f*.

rigmarole ['rigməroul] *n* (*long procedure*) trafila *f*; (*nonsense*) filastrocca *f*.

rigour ['rigə] *n* rigore *m*. **rigorous** *adj* rigoroso, rigido.

rim [rim] *n* orlo *m*, bordo *m*; (*of wheel*) cerchio *m*; (*of spectacles*) montatura *f*.

rind [raind] *n* (*fruit*) buccia *f*, scorza *f*; (*cheese*) crosta *f*.

ring¹ [riŋ] *n* anello *m*; (*enclosure*) recinto *m*, pista *f*; (*boxing*) quadrato *m*, ring *m* *invar*. *v* cingere, circondare. **ringlet** *n* (*curl*) ricciolo *m*.

*ring² [riŋ] *n* (*sound*) suono *m*, squillo *m*; (*inherent quality*) tono *m*; (*coll*) telefonata *f*, colpo di telefono *m*. *v* suonare; (*echo*) risonare, echeggiare; telefonare (a).

rink [riŋk] *n* pista di pattinaggio *f*.

rinse [rins] *v* sciacquare, risciacquare. *n* risciacquatura *f*; (*hair*) cachet *m*.

riot ['raiət] *n* rivolta *f*, sommossa *f*; (*uproar*) baccano *m*, fracasso *m*; (*profusion*) orgia *f*. **riot squad** squadra mobile *or* volante *f*. *v* insorgere, far baccano. **riotous** *adj* tumultuoso; (*noisy*) chiassoso, clamoroso; dissoluto.

rip [rip] *n* strappo *m*, squarcio *m*. *v* strappare, squarciare. **let rip** (*give vent to*) dare libero sfogo a.

ripe [raip] *adj* maturo. **ripen** *v* (*far*) maturare. **ripeness** *n* maturità *f*. **ripening** *n* maturazione *f*.

ripple ['ripl] *n* increspamento *m*, crespa *f*; (*sound*) mormorio *m*. *v* increspare, mormorare.

*rise [raiz] *v* sorgere; (*get up*) alzarsi, levarsi; (*increase*) aumentare, salire; (*swell*) gonfiarsi; (*rebel*) insorgere. *n* salita *f*; aumento *m*. **give rise to** causare.

risen ['rizn] *V* **rise**.

risk [risk] *v* rischiare, arrischiare, correre il rischio di. *n* rischio *m*. **at the risk of a** rischio di. **risky** *adj* rischioso.

rissole ['risoul] *n* polpetta *f*, crocchetta *f*.

rite [rait] *n* rito *m*.

ritual ['ritʃuəl] *nm*, *adj* rituale.

rival ['raivəl] *n*(*m*+*f*), *adj* rivale. *v* rivaleggiare, competere. **rivalry** *n* rivalità *f*.

river ['rivə] *n* fiume *m*.

rivet ['rivit] *n* rivetto *m*. *v* rivettare. **riveting** *adj* affascinante.

road [roud] *n* strada *f*, via *f*. **road-block** *n* posto di blocco *m*. **road sign** cartello stradale *m*. **road-works** *pl n* lavori stradali *m pl*. **roadworthy** *adj* atto a prendere la strada.

roam [roum] *v* vagare, errare.

roar [ro:] *v* (*wild beast*) ruggire, urlare; (*sea*) muggire. **roar with laughter** scoppiare dalle risa. *n* ruggito *m*, urlo *m*; muggito *m*; (*thunder*) rombo *m*; (*laughter*) scroscio *m*.

roast [roust] *v* arrostire; (*coffee*) tostare. *n* arrosto *m*.

rob [rob] *v* derubare, rapinare; (*plunder*) svaligiare. **robber** *n* ladro *m*, rapinatore *m*. **robbery** *n* rapina *f*. **armed robbery** rapina a mano armata *f*.

robe [roub] *n* abito lungo *m*, toga *f*.

robin ['robin] *n* pettirosso *m*.

robot ['roubot] *n* automa *m*.

robust [rə'bʌst] *adj* robusto.

rock¹ [rok] *n* roccia *f*, scoglio *m*; (*support*) rocca *f*. **on the rocks** (*coll: without money*) al verde; (*coll: with ice*) con ghiaccio. **rock-bottom** *adj* bassissimo. **rock-crystal** *n* cristallo di rocca *m*. **rock-salt** *n* salgemma *m*. **rocky** *adj* roccioso.

rock² [rok] *v* dondolare, oscillare; *(baby)* cullare. **off one's rocker** *(coll)* matto. **rocking-chair** *n* sedia a dondolo *f*. **rocking-horse** *n* cavallo a dondolo *m*.

rocket ['rokit] *n* razzo *m*; *(reprimand)* cicchetto *m*. *v (increase sharply)* andare alle stelle.

rod [rod] *n* bastone *m*, stecca *f*; *(fishing)* canna di pesca *f*; *(piston)* biella *f*.

rode [roud] *V* ride.

rodent ['roudənt] *nm, adj* roditore.

roe¹ [rou] *n (deer)* capriolo *m*.

roe² [rou] *n (hard)* uova di pesce *f pl*; *(soft)* latte di pesce *m*.

rogue [roug] *n (dishonest person)* mariolo *m*; *(rascal)* briccone *m*, furfante *m*. **roguery** *n* bricconeria *f*. **roguish** *adj* bricconesco; *(mischievous)* furbo.

role [roul] *n* ruolo *m*, funzione *f*.

roll [roul] *v* rullare; *(wave)* ondeggiare; *(rotate)* roteare; *(ship)* rollare. **be rolling in money** guazzare nel denaro. **roll out** *(pastry)* spianare. **roll up** arrotolare. *n* rotolo *m*; *(bread)* panino *m*. **roll-call** *n* appello *m*. **roller** *n* cilindro *m*, rullo *m*. **roller-skate** *n* schettino *m*, pattino a rotelle *m*. **rolling-pin** *n* matterello *m*.

romance [rou'mans] *n* romanzo (cavalleresco) *m*; *(medieval tale)* romanza *f*; *(love affair)* idillio *m*, avventura amorosa *f*. **romantic** *adj* romantico; *(fanciful)* romanzesco.

Romania [ru'meinjə] *n* Romania *f*. **Romanian** *n, adj* romeno, -a.

Rome [roum] *n* Roma *f*. **Roman** *n, adj* romano, -a. **Roman Catholic** *adj* cattolico (romano).

romp [romp] *v* giocare rumorosamente, ruzzare. **romp home** *(win easily)* vincere facilmente. **romp through** *(exam)* superare con facilità. *n* trambusto *m*; *(coll)* cagnara *f*.

roof [ruːf] *n, pl* **-s** tetto *m*. **hit the roof** *(coll)* andare su tutte le furie. **roof of the mouth** palato *m*.

rook [ruk] *n (bird)* corvo *m*; *(chess)* torre *f*; *(swindler)* truffatore, -trice *m, f. v* barare, truffare.

room [ruːm] *n* stanza *f*, sala *f*, camera *f*; *(space)* posto *m*, spazio *m*; opportunità *f*. **room temperature** temperatura ambiente *f. v* alloggiare. **roomy** *adj* spazioso, vasto.

roost [ruːst] *n (building)* pollaio *m*; *(pole)* posatoio *m*. **rule the roost** fare il gallo del pollaio. *v* appollaiarsi.

root¹ [ruːt] *n* radice *f*; *(cause)* fondo *m*. **root and branch** radicalmente. **root cause** causa prima *f*. **take root** mettere radice. *v* piantare, abbarbicare; *(become fixed)* mettere radici, radicare.

root² [ruːt] *v* grufolare; *(search)* frugacchiare. **root for** *(slang)* sostenere. **root out** scovare.

rope [roup] *n* corda *f*, fune *f*. **know the ropes** esser pratico, saperla lunga. **learn the ropes** familiarizzarsi.

rosary ['rouzəri] *n* rosario *m*.

rose¹ [rouz] *V* rise.

rose² [rouz] *n* rosa *f*. **rose-bush** *n* rosa *f*, rosaio *m*. **rosy** *adj* roseo.

rosé ['rouzei] *n* rosato *m*.

rosemary ['rouzməri] *n* rosmarino *m*.

rosette [rou'zet] *n* coccarda *f*, rosetta *f*.

roster ['rostə] *n* turno di servizio *m*; *(mil)* ruolino *m*.

rostrum ['rostrəm] *n* tribuna *f*, piattaforma *f*.

rot [rot] *v* putrefare, marcire; *(teeth, wood)* cariare. *n* putrefazione *f*; *(rotten matter)* marciume *m*; *(coll: nonsense)* sciocchezze *f pl*; declino *m*. **rotten** *adj* marcio; *(coll: annoying)* seccante.

rota ['routə] *n* turno (di servizio) *m*, lista *f*.

rotate [rou'teit] *v* rotare; *(crops)* avvicendare. **rotary** *adj* *(motion)* rotatorio; *(tech)* rotativo. **rotation** *n* rotazione *f*; avvicendamento *m*.

rouge [ruːʒ] *n* belletto *m*, rossetto *m*.

rough [rʌf] *adj* *(coarse)* ruvido; *(person)* rozzo; *(ground)* malagevole, irregolare; *(sea, weather)* agitato, tempestoso; approssimativo; *(unrefined)* greggio. **rough-and-ready** *adj* improvvisato. **rough-and-tumble** *n* zuffa *f*, mischia *f*. *v* **rough it** vivere primitivamente. **rough out** abbozzare. **roughen** *v* irruvidire. **roughness** *n* ruvidezza *f*.

roulette [ruː'let] *n* roulette *f*.

round [raund] *adj* tondo, rotondo; circolare; sferico. *prep* tutto intorno a. *n* tondo *m*, cerchio *m*; *(tour)* giro *m*; *(game)* partita *f*; *(boxing)* ripresa *f*; *(ammunition)* scarica *f*; *(applause)* salva *f. adv* in giro. **all year round** tutto l'anno. **show round** fare da guida a. *v* **round off**

completare. **round up** (number) arrotondare.

roundabout ['raundəbaut] n anello stradale m. adj indiretto, obliquo.

rouse [rauz] v destare. **rousing** adj stimolante.

route [ruːt] n strada f, rotta f. **en route** per strada.

routine [ruːˈtiːn] n uso m, abitudine f.

rove [rouv] v errare, vagabondare.

row¹ [rou] n fila f.

row² [rou] v remare. n remata f. **rowing boat** barca a remi f.

row³ [rau] n (quarrel) rissa f, lite f; (noise) chiasso m, baccano m. v litigarsi.

rowdy ['raudi] adj chiassoso, turbolento. n attaccabrighe m, f invar.

royal ['roiəl] adj reale, regio, regale. **royalist** n(m+f), adj realista. **royalties** pl n diritti d'autore m pl; (status) regalità f, dignità di re f.

rub [rʌb] v fregare, strofinare. **rub down** (clean) pulire fregando; (dry) asciugare fregando. **rub out** cancellare. **rub shoulders** venire in contatto.

rubber ['rʌbə] n gomma f, caucciù m.

rubbish ['rʌbiʃ] n (waste) immondizia f; (derog) robaccia f; (nonsense) sciocchezze f pl. **rubbish bin** pattumiera f.

rubble ['rʌbl] n frantumi m pl, macerie f pl.

ruby ['ruːbi] n rubino f. adj (color) rubino or vermiglio.

rucksack ['rʌksak] n sacco da montagna m, zaino m.

rudder ['rʌdə] n timone m.

rude [ruːd] adj (discourteous) scortese; (unmannerly) rozzo, grossolano; (sturdy) robusto. **rudeness** n scortesia f; grossolanità f; robustezza f.

rudiment ['ruːdimənt] n rudimento m.

rueful ['ruːfəl] adj triste, lamentevole.

ruff [rʌf] n gorgiera f.

ruffian ['rʌfiən] n ruffiano m, farabutto m.

ruffle ['rʌfl] v arruffare, increspare.

rug [rʌg] n tappeto m; (travelling) coperta da viaggio f; (bedside) scendiletto m.

rugby ['rʌgbi] n rugby m invar, palla ovale f.

rugged ['rʌgid] adj irregolare; rude.

ruin ['ruːin] n rovina f. v rovinare. **ruinous** adj rovinoso.

rule [ruːl] n regola f, norma f; (ruler)

regolo m. **as a rule** di regola or solito. v regolare, dirigere; decidere; (mark with lines) rigare. **rule out** escludere. **ruler** n sovrano m, governatore m; (school) regolo m. **ruling** n direttiva f, decisione f.

rum [rʌm] n rum m.

rumble ['rʌmbl] v rimbombare, brontolare; (stomach) gorgogliare; (coll: detect) scoprire. n brontolio m, gorgoglio m.

rummage ['rʌmidʒ] v frugare, rovistare.

rummy ['rʌmi] n ramino m.

rumour ['ruːmə] n diceria f, voce f. v far correre voce.

rump [rʌmp] n groppa f, culatta f. **rump steak** bisteca f.

*****run** [rʌn] n corsa f; (outing) gita f; serie f invar; durata f. **in the long run** a lungo andare. **on the run** in fuga. v correre; (flow) scorrere; funzionare; (colour) spandere; (stockings) smagliare; (manage) dirigere. **run away** or **off** fuggire. **runaway** n, adj fuggiasco, -a. **run down** (slow) rallentarsi; (car, etc.) investire; (disparage) parlare male di; (find) trovare. **run in** rodare. **run into** (encounter) incontrare per caso, imbattersi; (collide with) urtare; (amount to) raggiungere. **run out** (supplies, etc.) esaurirsi. **run over** (car, etc.) investire; (overflow) traboccare; (rehearse) ripassare. **runway** n pista di decollo or atterraggio f. **runner** n corridore m; (messenger) fattorino m; (carpet) passatoia f; (plant) pollone m. **runner bean** fagiolo (rampicante) m. **runner-up** n secondo arrivato, seconda arrivata m, f.

rung¹ [rʌŋ] n piolo m.

rung² [rʌŋ] V **ring²**.

running ['rʌniŋ] n corsa f; funzionamento m; (competition) gara f. **be in the running** aver possibilità di vincere. **make the running** fare l'andatura. adj funzionante; regolare; consecutivo.

rupture ['rʌptʃə] n rottura f; (med) ernia f. v rompere.

rural ['ruərəl] adj campestre, rurale.

rush¹ [rʌʃ] v precipitarsi, avventarsi; (convey with haste) precipitare, spostare in fretta. n corsa precipitosa f; (intense activity) trambusto m; (haste) fretta e furia f; (sudden coming) accesso m. **rush hour** ora di punta f.

rush² [rʌʃ] n (plant) giunco m.

rusk [rʌsk] n biscotto (non dolce) m.

Russia ['rʌʃə] n Russia f. **Russian** n, adj russo, -a.

rust [rʌst] n ruggine f. **rustproof** adj inossidabile. v arrugginirsi. **rusty** adj arrugginito, rugginoso; (out of practice) fuori d'esercizio.

rustic ['rʌstik] adj rustico.

rustle ['rʌsl] n fruscio m. v frusciare, stormire.

rut [rʌt] n solco m, carreggiata f; (fixed habit) abitudine fissa f.

ruthless ['ruːθlis] adj spietato, implacabile.

rye [rai] n segala f.

S

sabbatical [sə'batikəl] adj sabbatico.

sable ['seibl] n zibellino m. adj di zibellino.

sabotage ['sabətɑːʒ] n sabotaggio m. v sabotare. **saboteur** n sabotatore, -trice m, f.

sabre ['seibə] n sciabola f. **sabre-rattling** n minaccia di guerra f, bravata f.

saccharin ['sakərin] n saccarina f.

sachet ['saʃei] n sacchetto profumato m.

sack [sak] n sacco m; (coll; dismissal) licenziamento m. **get the sack** (coll) essere mandato a spasso. v (coll) mandare a spasso.

sacrament ['sakrəmənt] n sacramento m. **sacramental** adj sacramentale.

sacred ['seikrid] adj sacro, sacrosanto.

sacrifice ['sakrifais] n sacrificio m; (comm) perdita f. v sacrificare; (comm) vendere sottocosto.

sacrilege ['sakrəlidʒ] n sacrilegio m. **sacrilegious** adj sacrilego (m pl -ghi).

sad [sad] adj triste. **sadden** v rattristare. **sadness** n tristezza f.

saddle ['sadl] n sella f. v sellare.

sadism ['seidizəm] n sadismo m. **sadist** n sadico, -a m, f. **sadistic** adj sadico.

safe [seif] adj sicuro; (unharmed) salvo; innocuo. **safe and sound** sano e salvo. **safe-conduct** n salvacondotto m. **safeguard** v salvaguardare; proteggere. **safe keeping** custodia f. n cassaforte f. **safety** n sicurezza f, salvezza f. **safety-belt** n cintura di sicurezza f. **safety-catch** n sicura f. **safety-pin** n spillo di sicurezza m.

saffron ['safrən] n zafferano m.

sag [sag] v incurvarsi, piegarsi.

saga ['sɑːgə] n saga f.

sage[1] [seidʒ] n, adj saggio, -a. **sagacious** adj sagace, avveduto.

sage[2] [seidʒ] n (herb) salvia f.

Sagittarius [sadʒi'teəriəs] n Sagittario m.

sago ['seigou] n sagù m.

said [sed] V say.

sail [seil] v navigare; (leave) salpare. n vela f. **sailcloth** n tela olona f. **sailing** n vela f, sport della vela m. **sailing boat** barca a vela f. **sailor** n marinaio m.

saint [seint] n santo, -a m, f. adj santo. **saintly** adj santo, pio.

sake [seik] n beneficio m, interesse m, bene m. **for God's sake** per l'amor di Dio. **for the sake of** (in order to) tanto per. **for your own sake** per il tuo bene.

salad ['saləd] n insalata f.

salami [sə'lɑːmi] n salame m.

salary ['saləri] n stipendio m.

sale [seil] n vendita f; (clearance) liquidazione f, saldo m. **for or on sale** in vendita. **salesgirl** n commessa f. **salesman** n commesso m. **travelling salesman** commesso viaggiatore m.

saline ['seilain] adj salino. **salinity** n salinità f.

saliva [sə'laivə] n saliva f. **salivary** adj salivare. **salivate** v salivare.

sallow ['salou] adj giallastro, olivastro.

salmon ['samən] n salmone m.

salon ['salon] n salone m.

saloon [sə'luːn] n salone m; (ship) ritrovo per passeggeri m. **saloon car** berlina f.

salt [soːlt] n sale m. **salt-cellar** n saliera f. adj also **salty** salato, piccante. v salare.

salubrious [sə'luːbriəs] adj salubre.

salute [sə'luːt] n saluto m. v salutare.

salvage ['salvidʒ] n salvataggio m, ricupero m. v salvare, ricuperare.

salvation [sal'veiʃən] n salvezza f; (theology) salvazione f.

same [seim] adj stesso, medesimo; (unchanged) immutato. pron lo stesso, il medesimo. **all the same** (nevertheless) malgrado tutto. **at the same time** nello stesso tempo; (notwithstanding) con tutto ciò. **the same to you!** altrettanto! **sameness** n somiglianza f, uniformità f, monotonia f.

sample ['sɑːmpl] n campione m; (specimen) saggio m. v campionare; (test) assaggiare. **sampling** n campionatura f.

sanatorium [sanə'tɔːrɪəm] n sanatorio m.

sanctify ['saŋktɪfaɪ] v santificare, consacrare.

sanctimonious [saŋktɪ'məʊnɪəs] adj santocchio, santerello.

sanction ['saŋkʃən] n sanzione f. v sanzionare, sancire.

sanctity ['saŋktətɪ] n santità f.

sanctuary ['saŋktjʊərɪ] n santuario m; (refuge) asilo m, rifugio m.

sand [sand] n sabbia f. v (sprinkle) insabbiare; (smooth) smerigliare. **sand-blast** v pulire con un getto di sabbia. **sandpaper** n carta vetrata f. **sandy** adj (consistency) sabbioso; (colour) biondo rossiccio.

sandal ['sandl] n sandalo m.

sandwich ['sanwɪdʒ] n sandwich m invar, panino imbottito m. v inserire.

sane [seɪn] adj equilibrato, sano di mente.

sanity n sanità di mente f, equilibrio m.

sang [saŋ] V **sing**.

sanitary ['sanɪtərɪ] adj igienico, sanitario. **sanitary towel** n pannolino igienico m.

sank [saŋk] V **sink**.

sap¹ [sap] n (plant) linfa f.

sap² [sap] v (undermine) minare, indebolire.

sapphire ['safaɪə] n zaffiro m. adj zaffirino.

sarcasm ['sɑːkazəm] n sarcasmo m. **sarcastic** adj sarcastico.

sardine [sɑː'diːn] n sardina f.

Sardinia [sɑː'dɪnjə] n Sardegna f. **Sardinian** n, adj sardo, -a.

sardonic [sɑː'dɒnɪk] adj sardonico.

sash¹ [saʃ] n (scarf) sciarpa f.

sash² [saʃ] n (frame) telaio m. **sash-cord** n corda del contrappeso f. **sash-window** n finestra alla ghigliottina f.

sat [sat] V **sit**.

satchel ['satʃəl] n cartella f.

satellite ['satəlaɪt] nm, adj satellite. **satellite town** città satellite f.

satin ['satɪn] nm, adj raso.

satire ['sataɪə] n satira f. **satirical** adj satirico. **satirist** n satirista m, f.

satisfy ['satɪsfaɪ] v soddisfare. **satisfaction** n soddisfazione f. **satisfactory** adj soddisfacente.

saturate ['satʃəreɪt] v saturare. **saturated** adj saturo. **saturation** n saturazione f.

Saturday ['satədɪ] n sabato m.

sauce [sɔːs] n salsa f; (coll) impertinenza f. **saucy** adj impertinente, sfacciato. **sauciness** n impertinenza f, sfacciataggine f.

saucepan ['sɔːspən] n casseruola f, pentola f.

saucer ['sɔːsə] n piattino m, sottocoppa f.

sauerkraut ['sauəkraut] n sarcrauti m pl.

sauna [sɔːnə] n sauna f.

saunter ['sɔːntə] v girovagare, andare a passeggio, girare. n giro m.

sausage ['sɒsɪdʒ] n salsiccia f, salame m.

savage ['savɪdʒ] adj selvaggio; feroce, crudele. v assalire, ferire. **savagery** n selvatichezza f; ferocia f, crudeltà f.

save¹ [seɪv] v salvare; (keep) conservare; (put aside) risparmiare. **saver** n risparmiatore, -trice m, f. **saving** n economia f. **savings** pl n risparmi m pl.

save² [seɪv] prep (except) salvo, eccetto.

saviour ['seɪvjə] n liberatore, -trice m, f; (rel) redentore m.

savoury. ['seɪvərɪ] adj (appetizing) saporito, gustoso; (piquant) piccante. n piatto appetitoso m.

*****saw¹** [sɔː] n sega f. **sawdust** n segatura f. **sawmill** n segheria f. v segare.

saw² [sɔː] V **see¹**.

sawn [sɔːn] V **saw¹**.

saxophone ['saksəfəʊn] n sassofono m.

*****say** [seɪ] v dire; (declare) dichiarare, affermare. **I say!** senti! guarda un po'! (let's) **say** (as an estimate) mettiamo, facciamo. n **have no say** non aver voce. **have one's say** dire la sua. **saying** n massima f, motto m, proverbio m.

scab [skab] n crosta f; (biol) scabbia f, rogna f; (derog: non-striker) crumiro, -a m, f. **scabby** adj rognoso, scabbioso.

scaffold ['skafəld] n (execution) patibolo m. **scaffolding** n impalcatura f, ponteggio m; (theatre) palco m.

scald [skɔːld] n scottatura f. v scottare.

scale¹ [skeɪl] n (thin plate) lamina f; (of fish, etc.) scaglia f, squama f; tartaro m; incrostazione f. v squamare; incrostare. **scaly** adj squamoso.

scale² [skeɪl] n (music, math, etc.) scala f. **to scale** in proporzione. v (climb) scalare; (climb over) scavalcare. **scale down** ridurre proporzionalmente.

scales [skeɪlz] pl n bilancia f sing. **tip the scales** dare il crollo alla bilancia.

scallop ['skaləp] n (zool) pettine m; (shell) conchiglia f; (edging) dentellatura f.

scalp [skalp] n scalpo m. v scalpare.

scalpel ['skalpəl] n scalpello m.

scampi ['skampi] *pl n* scampi *m pl.*

scan [skan] *v* scrutare; *(radar, etc.)* analizzare, sondare; *(poetry)* scandire; *(glance at)* dare una scorsa a. **scanner** *n* analizzatore *m*, dispositivo di esplorazione *m.*

scandal ['skandl] *n* scandalo *m*; *(gossip)* maldicenza *f*, diceria *f*. **scandalmonger** *n* maldicente *m*, *f*. **scandalize** *v* scandalizzare. **scandalous** *adj* scandaloso.

scanty ['skanti] *adj also* **scant** scarso, insufficiente. **scantily dressed** vestito succintamente.

scapegoat ['skeipgout] *n* capro espiatorio *m.*

scar [skɑɪ] *n* cicatrice *f*, sfregio *m. v (mark)* sfregiare; *(heal)* cicatrizzare. **scarred** *adj* sfregiato.

scarce [skeəs] *adj* scarso, raro. **scarcely** *adv* appena. **scarcity** *n* scarsezza *f.*

scare [skeə] *n* paura *f*, panico *m. v* impaurire, spaventare. **be scared** avere paura. **be scared stiff** avere una paura matta. **scarecrow** *n* spauracchio *m*. **scaremonger** *n* allarmista *m*, *f.*

scarf [skɑːf] *n* sciarpa *f*; *(square)* foulard *m invar.*

scarlet ['skɑːlit] *adj* scarlatto. **scarlet fever** scarlattina *f*. **scarlet runner** fagiolo di Spagna *m.*

scathing ['skeiðiŋ] *adj* sprezzante, sdegnoso.

scatter ['skatə] *v* spargere, disperdere, diffondere. **scatterbrained** *adj* scervellato, distratto.

scavenge ['skavindʒ] *v (streets)* spazzare; *(zool)* nutrirsi di cadaveri. **scavenger** *n (street cleaner)* spazzino *m*; *(zool)* animale necrofago *m.*

scene [siːn] *n* scena *f*, spettacolo *m*. **scenario** *n* scenario *m.*

scenery ['siːnəri] *n (landscape)* paesaggio *m*, veduta *f*; *(theatre)* scenario *m.*

scent [sent] *n* profumo *m*, odore *m*; *(track)* pista *f*. **throw off the scent** far perdere la traccia. *v (detect)* fiutare; *(perfume)* profumare.

sceptic ['skeptik] *n* scettico, -a *m*, *f*. **sceptical** *adj* scettico. **scepticism** *n* scetticismo *m.*

sceptre ['septə] *n* scettro *m.*

schedule ['ʃedjuːl] *n* programma *m*; *(time-table)* orario *m*; lista *f*, specchietto *m*. **according to schedule** secondo il previsto

or programma. *v* programmare; *(list)* elencare.

scheme [skiːm] *n* schema *m*, progetto *m*, piano *m*; intrigo *(pl* -ghi) *m*, trama *f*. *v* progettare; tramare. **schematic** *adj* schematico.

schizophrenia [ˌskitsəˈfriːniə] *n* schizofrenia *f*. **schizophrenic** *n*, *adj* schizofrenico, -a.

scholar ['skolə] *n* persona erudita *f*, studioso, -a *m*, *f*; studente, -essa *m*, *f*. **scholarly** *adj* erudito, dotto. **scholarship** *n* erudizione *f*; studio *m*; *(award)* borsa di studio *f.*

scholastic [skəˈlastik] *adj* scolastico.

school[1] [skuːl] *n* scuola *f*. **schoolboy** *n* scolaro *m*. **schoolfellow** *n* compagno, -a di scuola *m*, *f*. **schoolgirl** *n* scolara *f*. **schoolmaster** *n* maestro *m*; insegnante *m*. **schoolmistress** *n* maestra *f*, insegnante *f*. *v* istruire, ammaestrare.

school[2] [skuːl] *n (of fish)* banco *m*, frotta *f.*

schooner ['skuːnə] *n* goletta *f.*

sciatica [saiˈatikə] *n* sciatica *f*. **sciatic** *adj* sciatico.

science ['saiəns] *n* scienza *f*. **science fiction** fantascienza *f*. **scientific** *adj* scientifico. **scientist** *n* scienziato, -a *m*, *f.*

scissors ['sizəz] *pl n* forbici *f pl.*

scoff[1] [skof] *v (mock)* beffare, schernire. *n* beffa *f.*

scoff[2] [skof] *v (coll: eat)* pappare.

scold [skould] *v* sgridare, rimproverare. **scolding** *n* sgridata *f*, lavata di capo *f.*

scone [skon] *n* focaccia *f.*

scoop [skuːp] *n (kitchen)* mestolo *m*; *(dredge)* benna *f*; *(coll)* colpo *m. v* scavare. **scoop out** scodellare. **scoop up** raccogliere, tirar su.

scooter ['skuːtə] *n* motoretta *f*, scooter *m invar*; *(child's)* monopattino *m.*

scope [skoup] *n (extent)* portata *f*; opportunità *f*; possibilità *f*; *(space for activity)* campo libero *m.*

scorch [skoːtʃ] *n* scottatura *f*. *v* abbruciacchiare. **scorcher** *n (coll)* giornata caldissima *f.*

score [skoː] *n (sport)* punteggio *m*; *(account)* conto *m*; *(debt)* debito *m*; *(ground)* causa *f*; *(music)* partitura *f*. **scoreboard** *n* tabellone *m*. *v (sport)* segnare; *(points)* notare; marcare; *(notches)* intaccare; orchestrare. **score off** aver la meglio su.

161 **seal**

scorn [skɔːn] n disprezzo m, sdegno m. v sdegnare, sprezzare. **scornful** adj sdegnoso, sprezzante.

Scorpio ['skɔːpiou] n Scorpione m.

scorpion ['skɔːpiən] n scorpione m.

scotch [skɒtʃ] v sopprimere.

Scotland ['skɒtlənd] n Scozia f. **Scot** n scozzese m, f. **Scotch** n (whisky) scotch m invar, whisky scozzese m. **Scottish** or **Scots** adj scozzese.

scoundrel ['skaundrəl] n furfante m, mascalzone m.

scour[1] [skauə] v (clean) pulire sfregando; (rub) fregare, forbire.

scour[2] [skauə] v (search) perlustrare.

scout [skaut] v esplorare, perlustrare. n (mil) vedetta f; (boy) giovane esploratore m; osservatore m.

scowl [skaul] n cipiglio m, guardataccia f. v accigliarsi.

scramble ['skræmbl] v (move hastily) sgambettare; (climb) arrampicarsi; (struggle) azzuffarsi, battagliare; (radio, etc.) disturbare. **scrambled eggs** uova strapazzate f pl. n confusione f, parapiglia f; (struggle) lotta f.

scrap [skræp] n (small piece) pezzetto m, frammento m; (metal) rottame m. **scrapbook** n album m invar. **scraps** pl n rifiuti m pl; (leftovers) avanzi m pl, rimasugli m pl. v scartare, mettere fuori servizio. **scrappy** adj frammentario.

scrape [skreip] v raschiare, grattare. **scrape through** cavarsela; (exam) passare per il buco della serratura. **scrape together** racimolare, raccogliere. n (embarrassing situation) impaccio m.

scratch [skrætʃ] v graffiare, grattare; cancellare; (withdraw) ritirarsi. n graffiatura f. **from scratch** da zero. **up to scratch** all'altezza della situazione.

scrawl [skrɔːl] n scarabocchio m. v scarabocchiare.

scream [skriːm] v strillare. n strillo m; (coll: funny person) spasso m.

screech [skriːtʃ] v stridere, cigolare. n strido m (pl -a f).

screen [skriːn] n paravento m; (shelter) riparo m; (film, etc.) schermo m. v (hide) nascondere; (protect) proteggere; (check) vagliare; (cinema) proiettare.

screw [skruː] n vite f. **screwdriver** n cacciavite m invar. v avvitare. **screw up one's courage** farsi coraggio.

scribble ['skribl] n sgorbio m. v

scribacchiare. **scribbler** n scribacchino, -a m, f.

script [skript] n (handwriting) scrittura f; manuscritto m; (theatre) copione m.

Scripture ['skriptʃə] n Sacra Scrittura f, Bibbia f.

scroll [skroul] n (roll) rotolo m; (ornament) voluta f.

scrounge [skraundʒ] (coll) v scroccare. **scrounger** n scroccone, -a m, f.

scrub[1] [skrʌb] v lavare o pulire fregando forte. **scrubbing brush** spazzola dura f, spazzolone per lavare m.

scrub[2] [skrʌb] n (bush) macchia f.

scruffy ['skrʌfi] adj trasandato.

scruple ['skruːpl] n scrupolo m. **scrupulous** adj scrupoloso.

scrutiny ['skruːtəni] n esame accurato m. **scrutinize** v esaminare accuratamente.

scuffle ['skʌfl] n tafferuglio m. v azzuffarsi.

scullery ['skʌləri] n retrocucina f.

sculpt [skʌlpt] v scolpire. **sculptor** n scultore m. **sculptress** n scultrice f. **sculptural** adj scultorio. **sculpture** n scultura f.

scum [skʌm] n (on liquids) schiuma f; (on metals) scoria f; (worthless people) feccia f.

scurf [skəːf] n forfora f. **scurfy** adj forforoso.

scurrilous ['skʌriləs] adj scurrile.

scurvy ['skəːvi] n scorbuto m.

scuttle[1] ['skʌtl] n (for coal) secchio da carbone m.

scuttle[2] ['skʌtl] v (run) scorrazzare.

scuttle[3] ['skʌtl] v (sink) affondare.

scythe [saið] n falce f. v falciare.

sea [siː] n mare m. **at sea** in mare; perplesso. **by sea** per mare. **put out to sea** prendere il largo.

sea bed n fondo del mare m.

seafaring ['siːfeəriŋ] adj navigatore, -trice; marinaro. **seafarer** n navigatore m.

seafood ['siːfuːd] n frutti di mare m pl.

sea front n marina f.

seagoing ['siːgouiŋ] adj d'alto mare.

sea-gull n gabbiano m.

sea-horse n cavalluccio marino m.

seal[1] [siːl] n (stamp) sigillo m; chiusura f. v sigillare; (close) chiudere. **sealing wax** ceralacca f.

seal[2] [siːl] n (animal) foca f. **sealskin** n pelle di foca f.

sea-level n livello del mare m.
sea-lion n leone marino m.
seam [siːm] n cucitura f, giuntura f; (geol) vena f. v cucire.
seaman ['siːmən] n marinaio m.
search [səːtʃ] v frugare, rovistare. n (act) ricerca f; esame minuto m; (for something hidden) perquisizione f. **searchlight** n proiettore m. **search-party** n squadra di ricerca f. **search-warrant** n mandato di perquisizione m. **searching** adj (careful) minuzioso; (observing) indagatore, -trice m, f.
seashore ['siːʃoː] n spiaggia f, costa f.
seasick ['siːsik] adj be seasick aver il mal di mare. **seasickness** n mal di mare m.
seaside ['siːsaid] n at or to the seaside al mare.
season ['siːzn] n stagione f. **season ticket** abbonamento m. v (wood) stagionare; (spice) condire. **seasonable** adj (timely) opportuno. **seasoning** n condimento m.
seat [siːt] n sedile m; (chair) sedia f; (place) posto m; (coll: behind) sedere m; (location) sede f. **take a seat** accomodarsi. v (cause to sit) far sedere; (provide with seat) provvedere di posti (a sedere).
seaweed ['siːwiːd] n alga f.
seaworthy ['siːwəːði] adj atto a tenere il mare.

secluded [si'kluːdid] adj isolato, appartato. **seclusion** n isolamento m.
second ['sekənd] n secondo m; (day) due m; (gear) seconda f. adj secondo m. **on second thoughts** ripensandoci bene. **second-hand** adj di seconda mano. **second-rate** adj mediocre. **second sight** chiaroveggenza f.
secondary ['sekəndəri] adj secondario.
secret ['siːkrit] nm, adj segreto. **top secret** adj riservatissimo. **secrecy** n segretezza f. **secretive** adj riservato, reticente.
secretary ['sekrətəri] n segretario, -a m, f. **secretarial** adj segretariale. **secretariat** n segreteria f, segretariato m.
secrete [si'kriːt] v (biol) secernere; (conceal) celare. **secretion** n secrezione f.
sect [sekt] n setta f. **sectarian** adj settario.
section ['sekʃən] n sezione f, parte f.
sector ['sektə] n settore m.
secular ['sekjulə] adj secolare; profano; laico.
secure [si'kjuə] adj sicuro; solido. v mettere al sicuro, assicurare; garantire;

procurarsi. **security** n sicurezza f, garanzia f. **securities** pl n titoli m pl, obbligazioni f pl.
sedate [si'deit] adj pacato, posato. . v calmare, tranquillizzare. **sedative** n sedativo m; calmante m.
sediment ['sedimənt] n sedimento m. **sedimentation** n sedimentazione f.
seduce [si'djuːs] v sedurre. **seducer** n seduttore, -trice m, f. **seduction** n seduzione f. **seductive** adj seducente.
*see¹ [siː] v vedere. **see about** or to occuparsi di. **see home** accompagnare a casa. **see through** penetrare.
see² [siː] n (bishop's) diocesi f. **Holy See** Santa Sede f.
seed [siːd] n seme m; (collective) semenza f. **go to seed** (bot) sementire; (decay) scadere, declinare. v seminare. **seedling** n germoglio m, semenzale m. **seedy** adj (shabby) malconcio; indisposto.
*seek [siːk] v cercare.
seem [siːm] v sembrare, parere. **seeming** adj apparente.
seen [siːn] V see¹.
seep [siːp] v infiltrare.
seesaw ['siːsoː] n altalena (a bilico) f. adj oscillante. v altalenare.
seethe [siːð] v bollire; (be agitated) fremere. **seethe with rage** fremere di rabbia.
segment ['segmənt] n segmento m, sezione f.
segregate ['segrigeit] v segregare. **segregation** n segregazione f.
seize [siːz] v (grasp) afferrare; (by force) impadronirsi di; confiscare. **seize up** grippare, ingranarsi. **seizure** n confisca f; conquista f; (med) attacco m.
seldom ['seldəm] adv raramente, di rado.
select [sə'lekt] adj scelto, distinto. v scegliere. **selection** n selezione f, scelta f. **selective** adj selettivo. **selectivity** n selettività f.
self [self] n io m, persona f.
self-assured adj sicuro di sé. **self-assurance** sicurezza di sé f.
self-centred adj egocentrico, egoista.
self-confident adj sicuro di sé. **self-confidence** n fiducia in sé.
self-conscious adj impacciato. **self-consciousness** n impaccio m.
self-contained adj (not shared) indipendente; (uncommunicative) riservato; (self-sufficient) autosufficiente.

163   **septic**

self-critical *adj* autocritico. **self-criticism** *n* autocritica *f.*
self-defence *n* autodifesa *f*; *(law)* legittima difesa *f.*
self-discipline *n* autodisciplina *f.*
self-employed *adj* be self-employed lavorare in proprio.
self-evident *adj* manifesto, palese.
self-explanatory *adj* ovvio.
self-expression *n* espressione della propria personalità *f.*
self-government *n* autonomia *f.*
self-interest *n* interesse personale *m.*
selfish ['selfiʃ] *adj* egoista, egoistico. **selfishness** *n* egoismo *m.*
selfless ['selflis] *adj* altruista, altruistico. **selflessness** *n* altruismo *m.*
self-pity *n* autocommiserazione *f.*
self-portrait *n* autoritratto *m.*
self-possessed *adj* composto, padrone di sè.
self-preservation *n* conservazione *f.*
self-propelled *adj* che si muove per forza propria.
self-respect *n* amor proprio *m.* **self-respecting** *adj* dignitoso.
self-restraint *n* autocontrollo *m.*
self-righteous *adj* compiaciuto di sè stesso. **self-righteousness** *n* autocompiacimento *m.*
self-sacrifice *n* abnegazione *f.*
selfsame ['selfseim] *adj* identico, proprio lo stesso.
self-satisfied *adj* contento di sè. **self-satisfaction** *n* autocompiacimento *m.*
self-service *n* self-service *m invar.*
self-styled *adj* sedicente.
self-sufficient *adj* autosufficiente. **self-sufficiency** *n* autosufficienza *f.*
self-willed *adj* ostinato; *(wilful)* caparbio.
***sell** [sel] *v* vendere. **seller** *n* venditore, -trice *m, f.*
sellotape ® ['seləteip] *n* scotch ® *m invar,* nastro autoadesivo *m.*
semantic [sə'mantik] *adj* semantico. **semantics** *n* semantica *f.*
semaphore ['seməfoː] *n* semaforo *m.*
semen ['siːmən] *n* sperma *m.*
semibreve ['semibriːv] *n* semibreve *f.*
semicircle ['semisəːkl] *n* semicerchio *m.* **semicircular** *adj* semicircolare.
semicolon [semi'koulən] *n* punto e virgola *m.*
semifinal [semi'fainl] *n* semifinale *f.* **semifinalist** *n* semifinalista *m, f.*

seminar ['seminaː] *n* seminario *m.*
seminary ['seminəri] *n* seminario *m.*
semi-precious *adj* semiprezioso.
semiquaver ['semikweivə] *n* semicroma *f.*
semitone ['semitoun] *n* semitono *m.*
semolina [semə'liːnə] *n* semolino *m.*
senate ['senit] *n* senato *m.* **senator** *n* senatore *m.*
***send** [send] *v* mandare; *(dispatch)* spedire; trasmettere. **send for** *(person)* mandare a chiamare; *(thing)* mandare a prendere. **send in** sottoporre. **send on** *(readdress)* inoltrare. **sender** *n* mittente *m, f.*
senile ['siːnail] *adj* senile. **senility** *n* *(old age)* senilità *f*; *(mental infirmity)* senilismo *m.*
senior ['siːnjə] *adj* più anziano, maggiore. *n* anziano, -a *m, f*; superiore, -a *m, f.* **seniority** *n* anzianità *f.*
sensation [sen'seiʃən] *n* sensazione *f.* **cause a sensation** far sensazione *or* colpo. **sensational** *adj* sensazionale, che fa colpo.
sense [sens] *n* senso *m.* **take leave of one's senses** perder la ragione. **talk sense** parlare sensatamente. *v* intuire, capire.
sensible ['sensəbl] *adj* sensato, ragionevole; *(appreciable)* sensibile. **sensibility** *n* sensibilità *f.*
sensitive ['sensitiv] *adj* sensibile; delicato; *(physiology)* sensitivo. **sensitivity** *n* sensibilità *f*; suscettibilità *f*; delicatezza *f.*
sensual ['sensjuəl] *adj* sensuale. **sensuality** *n* sensualità *f.*
sensuous ['sensjuəs] *adj* gradevole ai sensi, voluttuoso.
sent [sent] *V* **send.**
sentence ['sentəns] *n* *(gramm)* frase *f*; *(law)* condanna *f*, pena *f.* **pass sentence** pronunciare (una) sentenza. *v* condannare.
sentiment ['sentimənt] *n* sentimento *m.* **sentimental** *adj* sentimentale. **sentimentality** *n* sentimentalità *f.*
sentry ['sentri] *n* sentinella *f.* **stand sentry** fare la guardia.
separate ['sepərət; *v* 'sepəreit] *adj* separato; distinto; indipendente. *v* separare. **separation** *n* separazione *f.*
September [sep'tembə] *n* settembre *m.*
septic ['septik] *adj* settico. **septicaemia** *n* setticemia *f.*

sequel ['siːkwəl] *n* seguito *m*; conseguenza *f*.

sequence ['siːkwəns] *n* successione *f*; (*math, cards*) sequenza *f*. **in sequence** in ordine successivo.

sequin ['siːkwin] *n* lustrino *m*.

serenade [serə'neid] *n* serenata *f*. *v* fare una serenata a.

serene [sə'riːn] *adj* sereno. **serenity** *n* serenità *f*.

sergeant ['saːdʒənt] *n* (*mil*) sergente *m*; (*police*) brigadiere *m*.

serial ['siəriəl] *n* (*novel*) romanzo a puntate *m*; (*play*) commedia a puntate *f*. *adj* (*in instalments*) a puntate; (*tech*) di *or* in serie. **serialize** *v* pubblicare *or* trasmettere a puntate.

series ['siəriːz] *n* serie *f*.

serious ['siəriəs] *adj* serio, grave. **are you serious?** dice sul serio? **seriousness** *n* serietà *f*.

sermon ['səːmən] *n* predica *f*.

serpent ['saːpənt] *n* serpente *m*. **serpentine** *adj* serpentino; (*winding*) serpeggiante.

serum ['siərəm] *n* siero *m*.

servant ['saːvənt] *n* domestico, -a *m*, *f*; servo, -a *m*, *f*.

serve [saːv] *v* servire. **it serves you right!** ti sta bene! te lo sei meritato!

service ['saːvis] *n* servizio *m*; (*disposal*) disposizione *f*; (*rel*) ufficio divino *m*. **of service** d'aiuto, utile. **service area/station** area/stazione di servizio *f*. *v* provvedere alla manutenzione di, controllare. **serviceable** *adj* pratico, funzionale.

serviette [saːvi'et] *n* tovagliolo *m*.

servile ['saːvail] *adj* servile. **servility** *n* servilità *f*.

session ['seʃən] *n* seduta *f*, sessione *f*.

*****set** [set] *adj* fisso; (*ready*) pronto; prescritto; deciso; preparato; (*prearranged*) stabilito. *n* serie *f*, assortimento *m*; (*theatre, etc.*) set *m invar*, scenario *m*; (*tennis*) set *m invar*, partita *f*. *v* (*place*) mettere, posare; (*fix*) fissare; (*solidify*) indurirsi, rapprendersi; (*sun*) tramontare; (*jewel*) incastonare; (*hair*) mettere in piega; (*bones*) mettere a posto. **set about** (*begin to*) accingersi a; (*attempt*) cercare di; (*coll*) attaccare. **set aside** *or* **by** mettere da parte. **set back** (*hinder*) impedire; (*delay*) ritardare. **setback** *n* regresso *m*, contrattempo *m*. **set**

free liberare. **set off** far esplodere; (*depart*) mettersi in viaggio; (*intensify*) mettere in risalto; compensare. **set out** partire. **set up** (*erect*) erigere; (*establish*) stabilire, metter su; (*prepare*) allestire.

setting *n* (*environment*) ambiente *m*; (*jewel*) montatura *f*; (*theatre*) scenario *m*, messa in scena *f*; (*music*) messa in musica *f*; (*sun*) tramonto *m*.

settee [se'tiː] *n* canapè *m*, sofà *m*.

settle ['setl] *v* fissare, determinare; (*pay*) regolare, saldare; (*compose*) sistemare; decidere. **settle down** stabilizzarsi; (*live*) stabilirsi. **settlement** *n* decisione *f*; saldo *m*; colonia *f*. **settler** *n* colonizzatore, -trice *m*, *f*.

seven ['sevn] *nm*, *adj* sette. **seventh** *nm*, *adj* settimo.

seventeen [sevn'tiːn] *nm*, *adj* diciassette. **seventeenth** *adj* diciassettesimo.

seventy ['sevnti] *nm*, *adj* settanta. **seventieth** *adj* settantesimo.

sever ['sevə] *v* staccare.

several ['sevrəl] *pron* parecchi, diversi. *adj* parecchi, diversi; separato; (*own*) proprio.

severe [sə'viə] *adj* severo; grave; (*weather*) rigido; (*pain, etc.*) violento, vivo. **severity** *n* severità *f*, rigore *m*; violenza *f*.

*****sew** [sou] *v* cucire. **sewing** *n* cucito *m*. **sewing machine** macchina da cucire *f*.

sewage ['sjuːidʒ] *n* acque di scolo *or* scarico *f pl*.

sewer ['sjuə] *n* fogna *f*. **sewerage** *n* fognatura *f*.

sewn [soun] *V* **sew**.

sex [seks] *n* sesso *m*. **sexual** *adj* sessuale. **sexuality** *n* sessualità *f*.

sextet [seks'tet] *n* sestetto *m*.

shabby ['ʃabi] *adj* (*of poor appearance*) malconcio, trasandato; (*badly worn*) logoro, frusto; (*contemptible*) meschino.

shack [ʃak] *n* baracca *f*.

shade [ʃeid] *n* ombra *f*; (*colour*) tinta *f*; (*lamp*) paralume *m*. *v* ombreggiare; (*protect*) proteggere (dalla luce); (*drawing*) sfumare. **shading** *n* sfumatura *f*.

shadow ['ʃadou] *n* ombra *f*. *v* ombreggiare; (*follow*) pedinare. **shady** *adj* ombreggiato; (*dubious*) disonesto, losco.

shaft [ʃaːft] *n* (*pole*) asta *f*; (*passageway*) condotto *m*; (*handle*) manico *m*; (*light*) fascio *m*; (*sarcasm*) frecciata *f*.

shaggy ['ʃagi] *adj* peloso, irsuto.

*shake [ʃeik] n scossa f. **no great shakes** di poco conto. v scuotere; agitare; (tremble) tremare; (disturb) fremere. **shake hands** stringere la mano. **shake off** liberarsi da. **shake-up** n riorganizzazione f. **shaky** adj tremolante; (insecure) malsicuro; precario.

shaken [ˈʃeikn] V **shake**.

shall [ʃal] aux translated by future tense.

shallot [ʃəˈlot] n scalogno m.

shallow [ˈʃalou] adj poco profondo, basso, superficiale. **shallows** pl n bassofondo (pl bassifondi) m sing.

sham [ʃam] adj finto, falso. n finzione f, inganno m. v fingere, simulare.

shambles [ˈʃamblz] n macello m.

shame [ʃeim] v svergognare. n vergogna f. **bring shame on** recar onta a, disonorare. **shamefaced** adj timido, vergognoso. **what a shame!** che peccato! **shameful** adj vergognoso. **shameless** adj svergognato, spudorato; (brazen) sfacciato. **shamelessness** n spudoratezza f, sfacciataggine f.

shampoo [ʃamˈpuː] n shampoo m invar. v shampoo one's hair lavarsi i capelli.

shamrock [ˈʃamrok] n trifoglio d'Irlanda m.

shanty[1] [ˈʃanti] n (hut) capanna f. **shanty town** baraccopoli f, bidonville (pl -s) f.

shanty[2] [ˈʃanti] n (song) canzone marinaresca f.

shape [ʃeip] n forma f; condizione f. **take shape** concretizzarsi, prender forma. v formare, dar forma a; modellare; adattare. **shapeless** adj informe, confuso. **shapely** adj ben fatto, bello.

share [ʃeə] n porzione f, parte f; (comm) azione f. **shareholder** n azionista m, f. v dividere; (jointly) condividere. **share in** prender parte a. **share out** distribuire.

shark [ʃaːk] n pescecane (pl pescicani) m.

sharp [ʃaːp] adj (cutting) tagliente; (not blunt) aguzzo; brusco; (distinct) netto; (flavour) aspro, piccante; acuto; (alert) sveglio; (biting) mordace; (shrewd) scaltro. adv bruscamente; (punctually) in punto. n (music) diesis m. **sharpen** v affilare; (pencil) far la punta a; rendere più acuto.

shatter [ˈʃatə] v (break into fragments) frantumare; (destroy) rovinare. **shattering** adj (coll) schiacciante.

shave [ʃeiv] n rasatura f. **have a close shave** cavarsela per un pelo. v farsi la

barba; (cut closely) radere, rasare. **shaving brush/soap** pennello/sapone da barba m. **shaving cream** crema da barba f.

shawl [ʃoːl] n scialle m.

she [ʃiː] pron ella, lei. **she who** colei che.

sheaf [ʃiːf] n fascio m; (cereals) covone m.

*shear [ʃiə] v tosare; (tech) spezzarsi; (deprive) privare. **shears** pl n cesoie f pl.

sheath [ʃiːθ] n guaina f. **sheathe** v rivestire; (sword) ringuainare.

*shed[1] [ʃed] v (let fall) versare; (lose) perdere. **shed light on** far luce su.

shed[2] [ʃed] n capannone m; (outhouse) capanna f, rimessa f.

sheen [ʃiːn] n lucentezza f.

sheep [ʃiːp] n pecora f. **sheep-dog** n (cane da) pastore m. **sheepish** adj timido.

sheer[1] [ʃiə] adj (mere) mero; assoluto; (steep) a piombo; trasparente.

sheer[2] [ʃiə] v cambiar rotta.

sheet [ʃiːt] n (bedding) lenzuolo m (pl -a f); (paper) foglio m; (iron, etc.) lamiera f; (glass) lastra f. **sheet lightning** lampeggio m.

shelf [ʃelf] n (support) mensola f, ripiano m; (ledge) sporgenza f; (rock) scogliera f. **set of shelves** scaffale m.

shell [ʃel] n (of egg, etc.) guscio m; (of fish) conchiglia f; (mil) proiettile m; (hollow casing) involucro m. **shellfish** n crostaceo m, mollusco m; (pl: as food) frutti di mare m pl. **shell-shock** n psicosi traumatica da guerra f. v (mil) bombardare; (eggs, etc.) sgusciare; (peas) sgranare.

shelter [ˈʃeltə] n riparo m, rifugio m; protezione f. **take shelter** ripararsi, rifugiarsi. v proteggere, dare asilo a.

shelve [ʃelv] v (put aside) mettere da parte; (postpone) rimandare, archiviare.

shepherd [ˈʃepəd] n pastore m. **shepherdess** n pastora f.

sheriff [ˈʃerif] n sceriffo m.

sherry [ˈʃeri] n sherry m invar.

shield [ʃiːld] n schermo m; (armour) scudo m. v proteggere.

shift [ʃift] v spostare, trasferire; (free oneself from) liberarsi da. **shift for oneself** fare da sè. n turno m; (change) cambiamento m; (artifice) espediente m. **shifting** adj instabile, mutevole; (sands) mobile. **shifty** adj malizioso.

shimmer [ˈʃimə] v luccicare. n luccichio m.

shin [ʃin] n stinco m.

*shine [ʃain] n splendore m. v brillare, risplendere; (polish) lustrare.

shingle [ʃiŋgl] n (roof) lastra di copertura f; (stone) ciottolo m; (extent of pebbles) ghiaia f.

shingles [ʃiŋglz] n erpete m; (coll) fuoco di Sant'Antonio m.

ship [ʃip] n nave f. shipowner n armatore m. shipshape adv in ordine perfetto. shipwreck n naufragio m. be shipwrecked naufragare. shipyard n cantiere navale m. v spedire. shipper n spedizioniere m.

shirk [ʃəːk] v evitare, scansare. shirker n scansafatiche m, f invar.

shirt [ʃəːt] n camicia f.

shit [ʃit] n (vulgar) merda f. v cacare.

shiver [ʃivə] v tremare, rabbrividire. n brivido m, tremito m. have the shivers (cold) avere i brividi; (fear) avere la tremarella.

shoal [ʃoul] n frotta f; (fish) banco m.

shock¹ [ʃok] n colpo m; (encounter) scontro m; (elec) scossa f; (med) shock m invar; impressione f. shock absorber ammortizzatore m. v colpire; disgustare; impressionare; dare una scossa a. shocking adj terribile; ripugnante, disgustoso.

shock² [ʃok] n (hair) chioma f.

shod [ʃod] V shoe.

shoddy [ʃodi] adj scadente.

*shoe [ʃuː] n scarpa f. shoe-lace n laccio delle scarpe m. shoemaker n calzolaio m. v (horse) ferrare.

shone [ʃon] V shine.

shook [ʃuk] V shake.

*shoot [ʃuːt] v tirare, sparare; (hit) ferire; (kill) uccidere; (film) girare; (bot) germogliare. n (plant) rampollo m, germoglio m; (spedizione di) caccia f. shooting n tiro m, caccia f; (firing) sparatoria f. shooting pain dolore lancinante m. shooting star stella filante f.

shop [ʃop] n negozio m, bottega f; (in factory, etc.) officina f. shopkeeper n negoziante m, f. shoplifter n taccheggiatore, -trice m, f. shoplifting n taccheggio m. shop-soiled adj sciupato. shop-window n vetrina f. shut up shop chiudere bottega. talk shop parlare d'affari. v fare gli acquisti, fare la spesa. shopper n acquirente m, f. shopping n acquisti m pl. go shopping fare la spesa. shopping bag borsa per la spesa f.

shore¹ [ʃoː] n sponda f, riva f. on shore a terra.

shore² [ʃoː] v shore up puntellare.

shorn [ʃoːn] V shear.

short [ʃoːt] adj (not long) corto; breve; (not tall) basso; brusco. adv bruscamente; (suddenly) di botto. in short in breve. nothing short of addirittura. run short scarseggiare. to cut a long story short a farla breve. n (film) short m invar, cortometraggio m. shortage n mancanza f, carenza f. shorten v accorciare, abbreviare. shortly adv presto.

shortbread [ʃoːtbred] n biscotto di pasta frolla m.

short-circuit n corto circuito m. v mettere in corto circuito.

shortcoming [ʃoːtkʌmiŋ] n difetto m.

short cut n scorciatoia f.

shorthand [ʃoːthand] n stenografia f. shorthand typist n stenodattilografo, -a m, f.

short list n rosa dei candidati f. v mettere nella rosa dei candidati.

short-lived adj di poca durata.

shorts [ʃoːts] pl n shorts m pl; calzoncini corti m pl.

short-sighted adj miope; (lacking foresight) imprevidente. short-sightedness n miopia f; imprevidenza f.

short story n novella f.

short-tempered adj irascibile.

short-term adj a breve scadenza.

short-wave adj a onde corte.

shot¹ [ʃot] V shoot.

shot² [ʃot] n sparo m, colpo m; (pellet) pallottola f; (pellets) pallini di piombo m pl; (person) tiratore m; (phot) istantanea f; (film) ripresa f. off like a shot via come un bolide. shotgun n fucile da caccia m.

should¹ [ʃud] aux translated by conditional tense.

should² [ʃud] aux translated by conditional tense of dovere.

shoulder [ʃouldə] n spalla f; (road) banchina f. give the cold shoulder trattare con freddezza. shoulder-blade n scapola f. shoulder-strap n spallina f. v caricarsi sulle spalle; (assume as burden) addossarsi.

shout [ʃaut] v gridare, urlare. n grido m (pl -a f), urlo m (pl -a f). shout at sgridare, alzar la voce con. shout down far tacere a forza di grida.

shove [ʃʌv] *n* spinta *f.* *v* spingere.

shovel [ʃʌvl] *v* spalare. *n* pala *f.* **shovelful** *n* palata *f.*

***show** [ʃou] *n* (*display*) mostra *f*, esposizione *f*; (*theatre*) spettacolo *m*; apparenza *f*; ostentazione *f.* **give the show away** rivelare tutto. **run the show** essere in controllo. **show business** mondo dello spettacolo *m.* **show-case** *n* vetrina *f*; **show-down** *n* (*final reckoning*) resa dei conti *f.* **showman** *n* (*theatre*) impresario *m*; showman *m invar.* **show-room** *n* sala d'esposizione *f. v* mostrare, manifestare, indicare, dimostrare. **show off** ostentare, darsi delle arie. **show up** (*reveal*) svelare; (*display*) far risaltare; (*appear*) presentarsi.

shower [ʃauə] *n* (*bath*) doccia *f*; (*rain*) acquazzone *m*; (*blows*) grandine *f.* **have a shower** fare la doccia. *v* **shower with** tempestare di, inondare di.

shown [ʃoun] *V* show.

shrank [ʃraŋk] *V* shrink.

shred [ʃred] *n* (*piece torn off*) brandello *m*; (*bit, scrap*) briciolo *m. v* fare a brandelli *or* pezzetti.

shrew [ʃruː] *n* (*woman*) bisbetica *f*; (*zool*) toporagno *m.*

shrewd [ʃruːd] *adj* accorto, scaltro. **shrewdness** *n* accortezza *f*, scaltrezza *f.*

shriek [ʃriːk] *v* strillare. *n* strillo *m.*

shrill [ʃril] *adj* stridulo, acuto.

shrimp [ʃrimp] *n* gamberetto *m.*

shrine [ʃrain] *n* santuario *m*, reliquario *m*, tempio *m.*

***shrink** [ʃriŋk] *v* (*become tight*) restringersi; (*withdraw*) ritirarsi; (*become less*) ridursi. **shrink from** rifuggire da. **shrinkage** *n* restringimento *m.*

shrivel [ʃrivl] *v* raggrinzirsi.

shroud [ʃraud] *n* lenzuolo funebre *m*; (*mist*) velo *m. v* avvolgere.

Shrove Tuesday [ʃrouv] *n* martedì grasso *m.*

shrub [ʃrab] *n* arbusto *m.*

shrug [ʃrag] *v* scrollare (le spalle). **shrug off** (*minimize*) prendere alla leggera; (*shake off*) scrollarsi di dosso. *n* scrollata (di spalle) *f.*

shrunk [ʃraŋk] *V* shrink.

shudder [ʃadə] *n* brivido *m*, tremito *m. v* rabbrividire.

shuffle [ʃafl] *v* mettere in disordine; rimaneggiare; (*cards*) mescolare; (*feet*) strascicare.

shun [ʃan] *v* scansare, sfuggire (a).

shunt [ʃant] *v* (*rail*) smistare; (*get rid of*) mettere da parte; (*elec*) shuntare. *n* (*rail*) scambio *m*; (*elec*) shunt *m invar.*

***shut** [ʃat] *adj* chiuso. *v* chiudere. **shut down** (*work*) sospendere l'attività. **shut off** bloccare, sottrarsi a. **shut out** non lasciar entrare. **shut up** star zitto.

shutter [ʃatə] *n* (*window*) persiana *f*; (*phot*) otturatore *m.*

shuttle [ʃatl] *n* spola *f*, navetta *f.* **shuttlecock** *n* volano *m.* **shuttle service** servizio di spola *m*, servizio pendolare *m.*

shy [ʃai] *adj* timido, schivo. *v* (*horse*) scartare. **shy from** rifuggire da; (*shun*) schivare. **shyness** *n* timidezza *f*, diffidenza *f.*

sick [sik] *adj* malato; (*fed up*) stanco, stufo. **be sick** essere malato, star male; vomitare. **feel sick** sentirsi male, avere la nausea. **make sick** (*infuriate*) mandare in bestia; disgustare; far vomitare. **sick-bay** *n* infermeria *f.* **sicken** *v* ammalarsi. **sickening** *adj* nauseabondo, disgustante. **sickness** *n* malattia *f.*

sickle [sikl] *n* falce *f.*

side [said] *n* lato *m*, fianco *m*; (*lake, etc.*) riva *f*; (*in battle, quarrel, etc.*) partito *m*, parte *f.* **on the other side** d'altra parte. **sideboard** *n* credenza *f.* **side-issue** *n* questione secondaria *f.* **sidelight** *n* (*mot*) luce di posizione *f.* **sidelong** *adj* di traverso, furtivo. **sidestep** *v* schivare. **side-street** *n* via laterale *f.* **sidetrack** *v* distrarre. **sideways** *adv* lateralmente; obliquamente. *v* **side with** essere dalla parte di. **siding** *n* binario di raccordo *m.*

sidle [saidl] *v* andare a sghembo. **sidle up to** accostarsi furtivamente a.

siege [siːdʒ] *n* assedio *m.* **lay siege** assediare. **raise the siege** togliere l'assedio.

sieve [siv] *n* setaccio *m. v* setacciare.

sift [sift] *v* setacciare; (*examine*) vagliare.

sigh [sai] *v* sospirare. *n* sospiro *m.*

sight [sait] *n* vista *f*; (*coll*) spettacolo *m*; (*tech*) mirino *m.* **catch sight of** intravedere. **know by sight** conoscere di vista. **lose sight of** perdere di vista. **sights** *pl n* luoghi d'interesse *m pl.* **sightseeing** *n* turismo *m.*

sign [sain] *n* segno *m*, cenno *m*; (*inscription*) insegna *f*, segnale *m*; (*trace*) traccia *f.* **signpost** *n* indicatore *m. v* firmare, ratificare. **sign off** ritirarsi. **sign on** (*employ*) assumere; (*commit oneself*) impegnarsi.

signal ['signəl] n segnale m. v segnalare.

signature ['signətʃə] n firma f. **signatory** n firmatario, -a m, f.

signify ['signifai] v significare; (*mean*) voler dire; (*be of consequence*) importare. **significance** n importanza f; (*meaning*) significato m. **significant** adj significativo, espressivo.

silence ['sailəns] n silenzio m. v ridurre al silenzio, far tacere; (*put to rest*) porre fine a. **silencer** n silenziatore m.

silent ['sailənt] adj silenzioso; tacito; muto. **keep silent** tacere, rimaner zitto.

silhouette [silu'et] n silhouette (pl -s) f.

silk [silk] n seta f. **silkworm** n baco da seta m. **silken** adj di seta. **silky** adj di seta; (*lustrous*) lucido; (*smooth*) morbido.

sill [sil] n (*window*) davanzale m.

silly ['sili] adj sciocco. **silliness** n sciocchezza f.

silt [silt] n limo m. v **silt up** insabbiarsi.

silver ['silvə] n argento m; (*cutlery, etc.*) argenteria f. adj d'argento, argenteo. v argentare.

similar ['similə] adj simile. **similarity** n somiglianza f.

simile ['simili] n (*figure of speech*) similitudine f; (*example*) paragone m.

simmer ['simə] v sobbollire.

simple ['simpl] adj semplice. **simpleton** n sempliciotto, -a m, f. **simplicity** n semplicità f. **simplification** n semplificazione f. **simplify** v semplificare.

simulate ['simjuleit] v simulare, fingere. **simulation** n simulazione f, finzione f.

simultaneous [,siməl'teinjəs] adj simultaneo.

sin [sin] n peccato m. v peccare. **sinful** adj peccaminoso. **sinner** n peccatore, -trice m, f.

since [sins] adv (*from then*) da allora; (*subsequently*) poi; (*ago*) fa. prep da. conj (*period*) da quando; dacchè; (*because*) poichè.

sincere [sin'siə] adj sincero. **sincerity** n sincerità f.

sinew ['sinjuː] n tendine m; (*force*) nerbo m.

****sing** [siŋ] v cantare. **singer** n cantante m, f. **singing** n canto m.

singe [sindʒ] v strinare; (*scorch*) bruciacchiare.

single ['siŋgl] adj (*one only*) singolo; solo; (*unmarried*) celibe. **single-breasted** adj a un petto. **single file** fila indiana f. **single-handed** adj (*unaided*) solo, senza aiuto. **single-minded** adj deciso, fermo, tenace. **single mindedness** n fermezza f, tenacia f. **single ticket** biglietto di andata solo m. n singolo m. v **single out** scegliere.

singular ['siŋgjulə] n, adj singolare.

sinister ['sinistə] adj (*ominous*) di cattivo augurio.

****sink** [siŋk] n lavandino m. v (*submerge, go under*) affondare; (*go down*) calare, abbassarsi.

sinuous ['sinjuəs] adj tortuoso.

sinus ['sainəs] n seno m; (*nasal*) seno paranasale m. **sinusitis** n sinusite f.

sip [sip] n sorso m. v sorseggiare, bere a piccoli sorsi.

siphon ['saifən] n sifone m. v travasare con un sifone.

sir [səː] n signore m.

siren ['saiərən] n sirena f.

sirloin ['səːloin] n lombata f.

sister ['sistə] n sorella f; (*nursing*) infermiera capo sala f; (*rel*) suora f. **sister-in-law** n cognata f.

****sit** [sit] v sedere; posare; (*garment*) cadere; (*exam*) dare; (*be convened*) essere in seduta. **sit down** sedersi, mettersi a sedere. **sit on the fence** non prendere partito. **sit tight** non lasciarsi smuovere. **sitting** n seduta f. **sitting room** salotto m.

site [sait] n posizione f; (*building*) cantiere edile m. v situare.

situation [sitju'eiʃən] n situazione f; (*post*) posizione f. **situated** adj situato.

six [siks] nm, adj sei. **sixth** nm, adj sesto.

sixteen [siks'tiːn] nm, adj sedici. **sixteenth** nm, adj sedicesimo.

sixty ['siksti] nm, adj sessanta. **sixtieth** nm, adj sessantesimo.

size[1] [saiz] n dimensione f, grandezza f; (*garments*) misura f, taglia f. v **size up** valutare. **sizeable** adj notevole.

size[2] [saiz] n (*glue*) bozzima f. v imbozzimare.

sizzle ['sizl] v sfriggere. n sfrigolio m.

skate[1] [skeit] n pattino m. v pattinare. **skater** n pattinatore, -trice m, f. **skating** n pattinaggio m.

skate[2] [skeit] n (*fish*) razza f.

skeleton ['skelitn] n scheletro m.

sketch [sketʃ] n abbozzo m; (theatre) bozzetto m. v abbozzare; delineare. **sketchbook** n albo di or per schizzi m. **sketchy** adj impreciso, superficiale.

skewer ['skjuə] n spiedo m.

ski [skiː] n sci m. **ski-lift** n sciovia f. v sciare. **skier** n sciatore, -trice m, f. **skiing** n sci m.

skid [skid] v slittare; (car) sbandare; (plane) derapare. n slittamento m; sbandamento m.

skill [skil] n abilità f, destrezza f. **skilful** adj abile, esperto. **skilled** adj abile, esperto; (worker) specializzato.

skim [skim] v (milk) scremare; (glide over) rasentare. **skim over** sfiorare; (reading) sfogliare.

skimp [skimp] v (food, expense, etc.) lesinare, risparmiare; (person) tenere a stecchetto; (scrimp) fare economia. **skimpy** adj (scanty) scarso; (mean) tirchio.

skin [skin] n pelle f; (fruit) buccia f, scorza f; (film) pellicola f; (colouring) carnagione f. **by the skin of one's teeth** per il rotto della cuffia. **skin-deep** adj superficiale. **skin-diving** n pesca subacquea f. **skinflint** n spilorcio m. **skin-graft** n innesto epidermico m. v sbucciare; (animals) scorticare. **skinny** adj magro, ossuto.

skip [skip] v saltare; (leap) balzellare. n balzo m.

skipper ['skipə] n capitano m.

skirmish ['skəːmiʃ] n scaramuccia f. v scontrarsi.

skirt [skəːt] n gonna f, sottana f. v costeggiare; (edge) orlare. **skirting board** zoccolo m.

skittle [skitl] n birillo m.

skull [skʌl] n cranio m, teschio m. **skullcap** n calotta f, papalina f.

skunk [skʌŋk] n moffetta f; (coll) farabutto m.

sky [skai] n cielo m. **blow sky-high** far saltare per aria. **sky-blue** adj celeste. **skylark** n allodola f. **skylight** n lucernario m. **skyline** n profilo m, orizzonte m. **skyscraper** n grattacielo m.

slab [slab] n piastra f; (thick piece) fetta f.

slack [slak] adj (loose) lento; (inactive) fiacco; (negligent) indolente. n (rope) imbando m; (comm) attività ridotta f. v (neglect duty) trascurare. **slacken** v rallentare.

slacks [slaks] pl n calzoni sportivi m pl.

slag [slag] n scoria f.

slalom ['slaːləm] n slalom m.

slam [slam] v sbattere. n (bridge) slam m invar.

slander ['slaːndə] n diffamazione f. v diffamare. **slanderer** n diffamatore, -trice m, f. **slanderous** adj diffamatorio.

slang [slaŋ] n gergo m. v vituperare. **slanging match** battibecco m.

slant [slaːnt] v inclinare, inclinarsi; (news) presentare in modo tendenzioso. n (slope) inclinazione f; (point of view) punto di vista m; (bias) tendenza f.

slap [slap] n schiaffo m; (rebuke) rabbuffo m. **slap in the face** insulto m, umiliazione f. **slap on the back** felicitazione f. v schiaffeggiare. **slap-bang** adv (right) in pieno; (suddenly) di colpo. **slapdash** adj fatto a casaccio, abborracciato. **slap-happy** adj incosciente.

slash [slaʃ] v tagliare, squarciare. n taglio m.

slat [slat] n stecca f, assicella f.

slate [sleit] n lavagna f; (geol) ardesia f. **have a clean slate** aver la fedina pulita. **wipe the slate clean** ricominciare dimenticando il passato.

slaughter ['slɔːtə] n macello m; (massacre) strage f. v macellare, far strage di. **slaughterhouse** n macello m.

slave [sleiv] n schiavo, -a m, f. **slave-driver** n negriero, -a m, f. **slave labour** lavori forzati m pl. v sgobbare.

sledge [sledʒ] n slitta f.

sledgehammer ['sledʒ,hamə] n mazza f. **sledgehammer blow** mazzata f.

sleek [sliːk] adj (glossy) lucido; (smooth) liscio; (soft) morbido; (unctuous) mellifluo.

*****sleep** [sliːp] n sonno m. **go to sleep** addormentarsi, prendere sonno. **have a good sleep** fare una bella dormita. v dormire; (accommodate) alloggiare. **sleep on something** v dormirci su. **sleeper** n dormiente m, f; (timber beam) traversina f; (on train) vagone letto m. **be a heavy/light sleeper** avere il sonno pesante/leggero. **sleeping bag** sacco a pelo m. **sleeping partner** (econ) socio accomandante m. **sleeping pill** sonnifero m. **sleepless** adj insonne. **sleepy** adj sonnolento.

sleet [sliːt] n nevischio m.

sleeve [sliːv] *n* manica *f*; *(tech)* manicotto *m*; *(record)* copertina *f*. **up one's sleeve** di riserva.

sleigh [slei] *n* slitta *f*. *v* andare in slitta.

slender ['slendə] *adj* snello; *(small)* esiguo, scarso.

slept [slept] *V* sleep.

slice [slais] *n* fetta *f*; parte *f*, porzione *f*; *(spatula)* paletta *f*. *v* affettare, tagliare a fette; *(sport)* tagliare.

slick [slik] *adj* *(sleek)* lucido; *(coll: smooth)* untuoso; *(coll: shrewd)* spigliato, scaltro.

slid [slid] *V* slide.

*****slide** [slaid] *n* *(inclined plane)* scivolo *m*; *(microscope)* vetrino *m*; *(phot)* diapositiva *f*; *(hair)* fibbia *f*; *(act of sliding)* scivolata *f*. **slide-rule** *n* regolo calcolatore *m*. *v* scivolare. **let slide** lasciar correre. **sliding scale** scala mobile *f*.

slight [slait] *adj* leggero; *(frail)* esile. *n* affronto *m*, dispetto *m*, mancanza di rispetto *f*. *v* mancare di rispetto, ignorare.

slim [slim] *adj* magro, snello; *(poor)* povero; *(scant)* minimo. *v* dimagrare. **slimming** *adj* dimagrante.

slime [slaim] *n* melma *f*; *(secretion)* bava *f*. **slimy** *adj* melmoso; bavoso; *(servile)* untuoso.

*****sling** [sliŋ] *n* *(weapon)* fionda *f*; *(bandage)* benda *f*, fascia *f*; *(rifle)* cinghia *f*; *(hoist)* braca *f*. **have one's arm in a sling** portare un braccio al collo. *v* *(throw)* lanciare, gettare; *(suspend)* sospendere.

*****slink** [sliŋk] *v* sgattaiolare.

slip [slip] *n* errore *m*, svista *f*; *(garment)* sottana *f*; *(skid)* scivolata *f*; *(plant)* rampollo *m*; *(of paper)* pezzetto *m*. **slip of the tongue** lapsus linguae *m invar*. *v* scivolare. **let slip** lasciar scappare. **slip away** andarsene. **slip-knot** *n* nodo scorsoio *m*. **slip-road** *n* raccordo *m*. **slip up** fare uno sbaglio, prendere una papera.

slipper ['slipə] *n* pantofola *f*, ciabatta *f*.

slippery ['slipəri] *adj* scivoloso.

*****slit** [slit] *n* taglio *m*, fessura *f*. *v* tagliare, squarciare.

slither ['sliðə] *v* scivolare.

slobber ['slobə] *v* sbavare.

sloe [slou] *n* *(fruit)* prugnola *f*; *(tree)* prugnolo *m*.

slog [slog] *v* *(walk)* avanzare a fatica; *(toil)* faticare. *n* camminata dura *f*; faticata *f*.

slogan ['slougən] *n* motto *m*, slogan *m invar*.

slop [slop] *v* versare; *(spill over)* traboccare. **slops** *pl n* *(food)* pappa *f sing*; *(dirty water)* lavatura *f sing*.

slope [sloup] *n* pendio *m*. *v* inclinarsi, pendere. **sloping** *adj* inclinato, obliquo.

sloppy ['slopi] *adj* *(wet)* bagnato; *(careless)* abborracciato; *(untidy)* scatto; *(sentimental)* sentimentale.

slot [slot] *n* fessura *f*, apertura *f*. **slot-machine** *n* *(vending)* apparecchio a gettoni *m*; *(gambling)* slot-machine *m invar*. *v* **slot into** incanalare.

slouch [slautʃ] *v* *(walk)* camminare dinoccolato; *(droop)* languire. *n* andatura dinoccolata *f*.

slovenly ['slʌvnli] *adj* sciatto, trascurato.

slow [slou] *adj* lento; *(late)* tardo; *(clock)* indietro *invar*. *adv* piano, adagio. *v* **slow down** rallentare.

slug [slʌg] *n* lumaca *f*.

sluggish ['slʌgiʃ] *adj* lento, inerte.

sluice [sluːs] *n* chiusa *f*. *v* *(flush)* lavare abbondantemente.

slum [slʌm] *n* quartiere povero *or* basso *m*; *(tumbledown house)* tugurio *m*, catapecchia *f*.

slumber ['slʌmbə] *v* sonnecchiare. *n* *(heavy)* dormita *f*; *(light)* dormiveglia *m invar*.

slump [slʌmp] *n* crollo *m*, caduta *f*. *v* cadere, crollare.

slung [slʌŋ] *V* sling.

slunk [slʌŋk] *V* slink.

slur [sləː] *v* *(speech)* biascicare; *(disparage)* denigrare; *(music)* legare. **slur over** passar sopra a. *n* affronto *m*; *(blot)* macchia *f*.

slush [slʌʃ] *n* melma *f*. **slushy** *adj* melmoso.

slut [slʌt] *n* *(immoral)* sgualdrina *f*; *(slovenly)* sciattona *f*.

sly [slai] *adj* astuto, scaltro. **on the sly** in sordina.

smack[1] [smak] *n* *(hit)* schiaffo *m*; *(sound)* schiocco *m*; *(kiss)* bacione *m*. **smack in the eye** *(snub)* rabbuffo *m*; *(disappointment)* delusione *f*. *v* schiaffeggiare, schioccare. **smack one's lips** leccarsi i baffi.

smack[2] [smak] *n* sapore *m*. *v* **smack of** *(taste)* sapere di; *(suggest)* ricordare.

small [smoːl] *adj* piccolo; *(low)* basso; *(humble)* umile; insignificante. **small change** spiccioli *m pl*. **small fry** persone di poco conto f pl. **small-minded** adj gretto. **smallpox** n vaiolo m. **small talk** chiacchera f. cicaleccio m.

smart [smɑːt] adj (sharp) acuto; intelligente; (shrewd) sveglio; elegante; brillante. v bruciare, sentire un vivo dolore. **smarten** v abbellirse, ravvivarsi.

smash [smæʃ] n (collision) scontro m; (ruin) rovina f, disastro m; (tennis) smash m invar. **smash-and-grab raid** (coll) spaccata f. v (shatter) fracassare; (destroy) annientare. **smashing** adj (coll) magnifico.

smear [smɪə] n (grease) ungere; (daub) spalmare; (soil) macchiare; (defame) calunniare n macchia f; (slur) calunnia f.

*****smell** [smel] n odore m, profumo m; (faculty) odorato m. v sentire l'odore di; (perceive) fiutare; (stink) puzzare. **smell a rat** fiutare un imbroglio. **smell of** aver odore di.

smelt [smelt] V smell.

smile [smail] n sorriso m. v sorridere.

smirk [smɜːk] n sorriso compiaciuto m. v sorridere con aria compiaciuta.

smock [smok] n camiciotto m; (artists') blusa f. **smocking** n nido d'ape m, punto smock m.

smog [smog] n smog m invar.

smoke [smouk] n fumo m. **smoke-screen** n cortina di fumo f. **smoke-stack** n fumaiolo m. v fumare; (cure) affumicare. **smokeless** adj senza fumo. **smoker** n (person) fumatore, -trice m, f; (compartment) scompartimento per fumatori m. **smoky** adj fumoso, che sa di fumo.

smooth [smuːð] adj (not rough) liscio; (unruffled) calmo; (not harsh) gradevole. v lisciare, spianare, facilitare.

smother ['smʌðə] v soffocare, sopprimere.

smoulder ['smouldə] v covare (sotto la cenere).

smudge [smʌdʒ] n sgorbio m. v sgorbiare.

smug [smʌg] adj soddisfatto di sé.

smuggle ['smʌgl] v smuggle in/out far entrare/uscire di contrabbando. **smuggler** n contrabbandiere, -a m, f. **smuggling** n contrabbando m.

snack [snæk] n (light meal) spuntino m.

snag [snæg] n (impediment) intoppo m. v (stocking) smagliare.

snail [sneil] n chiocciola f, lumaca f.

snake [sneik] n serpente m.

snap [snæp] n (noise) schioccare; (break suddenly) spezzarsi; (phot) scattare. **snap**

out of it riprendersi. **snap up** non lasciarsi sfuggire. n schiocco m; rottura improvvisa f; (sudden bite) morsicata f; (phot) istantanea f; (short spell) ondata f. **snapdragon** n bocca di leone f. adj istantaneo. **snappy** adj irritabile; (lively) vivace.

snare [snɛə] n laccio m, lacciolo m. v prendere al laccio; accalappiare.

snarl¹ [snɑːl] v (growl) ringhiare. n ringhio m.

snarl² [snɑːl] n (tangle) groviglio m. v aggrovigliare.

snatch [snætʃ] v ghermire, aggiuntare. n strappo m; (scrap) frammento m.

sneak [sniːk] v muoversi furtivamente; (coll: steal) squagliarsela; (slang: tell tales) spifferare. n (coll) spifferone, -a m, f; (despicable person) vigliacco, -a m, f. **sneakers** pl n scarpe da tennis o ginnastica f pl.

sneer [snɪə] n (derisory) ghigno m; (contemptuous) sogghigno m. v ghignare; sogghignare. **sneer at** canzonare, burlarsi di.

sneeze [sniːz] n starnuto m. v starnutire. **sneeze at** (coll) sprezzare.

sniff [snif] n annusare, fiutare; aspirare col naso. n annusata f, fiuto m.

snigger ['snigə] v ridere sotto i baffi, ridacchiare. n ghigno m.

snip [snip] v tagliuzzare; (cut off) spuntare. n (piece) ritaglio m; (bargain) occasione f.

snipe [snaip] n (bird) beccaccino m. v sparare di sorpresa. **sniper** n tiratore scelto che spara di soppiatto m.

snivel ['snivl] v moccicare; (whine) frignare. **sniveller** n moccioso, -a m, f; frignone, -a m, f.

snob [snob] n snob m, f invar.

snoop [snuːp] v curiosare.

snooty ['snuːti] adj (coll) sdegnoso, altezzoso.

snooze [snuːz] v sonnecchiare. n pisolino m.

snore [snɔː] v russare, ronfare.

snorkel ['snɔːkəl] n respiratore a tubo m.

snort [snɔːt] n sbuffata f. v sbuffare.

snout [snaut] n muso m; (pig) grugno m; (nozzle) becco m.

snow [snou] n neve f. **snowball** n palla di neve f. **snowbound** adj bloccato dalla neve. **snow-drift** n cumulo or banco di neve m. **snowdrop** n bucaneve m invar.

snowfall n nevicata f. **snowflake** n fiocco di neve m. **snowman** n pupazzo di neve m. **snow-plough** n spazzaneve m invar.

snowstorm n tormenta f. v nevicare.

snowy adj nevoso; (colour) niveo, candido.

snub [snʌb] n rabbuffo m, affronto m. v trattare con disprezzo. **snub-nosed** adj camuso.

snuff¹ [snʌf] v fiutare, aspirare. n tabacco da fiuto m. **snuffbox** n tabacchiera f.

snuff² [snʌf] v snuff it (coll: die) crepare. **snuff out** spegnere.

snug [snʌg] adj (comfortable) comodo; (cosy) intimo; (close-fitting) aderente.

snuggle ['snʌgl] v rannicchiarsi; (cuddle) coccolare.

so [sou] adv così, tanto; (to that extent) talmente. conj perciò, quindi. **and so on** eccetera. **if so** in tal caso. **in so far as** per quanto. **so-called** adj cosiddetto. **so far** finora. **so long as** finché. **so much** tanto. **so-so** adv discretamente, così così. **so to speak** per così dire.

soak [souk] v inzuppare, imbevere. **be soaked through** essere bagnato fradicio. **soak in** penetrare. **soak up** assorbire.

soap [soup] n sapone m. **soap-dish** n portasapone m invar. **soap flakes/powder** sapone in scaglie/polvere m. **soap-suds** n saponata f sing. v insaponare. **soapy** adj (covered with soap) insaponato; (like soap) saponoso.

soar [soɪ] v librarsi; (rise) salire.

sob [sob] n singhiozzo m. v singhiozzare.

sober ['soubə] adj sobrio, calmo. v **sober down** calmarsi. **sober up** smaltire una sbornia. **sobriety** n moderatezza f, serietà f.

soccer ['sokə] n calcio m, football m invar.

sociable ['souʃəbl] adj socievole. **sociability** n socievolezza f.

social ['souʃəl] adj (of a community) sociale; (disposition) socievole; (of polite society) mondano. **social security** previdenza sociale f. **social worker** assistente sociale m. **socialism** n socialismo m. **socialist** n(m+f), adj socialista.

society [sə'saiəti] n società f, compagnia f.

sociology [sousi'olədʒi] n sociologia f. **sociological** adj sociologico. **sociologist** n sociologo, -a.

sock¹ [sok] n (short) calzino m; (long) calza f.

sock² [sok] (slang) n colpo m. v picchiare; (punch) prendere a pugni.

socket ['sokit] n cavità f; (eye) orbita f, occhiaia f; (elec) presa f.

soda ['soudə] n (water) seltz m invar; (sodium carbonate) soda f; soda caustica f.

sodden ['sodn] adj fradicio.

sofa ['soufə] n sofà m invar.

soft [soft] adj (not hard) molle; (not rough) morbido, soffice; (pleasant) mite, dolce; (soothing) tenero; (water) dolce. adv piano. **soften** v ammorbidire, intenerirsi. **softly** adv pian piano, adagio, dolcemente.

soggy ['sogi] adj fradicio, inzuppato.

soil¹ [soil] n suolo m, terra f.

soil² [soil] v sporcare, insudiciare.

solar ['soulə] adj solare.

sold [sould] V **sell**.

solder ['soldə] n saldatura f. v saldare. **soldering iron** saldatore m.

soldier ['souldʒə] n soldato m. v **soldier on** tirare avanti.

sole¹ [soul] adj solo, unico.

sole² [soul] n (foot) pianta f; (shoe, tech) suola f.

sole³ [soul] n (fish) sogliola f.

solemn ['soləm] adj solenne, serio.

solicitor [sə'lisitə] n avvocato, -essa m, f.

solicitous [sə'lisitəs] adj premuroso.

solid ['solid] adj solido, sodo, compatto; (sound) serio. n (corpo) solido m. **solidarity** n solidarietà f. **solidity** n solidità f; serietà f.

solitary ['solitəri] adj solitario, solo, isolato. **solitary confinement** n reclusione or segregazione cellulare f.

solitude ['solitjuːd] n solitudine f, isolamento m.

solo ['soulou] n assolo m. adj solo, solitario. **soloist** n solista m, f.

solstice ['solstis] n solstizio m.

soluble ['soljubl] adj solubile.

solution [sə'luːʃən] n soluzione f.

solve [solv] v risolvere. **solvent** nm, adj solvente. **solvency** n solvenza f.

sombre ['sombə] adj tetro, fosco.

some [sʌm] adj del, della; (pl) dei, delle; qualche; (certain) alcuni, -e; (before verb) ne. **somebody** or **someone** pron qualcuno. **somebody else** qualcun altro. **some day** un bel giorno. **somehow**

adv in qualche modo, in un modo o in un altro. **some ... some ... gli uni ... gli altri ... . something** *pron* qualcosa. **something else** qualcos'altro. **sometime** *adv* un giorno o l'altro, presto o tardi. **sometimes** *adv* qualche volta; *(now and then)* di tanto in tanto. **somewhat** *adv* piuttosto. **somewhere** *adv* in qualche parte. **somewhere else** altrove.

somersault ['sʌməsɔːlt] *n* capriola *f*, salto mortale *m*. *v* fare una capriola, fare un salto mortale.

son [sʌn] *n* figlio *m*. **son-in-law** *n* genero *m*.

sonata [sə'nɑːtə] *n* sonata *f*.

song [sɒŋ] *n* canzone *f*; *(act of singing)* canto *m*. **for a song** per una sciocchezza.

sonic ['sɒnik] *adj* sonico. **sonic bang or boom** boato sonico *m*.

sonnet ['sɒnit] *n* sonetto *m*.

soon [suːn] *adv* presto, tra poco. **as soon as** appena. **how soon?** fra quanto tempo? **soon after** subito dopo. **too soon** in anticipo. **very soon** tra breve, quanto prima. **no sooner said than done** detto fatto. **sooner or later** presto o tardi, prima o poi.

soot [sut] *n* fuliggine *f*. **sooty** *adj* fuligginoso.

soothe [suːð] *v* calmare, mitigare.

sophisticated [sə'fistikeitid] *adj* raffinato, sofisticato.

sopping ['sɒpiŋ] *adj* fradicio.

soprano [sə'prɑːnou] *n* soprano *m*, *f*.

sordid ['sɔːdid] *adj* sordido.

sore [sɔː] *adj* doloroso. **sore throat** mal di gola *m*. *n* piaga *f*, ulcera *f*.

sorrow ['sɔrou] *n* dolore *m*, dispiacere *m*; *(cause of regret)* rincrescimento *m*. **sorrowful** *adj* triste, addolorato; *(distressing)* penoso.

sorry ['sɔri] *adj* dolente, spiacente, triste; *(wretched)* meschino, miserabile. **feel sorry for** compatire. **I'm sorry** mi dispiace *or* rincresce. *interj* pardon! scusi! scusate!

sort [sɔːt] *n* sorta *f*, specie *f* *invar*. **a good sort** una brava persona *f*. **out of sorts** giù di giri. *v* classificare, raggruppare. **sort out** smistare; *(choose)* scegliere.

soufflé ['suːflei] *n* soufflé *m* *invar*.

sought [sɔːt] *V* seek.

soul [soul] *n* anima *f*, spirito *m*.

sound¹ [saund] *n* suono *m*; *(noise)* rumore

m. **sound effect** effetto sonoro *m*. **soundproof** *adj* fonoassorbente, impenetrabile al suono. **sound-track** *n* colonna sonora *f*. *v* suonare; *(seem)* sembrare.

sound² [saund] *adj* *(not damaged)* sano; valido, legittimo; *(sleep, etc.)* profondo.

sound³ [saund] *n* *(med)* sonda *f*. *v* sondare; *(naut)* scandagliare.

soup [suːp] *n* minestra *f*; *(broth)* brodo *m*; *(with bread)* zuppa *f*. **be in the soup** trovarsi nei pasticci. **soup-ladle** *n* cucchiaione *m*. **soup-plate** *n* fondina *f*.

sour [sauə] *adj* acido; *(tart, harsh)* acerbo, agro.

source [sɔːs] *n* sorgente *f*, origine *f*.

south [sauθ] *n* sud *m*; *(of country)* meridione *m*. *adj also* **southern, southerly** del sud; meridionale. *adv* *(direction)* verso sud; *(location)* al sud; *(origin)* dal sud. **south-east** *n* sudest *m*. **South Pole** polo sud *m*. **south-west** *n* sudovest *m*. **southernmost** *adj* il più a sud.

souvenir [suvə'niə] *n* ricordo *m*.

sovereign ['sɔvrin] *n*, *adj* sovrano, -a. **sovereignty** *n* sovranità *f*.

*ᵃ***sow¹** [sou] *v* seminare; disseminare.

sow² [sau] *n* scrofa *f*.

sown [soun] *V* sow¹.

soya ['sɔiə] *n* soia *f*.

spa [spɑː] *n* terme *f* *pl*, stazione termale *f*.

space [speis] *n* spazio *m*. *v* scaglionare; *(printing)* spaziare. **spaceman** *n* astronauta *m*. **spaceship** *n* astronave *f*. **spacious** *adj* ampio, spazioso.

spade [speid] *n* badile *m*, vanga *f*. **call a spade a spade** dire pane al pane.

spades [speidz] *pl* *n* *(cards)* picche *f* *pl*.

Spain [spein] *n* Spagna *f*. **Spaniard** *n* spagnolo, -a *m*, *f*. **Spanish** *nm*, *adj* spagnolo.

span [span] *n* *(hand)* spanna *f*; *(bridge)* arco *m*; *(extent)* portata *f*; *(time)* durata *f*. *v* stendersi attraverso.

spaniel ['spanjəl] *n* spaniel *m* *invar*.

spank [spaŋk] *v* sculacciare.

spanner ['spanə] *n* chiave *f*; *(adjustable)* chiave inglese *f*.

spare [speə] *adj* di riserva *or* scorta; *(surplus)* in più, disponibile; frugale; *(lean)* magro. **spare part** pezzo di ricambio *m*. **spare room** camera in più *f*. **spare time** tempo disponibile *m*. **spare wheel** ruota di scorta *f*. *v* *(not harm)* risparmiare; *(do without)* fare a meno di. **spare no**

expense non badare a spese. **sparing** adj parco, sobrio, limitato.

spark [spɑːk] n scintilla f; (gleam) barlume m. v emettere scintille, scintillare; (elec) accendere. **sparking-plug** n candela (d'accensione) f.

sparkle ['spɑːkl] n scintilla f, splendore m. v scintillare, brillare, risplendere. **sparkling** adj brillante; (wine) spumante.

sparrow ['sparou] n passero m.

sparse [spɑːs] adj rado, scarso. **sparsely** adv poco.

spasm ['spazəm] n accesso m; (muscular) spasmo m. **spasmodic** adj spasmodico.

spastic ['spastik] n, adj spastico, -a.

spat [spat] V **spit**[1].

spate [speit] n piena f.

spatial ['speiʃl] adj spaziale.

spatula ['spatjulə] n spatola f.

spawn [spoːn] n (zool) uova f pl; (brood) progenie f. v deporre uova; (give rise to) generare, produrre (in abbondanza); (derog) figliare.

****speak** [spiːk] v parlare. **so to speak** per così dire. **speaking of** a proposito di. **speak out** parlare apertamente. **speak up** (loudly) parlare ad alta voce, parlare più forte. **speak up for** parlare a favore di. **strictly speaking** per essere precisi. **speaker** n oratore m; (pol) presidente m; (hi-fi) cassa acustica.

spear [spiə] n lancia f. v trafiggere.

special ['speʃəl] adj speciale, particolare; straordinario. **specialist** n specialista m, f. **speciality** n specialità f. **specialization** n specializzazione f. **specialize** v specializzare.

species ['spiːʃiːz] n specie f invar, genere m.

specify ['spesifai] v specificare, precisare. **specific** adj specifico, preciso. **specification** n specificazione f; (detailed description) specifica f.

specimen ['spesimin] n esemplare m, modello m; (for test) campione m.

speck [spek] n (spot) macchia f; (particle) granello m. **speckle** n macchia f, chiazza f. **speckled** adj chiazzato.

spectacle ['spektəkl] n spettacolo m. **spectacles** pl n occhiali m pl. **spectacled** adj occhialuto.

spectator [spek'teitə] n spettatore, -trice m, f.

spectrum ['spektrəm] n spettro m.

speculate ['spekjuleit] v speculare,

meditare. **speculation** n speculazione f. **speculative** adj speculativo. **speculator** n speculatore, -trice m, f.

sped [sped] V **speed**.

speech [spiːtʃ] n (faculty) parola f; discorso m. **speechless** adj muto, senza parole.

****speed** [spiːd] n velocità f. **at full speed** a tutta corsa, a velocità massima. **speedboat** n fuoribordo m. **speed limit** limite di velocità m. **speedometer** n tachimetro m. v andare in fretta. **speed up** accelerare. **speedy** adj veloce; (ready) pronto.

****spell**[1] [spel] v (read) compitare, sillabare; (write) scrivere; significare. **spelling** n ortografia f.

spell[2] [spel] n (magic) incanto m, incantesimo m; fascino m. **cast a spell** incantare. **spellbind** v affascinare.

spell[3] [spel] n periodo m; (work) turno m; (bout) attacco m.

spelt [spelt] V **spell**[1].

****spend** [spend] v spendere; (employ) impiegare, dedicare; (time) trascorrere, passare; (consume) esaurire. **spendthrift** n, adj prodigo, -a.

spent [spent] V **spend**.

sperm [spəːm] n sperma m.

spew [spjuː] n vomito m. v vomitare.

sphere [sfiə] n sfera f. **spherical** adj sferico.

spice [spais] n (cookery) spezie f invar; (flavour) gusto m, sapore m. v condire (con spezie); dar gusto or interesse a. **spicy** adj piccante, aromatico; salace.

spider ['spaidə] n ragno m. **spider's web** ragnatela f.

spike [spaik] n punta f, chiodo m. v inchiodare; (frustrate) rendere inservibile.

****spill** [spil] v spandere, versare. **spill over** traboccare.

spilt [spilt] V **spill**.

****spin** [spin] v (thread) filare; (rotate) (far) girare. **spin-drier** n centrifuga f, idroestrattore m. **spin-dry** v asciugare con la centrifuga. **spin out** prolungare. **spin a yarn** raccontare una frottola. n rotazione f; (phys) spin m invar; (short trip) giro m.

spinach ['spinidʒ] n spinaci m pl.

spindle ['spindl] n fuso m. **spindly** adj esile, affusolato.

spine [spain] n (anat) spina dorsale f; (book) dorso m. **spinal** adj spinale,

vertebrale. **spine-chilling** adj agghiacciante. **spineless** adj smidollato, debole.
spinster ['spinstə] n nubile f; (coll) zitella f.
spiral ['spaiərəl] n spirale f. adj a spirale. **spiral staircase** scala a chiocciola f.
spire ['spaiə] n guglia f.
spirit ['spirit] n spirito m; (drink) superalcolico m. **be in high spirits** avere il morale alto; essere allegro. **spirit-level** n livella a bolla d'aria f. **that's the spirit!** così va bene! **spirited** adj vivace, vigoroso. **spiritless** adj (without vigour) fiacco; (not lively) abbattuto. **spiritual** adj spirituale. **spiritualism** n spiritismo m; (philos) spiritualismo m. **spiritualist** n spiritista m, f.
*****spit**[1] [spit] v sputare; (rain) piovigginare; (cat) soffiare. **the spitting image of ...** ... nato e sputato. n also **spittle** sputo m, saliva f.
spit[2] [spit] n (skewer) spiedo m; (land) lingua di terra f. v (skewer) infilzare.
spite [spait] n dispetto m. **in spite of** nonostante, malgrado. v far dispetto a; (annoy) indispettire. **spiteful** adj dispettoso, maligno.
splash [splæʃ] v (spatter) spruzzare; (mark with colour) macchiare, chiazzare. n spruzzata f; (sound) tonfo m; (liquid splashed) spruzzo m; (patch) macchia f; (showy display) sfoggio m.
spleen [spliːn] n (med) milza f; (peevishness) malumore m. **vent one's spleen on** sfogarsi su.
splendid ['splendid] adj splendido, stupendo. **splendour** n splendore m.
splice [splais] v (rope) impiombare; (tape) giuntare. n impiombatura f; giuntura f.
splint [splint] n stecca f.
splinter ['splintə] n scheggia f. v frantumarsi.
*****split** [split] v (cleave) spaccare; dividere, separare. **split hairs** cavillare. **split on** (coll) denunciare. **split up** dividersi, suddividere. n fenditura f; (into fractions) scissione f; separazione f. adj spaccato.
splutter ['splʌtə] v (spit) sputacchiare; (talk confusedly) farfugliare; (splash) spruzzare; (engine) scoppiettare.
*****spoil** [spoil] v rovinare, sciupare; (indulge) viziare. **be spoiling for** aver una gran voglia di. **spoil-sport** n guastafeste m, f invar. **spoils** pl n spoglie f pl.
spoilt [spoilt] V **spoil**.

spoke[1] [spouk] V **speak**.
spoke[2] [spouk] n raggio m; (rung) piolo m. **put a spoke in someone's wheel** mettere un bastone fra le ruote a qualcuno.
spoken ['spoukn] V **speak**.
spokesman ['spouksmən] n portavoce m, f invar.
sponge [spʌndʒ] n spugna f. **sponge-cake** n pan di Spagna m. **throw in the sponge** gettare la spugna. v lavare con la spugna; (coll: cadge) scroccare. **sponger** n scroccone, -a m, f. **spongy** adj spugnoso.
sponsor ['sponsə] n garante m, f; (TV, etc.) finanziatore, -trice m, f. v essere garante di; rendersi responsabile di; finanziare; (lend support) patrocinare. **sponsorship** n garanzia f; finanziamento m.
spontaneous [spon'teinjəs] adj spontaneo. **spontaneity** n spontaneità f.
spool [spuːl] n rocchetto m.
spoon [spuːn] n cucchiaio m. **spoonfeed** v scodellare la pappa a. **spoonful** n cucchiaiata f.
sporadic [spə'rædik] adj isolato.
sport [spoːt] n sport m invar; (jesting) scherzo m. **be a sport!** sii bravo! **sportsman** n sportivo m. **sportsmanship** n abilità sportiva f; spirito sportivo m. **sportswoman** n sportiva f. v (display) sfoggiare. **sporting** adj sportivo. **sporting chance** possibilità di successo f.
spot [spot] n (mark) macchia f, puntino m; (pimple) piccolo foruncolo m; (place) posto m, località f. **on the spot** sul posto. **spot check** controllo saltuario m. **spotlight** n riflettore m. v macchiare, punteggiare; (see) riconoscere, scoprire, osservare. **spotless** adj immacolato. **spotter** n osservatore, -trice m.
spouse [spaus] n sposo, -a m, f, coniuge m, f.
spout [spaut] n becco m, beccuccio m; (chute) scivolo m; (jet) getto m. **up the spout** (lost) perduto; (in a bad way) ridotto male. v (discharge) scaricare, gettare; (gush out) scaturire; (coll: talk) declamare.
sprain [sprein] v (strain) storcere; (wrench) slogare. n storta f; slogatura f.
sprang [spræŋ] V **spring**.
sprawl [sproːl] v stendersi lungo disteso; (spread out) estendersi. **send sprawling** mandare a gambe all'aria.

spray¹ [sprei] *n* (*jet*) spruzzo *m*; (*appliance*) spray *m invar*, atomizzatore *m*; (*hail*) raffica *f*. *v* spruzzare, atomizzare; (*scatter*) spargere.

spray² [sprei] *n* (*branch*) frasca *f*.

*spread [spred] *v* (*lay out*) stendere; (*distribute*) spargere; (*disseminate*) diffondere; (*apply layer*) spalmare. *n* estensione *f*, diffusione *f*; (*cover*) coperta *f*; (*coll: feast*) banchetto *m*.

spree [spriː] *n* baldoria *f*.

sprig [sprig] *n* ramoscello *m*.

sprightly ['spraitli] *adj* vivace.

*spring [sprin] *v* (*rise suddenly*) saltare, balzare; (*move rapidly*) scattare. **spring a leak** aprire una falla. **spring from** derivare *or* provenire da. **spring up** (*arise*) nascere; (*originate*) sorgere; (*jump up*) balzare; (*come forth*) spuntare. *n* (*beginning*) origine *f*; (*source of water*) sorgente *f*; (*season*) primavera *f*; (*coil*) molla *f*. *adj* primaverile, giovane. **spring-board** *n* trampolino *m*. **spring onion** cipollina *f*.

sprinkle ['sprinkl] *v* spargere, cospargere; (*liquid*) spruzzare. **sprinkler** *n* (*watering can*) annaffiatoio *m*; (*fire*) nebulizzatore (antincendio) *m*. **sprinkling** *n* (*of knowledge*) infarinatura *f*.

sprint [sprint] *n* (*sport*) sprint *m invar*; volata *f*. *v* correre di volata, scattare. **sprinter** *n* sprinter *m*, *f invar*, velocista *m*, *f*.

sprout [spraut] *v* germogliare. *n* germoglio *m*. **Brussels sprouts** cavolini di Bruxelles *m pl*.

spruce [spruːs] *n* abete *m*.

sprung [sprʌŋ] *V* **spring**.

spun [spʌn] *V* **spin**.

spur [spəː] *n* sprone *m*. **on the spur of the moment** lì per lì. *v* **spur on** incitare.

spurious ['spjuəriəs] *adj* falso, spurio.

spurn [spəːn] *v* sdegnare; rifiutare.

spurt [spəːt] *n* (*gush*) getto improvviso *m*, zampillo *m*; (*burst*) scatto *m*; (*effort*) sforzo *m*. *v* zampillare.

spy [spai] *n* spia *f*. *v* spiare, fare la spia. **spying** *n* spionaggio *m*.

squabble ['skwobl] *v* litigare, bisticciarsi. *n* alterco *m*, bisticcio *m*, lite *f*.

squad [skwod] *n* squadra *f*.

squadron ['skwodrən] *n* squadriglia *f*.

squalid ['skwolid] *adj* squallido.

squall [skwɔːl] *n* raffica *f*.

squander ['skwondə] *v* sprecare, sperperare. **squanderer** *n* sprecone, -a *m*, *f*.

square [skweə] *n* quadrato *m*; (*street*) piazza *f*; (*instrument*) squadra *f*. *adj* quadro; (*math*) quadrato; (*corner*) ad angolo retto; perpendicolare; (*settled*) saldato; (*straightforward*) diretto, netto. **square meal** pasto sostanzioso *m*. *v* (*math*) quadrare; (*accounts*) saldare; (*regulate*) mettere a punto; (*coll: bribe*) corrompere. **square up to** affrontare.

squash [skwoʃ] *v* schiacciare, spremere; (*suppress*) sopprimere; ridurre al silenzio, umiliare. *n* (*drink*) spremuta *f*; (*sport*) squash *m invar*; (*crowd*) ressa *f*.

squat [skwot] *v* rannicchiarsi, accovacciarsi; (*occupy illegally*) occupare abusivamente. *adj* tarchiato, tozzo.

squawk [skwoːk] *v* schiamazzare. *n* schiamazzo *m*.

squeak [skwiːk] *v* stridere, cigolare. *n* strido *m*, cigolio *m*. **have a narrow squeak** scamparla bella.

squeal [skwiːl] *v* strillare; (*coll: complain*) protestare. *n* strillo *m*.

squeamish ['skwiːmiʃ] *adj* schizzinoso, schifiltoso.

squeeze [skwiːz] *v* (*press*) spremere; (*force*) pigiare; (*embrace*) stringere; (*press together*) comprimere. *n* stretta *f*; (*crowd*) calca *f*; (*comm*) restrizioni *f pl*.

squid [skwid] *n* calamaro *m*, seppia *f*.

squiggle ['skwigl] *n* sgorbio *m*. *v* sgorbiare.

squint [skwint] *v* (*be cross-eyed*) essere guercio *or* strabico; (*glance sideways*) guardare di traverso. *n* sguardo torto *m*, strabismo *m*. **squint-eyed** *adj* guercio, strabico.

squire ['skwaiə] *n* gentiluomo *m*, proprietario di terre *m*.

squirm [skwəːm] *v* (*wriggle*) dimenarsi, contorcersi; (*feel embarrassed*) essere sulle spine.

squirrel ['skwirəl] *n* scoiattolo *m*.

squirt [skwəːt] *v* schizzare. *n* (*jet*) schizzo *m*; (*syringe*) schizzetto *m*; (*derog*) ometto *m*, tizio *m*.

stab [stab] *v* pugnalare, accoltellare. **stab in the back** pugnalare alle spalle. *n* pugnalata *f*, coltellata *f*; (*try*) tentativo *m*. **have a stab at** tentare di.

stabilize ['steibilaiz] *v* stabilizzare. **stabilization** *n* stabilizzazione *f*. **stabilizer** *n* stabilizzatore *m*.

stable¹ ['steibl] n stalla f; (racing) scuderia f.

stable² ['steibl] adj stabile; (firm) saldo; permanente. **stability** n stabilità f, fermezza f.

staccato [stə'kartou] adj staccato.

stack [stak] n (heap) catasta f, mucchio m; (chimney) fumaiolo m. v accatastare, ammucchiare.

stadium ['steidiəm] n stadio m.

staff [staf] n (stick) bastone m; (flag-pole) asta f; (personnel) personale m; (mil) stato maggiore m. v fornire di personale, impiegare.

stag [stag] n cervo m. **stag-beetle** n cervo volante m.

stage [steidʒ] n (phase) fase f; (lap) tappa f; periodo m, momento m; teatro m; (platform) palcoscenico m. **at this stage** a questo punto. **go on the stage** fare l'attore. **stage-coach** n diligenza f. **stage-craft** n scenotecnica f. **stage fright** timor panico m. **stage-manager** n direttore di scena m. v rappresentare, mettere in scena. **staging** n messa in scena f.

stagger ['stagə] v barcollare; (shock) colpire, impressionare; (arrange) scaglionare. **staggering** adj sconcertante.

stagnant ['stagnənt] adj stagnante, inattivo. **stagnate** v ristagnare. **stagnation** n ristagno m.

staid [steid] adj posato, serio.

stain [stein] n macchia f; tinta f, colore m. **stain remover** smacchiatore m. v macchiare; colorire. **stainless steel** acciaio inossidabile m.

stair [steə] n (step) scalino m, gradino m. **staircase** n scala f. **stairs** pl n scale f pl.

stake¹ [steik] n (post) palo m; (execution) rogo m. v (support) palare. **stake out** cintare. **stake out a claim** reclamare.

stake² [steik] n (bet) posta f, scommessa f. **at stake** in gioco. v mettere in gioco, scommettere. **stake one's life** scommettere l'osso del collo.

stale [steil] adj vecchio, stantio; (bread) raffermo.

stalemate ['steilmeit] n stallo m; (deadlock) punto morto m. **reach stalemate** giungere a una posizione di stallo.

stalk¹ [stok] n stelo m, gambo m.

stalk² [stok] v (follow) inseguire furtivamente; (stride haughtily) camminare impettito.

stall¹ [stol] n banco m, chiosco m; (newspapers) edicola f; (theatre) poltrona di platea f. **stalls** pl n (theatre) platea f sing. v (engine) imballare, (aeroplane) picchiare; (stop) fermarsi.

stall² [stol] v (delay) tirar per le lunghe; (act evasively) cercar pretesti.

stallion ['staljən] n stallone m.

stamina ['staminə] n vigore m, capacità di resistenza f.

stammer ['stamə] v balbettare. n balbuzie f. **stammerer** n balbuziente m, f.

stamp [stamp] v marcare, imprimere; (envelope) affrancare; (print on) timbrare; (documents) bollare; (with foot) pestare. n (impression) impronta f; marchio m; (document) bollo m; (postage) francobollo m; (implement) stampiglia f; (rubber) timbro m. **stamp out** domare, annientare. n filatelico, -a m, f.

stampede [stam'piid] n fuga precipitosa f. v fuggire in disordine.

*****stand** [stand] n posizione f; (platform) tribuna f; (exhibition) stand m invar; (music, etc.) leggio m. v stare, essere; (be upright) stare in piedi; (remain) restare; (tolerate) sopportare, tollerare. **stand by** (wait) rimanere in attesa; (help) aiutare; (remain faithful) restar fedele a. **stand-by** n riserva f, scorta f. **stand for** significare; (support) sostenere. **stand-in** n controfigura f. **stand-offish** adj riservato. **stand out** (project) spiccare; (be conspicuous) risaltare. **standstill** n arresto m, fermata f. **come to a standstill** fermarsi. **stand up** alzarsi. **stand up for** prender le parte di. **stand up to** resistere a.

standard ['standəd] n standard m invar, modello m, campione m; (level) livello m; (flag) stendardo m, bandiera f. adj standard invar, normale. **standard lamp** torciera f, piantana f.

standing ['standin] n posizione f, reputazione f; (period) durata f. adj fermo, fisso; permanente; abituale; (upright) in piedi. **leave standing** abbandonare sul posto.

stank [stank] V stink.

stanza ['stanzə] n strofa f.

staple¹ ['steipl] n graffa f; (stationery) punto metallico m. v graffare; cucire (con punti metallici). **stapler** n cucitrice f.

staple² ['steipl] n prodotto principale m; (textile) fiocco m. adj principale, base invar.

star [stɑː] *n* stella *f*; (*actor*) divo, -a *m, f*. **starfish** *n* stella di mare *f*. *adj* principale. *v* (*cinema, etc.*) primeggiare. **starry** *adj* stellato. **starry-eyed** *adj* (*coll*) ingenuo.

starboard ['stɑːbəd] *n* dritta *f*.

starch [stɑːtʃ] *n* amido *m*, fecola *f*. *v* inamidare. **starchy** *adj* (*food*) ricco d'amido; (*manner*) rigido.

stare [steə] *v* fissare; (*gaze fixedly*) sgranare gli occhi. **stare in the face** (*be obvious*) saltare agli occhi, essere ovvio. *n* sguardo fisso *m*.

stark [stɑːk] *adj* rigido; (*bleak*) brullo. **stark mad** matto da legare. **stark naked** completamente nudo, nudo nato.

starling ['stɑːliŋ] *n* storno *m*, stornello *m*.

start [stɑːt] *n* (*beginning*) inizio *m*; (*point of departure*) partenza *f*; (*sudden movement*) soprassalto *m*; (*lead*) vantaggio *m*. **by fits and starts** a sbalzi. *v* iniziare, cominciare; partire; (*jump*) sussultare; (*set in motion*) mettere in moto. **to start with** per cominciare. **starter** *n* starter *m* *invar*, motorino d'avviamento *m*.

startle ['stɑːtl] *v* (*far*) trasalire, sbigottire. **startling** *adj* sorprendente.

starve [stɑːv] *v* affamare; (*to death*) (*far*) morire di fame; (*be very hungry*) soffrire la fame. **starve of** (*far*) soffrire per mancanza di. **starvation** *n* fame *f*.

state [steit] *n* stato *m*; pompa *f*; (*coll*) ansietà *f*. **statesman** *n* uomo di stato *m*. *adj* statale; solenne. *v* dichiarare, affermare; specificare; indicare. **stateless** *adj* apolide. **stately** *adj* solenne, maestoso. **statement** *n* affermazione *f*, dichiarazione *f*; (*bank, etc.*) estratto conto *m*.

static ['statik] *adj* fisso, statico. **statics** *n* statica *f*.

station ['steiʃən] *n* stazione *f*; (*headquarters*) sede *f*; (*rank*) condizione sociale *f*. **station-master** *n* capostazione (*pl* capistazione) *m*. **station-wagon** *n* (*US*) giardinetta *f*. *v* appostare, collocare.

stationary ['steiʃənəri] *adj* fermo; costante, fisso.

stationer ['steiʃənə] *n* cartolaio, -a *m, f*. **stationer's** *n* cartoleria *f*. **stationery** *n* oggetti di cancelleria *m pl*.

statistics [stə'tistiks] *n* statistica *f*. **statistical** *adj* statistico. **statistician** *n* statistico, -a *m, f*.

statue ['statjuː] *n* statua *f*.

stature ['statʃə] *n* statura *f*.

status ['steitəs] *n* posizione sociale *f*, rango *m*, prestigio *m*.

statute ['statjuːt] *n* decreto *m*, legge *f*.

staunch [stɔːntʃ] *adj* fedele, leale. *v* stagnare.

stay [stei] *n* soggiorno *m*; arresto *m*; (*law*) sospensione *f*. *v* (*remain*) restare, rimanere; (*on holiday, etc.*) soggiornare; (*at hotel*) alloggiare (in); (*stop*) sostare; sospendere. **stay in** non uscire, restare a casa. **stay on** trattenersi. **stay out** rimaner fuori, non rientrare.

steadfast ['stedfɑːst] *adj* fermo, saldo.

steady ['stedi] *adj* fermo, stabile; (*responsible*) serio; regolare; costante. *v* reggersi, tener fermo; calmare.

steak [steik] *n* (*meat*) bistecca *f*; (*fish*) trancia *f*.

***steal** [stiːl] *v* rubare. **steal away** andarsene di nascosto. **steal a march on** prevenire.

stealthy ['stelθi] *adj* clandestino. **stealthily** *adv* di nascosto *or* soppiatto.

steam [stiːm] *n* vapore *m*; (*coll: energy*) carica *f*. **let off steam** sfogarsi. *v* emettere vapore; (*cook*) cucinare a vapore. **steam up** appannarsi. **steamer** *n* (*boat*) piroscafo *m*; (*cookery*) pentola a vapore *f*. **steamy** *adj* pieno di vapore.

steam-roller *n* rullo compressore *m*; (*coll*) forza irresistibile *f*. *v* sopraffare.

steel [stiːl] *n* acciaio *m*. *v* indurire. **steely** *adj* d'acciaio, inflessibile.

steep[1] [stiːp] *adj* (*sheer*) ripido; (*coll: unreasonable*) eccessivo.

steep[2] [stiːp] *v* (*soak*) inzuppare; (*tech*) macerare.

steeple ['stiːpl] *n* (*spire*) guglia *f*; (*tower*) campanile *m*.

steer[1] [stiə] *n* (*ox*) manzo *m*.

steer[2] [stiə] *v* guidare, dirigere. **steer clear of** evitare. **steering-wheel** *n* volante *m*.

stem[1] [stem] *n* (*stalk*) gambo *m*; (*of pipe*) cannello; (*branch*) ramo *m*; (*of word*) radice *f*. *v* **stem from** derivare da.

stem[2] [stem] *v* contenere, arginare.

stench [stentʃ] *n* puzzo *m*.

stencil ['stensl] *n* (*device*) stampino *m*; (*duplicating machine*) ciclostile *m*. *v* stampinare; ciclostilare.

step [step] *n* passo *m*; (*stair*) gradino *m*; (*measure*) provvedimento *m*. **out of step** non conforme. **step by step** un poco alla volta, per gradi. **step-ladder** *n* scala a libretto *f*, scaleo *m*. **watch one's step**

stare attenti. v fare un passo; (walk) camminare. step down scendere; (retire) ritirarsi. step in entrare; intervenire. step up salire; aumentare; accelerare.

stepbrother ['stepbrʌðə] n fratellastro m.
stepdaughter ['stepdɔttə] n figliastra f.
stepfather ['stepfaɪðə] n patrigno m.
stepmother ['stepmʌðə] n matrigna f.
stepsister ['stepsistə] n sorellastra f.
stepson ['stepsʌn] n figliastro m.

stereo ['steriou] adj stereo. stereophonic adj stereofonico.

stereotype ['steriətaip] n cliché m; (tech) stereotipia f. stereotyped adj (trite) stereotipato; (tech) stereotipo.

sterile ['sterail] adj sterile. sterility n sterilità f. sterilization n sterilizzazione f. sterilize v sterilizzare.

sterling ['stɜːlin] n sterlina f. adj genuino.
stern¹ [stəːn] adj (harsh) severo; (strict) rigoroso.
stern² [stəːn] n (ship) poppa f.

stethoscope ['steθəskoup] n stetoscopio m.

stew [stjuː] n spezzatino m, stufato m. be in a stew essere preoccupato or turbato. v cuocere (a fuoco lento).

steward ['stjuəd] n amministratore, -trice m, f; (ship) cameriere di bordo m, steward m invar. stewardess n stewardess f invar, assistente di volo f. stewardship n gestione f; (office) carica di amministratore f.

stick¹ [stik] n (wood) bastone m; (celery, etc.) gambo m; (small rod) bastoncino m. be in a cleft stick non sapere che pesci pigliare.

*stick² [stik] v attaccare, appiccicare; (stab) ficcare; (remain) rimanere. stick it out tener duro. stick out (be conspicuous) saltare agli occhi; (put out) tirar fuori. stick to (not digress) attenersi a, non divagare da; (remain loyal) restar fedele a. stick up for difendere, battersi per. sticky adj attaccaticcio; adesivo; (weather) pesante; (coll; difficult) complesso.

stickler ['stiklə] n pignolo, -a m, f. stickler for . . . persona ligia a . . .

stiff [stif] adj rigido; (hard to move, difficult) duro; (formal) freddo. adv (coll) a morte. stiffen v irrigidire. stiffness n rigidezza f; durezza f.

stifle ['staifl] v soffocare.

stigma ['stigmə] n segno m, marchio m; (disgrace) stigma m.

stile [stail] n scaletta f.
still¹ [stil] adj (quiet) tranquillo; (motionless) immobile. adv ancora, tuttora. stillborn adj nato morto. in silenzio m; (phot) posa f. v calmare. stillness n silenzio m, tranquillità f.
still² [stil] n distilleria f; (retort) storta f.
stilt [stilt] n trampolo m; (building) palafitta f. stilted adj artificiale; (pompous) ampolloso.

stimulus ['stimjuləs] n pl -li stimolo m. stimulant nm, adj stimolante. stimulate v stimolare. stimulation n stimolo m.

*sting [stiŋ] v (wound) pungere; (incite) spronare; (coll: cheat) truffare. n puntura f; (pang) morso m; (incitement) sprone m.

stingy ['stindʒi] adj tirchio, spilorcio. stinginess n tirchieria f, spilorceria f.

*stink [stiŋk] n puzzo m. v puzzare. stinking adj puzzolente, fetente.

stint [stint] n dovere m, periodo di lavoro m. v risparmiare, fare economia.

stipulate ['stipjuleit] v pattuire, convenire. stipulation n patto m, condizione f, convenzione f.

stir [stəː] v mescolare, agitare; (budge) muoversi. stir up eccitare, incitare. n (excitement) scalpore m; confusione f. stirring adj (touching) commovente; eccitante.

stirrup ['stirəp] n staffa f.

stitch [stitʃ] n (sewing) punto m; (knitting) maglia f. v cucire; (sew on) attaccare; (med) suturare.

stoat [stout] n ermellino m.

stock [stok] n (goods) provvista f, stock m invar, riserva f; (standing) credito m; famiglia f; (cookery) brodo m. stockbroker n agente di cambio m. stock exchange borsa valori f. stockholder n azionista m, f. stockpile v far scorta di. stocks and shares titoli m pl. stocktaking n inventario m. v (supply) fornire, rifornire; tenere in magazzino.

stocking ['stokin] n calza f.
stocky ['stoki] adj tarchiato, tozzo.
stodge [stodʒ] n (coll) in (food) cibo pesante m; (dull matter) mattone m. stodgy adj pesante; (tedious) noioso.

stoical ['stouikl] adj stoico. stoic n stoico, -a m, f.

stoke [stouk] v alimentare. stoke up rimpinzarsi. stoker n fuochista m.

stole¹ [stoul] V **steal.**

stole² [stoul] n stola f.

stolen ['stoulən] V **steal.**

stomach ['stʌmək] n stomaco m. **stomach-ache** n mal di stomaco m. v (tolerate) sopportare.

stone [stoun] n pietra f; (pebble) sasso m; (fruit) nocciolo m; (med) calcolo m. **a stone's throw from** a due passi da. **stone-deaf** adj sordo come una campana. **stonemason** n muratore m. **stoneware** n gres m invar. v prendere a sassate; (fruit) snocciolare.

stood [stud] V **stand.**

stool [stuːl] n sgabello m. **stool-pigeon** n spia f.

stoop [stuːp] v curvare, chinarsi; (condescend) abbassarsi. n **walk with a stoop** camminar curvo.

stop [stop] n (halt) sosta f, fermata f; (punctuation) punto m; (organ) registro m. v finire, smettere; (halt) fermare; (prevent) impedire; (withhold) trattenere; (block) turare. **stop-press** n ultimissime f pl. **stop-watch** n cronometro a scatto m. **stoppage** n fermata f, arresto m; sospensione f; (med) blocco m. **stopper** n (bung) tappo m.

store [stoː] n (supply) provvista f, riserva f; (shop) bottega f; (warehouse) magazzino m. **storekeeper** n magazziniere m. v fare provviste di; conservare; accumulare; mettere in magazzino. **storage** n immagazzinamento m; (comm) magazzinaggio m.

storey ['stoːri] n piano m.

stork [stoːk] n cicogna f.

storm [stoːm] n tempesta f; (thunder) temporale m. v (rage) infuriarsi; (rush) precipitarsi; (mil) prendere d'assalto. **stormy** adj burrascoso.

story ['stoːri] n storia f, racconto m; (news) fatto di cronaca m.

stout [staut] adj (fat) grasso; intrepido; robusto.

stove [stouv] n stufa f; (cooker) cucina f.

stow [stou] v stivare; (fill) riempire (di). **stow away** mettere da parte; (on boat, etc.) imbarcarsi clandestinamente. **stowaway** n passeggero clandestino m. **stowage** n stivaggio m.

straddle ['stradl] v stare a cavalcioni, cavalcare.

straggle ['stragl] v disperdersi; (lag behind) rimanere indietro. **straggler** n ritardatario, -a m, f.

straight [streit] adj diritto; (open) franco, aperto. adv diritto, in linea retta; (directly) direttamente. **straight away** subito. **straightforward** adj franco, aperto; onesto; semplice. **straighten** v raddrizzare; (order) assettare.

strain¹ [strein] v filtrare, passare; (force) sforzare; (sprain) storcere. n sforzo m, tensione f; (med) storta f; (tune) melodia f. **strained** adj forzato; filtrato. **strainer** n filtro m, colino m.

strain² [strein] n (race) stirpe f, famiglia f.

strait [streit] n (geog) stretto m. **straits** pl n difficoltà f pl. adj **strait-laced** adj rigoroso, puritano.

strand¹ [strand] n (hair) ciocca f; (rope) fune f.

strand² [strand] n (shore) spiaggia f, sponda f. v arenare, incagliarsi.

strange [streindʒ] adj strano, misterioso; (unaccountable) inspiegabile. **stranger** n sconosciuto, -a m, f; estraneo, -a m, f; (foreigner) straniero, -a m, f.

strangle ['strangl] v strangolare. **strangulation** n strangolamento m.

strap [strap] n cinghia f; (on garment) spallina f; (watch) cinturino m. v **strap up** assicurare con cinghia; (med) fissare con cerotto. **strapping** adj robusto.

strategy ['stratədʒi] n strategia f. **strategic** adj strategico.

stratum ['straːtəm] n, pl -**ta** strato m.

straw [stroː] n paglia f; (drinking) cannuccia f.

strawberry ['stroːbəri] n fragola f.

stray [strei] v (lose one's way) smarrirsi; (roam) vagare. **stray from** deviare or allontanarsi da. adj (animal) randagio; (lost) smarrito; (occasional) isolato.

streak [striːk] n (mark) riga f, striscia f; (vein) vena f; (lightning) lampo m. v striare; venare; (rush) filare.

stream [striːm] n corso d'acqua m; (brook) ruscello m; corrente f. **streamline** v sveltire. **streamlined** adj aerodinamico, sveltito. v grondare, riversarsi. **streaming cold** forte raffreddore m.

street [striːt] n strada f, via f. **street-cleaner** n spazzino m. **street-light** n lampione m. **the man in the street** l'uomo qualunque m.

strength [strenθ] n forza f; intensità f;

validità f; (mil) effettivo m. **strengthen** v rinforzare; (give weight to) convalidare.

strenuous ['strenjuəs] adj energico, fervente; (activity) arduo, duro.

stress [stres] n tensione f; pressione f, spinta f; (emphasis) rilievo m; accento m; (med) stress m invar. v mettere in rilievo, sottolineare; accentare; sottoporre a tensione.

stretch [stretʃ] v (pull) tirare; (extend) stendere; (reach) estendersi. **stretch one's legs** sgranchirsi le gambe. **stretch out** allungare, sdraiarsi. n (expanse) tratto m; (time) periodo m. **stretcher** n barella f, lettiga f.

stricken ['strikən] adj colpito.

strict [strikt] adj severo, rigoroso; esatto; (absolute) stretto.

*****stride** [straid] v camminare a grandi passi. n passo m. **take in one's stride** (do easily) superare con facilità; (adjust to) prendersela con calma.

strife [straif] n lotta f, conflitto m.

*****strike** [straik] v colpire; (deal a blow) battere; (match) accendere; (oil) scoprire; (not work) scioperare. **strike home** colpire nel segno. **strike off** radiare. **strike up** (enter upon) stringere. n sciopero m; (discovery) scoperta f. **striking** adj sorprendente, impressionante.

*****string** [strin] n spago m, corda f; (series) fila f. **pull strings** manovrare, raccomandare. **strings** pl n (music) strumenti a corda m pl. v (music) incordare; (racket) mettere le corde a; (beads) infilare.

stringent ['strindʒənt] adj rigoroso, severo.

strip¹ [strip] v spogliare, denudare; (car, etc.) smontare; (paint) togliere. **strip** of privare di. **strip-tease** n spogliarello m.

strip² [strip] n striscia f, nastro m; (comic) fumetto m.

stripe [straip] n riga f, striscia f; (mil) gallone m. **striped** adj a righe or strisce.

*****strive** [straiv] v (try hard) sforzarsi, adoperarsi; (struggle) lottare.

striven ['strivn] V **strive**.

strode [stroud] V **stride**.

stroke¹ [strouk] n colpo m; (mark) sbarra f; (swimming) bracciata f; (med) colpo apoplettico m; (clock) tocco m; (tech) corsa f. **stroke of genius** lampo di genio m. **stroke of lightning** fulmine m.

stroke² [strouk] v accarezzare, lisciare.

stroll [stroul] n passeggiatina f. **go for a stroll** andare a far quattro passi. v girovagare.

strong [stron] adj forte, robusto, resistente. **stronghold** n roccaforte f. **strong language** parole grosse f pl. **strong-minded** adj risoluto. **strong point** forte m.

strove [strouv] V **strive**.

struck [strʌk] V **strike**.

structure ['strʌktʃə] n struttura f. **structural** adj strutturale.

struggle ['strʌgl] n (fight) lotta f; (effort) sforzo m. v lottare; sforzarsi.

strum [strʌm] v strimpellare.

strung [strʌn] V **string**.

strut¹ [strʌt] v (prance) camminare impettito.

strut² [strʌt] n (support) puntone m.

stub [stʌb] n (cigarette, pencil, etc.) mozzicone m; (cheque) matrice f; (tree) ceppo m. v urtare. **stub out** spegnere.

stubble ['stʌbl] n stoppia f; (beard) barba ispida f. **stubbly** adj pieno di stoppie; ispido.

stubborn ['stʌbən] adj ostinato, testardo. **stubbornness** n ostinatezza f, testardaggine f.

stuck [stʌk] V **stick¹**.

stud¹ [stʌd] n (ornament) borchia f; (nail) ribattino m; (button) bottoncino m. v guarnire di borchie; (jewel) tempestare.

stud² [stʌd] n scuderia f. **stud-horse** n stallone m.

student ['stjuːdənt] n (pupil) studente, -essa m, f; (scholar) studioso, -a m, f.

studio ['stjuːdiou] n studio m.

study ['stʌdi] n studio m. v studiare; esaminare attentamente. **studied** adj studiato, premeditato. **studious** adj studioso, attento, premuroso.

stuff [stʌf] n roba f; (substance) sostanza f; (fabric) tessuto m. **know one's stuff** sapere il fatto proprio. v (cookery) farcire; (animal) imbalsamare; (fill) imbottire. **stuffing** n imbottitura f; (cookery) ripieno m. **stuffy** adj soffocante; (tedious) noioso; (blocked up) intasato; (prim) rigido, conservatore.

stumble ['stʌmbl] v inciampare, fare un passo falso; (speech) impaperarsi. **stumbling block** ostacolo m.

stump [stʌmp] n (tree) ceppo m; (limb) moncone m.

stun [stʌn] v stordire; (astound) sbalordire. **stunning** adj sbalorditivo, stupefacente.

stung [stʌŋ] V **sting**.

stunk [stʌŋk] V **stink**.

stunt[1] [stʌnt] v arrestare la crescita di.

stunt[2] [stʌnt] n bravata f; acrobazia f; trovata pubblicitaria f.

stupid ['stjuːpid] adj stupido, sciocco. **stupidity** n stupidità f.

stupor ['stjuːpə] n stupore m, torpore m.

sturdy ['stəːdi] adj vigoroso, robusto. **sturdiness** n vigoria f.

sturgeon ['stəːdʒən] n storione m.

stutter ['stʌtə] n balbuzie f. v balbettare. **stutterer** n balbuziente m, f.

sty [stai] n porcile m.

stye [stai] n orzaiolo m.

style [stail] n stile m. **stylish** adj elegante. **stylist** n stilista m, f.

stylus ['stailəs] n puntina f.

suave [swɑːv] adj cortese, affabile.

subconscious [sʌb'konʃəs] nm, adj subcosciente.

subcontract [sʌbkən'trakt] n subappalto m. v dare in subappalto.

subdivision [ˌsʌbdi'viʒən] n suddivisione f. **subdivide** v suddividere.

subdue [səb'djuː] v (conquer) soggiogare; (repress) reprimere; (reduce intensity) attenuare. **subdued** adj inibito; intimidito; attenuato.

subject [n 'sʌbdʒikt; v səb'dʒekt] n soggetto m, argomento m; (study) materia f; (pol) suddito, -a m, f. adj **subject to** soggetto a. v (bring under control) sottomettere; (expose) esporre, sottoporre. **subjective** adj soggettivo. **subjectivity** n soggettività f.

subjunctive [səb'dʒʌŋktiv] nm, adj congiuntivo.

*****sublet** [ˌsʌb'let] v subaffittare.

sublimate ['sʌblimeit] v sublimare. n sublimato m. **sublimation** n sublimazione f.

sublime [sə'blaim] adj sublime.

submarine ['sʌbməriːn] n sottomarino m.

submerge [səb'məːdʒ] v sommergere. **submersion** n sommersione f.

submit [səb'mit] v (yield) sottomettersi, rassegnarsi; deferire; (present) sottoporre. **submission** n sottomissione f, rassegnazione f; (theory) tesi f.

subnormal [sʌb'noːməl] adj subnormale.

subordinate [sə'bɔːdinət] adj subordinato, inferiore. n subalterno m. v subordinare. **subordination** n subordinazione f.

subscribe [səb'skraib] v sottoscrivere, aderire; (newspapers, etc.) abbonarsi. **subscriber** n abbonato, -a m, f. **subscription** n abbonamento m; (dues) quota f; (fund raised) sottoscrizione f.

subsequent ['sʌbsikwənt] adj successivo, susseguente.

subservient [səb'səːviənt] adj subordinato; (servile) umile.

subside [səb'said] v decrescere, diminuire; (give way) cedere, avvallare; (abate) quietarsi. **subsidence** n avvallamento m.

subsidiary [səb'sidiəri] adj sussidiario; (comm) consociato.

subsidize ['sʌbsidaiz] v sovvenzionare. **subsidy** n sovvenzione f.

subsist [səb'sist] v sostentarsi. **subsistence** n sostentamento m. **subsistence money** acconto paga m, trasferta f.

substance ['sʌbstəns] n sostanza f, materia f; realtà f; (wealth) beni m pl. **substantial** adj sostanziale; (meal) sostanzioso; (considerable) notevole.

substitute ['sʌbstitjuːt] n (p. .) sostituto, -a m, f; (thing) surrogato m. v sostituire, rimpiazzare. **substitution** n sostituzione f.

subterfuge ['sʌbtəfjuːdʒ] n sotterfugio m.

subterranean [sʌbtə'reiniən] adj sotterraneo.

subtitle ['sʌbtaitl] n sottotitolo m.

subtle ['sʌtl] adj sottile, delicato; astuto, ingegnoso. **subtlety** n sottigliezza f, finezza f; astuzia f.

subtract [səb'trakt] v dedurre, sottrarre. **subtraction** n sottrazione f.

suburb ['sʌbəːb] n sobborgo m. **suburban** adj suburbano.

subvert [səb'vəːt] v sovvertire. **subversion** n sovversione f. **subversive** n, adj sovversivo, -a.

subway ['sʌbwei] n sottopassaggio m; (US) metropolitana f.

succeed [sək'siːd] v riuscire; (be successful) aver successo; (follow) succedere. **success** n successo m, buona riuscita f. **successful** adj (person) che ha successo; vittorioso; prospero, arrivato; (thing) riuscito. **succession** n successione f. **successive** adj successivo. **successor** n successore m.

succinct [sək'siŋkt] adj succinto.

succulent ['sʌkjulənt] *adj* succulento.
succumb [sə'kʌm] *v* soccombere.
such [sʌtʃ] *adj* tale; (*like*) del genere, simile. *adv* così. **such and such** tale e tale. **such as** come. **such as it is** così com'è.
suck [sʌk] *v* succhiare; (*breast*) poppare. **suck up** assorbire; (*slang*) fare il leccapiedi.
sucker ['sʌkə] *n* (*plant*) pollone *m*; (*device*) ventosa *f*; (*slang: fool*) gonzo *m*.
suckle ['sʌkl] *v* allattare.
suction ['sʌkʃən] *n* aspirazione *f*. **suction pump** pompa aspirante *f*.
sudden ['sʌdən] *adj* improvviso, subitaneo. **all of a sudden** ad un tratto, all'improvviso.
suds [sʌdz] *pl n* saponata *f sing*.
sue [suː] *v* (*law*) citare, chiamare in giudizio, querelare. **sue for peace** chiedere or sollecitare la pace.
suede [sweid] *nm. adj* scamosciato.
suet ['suːit] *n* grasso di rognone *m*.
suffer ['sʌfə] *v* soffrire, patire; tollerare; (*undergo*) subire. **on sufferance** per tacita tolleranza. **suffering** *n* sofferenza *f*, dolore *m*.
sufficient [sə'fiʃənt] *adj* sufficiente. **sufficiency** *n* sufficienza *f*.
suffix ['sʌfiks] *n* suffisso *m*.
suffocate ['sʌfəkeit] *v* soffocare. **suffocation** *n* soffocazione *f*.
sugar ['ʃugə] *n* zucchero *m*. **sugar-beet** *n* barbabietola (da zucchero) *f*. **sugar-cane** *n* canna da zucchero *f*. **sugary** *adj* zuccherino, mellifluo.
suggest [sə'dʒest] *v* suggerire; proporre. **suggestible** *adj* suggestionabile. **suggestion** *n* suggerimento *m*; proposta *f*; (*psych*) suggestione *f*.
suicide ['suisaid] *n* (*deed*) suicidio *m*; (*person*) suicida *m, f*. **commit suicide** suicidarsi. **suicidal** *adj* suicida.
suit [suːt] *n* (*garment*) abito *m*; (*law*) causa *f*; (*cards*) seme *m*, colore *m*; (*request*) preghiera *f*. **follow suit** seguire l'esempio; (*cards*) rispondere a colore. **suitcase** *n* valigia *f*. *v* accontentare, convenire a, soddisfare. **suit yourself!** fa come ti pare! **suitable** *adj* adatto; conveniente, opportuno. **suitability** *n* convenienza *f*.
suite [swiːt] *n* (*music*) suite *f invar*; (*retinue*) seguito *m*; (*furniture*) mobilia *f invar*; (*rooms*) fuga di stanze *f*.

sulk [sʌlk] *v* tenere il broncio. **sulky** *adj* imbronciato.
sullen ['sʌlən] *adj* accigliato, imbronciato.
sulphur ['sʌlfə] *n* zolfo *m*.
sultan ['sʌltən] *n* sultano *m*.
sultana [sʌl'tɑːnə] *n* uva sultanina *f*.
sultry ['sʌltri] *adj* afoso; (*person*) eccitante.
sum [sʌm] *n* somma *f*, addizione *f*; (*amount*) importo *m*, totale *m*. **do sums** far calcoli. *v* **sum up** riassumere. **summing-up** *n* riassunto *m*, riepilogo (*pl* -ghi) *m*.
summarize ['sʌməraiz] *v* riassumere. **summary** *nm, adj* sommario.
summer ['sʌmə] *n* estate *f*. *adj* d'estate, estivo.
summit ['sʌmit] *n* cima *f*, vertice *m*.
summon ['sʌmən] *v* convocare; (*law*) citare, chiamare in giudizio. **summon up courage** farsi coraggio.
summons ['sʌmənz] *v* citare in giudizio. citazione *f*. **answer a summons** presentarsi in giudizio.
sumptuous ['sʌmptʃuəs] *adj* sontuoso.
sun [sʌn] *n* sole *m*. *v* **sun oneself** prendere il sole. **sunny** *adj* soleggiato; (*cheerful*) allegro.
sunbathe ['sʌnbeið] *v* fare i bagni di sole. **sunbathing** *n* bagni di sole *m pl*.
sunburn ['sʌnbəːn] *n* (*pain*) scottatura solare *f*, eritema solare *m*; (*tan*) abbronzatura *f*. **sunburnt** *adj* scottato dal sole; abbronzato.
Sunday ['sʌndi] *n* domenica *f*.
sundial ['sʌndaiəl] *n* meridiana *f*.
sundry ['sʌndri] *adj* diversi, parecchi. **all and sundry** tutti quanti.
sunflower ['sʌnflauə] *n* girasole *m*.
sung [sʌŋ] *V* **sing**.
sun-glasses ['sʌnglɑːsiz] *pl n* occhiali da sole *m pl*.
sunk [sʌŋk] *V* **sink**.
sunlight ['sʌnlait] *n* luce del sole *f*.
sunrise ['sʌnraiz] *n* alba *f*.
sunset ['sʌnset] *n* tramonto *m*.
sunshine ['sʌnʃain] *n* sole *m*; (*good weather*) bel tempo *m*. **sunshine roof** tetto scorrevole *m*.
sunstroke ['sʌnstrouk] *n* colpo di sole *m*, insolazione *f*.
sun-tan ['sʌntan] *n* abbronzatura *f*.
super ['suːpə] *adj* (*coll*) magnifico.
superannuation [ˌsuːpərænjuˈeiʃən] *n*

(retirement) collocamento a riposo *m*; *(pension)* vitalizio *m*.

superb [su'pɜtb] *adj* superbo, magnifico.

supercilious [,suɪpɔ'siliəs] *adj* altero, borioso.

superficial [,suɪpɔ'fiʃəl] *adj* superficiale.

superfluous [su'pɜtfluəs] *adj* superfluo.

superhuman [suɪpɔ'hjuɪmən] *adj* sovrumano.

superimpose [,suɪpɔrim'pouz] *v* sovrapporre.

superintendent [,suɪpɔrin'tendənt] *n* soprintendente *m*; *(police)* commissario *m*.

superior [suɪpiəriə] *adj* superiore. *n* superiore, -a *m, f*. **superiority** *n* superiorità *f*.

superlative [su'pɜtlətiv] *nm, adj* superlativo.

supermarket ['suɪpɔ,maɪkit] *n* supermercato *m*.

supernatural [,suɪpɔ'natʃərəl] *nm, adj* soprannaturale.

supersede [,suɪpɔ'siɪd] *v* rimpiazzare, sostituire.

supersonic [,suɪpɔ'sonik] *adj* supersonico.

superstition [suɪpɔ'stiʃən] *n* superstizione *f*. **superstitious** *adj* superstizioso.

supervise ['suɪpɔvaiz] *v* sorvegliare, soprintendere. **supervision** *n* sorveglianza *f*, soprintendenza *f*. **supervisor** *n* soprintendente *m, f*, sorvegliante *m, f*, ispettore, -trice *m, f*.

supper ['sʌpə] *n* cena *f*. **have supper** cenare.

supple ['sʌpl] *adj* flessibile; agile. **suppleness** *n* flessibilità *f*; agilità *f*.

supplement ['sʌpləmənt] *n* supplemento *m*, aggiunta *f*. *v* completare, integrare. **supplementary** *adj* supplementare.

supply [sɔ'plai] *n* provvista *f*, rifornimento *m*; *(econ)* offerta *f*. *v* provvedere, fornire. **supplier** *n* fornitore *m*.

support [sɔ'pɔtt] *n* appoggio *m*, sostegno *m*. **means of support** mezzi di sostentamento *m pl*. *v* reggere, sostenere; *(keep)* mantenere; *(tolerate)* sopportare.

suppose [sɔ'pouz] *v* supporre; *(think)* ritenere, pensare. **supposed** *adj* presunto. **be supposed to** dovere. **supposedly** *adv* per supposizione. **supposing** *conj* supponiamo che. **supposition** *n* supposizione *f*.

suppository [sɔ'pozitri] *n* supposta *f*.

suppress [sɔ'pres] *v* sopprimere; *(check)* soffocare; *(hide)* nascondere.

supreme [su'priɪm] *adj* supremo, massimo. **supremacy** *n* supremazia *f*.

surcharge ['sɜtʃaɪdʒ] *n* soprattassa *f*.

sure [ʃuə] *adj* certo, sicuro. **make sure** assicurarsi.

surety ['ʃuərəti] *n* certezza *f*; garanzia *f*. **stand surety for** farsi garante per.

surf [sɜtf] *n* frangente *m*, risacca *f*. **surfing** *n* surfing *m invar*, sport dell'acquaplano *m*.

surface ['sɜtfis] *n* superficie *f*, faccia *f*. *adj* superficiale, esterno. *v* venire a galla, affiorare.

surfeit ['sɜtfit] *n* eccesso *m*.

surge [sɜtdʒ] *n* ondata *f*, riflusso *m*. *v* fluttuare, rifluire.

surgeon ['sɜtdʒən] *n* chirurgo *m*. **surgery** *n* *(subject)* chirurgia *f*; *(consulting room)* gabinetto medico *m*, infermeria *f*. **surgical** *adj* chirurgico.

surly ['sɜtli] *adj* scontroso.

surmount [sə'maunt] *v* superare.

surname ['sɜtneim] *n* cognome *m*.

surpass [sə'paɪs] *v* sorpassare, superare.

surplus ['sɜtpləs] *n* eccesso *m*, avanzo *m*, residuato *m*.

surprise [sə'praiz] *n* sorpresa *f*; *(astonishment)* stupore *m*, meraviglia *f*. **take by surprise** *(amaze)* stupire; *(come upon unawares)* cogliere all'improvviso. *adj* *(unexpected)* inaspettato. *v* sorprendere; cogliere all'improvviso; stupire.

surrealism [sə'riəlizəm] *n* surrealismo *m*. **surrealist** *n(m+f)*, *adj* surrealista.

surrender [sə'rendə] *v* cedere; *(mil)* arrendersi. *n* resa *f*.

surreptitious [,sʌrəp'tiʃəs] *adj* furtivo, clandestino.

surround [sə'raund] *v* circondare; *(encircle)* accerchiare. *n* bordura *f*. **surrounding** *adj* circostante. **surroundings** *pl n* dintorni *m pl*; *(environment)* ambiente *m sing*.

survey ['sɜtvei *o* sə'vei] *n* quadro generale *m*; *(official examination)* perizia *f*; rapporto *m*, valutazione *f*; *(of land)* agrimensura *f*; *(geog)* rilievo topografico *m*; *(poll)* sondaggio *m*. *v* esaminare, fare una perizia di; prendere i rilievi di. **surveyor** *n* ispettore, -trice *m, f*; *(land)* agrimensore *m*; *(house)* geometra *m, f*; *(geog)* topografo, -a *m, f*.

swipe

survive [sə'vaiv] v sopravvivere. **survival** n sopravvivenza f. **survivor** n superstite m, f.

susceptible [sə'septəbl] adj suscettibile; predisposto. **susceptibility** n suscettibilità f; predisposizione f.

suspect [sə'spekt; n, adj 'sʌspekt] v sospettare; (surmise) dubitare. n persona sospetta f. adj sospetto.

suspend [sə'spend] v sospendere. **suspense** n incertezza f, apprensione f. **in suspense** in sospeso. **suspension** n sospensione f. **suspension bridge** ponte sospeso m.

suspicion [sə'spiʃən] n sospetto m, dubbio m. **suspicious** adj (distrustful) sospettoso, diffidente; (questionable) sospetto.

sustain [sə'stein] v sostenere; (injury, etc.) subire.

swab [swɔb] n tampone m; (sample) prelievo m.

swagger ['swagə] v (strut) pavoneggiarsi; (boast) boriarsi, grandeggiare. n boria f, andatura spavalda f.

swallow[1] ['swɔlou] v inghiottire, ingoiare; (coll: believe) bere; (suppress) reprimere. n gorgata f.

swallow[2] ['swɔlou] n (bird) rondine f.

swam [swam] V swim.

swamp [swɔmp] n palude f. v (flood) inondare, allagare; (overwhelm) travolgere.

swan [swɔn] n cigno m.

swank [swaŋk] (coll) v darsi delle arie. n boria f.

swap or **swop** [swɔp] n scambio m. v scambiare.

swarm [swɔːm] n (bees) sciame m; (crowd) folla f. v sciamare; (throng) accalcarsi; (teem) brulicare.

swarthy ['swɔːði] adj di carnagione scura.

swat [swɔt] v schiacciare.

sway [swei] v oscillare, vacillare; inclinare; influenzare. n oscillazione f. **hold sway over** esercitare potere su.

***swear** [sweə] v (declare solemnly) giurare; (curse) bestemmiare. **swear by** giurare su. **swear in** far prestare giuramento, insediare. **swear-word** n. bestemmia f.

sweat [swet] v sudare. n sudore m. **sweat-shirt** n argentina f. **sweater** n maglione m.

swede [swiːd] n ravizzone m.

Sweden ['swiːdn] n Svezia f. **Swede** n svedese m, f. **Swedish** nm, adj svedese.

***sweep** [swiːp] v spazzare; (view) percorrere. **sweep aside** scartare. **sweep the board** far piazza pulita. **sweep** n spazzata f; curva f; (chimney) spazzacamino m. **sweeping** adj radicale, di lunga portata. **sweeping statement** asserzione gratuita f.

sweet [swiːt] adj dolce; fresco; (smell) profumato; (sound) armonioso; (temper) amabile, carino. n caramella f; (dessert) dolce m. **sweet-and-sour** adj agrodolce. **sweetbread** n animella f. **sweetheart** n amoroso, -a m, f. **sweet pea** pisello odoroso m. **sweeten** v addolcire; alleviare. **sweetener** n dolcificante m; (bribe) bustarella f. **sweetness** n dolcezza f; (taste) sapore dolce m.

***swell** [swel] v aumentare, gonfiarsi. n (sea) ondata f. **swelling** n gonfiore m, tumore m, tumefazione f.

swelter ['sweltə] v soffocare or morire dal caldo. **sweltering** adj soffocante.

swept [swept] V sweep.

swerve [swəːv] v (change direction abruptly) scartare; deviare, scostarsi. n scarto m; deviazione f.

swift [swift] adj lesto; (prompt) pronto. n rondone m.

swig [swig] v tracannare. n sorso m.

swill [swil] v (swig) tracannare; (rinse) risciacquare. n (rubbish) rifiuti m pl; (slops) intruglio m; (for pigs) broda (per maiali) f.

***swim** [swim] v nuotare. n nuotata f. **go for a swim** andare a nuotare. **in the swim** attivo. **swimmer** n nuotatore, -trice m, f. **swimming** n nuoto m. **swimming costume** costume da bagno m. **swimming pool** or **baths** piscina f. **swimming trunks** calzoncini da bagno m pl.

swindle ['swindl] v truffare, imbrogliare. n truffa f. **swindler** n truffatore, -trice m, f, imbroglione, -a m, f.

swine [swain] n maiale m, porco (pl -ci) m.

***swing** [swiŋ] v dondolare, oscillare; (club, etc.) vibrare; influenzare. **swing open** spalancarsi. **swing round** voltarsi di scatto. n oscillazione f, ritmo m; (in playground) altalena f. **in full swing** in piena attività. **swing-door** n porta a due battenti f.

swipe [swaip] (coll) n botta f. v dare una botta (a); (steal) fregare.

swirl [swɔːl] v turbinare. n turbine m.

swish [swiʃ] v (sound) sibilare; (move) brandire; (rustle) frusciare. n (whip) sferza f; (sound) sibilo m.

Swiss [swis] n, adj svizzero, -a.

switch [switʃ] n (elec) interruttore m; (whip) sferza f; (change) svolta f, cambiamento m. **switchback** n montagne russe f pl. **switchboard** n tavolo di controllo m; (phone) centralino m. v spostare, scambiare. **switch off** spegnere. **switch on** accendere. **switch over** commutare.

Switzerland ['switsələnd] n Svizzera f.

swivel ['swivl] n perno m. **swivel chair** sedia girevole f. v girare, rotare.

swollen ['swoulən] V **swell**. adj gonfio.

swoop [swuːp] v piombare, avventarsi. n calata improvvisa f. **at one fell swoop** d'un sol colpo.

swop V **swap**.

sword [sɔːd] n spada f. **cross swords** (fight) battersi; (argue) venire alle mani. **swordfish** n pesce spada m.

swore [swɔː] V **swear**.

sworn [swɔːn] V **swear**.

swot [swot] (coll) v sgobbare. n secchione, -a m, f.

swum [swʌm] V **swim**.

swung [swʌŋ] V **swing**.

sycamore ['sikəmɔː] n sicomoro m.

syllable ['siləbl] n sillaba f.

syllabus ['siləbəs] n programma m, prospetto m.

symbol ['simbl] n simbolo m. **symbolic** adj simbolico. **symbolism** n simbolismo m. **symbolize** v simboleggiare.

symmetry ['simitri] n simmetria f. **symmetrical** adj simmetrico.

sympathy ['simpəθi] n simpatia f, comprensione f; compassione f. **sympathetic** adj simpatico, simpatizzante; compassionevole. **sympathetic to** favorevole a, ben disposto verso. **sympathize** v simpatizzare; essere d'accordo; compatire. **sympathizer** n simpatizzante m, f.

symphony ['simfəni] n sinfonia f. **symphony orchestra** orchestra sinfonica f. **symphonic** adj sinfonico.

symposium [sim'pouziəm] n simposio m.

symptom ['simptəm] n sintomo m. **symptomatic** adj sintomatico.

synagogue ['sinəgog] n sinagoga f.

synchromesh ['siŋkroumeʃ] n sincronizzatore m.

synchronize ['siŋkrənaiz] v sincronizzare.

syndicate ['sindikit] n sindacato m.

syndrome ['sindroum] n sindrome f.

synod ['sinəd] n sinodo m.

synonym ['sinənim] n sinonimo m. **synonymous** adj sinonimo.

synopsis [si'nopsis] n, pl **-ses** sinossi f; (film, etc.) sinopsi f. **synoptic** adj sinottico.

syntax ['sintaks] n sintassi f. **syntactic** adj sintattico.

synthesis ['sinθisis] n, pl **-ses** sintesi f. **synthesize** v sintetizzare. **synthetic** adj sintetico.

syphilis ['sifilis] n sifilide f.

syringe [si'rindʒ] n siringa f. v siringare; (inject) iniettare.

syrup ['sirəp] n sciroppo m; (golden) melassa f. **syrupy** adj sciropposo.

system ['sistəm] n sistema m. **systematic** adj sistematico.

T

tab [tab] n cartellino m, etichetta f. **keep tabs on** tener d'occhio.

tabby ['tabi] n (gatto) soriano or tigrato m.

table ['teibl] n tavola f; (with modifier) tavolo m; (multiplication) tavola pitagorica f; (synopsis) tabella f. **lay/clear the table** apparecchiare/sparecchiare la tavola. **table-cloth** n tovaglia f. **table-mat** n sottopiatto m. **table-napkin** n tovagliolo m. **tablespoon** n cucchiaio da tavola m; (spoonful) cucchiaiata f. **table tennis** tennis da tavola m. **turn the tables** rovesciare le posizioni. v intavolare.

table d'hôte [taːblə'dout] adj a prezzo fisso.

tablet ['tablit] n tavoletta f; (med) pastiglia f.

taboo [tə'buː] nm, adj tabù.

tabulate ['tabjuleit] v presentare in forma sinottica.

tacit ['tasit] adj tacito.

tack [tak] n (pin) puntina f; (naut) bordata f; (stitch) punto lungo m. **get down to brass tacks** venire ai fatti. v (sewing) imbastire; (sailing) bordeggiare. **tack on** aggiungere. **tacking** n imbastitura f. **tacky** adj appiccicaticcio, appiccicoso.

tackle ['takl] n attrezzatura f; (fishing) arnesi da pesca m pl; (hoisting) paranco m; (football) carica f; (rugby) placcaggio m. v venire alle prese con, affrontare; caricare; placcare.

tact [takt] n tatto m, riguardo m. **tactful** adj riguardoso, diplomatico. **tactless** adj mancante di riguardo, senza tatto.

tactics ['taktiks] pl n tattica f sing. **tactical** adj tattico. **tactician** n tattico, -a m, f.

tadpole ['tadpoul] n girino m.

taffeta ['tafitə] n taffettà m.

tag [tag] n (stub) talloncino m; (label) etichetta f, cartellino m; (refrain) ritornello m; (saying) locuzione f. v **tag along** seguire. **tag on** aggiungere.

tail [teil] n coda f. **tail-board** n ribalta f. **tail-end** n finalino m. **tail-light** n fanalino m. **tails** pl n (dress) frac m invar; (coin) croce f sing.

tailor ['teilə] n sarto, -a m, f. **tailoring** n mestiere del sarto m.

taint [teint] n tara f, traccia di marcio f. v (spoil) guastare, contaminare. **tainted** adj tarato.

*****take** [teik] v prendere; (carry, convey) portare; (require) volerci; (bath, walk, etc.) fare. **take after** assomigliare a. **take back** riportare. **take care** badare, far attenzione. **take care of** curarsi di. **take down** tirar giù; (dictation) prender nota di. **take in** -(visitors) dare alloggio a; (reduce) stringere; (understand) comprendere; (deceive) ingannare. **take off** (remove) togliere; (aero) decollare; (mimic) parodiare. **take-off** n decollo m; caricatura f. **take on** assumere; (fight) affrontare. **take out** tirar fuori; accompagnare. **take over** (assume control) rilevare. **take-over** n rilievo m. **take place** accadere, aver luogo. **take to** affezionarsi a; (addict) darsi a.

taken ['teikn] V take.

talcum powder ['talkəm] n talco in polvere m; borotalco m.

tale [teil] n storia f, racconto m; (gossip) diceria f.

talent ['talənt] n talento m; (gift) dote f; (aptitude) attitudine f. **talented** adj dotato.

talk [tɔːk] n discorso m, conversazione f; (lecture) conferenza f; (chat) chiacchierata f. v parlare; conversare; chiacchierare. **talk about** parlare di. **talk nonsense** dire sciocchezze. **talk over** discutere. **talk**

round persuadere. **talk sense** dire cose sensate. **talkative** adj loquace.

tall [tɔːl] adj alto. **tallboy** n canterano m. **tall order** impresa difficile f. **tall story** storia inverosimile f, frottola f.

tally ['tali] n (score) punteggio m; (account) conto m; (label) etichetta f, scontrino m. v corrispondere; coincidere (con).

talon ['talən] n artiglio m.

tambourine [tambə'riːn] n tamburello m.

tame [teim] adj docile, domestico. v addomesticare, domare.

tamper ['tampə] v **tamper with** alterare, falsificare; (meddle) ingerirsi in; (bribe) subornare.

tampon ['tampon] n tampone m.

tan [tan] v (leather) conciare; (sun) abbronzare. n (colour) castano m; abbronzatura f. adj castano.

tandem ['tandəm] n tandem m invar. **in tandem** in tandem.

tangent ['tandʒənt] n tangente f. **fly off at a tangent** pigliare un dirizzone.

tangerine [tandʒə'riːn] n mandarino m.

tangible ['tandʒəbl] adj tangibile.

tangle ['tangl] n groviglio m, confusione f. v ingarbugliare, imbrogliare. **tangle with** (fight) lottare con or contro.

tank [tank] n serbatoio m; (pool) vasca f; (mil) carro armato m. **tanker** n (ship) nave cisterna f; (lorry) autocisterna f.

tankard ['tankəd] n boccale m.

tantalize ['tantəlaiz] v tormentare.

tantamount ['tantəmaunt] adj **be tantamount to** equivalere a, essere come.

tantrum ['tantrəm] n accesso d'ira m, bizza f. **have tantrums** fare le bizze.

tap¹ [tap] v (strike) picchiare, dare un colpetto a; (knock) bussare. n colpetto m.

tap² [tap] n rubinetto m; (on cask) spina f, cannella f. **on tap** (beer) alla spina; (ready) a disposizione, pronto. v (draw off) spillare; (phone) intercettare; utilizzare.

tape [teip] n nastro m. **red tape** burocrazia f. **tape-measure** n metro m. **tape-recorder** n registratore a nastro m. v (tie) allacciare; (record) registrare.

taper ['teipə] v affusolare, assottigliarsi. **taper off** finire a punta. n cerino m, candela sottile f. **tapering** adj affusolato, a punta.

tapestry ['tæpəstri] n arazzo m, tappezzeria f.

tapioca [tæpi'oukə] n tapioca f.

tar [tɑː] n catrame m. v incatramare.

tarantula [tə'ræntjulə] n tarantola f.

target ['tɑːgit] n bersaglio m, obiettivo m.

tariff ['tærif] n tariffa f.

tarmac ['tɑːmæk] n macadam al catrame; (runway) pista f.

tarnish ['tɑːniʃ] v annerire, offuscare; (stain) macchiare. n annerimento m; macchia f.

tarpaulin [tɑː'pɔːlin] n copertone m.

tarragon ['tærəgən] n dragoncello m.

tart¹ [tɑːt] adj aspro, agro. **tartness** n asprezza f.

tart² [tɑːt] n torta f, crostata f; (slang) puttana f.

tartan ['tɑːtən] n tartan m invar, tessuto scozzese m.

tartar ['tɑːtə] n tartaro m. **cream of tartar** cremor di tartaro f.

task [tɑːsk] n compito m, dovere m. **take to task** rimproverare.

tassel ['tæsəl] n nappa f, nappina f.

taste [teist] n gusto m, sapore m; (liking) amore m, apprezzamento m; (small sample) assaggio m. v assaggiare, gustare. **taste of** sapere di. **tasteful** adj squisito, di buon gusto. **tasteless** adj insipido; di cattivo gusto. **tasty** adj saporito, appetitoso.

tattered ['tætəd] adj stracciato, a brandelli.

tattoo¹ [tə'tuː] n tatuaggio m. v tatuare.

tattoo² [tə'tuː] n (mil) ritirata f.

taught [tɔːt] V **teach**.

taunt [tɔːnt] v rinfacciare, schernire. n derisione f, scherno m.

Taurus ['tɔːrəs] n Toro m.

taut [tɔːt] adj teso.

tavern ['tævən] n osteria f, trattoria f, taverna f.

tawdry ['tɔːdri] adj vistoso, volgare.

tax [tæks] n tassa f, imposta f. **tax-collector** n esattore fiscale m. **tax evasion** evasione fiscale f. **taxpayer** n contribuente m, f. v tassare, imporre una tassa su; (make demands) mettere alla prova. **taxation** n tassazione f, tasse f pl.

taxi ['tæksi] n tassì m. **taxi-driver** n tassista m, f. **taxi rank** posteggio (per tassi) m. v (aero) rullare.

tea [tiː] n tè m. **teacup** n tazza da tè f. **teapot** n teiera f. **teaspoon** n cucchiaino m. **tea-towel** n canovaccio m.

***teach** [tiːtʃ] v insegnare. **teacher** n insegnante m, f; (primary school) maestro, -a m, f; (secondary school, university) professore, -essa m, f. **teaching** n insegnamento m. **teachings** pl n dottrina f sing, precetti m pl.

teak [tiːk] n tek m.

team [tiːm] n squadra f; (animals) tiro m. **teamwork** n affiatamento m. v **team up with** mettersi insieme a, collaborare con.

***tear¹** [teə] n strappo m. v strappare. **be torn between** dibattersi tra. **tear off** strappar via; (run) scappar via. **tear up** stracciare. **tearing** adj impetuoso, terribile.

tear² [tiə] n lacrima f. **burst into tears** scoppiare in lacrime. **in tears** sciolto in lacrime. **tear-gas** n gas lacrimogeno m. **tearful** adj lacrimoso.

tease [tiːz] v stuzzicare, canzonare; irritare.

teat [tiːt] n (nipple) capezzolo m; (rubber) tettarella f.

technical ['teknikəl] adj tecnico. **technicality** n tecnicismo m. **technician** n tecnico, -a m, f. **technique** n tecnica f. **technological** adj tecnologico. **technologist** n tecnologo, -a m, f. **technology** n tecnologia f.

teddy bear ['tedi,beə] n orsacchiotto m.

tedious ['tiːdiəs] adj noioso. **tedium** n noia f.

tee [tiː] n tee m invar. v **tee off** cominciare (dal tee). **tee up** preparare, collocare sul tee.

teem [tiːm] v (rain) grondare. **teem with** formicolare or brulicare di.

teenage ['tiːneidʒ] adj adolescente. **teenager** n adolescente m, f.

teeth [tiːθ] V **tooth**.

teethe [tiːð] v mettere i denti. **teething** n dentizione f. **teething-ring** n dentaruolo m. **teething troubles** difficoltà iniziali f pl.

teetotal [tiː'toutl] adj astemio. **teetotaller** n astemio, -a m, f.

telecommunications [,telikəmjuːni'keiʃənz] pl n telecomunicazioni f pl.

telegram ['teligræm] n telegramma m.

telegraph ['teligrɑːf] n telegrafo m. v telegrafare. **telegraphic** adj telegrafico.

telepathy [tə'lepəθi] n telepatia f. **telepathic** adj telepatico.

telephone ['telifoun] *n* telefono *m. v* telefonare. **telephone box** cabina telefonica *f.* **telephone call** telefonata *f,* colpo di telefono *m.* **telephone exchange** centralino *m.* **telephone operator** telefonista *m, f.*

teleprinter ['teliprintə] *n* telescrivente *f.*

telescope ['teliskoup] *n* telescopio *m. v* incastrare, far scorrere l'uno nell'altro; (*shorten*) condensare. **telescopic** *adj* telescopico.

television ['teliviʒən] *n* televisione *f.* **television screen** video *m.* **television set** televisore *m.* **televise** *v* teletrasmettere, trasmettere per televisione.

telex ['teleks] *n* telex *m. v* trasmettere per telex.

*****tell** [tel] *v* dire, raccontare; distinguere. **tell off** (*scold*) sgridare. **telling-off** *n* ramanzina *f,* sgridata *f.* **telling** *adj* efficace, indicativo.

temper ['tempə] *n* (*mood*) umore *m,* disposizione *f;* (*metal*) tempra *f.* **keep one's temper** contenersi, rimaner calmo. **lose one's temper** arrabbiarsi, andare in collera. *v* moderare, temperare; (*metal*) temprare.

temperament ['tempərəmənt] *n* temperamento *m,* indole *f.* **temperamental** *adj* capriccioso.

temperate ['tempərət] *adj* temperato.

temperature ['temprətʃə] *n* temperatura *f.* **have a temperature** (*med*) avere la febbre.

tempestuous [tem'pestjuəs] *adj* tempestoso, burrascoso.

temple[1] ['templ] *n* (*rel*) tempio *m.*

temple[2] ['templ] *n* (*anat*) tempia *f.*

tempo ['tempou] *n* tempo *m;* ritmo *m,* andamento *m.*

temporary ['tempərəri] *adj* temporaneo.

tempt [tempt] *v* tentare. **temptation** *n* tentazione *f.* **tempter** *n* tentatore *m.* **tempting** *adj* allettante, seducente; (*food*) appetitoso. **temptress** *n* tentatrice *f.*

ten [ten] *nm, adj* dieci. **tenth** *nm, adj* decimo.

tenable ['tenəbl] *adj* sostenibile, tenibile.

tenacious [tə'neiʃəs] *adj* tenace, ostinato; (*persistent*) accanito. **tenacity** *n* tenacia *f,* ostinazione *f;* accanimento *m.*

tenant ['tenənt] *n* inquilino, -a *m, f.* **tenancy** *n* affitto *m.*

tend[1] [tend] *v* (*be inclined*) tendere. **tendency** *n* tendenza *f,* inclinazione *f.* **tendentious** *adj* tendenzioso.

tend[2] [tend] *v* (*care for*) curare, assistere, soccorrere.

tender[1] ['tendə] *adj* tenero, delicato; (*affectionate*) affettuoso; (*sensitive*) sensibile. **tenderness** *n* tenerezza *f;* affettuosità *f.*

tender[2] ['tendə] *n* offerta *f;* (*comm*) preventivo *m,* appalto *m. v* offrire; appaltare, preventivare. **tender one's resignation** dare *or* rassegnare le dimissioni.

tendon ['tendən] *n* tendine *m.*

tendril ['tendril] *n* viticcio *m.*

tenement ['tenəmənt] *n* casamento *m,* casa popolare *f.*

tennis ['tenis] *n* tennis *m.* **tennis-ball/racket** *n* palla/racchetta da tennis *f.* **tennis-court** *n* campo da tennis *m.* **tennis player** giocatore, -trice di tennis *m, f.*

tenor ['tenə] *n* tenore *m.*

tense[1] [tens] *adj* teso, rigido. **tension** *n* tensione *f;* (*mech*) trazione *f.*

tense[2] [tens] *n* tempo *m.*

tent [tent] *n* tenda *f.*

tentacle ['tentəkl] *n* tentacolo *m.*

tentative ['tentətiv] *adj* di prova, sperimentale; (*hesitant*) titubante.

tenterhooks ['tentəhuks] *pl n* **on tenterhooks** sulle spine.

tenuous ['tenjuəs] *adj* tenue.

tenure ['tenjuə] *n* tenuta *f,* possesso *m,* esercizio *m.*

tepid ['tepid] *adj* tiepido.

term [təim] *n* termine *m;* durata *f;* (*school*) trimestre *m.* **come to terms with** venire a patti con. **terms** *pl n* tariffa *f sing;* condizioni *f pl;* (*footing*) relazioni *f pl.*

terminal ['təiminəl] *n* (*elec*) terminale *m;* (*aero*) terminal *m invar. adj* finale, estremo.

terminate ['təimineit] *v* terminare, porre termine a. **termination** *n* (*act*) terminazione *f;* (*end*) termine *m,* conclusione *f.*

terminology [təimi'noləd͡ʒi] *n* terminologia *f.*

terminus ['təiminəs] *n* stazione di testa *f,* capolinea (*pl* capilinea) *m.*

terrace ['terəs] *n* terrazzo *m;* (*row of houses*) fila di case *f.*

terrain [tə'rein] *n* terreno *m.*

terrestrial [tə'restriəl] *adj* terrestre.

terrible ['terəbl] *adj* terribile, spaventoso.

terrier ['teriə] *n* terrier *m invar.*

terrific [təˈrifik] *adj* (*coll*) tremendo, fantastico.

terrify [ˈterifai] *v* atterrire. **be terrified** avere una paura matta. **terrifying** *adj* spaventoso.

territory [ˈteritəri] *n* territorio *m*. **territorial** *adj* territoriale.

terror [ˈterə] *n* terrore *m*. **terror-stricken** *adj* terrorizzato, atterrito. **terrorism** *n* terrorismo *m*. **terrorist** *n* terrorista *m, f*. **terrorize** *v* terrorizzare.

test [test] *n* prova *f*; esame *m*; analisi *f*; (*psych*) test *m invar*; (*industry*) collaudo *m*. **test-tube** *n* provetta *f*. *v* provare; esaminare; analizzare; collaudare.

testament [ˈtestəmənt] *n* testamento *m*.

testicle [ˈtestikl] *n* testicolo *m*.

testify [ˈtestifai] *v* testimoniare, attestare.

testimonial [testiˈmouniəl] *n* benservito *m*, attestato di buona condotta *m*.

testimony [ˈtestiməni] *n* testimonianza *f*, deposizione *f*; (*proof*) prova *f*.

tetanus [ˈtetənəs] *n* tetano *m*.

tether [ˈteðə] *v* impastoiare. *n* pastoia *f*. **be at the end of one's tether** non poterne più, essere agli sgoccioli.

text [tekst] *n* testo *m*. **textbook** *n* libro di testo *m*. **textual** *adj* testuale.

textile [ˈtekstail] *nm, adj* tessile.

texture [ˈtekstjuə] *n* struttura *f*; (*surface*) grana *f*.

Thames [temz] *n* Tamigi *m*.

than [ðan] *conj* di, che.

thank [θaŋk] *v* ringraziare. **thank you** grazie. **thanks** *pl n* grazie *f pl*. **thanks to** grazie a. **thankful** *adj* riconoscente, grato.

that [ðat] *adj, pron* quel(lo), quella. that is cioè. **that's all!** ecco tutto! *adv* talmente. *conj* che.

thatch [θatʃ] *n* (copertura di) paglia *f*. *v* coprire di paglia.

thaw [θɔː] *n* disgelo *m*. *v* disgelare.

the [ðə] *art* il or lo, la; (*pl*) i or gli, le.

theatre [ˈθiətə] *n* teatro *m*; (*hospital*) sala operatoria *f*. **theatrical** *adj* teatrale.

theft [θeft] *n* furto *m*.

their [ðeə] *adj* (il) loro, (la) loro; (*pl*) (i) loro, (le) loro.

theirs [ðeəz] *pron* il loro, la loro; (*pl*) i loro, le loro.

them [ðem] *pron* (*before verb*) li, le; (*after verb or prep*) loro. **both of them** tutti e due. **none of them** nessuno di loro.

theme [θiːm] *n* tema *m*. **theme song** sigla (musicale) *f*. **thematic** *adj* tematico.

themselves [ðəmˈselvz] *pron* loro stessi, -e; (*reflexive*) si; (*after prep*) sè stessi, -e.

then [ðen] *adv* (*at that time*) allora; (*next in time*) poi, dopo. **by then** a quel punto. **now and then** di tanto in tanto. *conj* dunque, allora. *adj* di allora.

theology [θiˈolədʒi] *n* teologia *f*. **theologian** *n* teologo *m*. **theological** *adj* teologico.

theorem [ˈθiərəm] *n* teorema *m*.

theory [ˈθiəri] *n* teoria *f*. **theoretical** *adj* teorico.

therapy [ˈθerəpi] *n* terapia *f*. **therapeutic** *adj* terapeutico. **therapist** *n* terapista *m, f*.

there [ðeə] *adv* lì, là; (*to that place*) ci, vi. **thereabouts** *adv* da quelle parti, all'incirca. **thereafter** *adv* quindi, in seguito. **there are** ci sono. **thereby** *adv* così, in tal modo. **therefore** *adv* dunque, perciò, quindi. **there is** c'è; (*calling attention*) ecco. **there it is!** eccolo! **thereupon** *adv* quindi, subito dopo.

thermal [ˈθəːml] *adj* termico; (*waters*) termale.

thermodynamics [θəːmoudaiˈnamiks] *n* termodinamica *f*.

thermometer [θəˈmomitə] *n* termometro *m*.

thermonuclear [θəːmouˈnjukliə] *adj* termonucleare.

thermos ® [ˈθəːmos] *n* thermos ® *m invar*.

thermostat [ˈθəːməstat] *n* termostato *m*.

these [ðiːz] *pron, adj* questi, -e.

thesis [ˈθiːsis] *n, pl* -ses tesi *f*.

they [ðei] *pron* essi, -e, loro.

thick [θik] *adj* spesso; (*hair*) folto; (*fog*) fitto; stupido. **thick as thieves** amici per la pelle. **thickset** *adj* (*heavily built*) tarchiato; (*dense*) folto, fitto. **thick-skinned** *adj* insensibile. **through thick and thin** nella buona e nella cattiva sorte. **thicken** *v* addensare, ispessire, infittire. **thickness** *n* spessore *m*; (*layer*) strato *m*.

thief [θiːf] *n* ladro, -a *m, f*. **thieve** *v* rubare. **thieving** *n* ruberia *f*, il rubare *m*.

thigh [θai] *n* coscia *f*.

thimble [ˈθimbl] *n* ditale *m*.

thin [θin] *adj* sottile, fine; (*lean*) magro; (*not dense*) rado, sparso; (*weak*) debole. *v* diradare; (*lose weight*) dimagrare. **thinner** *n* diluente *m*.

thing [θiŋ] *n* cosa *f*, oggetto *m*. **for one thing ... for another ...** anzitutto ... e poi .... **things** *pl n* (*implements, possessions etc.*) roba *f sing*, cose *f pl*.

*think [θiŋk] v pensare; (believe) credere, ritenere; (imagine) figurarsi. **thinker** n pensatore, -trice m, f.

thinking ['θiŋkiŋ] adj pensante, ragionevole. n pensiero m, il ragionare m. **to my way of thinking** a mio avviso.

third [θəɪd] nm, adj terzo. **third party** terzi m pl.

thirst [θəɪst] n sete f. v aver sete. **thirst for** or **after** bramare. **thirsty** adj assetato. **be thirsty** aver sete.

thirteen [θəɪ'tiɪn] nm, adj tredici. **thirteenth** nm, adj tredicesimo.

thirty ['θəɪti] nm, adj trenta. **thirtieth** nm, adj trentesimo.

this [ðis] pron, adj questo, -a.

thistle ['θisl] n cardo m.

thorn [θoɪn] n spina f; (shrub) spino m. **thorny** adj spinoso.

thorough ['θʌrə] adj accurato; profondo; radicale; diligente. **thoroughly** adv a fondo.

thoroughbred ['θʌrəbred] n purosangue m. adj di razza, di puro sangue.

thoroughfare ['θʌrəfeə] n via f, passaggio m.

those [ðouz] pron, adj quei or quegli, quelle.

though [ðou] conj (in spite of) sebbene, benchè; (yet, still) tuttavia, pure. **as though** come se. **even though** anche se. **it looks as though** sembra che.

thought [θoɪt] V **think**. n pensiero m; idea f. **on second thoughts** ripensandoci (su). **thoughtful** adj (reflective) pensoso; (thought out) profondo; (considerate) premuroso, sollecito; (careful) attento, prudente. **thoughtless** adj (careless) imprudente; (heedless) sbadato; (unthinking) avventato; (inconsiderate) irrispettoso.

thousand ['θauzənd] adj mille. n mille m invar, migliaio (pl -a) m. **thousandth** nm, adj millesimo.

thrash [θraʃ] v battere, bastonare. **thrash out** discutere a fondo. **thrashing** n (defeat) batosta f; (beating) botte f pl.

thread [θred] n filo m; (screw) filetto m, passo m. v infilare; filettare. **threadbare** adj logoro.

threat [θret] n minaccia f. **threaten** v minacciare. **threatening** adj minaccioso; (letter) minatorio.

three [θriɪ] nm, adj tre. **three-cornered** adj triangolare, a tre punte. **three-dimensional** adj tridimensionale. **three-ply** adj (wood) a tre strati; (wool) a tre capi. **three-quarter** adj a tre quarti. **three-speed** adj a tre marce.

thresh [θreʃ] v (corn, etc.) trebbiare; battere. **threshing** n trebbiatura f.

threshold ['θreʃould] n soglia f.

threw [θruɪ] V **throw**.

thrift [θrift] n frugalità f, economia f. **thrifty** adj frugale, parsimonioso. **be thrifty** fare economia.

thrill [θril] n brivido m, fremito m; (excitement) emozione f. v far rabbrividire; emozionare; entusiasmare. **be thrilled with** essere entusiasta di. **thriller** n (book, film) giallo m. **thrilling** adj emozionante, eccitante.

thrive [θraiv] v fiorire, riuscire. **thrive on** approfittare di. **thriving** adj prospero, fiorente.

throat [θrout] n gola f. **have a sore throat** aver mal di gola. **throaty** adj gutturale.

throb [θrob] v battere, palpitare. n battito m, palpito m. **throbbing** adj palpitante, pulsante.

throes [θrouz] pl n **in the throes of** alle prese con.

thrombosis [θrom'bousis] n trombosi f.

throne [θroun] n trono m.

throng [θroŋ] n folla f, calca f. v affollarsi, stiparsi.

throttle [θrotl] v strozzare; (suppress) soffocare; (mot) regolare. n (valve) valvola a farfalla f.

through [θruɪ] adj diretto, di transito; finito. adv da una parte all'altra; (to the end) fino alla fine. prep da, per; (place) attraverso; (time) durante; (by means of) tramite, per mezzo di; (past) al di là di. **get through** (phone) ottenere la comunicazione; (finish) sbrigare. **throughout** adv completamente; (time) durante; (always) sempre.

*throw [θrou] n lancio m, tiro m. v lanciare, gettare; (coll: confuse) lasciare perplesso, sconcertare. **throw away** buttar via. **throwaway** adj (casual) spigliato; (remark) lasciato cadere; (to be discarded) da buttar via. **throw in** buttar dentro; (sport) rimettere in gioco; (include) comprendere. **throw out** buttar fuori, mettere alla porta; (put forward) dare. **throw up** lanciare in aria; (be sick) rigettare.

thrown [θroun] *V* throw.

thrush¹ [θrʌʃ] *n* (*bird*) tordo *m*.

thrush² [θrʌʃ] *n* (*med*) mughetto *m*.

*thrust** [θrʌst] *n* spinta *f*, botta *f*; (*mil*) attacco *m*. *v* spingere, ficcare, lanciarsi. **thrust oneself on** imporsi a.

thud [θʌd] *n* tonfo *m*.

thug [θʌg] *n* delinquente *m*.

thumb [θʌm] *n* pollice *m*. **thumbmark** *n* impronta digitale *f*. *v* **thumb a lift** fare l'autostop.

thump [θʌmp] *n* tonfo *m*. *v* picchiare, battere.

thunder ['θʌndə] *n* tuono *m*. **thunderbolt** *n* fulmine *m*. **thunderstorm** *n* temporale *m*. **thunderstruck** *adj* sbalordito. *v* tuonare. **thundering** *adj* (*coll*) enorme. **thundery** *adj* temporalesco; (*menacing*) minaccioso.

Thursday ['θəːzdi] *n* giovedi *m*.

thus [δʌs] *adv* cosi.

thwart [θwoːt] *v* frustrare.

thyme [taim] *n* timo *m*.

thyroid ['θairoid] *n* tiroide *f*.

tiara [ti'aːrə] *n* diadema *m*.

tick¹ [tik] *n* (*sound*) tictac *m invar*, ticchettio *m*; (*mark*) contrassegno *m*, visto *m*; (*moment*) attimo *m*. *v* ticchettare, fare tictac; contrassegnare, vistare. **tick off** (*coll*: *scold*) sgridare. **ticking-off** *n* (*coll*) lavata di capo *f*. **tick over** (*engine*) girare in folle.

tick² [tik] *n* (*insect*) zecca *f*, acaro *m*.

ticket ['tikit] *n* biglietto *m*; (*label*, *counterfoil*) scontrino *m*. **ticket collector** bigliettario, -a *m*, *f*. **ticket office** biglietteria *f*.

tickle ['tikl] *v* solleticare; (*make itch*) fare il solletico; (*gratify*) lusingare; (*amuse*) divertire. *n* irritazione *f*; (*itch*) prurito *m*. **ticklish** *adj* (*person*) che sente il solletico; (*tricky*) delicato, scabroso.

tide [taid] *n* marea *f*, corrente *f*. **tidemark** *n* battigia *f*. *v* **tide over** superare.

tidy ['taidi] *adj* ordinato; (*neat*) ben curato o tenuto; (*coll*: *considerable*) bello. *v* mettere in ordine. **tidy up** far pulizia. **tidiness** *n* ordine *m*.

tie [tai] *v* legare; (*join*) attaccare; (*lace up*) allacciare; (*sport*) pareggiare. **tie down** limitare, obbligare. **tie up** (*property*, *capital etc*.) vincolare. *n* legame *m*; (*neck*) cravatta *f*; (*bond*) vincolo *m*; pareggio *m*; (*music*) legatura *f*.

tier [tiə] *n* (*row*) fila *f*; (*rank*) gradino *m*; (*layer*) strato *m*.

tiger ['taigə] *n* tigre *f*.

tight [tait] *adj* stretto; (*fitting closely*) aderente; (*taut*) teso; (*coll*: *drunk*) brillo; (*coll*: *mean*) tirchio. **in a tight corner** con le spalle al muro. *adv* **hold tight** stringere, tenersi fermo. **sit tight** non muoversi. **tighten** *v* stringere, serrare.

tights *pl n* collant *m invar*.

tile [tail] *n* (*roof*) tegola *f*, (*floor*, *wall*) piastrella *f*, mattonella *f*. *v* coprire con tegole *o* piastrelle.

till¹ [til] *V* until.

till² [til] *n* cassa *f*.

till³ [til] *v* coltivare; (*plough*) arare.

tiller ['tilə] *n* (*rudder*) barra del timone *f*.

tilt [tilt] *v* inclinare. *n* inclinazione *f*. **at full tilt** di gran carriera, a tutta velocità.

timber ['timbə] *n* legname *m*; (*beam*) trave *f*. **timbered** *adj* costruito in legno, coperto di legno; (*wooded*) alberato.

time [taim] *n* tempo *m*, periodo *m*; (*occasion*) volta *f*; (*clock*) ora *f*; (*epoca*) *f*. **for a long time** (*past*) da molto tempo; (*future*) per molto tempo. **for the time being** per ora. **from time to time** ogni tanto, di quando in quando. **have a good time** divertirsi. **in time** a tempo; (*eventually*) alla fine. **one at a time** uno alla volta. **on time** in orario. **take one's time** fare con comodo. **time bomb** bomba a orologeria *f*. **timekeeper** *n* (*sport*) cronometrista *m*; (*overseer*) controllore *m*. **time-signal** *n* segnale orario *m*. **timetable** *n* orario *m*. *v* misurare il tempo; (*sport*) cronometrare; (*choose moment*) scegliere il momento. **timeless** *adj* eterno, permanente. **timely** *adj* opportuno, tempestivo.

timid ['timid] *adj* timido. **timidity** *n* timidezza *f*.

tin [tin] *n* (*metal*) stagno *m*; (*can*) latta *f*, scatola *f*. **tin-opener** *n* apriscatole *m invar*. *v* inscatolare; stagnare. **tinny** *adj* (*sound*) metallico.

tinge [tindʒ] *n* sfumatura *f*, tocco *m*. *v* **tinged with** misto a.

tingle ['tingl] *v* formicolare. *n* formicolio *m*, prurito *m*.

tinker ['tinkə] *v* (*repair*) rabberciare, rattoppare; (*busy oneself*) affaccendarsi.

tinkle ['tinkl] *v* (far) tintinnare, squillare. *n* tintinnio *m*, squillo *m*.

tinsel ['tinsəl] *n* orpello *m*.

tint [tint] *n* tono *m*, tinta *f*. *v* colorire.

tiny ['taini] *adj* piccino, minuto.

tip¹ [tip] *n* (*end*) punta *f*, estremità *f*; (*summit*) cima *f*. tiptoe *v* camminare in punta di piedi. on tiptoe in punta di piedi.

tip² [tip] *v* (*topple*) rovesciare; (*dump*) scaricare. *n* luogo di scarico *m*.

tip³ [tip] *v* (*money*) mancia *f*; (*hint*) consiglio *m*; informazione riservata *f*. *v* dare la mancia. tip off avvertire, prevenire.

tipsy ['tipsi] *adj* (*coll*) brillo. get tipsy ubriacarsi leggermente.

tire¹ ['taiə] *v* stancarsi, stancare; (*get fed up*) stufarsi. tired *adj* stanco; (*fed up*) stufo. tireless *adj* infaticabile; (*unceasing*) indefesso. tiresome *adj* noioso, seccante. tiring *adj* faticoso.

tire² (*US*) *V* tyre.

tissue ['tiʃuː] *n* tessuto *m*; (*handkerchief*) fazzoletto di carta *m*. tissue paper carta velina *f*.

tit [tit] *n* (*bird*) cincia *f*.

title ['taitl] *n* titolo *m*; (*law*) diritto *m*. title-page *n* frontespizio *m*. title-role *n* parte principale *f*. *v* intitolare.

to [tu] *prep* a, in; (*in order to*) per; (*towards*) verso; da. *adv* to and fro avanti e indietro. to-do *n* (*coll*) trambusto *m*.

toad [toud] *n* rospo *m*. toadstool *n* fungo *m*.

toast [toust] *n* (*bread*) toast *m invar*; (*speech, drink*) brindisi *m*. drink a toast to bere alla salute di. *v* tostare. toaster *n* tostapane *m invar*.

tobacco [tə'bakou] *n* tabacco *m*. tobacconist *n* tabaccaio, -a *m, f*.

toboggan [tə'bogən] *n* toboga *m invar*. *v* andare in toboga.

today [tə'dei] *adv* oggi; (*nowadays*) oggigiorno. a week/fortnight today oggi a otto/quindici. *n* oggi *m*.

toddler ['todlə] *n* bambino, -a *m, f*, piccino, -a *m, f*. toddle *v* sgambettare.

toe [tou] *n* dito del piede *m*; (*shoe*) punta *f*. tread on someone's toes pestare i piedi a qualcuno.

toffee ['tofi] *n* caramella mou *f*.

together [tə'geðə] *adv* insieme, assieme. together with insieme con, assieme a.

toil [toil] *n* fatica *f*. *v* faticare.

toilet ['toilit] *n* (*lavatory*) gabinetto *m*; (*dressing, etc.*) toilette (*pl* -s) *f*, toletta *f*. toilet-paper *n* carta igienica *f*. toilet water acqua da toletta *f*.

token ['toukən] *n* segno *m*, simbolo *m*; (*gift*) omaggio *m*; (*coin*) gettone *m*.

Tokyo ['toukiou] *n* Tokio *f*.

told [tould] *V* tell.

tolerate ['toləreit] *v* tollerare, sopportare. tolerable *adj* tollerabile. tolerance *n* tolleranza *f*. tolerant *adj* tollerante.

toll¹ [toul] *n* pedaggio *m*; (*duty*) dazio *m*.

toll² [toul] *n* (*bell*) rintocco *m*. *v* rintoccare.

tomato [tə'maːtou] *n* pomodoro *m*. tomato juice/paste succo/estratto di pomodoro *m*. tomato sauce salsa di pomodoro *f*.

tomb [tuːm] *n* tomba *f*. tombstone *n* pietra tombale *f*.

tomorrow [tə'morou] *nm, adv* domani. the day after tomorrow dopodomani. tomorrow morning domattina. tomorrow week domani a otto.

ton [tʌn] *n* tonnellata *f*. tonnage *n* tonnellaggio *m*.

tone [toun] *n* tono *m*. *v* armonizzare. tone down attenuare, smorzare. tonality *n* tonalità *f*.

tongs [toŋz] *pl n* pinza *f sing*; (*fire*) molle *f pl*.

tongue [tʌŋ] *n* lingua *f*. hold one's tongue star zitto, tacere. tongue-tied *adj* ammutolito; (*speech defect*) scilinguato.

tonic ['tonik] *n* ricostituente *m*; (*water*) acqua brillante *f*; (*music*) tonica *f*. *adj* tonico.

tonight [tə'nait] *adj* (*evening*) stasera; (*night*) stanotte.

tonsil ['tonsil] *n* tonsilla *f*. tonsillitis *n* tonsillite *f*.

too [tuː] *adv* (*also*) anche, pure; (*moreover*) inoltre; (*more than enough*) troppo. too many troppi. too much troppo.

took [tuk] *V* take.

tool [tuːl] *n* attrezzo *m*, arnese *m*; strumento *m*. tool-shed *n* ripostiglio per attrezzi *m*. tools of the trade ferri del mestiere *m pl*. *v* lavorare.

tooth [tuːθ] *n, pl* teeth dente *m*. have a sweet tooth essere ghiotto di dolci. have a tooth out farsi cavare un dente. in the teeth of (*in defiance of*) a dispetto di; (*in the presence of*) in cospetto di. toothache *n* mal di denti *m*. tooth-brush *n* spazzolino da denti *m*. toothpaste *n* dentifricio *m*. toothpick *n* stuzzicadenti *m*. toothless *adj* sdentato.

top¹ [top] n (*highest point*) cima f, vertice m; (*leading position*) testa f, capo m; (*lid*) coperchio m. **at the top of one's voice** a voce altissima; (*shouting*) a squarciagola. **from top to toe** da capo a piedi. **on top of** (*upon*) sopra, su; (*at the head of*) in testa a; (*following*) dopo, in seguito a. adj (*uppermost*) superiore, ultimo; (*greatest*) più alto; (*foremost*) principale. **at top speed** a velocità massima. **top-heavy** adj sovraccarico (m pl -chi); (*unbalanced*) sbilanciato. **topsoil** n terriccio m. v sorpassare, superare; (*be above*) sovrastare a; (*prune*) scapezzare. **top up** v riempire. **topless** adj (*dress*) a petto scoperto. **topmost** adj il più alto.

top² [top] n (*toy*) trottola f.

topaz ['toupæz] n topazio m.

topic ['topik] n argomento m. **topical** adj di attualità.

topography [tə'pogrəfi] n topografia f.

topple ['topl] v (*far*) cadere or crollare.

topsy-turvy [topsi'tɜːvi] adv sottosopra.

torch [tɔːtʃ] n fiaccola f, (*electric*) lampadina tascabile f, torcia elettrica f.

tore [tɔː] V tear¹.

torment ['tɔːment; v tɔː'ment] n supplizio m, tortura f. v tormentare, angosciare.

torn [tɔːn] V tear¹.

tornado [tɔː'neidou] n tornado m, turbine m.

torpedo [tɔː'piːdou] n siluro m, torpedine f. v silurare. **torpedo-boat** n torpediniera f.

torrent ['torənt] n torrente m. **torrential** adj torrenziale.

torso ['tɔːsou] n torso m.

tortoise ['tɔːtəs] n tartaruga f. **tortoise-shell** nf, adj tartaruga.

tortuous ['tɔːtʃuəs] adj tortuoso.

torture ['tɔːtʃə] n tortura f. v torturare.

Tory ['tɔːri] n, adj (*coll*) conservatore, -trice.

toss [tos] v (*throw*) lanciare; (*pitch*) sballottare; (*move restlessly*) agitarsi. **toss aside** buttar via. **toss back** rilanciare. **toss up** (*coin*) far testa o croce; tirare a sorte. **toss-up** n questione di fortuna f. n **toss of the head** scrollata del capo f.

tot¹ [tot] n (*child*) bimbo, -a m, f, piccino, -a m, f; (*drink*) bicchierino m.

tot² [tot] v **tot up** sommare, fare la somma di.

total ['toutəl] n totale m, ammontare m.

adj totale, globale. v (*add up*) fare la somma di; (*add up to*) ammontare a.

totter ['totə] v barcollare, vacillare. **tottering** adj barcollante; (*shaky*) malsicuro.

touch [tʌtʃ] n (*sense*) tatto m; contatto m; (*music, painting*) tocco m; (*hint*) accenno m; (*med*) attacco leggero m. **touchstone** n pietra di paragone f, criterio m. v toccare; (*lightly*) sfiorare; (*handle*) maneggiare, tastare; (*move*) commuovere. **touch-and-go** adj rischioso. **touch down** (*plane*) atterrare. **touch up** ritoccare, ripassare. **touch wood!** tocca ferro! **touched** adj commosso. **touching** adj commovente; adiacente. **touchy** adj permaloso.

tough [tʌf] adj (*hard*) duro; (*hardy*) tenace; robusto; resistente; difficile. n teppista m. **toughen** v indurire, rinforzare. **toughness** n robustezza f; durezza f; resistenza f.

toupee ['tuːpei] n toupet m invar, parrucca f.

tour [tuə] n giro m, viaggio m; (*theatre, sport*) tournée (pl -s) f. v viaggiare, fare un giro; fare una tournée. **tourism** n turismo m. **tourist** n turista m, f.

tournament ['tuənəmənt] n torneo m.

tow¹ [tou] n (*hemp*) stoppa f.

tow² [tou] v rimorchiare. n **in tow** da rimorchio. **tow-rope** n rimorchio m. **tow-path** n alzaia f.

towards [tə'wɔːdz] prep verso, incontro a.

towel ['tauəl] n asciugamano m. v asciugarsi. **towelling** n spugna f.

tower ['tauə] n torre f. v elevarsi. **tower above** dominare. **towering** adj dominante; (*very great*) smisurato; violento.

town [taun] n città f; (*smaller*) cittadina f. **go to town** andare in città; (*do thoroughly*) mettercela tutta. **town clerk** segretario comunale m. **town hall** municipio m. **town planner** urbanista m, f. **town planning** urbanistica f.

toxic ['toksik] adj tossico. **toxicity** n tossicità f.

toy [toi] n giocattolo m. v (*play*) giocherellare; (*trifle*) dilettarsi.

trace [treis] n traccia f. v (*indicate, sketch*) tracciare; (*follow, discover*) rintracciare. **traceable** adj rintracciabile.

track [træk] n (*footpath*) sentiero m; (*mark, trace*) traccia f, orma f; (*sport*) pista f; (*set course*) percorso m; (*record*) banda f. **keep track of** seguire. **off the**

trap

beaten **track** fuori mano. **on the right track** sulla strada buona. *v* inseguire. **track down** scovare.

tract¹ [trækt] *n* (*region*) zona *f*; (*anat*) apparato *m*.

tract² [trækt] *n* (*treatise*) trattato *m*; (*pamphlet*) manifesto *m*.

tractor ['træktə] *n* trattore *m*.

trade [treid] *n* (*work*) mestiere *m*; commercio *m*, traffico *m*; (*business*) affari *m pl*. **trademark** *n* marchio depositato *m*. **tradesman** *n* fornitore *m*, esercente *m*, negoziante *m*. **trade union** sindacato *m*. **trade unionist** sindacalista *m*, *f*. *v* fare affari, commerciare. **trade on** approfittare di. **trader** *n* commerciante *m*, *f*.

trading ['treidiŋ] *n* commercio *m*. *adj* commerciale.

tradition [trə'diʃən] *n* tradizione *f*. **traditional** *adj* tradizionale.

traffic ['træfik] *n* traffico *m*. **traffic jam** intasamento *or* ingorgo (del traffico) *m*. **traffic-light** *n* semaforo *m*. *v* trafficare.

tragedy ['trædʒədi] *n* tragedia *f*. **tragic** *adj* tragico.

trail [treil] *n* traccia *f*, pista *f*. *v* (*follow*) inseguire; (*drag*) trascinare. **trailer** *n* rimorchio *m*.

train [trein] *n* (*rail*) treno *m*; (*dress*) strascico *m*; (*following*) seguito *m*; serie *f*. **train of events** svolgimento *m*. *v* (*teach*) istruire; (*impart skill*) addestrare, ammaestrare; (*sport*) allenare. **trainee** *n* allievo, -a *m*, *f*; (*apprentice*) apprendista *m*, *f*. **trainer** *n* allenatore, -trice *m*, *f*. **training** *n* addestramento *m*; allenamento *m*.

trait [treit] *n* caratteristica *f*.

traitor ['treitə] *n* traditore *m*. **traitress** *n* traditrice *f*. **turn traitor** passare al nemico.

tram [træm] *n* tram *m invar*.

tramp [træmp] *n* (*person*) vagabondo *m*; (*walk*) passeggiata *f*; (*sound*) calpestio *m*. *v* vagabondare, percorrere a piedi.

trample ['træmpl] *v* calpestare. **trample on** pestare.

trampoline ['træmpəlin] *n* trampolino *m*.

trance [trains] *n* trance *f invar*; (*daze*) stupore *m*.

tranquil ['træŋkwil] *adj* sereno, calmo. **tranquillity** *n* serenità *f*, calma *f*. **tranquillizer** *n* tranquillante *m*, sedativo *m*.

transact [tran'zækt] *v* **transact business**

trattare, entrare in trattative. **transaction** *n* affare *m*, trattativa *f*.

transcend [tran'send] *v* trascendere, superare. **transcendental** *adj* trascendentale.

transcribe [tran'skraib] *v* trascrivere. **transcript** *or* **transcription** *n* trascrizione *f*.

transept ['transept] *n* transetto *m*.

transfer ['transfɜ; *v* trans'fɜ] *n* trasferimento *m*; (*design*) decalcomania *f*. *v* trasferire; (*drawing*) riportare. **transferable** *adj* trasferibile.

transform [trans'fɔrm] *v* trasformare. **transformation** *n* trasformazione *f*, mutamento *m*; (*phys*) conversione *f*. **transformer** *n* trasformatore *m*.

transfuse [trans'fjuz] *v* trasfondere. **transfusion** *n* trasfusione *f*.

transgress [trans'gres] *v* trasgredire. **transgression** *n* trasgressione *f*, infrazione *f*.

transient ['tranziənt] *adj* transitorio, passeggero; (*phys*) transiente.

transistor [tran'zistə] *n* transistor *m invar*, transistore *m*. **transistorize** *v* transistorizzare.

transit ['transit] *n* passaggio *m*, transito *m*. **in transit** durante il trasporto, in transito. *adj* di passaggio *or* transito.

transition [tran'ziʃən] *n* transizione *f*; (*music*) modulazione *f*.

transitive ['transitiv] *adj* transitivo.

translate [trans'leit] *v* tradurre. **translation** *n* traduzione *f*. **translator** *n* traduttore, -trice *m*, *f*.

translucent [trans'lusnt] *adj* semitrasparente, traslucido.

transmit [tranz'mit] *v* trasmettere. **transmission** *n* trasmissione *f*. **transmitter** *n* (*radio set*) trasmettitore *m*; (*station*) trasmittente *f*.

transparent [trans'peərənt] *adj* trasparente. **transparency** *n* trasparenza *f*; (*phot*) diapositiva *f*.

transplant [trans'plaint; *n* 'transplaint] *v* trapiantare. *n* trapianto *m*.

transport ['transpɔrt; *v* trans'pɔrt] *n* trasporto *m*. *v* trasportare. **transportation** *n* trasporto *m*.

transpose [trans'pouz] *v* trasporre. **transposition** *n* trasposizione *f*.

transverse ['tranzvɜis] *adj* traverso, trasversale.

trap [træp] *n* trappola *f*; (*trick*) tranello

m; (vehicle) carrozzetta f. **trapdoor** n trabocchetto m. v prendere in trappola.
trapeze [trə'piːz] n trapezio m.
trash [traʃ] n (rubbish) robaccia f; rifiuti m pl; (nonsense) sciocchezze f pl. **trashy** adj di nessun valore.
trauma ['trɔːmə] n trauma m. **traumatic** adj traumatico.
travel ['travl] n viaggiare m, viaggi m pl. **travel agency** agenzia di viaggi f. v viaggiare. **traveller** n viaggiatore, -trice m, f. **traveller's cheque** assegno turistico m.
travesty ['travəsti] n travestimento m, parodia f.
trawl [trɔːl] n strascico (pl -chi) m. v pescare con strascico. **trawler** n peschereccio m.
tray [trei] n vassoio m.
treachery ['tretʃəri] n tradimento m, perfidia f. **treacherous** adj traditore, -trice, perfido; (unreliable) falso; (dangerous) pericoloso.
treacle ['triːkl] n melassa f.
*tread [tred] v (trample) calcare, calpestare; (walk) camminare. n passo m; (stair) gradino m; (tyre) battistrada m invar.
treason ['triːzn] n tradimento m.
treasure ['treʒə] n tesoro m. v (cherish) aver caro; (prize) apprezzare; (retain carefully) tener caro. **treasurer** n tesoriere, -a m, f. **treasury** n tesoreria f. **Treasury** n Ministero del Tesoro m.
treat [triːt] v trattare; (med) curare. n piacere m. **treatment** n trattamento m.
treatise ['triːtiz] n trattato m, dissertazione f.
treaty ['triːti] n trattato m.
treble ['trebl] adj triplo, triplice; di soprano. n soprano. v triplicare. adv tre volte tanto.
tree [triː] n albero m.
trek [trek] v viaggiare (scomodamente). n viaggio (scomodo) m, migrazione f.
trellis ['trelis] n pergolato m, graticcio m.
tremble ['trembl] v tremare; (be agitated) fremere. n tremito m; fremito m.
tremendous [trə'mendəs] adj enorme; (coll) straordinario.
tremor ['tremə] n tremore m.
trench [trentʃ] n (ditch) fosso m; (mil) trincea f. **trenchant** adj tagliente, caustico.
trend [trend] n tendenza f; direzione f; (fashion) moda f. **trendy** adj di moda.

trespass ['trespəs] v trasgredire; (rel) peccare. n trasgressione f; peccato m.
trestle ['tresl] n trespolo m.
trial ['traiəl] n (law) processo m; (test) esame m, prova f; (trouble) disperazione f, dolore m. **by trial and error** (a) tentoni.
triangle ['traiaŋgl] n triangolo m. **triangular** adj triangolare.
tribe [traib] n tribù f. **tribal** adj tribale. **tribesman** n membro di tribù m.
tribunal [trai'bjuːnl] n tribunale m.
tributary ['tribjutəri] nm, adj tributario.
tribute ['tribjuːt] n tributo m, omaggio m. **pay tribute to** rendere omaggio a.
trick [trik] n espediente m; (prank) tiro m; (artifice) trucco m; (cards) bazza f. **confidence trick** truffa all'americana f. **do the trick** ottenere l'effetto voluto. v ingannare, abbindolare. **trickery** n inganno m. **tricky** adj (crafty) furbo; complicato, delicato.
trickle ['trikl] v gocciolare. n gocciolio m; flusso irregolare m. **trickle of water** filo d'acqua m.
tricycle ['traisikl] n triciclo m.
trifle ['traifl] n sciocchezza f, inezia f; (food) zuppa inglese f. **a trifle** (a little) un po', alquanto. v scherzare. **trifling** adj insignificante.
trigger ['trigə] n grilletto m. v **trigger off** far scattare.
trigonometry [trigə'nɔmətri] n trigonometria f.
trill [tril] n trillo m. v trillare; (continuous) trilleggiare.
trilogy ['trilədʒi] n trilogia f.
trim [trim] adj ordinato, ben messo or tenuto, assettato. n assetto m; (ornament) guarnizione f. v (neaten) assettare; guarnire; (hair) spuntare. **trimmings** pl n guarnizioni f pl.
trinket ['triŋkit] n gingillo m.
trio ['triːou] n trio m.
trip [trip] n (excursion) gita f; (journey) viaggio m; (stumble) passo falso m. v (step lightly) saltellare; (stumble) inciampare. **trip up** far cadere, fare lo sgambetto, inciampare. **tripper** n escursionista m, f.
tripe [traip] n trippa f.
triple ['tripl] adj triplo, triplice. v triplicare. **triplet** n trigemino, -a m, f.

tripod ['traipod] n cavalletto m. treppiede m.

trite [trait] adj banale. comune.

triumph ['traiʌmf] n trionfo m. v trionfare, esultare. **triumphant** adj trionfante.

trivial ['trivial] adj insignificante, banale. **triviality** n affare di nessuna importanza m.

trod [trod] V tread.

trodden ['trodn] V tread.

trolley ['troli] n carrello m.

trombone [trom'boun] n trombone m.

troop [truːp] n banda f. gruppo m; (mil) truppa f. v **troop along** sfilare. **troop in/out** entrare/uscire in gruppo.

trophy ['troufi] n trofeo m.

tropic ['tropik] n tropico m. **tropical** adj tropicale.

trot [trot] v trottare. n trotto m, trottata f. **on the trot** (coll) di seguito. **trotter** n (horse) trottatore m; (pig's foot) zampa f.

trouble ['trʌbl] n disturbo m; difficoltà f; (unpleasantness) dispiacere m; preoccupazione f; (annoyance) fastidio m. **make trouble** creare guai. **the trouble is** il guaio è. **troublemaker** n sobillatore, -trice m, f. v disturbare, dare fastidio. **troubled** adj turbato, preoccupato, agitato. **troublesome** adj noioso, fastidioso.

trough [trof] n trogolo m; (drinking) abbeveratoio m.

trousers ['trauzəz] pl n calzoni m pl, pantaloni m pl.

trout [traut] n trota f.

trowel ['trauəl] n (plastering) cazzuola f; (gardening) vanghetto m.

truant ['truːənt] n **play truant** marinare la scuola; (shirk duty) batter la fiacca.

truce [truːs] n tregua f.

truck [trʌk] n autocarro m, camion m.

trudge [trʌdʒ] v trascinarsi, camminare a stento.

true [truː] adj vero; corretto; genuino; (mech) centrato. **come true** avverarsi. **hold true for** valere per.

truffle ['trʌfl] n tartufo m.

trump [trʌmp] n briscola f; (bridge) atout m invar. **trump card** (coll) forte m. v (cards) tagliare; (beat) battere. **trump up** fabbricare.

trumpet ['trʌmpit] n tromba f. **blow one's own trumpet** vantare i propri meriti. v (proclaim loudly) strombazzare; (elephant) barrire.

truncheon ['trʌntʃən] n manganello m, bastone m.

trunk [trʌŋk] n tronco m; (chest) baule m; torso m; (elephant) proboscide f. (car)|portabagagli m **trunk call** telefonata interurbana f. **trunk road** strada maestra or statale f. **trunks** pl n calzoncini m pl.

truss [trʌs] v legare. n (framework) travatura f; (bundle) fastello f; (med) cinto erniario m.

trust [trʌst] n fiducia f; (hope) fede f; (law) fedecommesso m; (comm) trust m invar. **trustworthy** adj degno di fiducia, fidato. v fidarsi di, aver fiducia in; (hope) augurarsi. **trustee** n fedecommissario m; curatore, -trice m, f. **trusty** adj fedele, leale.

truth [truːθ] n verità f, vero m. **truthful** adj veritiero, sincero.

try [trai] v tentare; (test) provare; (law) giudicare, processare; (taste) assaggiare. **try on** provare. n tentativo m; (rugby) meta f. **trying** adj difficile; (distressing) penoso; (irritating) seccante.

tsar [zaː] n zar m invar.

T-shirt ['tiːʃəːt] n magiletta f.

tub [tʌb] n tino m; (bath) vasca f. **tubby** adj grassoccio.

tuba ['tjuːbə] n tuba f.

tube [tjuːb] n tubo m; (for toothpaste, etc.) tubetto m; (rail) metropolitana f. **inner tube** n camera d'aria f. **tubing** n tubo m. **tubular** adj tubolare.

tuber ['tjuːbə] n tubero m.

tuberculosis [tjubəːkju'lousis] n tubercolosi f.

tuck [tʌk] n piega f, rimbocco m. **tuck-shop** n spaccio di dolciumi m. v (thrust into) stipare; (needlework) rimboccare. **tuck in** ripiegare; (coll: eat) pappare, farsi una mangiata. **tuck up in bed** mettere a letto, coricare.

Tuesday ['tjuːzdi] n martedì m.

tuft [tʌft] n ciuffo m, fiocco m.

tug [tʌg] v(pull) tirare, dare uno strappo a; (drag) trascinare. n strappo m; (boat) rimorchiatore m.

tuition [tju'iʃən] n insegnamento m, istruzione f.

tulip ['tjuːlip] n tulipano m.

tumble ['tʌmbl] y cascare, ruzzolare; (somersault) fare un capitombolo. **tumble down** crollare. n caduta f, capitombolo m. **tumbler** n (glass) bicchiere m.

tummy ['tʌmi] (coll) n pancia f. **tummy-ache** n mal di pancia m.

tumour ['tjuːmə] n tumore m.

tumult ['tjuːmʌlt] n tumulto m. **tumultuous** adj tumultuoso.

tuna ['tjuːnə] n also **tunny** tonno m.

tune [tjuːn] n motivo m; melodia f, aria f. **call the tune** essere in comando. **in tune** in tono, intonato. **out of tune** fuori tono, stonato. **sing out of tune** stonare. **to the tune of** alla bellezza di. v accordare; (radio) sintonizzare. **tuner** n sintonizzatore m.

tunic ['tjuːnik] n tunica f.

tunnel ['tʌnl] n tunnel m invar, traforo m. v traforare.

tunny ['tʌni] V **tuna**.

turban ['təːbən] n turbante m.

turbid ['təːbid] adj torbido.

turbine ['təːbain] n turbina f.

turbot ['təːbət] n rombo m.

turbulent ['təːbjulənt] adj turbolento. **turbulence** n turbolenza f.

tureen [tə'riːn] n zuppiera f.

turf [təːf] n zolla erbosa f; (sod) piota f; (peat) torba f; (horse-racing) ippica f. v piotare. **turf out** (coll) buttar fuori.

turkey ['təːki] n tacchino m.

Turkey ['təːki] n Turchia f. **Turk** n turco, -a m, f. **Turkish** nm, adj turco.

turmeric ['təːmərik] n curcuma f.

turmoil ['təːmoil] n scompiglio m, confusione f.

turn [təːn] v girare, voltare; (change) cambiare; (change direction) svoltare. **turn against** alienare, ribellarsi a. **turn away** voltarsi da parte, guardar via; (refuse admission) mandar via. **turncoat** n rinnegato, -a m, f. **turn down** (fold) risvoltare; (lower) abbassare; (reject) rifiutare. **turn into** far diventare, convertire in. **turn off** (stop flow) chiudere; (switch off) spegnere; (change direction) voltare. **turn on** (start flow) aprire; (switch on) accendere; (coll) eccitare; (attack) aggredire. **turn out** (switch off) spegnere; produrre; (send away) cacciar via; (empty) vuotare; risultare; (clothe) vestire. **turn over** rovesciare. **turnover** n (comm) giro d'affari m; (cookery) pasticcio m. **turnstile** n tornello m. **turntable** n (records) giradischi m invar; (rail) piattaforma girevole f. **turn up** (arrive) capitare; (come to light) ricomparire;

(increase intensity) alzare; (occur) succedere. n giro m, rivoluzione f; (change of direction) svolta f; (in rota, game, etc.) turno m. **turning** n curva f, svolta f. **turning point** momento critico or decisivo m.

turnip ['təːnip] n rapa f.

turpentine ['təːpəntain] n trementina f; (oil) essenza di trementina f.

turquoise ['təːkwoiz] n (stone) turchese f; (colour) turchese m. adj turchese.

turret ['tʌrit] n torretta f.

turtle ['təːtl] n testuggine f, tartaruga f. **turn turtle** cappottare, capovolgersi. **turtle-dove** n tortora f.

Tuscany ['tʌskəni] n Toscana f. **Tuscan** n, adj toscano, -a.

tusk [tʌsk] n zanna f.

tussle ['tʌsl] n zuffa f. v venire alle mani, azzuffarsi.

tutor ['tjuːtə] n insegnante (privato) m; (coach) ripetitore, -trice m, f. **tutorial** n periodo di istruzione (privata) m.

tuxedo [tʌk'siːdou] n smoking m invar.

tweed [twiːd] n tweed m invar, tessuto di lana scozzese m.

tweezers ['twiːzəz] pl n pinzette f pl.

twelve [twelv] nm, adj dodici. **twelfth** nm, adj dodicesimo.

twenty ['twenti] nm, adj venti. **twentieth** nm, adj ventesimo.

twice [twais] adv due volte; (doubly) il doppio.

twiddle ['twidl] v (far) girare. **twiddle one's thumbs** tener le mani in mano.

twig [twig] n ramoscello m.

twilight ['twailait] n crepuscolo m, penombra f.

twin [twin] n, adj gemello, -a. **twin beds** letti gemelli m pl.

twine [twain] n spago m, corda f. v attorcigliare.

twinge [twindʒ] n spasimo m.

twinkle ['twinkl] v scintillare, luccicare; (wink) ammiccare, strizzare l'occhio. n luccichio m; strizzata d'occhio f.

twirl [twəːl] v girare rapidamente, piroettare.

twist [twist] v torcere, intrecciare; (sprain) slogarsi; alterare. n movimento rotatorio m; (curve) svolta f; (thread) filo ritorto m. **twister** n (cheat) imbroglione, -a m, f.

twit [twit] n (coll) scemo, -a m, f.

twitch [twitʃ] v (jerk) strappare, dare uno strattone; (body) storcere. n contorsione f, spasimo m. **twitching** adj convulsivo.

twitter ['twitə] v cinguettare. n cinguettio m.

two [tuː] nm, adj due. **in twos** due a due. **two-faced** adj falso. **two-piece** n (garment) duepezzi m invar. **two-seater** adj a due posti. **two-way** adj a doppio senso; (elec) bipolare.

tycoon [tai'kuːn] n magnate m.

type [taip] n tipo m, genere m; (print) carattere m. **typescript** n dattiloscritto m. **typesetter** n compositore m. **typewriter** n macchina da scrivere f. **typewritten** adj scritto a macchina, dattiloscritto. v dattilografare. **typical** adj tipico, caratteristico. **typify** v servire da esempio, simbolizzare. **typist** n dattilografo, -a m, f.

typhoid ['taifoid] n tifo m.

typhoon [tai'fuːn] n tifone m.

typographical [ˌtaipə'grafikl] adj tipografico.

tyrant ['taiərənt] n tiranno m. **tyrannical** adj tirannico. **tyranny** n tirannia f.

tyre or US **tire** ['taiə] n gomma f, copertone m.

U

ubiquitous [juː'bikwitəs] adj onnipresente.

udder ['ʌdə] n mammella f.

ugly ['ʌgli] adj (not pretty) brutto; (not agreeable) antipatico, sgradevole; (vicious) vile. **ugliness** n bruttezza f.

ulcer ['ʌlsə] n ulcera f.

ulterior [ʌl'tiəriə] adj ulteriore. **ulterior motive** secondo fine m.

ultimate ['ʌltimət] adj finale, definitivo, assoluto. **ultimately** adv alla fine. **ultimatum** n ultimatum m invar.

ultraviolet [ˌʌltrə'vaiələt] adj ultravioletto.

umbilical [ʌm'bilikəl] adj ombilicale.

umbrella [ʌm'brelə] n ombrello m.

umpire ['ʌmpaiə] n arbitro m. v arbitrare.

umpteen [ˈʌmp'tiːn] adj (coll) innumerevole. **umpteenth** adj ennesimo.

unable [ʌn'eibl] adj incapace. **be unable to** non potere.

unacceptable [ʌnək'septəbl] adj inaccettabile.

unaccompanied [ʌnə'kʌmpənid] adj solo, non accompagnato.

unaccountable [ʌnə'kauntəbl] adj inspiegabile.

unaccustomed [ʌnə'kʌstəmd] adj (not used to) poco abituato; (unusual) insolito.

unadulterated [ʌnə'dʌltəreitid] adj sincero.

unanimous [juː'nanıməs] adj unanime.

unapproachable [ʌnə'prəutʃəbl] adj inaccessibile.

unarmed [ʌn'aːmd] adj disarmato.

unashamed [ʌnə'ʃeimd] adj svergognato, senza vergogna.

unattainable [ʌnə'teinəbl] adj irraggiungibile.

unattractive [ʌnə'traktiv] adj poco attraente, antipatico.

unauthorized [ʌn'oːθəraizd] adj non autorizzato, illecito.

unavoidable [ʌnə'vɔidəbl] adj inevitabile.

unaware [ʌnə'weə] adj ignaro. **be unaware of** ignorare. **unawares** adv di sorpresa.

unbalanced [ʌn'balənst] adj squilibrato.

unbearable [ʌn'beərəbl] adj insopportabile.

unbelievable [ʌnbi'liːvəbl] adj incredibile.

*****unbend** [ʌn'bend] v raddrizzare. **unbending** adj rigido, inflessibile.

unbiased [ʌn'baiəst] adj imparziale.

unbreakable [ʌn'breikəbl] adj infrangibile.

unbridled [ʌn'braidld] adj sfrenato.

unbroken [ʌn'brəukn] adj intatto; ininterrotto; (not beaten) imbattuto.

unbutton [ʌn'bʌtn] v sbottonare.

uncalled-for [ʌn'kɔːldfɔː] adj immeritato, gratuito.

uncanny [ʌn'kani] adj strano, misterioso.

uncertain [ʌn'səːtn] adj incerto, dubbio. **uncertainty** n incertezza f.

unchanged [ʌn'tʃeindʒd] adj immutato, invariato.

uncharitable [ʌn'tʃaritəbl] adj aspro, crudele.

uncivilized [ʌn'sivilaizd] adj barbaro.

uncle ['ʌŋkl] n zio m.

uncomfortable [ʌn'kʌmfətəbl] adj scomodo. **feel uncomfortable** sentirsi a disagio.

uncommon [ʌn'komən] adj poco comune, insolito.

uncompromising [ʌn'komprəmaizıŋ] adj intrattabile, intransigente.

unconditional [ʌnkən'diʃənl] adj incondizionale, senza riserve, categorico.

unconscious [ʌnˈkɔnʃəs] adj (*unaware*) inconscio, inconsapevole; (*med*) privo di coscienza. n inconscio m. **become unconscious** svenire, perdere conoscenza. **be unconscious of** essere ignaro di, non accorgersi di. **unconsciously** adv senza rendersene conto.

uncontrollable [ʌnkənˈtrouləbl] adj incontrollabile, irreprimibile.

unconventional [ʌnkənˈvenʃənl] adj anticonformista; non convenzionale.

unconvincing [ʌnkənˈvinsiŋ] adj poco convincente. **unconvinced** adj non convinto, poco persuaso.

uncooked [ʌnˈkukt] adj crudo, non cotto.

uncouth [ʌnˈkuːθ] adj rozzo, grossolano.

uncover [ʌnˈkʌvə] v scoprire, rivelare, esporre.

uncut [ʌnˈkʌt] adj non tagliato, integro.

undecided [ʌndiˈsaidid] adj indeciso, irresoluto.

undeniable [ʌndiˈnaiəbl] adj innegabile, incontestabile.

under [ˈʌndə] adv, prep sotto, al di sotto (di). **be under the weather** sentirsi poco bene. **under age** minorenne. **under lock and key** sottochiave. **under one's breath** sottovoce. **under the circumstances** in queste circostanze.

undercharge [ʌndəˈtʃɑːdʒ] v far pagare meno del dovuto, non far pagare abbastanza.

underclothes [ˈʌndəklouðz] pl n biancheria intima f sing.

undercoat [ˈʌndəkout] n (*paint*) prima mano f.

undercover [ʌndəˈkʌvə] adj segreto.

*****undercut** [ʌndəˈkʌt] v (*comm*) offrire a un prezzo inferiore a.

underdeveloped [ʌndədiˈveləpt] adj sottosviluppato.

underdog [ˈʌndədog] n vittima f, persona che ha la peggio f.

underdone [ʌndəˈdʌn] adj (*meat*) al sangue.

underestimate [ʌndərˈestimeit] v sottovalutare.

underexpose [ʌndərikˈspouz] v sottoesporre.

underfoot [ʌndəˈfut] adv sotto i piedi.

*****undergo** [ʌndəˈgou] v subire, sopportare.

undergraduate [ʌndəˈgrædjuət] n studente universitario, studentessa universitaria m, f.

underground [ˈʌndəgraund;

adv ʌndəˈgraund] adj sotterraneo; (*secret*) segreto; clandestino. **underground passage** sottopassaggio m. adv sottoterra. n resistenza f; (*railway*) metropolitana f.

undergrowth [ˈʌndəgrouθ] n boscaglia f, macchia f.

underhand [ʌndəˈhand] adj clandestino; (*dubious*) losco.

*****underlie** [ʌndəˈlai] v sottostare a; essere alla base di.

underline [ʌndəˈlain] v sottolineare.

undermine [ʌndəˈmain] v minare, insidiare.

underneath [ʌndəˈniːθ] adv, prep sotto, al di sotto (di).

undernourished [ʌndəˈnʌriʃt] adj malnutrito.

underpants [ˈʌndəpants] pl n mutande f pl.

underpass [ˈʌndəpɑːs] n sottopassaggio m.

underprivileged [ʌndəˈprivilidʒd] adj non privilegiato, derelitto.

underrate [ʌndəˈreit] v sottovalutare.

understaffed [ʌndəˈstɑːft] adj a corto di personale or manodopera.

*****understand** [ʌndəˈstand] v capire, comprendere; (*realize*) rendersi conto; (*believe*) credere. **understandable** adj comprensibile.

understanding [ʌndəˈstandiŋ] n comprensione f; (*knowledge*) conoscenza f; (*agreement*) accordo m. **on the understanding that** a condizione or premesso che. adj comprensivo, indulgente.

understate [ʌndəˈsteit] v minimizzare, attenuare. **understatement** n atto del minimizzare m.

understudy [ˈʌndəstʌdi] v sostituire. n sostituto, -a m, f, attore, -trice supplente m, f.

*****undertake** [ʌndəˈteik] v intraprendere; (*accept obligation*) impegnarsi; (*warrant*) garantire. **undertaker** n imprenditore di pompe funebri m, becchino m. **undertaking** n impresa f; (*pledge*) impegno m, promessa f.

undertone [ˈʌndətoun] n fondo m, senso occulto m. **in an undertone** a bassa voce.

underwear [ˈʌndəwea] n biancheria or maglieria intima f.

underwater [ˈʌndəwɔːtə; adv ʌndəˈwɔːtə] adj subacqueo. adv sott'acqua.

underweight [ʌndəˈweit] adj di peso insufficiente.

underworld [ˈʌndəwəːld] n (myth) inferno m; (crime) malavita f.

✝underwrite [ˌʌndəˈrait] v sottoscrivere; (support) sostenere; (finance) garantire; (insurance) riassicurare. **underwriter** n riassicuratore m, garante di una emissione m.

undesirable [ˌʌndiˈzaiərəbl] adj indesiderabile, sgradito.

undignified [ʌnˈdignifaid] adj poco dignitoso.

✝undo [ʌnˈduː] v disfare, sciogliere, annullare; rovinare. **leave undone** tralasciare di fare. **undoing** n rovina f.

undoubted [ʌnˈdautid] adj indubbio, incontestato, certo.

undress [ʌnˈdres] v svestire, spogliarsi.

undue [ʌnˈdjuː] adj indebito, eccessivo.

undulate [ˈʌndjuleit] v ondeggiare.

unearth [ʌnˈəːθ] v scoprire, dissotterrare. **unearthly** adj (ghostly) spettrale; (coll) assurdo.

uneasy [ʌnˈiːzi] adj turbato, imbarazzato, a disagio.

uneducated [ʌnˈedjukeitid] adj ignorante, senza coltura.

unemployed [ˌʌnemˈploid] adj disoccupato. **the unemployed** i disoccupati m pl. **unemployment** n disoccupazione f.

unending [ʌnˈendiŋ] adj interminabile, che non finisce più.

unequal [ʌnˈiːkwəl] dj disuguale; (unevenly matched) impari. **unequal to** non all'altezza di. **unequalled** adj senza pari.

uneven [ʌnˈiːvn] adj (not level) irregolare; ineguale; (odd) dispari.

unexpected [ˌʌneksˈpektid] adj inatteso.

unfailing [ʌnˈfeiliŋ] adj infallibile, immancabile.

unfair [ʌnˈfeə] adj ingiusto; (dishonest) sleale; (sport) non sportivo. **unfairness** n ingiustizia f; slealtà f.

unfaithful [ʌnˈfeiθfəl] adj infedele, disonesto; inesatto. **unfaithfulness** n infedeltà f.

unfamiliar [ˌʌnfəˈmiljə] adj (not conversant) poco familiare or pratico; (not well-known) poco conosciuto or noto.

unfasten [ʌnˈfaːsn] v slegare, sciogliere, disfare.

unfavourable [ʌnˈfeivərəbl] adj sfavorevole.

unfit [ʌnˈfit] adj (unsuitable) inadatto, non idoneo; (unable) inabile; (unwell) indisposto.

unfold [ʌnˈfould] v (open out) schiudere; (develop) sviluppare; (reveal) rivelare.

unforeseen [ˌʌnfɔːˈsiːn] adj imprevisto. **unforeseeable** adj imprevedibile.

unfortunate [ʌnˈfɔːtʃənət] adj sfortunato, disgraziato; (unsuitable, unhappy) infelice. **unfortunately** adv purtroppo.

unfriendly [ʌnˈfrendli] adj freddo; ostile.

unfurnished [ʌnˈfəːniʃd] adj non ammobiliato.

ungrateful [ʌnˈgreitful] adj ingrato.

unguarded [ʌnˈgaːdid] adj incustodito, indifeso; imprudente, indiscreto.

unhappy [ʌnˈhapi] adj infelice, triste; inopportuno; (infelicitous) poco felice. **unhappily** adv sfortunatamente. **unhappiness** n infelicità f, tristezza f.

unhealthy [ʌnˈhelθi] adj malsano; (morbid) morboso.

unhurried [ʌnˈhʌrid] adj calmo, senza fretta.

unhurt [ʌnˈhəːt] adj incolume.

unicorn [ˈjuːnikɔːn] n unicorno m.

uniform [ˈjuːnifɔːm] adj uniforme, costante. n uniforme f, divisa f. **uniformity** n uniformità f.

unify [ˈjuːnifai] v unificare. **unification** n unificazione f.

unilateral [ˌjuːniˈlatərəl] adj unilaterale.

unimaginable [ˌʌniˈmadʒinəbl] adj inconcepibile. **unimaginative** adj poco immaginativo.

unimpaired [ˌʌnimˈpeəd] adj intatto, in pieno vigore.

uninhabited [ˌʌninˈhabitid] adj disabitato, deserto. **uninhabitable** adj inabitabile.

unintentional [ˌʌninˈtenʃənl] adj involontario.

uninterested [ʌnˈintristid] adj disinteressato. **uninteresting** adj poco interessante, noioso.

union [ˈjuːnjən] n unione f, unificazione f; associazione f; (trade) sindacato f; (tech) collegamento m.

unique [juːˈniːk] adj unico, solo.

unison [ˈjuːnisn] n unisono m. **in unison** all'unisono.

unit [ˈjuːnit] n unità f; (whole) insieme m.

unite [juːˈnait] v unire, combinare, congiungere. **united** adj unito. **United Kingdom** Regno Unito m. **United Nations** Nazioni Unite f pl. **United States of America** Stati Uniti d'America m pl.

unity ['juːniti] *n* unità *f.*

universe ('juːnivəːs] *n* universo *m.* **universal** *adj* universale.

university [juːni'vəːsəti] *n* università *f. adj* universitario.

unjust [ʌn'dʒʌst] *adj* ingiusto.

unkempt [ʌn'kempt] *adj* spettinato; (*untidy*) sciatto.

unkind [ʌn'kaind] *adj* poco gentile; crudele.

unknown [ʌn'noun] *adj* sconosciuto, ignoto. *n* ignoto *m*; (*math*) incognita *f.* **unknown to** all'insaputa di.

unlawful [ʌn'lɔːfəl] *adj* illegale; illecito.

unless [ʌn'les] *conj* a meno che non, se non.

unlike [ʌn'laik] *adj* dissimile or diverso (da). **be unlike** non rassomigliarsi. **not unlike** assai simile a. *prep* a differenza di, all'inverso di.

unlikely [ʌn'laikli] *adj* improbabile, inverosimile.

unload [ʌn'loud] *v* scaricare, liberarsi di.

unlock [ʌn'lok] *v* aprire.

unlucky [ʌn'lʌki] *adj* sfortunato, disgraziato.

unmarried [ʌn'marid] *adj* non sposato; (*bachelor*) celibe; (*spinster*) nubile. **unmarried mother** ragazza madre *f.*

unmistakable [ʌnmi'steikəbl] *adj* inequivocabile, manifesto.

unnatural [ʌn'natʃərəl] *adj* contro natura; (*lacking natural feelings*) snaturato, disumano; anormale; forzato.

unnecessary [ʌn'nesəsəri] *adj* inutile, non necessario.

unnoticed [ʌn'noutist] *adj* inavvertito.

unobtainable [ʌnəb'teinəbl] *adj* irreperibile.

unoccupied [ʌn'okjupaid] *adj* libero, vacante, vuoto.

unofficial [ʌnə'fiʃəl] *adj* ufficioso.

unopposed [ʌnə'pouzd] *adj* incontrastato.

unpack [ʌn'pak] *v* (*case*) disfare (le valige); (*contents*) disimballare.

unpaid [ʌn'peid] *adj* non retribuito or rimunerato; (*debt, etc.*) non saldato or pagato.

unpardonable [ʌn'paːdnəbl] *adj* imperdonabile.

unpleasant [ʌn'pleznt] *adj* spiacevole, sgradevole, antipatico. **unpleasantness** *n* spiacevolezza *f*; (*disagreement*) dissenso *m.*

unpopular [ʌn'popjulə] *adj* impopolare. **be unpopular with** esser malvisto da.

unprecedented [ʌn'presidentid] *adj* inaudito, senza precedenti.

unpredictable [ʌnprə'diktəbl] *adj* imprevedibile.

unqualified [ʌn'kwolifaid] *adj* non qualificato; senza diploma; categorico, assoluto.

unquestionable [ʌn'kwestʃənəbl] *adj* indiscutibile, fuori questione. **unquestioned** *adj* indiscusso, incontestato.

unravel [ʌn'ravəl] *v* sciogliere, sbrogliare; (*clear*) chiarire.

unreadable [ʌn'riːdəbl] *adj* illeggibile; (*tedious*) noioso.

unreal [ʌn'riəl] *adj* irreale.

unreasonable [ʌn'riːzənəbl] *adj* irragionevole.

unrecognizable [ʌn,rekəg'naizəbl] *adj* irriconoscibile.

unrelenting [ʌnri'lentiŋ] *adj* inesorabile; (*dogged*) accanito.

unreliable [ʌnri'laiəbl] *adj* da non fidarsene; (*news*) inattendibile.

unrepentant [ʌnri'pentənt] *adj* impenitente.

unrest [ʌn'rest] *n* agitazione *f*, fermento *m.*

unripe [ʌn'raip] *adj* immaturo, acerbo.

unruly [ʌn'ruːli] *adj* indisciplinato, turbolento.

unsafe [ʌn'seif] *adj* malsicuro, pericoloso.

unsatisfactory [ʌnsatis'faktəri] *adj* poco soddisfacente, che lascia desiderare.

unsavoury [ʌn'seivəri] *adj* sgradevole; (*coll*) disgustoso, poco pulito.

unscrew [ʌn'skruː] *v* svitare.

unscrupulous [ʌn'skruːpjuləs] *adj* senza scrupoli.

unselfish [ʌn'selfiʃ] *adj* altruistico.

unsettle [ʌn'setl] *v* turbare; disturbare; sconcertare. **unsettled** *adj* (*weather*) variabile; (*account*) non saldato; (*not fixed*) non sistemato; (*uncertain*) incerto.

unsightly [ʌn'saitli] *adj* brutto, spiacevole a vedersi.

unskilled [ʌn'skild] *adj* inesperto, non qualificato. **unskilled worker** *n* manovale *m.*

unsociable [ʌn'souʃəbl] *adj* poco socievole, scontroso.

unsound [ʌn'saund] *adj* imperfetto, difettoso; erroneo; (*ill-founded*) poco profondo.

unspeakable [ʌnˈspiːkəbl] *adj* indicibile, inesprimibile; (*very bad*) inqualificabile.

update [ʌpˈdeit] *v* aggiornare.

unstable [ʌnˈsteibl] *adj* instabile.

unsteady [ʌnˈstedi] *adj* malfermo, instabile; incostante; (*wavering*) traballante, barcollante.

unsuccessful [ʌnsəkˈsesfəl] *adj* non or mal riuscito, sfortunato, fallito.

unsuitable [ʌnˈsuːtəbl] *adj* inadatto; inopportuno; sconveniente. **unsuited** *adj* non idoneo, disadatto, sconvenevole.

unsure [ʌnˈʃuə] *adj* malsicuro, incerto.

untangle [ʌnˈtæŋgl] *v* districare.

unthinkable [ʌnˈθiŋkəbl] *adj* inconcepibile, assurdo.

untidy [ʌnˈtaidi] *adj* disordinato, trascurato. **untidiness** *n* disordine *m*. trascuratezza *f*.

untie [ʌnˈtai] *v* sciogliere, slegare.

until [ənˈtil] *prep* fino a; (*before*) prima di. *conj* finchè, fino a quando; fino al momento in cui.

untimely [ʌnˈtaimli] *adj* inopportuno, intempestivo, prematuro.

untrue [ʌntəˈwɔːd] *adj* disgraziato.

untrue [ʌnˈtruː] *adj* non vero, falso, erroneo; infedele; inesatto.

unusual [ʌnˈjuːʒuəl] *adj* insolito, straordinario, eccezionale.

unwanted [ʌnˈwontid] *adj* indesiderato, superfluo.

unwelcome [ʌnˈwelkəm] *adj* (*person*) malaccolto; (*news, etc.*) sgradito, spiacevole.

unwell [ʌnˈwel] *adj* indisposto, ammalato.

unwieldy [ʌnˈwiːldi] *adj* ingombrante.

unwilling [ʌnˈwiliŋ] *adj* restio, riluttante; (*given reluctantly*) dato controvoglia.

unwind [ʌnˈwaind] *v* dipanare; (*relax*) rilassarsi.

unwise [ʌnˈwaiz] *adj* imprudente, insensato.

unwittingly [ʌnˈwitiŋli] *adv* senza saperlo, per inavvertenza.

unworthy [ʌnˈwɔːði] *adj* indegno. **unworthy** of che non merita.

unwrap [ʌnˈræp] *v* disfare.

up [ʌp] *adv* su; (*erect*) in piedi; (*out of bed*) alzato. **be up against** essere alle prese con. **be up to** (*capable of*) essere all'altezza di; (*mischief*) tramare. **up here** quassù. **up there** lassù. **up to** fino a. **what's up?** cosa succede? *prep* su, su per. *n* **ups and downs** alti e bassi *m pl*.

upbringing [ˈʌpbriŋiŋ] *n* educazione *f*.

update [ʌpˈdeit] *v* aggiornare.

upheaval [ʌpˈhiːvl] *n* commozione *f*, sconvolgimento *m*.

uphill [ʌpˈhil] *adv* in salita, in su. *adj* in salita, ascendente; difficile.

***uphold** [ʌpˈhould] *v* sostenere, appoggiare.

upholster [ʌpˈhoulstə] *v* tappezzare. **upholsterer** *n* tappezziere *m*. **upholstery** *n* tappezzeria *f*.

upkeep [ˈʌpkiːp] *n* mantenimento *m*, manutenzione *f*.

uplift [ʌpˈlift] *v* edificare, incoraggiare. *n* edificazione *f*, incoraggiamento *m*.

upon [əˈpon] *prep* su, sopra.

upper [ˈʌpə] *adj* superiore, più alto. **get the upper hand** prevalere. *n* tomaia *f*. **be on one's uppers** essere alle strette. **uppermost** *adj* il più alto.

upright [ˈʌprait] *adj* verticale, in piedi; (*righteous*) retto, onesto.

uprising [ˈʌpraiziŋ] *n* insurrezione *f*.

uproar [ˈʌprɔː] *n* tumulto, fracasso. **uproarious** *adj* tumultuoso, chiassoso. **uproariously funny** da crepar dal ridere.

uproot [ʌpˈruːt] *v* sradicare.

***upset** [ʌpˈset; *n* ˈʌpset] *v* sconvolgere, disturbare; (*knock over*) rovesciare. *adj* sconvolto, turbato; rovesciato. *n* disturbo *m*, contrattempo *m*. **upsetting** *adj* turbante, preoccupante.

upshot [ˈʌpʃot] *n* conclusione *f*, effetto *m*.

upside down [ʌpsaiˈdaun] *adv*, *adj* sottosopra, in disordine.

upstairs [ʌpˈsteəz] *adv* di sopra, al piano superiore.

upstream [ʌpˈstriːm] *adv* a monte, controcorrente.

uptight [ˈʌptait] *adj* (*coll*) nervoso.

up-to-date [ʌptəˈdeit] *adj* aggiornato, di moda.

upward [ˈʌpwəd] *adj* in salita, rivolto in alto. **upwards** *adv* in su, in alto; (*more*) più.

uranium [juˈreiniəm] *n* uranio *m*.

urban [ˈəːbən] *adj* urbano.

urchin [ˈəːtʃin] *n* monello, -a *m, f*.

urge [əːdʒ] *n* sprone *m*, impulso *m*. *v* esortare, spingere; insistere.

urgent [ˈəːdʒənt] *adj* urgente. **urgency** *n* urgenza *f*.

urine [ˈjuːrin] *n* orina *f*. **urinal** *n* orinatoio *m*. **urinary** *adj* urinario. **urinate** *v* orinare.

urn [əin] *n* urna *f*.

us [ʌs] *pron* ci, ce; *(after prep)* noi.

usage ['juːzidʒ] *n* uso *m*, usanza *f*.

use [juːs; *v* juːz] *n* uso *m*, impiego (*pl* -ghi) *m*; utilità *f*. **it's no use!** è inutile! **what's the use?** a cosa serve? *v* usare, impiegare, adoperare. **use up** consumare. **used** *adj* (*car*) d'occasione. **be used to** essere abituato a. **useful** *adj* utile. **useless** *adj* inutile.

usher ['ʌʃə] *n* usciere *m*. *v* **usher in** far entrare, introdurre. **usherette** *n* maschera *f*.

usual ['juːzuəl] *adj* solito, usuale. **as usual** come di solito. **usually** *adv* di solito, generalmente.

usurp [juˈzəːp] *v* usurpare.

utensil [juˈtensl] *n* utensile *m*, arnese *m*.

uterus ['juːtərəs] *n* utero *m*.

utility [juˈtiləti] *n* utilità *f*, vantaggio *m*; servizio pubblico *m*. **utilize** *v* utilizzare.

utmost ['ʌtmoust] *adj* massimo, supremo. *n* massimo *m*, possibile *m*. **do one's utmost** fare del proprio meglio.

utter¹ ['ʌtə] *v* (*say*) pronunciare, emettere.

utter² ['ʌtə] *adj* (*absolute*) completo, assoluto.

U-turn ['juːtəːn] *n* cambio di direzione *m*.

V

vacant ['veikənt] *adj* libero, vuoto; vacuo. **vacancy** *n* (*job*) posto libero *m*; (*room*) camera libera *f*. **vacate** *v* lasciar libero, sgomberare.

vaccine ['vaksiːn] *n* vaccino *m*. **vaccinate** *v* vaccinare. **vaccination** *n* vaccinazione *f*.

vacuum ['vakjum] *n* vuoto *m*. **vacuum cleaner** *n* aspirapolvere *m invar*. **vacuum flask** *n* thermos *m invar*.

vagina [vəˈdʒainə] *n* vagina *f*. **vaginal** *adj* vaginale.

vagrant ['veigrənt] *n, adj* vagabondo, -a. **vagrancy** *n* vagabondaggio *m*.

vague [veig] *adj* vago.

vain [vein] *adj* (*worthless*) vano, inutile; (*conceited*) vanitoso. **in vain** invano.

valiant ['valiənt] *adj* valoroso.

valid ['valid] *adj* (*ticket, etc.*) valevole; (*sound*) valido. **validity** *n* validità *f*.

valley ['vali] *n* valle *f*.

value ['valjuː] *n* valore *m*. *v* valutare, stimare; dare importanza a. **valuable** *adj* prezioso, di valore. **valuables** *pl n* valori *m pl*, oggetti di valore *m pl*.

valve [valv] *n* valvola *f*.

vampire ['vampaiə] *n* vampiro *m*.

van¹ [van] *n* (*vehicle*) furgone *m*, camion *f*.

van² [van] *n* (*forefront*) avanguardia *f*.

vandal ['vandl] *n* vandalo *m*. **vandalism** *n* vandalismo *m*.

vanilla [vəˈnilə] *n* vaniglia *f*.

vanish ['vaniʃ] *v* sparire.

vanity ['vanəti] *n* vanità *f*.

vapour ['veipə] *n* vapore *m*. **vaporize** *v* vaporizzare.

variance ['veəriəns] *n* variazione *f*. **at variance** in disaccordo.

varicose veins ['varikous] *pl n* vene varicose *f pl*.

variety [vəˈraiəti] *n* varietà *f*, diversità *f*.

various ['veəriəs] *adj* vario, diverso.

varnish ['vaːniʃ] *n* vernice *f*, lacca *f*. *v* verniciare, laccare.

vary ['veəri] *v* variare; modificare; differire. **variant** *n* variante *f*. **variation** *n* variazione *f*. **varied** *adj* vario, svariato.

vase [vaːz] *n* vaso *m*.

vasectomy [vəˈsektəmi] *n* vasectomia *f*.

vast [vaːst] *adj* vasto, immenso.

vat [vat] *n* tino *m*.

Vatican ['vatikən] *n* Vaticano *m*. **Vatican City** la Città del Vaticano *f*.

vault¹ [voːlt] *n* volta *f*; (*cellar*) cantina *f*; (*safe*) camera di sicurezza *f*.

vault² [voːlt] *v* saltare, volteggiare. *n* salto *m*.

veal [viːl] *n* vitello *m*.

veer [viə] *v* virare, cambiar direzione.

vegetable ['vedʒtəbl] *n* ortaggio *m*, verdura *f*. *adj* vegetale; (*food*) di verdura. **vegetarian** *n, adj* vegetariano, -a. **vegetate** *v* vegetare. **vegetation** *n* vegetazione *f*.

vehement ['viːəmənt] *adj* violento, impetuoso.

vehicle ['viːəkl] *n* veicolo *m*; (*means*) mezzo *m*.

veil [veil] *n* velo *m*. *v* velare; (*hide*) nascondere.

vein [vein] *n* vena *f*; (*leaf, marking*) venatura *f*.

velocity [vəˈlosəti] *n* velocità *f*.

velvet ['velvit] *n* velluto *m*. **velvety** *adj* vellutato.

vending machine ['vendiŋ] n distributore automatico m.

veneer [və'niə] n piallaccio m; (superficial layer) vernice f.

venerate ['venəreit] v venerare. **venerable** adj venerabile.

venereal disease [və'niəriəl] n malattia venerea f.

Venetian blind [və'ni:ʃən] n veneziana f.

vengeance ['vendʒəns] n vendetta f. **with a vengeance** (unexpectedly) in modo insospettato; (with violence) violentemente.

Venice ['venis] n Venezia f.

venison ['venisn] n cacciagione f.

venom ['venəm] n veleno m; (spite) malignità f, cattiveria f. **venomous** adj velenoso; maligno, cattivo.

vent [vent] n (outlet) apertura f, sbocco m. **give vent to** sfogare. v esprimere, sfogare.

ventilate ['ventileit] v ventilare. **ventilation** n ventilazione f.

venture ['ventʃə] n impresa (rischiosa) f, avventura f. v azzardare, arrischiare.

venue ['venju:] n sede f; (place) posto m.

verb [və:b] n verbo m. **verbal** adj verbale. **verbatim** adj parola per parola.

verdict ['və:dikt] n verdetto m, giudizio m.

verge [və:dʒ] n orlo m, limite m. **on the verge of** sul punto di. v **verge on** tendere a, avvicinarsi a.

verify ['verifai] v verificare, confermare. **verification** n verifica f.

vermin ['və:min] pl n animali nocivi m pl, parassiti m pl; (scum) feccia f sing.

vermouth ['və:məθ] n vermut m invar.

vernacular [və'nakjulə] adj indigeno, dialettale; volgare. n **in the vernacular** in volgare.

versatile ['və:sətail] adj versatile, eclettico.

verse [və:s] n verso m; (poem) poesia f. **in verse** in versi.

version ['və:ʃən] n versione f.

versus ['və:səs] prep contro.

vertebra ['və:tibrə] n, pl -brae vertebra f. **vertebral** adj vertebrale. **vertebrate** nm, adj vertebrato.

vertical ['və:tikl] nf, adj verticale.

vertigo ['və:tigou] n vertigini f pl.

very ['veri] adv molto, assai. **the very next day** proprio il giorno dopo. adj proprio; esatto; (same) stesso; (mere) solo.

vessel ['vesl] n (container) recipiente m, vaso m; (ship) nave f, bastimento m.

vest [vest] n maglia f, maglietta f. v conferire, assegnare.

vestige ['vestidʒ] n vestigio m, traccia f.

vestry ['vestri] n sagrestia f.

vet [vet] (coll) v controllare, esaminare. n veterinario, -a m, f.

veteran ['vetərən] n veterano m; (mil) reduce m.

veterinary ['vetərinəri] adj veterinario. **veterinary surgeon** n veterinario, -a m, f.

veto ['vi:tou] n veto m.

vex [veks] v vessare, irritare. **vexed question** argomento dibattuto m.

via [vaiə] prep per, attraverso, tramite.

viable ['vaiəbl] adj vitale, capace a vivere; (workable) praticabile, possibile; (road) transitabile. **viability** n praticabilità f; (biol) vitalità f.

viaduct ['vaiədʌkt] n viadotto m.

vibrate [vai'breit] v (far) vibrare. **vibration** n vibrazione f.

vicar ['vikə] n parroco m, vicario m. **vicarage** n parrocchia f.

vicarious [vi'keəriəs] adj vicario.

vice¹ [vais] n (evil) vizio m; (fault) difetto m.

vice² [vais] n (tool) morsa f.

vice-chancellor [vais'tʃa:nsələ] n (university) rettore m.

vice-president [vais'prezidənt] n vice-presidente m.

vice versa [vaisi'və:sə] adv viceversa.

vicinity [vi'sinəti] n vicinanza f, prossimità f; (neighbourhood) vicinanze f pl, dintorni m pl.

vicious ['viʃəs] adj (bad) cattivo; (crude) crudele, maligno. **vicious circle** circolo vizioso m.

victim ['viktim] n vittima f. **fall victim to** essere preda a. **victimize** v perseguitare or punire ingiustamente; sacrificare.

victory ['viktəri] n vittoria f. **victorious** adj vittorioso.

video-tape ['vidiouteip] n video-cassetta f.

vie [vai] v gareggiare.

Vienna [vi'enə] n Vienna f.

view [vju:] n vista f; (scene, opinion) veduta f. **in view of** in vista di; (considering) dato; (on account of) grazie a, a causa di; **on view** esposto. **viewfinder** n mirino m. **viewpoint** n punto di vista m. **with a view to** allo scopo di. v vedere;

osservare; ispezionare. **viewer** *n* spettatore, -trice *m, f*; telespettatore, -trice *m, f*.

vigil ['vidʒil] *n* veglia *f*; vigilia *f*. **vigilant** *adj* vigile.

vigour ['vigə] *n* vigore *m*. **vigorous** *adj* vigoroso; robusto.

vile [vail] *adj* vile, spregevole.

villa ['vilə] *n* villa *f*.

village ['vilidʒ] *n* villaggio *m*, paese *m*. **villain** ['vilən] *n* farabutto *m*, villano *m*.

vindicate ['vindikeit] *v* rivendicare, giustificare; (*exonerate*) discolpare. **vindication** *n* rivendicazione *f*, giustificazione *f*; discolpa *f*.

vindictive [vin'diktiv] *adj* vendicativo, malevolo.

vine [vain] *n* vite *f*. **vineyard** *n* vigna *f*.

vinegar ['vinigə] *n* aceto *m*.

vintage ['vintidʒ] *n* vendemmia *f*; (*year*) annata *f*. *adj* (*wine*) pregiato *f*; (*car*) d'epoca.

vinyl ['vainil] *adj* vinilico.

viola [vi'oulə] *n* viola *f*.

violate ['vaiəleit] *v* violare, trasgredire. **violation** *n* violazione *f*, trasgressione *f*.

violence ['vaiələns] *n* violenza *f*. **violent** *adj* violento.

violet ['vaiəlit] *n* (*colour*) (color) viola *m*, violetto *m*; (*flower*) viola *f*, violetta *f*. *adj* viola *invar*, violetto.

violin [vaiə'lin] *n* violino *m*. **violinist** *n* violinista *m, f*.

viper ['vaipə] *n* vipera *f*.

virgin ['vəːdʒin] *nf, adj* vergine *f*. **virginity** *n* verginità *f*.

Virgo ['vəːgou] *n* Vergine *f*.

virile ['virail] *adj* virile. **virility** *n* virilità *f*.

virtual ['vəːtʃuəl] *adj* effettivo, in pratica.

virtue ['vəːtʃuː] *n* virtù *f*; (*admirable quality*) pregio *m*. **by virtue of** in virtù di, grazie a. **virtuoso** *n* virtuoso, -a *m, f*. **virtuous** *adj* virtuoso.

virulent ['virələnt] *adj* virulento. **virulence** *n* virulenza *f*.

virus ['vaiərəs] *n* virus *m invar*. **viral** *adj* virale.

visa ['viːzə] *n* visto *m*.

viscount ['vaikaunt] *n* visconte *m*. **viscountess** *n* viscontessa *f*.

viscous ['viskəs] *adj* viscoso. **viscosity** *n* viscosità *f*.

visible ['vizəbl] *adj* visibile; (*obvious*) evidente. **visibility** *n* visibilità *f*.

vision ['viʒən] *n* visione *f*; (*wisdom*) sagacia *f*. **visionary** *n, adj* visionario, -a.

visit ['vizit] *n* visita *f*. *v* visitare; (*person*) fare una visita a, andare a trovare; (*place*) andare a vedere; (*doctor*) consultare. **visitor** *n* visitatore, -trice *m, f*; (*guest*) ospite *m, f*.

visor ['vaizə] *n* visiera *f*.

visual ['viʒuəl] *adj* visivo, visuale. **visualize** *v* immaginare, concepire.

vital ['vaitl] *adj* vitale, essenziale; capitale. **vitality** *n* vitalità *f*.

vitamin ['vitəmin] *n* vitamina *f*.

vivacious [vi'veiʃəs] *adj* vivace, animato. **vivacity** *n* vivacità *f*.

vivid ['vivid] *adj* vivido, vivace.

vixen ['viksn] *n* volpe femmina *f*.

vocabulary [və'kabjuləri] *n* vocabolario *m*.

vocal ['voukəl] *adj* vocale; orale.

vocation [vou'keiʃən] *n* vocazione *f*; professione *f*; (*role*) funzione *f*. **vocational** *adj* vocazionale, professionale.

vociferous [və'sifərəs] *adj* rumoroso, chiassoso.

vodka ['vodkə] *n* vodka *f*.

voice [vois] *n* voce *f*. *v* esprimere, formulare, manifestare.

void [void] *nm, adj* vuoto. *v* vuotare; (*law*) annullare.

volatile ['volətail] *adj* (*chem*) volatile; capriccioso; (*unpredictable*) imprevedibile; esplosivo.

volcano [vol'keinou] *n* vulcano *m*. **volcanic** *adj* vulcanico.

volley ['voli] *n* raffica *f*, scarica *f*; (*tennis*) volata *f*. **volleyball** *n* pallavolo *f*.

volt [voult] *n* volt *m invar*. **voltage** *n* tensione *f*, voltaggio *m*.

volume ['voljum] *n* volume *m*. **voluminous** *adj* voluminoso.

volunteer [volən'tiə] *n* volontario, -a *m, f*. *v* offrirsi volontariamente; (*mil*) arruolarsi volontario; (*offer*) dare *or* offrire spontaneamente. **voluntary** *adj* volontario.

voluptuous [və'lʌptʃuəs] *adj* voluttuoso, sensuale.

vomit ['vomit] *v* vomitare. *n* vomito *m*.

voodoo ['vuːduː] *n* vudù *m*.

voracious [və'reiʃəs] *adj* vorace, insaziabile. **voracity** *n* voracità *f*.

vote [vout] *n* voto *m*, diritto di voto *m*, suffragio *m*. *v* votare, dare il proprio voto; (*agree generally*) convenire. **voter** *n* elettore, -trice *m, f*.

vouch [vautʃ] *v* **vouch for** garantire, attestare. **vouchsafe** *v* degnarsi di dare, concedere.

voucher ['vautʃə] *n* buono *m*, tagliando *m*.

vow [vau] *n* voto *m*, giuramento *m*. *v* giurare; fare voto di.

vowel ['vauəl] *n* vocale *f*.

voyage ['vɔiidʒ] *n* viaggio *m*, escursione *f*; (*crossing*) traversata *f*. *v* viaggiare; attraversare.

vulgar ['vʌlgə] *adj* volgare. **vulgarity** *n* volgarità *f*. **vulgarize** *v* divulgare, volgarizzare; (*debase*) degradare.

vulnerable ['vʌlnərəbl] *adj* vulnerabile.

vulture ['vʌltʃə] *n* avvoltoio *m*.

W

wad [wod] *n* tampone *m*; pacchetto *m*; (*roll*) rotolo *m*. **wadding** *n* (*padding*) imbottitura *f*.

waddle ['wodl] *v* camminare dondolandosi. *n* andatura dondolante *f*.

wade [weid] *v* guadare, avanzare con fatica. **wader** *n* (*bird*) trampoliere *m*.

wafer ['weifə] *n* cialda *f*, wafer *m invar*; (*church*) ostia *f*.

waft [woft] *v* diffondere. *n* zaffata *f*.

wag [wag] *v* agitare, scuotere; (*tail*) dimenare. **set tongues wagging** suscitare pettegolezzi.

wage [weidʒ] *n* salario *m*, paga *f*. *v* **wage war** muover guerra.

wager ['weidʒə] *n* scommessa *f*. *v* scommettere.

wagon ['wagən] *n* vagone *m*, carrozza *f*. **be on the wagon** (*coll*) essere astemio.

waif [weif] *n* senzatetto *m invar*; (*foundling*) trovatello, -a *m, f*.

wail [weil] *n* gemito *m*, lamento *m*. *v* gemere, emettere un lamento.

waist [weist] *n* vita *f*. **waistcoat** *n* gilè *m*. **waistline** *n* misura *or* circonferenza della vita *f*.

wait [weit] *v* aspettare, attendere; servire, sostare. *n* attesa *f*; sosta *f*. **lie in wait** stare in agguato. **waiter** *n* cameriere *m*. **waiting-room** *n* sala d'aspetto *f*. **waitress** *n* cameriera *f*.

waive [weiv] *v* rinunciare. **waiver** *n* rinuncia *f*; (*document*) atto di rinuncia *m*.

***wake¹** [weik] *v* *also* **wake up** svegliare, svegliarsi. *n* veglia *f*.

wake² [weik] *n* scia *f*. **in the wake of** subito dopo, nella scia di.

Wales [weilz] *n* Galles *m*.

walk [wɔːk] *v* camminare; (*go on foot*) andare a piedi. **walk in** entrare. **walk out on** piantare. **walkover** *n* vittoria incontestata *or* facile *f* in cammino *m*, passeggiata *f*; (*gait*) passo *m*. **walker** *n* camminatore, -trice *m, f*; (*sport*) podista *m, f*.

wall [wɔːl] *n* muro *m*; (*internal*) parete *f*. **wallpaper** *n* carta da parati *f*.

wallet ['wolit] *n* portafoglio *m*.

wallop ['woləp] (*coll*) *v* (*thrash*) battere, picchiare. *n* (*blow*) colpo violento *m*.

wallow ['wolou] *v* sguazzare.

walnut ['wɔːlnʌt] *n* (*tree*) noce *m*; (*fruit*) noce *f*.

walrus ['wɔːlrəs] *n* tricheco *m*. **walrus moustache** baffi spioventi *m pl*.

waltz [wɔːlts] *n* valzer *m invar*. *v* ballare il valzer. **waltz through** (*coll*) superare facilmente.

wand [wond] *n* bacchetta *f*.

wander ['wondə] *v* vagare, girare; (*stray*) allontanarsi, delirare.

wane [wein] *v* calare, declinare. *n* declino *m*; (*moon*) calare *m*.

wangle ['wangl] (*coll*) *n* trucco *m*, intrigo (*pl* -ghi) *m*. *v* procurare con astuzia.

want [wont] *v* volere, desiderare, aver voglia di; (*lack*) mancare di; (*ought*) dovere. *n* (*need*) bisogno *m*, esigenza *f*; (*deficiency*) mancanza *f*. **wanted** *adj* (*asked for*) richiesto; (*police*) ricercato; (*advertisement*) cercasi.

wanton ['wontən] *adj* deliberato, gratuito, sfrenato. *n* libertino *m*, sgualdrina *f*.

war [wɔː] *n* guerra *f*. **warfare** *n* guerra *f*. **warmonger** *n* guerrafondaio *m*. **wartime** *n* tempo di guerra *m*. *v* far guerra, combattere.

warble ['wɔːbl] *n* trillo *m*. *v* trillare. **warbler** *n* uccello canoro *m*.

ward [wɔːd] *n* (*district*) distretto *m*; (*hospital*) corsia *f*, padiglione *m*; (*law*) pupillo, -a *m, f*. *v* **ward off** parare, scansare.

warden ['wɔːdn] *n* guardiano, -a *m, f*, custode *m, f*.

warder ['wɔːdə] *n* carceriere, -a *m, f*.

wardrobe ['wɔɪdroub] *n* guardaroba *m invar*; (*cupboard*) armadio *m*.

warehouse ['weəhaus] *n* magazzino *m*.

warm [wɔɪm] *adj* caldo; cordiale, caloroso; (*lively*) animato; (*enthusiastic*) ardente. **be warm** aver caldo. **get warm** scaldarsi. *v* riscaldare. **warmth** *n* caldo *m*; calore *m*; animazione *f*; ardore *m*.

warn [wɔɪn] *v* mettere in guardia, ammonire; (*notify*) avvertire, preavvisare. **warning** *n* ammonimento *m*; preavviso *m*; allarme *m*.

warp [wɔɪp] *v* deformare. *n* ordito *m*.

warrant ['wɔrənt] *n* autorizzazione *f*, diritto *m*; (*law*) mandato *m*. *v* autorizzare; giustificare; garantire. **warranty** *n* (*comm*) garanzia *f*.

warren ['wɔrən] *n* (*rabbit*) garenna *f*.

warrior ['wɔriə] *n* guerriero *m*. **unknown warrior** *n* milite ignoto *m*.

Warsaw ['wɔɪsɔɪ] *n* Varsavia *f*.

wart [wɔɪt] *n* verruca *f*.

wary ['weəri] *adj* diffidente, cauto. **be wary of** diffidare di; guardarsi dal.

was [wɔz] *V* be.

wash [wɔʃ] *v* lavare. **wash away** portare via; (*obliterate*) cancellare. **wash-basin** *n* lavandino *m*. **wash-out** *n* (*slang*) fiasco *m*. **wash up** lavare i piatti. *n* lavata *f*; (*clothes, etc.*) bucato *m*; (*painting*) acquerello *m*, guazzo *m*. **have a wash** lavarsi. **washable** *adj* lavabile. **washing** *n* bucato *m*. **washing-machine** *n* lavatrice automatica *f*.

washer ['wɔʃə] *n* rondella *f*.

wasp [wɔsp] *n* vespa *f*.

waste [weist] *v* sprecare, sciupare. **waste away** deperire. *n* spreco *m*; (*rubbish*) immondizia *f*; (*scrap*) scarti *m pl*, cascami *m pl*; (*geog*) deserto *m*. **waste-paper basket** cestino da rifiuti *m*. **waste-pipe** *n* tubo di scarico *m*. **wasteful** *adj* dispendioso, sprecone.

watch [wɔtʃ] *v* guardare, osservare; (*as spectator*) assistere a; (*keep an eye on*) tener d'occhio. **watch out** stare attento. **watch over** sorvegliare. *n* (*time*) orologio *m*; osservazione *f*; guardia *f*, sorveglianza *f*. **keep watch** fare la guardia. **watch-dog** *n* cane da guardia *m*. **watchful** *adj* vigile.

water ['wɔɪtə] *n* acqua *f*. *v* annaffiare, irrigare. **water down** diluire; moderare, attenuare. **watery** *adj* acquoso; (*colour*) scialbo.

water-closet *n* gabinetto *m*.

water-colour *n* acquerello *m*.

watercress ['wɔɪtəkres] *n* crescione *m*.

waterfall ['wɔɪtəfɔɪl] *n* cascata *f*.

waterfront ['wɔɪtəfrʌnt] *n* lungomare *m*; (*wharf*) zona portuale *f*.

watering-can *n* annaffiatoio *m*.

water-lily *n* ninfea *f*.

waterlogged ['wɔɪtəlɔgd] *adj* saturo d'acqua; (*ground*) acquitrinoso.

water-melon *n* cocomero *m*.

water-mill *n* mulino ad acqua *m*.

water polo *n* pallanuoto *f*.

waterproof ['wɔɪtəpruf] *nm*, *adj* impermeabile. *v* impermeabilizzare.

watershed ['wɔɪtəʃed] *n* spartiacque *m invar*.

water-ski *n* sci nautico *m*. *v* fare dello sci nautico. **water-skiing** *n* sci nautico *m*.

watertight ['wɔɪtətait] *adj* stagno; (*irrefutable*) inconfutabile.

water-way *n* corso navigabile *m*.

waterworks ['wɔɪtəwɜɪks] *n* impianto idrico *m*. **turn on the waterworks** (*coll*) mettersi a piangere.

watt [wɔt] *n* watt *m invar*. **wattage** *n* wattaggio *m*.

wave [weiv] *n* onda *f*; (*surge*) ondata *f*; (*sign*) cenno *m*. **waveband** *n* gamma di lunghezze d'onda *f*. *v* sventolare, far segno con; (*hair*) ondulare. **wave aside** scartare. **wavy** *adj* (*hair*) ondulato; (*line*) ondeggiante.

waver ['weivə] *v* (*vacillate*) titubare, esitare.

wax[1] [waks] *n* cera *f*. *v* dar la cera a, lucidare.

wax[2] [waks] *v* (*increase*) crescere; (*become*) diventare.

way [wei] *n* (*manner*) modo *m*; (*respect*) rispetto *m*, particolare *m*; (*street*) strada *f*; passaggio *m*. **by the way** a proposito. **give way** cedere; (*traffic*) dare la precedenza. **in a way** in un certo modo. **make way for** fare largo a. **out of the way** (*place*) fuori strada; (*unusual*) fuori del comune. **way in** entrata *f*. **way out** uscita *f*.

*****waylay** [wei'lei] *v* abbordare; (*ambush*) tendere un agguato a.

wayward ['weiwəd] *adj* capriccioso, ribelle.

we [wiɪ] *pron* noi.

weak [wiːk] *adj* debole. **weaken** *v* indebolire. **weakling** *n* persona debole *f*. **weakness** *n* debolezza *f*; (*inclination*) debole *m*.

wealth [welθ] *n* ricchezza *f*; abbondanza *f*. **wealthy** *adj* ricco.

wean [wiːn] *v* svezzare.

weapon ['wepən] *n* arma *f*.

***wear** [weə] *v* portare, indossare; (*deteriorate*) consumare; (*last*) durare. **wear off** passare, dissiparsi. **wear out** consumare, indebolire; (*tire*) stancare. *n* (*use*) uso *m*; (*clothing*) abiti *m pl*, abbigliamento *m*; (*deterioration*) usura *f*.

weary ['wiəri] *adj* stanco, stufo. *v* stancare, stufare.

weasel ['wiːzl] *n* donnola *f*.

weather ['weðə] *n* tempo *m*. **weather-beaten** *adj* segnato dalle intemperie. **weather forecast** bollettino meteorologico *m*. *v* (*expose*) esporre all'aria, stagionare; (*overcome*) superare.

***weave** [wiːv] *v* tessere; (*devise*) ordire. *n* armatura *f*. **weaver** *n* tessitore *m*. **weaving** *n* tessitura *f*.

web [web] *n* tessuto *m*; (*spider*) ragnatela *f*. **webbed foot** piede palmato *m*.

wedding ['wediŋ] *n* matrimonio *m*; (*ceremony*) nozze *f pl*. **wedding-dress** *n* abito nuziale *m*. **wedding-ring** *n* fede *f*.

wedge [wedʒ] *n* cuneo *m*. *v* incuneare, incastrare.

Wednesday ['wenzdi] *n* mercoledì *m*.

weed [wiːd] *n* erbaccia *f*, malerba *f*. **weedkiller** *n* erbicida *m*. *v* diserbare, sarchiare. **weedy** *adj* coperto di erbacce; (*person*) sparuto.

week [wiːk] *n* settimana *f*. **weekday** *n* giorno feriale *or* lavorativo *m*. **weekend** *n* fine settimana *f*, week-end *m invar*.

weekly ['wiːkli] *nm, adj* settimanale. *adv* ogni settimana.

weep [wiːp] *v* piangere. **weeping** *n* pianto *m*. **weeping willow** salice piangente *m*. **weepy** *adj* (*coll*) lacrimoso, sentimentale.

weigh [wei] *v* pesare; (*have importance*) valere. **weigh anchor** salpare. **weighbridge** *n* pesa a ponte *f*, pesa pubblica *f*. **weigh up** soppesare, valutare. **weight** *n* peso *m*. **carry weight** aver peso. **lose weight** dimagrire. **put on weight** ingrassare. **weighty** *adj* pesante; importante.

weird [wiəd] *adj* strano, misterioso.

welcome ['welkəm] *interj* benvenuto! **welcome home!** ben tornato! *n* benvenuto

m, buona *or* cordiale accoglienza *f*. *adj* benvenuto, gradito. *v* accogliere; (*greet*) dare il benvenuto a; (*accept gladly*) gradire.

weld [weld] *v* saldare. *n* saldatura *f*.

welfare ['welfeə] *n* benessere *m*; assistenza sociale *f*. **welfare worker** *n* assistente sociale *m, f*.

well[1] [wel] *n* pozzo *m*; (*stairs*) tromba *f*.

well[2] [wel] *adv* bene. *interj* beh! allora! **as well** (*also*) anche.

well-behaved *adj* educato, beneducato.

well-being *n* benessere *m*, bene *m*.

well-bred *adj* educato, beneducato.

well-built *adj* ben costruito.

wellingtons ['weliŋtənz] *pl n* stivali impermeabili *m pl*, stivali di gomma *m pl*.

well-known *adj* ben noto.

well-meaning *adj* ben intenzionato. **well-meant** *adj* fatto a fin di bene.

well-off *adj* benestante, agiato.

well-paid *adj* ben pagato *or* retribuito.

well-read *adj* colto.

well-spoken *adj* che parla bene.

well-to-do *adj* benestante, abbiente.

well-worn *adj* logoro; (*hackneyed*) trito.

Welsh [welʃ] *n(m+f)*, *adj* gallese.

went [went] *V* go.

wept [wept] *V* weep.

were [wəː] *V* be.

west [west] *n* ovest *m*, occidente *m*. *adv also* **westward(s)** verso ovest, in direzione ovest.

western ['westən] *adj* occidentale, dell'ovest. *n* (*film*) western *m*.

wet [wet] *adj* bagnato, umido; (*rainy*) piovoso; (*paint, ink, etc*.) fresco. **wet blanket** guastafeste *m, f invar*. **wet through** bagnato fradicio; (*person*) bagnato fino alle ossa. *v* bagnare.

whack [wak] (*coll*) *n* colpo *m*; (*part*) fetta *f*. *v* colpire. **be whacked** essere sfinito.

whale [weil] *n* balena *f*. **have a whale of a time** (*coll*) divertirsi un mondo. **whaling** *n* caccia alla balena *f*.

wharf [woːf] *n* banchina *f*, scalo *m*.

what [wot] *pron* (che) cosa; (*relative*) quello che. *adj* che, quale. **what a ... !** che ... ! **what for?** perché? **what is the matter?** cosa c'è? cosa succede?

whatever [wot'evə] *pron* qualsiasi *or* qualunque cosa. *adj* qualsiasi, qualunque. **none whatever** nessuno. **nothing whatever** assolutamente nulla.

wheat [wiːt] n grano m, frumento m.

wheel [wiːl] n ruota f; (pottery) tornio m; (steering) volante m. **wheelbarrow** n carretta f, carriola f. **wheelchair** n sedia a rotelle f. v (make turn) far ruotare; (push) spingere.

wheeze [wiːz] v ansimare. n respiro affannoso m.

whelk [welk] n buccino m.

when [wen] adv quando. conj quando; (after which) appena; (whereas) mentre. **whenever** adv qualora, ogni volta che.

where [weə] conj, adv dove. **whereabouts** adv dove, da che parte. **whereas** conj mentre. **whereby** conj, adv onde, per cui. **whereupon** conj dopoché, dal momento che. **wherever** conj dovunque. **wherewithal** n necessario m.

whether [weðə] conj se.

which [witʃ] pron quale; (relative) il quale, la quale; che. adj quale. **which way?** da che parte?

whichever [witʃevə] adj qualunque, qualsiasi. pron quello che; (person) chiunque.

whiff [wif] n buffata f, zaffata f.

while [wail] conj mentre. n momento m. **a long while ago** molto tempo fa.

whim [wim] n capriccio m.

whimper [wimpə] v piagnucolare. n piagnucolio m.

whimsical [wimzikl] adj bizzarro, eccentrico.

whine [wain] v gemere; (complain) uggiolare. n uggiolio m, gemito m.

whip [wip] n frusta f. **whip-round** (coll) colletta f. v frustare; (cookery) frullare. **whipped cream** panna montata f.

whippet [wipit] n levriere inglese m.

whirl [wəil] v turbine m, giro vertiginoso m. **whirlpool** n vortice m. **whirlwind** n turbine m, tromba d'aria f. v girare (rapidamente).

whisk [wisk] v (dust) spolverare; (cookery) frullare. n piumino m; frullino m.

whisker [wiskə] n pelo m. **whiskers** pl n basette f pl; (moustache, cat) baffi m pl.

whisky [wiski] n whisky m invar.

whisper [wispə] v bisbigliare, mormorare. n bisbiglio m, mormorio m.

whist [wist] n whist m invar.

whistle [wisl] v fischiare; (tune) fischiettare. n (sound) fischio m; (instrument) fischietto m.

white [wait] n bianco m. adj bianco.

whitebait pl n bianchetti m pl. **whiten** v imbiancare.

whitewash [waitwoʃ] n intonaco m; (cover-up) riabilitazione f. v imbiancare, intonacare; (cover up) scolpare.

whiting [waitiŋ] n (fish) merlango m.

Whitsun [witsn] n Pentecoste f.

whizz [wiz] v (hum) sibilare; (move) guizzare.

who [huː] pron chi; (relative) che, il quale, la quale. **whoever** pron chiunque.

whole [houl] n totale m, insieme m. **as a whole** nell'insieme. **on the whole** tutto considerato, in fin dei conti. adj intero, tutto; intatto. **wholehearted** adj generoso. **wholemeal** adj integrale. **wholesale** adv all'ingrosso. **wholesaler** n grossista m, f. **wholesome** adj sano.

whom [huːm] pron che; (relative) il quale, la quale; (after prep) cui.

whooping cough [huːpiŋ] n pertosse f.

whore [hoː] n (derog) puttana f.

whose [huːz] pron di chi. adj di cui; (relative) il cui, la cui.

why [wai] adv, conj perché, per cui.

wick [wik] n stoppino m.

wicked [wikid] adj cattivo, malvagio. **wickedness** n cattiveria f, malvagità f.

wicker [wikə] n vimini m pl.

wicket [wikit] n porta f, sportello m. **a sticky wicket** una situazione scabrosa.

wide [waid] adj largo; (spacious) ampio. adv lontano. **open wide** v spalancare. **wide apart** spaziati. **wide awake** completamente sveglio; (alert) vigilante. **wide open** spalancato. **widespread** adj esteso, diffuso. **widen** v estendere, allargare.

widow [widou] n vedova f. **widower** n vedovo m.

width [widθ] n larghezza f; (cloth) altezza f.

wield [wiːld] v (weapon) brandire; (power) esercitare.

wife [waif] n moglie f.

wig [wig] n parrucca f.

wiggle [wigl] v dimenare.

wild [waild] adj selvatico; (animal, place) selvaggio; (unrestrained) feroce. **spread like wildfire** divampare velocemente. **wild with anger** fuori di sé dalla rabbia. **wild with joy** folle di gioia.

wilderness [wildənəs] n deserto m, solitudine f.

wilful [wilfəl] adj intenzionale; premeditato; ostinato.

will¹ [wil] *aux translated by future tense.*

will² [wil] *n* volontà *f*; *(law)* testamento *m*. **against one's will** malvolentieri, controvoglia. **at will** a piacere.

willing ['wiliŋ] *adj (disposed)* disposto; *(ready)* pronto, volonteroso. **willingness** *n* prontezza *f*; buona volontà *f*.

willow ['wilou] *n* salice *m*.

wilt [wilt] *v* appassire.

***win** [win] *v* vincere. **win back** riguadagnare. *n* vittoria *f*; *(games)* vincita *f*. **winner** *n* vincitore *m*.

wince [wins] *v* trasalire. *n* sussulto *m*, trasalimento *m*.

winch [wintʃ] *n* argano *m*. *v* **winch up** sollevare con l'argano.

wind¹ [wind] *n* vento *m*; *(breath)* fiato *m*. **get wind of** aver sentore di, fiutare. *v* sfiatare. **windy** *adj* esposto al vento.

***wind²** [waind] *v (twist)* serpeggiare. **wind up** *(roll up)* avvolgere; concludere; *(end up)* andare a finire; *(clock)* caricare; *(business)* liquidare.

wind-cheater *n* giacca a vento *f*.

windfall ['windfɔl] *n* frutto fatto cadere dal vento *m*; fortuna inaspettata *f*.

windlass ['windləs] *n* verricello *m*.

windmill ['wind,mil] *n* mulino a vento *m*.

window ['windou] *n* finestra *f*; *(train)* finestrino *m*; *(car)* cristallo *m*; *(cashier's)* sportello *m*. **French window** *n* portafinestra *f*. **window-dressing** *n* mostra *f*; *(show)* bella mostra *f*, inganno *m*. **window-sill** *n* davanzale *m*.

windpipe ['windpaip] *n* trachea *f*.

windshield ['windʃild] *n* parabrezza *m invar*. **windshield wiper** tergicristallo *m*.

windswept ['windswept] *adj* battuto dai venti.

wine [wain] *n* vino *m*. **wineglass** *n* bicchiere da vino *m*. **wine list** carta dei vini *f*.

wing [wiŋ] *n* ala *f*. **in the wings** *(theatre)* tra le quinte. **wingspan** *n* apertura alare *f*.

wink [wiŋk] *v* strizzare l'occhio, ammiccare. *n (signal)* cenno *m*; *(instant)* attimo *m*. **have forty winks** schiacciare un pisolino.

winkle ['wiŋkl] *n* chiocciola di mare *f*.

winter ['wintə] *n* inverno *m*. **wintry** *adj* invernale.

wipe [waip] *v* strofinare; *(dry)* asciugare. **wipe away** *or* **off** cancellare, allontanare. **wipe out** eliminare; *(debts, etc.)*

liquidare; *(annihilate)* annientare. **wiper** *n* strofinaccio *m*; *(windscreen)* tergicristallo *m*.

wire [waiə] *n* filo *m*; telegramma *m*. **wireless** *n* radio *f invar*. *v (elec)* montare; *(fasten)* legare con filo metallico; telegrafare. **wiry** *adj* secco, nerboruto.

wisdom ['wizdəm] *n* saggezza *f*. **wisdom tooth** *n* dente del giudizio *m*.

wise [waiz] *adj* saggio. **wisecrack** *n* battuta *f*.

wish [wiʃ] *n* desiderio *m*, voglia *f*. **wishes** *pl n* auguri *m pl*. *v* desiderare, volere; *(greeting)* augurare. **wishful thinking** pio desiderio *m*.

wisp [wisp] *n (hair)* ciocca *f*; *(smoke)* filo *m*.

wistful ['wistfəl] *adj* pensoso, malinconico.

wit [wit] *n* spirito *m*; arguzia *f*, intelligenza *f*; *(person)* uomo di spirito *m*. **be at one's wits' end** non saper più cosa fare. **live by one's wits** vivere di espedienti.

witch [witʃ] *n* strega *f*. **witchcraft** *n* stregoneria *f*. **witch-doctor** *n* stregone *m*.

with [wið] *prep* con; *(together with)* insieme a; *(because of)* per, a causa di.

***withdraw** [wið'drɔː] *v* ritirare; *(cash)* prelevare. **withdrawal** *n* ritiro *m*; *(mil)* ritirata *f*; prelevamento *m*.

wither ['wiðə] *v (lose freshness)* appassire; atrofizzare; *(decay)* avvizzire.

***withhold** [wið'hould] *v* trattenere; *(hide)* nascondere.

within [wi'ðin] *adv* dentro. *prep* entro, in. **within reach** a portata.

without [wi'ðaut] *prep* senza. *adv* fuori. **do without** fare a meno (di).

***withstand** [wið'stand] *v* resistere a.

witness ['witnis] *n (evidence)* testimonianza *f*; *(person)* testimone *m*, *f*. *v* testimoniare, attestare.

witty ['witi] *adj* spiritoso, arguto.

wizard ['wizəd] *n* mago *m*.

wobble ['wobl] *v* vacillare, traballare.

woke [wouk] *V* **wake¹**.

woken ['woukn] *V* **wake¹**.

wolf [wulf] *n* lupo *m*. **cry wolf** gridare al lupo. *v* divorare.

woman ['wumən] *n*, *pl* **women** donna *f*. **old woman** *n* vecchia *f*. **young woman** giovane *f*. **womanly** *adj* femminile.

womb [wuːm] *n* utero *m*.

won [wʌn] *V* win.

wonder ['wʌndə] *n* meraviglia *f*; miracolo *m. v* meravigliarsi; *(ask oneself)* domandarsi. **wonderful** *adj* meraviglioso.

wood [wud] *n (material)* legno *m*; *(as fuel)* legna *f*; *(forest)* bosco *m*. **wooden** *adj* di legno; rigido. **woody** *adj (wooded)* boscoso; *(tough)* legnoso.

woodcock ['wudkok] *n* beccaccia *f*.

woodcut ['wudkʌt] *n* silografia *f*, incisione su legno *f*.

woodland ['wudlənd] *n* boscaglia *f*.

woodpecker ['wudpekə] *n* picchio *m*.

wood-pigeon *n* colombaccio *m*.

wood-wind *n* strumenti a fiato *m pl*.

woodwork ['wudwətk] *n (carpentry)* lavoro in legno *m*, falegnameria *f*; *(wooden parts)* parti in legno *f pl*.

woodworm ['wudwətm] *n* tarlo *m*.

wool [wul] *n* lana *f*. **dyed in the wool** *adj* radicato, convinto. **woollen** *adj* di lana; *(industry)* laniero. **woolly** *adj* di lana, lanoso; confuso.

word [wətd] *n* parola *f*. **in other words** altrimenti detto. **word for word** alla lettera. *v* esprimere, redigere. **wording** *n* espressione *f*, formulazione *f*.

wore [wot] *V* wear.

work [wətk] *n* lavoro *m*; *(toil)* fatica *f*; *(product)* opera *f*. **workman** *n* operaio *m*. **works** *n (factory)* fabbrica *f*, stabilimento *m*. **workshop** *n* officina *f. v* lavorare; *(machine, etc.)* (far) funzionare. **work out** risolvere; risultare. **worker** *n* lavoratore, -trice *m, f*, operaio, -a *m, f*. **working** *n* operazione *f*, funzionamento *m*. **working class** classe operaia *f*. **working order** buon ordine *m*.

world [wətld] *n* mondo *m*. **world war** guerra mondiale *f*. **world-wide** *adj* mondiale, universale. **worldly** *adj* temporale; mondano.

worm [wətm] *n* verme *m. v* insinuarsi.

worn [wotn] *V* wear.

worry ['wʌri] *n* preoccupazione *f*, ansia *f. v* preoccupare; molestare. **worrying** *adj* preoccupante.

worse [wəts] *adj* peggio, peggiore. *nm, adv* peggio. **from bad to worse** di male in peggio. **get worse** peggiorare. **worsen** *v* peggiorare.

worship ['wətʃip] *n* adorazione *f*, omaggio *m*; *(rel)* culto *m*, servizio religioso *m. v* adorare; andare a messa, andare in chiesa.

worst [wətst] *adj* peggiore, il più brutto. *nm, adv* peggio.

worsted ['wustid] *nm, adj* pettinato.

worth [wətθ] *adj* **be worth** valere. **be worthless** non valere nulla. **be worthwhile** valere la pena. *n* merito *m*, valore *m*. **worthy** *adj* degno.

would [wud] *aux translated by conditional or imperfect tense.*

wound[1] [wuind] *n* ferita *f. v* ferire; offendere. **wounded** *adj* ferito.

wound[2] [waund] *V* wind[2].

wove [wouv] *V* weave.

woven ['wouvn] *V* weave.

wrangle ['rangl] *v* litigare, disputare. *n* lite *f*, disputa *f*.

wrap [rap] *v (envelop)* avvolgere; *(cover)* coprire; *(parcel)* incartare. *n (shawl)* scialle *m*; *(dressing-gown)* vestaglia *f*. **wrapper** *n* involucro *m*; *(book)* copertina *f*.

wreath [riːθ] *n* ghirlanda *f*, corona *f*. **wreathe** *v* incoronare. **wreathed in smiles** raggiante.

wreck [rek] *n (ship)* naufragio *m*; *(ruin)* relitto *m*, rovina *f. v* rovinare; demolire; naufragare. **wreckage** *n* rottami *m pl*.

wren [ren] *n* scricciolo *m*.

wrench [rentʃ] *v* storcere. **wrench open** forzare. *n (movement)* strappo *m*; *(injury)* storta *f*; *(spanner)* chiave *f*.

wrestle ['resl] *v* lottare. **wrestling** *n* lotta *f*.

wretch [retʃ] *n (unfortunate)* disgraziato, -a *m, f*; *(despicable)* incosciente *m, f*. **wretched** *adj* disgraziato, miserabile; *(pitiful)* pietoso.

wriggle ['rigl] *v* dimenarsi.

*****wring** [rin] *v* torcere. **wring out** strizzare. **wringer** *n* strizzatoio *m*. **wringing wet** fradicio.

wrinkle ['rinkl] *n* crespa *f*; *(face)* ruga *f. v* increspare; corrugare.

wrist [rist] *n* polso *m*.

writ [rit] *n* mandato *m*.

*****write** [rait] *v* scrivere. **write down** trascrivere, registrare. **write off** *(comm)* cancellare. **writer** *n* scrittore, -trice *m, f*. **writing** *n* calligrafia *f. n* scritti *m pl*. **writings** *pl n* scritti *m pl*.

writhe [raið] *v* contorcersi.

written ['ritn] *V* write.

wrong [ron] *adv* male. *adj (not moral)* peccato; *(incorrect)* sbagliato. **be wrong** *(person)* aver torto, sbagliarsi. *n* torto *m*; ingiustizia *f*; *(law)* violazione *f. v* far torto. a, maltrattare. **wrongful** *adj* ingiustificato.

wrote [rout] *V* **write**:

wrought iron [,rout'aiən] *n* ferro battuto *m*.

wrung [rʌŋ] *V* **wring**.

wry [rai] *adj* ironico, perverso; (*askance*) di sbieco.

X

xenophobia [zenə'foubiə] *n* xenofobia *f*. **xenophobic** *adj* xenofobo.

Xmas ['krisməs] *V* **Christmas**.

X-ray ['eksrei] *n* raggio X *m*; (*photo*) radiografia *f*. *v* radiografare.

xylophone ['zailəfoun] *n* xilofono *m*.

Y

yacht [jot] *n* panfilo *m*. **yachting** *n* velismo *m*.

yank [jaŋk] *v* (*coll*) dare uno strattone a, tirare con violenza.

yap [jap] *v* guaire. *n* guaito *m*.

yard [jaːd] *n* cortile *m*; (*site*) cantiere *m*; (*railway*) scalo merci *m*. **yardstick** *n* (*measure*) metro *m*; (*standard*) pietra di paragone *f*.

yarn [jaːn] *n* (*thread*) filo *m*, filato *m*; storia *f*.

yawn [joːn] *v* sbadigliare. *n* sbadiglio *m*.

year [jiə] *n* anno *m*, annata *f*. **year-book** *n* annuario *m*. **yearly** *adj* annuo, annuale.

yearn [jəːn] *v* languire. **yearn for** bramare, desiderare vivamente. **yearning** *n* vivo desiderio *m*, brama *f*.

yeast [jiːst] *n* lievito *m*.

yell [jel] *v* gridare, urlare. *n* grido *m*, urlo *m*.

yellow ['jelou] *adj* giallo; (*coll: cowardly*) vigliacco. *n* giallo *m*. *v* ingiallire. **yellowy** *adj* giallastro.

yelp [jelp] *v* (*dog*) uggiolare. **yelp with pain** gridare per il dolore. *n* uggiolio *m*; grido di dolore *m*.

yes [jes] *nm, adv* sì.

yesterday ['jestədi] *nm, adv* ieri.

yet [jət] *adv* ancora; (*already*) già. *conj* ma, tuttavia. **as yet** finora.

yew [juː] *n* tasso *m*.

yield [jiːld] *v* produrre; (*surrender*) cedere; (*profit, interest, etc.*) rendere, fruttare. *n* frutto *m*, prodotto *m*; (*tech*) resa *f*; (*finance*) reddito *m*; (*harvest*) raccolto *m*.

yoga ['jougə] *n* yoga *m*.

yoghurt ['jogət] *m* iogurt *m*.

yoke [jouk] *n* giogo *m*; (*dress*) carrè *m*.

yolk [jouk] *n* tuorlo *m*.

you [juː] *pron* (*subject: fam*) tú; (*subject: pl*) voi; (*subject: fml*) Lei; (*direct object*) ti, vi, la; (*indirect object*) ti *or* te, vi *or* ve, le; (*after prep*) te, voi, Lei. **if I were you** se fossi in te.

young [jʌŋ] *adj* giovane. **youngster** *n* (*child*) bambino, -a *m, f*; (*youth*) ragazzo, -a *m, f*.

your [joː] *adj* (*fam*) (il) tuo, (la) tua, (i) tuoi, (le) tue; (*pl*) (il) vostro, (la) vostra, (i) vostri, (le) vostre; (*fml*) (il) suo, (la) sua, (i) suoi, (le) sue.

yours [joːz] *pron* (*fam*) il tuo, la tua, i tuoi, le tue; (*pl*) il vostro, la vostra, i vostri, le vostre; (*fml*) il suo, la sua, i suoi, le sue.

yourself [jə'self] *pron* (*fam*) tu stesso; (*fml*) Lei stesso; (*reflexive*) ti, si; (*after prep*) te stesso, Lei stesso.

yourselves [jə'selvz] *pron* voi stessi; (*reflexive*) vi.

youth [juːθ] *n* gioventù *f*; (*boy*) giovane *m*.

Yugoslavia [juːgou'slaːvjə] *n* Iugoslavia *f*. **Yugoslav** *n, adj* iugoslavo, -a.

Z

zeal [ziːl] *n* zelo *m*. **zealous** *adj* zelante.

zebra ['zebrə] *n* zebra *f*. **zebra crossing** passaggio zebrato *m*.

zero ['ziərou] *n* zero *m*. *v* mettere a zero, azzerare.

zest [zest] *n* (*enjoyment*) gusto *m*, entusiasmo *m*; (*piquancy*) nota piccante *f*.

zigzag ['zigzag] *nm, adj* zigzag. *v* andare a zigzag, serpeggiare.

zinc [ziŋk] *n* zinco *m*.

zip [zip] *n* chiusura *or* cerniera lampo *f*. *v* **zip up** chiudere la (cerniera) lampo.

zodiac ['zoudiak] *n* zodiaco *m*.

zone [zoun] *n* zona *f*.

zoo [zuː] *n* giardino zoologico *m*, zoo *m invar*. **zoologist** *n* zoologo, -a *m, f.* **zoology** *n* zoologia *f.*

zoom [zuːm] *v* (*noise*) ronzare; (*aircraft*) salire in candela; (*film*) zumare. *n* ronzio *m*. **zoom lens** zoom *m invar*, obiettivo zoom *m*.

Italian–Inglese

A

a, ad [a, ad] *prep* to; (*stato in luogo*) at, in; (*prezzo, ora, età*) at. **a 10 metri da** 10 metres away from. **a due a due** two by two. **a le dozzina** by the dozen. **andare a casa** go home. **100 km all'ora** 100 km an hour.

abate [a'bate] *sm* abbot.

abbagliare [abba'λare] *v* dazzle.

abbaiare [abba'jare] *v* bark. **abbaiata** *sf* bark.

abbaino [abba'ino] *sm* attic, garret.

abbandonare [abbando'nare] *v* abandon, leave. **abbandonarsi a** (*darsi senza ritegno*) indulge in; give in to. **abbandono** *sm* neglect; desertion.

abbassare [abbas'sare] *v* lower, reduce. **abbasso** *avv* down. **abbasso ...** ! *inter* down with ... !

abbastanza [abbas'tantsa] *avv* enough.

abbattere [ab'battere] *v* knock down, fell; (*uccidere*) kill; (*deprimere*) depress. **abbattersi** *v* become disheartened.

abbazia [abba'tsia] *sf* abbey.

abbellire [abbel'lire] *v* embellish, adorn.

abbiente [ab'bjente] *agg* prosperous, well-to-do.

abbigliare [abbi'λare] *v* dress. **abbigliamento** *sm* clothes *pl*; (*modo*) dress.

abboccare [abbok'kare] *v* bite. **abboccato** *agg* (*vino*) medium sweet.

abbonarsi [abbo'narsi] *v* subscribe; take out a season ticket (for). **abbonamento** *sm* subscription; season ticket. **abbonato, -a** *sm, sf* subscriber; ticket-holder.

abbondare [abbon'dare] *v* be plentiful, abound. **abbondante** *agg* plentiful, abundant. **abbondanza** *sf* abundance, plenty.

abbordare [abbor'dare] *v* approach; (*introdurre*) broach.

abborracciare [abborrat'tʃare] *v* botch.

abbottonare [abbotto'nare] *v* button up.

abbozzare [abbot'tsare] *v* sketch, outline. **abbozzare un sorriso** give a faint smile. **abbozzo** *sm* sketch.

abbracciare [abbrat'tʃare] *v* embrace. **abbraccio** *sm* embrace, hug.

abbreviare [abbre'vjare] *v* abbreviate, shorten. **abbreviazione** *sf* abbreviation.

abbronzare [abbron'dzare] *v* tan. **abbronzatura** *sf* (sun-)tan.

abbrustolire [abbrusto'lire] *v* toast.

abbuono [ab'bwɔno] *sm* allowance; (*sport*) handicap.

abdicare [abdi'kare] *v* abdicate. **abdicazione** *sf* abdication.

aberrazione [aberra'tsjone] *sf* aberration.

abete [a'bete] *sm* fir(-tree). **abete rosso** spruce.

abietto [a'bjetto] *agg* abject. **abiezione** *sf* low spirits *pl*.

abile ['abile] *agg* clever, good (at); (*adatto*) suitable. **abilità** *sf* cleverness, skill; (*destrezza*) dexterity.

abilitare [abili'tare] *v* train; (*a una professione*) qualify. **abilitazione** *sf* qualification, diploma.

abisso [a'bisso] *sm* abyss.

abitare [abi'tare] *v* live. **abitante** *s(m+f)* inhabitant. **abitazione** *sf* home, dwelling.

abitato [abi'tato] *agg* inhabited. *sm* built-up area; (*villaggio*) hamlet.

abito ['abito] *sm* suit; dress; (*rel, abitudine*) habit. **abituale** *agg* customary, usual; habitual.

abituarsi [abitu'arsi] *v* **abituarsi a** get used to, become accustomed to.

abitudine [abi'tudine] *sf* habit, custom. **avere l'abitudine di** be in the habit of. **d'abitudine** as a rule.

abolire [abo'lire] *v* abolish. **abolizione** *sf* abolition.

abominevole [abomi'nevole] *agg* abominable.

aborigeno [abo'ridʒeno] *sm* aborigine. *agg* aboriginal.

aborrire [abor'rire] *v* abhor, loathe.

abortire [abor'tire] *v* miscarry; fail. **aborto** *sm* miscarriage. **aborto procurato** abortion.

abrasivo [abra'zivo] *sm, agg* abrasive. **abrasione** *sf* abrasion.

abside ['abside] *sf* apse.

abusare [abu'zare] *v* abuse. **abusivo** *agg* unauthorized, improper. **abuso** *sm* abuse.

accademia [akka'dɛmja] *sf* academy. **accademico** *sm, agg* academic.

*****accadere** [akka'dere] *v* happen. **accaduto** *sm* occurrence.

accampare [akkam'pare] *v* camp; (*avanzare*) put forward. **accampamento** *sm* camp.

accanirsi [akka'nirsi] *v* rage; persist. **accanito** *agg* (*ostinato*) dogged, stubborn; (*spietato*) merciless; (*violento*) fierce.

accanto [ak'kanto] *avv* nearby; (*casa*) next door. **accanto a** next to, near to, beside.

accantonare [akkanto'nare] *v* set aside.

accaparrare [akkapar'rare] *v* corner.

accappatoio [akkappa'tojo] *sm* bathrobe.

accarezzare [akkaret'tsare] *v* caress, stroke.

accasciare [akka'ʃare] *v* crush. **accasciarsi** *v* collapse.

accattone [akkat'tone], -a *sm, sf* scrounger.

accavallare [akkaval'lare] *v* (*sovrapporre*) overlap; (*accumulare*) pile up; (*incrociare*) cross.

accecare [attʃe'kare] *v* blind; block up. **accecante** *agg* blinding.

*****accedere** [at'tʃedere] *v* accede.

accelerare [attʃele'rare] *v* accelerate, speed up. **accelerato** *sm* local train. **acceleratore** *sm* accelerator. **accelerazione** *sf* acceleration.

*****accendere** [at'tʃɛndere] *v* light; (*luce, radio*) switch on, turn on. **accendino** *sm* (*fam*) lighter.

accennare [attʃen'nare] *v* make a sign, nod; refer to, hint at, touch on. **accenno** *sm* indication, mention.

accensione [attʃen'sjone] *sf* ignition.

accento [at'tʃento] *sm* accent, stress; tone. **accentare** *v* accent.

accentrare [attʃen'trare] *v* centralize, concentrate.

accentuare [attʃentu'are] *v* stress; (*aumentare*) heighten.

accerchiare [attʃer'kjare] *v* encircle. **accerchiamento** *sm* encirclement.

accertare [attʃer'tare] *v* verify, ascertain; (*dir*) establish. **accertamento** *sm* verification; establishment.

acceso [at'tʃezo] *agg* alight, switched on; (*colore*) vivid; (*eccitato*) burning.

accessibile [attʃes'sibile] *agg* (*luogo*) accessible; (*persona*) approachable.

accesso [at'tʃɛsso] *sm* access; (*med*) attack, fit.

accessorio [attʃes'sɔrjo] *agg* complementary, secondary. *sm* accessory, fitting.

accetta [at'tʃetta] *sf* hatchet.

accettare [attʃet'tare] *v* accept; admit. **accettabile** *agg* acceptable. **accettazione** *sf* acceptance; (*sala*) reception. **bene accetto** welcome. **male accetto** unwelcome.

acchiappare [akkjap'pare] *v* catch, grab (hold of), seize.

acciaio [at'tʃajo] *sm* steel. **acciaieria** *sf* steelworks.

accidente [attʃi'dɛnte] *sm* accident, mishap. **mandare un accidente a** (*fam*) curse. **non capire un accidente** not understand a thing. **accidenti!** *inter* my goodness! (*ira*) damn it! **accidenti a lui!** blast him! **accidentale** *agg* accidental.

acciglliarsi [attʃiʎ'ʎarsi] *v* frown. **accigliato** *agg* frowning.

*****accingersi** [at'tʃindʒersi] *v* **accingersi a** set about; be on the point of.

acciuffare [attʃuf'fare] *v* seize.

acciuga [at'tʃuga] *sf* anchovy.

acclamare [akkla'mare] *v* acclaim. **acclamazione** *sf* acclamation.

acclimatare [akklima'tare] *v* acclimatize.

*****accludere** [ak'kludere] *v* enclose.

accoccolarsi [akkokko'larsi] *v* squat.

*****accogliere** [ak'kɔʎʎere] *v* receive, accept, welcome; contain. **accoglienza** *sf* welcome, reception.

accomodare [akkomo'dare] *v* (*riparare*) mend, fix; (*mettere in ordine*) arrange, tidy; (*sistemare*) settle. **accomodarsi** *v* make oneself comfortable; take a seat; (*mettersi d'accordo*) agree. **accomodamento** *sm* agreement; compromise. **accomodante** *agg* accommodating.

accompagnare [akkompa'nare] v accompany. **accompagnatore, -trice** sm, sf escort; (musica) accompanist.

acconciare [akkon'tʃare] v prepare; arrange. **acconciarsi i capelli** do one's hair. **acconciatura** sf hair-style.

*****accondiscendere** [akkondi'ʃendere] v comply (with); condescend.

acconsentire [akkonsen'tire] v consent; acquiesce.

accoppare [akkop'pare] v (fam) kill, slaughter.

accorciare [akkor'tʃare] v shorten.

accordare [akkor'dare] v (uniformare) match; harmonize; (concedere) grant; (musica) tune. **accordarsi** v agree.

accordo [ak'kordo] sm agreement. **essere or andare d'accordo** agree. **d'accordo!** agreed!

*****accorgersi** [ak'kordʒersi] v notice. **accorgimento** sm expedient, stratagem.

*****accorrere** [ak'korrere] v come running, rush.

accorto [ak'korto] agg shrewd. **fare accorto** warn, caution. **stare accorto be** wary. **accortezza** sf shrewdness.

accostare [akkos'tare] v approach. **accosto** avv near.

accovacciarsi [akkovat'tʃarsi] v crouch, huddle.

accreditare [akkredi'tare] v accredit.

*****accrescere** [ak'kreʃere] v increase.

accumulare [akkumu'lare] v accumulate, heap. **accumulatore** sm accumulator.

accurato [akku'rato] agg accurate, thorough. **accuratezza** sf thoroughness, care.

accusare [akku'zare] v accuse; (notificare) acknowledge. **accusa** sf accusation, charge.

acerbo [a'tʃerbo] agg (immaturo) unripe; (aspro) sour.

acero ['atʃero] sm maple.

aceto [a'tʃeto] sm vinegar.

acido [a'tʃido] sm acid, sour. **acidità** sf acidity.

acne ['akne] sf acne.

acqua ['akkwa] sf water. **acqua ossigenata** hydrogen peroxide. **acqua in bocca!** keep mum!

acquaforte [akkwa'fɔrte] sf, pl **acqueforti** etching.

acquaio [ak'kwajo] sm kitchen sink.

acquaragia [akkwa'radʒa] sf turpentine, turps.

acquario [ak'kwarjo] sm aquarium.

acquatico [ak'kwatiko] agg aquatic, water.

acquavite [akkwa'vite] sf rough brandy.

acquazzone [akkwat'tsone] sm shower.

acquedotto [akkwe'dotto] sm aqueduct.

acquerello [akkwe'rello] sm water-colour.

acquistare [akkwis'tare] v buy; (ottenere) acquire; (guadagnare) gain. **acquistarsi fama di** gain the reputation of. **acquisto** sm purchase. **buon acquisto** bargain.

acquoso [ak'kwozo] agg watery; (terreno) marshy.

acre ['akre] agg acrid, sharp.

acrilico [a'kriliko] agg acrylic.

acrobata [a'krɔbata] s(m+f) acrobat. **acrobatico** agg acrobatic. **acrobazia** sf acrobatics pl.

aculeo [a'kuleo] sm sting.

acustica [a'kustika] sf acoustics pl. **acustico** agg acoustic. **apparecchio acustico** sm hearing-aid.

acuto [a'kuto] agg acute, intense; (aguzzo) pointed; (perspicace) shrewd. sm (musica) top note.

ad V a.

adagiarsi [ada'dʒarsi] v lie down.

adagio [a'dadʒo] avv slowly; gently. sm (musica) slow movement, adagio.

adattabile [adat'tabile] agg adaptable. **adattabilità** sf adaptability.

adattare [adat'tare] v adapt. **adattarsi** v adapt oneself, resign oneself. **adatto** agg suitable (for); (qualificato) suited (to).

addebitare [addebi'tare] v charge.

addensare [adden'sare] v thicken; (raccogliere) gather.

addestrare [addes'trare] v train. **addestramento** sm training.

addetto [ad'detto] agg employed (in); destined (for), intended (for); assigned. sm (pol) attaché.

addietro [ad'djetro] avv (fa) ago; (prima) before.

addio [ad'dio] inter goodbye, farewell. sm parting, farewell.

addirittura [addirit'tura] avv (persino) even; (direttamente) straight away; absolutely.

additare [addi'tare] v point at; (mostrare) point out, show.

additivo [addi'tivo] sm additive.

addizionare [additsjo'nare] v add up. **addizionale** agg additional. **addizione** sf addition.

addolcire [addol'tʃire] v sweeten; (*mitigare*) soften.

addolorare [addolo'rare] v distress.

addome [ad'dɔme] sm abdomen. **addominale** agg abdominal.

addomesticare [addomesti'kare] v tame.

addormentare [addormen'tare] v put to sleep. **addormentarsi** v fall asleep, go to sleep. **addormentato** agg sleeping; (*di mente*) dull; (*intorpidito*) numb.

addossare [addos'sare] v lean; (*mettere a carico*) saddle with. **addossarsi** v shoulder.

addosso [ad'dɔsso] avv, prep on. **d'addosso** off. **essere uno addosso all'altro** be crowded together.

***addurre** [ad'durre] v advance, put forward; produce.

adeguare [ade'gware] v adjust.

adempiere [a'dempjere] v also **adempire** carry out.

adenoidi [ade'nɔidi] sf pl adenoids pl.

aderire [ade'rire] v adhere, stick. **aderire a** comply with; accept; (*associarsi*) join. **aderente** agg close; (*abito*) close-fitting. **aderenza** sf adhesion. **aderenze** sf pl (*fam*) contacts pl.

adescare [ades'kare] v lure.

adesione [ade'zjone] sf adhesion; (*consenso*) assent; support. **adesivo** sm, agg adhesive.

adesso [a'dɛsso] avv now; nowadays; (*poco fa*) just (now); (*fra poco*) any minute (now). **per adesso** for the time being.

adiacente [adja'tʃente] agg adjacent. **adiacente a** next to.

adibire [adi'bire] v turn (into).

adirarsi [adi'rarsi] v get angry.

adito [a'dito] sm entry. **dare adito a** give rise to.

adocchiare [adok'kjare] v spot.

adolescente [adole'ʃente] agg adolescent. s(m+f) adolescent, teenager. **adolescenza** sf adolescence.

adombrare [adom'brare] v shade; (*celare*) hide. **adombrarsi** v take umbrage; (*cavalli*) shy.

adoperare [adope'rare] v use. **adoperarsi** v do one's best.

adorare [ado'rare] v adore, worship. **adorabile** agg adorable. **adoratore, -trice** sm, sf admirer. **adorazione** sf worship.

adornare [ador'nare] v adorn, decorate. **adorno** agg adorned, decked out.

adottare [adot'tare] v adopt, foster. **adottivo** agg adoptive. **adozione** sf adoption.

adrenalina [adrena'lina] sf adrenaline.

adulazione [adula'tsjone] sf flattery. **adulare** v flatter. **adulatore, -trice** sm, sf flatterer.

adulterare [adulte'rare] v adulterate; (*corrompere*) debase.

adultero [a'dultero], -a sm, sf adulterer. **-ess.** agg adulterous. **adulterio** sm adultery.

adulto [a'dulto], -a s, agg adult, grown-up.

adunare [adu'nare] v assemble. **adunanza** sf assembly. **adunata** sf meeting, gathering; (*mil*) parade.

aerare [ae'rare] v air, ventilate. **aeratore** sm ventilator.

aereo [a'ɛreo] agg aerial, air. sm aeroplane.

aerodinamica [aerodi'namika] sf aerodynamics. **aerodinamico** agg streamlined.

aerodromo [ae'rɔdromo] sm aerodrome.

aerolinea [aero'linea] sf airline.

aeronautica [aero'nautika] sf aeronautics; aviation; (*mil*) air-force. **aeronautico** agg aeronautical.

aeroplano [aero'plano] sm aeroplane, aircraft. **aeroplano a reazione** jet. **aeroplano di bombardamento** bomber. **aeroplano di combattimento** fighter.

aeroporto [aero'porto] sm airport.

aerosol [aero'sɔl] sm invar aerosol.

afa [a'fa] sf oppressive heat.

affabile [af'fabile] agg affable. **affabilità** sf affability.

affaccendarsi [affattʃen'darsi] v busy oneself. **affaccendato** agg busy.

affacciarsi [affat'tʃarsi] v show oneself, appear.

affamato [affa'mato] agg starving; (*bramoso*) eager (for). **affamare** v reduce to starvation.

affannare [affan'nare] v worry. **affannarsi** v do one's utmost. **affanno** sm (*difficoltà di respiro*) breathlessness; anxiety, worry. **affannoso** agg difficult.

affare [af'fare] sm affair, business; (*questione*) matter; (*fam*) thing; (*acquisto vantaggioso*) bargain. **affari** sm pl (*comm*) business sing. **affarista** s(m+f) speculator.

affascinare [affaʃi'nare] v fascinate, charm.

affastellare [affastel'lare] v tie in bundles; (*ammucchiare*) pile up; (*frasi, ecc.*) string together.

affaticare [affati'kare] v tire, strain.

affatto [af'fatto] *avv* quite; (*con negazione*) at all.

affermare [affer'mare] v affirm; assert. affermarsi v be successful.

afferrare [affer'rare] v seize, grab, clutch at.

affettare¹ [affet'tare] v affect, pretend. affettato *agg* affected; mannered.

affettare² [affet'tare] v slice. affettato *sm* sliced salami *or* ham.

affetto¹ [af'fetto] *sm* affection, feeling. affettuoso *agg* affectionate, loving.

affetto² [af'fetto] *agg* affected (by); (*med*) suffering (from).

affezionarsi [affetsjo'narsi] v become fond (of). affezionato *agg* fond, devoted. affezione *sf* fondness, affection; (*med*) disorder.

affibbiare [affib'bjare] v saddle with.

affidare [affi'dare] v entrust. affidare alla memoria commit to memory. affidamento *sm* trust. dare affidamento inspire confidence. fare affidamento su rely on.

*affiggere [af'fiddʒere] v affix; (*manifesto*) put up.

affilare [affi'lare] v sharpen.

affiliare [affi'ljare] v (*dir*) foster; (*iscrivere*) enrol.

affinché [affin'ke] *cong* so that, in order that.

affinità [affini'ta] *sf* affinity. affine *agg* related. affini *sm pl* in-laws *pl*.

affissione [affis'sjone] *sf* bill-posting.

affisso [af'fisso] *agg* exhibited. *sm* poster, bill.

affittare [affit'tare] v rent, lease; (*dare in affitto*) let. affitto *sm* (*prezzo*) rent; (*locazione*) lease.

*affliggere [af'fliddʒere] v afflict. affliggersi v grieve, worry. afflizione *sf* affliction.

*affluire [afflu'ire] v flow; (*gente*) flock. affluente *sm* (*geog*) tributary. affluenza *sf* flow; (*di gente*) influx. afflusso *sm* flow.

affogare [affo'gare] v drown. uovo affogato *sm* poached egg.

affollare [affol'lare] v crowd. affollamento *sm* (*atto*) crowding; (*folla*) crowd.

affondare [affon'dare] v sink.

affrancare [affran'kare] v stamp. affrancatura *sf* postage.

affranto [af'franto] *agg* distraught.

affresco [af'fresko] *sm* fresco.

affrettare [affret'tare] v hurry, speed up.

affrontare [affron'tare] v face. affronto *sm* affront.

affumicare [affumi'kare] v (*annerire*) blacken (with smoke); (*gastr*) smoke; (*snidare*) smoke out. affumicato *agg* smoked.

afoso [a'fozo] *agg* sultry.

Africa ['afrika] *sf* Africa. africano, -a *s, agg* African.

agenda [a'dʒɛnda] *sf* diary.

agente [a'dʒɛnte] *sm* agent. agente delle tasse tax inspector. agente di polizia police officer.

agenzia [adʒen'tsia] *sf* agency.

agevole [a'dʒevole] *agg* easy. agevolare v facilitate. agevolazione *sf* concession.

agganciare [aggan'tʃare] v fasten, hook up.

aggettivo [addʒet'tivo] *sm* adjective.

agghiacciare [aggjat'tʃare] v freeze. far agghiacciare il sangue make one's blood run cold.

aggiornare [addʒor'nare] v bring up to date; (*rinviare*) postpone. aggiornato *agg* up-to-date.

aggirarsi [addʒi'rarsi] v aggirarsi su (*approssimarsi*) be about or around.

aggiudicare [addʒudi'kare] v award.

*aggiungere [ad'dʒundʒere] v add. aggiungersi v join. aggiunta *sf* addition. aggiuntivo *agg* additional. aggiunto *sm* assistant.

aggiustare [addʒus'tare] v repair, adjust; (*ordinare*) tidy, arrange.

aggrappare [aggrap'pare] v clutch. aggrapparsi a cling to.

aggravare [aggra'vare] v make worse. aggravarsi v deteriorate.

aggredire [aggre'dire] v attack.

aggregare [aggre'gare] v aggregate. aggregato *sm*, *agg* aggregate.

aggressione [aggres'sjone] *sf* aggression, attack. aggressivo *agg* aggressive. aggressore *sm* aggressor, assailant.

aggrottare [aggrot'tare] v aggrottare le ciglia frown, knit one's brows.

aggruppare [aggrup'pare] v group.

agguato [ag'gwato] *sm* ambush, trap. stare in agguato lie in wait.

agiato [a'dʒato] *agg* well-off. agiatezza *sf* prosperity.

agile ['adʒile] *agg* agile, nimble. **agilità** *sf* agility.

agio ['adʒo] *sm* comfort, ease; (*di tempo*) leisure; (*mec*) play. **sentire a proprio agio** feel at ease.

agire [a'dʒire] *v* act; (*comportarsi*) behave; (*dir*) take legal action.

agitare [adʒi'tare] *v* wave, shake; (*incitare*) stir. **agitato** *agg* agitated, disturbed. **agitatore, -trice** *sm, sf* agitator.

agli ['aʎi] *prep* + *art* a **gli**.

aglio ['aʎo] *sm* garlic.

agnello [a'nɛllo] *sm* lamb.

agnostico [a'nɔstiko], **-a** *s, agg* agnostic.

ago ['ago] *sm* needle. **ago da calza** knitting-needle. **lavoro ad ago** *sm* needlework.

agonia [ago'nia] *sf* agony. **agonizzare** *v* agonize, suffer anguish.

agonismo [ago'nizmo] *sm* fighting spirit.

agopuntura [agopun'tura] *sf* acupuncture.

agosto [a'gosto] *sm* August.

agrario [a'grarjo] *sm* land-owner. *agg* agrarian, agricultural. **riforma agraria** *sf* land reform. **agraria** *sf* agricultural science.

agricoltore [agrikol'tore] *sm* farmer.

agrifoglio [agri'foʎʎo] *sm* holly.

agro ['agro] *agg* sour, sharp, tart.

agrumi [a'grumi] *sm pl* citrus fruit *pl*.

aguzzare [agut'tsare] *v* sharpen.

ahimé [ai'mɛ] *inter* alas!

ai ['ai] *prep* + *art* a **i**.

Aia ['aja] *sf* **L'Aia** The Hague.

airone [ai'rone] *sm* heron.

aiuola [a'jwɔla] *sf* flower-bed.

aiutare [aju'tare] *v* help. **aiuto** *sm* help, aid; assistant.

aizzare [ait'tsare] *v* incite, provoke.

al [al] *prep* + *art* a **il**.

ala ['ala] *sf* wing; (*di cappello*) brim. **apertura alare** *sf* wing-span.

alabastro [ala'bastro] *sm* alabaster.

alano [a'lano] *sm* Great Dane.

alba ['alba] *sf* dawn. **albeggiare** *v* dawn.

albatro [al'batro] *sm* albatross.

albergare [alber'gare] *v* give hospitality to; shelter, harbour.

albergo [al'bɛrgo] *sm* hotel. **albergatore** *sm* innkeeper. **alberghiero** *agg* hotel.

albero [al'bɛro] *sm* tree; (*mar*) mast. **albero a camme** camshaft.

albicocca [albi'kɔkka] *sf* apricot. **albicocco** *sm* apricot tree.

albo ['albo] *sm* roll, register; (*tavola*) notice-board. .

album ['album] *sm* album.

alcali ['alkali] *sm* alkali. **alcalino** *agg* alkaline.

alchimia [alki'mia] *sf* alchemy. **alchimista** *sm* alchemist.

alcool ['alkool] *sm* alcohol.

alcolismo [alko(o)'lizmo] *sm* alcoholism. **alco(o)lici** *sm pl* alcoholic drinks *pl*, spirits *pl*. **alco(o)lico** *agg* alcoholic. **alco(o)lizzato, -a** *sm, sf* alcoholic.

alcunché [alkun'ke] *pron* something, anything.

alcuno [al'kuno] *agg* some, any, a few. *pron* anyone, anybody. **alcuni** *pron* some, a few.

alfabeto [alfa'bɛto] *sm* alphabet.

alfiere¹ [al'fjere] *sm* (*portabandiera*) standard-bearer; (*fig*) forerunner.

alfiere² [al'fjere] *sm* (*scacchi*) bishop.

alfine [al'fine] *avv* in the long run.

alga ['alga] *sf* alga.

algebra [al'dʒebra] *sf* algebra.

aliante [ali'ante] *sm* glider. **aliantista** *s(m + f)* glider-pilot.

alibi ['alibi] *sm* alibi.

alice [a'litʃe] *sf* anchovy.

alienare [alje'nare] *v* alienate. **alienato** *agg* alienated; (*pazzo*) insane. **alienazione** *sf* alienation; (*pazzia*) madness.

alieno [a'ljɛno] *agg* alien, foreign.

alimentare [alimen'tare] *agg* alimentary. *v* feed. **alimentari** *sm pl* foodstuffs *pl*. **alimentazione** *sf* feeding; (*tec*) feed. **alimenti** *sm pl* alimony *sing*. **alimento** *sm* food.

aliquota [a'likwota] *sf* quota, share.

aliscafo [alis'kafo] *sm* hydrofoil.

alito ['alito] *sm* breath.

all' [all] *prep* + *art* a **l'**.

alla ['alla] *prep* + *art* a **la**.

allacciare [allat'tʃare] *v* tie up, fasten; (*amicizia, relazioni*) establish; (*tec*) connect.

allagare [alla'gare] *v* flood. **allagamento** *sm* flooding.

allargare [allar'gare] *v* broaden; (*sport*) open up.

allarmare [allar'mare] *v* alarm. **allarme** *sm* alarm. **allarmista** *s(m + f)* scaremonger, alarmist. **allarmistico** *agg* alarmist.

alle ['alle] *prep* + *art* a **le**.

alleanza [alle'antsa] *sf* alliance. **alleare** *v* ally.

alleato [alle'ato], **-a** *agg* allied. *sm, sf* ally.

allegare¹ [alle'gare] *v* enclose.

allegare² [alle'gare] *v* advance, put forward.

alleggerire [alleddʒe'rire] *v* lighten; (*sofferenza*) ease.

allegoria [allego'ria] *sf* allegory. **allegorico** *agg* allegorical.

allegro [al'legro] *agg* cheerful, merry. *sm* (*musica*) fast movement, allegro. **allegria** *sf* gaiety, fun, cheerfulness.

allenare [alle'nare] *v* train, coach. **allenatore**, **-trice** *sm, sf* trainer, coach.

allentare [allen'tare] *v* loosen. **allentare il passo** slow down.

allergia [aller'dʒia] *sf* allergy. **allergico** *agg* allergic.

allestire [alles'tire] *v* prepare, get ready; (*teatro*) stage; (*arredare*) fit out, equip. **allestimento** *sm* preparation; staging; fitting out.

allettare [allet'tare] *v* entice, tempt. **allettante** *agg* enticing, tempting.

allevare [alle'vare] *v* (*bambini*) bring up; (*animali*) breed, keep; (*piante*) grow. **allevamento** *sm* bringing up; (*educazione*) upbringing; (*cavalli*) stud farm; (*cani*) kennels *pl*. **allevatore**, **-trice** *sm, sf* breeder.

alleviare [alle'vjare] *v* relieve, alleviate.

allibratore [allibra'tore] *sm* bookmaker.

allievo [al'ljevo], **-a** *sm, sf* pupil, student; (*apprendista*) trainee. **allievo ufficiale** (*mil*) cadet.

alligatore [alliga'tore] *sm* alligator.

allineare [alline'are] *v* line up; (*adeguare*) adjust. **allineamento** *sm* alignment, coming into line.

allo [al'lo] *prep + art* **a lo**.

allocco [al'lokko] *sm* tawny owl.

allodola [al'lɔdola] *sf* lark.

alloggiare [allod'dʒare] *v* house, put up; (*mil*) billet; (*prendere alloggio*) stay, lodge. **alloggio** *sm* accommodation; lodgings *pl*.

allontanare [allonta'nare] *v* move away; (*tener lontano*) keep away; (*pericolo, ecc.*) avert; (*licenziare*) dismiss. **allontanarsi** *v* go away, leave. **allontanamento** *sm* removal.

allora [al'lora] *avv* then; in that case. **da allora** since then, from that time on. **fino allora** until then.

alloro [al'lɔro] *sm* laurel; (*gastr*) bay leaf.

alluce [al'lutʃe] *sm* big toe.

allucinazione [allutʃina'tsjone] *sf* hallucination. **allucinare** *v* hallucinate; (*abbagliare*) dazzle.

*alludere [al'ludere] *v* allude, hint (at).

alluminio [allu'minjo] *sm* aluminium.

allungare [allun'gare] *v* lengthen, stretch; (*diluire*) water down; *pass.* **allungare gli orecchi** strain one's ears. **allungare il muso** (*fam*) make a long face. **allungare la strada** go the long way round. **allungamento** *sm* extension, lengthening.

allusione [allu'zjone] *sf* allusion.

almeno [al'meno] *avv* at least; if only.

Alpi [alpi] *sf pl* **le Alpi** the Alps *pl*. **alpino** *agg* alpine.

alpinismo [alpi'nizmo] *sm* mountaineering.

alquanto [al'kwanto] *pron, agg* some; a fair amount of. **alquanti** *pron, agg* several; a number of. *avv* somewhat, rather.

alt [alt] *sm, inter* stop.

altalena [alta'lena] *sf* (*sospesa*) swing; (*a bilico*) see-saw; (*fig*) ups and downs *pl*.

altare [al'tare] *sm* altar.

alterare [alte'rare] *v* alter, change; (*falsificare*) forge; (*svisare*) distort; (*turbare*) upset, make angry; (*andare a male*) go off, spoil. **alterazione** *sf* alteration; forgery; deterioration.

alternare [alter'nare] *v* alternate; (*agric*) rotate. **alternarsi** *v* take turns. **alternativa** *sf* alternative. **alternato** *agg* alternating. **alterno** *agg* alternating, alternate.

altero [al'tero] *agg* haughty.

altezza [al'tettsa] *sf* height; (*profondità*) depth; (*di tessuto*) width; (*quota*) altitude; nobility; (*titolo*) Highness. **essere all'altezza di** be equal to, be up to.

altitudine [alti'tudine] *sf* height, altitude.

alto ['alto] *agg* high; (*statura*) tall; (*tessuto*) wide; (*suono forte*) loud; (*suono acuto*) shrill; (*profondo*) deep; (*geog*) northern; (*nobile*) lofty; (*di grado elevato*) high-ranking. *avv* high. *sm* top, upper part. **alti e bassi** ups and downs *pl*.

altoforno [alto'forno] *sm, pl* **altiforni** blast furnace.

altoparlante [altopar'lante] *sm* loudspeaker.

altopiano [alto'pjano] *sm, pl* **altipiani** plateau.

altrettanto [altret'tanto] *pron, agg* as much *or* many (again); (*medesimo*) the same. **altrettanto ... quanto** ... as ... as ... . *avv* as, as much.

altri ['altri] *pron* others *pl*, another (person), someone else.

altro ['altro] *agg* other; another; (*in più*) more; (*ulteriore*) further; (*prossimo*) next. *pron* other (one), another (one); (*persona*) somebody else. **cos'altro?** what else? **l'un l'altro** one another, each other. **l'uno e l'altro** both. **nè l'uno nè l'altro** neither. **nessun'altro** nobody else. **nient'altro** nothing else. **non altro che** nothing but. **più che altro** more than anything. **qualcos'altro** something else. **se non altro** at least. **senz'altro** certainly. **tra l'altro** among other things. **tutt'altro!** far from it!

altronde [al'tronde] *avv* **d'altronde** on the other hand, however.

altrove [al'trove] *avv* elsewhere.

altrui [al'trui] *agg invar* other people's, someone else's.

altruista [altru'ista] *s(m+f)* altruist, unselfish person. **altruismo** *sm* altruism, unselfishness. **altruistico** *agg* unselfish, altruistic.

alunno [a'lunno], **-a** *sm, sf* pupil.

alveare [alve'are] *sm* beehive.

alzaia [al'tsaja] *sf* tow-line; (*strada*) towpath.

alzare [al'tsare] *v* raise, lift; (*raccogliere*) pick up; (*carte da gioco*) cut. **alzarsi** *v* get up, rise. **alzare le spalle** shrug one's shoulders.

amaca [a'maka] *sf* hammock.

amalgamare [amalga'mare] *v* amalgamate, combine. **amalgama** *sm* amalgam.

amante [a'mante] *s(m+f)* lover. *agg* fond (of), keen (on).

amare [a'mare] *v* love, like. **amato** *agg* beloved. **amatore** *sm* lover; (*conoscitore*) connoisseur.

amarena [ama'rena] *sf* sour cherry, black cherry.

amaro [a'maro] *agg* bitter; (*doloroso*) painful. *sm* bitterness; (*bibita*) bitters *pl*. **amarezza** *sf* bitterness.

ambasciata [amba'ʃata] *sf* embassy; message. **ambasciatore**, **-trice** *sm, sf* ambassador, ambassadress.

ambedue [ambe'due] *pron, agg* both.

ambidestro [ambi'dɛstro] *agg* ambidextrous.

ambientarsi [ambjen'tarsi] *v* accustom oneself, settle down. **ambiente** *sm* environment, milieu; atmosphere. **temperatura ambiente** *sf* room temperature.

ambiguo [am'biguo] *agg* ambiguous; (*equivoco*) dubious; (*fam*) shady. **ambiguità** *sf* ambiguity; duplicity.

ambito[1] ['ambito] *sm* limits *pl*; sphere.

ambito[2] [am'bito] *agg* longed-for, coveted. **ambire** *v* covet.

ambivalente [ambiva'lɛnte] *agg* ambivalent.

ambizione [ambi'tsjone] *sf* ambition. **ambizioso** *agg* ambitious.

ambo ['ambo] *agg* both.

ambra ['ambra] *sf, agg* amber. **ambra grigia** ambergris.

ambulante [ambu'lante] *agg* wandering. **biblioteca ambulante** *sf* mobile library. **venditore ambulante** *sm* pedlar.

ambulanza [ambu'lantsa] *sf* ambulance; (*infermeria mobile*) field hospital.

ambulatorio [ambula'tɔrjo] *sm* outpatients' department, clinic.

ameba [a'mɛba] *sf* amoeba.

ameno [a'meno] *agg* agreeable; (*divertente*) entertaining.

America [a'mɛrika] *sf* America. **americano**, **-a** *s, agg* American.

ametista [ame'tista] *sf* amethyst.

amianto [a'mjanto] *sm* asbestos.

amichevole [ami'kevole] *agg* friendly.

amico [a'miko], **-a** *sm, sf* friend. *agg* friendly. **amicizia** *sf* friendship.

amido ['amido] *sm* starch.

ammaccare [ammak'kare] *v* dent. **ammaccatura** *sf* dent.

ammaestrare [ammaes'trare] *v* teach, train. **ammaestramento** *sm* teaching, training.

ammalarsi [amma'larsi] *v* fall ill.

ammansire [amman'sire] *v* tame, subdue.

ammassare [ammas'sare] *v* amass.

ammazzare [ammat'tsare] *v* kill, murder.

ammenda [am'menda] *sf* (*dir*) fine. **fare ammenda di** make amends for.

*****ammettere** [am'mettere] *v* admit; permit; suppose; take for granted. **ammesso che** given that.

ammezzato [ammed'dzato] *agg* mezzanine. *sm* mezzanine floor.

ammiccare [ammik'kare] *v* wink (at).

amministrare [amminis'trare] *v* administer, manage, run. **amministrativo** *agg* administrative. **amministratore**, **-trice** *sm, sf* director. **amministratore delegato** managing director. **amministrazione** *sf* administration, management. **consiglio d'amministrazione** *sm* board of directors.

ammiraglio [ammi'raʎo] *sm* admiral. **ammiragliato** *sm* admiralty.

ammirare [ammi'rare] *v* admire. **ammiratore, -trice** *sm, sf* admirer, fan. **ammirazione** *sf* admiration. **ammirevole** *agg* admirable.

ammissibile [ammis'sibile] *agg* admissible, acceptable.

ammissione [ammis'sjone] *sf* admission, admittance. **esame d'ammissione** *sm* entrance examination. **tassa d'ammissione** *sf* entrance fee.

ammobiliare [ammobi'ʎare] *v* furnish.

ammollare¹ [ammol'lare] *v* soften; (*nell'acqua*) soak.

ammollare² [ammol'lare] *v* let go, slacken.

ammoniaca [ammo'niaka] *sf* ammonia.

ammonire [ammo'nire] *v* warn; reprimand. **ammonimento** *sm* warning; reproof.

ammontare [ammon'tare] *sm, v* amount.

ammorbidire [ammorbi'dire] *v* soften.

ammortire [ammor'tire] *v* deaden.

ammucchiare [ammuk'kjare] *v* pile up.

ammuffire [ammuf'fire] *v* go mouldy. **ammuffito** *agg* mouldy.

ammutinamento [ammutina'mento] *sm* mutiny.

amnistia [amnis'tia] *sf* amnesty.

amo [amo] *sm* hook. **abboccare all'amo** swallow the bait.

amorale [amo'rale] *agg* amoral.

amore [a'more] *sm* love; (*persona graziosa*) darling. **amor proprio** self-respect. **per amore di** for the sake of. **amoroso** *agg* loving.

ampère [ã'pɛr] *sm invar* ampere, amp.

ampio [ampjo] *agg* wide, spacious; (*abbondante*) full.

amplificare [amplifi'kare] *v* amplify, enlarge. **amplificatore** *sm* amplifier.

ampolloso [ampol'loso] *agg* pompous.

amputare [ampu'tare] *v* amputate. **amputazione** *sf* amputation.

anacronismo [anakro'nizmo] *sm* anachronism.

anagrafe [a'nagrafe] *sf* register office.

anagramma [ana'gramma] *sm* anagram.

analcolico [anal'kɔliko] *agg* non-alcoholic. *sm* soft drink.

anale [a'nale] *agg* anal.

analfabeta [analfa'bɛta] *agg, s(m+f)* illiterate. **analfabetismo** *sm* illiteracy.

analgesico [anal'dʒeziko] *agg, sm* analgesic.

analizzare [analid'dzare] *v* analyse. **analisi** *sf* analysis (*pl* -ses). **in ultima analisi** when all is said and done. **analista** *s(m+f)* analyst. **analitico** *agg* analytic.

analogo [a'nalogo] *agg, m pl* -ghi analogous. **analogia** *sf* analogy.

ananas ['ananas] *sm* pineapple.

anarchico [a'narkiko], **-a** *agg* anarchic(al). *sm, sf* anarchist. **anarchia** *sf* anarchy.

anatema [ana'tɛma] *sm* anathema.

anatomia [anato'mia] *sf* anatomy. **anatomia patologica** pathology. **anatomico** *agg* anatomical. **anatomista** *s(m+f)* anatomist.

anatra ['anatra] *sf* duck. **anatroccolo** *sm* duckling.

anca ['anka] *sf* hip.

anche ['anke] *cong* too, as well, also; (*inoltre*) besides; (*perfino*) even.

ancora¹ ['ankora] *sm* anchor. **ancoraggio** *sm* moorings *pl*. **ancorare** *v* anchor.

ancora² [an'kora] *avv* still; (*in frasi negative*) yet; (*di nuovo*) again; (*un altro*) another; (*persino*) even. **ancora un po'** a little more; (*tempo*) a little longer.

****andare** [an'dare] *v* go; (*funzionare*) work, run; (*calzare*) fit; (*essere adatto*) suit; (*dovere*) must be, have to be. **a lungo andare** in the long run. **andare a genio** be to one's liking. **andare a piedi** walk. **andare a spasso** go for a walk. **andare avanti** proceed, progress, go on. **andar bene** go well; fit; (*salute*) be well. **andare in bicicletta** cycle. **andare incontro a** go towards, go and meet. **andarsene** go away, leave.

andata [an'data] *sf* **biglietto d'andata** *sm* single ticket.

andirivieni [andiri'vjeni] *sm* coming and going; (*risposta evasiva*) prevarication.

andito [an'dito] *sm* passage.

aneddoto [a'neddoto] *sm* anecdote.

anelare [ane'lare] *v* pant; (*aspirare*) yearn (for). **anelante** *agg* panting, out of breath.

anello [a'nello] *sm* ring. **anello matrimoniale/di fidanzamento** wedding/engagement ring.

anemia [ane'mia] *sf* anaemia. **anemico** *agg* anaemic.

anemone [a'nɛmone] *sm* anemone.

anestetico [anes'tɛtiko] *agg, sm* anaesthetic. **anestesia** *sf* anaesthesia. **anestetista** *s(m+f)* anaesthetist.

anfetamina [anfeta'mina] sf ampheta-mine.

anfibio [an'fibjo] sm, agg amphibian.

angariare [anga'rjare] v harass.

angelica [an'dʒɛlika] sf angelica.

angelo ['andʒelo] sm angel; (pesce) angel-fish. **angelo custode** guardian angel. **angelico** agg angelic.

anglicano [angli'kano], -a s, agg Anglican. **anglicanesimo** sm Anglican-ism.

angolo ['angolo] sm corner; (geom, ecc.) angle. **angolare** agg angular. **pietra angolare** sf cornerstone.

angoscia [an'gɔʃa] sf anxiety, anguish. **angosciare** v distress. **angoscioso** agg dis-tressed; distressing.

anguilla [an'gwilla] sf eel.

anguria [an'gurja] sf water-melon.

anice ['anitʃe] sm aniseed.

anima ['anima] sf soul; (parte centrale) core; (fervore) heart; (di arma da fuoco) bore. **rodersi l'anima** torment oneself.

animale [ani'male] sm animal; (persona) brute. agg animal.

animare [ani'mare] v animate; stimulate. **animato** agg animate; (vivace) spirited. **disegno or cartone animato** sm cartoon. **essere animato da** be inspired by.

animo ['animo] sm mind; (cuore, coraggio) heart; (carattere) nature. **farsi animo** pluck up courage. **in fondo all'animo** at the back of one's mind. **mettersi l'animo in pace** resign oneself. **stato d'animo** sm mood.

animosità [animozi'ta] sf animosity, spite.

annacquare [annak'kware] v water down.

annaffiare [annaf'fjare] v water.

annali [an'nali] sm pl annals pl.

annata [an'nata] sf year; (raccolto) crop; (di vino) vintage; (importo) income.

annebbiare [anneb'bjare] v become fog-gy; (fig) dim, cloud.

annegare [anne'gare] v drown. **annega-mento** sm drowning.

*****annettere** [an'nɛttere] v (pol) annex; attach. **annesso** sm annexe, appendage.

annichilare [anniki'lare] v annihilate, destroy.

annientare [annjen'tare] v annihilate, destroy. **annientamento** sm (total) destruction.

anniversario [anniver'sarjo] sm, agg anni-versary.

anno ['anno] sm year. **anno bisestile** leap-year. **anno luce** light-year.

annodare [anno'dare] v knot or tie (together).

annoiare [anno'jare] v bore.

annotare [anno'tare] v note, jot down; (postillare) annotate.

annoverare [annove'rare] v number; enu-merate.

annuale [annu'ale] agg annual, yearly.

annuario [annu'arjo] sm yearbook.

annuire [annu'ire] v nod in agreement; (acconsentire) agree.

annullare [annul'lare] v cancel; (matrimonio) annul; (legge) repeal. **annullamento** sm cancellation; annul-ment; repeal.

annunciare [annun'tʃare] v announce; (precorrere) herald. **annunciatore, -trice** sm, sf announcer. **annuncio** sm announcement, notice; (pubblicità) advertisement.

Annunciazione [annuntʃa'tsjone] sf Annunciation.

annuo ['annuo] agg yearly, annual.

annusare [annu'zare] v sniff; (intuire) smell.

annuvolare [annuvo'lare] v cloud (over).

ano ['ano] sm anus.

anodo ['anodo] sm anode.

anomalia [anoma'lia] sf anomaly. **anomalo** agg anomalous.

anonimo [a'nɔnimo] agg anonymous. **società anonima** sf limited company.

anormale [anor'male] agg abnormal. **anormalità** sf abnormality.

ansare [an'sare] v puff, pant.

ansia ['ansja] sf anxiety; (angoscia) dread; (desiderio) longing. **ansioso** agg anxious; longing; (impaziente) restless.

antagonismo [antago'nizmo] sm antago-nism. **antagonista** s(m+f) adversary.

antartico [an'tartiko] agg antarctic.

antenato [ante'nato] sm forefather, ances-tor.

antenna [an'tenna] sf (zool) antenna; (radio, TV) aerial.

anteprima [ante'prima] sf preview.

anteriore [ante'rjore] agg (nel tempo) pre-ceding, previous; (nello spazio) front, fore.

antiabbagliante [antiabba'ʎante] agg anti-dazzle. **fari antiabbagliantii** sm pl dipped headlights pl.

antiaereo [antia'ereo] *agg* anti-aircraft.

antibiotico [antibi'ɔtiko] *agg, sm* antibiotic.

anticamera [anti'kamera] *sf* lobby, waiting-room. **fare anticamera** be kept waiting. **far fare anticamera** keep waiting.

antichità [antiki'ta] *sf* antiquity; *(oggetto)* antique.

anticiclone [antitʃi'klone] *sm* anticyclone.

anticipare [antitʃi'pare] *v* anticipate; advance; pay in advance. **anticipato** *agg* advanced; *(prima del tempo)* in advance. **anticipazione** *sf* anticipation; *(soldi)* advance.

anticipo [an'titʃipo] *sm* advance, deposit. **in anticipo** early; *(orologio)* fast.

antico [an'tiko] *agg, m pl* -**chi** old; ancient; antique. **all'antica** *agg* old-fashioned.

anticoncezionale [antikontʃetsjo'nale] *agg, sm* contraceptive.

anticonformista [antikonfor'mista] *agg, s(m+f)* non-conformist.

anticongelante [antikondʒe'lante] *sm* anti-freeze.

anticorpo [anti'kɔrpo] *sm* antibody.

antidoto [an'tidoto] *sm* antidote.

antifecondativo [antifekonda'tivo] *sm, agg* contraceptive.

antifurto [anti'furto] *sm* burglar alarm.

antilope [an'tilope] *sf* antelope.

antincendio [antin'tʃendjo] *agg* **equipaggiamento antincendio** fire-fighting equipment.

antiorario [antio'rarjo] *agg* anti-clockwise.

antipasto [anti'pasto] *sm* hors d'oeuvre, starter.

antipatia [antipa'tia] *sf* dislike, antipathy. **prendere in antipatia** take a dislike to. **antipatico** *agg* disagreeable, unpleasant.

antiquario [anti'kwarjo] *sm* antique dealer. **antiquariato** *sm* antique trade; *(negozio)* antique shop.

antiquato [anti'kwato] *agg (fuori moda)* old-fashioned; *(disusato)* obsolete.

antisemita [antise'mita] *s(m+f)* anti-Semite. *agg* anti-Semitic. **antisemitismo** *sm* anti-Semitism.

antisettico [anti'settiko] *sm, agg* antiseptic.

antisociale [antiso'tʃale] *agg* antisocial.

antistaminico [antista'miniko] *sm* antihistamine.

antitesi [an'titezi] *sf* antithesis *(pl* -ses).

antologia [antolo'dʒia] *sf* anthology.

antro ['antro] *sm* cave.

antropologia [antropolo'dʒia] *sf* anthropology. **antropologico** *agg* anthropological. **antropologo, -a** *sm, sf* anthropologist.

anulare [anu'lare] *agg* annular, ring-shaped. *sm* ring-finger.

anzi ['antsi] *cong* on the contrary; *(invece)* as a matter of fact; *(o meglio)* or better, better still; *(di più)* indeed.

anziano [an'tsjano] *-a agg* elderly; aged; senior. *sm, sf* elderly person.

anziché [antsi'ke] *cong (piuttosto)* rather than; *(invece)* instead of.

anzitutto [antsi'tutto] *avv* above all, first of all.

apatia [apa'tia] *sf* apathy.

ape ['ape] *sf* bee.

aperitivo [aperi'tivo] *sm* aperitif.

aperto [a'pɛrto] *agg* open; *(pronto)* quick. **all'aperto** in the open, outdoors.

apice ['apitʃe] *sm* apex, top.

apocrifo [a'pɔkrifo] *agg* apocryphal.

apolide [a'polide] *agg* stateless.

apostolo [a'postolo] *sm* apostle. **apostolico** *agg* apostolic.

apostrofo [a'postrofo] *sm* apostrophe.

appagare [appa'gare] *v* satisfy.

appalto [ap'palto] *sm* contract.

appannare [appan'nare] *v (vista)* dim, blur; *(vetri)* mist up.

apparato [appa'rato] *sm* show, display; *(tec)* machinery; *(biol)* system, apparatus. **apparato scenico** set.

apparecchiare [apparek'kjare] *v* prepare. **apparecchiare la tavola** lay the table. **apparecchio** *sm* set; device, instrument, appliance; *(fam)* (aero)plane; *(fam)* (tele)phone.

apparenza [appa'rentsa] *sf* appearance. **apparente** *agg* apparent. **apparentemente** *avv* apparently; *(a prima vista)* to all appearances.

****apparire** [appa'rire] *v* appear; *(sembrare)* look, seem. **appariscente** *agg* striking.

appartamento [apparta'mento] *sm* flat, apartment.

appartare [appar'tare] *v* put aside. **appartarsi** *v* withdraw. **appartato** *agg* secluded.

****appartenere** [apparte'nere] *v* belong.

****appassionare** [appassjo'nare] *v* move, arouse passion; arouse interest. **appassionarsi per** be very fond of.

appena [ap'pena] *avv* barely, hardly; (*soltanto*) only; (*solo un po'*) only just; (*da poco*) just (recently). *cong* appena ... che ... no sooner ... than ....

*appendere [ap'pendere] *v* hang.

appendice [appen'ditʃe] *sm* appendix. appendicite *sf* appendicitis.

appetito [appe'tito] *sm* appetite. aver appetito have an appetite, be hungry. appetitoso *agg* appetizing; tempting.

appianare [appja'nare] *v* level; (*dissidio, ecc.*) smooth (over), settle.

appiccare [appik'kare] *v* (*appendere*) hang; (*cominciare*) set off. appiccar fuoco a set fire to.

appiccicare [appittʃi'kare] *v* stick. appiccicaticcio *agg* sticky.

appigionare [appidʒo'nare] *v* let.

appioppare [appjop'pare] *v* give; (*affibbiare*) saddle with.

appisolarsi [appizo'larsi] *v* doze.

applaudire [applau'dire] *v* applaud. applauso *sm* applause.

applicare [appli'kare] *v* apply. applicazione *sf* application; concentration; (*dir*) enforcement. applique *sf*, *pl* -s wall-bracket.

appoggiare [appod'dʒare] *v* lean; (*posare*) lay; (*fondare*) base; (*favorire*) support. appoggio *sm* support.

*apporre [ap'porre] *v* affix, append.

apportare [appor'tare] *v* bring about, produce. apporto *sm* contribution.

apposito [ap'pozito] *agg* special; (*adatto*) suitable. appositamente *avv* suitably; (*apposta*) deliberately; (*espressamente*) specially.

apposta [ap'posta] *avv* deliberately, on purpose, specially. *agg invar* special.

*apprendere [ap'prendere] *v* learn. apprendista *s(m+f)* apprentice, learner. apprendistato *sm* apprenticeship.

apprensione [appren'sjone] *sm* apprehension, concern. apprensivo *agg* apprehensive, uneasy.

appresso [ap'presso] *avv* close by, at hand; (*con sè*) with one; (*in sequito*) later. *prep* close to; (*dietro*) close behind. *agg invar* following.

apprestare [appres'tare] *v* prepare; (*porgere*) bring.

apprezzare [appret'tsare] *v* appreciate. apprezzamento *sm* appreciation; (*giudizio*) opinion; (*osservazione*) remark.

approfittare [approfit'tare] *v* profit (by), take advantage (of).

approfondire [approfon'dire] *v* deepen; (*studiare*) probe, go into.

approntare [appron'tare] *v* get ready.

approssimativo [approssima'tivo] *agg* approximate, rough. approssimare *v* approximate. approssimarsi (a) approach. approssimazione *sf* approximation.

approvare [appro'vare] *v* approve (of). approvazione *sf* approval.

appuntamento [appunta'mento] *sm* appointment; (*fam*) date.

appunto¹ [ap'punto] *sm* note; (*osservazione*) remark. muovere *or* fare un appunto a blame, find fault with.

appunto² [ap'punto] *avv* precisely, just.

appurare [appu'rare] *v* verify.

aprile [a'prile] *sm* April.

*aprire [a'prire] *v* open; (*luce, radio, ecc.*) switch on. apribottiglie *sm invar* bottle-opener. apriscatole *sm invar* tin-opener.

aquila ['akwila] *sf* eagle. aquilone *sm* kite.

Arabia [a'rabja] *sf* Araòia. arabo, -a *s*, *agg* Arab; *sm* (*lingua*) Arabic.

arachide [a'rakide] *sf* ground-nut, peanut.

aragosta [ara'gosta] *sf* lobster.

araldo [a'raldo] *sm* herald. araldica *sf* heraldry. araldico *agg* heraldic.

arancio [a'rantʃo] *sm* orange tree. *agg invar* (*colore*) orange. arancia *sf* orange. arancione *sm*, *agg invar* orange.

arare [a'rare] *v* plough. aratro *sm* plough.

arazzo [a'rattso] *sm* tapestry.

arbitrare [arbi'trare] *v* arbitrate; (*sport*) referee. arbitro *sm* referee, umpire.

arbitrio [ar'bitrjo] *sm* will. arbitrario *agg* arbitrary.

arbusto [ar'busto] *sm* bush.

arca ['arka] *sf* ark.

arcaico [ar'kaiko] *agg* archaic.

arcata [ar'kata] *sf* arcade; (*di ponte*) span; (*anat*) arch.

archeologia [arkeolo'dʒia] *sf* archaeology. archeologico *agg* archaeological. archeologo, -a *sm*, *sf* archaeologist.

archetipo [ar'kɛtipo] *sm* archetype. *agg* archetypal.

archetto [ar'ketto] *sm* bow.

architetto [arki'tetto] *sm* architect. architettonico *agg* architectural. architettura *sf* architecture.

archivio [ar'kivjo] *sm* archives *pl*; (*comm*) file. archiviare *v* (place on) file;

(*questione*, *ecc.*) pigeon-hole. **archivista** *s(m+f)* archivist; (*comm*) filing clerk.

arciduca [artʃi'duka] *sm* archduke.

arciere [ar'tʃɛre] *sm* archer.

arcigno [ar'tʃiɲo] *agg* sullen.

arcipelago [artʃi'pelago] *sm*, *pl* -ghi archipelago.

arcivescovo [artʃi'veskovo] *sm* archbishop. **arcivescovado** *sm* archbishop's palace; (*dignità*) archbishopric.

arco ['arko] *sm* bow; (*anat*, *arch*) arch; (*geom*) arc. **quartetto d'archi** *sm* string quartet. **strumenti ad arco** *sm pl* strings *pl*. **tiro all'arco** *sm* archery.

arcobaleno ['arkobaleno] *sm* rainbow.

arcuato [arku'ato] *agg* arched. **dalle gambe arcuate** bow-legged.

****ardere** ['ardere] *v* burn. **ardente** *agg* burning; (*colore*) fiery; (*appassionato*) ardent.

ardesia [ar'dɛzja] *sf* slate.

ardire [ar'dire] *v* dare. **ardito** *agg* bold, daring; risky. **ardore** *sm* (*calore*) heat; passion.

arduo [ar'duo] *agg* arduous, laborious; (*ripido*) steep.

area ['area] *sf* area; (*terreno*) land, ground.

arena[1] [a'rɛna] *sf* arena.

arena[2] [a'rɛna] *sf* (*sabbia*) sand. **arenaria** [are'narja] *sf* sandstone. **arenarsi** [are'narsi] *v* run aground; (*fermarsi*) come to a standstill.

argano ['argano] *sm* winch; (*mar*) capstan.

argentina [ardʒen'tina] *sf* polo-neck sweater.

argento [ar'dʒɛnto] *sm* silver. **argento vivo** quicksilver. **argentare** *v* silver(-plate). **argentato** *agg* silver-plated; (*colore*) silver. **argenteria** *sf* silver, silverware.

argilla [ar'dʒilla] *sf* clay.

argine ['ardʒine] *sm* embankment; barrier. **arginare** *v* stem, check.

argomento [argo'mento] *sm* argument, reason; (*materia*) subject, topic. **argomentare** *v* discuss, argue.

arguto [ar'guto] *agg* (*spiritoso*) witty, shrewd. **arguzia** *sf* wit, humour; shrewdness.

aria ['arja] *sf* air; (*aspetto*) look; (*musica*) tune; (*opera*) aria. **all'aria aperta** in the open, out-of-doors. **corrente d'aria** *sf* draught. **darsi delle arie** put on airs.

arido ['arido] *agg* dry, arid.

arieggiare [arjed'dʒare] *v* air.

ariete [a'rjɛte] *sm* ram. **Ariete** *sm* Aries.

aringa [a'ringa] *sf* herring.

arioso [a'rjozo] *agg* airy.

aristocratico [aristo'kratiko], **-a** *sm*, *sf* aristocrat. *agg* aristocratic. **aristocrazia** *sf* aristocracy.

aritmetica [arit'metika] *sf* arithmetic. **aritmetico** *agg* arithmetic(al).

armadio [ar'madjo] *sm* cupboard; (*per abiti*) wardrobe.

armare [ar'mare] *v* arm; (*mar*) rig up; reinforce. **armarsi** *v* take up arms; (*provvedersi*) arm oneself. **arma** *sf*, *pl* -**i** weapon, arms *pl*; (*mil*) force. **armamento** *sm* armament; (*tec*) equipment.

armata [ar'mata] *sf* army; (*flotta*) fleet. **armato** [ar'mato] *agg* armed; equipped. **armatura** [arma'tura] *sf* scaffolding; (*elett*) armature.

armonia [armo'nia] *sf* harmony. **in armonia con** in keeping with. **armonica** *sf* harmonics. **armonica a bocca** mouthorgan. **armonico** *agg* harmonic. **armonioso** *agg* melodious. **armonizzare** *v* harmonize; (*colori*, *ecc.*) match.

arnese [ar'neze] *sm* tool; gadget. **arnese da cucina** kitchen utensil. **bene/male in arnese** in good/poor shape.

arnia ['arnja] *sf* beehive.

aroma [a'roma] *sm* aroma; aromatic herb, spice. **aromatico** *agg* aromatic.

arpa ['arpa] *sf* harp. **arpeggio** *sm* arpeggio. **arpista** *s(m+f)* harpist.

arpione [ar'pjone] *sm* hook; (*arma*) harpoon; (*cardine*) hinge.

arrabbiarsi [arrab'bjarsi] *v* become angry or annoyed. **far arrabbiare** annoy, anger. **arrabbiato** *agg* angry; (*cane*) rabid; (*furioso*) enraged.

arraffare [arraf'fare] *v* snatch.

arrampicarsi [arrampi'karsi] *v* climb (up). **arrampicata** *sf* climbing, climb.

arrangiare [arran'dʒare] *v* (*aggiustare*) mend; improvise; (*fam*) fix; (*musica*) arrange. **arrangiarsi** *v* manage; come to an agreement.

arrecare [arre'kare] *v* cause, bring about.

arredare [arre'dare] *v* furnish. **arredamento** *sm* furnishing; (*mobilio*) furniture. **arredatore**, **-trice** *sm*, *sf* interior decorator; (*cinema*) set decorator.

****arrendersi** [ar'rendersi] *v* surrender, give oneself up. **arrendevole** *agg* yielding.

arrestare [arres'tare] v stop; (dir) arrest. **arresto** sm stop, stoppage; arrest. **arresto cardiaco** heart failure.

arretrato [arre'trato] agg behind; (non fatto) outstanding, overdue; (non sviluppato) backward; (numero di rivista, ecc.) back. **arretrati** sm pl arrears pl; (di paga) back-pay sing.

arricchire [arrik'kire] v enrich. **arricchirsi** become rich.

arricciare [arrit'tʃare] v curl. **arricciare il naso** pull a face. **arricciare il pelo** bristle.

arringa [ar'ringa] sf address.

arrischiare [arris'kjare] v risk, venture. **arrischiato** agg risky; (imprudente) rash.

arrivare [arri'vare] v arrive; succeed; (capitare) happen. **arrivare a** (riuscire) manage to; (giungere) reach, get to; (essere ridotto a) be reduced to. **arrivare fino a** reach, get as far as. **ben arrivato!** welcome! **arrivo** sm arrival.

arrivederci [arrive'dertʃi] inter goodbye! (fam) see you!

arrogante [arro'gante] agg arrogant. **arroganza** sf arrogance.

arrossire [arros'sire] v blush.

arrostire [arros'tire] v roast. **arrosto** sm, agg invar roast.

arrotare [arro'tare] v sharpen. **arrotino** sm knife-grinder.

arrotolare [arroto'lare] v roll up.

arrotondare [arroton'dare] v round off.

arroventato [arroven'tato] agg red-hot.

arruffare [arruf'fare] v ruffle; (confondere) muddle.

arrugginirsi [arruddʒi'nirsi] v rust. **arrugginito** agg rusty.

arruolare [arrwo'lare] v enlist.

arsenale [arse'nale] sm arsenal; (mar) (naval) dockyard.

arsenico [ar'sɛniko] sm arsenic.

arso ['arso] agg burnt, parched.

arte ['arte] sf art; (attività) craft; (abilità) skill; (astuzia) cunning. **ad arte** on purpose; (con artifizio) cunningly. **artefice** sm craftsman.

arteria [ar'tɛria] sf artery. **arteria di traffico** main road, thoroughfare.

artico ['artiko] agg arctic.

articolare [artiko'lare] v articulate; (suddividere) split up.

articolo [ar'tikolo] sm article. **articoli** sm pl goods pl. **articolo di cronaca** news item. **articolo di fondo** leading article, leader.

artificiale [artifi'tʃale] agg artificial.

artificio [arti'fitʃo] sm stratagem, device. **fuochi d'artificio** sm pl fireworks pl.

artigiano [arti'dʒano] sm craftsman. **artigianato** sm craftsmanship; (prodotti) handicraft; (classe) craftsmen pl.

artiglieria [artiʎe'ria] sf artillery.

artiglio [ar'tiʎo] sm claw, talon. **cadere negli artigli di** fall into the clutches of.

artista [ar'tista] s(m+f) artist. **artistico** artistic.

arto ['arto] sm limb.

artrite [ar'trite] sf arthritis.

asbesto [az'bɛsto] sm asbestos.

ascella [a'ʃella] sf armpit.

***ascendere** [a'ʃendere] v rise.

ascensore [aʃen'sore] sm elevator.

ascesa [a'ʃeza] sf also **ascensione** ascent, climb.

ascesso [a'ʃɛsso] sm abscess.

asceta [a'ʃɛta] s(m+f) ascetic. **ascetico** agg ascetic. **ascetismo** sm asceticism.

ascia ['aʃa] sf axe.

asciugare [aʃu'gare] v dry. **asciugamano** sm towel. **asciugatoio** sm bath towel. **carta asciugante** sf blotting-paper.

asciutto [a'ʃutto] agg dry. **essere all'asciutto** (salvo) be safe; (al verde) be broke. **pasta asciutta** sf pasta.

ascoltare [askol'tare] v listen (to); heed, pay attention (to); (lezioni, messa, ecc.) attend. **ascoltatore, -trice** sm, sf listener. **dare ascolto a** pay attention to.

asfalto [as'falto] sm asphalt. **asfaltare** v asphalt.

Asia ['azja] sf Asia. **asiatico** sm, agg Asian, Asiatic.

asilo [a'zilo] sm refuge, shelter; (pol) asylum. **asilo infantile** kindergarten, nursery school. **dare asilo a** shelter.

asino ['azino] sm ass, donkey. **asineria** sf stupidity. **asinino** agg asinine. **tosse asinina** sf whooping cough.

asma ['azma] sm asthma. **asmatico** agg asthmatic.

asola ['azola] sf buttonhole.

asparago [as'parago] sm asparagus.

aspettare [aspet'tare] v await, wait (for). **aspettare con desiderio** look forward to. **aspettare un bambino** be expecting a baby. **aspettativa** sf expectation; (licenza) leave of absence.

aspetto[1] [as'petto] sm appearance, look. **sotto questo aspetto** from this point of view.

aspetto² [as'petto] *sm* waiting. **sala d'aspetto** *sf* waiting-room.

aspirare [aspi'rare] *v* inhale, breathe in; (*desiderare*) aspire. **aspirapolvere** *sm invar* vacuum cleaner.

aspirina [aspi'rina] *sf* aspirin.

asportare [aspor'tare] *v* remove, take away.

aspro ['aspro] *agg* sour, tart; (*vino*) rough; (*suono*) harsh; (*clima*) raw; (*fig*) hard. **asprezza** *sf* sourness; harshness.

assaggiare [assad'dʒare] *v* taste, try. **assaggio** *sm* taste; (*campione*) sample.

assai [as'sai] *avv* very; (*very*) much; (*abbastanza*) enough.

assalire [assa'lire] *v* assail, attack.

assalto [as'salto] *sm* attack.

assassinare [assassi'nare] *v* murder. **assassinio** *sm* murder. **assassino, -a** *sm, sf* murderer, murderess.

asse¹ ['asse] *sm* axis; (*mec*) axle.

asse² ['asse] *sf* (*tavola*) board, plank. **asse da stiro** ironing-board.

assediare [asse'djare] *v* besiege. **assedio** *sm* siege. **stato d'assedio** *sm* state of emergency.

assegnare [asse'ɲare] *v* assign, allot. **assegnazione** *sf* allocation.

assegno [as'seɲno] *sm* check. **assegno circolare** banker's draft. **assegno in bianco** blank check. **assegno sbarrato** crossed check. **assegno turistico** traveller's check.

assemblea [assem'blɛa] *sf* assembly, meeting.

assenso [as'sɛnso] *sm* assent, agreement.

assente [as'sɛnte] *agg* absent. **assentarsi** *v* absent oneself, stay away. **assenteismo** *sm* absenteeism. **assenza** *sf* absence; (*mancanza*) lack.

assentire [assen'tire] *v* assent, approve.

asserire [asse'rire] *v* assert, affirm. **asserzione** *sf* assertion, statement.

assessore [asses'sore] *sm* (*dir*) assessor; (*comunale*) councillor.

assestare [asses'tare] *v* arrange, settle.

assetato [asse'tato] *agg* thirsty.

assettare [asset'tare] *v* tidy, put in order.

assicurare [assiku'rare] *v* assure; (*dir*) insure; (*rendere certo*) ensure; (*procurare*) secure; (*lettera*) register. **assicurarsi** *v* take out insurance. **assicuratore** *sm* underwriter. **assicurazione** *sf* insurance.

assiduo [as'siduo] *agg* assiduous.

assieme [as'sjeme] *avv* together.

assieparsi [assje'parsi] *v* crowd (round).

assillare [assil'lare] *v* pester.

assimilare [assimi'lare] *v* assimilate. **assimilazione** *sf* assimilation.

Assise [as'size] *sf* **corte d'Assise** *sf* Assizes *pl*.

assistente [assis'tɛnte] *s(m+f)* assistant; (*universitario*) lecturer; (*di volo*) steward, stewardess. **assistente sociale** social worker. **assistenza** *sf* assistance; (*sociale*) welfare.

*****assistere** [as'sistere] *v* (*aiutare*) assist, help; be present at; (*sport*) watch; (*lezione*) attend.

asso [asso] *sm* ace; champion. **piantare in asso** leave in the lurch.

associare [asso'tʃare] *v* associate, join. **associarsi** *v* join; become a partner *or* member. **associazione** *sf* association, society; (*comm*) partnership.

assoggettare [assoddʒet'tare] *v* subject.

assoluto [asso'luto] *agg* absolute, complete.

*****assolvere** [as'sɔlvere] *v* (*rel*) absolve; (*dir*) discharge, acquit. **assoluzione** *sf* absolution; discharge, acquittal. **assolvimento** *sm* fulfilment.

assomigliare [assomi'ʎare] *v* resemble.

assonnato [asson'nato] *agg* sleepy; (*torpido*) sluggish.

assopirsi [asso'pirsi] *v* nod off; calm *or* cool down.

assorbire [assor'bire] *v* absorb. **assorbente** *agg* absorbent. **assorbente (igienico)** *sm* sanitary towel. **carta assorbente** *sf* blotting-paper.

assordare [assor'dare] *v* deafen; (*attutire un suono*) deaden.

assortire [assor'tire] *v* sort out. **assortimento** *sm* assortment.

*****assuefare** [assue'fare] *v* accustom.

*****assumere** [as'sumere] *v* assume; (*personale*) take on, engage; (*procurarsi*) obtain.

assunzione [assun'tsjone] *sf* engagement; (*di un obbligo*) undertaking; (*elevazione*) ascent; (*filos*) assumption. **Assunzione** *sf* (*rel*) Assumption.

assurdo [as'surdo] *agg* absurd, preposterous. *sm* absurdity.

asta ['asta] *sf* pole; (*mec*) rod; (*scrittura*) stroke. **a mezz'asta** at half-mast. **vendita all'asta** *sf* auction.

astante [as'tante] *s(m+f)* bystander.
astemio [as'tɛmjo], **-a** *sm*, *sf* teetotaller. *agg* teetotal.
*****astenersi** [aste'nersi] *v* abstain, refrain.
asterisco [aste'risko] *sm* asterisk.
astinenza [asti'nɛntsa] *sf* abstinence.
astio ['astjo] *sm* rancour, resentment. **portar astio** bear a grudge.
*****astrarre** [as'trarre] *v* abstract. **astratto** *sm*, *agg* abstract. **astrazione** *sf* abstraction.
astro ['astro] *sm* star.
astrologia [astrolo'dʒia] *sf* astrology. **astrologico** *agg* astrological. **astrologo, -a** *sm*, *sf* astrologer.
astronauta [astro'nauta] *s(m+f)* astronaut.
astronomia [astrono'mia] *sf* astronomy. **astronomico** *agg* astronomic(al). **astronomo, -a** *sm*, *sf* astronomer.
astuccio [as'tuttʃo] *sm* case.
astuto [as'tuto] *agg* astute, shrewd. **astuzia** *sf* shrewdness, cunning; (*azione*) trick.
Atene [a'tɛne] *sf* Athens. **ateniese** *s(m+f)*, *agg* Athenian.
ateo ['ateo], **-a** *sm*, *sf* atheist. *agg* atheistic.
atlante [at'lante] *sm* atlas.
atlantico [at'lantiko] *agg* Atlantic.
atleta [at'lɛta] *s(m+f)* athlete. **atletica** *sf* athletics. **atletico** *agg* athletic.
atmosfera [atmos'fɛra] *sf* atmosphere. **atmosferico** *agg* atmospheric.
atomo ['atomo] *sm* atom. **atomico** *agg* atomic.
atrio ['atrjo] *sm* (entrance) hall, lobby.
atroce [a'trɔtʃe] *agg* dreadful, terrible; (*feroce*) cruel. **atrocità** *sf* atrocity.
attaccare [attak'kare] *v* attach, fasten; (*appendere*) hang (up); (*incollare*) stick (on); apply; pass on; (*assalire, corrodere*) attack; (*iniziare*) begin. **attaccabottoni** *s(m+f)* *inv* (*fam*) bore. **attaccabrighe** *s(m+f)* *inv* (*fam*) troublemaker. **attaccapanni** *sm* (*gruccia*) coat-hanger; (*mobilia*) coat-rack. **attaccar briga** or **lite** pick a quarrel. **attaccaticcio** *agg* sticky. **attacco** *sm* attack; (*inizio*) opening; (*giuntura*) joint, fastening; (*eletl*) plug.
attecchire [attek'kire] *v* (*radicarsi*) take root; (*diffondersi*) catch on.
atteggiare [atted'dʒare] *v* assume. **atteggiarsi** *v* pose. **atteggiamento** *sm* attitude, expression.

*****attendere** [at'tɛndere] *v* await, wait (for); (*dedicarsi*) devote oneself to, look after. **attendibile** *agg* reliable, trustworthy.
*****attenersi** [atte'nersi] *v* **attenersi a** keep to.
attentato [atten'tato] *sm* attack; attempted murder or assassination.
attento [at'tɛnto] *agg* attentive, alert; careful. **stare attento** pay attention, mind. *inter* careful! mind! look out!
attenzione [atten'tsjone] *sf* attention, care. **fare attenzione a** pay attention to.
atterrare [atter'rare] *v* (*di aereo*) land; (*gettare a terra*) knock down. **atterraggio** *sm* landing.
attesa [at'teza] *sf* wait; (*aspettativa*) expectation.
attestare [attes'tare] *v* certify, attest. **attestato** *sm* certificate, testimonial.
attiguo [at'tiguo] *agg* adjoining.
attimo ['attimo] *sm* instant, moment.
attirare [atti'rare] *v* attract, draw.
attitudine[1] [atti'tudine] *sf* (*disposizione*) aptitude, bent.
attitudine[2] [atti'tudine] *sf* attitude.
attivare [atti'vare] *v* activate, bring into action.
attivo [at'tivo] *agg* active; (*diligente*) busy. **bilancio attivo** *sm* credit balance. *sm* asset.
attizzare [attit'tsare] *v* poke; (*fig*) stir up.
atto[1] ['atto] *agg* suitable, fit.
atto[2] ['atto] *sm* action, act; gesture; (*dir*) deed. **atto di accusa** indictment. **atto di citazione** summons. **atto di nascita/morte** birth/death certificate. **atto matrimoniale** marriage certificate. **dare atto** give notice. **in atto** in progress.
attonito [at'tonito] *agg* astonished.
attorcigliare [attortʃi'ʎare] *v* twist.
attore [at'tore] *sm* actor; (*dir*) plaintiff.
attorniare [attor'njare] *v* surround.
attorno [at'torno] *avv* round, around, about. **guardarsi attorno** look round; (*fig*) be wary. **qui attorno** hereabouts.
*****attrarre** [at'trarre] *v* attract. **attrattiva** *sf* attraction, fascination. **attrazione** *sf* attraction.
attraversare [attraver'sare] *v* cross; go through. **attraversamento** *sm* crossing.
attrezzo [at'trettso] *sm* tool, appliance. **attrezzi** *sm pl* equipment *sing*; kitchen utensils *pl*; (*teatro*) props *pl*. **attrezzare** *v*

equip; furnish. **attrezzatura** *sf* equipment.

attribuire [attribu'ire] *v* ascribe, attribute; *(assegnare)* award. **attributo** *sm* attribute.

attrice [at'tritʃe] *sf* actress.

attrito [at'trito] *sm* friction.

attuale [attu'ale] *agg* present, current; *(valido)* topical; *(filos)* actual. **attualmente** *avv* at present.

attualità [attuali'ta] *sf* topicality. *sf pl* news *sing*, current events *pl*. **di attualità** topical; *(di moda)* fashionable. **tornare di attualità** come back into fashion.

attuare [attu'are] *v* carry out, put into effect. **attuarsi** *v* come true, be fulfilled.

attutire [attu'tire] *v* mitigate; *(suono)* muffle.

audace [au'datʃe] *agg* daring, bold; risky, rash. **audacia** *sf* boldness, daring.

audiovisivo [audjovi'zivo] *agg* audio-visual.

auditorio [audi'torjo] *sm* auditorium, studio.

audizione [audi'tsjone] *sf* audition; *(dir)* hearing.

augurare [augu'rare] *v* wish. **augurarsi** *v* hope. **augurio** *sm* wish; *(presagio)* omen.

aula ['aula] *sf* classroom; *(università)* lecture theatre; courtroom.

aumentare [aumen'tare] *v* increase. **aumentare di peso** put on weight. **aumento** *sm* increase.

aureo ['aureo] *agg* golden.

aureola [au'rɛola] *sf* halo.

aurora [au'rora] *sf* dawn.

ausiliare [auzi'ljare] *sm*, *agg also* **ausiliario** auxiliary.

austero [aus'tɛro] *agg* austere.

Australia [aus'tralja] *sf* Australia. **australiano**, **-a** *s*, *agg* Australian.

Austria ['austrja] *sf* Austria. **austriaco**, **-a** *s*, *agg* Austrian.

autarchia [autar'kia] *sf* self-sufficiency. **autarchico** *agg* self-sufficient.

autentico [au'tɛntiko] *agg* authentic, genuine. **autenticare** *v* authenticate.

autista[1] [au'tista] *s(m+f)* driver. **autista di piazza** taxi-driver.

autista[2] [au'tista] *agg* autistic.

auto ['auto] *sf* (*fam*) car.

autobiografia [autobiogra'fia] *sf* autobiography. **autobiografico** *agg* autobiographical.

autoblinda [auto'blinda] *sf* armoured car.

autobus ['autobus] *sm* bus.

autocarro [auto'karro] *sm* truck.

autocolonna [autoko'lonna] *sf* convoy.

autocontrollo [autokon'trollo] *sm* self-control.

autocratico [auto'kratiko] *agg* autocratic.

autodidatta [autodi'datta] *s(m+f)* self-taught person.

autofurgone [autofur'gone] *sm* van.

autolettiga [autolet'tiga] *sf* ambulance.

autolinea [auto'linea] *sf* bus route.

automa [au'tɔma] *sm* automaton, robot.

automatico [auto'matiko] *agg* automatic. **distributore automatico** slot-machine. **automatizzare** *v* automate.

automezzo [auto'mɛddzo] *sm* motor vehicle.

automobile [auto'mobile] *sf* car. **automobilismo** *sm* motoring. **automobilista** *s(m+f)* motorist. **automobilistico** *agg* motor.

autonomo [au'tɔnomo] *agg* autonomous. **autonomia** *sf* autonomy.

autopsia [autop'sia] *sf* post-mortem, autopsy.

autore [au'tore], **-trice** *sm*, *sf* author; artist.

autorevole [auto'revole] *agg* authoritative.

autorimessa [autori'messa] *sf* garage.

autorità [autori'ta] *sf* authority. **autoritario** *agg* authoritarian.

autoritratto [autori'tratto] *sm* self-portrait.

autorizzare [autorid'dzare] *v* authorize. **autorizzazione** *sf* authorization; permit.

autostop [autos'tɔp] *sm invar* hitch-hiking. **fare l'autostop** hitch-hike.

autostrada [autos'trada] *sf* expressway.

autosufficiente [autosuffi'tʃɛnte] *agg* self-sufficient.

autotreno [auto'treno] *sm* articulated lorry.

autoveicolo [autove'ikolo] *sm* motor vehicle.

autunno [au'tunno] *sm* autumn. **autunnale** *agg* autumnal.

avambraccio [avam'brattʃo] *sm* forearm.

avanguardia [avan'gwardja] *sf* forefront; *(mil)* vanguard; *(arte)* avant-garde.

avanti [a'vanti] *avv* forward, ahead; *(prima)* before. **andare avanti** go forward, proceed. **avanti** *a* before, in front of. **avanti e indietro** backwards and forwards, to and fro. **d'ora in avanti** from now on. **tirare avanti** *(fam)* scrape along.

get by. *inter* come in! (*andiamo*) come now!

avantieri [avan'tjɛri] *avv* the day before yesterday.

avanzare[1] [avan'tsare] *v* advance; (*presentare*) put forward. **avanzata** *sf* advance.

avanzare[2] [avan'tsare] *v* be owed; remain, be left over. **avanzo** *sm* remainder; (*cibo*) left-overs *pl*.

avaro [a'varo], **-a** *agg* mean. *sm*, *sf* miser. **avarizia** *sf* meanness, stinginess.

avena [a'vena] *sf* oats *pl*. **farina d'avena** *sf* oatmeal.

avere [a'vere] *v* have; get. **aver caldo/freddo** be hot/cold. **aver fame/sete** be hungry/thirsty. **aver fretta** be in a hurry. **aver paura/sonno** be afraid/sleepy. *sm* (*comm*) credit; belongings *pl*; property.

aviazione [avja'tsjone] *sf* aviation, flying; (*arma*) air-force. **aviatore, -trice** *sm*, *sf* aviator, pilot.

avido ['avido] *agg* avid, eager.

aviolinea [avjo'linea] *sf* airline.

avo ['avo] *sm* (*nonno*) grandfather; (*antenato*) forefather, ancestor. **avito** *agg* ancestral.

avocado [avo'kado] *sm* avocado.

avorio [a'vorjo] *sm* ivory.

avvampare [avvam'pare] *v* blaze, flare up.

avvantaggiare [avvantad'dʒare] *v* profit, benefit.

avvedersi [avve'dersi] *v* become aware.

avvelenare [avvele'nare] *v* poison. **avvelenamento** *sm* poisoning. **avvelenatore, -trice** *sm*, *sf* poisoner.

avvenire [avve'nire] *v* happen. *sm* future. **avvenimento** *sm* event, occurrence.

avventato [avven'tato] *agg* rash, reckless. **avventare** *v* hurl; (*azzardare*) venture.

avventore [avven'tore], **-a** *sm*, *sf* patron, regular customer.

avventurare [avventu'rare] *v* venture, risk. **avventura** *sf* adventure; (*amorosa*) love affair. **avventuriere** *sm* adventurer.

avverbio [av'verbjo] *sm* adverb.

avversario [avver'sarjo], **-a** *sm*, *sf* adversary, opponent. *agg* opposing.

avversione [avver'sjone] *sf* dislike, aversion.

avversità [avversi'ta] *sf* adversity.

avverso [av'vɛrso] *agg* adverse; opposing.

avvertire [avver'tire] *v* (*osservare*) notice; (*percepire*) feel; (*ammonire*) warn; (*avvisare*) inform. **avvertenza** *sf* warning, notice; (*attenzione*) care; (*istruzioni*) directions *pl*.

avvezzare [avvet'tsare] *v* (*educare*) train; (*abituare*) accustom.

avviare [avvi'are] *v* start (up), set going; (*comm*) set up; direct. **scuola d'avviamento** *sf* training college, technical college. **avviato** *agg* under way; (*prospero*) thriving.

avvicinare [avvitʃi'nare] *v* approach; (*portar vicino*) bring near.

avvilire [avvi'lire] *v* disgrace; (*scoraggiare*) dishearten; humiliate. **avvilito** *agg* downhearted; demoralized.

avviluppare [avvilup'pare] *v* entangle; (*avvolgere*) wrap up.

avvincente [avvin'tʃɛnte] *agg* fascinating.

avvisare [avvi'zare] *v* let know, advise; (*ammonire*) warn. **avviso** *sm* notice, note; announcement; (*pubblicità*) advertisement; opinion. **avviso circolare** circular. **come d'avviso** as advised.

avvizzire [avvit'tsire] *v* wither.

avvocato [avvo'kato] *sm* lawyer, barrister, solicitor; advocate, champion. **avvocatura** *sf* legal profession.

avvolgere [av'voldʒere] *v* envelop, wrap up; (*arrotolare*) roll up, wind.

avvoltoio [avvol'tojo] *sm* vulture.

azalea [adza'lea] *sf* azalea.

azienda [a'dzjenda] *sf* firm, business, company; (*impresa*) undertaking. **azienda agricola** farm. **aziendale** *agg* business.

azione [a'tsjone] *sf* action; (*atto*) deed; (*mec*) movement, motion; (*dir*) lawsuit; (*comm*) share. **azionista** *s(m+f)* shareholder.

azoto [a'dzɔto] *sm* nitrogen.

azzardare [addzar'dare] *v* risk, venture. **azzardarsi** *v* dare. **azzardato** *agg* risky, rash. **azzardo** *sm* risk.

azzuffarsi [addzuf'farsi] *v* brawl, come to blows.

azzurro [ad'dzurro] *agg*, *sm* (sky) blue.

B

babbo ['babbo] *sm (fam)* dad, daddy.
babbuino [babbu'ino] *sm* baboon.
babordo [ba'bordo] *sm* port.
bacca ['bakka] *sf* berry.
baccalà [bakka'la] *sm* dried salt cod.
baccano [bak'kano] *sm* row, din, uproar.
baccello [bat'tʃɛllo] *sm* pod.
bacchetta [bak'ketta] *sf* rod, stick; *(musica)* baton.
baciare [ba'tʃare] *v* kiss. **bacio** *sm* kiss.
bacino [ba'tʃino] *sm* basin; *(anat)* pelvis.
baco ['bako] *sm* larva; *(da seta)* silkworm.
bada ['bada] *sf* **tenere a bada** hold at bay.
badare [ba'dare] *v* **badare a** pay attention to, take care to. **badare di** be careful to. **senza badare a** regardless of.
badessa [ba'dessa] *sf* abbess.
badia [ba'dia] *sf* abbey.
badile [ba'dile] *sm* spade.
baffo ['baffo] *sm* **farsene un baffo** *(fam)* not care a damn. **baffi** *sm pl* moustache *sing.* **leccarsi i baffi** lick one's lips. **ridere sotto i baffi** laugh up one's sleeve.
bagaglio [ba'gaʎʎo] *sm* baggage. **bagagliaio** *sm (ferr)* luggage van; *(auto)* boot. **deposito bagagli** *sm* left luggage.
bagattella [bagat'tɛlla] *sf (gioco)* bagatelle; *(inezia)* trifle.
bagliore [ba'ʎore] *sm* flash.
bagnare [ba'ɲare] *v* wet. **bagnato** *agg* wet.
bagnino [ba'ɲino] *sm* beach attendant, lifeguard.
bagno ['baɲo] *sm* bath; *(locale)* bathroom. **fare il bagno** take a bath. **bagnante** *s(m+f)* bather. **bagnomaria** *sm* bainmarie.
baia ['baja] *sf (geog)* bay.
baionetta [bajo'netta] *sf* bayonet.
balbettare [balbet'tare] *v* stammer.
balbuziente [balbut'tsjɛnte] *s(m+f)* stammerer.
balcone [bal'kone] *sm* balcony. **balconata** *sf (teatro, ecc.)* gallery.
baldacchino [baldak'kino] *sm* canopy; *(rel)* baldachin.
baldanza [bal'dantsa] *sf* self-confidence; audacity. **baldanzoso** *agg* self-confident; audacious.
baldoria [bal'dɔrja] *sf* merrymaking. **far baldoria** make merry.
balena [ba'lena] *sf* whale.
balenare [bale'nare] *v* flash (with lightning); *(apparire improvvisamente)* come in a flash. **baleno** *sm* flash.

balia¹ ['balja] *sf* nurse.
balia² [ba'lia] *sf* **in balia di** in the power of, at the mercy of.
balistica [ba'listika] *sf* ballistics. **balistico** *agg* ballistic.
balla ['balla] *sf (involto)* bale; *(frottola)* fib, lie.
ballare [bal'lare] *v* dance.
ballata [bal'lata] *sf* ballad.
ballerino [balle'rino], **-a** *sm, sf* balletdancer.
balletto [bal'letto] *sm* ballet.
ballo ['ballo] *sm* ball; dance. **essere in ballo** be at stake.
ballottaggio [ballottad'dʒo] *sm* ballot. **ballottare** *v* ballot.
balneare [balne'are] *agg* bathing.
balocco [ba'lɔkko] *sm* toy, plaything.
balordo [ba'lordo] *agg* senseless, absurd; *(tonto)* dull.
balsamo ['balsamo] *sm* balsam; *(lenimento)* balm.
balza ['baltsa] *sf (rupe)* cliff; *(frangia)* fringe.
balzare [bal'tsare] *v* bounce, leap.
bambagia [bam'badʒa] *sf* cotton wool. **tenere nella bambagia** pamper, spoil.
bambinaia [bambi'naja] *sf* (children's) nurse, nanny.
bambino [bam'bino], **-a** *sm, sf* child *(pl* -ren). **bambinata** *sf* childishness. **bambinesco** *adj* puerile.
bamboccio [bam'bottʃo] *sm (sciocco-ne)* simpleton; *(fantoccio)* rag-doll; *(bambino)* bonny child.
bambola ['bambola] *sf* doll.
bambù [bam'bu] *sm* bamboo.
banale [ba'nale] *adj* banal.
banana [ba'nana] *sf* banana. **banano** *sm* banana tree.
banca ['banka] *sf* bank. **bancario** *agg* bank, banking. **banchiere** *sm* banker.
bancarella [banka'rella] *sf* barrow, stall.
bancarotta [banka'rotta] *sf* bankruptcy.
banchetto [ban'ketto] *sm* banquet. **banchettare** *v* banquet, feast.
banchina [ban'kina] *sf (porto)* wharf, quay; *(stazione)* platform.
banco ['banko] *sm* bench; *(di vendita)* counter; *(banca)* bank. **bancogiro** *sm* giro. **banconota** *sf* banknote.
banda¹ ['banda] *sf (lato)* side.
banda² ['banda] *sf (striscia)* stripe; *(radio)* band. **banda sonora** sound-track.

banda[1] ['banda] *sf* group, band; (*delinquenti*) gang.

bandiera [ban'djɛra] *sf* flag, banner. **bandiera di comodo** flag of convenience. **banderuola** *sf* pennant; (*ventaruola*) weather-vane; (*girella*) fickle person.

bandire [ban'dire] *v* proclaim; (*esiliare*) banish. **bandito** *sm* bandit. **banditore** *sm* town-crier. **bando** *sm* proclamation; banishment.

bangio ['bandʒo] *sm invar* banjo.

bar [bar] *sm invar* bar, café.

bara ['bara] *sf* bier, coffin. **aver un piede nella bara** have one foot in the grave.

baracca [ba'rakka] *sf* hut. **mandare avanti la baracca** carry on. **piantare baracca e burattini** abandon everything. **baraccone** *sm* stall, stand.

baraonda [bara'onda] *sf* hubbub, confusion.

barare [ba'rare] *v* cheat. **baro** *sm* cheat.

barattare [barat'tare] *v* barter. **baratto** *sm* barter, exchange.

barattolo [ba'rattolo] *sm* jar, tin.

barba ['barba] *sf* beard. **che barba!** what a bore! **barbuto** *adj* bearded.

barbabietola [barba'bjɛtola] *sf* beetroot.

barbaro ['barbaro] *sm* barbarian. *adj* barbarous.

barbiere [bar'bjɛre] *sm* barber.

barbiturato [barbitu'rato] *sm* barbiturate.

barca ['barka] *sf* boat. **barca a remi** rowing-boat. **barca a vela** sailing-boat. **barca a motore** motor boat. **barcamenarsi** *v* manage.

barcollare [barkol'lare] *v* totter, stagger.

bardare [bar'dare] *v* harness.

barella [ba'rella] *sf* stretcher. **barelliere** *sm* stretcher-bearer.

barile [ba'rile] *sm* barrel, cask.

barista [ba'rista] *sm* barman. *sf* barmaid.

baritono [ba'ritono] *sm* baritone.

barlume [bar'lume] *sm* glimmer.

barocco [ba'rokko] *sm*, *agg* baroque.

barometro [ba'rometro] *sm* barometer.

barone [ba'rone] *sm* baron; (*dell'industria*) tycoon. **baronessa** *sf* baroness.

barra ['barra] *sf* bar, rod.

barricare [barri'kare] *v* barricade. **barricata** *sf* barricade.

barriera [bar'rjɛra] *sf* barrier.

baruffa [ba'ruffa] *sf* brawl.

barzelletta [bardzel'letta] *sf* joke, funny story.

bascula ['baskula] *sf* weighing machine.

base ['baze] *sf* basis (*pl* -ses); (*tec*) base. **a base di** made up of. **in base a** on the basis of. **basamento** *sm* pedestal; foundation. **basare** *v* base, found.

basetta [ba'zetta] *sf* sideburn.

basilica [ba'zilika] *sf* basilica.

basilico [ba'ziliko] *sm* basil.

basso ['basso] *agg* low, low-lying; (*poco profondo*) shallow. *avv* low, low down. *sm* (*musica*) bass. **a basso ... !** down with ... !

bassofondo [basso'fondo] *sm* shallows *pl*. **bassifondi** *sm pl* (*quartieri*) slums *pl*; (*strati sociali*) underworld *sing*.

bassotto [bas'sotto] *sm* dachshund.

bastardo [bas'tardo], **-a** *s*, *agg* bastard; (*non di razza*) mongrel.

bastare [bas'tare] *v* suffice, be enough. **basta!** *inter* enough! (*silenzio*) quiet! **basta che** provided that.

bastimento [basti'mento] *sm* ship.

bastonare [basto'nare] *v* beat, cane. **bastonata** *sf* caning, beating.

bastone [bas'tone] *sm* stick, cane; golf-club. **bastone da passeggio** walking stick.

battaglia [bat'taʎa] *sf* battle; campaign. **cavallo di battaglia** hobby-horse.

battaglio [bat'taʎʎo] *sm* (*campana*) clapper; (*porta*) door-knocker.

battaglione [batta'ʎone] *sm* battalion.

battello [bat'tɛllo] *sm* boat.

battere ['battere] *v* beat. **battere a macchina** type. **battere le mani** clap (one's hands). **in un batter d'occhio** in a flash. **senza batter ciglio** without batting an eyelid.

batteria [batte'ria] *sf* battery; (*sport*) heat; (*insieme*) set.

batterio [bat'terjo] *sm* bacterium (*pl* -a). **batteriologia** *sf* bacteriology. **batteriologo**, **-a** *sm*, *sf* bacteriologist.

battesimo [bat'tezimo] *sm* baptism, christening. **battesimale** *adj* baptismal. **battezzare** *v* baptize, christen.

battibecco [batti'bekko] *sm* quarrel.

batticuore [batti'kwore] *sm* avere il **batticuore** have palpitations. **far venire il batticuore** make anxious.

battimani [batti'mani] *sm* applause.

battistero [battis'tero] *sm* baptistry.

battito ['battito] *sm* beat, pulsation.

battitore [batti'tore] *sm* (*sport*) server, striker; (*caccia*) beater.

battuta [bat'tuta] *sf (colpo)* blow; *(spiritosaggine)* witty remark; *(musica)* beat; *(sport)* service.

batuffolo [ba'tuffolo] *sm* wad.

baule [ba'ule] *sm* trunk. **fare i bauli** *(fam)* go away.

bava ['bava] *sf* dribble.

bavaglino [bavaʎino] *sm* bib.

bavaglio [ba'vaʎo] *sm* gag. **mettere il bavaglio a** gag.

bavero ['bavero] *sm* collar.

bazzicare [battsi'kare] *v* associate with; frequent.

beatitudine [beati'tudine] *sf* beatitude.

beato [be'ato] *agg* blessed. **beato te!** lucky you!

bebè [be'bɛ] *sm* baby.

beccaccia [bek'kattʃa] *sf* woodcock. **beccaccino** *sm* snipe.

beccare [bek'kare] *v* peck; *(fam)* catch, collar.

becchino [bek'kino] *sm* undertaker; gravedigger.

becco¹ ['bekko] *sm* beak; *(bruciatore)* burner.

becco² ['bekko] *sm (caprone)* goat; *(cornuto)* cuckold.

Befana [be'fana] *sf* Epiphany.

beffare [bef'fare] *v* mock. **beffarsi di** make fun of. **beffa** *sf* jest, practical joke.

begli ['beʎi] *V* **bello.**

bei ['bɛi] *V* **bello.**

bel ['bɛl] *V* **bello.**

belare [be'lare] *v* bleat.

Belgio ['bɛldʒo] *sm* Belgium. **belga** *s(m+f)*, *agg*, *m pl* -**gi** Belgian.

belletto [bel'letto] *sm* make-up, rouge.

bellezza [bel'lettsa] *sf* beauty. **che bellezza!** how lovely!

bello ['bɛllo] *agg* beautiful; fine; fair. **il bello è che** the odd thing is (that). **nel bel mezzo** right in the middle. **oh bella!** you don't say! **questa à bella!** *(ironico)* that's a good one! **sul più bello** at the crucial moment.

belva ['belva] *sf* wild animal.

bemolle [be'mɔlle] *sm (musica)* flat.

benché [ben'ke] *cong* although.

bendare [ben'dare] *v (fasciare)* bandage; *(coprire gli occhi)* blindfold. **benda** *sf* bandage; blindfold.

bene ['bɛne] *avv* well. **star bene** feel well; *(abito)* suit. **va bene** all right. *sm* good; *(amore)* love; wealth, property. **beni di consumo** consumer goods *pl.* **voler bene**

a be fond of. **benino** *avv* fairly well, reasonably.

*****benedire** [bene'dire] *v* bless, consecrate. **benedetto** *agg* blessed. **benedetti voi!** lucky you!

beneducato [benedu'kato] *agg* well-mannered.

beneficenza [benefi'tʃɛntsa] *sf* charity.

beneficio [bene'fitʃo] *sm* profit; advantage. **benefico** *agg* beneficial.

benessere [be'nɛssere] *sm* well-being, welfare.

benestante [benes'tante] *agg* comfortably off, well-to-do. **benestare** *sm* well-being; *(autorizzazione)* consent.

benevolo [be'nɛvolo] *agg* kindly, well-disposed.

beninteso [benin'tezo] *avv* naturally, of course.

benvenuto [benve'nuto] *sm, agg* welcome. **dare il benvenuto a** welcome.

benzina [ben'dzina] *sf* gasoline. **far benzina** fill up. **distributore di benzina** *sm* gasoline station or pump.

*****bere** ['bere] *v* drink.

bernoccolo [ber'nokkolo] *sm* bump; *(disposizione)* flair.

berretto [ber'retto] *sm* cap, hat.

bersaglio [ber'saʎo] *sm* target.

bestemmia [bes'temmja] *sf* swear-word, curse. **bestemmiare** *v* swear, curse.

bestia ['bɛstja] *sf* animal, beast; ignoramus. **bestiale** *agg* bestial, brutal; *(fam: intenso)* beastly.

bestiame [bes'tjame] *sm* livestock.

betoniera [beto'njera] *sf* cement-mixer.

bettola ['bettola] *sf* low dive.

betulla [be'tulla] *sf* birch.

bevanda [be'vanda] *sf* drink, beverage. **bevibile** *agg* drinkable.

biada ['bjada] *sf* fodder, forage.

biancheria [bjanke'ria] *sf (indumenti intimi)* underwear; *(da casa)* linen. **bianchetti** [bjan'ketti] *sm pl* whitebait *pl.*

bianchetto [bjan'ketto] *sm* whitewash.

bianco ['bjanko] *agg* white; *(non scritto)* blank. *sm* white.

biancospino [bjanko'spino] *sm* hawthorn.

biascicare [bjaʃi'kare] *v (cibo)* munch; *(parole)* mumble.

biasimare [bjazi'mare] *v* blame. **biasimo** *sm* blame.

Bibbia ['bibbja] *sf* Bible. **biblico** *agg* biblical.

bibita [bi'bita] sf (soft) drink, beverage.
bibliografia [bibljogra'fia] sf bibliography. **bibliografico** agg bibliographical. **bibliografo, -a** sm, sf bibliographer.
biblioteca [bibljo'tɛka] sf library. **bibliotecario, -a** sm, sf librarian.
bicchiere [bik'kjɛre] sm glass, tumbler.
bicicletta [bitʃi'kletta] sf bicycle. **andare in bicicletta** cycle.
bicipite [bi'tʃipite] sm biceps.
bidè [bi'dɛ] sm bidet.
bidone [bi'done] sm drum, can.
bieco ['bjɛko] agg **guardare con occhio bieco** look askance at.
biennale [bien'nale] agg biennial. sf biennial event.
bietta ['bjetta] sf wedge.
biforcarsi [bifor'karsi] v branch off, fork. **biforcazione** sf fork, junction.
bigamia [biga'mia] sf bigamy. **bigamo** sm bigamist.
bighellonare [bigello'nare] v idle; (girellare) saunter.
bigio ['bidʒo] agg grey; (tempo) dull.
bigliardo [biʎ'Aardo] sm billiards.
biglietto [biʎ'Aetto] sm ticket; note; card. **bigliettaio, -a** sm, sf conductor. **biglietteria** sf booking-office.
bigodino [bigo'dino] sm curler, roller.
bigotto [bi'gɔtto], **-a** sm, sf bigot. agg bigoted.
bilancia [bi'lantʃa] sf scales pl; (comm) balance. **Bilancia** sf Libra. **bilanciare** v balance; (pesare) weigh.
bilancio [bi'lantʃo] sm balance sheet; budget.
bile ['bile] sf bile.
bilico ['biliko] sm **in bilico** in the balance.
bilingue [bi'lingwe] agg bilingual.
bilione [bi'ljone] sm a thousand millions.
bimbo ['bimbo], **-a** sm, sf child (pl -ren).
bimensile [bimen'sile] agg fortnightly.
binario [bi'narjo] agg binary. sm rails pl, railway line.
binocolo [bi'nɔkolo] sm binoculars pl.
biochimico [bio'kimiko], **-a** agg biochemical. sm, sf biochemist. sf (scienza) biochemistry.
biografia [biogra'fia] sf biography. **biografico** agg biographical. **biografo, -a** sm, sf biographer.
biologia [biolo'dʒia] sf biology. **biologico** agg biological. **biologo, -a** sm, sf biologist.

biondo ['bjondo] agg blond, fair-haired.
birbante [bir'bante] sm rascal, knave.
birbone [bir'bone] sm rogue, scamp.
birichino [biri'kino], **-a** sm, sf imp, mischievous child. agg impish, cheeky. **birichinata** sf childish prank.
birillo [bi'rillo] sm skittle.
birra ['birra] sf beer. **birreria** sf public house.
bis [bis] inter encore! **dare il bis** give an encore.
bisaccia [bi'zattʃa] sf knapsack, saddle-bag.
bisbetico [biz'betiko] agg cantankerous, peevish.
bisbigliare [bizbi'ʎare] v whisper. **bisbiglio** sm whisper.
biscia ['biʃa] sf snake.
biscotto [bis'kɔtto] sm biscuit.
bisestile [bizes'tile] agg **anno bisestile** leap-year.
bisognare [bizo'ɲare] v be necessary. **bisogno** sm need, requirement. **aver bisogno di** need. **non c'è bisogno** there is no need. **bisognoso** agg needy.
bistecca [bis'tekka] sf steak.
bisticciare [bistit'tʃare] v quarrel. **bisticcio** sm quarrel.
bistrattare [bistrat'tare] v ill-treat.
bitorzolo [bi'tortsolo] sf pimple.
bivio ['bivjo] sm junction, fork.
bizzarro [bid'dzarro] agg strange, odd.
bizzeffe [bid'dzeffe] avv **a bizzeffe** galore.
blandire [blan'dire] v caress, entice. **blandizie** sf pl flattery sing.
blando ['blando] agg bland, mellow.
blasfemo [blas'fɛmo] agg blasphemous.
blatta ['blatta] sf cockroach.
blesità [blezi'ta] sf lisp. **parlar bleso** lisp.
bloccare [blok'kare] v block, blockade. **blocco** sm block; (massa) lump; blockade; (ostruzione) blockage. **in blocco** in bulk.
blu [blu] agg blue. **bluastro** agg bluish.
blusa ['bluza] sf blouse.
boa¹ ['boa] sm invar (zool) boa.
boa² sf (mar) buoy.
boato [bo'ato] sm roar, rumble. **boato sonico** sonic bang.
bobina [bo'bina] sf bobbin, reel.
bocca ['bokka] sf mouth; (apertura) opening. **in bocca al lupo!** good luck!
boccale [bok'kale] sm tankard.
boccata [bok'kata] sf mouthful.

bocchino [bok'kino] *sm* mouthpiece; cigarette-holder.

boccia ['bɔttʃa] *sf* (*sport*) bowl; (*vaso*) decanter; (*bot*) bud.

bocciare [bot'tʃare] *v* (*dir*) repeal; (*esami*) fail.

boccio ['bɔttʃo] *sm also* **bocciolo** bud.

boccone [bok'kone] *sm* mouthful.

bocconi [bok'koni] *avv* prone, flat on one's face.

bofonchiare [bofon'kjare] *v* snort.

boia ['bɔja] *sm invar* executioner. **boiata** *sf* (*fam*) rubbish.

boicottare [boikot'tare] *v* boycott. **boicottaggio** *sm* boycott.

bolide ['bɔlide] *sm* fire-ball. **andare come un bolide** go like a bomb. **passare come un bolide** flash past.

bolla¹ ['bolla] *sf* bubble; (*med*) blister.

bolla² ['bolla] *sf* (*sigillo*) seal; (*papale*) bull; (*comm*) bill.

bollare [bol'lare] *v* seal, stamp.

bolletta [bol'letta] *sf* (*comm*) bill, receipt. **essere in bolletta** (*fam*) be broke. **bollettino** *sm* bulletin, bill.

bollire [bol'lire] *v* boil. **bollente** *agg* boiling. **bollito** *sm* boiled meat. **bollitore** *sm* kettle.

bollo ['bollo] *sm* stamp, seal. **bollo di circolazione** tax disc.

bomba ['bomba] *sf* bomb.

bombardare [bombar'dare] *v* bomb, shell. **bombardamento** *sm* bombardment, shelling.

bombetta [bom'betta] *sf* bowler hat.

bombola ['bombola] *sf* gas cylinder.

bonario [bo'narjo] *agg* good-natured.

bontà [bon'ta] *sf* goodness.

borbottare [borbot'tare] *v* mutter; rumble.

bordello [bor'dello] *sm* brothel; (*confusione*) uproar.

bordo ['bordo] *sm* (*mar*) side; (*orlo*) border, edge. **a bordo** on board. **giornale di bordo** *sm* (ship's) log. **virare di bordo** (*mar*) tack.

borghese [bor'geze] *agg* bourgeois, middle-class; civilian. *s(m+f)* middle-class person; civilian. **in borghese** in civilian or plain clothes. **borghesia** *sf* middle class, bourgeoisie.

borgo ['borgo] *sm* (*paesello*) hamlet; (*sobborgo*) suburb.

boria ['bɔrja] *sf* conceit, arrogance. **metter**

su boria put on airs. **borioso** arrogant, conceited.

borotalco [boro'talko] *sm invar* talcum powder.

borsa¹ ['borsa] *sf* bag; (*della spesa*) shopping bag; (*per documenti*) brief-case; (*diplomatica*) attaché case; (*dell'acqua*) hot-water bottle. **borsa di studio** scholarship, grant. **borsaiolo** *sm* pickpocket. **borsetta** *sf* handbag. **borsista** *s(m+f)* scholarship-holder.

borsa² ['borsa] *sf* (*comm*) stock exchange. **borsa nera** black market. **borsista** *sm* stockbroker.

bosco ['bosko] *sm* wood, forest. **boscaglia** *sf* thicket. **boschereccio** *agg* woody. **boschetto** *sm* grove. **boscoso** *agg* wooded.

botanico [bo'taniko], **-a** *agg* botanical. *sm, sf* botanist. *sf* botany.

botta ['botta] *sf* blow. **fare a botte** come to blows. **dare le botte** a spank, slap.

botte ['botte] *sf* cask, barrel.

bottega [bot'tega] *sf* shop; (*laboratorio*) workshop. **bottegaio, -a** *sm, sf* shopkeeper. **botteghino** *sm* small shop; (*teatro*) box-office.

bottiglia [bot'tiʎa] *sf* bottle.

bottone [bot'tone] *sm* button. **attaccare un bottone a** (*fam*) buttonhole. **bottoni gemelli** *sm* cuff-links *pl*.

bozza ['bɔttsa] *sf* draft, sketch; (*stampa*) galley proof. **bozzetto** *sm* sketch.

bozzolo ['bottsolo] *sm* cocoon.

braccetto [brat'tʃetto] *sm* **a braccetto** arm in arm.

braccialetto [brattʃa'letto] *sm* bracelet.

bracciante [brat'tʃante] *sm* labourer.

bracciata [brat'tʃata] *sf* armful.

braccio ['brattʃo] *sm, pl* **-a** *f in anat* sense arm. **prendere in braccio** take into one's arms. **bracciolo** *sm* (*sedia*) arm.

braciola [bra'tʃɔla] *sf* chop.

bramare [bra'mare] *v* yearn or long for. **brama** *sf* longing, strong desire.

branchia ['brankja] *sf* gill.

branco ['branko] *sm* flock, drove, herd.

brancolare [branko'lare] *v* grope.

branda ['branda] *sf* camp-bed.

brandello [bran'dello] *sm* shred, tatter.

brandire [bran'dire] *v* brandish.

brano ['brano] *sm* (*pezzo*) shred, piece; (*frammento di opera*) passage, extract.

branzino [bran'dzino] *sm* sea bass.

brasare [bra'zare] *v* braise. **brasato** *sm* braised beef.

bravo ['bravo] *agg* good; capable; *(dabbene)* decent. *inter* well done! **bravura** *sf* skill.

breccia ['brettʃa] *sf* breach.

bretelle [bre'tɛlle] *sf pl* braces *pl*.

breve ['brɛve] *agg* brief, short. *sf* breve. **per farla breve** to cut a long story short. **tra breve** shortly. **brevità** *sf* brevity.

brevetto [bre'vetto] *sm* patent. **brevettare** *v* patent.

brezza ['brettsa] *sf* breeze.

bricco ['brikko] *sm* jug, pot.

briccone [brik'kone] *sm* knave, rascal. *agg* knavish, mischievous.

briciola ['britʃola] *sf* crumb. **briciolo** *sm* tiny piece, morsel.

bridge ['bridʒ] *sm invar (carte)* bridge.

briga ['briga] *sf* trouble. **attaccar briga** pick a quarrel. **darsi** *or* **prendersi la briga di** go to the trouble of.

brigadiere [briga'djere] *sm* sergeant-major; *(generale)* brigadier.

brigante [bri'gante] *sm* brigand, bandit.

brigata [bri'gata] *sf* company, group; *(mil)* brigade; *(uccelli)* flock.

briglia ['briʎa] *sf* bridle. **tenere in briglia** rein in, restrain.

brillare [bril'lare] *v* shine, sparkle, glitter. **brillante** *agg* sparkling, brilliant. **brillo** *agg* tipsy.

brina ['brina] *sf* rime, hoar-frost.

brindare [brin'dare] *v* **brindare a drink to,** toast.

brindello [brin'dɛllo] *sm* shred, tatter.

brindisi [brindizi] *sm* toast. **fare un brindisi a** drink to, toast.

brio ['brio] *sm* liveliness, vivacity.

britannico [bri'tanniko], **-a** *agg* British. *sm, sf* Briton, British person.

brivido ['brivido] *sm* shudder, shiver. **aver dei brividi** shudder, shiver.

brocca ['brɔkka] *sf* jug, pitcher.

broccolo ['brɔkkolo] *sm* broccoli.

brodo ['brɔdo] *sm* broth, soup. **tutto fa brodo** it is all grist to the mill.

broglio ['brɔʎo] *sm* malpractice, racket.

bronchite [bron'kite] *sf* bronchitis.

broncio ['brontʃo] *sm* **tenere** *or* **portare il broncio** sulk.

brontolare [bronto'lare] *v* mutter, grumble. **brontolone, -a** *sm, sf* grumbler.

bronzo ['brondzo] *sm* bronze.

bruciapelo [brutʃa'pelo] *sm* **a bruciapelo** point-blank.

bruciare [bru'tʃare] *v* burn, scorch. **bruciare le tappe** hurry. **bruciatura** *sf* burn, scald. **bruciore** *sm* burning sensation, intense desire.

bruco ['bruko] *sm* larva, caterpillar.

brufolo ['brufolo] *sm* pimple.

brughiera [bru'gjera] *sf* heath, moor.

brulicare [bruli'kare] *v* swarm, crawl, teem. **brulichio** *sm* swarming, teeming.

brullo ['brullo] *agg* bleak; barren.

bruno ['bruno] *agg* brown; dark.

brusco ['brusko] *agg* sharp; brusque, harsh; *(improvviso)* sudden.

brusio [bru'zio] *sm* bustle, hum.

bruto ['bruto] *sm, agg* brute. **brutale** *agg* brutal.

brutto ['brutto] *agg* ugly, plain; *(non buono)* bad. **avere brutta cera** look poorly. **far brutta figura** cut a sorry figure, disgrace oneself. **il brutto è che** the worst is (that), the difficulty is (that).

buca ['buka] *sf* hole, pit. **buca delle lettere** *sf* letter-box. **bucare** *v* make a hole in; *(biglietto)* punch; *(gomma)* puncture. **bucatura** *sf* puncture.

bucaneve [buka'neve] *sm invar* snowdrop.

bucato [bu'kato] *sm* washing. **fare il bucato** do the washing.

buccia ['buttʃa] *sf* peel, skin, rind.

buco ['buko] *sm* hole. **buco nell'acqua** failure.

buddismo [bud'dizmo] *sm* Buddhism. **buddista** *s(m+f)*, *agg* Buddhist.

budello [bu'dɛllo] *sm* gut.

budino [bu'dino] *sm* pudding.

bue ['bue] *sm, pl* **buoi** ox *(pl* -en); *(carne)* beef.

bufalo ['bufalo], **-a** *sm, sf* buffalo.

bufera [bu'fera] *sf* gale, blizzard.

buffè [buf'fɛ] *sm invar (credenza)* sideboard; *(gastr)* buffet.

buffo ['buffo] *agg* comic(al), amusing. *sm (teatro)* comic. **il buffo è che** the odd thing is (that).

bugia¹ [bu'dʒia] *sf* lie. **dire bugie** tell lies. **bugiardo, -a** *sm, sf* liar.

bugia² [bu'dʒia] *sf* candlestick.

buio ['bujo] *sm, agg* dark. **al buio** in the dark. **buio pesto** pitch-dark.

bulbo ['bulbo] *sm* bulb. **bulbo oculare** eyeball.

Bulgaria [bulga'ria] *sf* Bulgaria. **bulgaro, -a** *s, agg* Bulgarian.

bullone [bul'lone] *sm* bolt.

buono¹ [ˈbwɔno], **-a** agg good; kind; (giusto) right. **a buon conto** apropos. **a buon mercato** cheap(ly). **buoncostume** sm good conduct. **buongustaio, -a** sm, sf gourmet. **buongusto** sm good taste. **buono a nulla** sm, agg good-for-nothing. **buonsenso** sm good sense. **con le buone o con le cattive** by hook or by crook. sm, sf good person.

buono² [ˈbwɔno] sm (documento) bond, coupon, voucher.

buonora [bwoˈnora] sf **alla buonora!** at last! **di buonora** early.

burattino [buratˈtino] sm puppet.

burbero [ˈburbero], **-a** agg grumpy, gruff. sm, sf grumpy person.

burlare [burˈlare] v make a fool of; (scherzare) joke. **burlarsi di** make fun of. **burla** sf joke, jest.

burocrate [buˈrokrate] sm bureaucrat. **burocratico** agg bureaucratic. **burocrazia** sf bureaucracy; (fam) red tape.

burrasca [burˈraska] sf blizzard, storm. **burrascoso** agg stormy.

burro [ˈburro] sm butter.

burrone [burˈrone] sm ravine.

bussare [busˈsare] v knock.

bussola [ˈbussola] sf compass.

busta [ˈbusta] sf envelope.

bustarella [bustaˈrella] sf bribe.

busto [ˈbusto] sm bust; (indumento) corset.

buttare [butˈtare] throw. **buttar giù** (cibo) gulp down; (scritto) jot down; (gastr) put in boiling water.

C

cabina [kaˈbina] sf (aero, mar) cabin; (telefono, ecc.) booth; (ascensore) cage.

cablogramma [kabloˈgramma] sm cable.

cacao [kaˈkao] sm cocoa.

cacare [kaˈkare] v (volg) shit.

caccia¹ [ˈkattʃa] sf hunt, chase; (ricerca) pursuit, search. **a caccia di** in search of. **caccia grossa** big game. **dar la caccia** pursue.

caccia² [ˈkattʃa] sm invar (aero) fighter; (mar) destroyer.

cacciagione [kattʃaˈdʒone] sf game.

cacciare [katˈtʃare] v hunt; (espellere) throw or drive out; (introdurre) thrust; (mettere) stick, put.

cacciavite [kattʃaˈvite] sm screwdriver.

cachi [ˈkaki] agg, sm khaki.

cacio [ˈkatʃo] sm cheese.

cactus [ˈkaktus] sm cactus.

cadauno [kadaˈuno] agg, pron each.

cadavere [kaˈdavere] sm corpse.

*cadere [kaˈdere] v fall; (aero) crash. **cader dalle nuvole** be dumbfounded. **lasciar cadere** drop. **caduta** sf fall; (aero) crash.

cadetto [kaˈdetto] sm younger son; (mil) cadet.

caffè [kafˈfɛ] sm coffee; (locale) café. **caffettiera** sf coffee-pot; (macchina) coffee-maker.

caffeina [kaffeˈina] sf caffeine.

cafone [kaˈfone] sm (fam) lout.

cagionare [kadʒoˈnare] v cause. **cagione** sf cause, reason. **a cagion di** on account of, owing to.

cagna [ˈkaɲa] sf bitch.

cagnara [kaˈɲara] sf (fam) row, uproar.

calabrone [kalaˈbrone] sm hornet.

calamaio [kalaˈmajo] sm inkstand, inkwell.

calamaro [kalaˈmaro] sm squid.

calamita [kalaˈmita] sf magnet.

calamità [kalamiˈta] sf calamity.

calare [kaˈlare] v lower, let down; (maglia) decrease, cast off; (scendere) go down; (abbassarsi) drop. **calata** sf descent; (banchina) quay.

calcagno [kalˈkaɲo] sm heel. **stare alle calcagna di** follow closely.

calcare¹ [kalˈkare] v press (hard); (disegno) trace. **calco** sm (impronta di rilievo) cast; (disegno) tracing.

calcare² [kalˈkare] sm limestone.

calce [ˈkaltʃe] sf lime.

calcestruzzo [kaltʃesˈtruttso] sm concrete.

calcio¹ [ˈkaltʃo] sm (chim) calcium.

calcio² [ˈkaltʃo] sm (fucile) rifle butt.

calcio³ [ˈkaltʃo] sm kick; (sport) football. **calcio di rigore** penalty (kick). **dare un calcio** kick.

calcolare [kalkoˈlare] v calculate; consider. **calcolatore, -trice** sm, sf calculator, computer.

calcolo¹ [ˈkalkolo] sm calculation; (congettura) reckoning; (mat) calculus. **a calcoli fatti** all things considered.

calcolo² [ˈkalkolo] sm (med) calculus, stone.

caldaia [kal'daja] *sf* boiler.

caldo ['kaldo] *agg* warm; (*molto*) hot. *sm* warmth; heat. **aver** *or* **far caldo** be hot.

caleidoscopio [kaleido'skɔpjo] *sm* kaleidoscope.

calendario [kalen'darjo] *sm* calendar.

calibro ['kalibro] *sm* calibre; (*mec*) gauge; (*strumento*) callipers *pl*.

calice ['kalitʃe] *sm* goblet; (*rel*) chalice; (*bot*) calyx.

caligine [ka'lidʒine] *sf* fog.

calligrafia [kalligra'fia] *sf* handwriting.

callo ['kallo] *sm* corn. **callifugo** *sm, pl* -ghi corn-plaster.

calmare [kal'mare] *v* calm; ease. **calmarsi** *v* calm down. **calma** *sf* calm, tranquillity. **perdere la calma** lose one's temper. **prendersela con calma** take it easy. **calmante** *sm* sedative. **calmo** *agg* calm.

calore [ka'lore] *sm* heat; (*cordialità*) warmth.

caloria [kalo'ria] *sf* calorie.

calorifero [kalo'nifero] *sm* radiator.

caloroso [kalo'rozo] *agg* warm.

calpestare [kalpes'tare] *v* trample on.

calunnia [ka'lunnja] *sf* calumny; (*diffamazione orale*) slander; (*scritta*) libel. **calunniare** *v* slander; libel.

calvo ['kalvo] *agg* bald. **calvizie** *sf* baldness.

calza ['kaltsa] *sf* (*corta*) sock; (*lunga*) stocking. **fare la calza** knit. **ferro da calza** *sm* knitting-needle.

calzare [kal'tsare] *v* put on; (*portare*) wear; (*convenire*) fit. **calzatura** *sf* footwear.

calzolaio [kaltso'lajo] *sm* shoemaker. **calzoleria** *sf* shoe shop.

calzoni [kal'tsoni] *sm pl* trousers *pl*.

camaleonte [kamale'onte] *sm* chameleon.

cambiale [kam'bjale] *sf* bill of exchange.

cambiare [kam'bjare] *v* change. **cambiar casa** move. **tanto per cambiare** just for a change. **cambiamento** *sm* change.

cambio [kam'bjo] *sm* change; (*econ*) exchange; (*auto*) transmission, gearbox.

camera [kamera] *sf* room; (*da letto*) bedroom; (*assemblea, tec*) chamber. **camera d'aria** (*pneumatico*) inner tube. **musica da camera** *sf* chamber music.

camerata[1] [kame'rata] *sf* dormitory.

camerata[2] [kame'rata] *s(m+f)* comrade; (*fam*) mate.

cameriera [kame'rjera] *sf* (*albergo*) chamber-maid; (*ristorante*) waitress; (*domestica*) maid.

cameriere [kame'rjere] *sm* (*ristorante*) waiter; servant.

camicia [ka'mitʃa] *sf* shirt; (*da donna*) blouse; (*tec*) jacket. **camicia da notte** night-gown. **camicia di forza** strait-jacket. **camiciola** *sf* (*maglia*) vest; T-shirt.

camino [ka'mino] *sm* fireplace; chimney.

camion [ka'mjon] *sm invar* truck **camioncino** *sm* van.

cammello [kam'mello] *sm* camel.

camminare [kammi'nare] *v* walk; (*procedere*) go. **camminata** *sf* walk.

cammino [kam'mino] *sm* way; (*percorso*) journey; (*sentiero*) path. **mettersi in cammino** set out.

camorra [ka'morra] *sf* racket. **camorrista** *s(m+f)* racketeer.

camoscio [ka'moʃo] *sm* chamois; (*pelle*) chamois leather.

campagna [kam'paɲa] *sf* country; (*paesaggio*) countryside; (*terreno*) land; (*villeggiatura*) holidays *pl*; (*mil, propaganda, ecc.*) campaign. **campagnolo** *agg* rural, country.

campana [kam'pana] *sf* bell; (*di lampada*) lampshade. **campanello** *sm* bell. **campanile** *sm* bell tower.

campare [kam'pare] *v* live.

campeggiare [kamped'dʒare] *v* camp. **campeggio** *sm* camping; (*terreno*) campsite.

campestre [kam'pestre] *agg* rural, country.

campione [kam'pjone] *sm* (*sport, difensore*) champion; (*piccola quantità*) sample; (*di tessuto*) pattern. **campionario** *sm* sample collection; pattern book. **campionessa** *sf* champion.

campo ['kampo] *sm* field. **campo di golf** golf-course. **campo di tennis** tennis court.

camposanto [kampo'santo] *sm* cemetery.

camuffamento [kamuffa'mento] *sm* disguise; (*mil*) camouflage. **camuffare** *v* disguise; camouflage.

camuso [ka'muzo] *agg* snub-nosed.

Canada [ka'nada] *sm* Canada. **Canadese** *s(m+f), agg* Canadian.

canaglia [ka'naʎa] *sf* scoundrel; (*marmaglia*) rabble.

canale [ka'nale] *sm* canal; (*radio, TV*) channel. **Canale della Manica** (English)

Channel. **canale di scarico** drain. **canale di scolo** gutter.

canapa ['kanapa] *sf* hemp.

canapè [kana'pɛ] *sm* (*mobile*) settee; (*tartina*) canapé.

canarino [kana'rino] *sm* canary. *agg* canary yellow.

cancellare [kantʃel'lare] *v* cancel, wipe out; (*con gomma*) rub out; (*con penna*) cross out.

cancelliere [kantʃel'ljere] *sm* chancellor. **cancelleria** *sf* chancellery, chancery; (*cartoleria*) stationery.

cancello [kan'tʃɛllo] *sm* gate. **cancellata** *sf* railings *pl*.

cancro [kan'kro] *sm* cancer. **Cancro** *sm* Cancer.

cancrena [kan'krena] *sf* gangrene.

candeggiare [kanded'dʒare] *v* bleach. **candeggina** *sf* bleach.

candela [kan'dela] *sf* candle; (*auto*) sparking-plug. **precipitare in candela** do a nose-dive. **candelabro** *sm* candlestick; (*a bracci*) candelabra.

candidato [kandi'dato], **-a** *sm*, *sf* candidate. **candidatura** *sf* candidature.

candido ['kandido] *agg* spotless, snow-white; (*sincero*) candid.

candito [kan'dito] *agg* candied, crystallized.

cane ['kane] *sm* dog. **cane bastardo** mongrel. **cane da guardia** watch-dog. **cane da salotto** lap-dog.

canestro [ka'nestro] *sm* basket.

canguro [kan'guro] *sm* kangaroo.

canicola [ka'nikola] *sf* heat-wave.

canile [ka'nile] *sm* kennel.

canino [ka'nino] *agg* canine.

canna ['kanna] *sf* cane; (*pianta*) reed; (*fucile*) barrel; (*bicicletta*) cross-bar; (*pesca*) rod; (*tubo, organo*) pipe. **cannello** *sm* tube; (*per saldare*) blowpipe.

cannella [kan'nella] *sf* cinnamon.

cannibale [kan'nibale] *sm* cannibal.

cannocchiale [kannok'kjale] *sm* telescope.

cannone [kan'none] *sm* cannon. **cannonata** *sf* cannon shot. **è una cannonata!** (*fam*) it's terrific!

cannuccia [kan'nuttʃa] *sf* (*per bibite*) (drinking) straw; (*di pipa*) stem.

canoa [ka'nɔa] *sf* canoe.

canone ['kanone] *sm* canon; (*soldi dovuti*) fee; (*per affitto*) rent.

canonico [ka'nɔniko] *agg* canonical. **diritto canonico** *sm* canon law. **canonica** *sf* rectory.

canonizzare [kanonid'dzare] *v* canonize.

canottaggio [kanot'taddʒo] *sm* rowing. **canottiere** *sm* oarsman.

canottiera [kanot'tjera] *sf* T-shirt.

canotto [ka'nɔtto] *sm* rowing-boat; (*di salvataggio*) lifeboat.

canovaccio [kano'vattʃo] *sm* (*per stoviglie*) dishcloth; (*teatro*) plot.

cantare [kan'tare] *v* sing; (*del gallo*) crow; (*cinguettare*) chirp; (*fam: fare la spia*) squeal. **cantata** *sf* singsong; (*musica*) cantata. **canterellare** or **canticchiare** *v* hum.

cantiere [kan'tjere] *sm* yard; (*mar*) shipyard, dockyard.

cantilena [kanti'lena] *sf* singsong.

canto¹ ['kanto] *sm* song; (*poesia*) lyric; (*liturgia*) chant. **canto popolare** folksong.

canto² ['kanto] *sm* (*angolo*) corner; (*parte*) side. **da canto** aside. **d'altro canto** on the other hand. **da un canto** in a way.

cantone¹ [kan'tone] *sm* corner. **cantonata** *sf* (street-)corner; (*errore*) blunder. **prendere una cantonata** blunder.

cantone² [kan'tone] *sm* (*geog*) canton.

cantoniere [kanto'njere] *sm* (*ferr*) signalman.

canuto [ka'nuto] *agg* white-haired.

canzonare [kantso'nare] *v* make fun of, tease, mock. **canzonatore, -trice** *sm*, *sf* mocker. **canzonatura** *sf* mockery.

canzone [kan'tsone] *sf* song; (*discorso noioso*) old story. **canzonetta** *sf* pop song.

caos ['kaos] *sm* chaos. **caotico** *agg* chaotic.

capace [ka'patʃe] *agg* (*abile*) capable; (*in grado di*) able. **capacità** *sf* capacity; ability.

capanna [ka'panna] *sf* hut. **capannone** *sm* shed; (*aero*) hangar.

caparbio [ka'parbjo] *agg* stubborn.

caparra [ka'parra] *sf* deposit.

capello [ka'pello] *sm* hair. **capelli** *sm pl* hair *sing*. **averne fin sopra i capelli (di)** be heartily sick (of). **capelluto** *agg* hairy. **cuoio capelluto** *sm* scalp.

capezzale [kapet'tsale] *sm* **al capezzale di** at the bedside.

capezzolo [ka'pettsolo] *sm* nipple.

capire [ka'pire] *v* understand; (*rendersi*

conto) realize. **farsi capire** make oneself understood. **si capisce** naturally.

capitale [kapi'tale] *sm* (*econ*) capital. *sf* capital (city). *agg* capital. fundamental; (*principale*) main. **capitalismo** *sm* capitalism. **capitalista** *s*(*m*+*f*), *agg* capitalist.

capitano [kapi'tano] *sm* captain.

capitare [kapi'tare] *v* (*giungere*) turn up; (*presentarsi*) arise, come up; (*accadere*) happen. **capitar bene** strike lucky. **dove capita** anywhere.

capitello [kapi'tɛllo] *sm* capital.

capitolo [ka'pitolo] *sm* chapter. **aver voce in capitolo** have a say in the matter.

capo ['kapo] *sm* head; (*pezzo*) item; (*geog*) cape. **da capo** again, from the beginning. **da capo a fondo** from top to bottom. **da un capo all'altro** from one end to the other. **in capo a** within. **per sommi capi** briefly, in short. **venire a capo di** get to the bottom of.

capobanda [kapo'banda] *sm invar* ringleader; (*musica*) bandmaster.

capodanno [kapo'danno] *sm* New Year's Day.

capofitto [kapo'fitto] *agg* **a capofitto** headlong; (*con massimo impegno*) wholeheartedly.

capogiro [kapo'dʒiro] *sm* giddiness, dizzy spell. **fare venire il capogiro a** make dizzy.

capolavoro [kapola'voro] *sm* masterpiece.

capolinea [kapo'linea] *sm, pl* **capilinea** terminus.

capoluogo [kapo'lwɔgo] *sm, pl* -**ghi** main town, capital.

capomastro [kapo'mastro] *sm* foreman.

capoofficina [kapoofi'tʃina] *sm, pl* **capiofficina** foreman.

caporale [kapo'rale] *sm* corporal.

caposala [kapo'sala] *s*(*m*+*f*), *pl* **capisala, caposala** (*fabbrica*) foreman; (*albergo*) head-waiter; (*ospedale*) ward sister.

capostazione [kaposta'tsjone] *sm, pl* **capistazione** station-master.

capotare [kapo'tare] *v* (*auto*) overturn; (*mar*) capsize.

capote [ka'pɔt] *sf, pl* -**s** (*auto*) hood.

capotreno [kapo'treno] *sm* guard.

*****capovolgere** [kapo'vɔldʒere] *v* overturn; (*fig*) turn upside down, reverse; (*mar*) capsize. **capovolgimento** *sm* reversal.

cappa ['kappa] *sf* cloak; (*di camino*) hood.

cappella¹ [kap'pɛlla] *sf* chapel. **cappellano** *sm* chaplain.

cappella² [kap'pɛlla] *sf* (*di fungo*) cap.

cappello [kap'pɛllo] *sm* hat. **cappellaio** *sm* hatter.

cappero ['kappero] *sm* caper. **capperi!** *inter* gosh! good heavens!

cappotta [kap'pɔtta] *sf* (*auto*) hood.

cappotto [kap'pɔtto] *sm* coat; (*bridge*) slam.

cappuccino [kapput'tʃino] *sm* coffee with milk, cappuccino; (*rel*) Capuchin friar.

cappuccio [kap'puttʃo] *sm* hood; (*tec*) cap; (*rel*) cowl.

capra ['kapra] *sf* goat. **capretto** *sm* kid. **capro** *sm* he-goat. **capro espiatorio** scapegoat.

capriccio [ka'prittʃo] *sm* whim, fancy. **fare i capricci** have tantrums.

Capricorno [kapri'kɔrno] *sm* Capricorn.

caprifoglio [kapri'fɔʎʎo] *sm* honeysuckle.

capriola¹ [kapri'ɔla] *sf* somersault, jump.

capriola² [kapri'ɔla] *sf* (*zool*) roe deer. **capriolo** *sm* roebuck.

capsico [kap'siko] *sm* capsicum.

capsula ['kapsula] *sf* capsule; (*di dente*) crown.

carabiniere [karabi'njere] *sm* policeman, soldier in police corps.

caraffa [ka'raffa] *sf* carafe, jug.

caramella [kara'mɛlla] *sf* sweet. **caramellato** *agg* candied; (*zucchero*) caramelized.

carato [ka'rato] *sm* carat.

carattere [ka'rattere] *sm* (*indole*) nature; (*forza, lettera*) character; characteristic; (*teatro*) role; type. **caratteristica** *sf* characteristic, (*distinctive*) feature; (*tec*) specification. **caratteristico** *agg* typical, distinctive.

carboidrato [karboi'drato] *sm* carbohydrate.

carbonchio [kar'bonkjo] *sm* carbuncle; (*vet*) anthrax; (*agric*) blight.

carbone [kar'bone] *sm* coal. **carbone coke** coke. **carbone di legna** charcoal. **carboncino** *sm* (*disegno*) charcoal.

carbonio [kar'bɔnjo] *sm* carbon.

carburante [karbu'rante] *sm* fuel.

carburatore [karbura'tore] *sm* carburettor.

carcassa [kar'kassa] *sf* carcass; (*fam*) wreck.

carcere ['kartʃere] *sm* prison, jail. **carcerato, -a** *sm, sf* prisoner. **carceriere, -a** *sm, sf* jailer.

carciofo [kar'tʃɔfo] *sm* artichoke.

cardiaco [kar'diako] *agg* cardiac. **attacco cardiaco** *sm* heart attack. **cardiologo, -a** *sm, sf* heart specialist, cardiologist.

cardinale [kardi'nale] *sm, agg* cardinal.

cardine ['kardine] *sm* hinge; *(fig)* cornerstone.

cardo ['kardo] *sm (bot)* thistle.

carena [ka'rɛna] *sf* hull. **(bacino di) carenaggio** *sm* dry dock.

carestia [kares'tia] *sf* famine.

carezzare [karet'tsare] *v* stroke, caress. **carezza** *sf* caress. **fare le carezze** a pat, stroke.

cariarsi [ka'rjarsi] *v* decay.

carica ['karika] *sf (impiego)* position; *(ufficio pubblico)* office; *(mil, elett)* charge; *(sport)* tackle.

caricare [kari'kare] *v* load; *(riempire)* fill; *(mil, elett)* charge; *(sport)* tackle; *(orologio, molla)* wind up.

caricatura [karika'tura] *sf* caricature.

carico ['kariko] *sm, pl -chi (di nave)* cargo; *(peso)* burden; *(tec)* load. **a carico di** *(contro)* against; *(a spese di)* at the expense of, chargeable to. **testimone a carico** witness for the prosecution. *agg* loaded, filled (with), full (of).

carie ['karje] *sf (dentaria)* tooth decay; *(di legno, cereali, ecc.)* rot.

carino [ka'rino] *agg* lovely, charming.

carità [kari'ta] *sf* charity; *(misericordia)* compassion. **aver carità di** take pity on. **fare la carità** give alms. **per carità!** God forbid!

carlinga [kar'linga] *sf* fuselage.

carnagione [karna'dʒone] *sf* complexion, skin.

carne ['karne] *sf* flesh; *(alimento)* meat. **carne di manzo/maiale/vitello** beef/pork/veal. **carnale** *agg* carnal. **carnoso** *agg* fleshy.

carneficina [karnefi'tʃina] *sf* slaughter. **carnefice** *sm* executioner.

carnevale [karne'vale] *sm* carnival.

carnivoro [kar'nivoro] **, -a** *sm, sf* carnivore. *agg* carnivorous.

caro ['karo] *agg* dear. **aver caro** hold dear. **pagar caro** pay a lot for; *(fig)* pay dearly for. **cari** *sm pl* loved ones *pl*.

carogna [ka'roɲa] *sf* carrion; *(fam)* bastard, sod.

carosello [karo'zɛllo] *sm* merry-go-round.

carota [ka'rɔta] *sf* carrot.

carovana [karo'vana] *sf* caravan; procession.

carpione [kar'pjone] *sm* **in carpione** soused.

carponi [kar'poni] *avv* on all fours.

carrabile [kar'rabile] *agg* **passo carrabile** *sm* passageway.

carreggiata [karred'dʒata] *sf* carriageway, track. **rimettersi in carreggiata** catch up. **uscire di carreggiata** go off the road; *(fig)* go astray.

carrello [kar'rello] *sm (vagoncino)* trolley; *(mec)* (under-)carriage.

carretta [kar'retta] *sf* cart.

carriera [kar'rjɛra] *sf* career; *(velocità)* full speed. **fare carriera** get on, make good.

carriola [kar'rjɔla] *sf* wheelbarrow.

carro ['karro] *sm (a quattro ruote)* wagon; *(a due ruote)* cart. **carro armato** armoured vehicle, tank. **carro attrezzi** breakdown van. **carro funebre** hearse. **carro merci** goods wagon.

carrozza [kar'rottsa] *sf* coach. **carrozza letto** sleeping-car, sleeper. **in carrozza!** all aboard!

carrucola [kar'rukola] *sf* pulley.

carta ['karta] *sf* paper; *(geog)* map; *(da gioco, documento)* card; *(statuto)* charter. **carta asciugante** *o* **assorbente** blotting paper. **carta carbone** carbon paper. **carta da parati** wallpaper. **cartapecora** *sf* parchment. **cartapesta** *sf* papier mâché. **cartastraccia** *sf* waste paper.

cartella [kar'tella] *sf (custodia per fogli)* folder; *(busta di pelle)* brief-case; *(per scolari)* satchel; *(scheda)* card, file. **cartellino** [kartel'lino] *sm* tag.

cartello [kar'tello] *sm (insegna)* sign; *(indicatore)* signpost, road sign; *(avviso)* notice, poster. **cartellone** *sm* poster.

cartilagine [karti'ladʒine] *sf* cartilage.

cartolaio [karto'lajo], **-a** *sm, sf* stationer. **cartoleria** *sf* stationer's (shop).

cartolina [karto'lina] *sf* postcard.

cartone [kar'tone] *sm* cardboard; *(disegno)* cartoon. **cartoni animati** *(cinema)* cartoons *pl*. **cartoncino** *sm* card.

cartuccia [kar'tuttʃa] *sf* cartridge.

casa ['kaza] *sf (edificio, dinastia)* house; *(comm)* firm. **a casa** *(stato in' luogo)* at home; *(moto a luogo)* home. **a casa del diavolo** off the beaten track. **cambiar casa** move house. **casa di cura** nursing home. **casa popolare** council house.

casalinga [kaza'linga] *sf* housewife. **casalinghi** *sm pl* household goods *pl.* **casalingo** *agg* domestic; (*semplice*) homely, plain.

cascame [kas'kame] *sm* waste.

cascare [kas'kare] *v* fall; (*capelli, denti*) fall out; (*muri, ecc.*) fall down. **cascata** *sf* fall; (*d'acqua*) waterfall; (*perle, ecc.*) cascade.

cascina [ka'ʃina] *sf* dairy farm; (*casa colonica*) farmhouse.

casco ['kasko] *sm* helmet; (*parrucchieri*) hair-drier.

caseggiato [kazed'dʒato] *sm* block of buildings.

casella [ka'zella] *sf* (*riquadro*) square; (*scompartimento*) compartment. **casella postale** post-office box. **casellario** *sm* (*mobile*) filing cabinet; (*ufficio*) registry.

casello [ka'zɛllo] *sm* (*ferr*) signal-box; (*autostrada*) toll-booth.

caserma [ka'zɛrma] *sf* barracks *pl.*

casino [ka'zino] *sm* (*fam: confusione*) row, racket; (*postribolo*) brothel; (*casa signorile*) lodge.

casinò [kazi'nɔ] *sm* casino.

caso ['kazo] *sm* case; (*affare*) matter; (*combinazione, destino*) chance; possibility. **a caso** at random. **fare caso a** heed, attach importance to. **in caso** in case. **in caso diverso** *or* **contrario** otherwise. **in ogni caso** in any case, at any rate. **per caso** by chance. **poniamo il caso** let us suppose.

cassa ['kassa] *sf* case, box; (*istituzione*) fund; (*dove si paga*) cash desk. **cassa da morto** coffin. **cassa pronta** ready cash. **libro di cassa** cash-book.

casseruola [kasse'rwɔla] *sf* casserole, saucepan.

cassetta [kas'setta] *sf* box; (*teatro*) takings *pl.* **cassetto** *sm* drawer. **cassettone** *sm* chest of drawers.

cassiere [kas'sjɛre], **-a** *sm, sf* cashier.

casta ['kasta] *sf* caste.

castagno [kas'taɲo] *sm* chestnut tree; (*colore*) chestnut. *agg* chestnut. **castagna** *sf* chestnut. **castagnola** *sf* (*petardo*) cracker.

castello [kas'tɛllo] *sm* castle; (*impalcatura*) scaffolding. **castello di poppa** quarterdeck. **castello di prua** forecastle.

castigare [kasti'gare] *v* punish. **castigo** *sm, pl* **-ghi** punishment.

casto ['kasto] *agg* chaste. **castità** *sf* chastity.

castoro [kas'tɔro] *sm* beaver.

castrare [kas'trare] *v* castrate, geld. **castrato** *sm* (*carne*) lamb.

casuale [kazu'ale] *agg* fortuitous, accidental; (*dir*) contingent. **casualmente** *avv* by chance.

catacomba [kata'komba] *sf* catacomb.

catafascio [kata'faʃo] *sm* **andare a catafascio** go to rack and ruin.

catalizzatore [katalidzza'tore] *sm* catalyst. *agg* catalytic.

catalogo [ka'talogo] *sm, pl* **-ghi** catalogue, list. **catalogare** *v* catalogue, list.

catapulta [kata'pulta] *sf* catapult; (*missili*) launcher. **catapultare** *v* launch.

catarifrangente [katarifran'dʒɛnte] *sm* reflector.

catarro [ka'tarro] *sm* catarrh.

catasta [ka'tasta] *sf* pile.

catastrofe [ka'tastrofe] *sf* catastrophe. **catastrofico** *agg* catastrophic.

categoria [katego'ria] *sf* category, class. **categorico** *agg* categorical, absolute, explicit.

catena [ka'tena] *sf* chain. **catena di montaggio** assembly line. **catenaccio** *sm* bolt; (*fam: macchina vecchia*) old crock; (*sport*) defensive tactics *pl.*

cateratta [kate'ratta] *sf* cataract; (*chiusa*) floodgate.

catetere [kate'tɛre] *sm* catheter.

catino [ka'tino] *sm* basin. **piovere a catinelle** rain cats and dogs.

catodo ['katodo] *sm* cathode.

catrame [ka'trame] *sm* tar.

cattedra ['kattedra] *sf* (*tavola*) desk; (*ufficio di insegnante*) teaching post; (*carica universitaria*) chair.

cattedrale [katte'drale] *sf* cathedral.

cattivarsi [katti'varsi] *v* win, gain.

cattivo [kat'tivo] *agg* bad; (*in senso morale*) wicked; (*scortese*) nasty; (*capriccioso*) naughty. **cattiveria** *sf* wickedness, naughtiness; (*parole cattive*) spiteful remark.

cattolico [kat'toliko], **-a** *s, agg* Catholic. **Cattolicesimo** *sm* Catholicism.

catturare [kattu'rare] *v* capture, arrest. **cattura** *sf* capture, arrest.

caucciù [kaut'tʃu] *sm* rubber.

causa ['kauza] *sf* cause; (*dir*) lawsuit.

action. **a causa di** because of, on account of. **fare causa a** sue. **causale** *agg* causal.

causare [kau'zare] *v* cause, give rise to, bring about.

caustico ['kaustiko] *agg* caustic.

cauto ['kauto] *agg* cautious, careful. **cautela** *sf* caution; *(precauzione)* care.

cauzione [kau'tsjone] *sf (caparra)* security, bail. **rilasciare su cauzione** release on bail. **cauzionare** *v* pay a deposit.

cava ['kava] *sf* quarry.

cavalcare [kaval'kare] *v* ride; *(ponte)* span. **cavalcata** *sf* ride. **cavalcavia** *sm invar* flyover. **a cavalcioni** astride.

cavaliere [kava'ljere] *sm* knight; *(chi cavalca)* rider.

cavalleria [kavalle'ria] *sf (mil)* cavalry; *(medievale, cortesia)* chivalry. **cavalleresco** *agg* chivalrous. **cavallerizza** *sf* horsewoman; *(maneggio)* riding school. **cavallerizzo** *sm* horseman; *(chi insegna)* riding master.

cavalletta [kaval'letta] *sf* grasshopper.

cavalletto [kaval'letto] *sm (sostegno)* trestle, stand; *(da pittore)* easel.

cavallo [ka'vallo] *sm* horse; *(scacchi)* knight. **a cavallo** on horseback. **a cavallo di** astride, straddling. **andare a cavallo** ride. **cavallo dei pantaloni** crotch. **cavalla** *sf* mare. **cavallina** *sf* filly. **correre la cavallina** sow one's wild oats.

cavare [ka'vare] *v* draw or pull out. **cavarsela** *v* get by, manage. **cavarsi** *v (togliersi)* take off. **cavatappi** *sm invar* corkscrew.

caverna [ka'vɛrna] *sf* cave. **cavernoso** *agg* cavernous, hollow.

cavia ['kavja] *sf* guinea pig.

caviale [ka'vjale] *sm* caviar.

caviglia [ka'viʎʎa] *sf* ankle.

cavillare [kavil'lare] *v* quibble.

cavo¹ ['kavo] *sm*, *agg (vuoto)* hollow.

cavo² ['kavo] *sm* cable.

cavolo ['kavolo] *sm* cabbage. **cavoli di Bruxelles** Brussels sprouts *pl.* **cavolfiore** *sm* cauliflower. **testa di cavolo** *(fam)* clot.

cazzo ['kattso] *sm (volg)* prick.

cazzotto [kat'tsɔtto] *sm (fam)* punch. **fare a cazzotti** fight.

ce [tʃe] *V* ci.

cece ['tʃetʃe] *sm* chick-pea.

cecità [tʃetʃi'ta] *sf* blindness.

Cecoslovacchia [tʃekozlo'vakkja] *sf* Czechoslovakia. **ceco(slovacco)** *-a s, agg* Czech(oslovak).

cedere ['tʃedere] *v* yield; *(trasferire)* hand

over; *(piegarsi)* give way. **cedere il passo** make way. **cedere il posto** give up one's seat.

cedola ['tʃedola] *sf (scontrino)* coupon; *(di titolo)* dividend voucher.

cedro¹ ['tʃedro] *sm (agrume)* citron.

cedro² ['tʃedro] *sm (conifera)* cedar.

ceffone [tʃef'fone] *sm* slap (in the face).

celare [tʃe'lare] *v* conceal, hide.

celebrare [tʃele'brare] *v* celebrate.

celebre ['tʃelebre] *agg* famous. **celebrità** *sf* fame; *(persona)* celebrity.

celere ['tʃelere] *agg* rapid. *sf* flying squad.

celeste [tʃe'leste] *agg, sm* sky-blue.

celibe ['tʃelibe] *agg* single. *sm* bachelor.

cella ['tʃella] *sf* cell. **cella frigorifera** cold storage.

cellula ['tʃellula] *sf* cell.

cellulosa [tʃellu'loza] *sf* cellulose.

cemento [tʃe'mento] *sm* cement. **cemento armato** reinforced concrete. **cementare** *v* cement.

cena ['tʃena] *sf* supper, dinner. **cenare** *v* have supper or dinner.

cencio ['tʃentʃo] *sm* rag; *(per stoviglie)* dishcloth; *(per spolverare)* duster. **cencioso** *agg* ragged, tattered.

cenere ['tʃenere] *sf* ash. **Ceneri** *sf pl* Ash Wednesday *sing.*

cenno ['tʃenno] *sm* sign, gesture; *(col capo)* nod; *(con gli occhi)* wink; *(con la mano)* wave; *(allusione)* mention.

censimento [tʃensi'mento] *sm* census.

censurare [tʃensu'rare] *v (biasimare)* censure; *(sottoporre a censura)* censor. **censura** *sf* censorship; *(riprovazione)* censure.

centenario [tʃente'narjo], *-a sm, sf* centenarian. *sm (ricorrenza)* centenary. *agg* hundred-year-old.

centesimo [tʃen'tezimo] *sm* hundredth; *(soldo)* cent. *agg* hundredth.

centigrado [tʃen'tigrado] *agg* centigrade.

centimetro [tʃen'timetro] *sm* centimetre; *(nastro per misurare)* tape-measure.

cento ['tʃento] *agg, sm* hundred. **per cento** per cent. **centinaio** *sm, pl* **-a** *f* hundred; *(circa cento)* about a hundred. **a centinaia** by the hundred, in hundreds.

centrale [tʃen'trale] *agg* central, principal. *sf (deposito)* main depot; *(del telefono)* exchange; *(di energia)* power station; *(di amministrazione)* head office. **centralino** *sm* switchboard. **centralinista** *s(m+f)* switchboard operator.

centro ['tʃɛntro] *sm* centre; *(mezzo)* middle; *(luogo di soggiorno)* resort; *(fam: colpo centrato)* bull's-eye.

ceppo ['tʃeppo] *sm (razza)* stock; *(base di albero)* stump; *(pezzo di legno)* block; *(auto)* brake-block. **ceppi** *sm pl* fetters *pl*.

cera¹ ['tʃera] *sf* wax; *(per lucidare)* polish. **dare la cera** wax. **ceralacca** *sf* sealing-wax.

cera² ['tʃera] *sf (aspetto)* air, expression. **aver buona/brutta cera** look well/ill. **far buona cera** a welcome heartily.

ceramica [tʃe'ramika] *sf (oggetto)* piece of pottery; *(materiale)* earthenware; *(arte)* pottery. **ceramiche** *sf pl* pottery *sing*. **ceramista** *s(m+f)* potter.

cercare [tʃer'kare] *v* look for, search for; *(nei libri)* look up; *(tentare)* try; *(volere)* want. **cerca** *sf* search; *(questua)* begging.

cerchia ['tʃerkja] *sf* circle.

cerchio ['tʃerkjo] *sm* circle; *(giocattolo, di botte)* hoop. **fare cerchio intorno a** circle round.

cereale [tʃere'ale] *sm*, *agg* cereal.

cerebrale [tʃere'brale] *agg* cerebral.

cerimonia [tʃeri'mɔnja] *sf* ceremony. **far cerimonie** stand on ceremony. **senza cerimonie** without fuss. **cerimoniale** *sm*, *agg* ceremonial.

cerino [tʃe'rino] *sm (candela)* taper; *(fiammifero)* wax match.

cerniera [tʃer'njɛra] *sf* hinge; *(di borsetta)* clasp. **cerniera lampo** zip fastener.

cernita ['tʃernita] *sf* choice.

cero ['tʃero] *sm (church)* candle.

cerotto [tʃe'rɔtto] *sm* plaster.

certezza [tʃer'tettsa] *sf* certainty.

certificare [tʃertifi'kare] *v* certify. **certificato** *sm* certificate.

certo ['tʃɛrto] *agg* certain. *avv* certainly. **dare** *or* **sapere per certo** know for a fact. **tenere per certo** have no doubts about. **certuni** *(di certe)* some (people).

cervello [tʃer'vɛllo] *sm* brain; *(intelligenza, cibo)* brains *pl*. **dare al cervello** go to one's head.

cervo ['tʃɛrvo] *sm* deer, stag. **cervo volante** *(insetto)* stag beetle; *(aquilone)* kite. **cerva** *sf* deer, doe, hind.

cesello [tʃe'zɛllo] *sm (strumento)* engraving tool, small chisel. **cesellare** *v* engrave, chisel; *(fare con cura)* polish.

cesoie [tʃe'zɔje] *sf pl* shears *pl*.

cespo ['tʃɛspo] *sm (di erbe)* tuft; *(di fiori)* cluster. **cespo di lattuga** head of lettuce.

cespuglio [tʃes'puʎo] *sm* shrub, bush.

cessare [tʃes'sare] *v* cease, stop. **cessate il fuoco** *sm* cease-fire. **cessazione** *sf* cessation; *(comm)* termination, stoppage.

cessione [tʃes'sjone] *sf* relinquishment; *(dir)* transfer, assignment.

cesso [tʃesso] *sm (fam)* loo, lavatory.

cesta ['tʃesta] *sf* basket.

cestino [tʃes'tino] *sm* waste-paper basket; *(da lavoro)* work-basket. **cestino da viaggio** packed lunch. **cestinare** *v* throw away; *(scritti)* reject.

cesto ['tʃesto] *sm* basket.

ceto ['tʃeto] *sm* class.

cetriolo [tʃetri'ɔlo] *sm* cucumber. **cetriolino** *sm* gherkin.

che¹ [ke] *pron (persone: soggetto)* who; *(persone: oggetto)* whom, that; *(cose)* which, that; *(quando)* when; *(dove)* where; *(interrogativo)* what; *(indefinito)* something. *inter* what! *(come)* how! *agg (quale)* what; *(numero limitato)* which. **non è un gran che** it's nothing much.

che² [ke] *cong* that; *(comparativa)* than; *(quando)* when; *(dopo)* after; *(eccettuativa)* but.

checché [ke'ke] *pron* whatever.

chi [ki] *pron (soggetto)* who; *(oggetto)* whom; *(colui che)* he who; *(colei che)* she who; *(coloro che)* those who; *(chiunque)* whoever. **chi ... chi ...** some ... others .... **di chi** whose.

chiacchierare [kjakkje'rare] *v* chat. **chiacchiera** *sf* chat; *(discorso inutile)* idle talk. **far due** *or* **quattro chiacchiere** chat. **chiacchierata** *sf* chat.

chiacchierone [kjakkje'rone], **-a** *agg* talkative; *(pettegolo)* gossipy. *sm*, *sf* chatterbox, gossip.

chiamare [kja'mare] *v* call; *(far venire)* send for; *(al telefono)* ring (up). **chiamare in giudizio** sue. **chiamare sotto le armi** call up. **chiamata** *sf* call. **chiamata in giudizio** summons. **chiamata urbana/interurbana** local/trunk call.

chiarire [kja'rire] *v* clarify; *(spiegare)* explain.

chiaro ['kjaro] *agg* clear; *(luminoso)* bright; *(non scuro)* light. *sm* light. *avv* clearly, distinctly. **chiaro e tondo** blunt. **mettere in chiaro** clear up.

chiasso ['kjasso] *sm* noise, racket, row. **far chiasso** kick up a row. **chiassoso** *agg* rowdy, noisy; *(colore)* loud.

chiavare [kja'vare] v (*volg*) screw, fuck.

chiave ['kjave] *sf* key; (*tec*) spanner; (*segno musicale*) clef. **chiave apritutto** master key. **chiave inglese** adjustable spanner.

chiavistello [kjavis'tɛllo] *sm* bolt, latch.

chiazzare [kjat'tsare] v spot; (*con colori diversi*) mottle. **chiazza** *sf* spot; (*sulla pelle*) patch, blotch. **chiazzato** *agg* spotty; blotchy; mottled.

chicco ['kikko] *sm* grain; (*di caffè*) bean; (*d'uva*) grape; (*di grandine*) hailstone; (*del rosario*) bead.

***chiedere** ['kjɛdere] v ask; (*per avere*) ask for; (*di diritto*) demand; (*vivamente*) beg; (*richiedere*) require; (*prezzo*) charge. **chiedersi** v wonder.

chiesa ['kjɛza] *sf* church.

chiglia ['kiʎa] *sf* keel.

chilo ['kilo] *sm* kilo.

chilometro [ki'lɔmetro] *sm* kilometre.

chimera [ki'mɛra] *sf* chimera.

chimico ['kimiko] *agg* chemical. *sm* chemist. **chimica** *sf* (*scienza*) chemistry; (*persona*) chemist.

china[1] ['kina] *sf* slope; decline.

china[2] ['kina] *sf* **inchiostro di china** *sm* Indian ink.

chinare [ki'nare] v bend; (*occhi*) lower. **chinarsi** v stoop.

chincaglieria [kinkaʎe'ria] *sf* fancy goods *pl*.

chiocciare [kjot'tʃare] v cluck; (*covare*) brood. **chioccia** *sf* broody hen.

chiocciola [ki'ɔttʃola] *sf* snail; (*anat*) cochlea. **scala a chiocciola** *sf* spiral staircase.

chiodo ['kjɔdo] *sm* nail; fixed idea; (*fam*) debt. **chiodato** *agg* nailed; (*scarpe*) hobnailed.

chioma ['kjɔma] *sf* hair.

chiosco ['kjɔsko] *sm* kiosk, stall.

chiostro ['kjɔstro] *sm* cloister.

chiromante [kiro'mante] *s(m+f)* fortuneteller. **chiromanzia** *sf* fortune-telling.

chirurgia [kirur'dʒia] *sf* surgery. **chirurgico** *agg* surgical. **chirurgo** *sm* surgeon.

chissà [kis'sa] *avv* who knows, goodness knows; (*forse*) perhaps.

chitarra [ki'tarra] *sf* guitar.

***chiudere** ['kjudere] v close, shut; (*a chiave*) lock (up); (*sbattendo*) slam; (*spegnere*) turn or switch off; (*tappare*)

stop up; (*recingere*) enclose. **chiudere bottega** shut up shop. **chiuder dentro** shut in. **chiudere in attivo/perdita** show a profit/loss.

chiunque [ki'unkwe] *pron* whoever; (*qualunque persona*) anyone.

chiusa ['kjuza] *sf* (*parte finale*) close; (*recinto*) enclosure; (*sbarramento artificiale*) lock; (*diga*) dam.

chiuso ['kjuzo] *agg* closed, shut.

chiusura [kju'zura] *sf* (*termine*) end; (*serratura*) fastener; (*il chiudere*) closing, shut-down.

ci [tʃi], **ce** *pron* (*a noi*) to us; (*riflessivo*) ourselves; (*reciproco*) each other; (*impersonale*) one; (*di ciò*) about it or that. **ci conto su** I'm counting on it. **ci penso io** I'll think about it. *avv* (*lì*) there; (*qui*) here.

ciabatta [tʃa'batta] *sf* slipper.

cialda ['tʃalda] *sf* waffle; (*cialdino*) wafer.

ciambella [tʃam'bɛlla] *sf* (*pasta*) doughnut; (*cuscino*) rubber ring; (*di salvataggio*) lifebuoy.

ciambellano [tʃambel'lano] *sm* chamberlain.

cianciare [tʃan'tʃare] v prattle away, talk idly.

cianfrusaglia [tʃanfru'zaʎa] *sf* knickknack, junk.

cianuro [tʃa'nuro] *sm* cyanide.

ciao ['tʃao] *inter* (*incontrandosi*) hello! (*congedandosi*) cheerio! goodbye!

ciarlare [tʃar'lare] v chatter, chat. **ciarla** *sf* (*chiacchiera*) chat; (*pettegolezzo*) gossip.

ciarlatano [tʃarla'tano] *sm* charlatan.

ciascuno [tʃas'kuno] *agg* each; (*ogni*) every. *pron* each one; (*ognuno*) everyone.

cibare [tʃi'bare] v feed. **cibo** *sm* food.

cicala [tʃi'kala] *sf* cicada.

cicalino [tʃika'lino] *sm* buzzer.

cicatrice [tʃika'tritʃe] *sf* scar.

cicca [tʃi'kka] *sf* (*mozzicone*) fag end. **non valere una cicca** be not worth a thing.

cicchetto [tʃik'ketto] *sm* (*bicchierino*) nip; (*rimprovero*) dressing-down.

cicerone [tʃitʃe'rone] *sm* (*tourist*) guide.

ciclamino [tʃikla'mino] *sm* cyclamen.

ciclismo [tʃi'klizmo] *sm* cycling. **ciclista** *s(m+f)* cyclist.

ciclo ['tʃiklo] *sm* cycle. **ciclico** *agg* cyclical.

ciclomotore [tʃiklomo'tore] *sm* moped.

ciclone [tʃi'klone] *sm* cyclone.

cicogna [tʃi'koɲa] sf stork.

cicoria [tʃi'korja] sf chicory. **cicoria belga** endive.

cicuta [tʃi'kuta] sf hemlock.

cieco ['tʃɛko], **-a** agg blind. sm, sf blind person.

cielo ['tʃɛlo] sm sky; (sede divina) heaven. **a cielo aperto** in the open. **per amor del cielo!** for heaven's sake!

cifra ['tʃifra] sf figure, number; (somma) amount; (codice segreto) cipher.

ciglio ['tʃiλλo] sm, pl -a f in anat sense eyelash; (bordo) edge. **non batter ciglio** not bat an eyelash.

cigno ['tʃiɲo] sm swan.

cigolare [tʃigo'lare] v creak, squeak. **cigolio** sm creaking, squeaking.

cilecca [tʃi'lekka] sf far cilecca misfire.

ciliegia [tʃi'ljɛdʒa] sf cherry. **ciliegio** sm cherry tree.

cilindro [tʃi'lindro] sm cylinder; (rullo) roller; (cappello) top hat.

cima ['tʃima] sf top, summit. **da cima a fondo** from top to bottom. **cimare** v (piante) trim, clip; (tessuti) shear.

cimelio [tʃi'mɛljo] sm (oggetto prezioso) treasure; (ricordo) relic, memento.

cimice ['tʃimitʃe] sf bedbug.

ciminiera [tʃimi'njɛra] sf chimney.

cimitero [tʃimi'tɛro] sm cemetery.

cimurro [tʃi'murro] sm distemper.

Cina ['tʃina] sf China. **cinese** agg, s(m+f) Chinese.

cincia ['tʃintʃa] sf tit(mouse). **cinciallegra** sf (great) tit.

cincin [tʃin'tʃin] inter cheers!

cinema ['tʃinema] sm invar cinema. **cinematografico** agg film. **cinematografo** sm cinema.

cinetico [tʃi'nɛtiko] agg kinetic. **cinetica** sf kinetics.

*****cingere** ['tʃindʒere] v surround, encircle. **cingere d'assedio** besiege.

cinghia ['tʃingja] sf belt.

cinghiale [tʃin'gjale] sm (wild) boar; (pelle) pigskin.

cinguettare [tʃingwet'tare] v twitter. **cinguettio** sm twittering.

cinico ['tʃiniko], **-a** agg cynical. sm, sf cynic. **cinismo** sm cynicism.

cinquanta [tʃin'kwanta] sm, agg fifty. **cinquantesimo** sm, agg fiftieth.

cinque ['tʃinkwe] sm, agg five.

cintura [tʃin'tura] sf belt; (giro della vita)

waist. **cintura di sicurezza** safety-belt. **cinturino** sm strap.

ciò [tʃɔ] pron this, that. **ciò che** what. **ciò detto** having said this. **ciònondimeno** or **ciònonostante** nevertheless, just the same. **con ciò** therefore. **e con ciò?** so what?

cioccolata [tʃokko'lata] sf chocolate; (bevanda) (drinking) chocolate. **cioccolatino** sm (piece of) chocolate. **cioccolato** sm chocolate.

cioè [tʃo'ɛ] avv that is; (o piuttosto) or better.

ciondolo ['tʃondolo] sm pendant. **ciondolare** v dangle; (bighellonare) hang about.

ciotola ['tʃotola] sf bowl.

ciottolo ['tʃottolo] sm pebble.

cipiglio [tʃi'piλλo] sm frown.

cipolla [tʃi'polla] sf onion.

cipresso [tʃi'prɛsso] sm cypress.

cipria ['tʃiprja] sf powder.

Cipro ['tʃipro] sm Cyprus. **cipriota** agg, s(m+f) Cypriot.

circa ['tʃirka] prep (riguardo a) about, concerning. avv (pressappoco) about, approximately.

circo ['tʃirko] sm circus.

circolare[1] [tʃirko'lare] sf, agg circular. **assegno circolare** sm banker's draft.

circolare[2] [tʃirko'lare] v circulate. **circolatorio** agg circulatory. **circolazione** sf circulation.

circolo ['tʃirkolo] sm circle.

*****circoncidere** [tʃirkon'tʃidere] v circumcise. **circoncisione** sf circumcision.

circondare [tʃirkon'dare] v surround.

circonferenza [tʃirkonfe'rentsa] sf circumference.

circonvallazione [tʃirkonvalla'tsjone] sf ring-road.

*****circoscrivere** [tʃirkos'krivere] v circumscribe.

circostante [tʃirkos'tante] agg surrounding.

circostanza [tʃirkos'tantsa] sf circumstances pl; (condizione particolare) occurrence. **di circostanza** fitting.

circuito [tʃir'kuito] sm circuit; (sport) (race-)track.

cisterna [tʃis'tɛrna] sf cistern; (serbatoio) tank. **nave cisterna** sf tanker.

citare [tʃi'tare] v (riportare parole) quote; (nominare) cite; (dir: convocare) summon(s). **citazione** sf quotation; summons.

citofono [tʃi'tɔfono] *sm* (*fam*) intercom.

città [tʃit'ta] *sf* town, city. **cittadina** *sf* small town; (*persona*) citizen. **cittadinanza** *sf* citizenship, nationality; (*popolazione*) people. **cittadino** *sm* citizen.

ciuco ['tʃuko] *sm* donkey.

ciuffo ['tʃuffo] *sm* tuft.

ciurma ['tʃurma] *sf* crew; (*ciurmaglia*) riffraff.

civetta [tʃi'vetta] *sf* (*uccello*) owl; (*donna*) flirt. **civettare** *v* flirt.

civico ['tʃiviko] *agg* civic.

civile [tʃi'vile] *agg* civil; (*non militare*) civilian; (*incivilito*) civilized. **civilizzare** *v* civilize. **civismo** *sm* public spirit.

civiltà [tʃivil'ta] *sf* civilization; (*cortesia*) good breeding.

clacson [klakson] *sm invar* horn, hooter.

clamore [kla'more] *sm* clamour; (*fig*) outcry, sensation. **clamoroso** *agg* noisy, sensational.

clandestino [klandes'tino] *agg* clandestine.

clarinetto [klari'netto] *sm* clarinet.

classe ['klasse] *sf* class; (*scuola*) form.

classico ['klassiko] *agg* classic, classical; typical. *sm* classic.

classificare [klassifi'kare] *v* classify. **classificatore** *sm* file. **classificazione** *sf* classification.

classismo [klas'sizmo] *sm* class-consciousness. **classista** *agg* class-conscious.

clausola [klauzola] *sf* clause.

claustrofobia [klaustrofo'bia] *sf* claustrophobia.

clavicembalo [klavi'tʃembalo] *sm* harpsichord.

clavicola [kla'vikola] *sf* collar-bone.

clemenza [kle'mentsa] *sf* clemency; (*tempo*) mildness. **clemente** *agg* mild, clement.

cleptomane [klep'tɔmane] *s(m+f)*, *agg* kleptomaniac. **cleptomania** *sf* kleptomania.

clero ['klɛro] *sm* clergy. **clericale** *agg* clerical.

cliché [kli'ʃe] *sm* (*stampa*) block; (*luogo comune*) cliché.

cliente [kli'ente] *s(m+f)* (*di negozio*) customer; (*di professionista*) client; (*di albergo*) guest. **cliente abituale** patron. **clientela** *sf* customers *pl*, clientele; (*di professionista*) practice.

clima ['klima] *sm* climate. **climatico** *agg* climatic.

clinica ['klinika] *sf* clinic. **clinico** *agg* clinical.

cloro ['klɔro] *sm* chlorine.

clorofilla [kloro'filla] *sf* chlorophyll.

cloroformio [kloro'fɔrmjo] *sm* chloroform.

cloruro [klo'ruro] *sm* chloride.

coabitare [koabi'tare] *v* cohabit.

coagulare [koagu'lare] *v* coagulate; (*latte*) curdle; (*sangue*) clot. **coagulazione** *sf* coagulation; curdling; clotting.

coalizione [koali'tsjone] *sf* coalition. **coalizzarsi** *v* unite.

coatto [ko'atto] *agg* compulsory.

cobalto [ko'balto] *sm* cobalt.

cobra ['kɔbra] *sm invar* cobra.

cocaina [koka'ina] *sf* cocaine. **cocainomane** *s(m+f)* cocaine addict.

coccarda [kok'karda] *sf* rosette.

cocchio ['kɔkkjo] *sm* carriage, coach. **cocchiere** *sm* coachman.

coccinella [kottʃi'nella] *sf* ladybird.

coccio ['kɔttʃo] *sm* (*terracotta*) earthenware; (*rottame*) piece, crock.

cocciuto [kot'tʃuto] *agg* stubborn, pigheaded. **cocciutaggine** *sf* stubbornness, pig-headedness.

cocco[1] ['kɔkko], **-a** *sm*, *sf* (*fam: amore*) pet, darling.

cocco[2] ['kɔkko] *sm* coconut tree *or* palm. **noce di cocco** *sf* coconut.

coccodrillo [kokko'drillo] *sm* crocodile.

cocente [ko'tʃente] *agg* burning, scorching.

cocomero [ko'kɔmero] *sm* water-melon.

cocuzzolo [ko'kuttsolo] *sm* tip.

coda ['koda] *sf* tail; (*fila*) queue; (*musica*) coda. **con la coda dell'occhio** out of the corner of one's eye. **fare la coda** queue (up).

codardo [ko'dardo] *agg* cowardly.

codeina [kode'ina] *sf* codeine.

codesto [ko'desto] *agg* that. *pron* that (one).

codice ['kɔditʃe] *sm* code. **codice della strada** highway code.

coefficiente [koeffi'tʃente] *sm* coefficient; (*causa*) contributory factor.

coerente [koe'rente] *agg* coherent; (*fig*) consistent.

coesistere [koe'zistere] *v* coexist. **coesistenza** *sf* coexistence.

coetaneo [koe'taneo], **-a** *s*, *agg* contemporary.

cofano ['kɔfano] *sm* (*auto*) bonnet; (*forziere*) chest.

*****cogliere** ['kɔʎere] *v* (*staccare*) pick; (*sorprendere, capire*) catch; (*colpire*) hit. **cogliere la palla al balzo** seize the opportunity.

coglione [koʎoɲe] *sm* (*volg*) testicle; (*sciocco*) fool. **coglioneria** *sf* foolishness.

cognato [koɲnato] *sm* brother-in-law. **cognata** *sf* sister-in-law.

cognizione [koɲitsjone] *sf* knowledge; (*dir*) cognizance.

cognome [koɲnome] *sm* surname.

coi ['koi] *prep + art* con i.

*****coincidere** [koin'tʃidere] *v* coincide. **coincidenza** *sf* coincidence; (*treno, ecc.*) connection.

*****coinvolgere** [koin'vɔldʒere] *v* involve.

coito ['kɔito] *sm* coitus, sexual intercourse.

col [kol] *prep + art* con il.

colare [ko'lare] *v* (*filtrare*) sieve, strain; (*gocciolare*) drip, trickle; (*fondere*) melt, cast; (*a picco*) sink. **colabrodo** or **colapasta** *sm invar* strainer, colander. **colatoio** *sm* strainer. **colino** *sm* sieve.

colazione [kola'tsjone] *sf* (*del mattino*) breakfast; (*di mezzogiorno*) lunch. **far colazione** (have) breakfast; (have) lunch.

colei [ko'lei] *pron* (*soggetto*) she; (*oggetto*) her. **colei che** (she) who.

colera [ko'lera] *sm invar* cholera.

colesterolo [koleste'rɔlo] *sm* cholesterol.

coll' [koll] *prep + art* con l'.

colla ['kɔlla] *sf* glue, paste.

collaborare [kollabo'rare] *v* collaborate; (*giornale*) contribute. **collaboratore, -trice** *sm, sf* collaborator; contributor. **collaborazione** *sf* collaboration; contribution.

collana [kol'lana] *sf* necklace; (*raccolta*) collection.

collants [kol'lã] *sm pl* tights *pl*.

collare [kol'lare] *sm* collar.

collasso [kol'lasso] *sm* collapse. **collasso cardiaco** heart failure.

collaterale [kollate'rale] *agg* collateral.

collaudare [kollau'dare] *v* test. **collaudo** *sm* test.

colle¹ ['kɔlle] *sm* (*altura*) hill.

colle² ['kɔlle] *sm* (*valico*) pass.

collega [kol'lɛga] *s(m+f)*, *m pl* -ghi colleague.

collegare [kolle'gare] *v* connect, link (up).

collegarsi *v* (*telefono*) get through. **collegamento** *sm* connection; link; (*mil*) liaison.

collegio [kol'lɛdʒo] *sm* college; (*convitto*) boarding school; (*consiglio*) board. **collegio di difesa** counsel for the defence. **collegio elettorale** constituency.

collegiale [kolle'dʒale] *s(m+f)* boarder. *agg* (*collettivo*) corporate, collective; (*di collegio*) college, boarding-school.

collera ['kɔllera] *sf* anger, rage.

colletta [kol'letta] *sf* collection.

collettivo [kollet'tivo] *agg* collective.

colletto [kol'letto] *sm* collar.

collettore [kollet'tore] *sm* collector; (*tec*) manifold.

collezionare [kolletsjo'nare] *v* collect. **collezione** *sf* collection.

collina [kol'lina] *sf* hill.

collisione [kolli'zjone] *sf* collision.

collo¹ ['kɔllo] *sm* neck. **collo del piede** instep.

collo² ['kɔllo] *sm* (*pacco*) parcel, package; (*bagaglio*) item of luggage.

collocare [kollo'kare] *v* place. **collocare a riposo** retire, pension off. **collocamento** *sm* (*occupazione*) employment, job; (*il collocare*) placing, setting; (*vendita*) sale. **collocamento a riposo** retirement. **ufficio di collocamento** *sm* employment exchange.

colloide [kol'lɔide] *sm* colloid. *agg* colloidal.

colloquio [kol'lɔkwjo] *sm* conversation, talk; (*intervista*) interview; (*esame*) oral (examination).

colmare [kol'mare] *v* fill; (*fino all'orlo*) fill to the brim; (*coprire di*) shower. **colmo** *sm* top, summit; (*culmine*) height; (*situazione paradossale*) last straw, limit.

colombo [ko'lombo], **-a** *sm, sf* dove, pigeon. **colombaia** *sf* dovecote.

colonia [ko'lɔnja] *sf* colony; (*per bambini*) holiday camp; (*per lavoro*) settlement. **coloniale** *agg* colonial.

colonna [ko'lonna] *sf* column; (*sostegno*) pillar; (*fila*) line, queue. **colonna vertebrale** spinal column, backbone.

colonnello [kolon'nɛllo] *sm* colonel.

colore [ko'lore] *sm* colour; (*sostanza colorante*) paint, dye, tint; (*carte da gioco*) suit. **farne di tutti i colori** get up to all sorts of mischief. **colorante** *sm* dye. **colorare** *v* colour.

colorire [kolo'rire] v colour; (arrossire) blush.

colorito [kolo'rito] sm (carnagione) complexion; (tinta) colour(ing). agg colourful.

coloro [ko'loro] pron (soggetto) they; (oggetto) them. **coloro che** (those) who.

colossale [kolos'sale] agg colossal, tremendous. **colosso** sm (statua) colossus; (uomo) giant.

colpa ['kolpa] sf fault; (colpevolezza) guilt; (peccato) sin. **dare la colpa** a blame. **per colpa di** through, because of. **prendersi la colpa** take the blame.

colpevole [kol'pevole] agg (persona) guilty; (azione) culpable. s(m + f) culprit. **dichiararsi colpevole** plead guilty.

colpire [kol'pire] v hit, strike.

colpo ['kolpo] sm stroke, blow; (arma da fuoco) shot; (impresa) move, raid. **colpo d'aria** draught. **far colpo** impress, cause a stir, make a hit.

coltello [kol'tɛllo] sm knife. **coltellata** sf stab.

coltivare [kolti'vare] v cultivate; (far crescere) grow. **coltivatore** sm grower. **coltivazione** sf cultivation; growing.

colto[1] ['kolto] agg cultivated, cultured.

coltura [kol'tura] sf cultivation; (allevamento) breeding; (med) culture.

colui [ko'lui] pron (soggetto) he; (oggetto) him. **colui che** (he) who.

coma ['kɔma] sm invar coma. **comatoso** agg comatose.

comandare [koman'dare] v (reggere comando) be in command, command; (chiedere) order; (mec) control. **comandamento** sm commandment. **comandante** sm commander. **comando** sm command; (sede) headquarters; (mec) control, drive. **comando a distanza** remote control.

combaciare [komba'tʃare] v coincide.

combattere [kom'battere] v fight. **combattente** sm serviceman. **combattimento** sm fight. **combattivo** agg pugnacious. **combattuto** agg undecided, torn.

combinare [kombi'nare] v combine; (mettere d'accordo) agree; (concludere) arrange, bring off, achieve. **combinazione** sf combination; (caso) chance.

combustibile [kombus'tibile] sm fuel. agg combustible.

combustione [kombus'tjone] sf combustion.

come ['kome] avv as; (somiglianza) like; (in qual modo) how.

comedone [kome'done] sm blackhead.

cometa [ko'meta] sf comet.

comico ['kɔmiko], -a sm, sf comic, comedian. agg comic(al), funny; (commedia) dramatic.

comignolo [ko'miɲolo] sm chimney-pot.

cominciare [komin'tʃare] v begin, start. **a cominciare da** from.

comitato [komi'tato] sm committee.

comitiva [komi'tiva] sf party.

comizio [ko'mitsjo] sm meeting.

commedia [kom'mɛdja] sf play, comedy; (finzione) play-acting, sham; (scena comica) farce. **commediante** s(m + f) (fam) ham; (ipocrita) humbug. **commediografo** sm playwright.

commemorare [kommemo'rare] v commemorate. **commemorativo** agg memorial.

commentare [kommen'tare] v comment (on). **commentario** sm commentary. **commentatore, -trice** sm, sf commentator. **commento** sm comment; (radio) commentary.

commercio [kom'mɛrtʃo] sm trade, commerce. **commercio all'ingrosso/al minuto** wholesale/retail trade. **mettere in commercio** put on sale.

commesso [kom'messo], -a sm, sf (di negozio) (shop) assistant; (d'ufficio) clerk. **commesso viaggiatore** travelling salesman.

commestibile [kommes'tibile] agg edible. **commestibili** sm pl foodstuffs pl, provisions pl.

*****commettere** [kom'mettere] v (fare) commit; (mettere insieme) fit together, join; (ordinare) commission.

commissariato [kommissa'rjato] sm (polizia) police station. **commissario** sm (polizia) police inspector; (sovietico) commissar; (amministratore) commissioner.

commissione [kommis'sjone] sf commission; (incombenza) errand; (ordinazione) order; (comitato) board. **fare delle commissioni** go shopping.

commosso [kom'mɔsso] agg moved, touched.

commozione [kommo'tsjone] sf deep feelings pl; (med) concussion.

*****commuovere** [kom'mwɔvere] v move,

touch. **commovente** agg moving, touching.

commutare [kommu'tare] v commute.

comò [ko'mɔ] sm chest of drawers.

comodino [komo'dino] sm bedside table.

comodo ['kɔmodo] sm convenience. agg comfortable; (opportuno) convenient; (utile) useful, handy. **far comodo** be useful or handy; (garbare) please, suit. **fare con comodo** take one's time. **comodare** v suit. **comodità** sf comfort.

compagnia [kompa'ɲia] sf company.

compagno [kom'paɲo], **-a** sm, sf companion, mate, friend. **compagno d'armi** fellow-soldier. **compagno di prigionia/viaggio** fellow-prisoner/traveller. **compagno di scuola** classmate.

***comparire** [kompa'rire] v appear. **comparsa** sf appearance; (film) extra.

compartimento [komparti'mento] sm compartment.

compassione [kompas'sjone] sf pity. **far compassione** arouse pity. **per compassione** out of pity. **compassionevole** agg (che fa compassione) pitiful; (che ha compassione) compassionate.

compasso [kom'passo] sm compasses pl.

compatire [kompa'tire] v be sorry for. **compatibile** agg compatible; (perdonabile) excusable.

compatriota [kompatri'ɔta] s(m+f) compatriot.

compatto [kom'patto] agg compact, dense; (fig) united. **compattezza** sf compactness; unity.

compendio [kom'pendjo] sm (riassunto) summary; (trattato) outline. **compendioso** agg brief.

compensare [kompen'sare] v compensate; (ricompensare) reward. (legno) **compensato** sm plywood. **compensazione** sf compensation; (econ) clearing. **compenso** sm compensation; reward. **in compenso** in return, in exchange.

competente [kompe'tɛnte] agg competent, qualified; (adeguato) fair. **competenza** sf experience, authority; (dir) competence.

competere [kom'pɛtere] v (spettare) be due; (gareggiare) compete, rival. **competitivo** agg competitive.

***compiacere** [kompja'tʃere] v please. **compiacersi** v be pleased, rejoice; congratulate; (degnarsi) be good enough. **compiaciuto** agg pleased, satisfied.

***compiangere** [kom'pjandʒere] v pity; (rimpiangere) mourn. **compianto** sm grief.

compiere ['kompjere] v (finire) complete; (adempiere) carry out, fulfil. **compiere ... anni** be ... years old. **compimento** sm fulfilment.

compilare [kompi'lare] v compile, draw up.

compito ['kompito] sm task; (dovere) duty; (scuola) homework.

compleanno [komple'anno] sm birthday.

complementare [komplemen'tare] agg complementary; (secondario) subsidiary. **complemento** sm complement; (gramm) object.

complesso [kom'plɛsso] agg complex; complicated. sm (insieme) whole; (industria) combine, group; (psic) complex; (musica) ensemble, band. **in complesso** (tutto sommato) on the whole; (in tutto) in all, altogether. **nel complesso as a whole**.

completo [kom'pleto] agg complete; (pieno) full (up); (assoluto) total. sm (abito) suit; (di maglia) twin set; (in generale) outfit. **al completo** (pieno) full up; (esaurito) sold out; (tutti presenti) in full force. **completare** v complete, finish.

complicare [kompli'kare] v complicate; (aggravare) worsen. **complicato** agg complicated, complex; (intricato) involved. **complicazione** sf complication.

complice ['komplitʃe] s(m+f) accomplice; (dir) accessory. **complice in adulterio** correspondent. **essere complice in** be a party to. **complicità** sf complicity.

complimento [kompli'mento] sm compliment. **complimenti** sm pl (cerimonie) ceremony sing; (ossequi) regards pl; (auguri) congratulations pl. **far complimenti** stand on ceremony. **complimentare** v compliment.

complotto [kom'plɔtto] sm plot. **complottare** v plot.

componente [kompo'nɛnte] agg component. s(m+f) component, member.

***comporre** [kom'porre] v (costituire) make up; (assestare) tidy; (mettere assieme) assemble, put together; (musica) compose; (atteggiare) put on. **comporre una lite** settle a quarrel.

comportare [kompor'tare] v (richiedere) involve; (portare con sè) imply; (consentire) permit. **comportarsi** v behave. **comportamento** sm behaviour.

compositore [kompozi'tore], **-trice** *sm, sf* (*musica*) composer; type-setter.

composizione [kompozi'tsjone] *sf* composition.

composto [kom'posto] *sm* compound, mixture. *agg* (*decoroso*) dignified; (*assestato*) neat; (*costituito*) made up (of), consisting (of); (*mat*) compound. **compostezza** *sf* self-possession; decorum; neatness.

comprare [komp'rare] *v* buy; (*corrompere*) bribe. **comprare all'ingrosso** buy wholesale. **compratore**, **-trice** *sm, sf* buyer.

*****comprendere** [kom'prɛndere] *v* include; (*capire*) understand. **comprensibile** *agg* understandable, intelligible. **comprensione** *sf* understanding. **comprensivo** *agg* (*che include*) inclusive, comprehensive; (*tollerante*) understanding. **compreso** *agg* inclusive; (*capito*) understood.

compressa [kom'pressa] *sf* tablet, pill; (*garza*) compress.

compressore [kompres'sore] *sm* compressor.

*****comprimere** [kom'primere] *v* compress; (*reprimere*) suppress.

*****compromettere** [kompro'mettere] *v* compromise. **compromesso** *sm* compromise. **compromettente** *agg* compromising.

comprovare [kompro'vare] *v* confirm.

compunto [kom'punto] *agg* contrite.

comune [ko'mune] *agg* common. *sm* commune, municipality; (*autorità*) town council. **avere in comune** share. **fuori del comune** uncommon, unusual.

comunicare [komuni'kare] *v* communicate, announce; (*malattia*) pass on; (*rel*) administer Communion. **comunicarsi** *v* spread; receive Communion. **comunicato** *sm* communiqué, bulletin. **comunicato stampa** press release.

comunione [komu'njone] *sf* community; (*rel*) (Holy) Communion.

comunismo [komu'nizmo] *sm* communism. **comunista** *s(m+f)*, *agg* communist.

comunità [komuni'ta] *sf* community.

comunque [ko'munkwe] *avv* (*in ogni modo*) anyhow, at any rate. *cong* however, no matter how.

con [kon] *prep* with; (*mezzo*) with, by.

conca ['konka] *sf* basin; (*valle*) depression.

concavo [kon'kavo] *agg* concave.

*****concedere** [kon'tʃedere] *v* grant, award; (*permettere*) allow.

concentrare [kontʃen'trare] *v* concentrate. **concentramento** *sm* concentration. **concentrato** *sm* concentrate.

concentrico [kon'tʃentriko] *agg* concentric.

concepire [kontʃe'pire] *v* conceive; (*capire*) understand; (*nutrire*) entertain, cherish. **concepibile** *agg* conceivable.

conceria [kontʃe'ria] *sf* tannery.

concernere [kon'tʃernere] *v* concern, regard. **per quanto mi concerne** as far as I am concerned.

concerto [kon'tʃerto] *sm* concert.

concessione [kontʃes'sjone] *sf* concession.

concetto [kon'tʃetto] *sm* concept, notion, idea.

concezione [kontʃe'tsjone] *sf* conception; (*pensiero*) concept.

conchiglia [kon'kiʎa] *sf* shell.

conciare [kon'tʃare] *v* (*pelli*) tan; (*tabacco*) cure; (*ridurre male*) get into a mess; spoil. **conciare per le feste** (*fam*) give a thrashing.

conciliare [kontʃi'ljare] *v* reconcile.

concilio [kon'tʃiljo] *sm* council.

concime [kon'tʃime] *sm* manure; (*artificiale*) fertilizer.

conciso [kon'tʃizo] *agg* concise, to the point.

concittadino [kontʃitta'dino], **-a** *sm, sf* fellow-citizen.

conclave [kon'klave] *sm* conclave.

*****concludere** [kon'kludere] *v* conclude; (*operare con profitto*) achieve. **conclusione** *sf* conclusion, result. **in conclusione** to sum up, in short. **conclusivo** *agg* final, conclusive; (*determinante*) decisive.

concordare [konkor'dare] *v* agree, fix. **concordato** *sm* agreement.

concorrente [konkor'rɛnte] *agg* concurrent; (*rivale*) competing. *s(m+f)* competitor; (*a un concorso*) candidate, applicant. **concorrenza** *sf* competition. **far concorrenza** compete (with).

*****concorrere** [kon'korrere] *v* contribute; (*gareggiare*) compete (for); (*convergere*) come together.

concorso [kon'korso] *sm* (*affluire*) concourse, gathering; contribution; contest, competition; (*esame*) competitive examination.

concreto [kon'krɛto] *sm, agg* concrete. **concretare** *v* get done.

condannare [kondan'nare] v condemn; (*dichiarare colpevole*) sentence. **condanna** sf conviction, sentence. **condannato, -a** sm, sf condemned person.

condensazione [kondensa'tsjone] sf condensation. **condensare** v condense.

condire [kon'dire] v season; (*insalata*) dress. **condimento** sm seasoning, dressing.

*condividere [kondi'videre] v share.

condizione [kondi'tsjone] sf condition. **condizioni** sf pl state sing; (*comm*) terms pl. **condizioni di vita** standard of living sing. **essere in condizione di** be able to. **mettere in condizione di** enable to. **condizionale** sm, agg conditional.

condoglianza [kondo'ʎantsa] sf condolence. **fare le condoglianze** express one's sympathy.

condonare [kondo'nare] v remit, condone. **condono** sm remission.

condotta [kon'dotta] sm (*comportamento*) conduct, behaviour; (*di un'azione, ecc.*) handling; (*tubazione*) piping.

*condurre [kon'durre] v (*portare*) lead; (*accompagnare*) take; (*auto*) drive; (*dirigere*) manage, run; (*eseguire, fis*) conduct; (*ridurre*) reduce. **condursi** v behave.

conduttore [kondut'tore] agg conducting. sm (*fis*) conductor; (*conducente*) driver. **conduttura** sf (*tubazione*) piping; (*condotto*) pipe.

confederazione [konfedera'tsjone] sf federation.

conferenza [konfe'rentsa] sf (*congresso*) conference; (*discorso*) lecture. **conferenza stampa** press conference. **conferenziere, -a** sm, sf lecturer, speaker.

conferire [konfe'rire] v award, confer; (*dare*) give.

confermare [konfer'mare] v confirm, **conferma** sf confirmation.

confessare [konfes'sare] v confess. **confessione** sf confession. **confessore** sm confessor.

confetto [kon'fetto] sm sugared almond. **confettura** sf preserve.

confezionare [konfetsjo'nare] v make up: **confezione** sf (*involucro*) wrapping; (*lavorazione*) manufacture. **confezioni** sf pl (*abiti pronti*) ready-made clothes pl.

confidare [konfi'dare] v trust, confide. **confidenza** sf confidence. **dar confidenza**

a be familiar with. **prendersi la confidenza** take the liberty. **confidenziale** agg confidential.

confinare [konfi'nare] v border (on); (*relegare*) confine; (*pol*) intern, banish. **confine** sm border.

confiscare [konfis'kare] v seize, confiscate. **confisca** sf seizure, confiscation.

conflitto [kon'flitto] sm conflict.

*confondere [kon'fondere] v confuse; (*scambiare*) mistake for; (*mettere in imbarrazzo*) embarrass. **confondersi** v become mixed up.

conformare [konfor'mare] v conform, adapt. **conforme a** agg in conformity with, true to. **conformista** s(m+f) conformist.

confortare [konfor'tare] v comfort, console. **confortevole** agg comforting; (*comodo*) comfortable. **conforto** sm comfort.

confrontare [konfron'tare] v compare; (*dir*) confront. **confronto** sm comparison; (*dir*) confrontation. **a confronto di** compared with. **senza confronto** far and away.

confusione [konfu'zjone] sf confusion; (*ressa*) bustle; (*chiasso*) din, turmoil. **confusione mentale** mental aberration. **confuso** agg confused, muddled; vague; (*turbato*) bewildered.

congedare [kondʒe'dare] v dismiss; (*mil*) discharge. **congedarsi** v say goodbye (to); take leave (of). **congedo** sm (*commiato*) leave; discharge.

congegno [kon'dʒeɲo] sm device, gadget. **congegnare** v plan, devise.

congelare [kondʒe'lare] v freeze. **congelatore** sm freezer.

congenito [kon'dʒenito] agg congenital.

congestionato [kondʒestjo'nato] agg congested; (*traffico*) blocked; (*viso*) flushed. **congestione** sf congestion; (*traffico*) jam.

*congiungere [kon'dʒundʒere] v (*unire*) join; (*collegare*) connect, link (up). **congiuntivite** sf conjunctivitis. **congiuntivo** sm subjunctive. **congiuntura** sf (*punto di unione*) joint; (*circostanza*) juncture; economic situation. **congiunzione** sf conjunction.

congiura [kon'dʒura] sf plot, conspiracy. **congiurato, -a** sm, sf plotter, conspirator.

congratularsi [kongratu'larsi] v congratulate.

congregare [kongre'gare] v congregate, gather. **congrega** sf band. **congregazione** sf congregation.

congresso [kon'grɛsso] sm congress.

congruo ['kongruo] agg adequate, fair.

coniare [ko'njare] v coin. **conio** sm coining; (impronta, qualità) stamp; (matrice) minting die.

conico ['kɔniko] agg conical.

conifero [ko'nifero] agg coniferous. **conifera** sf conifer.

coniglio [ko'niʎo] sm rabbit.

coniugare [konju'gare] v conjugate.

coniuge ['kɔnjudʒe] s(m+f) spouse. **coniugale** agg conjugal.

*connettere [kon'nɛttere] v connect, link; associate; (ragionare) think straight. **connessione** sf connection.

connotati [konno'tati] sm pl description sing, distinguishing features pl.

cono ['kɔno] sm cone.

*conoscere [ko'noʃere] v know; (fare la conoscenza) meet. **conoscere di fama/vista** know by reputation/sight. **conoscente** s(m+f) acquaintance. **conoscenza** sf knowledge; (conoscente) acquaintance; (coscienza) consciousness, senses pl. **conoscitore, -trice** sm, sf expert, connoisseur. **conosciuto** agg (well-)known, renowned.

conquistare [konkwis'tare] v conquer; (fig) gain. **conquista** sf conquest. **conquistatore, -trice** sm, sf conqueror.

consacrare [konsa'krare] v consecrate, dedicate.

consanguineo [konsan'gwineo], **-a** agg related (by blood). sm, sf blood relation.

consapevole [konsa'pevole] agg aware, conscious. **consapevolezza** sf awareness, consciousness.

consecutivo [konseku'tivo] agg consecutive; (seguente) following.

consegnare [konse'ɲare] v deliver, hand over; (mil) confine to barracks. **consegna** sf delivery; (merce ordinata) consignment; (custodia) care; (deposito) (safe) custody; (mil: ordine) order; (mil: punizione) confinement.

conseguire [konse'gwire] v. (ottenere) obtain, get; (raggiungere) achieve; (risultare) follow, ensue. **conseguenza** sf consequence, result; (malattia) aftereffect. **di conseguenza** consequently, as a result.

consenso [kon'sɛnso] sm approval; (accordo) agreement; (permesso) consent.

consentire [konsen'tire] v (essere d'accordo) agree; (accondiscendere) consent; (permettere) allow. **consenziente** agg consenting.

conservare [konser'vare] v keep, preserve. **conserva** sf preserve. **mettere in conserva** preserve; (in scatola) tin; (in bottiglia) bottle. **conservatore, -trice** s, agg conservative. **conservazione** sf preservation.

considerare [konside'rare] v consider; (guardare) examine; (stimare) esteem, think highly of; (tener conto) bear in mind. **consideratezza** sf caution. **considerato** agg careful, wary. **considerazione** sf (prudenza) caution; (risguardo) consideration; (stima) esteem, regard. **considerevole** agg considerable.

consigliare [konsi'ʎare] v advise, recommend. **consigliere** sm counsellor. **consigliere comunale** town councillor. **consigliere delegato** managing director. **consiglio** sm advice; (organo amministrativo) board; (ente pubblico) council; (colloquio) meeting. **consiglio d'amministrazione** board of directors.

*consistere [kon'sistere] v consist. **consistente** agg substantial; (convincente) sound. **consistenza** sf consistency; (fondamento) basis. **consistenza di cassa/magazzino** cash/stock in hand.

consolare [konso'lare] v console, comfort; (rallegrare) cheer (up). **consolazione** sf consolation, comfort; (piacere) delight.

console ['kɔnsole] sm consul. **consolare** agg consular. **consolato** sm consulate.

consolidare [konsoli'dare] v consolidate; (rinforzare) reinforce.

consonante [konso'nante] sf consonant.

consono ['kɔnsono] agg **consono a** in keeping with; in accordance with.

consorte [kon'sɔrte] s(m+f), agg consort.

consorzio [kon'sortsjo] sm partnership; (impresa commerciale, banca) consortium, trust; (imprese riunite) syndicate, cooperative.

constare [kon'stare] v consist. **a quanto mi consta** to my knowledge, as far as I know.

constatare [konsta'tare] v (notare) see; (accertare) ascertain, verify; (riconoscere) recognize. **constatazione** sf verification; recognition.

consueto [konsu'εto] *agg* (*solito*) usual; (*abituato*) used. **come di consueto** as usual. **di consueto** usually. **consuetudine** *sf* habit, custom.

consulente [konsu'lεnte] *s(m+f)*, *agg* consultant. **consulenza** *sf* advice. **consultare** *v* consult. **consultazione** *sf* consultation; (*biblioteca*) reference. **consultivo** *agg* consultative, advisory.

consumare[1] [konsu'mare] *v* consume, use up; (*logorare*) wear out; (*dissipare*) squander; (*mangiare*) eat. **consumazione** *sf* (*bibita*) drink; (*spuntino*) snack. **consumismo** *sm* consumer society. **consumo** *sm* consumption; (*spreco*) waste. **articoli di consumo** *sm pl* consumer goods *pl*.

consumare[2] [konsu'mare] *v* (*portare a compimento*) consummate. **consumazione** *sf* consummation.

consuntivo [konsun'tivo] *sm* balance sheet.

contabile [kon'tabile] *s(m+f)* bookkeeper; (*ragioniere*) accountant. **valore contabile** *sm* book value. **contabilità** *sf* bookkeeping; accountancy. **tenere la contabilità** keep the books.

contachilometri [kontaki'lɔmetri] *sm invar* mileometer; (*tachimetro*) speedometer.

contadino [konta'dino], **-a** *agg* (*della campagna*) rustic; (*dei contadini*) peasant. *sm*, *sf* peasant; (*agricoltore*) farmer.

contagioso [konta'dʒozo] *agg* contagious, catching. **contagiare** *v* infect, contaminate.

contagiri [konta'dʒiri] *sm invar* rev(olution) counter.

contaminare [kontami'nare] *v* contaminate.

contanti [kon'tanti] *sm pl* cash *sing*, ready money *sing*.

contare [kon'tare] *v* count; (*proporsi*) think. **contato** *agg* limited. **ho i giorni contati** my days are numbered. **ho i minuti contati** I have no time to waste. **contatore** *sm* meter.

contatto [kon'tatto] *sm* contact. **essere/mantenersi/mettersi in contatto** be/keep/get in touch.

conte ['konte] *sm* count. **contea** *sf* (*suddivisione amministrativa*) county; (*titolo, dominio di conti*) earldom. **contessa** *sf* countess.

conteggio [kon'teddʒo] *sm* count, counting. **conteggiare** *v* (*calcolare*) count; (*far pagare*) charge.

contegno [kon'teɲo] *sm* bearing, behaviour. **darsi** *or* **assumere un contegno** strike an attitude. **contegnoso** *agg* dignified, reserved.

contemplare [kontem'plare] *v* contemplate; consider, provide for. **contemplazione** *sf* contemplation.

contempo [kon'tεmpo] *sm* **nel contempo** in the meantime, meanwhile.

contemporaneo [kontempo'raneo], **-a** *sm*, *sf* contemporary. *agg* contemporary; simultaneous.

*•***contendere** [kon'tεndere] *v* dispute; (*litigarsi*) quarrel (over); oppose. **contendente** *s(m+f)* competitor.

*•***contenere** [konte'nere] *v* contain, hold; (*trattenere*) hold back. **contenersi** *v* (*dominarsi*) restrain oneself; (*comportarsi*) act. **contenitore** *sm* container.

contentare [konten'tare] *v* (*appagare*) satisfy; (*far contento*) please. **contentarsi** *v* be satisfied. **contentezza** *sf* satisfaction, contentment; (*gioia*) joy. **contento** *agg* (*soddisfatto*) pleased, satisfied; (*felice*) happy; (*allegro*) cheerful.

contenuto [konte'nuto] *sm* (*recipiente*) contents *pl*; (*argomento*) content. *agg* reserved, restrained.

contestare [kontes'tare] *v* contest; (*dir*) charge (with); (*impugnare*) challenge. **contestazione** *sf* dispute; notification.

contiguo [kon'tiguo] *agg* neighbouring, adjoining.

continente [konti'nεnte] *sm*, *agg* continent. **continentale** *agg* continental. **continenza** *sf* continence.

contingente [kontin'dʒεnte] *sm* quota; (*mil*) contingent. **contingenza** *sf* circumstance; contingency. **indennità di contingenza** *sf* cost of living allowance.

continuare [kontinu'are] *v* continue, carry on; (*riprendere*) resume; (*insistere*) keep on. **continuazione** *sf* continuation. **continuità** *sf* continuity. **continuo** *agg* endless; (*costante*) continual; (*ininterrotto*) continuous.

conto ['konto] *sm* account; (*somma da pagare*) bill; calculation. **a conti fatti** all things considered. **a (ogni) buon conto** in any case. **far conto che** *or* **di** suppose, imagine; (*proporsi*) intend. **fare conto su** rely on. **per conto di** on behalf of. **per**

conto mio as far as I'm concerned; (da solo) on my own. tener conto di make a note of; consider, take into account.

*contorcere [kon'tɔrtʃere] v twist. contorcersi v writhe. contorsione sf contortion. contorsionista s(m+f) contortionist.

contorno [kon'torno] sm (linea) outline; (gastr) vegetables pl, side-dish; (ornamento) surround, border.

contrabbandare [kontrabban'dare] v smuggle. contrabbando sm contraband, smuggling. merce di contrabbando sf smuggled goods pl.

contrabbasso [kontrab'basso] sm double-bass.

contraccambiare [kontrakkam'bjare] v reciprocate. in contraccambio di in return for.

contraccolpo [kontrak'kolpo] sm counter-blow; (fig) repercussion.

*contraddire [kontrad'dire] v contradict. contraddizione sf contradiction. spirito di contraddizione sm contrariness.

contraddittorio [kontraddit'tɔrjo] agg contradictory. sm (dir) cross-examination.

contraente [kontra'ente] agg contracting.

contraereo [kontra'ɛreo] agg anti-aircraft.

*contraffare [kontraf'fare] v imitate; (falsificare) forge, counterfeit. contraffattore, -trice sm, sf counterfeiter, forger; imitator. contraffazione sf forgery.

contralto [kon'tralto] sm contralto. agg alto.

*contrapporre [kontrap'porre] v oppose, contrast. contrapposizione sf opposition, contrast.

contrariare [kontra'rjare] v irritate, oppose.

contrario [kon'trarjo] agg opposite, contrary; (avverso) unfavourable. sm contrary, opposite. al contrario on the contrary. al contrario di unlike. essere contrario a be opposed to.

*contrarre [kon'trarre] v contract.

contrassegnare [kontrasse'ɲare] v mark. contrassegno sm mark.

contrastare [kontras'tare] v (ostacolare) bar, oppose; (essere in conflitto) clash; dispute. contrasto sm contrast; conflict.

contrattaccare [kontrattak'kare] v counter-attack. contrattacco sm counter-attack.

contrattempo [kontrat'tɛmpo] sm hitch.

contratto [kon'tratto] sm contract. contrattare v negotiate; (mercanteggiare) haggle.

contravvenzione [kontravven'tsjone] sf (violazione) infringement; (multa) fine. contravventore, -trice sm, sf offender.

contrazione [kontra'tsjone] sf contraction.

contribuire [kontribu'ire] v contribute. contribuente sm, sf taxpayer. contributo sm contribution; (dir) tax.

contristare [kontris'tare] v sadden.

contrito [kon'trito] agg contrite.

contro ['kontro] prep, avv against.

controbattere [kontro'battere] v rebut.

controbilanciare [kontrobilan'tʃare] v counterbalance.

controfirmare [kontrofir'mare] v countersign. controfirma sf countersignature.

controllare [kontrol'lare] v control; (esaminare) check. controllo sm control; (verifica) check; inspection. controllo delle nascite birth-control. controllore sm inspector.

contromano [kontro'mano] avv in the opposite direction.

contromarcia [kontro'martʃa] sf reverse (gear).

contropelo [kontro'pelo] avv against the grain.

controproducente [kontroprodu'tʃɛnte] agg self-defeating, counter-productive.

contrordine [kon'trordine] sm countermand. dare un contrordine countermand.

controsenso [kontro'sɛnso] sm nonsense, contradiction in terms.

controversia [kontro'vɛrsja] sf controversy. controverso agg controversial.

controvoglia [kontro'vɔʎa] avv unwillingly.

conturbare [kontur'bare] v perturb.

contusione [kontu'zjone] sf bruise. contuso agg bruised.

convalescenza [konvale'ʃɛntsa] sf convalescence. convalescente s(m+f), agg convalescent. convalescenziario sm convalescent home.

convalidare [konvali'dare] v confirm. convalida or convalidazione sf confirmation.

convegno [kon'veɲo] sm meeting, rendezvous. darsi convegno make a date; meet.

*convenire [konve'nire] v (venire insieme) come together, meet; (essere d'accordo) agree; (ammettere) admit; (essere vantaggioso) suit, pay, be worth it. conveniente *agg* (*vantaggioso*) favourable, reasonable; (*adatto, adeguato*) suitable. **convenienza** *sf* (*utilità*) convenience; (*decoro*) propriety; (*l'essere adatto*) suitability.

convento [kon'vɛnto] *sm* convent.

convenzione [konven'tsjone] *sf* (*patto*) agreement; (*uso*) custom, convention.

*convergere [kon'vɛrdʒere] v converge.
convergente *agg* converging.

conversare [konver'sare] *v* converse. **conversazione** *sf* conversation, talk.

conversione [konver'sjone] *sf* conversion; (*trasformazione*) change, turn(ing).

convertire [konver'tire] *v* convert, turn. **convertibile** *agg* convertible. **convertito, -a** *sm, sf* convert.

convesso [kon'vɛsso] *agg* convex.

*convincere [kon'vintʃere] v convince. **convincente** *agg* convincing. **convinto** *agg* (*persuaso*) convinced; (*dimostrato colpevole*) convicted; (*fedele*) staunch. **convinzione** *sf* conviction.

convitato [konvi'tato] *sm* guest.

convito [kon'vito] *sm* banquet.

convitto [kon'vitto] *sm* boarding-school.

convocare [konvo'kare] *v* convoke, convene; (*radunare*) call together, rally.

convoglio [kon'vɔʎo] *sm* convoy. **convoglio funebre** funeral procession. **convogliare** *v* (*scortare*) convoy; (*condurre, trasportare*) transport.

convulsione [konvul'sjone] *sf* convulsion. **convulsivo** *agg* convulsive. **convulso** *agg* convulsed.

cooperare [koope'rare] *v* cooperate, collaborate; contribute. **cooperativa** *sf* cooperative. **cooperazione** *sf* cooperation, collaboration.

coordinare [koordi'nare] *v* coordinate. **coordinata** *sf* coordinate.

coperchio [ko'perkjo] *sm* lid, cover.

coperta [ko'perta] *sf* (*drappo*) blanket; (*riparo*) cover. **copertina** *sf* (*quaderno*) cover; (*libro*) dust-jacket.

coperto[1] [ko'perto] *agg* covered; (*riparato*) sheltered; (*chiuso*) closed; (*nuvoloso*) overcast; (*nascosto*) concealed. **al coperto** under cover. **mettersi al coperto** shelter.

coperto[2] [ko'perto] *sm* (*a tavola*) place (-setting); (*prezzo*) cover charge. **copertone** [koper'tone] *sm* (*pneumatico*) tyre; (*telone*) tarpaulin.

copia ['kɔpja] *sf* copy; (*fig*) image. **bella/brutta copia** fair/rough copy. **copiare**

v copy. **carta copiativa** *sf* carbon paper. **matita copiativa** *sf* indelible pencil. **copiatura** *sf* copy; (*trascrizione*) copying. **copioso** [ko'pjozo] *agg* copious.

coppa ['kɔppa] *sf* cup; (*auto*) sump.

coppia ['kɔppja] *sf* couple. **a coppie** in pairs, in twos.

*coprire [ko'prire] v cover; (*nascondere*) hide. **coprire un rumore** drown a noise.

coraggio [ko'raddʒo] *sm* courage, bravery; (*sfacciataggine*) nerve; (*cuore*) heart. **farsi coraggio** pluck up courage. **perdere coraggio** lose heart. **coraggioso** *agg* courageous, brave; (*ardito*) bold.

corallo [ko'rallo] *sm* coral.

corazzare [korat'tsare] *v* armour. **corazza** *sf* armour. **corazzata** *sf* battleship.

corbelleria [korbelle'ria] *sf* (*detto*) nonsense; (*atto*) foolery.

corda ['kɔrda] *sf* cord; (*cordicella, musica*) string; (*fune*) rope; (*geom*) chord. **avere la corda al collo** have one's back to the wall. **essere giù di corda** feel low. **tagliar la corda** (*andarsene di soppiatto*) sneak off; (*fuggire*) cut and run.

cordiale [kor'djale] *agg* cordial, warm. **cordiali saluti** kind regards *pl*. **cordialità** *sf* friendliness.

cordoglio [kor'dɔʎo] *sm* grief. **esprimere il proprio cordoglio** offer one's condolences.

cordone [kor'done] *sm* cord; (*schieramento*) cordon.

coreografo [kore'ɔgrafo] *sm* choreographer. **coreografia** *sf* choreography.

coriandoli [ko'rjandoli] *sm pl* confetti *sing*.

coricare [kori'kare] *v* lay down; (*mettere a letto*) put to bed. **coricarsi** *v* lie down; go to bed.

cornacchia [kor'nakkja] *sf* crow.

cornamusa [korna'muza] *sf* bagpipes *pl*.

cornetto [kor'netto] *sm* (*musica*) cornet; (*telefono*) receiver.

cornice [kor'nitʃe] *sf* frame; (*ambiente*) setting; (*arch*) cornice.

corno ['kɔrno] *sm, pl* **-a** *f in zool sense* horn; (*ramificato*) antler; (*musica*) French horn. **corno da caccia** bugle. **corno inglese** cor anglais. **dire corna di** run down. **fare le corna** (*non essere fedele*) be unfaithful; (*gesto*) make a V-sign. **non capire un corno** not understand a thing. **non valere un corno** not be worth a brass farthing. **cornuto** *agg* horned.

coro ['kɔro] *sm* choir; (*canto*) chorus. **in coro** in chorus, all together.

corpo ['kɔrpo] *sm* body; (*mil., ecc.*) corps. **a corpo morto** headlong, whole-heartedly. **corpo a corpo** hand to hand. **corporatura** *sf* build. **corporeo** *agg* bodily.

corporazione [korpora'tsjone] *sf* guild, association.

corpulento [korpu'lento] *agg* stout.

corpuscolo [kor'puskolo] *sm* corpuscle.

corredo [kor'redo] *sm* outfit; (*mil*) equipment. **corredare** *v* fit out, equip; (*fig*) furnish (with).

*__**correggere**__ [kor'reddʒere] *v* correct; (*bevanda*) lace.

corrente [kor'rɛnte] *agg* current; (*che scorre*) running; (*andante*) common or garden. **essere/tenere al corrente** be/keep informed or up-to-date. **mettere al corrente** acquaint, inform. *sf* current, stream; (*tendenza, moda*) trend. **corrente d'aria** draught.

*__**correre**__ ['korrere] *v* run; (*veicoli*) go; (*circolare*) circulate. **correre dietro a** run after.

corretto [kor'retto] *agg* correct, right, exact. **correttezza** *sf* fairness; (*educazione*) propriety.

correzione [korre'tsjone] *sf* correction. **correzione di bozze** proof-reading.

corridoio [korri'dojo] *sm* passage, corridor.

corridore [korri'dore] *sm* runner; (*automobilista*) racing-driver; (*ciclista*) racing-cyclist. **cavallo corridore** *sm* racehorse.

corriera [kor'rjera] *sf* coach.

corriere [kor'rjere] *sm* messenger, courier; (*merci*) carrier; (*posta*) mail.

corrimano [korri'mano] *sm* handrail.

*__**corrispondere**__ [korris'pondere] *v* correspond; (*accordarsi*) agree; (*pagare*) pay; (*ricambiare*) reciprocate. **corrispondente** *s*(*m* + *f*) correspondent. **corrispondenza** *sf* correspondence; (*posta*) mail; (*conformità*) relation; (*somiglianza*) likeness.

corroborare [korrobo'rare] *v* corroborate; (*rinforzare*) strengthen.

*__**corrodere**__ [kor'rodere] *v* corrode. **corrosione** *sf* of corrosion.

*__**corrompere**__ [kor'rompere] *v* corrupt;

(*con denaro*) bribe; (*guastare*) spoil. **corrotto** *agg* corrupt.

corrucciarsi [korrut'tʃarsi] *v* be angered and upset (by).

corrugare [korru'gare] *v* crease, wrinkle. **corrugare la fronte** knit one's brow.

corruzione [korru'tsjone] *sf* corruption; (*con denaro*) bribery.

corsa ['korsa] *sf* (*gara*) race; (*azione*) racing; (*atletica*) running; (*percorso*) run. **andare di corsa** (be in a) hurry. **di gran corsa** in a great hurry, in great haste. **fare una corsa (da)** (*fam*) pop over or round (to).

corsia [kor'sia] *sf* (*teatro, ecc.*) gangway; (*ospedale*) ward; (*autostrada*) lane; (*tappeto*) runner.

corsivo [kor'sivo] *agg* italic. *sm* italics *pl*.

corso¹ ['korso] *sm* course; (*econ*) circulation; (*quotazione*) rate; (*strada principale*) high street. **in corso** in progress; (*in sospeso*) pending; (*corrente*) present.

corso² ['korso], **-a** *s*, *agg* Corsican.

corte ['kɔrte] *sf* court; (*cortile*) courtyard. **corte marziale** court-martial. **fare la corte (a)** (*ragazza*) court; (*lusingare*) play up (to). **corteggiare** *v* court. **corteggio** *sm* retinue.

corteccia [kor'tettʃa] *sf* (*albero*) bark; (*frutto*) rind; (*anat*) cortex.

corteo [kor'tɛo] *sm* procession.

cortese [kor'teze] *agg* polite, courteous; (*gentile*) kind. **cortesia** *sf* politeness, courtesy; kindness. **avere la cortesia di** be so kind as to. **per cortesia** (*per favore*) please, kindly; (*per ragioni di cortesia*) out of politeness.

cortile [kor'tile] *sm* courtyard; (*casa colonica*) farmyard. **animali da cortile** *sm pl* farmyard animals *pl*.

cortina [kor'tina] *sf* curtain. **cortina di ferro** iron curtain. **cortina di fumo** smoke-screen.

corto ['korto] *agg* short. **a farla corta** to come to the point. **essere a corto di** be short of.

corvo ['korvo] *sm* (*imperiale*) raven; (*comune*) rook.

cosa ['kɔza] *pron* what. **a cosa serve?** what is it for? *sf* thing; (*qualcosa*) something; (*faccenda*) matter. **a cose fatte** after the event. **cosa da nulla** nothing. **cosa da poco** trifle. **gran cosa** much. **qualsiasi** *o* **qualunque cosa** anything. **tante cose** (*augurio*) best wishes *pl*.

coscia ['kɔʃa] *sf* thigh; (*gastr*) leg.

cosciente [koʃ'ɛnte] *agg* aware. **coscienza** *sf* conscience; (*conoscenza*) consciousness; (*impegno*) conscientiousness. **avere la coscienza pulita/sporca** have a clear/guilty conscience. **in coscienza** morally, honestly. **coscienzioso** *agg* conscientious.

coscrizione [koskri'tsjone] *sf* draft, conscription. **coscritto** *sm* conscript, recruit.

così [ko'zi] *avv* (*in questo modo*) like this or that; (*tanto*) so; (*con agg qualificante un sostantivo*) such. **cong** so. **così ... come ...** as ... as .... **così così** so-so. **cosiddetto** *agg* so-called.

cosmetico [koz'metiko] *sm, agg* cosmetic. **cosmesi** *or* **cosmetica** *sf* beauty culture.

cosmo ['kɔzmo] *sm* cosmos. **cosmonauta** *s(m+f)* astronaut. **cosmonautica** *sf* astronautics.

cosmopolita [kozmo'polita] *s(m+f)*, *agg* cosmopolitan.

coso ['kɔzo] *sm* (*fam*) thingummy.

****cospargere** [kos'pardʒere] *v* strew.

cospicuo [kos'pikuo] *agg* conspicuous; (*grande*) considerable.

cospirare [kospi'rare] *v* plot.

costa ['kɔsta] *sf* coast, coastline; (*litorale*) shore; (*coltello, libro*) back; (*costola*) rib.

costà [kos'ta] *avv* (*over*) there.

costante [kos'tante] *agg* constant, firm; (*saldo*) steady. *sf* constant. **costanza** *sf* steadfastness, firmness.

costare [kos'tare] *v* cost. **costar caro** be expensive. **mi è costato caro** I have paid dearly for it.

costeggiare [kosted'dʒare] *v* skirt; (*costa*) follow the coast.

costei [kos'tɛi] *pron* this woman.

costellare [kostel'lare] *v* stud.

costellazione [kostella'tsjone] *sf* constellation.

costernare [koster'nare] *v* dismay.

costiero [kos'tjera] *agg* coastal.

costipato [kosti'pato] *agg* (*stitico*) constipated; (*fam: raffreddato*) having a bad cold.

costituire [kostitu'ire] *v* (*formare*) set up, form; (*dar luogo*) constitute; (*dichiarare*) appoint. **costituirsi** *v* (*presentarsi spontaneamente*) give oneself up. **costituirsi parte civile** take legal proceedings. **costituzione** *sf* constitution.

costo ['kɔsto] *sm* cost, price. **costoso** *agg* costly, dear.

costola ['kɔstola] *sf* rib.

costoro [kos'toro] *pron* these people.

****costringere** [kos'trindʒere] *v* force, compel.

****costruire** [kostru'ire] *v* build, construct. **costruzione** *sf* construction; (*edificio*) building.

costui [kos'tui] *pron* this man.

costume [kos'tume] *sm* (*usanza*) custom, use; (*condotta*) behaviour; (*indumento*) costume; (*abitudine personale*) habit. **il buon costume** morality.

costura [kos'tura] *sf* seam.

cotogna [ko'toɲa] *sf* quince.

cotoletta [koto'letta] *sf* cutlet.

cotone [ko'tone] *sm* cotton. **cotone idrofilo** cotton-wool. **cotoniero** *agg* cotton. **cotonificio** *sm* cotton mill.

cotta ['kɔtta] *sf* **prendere una cotta** (*fam*) fall in love.

cottimo ['kɔttimo] *sm* piece-work.

cotto ['kɔtto] *agg* cooked; (*carne*) done; (*in forno*) baked. **farne di cotte e di crude** be up to all sorts of tricks. **nè cotto nè crudo** neither one thing nor the other.

cottura [kot'tura] *sf* cooking; (*in forno*) baking.

covare [ko'vare] *v* hatch; (*fig*) brood over; (*sotto la cenere*) smoulder. **covata** *sf* brood.

covo ['kɔvo] *sm* lair, den.

cozza ['kɔttsa] *sf* mussel.

cozzare [kot'tsare] *v* collide *or* clash (with); (*con le corna*) butt. **cozzo** *sm* collision, clash; butt.

crampo ['krampo] *sm* cramp.

cranio ['kranjo] *sm* skull.

cratere [kra'tɛre] *sm* crater.

cravatta [kra'vatta] *sf* tie.

creanza [kre'antsa] *sf* (good) manners *pl*, breeding.

creare [kre'are] *v* create, give rise to; (*eleggere*) appoint. **creatore** *sm* maker, creator. **creatura** *sf* creature. **creazione** *sf* creation.

credenza[1] [kre'dɛntsa] *sf* belief (*pl* -s), opinion; (*fede*) faith; (*comm*) credit.

credenza[2] [kre'dɛntsa] *sf* (*mobile*) sideboard.

credere ['krɛdere] *v* believe; (*pensare*) think; (*aver fiducia*) trust. **credibile** *agg* credible, believable. **credibilità** *sf* credibility.

credito ['kredito] sm credit; (stima) esteem. **creditore** sm creditor.

credulo ['kredulo] agg credulous. **credulone, -a** sm, sf gullible person.

crema ['krɛma] sf cream. **cremoso** agg creamy.

cremare [kre'mare] v cremate. **crematorio** sm crematorium. **cremazione** sf cremation.

cremisi ['kremizi] agg, sm crimson.

cren ['krɛn] sm horse-radish.

crepare [kre'pare] v burst, crack; (fam: morire) die, kick the bucket. **crepacuore** sm heartbreak.

crepitare [krepi'tare] v crackle. **crepitio** sm crackle, crackling.

crepuscolo [kre'puskolo] sm twilight, dusk; decline.

*crescere ['kreʃere] v grow; (maturarsi) grow up; (aumentare) rise; (sovrabbondare) be left over. **crescita** sf growth.

crescione [kre'ʃone] sm (d'acqua) watercress; (inglese) mustard and cress.

cresima ['krɛzima] sf confirmation. **cresimare** v confirm.

crespa ['krɛspa] sf (ruga) wrinkle; (stoffa) crease; (piccola ondulazione) ripple. **crespo** ['krɛspo] agg frizzy. sm crepe.

cresta ['krɛsta] sf crest.

creta ['krɛta] sf clay.

cretino [kre'tino] , **-a** sm, sf idiot, fool. agg idiotic, foolish. **cretineria** sf stupidity; (discorso, azione) foolish thing.

cricca ['krikka] sf clique, gang.

cricco ['krikko] sm jack.

criceto [kri'tʃeto] sm hamster.

criminale [krimi'nale] agg, s(m+f) criminal. **crimine** sm crime. **criminoso** agg criminal.

criniera [kri'njɛra] sf mane.

cripta ['kripta] sf crypt.

crisalide [kri'zalide] sf chrysalis.

crisantemo [krizan'tɛmo] sm chrysanthemum.

crisi ['krizi] sf crisis (pl -ses); (med) fit, attack.

cristallizzare [kristallid'dzare] v crystallize.

cristallo [kris'tallo] sm crystal; (vetro) plate-glass, (window) pane. **cristallino** agg crystalline; pure, limpid.

cristiano [kris'tjano], **-a** agg Christian. sm, sf Christian; (essere umano) soul.

Cristo ['kristo] sm Christ. **non c'è cristo** (possibilità) there isn't a chance. **povero cristo** poor devil.

criterio [kri'tɛrjo] sm criterion (pl -a), norm; sense.

critico ['kritiko] agg critical. sm critic. **critica** sf criticism; (scritto) review; (persona) critic. **criticare** v criticize; review; (biasimare) blame.

crivellare [krivel'lare] v riddle. **crivello** sm sieve.

croccante [krok'kante] agg crisp. sm (dolce) praline.

crocchia ['krɔkkja] sf bun, chignon.

crocchio ['krɔkkjo] sm cluster.

croce ['krotʃe] sf cross. **a occhio e croce** roughly. **croce uncinata** swastika. **crocevia** sm invar crossroads. **fare a testa e croce** toss a coin. **punto a croce** sm cross-stitch.

crociare [kro'tʃare] v cross.

crociata [kro'tʃata] sf crusade. **crociato** sm crusader.

crocicchio [kro'tʃikkjo] sm crossroads.

crociera [kro'tʃɛra] sf cruise.

*crocifiggere [krotʃifid'dʒere] v crucify. **crocifisso** [krotʃi'fisso] sm crucifix. agg crucified.

croco ['krɔko] sm crocus.

crogiolarsi [krodʒo'larsi] v bask. **crogiolo** sm crucible; (fig) melting-pot.

crollare [krol'lare] v (cadere) collapse, slump; (spalle) shrug. **crollo** sm collapse, slump.

croma ['krɔma] sf quaver.

cromo ['krɔmo] sm (metallo) chromium. **giallo cromo** chrome yellow. **cromatura** sf chromium-plating.

cromosoma [kromo'sɔma] sm chromosome.

cronaca ['krɔnaka] sf (narrazione) chronicle; (radio, TV, stampa) news, review.

cronico ['krɔniko] agg chronic. sm chronic invalid.

cronista [kro'nista] s(m+f) reporter.

cronologico [krono'lɔdʒiko] agg chronological.

cronometro [kro'nɔmetro] sm chronometer, stop-watch. **cronometrare** v time.

crosta ['krɔsta] sf crust; (ferita) scab. **crostata** sf tart.

crostacei [kros'tatʃei] sm pl crustaceans pl, shellfish pl.

crucciare [krut'tʃare] v distress, worry.

cruciale [kru'tʃale] agg crucial.

cruciverba [krutʃi'vɛrba] *sm invar* crossword.

crudele [kru'dɛle] *agg* cruel; *(duro, aspro)* harsh; *(doloroso)* bitter. **crudeltà** *sf* cruelty; *(asprezza)* harshness.

crudo ['krudo] *agg* raw; *(rigido)* harsh; *(brusco)* crude; *(volgare)* coarse.

crumiro [kru'miro], **-a** *sm, sf* blackleg.

cruna ['kruna] *sf* eye (of a needle).

crusca ['kruska] *sf* bran.

cruscotto [krus'kɔtto] *sm* instrument panel; *(auto)* dashboard.

cubo ['kubo] *sm* cube. **cubico** *agg* cubic. **cubismo** *sm* cubism.

cuccagna [kuk'kaɲa] *sf (abbondanza)* plenty; *(allegria)* fun.

cuccetta [kut'tʃetta] *sf* couchette.

cucchiaio [kuk'kjajo] *sm* spoon; *(contenuto)* spoonful; *(da tavola)* tablespoon. **cucchiaino** *sm* teaspoon.

cucciolo [kuttʃolo] *sm* puppy.

cucina [ku'tʃina] *sf (luogo)* kitchen; *(atto del cucinare)* cooking; *(cibo)* food; *(apparecchio)* cooker. **cucina casalinga** home cooking. **cucinare** *v* cook.

cucire [ku'tʃire] *v* sew, stitch; *(con cucitrice)* staple. **cucirino** *sm* sewing thread. **cucito** *sm* sewing, needlework. **cucitrice** *sf (persona)* seamstress; *(apparecchio)* stapler. **cucitura** *sf* seam.

cuculo [kukulo] *sm* cuckoo.

cuffia ['kuffja] *sf* cap; bonnet; *(telefono, radio)* earphones *pl*, headphones *pl*.

cugino [ku'dʒino], **-a** *sm, sf* cousin.

cui ['kui] *pron (persone)* whom; *(cose)* which. **il cui, la cui,** ecc. whose. **in cui** *(quando)* when; *(dove)* where.

culla ['kulla] *sf* cradle. **cullare** *v* rock, lull. **cullarsi** *v (illudersi)* delude oneself.

culmine ['kulmine] *sm* summit, height. **culminare** *v* culminate.

culo ['kulo] *sm (fam)* bottom; *(volg)* arse.

culto ['kulto] *sm* worship; *(religione)* cult.

cultura [kul'tura] *sf* culture, learning; cultivation. **culturale** *agg* cultural.

cumulo [kumulo] *sm* pile, heap.

cuneo ['kuneo] *sm* wedge.

cunetta [ku'netta] *sf* gutter.

***cuocere** [kwɔtʃere] *v (cucinare)* cook; *(al forno)* bake; *(a lesso)* boil; *(alla griglia)* grill; *(arrosto)* roast; *(in umido)* stew; *(ceramica, ecc.)* fire. **cuocere a fuoco lento** simmer. **cuoco, -a** *sm, sf* cook.

cuoio [kwɔjo] *sm* leather; *(pelle)* hide.

cuoio capelluto scalp. **cuoio scamosciato** chamois leather, suede.

cuore ['kwore] *sm* heart. **di cuore** heartily. **di tutto cuore** with all one's heart. **mettersi il cuore in pace** set one's mind at rest. **nel cuore di** at the height of; *(notte)* at dead of. **senza cuore** heartless.

cupido ['kupido] *agg* greedy. **cupidigia** *sf* greed.

cupo ['kupo] *agg (profondo, suono)* deep; *(privo di luce, colore)* dark.

cupola ['kupola] *sf* dome.

cura ['kura] *sf* care; *(med)* cure, treatment. **curare** *v* look after, take care of; cure, treat. **curarsi** *v* mind *or* care about. **curativo** *agg* curative.

curatore [kura'tore], **-trice** *sm, sf* guardian. **curatela** *sf* guardianship.

curioso [ku'rjozo] *agg* curious; *(strano)* odd. **curiosità** *sf* curiosity. **curiosare** *v* pry.

curvare [kur'vare] *v* bend. **curvare il capo** bow one's head. **curva** *sf* bend, curve. **curvatura** *sf* curvature, sweep. **curvo** *agg* curved, bent.

cuscino [kuʃino] *sm* cushion; *(guanciale)* pillow. **cuscinetto** *sm (a sfere)* ball-bearing; *(a rulli)* roller-bearing. **stato di cuscinetto** *sm* buffer state.

custode [kus'tɔde] *s(m+f)* keeper, caretaker. **custodia** *sf* custody, care, safe keeping; *(astuccio)* case. **custodire** *v* keep; look after; *(sorvegliare)* guard.

cutaneo [ku'taneo] *agg* cutaneous, skin.

D

da [da] *prep* from; *(moto a luogo)* to; *(stato in luogo)* at; *(durata)* for; *(fin da)* since; *(causa)* of, from; *(segno distintivo)* with; *(come)* as, like. **da allora** since then. **da allora in poi** ever since. **da lontano** from afar. **da molto** for a long time. **da noi** at home; *(al mio paese)* in my country.

dabbasso [dab'basso] *avv* downstairs.

dabbene [dab'bene] *agg* decent, honest.

daccapo [dak'kapo] *avv (di nuovo)* again, once more; *(da principio)* from the beginning, all over again.

dacché [dak'ke] *cong* since.

dado ['dado] *sm* die *(pl* dice); *(gastr)* cube; *(mec)* nut.

daffare [daf'fare] *sm invar* work, business.

dagli[1] ['daʎi] *prep + art* **da gli**.

dagli[2] ['daʎi] *inter (forza)* go on! come on! *(noioso)* not again! pack it in!

dai ['dai] *prep + art* **da i**.

daino ['daino] *sm (fallow)* deer. **daina** *sf* doe. **pelle di daino** *sf* buckskin.

dal ['dal] *prep + art* **da il**.

dalia ['dalja] *sf* dahlia.

dall' [dall] *prep + art* **da l'**.

dalla ['dalla] *prep + art* **da la**.

dalle ['dalle] *prep + art* **da le**.

dallo ['dallo] *prep + art* **da lo**.

daltonismo [dalto'nizmo] *sm* colour-blindness. **daltonico** *agg* colour-blind.

dama ['dama] *sf* lady, noblewoman; *(gioco)* draughts; *(carta)* queen.

damasco [da'masko] *sm* damask.

dancing ['dansiŋ] *sm invar* dance-hall.

Danimarca [dani'marka] *sf* Denmark. **danese** *sm, agg* Danish; *s(m+f)* Dane.

dannare [dan'nare] *v* damn. **dannato, -a** *s, agg* damned. **dannazione** *sf* damnation; *(tormento)* trial.

danneggiare [danned'dʒare] *v (guastare)* damage; *(nuocere)* injure, harm. **danno** *sm* damage; injury, harm; *(pregiudizio)* detriment. **danno doloso** wilful damage. **dannoso** *agg* harmful.

danzare [dan'tsare] *v* dance. **danza** *sf* dancing; *(ballo)* dance. **danzatore, -trice** *sm, sf* dancer.

dappertutto [dapper'tutto] *avv* everywhere, all over the place.

dappoco [dap'pɔko] *agg invar* worthless; *(inetto)* good-for-nothing.

dappresso [dap'presso] *avv* close to, close up.

dapprima [dap'prima] *avv* at first.

dardeggiare [darded'dʒare] *v* dart. **dardo** *sm* dart.

***dare** ['dare] *v* give; *(avere come risultato)* make, come to; *(esame)* take; apply; *(colpire)* hit; *(fruttare)* yield. **dare ai** *or* **sui nervi a qualcuno** get on someone's nerves. **dare alla luce** give birth to. **dar da fare** a keep busy. **dar fine** a put an end to. **dare nell'occhio** catch the eye. **dare per scontato** take for granted. **dar retta** a listen to. **dare su** look out on to; *(affacciare)* face. **darsi a** *(dedicarsi)* devote oneself to; *(applicarsi)* go in for.

darsena ['darsena] *sf* dock.

data ['data] *sf* date. **di fresca data** recent. **di vecchia data** of long standing. **in che**

data? when? **datare** *v* date; *(risalire)* go back (to).

dato ['dato] *agg* given; *(in vista)* considering, in view of. **dato che** supposing that, as, since. *sm* data. **dato di fatto** fact. **datore** *sm* di lavoro employer.

dattero ['dattero] *sm (frutto)* date; *(albero)* date-palm.

dattilografo [datti'lɔgrafo], **-a** *sm, sf* typist. **dattilografare** *v* type.

davanti [da'vanti] *avv* in front. *sm, agg* front. **davanti a** in front of; *(dirimpetto)* facing; *(in presenza di)* before.

davanzale [davan'tsale] *sm* window-sill.

davvero [dav'vero] *avv* really. **dici davvero?** do you (really) mean it?

dazio ['datsjo] *sm (imposta)* duty; *(ufficio)* customs (office).

dea ['dea] *sf* goddess.

debito[1] ['debito] *agg* due.

debito[2] ['debito] *sm* debt; *(comm)* debit; *(dovere)* duty. **estinguere/fare un debito** settle/incur a debt. **sentirsi in debito** be indebted. **debitore** *sm* debtor.

debole ['debole] *agg* weak, feeble; *(luce, suono, speranza)* faint. *sm (persona)* weakling; *(punto)* weak point; *(inclinazione)* weakness, foible. **debolezza** *sf* weakness; *(difetto)* failing.

debuttare [debut'tare] *v* make one's debut. **debutto** *sm* debut.

decade ['dɛkade] *sf* ten days *pl*.

***decadere** [deka'dere] *v* decline. **decadere da** *(dir)* forfeit. **decadente** *agg* decadent. **decadenza** *sf* decline; *(dir)* forfeiture, lapse. **decaduto** *agg* impoverished; *(scaduto)* fallen into disuse.

decalcomania [dekalkoma'nia] *sf* transfer.

decano [de'kano] *sm* dean; *(diplomatico)* doyen.

decantare[1] [dekan'tare] *v (lodare)* sing the praises of.

decantare[2] [dekan'tare] *v (liquido)* decant.

decapitare [dekapi'tare] *v* behead.

deceduto [detʃe'duto] *agg* deceased.

decennio [de'tʃennjo] *sm* decade.

decente [de'tʃente] *agg* decent. **decenza** *sf* decency, propriety.

decentrare [detʃen'trare] *v* decentralize. **decentramento** *sm* decentralization.

decesso [de'tʃesso] *sm* death.

decibel [detʃi'bɛl] *sm invar* decibel.

***decidere** [de'tʃidere] *v* decide (on); *(risolvere, determinare)* settle. **decidersi**

make up one's mind; *(indursi)* bring one-self to.

deciduo [de'tʃiduo] *agg* deciduous.

decifrare [detʃi'frare] *v* decipher; *(fam)* make out.

decimale [detʃi'male] *agg, sm* decimal.

decimo ['dɛtʃimo] *sm, agg* tenth.

decina [de'tʃina] *sf* ten; *(circa dieci)* ten or so. **a decine** *(fig)* by the dozen.

decisione [detʃi'zjone] *sf* decision, resolution; *(dir)* ruling. **decisivo** *agg* decisive; *(prova)* conclusive; *(voto)* casting.

deciso [de'tʃizo] *agg (fermo)* decided, firm, resolute; *(definito, risolto)* settled, resolved; *(spiccato)* decided, marked. **decisamente** *avv* decidedly, definitely.

declamare [dekla'mare] *v* declaim; *(protestare)* rail.

declinare [dekli'nare] *v* decline. **declinazione** *sf (fis)* declination; *(gramm)* declension. **declino** *sm* decline.

declivio [de'klivjo] *sm* slope.

decollare [dekol'lare] *v* take off. **decollo** *sm* take-off.

*****decomporsi** [dekom'porsi] *v* disintegrate, decompose. **decomposizione** *sf* disintegration, decomposition.

decorare [deko'rare] *v* decorate. **decorazione** *sf* decoration.

decoro [de'kɔro] *sm* dignity; *(orgoglio)* pride. **decoroso** *agg* prope..

decorrere [de'korrere] *v* elapse. **con decorrenza da . . .** with effect from. **decorso** *sm (svolgimento)* course; *(periodo)* lapse.

decrepito [de'krepito] *agg* decrepit.

decrescente [dekre'ʃente] *agg* decreasing, diminishing; *(luna)* on the wane.

decreto [de'kreto] *sm* decree, order. **decreto di citazione** writ; *(testimone)* subpoena. **decretare** *v* decree, order; *(concedere)* award.

dedalo ['dɛdalo] *sm* maze.

dedicare [dedi'kare] *v* dedicate, devote; consecrate; *(intitolare)* name after. **dedicarsi a** *(occuparsi di)* take up, go in for. **dedica** *sf* dedication.

dedito ['dɛdito] *agg* devoted; *(assorbito)* engrossed (in); *(vizio)* addicted.

*****dedurre** [de'durre] *v* deduce; *(desumere)* infer; *(prendere, derivare)* take, draw; *(sottrarre)* deduct. **deduzione** *sf* deduction.

defalcare [defal'kare] *v* deduct.

deferire [defe'rire] *v* defer, refer. **deferire al tribunale** sue. **deferente** *agg* deferential.

deficiente [defi'tʃɛnte] *agg* deficient; insufficient; *(inferiore alla media)* backward; *(fam)* moronic. *s(m+f)* moron, half-wit. **deficienza** *sf* deficiency, lack; *(scarsità)* shortage; *(idiozia)* mental deficiency.

deficit ['dɛfitʃit] *sm invar* deficit. **bilancio deficitario** *sm* debit balance.

definire [defi'nire] *v* define; *(risolvere)* settle. **definitivo** *agg* definitive. **in definitiva** *(dopo tutto)* after all; to sum up; *(in fin dei conti)* all things considered. **definizione** *sf* definition; settlement.

deflazione [defla'tsjone] *sf* deflation. **deflazionare** *v* deflate. **deflazionistico** *agg* deflationary.

*****deflettere** [de'flettere] *v* deviate. **deflessione** *sf* deflection; deviation.

deformare [defor'mare] *v* deform, distort; *(mec)* warp; *(senso)* twist. **deformazione** *sf* deformation, distortion; warping. **deforme** *agg* deformed, misshapen; *(viso)* disfigured.

defunto [de'funto], **-a** *s, agg* deceased.

degenerare [dedʒene'rare] *v* degenerate. **degenerato, -a** *s, agg* degenerate.

degente [de'dʒɛnte] *agg* bedridden. **degenza** *sf (a letto)* stay in bed; *(in ospedale)* stay in hospital.

degli [de'ʎi] *prep + art* di gli.

degnare [de'ɲare] *v* deign; deem *or* consider worthy. **degnarsi di** condescend to. **degno** *agg* worthy, deserving. **degno di fiducia** trustworthy. **degno di lode** praiseworthy. **degno di nota** noteworthy.

degradare [degra'dare] *v* degrade. **degradazione** *sf* degradation.

degustare [degus'tare] *v* taste, sample.

dei[1] ['dei] *prep + art* di i.

dei[2] ['dei] *V* dio.

deificare [deifi'kare] *v* deify.

del [del] *prep + art* di il.

delatore [dela'tore], **-trice** *sm, sf* informer. **delazione** *sf* denouncement; *(fam)* tip-off.

delegare [dele'gare] *v* delegate. **delega** *sf (procura)* proxy; *(dir)* power of attorney. **delegato, -a** *sm, sf* delegate. **delegazione** *sf* delegation.

deleterio [dele'tɛrjo] *agg* harmful.

delfino [del'fino] *sm* dolphin.

deliberare [delibe'rare] *v* deliberate;

(*decidere*) resolve. **deliberato** *agg* determined, resolved. **deliberazione** *sf* deliberation, decision.

delicato [deli'kato] *agg* delicate; (*gusto*) refined. **delicatezza** *sf* delicacy; (*tatto*) tact; refinement.

delimitare [delimi'tare] *v* define, circumscribe. **delimitazione** *sf* demarcation.

delineare [deline'are] *v* sketch, outline. **delinearsi** *v* (*presentarsi*) appear, emerge; (*apparire*) loom up, take shape.

delinquente [delin'kwɛnte] *s(m+f)* delinquent, criminal; (*mascalzone*) rascal. **delinquenza** *sf* criminality.

deliquio [de'likwjo] *sm* **cadere in deliquio** faint. **essere in deliquio** be in a faint.

delirare [deli'rare] *v* be delirious; (*farneticare*) rave. **delirio** *sm* delirium; (*follia*) frenzy.

delitto [de'litto] *sm* crime; (*reato*) offence; (*grave*) felony; (*lieve*) misdemeanour. **delittuoso** *agg* criminal.

delizia [de'litsja] *sf* delight. **delizioso** *agg* delightful; (*sapore*) delicious.

dell' [dell] *prep + art* **di l'**.

della [della] *prep + art* **di la**.

delle [delle] *prep + art* **di le**.

dello [dello] *prep + art* **di lo**.

delta [delta] *sm invar* delta.

*****deludere** [de'ludere] *v* disappoint; (*render vano*) frustrate.

delusione [delu'zjone] *sf* disappointment. **deluso** *agg* disappointed.

demente [de'mɛnte] *agg* insane. *s(m+f)* lunatic. **demenza** *sf* madness, insanity; (*med*) dementia.

democratico [demo'kratiko], **-a** *sm, sf* democrat. *agg* democratic. **democrazia** *sf* democracy.

democristiano [demokris'tjano], **-a** *sm, sf* Christian Democrat. *agg* Christian Democratic.

demografia [demogra'fia] *sf* demography. **demografico** *agg* demographic.

demolire [demo'lire] *v* demolish. **demolizione** *sf* demolition.

demone ['dɛmone] *sm* demon; (*potenza ispiratrice*) genius; passion. **demonico** *agg* demonic.

demonio [de'monjo] *sm* devil. **brutto come il demonio** as ugly as sin. **demoniaco** *agg* demoniacal, devilish.

demoralizzare [demoralid'dzare] *v* demoralize. **demoralizzarsi** *v* lose heart.

denaro [de'naro] *sm* money; (*grossezza di filo*) denier. **denaro spicciolo** small change.

denigrare [deni'grare] *v* denigrate; (*fam*) run down. **denigratorio** *agg* disparaging. **denigrazione** *sf* denigration, disparagement.

denominatore [denomina'tore] *sm* denominator. **denominare** *v* name. **denominazione** *sf* naming; (*nome*) name. **denotare** [deno'tare] *v* denote, show.

denso ['dɛnso] *agg* dense, thick. **densità** *sf* density; (*spessore*) thickness.

dente ['dɛnte] *sm* tooth (*pl* teeth); (*ruota*) cog; (*forchetta*) prong. **a denti stretti** tight-lipped. **avere il dente avvelenato contro** have it in for. **dente del giudizio** wisdom tooth. **dente di latte** milk-tooth. **dente finto** false tooth. **dente sporgente** buck-tooth. **mettere i denti** teethe, cut one's teeth. **restare a denti asciutti** go hungry; (*fig*) go away empty-handed. **dentario** *agg* dental. **dentato** *agg* toothed.

dentellare [dentel'lare] *v* indent, notch. **dentellatura** *sf* indentation.

dentice ['dentitʃe] *sm* sea bream.

dentiera [den'tjɛra] *sf* denture.

dentifricio [denti'fritʃo] *sm* toothpaste.

dentista [den'tista] *s(m+f)* dentist.

dentro ['dentro] *avv* in; (*all'interno*) inside. *prep* in, inside; (*in casa*) indoors. **andar dentro** (*fam*) go to jail.

denunziare [denun'tsjare] *v* also **denunciare** denounce; (*riferire*) report; (*dichiarare*) declare; (*disdire*) terminate; (*rendere palese*) show. **denunzia** or **denuncia** *sf* report; (*accusa*) charge; declaration; notice of termination.

deodorante [deodo'rante] *agg, sm* deodorant.

deperire [depe'rire] *v* (*piante*) wither; (*animali*) waste away; (*persone*) get run down; (*cibi*) perish. **deperibile** *agg* perishable.

depilatorio [depila'torjo] *agg* depilatory. *sm* hair-remover.

dépliant [depli'ã] *sm, pl* **-s** leaflet.

deplorare [deplo'rare] *v* (*compiangere*) lament, regret; (*biasimare*) deplore, regret. **deplorevole** *agg* deplorable.

*****deporre** [de'porre] *v* put or set down, deposit, lay; (*testimoniare*) (bear) witness. **deporre in giudizio** give evidence. **deposizione** *sf* deposition, testimony.

deportare [depor'tare] v deport. **deportato, -a** sm, sf deportee. **deportazione** sf deportation.

deposito [de'pɔzito] sm deposit; (magazzino) warehouse, store. **deposito bagagli** left-luggage office. **depositare** v deposit. **depositario** sm trustee.

depravare [depra'vare] v deprave.

depredare [depre'dare] v plunder.

depresso [de'prɛsso] agg depressed. **depressione** sf depression. **depressivo** agg depressive, depressant.

deprezzare [depret'tsare] v depreciate. **deprezzamento** sm depreciation.

*__deprimere__ [de'primere] v depress. **deprimente** agg depressing.

depurare [depu'rare] v purify. **depuratore** sm purifier. **depurazione** sf purification.

deputare [depu'tare] v delegate. **deputato, -a** sm, sf deputy; delegate; Member of Parliament.

deragliare [dera'ʎare] v be derailed, go off the rails. **deragliamento** sm derailment.

derapare [dera'pare] v skid.

derelitto [dere'litto] -a agg forsaken. sm, sf down-and-out; (trovatello) foundling.

deretano [dere'tano] sm behind.

*__deridere__ [de'ridere] v laugh at, mock, deride. **derisione** sf derision, ridicule. **derisorio** agg derisory, laughable.

deriva [de'riva] sf **alla deriva** adrift. **andare alla deriva** drift.

derivare [deri'vare] v derive; (conseguire) follow, result; (sviare) divert. **derivata** sf (mat) derivative. **derivato** sm (chim) derivative; (sottoprodotto) by-product. **derivazione** sf derivation, origin. **collegare in derivazione** (elett, radio) shunt.

dermatite [derma'tite] sf dermatitis. **dermatologo, -a** sm, sf dermatologist.

derogare [dero'gare] v deviate (from), depart (from); (non osservare) not comply (with); (dir) waive. **deroga** sf departure. **in deroga a** notwithstanding; (dir) waiving. **derogabile** agg not binding.

derrate [der'rate] sf pl provisions pl; (alimentari) foodstuffs pl.

derubare [deru'bare] v rob.

*__descrivere__ [des'krivere] v describe. **descrittivo** agg descriptive. **non descrivibile** indescribable. **descrizione** sf description, account.

deserto [de'zɛrto] sm desert, wilderness.

agg (vuoto) deserted; (disabitato) uninhabited.

desiderare [deside'rare] v wish; (volere) want; (bramare) long for, desire. **lasciare a desiderare** leave to be desired. **desiderabile** agg desirable.

desiderio [dezi'dɛrjo] sm wish; (brama, rimpianto) longing, desire. **aver desiderio di** wish or want to. **pio desiderio** wishful thinking.

designare [dezi'ɲare] v designate; (denominare) call; (nominare, stabilire) appoint.

desinare [dezi'nare] sm lunch, dinner. v lunch, dine.

desinenza [dezi'nɛntsa] sf ending.

*__desistere__ [de'zistere] v desist. **desistere da** give up.

desolato [dezo'lato] agg (afflitto) distressed; (deserto) desolate; (devastato) desolated. **desolante** agg distressing. **desolazione** sf desolation; distress.

despota ['dɛspota] sm despot.

destare [des'tare] v awake, rouse; (suscitare) arouse, awaken. **destare meraviglia** cause wonder.

destinare [desti'nare] v destine; (assegnare) intend, assign; (dedicare) devote; (riservare) set aside; (indirizzare) address; decide. **destinatario, -a** sm, sf (lettera) addressee; (merci) consignee. **esser destinato a** (decretato dalla sorte) be bound or destined to; (condannato) be doomed to. **destinazione** sf destination. **destino** sm destiny, fate.

destituire [destitu'ire] v dismiss. **destituito** agg dismissed; (privo) devoid. **destituzione** sf dismissal.

desto ['desto] agg (sveglio) (wide-)awake; (vivace) lively.

destra ['destra] sf (lato) right, right-hand side; (mano) right hand; (pol) right (wing). **a destra** on or to the right. **tenere la destra** keep (to the) right.

destro ['destro] agg (lato) right(-hand); (abile) skilful, dextrous; (accorto) clever. **destrezza** sf ability, skill, dexterity. **destrorso** agg from left to right; (in senso orario) clockwise.

detenere [dete'nere] v hold; (trattenere in prigione) detain. **detenuto, -a** sm, sf detainee. **detenzione** sf detention. **detenzione abusiva** unlawful possession.

detergente [deter'dʒɛnte] sm, agg detergent.

deteriorare [deterjo'rare] v deteriorate. **deterioramento** sm deterioration.

determinare [determi'nare] v determine; (causare) bring about. **determinante** agg determining, decisive. **determinato** agg (preciso) definite, distinct; (stabilito) appointed; (noto) given; (particolare) special; (deciso) determined. **determinazione** sf determination.

deterrente [deter'rɛnte] sm, agg deterrent.

detersivo [deter'sivo] sm, agg detergent.

detestare [detes'tare] v detest, loathe. **detestabile** agg hateful, odious.

detonatore [detona'tore] sm detonator. **detonante** sm, agg explosive. **capsula detonante** sf percussion cap.

*detrarre [det'rarre] v deduct, take away; (nuocere a) detract (from).

detrimento [detri'mento] sm detriment, prejudice.

detrito [de'trito] sm debris; (geol) detritus.

dettagliare [detta'ʎare] v (particolareggiare) detail; (vendere al minuto) retail. **dettagliante** s(m+f) retailer. **dettaglio** sm detail; retail.

dettare [det'tare] v dictate. **dettar legge** lay down the law. **dettato** sm dictation.

detto ['detto] agg (già citato) above-mentioned, aforesaid; (chiamato) known as, alias. **detto fatto** no sooner said than done. **detto fra noi** between you and me. sm saying.

deturpare [detur'pare] v disfigure, deface.

devastare [devas'tare] v ravage, devastate. **devastazione** sf devastation, destruction. **devastatore** [devasta'tore] agg devastating, destructive. sm devastator, destroyer.

deviare [devi'are] v deviate; (spostare in altra direzione) divert. **deviazione** sf deviation; (fis) deflection; (traffico) diversion, detour.

devolvere [de'volvere] v devolve, assign.

devoto [de'voto] agg (rel) devout; (dedicato, affezionato) devoted. **devozione** sf devotion; devoutness.

di [di] prep of; (partitivo) some, any; (moto da luogo) from; (paragone) than.

diabete [dia'bɛte] sm diabetes. **diabetico, -a** s, agg diabetic.

diacono [di'akono] sm deacon.

diadema [dia'dɛma] sm diadem, tiara.

diaframma [dia'framma] sm diaphragm; (divisione) partition.

diagnosi ['djaɲozi] sf diagnosis (pl -ses). **fare la diagnosi di** diagnose.

diagonale [djago'nale] sf, agg diagonal.

diagramma [dia'gramma] sm diagram; (grafico) chart, curve.

dialetto [dia'lɛtto] sm dialect. **dialettale** agg dialect.

dialogo ['djalogo] sm, pl -ghi dialogue; (trattative) negotiations pl; (colloquio) conversation, talk.

diamante [dia'mante] sm diamond.

diametro [di'ametro] sm diameter. **diametrale** agg diametrical.

diamine ['djamine] inter heavens! **che diamine . . . !** what on earth . . . !

diapason [di'apazon] sm tuning fork; (tono) pitch; (estensione di voce) range.

diapositiva [diapozi'tiva] sf transparency, slide.

diario [di'arjo] sm diary, journal. **diario di bordo** log-book.

diarrea [diar'rɛa] sf diarrhoea.

diavolo ['djavolo] sm devil. **che diavolo . . . !** what the devil . . . ! **un buon diavolo** a good chap. **diavoleria** sf mischief. **diavoletto** sm imp; (bigodino) roller, curler.

dibattere [di'battere] v debate. **dibattersi** v struggle. **dibattimento** sm hearing. **dibattito** sm debate. **dibattuto** agg (discusso) controversial, vexed; (tormentato) troubled.

dicastero [dikas'tɛro] sm ministry.

dicembre [di'tʃɛmbre] sm December.

diceria [ditʃe'ria] sf rumour, gossip.

dichiarare [dikja'rare] v declare; (gioco di carte) bid. **dichiarazione** sf declaration; bid; (attestazione) statement; (amore) proposal. **dichiarazione dei redditi** tax return.

diciannove [ditʃan'nɔve] agg, sm nineteen. **diciannovesimo** sm, agg nineteenth.

diciassette [ditʃas'sɛtte] agg, sm seventeen. **diciassettesimo** sm, agg seventeenth.

diciotto [di'tʃɔtto] agg, sm eighteen. **diciottesimo** sm, agg eighteenth.

dicitura [ditʃi'tura] sf caption.

didascalia [didaska'lia] sf caption; (cinema) subtitle; (teatro) stage directions pl.

didattico [di'dattiko] agg didactic.

didentro [di'dɛntro] **al/dal didentro** on/from the inside.

didietro [di'djɛtro] *sm* behind.

dieci ['djɛtʃi] *sm, agg* ten.

diesis [di'ɛzis] *sm (musica)* sharp.

dieta ['djɛta] *sf* diet. **essere a dieta** be on a diet.

dietro ['djɛtro] *avv* behind. *prep (luogo)* behind; *(tempo)* after; *(su, in seguito a)* on. **dietro front** about turn.

difatti [di'fatti] *cong* in fact.

*****difendere** [di'fɛndere] *v* defend.

difensiva [difen'siva] *sf* defensive. **difensivo** *agg* defensive.

difensore [difen'sore] *sm* defender. **avvocato difensore** *sm* counsel for the defence.

difesa [di'feza] *sf* defence. **difesa legittima** self-defence. **senza difesa** defenceless. **stare sulla difesa** be on the defensive.

difeso [di'fezo] *agg (riparato)* sheltered; *(fortificato)* defended, protected.

difetto [di'fɛtto] *sm (mancanza)* lack; *(imperfezione)* defect, fault. **difettare** *v also* **far difetto** lack; *(venir meno)* fail; *(essere difettoso)* be defective *or* faulty. **difettoso** *agg* defective, faulty.

diffamare [diffa'mare] *v* denigrate; *(a voce)* slander; *(per iscritto)* libel. **diffamatorio** *agg* defamatory; slanderous; libellous. **diffamatore, -trice** *sm, sf* libeller; slanderer.

differente [diffe'rɛnte] *agg* different, unlike.

differenza [diffe'rɛntsa] *sf* difference. **a differenza di** unlike. **differenziale** *sm, agg* differential. **differenziare** *v* differentiate.

differire [diffe'rire] *v (rimandare)* defer; *(esser diverso)* differ, be different.

difficile [dif'fitʃile] *agg* difficult; *(improbabile)* unlikely; *(duro)* hard. *sm* difficulty. *s(m+f)* difficult person.

difficoltà [diffikol'ta] *sf* difficulty; *(ostacolo)* trouble. **difficoltoso** *agg* difficult.

diffidare [diffi'dare] *v (non fidarsi)* mistrust, be suspicious of; *(avvisare)* warn, caution. **diffida** *sf* warning, notice. **diffidente** *agg* suspicious. **diffidenza** *sf* suspicion.

*****diffondere** [dif'fondere] *v* spread; *(luce, calore, ecc.)* diffuse; *(dilungarsi)* dwell; *(comm)* promote.

diffusione [diffu'zjone] *sf* spreading, diffusion; *(giornali)* circulation. **diffuso** *agg* widespread; diffused; widely circulated; *(prolisso)* long-winded.

diga ['diga] *sf* dam, barrier.

digerire [didʒe'rire] *v* digest; *(assimilare)* take in; *(tollerare)* stand, bear; *(credere)* swallow. **digeribile** *agg* digestible. **digestione** *sf* digestion. **digestivo** *sm, agg* digestive.

digitale [didʒi'tale] *agg* **impronta digitale** *sf* finger-print.

digiunare [didʒu'nare] *v also* **stare a digiuno** fast. **digiuno** *sm* fast. **a digiuno** on an empty stomach. **essere a digiuno di** *(fig)* be without.

dignità [diɲi'ta] *sf* dignity; *(ufficio)* (high) rank. *sf pl* dignitaries *pl*. **dignitoso** *agg* dignified.

digredire [digre'dire] *v* digress.

digressione [digres'sjone] *sf* digression.

digrignare [digri'ɲare] *v* **digrignare i denti** gnash one's teeth; *(animali)* bare the teeth.

dilagare [dila'gare] *v* flood, spread. **dilagamento** *sm* flooding.

dilaniare [dila'njare] *v* rend.

dilapidare [dilapi'dare] *v* squander.

dilatare [dila'tare] *v* dilate, open (wide). **dilatazione** *sf* dilation.

dilatorio [dila'torjo] *agg* dilatory. **dilazione** *sf* delay, deferment.

dileguare [dile'gware] *v* dispel. **dileguarsi** *v* disappear, fade.

dilemma [di'lemma] *sm* dilemma.

dilettante [dilet'tante] *agg. s(m+f)* amateur. **dilettantesco** *agg* amateurish.

dilettare [dilet'tare] *v* delight; *(far divertire)* amuse. **dilettarsi** *v* delight in, enjoy.

diletto¹ [di'letto] *sm (piacere)* delight, pleasure; *(godimento)* enjoyment.

diletto² [di'letto] *agg* beloved; *(preferito)* favourite.

diligente [dili'dʒɛnte] *agg (che lavora)* industrious; *(accurato)* conscientious; painstaking.

diligenza¹ [dili'dʒɛntsa] *sf* industry, conscientiousness. **con diligenza** conscientiously.

diligenza² [dili'dʒɛntsa] *sf (carrozza)* stage-coach.

diluire [dilu'ire] *v* dilute; *(allungare con acqua)* water down; *(vernice, ecc.)* thin (down).

dilungarsi [dilun'garsi] *v (andar per le lunghe)* talk at length, dwell.

diluvio [di'luvjo] *sm* flood, deluge.

dimagrire [dima'grire] *v also* **dimagrare** lose weight; *(di proposito)* slim; *(far sembrare snello)* make look slimmer.

dimenare [dime'nare] *v* wave (about); *(coda)* wag. **dimenarsi** *v* fidget, toss about.

dimensione [dimen'sjone] *sf* dimension. **a due/tre dimensioni** two/three-dimensional.

dimenticare [dimenti'kare] *v* forget; *(perdonare)* forget about; *(trascurare)* neglect. **dimenticarsi** *(di)* forget (about). **dimentico** *agg, m pl* **-chi** forgetful; *(noncurante)* oblivious.

dimestichezza [dimesti'kettsa] *sf* familiarity. **aver dimestichezza con** be familiar with.

dimettere [di'mettere] *v* discharge; *(licenziare)* dismiss. **dimettersi** *v* resign.

dimezzare [dimed'dzare] *v* halve.

diminuire [diminu'ire] *v* diminish, reduce; *(calare)* drop; *(lavoro a maglia)* cast off, decrease. **diminuire di peso** lose weight. **diminuire di prezzo** cost less. **diminuire di valore** fall in value, be worth less. **diminutivo** *agg* diminutive. **diminuzione** *sf* decrease; drop, cut, fall.

dimissione [dimis'sjone] *sf* resignation. **dare** *or* **rassegnare le dimissioni** resign. **dimissionario** *agg* outgoing.

dimorare [dimo'rare] *v* stay, live. **dimora** *sf (abitazione)* home, abode; *(soggiorno)* stay, residence.

dimostrare [dimos'trare] *v* demonstrate; *(manifestare)* show, display; prove. **dimostrabile** *agg* demonstrable. **dimostrante** *s(m+f)* demonstrator. **dimostrativo** *agg* demonstrative. **dimostratore, -trice** *sm, sf* demonstrator. **dimostrazione** *sf* demonstration; *(prova)* proof.

dinamica [di'namika] *sf* dynamics. **dinamico** *agg* dynamic, forceful.

dinamite [dina'mite] *sf* dynamite.

dinamo ['dinamo] *sf invar* dynamo.

dinanzi [di'nantsi] *avv* ahead, forward. *agg invar (dirimpetto)* facing; *(precedente)* previous. *prep* **dinanzi a** *(davanti a)* in front of; *(dirimpetto)* opposite; in the presence of, before.

dinastia [dinas'tia] *sf* dynasty. **dinastico** *agg* dynastic.

dinoccolato [dinokko'lato] *agg* shambling. **camminare dinoccolato** *v* slouch.

dinosauro [dino'sauro] *sm* dinosaur.

dintorno [din'torno] *avv* around, about.

dintorni *sm pl* outskirts *pl*, surroundings *pl*.

dio ['dio] *sm, pl* **dei** god. **come un dio** wonderfully, beautifully.

diocesi ['diot∫ezi] *sf* diocese.

diodo ['diodo] *sm* diode.

dipanare [dipa'nare] *v* unravel.

dipartimento [diparti'mento] *sm* department, district.

dipendente [dipen'dɛnte] *s(m+f) (impiegato)* employee. *agg* dependent, subordinate. **dipendenza** *sf* dependence; *(edificio)* annexe; *(filiale)* branch. **essere alle dipendenze di** be in the employ of.

*****dipendere** [di'pendere] *v* depend (on); *(derivare)* be due (to), be caused (by). **dipende!** that depends! **dipende da te!** it is up to you!

*****dipingere** [di'pindʒere] *v* paint; *(rappresentare)* depict. **dipingersi** *v (truccarsi)* make up. **dipinto** *sm* painting.

diploma [di'plɔma] *sm* diploma, certificate, qualification. **diplomarsi** *v* obtain a certificate, qualify.

diplomatico [diplo'matiko], **-a** *agg* diplomatic. *sm, sf* diplomat. **diplomazia** *sf* diplomacy.

diporto [di'porto] *sm* pleasure, pastime.

diradare [dira'dare] *v* thin; *(nebbia)* clear.

diramare [dira'mare] *v* issue, broadcast. **diramarsi** *v* branch out *or* off. **diramazione** *sf* branch; *(comunicato, ecc.)* broadcasting, circulation.

*****dire** ['dire] *v* say; *(raccontare, ordinare)* tell; *(significare)* mean. **a chi lo dici!** don't I know! **aver da dire su** find fault with. **è tutto dire** which is saying a lot. **inutile dire** it goes without saying. *sm* speech, words *pl*. **a dire di tutti** by all accounts. **oltre ogni dire** beyond all description.

diretto [di'rɛtto] *agg* direct; *(inteso)* meant, destined; *(guidato)* conducted. *sm (ferr)* through train. **direttissimo** *sm (ferr)* express train. **direttiva** *sf* directive; *(condotta)* policy. **direttivo** *agg (che dirige)* guiding; *(proprio alla direzione)* managerial. **direttore** *sm* manager; *(scuola)* headmaster; *(giornale)* editor; *(orchestra)* conductor. **direttrice** *sf* manageress; headmistress.

direzione [diret'tsjone] *sf* direction; *(il dirigere)* management, administration; *(sede)* head office. **assumere la direzione**

take charge. **in che direzione?** which way?

*__dirigere__ [di'ridʒere] v direct; (*rivolgere*) address; (*guidare*) lead; (*amministrare*) manage; (*giornale*) edit; (*orchestra*) conduct. **dirigersi verso** go towards, head for. **dirigibile** *sm* airship.

dirimpetto [dirim'petto] *agg invar, avv* opposite.

diritto¹ [di'ritto] *agg* (*non curvo*) straight; (*eretto, onesto*) upright; (*fam: astuto*) crafty; (*fam: accorto*) shrewd; (*destro*) right(-hand). *avv* straight. **andar diritto** go straight ahead *or* on. *sm* (*moneta*) obverse; (*lato buono*) good side; (*tennis*) forehand.

diritto² [di'ritto] *sm* (*legge*) law; (*pretesa*) right; (*tassa*) due, duty. **a buon diritto** with good cause. **diritti d'autore** copyright *sing*; (*compenso*) royalties *pl*. **diritto acquisito** vested interest.

diroccato [dirok'kato] *agg* dilapidated.

dirottare [dirot'tare] v divert; change course.

dirotto [di'rotto] *agg* (*pianto*) copious; (*pioggia*) pouring.

disabitato [dizabi'tato] *agg* uninhabited.

disabituare [dizabitu'are] v wean.

disaccordo [dizak'kordo] *sm* disagreement; variance. **essere** *or* **trovarsi in disaccordo su** disagree on, be at variance over.

disadatto [diza'datto] *agg* ill-suited.

disadorno [diza'dorno] *agg* bare.

disagevole [diza'dʒevole] *agg* uncomfortable.

disagio [di'zadʒo] *sm* (*imbarazzo*) uneasiness; (*mancanza di comodità*) discomfort. **essere a disagio** be ill at ease. **sentirsi a disagio** feel uneasy. **disagiato** *agg* uncomfortable; (*duro*) hard.

disamorarsi [dizamo'rarsi] v become estranged (from), cease to care (for).

disapprovare [dizappro'vare] v disapprove. **disapprovazione** *sf* disapproval.

disappunto [dizap'punto] *sm* disappointment.

disarmare [dizar'mare] v disarm; (*smantellare*) dismantle; (*edificio*) remove the scaffolding from. **disarmo** *sm* disarmament.

disarmonia [dizarmo'nia] *sf* discord.

disastro [di'zastro] *sm* disaster; (*incidente*) crash; (*fam: insuccesso*) utter failure.

combinare un disastro (*fam*) make a mess. **disastroso** *agg* disastrous.

disattento [dizat'tento] *agg* inattentive; (*sbadato*) careless. **disattenzione** *sf* carelessness; (*errore*) slip. **per disattenzione** through an oversight.

disavanzo [diza'vantso] *sm* deficit.

disavventura [dizavven'tura] *sf* misfortune.

disbrigo [diz'brigo] *sm, pl* **-ghi** settlement, dispatch.

discapito [dis'kapito] *sm* **a discapito di** at the cost of, to the prejudice of.

*__discendere__ [di'ʃendere] v descend; (*andar giù*) go down; (*venir giù*) come down. **discendente** *s*(*m+f*) descendant. **discendenza** *sf* descent; (*collettivo*) offspring. **discensore** *sm* lift.

discepolo [di'ʃepolo] *sm* disciple.

discernere [di'ʃernere] v discern; distinguish.

discesa [di'ʃesa] *sf* descent; (*declivio*) slope. **discesa in picchiata** nose-dive. **in discesa** downhill.

*__dischiudere__ [dis'kjudere] v open; (*svelare*) disclose.

*__disciogliere__ [di'ʃɔʎere] v dissolve; (*liquefare*) melt.

disciplinare [diʃipli'nare] v discipline, control. *agg* disciplinary. **disciplina** *sf* discipline. **disciplinato** *agg* (well-)disciplined, orderly.

disco ['disko] *sm* disc; (*grammofono*) record; (*sport*) discus; (*hockey*) puck; (*telefono*) dial. **disco rosso/verde** red/green light.

discolo ['diskolo] *agg* mischievous.

discolpare [diskol'pare] v clear. **discolpa** *sf* justification, defence.

*__disconoscere__ [disko'noʃere] v refuse to acknowledge.

discontinuo [diskon'tinuo] *agg* discontinuous; (*non regolare*) erratic.

discorde [dis'korde] *agg also* **discordante** discordant; (*contrastante*) conflicting; (*stonante*) clashing. **discordare** v disagree; conflict; clash. **discordia** *sf* disagreement.

*__discorrere__ [dis'korrere] v talk. **discorrere del più e del meno** talk about this and that. **e via discorrendo** and so on.

discorso [dis'korso] *sm* conversation, talk; (*in pubblico, gramm*) speech. **cambiare discorso** change the subject. **senza tanti discorsi** quite frankly. **tenere**

un discorso make a speech, give an address.

discoteca [disko'tɛka] sf (*locale*) discotheque; record collection.

discreto [dis'krɛto] agg fair, reasonable; (*non importuno*) tactful, discreet; (*separato*) discrete. **discretamente** avv moderately well. **discrezionale** agg discretionary. **discrezione** sf discretion, moderation, tact.

discriminazione [diskrimina'tsjone] sf discrimination. **discriminare** v discriminate; (*dir*) extenuate.

discussione [diskus'sjone] sf discussion, debate; (*litigio*) argument. **mettere in discussione** discuss, debate; (*in dubbio*) question.

discusso [dis'kusso] agg discussed, controversial.

*****discutere** [dis'kutere] v discuss, debate; (*litigare*) argue. **discutibile** agg debatable, questionable.

disdegnare [dizde'ɲare] v disdain, scorn. **disdegno** sm disdain, scorn.

*****disdire** [diz'dire] v (*annullare*) cancel; (*negare*) deny; (*ritrattare*) withdraw, take back; (*mentire*) refute. **disdetta** sf notice; (*sfortuna*) bad luck; cancellation.

disegnare [dize'ɲare] v draw; (*progettare*) design, sketch; (*delineare*) outline. **disegnatore** sm draughtsman. **disegno** sm drawing; (*schizzo*) sketch; (*progetto*) design, plan; (*abbozzo*) outline. **a disegni** patterned. **disegno animato** (*cinema*) cartoon. **disegno di legge** bill.

diseredare [dizere'dare] v disinherit. **diseredato, -a** s, agg destitute.

disertare [dizer'tare] v desert. **disertore** sm deserter. **diserzione** sf desertion.

*****disfare** [dis'fare] v undo; (*smontare*) take to pieces; (*valigia*) unpack; (*sciogliere*) melt. **disfatta** sf defeat. **disfattismo** sm defeatism. **disfattista** s(m+f), agg defeatist.

disgelare [dizdʒe'lare] v thaw (out); (*frigorifero*) defrost. **disgelo** sm thaw.

*****disgiungere** [diz'dʒundʒere] v detach, separate.

disgraziato [dizgra'tsjato], -a agg unfortunate, unlucky; (*infelice*) wretched. sm, sf (*sventurato*) wretch; (*sciagurato*) scoundrel. **disgrazia** sf misfortune; (*incidente*) accident, mishap; (*sfavore*) disgrace; (*sfortuna*) bad luck.

disgregare [dizgre'gare] v break up. **disgregazione** sf break-up.

disguido [diz'gwido] sm (*equivoco*) misunderstanding; (*errore nel recapito*) mistake in delivery.

disgustare [dizgus'tare] v disgust. **disgusto** sm disgust, revulsion, loathing. **disgustoso** agg disgusting, loathsome, revolting.

disidratare [dizidra'tare] v dehydrate.

*****disilludere** [dizil'ludere] v disillusion, disenchant. **disillusione** sf disenchantment, disillusion.

disimpegnare [dizimpe'ɲare] v free, release; (*oggetto dato in pegno*) redeem; (*mil*) relieve. **disimpegnarsi** v (*cavarsela*) acquit oneself, manage. **disimpegno** sm (*adempimento*) fulfilment; (*politica*) disengagement.

disinfettare [dizinfet'tare] v disinfect. **disinfettante** sm disinfectant. **disinfezione** sf disinfection.

disintegrare [dizinte'grare] v disintegrate; (*fis*) split, decay.

disinteressarsi [dizinteres'sarsi] v take no interest (in). **disinteressato** agg disinterested; (*altruistico*) unselfish.

disinvolto [dizin'vɔlto] agg unconstrained, self-possessed; (*spigliato*) free and easy, casual; (*senza ritegno*) uninhibited. **disinvoltura** sf ease, casualness; self-possession.

disistima [dizis'tima] sf lack of esteem; (*disprezzo*) contempt.

dislivello [dizli'vɛllo] sm difference (in level); (*fig*) inequality.

dislocare [dizlo'kare] v displace; (*mil*) detach.

dismisura [dizmi'zura] sf **a dismisura** excessively.

disoccupato [dizokku'pato], -a s, agg unemployed. **disoccupazione** sf unemployment. **sussidio di disoccupazione** sm unemployment benefit; (*fam*) dole.

disonesto [dizo'nɛsto] agg dishonest; (*immorale*) dishonourable; (*impudico*) shameless. **disonestà** sf dishonesty; dishonourable behaviour; shamelessness.

disonorare [dizono'rare] v dishonour, disgrace. **disonore** sm dishonour, disgrace. **disonorevole** agg dishonourable, disgraceful, shameful.

disopra [di'sopra] avv above; (*al piano superiore*) upstairs. agg invar (*superiore*) upper; (*posto più in alto*) higher up;

upstairs. *sm invar* top, upper part. **al disopra di** (*più di*) more than; (*superiore a*) above all; (*più alto di*) above. **dal disopra** from above.

disordinare [dizordi'nare] *v* upset, turn upside down. **disordinato** *agg* untidy; confuso; (*sregolato*) disorderly. **disordine** *sm* disorder; (*confusione*) muddle.

disorientare [dizorjen'tare] *v* (*confondere*) confuse, bewilder. **disorientarsi** *v* lose one's bearings, become confused.

disossare [dizos'sare] *v* bone.

disotto [di'sotto] *avv* below, underneath; (*al piano inferiore*) downstairs. *agg invar* below; (*tra due*) lower; (*in fondo*) bottom; downstairs.

dispaccio [dis'pattʃo] *sm* dispatch.

disparato [dispa'rato] *agg* dissimilar, different.

dispari ['dispari] *agg* odd.

disparte [dis'parte] *avv* **in disparte** aside, to one side. **tenersi in disparte** keep at a distance.

dispensa [dis'pensa] *sf* distribution; (*mobile*) cupboard; (*locale*) pantry, larder; (*fascicolo*) number, issue; (*esonero*) exemption. **a dispense** in instalments. **dispensa ecclesiastica** dispensation. **dispensa universitaria** lecture notes *pl*. **dispensare** *v* dispense. **dispensario** *sm* clinic.

disperare [dispe'rare] *v* despair. **disperato** *agg* desperate. **disperazione** *sf* despair.

dispetto [dis'petto] *sm* spite; (*irritazione*) annoyance. **a dispetto di** despite. **fare un dispetto** annoy. **per dispetto** out of spite. **dispettoso** *agg* spiteful, annoying.

****dispiacere** [dispja'tʃere] *v* displease. **mi dispiace ...** (*non mi piace*) I don't like ... ; (*sono spiacente*) I'm sorry ... . **ti dispiace ... ?** do you mind ... ? *sm* (*rammarico*) regret; (*noia*) displeasure; (*fastidio*) trouble, worry.

disponibile [dispo'nibile] *agg* available; (*libero*) vacant. **posto disponibile** *sm* vacancy.

disponibilità [disponibili'ta] *sf* availability. *sf pl* assets *pl*.

****disporre** [dis'porre] *v* dispose; (*collocare in ordine, stabilire*) arrange; prepare; induce; order. **disporre di** have available,

have at one's disposal; (*avere*) have. **disporsi** *v* prepare, get ready; (*in fila*) line up.

dispositivo [dispozi'tivo] *sm* device.

disposizione [dispozi'tsjone] *sf* arrangement, layout; (*stato d'animo*) disposition; (*inclinazione*) bent; (*norma*) provision; (*comando*) order. **a disposizione** available.

disposto [dis'posto] *agg* arranged, laid out; (*pronto*) ready, willing; (*stabilito*) laid down.

disprezzare [dispret'tsare] *v* despise, scorn. **disprezzo** *sm* scorn, contempt.

disputare [dispu'tare] *v* dispute; (*litigare*) argue; (*contendere*) fight (over); strive (for); (*incontro*) play; (*corsa*) run. **disputa** *sf* dispute; (*lite*) argument.

dissanguare [dissan'gware] *v* bleed.

dissecare [disse'kare] *v* dissect.

disseccare [dissek'kare] *v* dry up.

disseminare [dissemi'nare] *v* scatter; (*diffondere*) spread.

dissenteria [dissente'ria] *sf* dysentery.

dissentire [dissen'tire] *v* dissent, disagree.

disseppellire [disseppel'lire] *v* unearth; (*esumare*) exhume.

dissertazione [disserta'tsjone] *sf* dissertation.

dissestare [disses'tare] *v* upset, unbalance. **dissestato** *agg* ruined; (*strada*) in poor condition; (*bilancio*) adverse.

dissetarsi [disse'tarsi] *v* quench one's thirst. **dissetante** *agg* thirst-quenching.

dissidente [dissi'dente] *s(m+f)*, *agg* dissident; (*rel*) non-conformist.

dissidio [dis'sidjo] *sm* disagreement; (*lite*) quarrel.

dissimile [dis'simile] *agg* different, unlike.

dissimulare [dissimu'lare] *v* dissimulate; (*fingere*) pretend; (*nascondere*) hide.

dissipare [dissi'pare] *v* dispute; (*sospetti, dubbi, ecc.*) dispel; (*sprecare*) squander.

dissociare [disso'tʃare] *v* dissociate. **dissociazione** *sf* dissociation.

dissoluto [disso'luto] *agg* dissolute.

dissoluzione [dissolu'tsjone] *sf* dissolution, break-up.

****dissolvere** [dis'solvere] *v* dispel; (*sciogliere*) dissolve.

dissotterrare [dissotter'rare] *v* unearth; (*esumare*) exhume.

****dissuadere** [dissua'dere] *v* dissuade, deter.

distaccare [distak'kare] *v* detach; (*sport:*

lasciar dietro) leave behind. **distaccarsi** v (*spiccare*) stand out; (*allontanarsi*) withdraw. **distaccamento** sm (*mil*) detachment. **distacco** sm detachment; (*separazione*) parting, separation; (*sport: vantaggio*) lead.

distante [dis'tante] *agg* distant, remote, far. *avv* far, far off. **distanza** *sf* distance; (*tempo*) interval.

**distare [dis'tare] v be far (from).

distendere [dis'tendere] v spread; (*allungare*) stretch; (*appendere*) hang (up); (*mettere giù*) lay; (*rilassare*) relax. **distendersi v lie down, relax.

distensione [disten'sjone] *sf* stretching; relaxation; (*pol*) détente. **distensivo** *agg* relaxing.

distesa [dis'teza] *sf* expanse; (*fila*) row. **disteso** [dis'tezo] *agg* (*teso*) stretched; (*coricato*) lying down; (*braccio*) outstretched; (*spiegato*) spread out; relaxed.

distillare [distil'lare] v distil. **distilleria** *sf* distillery.

distinguere [dis'tingwere] v distinguish, tell; (*contrassegnare*) mark; draw a distinction; (*riconoscere*) recognize. **distinguibile *agg* distinguishable; recognizable.

distinta [dis'tinta] *sf* list. **distinta delle spese** statement of expenses.

distintivo [distin'tivo] *agg* distinctive; (*atto a distinguere*) distinguishing. *sm* badge.

distinto [dis'tinto] *agg* distinct, different, separate; (*scelto, raffinato*) distinguished. **ben distinto** precise. **distinti saluti** yours faithfully.

distinzione [distin'tsjone] *sf* distinction. **fare una distinzione** make a distinction, discriminate. **senza distinzione** (*senza merito*) undistinguished; (*senza criterio*) indiscriminately; (*in modo equo*) impartially.

**distogliere [dis'toʎere] v divert, turn away.

distorsione [distor'sjone] *sf* distortion; (*med*) sprain.

distrarre [dis'trarre] v distract; (*divertire*) amuse. **distrarsi v amuse oneself; (*essere disattento*) be inattentive. **distratto** *agg* inattentive; (*assente*) absent-minded; (*sbadato*) careless. **distrazione** *sf* (*svago*) distraction, relaxation; (*sbadatezza*) carelessness; absent-mindedness; lack of attention.

distretto [dis'tretto] *sm* district.

distribuire [distribu'ire] v distribute; (*disporre*) arrange; (*assegnare*) hand out; (*le carte*) deal; (*posta*) deliver. **distributore** sm (*di accensione*) distributor; (*di benzina*) petrol pump, service station. **distribuzione** *sf* distribution; (*fornitura*) supply; arrangement; delivery. **distribuzione dei premi** prize-giving. **distribuzione dei ruoli** (*cinema*) casting.

districare [distri'kare] v disentangle; (*fig*) sort out. **districarsi** v extricate oneself.

distruggere [dis'truddʒere] v destroy, ruin. **distruttivo *agg* destructive. **distrutto** *agg* destroyed, ruined; (*fig*) broken. **distruzione** *sf* destruction, ruin.

disturbare [distur'bare] v disturb; (*molestare, seccare*) trouble, bother; (*recar fastidio*) inconvenience; (*radio*) jam. **disturbo** sm trouble; (*incomodo*) nuisance, inconvenience; (*indisposizione*) upset, disorder; (*radio*) jamming; atmospherics *pl*, interference. **recar disturbo** trouble, inconvenience.

disubbidire [dizubbi'dire] v disobey.

disuguale [dizu'gwale] *agg* unequal; (*non regolare*) irregular. **disuguaglianza** *sf* difference, disparity.

disunire [dizu'nire] v separate, divide.

disuso [di'zuzo] sm disuse. **andare** or **cadere in disuso** fall into disuse, become obsolete. **disusato** *agg* obsolete, out-of-date; (*fuori moda*) old-fashioned.

dito ['dito] sm, *pl* **-a** *f* finger. **dito anulare/indice/medio/mignolo** ring/ index/middle/little finger. **dito del piede** toe. **ditale** sm (*cucire*) thimble; (*guanto*) finger-stall.

ditta ['ditta] *sf* firm, company.

dittatore [ditta'tore] sm dictator. **dittatorio** *agg* dictatorial. **dittatura** *sf* dictatorship.

dittico ['dittiko] sm diptych.

dittongo [dit'tɔngo] sm diphthong.

diurno [di'urno] *agg* day(-time). **spettacolo diurno** sm matinee.

diva ['diva] *sf* (*film-*)star.

divagare [diva'gare] v digress, wander; (*distrarre*) distract.

divampare [divam'pare] v flare up, blaze.

divano [di'vano] sm divan, settee, couch.

diventare [diven'tare] v *also* **divenire** become, turn or grow (into). **diventar matto** go mad. **diventar pallido/rosso** go or turn pale/red.

divergere [di'vɛrdʒere] v diverge; (essere diverso) differ. **divergenza** sf divergence; difference.

diversi [di'vɛrsi] agg several. pron (parecchi) several (people); (alcuni) some (people).

diversivo [diver'sivo] agg diverting; distracting. sm diversion; distraction.

diverso [di'vɛrso] agg different; distinct, separate; (di genere diverso) various; (comm) sundry. **in caso diverso** otherwise. **diversamente** avv differently; (se no) otherwise. **diversità** sf difference, diversity.

divertente [diver'tɛnte] agg amusing, enjoyable. **divertimento** sm entertainment, amusement. **buon divertimento!** enjoy yourself! have a good time!

divertire [diver'tire] v amuse; (ricreare) entertain. **divertirsi** v enjoy oneself.

dividendo [divi'dɛndo] sm dividend.

*dividere [di'videre] v divide; (condividere) share. **dividersi** v separate, part, split (up).

divieto [di'vjɛto] sm prohibition. **divieto di sorpasso/sosta/transito** no overtaking/stopping/thoroughfare.

divinare [divi'nare] v divine; (prevedere) foretell.

divincolarsi [divinko'larsi] v wriggle.

divino [di'vino] agg sacred, holy; (sublime) divine, heavenly. **divinità** sf divinity.

divisa [di'viza] sf uniform; motto. **divisa estera** foreign currency.

divisibile [divi'zibile] agg divisible. **divisibilità** sf divisibility.

divisione [divi'zjone] sf division; (reparto) department.

diviso [di'vizo] agg divided, separated; (condiviso) shared. **divisore** sm divisor.

divisorio [divi'zɔrjo] sm partition. agg dividing.

divo ['divo] sm (film-)star.

divorare [divo'rare] v devour, eat up.

divorzio [di'vɔrtsjo] sm divorce. **divorziare** v divorce.

divulgare [divul'gare] v spread; (rivelare) divulge; (rendere accessibile) popularize. **divulgazione** sf spreading; (notizie) broadcasting; popularization.

dizionario [ditsjo'narjo] sm dictionary.

dizione [di'tsjone] sf diction.

doccia ['dottʃa] sf shower; (grondaia) gutter.

docente [do'tʃɛnte] s(m+f) lecturer, teacher.

docile ['dɔtʃile] agg docile, mild; (materiale) easily worked. **docilità** sf mildness, submissiveness; workability.

documento [doku'mento] sm document, paper. **documentare** v document. **documentario** agg, sm documentary. **documentazione** sf documentation; (dir) evidence.

dodici ['doditʃi] agg, sm twelve. **dodicesimo** sm, agg twelfth.

dogana [do'gana] sf customs. **doganale** agg customs. **doganiere** sm customs officer.

doge ['dɔdʒe] sm doge.

doglie ['dɔʎʎe] sf pl **doglie del parto** labour pains pl.

dogma ['dɔgma] sm dogma. **dogmatico** agg dogmatic.

dolce ['doltʃe] agg sweet; (mite) mild; (morbido) soft. sm sweet. **dolcezza** sf sweetness; mildness; softness.

*dolere [do'lere] v (far male) ache, hurt. **mi duole di** or **che ...** I regret that ..., I'm sorry that ....

dollaro ['dɔllaro] sm dollar.

dolo ['dɔlo] sm (dir) malice; (inganno) fraud.

dolore [do'lore] sm pain; (male fisico) ache; (sofferenza morale) sorrow; (rincrescimento) regret. **doloroso** agg painful; sorrowful.

domanda [do'manda] sf question; (richiesta) request; (scritta) application; (econ) demand; (dir) petition. **domandare** v (per sapere) ask; (per avere) ask for; (esigere) demand. **domandarsi** v wonder.

domani [do'mani] avv tomorrow. **a domani!** see you tomorrow! **domani a otto** tomorrow week. **domani l'altro** the day after tomorrow. **dopo** tomorrow; future. **un domani** one day.

domare [do'mare] v tame; (sedare) put down; (spegnere) put out; (frenare) curb. **domatore** sm tamer.

domattina [domat'tina] avv tomorrow morning.

domenica [do'menika] sf Sunday.

domestico [do'mɛstiko] agg domestic; (della casa) household, home. **apparecchio domestico** household appliance. sm servant. **domestica** sf maid. **domestichezza** sf familiarity.

domiciliarsi [domitʃi'ljarsi] v settle.

domicilio [domi'tʃiljo] sm domicile, home.

dominare [domi'nare] v dominate; (predominare) prevail; (frenare) control; (aver potestà) rule. **dominio** sm domination; rule; (territorio) domain; (proprietà) possession. **pubblico dominio** (proprietà) common property; (noto a tutti) common knowledge.

domino ['domino] sm (gioco) dominoes.

donare [do'nare] v give, present; (star bene) suit, become. **donatore, -trice** sm, sf donor. **donazione** sf donation, gift.

donde ['donde] avv (da dove) whence, from where; (di che) with which.

dondolare [dondo'lare] v swing, rock. **cavallo a dondolo** sm rocking-horse. **sedia a dondolo** sf rocking-chair.

donna ['dɔnna] sf woman (pl women); (domestica) maid, servant; (giochi) queen. **donnaiolo** sm philanderer. **donnesco** agg feminine.

donnola ['dɔnnola] sf weasel.

dono ['dono] sm gift.

dopo ['dopo] avv after; (poi) then, afterwards; (più tardi) later (on); (prossimo) next. **a dopo!** see you later! (prep) after; (tempo) since. **dopo che** since. **dopo di che** whereupon. **dopodomani** sm, avv the day after tomorrow. **dopotutto** avv after all. **molto tempo dopo** long after.

dopopranzo [dopo'prantso] avv after lunch. sm afternoon.

doppiare¹ [dop'pjare] v (cinema) dub. **doppiaggio** sm dubbing.

doppiare² [dop'pjare] v double; (sport) lap.

doppio ['doppjo] agg double; (insincero) two-faced; (duplice) dual, twofold. **a doppio petto** double-breasted. **fare il doppio gioco** double-cross. sm double, twice as much or many. **doppione** sm duplicate.

dorare [do'rare] v gild; (gastr) coat with egg. **doratura** sf gilding, gold-plating.

dormicchiare [dormik'kjare] v doze, snooze.

dormire [dor'mire] v sleep; (esser fermo) lie dormant. **dormita** sf good sleep.

dormitorio [dormi'tɔrjo] sm dormitory.

dormiveglia [dormi'veʌa] sm **essere nel dormiveglia** be half-asleep.

dorso ['dorso] sm back; (nuoto) backstroke.

dose ['dɔze] sf dose; quantity. **dose eccessiva** overdose. **rincarare la dose** (fam) pile it on. **dosaggio** sm dosage.

dosso ['dɔsso] sm back. **togliersi un peso di dosso** take a weight off one's mind.

dotare [do'tare] v endow, provide. **dotato** agg gifted; endowed or provided (with); (munito) equipped (with). **dotazione** sf equipment; (rendita) endowment. **dote** sf (matrimonio) dowry; (donazione) endowment; (qualità) gift.

dotto¹ ['dotto] agg scholarly, learned. sm scholar.

dotto² [dotto] sm (condotto) duct.

dottore [dot'tore], **-essa** sm, sf doctor.

dottrina [dot'trina] sf (cultura) learning; (teoria, insieme di principi) doctrine.

dove ['dove] avv where. cong (se) if; (mentre) whereas. **fin dove** as far as.

*dovere [do'vere] v must, have to; (esser lecito) may; (essere inevitabile) be bound to; (esser causato da) be due to; (al condizionale) should, ought to. **come si deve** properly; (persona) proper, decent. sm duty. **doveroso** agg right and proper; (obbligato) (duty-)bound. **dovuto** agg, sm due.

dovunque [do'vunkwe] avv (dappertutto) everywhere; (in qualsiasi luogo) anywhere. cong wherever.

dozzina [dod'dzina] sf dozen. **a dozzine** by the dozen. **da dozzina** cheap, poor.

dragare [dra'gare] v dredge; (mine) sweep. **draga** sf dredge, dredger. **dragamine** sm invar minesweeper.

drago ['drago] sm dragon; (aquilone) kite. **dragone** sm dragoon; (mil) dragon.

dramma ['dramma] sm play; tragedy. **drammatico** agg dramatic; (esagerato) theatrical. **drammatizzare** v dramatize. **drammaturgo** sm playwright, dramatist.

drappello [drap'pello] sm squad, band.

drappo ['drappo] sm cloth; (funebre) pall. **drappeggiare** v drape.

drastico ['drastiko] agg drastic.

drenare [dre'nare] v drain. **drenaggio** sm drainage.

dritta ['dritta] sf (mano) right (hand); (parte) right(-hand side); (mar) starboard.

dritto ['dritto] agg (fam) astute. sm (non rovescio) right side; (fam) crafty person, fast worker.

drizzare [drit'tsare] v (raddrizzare)

straighten; (*erigere*) erect. **drizzare le orecchie** prick up one's ears.

droga ['drɔga] *sf* drug; (*sostanza aromatica*) spice. **drogare** *v* drug, dope; spice. **drogarsi** *v* take drugs.

droghiere [dro'gjɛre], **-a** *sm*, *sf* grocer. **drogheria** *sf* grocer's shop. **articoli di drogheria** *sm pl* groceries *pl*.

dromedario [drome'darjo] *sm* dromedary.

dualismo [dua'lizmo] *sm* dualism.

dubbio ['dubbjo] *sm* doubt. **essere in dubbio** be in doubt, be uncertain. **mettere in dubbio** doubt, call in question. **senza dubbio** no doubt, doubtless. *agg also* **dubbioso** doubtful, uncertain; (*ambiguo*) dubious.

dubitare [dubi'tare] *v* doubt; (*essere in dubbio*) be in doubt; (*diffidare*) distrust. **non dubitare!** don't worry!

duca ['duka] *sm* duke.

duce ['dutʃe] *sm* leader.

duchessa [du'kessa] *sf* duchess.

due ['due] *sm*, *agg* two. **a due a due** two by two, in twos. **duepezzi** *sm invar* two-piece. **due punti** colon. **due volte** twice. **due volte tanto** twice as much or many. **nessuno dei due** neither of them. **tutti e due** both of them.

duello [du'ello] *sm* duel. **duellare** *v* duel. **duellista** *or* **duellante** *sm* duellist.

duetto [du'etto] *sm* duet.

duna ['duna] *sf* dune.

dunque ['dunkwe] *cong* (*nel discorso*) well, now then; (*perciò*) so, therefore, hence; (*rafforzativo*) then. *sm* **trovarsi al dunque** come to the crunch. **venire al dunque** come to the point.

duo ['duo] *sm invar* duo.

duodeno [duo'dɛno] *sm* duodenum. **duodenale** *agg* duodenal.

duomo ['dwɔmo] *sm* cathedral.

duplex ['dupleks] *sm invar* (*telefono*) party-line.

duplicare [dupli'kare] *v* duplicate. **duplicato** *agg*, *sm* duplicate. **duplicatore** *sm* duplicator, copier. **duplice** *agg* double.

durare [du'rare] *v* last; (*cibo*) keep; (*abiti*) wear; (*sopportare*) endure. **durata** *sf* length (of time), duration. **di breve durata** short(-lived), not lasting. **di lunga durata** lasting. **durata di una carica** term of office. **durevole** *agg* lasting.

duro ['duro] *agg* hard, tough. **aver la pelle dura** be thick-skinned. **aver la testa dura** be stubborn. **tener duro** hold out. **durezza** *sf* hardness. **durone** *sm* callus.

duttile ['duttile] *agg* ductile.

E

e [e], **ed** *cong* and; (*invece*) and then. **e ... e ...** both ... and .... **tutti e due** both (of them). **tutti e tre** all three (of them).

ebano ['ɛbano] *sm* ebony. **d'ebano** (*colore*) jet-black. **ebanista** *sm* cabinet-maker.

ebbene [eb'bɛne] *cong* well (then).

ebbro ['ɛbbro] *agg* intoxicated, drunk. **ebbrezza** *sf* intoxication; (*fig*) rapture, elation.

ebdomadario [ebdoma'darjo] *agg*, *sm* weekly.

ebete ['ɛbete] *agg* dull-witted.

ebollizione [ebolli'tsjone] *sf* boiling. **punto di ebollizione** *sm* boiling point.

ebraico [e'braiko] *agg* Jewish, Hebrew. *sm* (*lingua*) Hebrew.

ebreo [e'brɛo], **-a** *sm*, *sf* Jew. *agg* Jewish.

eccedere [et'tʃɛdere] *v* exceed; surpass. **eccedere i limiti** go too far.

*•**eccellere** [et'tʃɛllere] *v* excel, be outstanding. **eccellente** *agg* excellent. **eccellenza** *sf* excellence; (*titolo*) Excellency. **per eccellenza** par excellence.

eccentrico [et'tʃɛntriko] *agg*, *sm* eccentric. **eccentricità** *sf* eccentricity.

eccepibile [ettʃe'pibile] *agg* objectionable. **eccepire** *v* take exception (to), object (to).

eccesso [et'tʃɛsso] *sm* excess. **all'eccesso** excessively, to a fault. **eccesso di velocità** speeding. **eccessivo** *agg* excessive, exaggerated.

eccetera [et'tʃɛtera] etcetera, and so forth *or* on.

eccetto [et'tʃɛtto] *prep* except. **eccetto che** (*tranne che*) except for, but for; (*a meno che*) unless.

eccettuare [ettʃettu'are] *v* except, leave out.

eccezione [ettʃe'tsjone] *sf* exception. **ad eccezione di** except for. **eccezionale** *agg* exceptional.

eccidio [et'tʃidjo] *sm* slaughter.

eccitare [ettʃi'tare] *v* excite, stimulate; (*provocare*) stir up, rouse. **eccitamento** *sm* excitement; (*stimolo*) incitement. **eccitante** *sm* stimulant. **eccitazione** *sf* excitement.

ecclesiastico [ekkle'zjastiko] *agg* clerical, ecclesiastic(al). *sm* clergyman.

ecco ['ekko] *avv* this *or* that is; (*qui*) here is; (*lì*) there is. **ecco fatto** that is that. **ecco tutto** that is all.

eccome [ek'kome] *avv*, *inter* and how, certainly.

echeggiare [eked'dʒare] *v* echo; (*risonare*) resound.

eclettico [e'klettiko] *agg* eclectic.

eclissare [eklis'sare] *v* eclipse. **eclisse** *or* **eclissi** *sf* eclipse.

eco ['ɛko] *s(m+f)*, *pl* -i *m* echo. **echi di cronaca** gossip (column) *sing*. **far eco a** echo.

ecologia [ekolo'dʒia] *sf* ecology. **ecologico** *agg* ecological. **ecologo, -a** *sm*, *sf* ecologist.

economia [ekono'mia] *sf* economy; (*risparmio*) thrift, saving; (*scienza*) economics. **fare economie** economize, save. **economico** *agg* economic; (*a bassa spesa*) economical, cheap.

economizzare [ekonomid'dzare] *v* economize, save.

economo [e'kɔnomo] *sm* steward, supply officer.

ed [ed] *V* **e**.

edera ['edera] *sf* ivy.

edibile [e'dibile] *agg* edible.

edicola [e'dikola] *sf* bookstall.

edificare [edifi'kare] *v* (*erigere*) construct; (*stimolare al bene*) edify. **edificante** *agg* edifying. **edificio** *sm* building; (*fig*) structure.

edile [e'dile] *agg* building. *sm* builder. **edilizia** *sf* building trade. **edilizio** *agg* building.

Edimburgo [edim'burgo] *sf* Edinburgh.

editore [edi'tore], -**trice** *sm*, *sf* publisher. *agg* publishing. **edito** *agg* published.

editto [e'ditto] *sm* edict.

edizione [edi'tsjone] *sf* edition; (*tiratura*) issue.

educare [edu'kare] *v* educate; (*ammaestrare*) train. **educativo** *agg* educational. **educato** *agg* (*cortese*) polite. **bene/male educato** well-/ill-mannered. **educazione** *sf* education, upbringing; training; (*comportamento*) manners *pl*, breeding.

effeminato [effemi'nato] *agg* effeminate. **effeminatezza** *sf* effeminacy.

effervescente [efferve'ʃɛnte] *agg* effervescent, sparkling.

effetto [ef'fetto] *sm* effect; (*conseguenza*) result; impression; (*comm*) bill. **aver effetto** take effect. **dare effetto a** carry out. **fare effetto** work. **fare l'effetto di** give the impression of.

effettuare [effettu'are] *v* effect, bring about; (*realizzare*) carry out; (*fare*) make. **effettuabile** *agg* feasible. **effettuazione** *sf* execution.

efficace [effi'katʃe] *agg* effective, efficient. **efficacia** *sf* efficacy, effectiveness; force.

efficiente [effi'tʃɛnte] *agg* efficient. **efficienza** *sf* efficiency, effectiveness; (*mec*) working order.

effigie [ef'fidʒe] *sf* effigy; image.

effimero [ef'fimero] *agg* ephemeral.

effluente [efflu'ɛnte] *sm* effluent, sewage. **efflusso** *sm* outflow.

egida ['ɛdʒida] *sf* aegis.

Egitto [e'dʒitto] *sm* Egypt. **egiziano, -a** *s*, *agg* Egyptian. **egizio, -a** *s*, (ancient) Egyptian.

egli ['eʎi] *pron* he.

egocentrico [ego'tʃɛntriko] *agg* egocentric, self-centred.

egoista [ego'ista] *s(m+f)* egoist, selfish person. **egoistico** *agg* egoistic(al), selfish.

egotista [ego'tista] *s(m+f)* egotist, boaster. **egotistico** *agg* egotistic(al).

egregio [e'gredʒo] *agg* distinguished; (*in lettere*) dear.

eguale [e'gwale] *V* **uguale**.

egualitario [egwali'tarjo], -**a** *s*, *agg* egalitarian.

elettore [elet'tore] *sm* ejector. **sedile elettore** *sm* ejector seat.

elaborare [elabo'rare] *v* elaborate, devise; (*dati*) process. **elaborato** *agg* elaborate. **elaboratore** *sm* (*elettronico*) computer; (*dati*) processor. **elaborazione** *sf* preparation, formulation; (*dati*) processing.

elargire [elar'dʒire] *v* lavish.

elastico [e'lastiko] *agg* elastic; (*molleggiante*) springy; (*fig*) flexible; (*agile*) nimble. *sm* elastic; (*anello*) elastic band; (*materasso*) spring.

elefante [ele'fante] *sm* elephant. **elefantesco** *agg* elephantine.

elegante [ele'gante] *agg* elegant; (*vestito*) smart; (*fine*) graceful; (*ingegnoso*) neat. **eleganza** *sf* elegance; smartness, stylishness.

*eleggere [e'lɛddʒere] v elect, nominate. **eleggibile** agg eligible. **eleggibilità** sf eligibility.

elegia [ele'dʒia] sf elegy. **elegiaco** agg elegiac.

elemento [ele'mento] sm element; (individuo) fellow, individual. **elementare** agg elementary; (naturale) elemental.

elemosina [ele'mɔzina] sf alms, charity. **chiedere l'elemosina** beg. **fare l'elemosina** give alms.

elenco [e'lɛnko] sm list; (telefonico) directory; (iscritti) register. **elencare** v list; enumerate.

eletto [e'letto] agg chosen; (scelto) select; (nominato) elected.

elettorale [eletto'rale] agg electoral, election. **collegio elettorale** sm constituency. **propaganda elettorale** sf electioneering. **scheda/urna elettorale** sf ballot-paper/box. **elettorato** sm electorate; (diritto di alzare) franchise.

elettore [elet'tore], **-trice** sm, sf elector, voter; (di collegio elettorale) constituent.

elettrico [e'lɛttriko] agg electric(al). **elettricista** sm electrician. **elettricità** sf electricity.

elettrificare [elettrifi'kare] v electrify. **elettrificazione** sf electrification.

elettrizzare [elettrid'dzare] v electrify; (fig) thrill.

elettrodo [e'lɛttrodo] sm electrode.

elettrodomestico [elettrodo'mɛstiko] sm electric appliance.

elettrodotto [elettro'dotto] sm power line, mains.

elettrolisi [elet'trɔlizi] sf electrolysis. **elettrolitico** agg electrolytic.

elettrone [elet'trone] sm electron. **elettronica** sf electronics. **elettronico** agg electronic.

elettrotecnico [elettro'tɛkniko] sm electrical engineer.

elevare [ele'vare] v raise. **elevato** agg high; (fig) lofty. **elevazione** sf elevation; (atto di alzare) raising.

elezione [ele'tsjone] sf election. **elezioni politiche** general election sing.

elica ['elika] sf propeller. **elicottero** sm helicopter.

eliminare [elimi'nare] v eliminate; (escludere) rule out. **eliminatoria** sf (sport) qualifying round. **eliminazione** sf elimination; exclusion.

elio ['ɛljo] sm helium.

ella ['ella] pron she; (formula di cortesia) you.

ellisse [el'lisse] sf ellipse. **ellittico** agg elliptical.

elmetto [el'metto] sm also **elmo** helmet.

elogio [e'lɔdʒo] sm praise. **elogiare** v praise.

eloquente [elo'kwɛnte] agg eloquent; (significativo) meaningful. **eloquenza** sf eloquence.

elsa ['elsa] sf hilt.

*eludere [e'ludere] v elude, dodge, evade.

emaciato [ema'tʃato] agg emaciated.

emanare [ema'nare] v emanate; (diffondere) give off, send out; (promulgare) issue. **emanazione** sf emanation; promulgation.

emancipare [emantʃi'pare] v emancipate. **emancipazione** sf emancipation.

embargo [em'bargo] sm embargo.

emblema [em'blɛma] sm emblem; symbol, model. **emblematico** agg emblematic, symbolic.

embolia [embo'lia] sf embolism. **embolo** sm embolus.

embrione [embri'one] sm embryo. **embrionale** agg embryonic.

emendare [emen'dare] v amend. **emendamento** sm amendment.

emergenza [emer'dʒɛntsa] sf emergency.

*emergere [e'mɛrdʒere] v emerge; (distinguersi) stand out; (apparire) appear.

*emettere [e'mettere] v emit, give out; (ordine, azioni) issue; (giudizio) deliver; (grido) utter.

emicrania [emi'krania] sf migraine.

emigrare [emi'grare] v emigrate; (animali) migrate. **emigrante** s(m+f) emigrant. **emigrato, -a** sm, sf emigrant; (pol) exile. **emigrazione** sf emigration, migration; (econ) flight.

eminente [emi'nɛnte] agg eminent, distinguished; (elevato) high. **eminenza** sf eminence.

emisfero [emis'fero] sm hemisphere. **emisferico** agg hemispheric(al).

emissario¹ [emis'sarjo] sm (mandatario) emissary.

emissario² [emis'sarjo] sm (canale, ecc.) outlet.

emissione [emis'sjone] sf emission; (econ) issue. **emittente** agg issuing; (radio) transmitting.

279

equilibrare

emolliente [emol'ljente] *sm, agg* emollient.

emorragia [emorra'dʒia] *sf* haemorrhage, bleeding.

emorroidi [emor'rɔidi] *sf pl* piles *pl*.

emotivo [emo'tivo] *agg* emotional; *(impressionabile)* excitable; *(che provoca emozione)* emotive, thrilling.

emozione [emo'tsjone] *sf* emotion; excitement. **emozionante** *agg* exciting. **emozionare** *v* excite; *(commuovere)* move.

empio ['empjo] *agg* impious; *(crudele)* cruel.

empire [em'pire] *v* fill.

empirico [em'piriko] *agg* empirical.

emporio [em'pɔrjo] *sm* store.

emù [e'mu] *sm* emu.

emulare [emu'lare] *v* emulate. **emulazione** *sf* rivalry; *(dir)* nuisance.

emulsione [emul'sjone] *sf* emulsion.

enciclopedia [entʃiklope'dia] *sf* encyclopaedia. **enciclopedico** *agg* encyclopaedic.

encomio [en'kɔmjo] *sm* praise. **encomiabile** *agg* praiseworthy.

endemico [en'dɛmiko] *agg* endemic.

energia [ener'dʒia] *sf* energy. **energetico** *sm, agg* tonic. **energico** *agg* energetic; *(forte)* forceful, strong.

enfasi ['enfazi] *sf* emphasis (*pl* -ses). **enfatico** *agg* emphatic.

enfiare [en'fjare] *v* swell, inflate.

enigma [e'nigma] *sm* puzzle, riddle; *(mistero, persona misteriosa)* enigma, mystery. **enigmatico** *agg* puzzling; mysterious.

ennesimo [en'nɛzimo] *agg* nth; *(fam)* umpteenth.

enorme [e'norme] *agg* enormous, huge. **enormità** *sf (causa di indignazione)* enormity; *(errore)* blunder.

ente ['ente] *sm (filos)* being; *(azienda)* undertaking, concern; authority; *(istituzione)* body.

enteroclisi [entero'klizi] *sm* enema.

entità [enti'ta] *sf* entity; importance; *(consistenza)* extent.

entrambi [en'trambi] *agg, pron* both.

entrare [en'trare] *v* enter; *(andar dentro)* go in(to); *(con difficoltà)* get in(to); *(venir dentro)* come in(to); *(associarsi)* join. **entrare in ballo** come into play. **entrare in vigore** come into effect.

entrata [en'trata] *sf* entrance, entry; *(accesso)* admission. **entrate** *sf pl (redditi)* income *sing*, earnings *pl*; *(incassi)* receipts *pl*; *(di enti pubblici)* revenue *sing*.

entro ['entro] *prep* within; *(ora/data precisata)* by. **entro oggi** before the day is out.

entusiasmo [entu'zjazmo] *sm* enthusiasm. **entusiasmare** *v* thrill, excite. **entusiasta** *s(m+f)* enthusiast. **entusiastico** *agg* enthusiastic.

enumerare [enume'rare] *v* list. **enumerazione** *sf* listing; list.

enunciare [enun'tʃare] *v* enunciate; *(esprimere)* express; formulate.

enzima [en'dzima] *sm* enzyme.

epatite [epa'tite] *sf* hepatitis.

epico ['epiko] *agg* epic, heroic. **epica** *sf* epic poetry.

epidemia [epide'mia] *sf* epidemic. **epidemico** *agg* epidemic.

Epifania [epifa'nia] *sf* Epiphany; *(festa)* Twelfth Night.

epigramma [epi'gramma] *sm* epigram. **epigrammatico** *agg* epigrammatic.

epilessia [epiles'sia] *sf* epilepsy. **epilettico, -a** *s, agg* epileptic.

epilogo [e'pilogo] *sm, pl* -ghi epilogue; *(fig)* end, conclusion.

episodio [epi'zɔdjo] *sm* episode. **episodico** *agg* episodic; *(frammentario)* bitty; *(accidentale)* incidental; isolated.

epistola [e'pistola] *sf* epistle. **epistolare** *agg* epistolary.

epitaffio [epi'taffjo] *sm* epitaph.

epiteto [e'piteto] *sm* epithet.

epoca ['epoka] *sf* period; *(tempo)* time. **a quell'epoca** at that time. **che fa epoca** epoch-making. **da quell'epoca** from that time on, since then.

eppure [ep'pure] *cong* and yet.

epurare [epu'rare] *v* purge. **epurazione** *sf* purging; purge.

equanime [e'kwanime] *agg (imparziale)* fair; *(sereno)* even-tempered. **equanimità** *sf* fairness, equanimity.

equatore [ekwa'tore] *sm* equator. **equatoriale** *agg* equatorial.

equazione [ekwa'tsjone] *sf* equation.

equestre [e'kwestre] *agg* equestrian.

equilibrare [ekwili'brare] *v* balance. **equilibrio** *sm* balance, equilibrium; moderation, common sense; *(padronanza di sè)* poise. **perdere l'equilibrio** lose one's balance. **tenere in equilibrio** balance. **tenersi in equilibrio** keep one's balance. **equilibrista** *s(m+f)* acrobat.

equinozio [ekwi'nɔtsjo] sm equinox.

equipaggiare [ekwipad'dʒare] v (fornire) equip; (nave) man. **equipaggiamento** sm kit. **equipaggio** sm crew.

equiparare [ekwipa'rare] v level.

equitazione [ekwita'tsjone] sf (horse-)riding.

*****equivalere** [ekwiva'lere] v be equivalent, correspond. **equivalente** sm, agg equivalent.

equivoco [e'kwivoko] sm (errore) mistake; (malinteso) misunderstanding. **a scanso di equivoci** to avoid misunderstandings. agg ambiguous; (di dubbia moralità) questionable, shady. **non equivoco** unambiguous, straightforward.

equo ['ekwo] agg fair.

era ['era] sf era, age.

erario [e'rarjo] sm Treasury. **erariale** agg fiscal.

erba ['erba] sf grass; (gastr) herb. **in erba** green; (fig) budding. **erbaceo** agg herbaceous.

erbaccia [er'battʃa] sf weed.

erbicida [erbi'tʃida] sm herbicide, weedkiller.

erbivendolo [erbi'vendolo], **-a** sm, sf greengrocer.

erbivoro [er'bivoro] sm herbivore. agg herbivorous.

erede [e'rede] s(m+f) heir, heiress. **erede apparente** heir presumptive. **erede universale** sole heir.

eredità [eredi'ta] sf inheritance, heritage. **ereditare** v inherit. **ereditario** agg inherited, hereditary. **principe ereditario** sm crown prince. **ereditiera** sf heiress.

eremita [ere'mita] sm hermit. **eremitaggio** sm hermitage.

eretico [e'retiko], **-a** sm, sf heretic. agg heretical. **eresia** sf heresy; (fam: sproposito) rubbish.

eretto [e'rɛtto] agg erect, upright. **erettile** agg erectile.

erezione [ere'tsjone] sf erection.

ergastolo [er'gastolo] sm life imprisonment or sentence.

erica ['erika] sf heather.

*****erigere** [e'ridʒere] v raise, erect; (fondare, considerare) set up.

ermellino [ermel'lino] sm ermine; (bruno) stoat.

ermetico [er'mɛtiko] agg (aria) air-tight; (acqua) water-tight; obscure.

ernia ['ɛrnja] sf hernia, rupture.

*****erodere** [e'rodere] v erode.

eroe [e'rɔe] sm hero. **eroico** agg heroic. **eroina** sf heroine. **eroismo** sm heroism; (atto) heroic deed.

erogare [ero'gare] v distribute, deliver; (in donazione) donate. **erogazione** sf distribution, delivery; donation.

eroina [ero'ina] sf (stupefacente) heroin.

erosione [ero'zjone] sf erosion.

erotico [e'rɔtiko] agg erotic. **erotismo** sm eroticism.

erpete ['ɛrpete] sm herpes.

erpice ['ɛrpitʃe] sm harrow.

errare [er'rare] v (andare senza meta) roam, wander; (sbagliare) err, be mistaken. **erratico** agg erratic. **errato** agg incorrect. **se non vado errato** if I am not mistaken.

erroneo [er'rɔneo] agg erroneous, wrong.

errore [er'rore] sm mistake, error. **errore giudiziario** miscarriage of justice. **per errore** by mistake, in error.

erudito [eru'dito] agg erudite, learned. **erudizione** sf learning.

eruttare [erut'tare] v (ruttare) belch; (vulcano) erupt; (fig) spew out. **eruzione** sf eruption.

esacerbare [ezatʃer'bare] v exacerbate.

esagerare [ezadʒe'rare] v exaggerate; (caricare) overdo. **esagerazione** sf exaggeration.

esagono [e'zagono] sm hexagon. **esagonale** agg hexagonal.

esalare [eza'lare] v exhale, give off. **esalazione** sf exhalation.

esaltare [ezal'tare] v exalt; (lodare) extol; (entusiasmare) thrill, stir. **esaltato**, **-a** sm, sf fanatic, hot-head.

esame [e'zame] sm examination, test; (controllo) inspection, check. **dare un esame** take an examination. **prendere in esame** consider, take into consideration.

esaminare [ezami'nare] v examine, test, check.

esanime [e'zanime] agg lifeless.

esasperare [ezaspe'rare] v (irritare) exasperate; (inasprire) sharpen, increase. **esasperazione** sf exasperation; sharpening, increase.

esatto [e'zatto] agg exact; correct; accurate; punctual. avv (in punto) exactly. **esattezza** sf exactness; accuracy, precision.

esattore [ezat'tore] *sm* (*tassa*) collector. **esattoria** *sf* tax office.

esaudire [ezau'dire] *v* grant.

esaurire [ezau'rire] *v* exhaust, use up; (*vendere completamente*) sell out; (*condurre a termine*) complete. **esaurirsi** *v* (*debilitarsi*) wear oneself out.

esca ['eska] *sf* bait; (*fig*) lure; (*per accendere*) tinder. **dar esca** a fan, stir up.

escandescenza [eskande'ʃɛntsa] *sf* **dare in escandescenza** flare up; (*fam*) fly off the handle.

eschimese [eski'meze] *s(m+f)*, *agg* Eskimo.

esclamare [eskla'mare] *v* exclaim, cry out. **punto esclamativo** *sm* exclamation mark. **esclamazione** *sf* exclamation.

*escludere [es'kludere] *v* exclude. **esclusione** *sf* exclusion. **ad esclusione di** except.

esclusivo [esklu'zivo] *agg* exclusive. **esclusiva** *sf* (*comm*) exclusive or sole right; (*rappresentanza*) sole agency. **escluso** *agg* excluded, impossible; (*eccettuato*) except; (*non compreso*) exclusive of, not including.

escogitare [eskodʒi'tare] *v* devise, think up.

escursione [eskur'sjone] *v* excursion, trip; (*a macchina*) drive; (*a piedi*) hike. **escursionista** *s(m+f)* tripper; hiker.

esecutivo [ezeku'tivo] *sm*, *agg* executive.

esecutore [ezeku'tore], **-trice** *sm*, *sf* (*dir*) executor; (*musica*) performer; (*carnefice*) executioner.

esecuzione [ezeku'tsjone] *sf* execution, performance.

eseguire [eze'gwire] *v* carry out; (*musica*, *teatro*) perform; (*dir*) execute.

esempio [e'zɛmpjo] *sm* example; model. **ad** *or* **per esempio** for instance. **dare l'esempio** set an example.

esemplare [ezem'plare] *agg* exemplary. *sm* example, model; (*tipico*) specimen. **esemplificare** *v* exemplify, illustrate.

esentare [ezen'tare] *v* exempt. **esentarsi da** get out of. **esente** *agg* exempt, free. **esenzione** *sf* exemption.

esequie [e'zɛkwje] *sf pl* (*cerimonie*) funeral rites *pl*; funeral *sing*.

esercente [ezer'tʃɛnte] *s(m+f)* retailer; (*negoziante*) shopkeeper. **esercire** *v* manage, run.

esercitare [ezertʃi'tare] *v* practise; (*usare*)

exercise. **esercitazione** *sf* practice; exercise; (*mil*) drill. **esercizio** *sm* exercise; (*attività*) practice; (*azienda*) concern.

esibire [ezi'bire] *v* exhibit. **esibirsi** *v* (*dar spettacolo*) perform; (*mettersi in mostra*) show off. **esibizione** *sf* exhibition, show, display. **esibizionismo** *sm* exhibitionism. **esibizionista** *s(m+f)* exhibitionist.

*esigere [e'zidʒere] *v* require, need, demand. **esigente** *agg* exacting. **esigenza** *sf* requirement; (*necessità*) need; (*pretesa*) demand. **esiguo** *agg* meagre.

esilarante [ezila'rante] *agg* exhilarating.

esile ['ezile] *agg* slender; (*debole*) feeble.

esiliare [ezi'ljare] *v* exile. **esiliarsi** *v* go into exile. **esiliato, -a** *sm*, *sf* exile. **esilio** *sm* exile.

*esimere [e'zimere] *v* exempt, free.

esimio [e'zimjo] *agg* distinguished, outstanding.

esistenzialismo [ezistentsja'lizmo] *sm* existentialism. **esistenzialista** *s(m+f)*, *agg* existentialist.

esistere [e'zistere] *v* exist, be. **esistente** *agg* existing. **esistenza** *sf* existence. **esistenza di cassa/magazzino** (*comm*) cash/stock in hand.

esitare [ezi'tare] *v* hesitate. **esitazione** *sf* hesitation.

esito ['ezito] *sm* outcome; (*dramma*) denouement. **buon esito** success.

esodo [e'zɔdo] *sm* exodus.

esofago [e'zɔfago] *sm* oesophagus; gullet.

esonerare [ezone'rare] *v* exempt. **esonero** *sm* exemption.

esorbitante [ezorbi'tante] *agg* exorbitant.

esorcizzare [ezortʃid'dzare] *v* exorcise. **esorcismo** *sm* exorcism.

esordire [ezor'dire] *v* start out; (*artista*) make one's debut. **esordio** *sm* start, debut.

esortare [ezor'tare] *v* urge. **esortazione** *sf* exhortation, encouragement.

esoso [e'zɔzo] *agg* (*avido*) greedy; exorbitant; odious.

esoterico [ezo'tɛriko] *agg* esoteric.

esotico [e'zɔtiko] *agg* exotic.

*espandere [es'pandere] *v* expand, extend. **espandersi** *v* spread. **espansione** *sf* expansion; (*effusione d'affetto*) effusiveness. **espansivo** *agg* effusive; (*forza*) expansive.

espatriare [espa'trjare] *v* emigrate. **espatrio** *sm* expatriation.

espediente [espe'djɛnte] *sm* expedient, device; (*soluzione*) way out. **vivere di espedienti** live on one's wits.

*__espellere__ [es'pɛllere] *v* expel.

esperienza [espe'rjɛntsa] *sf* experience; experiment; (*conoscenza*) familiarity. **fare esperienza di** experience. **senza esperienza** inexperienced.

esperimento [esperi'mento] *sm* experiment; (*tentativo*) trial, test.

esperto [es'pɛrto], **-a** *sm*, *sf* expert, authority. *agg* expert (in); (*abile*) skilful (at); experienced (in).

espiare [espi'are] *v* expiate, atone. **capro espiatorio** *sm* scapegoat.

espletare [esple'tare] *v* accomplish.

esplicito [es'plitʃito] *agg* explicit. **esplicativo** *agg* explanatory.

*__esplodere__ [es'plɔdere] *v* explode. **far esplodere** explode, blow up.

esplorare [esplo'rare] *v* explore; (*investigare*) probe. **esploratore**, **-trice** *sm*, *sf* explorer; (*mil*) scout. **giovani esploratori** Boy Scouts *pl*. **esplorazione** *sf* exploration; (*mil*) reconnaissance.

esplosione [esplo'zjone] *sf* explosion.

esplosivo [esplo'zivo] *sm*, *agg* explosive.

esponente [espo'nɛnte] *sm* exponent; representative. **esponenziale** *agg* exponential.

*__esporre__ [es'porre] *v* expose; (*arrischiare*) risk; (*spiegare*) expound; (*mostrare*) exhibit, display.

esportare [espor'tare] *v* export. **esportatore**, **-trice** *sm*, *sf* exporter. **esportazione** *sf* export.

esposizione [espozi'tsjone] *sf* exhibition, show; (*spiegazione*) explanation; (*posizione*, *foto*) exposure.

esposto [es'posto] *agg* exhibited, displayed; exposed. *sm* statement.

espressione [espres'sjone] *sf* expression. **espressivo** *agg* expressive, eloquent.

espresso [es'prɛsso] *agg* express; (*manifestato*) expressed; (*dichiarato*) avowed, declared. **piatto espresso** *sm* specially prepared dish. *sm* (*lettera*) express letter; (*caffè*) espresso; (*ferr*) express train.

*__esprimere__ [es'primere] *v* express.

espulsione [espul'sjone] *sf* expulsion.

essa [essa] *pron* (*persona*: *soggetto*) she; (*persona*: *oggetto*) her; (*cosa*, *animale*) it.

esse [esse] *pron* (*soggetto*) they; (*oggetto*) them.

essenza [es'sɛntsa] *sf* essence. **essenziale** *agg* essential.

*__essere__ [ɛssere] *v* be; (*ausiliare con forma attiva*) have. *sm* being; (*fam*) person, creature; (*condizione*) existence.

essi ['essi] *pron* (*soggetto*) they; (*oggetto*) them.

essiccare [essik'kare] *v* dry. **essiccatoio** *sm* dryer.

esso ['esso] *pron* (*persona*: *soggetto*) he; (*persona*: *oggetto*) him; (*cosa*, *animale*) it.

est [est] *sm* east. **dell'est** east, eastern.

estasi ['estazi] *sf* ecstasy. **estatico** *agg* ecstatic.

estate [es'tate] *sf* summer. **estate di San Martino** Indian summer.

*__estendere__ [es'tɛndere] *v* extend, stretch; (*ampliare*) broaden. **estendersi** *v* (*stendersi*) stretch; (*diffondersi*) spread.

estensione [esten'sjone] *sf* extension; (*dimensione*) extent; (*distesa*) expanse; (*fig*, *musica*) range; (*significato*) wider sense.

estenuare [estenu'are] *v* exhaust. **estenuante** *agg* exhausting, wearing.

esteriore [este'rjore] *agg* outer, exterior, external. *sm* (*parte esterna*) outside; (*apparenze*) appearances *pl*.

esterno [es'tɛrno] *agg* external, outer, exterior. *sm* outside; (*scolaro*) day-boy; (*film*) exterior.

estero [es'tɛro] *agg* foreign. *sm* foreign countries *pl*. **all'estero** abroad.

esterrefatto [esterre'fatto] *agg* (*atterrito*) aghast, horrified; (*sbigottito*) amazed.

esteso [es'tezo] *agg* large, wide-ranging; (*fig*) thorough. **per esteso** in full.

estetica [es'tɛtika] *sf* aesthetics. **estetico** *agg* aesthetic.

estetista [este'tista] *s(m+f)* beauty specialist, beautician.

*__estinguere__ [es'tingwere] *v* put out; (*far svanire*) extinguish; (*econ*) wipe out; (*debito*) pay off; (*sete*) quench. **estinguersi** *v* die out. **estinto** *agg* extinguished; (*scomparso*) extinct. **estinzione** *sf* extinction; (*sete*) quenching; (*econ*) discharge.

estirpare [estir'pare] *v* eradicate.

estivo [es'tivo] *agg* summer.

*__estorcere__ [es'tortʃere] *v* extort. **estorsione** *sf* extortion.

estradare [estra'dare] *v* extradite. **estradizione** *sf* extradition.

estraneo [es'traneo] *agg* extraneous, unrelated (to), unconnected (with); *(alieno)* foreign. **essere estraneo a** have no part in. **mantenersi estraneo a** have nothing to do with, keep clear of. *sm* stranger; unauthorized person. **estraniare** *v* estrange.

*estrarre [es'trarre] *v* extract, draw (out); *(miniera)* mine; *(cava)* quarry. **estratto** *sm* extract; *(compendio)* abstract; *(stralcio)* excerpt. **estrazione** *sf* extraction.

estremo [es'trɛmo] *agg* extreme; *(ultimo)* final; *(grandissimo)* utmost. *sm* extreme; *(colmo)* height; *(estremità)* end, tip. **estremi** *sm pl* particulars *pl*; *(dir)* essential elements *pl*. **estremismo** *sm* extremism. **estremista** *s(m+f)* extremist.

estro [ˈɛstro] *sm* *(ghiribizzo)* whim, fancy; *(impulso)* inspiration; *(venereo)* heat. **estroso** *agg* whimsical, capricious; inspired.

estrogeno [es'trɔdʒeno] *sm* oestrogen.

estroverso [estro'vɛrso], **-a** *sm, sf* extrovert. *agg* extroverted.

estuario [estu'arjo] *sm* estuary.

esuberante [ezube'rante] *agg* exuberant. **esuberanza** *sf* exuberance.

esule [ˈɛzule] *s(m+f)* exile. **esulare** *v* lie outside, be beyond.

esultare [ezul'tare] *v* rejoice. **esultante** *agg* exultant.

esumare [ezu'mare] *v* exhume; *(fig)* unearth.

età [e'ta] *v* age. **all'età di dieci anni** at (the age of) ten. **età della ragione** age of discretion.

etere [ˈɛtere] *sm* ether.

eterno [e'tɛrno] *agg* eternal, everlasting; *(lunghissimo)* interminable. **eternità** *sm* eternity; *(molto tempo)* ages *pl*.

eterodosso [etero'dɔsso] *agg* heterodox.

eterogeneo [etero'dʒɛneo] *agg* heterogeneous.

etica [ˈetika] *sf* ethics. **etico** *agg* ethical.

etichetta¹ [eti'ketta] *sf* *(cartellino)* label.

etichetta² [eti'ketta] *sf* *(regole)* etiquette.

etimologia [etimolo'dʒia] *sf* etymology. **etimologico** *agg* etymological.

etnico [ˈɛtniko] *agg* ethnic.

ettaro [ˈɛttaro] *sm* hectare.

etto [ˈɛtto] *sm* hundred grams.

eucalipto [euka'lipto] *sm* eucalyptus.

eufemismo [eufe'mizmo] *sm* euphemism. **eufemistico** *agg* euphemistic.

eunuco [eu'nuko] *sm, pl* **-chi** eunuch.

Europa [eu'rɔpa] *sf* Europe. **europeo, -a** *s, agg* European.

eutanasia [eutana'zia] *sf* euthanasia.

evacuare [evaku'are] *v* evacuate.

*evadere [e'vadere] *v* escape (from); *(sbrigare)* dispatch; *(fattura)* settle; *(ordini)* execute; *(fisco)* avoid.

evanescente [evane'ʃɛnte] *agg* *(suono)* fading; *(fugace)* fleeting; *(crema)* vanishing.

evangelista [evandʒe'lista] *sm* evangelist. **evangelico** *agg* evangelical.

evaporare [evapo'rare] *v* evaporate. **evaporatore** *sm* humidifier. **evaporazione** *sf* evaporation.

evasione [eva'zjone] *sf* escape; *(fisco)* evasion; *(comm)* execution.

evasivo [eva'zivo] *agg* evasive.

evaso [e'vazo], **-a** *agg* escaped; *(comm)* dispatched, dealt with. *sm, sf* fugitive, escaped convict.

evento [e'vɛnto] *sm* event; *(eventualità)* eventuality. **in ogni evento** in any case, at all events.

eventuale [eventu'ale] *agg* possible, any. **eventualità** *sf* eventuality. **nell'eventualità di** *o* **che** in the event of. **eventualmente** *cong* if, in case.

evidente [evi'dɛnte] *agg* obvious, manifest, clear; *(irrefutabile)* unmistakable. **evidenza** *sf* *(chiarezza)* clarity, obviousness. **mettere in evidenza** stress, emphasize. **mettersi in evidenza** make oneself conspicuous, draw attention to oneself. **tenere un'evidenza** *(comm)* keep pending.

evitare [evi'tare] *v* avoid; *(non arrecare)* spare, save.

evo [ˈevo] *sm* **Medio Evo** Middle Ages *pl*.

evocare [evo'kare] *v* evoke.

evoluzione [evolu'tsjone] *sf* evolution. **evoluto** *agg* evolved, fully developed; advanced, progressive.

evviva [ev'viva] *inter* hurrah! **evviva ... !** long live ... !

extra [ˈɛkstra] *agg invar* *(qualità)* first-rate; *(fuori del previsto)* additional. *sm invar* extra.

F

fa [fa] *avv* ago.

fabbisogno [fabbi'zoɲo] *sm* requirements *pl*.

fabbrica ['fabbrika] *sf* factory; (*officina*) works; (*edificio*) building. **fabbricante** *sm* manufacturer. **fabbricare** *v* manufacture, produce; (*costruire*) build; (*inventare*) make up. **fabbricato** *sm* building. **fabbricazione** *sf* manufacture, production.

fabbro ['fabbro] *sm* (*ferraio*) (black)smith.

faccenda [fat'tʃɛnda] *sf* matter; (*caso, circostanza*) business. **faccende domestiche** housework *sing*.

facchino [fak'kino] *sm* porter. **facchinaggio** *sm* porterage. **facchinata** *sf* (*lavoro*) drudgery.

faccia ['fattʃa] *sf* face; (*lato*) side. **avere una bella/brutta faccia** look well/unwell. **di faccia** opposite. **faccia tosta** (*fam*) cheek, nerve. **in faccia** a opposite. **facciata** *sf* front; (*pagina*) side.

facezia [fa'tʃɛtsja] *sf* pleasantry; (*detto spiritoso*) witticism. **faceto** *agg* facetious, witty.

facile ['fatʃile] *agg* easy; (*incline*) easily moved, prone. **facilità** *sf* ease, facility; (*l'esser facile*) easiness; (*capacità*) aptitude. **con facilità** with ease, readily; (*lingua*) fluently.

facilitare [fatʃili'tare] *v* facilitate; (*aiutare*) help. **facilitazione** *sf* facilitation, making easy. **facilitazioni di pagamento** easy terms *pl*.

facoltà [fakol'ta] *sf* faculty; (*potere*) power. **facoltativo** *agg* optional. **facoltoso** *agg* wealthy.

faggio ['faddʒo] *sm* beech.

fagiano [fa'dʒano] *sm* pheasant.

fagiolo [fa'dʒɔlo] *sm* bean. **andare a fagiolo** (*fam*) suit. **fagiolino** *sm* French bean.

fagotto [fa'gɔtto] *sm* bundle; (*musica*) bassoon. **far fagotto** pack up.

falcata [fal'kata] *sf* step.

falce [faltʃe] *sf* sickle; (*manico lungo*) scythe.

falciare [fal'tʃare] *v* mow; (*fig*) mow down. **falciatrice** *sf* mower.

falco ['falko] *sm* hawk. **falcone** *sm* falcon; (*tec*) derrick.

falda ['falda] *sf* (*strato*) layer, sheet; (*di pendio*) foot; (*di cappello*) brim; (*di vestito*) skirt; (*di marsina*) tail.

falegname [fale'ɲame] *sm* joiner, carpenter. **falegnameria** *sf* (*arte*) joinery, carpentry; (*bottega*) joiner's shop.

falena [fa'lɛna] *sf* moth; (*cenere*) ash; (*persona fatua*) flighty person.

falla ['falla] *sf* leak. **aprire/chiudere una falla** spring/stop a leak.

fallace [fal'latʃe] *agg* fallacious.

fallire [fal'lire] *v* fail; (*non colpire*) miss; (*dir, comm*) go bankrupt. **fallimento** *sm* failure; bankruptcy.

fallito [fal'lito], **-a** *agg* unsuccessful. *sm, sf* bankrupt; (*fig*) failure.

fallo¹ ['fallo] *sm* (*errore*) fault; (*sport*) foul. **cogliere in fallo** find out. **essere in fallo** be at fault. **senza fallo** without fail, certainly.

fallo² ['fallo] *sm* (*membro virile*) phallus.

falò [fa'lo] *sm* bonfire.

falsare [fal'sare] *v* falsify; (*alterare*) distort. **falsario** *sm* (*documenti*) forger; (*monete*) counterfeiter.

falsariga [falsa'riga] *sf* (*modello*) pattern; (*norma*) lines *pl*.

falsificare [falsifi'kare] *v* falsify; (*arte*) fake. **falsificazione** *sf* falsification, faking; forgery, fake.

falso ['falso] *agg* false; (*falsificato*) counterfeit, faked, forged; (*fam*) bogus. *sm* (*non vero*) falsehood; (*reato*) forgery. **giurare il falso** commit perjury.

fama ['fama] *sf* fame, reputation.

fame ['fame] *sf* hunger; (*carestia*) famine. **aver fame** be hungry. **aver fame di** (*fig*) hunger for. **aver una fame da lupo** be ravenous. **fare la fame** go hungry. **morir di fame** starve to death; (*fig*) be starving.

famelico [fa'mɛliko] *agg* ravenous.

famigerato [famidʒe'rato] *agg* notorious.

famiglia [fa'miʎa] *sf* family. **in famiglia** at home.

familiare [fami'ljare] *agg* domestic; (*consueto, intimo*) familiar; (*semplice*) informal. *s(m + f)* (*parente*) relative. **familiarità** *sf* familiarity. **familiarizzarsi** *v* familiarize oneself.

famoso [fa'moso] *agg* famous, well-known; memorable.

fanale [fa'nale] *sm* lamp; (*auto*) light. **fanale anteriore** headlight. **fanale di coda** tail-light.

fanatico [fa'natiko], **-a** *agg* fanatical; (*fam: entusiasta*) wild (about). *sm, sf* fanatic; (*tifoso*) fan. **fanatismo** *sm* fanaticism.

fanciullo [fan'tʃullo], **-a** *sm, sf* child (*pl* -ren). **fanciullaggine** *sf* childish behaviour. **fanciullesco** *agg* childish, puerile;

(*innocente*) child-like. **fanciullezza** *sf*
childhood.

fandonia [fan'dɔnja] *sf* nonsense.

fanfara [fan'fara] *sf* (brass-)band; (*composizione*) fanfare. **fanfaronata** *sf* boasting. **fanfarone, -a** *sm, sf* boaster.

fango ['fango] *sm* mud. **fare i fanghi** take mud-baths. **fangoso** *agg* muddy.

fannullone [fannul'lone], **-a** *sm, sf* idler, loafer.

fantascienza [fanta'ʃɛntsa] *sf* science fiction.

fantasia [fanta'zia] *sf* fantasy; (*capriccio*) fancy; imagination. *agg* (*moda*) fancy, patterned.

fantasma [fan'tazma] *sm* ghost, phantom.

fantasticare [fantasti'kare] *v* daydream, dream up. **fantastico** *agg* fantastic; (*non reale*) fanciful, strange.

fante ['fante] *sm* (*mil*) infantryman; (*carte*) knave, jack. **fanteria** *sf* infantry. **fantino** *sm* jockey.

fantoccio [fan'tɔttʃo] *sm* puppet.

farabutto [fara'butto] *sm* rascal, rogue.

faraona [fara'ona] *sf* guinea-fowl.

farcire [far'tʃire] *v* stuff.

fardello [far'dello] *sm* burden.

*fare ['fare] *v* (*agire*) do; (*produrre*) make; (*essere*) be; (*avere*) have; (*un mestiere, ecc.*) go in for, practise; (*comportarsi*) play; (*orologio*) say. **farcela** *v* (*riuscire*) manage; (*resistere*) be able to go on. **far attenzione** pay attention. **far bene** do good. **far bene a** be good for. **far chiamare** send for. **far entrare** let in. **fare il pieno** (*auto*) fill up. **far male** (*dolere*) hurt, ache; (*nuocere*) be bad for; (*agire male*) do the wrong thing. **far notare** point out. **fare per** be about to. **far vedere** show. **farsi** *v* (*diventare*) become, grow into; (*convertirsi*) turn into; (*tempo*) get.

farfalla [far'falla] *sf* butterfly; (*falena*) moth. **nuoto a farfalla** *sm* butterfly stroke.

farina [fa'rina] *sf* flour. **farina gialla** maize meal. **farina integrale** wholemeal. **farinaceo** *agg* floury, starchy. **farinoso** *agg* floury, mealy; (*neve*) powdery.

faringe [fa'rindʒe] *sf* pharynx. **faringite** *sf* pharyngitis.

farmacia [farma'tʃia] *sf* (*negozio*) chemist's (shop); (*scienza*) pharmacy. **farmacista** *s(m+f)* chemist. **farmaco** *sm* medicine.

farneticare [farneti'kare] *v* rave.

faro ['faro] *sm* lighthouse; (*lume, fig*) beacon; (*auto*) headlight.

farragine [far'radʒine] *sf* muddle, jumble.

farsa ['farsa] *sf* farce.

fascia ['faʃa] *sf* band; (*benda*) bandage; (*uniforme*) sash; (*postale*) wrapper; (*zona*) strip.

fasciare [fa'ʃare] *v* wrap; (*bambini*) swaddle; (*ferita*) dress, bandage.

fascicolo [fa'ʃikolo] *sm* (*opuscolo*) pamphlet, booklet; (*numero*) issue.

fascino [fa'ʃino] *sm* charm, fascination.

fascio ['faʃo] *sm* bundle, bunch.

fascismo [fa'ʃizmo] *sm* fascism. **fascista** *s(m+f)*, *agg* fascist.

fase ['faze] *sf* phase; (*auto*) stroke.

fastidio [fas'tidjo] *sm* trouble; (*avversione*) dislike; (*cosa fastidiosa*) bother, inconvenience. **dar fastidio** trouble; (*molestare*) annoy, bother. **darsi fastidio** put oneself out. **fastidioso** *agg* troublesome, annoying.

fasto ['fasto] *sm* pomp.

fasullo [fa'zullo] *agg* (*fam*) bogus, phoney.

fata ['fata] *sf* fairy.

fatale [fa'tale] *agg* inevitable; (*funesto*) fatal; (*decisivo*) fateful; irresistible.

fatica [fa'tika] *sf* (*sforzo*) effort, labour; (*stanchezza, tec*) fatigue. **a fatica** with difficulty. **costar fatica** require an effort. **durare fatica** find it difficult. **reggere alla fatica** stand the strain. **faticare** *v* labour; (*stentare*) have difficulty. **faticoso** *agg* tiring.

fatta ['fatta] *sf* kind.

fattezze [fat'tettse] *sf pl* features *pl*.

fattibile [fat'tibile] *agg* feasible.

fatto[1] ['fatto] *agg* made, done. **a conti fatti** all things considered. **detto fatto** no sooner said than done. **fatto a macchina/mano** machine-/hand-made. **fatto su misura** tailor-made.

fatto[2] ['fatto] *sm* fact; (*avvenimento*) event; (*azione*) deed; (*affare*) business. **cogliere sul fatto** catch in the act. **dire il fatto suo** have one's say. **fatto compiuto** fait accompli. **fatto sta** the fact remains. **in fatto di** regarding.

fattore [fat'tore] *sm* factor; (*capo di fattoria*) steward.

fattoria [fatto'ria] *sf* farm, estate.

fattorino [fatto'rino] *sm* messenger; (*di negozio*) errand-boy; (*di autobus*) conductor.

fattura [fat'tura] *sf* (*confezione*) making; (*lavorazione*) construction, workmanship; (*conto*) bill; (*comm*) invoice. **fatturare** *v* (*comm*) invoice; (*manipolare*) doctor. **fatturato** *sm* turnover.

fatuo ['fatuo] *agg* foolish, fatuous.

fauci ['fautʃi] *sf pl* jaws *pl*; (*fig*) clutches *pl*.

fauna ['fauna] *sf* fauna.

fausto ['fausto] *agg* propitious.

fautore [fau'tore], **-trice** *sm, sf* supporter.

fava ['fava] *sf* broad bean.

favilla [fa'villa] *sf* spark. **far faville** sparkle, shine.

favo ['favo] *sm* honeycomb.

favola ['favola] *sf* fable, story. **favoloso** *agg* fabulous.

favore [fa'vore] *sm* favour; (*appoggio*) support. **di favore** (*biglietto*) complimentary; (*prezzo*) special. **per favore** please.

favoreggiare [favored'dʒare] *v* favour; (*dir*) aid and abet.

favorevole [favo'revole] *agg* favourable, in favour.

favorire [favo'rire] *v* favour; (*sostenere*) support; (*promuovere*) promote, foster. **favorito, -a** *s, agg* favourite. **favoritismo** *sm* favouritism.

fazione [fa'tsjone] *sf* faction, party. **fazioso** *agg* subversive.

fazzoletto [fattso'letto] *sm* handkerchief; (*da testa*) headsquare.

febbraio [feb'brajo] *sm* February.

febbre ['febbre] *sf* temperature, fever; (*fam*: *sulle labbra*) cold sore; (*brama*) lust, passion. **febbre da fieno** hay fever. **febbricitante** *agg* feverish.

feccia ['fettʃa] *sf* dregs *pl*.

feci ['fetʃi] *sf pl* faeces *pl*.

fecola ['fekola] *sf* starch.

fecondare [fekon'dare] *v* fertilize. **fecondazione** *sf* fertilization. **fecondazione artificiale** artificial insemination. **fecondità** *sf* fertility. **fecondo** *agg* fertile; prolific, fruitful.

fede ['fede] *sf* faith; (*fiducia*) confidence, trust; (*anello*) wedding ring; (*attestazione*) proof.

fedele [fe'dele] *agg* faithful, true. *s(m+f)* believer; (*seguace*) follower. **fedeltà** *sf* faithfulness, fidelity.

federa ['federa] *sf* pillow-case.

federale [fede'rale] *agg* federal.

federazione [federa'tsjone] *sf* federation, association.

fedina [fe'dina] *sf* police *or* criminal record.

fedine [fe'dine] *sf pl* side-whiskers *pl*.

fegato ['fegato] *sm* liver; (*coraggio*) guts *pl*. **mangiarsi il fegato** eat one's heart out.

felce [feltʃe] *sf* fern; (*comune*) bracken.

felice [fe'litʃe] *agg* happy; (*fortunato*) lucky. **felicità** *sf* happiness, bliss. **felicitarsi con** congratulate. **felicitazioni** *sf pl* congratulations *pl*.

felino [fe'lino] *agg* feline.

felpa ['felpa] *sf* plush.

feltro ['feltro] *sm* felt.

femmina ['femmina] *sf* female; (*figlia*) daughter. *agg* female. **femminismo** *sm* feminism, women's movement. **femminista** *s(m+f), agg* feminist.

femminile [femmi'nile] *agg* female; (*da donna*) feminine, womanly; (*gramm*) feminine. **scuola femminile** girls' school. *sm* feminine (gender). **femminilità** *sf* femininity.

femore ['femore] *sm* femur.

*****fendere** ['fendere] *v* split, pierce; (*solcare*) plough (through). **fenditura** *sf* cleft; (*fessura*) crack.

fenicottero [feni'kɔttero] *sm* flamingo.

fenomeno [fe'nɔmeno] *sm* phenomenon (*pl* -a); (*prodigio*) marvel. **fenomenale** *agg* phenomenal; (*eccezionale*) extraordinary, remarkable.

feretro ['feretro] *sm* coffin.

ferie ['ferje] *sf pl* holidays *pl*. **giorno feriale** *sm* weekday.

ferire [fe'rire] *v* wound, injure, hurt. **ferita** *sf* wound, injury; (*persona*) casualty. **ferito** *sm* casualty.

fermacarte [ferma'karte] *sm invar* (*a molla*) paper-clip; (*pesante*) paperweight.

fermaglio [fer'maʎo] *sm* clasp, clip.

fermare [fer'mare] *v* stop; (*arrestare*) check; (*fissare*) secure, fasten; (*prenotare*) book. **fermarsi** stop; (*rimanere*) stay. **fermata** *sf* stop; (*tappa*) stay; (*veicoli*) halt. **fermata facoltativa** request stop.

fermentare [fermen'tare] *v* ferment. **fermentazione** *sf* fermentation. **fermento** *sm* ferment; (*fig*) unrest.

fermo ['fermo] *agg* still; (*non in moto*) stationary; (*saldo*) firm, steady. **restar fermo** stand still; (*fig*) hold good. *sm* (*mec*) catch, fastener, lock; (*dir*) detention; (*sospensione*) stop.

feroce [fe'rotʃe] *agg* wild; (*crudele*) savage, ferocious; (*fig*) fierce. **ferocia** *sf* cruelty, ferocity.

ferragosto [ferra'gosto] *sm* mid-August holiday.

ferramenta [ferra'menta] *sf pl* ironmongery *sing*.

ferreo ['ferreo] *agg* iron.

ferro ['ferro] *sm* of iron. **essere ai ferri corti** be at loggerheads. **ferro battuto** wrought iron. **ferro da calza** knitting needle. **ferro di cavallo** horseshoe. **tocca ferro!** touch wood!

ferrovia [ferro'via] *sf* railway. **ferroviario** *agg* rail(way), train. **ferroviere** *sm* railwayman.

fertile ['fertile] *agg* fertile, fruitful. **fertilità** *sf* fertility, fruitfulness. **fertilizzante** *sm* fertilizer. **fertilizzare** *v* fertilize.

fervore [fer'vore] *sm* fervour. **fervente** *agg* fervent. **fervido** *agg* ardent; (*caloroso*) heartfelt; (*vivace*) lively.

fesso ['fesso] (*volg*) *agg, sm* idiot, fool. **fesseria** *sf* (*azione*) foolishness; (*parole*) nonsense; (*inezia*) trifle.

fessura [fes'sura] *sf* crack, slit; (*gettone, moneta*) slot.

festa ['festa] *sf* holiday; (*compleanno*) birthday; (*onomastico*) saint's day; (*festeggiamento*) celebration; (*ricevimento*) party. **far festa** (*non lavorare*) take a holiday, take time off; (*smettere il lavoro*) stop work; (*divertirsi*) make merry. **far festa a** give a warm welcome (to).

festeggiare [fested'dʒare] *v* celebrate; (*far festa*) give a hearty welcome (to). **festeggiamenti** *sm pl* festivities *pl*. **festeggiamento** *sm* celebration.

festività [festivi'ta] *sf* festivity, holiday. **festivo** *agg* (*della domenica*) Sunday; (*non-feriale*) holiday.

festone [fes'tone] *sm* festoon; (*ricamo*) scallop.

fetente [fe'tɛnte] *sm* (*volg*) stinker, scoundrel. *agg also* **fetido** stinking, foul. **fetore** *sm* stench.

feticcio [fe'tittʃo] *sm* fetish.

feto ['feto] *sm* foetus.

fetta ['fetta] *sf* slice. **tagliare a fette** slice, cut into slices. **fettuccia** *sf* (*nastro*) tape, ribbon. **fettuccine** *sf pl* noodles *pl*.

feudale [feu'dale] *agg* feudal. **feudalesimo**

sm feudalism. **feudo** *sm* feud; (*proprietà terriera*) lands *pl*; (*fig*) domain.

fiaba ['fjaba] *sf* story, (fairy) tale.

fiacca ['fjakka] *sf* (*stanchezza*) weariness; (*pigrizia*) laziness; (*svogliatezza*) listlessness. **battere la fiacca** (*fam: stare in ozio*) kick one's heels; (*agire svogliatamente*) be sluggish. **fiaccare** *v* (*indebolire*) weaken; (*spossare*) wear out; (*spezzare*) break. **fiacco** *agg* (*debole*) weak; (*stanco*) exhausted, weary.

fiaccola ['fjakkola] *sf* torch. **alla luce di fiaccole** by torchlight.

fiala ['fjala] *sf* phial, medicine bottle.

fiamma ['fjamma] *sf* flame; (*improvvisa, irregolare*) flare; (*molto viva*) blaze. **in fiamme** on fire. **nuovo fiammante** brand-new. **fiammata** *sf* blaze, flare.

fiammeggiare [fjammed'dʒare] *v* blaze, flame.

fiammifero [fjam'mifero] *sm* match.

fiammingo [fjam'mingo] *agg* Flemish.

fiancheggiare [fjanked'dʒare] *v* flank; (*sostenere*) help.

fianco ['fjanko] *sm* side; (*mil*) flank. **di fianco a** (*vicino*) next to, by; (*lungo*) alongside.

fiasco ['fjasko] *sm* flask, (straw-covered) bottle; (*insuccesso*) flop. **far fiasco** flop.

fiatare [fja'tare] *v* breathe. **fiato** *sm* breath. **fiati** *sm pl* woodwind *pl*. **senza fiato** out of breath. **strumenti a fiato** *sm pl* wind instruments *pl*. **tutto d'un fiato** in one go.

fibbia ['fibbja] *sf* buckle.

fibra ['fibra] *sf* fibre; (*fig*) constitution.

ficcare [fik'kare] *v* poke, stick; (*fam: mettere*) put. **ficcanaso** *sm* busybody.

fico ['fiko] *sm* fig. **fico d'India** prickly pear. **non m'importa un fico** (*secco*) (*fam*) I couldn't care less. **non valere un fico** be worthless.

fidanzarsi [fidan'tsarsi] *v* get engaged. **fidanzamento** *sm* engagement. **fidanzato, -a** *sm, sf* fiancé, -e.

fidarsi [fi'darsi] *v* (*aver fiducia*) rely (on), trust; (*osare*) trust oneself, dare.

fido ['fido] *sm* (*econ*) credit.

fiducia [fi'dutʃa] *sf* trust, confidence. **aver fiducia in** trust. **di fiducia** (*fidato*) reliable, trustworthy; responsible. **fiduciario** *sm* (*official*) representative; (*dir*) trustee. **fiducioso** *agg* trusting.

fiele ['fjɛle] *sm* bile; (*fig*) ill-will.

fieno ['fjɛno] *sm* hay.

fiera ['fjɛra] *sf* fair; (*mostra*) exhibition; (*di beneficienza*) bazaar.

fiero ['fjɛro] *agg* (*orgoglioso*) proud; (*audace*) bold, spirited; (*feroce, violento*) fierce; (*austero*) severe. **fierezza** *sf* pride; boldness.

fifa ['fifa] (*fam*) *sf* fear. **aver fifa** be afraid. **fifone, -a** *sm, sf* coward.

figliastro [fi'ʎastro] *sm* stepson. **figliastra** *sf* stepdaughter.

figlio ['fiʎo] *sm* son; (*fig: frutto*) result, product. **figli** *sm pl* children *pl*. **figlia** *sf* daughter; (*comm*) counterfoil. **figliare** *v* give birth. **figliata** *sf* litter.

figlioccio [fi'ʎottʃo] *sm* godson. **figlioccia** *sf* goddaughter.

figliolo [fi'ʎɔlo] *sm* (*figlio*) son; (*ragazzo*) boy, young man; (*fam*) chap. **figliola** *sf* (*figlia*) daughter; (*ragazza*) girl. **figliolanza** *sf* offspring.

figura [fi'gura] *sf* figure; (*aspetto*) shape; (*illustrazione*) picture; (*tavola*) plate. **far bella figura** show up to advantage; make a good impression; (*riuscir bene*) do well. **far brutta figura** cut a sorry figure, disgrace oneself.

figurare [figu'rare] *v* represent, portray; (*simboleggiare*) stand for; (*mostrare*) pretend; (*risultare*) appear; (*far figura*) look smart. **figurarsi** *v* imagine. **figurati!** *inter* (*altro che*) of course! you bet! **figurina** *sf* figurine; (*cartoncino*) card. **figurino** *sm* fashion-plate; (*giornale*) fashion magazine. **figuro** *sm* shady character.

fila ['fila] *sf* row, line; (*coda*) queue; (*serie*) string. **di fila** (*di seguito*) in succession, in a row; (*senza interruzione*) on end, non-stop. **in fila indiana** in single file. **mettere in fila** line up. **mettersi in fila** queue up.

filantropo [fi'lantropo], **-a** *sm, sf* philanthropist. **filantropico** *agg* philanthropic.

filare [fi'lare] *v* spin; (*cavo, catena*) pay out; (*correre*) run, speed along.

filarmonico [filar'mɔniko] *agg* philharmonic.

filastrocca [filas'trɔkka] *sf* (*per bambini*) nursery rhyme; (*storia lunga*) tedious list, rigmarole.

filatelia [filate'lia] *sf* stamp-collecting, philately. **filatelico** *agg* stamp. **filatelista** *s(m + f)* stamp collector.

filatura [fila'tura] *sf* (*industria*) spinning; (*filanda*) spinning mill.

filetto [fi'letto] *sm* (*gastr*) fillet; border; (*filo sottile, mec*) thread; (*tipografia*) rule. **filettare** *v* (*ornare*) decorate; (*bordare*) edge; (*mec*) thread. **filettatura** *sf* edging, braid; threading.

filiale [fi'ljale] *sf* branch. *agg* filial.

filibustiere [filibus'tjɛre] *sm* pirate; (*imbroglione*) rogue.

filigrana [fili'grana] *sf* filigree; (*carta*) watermark.

film [film] *sm invar* film. **filmare** *v* film.

filo ['filo] *sm* thread; (*filato*) yarn; (*metallico*) wire; (*coltello*) edge; (*elettrico*) flex. **filo d'erba** blade of grass. **filo spinato** barbed wire. **lana a due/tre fili** *sf* two-/three-ply wool. **perdere il filo** (*discorso*) lose track; (*taglio*) become blunt. **per filo e per segno** in detail.

filodrammatico [filodram'matiko], **-a** *sm, sf* amateur actor, amateur actress. *agg* amateur theatrical.

filologo [fi'lologo], **-a** *sm, sf* philologist. **filologia** *sf* philology. **filologico** *agg* philological.

filone [fi'lone] *sm* seam, vein; (*pane*) French loaf; (*fig*) current, line.

filosofia [filozo'fia] *sf* philosophy. **filosofico** *agg* philosophical. **filosofo, -a** *sm, sf* philosopher.

filtrare [fil'trare] *v* filter. **filtro** *sm* filter; (*colino*) strainer.

filza ['filtsa] *sf* string.

finale [fi'nale] *agg* final; (*ultimo*) last. *sf* (*sport*) final; (*gramm*) ending. *sm* (*musica*) finale. **finalista** *s(m + f)* finalist. **finalità** *sf* (*scopo*) purpose, aim; (*filosofia*) finality.

finanza [fi'nantsa] *sf* finance; (*fam: risorse economiche*) finances *pl*. **finanze** *sf pl* (*entrate dello Stato*) public revenue *sing*. **guardia di finanza** *sf* customs officer.

finanziare [finan'tsjare] *v* finance. **finanziamento** *sm* financing; (*fondi*) funds *pl*. **finanziario** *agg* financial. **finanziatore, -trice** *sm, sf* backer. **finanziera** *sf* frock-coat.

finché [fin'ke] *cong* (*per tutto il tempo che*) as long as; (*fino a quando*) until, till.

fine[1] ['fine] *sf* end; (*libro, film, ecc.*) ending. *sm* end; (*scopo*) aim; (*esito*) conclusion. **alla fine** (*luogo*) at the end; (*tempo*) in the end; (*finalmente*) at last. **in fin dei conti** when all is said and done, in the end. **secondo fine** ulterior motive, hidden purpose. **senza fine** endless.

fine² ['fine] *agg* fine; (*signorile*) refined; (*acuto*) sharp; (*penetrante*) subtle. **finezza** *sf* fineness; (*raffinatezza*) finesse, polish; (*minuzie*) nicety.

fine-settimana [finesetti'mana] *s(m+f) invar* weekend.

finestra [fi'nɛstra] *sf* window.

***fingere** ['findʒere] *v* pretend; **fingersi** *v* pretend to be.

finire [fi'nire] *v* finish; (*smettere*) stop; (*terminare, sboccare*) end; (*capitare*) end up. **andare a finire** (*capitare*) get to; (*concludersi*) turn out, end up. **finimondo** *sm* pandemonium. **finissaggio** *sm* finish. **finitura** *sf* finishing off; finishing touches *pl*.

Finlandia [fin'landja] *sf* Finland. **finlandese** *sm*, *agg* Finnish; *s(m+f)* (*abitante*) Finn.

fino¹ ['fino] *agg* fine, delicate; (*acuto*) subtle.

fino² ['fino] *avv* (*persino*) even. **fino a** (*tempo*) until, up to; (*luogo*) as far as. **fino a che punto?** how far? **fin da** (*passato*) since, as far back as; (*presente, futuro*) (as) from. **fin dove?** how far? **fino in fondo** right down, to the (very) end.

finocchio [fi'nɔkkjo] *sm* (*bot*) fennel; (*volg*) queer, gay.

finora [fi'nora] *avv* up to now, so far.

finta ['finta] *sf* pretence, sham; (*sport*) feint. **far finta di** pretend.

finto ['finto] *agg* false; (*simulato*) bogus; (*non reale*) mock; artificial. **fintapelle** *sf* imitation leather.

finzione [fin'tsjone] *sf* pretence; (*falsità*) falsehood; (*illusione*) fiction.

fio ['fio] *sm* **pagare il fio** pay the price.

fioccare [fjok'kare] *v* (*neve*) fall; (*fig*) come down thick and fast.

fiocco ['fjɔkko] *sm* flake; (*batuffolo*) flock; (*fibra tessile*) staple; (*nastro*) bow. **coi fiocchi** first-class, magnificent. **fiocchi d'avena** oatflakes *pl*. **fiocco di neve** snowflake.

fioco ['fjɔko] *agg* faint; (*luce*) dim.

fionda ['fjonda] *sf* catapult, sling.

fiordo ['fjɔrdo] *sm* fjord.

fiore ['fjore] *sm* flower; (*di albero*) blossom; (*meglio*) cream; (*carte da gioco*) club. **a fiori** floral. **fior di quattrini** pots of money *pl*. **in fiore** in bloom, in blossom. **fiorente** *agg* (*di fiore*) flowering; (*fig*) thriving, flourishing.

fiorentino [fjoren'tino], **-a** *s*, *agg* Florentine.

fioretto [fjo'retto] *sm* (*sport*) foil; (*musica, discorso*) embellishment.

fiorire [fjo'rire] *v* flower, bloom, blossom. **fioritura** *sf* flowering, blossoming; (*fiori*) bloom, blossom.

Firenze [fi'rɛntse] *sf* Florence.

firma ['firma] *sf* signature. **firmare** *v* sign. **firmatario** *sm* signatory.

fisarmonica [fizar'mɔnika] *sf* accordion.

fiscale [fis'kale] *agg* fiscal, tax. **fisco** *sm* treasury, tax authorities *pl*.

fischiare [fis'kjare] *v* whistle; (*disapprovare*) boo, hiss. **fischiata** *sf* booing, hissing. **fischiettare** *v* whistle (softly). **fischietto** *sm* whistle. **fischio** *sm* whistle, boo, hiss.

fisica ['fizika] *sf* physics; (*scienziata*) physicist.

fisico ['fiziko] *agg* physical. *sm* (*corpo*) body; (*costituzione*) make-up; (*scienziato*) physicist.

fisima ['fizima] *sf* whim, fancy.

fisiologia [fizjolo'dʒia] *sf* physiology. **fisiologico** *agg* physiological. **fisiologo, -a** *sm*, *sf* physiologist.

fisionomia [fizjono'mia] *sf* expression.

fisioterapia [fizjotera'pia] *sf* physiotherapy. **fisioterapista** *s(m+f)* physiotherapist.

fissare [fis'sare] *v* fix; (*attaccare*) fasten; (*guardare fissamente*) stare (at), gaze (at); (*prenotare*) book. **fissarsi di** be set on. **fissazione** *sf* fixation.

fissato [fis'sato] *agg* obsessed. *sm* (*fam*) fanatic, maniac. **essere fissato** have a bee in one's bonnet.

fissione [fis'sjone] *sf* fission.

fitta ['fitta] *sf* (*dolore*) twinge, sharp pain.

fittizio [fit'titsjo] *agg* fictitious.

fitto¹ ['fitto] *agg* thick, dense; (*conficcato*) stuck, driven in; (*tessuto, ecc.*) close. *sm* thick, middle. **a capo fitto** headlong. **buio fitto** pitch dark.

fitto² ['fitto] *sm* (*affitto*) rent.

fiume ['fjume] *sm* river; (*fig*) flood, stream. **fiumana** *sf* torrent.

fiutare [fju'tare] *v* smell; (*annusare rumorosamente*) sniff; (*intuire*) scent. **fiutare un inganno** (*fam*) smell a rat. **fiuto** *sm* scent, nose. **al fiuto** straight off, instinctively. **aver fiuto di** get wind of.

flaccido ['flattʃido] *agg* flabby, limp.

flacone [fla'kone] *sm* small bottle.

flagellare [fladʒel'lare] v flagellate, whip. **flagello** sm scourge, whip.

flagrante [fla'grante] agg flagrant. **cogliere in flagrante** catch in the act, catch red-handed.

flanella [fla'nɛlla] sf flannel.

flauto ['flauto] sm flute. **flauto dolce** recorder. **flautista** s(m+f) flautist.

flebile ['flebile] agg (debole) faint, feeble; (lamentevole) mournful, melancholy.

flemma ['flɛmma] sf coolness, imperturbability. **flemmatico** agg cool, self-possessed, phlegmatic.

flessibile [fles'sibile] agg flexible, pliable; versatile. **flessibilità** sf flexibility, pliability; versatility. **flessione** sf bending; (diminuzione graduale) drop, fall; (ginnastica) bend.

flessuoso [flessu'ozo] agg supple, lithe. **flessuosità** sf suppleness.

*****flettere** ['flɛttere] v bend, bow; (membra) flex.

flipper ['flipper] sm invar pin-table.

flirt [flɜrt] sm invar (amore superficiale) flirtation; (persona) boy-friend, girl-friend. **flirtare** v flirt.

flora ['flora] sf flora.

florido ['florido] agg (prospero) flourishing, thriving; (colorito) ruddy, glowing with health.

floscio ['floʃo] agg floppy, limp.

flotta ['flotta] sf fleet. **flottiglia** sf flotilla.

fluido ['fluido] sm, agg fluid. **fluidità** sf fluidity; (scorrevolezza) fluency; instability.

fluire [flu'ire] v flow.

fluorescente [fluore'ʃɛnte] agg fluorescent. **fluorescenza** sf fluorescence.

fluoro ['fluɔro] sm fluorine.

flusso ['flusso] sm flow, stream. **flusso e riflusso** ebb and flow. **flusso di sangue dal naso** nosebleed.

fluttuare [fluttu'are] v fluctuate.

fobia [fo'bia] sf phobia; (fam) (pet) aversion.

foca ['fɔka] sf seal.

focaccia [fo'kattʃa] sf bun. **rendere pan per focaccia** give as good as one gets.

focale [fo'kale] agg focal.

foce ['fotʃe] sf mouth, outlet.

focena [fo'tʃɛna] sf porpoise.

focolaio [foko'lajo] sm (med) focus; (centro di diffusione) hotbed, breeding ground.

focolare [foko'lare] sm hearth; (fig) fireside, home.

focoso [fo'kozo] agg fiery; (ardente) burning.

fodera ['fɔdera] sf lining; (rivestimento) cover. **foderare** v line; cover. **fodero** sm sheath.

foga ['foga] sf rush; (ardore) heat.

foggia ['fɔddʒa] sf fashion; (forma) shape. **foggiare** v shape, form, fashion.

foglia ['fɔʎʎa] sf leaf. **mettere le foglie** come into leaf. **fogliame** sm foliage.

foglio ['fɔʎʎo] sm sheet; (giornale) paper; (banconota) note. **foglio di via** travel-warrant. **foglio volante** leaflet.

fogna ['fɔɲa] sf sewer. **fognatura** sf sewerage.

foia ['fɔja] sf heat. **essere in foia** be on heat.

foiata [fo'lata] sf gust.

folclore [fol'klore] sm folklore. **folcloristico** agg folk.

folgorare [folgo'rare] v flash; (inveire) rail; (colpire con fulmine) strike with lightning. **folgorare con lo sguardo** wither with a glance.

folla ['folla] sf crowd; (gran quantità) host.

folle ['folle] agg crazy; (pazzo) mad; (sciocco) foolish; (auto) neutral. **andare in folle** coast. **folletto** sm imp. **follia** sf madness, folly.

follicolo [fol'likolo] sm follicle.

folto ['folto] sm, agg thick.

fomentare [fomen'tare] v encourage; (eccitare) rouse. **fomento** sm (impacco caldo) poultice; (sprone) spur.

fonda ['fonda] sf anchorage.

fondamento [fonda'mento] sm, pl -a f in literal sense foundation. **fondamentale** agg fundamental, basic.

fondare [fon'dare] v found; (istituire) establish; base. **fondarsi su** be based on; (fare assegnamento) rely on. **fondatore, -trice** sm, f founder. **fondazione** sf foundation, establishment.

*****fondere** [fondere] v melt, fuse; (in una forma) cast, mould; (unire) blend, merge. **fonderia** [fonde'ria] sf foundry.

fondiario [fon'djarjo] agg land. **proprietà fondiaria** sf real estate.

fondina¹ [fon'dina] sf (di pistola) holster.

fondina² [fon'dina] sf (piatto) soup plate.

fondista [fon'dista] s(m+f) (sport) long

distance runner; (*giornalista*) leader writer.

fondo ['fondo] *agg* deep. *sm* bottom; (*feccia*) dregs *pl*; (*caffè*) grounds *pl*; (*estremità*) end; (*sfondo*) background; (*pittura*) primer; (*denaro*) fund; (*terreno*) estate. **a fondo** (*profondamente*) thoroughly; (*con tutte le forze*) wholeheartedly. **andare a fondo** sink. **andare a fondo di** get to the bottom of. **articolo di fondo** *sm* leading article. **dar fondo a** (*consumare*) use up. **fino in fondo** to the end. **fondo (di) cassa/magazzino** cash/stock in hand. **fondo stradale** road surface. **in fondo** (*sotto*) at or to the bottom; (*dietro*) at or to the back; (*in conclusione*) after all. **mandare a fondo** sink.

fonetica [fo'netika] *sf* phonetics. **fonetico** *agg* phonetic.

fontana [fon'tana] *sf* fountain.

fonte ['fonte] *sf* spring; (*fig*) source. *sm* (*battesimale*) font.

foraggiare [forad'dʒare] *v* forage. **foraggio** *sm* forage.

forare [fo'rare] *v* perforate; (*gomma*) puncture; (*al trapano*) bore. **foratura** *sf* perforation; puncture.

forbici ['fɔrbitʃi] *sf pl* scissors *pl*; (*da siepe, cesoie*) shears *pl*; (*da potatura*) secateurs *pl*. **forbicina** *sf* earwig.

forbire [for'bire] *v* clean; (*fig*) polish.

forca ['forka] *sf* pitchfork; (*patibolo*) gallows. **va alla** *or* **sulla forca!** (*fam*) get stuffed! **forcella** *sf* fork; (*volatili*) wishbone.

forchetta [for'ketta] *sf* fork. **una buona forchetta** a hearty eater. **forchettata** *sf* forkful.

forcina [for'tʃina] *sf* hairpin.

forcipe ['fɔrtʃipe] *sm* forceps *pl*.

forense [fo'rense] *agg* forensic.

foresta [fo'resta] *sf* forest.

forestiero [fores'tjero], **-a** *agg* foreign. *sm*, *sf* foreigner.

forfait¹ [for'fɛ] *sm invar* (*contratto*) flat rate. **a forfait** all-in.

forfait² [for'fɛ] *sm invar* (*sport*) withdrawal. **dichiarare forfait** scratch.

forfora ['forfora] *sf* dandruff.

forma ['forma] *sf* form, shape; (*stampo*) mould; (*del calzolaio*) last. **a forma di X** X-shaped.

formaggio [for'maddʒo] *sm* cheese.

formale [for'male] *agg* formal. **formalità** *sf* formality.

formare [for'mare] *v* form; (*modellare*) shape; (*costituire*) make up; (*numero telefonico*) dial. **formarsi un'idea** get an idea. **formato** *sm* format, size. **formazione** *sf* formation; (*addestramento*) training.

formica [for'mika] *sf* ant. **formicaio** *sm* antheap; (*fig*) teeming crowd.

formicolare [formiko'lare] *v* swarm; (*provare sensazione*) tingle. **formicolio** *sm* swarming; (*sensazione*) pins and needles.

formidabile [formi'dabile] *agg* remarkable; (*molto forte*) powerful, formidable.

formula ['formula] *sf* formula (*pl* -ae).

formulare [formu'lare] *v* formulate; (*avanzare*) put forward; (*esprimere*) express. **formulario** *sm* (*modulo*) form.

fornace [for'natʃe] *sf* kiln, furnace.

fornaio [for'najo], **-a** *sm*, *sf* baker.

fornire [for'nire] *v* supply, furnish. **ben fornito** well-stocked. **fornitore** *sm* supplier. **fornitura** *sf* supply.

forno ['forno] *sm* oven. **fornello** *sm* cooker.

foro¹ ['foro] *sm* (*buco*) hole.

foro² ['foro] *sm* (*tribunale*) (law-)court; (*gli avvocati*) the bar; (*Roma*) forum.

forse ['forse] *avv* perhaps, maybe; (*circa*) about. **in forse** in doubt.

forsennato [forsen'nato] *agg* crazy, mad.

forte ['fɔrte] *agg* strong; (*grande*) large; (*bravo*) good; (*suono*) loud; (*intenso*) heavy. *avv* (*con forza*) hard; (*assai*) very much; (*velocemente*) fast; (*a voce alta*) loud. *sm* (*specialità*) strong point; (*persona*) powerful person; (*mil*) fort.

fortezza [for'tettsa] *sf* (*mil*) fortress; (*forza morale*) strength.

fortificare [fortifi'kare] *v* strengthen, fortify. **fortificazione** *sf* fortification.

fortuito [for'tuito] *agg* fortuitous, chance.

fortuna [for'tuna] *sf* fortune; (*buona sorte*) luck; success. **di fortuna** (*improvvisato*) makeshift; emergency. **fortuna che** fortunately. **fortunato** *agg* fortunate, lucky.

foruncolo [fo'runkolo] *sm* boil.

forza ['fortsa] *sf* strength; (*potere, potenza*) power; (*fis, mil*) force. **a forza di** through, by dint of. **a tutta forza** with all one's strength. **bella forza!** there's nothing to it! **farsi forza** (*coraggio*) pluck up courage. **forza maggiore** force majeure, circumstances beyond one's control. **per forza** necessarily; (*controvoglia*) unwillingly. **per forza di cose** of necessity.

forzare [for'tsare] v force. **forzato** sm convict.

foschia [fos'kia] sf haze, mist.

fosco ['fosko] agg (scuro) dark; (tetro) gloomy.

fosfato [fos'fato] sm phosphate.

fosforescente [fosfore'ʃɛnte] agg phosphorescent. **fosforo** sm phosphorus.

fossa ['fossa] sf pit, hole; (cimitero) grave. **fossato** sm ditch; (mil) moat. **fossetta** sf dimple.

fossile ['fossile] sm, agg fossil.

fosso ['fosso] sm ditch. **saltare il fosso** (fig) take the plunge.

foto ['foto] sf invar (fam) snap, photo.

fotocopia [foto'kɔpja] sf photocopy.

fotogenico [foto'dʒɛniko] agg photogenic.

fotografare [fotogra'fare] v photograph. **fotografia** sf (tecnica) photography; (copia) photograph. **fotografico** agg photographic. **apparecchio fotografico** sm camera. **fotografo, -a** sm, sf photographer.

fottere ['fottere] v (volg) fuck. **fottuto** agg (spacciato) ruined, buggered.

fra [fra] prep (fra due) between; (fra più di due) among(st); (entro) in, within; (partitivo) of. **detto fra** (di) **noi** between ourselves. **fra l'altro** among other things; (inoltre) besides. **fra tutti** (tutti insieme) altogether, in all.

frac [frak] sm invar (fam) tails pl.

fracassare [frakas'sare] v smash. **fracassarsi** v break. **fracasso** sm (chiasso) racket, din, row; (scalpore) uproar.

fradicio [fra'ditʃo] agg (inzuppato) sopping (wet), wet through; (guasto) rotten. **ubriaco fradicio** dead drunk.

fragile ['fradʒile] agg fragile; (delicato) frail.

fragola ['fragola] sf strawberry.

fragore [fra'gore] sm din. **fragoroso** agg roaring, resounding.

fragrante [fra'grante] agg fragrant.

*****fraintendere** [frain'tɛndere] v misunderstand, misconstrue.

frammassone [frammas'sone] sm freemason. **frammassoneria** sf freemasonry.

frammento [fram'mento] sm fragment; (scheggia) splinter. **frammentario** agg fragmentary.

*****frammettersi** [fram'mettersi] v (interporsi) come between; (immischiarsi) meddle.

frammezzo [fram'mɛddzo] avv **frammezzo a** in the midst of.

frana ['frana] sf landslide. **franare** v slide down; (crollare) cave in.

francamente [franka'mente] avv frankly.

franchezza [fran'kettsa] sf frankness.

franchigia [fran'kidʒa] sf exemption. **in franchigia** (posta) post-free; (tassa) tax-free.

Francia ['frantʃa] sf France. **francese** sm, agg French; s(m+f) French person.

franco[1] ['franko] agg (schietto) frank, open; (disinvolto) (self-)confident; (libero) free (of), exempt (from). **in porto franco** (comm) carriage paid.

franco[2] ['franko] sm (moneta) franc.

francobollo [franko'bollo] sm (postage) stamp.

*****frangersi** [frand'ʒersi] v break. **frangente** sm (ondata) breaker; (crisi) spot, predicament.

frangia ['frandʒa] sf fringe.

frantumare [frantu'mare] v crush. **in frantumi** in or to pieces.

*****frapporre** [frap'porre] v interpose.

frase ['fraze] sf phrase; (periodo) sentence. **frase fatta** stock phrase.

frassino ['frassino] sm ash.

frastagliare [frastaʎ'ʎare] v indent.

frastornato [frastor'nato] agg dizzy.

frastuono [fras'twɔno] sm din, uproar.

frate ['frate] sm friar.

fratello [fra'tɛllo] sm brother. **fratellanza** sf brotherhood. **fratellastro** sm stepbrother.

fraterno [fra'tɛrno] agg brotherly, fraternal. **fraternizzare** v fraternize.

frattaglie [frat'taʎe] sf pl offal sing; (di pollame) giblets pl.

frattanto [frat'tanto] avv also **nel frattempo** meanwhile, in the meantime.

frattura [frat'tura] sf fracture; (fig) break. **fratturare** v fracture, break.

frazione [fra'tsjone] sf fraction; (borgata) hamlet. **frazionare** v split up.

freccia ['frettʃa] sf arrow; (auto) indicator. **frecciata** sf shaft.

freddo ['freddo] agg cold; (fig) cool, chilly. sm cold. **aver freddo** be cold, feel cold. **fa freddo** it is cold. **fa un freddo cane** it is bitterly cold. **morir di freddo** be dying of cold. **soffrire il freddo** feel the cold.

freddura [fred'dura] sf pun.

fregare [fre'gare] v rub; (per lucidare) polish; (per lavare) scrub; (fam: rubare) pinch, swipe; (volg: imbrogliare) cheat.

fregata sf rub(bing). **fregatura** sf (volg: imbroglio) swindle; (fam: contrattempo) wash-out, flop.

fregio ['fredʒo] sm ornament; (arch) frieze. **fregiare** v decorate.

fremere ['fremere] v quiver.

fremito ['fremito] sm quiver; (di emozione) thrill; (brivido) shudder.

frenare [fre'nare] v brake; (fig) restrain, control, check.

frenesia [frene'zia] sf frenzy. **frenetico** agg frenzied, raving.

freno ['freno] sm brake; (fig) check, restraint; (cavallo) bit. **allentare il freno** (fig) slacken the reins. **mordere il freno** champ at the bit. **stringere i freni** (fig) clamp down.

frequentare [frekwen'tare] v frequent, go to often; (scuola, ecc.) attend; (persone) mix with. **frequentatore, -trice** sm, sf regular. **frequente** agg frequent. **frequenza** sf frequency. **con frequenza** frequently.

fresa ['freza] sf also **fresatrice** cutter, milling machine.

fresco ['fresko] agg fresh; (leggermente freddo) cool. sm cool(ness); (freschezza) freshness; (pittura) fresco. **al fresco** in the cool; (prigione) in the cooler. **star fresco** (non guai) be in a mess; (sbagliarsi) kid oneself.

fretta ['fretta] sf hurry. **aver fretta** be in a hurry. **far fretta** a hurry. **fatto in fretta** rushed, hurried. **frettoloso** agg rushed, hasty.

***friggere** ['friddʒere] v fry; (scoppiettare bollendo) sizzle.

frigido ['fridʒido] agg cold, frigid. **frigidità** sf coldness, frigidity.

frigorifero [frigo'rifero] sm refrigerator. **frigo** sm invar (fam) fridge.

fringuello [frin'gwello] sm chaffinch.

frittata [frit'tata] sf omelette. **frittella** sf pancake.

fritto ['fritto] agg fried. sm fried food. **star fritto** (fam) be in trouble, be in for it. **frittura** sf (vivanda) fried food; (atto del friggere) frying.

frivolo ['frivolo] agg frivolous. **frivolezze** sf frivolity, trifle.

frizione [frit'tsjone] sf (massaggio) rubdown; (auto) clutch; (attrito) friction.

frizzare [frit'tsare] v tingle; (bevande) sparkle; (metallo rovente) hiss.

frodare [fro'dare] v defraud. **frode** sf fraud. **frodo** sm smuggling. **cacciare or pescare di frodo** poach. **cacciatore or pescatore di frodo** sm poacher.

frollare [frol'lare] v ripen. **frollo** agg ripe; (carne) tender; (selvaggina) high; (pasta) short.

fronda ['fronda] sf (leafy) branch; (fig) embellishment.

fronte ['fronte] sf (testa) forehead; (faccia) face; (parte anteriore) front; (arch) façade. sm (mil) front. **a fronte** (in faccia) facing. **di fronte** (dirimpetto) opposite; (da davanti) from the front. **far fronte a** face.

fronteggiare [fronted'dʒare] v face, stand up to.

frontespizio [frontes'pitsjo] sm title-page.

frontiera [fron'tjera] sf frontier, border.

fronzoli ['frondzoli] sm pl frills pl.

frotta ['frotta] sf flock, swarm.

frottola ['frottola] sf fib.

frugale [fru'gale] agg frugal.

frugare [fru'gare] v rummage, go through; (perquisire) search.

frullare [frul'lare] v whisk; (fig) whirl. **frullino** sm whisk.

frumento [fru'mento] sm wheat.

frusciare [fru'ʃare] v rustle.

frustare [frus'tare] v whip. **frusta** sf whip. **frustata** sf lash.

frustrazione [frustra'tsjone] sf frustration. **frustrare** v frustrate, thwart.

frutta ['frutta] sf fruit. **frutta cotta** stewed fruit. **fruttare** v bear fruit; yield; (rendere) bring in; (procurare) earn.

frutteto [frut'teto] sm orchard.

fruttifero [frut'tifero] agg fruitful; (redditizio) profitable.

fruttivendolo [frutti'vendolo], **-a** sm, sf fruiterer, greengrocer.

frutto ['frutto] sm fruit; (interesse) yield; (rendita) income; profit. **frutti di mare** seafood sing.

fu [fu] agg invar late, deceased.

fucilare [futʃi'lare] v shoot. **fucilata** sf shot. **fucilazione** sf execution. **fucile** sm rifle; (da caccia) shotgun.

fucina [fu'tʃina] sf forge.

fuco¹ ['fuko] sm (ape) drone.

fuco² ['fuko] sm (alga) fucus.

fucsia [fuksja] sf fuchsia.

fuga ['fuga] *sf* escape; *(musica)* fugue; *(serie)* suite. **mettere in fuga** put to flight. **prendere la fuga** take flight, flee, escape. **fugace** *agg* transient.

fuggire [fud'dʒire] *v* flee, escape, run away. **fuggiasco** *sm, agg* fugitive; *(profugo)* refugee.

fulcro ['fulkro] *sm* fulcrum; *(fig)* heart.

fuliggine [fu'liddʒine] *sf* soot. **fulligginoso** *agg* sooty.

fulminare [fulmi'nare] *v (dal fulmine)* strike (by lightning); *(dalla corrente)* electrocute; *(con uno sguardo)* wither; *(allibire)* dumbfound. **fulmine** *sm* lightning, thunderbolt. **un fulmine a ciel sereno** a bolt from the blue.

fumaiolo [fuma'jɔlo] *sm (casa)* chimney-pot; *(nave)* funnel, smoke-stack.

fumare [fu'mare] *v* smoke; *(emettere vapore)* steam. **fumata** *sf* smoke. **fumatore, -trice** *sm, sf* smoker.

fumetto [fu'metto] *sm* comic-strip. **fumettista** *s(m+f)* comic-strip writer.

fumo ['fumo] *sm* smoke. **andare in fumo** go up in smoke.

funambolo [fu'nambolo], **-a** *sm, sf* tight-rope walker.

fune ['fune] *sf* rope, cable; *(per bucato)* washing line.

funebre ['funebre] *agg* funeral; *(lugubre)* funereal.

funerale [fune'rale] *sm* funeral. **funereo** *agg* funereal.

funesto [fu'nɛsto] *agg* fatal; *(doloroso)* distressing.

fungo ['fungo] *sm* mushroom; *(non mangereccio)* toadstool; *(bot)* fungus (*pl* -gi).

funicolare [funiko'lare] *sf* funicular railway.

funivia [funi'via] *sf* cable-car.

funzionare [funtsjo'nare] *v* function, work. **funzionale** *agg* functional, practical. **funzionamento** *sm* operation, working.

funzionario [funtsjo'narjo] *sm* official; *(impiegato statale)* civil servant.

funzione [fun'tsjone] *sf* function; *(carica)* office; *(compito)* duty. **entrare in funzione** come into operation. **essere in funzione di . . .** act as . . . .

fuochista [fwo'kista] *sm* stoker.

fuoco ['fwɔko] *sm* fire; *(fis, mat, foto)* focus. **appiccare** *or* **dare fuoco a** set fire to. **a prova di fuoco** fireproof. **fuoco di Sant'Antonio** *(med)* shingles. **mettere a fuoco** *(foto)* focus. **prendere fuoco** catch fire.

fuorché [fwor'ke] *prep, cong* except.

fuori ['fwɔri] *avv* out; *(all'esterno)* outside. *prep also* **fuori di** *or* **da** out of. **esser fuori di sè** be beside oneself. **fuoribordo** *sm (motore)* outboard motor; *(barca)* motor boat. **fuori strada** *(veicoli)* off the road; *(fig)* on the wrong track. **mettere fuori combattimento** *(sport)* knock out; *(fig)* put out of the running.

furbo ['furbo] *agg* cunning, crafty. **furbacchione** *sm* cunning fellow. **furberia** *sf* cunning.

furetto [fu'retto] *sm* ferret.

furfante [fur'fante] *sm* rascal.

furgone [fur'gone] *sm (delivery)* van. **furgoncino** *sm* small (delivery) van.

furia ['furja] *sf (collera)* rage, fury; *(fretta)* rush, haste. **a furia di . . .** by dint of . . . . **furibondo** [furi'bondo] *agg* furious.

furioso [fu'rjozo] *agg* violent, furious.

furore [fu'rore] *sm* fury, rage.

furtivo [fur'tivo] *agg* furtive, stealthy.

furto ['furto] *sm* theft. **furto con scasso** burglary. **piccolo furto** petty theft, petty larceny.

fusa ['fuza] *sf pl* **fare le fusa** purr.

fuscello [fu'ʃɛllo] *sm* twig.

fusibile [fu'zibile] *agg* fusible. *sm (elett)* fuse.

fusione [fu'zjone] *sf* fusion; *(colata)* casting; *(scioglimento)* melting; *(fig)* merging; *(comm)* merger.

fuso¹ ['fuzo] *agg (liquefatto)* melted, molten; *(colato)* cast.

fuso² ['fuzo] *sm* spindle; *(ancora)* shank. **diritto come un fuso** *(eretto)* straight as a ramrod; *(difilato)* like a shot. **fuso orario** time zone.

fusoliera [fuzo'ljera] *sf* fuselage.

fustagno [fus'tano] *sm* fustian; *(a coste)* corduroy.

fustella [fus'tella] *sf (tec)* die.

fustigare [fusti'gare] *v* flog; *(fig)* lash out at.

fusto ['fusto] *sm* trunk; *(ossatura)* frame; *(barile)* barrel, cask; *(recipiente di metallo)* drum.

futile ['futile] *agg* futile; *(meschino)* petty.

futuro [fu'turo] *agg, sm* future.

G

gabbare [gab'bare] *v* cheat.

gabbia ['gabbja] *sf* cage. **gabbia degli imputati** dock.

gabbiano [gab'bjano] *sm* seagull.

gabinetto [gabi'netto] *sm* study, office; (*di medico*) surgery; (*WC*) toilet, lavatory; (*pol*) cabinet; (*di scienze*) laboratory.

gaffe ['gaf] *sf, pl* -s blunder. **fare una gaffe** (*fam*) put one's foot in it.

gagà [ga'ga] *sm* (*fam*) dandy.

gagliardo [ga'ʎardo] *agg* vigorous; (*robusto*) strapping; (*coraggioso*) brave. **gagliardetto** *sm* pennant, flag.

gaio ['gajo] *agg* cheerful.

gala ['gala] *sf* (*ricevimento*) feast. *sm* (*mar*) flags *pl*. *sf* (*stoffa*) frill; (*cravatta*) bow-tie.

galantuomo [galan'twɔmo] *sm* (*true*) gentleman, man of honour. **galante** *agg* gallant, courteous.

galassia [ga'lassja] *sf* galaxy.

galateo [gala'tɛo] *sm* etiquette, good manners *pl*.

galea [ga'lɛa] *sf* galley.

galeotto [gale'ɔtto] *sm* (*carcerato*) convict; (*furfante*) scoundrel; (*vogatore forzato*) galley slave.

galera [ga'lɛra] *sf* prison.

galla ['galla] *sf* **stare** *or* **rimanere a galla** float, keep afloat. **tenersi a galla** keep afloat; (*fig*) keep one's head above water. **venire a galla** come to the surface; (*fig*) come to light, emerge.

galleggiare [galled'dʒare] *v* float. **galleggiante** *agg* floating. *sm* float; (*tec*) ballcock.

galleria [galle'ria] *sf* gallery; (*traforo*) tunnel; (*passaggio sotterraneo*) subway; (*cinema, ecc.*) circle, balcony.

Galles ['galles] *sm* Wales. **gallese** *sm, agg* Welsh; *s(m+f)* Welsh person.

gallo ['gallo] *sm* cock. **galletto** *sm* cockerel; (*tec*) wing-nut. **gallina** *sf* hen.

gallone[1] [gal'lone] *sm* (*misura*) gallon.

gallone[2] [gal'lone] *sm* braid; (*mil*) stripe.

galoppare [galop'pare] *v* gallop. **galoppata** *sf* gallop; (*lavoro faticoso*) hard work. **galoppo** *sm* gallop.

galvanizzare [galvanid'dzare] *v* galvanize.

gamba ['gamba] *sf* leg. **andare a gambe all'aria** fall flat on one's back; (*fallire*) fail. **a tre gambe** three-legged. **darsela a gambe** take to one's heels. **gambe storte** bandy *or* bow legs *pl*. **in gamba** (*valente*) smart. *inter* take care!

gambero ['gambero] *sm* (*di acqua dolce*) crayfish; (*gamberetto*) shrimp; (*gamberone*) prawn. **rosso come un gambero** as red as a lobster.

gambo ['gambo] *sm* (*pianta*) stem, stalk; (*tec*) shank.

gamma ['gamma] *sf* range; (*lunghezza d'onda*) wave-band.

ganascia [ga'naʃa] *sf* jaw; (*freno*) brake-shoe.

gancio ['gantʃo] *sm* hook.

ganghero ['gangero] *sm* hinge. **essere fuori dai gangheri** be beside oneself. **uscire dai gangheri** lose one's head.

gara ['gara] *sf* competition; (*corsa*) race; (*comm*) tender.

garage [ga'raʒ] *sm, pl* -s garage.

garantire [garan'tire] *v* guarantee; (*rendersi garante*) vouch for; (*assicurare*) assure. **essere garante per** *or* **di** vouch for. **rendersi garante per** (*dir*) stand bail for.

garanzia [garan'tsia] *sf* guarantee.

garbare [gar'bare] *v* please, suit. **garbato** *agg* polite, well-mannered. **garbo** *sm* (*maniera*) good manners *pl*, politeness; (*gentilezza*) charm.

garbuglio [gar'buʎo] *sm* muddle.

gareggiare [gared'dʒare] *v* compete.

gargarismo [garga'rizmo] *sm* gargle. **fare i gargarismi** gargle.

garitta [ga'ritta] *sf* cabin; (*mil*) sentry-box.

garofano [ga'rɔfano] *sm* carnation. **chiodo di garofano** *sm* clove.

garrire [gar'rire] *v* twitter. **garrito** *sm* twitter.

garrulo ['garrulo] *agg* (*uccello*) twittering; (*persona loquace*) garrulous.

garza ['gardza] *sf* gauze.

garzone [gar'dzone] *sm* boy, mate.

gas ['gas] *sm* gas. **a gas gas. gas asfissiante/esilarante** poison/laughing gas. **gassoso** *agg* gaseous.

gasolio [ga'zɔljo] *sm* fuel oil, diesel fuel.

gassosa [gas'soza] *sf* fizzy drink, lemonade.

gastrico ['gastriko] *agg* gastric.

gastronomia [gastrono'mia] *sf* gastronomy, cooking. **gastronomico** *agg* gastronomic(al). **gastronomo** *sm* (*buongustaio*) gourmet.

gattabuia [gatta'buja] *sf* (*fam*) clink.

gatto ['gatto] *sm* cat. **gatta** *sf* she-cat. **comprare una gatta nel sacco** buy a pig in a poke. **gatta ci cova!** I smell a rat! **una gatta da pelare** a tricky job to do. **gattino** *sm* kitten; (*bot*) catkin.

gazza ['gaddza] *sf* magpie.

gazzarra [gad'dzarra] *sf* uproar, row.

gazzella [gad'dzɛlla] *sf* gazelle.

gazzetta [gad'dzetta] *sf* gazette.

gelare [dʒe'lare] *v* freeze. **gelata** *sf* (hard) frost.

gelatina [dʒela'tina] *sf* gelatine.

gelato [dʒe'lato] *agg* frozen. ◊ *sm* ice-cream. **gelataio** *sm* ice-cream vendor. **gelateria** *sf* ice-cream shop *or* parlour.

gelido ['dʒɛlido] *agg* icy.

gelo ['dʒɛlo] *sm* frost; intense cold; (*sensazione*) chill.

gelone [dʒe'lone] *sm* chilblain.

gelosia¹ [dʒelo'zia] *sf* jealousy; (*cura attenta*) great care.

gelosia² [dʒelo'zia] *sf* (*finestra*) blind.

geloso [dʒe'lozo] *agg* jealous.

gelso ['dʒɛlso] *sm* (*mora*) mulberry; (*albero*) mulberry-tree.

gelsomino [dʒelso'mino] *sm* jasmine.

gemello [dʒe'mɛllo] *sm, agg* twin. **gemelli** *sm pl* (*di polsino*) cuff-links *pl*. **Gemelli** *sm pl* Gemini *sing*.

gemere [dʒe'mere] *v* groan; (*colare*) drip, ooze; (*tubare*) coo. **gemito** *sm* groan.

gemma [dʒemma] *sf* gem; (*bot*) bud.

gene ['dʒɛne] *sm* gene.

genealogia [dʒenealo'dʒia] *sf* (*scienza*) genealogy; (*stirpe*) pedigree. **albero genealogico** *sm* family tree.

generale [dʒene'rale] *sm*, *agg* general. **in generale** in general; (*di solito*) as a rule.

generalizzare [dʒeneralid'dzare] *v* generalize. **generalizzazione** *sf* generalization.

generare [dʒene'rare] *v* generate, produce. **generazione** *sf* generation.

genere ['dʒɛnere] *sm* kind, type; (*tipo di merce*) product, article; (*stile*) genre; (*gramm*) gender. **d'ogni genere** of all kinds. **il genere umano** mankind. **nel suo genere** in his way.

generico [dʒe'nɛriko] *agg* generic; general.

genero ['dʒɛnero] *sm* son-in-law.

generoso [dʒene'rozo] *agg* generous; (*vino*) full-bodied; (*cavallo*) thorough-bred.

genetica [dʒe'nɛtika] *sf* genetics. **genetico** *agg* genetic. **genetista** *s(m+f)* geneticist.

gengiva [dʒen'dʒiva] *sf* gum. **gengivite** *sf* gingivitis.

geniale [dʒe'njale] *agg* ingenious, clever. **genialità** *sf* brilliance.

genio¹ ['dʒɛnjo] *sm* genius; (*disposizione*) talent, gift; (*inclinazione*) taste. **andare a genio** be to one's liking, suit.

genio² [dʒɛnjo] *sm* (*mil*) engineers *pl*.

genitali [dʒeni'tali] *sm pl* genitals *pl*.

genitore [dʒeni'tore] *sm* parent.

gennaio [dʒen'najo] *sm* January.

Genova [dʒɛnova] *sf* Genoa. **genovese** *agg, s(m+f)* Genoese.

gente [dʒɛnte] *sf* people *pl*.

gentile [dʒen'tile] *agg* kind; (*cortese*) polite; delicate. **gentilezza** *sf* kindness; politeness; (*atto gentile*) favour. **gentiluomo** *sm* (*nobile*) nobleman; (*persona retta*) gentleman.

genuino [dʒenu'ino] *agg* genuine, natural; authentic. **genuinità** *sf* authenticity, naturalness, spontaneity.

genziana [dʒen'tsjana] *sf* gentian.

geografia [dʒeogra'fia] *sf* geography. **geografico** *agg* geographical. **atlante geografico** *sm* atlas. **carta geografica** *sf* map. **geografo, -a** *sm, f* geographer.

geologia [dʒeolo'dʒia] *sf* geology. **geologico** *agg* geological. **geologo, -a** *sm, f* geologist.

geometra [dʒe'ometra] *s(m+f)* surveyor.

geometria [dʒeome'tria] *sf* geometry. **geometrico** *agg* geometrical.

geranio [dʒe'ranjo] *sm* geranium.

gerarchia [dʒerar'kia] *sf* hierarchy. **gerarca** *sm* (*rel*) hierarch; (*capo*) leader. **gerarchico** *agg* hierarchical. **per via gerarchica** through official channels.

gerente [dʒe'rɛnte] *sm* manager.

gergo ['dʒɛrgo] *sm* slang, jargon.

geriatria [dʒerja'tria] *sf* geriatrics. **geriatrico** *agg* geriatric.

Germania [dʒer'manja] *sf* Germany. **germanico** *agg* German.

germe ['dʒɛrme] *sm* germ. **germinare** *v* germinate.

germogliare [dʒermoʎ'ʎare] *v* bud, sprout; (*fig*) germinate. **germoglio** *sm* shoot; (*origine*) germ.

gesso ['dʒɛsso] *sm* (*minerale*) gypsum; (*da disegno*) chalk; (*a pronta presa*) plaster (of Paris); (*opera*) plaster cast.

gesta ['dʒɛsta] *sf pl* (noble) deeds *pl*, feats *pl*.

gesticolare [dʒestiko'lare] *v* gesticulate.

gestire [dʒes'tire] *v* manage, run. **gestione** *sf* management.

gesto ['dʒɛsto] *sm* gesture; (*azione*) deed; (*del capo*) nod; (*della mano*) wave.

Gesù [dʒe'zu] *sm* Jesus.

gesuita [dʒezu'ita] *sm* Jesuit. **gesuitico** *agg* Jesuitical.

gettare [dʒet'tare] *v* throw; (*emettere*) let out; (*tec*) cast. **gettare i soldi dalla finestra** throw money down the drain. **gettare le fondamenta** lay the foundations. **gettar luce su ...** cast light on .... **gettata** *sf* cast; (*di reti*) casting.

getto ['dʒɛtto] *sm* (*lancio*) throw; (*di liquido o gas*) jet; (*metallo, ecc.*) casting.

gettone [dʒet'tone] *sm* counter, token.

ghermire [ger'mire] *v* clutch, grab.

ghetto ['getto] *sm* ghetto.

ghiacciaia [gjat'tʃaja] *sf* ice-box.

ghiacciaio [gjat'tʃajo] *sm* glacier.

ghiacciare [gjat'tʃare] *v* freeze. **ghiacciata** *sf* drink with crushed ice.

ghiaccio ['gjattʃo] *sm* ice. **di ghiaccio** (*freddissimo*) ice-cold, frozen; (*fig*) icy. **ghiacciolo** *sm* icicle; (*gelato*) ice lolly.

ghiaia ['gjaja] *sf* gravel.

ghianda ['gjanda] *sf* acorn.

ghiandaia [gjan'daja] *sf* jay.

ghiandola ['gjandola] *sf* gland. **ghiandolare** *agg* glandular.

ghigliottina [giʎot'tina] *sf* guillotine. **ghigliottinare** *v* guillotine.

ghignare [gi'ɲare] *v* sneer. **ghigno** *sm* sneer, smirk.

ghiotto ['gjotto] *agg* greedy; (*appetitoso*) inviting. **ghiottone, -a** *sm, sf* glutton, greedy person. **ghiottoneria** *sf* (*golosità*) gluttony; (*cibo ghiotto*) titbit.

ghiribizzo [giri'bittso] *sm* fancy, whim.

ghirigoro [giri'gɔro] *sm* flourish.

ghirlanda [gir'landa] *sf* garland, wreath.

ghiro ['giro] *sm* dormouse. **dormire come un ghiro** sleep like a log.

ghisa ['giza] *sf* cast iron.

già [dʒa] *avv* already; (*un tempo*) once; (*ex*) formerly.

giacca ['dʒakka] *sf* coat; (*giacchetta*) jacket.

giacché [dʒak'ke] *cong* as, since.

giacchetta [dʒak'ketta] *sf* jacket.

***giacere** [dʒa'tʃere] *v* lie; (*in sospeso*) be in abeyance. **mettersi a giacere** lie down. **giacenza** *sf* abeyance; (*merce*) (unsold) stock; (*econ*) deposit. **giacimento** *sm* deposit.

giacinto [dʒa'tʃinto] *sm* hyacinth.

giada ['dʒada] *sf* jade.

giaggiolo [dʒad'dʒɔlo] *sm* iris.

giaguaro [dʒa'gwaro] *sm* jaguar.

giallo ['dʒallo] *agg* yellow. *sm* (*colore*) yellow; (*libro, film*) thriller. **giallo d'uovo** (egg) yolk. **giallastro** *agg* yellowish, sallow. **giallognolo** *agg* pale yellow, yellowish.

giammai [dʒam'mai] *avv* never. **se giammai** if ever.

Giappone [dʒap'pone] *sm* Japan. **giapponese** *s(m+f)*, *agg* Japanese.

giardinetta [dʒardi'netta] *sf* estate car.

giardino [dʒar'dino] *sm* garden. **giardino d'infanzia** kindergarten, nursery school. **giardino zoologico** zoo. **giardinaggio** *sm* gardening. **giardiniere, -a** *sm, sf* gardener.

giarrettiera [dʒarret'tjɛra] *sf* suspender, garter.

giavellotto [dʒavel'lɔtto] *sm* javelin.

Gibilterra [dʒibil'terra] *sf* Gibraltar.

gigante [dʒi'gante] *sm, agg* giant. **gigantesco** *agg* gigantic, huge.

gigione [dʒi'dʒone] *sm* ham (actor). **fare il gigione** ham.

giglio ['dʒiʎo] *sm* lily.

gilè [dʒi'lɛ] *sm* waistcoat.

ginecologo [dʒine'kɔlogo], **-a** *sm, sf* gynaecologist. **ginecologia** *sf* gynaecology. **ginecologico** *agg* gynaecological.

ginepro [dʒi'nepro] *sm* juniper.

ginestra [dʒi'nɛstra] *sf* broom. **ginestrone** *sm* furze, gorse.

Ginevra [dʒi'nevra] *sf* Geneva.

gingillarsi [dʒindʒil'larsi] *v* (*divertirsi*) amuse oneself; (*perder tempo*) hang about.

ginnasio [dʒin'nazjo] *sm* secondary school.

ginnastica [dʒin'nastika] *sf* (*sport*) gymnastics; (*esercizi*) physical exercises *pl*.

ginocchio [dʒi'nɔkkjo] *sm pl* **-a** *f* knee. **ginocchioni** *avv* also **in ginocchio** on one's knees.

giocare [dʒo'kare] *v* play; (*in borsa*) gamble (on the Stock Exchange); (*scommettere*) bet. **giocata** *sf* (*partita*) game;

(*puntata*) stake, bet. **giocatore, -trice** *sm,* *sf* player; (*d'azzardo*) gambler.

giocattolo [dʒo'kattolo] *sm* toy.

giocherellare [dʒokerel'lare] *v* toy.

giochetto [dʒo'ketto] *sm* (*passatempo*) pastime; (*tranello*) trick; (*lavoro facile*) child's play.

gioco ['dʒɔko] *sm* (*divertimento, tec*) play; (*con regole, partita*) game; (*vizio*) gambling; (*combinazione di carte*) hand; (*posta*) stake; (*beffa*) trick. **entrare in gioco** come into play. **fare il doppio gioco** double-cross. **mettere in gioco** (*far agire*) bring into action; (*rischiare*) stake.

giocoliere [dʒoko'ljere] *sm* juggler.

giocondo [dʒo'kondo] *agg* cheerful, merry.

giogo ['dʒogo] *sm* yoke; (*valico*) pass; (*cima allungata*) ridge.

gioia¹ ['dʒɔja] *sf* joy, delight.

gioia² ['dʒɔja] *sf* (*gemma*) jewel.

gioire [dʒo'ire] *v* rejoice. **gioioso** *agg* joyful.

giornalaio [dʒorna'lajo], **-a** *sm, sf* newsagent.

giornale [dʒor'nale] *sm* (*quotidiano*) newspaper; (*registro*) journal; diary. **giornale di bordo** log(-book). **giornale radio** news (bulletin).

giornaliero [dʒorna'ljero] *agg* daily.

giornalismo [dʒorna'lizmo] *sm* journalism. **giornalista** *s(m+f)* journalist.

giornata [dʒor'nata] *sf* day. **a giornata** by the day. **di giornata** (*fresco*) fresh; (*di turno*) on duty. **donna a giornata** daily (woman). **vivere alla giornata** live from day to day.

giorno ['dʒorno] *sm* day. **a giorni** (*tra breve*) soon; (*a intervalli*) sometimes. **al giorno** a day. **al giorno d'oggi** nowadays. **che giorno è?** (*data*) what is the date? (*della settimana*) what day (of the week) is it? **da un giorno all'altro** (*improvvisamente*) suddenly; (*tra poco*) any day now. **di giorno** by day. **giorno festivo** holiday. **giorno libero** day off. **punto a giorno** hem-stitch. **un giorno o l'altro** one of these days.

giostra ['dʒɔstra] *sf* (*fiera*) merry-go-round; (*torneo*) tournament.

giovane ['dʒovane] *agg* young; (*giovanile*) youthful; (*non stagionato*) new. *sm* (*giovanotto*) young man, youth. *sf* young woman, girl. **giovanile** *agg* youthful, juvenile.

giovare [dʒo'vare] *v* help, do good.

giovedì [dʒove'di] *sm* Thursday.

giovenca [dʒo'venka] *sf* heifer.

gioventù [dʒoven'tu] *sf* youth; (*i giovani*) young people *pl.*

giovevole [dʒo'vevole] *agg* useful.

gioviale [dʒo'vjale] *agg* genial, jolly.

giovinezza [dʒovi'nettsa] *sf* (*gioventù*) youth; (*qualità*) youthfulness. **seconda giovinezza** second childhood.

giradischi [dʒira'diski] *sm invar* record player.

giradito [dʒira'dito] *sm* whitlow.

giraffa [dʒi'raffa] *sf* giraffe.

giramento [dʒira'mento] *sm* **giramento di capo** dizzy spell; (*fit of*) dizziness.

girandola [dʒi'randola] *sf* (*fuochi d'artificio*) Catherine wheel; (*giocattolo*) toy windmill; (*fig*) fickle person.

girare [dʒi'rare] *v* turn; (*scansare*) get round, avoid; (*percorrere viaggiando*) travel, tour; (*andare da un posto all'altro*) go around; (*comm*) endorse; (*cinema*) shoot, take; (*camminare senza meta*) wander about; circulate. **girare a vuoto** (*mec*) idle. **mi gira la testa** I feel dizzy or giddy.

girarrosto [dʒirar'rɔsto] *sm* spit.

girasole [dʒira'sole] *sm* sunflower.

girino [dʒi'rino] *sm* tadpole.

giro ['dʒiro] *sm* turn; (*pista*) lap; (*percorso*) round; (*viaggio*) tour; (*passeggiata a piedi*) stroll, walk; (*in macchina*) drive; (*in bicicletta, a cavallo*) ride; (*periodo*) course, space; circulation; (*mec*) revolution. **andare in giro** go round. **essere in giro** (*fuori*) be out; (*in qualche posto*) be somewhere. **giro collo** neck. **giro d'affari** turnover. **giro d'orizzonte** survey. **giro manica** armhole. **guardarsi in giro** look around. **prendere in giro** make fun of.

gironzolare [dʒironzo'lare] *v* stroll, wander (about).

girovago [dʒi'rɔvago] *sm, pl* **-ghi** vagabond, tramp. *agg* wandering. **girovagare** *v* stroll, wander (about).

gita ['dʒita] *sf* excursion, trip. **fare una gita** make an excursion, go on a trip.

giù [dʒu] *avv* down; (*dabbasso*) downstairs. **andare su e giù** (*salire e scendere*) go up and down; (*avanti e indietro*) go to and fro. **giù di lì** thereabouts. **in giù** (*moto*) down; (*stato*) low; (*in meno*) under. **su per giù** thereabouts.

giubba ['dʒubba] *sf* jacket; *(mil)* tunic. **giubbotto di salvataggio** *sm* life-jacket.

giubilare [dʒubi'lare] *v* rejoice.

giubileo [dʒubi'lɛo] *sm* jubilee.

giudaismo [dʒuda'izmo] *sm* Judaism.

giudicare [dʒudi'kare] *v* judge; *(ritenere)* consider. **a giudicare da** judging by. **passare in giudicato** be beyond recall, be final.

giudice ['dʒuditʃe] *sm* judge. **giudice istruttore** examining magistrate.

giudiziario [dʒudit'tsjarjo] *agg* judicial.

giudizio [dʒu'ditsjo] *sm* judgment; *(parere)* opinion; *(dir)* sentence, verdict; *(buon senso)* common sense. **aver giudizio** be sensible. **citare in giudizio** summon. **comparire in giudizio** appear before a court. **dente del giudizio** *sm* wisdom tooth. **far giudizio** behave oneself. **rinviare a giudizio** commit for trial. **giudizioso** *agg* sensible.

giugno ['dʒuɲo] *sm* June.

giulivo [dʒu'livo] *agg* merry.

giullare [dʒul'lare] *sm (cantastorie)* minstrel; *(buffone)* clown.

giunco ['dʒunko] *sm* rush.

***giungere** ['dʒundʒere] *v* arrive (at), reach; *(riuscire)* manage; *(arrivare al punto di)* go so far as. **mi è giunto** I have received. **mi giunge nuovo** it is news to me.

giungla ['dʒungla] *sf* jungle.

giunta¹ ['dʒunta] *sf* addition; *(peso)* makeweight; *(sartoria)* insert. **giuntare** *v (unire)* join; *(cucire)* sew together; *(cinema, nastro)* splice.

giunta² ['dʒunta] *sf (comitato)* council; *(mil)* junta.

giunto ['dʒunto] *sm* joint.

giuntura [dʒun'tura] *sf* joint; *(accoppiamento)* coupling.

giunzione [dʒun'tsjone] *sf* junction; *(giunto)* joint.

giurare [dʒu'rare] *v* swear. **giuramento** *sm* oath. **giuramento falso** *(spergiuro)* perjury. **mancare al giuramento** break an oath. **prestar giuramento** swear, take an oath.

giurato [dʒu'rato], **-a** *sm, sf* juror. *agg* sworn.

giuria [dʒu'ria] *sf* jury.

giuridico [dʒu'ridiko] *agg* legal.

giurisdizione [dʒurizdit'tsjone] *sf* jurisdiction.

***giustapporre** [dʒustap'porre] *v* juxtapose. **giustapposizione** *sf* juxtaposition.

giustezza [dʒus'tettsa] *sf* correctness; *(esattezza)* precision.

giustificare [dʒustifi'kare] *v* justify. **giustificazione** *sf* justification; *(scusa)* excuse.

giustizia [dʒus'tittsja] *sf* justice; *(equità)* fairness. **assicurare alla giustizia** bring to justice. **fare** *or* **rendere giustizia** do justice.

giusto ['dʒusto] *agg* just; *(equo)* fair; *(legittimo)* rightful; *(corretto)* right. *avv* *(proprio, appena)* just; *(esattamente)* correctly. *sm (persona)* righteous man.

glaciale [gla'tʃale] *agg* glacial; *(fig)* icy.

gladiolo [gla'djolo] *sm* gladiolus.

glassa ['glassa] *sf* icing. **glassare** *v* ice.

gli¹ [ʎi] *art* the.

gli² [ʎi] *pron (persona)* (to) him; *(cosa, animale)* (to) it.

glicerina [glitʃe'rina] *sf* glycerine.

glicine ['glitʃine] *sm* wisteria.

globo ['globo] *sm* globe. **globo oculare** eyeball.

globulo ['globulo] *sm* globule; *(med)* corpuscle. **globulare** *agg* globular.

gloria ['glorja] *sf* glory; *(vanto)* pride. **gloriarsi** *v* glory (in); *(vantarsi)* boast (of).

glorificare [glorifi'kare] *v* glorify.

glucosio [glu'kɔzjo] *sm* glucose.

gnomo ['ɲɔmo] *sm* gnome.

gnomone [ɲo'mone] *sm* sundial.

gobba ['gobba] *sf* hump.

gobbo ['gobbo], **-a** *sm, sf* hunchback. *agg* hunchbacked.

goccia ['gottʃa] *sf* drop. **goccia a goccia** drop by drop; *(fig)* little by little. **una goccia nel mare** a drop in the ocean. **gocciolare** *v* drip.

***godere** [go'dere] *v* enjoy; *(rallegrarsi)* rejoice. **godimento** *sm* enjoyment; *(piacere)* pleasure.

goffo ['goffo] *agg* awkward, clumsy. **goffaggine** *sf* awkwardness, clumsiness; *(atto)* clumsy action; *(parola)* blunder.

gol [gɔl] *sm invar* goal.

gola ['gola] *sf* throat; *(golosità)* greed, gluttony. **aver l'acqua alla gola** be in deep water. **far gola** tempt.

golf¹ [gɔlf] *sm invar (sport)* golf.

golf² [gɔlf] *sm invar (maglione)* sweater, jumper; *(con bottoni)* cardigan.

golfo ['golfo] *sm* gulf.

goliardo [go'ljardo] *sm* (university) student. **goliardico** *agg* university.

goloso [go'lozo] *agg* greedy. **golosità** *sf* greediness, gluttony.

golpe[1] ['golpe] *sf* smut, blight.

golpe[2] ['golpe] *sm* coup (d'état).

gomito ['gomito] *sm* elbow. **gomitata** *sf* dig with the elbow. **farsi avanti a (forza di) gomitate** elbow one's way forward.

gomitolo [go'mitolo] *sm* ball.

gomma ['gomma] *sf* rubber; (*colla*) gum; (*pneumatico*) tyre. **gommapiuma** *sf* foam rubber. **gommato** *agg* rubberized; gummed. **gommoso** *agg* rubbery.

gondola ['gondola] *sf* gondola. **gondoliere** *sm* gondolier.

gonfalone [gonfa'lone] *sm* banner, standard.

gonfiare [gon'fjare] *v* swell (up); (*riempire di gas, ecc.*) inflate, blow up; (*montare*) puff up; exaggerate. **gonfiatura** *sf* blowing up, swelling up; (*gonfiore*) swelling; exaggeration. **gonfio** *agg* swollen, inflated. **gonfiore** *sm* swelling.

gong ['gɔŋ] *sm invar* gong.

gonna ['gonna] *sf also* **gonnella** skirt.

gonorrea [gonor'rɛa] *sf* gonorrhea.

gonzo ['gondzo] *sm* simpleton.

gorgheggiare [gorged'dʒare] *v* trill, warble. **gorgheggio** *sm* trill, warble; (*di uccello*) warbling.

gorgo ['gorgo] *sm* whirlpool.

gorgogliare [gorgo'ʎare] *v* gurgle; (*intestino*) rumble. **gorgoglio** *sm* rumble; gurgle.

gorilla [go'rilla] *sm invar* gorilla.

gotico ['gɔtiko] *agg* Gothic.

gotta ['gotta] *sf* gout.

governante [gover'nante] *sf* (*incaricata della casa*) housekeeper; (*istitutrice*) governess.

governare [gover'nare] *v* govern; (*dirigere*) run; (*dominare*) rule; (*pilotare*) steer. **governativo** *agg* government, governmental. **governatore** *sm* governor. **governo** *sm* government; (*dominio*) rule; (*amministrazione*) management. **governo della casa** housekeeping.

gozzo ['goddzo] *sm* crop; (*med*) goitre. **averlo nel** *or* **sul gozzo** be unable to swallow.

gozzovigliare [goddzovi'ʎare] *v* revel, go on a spree.

gracchiare [grak'kjare] *v* croak.

gracidare [gratʃi'dare] *v* croak.

gracile ['gratʃile] *agg* frail. **gracilità** *sf* frailty.

gradasso [gra'dasso] *sm* boaster, braggart. **fare il gradasso** boast, brag.

gradazione [grada'tsjone] *sf* gradation; (*sfumatura*) shade. **gradazione alcolica** alcoholic strength.

gradevole [gra'devole] *agg* agreeable.

gradiente [gra'djɛnte] *sm* gradient.

gradimento [gradi'mento] *sm* (*approvazione*) liking; (*piacere*) pleasure.

gradino [gra'dino] *sm* step. **gradinata** *sf* flight of steps.

gradire [gra'dire] *v* (*trovar piacevole*) find agreeable; (*accogliere con gioia*) welcome; (*accettare*) accept; (*nelle richieste*) like.

grado[1] ['grado] *sm* degree; (*mil, rango*) rank. **a gradi** step by step. **avanzare di grado** be promoted. **essere in grado di** be able to.

grado[2] ['grado] *sm* **di buon grado** willingly.

graduale [gradu'ale] *agg* gradual.

graduare [gradu'are] *v* graduate. **graduatoria** *sf* (*elenco*) list; (*ordine*) classification.

graffa ['graffa] *sf* bracket; (*fermaglio*) (paper-)clip.

graffiare [graf'fjare] *v* scratch. **graffiatura** *sf* scratch. **graffio** *sm* scratch.

grafico [gra'fico] *agg* graphic. *sm* (*diagramma*) chart, graph; (*persona*) graphic artist.

grafologo [gra'fɔlogo], -**a** *sm*, *sf* graphologist.

gramigna [gra'miɲa] *sf* couch-grass; (*malerba*) weed. **attaccarsi come la gramigna** cling like a leech.

grammatico [gram'matiko] *agg* grammatical. *sm* grammarian. **grammatica** *sf* grammar; (*persona*) grammarian.

grammo ['grammo] *sm* gram.

grammofono [gram'mɔfono] *sm* gramophone.

grana[1] ['grana] *sf* (*struttura*) grain. *sm* (*formaggio*) Parmesan (cheese).

grana[2] ['grana] *sf* (*seccatura*) nuisance. **piantare una grana** make trouble.

granaglie [gra'naʎe] *sf pl* cereals *pl*.

granaio [gra'najo] *sm* barn; (*zona produttrice di grano*) granary; (*locale sottotetto*) loft.

granata[1] [gra'nata] *sf* (*scopa*) broom.

granata[2] [gra'nata] *sf* (*mil*) grenade.

granata[3] [gra'nata] *sf* (*frutto*) pomegranate; (*pietra*) garnet.

Gran Bretagna [gran bre'taɲa] *sf* Great Britain.

grancassa [gran'kassa] *sf* (*musica*) bass drum. **batter la grancassa** blow one's own trumpet.

granchio ['grankjo] *sm* crab. **prendere un granchio** make a blunder.

grande ['grande] *agg* big; (*ampio, numeroso*) large; (*largo*) wide; (*adulto*) grown-up. **in grande** on a large scale. **in gran parte** largely. **non ... un gran che** not ... much.

grandeggiare [granded'dʒare] *v* (*emergere*) tower, stand out; (*darsi arie*) show off.

grandezza [gran'dettsa] *sf* (*dimensione, taglia*) size; (*altezza*) height; (*larghezza*) width; (*ampiezza*) breadth; (*fig*) greatness; (*mat, fis*) magnitude.

grandinare [grandi'nare] *v* hail. **grandine** *sf* hail. **chicco di grandine** *sm* hailstone.

grandioso [gran'djozo] *agg* grand.

granduca [gran'duka] *sm, pl* -chi grand duke. **granducato** *sm* grand duchy. **granduchessa** *sf* grand duchess.

granello [gra'nello] *sm* grain; (*di frutta*) pip. **granello di pepe** peppercorn.

granita [gra'nita] *sf* crushed-ice drink.

granito [gra'nito] *sm* granite.

grano ['grano] *sm* (*granello*) grain; (*frumento*) wheat; (*cereale in genere*) corn, cereal.

granturco [gran'turko] *sm* maize.

granulo ['granulo] *sm* granule. **granulare** *agg* granular.

grappolo ['grappolo] *sm* bunch.

grasso ['grasso] *agg* fat; (*unto*) greasy, oily; (*che contiene grasso*) fatty. *sm* fat; (*sostanza untuosa*) grease. **grassoccio** *agg* plump.

grata ['grata] *sf* grating, grille. **gratella** *sf* grill.

graticcio [gra'tittʃo] *sm* trellis.

graticola [gra'tikola] *sf* grill.

gratifica [gra'tifika] *sf* bonus.

gratis ['gratis] *agg* free. *avv* for nothing, for love.

gratitudine [grati'tudine] *sf* gratitude.

grato ['grato] *agg* grateful, obliged; (*gradevole*) pleasant; (*gradito*) welcome.

grattacapo [gratta'kapo] *sm* worry, headache.

grattacielo [gratta'tʃelo] *sm* skyscraper.

grattare [grat'tare] *v* scratch; (*grattugiare*)

grate; (*raschiare*) scrape; (*fam: rubare*) pinch.

grattugiare [grattu'dʒare] *v* grate. **grattugia** *sf* grater.

gratuito [gra'tuito] *agg* free; (*non retribuito*) unpaid; (*ingiustificato*) gratuitous; (*infondato*) unfounded.

gravare [gra'vare] *v* burden.

grave ['grave] *agg* (*serio*) grave; (*pesante*) heavy; (*malattia*) serious; (*perdita*) grievous. **gravità** *sf* gravity. **gravoso** *agg* hard, onerous.

gravido ['gravido] *agg* pregnant. **gravidanza** *sf* pregnancy.

grazia ['gratsja] *sf* grace; (*fascino*) charm; (*clemenza*) pardon; (*favore*) favour. **grazie** *sm pl*, *inter* thanks. **grazie a** thanks to.

Grecia ['grɛtʃa] *sf* Greece. **greco, -a** *s, agg, m pl* -**ci** Greek. **naso greco** *sm* Grecian nose.

gregge ['greddʒe] *sm* flock, herd.

greggio ['greddʒo] *agg* raw, crude.

grembiule [grem'bjule] *sm* apron; (*con petto*) pinafore; (*con maniche*) overall.

grembo ['grembo] *sm* lap.

gremire [gre'mire] *v* fill (up). **gremirsi** *v* get crowded.

gres ['grɛs] *sm* stoneware.

gretto ['gretto] *agg* mean; (*idea, animo*) narrow-minded. **grettezza** *sf* meanness; narrow-mindedness.

gridare [gri'dare] *v* shout; (*strillare*) yell, scream. **gridare aiuto** call for help. **grido** *sm, pl* -**a** *f* shout; cry; scream, yell. **di grido** (*noto*) famous; (*di moda*) fashionable. **l'ultimo grido** the latest fashion, the last word.

griffa ['griffa] *sf* claw.

grigio ['gridʒo] *agg* grey; (*fig*) drab. *sm* grey. **grigiastro** *agg* greyish. **grigiore** *sm* greyness; (*fig*) drabness. **grigioverde** *sm*, *agg* grey-green, khaki.

griglia ['griʎa] *sf* grill; (*saracinesca*) shutter; (*schermo*) grille; (*radio*) grid; (*focolare*) grate.

grilletto [gril'letto] *sm* trigger.

grillo ['grillo] *sm* cricket; (*capriccio*) whim. **gli è saltato il grillo di** he got it into his head to.

grimaldello [grimal'dello] *sm* jemmy.

grinza ['grintsa] *sf* crease; (*ruga*) wrinkle. **non fare una grinza** (*calzare bene*) fit perfectly; (*filare bene*) be flawless.

gripparsi [grip'parsi] *v* (*auto*) seize up.

grondaia [gron'daja] *sf* gutter.

grondare [gron'dare] *v* drip; (*abbondantemente*) pour.

groppa ['grɔppa] *sf* back.

grossa ['grɔssa] *sf* (*comm*) gross. **dormire della grossa** sleep like a log.

grossezza [gros'settsa] *sf* (*volume*) bulk, size; (*spessore*) thickness.

grossista [gros'sista] *s(m+f)* wholesaler.

grosso ['grɔsso] *agg* large, big; (*spesso*) thick; (*non raffinato*) coarse; serious. **dirle grosse** tell fibs. **farne di grosse** cause all sorts of trouble. **grossolano** *agg* coarse, rough.

grotta ['grɔtta] *sf* cave; grotto.

grottesco [grot'tesko] *agg* grotesque.

groviera [gro'vjɛra] *s(m+f)* also **gruviera** (*formaggio*) gruyère.

groviglio [gro'viʎo] *sm* tangle; (*confusione*) mess.

gru [gru] *sf* crane.

gruccia ['gruttʃa] *sf* crutch; (*attaccapanni*) coat-hanger.

grugnire [gru'ɲire] *v* grunt. **grugnito** *sm* grunt.

grugno ['gruɲo] *sm* (*maiale*) snout; (*fam: muso*) mug.

grullo ['grullo] *agg* foolish.

grumo ['grumo] *sm* clot.

gruppo ['gruppo] *sm* group; (*mec*) unit.

gruviera [gru'vjɛra] *V* **groviera**.

gruzzolo ['gruttsolo] *sm* pile; (*risparmi*) nest-egg.

guadagnare [gwada'ɲare] *v* earn; (*ottenere*) gain; (*vincere*) win; (*raggiungere*) reach; (*risparmiare*) save.

guadagno [gwa'daɲo] *sm* (*retribuzione*) earnings *pl*; profit; advantage.

guado ['gwado] *sm* ford. **guadare** *v* wade.

guaina [gwa'ina] *sf* sheath.

guaio ['gwajo] *sm* trouble. **guai** *inter* woe betide you, us, etc.

guaire [gwa'ire] *v* whine, yelp. **guaito** *sm* whine, yelp.

guancia ['gwantʃa] *sf* cheek. **guanciale** *sm* pillow.

guanto ['gwanto] *sm* glove. **calzare come un guanto** fit like a glove. **gettare il guanto** throw down the gauntlet. **trattare coi guanti** treat with kid gloves.

guardaboschi [gwarda'boski] *sm* forester.

guardacaccia [gwarda'kattʃa] *sm invar* gamekeeper.

guardacoste [gwarda'kɔste] *sm invar* coastguard.

guardalinee [gwarda'linee] *sm invar* (*sport*) linesman.

guardamano [gwarda'mano] *sm invar* (*sciabola*) hilt; (*fucile*) guard; (*guanto*) protective glove.

guardare [gwar'dare] *v* look (at); (*affacciarsi*) look out; face; (*dare un'occhiata*) have a look; (*custodire*) look after, mind; (*stare a vedere*) watch; (*considerare*) view; (*cercare*) try to, be careful to. **andare a guardare** have a look. **Dio ne guardi!** God forbid! **guarda che roba!** just look at that! **guardar di sbieco** *or* **traverso** look askance (at). **guardare fisso** stare, gaze (at). **guarda un po'!** well, well!

guardaroba [gwarda'roba] *sm invar* (*luogo*) cloakroom; (*armadio*) wardrobe. **guardarobiera** *sf* cloakroom attendant.

guardarsi [gwar'darsi] *v* look at oneself. **guardarsi intorno** look around. **guardarsi da** (*fare attenzione a*) beware of; (*astenersi da*) refrain from. **me ne guardo bene!** heaven forbid!

guardata [gwar'data] *sf* look, glance.

guardavia [gwarda'via] *sm invar* guard-rail.

guardia ['gwardja] *sf* (*custodia*) watch, guard; (*turno*) duty; (*custode*) keeper, watchman; (*sentinella*) sentry; (*sport*) guard. **essere di guardia** be on duty; (*mil*) be on guard duty. **fare la guardia** (*sorvegliare*) guard, watch; (*badare*) watch over. **guardia di finanza** (*corpo*) Customs *pl*; (*singolo*) Customs officer. **mettere in guardia** warn. **guardiano** *sm* keeper, guardian.

guardingo [gwar'dingo] *agg* cautious, wary.

guarire [gwa'rire] *v* cure; (*rimettersi in salute*) recover; (*ferita*) heal. **guarigione** *sf* recovery; healing.

guarnigione [gwarni'dʒone] *sf* garrison.

guarnire [gwar'nire] *v* decorate; (*vestiario*) trim; (*gastr*) garnish; (*corredare*) equip; (*mil*) garrison. **guarnizione** *sf* decoration, trimming, garnish; (*tec*) packing; (*auto*) gasket.

guastafeste [gwasta'feste] *s(m+f) invar* spoilsport.

guastamestieri [gwastames'tjeri] *s(m+f) invar* bungler; (*fam*) menace.

guastare [gwas'tare] *v* spoil; (*rovinare*) ruin, damage. **guastarsi** *v* (*cibi*) go bad; (*mec*) break down; (*tempo*) change for the worse. **guasto** *agg* (*cibo*) bad, rotten; (*mec*) broken; (*salute, ecc.*) bad.

guazzabuglio [gwattsa'buʎo] *sm* hotchpotch, jumble.

guazzare [gwat'tsare] *v* splash about; (*fig*) wallow. **guazzo** *sm* pool; (*pittura*) gouache.

guercio ['gwertʃo] *agg* cross-eyed.

guerra ['gwerra] *sf* war; (*il guerreggiare*) warfare. **far guerra** wage war. **guerra mondiale** world war. **guerrafondaio** *sm*, *sf* warmonger.

guerreggiare [gwerred'dʒare] *v* fight.

guerresco [gwer'resko] *agg* (*bellicoso*) warlike; (*di guerra*) war.

guerriero [gwer'rjɛro] *agg* (*bellicoso*) warlike; (*combattivo*) aggressive. *sm* warrior.

guerriglia [gwer'riʎa] *sf* guerrilla warfare. **guerrigliero** *sm* guerrilla.

gufo ['gufo] *sm* owl.

guglia ['guʎa] *sf* (*arch*) spire; (*geog*) pinnacle.

guida ['gwida] *sf* guide; (*direzione, comando*) guidance, leadership; (*tappeto*) runner; (*elenco*) directory; (*auto*) drive, driving; (*comandi*) controls *pl*. **esame (di) guida** driving test. **guida a destra/sinistra** right-/left-hand drive. **scuola (di) guida** *sf* driving school.

guidare [gwi'dare] *v* guide; (*dirigere, comandare*) lead; (*auto*) drive; (*aero*) fly; (*nave*) steer; (*moto*) ride. **guidatore, -trice** *sm*, *sf* driver.

guinzaglio [gwin'tsaʎo] *sm* leash, lead. **mettere il guinzaglio** (*fig*) keep a tight rein (on). **tenere al guinzaglio** keep on a leash.

guisa ['gwiza] *sf* **a** or **in guisa di** in the manner of, like.

guizzare [gwit'tsare] *v* (*lampo*) flash; (*pesci*) dart; (*sfuggire*) wriggle; (*fiamma*) flicker. **guizzo** *sm* flash; dart; flicker.

guscio ['guʃo] *sm* shell; (*legumi*) pod.

gustare [gus'tare] *v* taste; (*trovar buono*) enjoy. **gusto** *sm* taste; (*piacere*) enjoyment. **con gusto** tastefully. **di gusto** heartily. **non aver gusto** be tasteless. **prenderci gusto** take a liking (to). **senza gusto** tasteless.

gutturale [guttu'rale] *agg* guttural.

H

hascisc [a'ʃiʃ] *sm* hashish.
hockey ['hɔki] *sm* hockey.

I

i [i] *art* the.

iattanza [jat'tantsa] *sf* arrogance.

ibernazione [iberna'tsjone] *sf* hibernation. **ibernare** *v* hibernate.

ibrido ['ibrido] *sm*, *agg* hybrid.

Iddio [id'dio] *sm* God.

idea [i'dɛa] *sf* idea; opinion; (*proposito*) intention. **cambiare idea** change one's mind. **dare l'idea** give the impression.

ideale [ide'ale] *sm*, *agg* ideal. **idealismo** *sm* idealism. **idealista** *s(m+f)* idealist. **idealistico** *agg* idealistic.

identico [i'dɛntiko] *agg* identical.

identificare [identifi'kare] *v* identify. **identificazione** *sf* identification.

identità [identi'ta] *sf* identity.

ideologia [ideolo'dʒia] *sf* ideology. **ideologico** *agg* ideological.

idillio [i'dilljo] *sm* idyll. **idillico** *agg* idyllic.

idioma [i'djɔma] *sm* language. **frase idiomatica** *sf* idiom.

idiota [i'kjɔta] *s(m+f)* idiot, fool. *agg* idiotic, stupid.

idiotismo [idjo'tizmo] *sm* (*lingua*) idiom; (*med*) idiocy.

idiozia [idjo'tsia] *sf* idiocy; stupidity.

idolo ['idolo] *sm* idol. **idoleggiare** *v* idolize.

idoneo [i'dɔneo] *agg* fit, suitable; (*capace*) able. **non idoneo** unfit, unsuitable. **idoneità** *sf* ability, suitability.

idrante [i'drante] *sm* hydrant. **idratante** *agg* (*crema*) moisturizing.

idraulico [i'drauliko] *agg* hydraulic. *sm* plumber. **idraulica** *sf* hydraulics.

idroelettrico [idroe'lettriko] *agg* hydroelectric.

idroestrattore [idroestrat'tore] *sm* spindrier.

idrofilo [i'drɔfilo] *agg* **cotone idrofilo** *sm* cotton-wool.

idrofobia [idro'fəbia] *sf* rabies, hydrophobia. **idrofobo** *agg* rabid, hydrophobic.

idrogeno [i'drədʒɛno] *sm* hydrogen.

idrosci [idro'ʃi] *sm* water-skiing.

idrovolante [idrovo'lante] *sm* seaplane.

iena ['jɛna] *sf* hyena.

ieri ['jɛri] *avv*, *sm* yesterday. **ieri l'altro** the day before yesterday. **tutto ieri** all day yesterday.

iettatore [jetta'tore] *sm* jinx. **iettatura** *sf* bad luck; (*malocchio*) evil eye.

igiene [i'dʒɛne] *sf* hygiene. **igienico** *agg* hygienic; (*sano*) healthy. **assorbente igienico** *sm* sanitary towel. **carta igienica** *sf* toilet paper.

iglù [i'glu] *sm* igloo.

ignaro [i'ɲaro] *agg* unaware, ignorant.

ignobile [i'ɲəbile] *agg* mean, base.

ignominia [iɲo'minja] *sf* disgrace.

ignorante [iɲo'rante] *agg* ignorant; (*non colto*) uneducated. *s(m+f)* ignoramus. **ignoranza** *sf* ignorance.

ignorare [iɲo'rare] *v* (*non sapere*) not know; (*trascurare, fingere di non conoscere*) ignore.

ignoto [i'ɲɔto] *agg* unknown. *sm* (*concetto*) unknown; (*persona*) unknown person.

ignudo [i'ɲudo] *agg* naked.

il [il] *art* the.

ilare ['ilare] *agg* cheerful. **ilarità** *sf* (*allegria*) cheerfulness; (*riso*) hilarity.

illecito [il'letʃito] *agg* illicit, unlawful.

illegale [ille'gale] *agg* illegal, unlawful. **illegalità** *sf* illegality.

illeggibile [illed'dʒibile] *agg* illegible; (*fig*) unreadable.

illegittimo [ille'dʒittimo] *agg* illegitimate. **illegittimità** *sf* illegitimacy.

illeso [il'lɛzo] *agg* unhurt.

illibato [illi'bato] *agg* pure, chaste.

illimitato [illimi'tato] *agg* unlimited, boundless.

illogico [il'lɔdʒiko] *agg* illogical, unsound. **illogicità** *sf* illogicality.

*****illudere** [il'ludere] *v* deceive, fool. **illudersi** *v* delude oneself.

illuminare [illumi'nare] *v* light, illuminate; (*rischiarare*) light up; (*mostrare la verità*) enlighten; (*a giorno*) floodlight. **illuminazione** *sf* illumination, lighting. **illuminismo** *sm* Enlightenment.

illusione [illu'zjone] *sf* illusion; impression. **farsi (delle) illusioni** delude oneself;

(*fam*) kid oneself. **non farsi (delle) illusioni** have no illusions. **illusionista** *s(m+f)* conjurer.

illusorio [illu'zɔrjo] *agg* illusory, vain.

illustrare [illus'trare] *v* illustrate; (*spiegare*) explain. **illustrativo** *agg* explanatory. **illustrato** *agg* illustrated. **illustratore, -trice** *sm*, *sf* illustrator. **illustrazione** *sf* illustration, explanation.

illustre [il'lustre] *agg* famous, illustrious. **illustre ignoto** *sm* nobody.

imbaccucare [imbakuk'kare] *v* wrap up.

imballare¹ [imbal'lare] *v* pack; (*involucro*) wrap; (*in scatole*) box; (*in casse*) crate. **imballaggio** *sm* packing; wrapping; boxing; crating.

imballare² [imbal'lare] *v* (*auto*) race.

imbalsamare [imbalsa'mare] *v* embalm. **imbalsamatore, -trice** *sm*, *sf* embalmer; (*di animali*) taxidermist.

imbambolato [imbambo'lato] *agg* bewildered.

imbandierare [imbandje'rare] *v* deck with flags.

imbandire [imban'dire] *v* prepare.

imbarazzare [imbarat'tsare] *v* embarrass; (*impedire*) hamper; (*ostacolare*) block, hinder. **imbarazzo** *sm* embarrassment; (*impaccio*) hindrance, trouble. **essere in imbarazzo** be in a difficult situation, be in a fix; (*scelta difficile*) be in a quandary. **mettere in imbarazzo** (*in situazione difficile*) put in a spot; (*a disagio*) make ill at ease.

imbarcare [imbar'kare] *v* take aboard. **imbarcarsi** *v* embark. **imbarcazione** *sf* craft, boat. **imbarco** *sm* embarkation; (*merci*) shipment.

imbastire [imbas'tire] *v* (*cucire*) tack; (*tracciare sommariamente*) draw up, outline.

imbattersi [im'battersi] *v* come across; (*fam*) bump into.

imbattibile [imbat'tibile] *agg* invincible, unbeatable.

imbavagliare [imbava'ʎare] *v* gag.

imbecille [imbe'tʃille] *agg* stupid, idiotic. *s(m+f)* fool, idiot; (*med*) imbecile.

imbellettare [imbellet'tare] *v* make up; (*fig*) embellish.

imbellire [imbel'lire] *v* beautify.

imbevuto [imbe'vuto] *agg* steeped (in), imbued (with).

imbiancare [imbjan'kare] *v* whiten; (*muri*)

whitewash; (*candeggiare*) bleach. **imbianchino** *sm* house-painter.

imbizzarrirsi [imbiddzar'rirsi] *v* get excited.

imboccare [imbok'kare] *v* (*cibo*) feed; (*suggerire*) prompt; enter; (*portare alla bocca*) put to one's mouth. **imboccatura** *sf* mouth; entrance; (*bocchino*) mouthpiece.

imbonire [imbo'nire] *v* entice, talk into buying. **imbonimento** *sm* (*discorso*) salestalk; (*elogio immeritato*) build-up.

imboscata [imbos'kata] *sf* ambush. **imboscato** *sm* shirker, (draft-)dodger.

imbottigliare [imbotti'ʎare] *v* bottle; (*mil*) blockade; (*traffico*) jam.

imbottire [imbot'tire] *v* stuff; (*sarto*) pad, wad. **coperta imbottita** *sf* quilt. **panino imbottito** *sm* sandwich. **imbottitura** *sf* stuffing; padding; wadding.

imbrattare [imbrat'tare] *v* soil, dirty.

imbrigliare [imbri'ʎare] *v* bridle.

imbroccare [imbrok'kare] *v* (*azzeccare*) get right.

imbrogliare [imbro'ʎare] *v* (*gabbare*) cheat; (*mettere in disordine*) mix up, muddle up; (*ingarbugliare*) tangle (up). **imbroglio** *sm* (*faccenda confusa*) muddle, mess; (*groviglio*) tangle; (*raggiro*) trick, swindle. **imbroglione, -a** *sm, sf* cheat, trickster, swindler.

imbronciarsi [imbron'tʃarsi] *v* sulk; (*cielo*) cloud over.

imbrunire [imbru'nire] *v* darken, get dark. *sm* nightfall.

imbruttire [imbrut'tire] *v* spoil.

imbucare [imbu'kare] *v* post.

imburrare [imbur'rare] *v* butter.

imbuto [im'buto] *sm* funnel.

imitare [imi'tare] *v* imitate. **imitazione** *sf* imitation.

immagazzinare [immagaddzi'nare] *v* store.

immaginare [immadʒi'nare] *v* imagine. **s'immagini!** (*tutt'altro*) not in the least! (*certamente*) by all means! **immaginario** *agg* imaginary. **immaginazione** *sf* imagination.

immagine [im'madʒine] *sf* image; (*figura, ritratto*) picture. **immagine riflessa** reflection.

immancabile [imman'kabile] *agg* unfailing, certain.

immangiabile [imman'dʒabile] *agg* inedible, uneatable.

immatricolarsi [immatriko'larsi] *v* register, enrol.

immaturo [imma'turo] *agg* unripe; (*fig*) immature; (*prematuro*) untimely.

immedesimarsi [immedezi'marsi] *v* identify oneself (with).

immediato [imme'djato] *agg* immediate. **immediatamente** *avv* immediately; directly; (*subito*) at once.

immemorabile [immemo'rabile] *agg* immemorial.

immemore [im'mɛmore] *agg* heedless, forgetful.

immenso [im'mɛnso] *agg* huge, vast; enormous. **immensità** *sf* hugeness, immensity; (*gran numero*) mass, enormous number.

*****immergere** [im'mɛrdʒere] *v* immerse; (*intingere*) dip; (*con forza, tuffare*) plunge; (*sottomarino*) submerge. **immersione** *sf* immersion; (*tuffo*) dive.

immeritato [immeri'tato] *agg* undeserved.

immeritevole *agg* undeserving.

*****immettere** [im'mettere] *v* admit, introduce.

immigrare [immi'grare] *v* immigrate. **immigrante** *s(m+f)*, *agg* immigrant. **immigrato, -a** *s, agg* immigrant. **immigrazione** *sf* immigration.

imminente [immi'nɛnte] *agg* imminent. **imminenza** *sf* imminence.

immischiare [immis'kjare] *v* involve, mix up. **immischiarsi** *v* get involved, interfere.

immobile [im'mɔbile] *agg* (*che non si muove*) motionless, still; (*che non si può muovere*) immovable. **società immobiliare** *sf* building society. **immobilità** *sf* immobility, stillness. **beni immobili** *sm pl* real estate *sing*.

immobilizzare [immobilid'dzare] *v* immobilize; (*econ*) tie up.

immoderato [immode'rato] *agg* excessive. **immoderatezza** *sf* excessiveness; (*smoderatezza*) lack of moderation.

immodesto [immo'desto] *agg* conceited, immodest.

immolare [immo'lare] *v* sacrifice.

immondo [im'mondo] *agg* filthy. **immondezzaio** *sm* rubbish dump. **immondizia** *sf* (*sporcizia*) filth; (*spazzatura*) rubbish, garbage.

immorale [immo'rale] *agg* immoral.

immortale [immor'tale] *agg* immortal. **immortalare** *v* immortalize. **immortalità** *sf* immortality.

immune [im'mune] *agg* immune, free. **immunità** *sf* immunity. **immunizzare** *v* immunize.

immutabile [immu'tabile] *agg* immutable, unchangeable; (*costante*) unswerving. **immutabilità** *sf* immutability; firmness. **immutato** *agg* unchanged, unfailing.

impacchettare [impakket'tare] *v* parcel up, package.

impacciare [impat'tʃare] *v* hamper, hinder. **impaccio** *sm* obstacle, hindrance; (*situazione imbarazzante*) fix, predicament. **impacciato** *agg* awkward; (*imbarazzato*) ill at ease; (*goffo*) clumsy.

impadronirsi [impadro'nirsi] *v* **impadronirsi di** seize, take possession of; (*imparare a fondo*) master.

impagabile [impa'gabile] *agg* invaluable, priceless.

impalcatura [impalka'tura] *sf* (*struttura provvisoria*) scaffolding; (*struttura di sostegno*) framework; (*cervo*) antlers *pl*.

impallidire [impalli'dire] *v* turn pale; (*fig*) fade; (*offuscarsi*) grow dim.

impanare[1] [impa'nare] *v* (*mec*) thread.

impanare[2] [impa'nare] *v* (*gastr*) dip in breadcrumbs.

impannata [impan'nata] *sf* window-frame.

impantanarsi [impanta'narsi] *v* get bogged down.

imparare [impa'rare] *v* learn. **imparare a memoria** learn by heart.

impareggiabile [impared'dʒabile] *agg* incomparable.

impari ['impari] *agg invar* unequal.

impartire [impar'tire] *v* give, impart.

imparziale [impar'tsjale] *agg* impartial, unbiased; (*giusto*) fair.

impassibile [impas'sibile] *agg* impassive, unmoved.

impastare [impas'tare] *v* (*pane*) knead; (*lavorare*) mix; (*incollare*) paste. **impastatrice** *sf* mixer. **impasto** *sm* mixture.

impatto [im'patto] *sm* impact.

impaurire [impau'rire] *v* frighten.

impaziente [impa'tsjente] *agg* impatient; (*desideroso*) anxious. **impazientirsi** *v* lose one's patience.

impazzare [impat'tsare] *v* be in full swing; (*gastr*) curdle. **all'impazzata** wildly.

impazzire [impat'tsire] *v* go mad. **far impazzire** drive mad.

impeccabile [impek'kabile] *agg* impeccable.

impedire [impe'dire] *v* prevent; (*sbarrare*) block; (*impacciare*) hinder. **impedimento** *sm* impediment; obstacle; (*l'impedire*) prevention.

impegnare [impe'ɲare] *v* (*dare in pegno*) pledge; (*tenere impegnato*) engage; (*obbligare*) bind; (*tenere occupato*) take up; (*prenotare*) book. **impegnarsi** *v* undertake, strive. **impegnativo** *agg* (*lavoro*) exacting, demanding; (*promessa*) binding. **impegnato** *agg* engaged; (*vincolato*) pledged; (*pol*) committed. **impegno** *sm* engagement; obligation; commitment; (*zelo*) eagerness, enthusiasm.

impenetrabile [impene'trabile] *agg* impenetrable, impervious.

impenitente [impeni'tente] *agg* unrepentant. **scapolo impenitente** *sm* confirmed bachelor.

impennarsi [impen'narsi] *v* flare up; (*cavallo*) rear (up); (*aereo*) go into a climb.

impensabile [impen'sabile] *agg* unthinkable.

impensato [impen'sato] *agg* unforeseen.

impensierirsi [impensje'rirsi] *v* worry.

imperativo [impera'tivo] *sm, agg* imperative. **imperare** *v* rule.

imperatore [impera'tore] *sm* emperor. **imperatrice** *sf* empress.

impercettibile [impertʃet'tibile] *agg* imperceptible.

imperdonabile [imperdo'nabile] *agg* unforgivable.

imperfetto [imper'fetto] *agg* faulty, defective. *sm* imperfect (tense). **imperfezione** *sf* defect.

imperioso [impe'rjozo] *agg* imperious; (*ineluttabile*) pressing, impelling.

impermalirsi [imperma'lirsi] *v* take umbrage, take offence.

impermeabile [imperme'abile] *sm* raincoat. *agg* impervious; (*all'acqua*) waterproof; (*all'aria*) airtight. **impermeabilizzare** *v* waterproof.

imperniare [imper'ɲare] *v* hinge; (*fondare*) base.

impero [im'pero] *sm* (*territorio*) empire; (*autorità*) rule.

imperscrutabile [imperskru'tabile] *agg* inscrutable.

impersonale [imperso'nale] *agg* impersonal.

impersonare [imperso'nare] v (simboleggiare) personify; (attore) impersonate. impersonarsi v be the personification (of).

imperterrito [imper'territo] agg undaunted; unperturbed.

impertinente [imperti'nɛnte] agg impertinent, cheeky.

imperturbabile [impertur'babile] agg unruffled, imperturbable, calm. imperturbato agg unperturbed, unruffled.

impeto ['impeto] sm impetus, force; (accesso) outburst. agire d'impeto act on impulse.

impettito [impet'tito] agg stiff, erect. camminare impettito strut.

impetuoso [impe'twozo] agg impetuous.

impiallacciato [impjallat'tʃato] agg veneered. impiallacciatura sf veneer.

impiantare [impjan'tare] v set up; (fondare) establish; (tec) install. impianto sm plant, installation; (fondazione) establishment.

impiantito [impjan'tito] sm flooring.

impiastrare [impjas'trare] v smear. impiastro sm (cataplasma) poultice; (persona uggiosa) bore.

impiccare [impik'kare] v hang. impiccato sm hanged man.

impicciare [impit'tʃare] v be in the way, hamper. impicciarsi v meddle, interfere. impiccio [im'pittʃo] sm (ostacolo) hindrance; (guaio) mess, trouble. essere d'impiccio v be in the way.

impiegare [impje'gare] v employ; spend. impiegatizio agg clerical. impiegato, -a sm, sf employee; (funzionario) official. impiegati pl (collettivo) staff sing, personnel sing.

impiego [im'pjɛgo] sm, pl -ghi use; (denaro) investment; (posto, occupazione) employment, job.

impietrito [impje'trito] agg petrified.

impigliarsi [impiʎ'ʎarsi] v get entangled, get mixed up.

impiparsi [impi'parsi] v (fam) not care a damn.

implacabile [impla'kabile] agg implacable.

implicare [impli'kare] v (coinvolgere) involve; (comportare) imply, entail. implicito [im'plitʃito] agg implicit.

implorare [implo'rare] v implore, entreat.

impolverare [impolve'rare] v cover with dust.

imponderabile [imponde'rabile] agg imponderable.

imponente [impo'nɛnte] agg imposing, impressive.

imponibile [impo'nibile] agg taxable. sm taxable income.

impopolare [impopo'lare] agg unpopular. impopolarità sf unpopularity.

*imporre [im'porre] v impose; (costringere) oblige; (ordinare) order; (comportare) involve. imporsi v (farsi valere) assert oneself; (incontrar favore) go down well; (rendersi necessario) become necessary.

importante [impor'tante] agg important. sm important thing, main point. importanza sf importance. di nessuna importanza unimportant.

importare [impor'tare] v (aver peso) matter; (comportare) involve; (introdurre dall'estero) import. non importa! it doesn't matter! never mind! non me ne importa niente! (fam) I couldn't care less!

importazione [importa'tsjone] sf import; (atto) importation.

importo [im'porto] sm amount.

importunare [importu'nare] v trouble, bother. importuno agg troublesome, tiresome, boring.

imposizione [impozi'tsjone] sf imposition.

impossessarsi [imposses'sarsi] v get hold of, seize.

impossibile [impos'sibile] agg impossible. fare l'impossibile do all one can. impossibilità sf impossibility.

imposta[1] [im'posta] sf (finestra) shutter.

imposta[2] [im'posta] sf (econ) tax, duty.

impostare[1] [impos'tare] v (spedire) post.

impostare[2] [impos'tare] v (avviare) get under way; (questione, ecc.) set out, state; (nave) lay down; (voce) pitch. impostazione sf approach.

impostore [impos'tore] sm imposter.

impotente [impo'tɛnte] agg powerless; (med) impotent. impotenza sf powerlessness; impotence.

impoverire [impove'rire] v impoverish. impoverimento sm impoverishment.

impraticabile [imprati'kabile] agg (strada) impassable; (campo sportivo) unfit for play.

impratichirsi [imprati'kirsi] v practise.

imprecare [impre'kare] v curse. **imprecazione** sf curse.

impreciso [impre't∫izo] agg (inesatto) inaccurate; (indeterminato) imprecise, vague. **imprecisabile** agg indefinable. **imprecisione** sf inaccuracy; vagueness.

impregnare [impre'nare] v impregnate; (fig) imbue; (inzuppare) soak.

imprenditore [imprendi'tore] sm contractor; entrepreneur. **imprenditore di pompe funebri** undertaker. **imprenditore edile** building contractor. **piccolo imprenditore** tradesman.

impreparato [imprepa'rato] agg unprepared; (lavoro) untrained. **impreparazione** sf unpreparedness; lack of training.

impresa [im'preza] sf undertaking, enterprise; (azienda) concern, firm; (azione) deed; (azione pericolosa) exploit. **impresario** sm entrepreneur; (theatre) manager, impresario.

imprescindibile [impre∫in'dibile] agg that cannot be disregarded.

impressionare [impressjo'nare] v make an impression; (spaventare) frighten; (turbare) shock, upset; (foto) expose. **impressionarsi** v be upset, be shocked; be affected. **impressionabile** agg impressionable, easily affected; easily frightened. **impressionante** agg striking, impressive; frightening; upsetting.

impressione [impres'sjone] sf impression; sensation.

imprestare [impres'tare] v lend.

imprevidenza [imprevi'dentsa] sf lack of foresight. **imprevedibile** agg unforeseeable. **imprevidente** agg heedless.

imprevisto [impre'visto] agg unforeseen. **salvo imprevisti** if all goes well.

imprigionare [impridʒo'nare] v imprison.

*imprimere** [im'primere] v imprint, impress; (dare) impart; (pittura) prime.

improbabile [impro'babile] agg unlikely, improbable. **improbabilità** sf unlikelihood.

improduttivo [improdut'tivo] agg unproductive.

impronta [im'pronta] sf impression, mark, stamp. **impronta del piede** footprint. **impronta digitale** fingerprint. **improntare** v stamp. **all'impronto** at sight.

improprio [im'proprjo] agg (inadatto) inappropriate; (inopportuno) out of place; (mat) improper.

improrogabile [improro'gabile] agg termine improrogabile sm deadline.

improvvisare [improvvi'zare] v improvise. **improvvisamente** avv suddenly, all of a sudden. **improvvisata** sf surprise. **improvvisazione** sf improvisation.

imprudente [impru'dente] agg rash, imprudent. **imprudenza** sf imprudence. **commettere un'imprudenza** do something rash.

impudente [impu'dente] agg impudent.

impudico [impu'diko] agg, m pl -chi immodest.

impugnare[1] [impu'nare] v (contestare) challenge; (dir) contest.

impugnare[2] [impu'nare] v (afferrare) grasp. **impugnare le armi** take up arms. **impugnatura** sf handle; (spada) hilt; (racchetta) grip.

impulso [im'pulso] sm impulse. **dare impulso** boost. **impulsivo** agg impulsive.

impunemente [impune'mente] avv with impunity.

impunito [impu'nito] agg (delitto) unpunished.

impuntarsi [impun'tarsi] v refuse to budge, dig one's heels in.

impuro [im'puro] agg impure. **impurità** sf impurity.

imputare [impu'tare] v impute, attribute, ascribe; (dir) charge. **imputabile** agg attributable. **imputato, -a** sm, sf defendant, accused. **imputazione** sf charge.

imputridire [imputri'dire] v rot.

in [in] prep in; (su, sopra) on; (moto a luogo) to; (dentro) into; (moto per luogo) round, through; (entro) within; (durante) during.

inabile [in'abile] agg (non capace) unable, incapable; (non idoneo) unfit; (per infortunio) disabled; (dir) ineligible.

inabitabile [inabi'tabile] agg uninhabitable. **inabitato** agg uninhabited.

inaccessibile [inatt∫es'sibile] agg inaccessible.

inaccettabile [inatt∫et'tabile] agg unacceptable.

inadatto [ina'datto] agg unsuitable (for); (incapace) unfit (for).

inadeguato [inade'gwato] agg insufficient, inadequate.

inalare [ina'lare] v inhale.

inalienabile [:inalje'nabile] agg inalienable.

inalterabile [inalte'rabile] *agg* unchangeable. **inalterato** *agg* unchanged.

inamidare [inami'dare] *v* starch.

inammissibile [innammis'sibile] *agg* inadmissible.

inanimato [inani'mato] *agg* inanimate, lifeless.

inappagabile [innappa'gabile] *agg* insatiable. **inappagato** *agg* unsatisfied.

inapplicabile [inappli'kabile] *agg* inapplicable.

inarcare [inar'kare] *v* arch, bend. **inarcare le sopracciglia** raise one's eyebrows.

inargentare [inardʒen'tare] *v* silver.

inaridire [inari'dire] *v* dry up.

inaspettato [inaspet'tato] *agg* unexpected.

inasprire [inas'prire] *v* exacerbate, make worse.

inattendibile [inatten'dibile] *agg* unreliable.

inatteso [inat'tezo] *agg* unexpected.

inattivo [inat'tivo] *agg* idle.

inattuabile [inat'twabile] *agg* impracticable.

inaudito [inau'dito] *agg* (*non udito prima*) unheard of; incredible, extraordinary.

inaugurare [inaugu'rare] *v* inaugurate, open. **inaugurazione** *sf* inauguration, opening.

inavveduto [inavve'duto] *agg* thoughtless, careless.

inavvertenza [inavver'tɛntsa] *sf* carelessness, oversight.

incagliarsi [inka'ʎarsi] *v* (*mar*) run aground; (*fig*) get stuck.

incalcolabile [inkalko'labile] *agg* incalculable.

incalzare [inkal'tsare] *v* follow closely; (*fig*) press.

incamminare [inkammi'nare] *v* start (off). **incamminarsi** *v* set off; (*avviarsi*) be on the way (to).

incanalare [inkana'lare] *v* channel.

incantare [inkan'tare] *v* enchant, charm. **incantarsi** *v* (*rimanere intontito*) be in a daze; (*mec*) jam, break down. **incantato** *agg* enchanted; (*intontito*) dazed, spellbound. **incantatore, -trice** *sm, sf* charmer. **incantesimo** *sm* charm, spell. **incantevole** *agg* charming, enchanting.

incanto¹ [in'kanto] *sm* spell, magic. **stare d'incanto** suit perfectly.

incanto² [in'kanto] *sm* (*vendita*) auction.

incapace [inka'patʃe] *agg* incapable.

incapacità *sf* inability; (*fisica*) disability; (*dir*) incapacity.

incappare [inkap'pare] *v* run into, come up against.

incarcerare [inkartʃe'rare] *v* imprison, jail.

incaricare [inkari'kare] *v* charge, entrust; order. **incaricarsi** *v* take charge. **incaricato, -a** *sm, sf* person in charge; (*università*) lecturer; (*funzionario*) official.

incarico [in'kariko] *sm, pl* -chi task, assignment, charge.

incarnare [inkar'nare] *v* embody; (*personaggio*) impersonate.

incartare [inkar'tare] *v* wrap (up).

incasellare [inkazel'lare] *v* pigeon-hole.

incassare [inkas'sare] *v* (*riscuotere*) collect, cash; (*sport*) take; (*inserire*) embed. **incasso** *sm* collection; (*entrata*) takings *pl*.

incastellatura [inkastella'tura] *sf* (*impalcatura*) scaffolding; (*mec*) casing.

incastonare [inkasto'nare] *v* set, mount. **incastonatura** *sf* setting, mounting.

incastrare [inkas'trare] *v* wedge, drive; (*imprigionare*) jam, sandwich; (*falegnameria*) mortise. **incastro** *sm* joint; (*cavità*) hollow, recess; mortise.

incatenare [inkate'nare] *v* chain; (*fig*) tie.

incatramare [inkatra'mare] *v* tar.

incauto [in'kauto] *agg* incautious.

incavare [inka'vare] *v* hollow out. **incavo** *sm* hollow; (*scanalatura*) groove.

incendiare [intʃen'djare] *v* set on fire; (*fig*) fire.

incendiario [intʃen'djarjo] *agg* incendiary. *sm* arsonist, fire-raiser.

incendio [in'tʃendjo] *sm* fire. **bocca d'incendio** *sf* (fire) hydrant. **incendio doloso** arson.

incenerire [intʃene'rire] *v* burn down; (*fig*) wither.

incenso [in'tʃɛnso] *sm* incense.

incensurabile [intʃensu'rabile] *agg* beyond reproach. **essere incensurato** have a clean record.

inceppare [intʃep'pare] *v* obstruct, hamper.

incertezza [intʃer'tettsa] *sf* uncertainty; (*dubbio*) doubt; (*indecisione*) hesitation.

incerto [in'tʃerto] *agg* uncertain; dubious; (*indeciso*) hesitant; (*malsicuro*) unsure. *sm* uncertainty.

incespicare [intʃespi'kare] *v* stumble, trip up.

incessante [intʃes'sante] *agg* ceaseless, constant.

incesto [in'tʃesto] *sm* incest. **incestuoso** *agg* incestuous.

incettare [intʃet'tare] *v also* **fare incetto di** corner, buy up. **incetta** *sf* cornering.

inchiesta [in'kjesta] *sf* inquiry, investigation; (*giornalismo*) report; (*scandalo*) probe.

inchinare [inki'nare] *v* bow, bend; (*abbassare*) lower. **inchinarsi** *v* bend down, bow; (*donna*) curtsey. **inchino** *sm* bow, curtsey.

inchiodare [inkjo'dare] *v* nail.

inchiostro [in'kjostro] *sm* ink. **inchiostro di china** Indian ink.

inciampare [intʃam'pare] *v* stumble (over), trip up. **inciampo** *sm* obstacle, stumbling block.

incidente [intʃi'dɛnte] *sm* (*episodio*) incident; (*infortunio*) accident; (*disputa*) argument.

incidenza [intʃi'dɛntsa] *sf* incidence.

****incidere**[1] [in'tʃidere] *v* cut (into); carve; (*intagliare*) engrave; (*ad acquaforte*) etch; (*registrare*) record; (*med*) incise, lance. **incisione** *sf* incision; cut; engraving; etching; recording. **incisivo** *agg* incisive. **per inciso** by the way, incidentally. **incisore** *sm* engraver.

****incidere**[2] [in'tʃidere] *v* **incidere su** affect.

incinta [in'tʃinta] *agg* pregnant.

incipriare [intʃi'prjare] *v* powder.

incitare [intʃi'tare] *v* incite. **incitamento** *sm* incitement, spur.

incivile [intʃi'vile] *agg* uncivilized; (*villano*) boorish, uncivil.

incivilire [intʃivi'lire] *v* civilize.

inclemente [inkle'mente] *agg* harsh.

inclinare [inkli'nare] *v* incline; (*propendere*) tend, be inclined. **inclinazione** *sf* inclination; (*pendenza*) slope; (*disposizione d'animo*) leaning; (*simpatia*) liking; (*strada*) gradient. **incline** *agg* prone.

****includere** [in'kludere] *v* (*comprendere*) include; (*accludere*) enclose; (*implicare*) imply. **inclusione** *sf* inclusion. **incluso** *agg* included; (*comm*) inclusive.

incoerente [inkoe'rɛnte] *agg* incoherent; (*fig*) inconsistent.

incognita [in'kɔɲita] *sf* (*matematica*) unknown; (*fatto imprevedibile*) unknown factor, uncertainty; (*persona*) mystery, dark horse.

incognito [in'kɔɲito] *agg* unknown. *sm* incognito; (*ignoto*) unknown.

incollare [inkol'lare] *v* (*attaccare*) glue; (*spalmare*) paste.

incolore [inko'lore] *agg* colourless.

incolpare [inkol'pare] *v* blame.

incolto [in'kolto] *agg* (*non coltivato*) uncultivated; (*trascurato*) untidy; (*privo di cultura*) uncultured.

incolume [in'kɔlume] *agg* unharmed.

incombente [inkom'bɛnte] *agg* (*imminente*) impending; (*spettante*) incumbent.

incominciare [inkomin'tʃare] *v* begin, start. (**tanto**) **per cominciare** to begin with.

incomodo [in'kɔmodo] *agg* (*disagevole*) uncomfortable; (*inopportuno*) inconvenient. *sm* trouble, inconvenience. **il terzo incomodo** the odd man out. **incomodare** *v* inconvenience, trouble.

incomparabile [inkompa'rabile] *agg* incomparable.

incompatibile [inkompa'tibile] *agg* incompatible. **incompatibilità** *sf* incompatibility.

incompetente [inkompe'tɛnte] *agg* incompetent. *s(m+f)* incompetent person.

incompiuto [inkom'pjuto] *agg* unfinished.

incompleto [inkom'pleto] *agg* incomplete.

incomprensibile [inkompren'sibile] *agg* incomprehensible. **incomprensibilità** *sf* incomprehensibility.

incompreso [inkom'prezo] *agg* misunderstood.

inconcepibile [inkontʃe'pibile] *agg* inconceivable.

inconciliabile [inkontʃi'ljabile] *agg* irreconcilable.

inconcludente [inkonklu'dɛnte] *agg* inconclusive.

incondizionato [inkonditsjo'nato] *agg* unconditional; (*pieno*) complete.

inconsapevole [inkonsa'pevole] *agg* unaware, unconscious.

inconscio [in'kɔnʃo] *agg* unconscious; (*persona*) unaware. *sm invar* unconscious.

inconsiderabile [inkonside'rabile] *agg* negligible. **inconsiderato** *agg* thoughtless. **inconsideratezza** *sf* thoughtlessness. **inconsistente** [inkonsis'tɛnte] *agg* flimsy; (*infondato*) groundless.

inconsolabile [inkonso'labile] *agg* inconsolable.

inconsueto [inkonsu'eto] *agg* unusual.

incontenibile [inkonte'nibile] *agg* uncontrollable.

incontentabile [inkonten'tabile] *agg* hard to please, exacting.

incontrare [inkon'trare] *v* meet; (*esser popolare*) be a success. **incontrar favore** find favour. **incontrarsi per caso** run into.

incontrario [inkon'trarjo] *sm* **all'incontrario** (*a rovescio*) the wrong way round.

incontrastato [inkontras'tato] *agg* unopposed.

incontro¹ [in'kontro] *sm* meeting; (*partita*) match; (*gioco*) game; (*favore*) reception, success. **incontro alla pari** (*sport*) tie, draw.

incontro² [in'kontro] *avv* towards. **all'incontro** on the contrary. **andare incontro a** go towards, approach; (*fig*) meet halfway.

incontrollabile [inkontrol'labile] *agg* uncontrollable.

inconveniente [inkonve'njente] *sm* drawback, snag.

incoraggiare [inkorad'dʒare] *v* encourage.

incorniciare [inkorni'tʃare] *v* frame.

incoronare [inkoro'nare] *v* crown. **incoronazione** *sf* coronation.

incorporare [inkorpo'rare] *v* incorporate, annex.

incorreggibile [inkorred'dʒibile] *agg* incorrigible.

*incorrere [in'korrere] *v* incur.

incorruttibile [inkorrut'tibile] *agg* incorruptible.

incosciente [inko'ʃente] *agg* unconscious; (*sconsiderato*) irresponsible.

incredibile [inkre'dibile] *agg* incredible, unbelievable.

incredulo [in'kredulo] *agg* incredulous, disbelieving.

incremento [inkre'mento] *sm* (*aumento*) increase; (*sviluppo*) growth, expansion; (*mat*) increment. **incrementare** *v* increase; (*far prosperare*) promote.

increspare [inkres'pare] *v* (*acqua*) ripple; (*capelli*) curl. **increspare la fronte** frown.

incrinare [inkri'nare] *v* crack.

incrociare [inkro'tʃare] *v* cross. **incrociatore** *sm* cruiser. **incrocio** *sm* crossing; (*accoppiamento*) cross-breeding; (*frutto*) cross, hybrid.

incrostato [inkros'tato] *agg* encrusted.

incubatrice [inkuba'tritʃe] *sf* incubator. **incubazione** *sf* incubation.

incubo ['inkubo] *sm* nightmare.

incudine [in'kudine] *sf* anvil.

inculcare [inkul'kare] *v* inculcate.

incuneare [inkune'are] *v* wedge.

incurabile [inku'rabile] *agg* incurable.

incurante [inku'rante] *agg* heedless, unconcerned.

incuriosire [inkurjo'zire] *v* arouse curiosity.

incursione [inkur'sjone] *sf* incursion, raid. **incursione aerea** air-raid.

incustodito [inkusto'dito] *agg* unattended.

indagare [inda'gare] *v* investigate, inquire into. **indagine** *sf* inquiry, investigation; (*scientifica*) research; (*studio*) survey.

indebitamente [indebita'mente] *avv* unduly; (*ingiustamente*) unlawfully.

indebitarsi [indebi'tarsi] *v* run into debt. **indebitato** *agg* indebted.

indebolire [indebo'lire] *v* weaken. **indebolimento** *sm* weakening; (*debolezza*) weakness.

indecente [inde'tʃente] *agg* indecent. **indecenza** *sf* indecency; (*vergogna*) disgrace.

indecifrabile [indetʃi'frabile] *agg* illegible.

indecisione [indetʃi'zjone] *sf* indecision.

indeciso [inde'tʃizo] *agg* undecided; (*non risolto, instabile*) unsettled.

indefesso [inde'fesso] *agg* tireless.

indefinibile [indefi'nibile] *agg* indefinable.

indefinito [indefi'nito] *agg* indefinite; (*non risolto*) unsettled.

indegno [in'deɲo] *agg* unworthy. **indegnità** *sf* base action.

indelicato [indeli'kato] *agg* tactless; indiscreet.

indemagliabile [indema'ʎabile] *agg* nonrun, ladder-proof.

indenne [in'denne] *agg* unharmed, unscathed.

indennità [indenni'ta] *sf* (*risarcimento*) allowance; (*dir*) indemnity. **indennizzare** *v* compensate. **indennizzo** *sm* compensation.

inderogabile [indero'gabile] *agg* binding, irrevocable.

indescrivibile [indeskri'vibile] *agg* indescribable.

indesiderabile [indeside'rabile] *agg* undesirable.

indeterminabile [indetermi'nabile] *agg* indeterminate, imprecise.

indi ['indi] *avv* (*dopo*) then; (*da quel luogo*) from there. **indi a poco** soon after.

India ['indja] *sf* India. **indiano, -a** *s, agg* Indian.

indiavolato [indjavo'lato] *agg* (*molto agitato*) wild; (*eccessivo*) awful; (*indemoniato*) frenzied.

indicare [indi'kare] *v* indicate, show; (*significare*) mean. **indicativo** *agg* indicative. **indicato** *agg* indicated; (*adatto*) suitable.

indicatore [indika'tore] *sm* indicator; (*tec*) gauge; (*stradale*) signpost.

indicazione [indika'tsjone] *sf* indication; (*dato, notizia*) information; (*istruzione per l'uso*) direction.

indice ['inditfe] *sm* index; (*dito*) index finger; (*tec*) pointer.

indietreggiare [indjetred'dʒare] *v* draw back, withdraw.

indietro [in'djetro] *avv* (*in arretrato*) in arrears; (*debole*) weak; (*moto*) back(wards).

indifeso [indi'fezo] *agg* undefended; (*fig*) defenceless.

indifferente [indiffe'rɛnte] *agg* indifferent; (*lo stesso*) all the same; (*che non interessa*) unimportant. **indifferenza** *sf* indifference, lack of interest.

indigeno [in'didʒeno] *sm, agg* native.

indigesto [indi'dʒesto] *agg* indigestible; (*non digerito*) undigested.

indignare [indi'ɲare] *v* fill with indignation.

indimenticabile [indimenti'kabile] *agg* unforgettable.

indipendente [indipen'dɛnte] *agg* independent. **indipendenza** *sf* independence.

*indire [in'dire] *v* announce; (*radunare*) call.

indiretto [indi'retto] *agg* indirect.

indirizzare [indirit'tsare] *v* address; (*rivolgere*) direct. **indirizzo** *sm* address; (*tendenza*) trend; direction.

indisciplinato [indiʃipli'nato] *agg* undisciplined.

indiscreto [indis'kreto] *agg* indiscreet.

indiscusso [indis'kusso] *agg* beyond dispute, incontrovertible.

indispensabile [indispen'sabile] *agg* indispensable, essential.

indispettire [indispet'tire] *v* irritate.

indisposizione [indispozi'tsjone] *sf* indisposition, slight illness. **indisposto** *agg* indisposed, unwell.

indistinto [indis'tinto] *agg* indistinct. **indistinguibile** *agg* indistinguishable.

indivia [in'divja] *sf* endive.

individuale [individu'ale] *agg* individual.

individuare [individu'are] *v* (*determinare*) locate; (*riconoscere*) single out; (*scoprire*) discover, recognize.

individuo [indi'viduo] *sm* person; (*spreg*) fellow, character.

indivisibile [indivi'zibile] *agg* indivisible. **indiviso** *agg* undivided.

indizio [in'ditsjo] *sm* sign, indication; (*dir*) (circumstantial) evidence.

indole ['indole] *sf* nature, character.

indolenzire [indolen'tsire] *v* make sore, make ache. **indolenzito** *agg* sore, aching.

indomani [indo'mani] *sm* **l'indomani** the following day.

indossare [indos'sare] *v* (*mettersi indosso*) put on; (*portare*) wear. **indossatrice** *sf* model. **indosso** *avv* on.

indotto [in'dotto] *agg* induced.

indovinare [indovi'nare] *v* guess. **indovinato** *agg* (*riuscito*) successful; (*che sta bene*) becoming. **indovinello** *sm* puzzle, riddle. **indovino, -a** *sm, sf* fortuneteller.

indù [in'du] *s(m+f)*, *agg* Hindu.

indubbio [in'dubbjo] *agg* certain, unmistakable.

indubitabile [indubi'tabile] *agg* unquestionable. **indubitato** *agg* certain, unquestioned.

indugiare [indu'dʒare] *v* delay; (*soffermarsi*) linger over. **indugio** *sm* delay.

indulgente [indul'dʒɛnte] *agg* lenient. **indulgenza** *sf* indulgence.

indumento [indu'mento] *sm* garment.

indurire [indu'rire] *v* harden. **indurimento** *sm* hardening.

*indurre [in'durre] *v* induce. **indurre in errore** mislead; (*fig*) lead astray. **indurre in tentazione** lead into temptation.

industria [in'dustrja] *sf* industry; (*attività industriale*) business.

industriale [indus'trjale] *agg* industrial. *sm* industrialist, manufacturer. **industrializzare** *v* industrialize. **industrializzazione** *sf* industrialization.

inebriare [inebri'are] v intoxicate.

inedito [in'edito] agg unpublished.

ineducato [inedu'kato] agg ill-mannered.

ineguale [ine'gwale] agg unequal; (non uniforme) uneven.

ineluttabile [inelut'tabile] agg relentless; (inevitabile) unavoidable.

inerente [ine'rɛnte] agg (riferentesi) concerning; (implicito) inherent.

inerme [i'nɛrme] agg unarmed; (senza difesa) defenceless.

inerpicarsi [inerpi'karsi] v scramble up.

inerte [i'nɛrte] agg inert. **inerzia** sf sluggishness; (fis) inertia.

inesatto [ine'zatto] agg (sbagliato) wrong, incorrect; (imprecise) inaccurate.

inesistente [inezis'tɛnte] agg non-existent.

inesorabile [inezo'rabile] agg inexorable.

inesperienza [insper'jɛntsa] sf inexperience.

inesperto [ines'pɛrto] agg inexperienced.

inesplicabile [inespli'kabile] agg inexplicable.

inespressivo [inespres'sivo] agg expressionless.

inesprimibile [inespri'mibile] agg indescribable.

inetto [i'nɛtto] agg inept, inadequate; (incapace) unsuited (to), incapable (of).

inevaso [ine'vazo] agg outstanding.

inevitabile [inevi'tabile] agg unavoidable.

inezia [i'nɛtsja] sf trifle.

infagottare [infagot'tare] v bundle up, wrap up.

infallibile [infal'libile] agg infallible. **infallibilità** sf infallibility.

infame [in'fame] agg infamous, vile. **infamia** sf infamy, disgrace.

infangare [infan'gare] v muddy.

infante [in'fante] s(m+f) infant, newborn baby. **infantile** agg childlike; (puerile) childish, infantile. **asilo infantile** sm nursery school. **infanzia** sf infancy, childhood.

infarcire [infar'tʃire] v stuff.

infarinare [infari'nare] v (dip in) flour. **infarinatura** sf coating of flour; (fig) smattering.

infastidire [infasti'dire] v bother, trouble.

infaticabile [infati'kabile] agg tireless.

infatti [in'fatti] cong in fact, as a matter of fact, indeed.

infatuarsi [infatu'arsi] v become infatuated (with); fall (for).

infausto [in'fausto] agg inauspicious, unlucky.

infedele [infe'dele] agg unfaithful.

infelice [infe'litʃe] agg unhappy; (inopportuno) unfortunate; (disgraziato) wretched, unlucky; (cattivo) bad. s(m+f) unhappy person, wretch.

inferiore [infe'rjore] agg lower; (di grado più basso) inferior; (numeri) below, less than. **inferiorità** sf inferiority.

inferire [infe'rire] v (arrecare) inflict, cause; (dedurre) infer.

infermeria [inferme'ria] sf infirmary. **infermiere, -a** sm, sf nurse. **infermità** sf illness. **infermo** agg invalid.

inferno [in'fɛrno] sm hell. **infernale** agg infernal, hellish.

inferriata [infer'rjata] sf grille.

infestare [infes'tare] v infest.

infettare [infet'tare] v infect; (fig) taint. **infettivo** agg infectious, catching. **infezione** sf infection.

infiacchire [infjak'kire] v weaken.

infiammare [infjam'mare] v set on fire; (eccitare, med) inflame. **infiammabile** agg inflammable. **infiammazione** sf inflammation.

infido [in'fido] agg untrustworthy.

infierire [infje'rire] v rage.

infilare [infi'lare] v thread, string; (introdurre) insert; (imboccare) turn into, take. **infilata** sf row, string.

infiltrarsi [infil'trarsi] v infiltrate.

infimo [i'nfimo] agg (the) lowest.

infine [in'fine] avv in the end, finally.

infinito [infi'nito] agg infinite; (interminabile) endless; (innumerevole) countless. sm infinity; (gramm) infinitive. **infinità** sf infinity; (gran numero) large number, crowd.

infischiarsi [infis'kjarsi] v not give a damn.

infisso [in'fisso] sm frame.

inflazione [infla'tsjone] sf inflation.

inflessibile [infles'sibile] agg inflexible. **inflessione** sf inflection.

*****infliggere** [in'fliddʒere] v inflict.

influenza [influ'ɛntsa] sf influence; (med) influenza, flu. **influenzare** v influence.

influire [influ'ire] v have an influence. **influire su** affect, influence. **influsso** sm influence.

infondato [infon'dato] agg groundless, unfounded.

*__infondere__ [in'fondere] v instil, inspire.

__informare__ [infor'mare] v inform, tell; (*plasmare*) form, shape. __informarsi__ v inquire, find out. __informazione__ sf information.

__informe__ [in'forme] agg shapeless.

__informicolirsi__ [informiko'lirsi] v have pins and needles.

__infortunio__ [infor'tunjo] sm accident.

__infossato__ [infos'sato] agg hollow.

*__inframmettersi__ [infram'mettersi] v interfere.

*__infrangere__ [in'frandʒere] v break. __infrangibile__ agg unbreakable.

__infrazione__ [infra'tsjone] sf infringement, breach.

__infreddarsi__ [infred'darsi] v catch a cold. __infreddatura__ sf cold.

__infrequente__ [infre'qwente] agg infrequent.

__infuori__ [in'fwori] avv __all'infuori di__ apart from, except.

__infuriare__ [infu'rjare] v rage. __infuriarsi__ v fly into a temper.

__ingannare__ [ingan'nare] v deceive; (*truffare*) cheat; (*essere infedele*) be unfaithful. __inganno__ sm deceit, deception, trick.

__ingarbugliarsi__ [ingarbu'ʎarsi] v get entangled.

__ingegnarsi__ [indʒe'narsi] v get by, manage.

__ingegnere__ [indʒe'nere] sm engineer. __ingegneria__ sf engineering.

__ingegno__ [in'dʒeno] sm genius, talent. __ingegnoso__ agg ingenious, clever.

__ingenuo__ [in'dʒenwo] agg ingenuous, naive. sm naive person. __fare l'ingenuo__ feign innocence; pretend not to understand.

__ingerirsi__ [indʒe'rirsi] v meddle, interfere.

__ingessare__ [indʒes'sare] v put in plaster.

__Inghilterra__ [ingil'terra] sf England.

__inghiottire__ [ingjot'tire] v swallow.

__inginocchiarsi__ [indʒinok'kjarsi] v kneel (down).

__ingiuria__ [in'dʒurja] sf offence; insult; (*fig*) damage. __ingiuriare__ v insult; (*oltraggiare*) offend. __ingiurioso__ agg insulting, offensive.

__ingiusto__ [in'dʒusto] agg unjust; unfair.

__inglese__ [in'gleze] sm (*persona*) Englishman; (*lingua*) English. sf Englishwoman. agg English. __filare all'inglese__ take French leave. __zuppa inglese__ sf trifle.

__ingoiare__ [ingo'jare] v gulp (down), swallow (down).

__ingolfarsi__ [ingol'farsi] v (*auto*) flood; (*debiti*) be swamped.

__ingombrare__ [ingomb'rare] v obstruct, get in the way.

__ingombro__ [in'gombro] agg cluttered (with). sm obstruction; (*spazio*) space.

__ingommare__ [ingom'mare] v stick.

__ingordo__ [in'gordo] agg greedy. __ingordigia__ sf greed.

__ingorgarsi__ [ingor'garsi] v be blocked up. __ingorgo__ sm obstruction; (traffic) jam.

__ingranare__ [ingra'nare] v engage; (*fam*) get on. __ingranaggio__ sm (*mec*) gear; (*fig*) works pl, mechanism.

__ingrandire__ [ingran'dire] v enlarge, magnify. __ingrandimento__ sm enlargement.

__ingrassare__ [ingras'sare] v fatten, make fat; (*ungere*) grease. __ingrassarsi__ v put on weight, get fat; (*arricchirsi*) profit.

__ingrato__ [in'grato] agg ungrateful; (*sgradevole*) thankless. __ingratitudine__ sf ingratitude.

__ingrediente__ [ingre'djente] sm ingredient.

__ingresso__ [in'gresso] sm entrance; admission.

__ingrossare__ [ingros'sare] v swell.

__ingrosso__ [in'grosso] avv __all'ingrosso__ wholesale.

__ingualcibile__ [ingwal'tʃibile] agg crease-resistant.

__inguaribile__ [ingwa'ribile] agg incurable.

__inguine__ ['ingwine] sm groin.

__inibire__ [ini'bire] v inhibit, forbid. __inibizione__ sf inhibition.

__iniettare__ [injet'tare] v inject. __iniezione__ sf injection.

__inimicizia__ [inimi'tʃitsja] sf enmity, hostility.

__inimitabile__ [inimi'tabile] agg inimitable.

__inimmaginabile__ [inimmadʒi'nabile] agg unimaginable.

__inintelligibile__ [inintelli'dʒibile] agg unintelligible.

__ininterrotto__ [ininter'rotto] agg uninterrupted, continuous.

__iniziale__ [ini'tsjale] agg initial. sf initial (letter).

__iniziare__ [ini'tsjare] v start, begin; (*avviare*) initiate. __iniziativa__ sf initiative, enterprise. __inizio__ sm beginning.

__innaffiare__ [innaf'fjare] v water.

__innalzare__ [innal'tsare] v raise.

__innamorarsi__ [innamo'rarsi] v fall in love (with).

innanzi [in'nantsi] *prep* before. **innanzi tutto** first of all; (*sopratutto*) above all. *avv* (*prima*) before; (*avanti*) on, ahead. **d'ora innanzi** from now on, henceforth.

innato [in'nato] *agg* innate.

innegabile [inne'gabile] *agg* undeniable.

innestare [innes'tare] *v* (*piante*) graft; insert; (*med*) inoculate. **innestare una marcia** (*auto*) put into gear. **innesto** *sm* graft; (*auto*) clutch; (*med*) inoculation.

inno ['inno] *sm* hymn. **inno nazionale** national anthem.

innocente [inno'tʃente] *agg* innocent. **dichiararsi innocente** (*dir*) plead not guilty. **innocenza** *sf* innocence.

innocuo [in'nɔkuo] *agg* innocuous, harmless.

innominabile [innomi'nabile] *agg* unmentionable.

innovare [inno'vare] *v* innovate. **innovatore**, **-trice** *sm*, *sf* innovator. **innovazione** *sf* innovation.

innumerevole [innume'revole] *agg* innumerable.

inoculare [inoku'lare] *v* inoculate.

inoffensivo [inoffen'sivo] *agg* inoffensive, harmless.

inoltrare [inol'trare] *v* send on, forward. **inoltrarsi** *v* advance.

inoltre [i'noltre] *avv* besides, furthermore.

inondare [inon'dare] *v* flood. **inondazione** *sf* flood.

inoperoso [inope'rozo] *agg* idle; (*econ*) unemployed.

inopportuno [inoppor'tuno] *agg* untimely; inopportune. **inopportunità** *sf* unsuitability; inappropriateness.

inorridire [inorri'dire] *v* horrify; be horrified.

inospitale [inospi'tale] *agg* inhospitable.

inosservato [inosser'vato] *agg* unobserved.

inossidabile [inossi'dabile] *agg* stainless.

inquadrare [inkwa'drare] *v* (*mettre in cornice*) frame; (*fig*) set; (*mil*) organize. **inquadratura** *sf* (*cine*, *TV*) shot.

inquietare [inkwje'tare] *v* worry. **inquietante** *agg* worrying. **inquieto** *agg* restless; (*preoccupato*) uneasy. **inquietudine** *sf* restlessness, worry.

inquilino [inkwi'lino], **-a** *sm*, *sf* tenant.

inquinare [inkwi'nare] *v* pollute. **inquinamento** *sm* pollution.

insabbiare [insab'bjare] *v* (*pratica*) shelve.

insalata [insa'lata] *sf* salad; (*confusione*) muddle. **insalatiera** *sf* salad-bowl.

insalubre [insa'lubre] *agg* unhealthy.

insanabile [insa'nabile] *agg* incurable.

insanguinare [insangwi'nare] *v* stain with blood.

insaputa [insa'puta] *sf* **all'insaputa di** without the knowledge of.

insaziabile [insa'tsjabile] *agg* insatiable.

inscatolare [inskato'lare] *v* tin, can.

inscenare [inʃe'nare] *v* stage.

insegna [in'seɲa] *sf* (*emblema*) insignia *pl*; (*stemma*) coat of arms; motto; (*cartello*) sign.

insegnare [inse'ɲare] *v* teach. **insegnamento** *sm* teaching, education. **insegnante** *s*(*m*+*f*) teacher.

inseguire [inse'gwire] *v* pursue, chase. **inseguimento** *sm* pursuit, chase.

insensato [insen'sato] *agg* senseless, foolish.

insensibile [insen'sibile] *agg* (*leggerissimo*) imperceptible, very slight; (*indifferente*) insensitive, unfeeling.

inseparabile [insepa'rabile] *agg* inseparable.

inserire [inse'rire] *v* insert. **inserirsi** *v* introduce oneself, appear. **inserto** *sm* supplement. **inserzione** *sf* insertion; (*pubblicitaria*) advertisement.

inservibile [inser'vibile] *agg* useless.

inserviente [inser'vjente] *s*(*m*+*f*) attendant.

insetto [in'setto] *sm* insect. **insetticida** *sm* insecticide.

insicuro [insi'kuro] *agg* insecure.

insidia [in'sidja] *sf* snare, trap; (*pericolo*) danger. **insidioso** *agg* insidious.

insieme [in'sjeme] *avv* together; (*allo stesso tempo*) at the same time. *sm* whole; (*abbigliamento*) outfit.

insigne [in'siɲe] *agg* notable, illustrious.

insignificante [insiɲifi'kante] *agg* insignificant, trivial.

insignire [insi'ɲire] *v* decorate, honour.

insincero [insin'tʃero] *agg* insincere.

insinuare [insinu'are] *v* insinuate, creep. **insinuazione** *sf* insinuation.

insipido [in'sipido] *agg* insipid, tasteless.

*insistere [in'sistere] *v* insist (on). **insistente** *agg* insistent; (*incessante*) persistent, ceaseless. **insistenza** *sf* insistence.

insocievole [insot'ʃevole] *agg* unsociable.

insoddisfatto [insoddis'fatto] *agg* dissatisfied.

insofferente [insoffe'rɛnte] *agg* intolerant, impatient.

insoffribile [insof'fribile] *agg* unbearable.

insolazione [insola'tsjone] *sf* sunstroke.

insolente [inso'lɛnte] *agg* insolent. **insolenza** *sf* insolence.

insolito [in'sɔlito] *agg* unusual, strange.

insolubile [inso'lubile] *agg* insoluble. **insoluto** *agg* unsolved; (*non pagato*) outstanding.

insomma [in'somma] *inter* well! now then! *avv* (*in conclusione*) in short, in other words.

insonnia [in'sɔnnja] *sf* insomnia, sleeplessness. **insonne** *agg* sleepless; (*fig*) indefatigable.

insopportabile [insoppor'tabile] *agg* unbearable, intolerable.

****insorgere** [in'sɔrdʒere] *v* rebel, rise (up against); protest.

insormontabile [insormon'tabile] *agg* insurmountable.

insospettato [insospet'tato] *agg* unexpected, unsuspected.

insostenibile [insoste'nibile] *agg* (*non difensibile*) untenable; (*non sopportabile*) unbearable.

insostituibile [insostitu'ibile] *agg* irreplaceable.

insperato [inspe'rato] *agg* undreamt of, unexpected.

inspiegabile [inspje'gabile] *agg* inexplicable.

installare [instal'lare] *v* install, establish. **installarsi** *v* settle (down). **installazione** *sf* installation.

insù [in'su] *avv* up.

insubordinato [insubordi'nato] *agg* insubordinate.

insuccesso [insut'tʃesso] *sm* failure.

insudiciare [insudi'tʃare] *v* soil, dirty.

insufficiente [insuffi'tʃɛnte] *agg* insufficient, inadequate. **insufficienza** *sf* insufficiency; (*mancanza*) shortage.

insulina [insu'lina] *sf* insulin.

insultare [insul'tare] *v* insult. **insulto** *sm* insult, abuse; (*accesso*) fit.

insuperabile [insupe'rabile] *agg* insuperable, insurmountable; (*imbattibile*) unbeatable.

insurrezione [insurre'tsjone] *sf* insurrection.

insussistente [insussis'tɛnte] *agg* non-existent, baseless.

intaccare [intak'kare] *v* attack; (*far tacche*) notch, nick; (*consumare*) eat into.

intagliare [inta'Áare] *v* carve, cut.

intangibile [intan'dʒibile] *agg* intangible.

intanto [in'tanto] *avv* meanwhile, in the meantime; (*fam: invece*) but, whereas, while.

intasare [inta'zare] *v* clog, block. **intasamento** *sm* obstruction, blockage.

intascare [intas'kare] *v* pocket.

intatto [in'tatto] *agg* intact.

intavolare [intavo'lare] *v* (*iniziare*) begin.

integrale [integ'rale] *agg* complete, total. **calcolo integrale** *sm* integral calculus. **pane integrale** *sm* wholemeal bread.

integrare [integ'rare] *v* integrate.

integro ['integro] *agg* complete; (*onesto*) upright. **integrità** *sf* integrity.

intelletto [intel'letto] *sm* intellect. **intellettuale** *s(m+f)*, *agg* intellectual.

intelligente [intelli'dʒɛnte] *agg* intelligent. **intelligenza** *sf* intelligence. **intelligibile** *agg* intelligible.

intemperie [intem'pɛrje] *sf pl* bad weather *sing*.

intempestivo [intempes'tivo] *agg* untimely. **intempestività** *sf* untimeliness.

intendente [inten'dɛnte] *sm* superintendent, administrator. **intendenza** *sf* administration.

****intendere** [in'tɛndere] *v* (*udire*) hear; (*comprendere*) understand; (*aver intenzione, volere*) intend; (*significare*) mean. **intendersi** *v* (*andar d'accordo*) agree, get on; (*essere competente*) be knowledgeable (about). **s'intende** of course, it goes without saying.

intenditore [intendi'tore], **-trice** *sm*, *sf* connoisseur, good judge.

intenso [in'tɛnso] *agg* intense. **intensificare** *v* intensify. **intensità** *sf* intensity.

intento [in'tɛnto] *agg* busy. *sm* object, end.

intenzione [inten'tsjone] *sf* of intention. **aver l'intenzione di** intend to. **bene/male intenzionato** *agg* well-/ill-disposed.

intercettare [intertʃet'tare] *v* intercept.

****interdire** [inter'dire] *v* (*proibire*) forbid; (*dir*) disqualify. **interdizione** *sf* ban, disqualification.

interessare [interes'sare] *v* interest; (*riguardare*) concern; (*stare a cuore*) matter. **interessarsi** *v* take an interest (in); (*prendersi cura*) look after, take care (of). **interessato** *agg* interested, concerned;

(oppportunistico) self-interested. **interesse** sm interest; (tornaconto) profit.

interferire [interfe'rire] v interfere. **interferenza** sf interference.

interiore [inte'rjore] agg inner, interior.

intermedio [inter'medjo] agg intermediate. **intermediario, -a** s, agg intermediary.

interminabile [intermi'nabile] agg endless, never-ending.

internare [inter'nare] v intern; (med) commit. **internamento** sm internment; commitment. **internato** sm (convitto) boarding school; (scolaro) boarder.

internazionale [internatsjo'nale] agg international.

interno [in'terno] agg inner, internal. sm inside, interior; (telefono) extension.

intero [in'tero] sm, agg whole. **per intero** in full.

interpellare [interpel'lare] v ask, consult.

interpretare [interpre'tare] v interpret, explain; (teatro, ecc.) play. **interpretazione** sf interpretation. **interprete** s(m + f) interpreter; (teatro, ecc.) actor, performer; (cantante) singer.

interrare [inter'rare] v inter, bury.

interrogare [interro'gare] v interrogate, question; examine, test; consult. **interrogatorio** sm examination; questioning. **interrogazione** sf interrogation; (domanda) question; (dir) questioning, examination.

*****interrompere** [inter'rompere] v interrupt, break (off).

interruttore [interrut'tore] sm switch.

interruzione [interru'tsjone] sf interruption, break.

interurbano [interur'bano] agg **chiamata** or **telefonata interurbana** sf trunk-call.

intervallo [inter'vallo] sm interval, break.

*****intervenire** [interve'nire] v intervene; (assistere) take part, attend; (med) operate. **intervento** sm intervention; operation.

intervista [inter'vista] sf interview. **intervistare** v interview. **intervistatore, -trice** sm, sf interviewer.

intesa [in'teza] sf agreement, understanding; (pol) entente. **inteso** agg (volto a un fine) intended, meant; (compreso) understood; (convenuto) agreed. **ben inteso** understood.

intestare [intes'tare] v head; (mettere a nome di) make out to. **intestatario, -a** sm, sf holder.

intestino [intes'tino] sm intestine.

intimare [inti'mare] v order; (dichiarare) declare.

intimidire [intimi'dire] v intimidate.

intimità [intimi'ta] sf intimacy; (ambiente intimo, fig) privacy.

intimo ['intimo] agg intimate; (interno) innermost. sm (amico) close friend; (anima) heart of hearts. **biancheria intima** sf underwear.

intimorire [intimo'rire] v intimidate, frighten.

*****intingere** [in'tindʒere] v dip.

intingolo [in'tingolo] sm (piatto) stew; (salsa) sauce, gravy.

intirizzire [intirit'tsire] v grow numb. **intirizzito** agg numb.

intitolare [intito'lare] v entitle; dedicate.

intollerabile [intolle'rabile] agg intolerable, unbearable.

intollerante [intolle'rante] agg intolerant.

intonaco [in'tɔnako] sm plaster. **intonacare** v plaster, whitewash.

intonare [into'nare] v (accordare) tune, (cominciare a cantare) intone, strike up; (armonizzare) match.

intontire [inton'tire] v daze.

intorno [in'torno] avv around; (circa) about; (argomento) on, about.

intorpidire [intorpi'dire] v grow numb.

intossicante [intossi'kante] agg poisoning. **intossicazione** sf poisoning.

intraducibile [intradu'tʃibile] agg untranslatable.

intralciare [intral'tʃare] v hold up, hinder. **intralcio** sm hindrance, obstacle.

intransigente [intransi'dʒente] agg intransigent.

intransitivo [intransi'tivo] agg intransitive.

*****intraprendere** [intra'prendere] v undertake, take on, begin. **intraprendente** agg enterprising. **intraprendenza** sf enterprise, initiative.

intrattabile [intrat'tabile] agg intractable; (fam) impossible, difficult.

*****intrattenere** [intratte'nere] v entertain. **intrattenersi** v linger; (indugiare su) dwell (on).

*****intravedere** [intrave'dere] v catch a glimpse (of); (intuire) sense.

intreccio [in'trettʃo] sm plaiting; (trama) plot. **intrecciare** v intertwine; (capelli) braid.

intrepido [in'trɛpido] *agg* intrepid, brave.
intrigo [in'trigo] *sm*, *pl* -**ghi** plot, intrigue.
  intrigare *v* plot, intrigue.
intrinseco [in'trinseko] *agg* intrinsic.
intriso [in'trizo] *agg* soaked.
*****introdurre** [intro'durre] *v* introduce;
  (*inserire*) insert; (*far entrare*) show in.
  introdotto *agg* (*conosciuto*) well-known,
  well-established; (*esperto*) well up in.
  introduzione *sf* introduction.
introito [in'trɔito] *sm* income; (*incasso*)
  takings *pl*.
*****intromettersi** [intro'mettersi] *v* meddle,
  intervene.
intronare [intro'nare] *v* deafen.
introspettivo [introspet'tivo] *agg* introspective.
introvabile [intro'vabile] *agg* unobtainable, not to be found.
introverso [intro'vɛrso], -**a** *s*, *agg* introvert.
intrusione [intru'zjone] *sf* intrusion.
  intruso, -**a** *sm*, *sf* intruder.
intuitivo [intui'tivo] *agg* intuitive. **intuire**
  v sense. **intuito** *sm* intuition, instinct,
  insight.
inumano [inu'mano] *agg* inhuman.
inumidire [inumi'dire] *v* moisten.
inusitato [inuzi'tato] *agg* uncommon.
inutile [i'nutile] *agg* useless; (*non necessario*) unnecessary.
invadente [inva'dɛnte] *agg* intrusive.
  s(*m*+*f*) busybody.
*****invadere** [in'vadere] *v* invade, flood.
invalido [in'valido], -**a** *agg* invalid; (*privo
  di valore*) null and void; (*mutilato*) disabled. *sm*, *sf* invalid; disabled person.
  invalidare *v* (*dir*) invalidate.
invano [in'vano] *avv* in vain. *agg* vain,
  useless.
invariabile [inva'rjabile] *agg* invariable,
  even. **invariato** *agg* unchanged.
invasione [inva'zjone] *sf* invasion.
invecchiare [invek'kjare] *v* age. **invecchia-
  mento** *sm* ageing.
invece [in'vetʃe] *avv* instead (of); (*mentre*)
  whereas, while.
invendibile [inven'dibile] *agg* unsaleable.
  invenduto *agg* unsold.
inventare [inven'tare] *v* invent. **inventore**
  sm inventor. **invenzione** *sf* invention.
inventario [inven'tarjo] *sm* inventory.
inverno [in'vɛrno] *sm* winter. **invernale**
  agg winter, wintry.
inverosimile [invero'simile] *agg* unlikely.

inverso [in'vɛrso] *agg* contrary, opposite;
  (*mat*) inverse. *sm* contrary, opposite.
  inversione *sf* inversion; (*tec*) reversal.
invertebrato [inverte'brato] *sm*, *agg* invertebrate.
investigare [investi'gare] *v* investigate.
investire [inves'tire] *v* (*comm*) invest;
  (*scontrare*) collide, hit; (*scontrare persone*) hit, run down. **investimento** *sm*
  investment; collision, crash.
invetriata [invetri'ata] *sf* (*porta*) glass-
  door; (*finestra*) window.
invettiva [invet'tiva] *sf* invective.
inviare [invi'are] *v* dispatch, send (off).
  inviato, -**a** *sm*, *sf* (*diplomatico*) envoy;
  (*giornale*) correspondent. **invio** *sm* dispatch.
invidiare [invi'djare] *v* envy. **invidia** *sf*
  envy. **invidioso** *agg* envious.
invigorire [invigo'rire] *v* invigorate,
  strengthen.
invincibile [invin'tʃibile] *agg* invincible.
invisibile [invi'zibile] *agg* invisible.
invitare [invi'tare] *v* invite. **invitato**, -**a** *sm*,
  sf guest. **invito** *sm* invitation.
invocare [invo'kare] *v* invoke, call for.
invogliare [invo'ʎare] *v* tempt.
*****involgere** [in'voldʒere] *v* wrap (up).
involontario [involon'tarjo] *agg* involuntary.
involtino [invol'tino] *sm* (*gastr*) roulade,
  olive.
involto [in'vɔlto] *sm* bundle, package.
involucro [in'vɔlukro] *sm* covering, wrapper.
invulnerabile [invulne'rabile] *agg* invul-
  nerable.
inzaccherare [indzakke'rare] *v* spatter
  with mud.
inzuppare [indzup'pare] *v* soak.
io ['io] *pron* I. *sm* self.
iodio ['jɔdjo] *sm* iodine.
ione ['jone] *sm* ion.
iperbole [i'pɛrbole] *sf* hyperbole.
  iperbolico *agg* exaggerated; (*mat*) hyper-
  bolic.
ipertensione [iperten'sjone] *sf* hyperten-
  sion. **iperteso** *agg* hypertensive.
ipnosi [ip'nɔzi] *sf* hypnosis. **ipnotico** *agg*
  hypnotic. **ipnotismo** *sm* hypnotism.
ipnotizzare [ipnotid'dzare] *v* hypnotize.
  ipnotizzatore, -**trice** *sm*, *sf* hypnotist.
ipocondriaco [ipokon'driako], -**a** *s*, *agg*
  hypochondriac. **ipocondria** *sf* hypochondria.

ipocrita [i'pokrita] s(m+f) hypocrite. **agg** hypocritical. **ipocrisia** sf hypocrisy.

ipoteca [ipo'tɛka] sf mortgage. **ipotecare** v mortgage.

ipotenusa [ipote'nuza] sf hypotenuse.

ipotesi [i'potezi] sf hypothesis (pl -ses). **nella migliore delle ipotesi** at best. **nella peggiore delle ipotesi** if the worst comes to the worst. **ipotetico** agg hypothetical.

ippica ['ippika] sf horse-racing. **ippico** agg horse.

ippocampo [ippo'kampo] sm sea-horse.

ippocastano [ippokas'tano] sm horse-chestnut.

ippodromo [ip'pɔdromo] sm racecourse.

ippopotamo [ippo'pɔtamo] sm hippopotamus.

ira ['ira] sf rage, anger. **irascibile** agg irascible.

iride ['iride] sf iris; (arcobaleno) rainbow.

Irlanda [ir'landa] sf Ireland. **irlandese** sm, agg Irish. **gli irlandesi** the Irish.

ironia [iro'nia] sf irony. **ironico** agg ironic(al).

irradiare [irra'djare] v radiate; (fig) irradiate.

irraggiungibile [irraddʒun'dʒibile] agg unattainable.

irragionevole [irradʒo'nevole] agg unreasonable.

irrazionale [irratsjo'nale] agg irrational.

irreale [irre'ale] agg unreal.

irregolare [irrego'lare] agg irregular. **irregolarità** sf irregularity.

irreperibile [irrepe'ribile] agg that cannot be found.

irrequieto [irre'kwjeto] agg restless.

irresistibile [irrezis'tibile] agg irresistible.

irresoluto [irrezo'luto] agg wavering, undecided. **irresolutezza** sf indecision, wavering.

irresponsabile [irrespon'sabile] agg irresponsible. **irresponsabilità** sf irresponsibility.

irrigare [irri'gare] v irrigate. **irrigazione** sf irrigation.

irrigidire [irridʒi'dire] v stiffen. **irrigidimento** sm stiffening; (fig) obstinacy.

irrimediabile [irrime'djabile] agg irreparable.

irrisorio [irri'zɔrjo] agg derisory, ridiculous.

irritare [irri'tare] v irritate; (dar fastidio) annoy. **irritabile** agg irritable. **irritante** agg irritating; (med) irritant. **irritazione** sf irritation.

irriverenza [irrive'rentsa] sf disrespect.

*irrompere [ir'rompere] v burst into; (riversarsi) pour into.

irsuto [ir'suto] agg shaggy, hairy.

irto ['irto] agg bristling (with).

*iscrivere [is'krivere] v enrol, register; (diventar socio) join. **iscritto** sm member. **iscrizione** sf registration, enrolment; (scritta) inscription.

Islanda [is'landa] sf Iceland. **islandese** sm, agg Icelandic; s(m+f) Icelander.

isola ['izola] sf island.

isolare [izo'lare] v isolate; (fis) insulate. **isolamento** sm isolation; insulation.

ispettore [ispet'tore], **-trice** sm, sf inspector.

ispezionare [ispetsjo'nare] v inspect. **ispezione** sf inspection.

ispirare [ispi'rare] v inspire.

issare [is'sare] v hoist.

istamina [ista'mina] sf histamine.

istante [is'tante] sm instant, moment. **istantanea** sf snapshot. **istantaneo** agg instantaneous.

istanza [is'tantsa] sf (domanda) application, petition.

isterico [is'tɛriko] agg hysterical. **attacco isterico** sm hysterics pl. **isteria** sf hysteria.

istigare [isti'gare] v instigate.

istillare [istil'lare] v instil.

istinto [is'tinto] sm instinct.

istituire [istitu'ire] v institute, establish.

istituto [isti'tuto] sm institute; (ente) institution, organization. **istituzione** sf institution.

istrice ['istritʃe] sm porcupine; (persona scontrosa) touchy person.

*istruire [istru'ire] v instruct, educate. **istruire un processo** (dir) prepare a case. **istruttore**, **-trice** sm, sf instructor, -tress, teacher. **giudice istruttore** sm examining magistrate. **istruttoria** sf (dir) examination. **istruttorio** agg preliminary. **istruzione** sf instruction, education, tuition.

Italia [i'talja] sf Italy. **italiano**, **-a** s, agg Italian.

itinerario [itine'rarjo] sm itinerary, route.

itterizia [itte'ritsja] sf jaundice.

Iugoslavia [jugo'slavja] sf Yugoslavia. **iugoslavo**, **-a** s, agg Yugoslav.

iuta ['juta] sf jute.

L

la¹ [la] *art* the.

la² [la] *pron* (*cosa, animale*) it; (*persona*) her; (*formula di cortesia*) you.

là [la] *avv* there. **di là** (*nell'altra stanza*) in the other room; (*da quella parte*) that way. **in là** (*oltre*) further. **va là!** come off it!

labbro ['labbro] *sm*, *pl* **-a** *f* in anat sense lip; (*orlo*) brim.

labirinto [labi'rinto] *sm* labyrinth, maze.

laboratorio [labora'tɔrjo] *sm* laboratory; (*industria*) workshop.

laborioso [labo'rjozo] *agg* laborious.

laburista [labu'rista] *agg* Labour.

lacca ['lakka] *sf* lacquer.

laccio ['lattʃo] *sm* noose; (*trappola*) snare, trap; (*legame*) tie. **laccio da scarpe** shoelace.

lacerare [latʃe'rare] *v* lacerate, tear.

lacrima ['lakrima] *sf* tear.

lacrimogeno [lakri'mɔdʒeno] *agg* **gas lacrimogeno** *sm* tear-gas.

lacuna [la'kuna] *sf* gap.

ladro ['ladro] *sm* thief. **al ladro!** stop thief! **vestito come un ladro** dressed like a tramp.

laggiù [lad'dʒu] *avv* down there.

lagnarsi [la'narsi] *v* complain. **lagna** *sf* bore.

lago ['lago] *sm* lake.

laico ['laiko] *agg* lay. *sm* layman.

lama¹ ['lama] *sf* blade. **lametta** *sf* razorblade.

lama² ['lama] *sm invar* (*zool*) llama.

lambiccarsi [lambik'karsi] *v* **lambiccarsi il cervello** rack one's brains.

lambire [lam'bire] *v* lick, lap.

lamentare [lamen'tare] *v* lament. **lamentarsi** (**di**) complain (about). **lamentela** *sf* complaint. **lamentevole** *agg* pitiful. **lamento** *sm* lament. **lamentoso** *agg* plaintive.

lamiera [la'mjera] *sf* sheet.

lamina ['lamina] *sf* thin layer; (*metallo*) foil. **laminare** *v* (*ridurre in lamine*) roll; (*coprire con lamine*) laminate. **laminato** *sm* laminate. **laminatoio** *sm* rolling-mill.

lampada ['lampada] *sf* lamp. **lampadario** *sm* chandelier. **lampadina** *sf* (light) bulb. **lampadina tascabile** torch.

lampeggiare [lamped'dʒare] *v* flash.

lampione [lam'pjone] *sm* lamp-post.

lampo ['lampo] *sm* flash; (*temporale*) lightning. **cerniera lampo** *sf* zip.

lampone [lam'pone] *sm* raspberry.

lampreda [lam'preda] *sf* lamprey.

lana ['lana] *sf* wool. **di lana** woollen. **industria laniera** *sf* wool industry. **lanificio** *sm* woollen mill.

lancetta [lan'tʃetta] *sf* hand.

lancia¹ ['lantʃa] *sf* (*arma*) lance.

lancia² ['lantʃa] *sf* (*barca*) launch. **lancia di salvataggio** lifeboat.

lanciare [lan'tʃare] *v* throw, fling; (*diffondere*) launch; (*bombe*) drop. **lanciafiamme** *sm invar* flame-thrower. **lanciamissili** *sm invar* rocket-launcher. **lanciare un grido** utter a cry. **lancio** *sm* throw, fling; launching.

languire [lan'gwire] *v* languish; (*diminuire di forza*) flag. **languido** *agg* languid.

lanterna [lan'tɛrna] *sf* lantern.

lanugine [la'nudʒine] *sf* down.

lapide ['lapide] *sf* (*sepolcrale*) tombstone; (*commemorativa*) memorial tablet.

lapis ['lapis] *sm* pencil.

lardo ['lardo] *sm* lard, dripping.

largo ['largo] *agg* wide, broad. **al largo di** away from, off. **far largo** a make room for. **larghezza** *sf* width, breadth; (*fig*) generosity.

larice ['laritʃe] *sm* larch.

laringe [la'rindʒe] *sf* larynx. **laringite** *sf* laryngitis.

larva ['larva] *sf* larva; (*spettro*) shadow.

lasciare [la'ʃare] *v* leave; (*permettere*) let. **lascito** *sm* legacy.

lascivo [la'ʃivo] *agg* lascivious.

laser ['lazer] *sm invar* laser.

lassativo [lassa'tivo] *sm*, *agg* laxative.

lasso ['lasso] *sm* (*periodo*) lapse. *agg* (*rilassato*) loose.

lassù [las'su] *avv* up there.

lastra ['lastra] *sf* plate; sheet.

lastricare [lastri'kare] *v* pave. **lastrico** *sm* pavement; (*miseria*) poverty.

latente [la'tɛnte] *agg* latent.

laterale [late'rale] *agg* lateral, side.

laterizi [late'ritsi] *sm pl* bricks *pl*, tiles *pl*.

latice [la'titʃe] *sm* latex.

latino [la'tino] *sm*, *agg* Latin.

latitante [lati'tante] *agg* fugitive. **rendersi latitante** abscond.

latitudine [lati'tudine] *sf* latitude.

lato¹ ['lato] *sm* side. **da un lato** ... **dall'altro** ... on the one hand ... on the other .... **d'altro lato** on the other hand.

lato² ['lato] *agg* **in senso lato** in a broad sense.

latrare [la'trare] *v* bark.

latrina [la'trina] *sf* latrine.

latta ['latta] *sf* (*lamiera*) tin, tinplate; (*recipiente*) tin, can.

lattaio [lat'tajo] *sm* milkman.

latte ['latte] *sm* milk. **latte magro** skimmed milk. **latteo** *agg* milky. **latteria** *sf* dairy. **lattiera** *sf* milk jug.

lattuga [lat'tuga] *sf* lettuce.

laurea ['laurea] *sf* degree. **laurearsi** *v* graduate. **laureato, -a** *sm, sf* graduate. **essere laureato in** ... have a degree in ....

lauro ['lauro] *sm* laurel.

lauto ['lauto] *agg* generous, sumptuous.

lava ['lava] *sf* lava.

lavabo [la'vabo] *sm* wash-basin.

lavaggio [la'vaddʒo] *sm* washing. **lavaggio a secco** dry-cleaning. **lavaggio del cervello** brain-washing.

lavagna [la'vaɲa] *sf* slate; (*scolastica*) blackboard.

lavanda¹ [la'vanda] *sf* (*bot*) lavender.

lavanda² [la'vanda] *sf* wash(ing).

lavandaia [lavan'daja] *sf* laundress, washer-woman.

lavanderia [lavande'ria] *sf* laundry; (*a gettoni*) launderette.

lavandino [lavan'dino] *sm* sink.

lavapiatti [lava'pjatti] *sm also* **lavastoviglie** *invar* dishwasher.

lavatrice [lava'tritʃe] *sf* washing machine.

lavare [la'vare] *v* wash. **lavare a secco** *v* dry-clean. **lavare il capo a** tell off. **lavarsi** *v* (have a) wash. **lavata di capo** *sf* telling-off. **lavatura** *sf* washing; (*acqua sporca*) dishwater.

lavativo [lava'tivo] *sm* (*fam*) bore, pain in the neck.

lavorare [lavo'rare] *v* work; (*con fatica*) labour; (*aziende, negozi, ecc.*) do business; (*il terreno*) till; (*teatro, ecc.*) act, play. **lavorativo** *agg* working. **lavorato** *agg* finished; (*metallo*) wrought; (*a macchina*) machined.

lavoratore [lavora'tore], **-trice** *sm, sf* worker. **lavoratore a cottimo** piece-worker.

lavorazione [lavora'tsjone] *sf* manufacture; (*fattura*) workmanship; work. **lavorazione in serie** mass-production.

lavoro [la'voro] *sm* work; (*occupazione*) job; (*teatro, ecc.*) play. **lavori di casa** *sm pl* housework *sing.* **lavoro a cottimo** *sm* piece-work. **lavoro straordinario** *sm* overtime.

lazzarone [laddza'rone] *sm* scoundrel.

le¹ [le] *art* the.

le² [le] *pron* (*persona*) (to) her; (*cosa, animale*) (to) it; (*formula di cortesia*) (to) you; (*pl*) them.

leale [le'ale] *agg* sincere; (*onesto*) fair. **lealtà** *sf* loyalty, fairness.

lebbroso [leb'brozo], **-a** *agg* leprous. *sm, sf* leper. **lebbra** *sf* leprosy.

leccare [lek'kare] *v* lick. **leccalecca** *sm invar* (*fam*) lollipop. **leccapiedi** *sm invar* (*fam*) bootlicker. **leccare i piedi a** lick the boots of. **leccornia** *sf* titbit, tasty morsel.

lecito ['letʃito] *agg* (*dir*) lawful; (*permesso*) allowed.

lega ['lega] *sf* league, alliance; (*metalli*) alloy.

legale [le'gale] *agg* legal; (*legittimo*) lawful. **medicina legale** *sf* forensic medicine. **numero legale** *sm* quorum. **ora legale** *sf* summer-time. **legalizzare** *v* legalize, certify.

legame [le'game] *sm* tie, bond; (*fig*) link; (*amoroso*) liaison.

legare [le'gare] *v* tie (up), bind; (*assicurare*) fasten. **matto da legare** crazy, mad as a hatter.

legato [le'gato] *agg* tied (up); (*libro*) bound; (*impacciato*) stiff. *sm* (*papale*) legate; (*testamento*) legacy.

legatura [lega'tura] *sf* binding.

legge ['leddʒe] *sf* law; (*votata dal parlamento*) act (of parliament); (*norma di condotta*) rule. **progetto di legge** *sm* bill. **proposta di legge** *sf* draft bill.

leggenda [led'dʒenda] *sf* legend; (*didascalia*) caption. **leggendario** *agg* legendary.

*leggere ['leddʒere] *v* read.

leggero [led'dʒero] *agg* light; (*lieve*) slight. **leggerezza** *sf* lightness; (*frivolezza*) levity; (*sconsideratezza*) thoughtlessness.

leggiadro [led'dʒadro] *agg* graceful, lovely.

leggibile [led'dʒibile] *agg* readable, legible.

leggio [led'dʒio] *sm* music stand; (*chiesa*) lectern.

legione [le'dʒone] *sf* legion.

legislazione [ledʒizla'tsjone] *sf* legislation. **legislatore** *sm* legislator.

legittimo [le'dʒittimo] *agg* lawful; (*tale per legge*) legitimate; proper; justifiable.

legna ['leɲa] *sf invar* firewood. **mettere legna al fuoco** add fuel to the fire.

legname [le'ɲame] *sm* timber; (*in tronchi*) logs *pl*.

legnata [le'ɲata] *sf* blow. **un sacco di legnate** *sm* (*fam*) a good hiding.

legno ['leɲo] *sm* wood. **di legno** wooden, wood. **lavoro in legno** *sm* woodwork; (*edilizia*) timberwork. **legno compensato** plywood. **legno impiallacciato** veneer.

lei ['lɛi] *pron* (*soggetto*) she; (*oggetto*) her; (*formula di cortesia*) you.

lembo ['lembo] *sm* (*orlo*) edge, border; (*striscia*) strip.

lemme lemme ['lemme 'lemme] *avv* (*fam*) very leisurely.

lena ['lena] *sf* vigour. **lavorare di buona lena** (*fam*) put one's back into it.

lente ['lɛnte] *sf* lens. **lente a contatto** contact lens. **lente d'ingrandimento** magnifying glass. **lenti** *sf pl* glasses *pl*.

lenticchia [len'tikkja] *sf* lentil.

lentiggine [len'tiddʒine] *sf* freckle. **lentigginoso** *agg* freckled.

lento ['lɛnto] *agg* slow; (*allentato*) loose. **lento a capire** slow in the uptake.

lenza ['lɛntsa] *sf* (*fishing-*)line.

lenzuolo [len'tswɔlo] *sm, pl* **-a** *f when referring to a pair* sheet.

leone [le'one] *sm* lion. **leonessa** *sf* lioness.

leopardo [leo'pardo] *sm* leopard.

lepido ['lɛpido] *agg* witty.

lepre ['lɛpre] *sf* hare. **lepre in salmì** jugged hare. **leporino** *sm* hare-lip.

lesbico ['lɛzbiko] *agg* lesbian. **lesbica** *sf* lesbian.

lesina [le'zina] *sf* awl; (*taccagneria*) (*fam*) meanness. **lesinare** *v* skimp.

lesione [le'zjone] *sf* injury; (*med*) lesion; (*danno*) damage. **parte lesa** *sf* injured party.

lessare [les'sare] *v* boil. **lesso** *sm* boiled meat.

lessico ['lɛssiko] *sm* lexicon; vocabulary.

lesto ['lɛsto] *agg* swift, quick. **lesto di lingua** glib. **lesto di mano** light-fingered. **lestofante** *sm* swindler.

letale [le'tale] *agg* lethal, deadly.

letame [le'tame] *sm* manure, dung; (*fig*)

filth. **letamaio** *sm* dung-heap; (*luogo sudicio*) pigsty.

letargico [le'tardʒiko] *agg* lethargic. **letargo** *sm* (*zool*) hibernation; (*med, torpore*) lethargy.

letizia [le'titsja] *sf* joy, gladness.

lettera ['lettera] *sf* letter. **alla lettera** literally; verbatim. **lettera d'accompagnamento/raccomandata** covering/registered letter. **lettera di sollecitazione** reminder. **lettera maiuscola/minuscola** capital/small letter.

letterario [lette'rarjo] *agg* literary.

letteratura [lettera'tura] *sf* literature.

lettiga [let'tiga] *sf* litter; (*barella*) stretcher.

letto ['lɛtto] *sm* bed.

lettore [let'tore], **-trice** *sm, sf* reader; (*universitario*) modern language lecturer.

lettura [let'tura] *sf* reading.

leucemia [leutʃe'mia] *sf* leukaemia.

leva[1] ['lɛva] *sf* (*mec*) lever; (*fig*) incentive. **far leva** lever. **far leva su** exploit, play on.

leva[2] ['lɛva] *sf* call-up; conscripts *pl*.

levante [le'vante] *sm* east.

levare [le'vare] *v* (*alzare*) raise, lift; (*togliere*) take away or off; (*estrarre*) pull out. **levare di mezzo** get rid of, remove. **levarsi** *v* (*alzarsi*) rise; (*dal letto*) get up. **levarsi la fame** satisfy one's hunger. **levarsi la sete** quench one's thirst. **levata della posta** *sf* mail collection. **levata del sole** *sf* sunrise.

levatoio [leva'tojo] *agg* **ponte levatoio** *sm* drawbridge.

levatrice [leva'tritʃe] *sf* midwife.

levigare [levi'gare] *v* smooth; polish; (*pomiciare*) rub down; (*con carta vetrata*) sand down.

levriere [le'vrjere] *sm* greyhound.

lezione [le'tsjone] *sf* lesson; class; (*durata*) period; (*universitaria*) lecture. **lezioso** [le'tsjozo] *agg* affected, mannered.

lezzo ['lɛttso] *sm* stench; (*sudiciume*) filth.

li [li] *pron* them.

lì [li] *avv* there. **giù di lì** thereabouts. **lì per lì** (*sul momento*) there and then; (*dapprima*) at first.

libbra ['libbra] *sf* pound.

libellula [li'bellula] *sf* dragonfly.

liberale [libe'rale] *sm* (*n* + *f*), *agg* liberal.

liberare [libe'rare] *v* free, liberate; (*salvare*) save, rescue. **liberazione** *sf* liberation; release.

libero ['libero] agg free; (sgombro) clear; exempt. **aria libera** sf open air. **libero pensatore** sm freethinker. **tempo libero** sm time off.

libertà [liber'ta] sf freedom, liberty. **giorno di libertà** sm day off. **libertà condizionata** probation. **libertà provvisoria** bail. **mettere in libertà** set free.

Libra ['libra] sf Libra.

libraio [li'brajo] sm bookseller. **libreria** sf (negozio) bookshop; (raccolta di libri) library; (casa editrice) publishers pl.

libro ['libro] sm book. **a libro** hinged. **libro di cassa** cash register. **libro giallo** thriller. **libro mastro** ledger. **libro nero** blacklist.

licenza [li'tʃentsa] sf licence, permission; (scuola) leaving certificate.

licenziare [litʃen'tsjare] v dismiss. **licenziamento** sm dismissal.

liceo [li'tʃɛo] sm secondary school, high school.

lichene [li'kɛne] sm lichen.

lido ['lido] sm shore.

lieto ['ljɛto] agg glad, happy.

lieve ['ljɛve] agg slight, light.

lievito ['ljɛvito] sm yeast; (fig) ferment.

lignaggio [liɲ'naddʒo] sm lineage, pedigree.

ligustro [li'gustro] sm privet.

lilla ['lilla] agg, sm invar lilac.

lima ['lima] sf file. **limare** v file. **limatura** sf filing; (polvere) filings pl.

limitare [limi'tare] v limit, restrict. **limitazione** sf limitation, restraint.

limite ['limite] sm limit; (confine) boundary. **caso limite** sm borderline case. **limitrofo** agg bordering.

limo ['limo] sm mud, slime.

limone [li'mone] sm (albero) lemon-tree; (frutto) lemon. **limonata** sf lemonade.

limpido ['limpido] agg clear.

lince ['lintʃe] sf lynx.

linciare [lin'tʃare] v lynch. **linciaggio** sm lynching.

lindo ['lindo] agg clean, tidy.

linea ['linea] sf line; (corpo umano) figure. **lineetta** sf dash.

lineamenti [linea'menti] sm pl features pl; (elementi essenziali) outlines pl.

lineare [line'are] agg linear, coherent; (di indirizzo stabile) unswerving.

linfa ['linfa] sf lymph; (bot) sap.

lingua ['lingwa] sf tongue; (linguaggio) language. **linguaggio** sm language.

linguista s(m + f) linguist. **linguistico** agg linguistic.

lino ['lino] sm (pianta) flax; (tessuto) linen. **olio di lino** sm linseed oil.

liocorno [lio'korno] sm unicorn.

liquefare [likwe'fare] v liquefy, melt. **liquefazione** sf liquefaction.

liquidare [likwi'dare] v liquidate; (conti) settle; (merci) sell off; (sciogliere) wind up. **liquidazione** sf liquidation, settlement; (svendita) clearance sale; winding-up; (indennità) leaving bonus. **liquidatore** sm receiver.

liquido ['likwido] sm, agg liquid, fluid.

liquirizia [likwi'ritsja] sf liquorice.

liquore [li'kwore] sm liqueur.

lira¹ ['lira] sf (moneta) lira. **lira sterlina** pound sterling.

lira² ['lira] sf (musica) lyre.

lirico ['liriko] agg lyrical; opera. **cantante lirico** s(m + f) opera singer. **dramma lirico** sm opera. **teatro lirico** sm opera house. **lirica** sf lyric poetry.

lisca ['liska] sf fish-bone.

lisciare [li'ʃare] v smooth. **liscio** agg smooth; (bevanda) neat. **andar liscio** go smoothly. **passarla liscia** get off scot-free.

liseuse [li'zóz] sf, pl -s bed-jacket.

liso ['lizo] agg worn.

lista ['lista] sf (striscia) strip; (elenco) list. **lista elettorale** electoral register. **listare** v border. **listino** sm list.

litania [lita'nia] sf litany.

lite ['lite] sf quarrel; (dir) (law)suit.

litigare [liti'gare] v quarrel. **litigio** sm quarrel, row. **litigioso** agg quarrelsome; (dir) contentious.

litorale [lito'rale] agg coastal. sm shore.

litro ['litro] sm litre.

liturgia [litur'dʒia] sf liturgy. **liturgico** agg liturgical.

liuto [li'uto] sm lute.

livellare [livel'lare] v level. **livella** sf level. **livellatore, -trice** sm, sf leveller.

livello [li'vello] sm level. **livello del mare** sea-level. **passaggio a livello** sm level crossing.

livido ['livido] agg livid. sm bruise.

Livorno [li'vorno] sf Leghorn.

livrea [li'vrea] sf livery.

lizza ['littsa] sf **entrare in lizza** compete.

lo¹ [lo] art the.

lo² [lo] pron (persona) him; (cosa, animale) it.

lobo ['lɔbo] sm lobe.

locale[1] [lo'kale] agg local.

locale[2] [lo'kale] sm room, spot. **locale notturno** night-club. **località** sf locality.

localizzare [lokalid'dzare] v (individuare) locate; (circoscrivere) localize.

locanda [lo'kanda] sf inn. **locandiere, -a** sm, sf innkeeper.

locatario [loka'tarjo] sm tenant.

locatore [loka'tore] sm landlord.

locazione [lokat'tsjone] sf lease, tenancy.

locomotiva [lokomo'tiva] sf locomotive, engine.

lodare [lo'dare] v praise. **lode** sf praise. **lodevole** agg praiseworthy.

logaritmo [loga'ritmo] sm logarithm.

loggia ['lɔddʒa] sf loggia; (massone) lodge. **loggione** sm gallery.

logica ['lɔdʒika] sf logic. **logico** agg logical.

logistica [lo'dʒistika] sf logistics. **logistico** agg logistic(al).

logorare [logo'rare] v wear out. **logoramento** sm wear; (mentale) strain. **logorio** sm wear and tear. **logoro** agg worn out.

Londra ['londra] sf London. **londinese** s(m+f) Londoner.

longevo [lon'dʒevo] agg long-lived. **longevità** sf longevity.

longitudine [londʒi'tudine] sf longitude. **longitudinale** agg longitudinal.

lontano [lon'tano] agg far, far away; (assente) absent; distant; vague. avv far. **lontananza** sf distance.

loquace [lo'kwatʃe] agg loquacious.

lordo ['lordo] agg (peso) gross; (sporco) filthy.

loro ['loro] pron (soggetto) they; (oggetto) them; (formula di cortesia) you; (di essi) theirs. agg their.

losco ['losko] agg sinister.

loto ['lɔto] sm lotus.

lotta ['lɔtta] sf struggle, fight; (sport) wrestling. **lottare** v struggle, fight; wrestle.

lotteria [lotte'ria] sf lottery.

lotto ['lɔtto] sm portion; (comm) lot; lottery.

lozione [lo'tsjone] sf lotion.

lubrificante [lubrifi'kante] agg lubricating. sm lubricant. **lubrificare** v lubricate. **lubrificazione** sf lubrication.

lucchetto [luk'ketto] sm padlock.

luccicare [luttʃi'kare] v shine, sparkle.

luccio [luttʃo] sm pike.

lucciola ['luttʃola] sf firefly.

luce ['lutʃe] sf light.

lucernario [lutʃer'narjo] sm skylight.

lucertola [lu'tʃertola] sf lizard.

lucidare [lutʃi'dare] v polish.

lucido ['lutʃido] agg shiny, glossy; (fig) lucid. sm polish.

luglio ['luʎo] sm July.

lugubre ['lugubre] agg lugubrious.

lui ['lui] pron (soggetto) he; (oggetto) him.

lumaca [lu'maka] sf snail; (persona) slowcoach.

lume ['lume] sm light; lamp. **far lume su** throw light on.

luminoso [lumi'nozo] agg bright, shining.

luna ['luna] sf moon. **avere la luna** be in a bad mood. **luna di miele** honeymoon. **luna-park** sm invar fun-fair. **lunare** agg lunar. **sbarcare il lunario** make ends meet.

lunedì [lune'di] sm Monday.

lungo[1] ['lungo] agg long; (alto) tall; (lento) slow; (diluito) weak. **alla lunga** in the long run. **a lungo** (for) long. **di gran lunga** by far. **lunghezza** sf length.

lungo[2] ['lungo] prep along. **lungomare** sm seashore.

luogo ['lwɔgo] sm place. **aver luogo** take place. **fuori luogo** out of place. **in luogo di** instead of. **luogotenente** sm lieutenant.

lupo ['lupo] sm wolf. **lupa** sf she-wolf.

luppolo ['luppolo] sm hop.

lurido ['lurido] agg filthy.

lusingare [luzin'gare] v flatter; (illudere) delude. **lusinga** sf flattery; delusion. **lusinghiero** agg flattering, alluring.

Lussemburgo [lussem'burgo] sm Luxembourg.

lusso ['lusso] sm luxury. **di lusso** luxury, de luxe. **lussuoso** agg luxurious.

lustrare [lus'trare] v polish. **lustrino** sm sequin. **lustro** sm polish, sheen; lustre.

lutto ['lutto] sm mourning; (dolore) grief.

M

ma [ma] cong but. **macché!** inter (neanche per sogno) of course not! not on your life! **ma davvero?** really? **ma no!** of course not! **ma sì!** of course!

macabro ['makabro] *agg* macabre.

maccheroni [makke'roni] *sm pl* macaroni *sing.*

macchia[1] ['makkja] *sf* spot; stain.

macchia[2] ['makkja] *sf (arbusti)* bush.

macchiare [mak'kjare] *v* stain. **caffè macchiato** *sm* coffee with a dash of milk.

macchietta [mak'kjetta] *sf (persona)* character.

macchina ['makkina] *sf* machine; *(automobile)* car. **macchina da scrivere** typewriter. **macchina fotografica** camera.

macchinare [makki'nare] *v* plot.

macchinario [makki'narjo] *sm* machinery.

macchinista [makki'nista] *s(m + f)* machinist; *(ferr)* engine driver.

macedonia [matʃe'dɔnja] *sf* fruit salad.

macellare [matʃel'lare] *v* slaughter. **macelleria** *sf* butcher's shop. **macellaio** *sm* butcher. **macello** *sm* slaughterhouse; *(fig)* shambles.

macerare [matʃe'rare] *v* soak; macerate.

macerie [ma'tʃɛrje] *sf pl* ruins *pl.*

macina ['matʃina] *sf* millstone, grindstone. **macinare** *v* grind. **macinino** *sm (da caffè)* coffee-mill; *(da pepe)* pepper-mill.

madido ['madido] *agg* soaking wet.

Madonna [ma'donna] *sf* **la Madonna** the Virgin Mary.

madornale [mador'nale] *agg* gross.

madre ['madre] *sf* mother; *(comm)* counterfoil. **madreperla** *sf* mother-of-pearl.

madrigale [madri'gale] *sm* madrigal.

maestà [mae'sta] *sf* majesty. **maestoso** *agg* majestic; imposing.

maestro [ma'ɛstro] *sm* master; teacher. *agg* principal, main. **colpo maestro** *sm* master-stroke. **maestra** *sf* mistress; teacher. **maestranze** *sf pl* work force *sing.*

mafia ['mafja] *sf* mafia. **mafioso, -a** *sm, sf* member of the Mafia.

magagna [ma'gaɲa] *sf* flaw, fault.

magari [ma'gari] *inter* most certainly! *(oh se ...)* if only .... *avv (forse)* perhaps; *(perfino)* even.

magazzino [magad'dzino] *sm* store, warehouse. **magazzinaggio** *sm* warehousing. **magazziniere** *sm* warehouseman.

maggio [maddʒo] *sm* May.

maggiorana [maddʒo'rana] *sf* marjoram.

maggioranza [maddʒo'rantsa] *sf* majority.

maggiore [mad'dʒore] *agg (m + f),* sm major; *(più grande)* greater, larger; *(più vecchio)* older; *(di due fratelli)* elder; *(superlativo)* greatest, oldest, eldest. *sm* major. **andare per la maggiore** be a hit.

maggiorenne [maddʒo'rɛnne] *agg* of age. *s(m + f)* major.

maggiormente [maddʒor'mente] *avv* (all the) more; *(di più)* most.

magia [ma'dʒia] *sf* magic. **magico** *agg* magic(al).

magistero [madʒis'tɛro] *sm* teaching (profession). **scuola di magistero** *sf* college of education. **magistrale** *agg (di maestro)* magisterial; *(da maestro)* masterly.

magistrato [madʒis'trato] *sm* magistrate.

maglia ['maʎa] *sf* stitch; *(rete)* mesh; *(indumento intimo)* vest; T-shirt; *(maglione)* jersey. **fare la maglia** knit. **lavoro a maglia** *sm* knitting. **maglieria** *sf* knitwear. **maglione** *sm* jersey, pullover.

magnanimo [ma'nanimo] *agg* magnanimous.

magnete [ma'ɲɛte] *sm (auto)* magneto; *(calamita)* magnet. **magnetismo** *sm* magnetism.

magnetofono [maɲe'tɔfono] *sm* taperecorder.

magnifico [ma'ɲifiko] *agg* magnificent, splendid. **magnificenza** *sf* magnificence.

magnolia [ma'nɔlja] *sf* magnolia.

mago ['mago] *sm (stregone)* sorcerer; *(illusionista)* magician.

magro ['magro] *agg* thin; *(fig)* meagre; *(povero di grasso)* lean. **magra** *sf (fiume)* low level; *(fig)* shortage.

mai ['mai] *avv* never, ever. **caso o se mai** in case, if ever. **come mai** how (on earth).

maiale [ma'jale] *sm* pig; *(carne)* pork.

maionese [majo'neze] *sf* mayonnaise.

mais ['mais] *sm* maize.

maiuscolo [ma'juskolo] *agg* capital. **maiuscola** *sf* capital (letter).

malaccorto [malak'kɔrto] *agg* ill-advised.

malafede [mala'fede] *sf* bad faith.

malandato [malan'dato] *agg* in bad condition.

malanno [ma'lanno] *sm* misfortune, trouble.

malapena [mala'pena] *sf* **a malapena** scarcely.

malaria [ma'larja] *sf* malaria.

malato [ma'lato] *-a agg* sick, ill. *sm, sf* sick person, patient. **malattia** *sf* illness, disease.

malavita [mala'vita] *sf* underworld.

malavoglia [mala'voʎa] *sf* reluctance.

malavveduto [malavve'duto] *agg* unwise.

malconcio [mal'kontʃo] *agg* shabby.

malcontento [malkon'tɛnto] *agg* dissatisfied. *sm* dissatisfaction.

maldestro [mal'dɛstro] *agg* awkward.

maldicente [maldi'tʃɛnte] *agg* slanderous.

male ['male] *avv* (*non bene*) badly; (*in modo non buono*) ill; (*in modo imperfetto*) not well; (*indisposto*) unwell. **sentirsi male** feel unwell or ill. *sm* evil; (*dolore*) pain. **andare a male** go bad. **di male in peggio** from bad to worse. **far male** hurt. **mal di denti** toothache. **mal di gola** sore throat. **mal di mare** sea-sickness. **mal di testa** headache.

°maledire [male'dire] *v* curse, damn. **maledizione** *sf* curse.

maleducato [maledu'kato] *agg* ill-mannered, rude.

malefico [ma'lɛfiko] *agg* harmful.

malerba [ma'lɛrba] *sf* weed.

malessere [ma'lɛssere] *sm* malaise.

malevolo [ma'lɛvolo] *agg* hostile.

malfamato [malfa'mato] *agg* ill-famed.

malfatto [mal'fatto] *agg* badly made.

malfattore [malfat'tore] *sm* evil-doer.

malfermo [mal'fermo] *agg* unsteady.

malfido [mal'fido] *agg* unreliable.

malgrado [mal'grado] *prep* notwithstanding, in spite of.

malia [ma'lia] *sf* charm. **maliardo** *agg* bewitching.

maligno [ma'liɲo] *agg* spiteful; (*med*) malignant.

malinconia [malinko'nia] *sf* melancholy, gloom. **malinconico** *agg* gloomy, dismal.

malincuore [malin'kwɔre] *avv* **a malincuore** reluctantly, half-heartedly.

malinteso [malin'tezo] *agg* misunderstood, mistaken. *sm* misunderstanding.

malizia [ma'litsja] *sf* cunning, malice. **malizioso** *agg* malicious, cunning.

mallevadore [malleva'dore] *sm* guarantor, surety.

malmenare [malme'nare] *v* manhandle.

malnutrito [malnu'trito] *agg* undernourished.

malora [ma'lora] *sf* ruin. **andare in malora** (*fam*) go to the dogs. **va in malora!** (*al diavolo*) go to hell!

malsano [mal'sano] *agg* unhealthy.

malsicuro [malsi'kuro] *agg* unsafe.

malta ['malta] *sf* mortar.

maltempo [mal'tempo] *sm* bad weather.

malto ['malto] *sm* malt.

maltrattare [maltrat'tare] *v* ill-treat. **maltrattamento** *sm* ill-treatment.

malumore [malu'more] *sm* bad temper.

malva ['malva] *sm invar* (*colore*) mauve. *sf* (*bot*) mallow.

malvagio [mal'vadʒo] *agg* wicked.

malversare [malver'sare] *v* embezzle. **malversatore, -trice** *sm, sf* embezzler. **malversazione** *sf* embezzlement.

malvisto [mal'visto] *agg* unpopular.

malvivente [malvi'vɛnte] *sm* crook.

malvolentieri [malvolen'tjɛri] *avv* reluctantly.

mamma ['mamma] *sf* mother, mum(my). **mamma mia!** good gracious!

mammella [mam'mɛlla] *sf* breast.

mammifero [mam'mifero] *sm* mammal.

mammola ['mammola] *sf* violet.

manata [ma'nata] *sf* handful.

mancare [man'kare] *v* (*aver difetto*) lack; (*essere assente*) be missing; (*fallire, sentire la mancanza*) miss. **ci mancherebbe altro!** that would be the limit! **mancare alla parola** not keep one's word. **sentirsi mancare** feel faint.

mancia ['mantʃa] *sf* tip. **dar la mancia** tip.

mancino [man'tʃino], **-a** *sm, sf* left-hander. *agg* left-handed, left. **colpo mancino** *sm* underhand trick.

mandare [man'dare] *v* send. **mandare a fondo** sink. **mandare avanti** run. **mandar giù** (*cibo*) swallow. **mandar via** dismiss.

mandarino[1] [manda'rino] *sm* (*cinese*) mandarin.

mandarino[2] [manda'rino] *sm* (*albero*) mandarin tree; (*frutto*) mandarin, tangerine.

mandato [man'dato] *sm* commission; (*pol*) mandate; (*dir*) warrant.

mandibola [man'dibola] *sf* jaw.

mandolino [mando'lino] *sm* mandolin.

mandorla ['mandorla] *sf* almond. **mandorlo** *sm* almond-tree.

mandria ['mandrja] *sf* herd, flock.

mandrino [man'drino] *sm* (*tec*) spindle, mandrel.

maneggiare [maned'dʒare] *v* handle. **maneggio** *sm* handling; (*addestramento cavalli*) riding-school; (*intrigo*) plot.

manette [ma'nette] *sf pl* handcuffs *pl*.

mangano ['mangano] *sm* mangle.

mangereccio [mandʒe'rettʃo] *agg* edible.

mangiare [man'dʒare] *v* eat; (*corrodere*) eat into; (*dissipare*) squander; (*carte, scacchi, ecc.*) take. **dar da mangiare a**

feed. **far da mangiare** prepare a meal. **mangiare la foglia** smell a rat. **mangiarsi il fegato** fret. *sm* food.

mangiatoia [mandʒa'toja] *sf* manger.

mangime [man'dʒime] *sm* fodder.

maniaco [ma'niako], **-a** *agg* maniacal. *sm, sf* maniac. **mania** *sf* mania.

manica [manika] *sf* sleeve. **senza maniche** sleeveless.

manichino [mani'kino] *sm* mannequin, (tailor's) dummy.

manico ['maniko] *sm* handle; (violino, ecc.) neck.

manicomio [mani'kɔmjo] *sm* lunatic asylum.

maniera [ma'njera] *sf* manner.

manifattura [manifat'tura] *sf* manufacture.

manifestare [manifes'tare] *v* show; express; (pol) demonstrate. **manifestazione** *sf* display, show; expression; demonstration.

manifesto[1] [mani'fɛsto] *sm* poster, bill; (pol) manifesto. **manifestino** *sm* leaflet.

manifesto[2] [mani'fɛsto] *agg* clear, manifest.

maniglia [ma'niʎa] *sf* handle.

manipolare [manipo'lare] *v* manipulate.

mano ['mano] *sf, pl* **-i** hand; (strato) coat. **alla mano** ready, to hand. **a portata di mano** within reach. **dar** or **stringere la mano** a shake hands with. **di prima/seconda mano** first-/second-hand. **far man bassa** make a clean sweep. **fuori mano** outlying, off the beaten track. **man mano che** as. **mettere le mani avanti** take precautions. **sotto mano** handy.

manodopera [mano'dɔpera] *sf invar* labour, workforce.

*****manomettere** [mano'mettere] *v* tamper with, violate.

manopola [ma'nɔpola] *sf* (manubrio) hand-grip; (guanto) mitten; (radio, ecc.) knob.

manoscritto [mano'skritto] *sm* manuscript. *agg* handwritten.

manovale [mano'vale] *sm* labourer.

manovella [mano'vɛlla] *sf* handle, crank.

manovrare [manov'rare] *v* handle, manoeuvre. **manovra** *sf* manoeuvre.

mansione [man'sjone] *sf* function, duty.

mansueto [mansu'eto] *agg* gentle, meek.

mantello [man'tɛllo] *sm* coat, cloak.

*****mantenere** [mante'nere] *v* maintain, keep. **mantenimento** *sm* maintenance.

mantice ['mantitʃe] *sm* bellows *pl.*

manto ['manto] *sm* cloak, mantle.

manuale [manu'ale] *agg, sm* manual.

manubrio [ma'nubrjo] *sm* handlebar.

manutenzione [manuten'tsjone] *sf* maintenance, upkeep; (auto) servicing.

manzo ['mandzo] *sm* (animale) steer; (carne) beef.

mappa ['mappa] *sf* map. **mappamondo** *sm* globe.

maratona [mara'tona] *sf* marathon.

marca ['marka] *sf* brand.

marcare [mar'kare] *v* mark; (sport) score; accentuate.

marchese [mar'keze] *sm* marquis. **marchesa** *sf* marchioness.

marchio ['markjo] *sm* mark; (comm) trade-mark. **marchio depositato** registered trade-mark.

marcia[1] ['martʃa] *sf* march; (auto) gear; (sport) walking. **fare marcia indietro** reverse; (fig) back out. **mettere in marcia** get going, set off.

marcia[2] ['martʃa] *sf* (materia) pus.

marciapiede [martʃa'pjede] *sm* pavement.

marciare [mar'tʃare] *v* march; (sport) walk; (fam: funzionare) work.

marcio ['martʃo] *agg* rotten; (fig) corrupt. *sm* rottenness; rotten part.

marcire [mar'tʃire] *v* rot, go bad. **marciume** *sm* rot.

marco[1] ['marko] *sm* mark.

mare ['mare] *sm* sea; (grande quantità) host. **alto mare** high sea. **essere in alto mare** (fig) be floundering, be at sea. **mare agitato** or **mosso** rough sea. **maretta** *sf* choppy sea.

marea [ma'rɛa] *sf* tide.

maresciallo [mareʃʃallo] *sm* (sottufficiale) sergeant major; (ufficiale) field-marshal.

margarina [marga'rina] *sf* margarine.

margherita [marge'rita] *sf* daisy.

margine ['mardʒine] *sm* edge, border; (fig) margin.

marina [ma'rina] *sf* navy. **marinaio** *sm* sailor.

marinare [mari'nare] *v* marinate. **marinare la scuola** play truant.

marionetta [marjo'netta] *sf* puppet.

maritare [mari'tare] *v* marry; (mescolare) mix. **maritarsi** *v* get married.

*****marito** [ma'rito] *sm* husband.

marittimo [ma'rittimo] *agg* sea; maritime.

marmaglia [mar'maʎa] sf rabble.
marmellata [marmel'lata] sf jam; (di agrumi) marmalade.
marmo ['marmo] sm marble.
marra ['marra] sf hoe.
marrone [mar'rone] sm chestnut. agg brown.
marsupiale [marsu'pjale] sm, agg marsupial.
martedì [marte'di] sm Tuesday.
martellare [martel'lare] v hammer; (fig) pound. **martellata** sf hammer-blow; (fig) heavy blow. **martello** sm hammer; (porta) knocker; (orologio) striker.
martinetto [marti'netto] sm jack.
martin pescatore [mar'tin peska'tore] sm kingfisher.
martire ['martire] s(m+f) martyr. **martirio** sm martyrdom. **martoriare** v torture.
marxismo [mark'sizmo] sm Marxism. **marxista** s(m+f), agg Marxist.
marzapane [martsa'pane] sm marzipan.
marziale [mar'tsjale] agg martial.
marzo ['martso] sm march.
mascalzone [maskal'tsone] sm rascal, scoundrel. **mascalzonata** sf nasty trick.
mascara [mas'kara] sm mascara.
mascella [ma'ʃella] sf jaw.
maschera ['maskera] sf mask; (travestimento) disguise; (cinema, teatro) usherette. **mascherare** v mask; (con costumi) dress up; (celare) disguise; (schermare) screen; (mimetizzare) camouflage.
maschile [mas'kile] agg male; (gramm) masculine; (per ragazzi) boys'; (per uomini) men's.
maschio ['maskjo] sm male; (ragazzo) boy.
masochismo [mazo'kizmo] sm masochism. **masochista** s(m+f) masochist.
massa ['massa] sf mass; (gran numero) heap, lot; (elett) earth.
massacrare [massa'krare] v massacre. **massacro** sm massacre.
massaggiare [massad'dʒare] v massage. **massaggio** sm massage.
massaia [mas'saja] sf housewife.
masserizie [masse'ritsje] sf pl fixtures and fittings pl.
massiccio [mas'sittʃo] agg solid.
massima ['massima] sf maxim; (norma) rule. **di massima** general, informal. **in linea di massima** as a general rule, on the whole.
massimo ['massimo] agg greatest;

(estremo) utmost; (il più alto) highest; (il migliore) best; (fis) maximum. sm maximum; (tutto ciò che) most; (meglio) best.
massone [mas'sone] sm freemason. **massoneria** sf freemasonry.
masticare [masti'kare] v chew; (borbottare) mutter. **gomma da masticare** sf chewing gum.
mastice ['mastitʃe] sm mastic; (per vetri) putty.
mastino [mas'tino] sm mastiff.
mastro ['mastro] sm ledger.
matassa [ma'tassa] sf skein, hank.
matematico [mate'matiko], **-a** agg mathematical. sm, sf mathematician. sf mathematics.
materasso [mate'rasso] sm mattress. **materassino** (pneumatico) sm air-bed.
materia [ma'tɛrja] sf matter; substance; (argomento, disciplina) subject; (fam: marcia) pus. **entrare in materia** broach a subject. **materia prima** raw material.
materiale [mate'rjale] sm, agg material. **materialismo** sm materialism. **materialista** s(m+f) materialist.
materno [ma'tɛrno] agg maternal, motherly. **scuola materna** sf nursery school. **maternità** sf motherhood; (ospedale) maternity hospital.
matita [ma'tita] sf pencil.
matriarcale [matriar'kale] agg matriarchal.
matrice [ma'tritʃe] sf matrix; (modulo) counterfoil.
matricola [ma'trikola] sf register; (numero) serial number; (studente) freshman. **matricolare** v register.
matrigna [ma'trinja] sf stepmother.
matrimonio [matri'monjo] sm marriage, matrimony; (festa nuziale) wedding. **matrimoniale** agg matrimonial. **letto matrimoniale** sm double bed.
matta ['matta] sf (carte) joker.
mattatoio [matta'tojo] sm slaughterhouse.
matterello [matte'rɛllo] sm rolling-pin.
mattina [mat'tina] sf morning. **mattinata** sf morning; (teatro) matinée. **mattiniero** agg early rising.
matto ['matto] agg mad. **andar matto per** be crazy about. **matto da legare** mad as a hatter. **scacco matto** checkmate.
mattone [mat'tone] sm brick; (fam: noioso) bore. **mattonella** sf tile; (biliardo) cushion.

mattutino [mattu'tino] *agg* morning.

maturare [matu'rare] *v* mature, ripen; *(med)* come to a head. **maturazione** *sf* ripening. **maturità** *sf* maturity. **esame di maturità** *sm* school-leaving examination, A level(s). **maturo** *agg* ripe; mature.

mausoleo [mauzo'lɛo] *sm* mausoleum.

mazza ['mattsa] *sf* club; *(martello)* sledgehammer. **mazzata** *sf* heavy blow.

mazzo ['mattso] *sm* bunch; *(carte)* pack. **fare il mazzo** shuffle the cards or pack.

me [me] *pron* me. *V* **mi.**

meccanico [mek'kaniko] *agg* mechanical. *sm* mechanic. **meccanica** *sf* mechanics. **meccanismo** *sm* mechanism, works. **meccanizzare** *v* mechanize. **meccanizzazione** *sf* mechanization.

meccanografico [mekkano'grafiko] *agg* data processing.

medaglia [me'daʎa] *sf* medal. **medaglione** *sm* medallion; *(gioiello)* locket.

medesimo [me'dezimo] *agg* same.

media ['mɛdja] *sf* mean, average; *(scuola)* secondary school. **fare la media di** average.

mediana [me'djana] *sf* median. **mediano** *agg* median, medial.

mediante [me'djante] *prep* through, by (means of).

mediatore [medja'tore], **-trice** *sm, sf* intermediary; *(comm)* broker. **mediazione** *sf* mediation; brokerage.

medicare [medi'kare] *v* treat; *(ferita)* dress. **medicina** *sf* medicine.

medicinale [meditʃi'nale] *agg* medicinal. *sm* medicine.

medico ['mɛdiko] *sm* doctor, physician. *agg* medical. **medico chirurgo** surgeon. **medico condotto** medical officer. **medico generico** general practitioner.

medievale [medje'vale] *agg* medieval.

medio ['mɛdjo] *agg* middle; average; *(scuola)* secondary. *sm* middle finger.

mediocre [me'djɔkre] *agg* mediocre, poor.

meditare [medi'tare] *v* meditate, ponder. **meditazione** *sf* meditation.

mediterraneo [mediter'raneo] *sm, agg* Mediterranean.

medium ['mɛdjum] *s(m+f)* *invar* medium.

medusa [me'duza] *sf* jelly-fish.

megafono [me'gafono] *sm* loudspeaker.

megera [me'dʒɛra] *sf* harridan.

meglio ['mɛʎo] *agg, avv* *(comparativo)* better; *(superlativo)* best. *sm* best. **alla meglio** as well as possible. **tanto meglio!** so much the better!

mela ['mela] *sf* apple. **mela cotogna** quince. **melo** *sm* apple-tree.

melagrana [mela'grana] *sf* pomegranate. **melograno** *sm* pomegranate tree.

melanzana [melan'dzana] *sf* aubergine, egg-plant.

melassa [me'lassa] *sf* treacle, molasses.

melma ['mɛlma] *sf* slime.

melodia [melo'dia] *sf* melody. **melodico** *agg* melodious. **melodioso** *agg* melodious, sweet-sounding.

melodramma [melo'dramma] *sm* melodrama.

melone [me'lone] *sm* melon.

membrana [mem'brana] *sf* membrane; *(acustica)* diaphragm.

membro ['mɛmbro] *sm, pl* **-a** *f* in collective sense member; *(anat)* limb.

memoria [me'mɔrja] *sf* memory; *(oggetto ricordo)* souvenir; *(scritto)* memoir. **a memoria** by heart. **prendere memoria di** make a note of. **memoriale** *sm* memorial; petition; *(raccolta di documenti)* record. **memorizzare** *v* memorize.

menare [me'nare] *v* lead; *(portare)* take, bring; *(assestare)* strike. **a menadito** at one's fingertips.

mendicare [mendi'kare] *v* beg. **mendicante** *s(m+f)* beggar.

meno ['meno] *avv* *(comparativo)* less; *(superlativo)* least; *(mat)* minus. *agg invar* *(minore)* less; *(in minor numero)* fewer. *prep* *(eccetto)* but (for), except (for). **a meno che** unless. **fare a meno di** do without. **meno male!** thank goodness! **o meno** *(o no)* or not. **tanto meno** let alone. **venir meno** *(svenire)* faint; *(mancare)* fail. **venir meno alla parola** break one's word. **sm invar** *(the)* least. **i meno** *sm pl* *(the)* minority *sing.*

menomare [meno'mare] *v* diminish; *(danneggiare)* injure, disable. **menomato, -a** *s, agg* disabled.

menopausa [meno'pauza] *sf* menopause.

mensa ['mɛnsa] *sf* table; refectory; *(mil)* mess.

mensile [men'sile] *agg* monthly. *sm* *(giornale)* monthly; *(paga)* monthly pay.

mensola ['mɛnsola] *sf* bracket, shelf; *(caminetto)* mantelpiece.

menta ['mɛnta] *sf* mint; *(peperina)* peppermint; *(romana)* spearmint.

mente ['mente] *sf* mind; intellect. **venire in mente** occur; come to mind. **mentale** *agg* mental. **mentalità** *sf* mentality.

mentire [men'tire] *v* lie. **mentito** *agg* false.

mento ['mento] *sm* chin.

mentre ['mentre] *cong* while, as; (*laddove*) whereas.

menu [mə'ny] *sm* menu.

menzionare [mentsjo'nare] *v* mention. **menzione** *sf* mention.

menzogna [men'dzoɲa] *sf* lie. **menzognero** *agg* lying, false.

meraviglia [mera'viʎa] *sf* wonder, marvel; (*stupore*) surprise. **a meraviglia** wonderfully. **meravigliare** *v* surprise, amaze. **meraviglioso** *agg* marvellous, wonderful.

mercante [mer'kante] *sm* merchant, trader. **mercanteggiare** *v* trade, deal; (*contrattare*) haggle, bargain. **mercantile** *agg* mercantile. **nave mercantile** *sf* merchant ship.

mercanzia [merkan'tsia] *sf* merchandise, goods *pl*.

mercato [mer'kato] *sm* market. **a buon mercato** cheap, inexpensive.

merce ['mertʃe] *sf* merchandise, goods *pl*; (*in magazzino*) stock.

mercenario [mertʃe'narjo] *agg*, *sm* mercenary.

merciaio [mer'tʃajo], **-a** *sm*, *sf* haberdasher. **merceria** *sf* haberdashery.

mercoledì [merkole'di] *sm* Wednesday.

mercurio [mer'kurjo] *sm* mercury.

merda ['merda] *sf* (*volg*) shit.

merenda [me'renda] *sf* (afternoon) snack, tea.

meridiano [meri'djano] *sf* (*geog*) meridian. *agg* (*di mezzogiorno*) midday. **meridiana** *sf* (*geog*) meridian line; (*orologio solare*) sundial.

meridionale [meridjo'nale] *agg* southern, south. *s(m+f)* southerner. **meridione** *sm* south.

meringa [me'ringa] *sf* meringue.

meritare [meri'tare] *v* deserve, merit. **meritevole** *agg* deserving, worthy.

merito ['merito] *sm* merit. **a pari merito** equal. **in merito a** regarding, as to, about. **per merito di** thanks to.

merletto [mer'letto] *sm* lace.

merlo ['merlo] *sm* blackbird; (*sempliciotto*) fool.

merluzzo [mer'luttso] *sm* cod; (*nasello*) hake.

mero ['mero] *agg* mere.

meschino [mes'kino] *agg* wretched, mean.

mescolare [mesko'lare] *v* mix; (*unire*) blend. **mescolatore, -trice** *sm, sf* mixer.

mese ['meze] *sm* month.

messa[1] ['messa] *sf* (*rel*) Mass. **messale** *sm* missal.

messa[2] ['messa] *sf* (*il mettere*) placing, putting.

messaggio [mes'saddʒo] *sm* message. **messaggero** *sm* messenger; (*fig*) herald.

messo ['messo] *sm* usher.

mestiere [mes'tjere] *sm* job, trade; (*manuale*) craft; profession. **di mestiere** by profession. **essere del mestiere** be an expert. **ferri del mestiere** *sm pl* tools of the trade *pl*.

mesto ['mesto] *agg* sad, mournful. **mestizia** *sf* sadness.

mestolo ['mestolo], **-a** *sm, sf* ladle, kitchen spoon.

mestruazione [mestrua'tsjone] *sf* menstruation; (*fam*) period. **mestruale** *agg* menstrual.

meta ['meta] *sf* goal, aim; destination; (*rugby*) try.

metà [me'ta] *sf* half; (*centro*) middle. **a metà strada** half-way. **fare a metà** halve; (*fam*) go halves.

metabolismo [metabo'lizmo] *sm* metabolism. **metabolico** *agg* metabolic.

metafisico [meta'fiziko], **-a** *agg* metaphysical. *sm, sf* metaphysician. *sf* metaphysics.

metafora [me'tafora] *sf* metaphor, figure of speech. **metaforico** *agg* metaphorical.

metallo [me'tallo] *sm* metal. **metallico** *agg* metallic. **metallurgia** *sf* metallurgy.

metamorfosi [meta'morfozi] *sf* metamorphosis, transformation.

metano [me'tano] *sm* methane.

meteora [me'teora] *sf* meteor. **meteorico** *agg* meteoric.

meteorologia [meteorolo'dʒia] *sf* meteorology. **meteorologico** *agg* meteorological, weather. **bollettino meteorologico** *sm* weather report. **previsioni meteorologiche** *sf pl* weather forecast *sing*.

meticcio [me'tittʃo], **-a** *s, agg* half-caste.

meticoloso [metiko'lozo] *agg* meticulous.

metodista [meto'dista] *s(m+f)*, *agg* methodist.

metodo ['metodo] *sm* method. **metodico** *agg* methodical.

metro ['metro] sm metre; (per misurare) rule; (a nastro) tape-measure. **metrico** agg (misura) metric; (poesia) metrical.

metropoli [me'tropoli] sf metropolis. **metropolitana** sf underground (railway).

*****mettere** ['mettere] v put; place; lay (down); (indossare) put on, wear; (supporre) suppose. **mettersi sotto** get down to it.

mezzo [meddzo] agg half; (medio) middle. **mezzogiorno** sm noon, midday; (geog) south. sm half; (centro) middle; (strumento) means. **a** or **per mezzo di** by, through. **mezzi** pl means pl. avv half; (quasi) nearly. **andarci di mezzo** (avere la peggio) suffer for it; (essere in gioco) be at stake. **togliere di mezzo** get rid of.

mi [mi], **me** pron (to) me; (riflessivo) myself.

miagolare [mjago'lare] v mew, miaow. **miagolio** sm mewing.

mica¹ ['mika] avv (fam) at all.

mica² ['mika] sf mica.

miccia ['mittʃa] sf fuse.

microbo ['mikrobo] sm microbe.

microcosmo [mikro'kozmo] sm microcosm.

microfilm ['mikrofilm] sm invar microfilm.

microfono [mi'krɔfono] sm microphone; (telefono) mouthpiece.

microscopio [mikro'skɔpjo] sm microscope. **microscopico** agg microscopic.

microsolco [mikro'sɔlko] sm microgroove; (disco a 33 giri) LP; (disco a 45 giri) EP.

midollo [mi'dollo] sm marrow; (bot) pith. **bagnato fino al midollo** soaked to the skin. **fino al midollo** to the core. **midollo spinale** spinal cord.

miele ['mjɛle] sm honey.

mietere ['mjetere] v reap, harvest; (uccidere) mow down. **mietitore, -trice** sm, sf reaper, harvester. **mietitrebbiatrice** sf combine harvester. **mietitura** sf reaping, harvesting; (periodo, messe) harvest.

migliaio [mi'ʎajo] sm, pl -a f thousand; (circa mille) about a thousand.

miglio¹ ['miʎo] sm, pl -a f mile.

miglio² ['miʎo] sm (bot) millet.

migliore [mi'ʎore] agg (comparativo) better; (superlativo) best. sm best.

mignolo ['miɲolo] sm (della mano) little finger; (del piede) little toe.

migrare [mi'grare] v migrate. **migratorio** agg migratory. **migrazione** sf migration.

milione [mi'ljone] sm million. **milionesimo** sm, agg millionth.

militare [mili'tare] agg military. sm soldier. v militate. **militarismo** sm militarism. **militarista** s(m+f), agg militarist. **milite** ['milite] sm soldier, warrior. **milizia** sf (corpo armato) militia.

millantare [millan'tare] v boast. **millantato credito** sm false pretences pl. **millantatore, -trice** sm, sf braggart, show-off. **millanteria** sf boasting.

mille ['mille] agg, sm thousand. **millennio** sm millennium. **millesimo** agg, sm thousandth.

milligrammo [milli'grammo] sm milligram.

millimetro [mil'limetro] sm millimetre.

mimetizzare [mimetid'dzare] v camouflage. **mimetizzazione** sf camouflage.

mimica ['mimika] sf mime. **mimico** agg mimic. **mimo** sm mime; (uccello) mocking-bird.

mina ['mina] sf mine; (di matita) lead. **minare** v mine; (insidiare) undermine. **minatore** sm miner.

minaccia [mi'nattʃa] sf threat. **minacciare** v threaten. **minaccioso** agg threatening.

minareto [mina'reto] sm minaret.

minerale [mine'rale] agg, sm mineral.

minerario [mine'rarjo] agg mining.

minestra [mi'nestra] sf soup.

mingherlino [minger'lino] agg skinny.

miniatura [minja'tura] sf miniature.

miniera [mi'njera] sf mine.

minimo ['minimo] agg (il più piccolo) least, smallest, slightest; (più basso) minimum; (piccolissimo) very small, very slight; (molto basso) very low. sm minimum; (la minima cosa) least.

ministero [mini'stero] sm (pol) ministry. **pubblico ministero** public prosecutor.

ministro [mi'nistro] sm minister.

minore [mi'nore] s(m+f), agg (più piccolo) less, smaller; (più basso) lower; (più giovane) younger; (superlativo) least, lowest, youngest; (mat, musica) minor. **minorità** sf minority.

minorenne [mino'renne] s(m+f) minor. agg under age.

minuetto [minu'etto] sm minuet.

minuscolo [mi'nuskolo] agg small, diminutive. **minuscola** sf small letter.

minuta [mi'nuta] *sf* draft.
minuto[1] [mi'nuto] *agg* small, minute; detailed. **al minuto** retail. **vendere al minuto** retail.
minuto[2] [mi'nuto] *sm* (*primo*) minute. **minuto secondo** second. **spaccare il minuto** be dead on time.
mio ['mio], *m pl* **miei** *agg* my. *pron* mine.
miope [mi'ope] *agg* short-sighted. **miopia** *sf* short-sightedness.
mira ['mira] *sf* aim.
miracolo [mi'rakolo] *sm* miracle. **miracoloso** *agg* miraculous.
miraggio [mi'raddʒo] *sm* mirage.
mirare [mi'rare] *v* aim; (*prendere mira*) take aim. **mirino** *sm* sight; (*foto*) viewfinder.
mirtillo [mir'tillo] *sm* bilberry. **mirtillo rosso** cranberry.
miscela [mi'ʃela] *sf* mixture; (*caffè, tè, tabacco*) blend. **miscelare** *v* mix, blend.
mischia ['miskja] *sf* fray.
mischiare [mis'kjare] *v* mix; (*carte*) shuffle.
miscuglio [mis'kuʎo] *sm* mixture.
miseria [mi'zɛrja] *sm* poverty; (*inezia*) pittance; squalor. **miserabile** *agg* miserable, wretched.
misericordia [mizeri'kɔrdja] *sf* mercy. **senza misericordia** merciless; (*spietato*) ruthless.
misero ['mizero] *agg* poor, wretched.
missile ['missile] *sm* missile.
missione [mis'sjone] *sf* mission. **missionario, -a** *s, agg* missionary.
mistero [mis'tero] *sm* mystery. **misterioso** *agg* mysterious.
mistico ['mistiko], **-a** *agg* mystical. *sm, sf* mystic. **misticismo** *sm* mysticism.
misto ['misto] *agg* mixed.
misura [mi'zura] *sf* measure; (*taglia, dimensione*) size; (*atto e modo del misurare*) measurement; moderation. **fatto su misura** made to measure. **prendere delle misure** take steps.
misurare [mizu'rare] *v* measure; limit; (*indumenti*) try on. **misurato** *agg* measured, moderate.
mite ['mite] *agg* mild, moderate.
mito ['mito] *sm* myth. **mitico** *agg* mythical. **mitologia** *sf* mythology. **mitologico** *agg* mythological.
mitra[1] ['mitra] *sf* (*rel*) mitre.

mitra[2] ['mitra] *sm invar* tommy-gun.
mitragliatrice [mitraʎʎa'tritʃe] *sf* machine-gun. **mitragliamento** *sm* machine-gun fire; (*fig*) bombarding. **mitragliare** *v* machine-gun; (*fig*) bombard.
mittente [mit'tɛnte] *s(m+f)* sender.
mobile ['mobile] *agg* mobile, moving; movable. **squadra mobile** *sf* flying squad. *sm* piece of furniture. **mobili** *sm pl* furniture *sing*.
mobilia [mo'bilja] *sf* furnishings *pl*; (*mobili*) furniture.
mobiliare [mobi'ljare] *agg* movable. *v* furnish.
mobilitare [mobili'tare] *v* mobilize. **mobilitazione** *sf* mobilization.
mocassino [mokas'sino] *sm* moccasin.
moccolo ['mɔkkolo] *sm* candle-end. **reggere il moccolo** play gooseberry. **tirare dei moccoli** (*fam*) swear.
moda ['mɔda] *sf* fashion. **di** *or* **alla moda** in fashion, fashionable. **fuori moda** out of fashion. **passare di moda** go out of fashion.
modalità [modali'ta] *sf* procedure, formality.
modellare [model'lare] *v* model. **modella** *sf* model. **modello** *sm* model; (*disegno*) pattern.
moderare [mode'rare] *v* moderate, lower; control. **moderatore** *sm* moderator; (*TV, radio*) chairman. **moderazione** *sf* moderation, restraint.
moderno [mo'dɛrno] *agg* modern; (*al passo coi tempi*) up-to-date. **modernizzare** *v* modernize, bring up-to-date.
modestia [mo'dɛstja] *sf* modesty. **modesto** *agg* modest, unassuming; (*umile*) humble.
modificare [modifi'kare] *v* modify, alter. **modifica** *sf* alteration, modification.
modista [mo'dista] *sf* milliner.
modo ['mɔdo] *sm* manner, way; opportunity; (*gramm*) mood. **ad ogni modo** anyhow, in any case. **di modo che** (*affinché*) so that; (*e così*) and so. **in modo da** so that. **in qualche modo** somehow. **modo di dire** expression, idiom. **modo di fare** manner. **per modo di dire** so to speak.
modulare [modu'lare] *v* modulate.
modulo ['mɔdulo] *sm* form; (*mat, tec*) modulus.
mogano ['mɔgano] *sm* mahogany.
mogio ['mɔdʒo] *agg* downhearted.

moglie ['moʎe] sf wife.

moina [mo'ina] sf **fare moine** coax.

molare [mo'lare] v grind. agg molar. **pietra molare** sf millstone. **mola** sf grinding wheel.

mole ['mɔle] sf pile, mass; (grandezza) size.

molecola [mo'lɛkola] sf molecule.

molesto [mo'lɛsto] agg troublesome, annoying. **molestare** v trouble, annoy. **molestia** sf annoyance, nuisance.

molla ['mɔlla] sf spring; (stimolo) mainspring. **molle** sf pl tongs pl. **mollare** v (lasciar andare) let go; (allentare) loosen, slacken. **molleggiato** agg sprung. **molletta** sf (biancheria) (clothes-)peg; (capelli) hair-pin.

molle ['mɔlle] agg soft; (bagnato) wet; (debole) weak. **mettere in molle** steep.

mollusco [mol'lusko] sm mollusc.

molo ['mɔlo] sm jetty; (banchina) wharf.

molteplice [mol'teplitʃe] agg manifold; varied.

moltiplicare [moltipli'kare] v multiply.

moltitudine [molti'tudine] sm multitude, host.

molto ['molto] agg a lot of, lots of, much; (pl) many; (tempo) long. avv much, a lot; (con agg e avv positivi) very. pron. a lot, much; (pl) many.

momento [mo'mento] sm moment. **a momenti** (tra poco) shortly; (quasi) almost. **al momento d'oggi** nowadays. **dal momento che** since.

monaca ['mɔnaka] sf nun. **monaco** sm monk.

Monaco ['mɔnako] sf (principato) Monaco; (di Baviera) Munich.

monarca [mo'narka] sm monarch, king. **monarchia** sf monarchy. **monarchico, -a** sm, sf monarchist.

monastero [monas'tɛro] sm monastery. **monastico** agg monastic.

monco ['monko] agg maimed. **essere monco di** ... have ... missing. **moncherino** sm stump.

mondezzaio [mondet'tsajo] sm rubbish heap; (ambiente sudicio) pigsty. **mondare** v (sbucciare) peel; (togliere erbacce) weed.

mondo ['mondo] sm world. **mandare all'altro mondo** (fam) send to hell. **mettere al mondo** give birth to. **vivere nel mondo della luna** have one's head in the

clouds. **mondiale** agg world; (diffuso) world-wide.

monello [mo'nɛllo] sm urchin. **monelleria** sf prank.

moneta [mo'neta] sf coin; (denaro) money; (spicciola) (small) change. **monetario** agg monetary.

monito ['mɔnito] sm warning.

monocolore [monoko'lore] agg plain; (pol) one-party.

monocromo [mo'nɔkromo] agg, sm monochrome.

monogamo [mo'nɔgamo], -a agg monogamous. sm, sf monogamist. **monogamia** sf monogamy.

monolitico [mono'litiko] agg monolithic.

monologo [mo'nɔlogo] sm, pl -ghi monologue.

monopolio [mono'poljo] sm monopoly. **monopolizzare** v monopolize.

monoteismo [monote'izmo] sm monotheism.

monotono [mo'nɔtono] agg monotonous. **monotonia** sf monotony.

monsone [mon'sone] sm monsoon.

monta ['monta] sf (accoppiamento) mounting; (luogo) stud-farm; (modo di cavalcare) riding.

montacarichi [monta'kariki] sm goods lift.

montaggio [mon'taddʒo] sm assembly; (cinema) editing.

montagna [mon'taɲa] sf mountain. **montagne russe** switchback sing.

montare [mon'tare] v (salire) climb; (tec) assemble; (incorniciare) mount; (film) edit; (macchina) get in(to). **montare a cavallo** get on a horse; (cavalcare) ride. **montatura** sf assembly; (occhiali) frame; (pubblicitaria) stunt.

monte ['monte] sm mountain; (davanti a nome) Mount. **a monte** above, upstream. **andare a monte** fall through. **mandare a monte** upset; (disdire) cancel. **monte di pietà** pawnshop. **monte premi** jackpot. **montuoso** agg mountainous.

montone [mon'tone] sm ram; (carne) mutton.

monumento [monu'mento] sm monument. **monumentale** agg monumental.

mora ['mɔra] sf (gelso) mulberry; (rovo) blackberry.

morale [mo'rale] agg moral. sf (dottrina) ethics pl; morality, morals pl; (insegnamento) moral. sm morale. **essere su/giù**

di **morale** be cheerful/depressed. **moralizzare** v moralize.

morbido ['mɔrbido] agg soft.

morbillo [mor'billo] sm measles.

morbo ['mɔrbo] sm disease. **morboso** agg morbid; pathological.

*mordere** ['mɔrdere] v bite; (afferrare) grip. **mordere il freno** strain at the leash. **mordace** agg biting, caustic.

morfina [mor'fina] sf morphine.

morigerato [moridʒe'rato] agg sober, clean-living.

*morire** [mo'rire] v die. **avere una fame/sete da morire** be terribly hungry/thirsty.

mormorare [mormo'rare] v murmur. **mormorio** sm murmur.

moro[1] ['mɔro] agg dark; (nero) black; (carnagione) swarthy; (capelli) brown.

moro[2] ['mɔro] sm (gelso) mulberry.

morsa ['mɔrsa] sf vice. **morsetto** sm clamp; (elett) terminal.

morsicare [morsi'kare] v gnaw, bite. **morso** sm bite; (fig) sting; (cavallo) bit.

mortaio [mor'tajo] sm mortar.

mortale [mor'tale] agg mortal; (implacabile) deadly. **mortalità** sf mortality.

morte ['mɔrte] sf death.

morto ['mɔrto] agg dead. sm dead person; (carte) dummy. **fare il morto** float (on one's back).

mosaico [mo'zaiko] sm mosaic.

mosca ['moska] sf fly; (barbetta) goatee. **mosca cieca** blindman's buff. **moscerino** sm small fly.

Mosca ['moska] sf Moscow.

moscato[1] [mos'kato] agg muscat(el). **noce moscata** sf nutmeg.

moscato[2] [mos'kato] agg (cavallo) dappled.

moschea [mos'kɛa] sf mosque.

moschetto [mos'ketto] sm musket. **moschettiere** sm musketeer.

mossa ['mɔssa] sf movement; (fig) move. **mosso** ['mɔsso] agg (mare) rough; (capelli) wavy.

mostarda [mos'tarda] sf mustard.

mostrare [mos'trare] v show. **mostra** sf show, exhibition; ostentation; (campione) sample. **mettere in mostra** display. **mostro** ['mɔstro] sm monster. **mostruosità** sf monstrosity. **mostruoso** agg monstrous.

motivo [mo'tivo] sm ground, reason; (disegno, musica) motif. **motivare** v motivate. **motivazione** sf motivation.

moto[1] ['mɔto] sm motion; (sommossa) rebellion. **mettere in moto** set in motion, start (up).

moto[2] ['mɔto] sf (fam) motor-bike.

motocicletta [mototʃik'letta] sf motorcycle. **motociclista** s(m + f) motor-cyclist.

motore [mo'tore] sm engine. agg motor. **albero motore** sm crankshaft. **motorino d'avviamento** sm starter (motor).

motoscafo [moto'skafo] sm motor-boat.

motto ['mɔtto] sm motto; (detto) saying.

movimento [movi'mento] sm movement; activity. **movimentato** agg lively, busy.

mozione [mo'tsjone] sf motion.

mozzare [mot'tsare] v cut off; (coda) dock. **mozzare il fiato** take one's breath away.

mozzicone [mottsi'kone] sm butt.

mucca ['mukka] sf cow.

mucchio ['mukkjo] sm heap.

muco ['muko] sm mucus. **mucosa** sf mucous membrane.

muda ['muda] sf moulting.

muffa ['muffa] sf mould. **muffoso** agg mouldy.

muggire [mud'dʒire] v also **mugghiare** bellow; (mare) roar; (vento) howl.

mughetto [mu'getto] sm lily of the valley.

mugnaio [mu'najo] sm miller.

mugolare [mugo'lare] v howl, whine.

mulattiera [mulat'tjera] sf (mule-)track.

mulino [mu'lino] sm mill; (a vento) windmill. **mulinello** sm whirlpool; (pesca) reel.

mulo ['mulo] sm mule.

multa ['multa] sf fine.

multicolore [multiko'lore] agg multicoloured.

multiplo ['multiplo] agg, sm multiple.

mummia ['mummja] sf mummy. **mummificare** v mummify.

*mungere** ['mundʒere] v milk.

municipio [muni'tʃipjo] sm (comune) municipality; (sede) town hall. **municipale** agg municipal.

munire [mu'nire] v supply; fortify.

munizione [muni'tsjone] sf munitions pl; (military) stores pl. **munizioni** sf pl ammunition sing.

*muovere** ['mwɔvere] v move.

muraglia [mu'raʎa] sf wall.

muratore [mura'tore] sm bricklayer.

muro ['muro] sm wall. **mura** sf pl city

walls *pl.* **parlare al muro** talk to a brick wall.

musa ['muza] *sf* muse.

muschio¹ ['muskjo] *sm (bot)* moss. **muscoso** *agg* mossy.

muschio² ['muskjo] *sm (odore)* musk.

muscolo ['muskolo] *sm* muscle.

museo [mu'zɛo] *sm* museum.

museruola [muze'rwɔla] *sf* muzzle.

musica ['muzika] *sf* music. **musicale** *agg* musical, music. **musicista** *s(m+f)* musician.

muso ['muzo] *sm* snout; *(spreg)* mug. **mettere il muso lungo** pull a long face.

mussolina [musso'lina] *sf* muslin.

mutande [mu'tande] *sf pl also* **mutandine** *(da donna)* panties *pl*; *(da uomo)* underpants *pl*; *(da bagno)* swimming trunks *pl*.

mutare [mu'tare] *v* change; *(fare la muta)* shed. **mutabile** *or* **mutevole** *agg* changeable; *(fig)* fickle. **mutamento** *sm* change. **mutazione** *sf* mutation.

mutilare [muti'lare] *v* maim, mutilate. **mutilato, -a** *sm, sf* disabled person.

muto ['muto], **-a** *agg* silent; *(affetto da mutismo)* dumb. *sm, sf* mute. **linguaggio dei muti** *sm* deaf-and-dumb language.

mutuo ['mutuo] *agg* mutual. *sm* loan. **mutuo ipotecario** mortgage. **mutus** *sf* insurance.

N

nafta ['nafta] *sf* fuel oil.

nailon ['nailon] *sm invar* nylon.

nanna ['nanna] *sf* **fare la nanna** *(fam)* sleep.

nano ['nano], **-a** *s, agg* dwarf.

Napoli ['napoli] *sf* Naples. **napoletano, -a** *s, agg* Neapolitan.

nappa ['nappa] *sf* tassel; *(fam: naso)* conk; *(pelle)* nappa.

narciso [nar'tʃizo] *sm* narcissus; *(giunchiglia)* daffodil.

narcotico [nar'kɔtiko] *agg, sm* narcotic. **narcosi** *sf* narcosis.

narice [na'ritʃe] *sf* nostril.

narrare [nar'rare] *v* tell. **narrativa** *sf* fiction. **narrazione** *sf* tale.

*****nascere** [na'ʃere] *v* be born; *(fig)* (a)rise, start (up). **far nascere** give rise to. **nascita** *sf* birth. **atto di nascita** *sm* birth certificate.

*****nascondere** [nas'kondere] *v* hide. **nascondiglio** *sm* hide-out. **nascondino** *sm* hide-and-seek.

nascosto [nas'kosto] *agg* hidden.

nasello [na'zɛllo] *sm* hake.

naso ['nazo] *sm* nose. **cacciare** *or* **ficcare il naso (in)** poke one's nose (into).

nastro ['nastro] *sm* ribbon; *(tec)* tape. **nastro sonoro** sound-track. **nastro trasportatore** conveyor belt.

nasturzio [nas'turtsjo] *sm* nasturtium.

natale [na'tale] *agg* native. **Natale** *sm* Christmas. **natalizio** *agg* Christmas. **giorno natalizio** *sm* birthday.

natatoia [nata'toja] *sf* flipper, fin.

natica ['natika] *sf* buttock.

nativo [na'tivo] *agg* native.

nato ['nato] *agg* born. **appena nato** new-born. **... nato e sputato** the (spitting) image of .... **nato morto** stillborn.

natura [na'tura] *sf* nature. **naturale** *agg* natural. **naturalezza** *sf* spontaneity; simplicity. **naturalistico** *agg* naturalistic.

naturalizzare [naturalid'dzare] *v* naturalize. **naturalizzazione** *sf* naturalization.

naufragio [nau'fradʒo] *sm* shipwreck; *(fig)* wreck. **naufragare** *v* be shipwrecked; *(fig)* come to grief. **naufrago, -a** *sm, sf* survivor.

nausea ['nauzea] *sf* nausea. **dare la nausea a** make sick. **provar nausea** feel sick. **nauseante** *agg* nauseating, sickening. **nauseato** *agg* nauseated, sickened.

nautico ['nautiko] *agg* nautical. **sport nautici** *sm pl* water sports *pl*.

navata [na'vata] *sf (centrale)* nave; *(laterale)* aisle.

nave ['nave] *sf* ship. **nave cisterna** tanker. **nave di salvataggio** lifeboat. **nave traghetto** ferry. **navale** *agg* naval. **navalmeccanica** *sf* shipbuilding. **navalmeccanico** *sm* shipyard worker.

navetta [na'vetta] *sf* shuttle.

navigare [navi'gare] *v* sail, navigate. **navigatore** *sm* navigator. **navigazione** *sf* navigation.

nazionalizzare [natsjonalid'dzare] *v* nationalize. **nazionalizzazione** *sf* nationalization.

nazione [na'tsjone] *sf* nation. **nazionale** *agg* national; *(econ)* domestic. **nazionalismo** *sm* nationalism. **nazionalista** *s(m+f)*, *agg* nationalist. **nazionalità** *sf* nationality.

nazismo [na'dzizmo] *sm* Nazism, National Socialism. **nazista** *s(m+f)*, *agg* Nazi.
ne [ne] *pron* of it *or* them, about it *or* them; (*partitivo*) some, any. *avv* from there.
nè [ne] *cong* neither, nor; (*con altra negazione*) either. **nè ... nè** ... neither ... nor ....
neanche [ne'anke] *avv*, *cong*, *also* **nemmeno**, **neppure** neither; either; (*rafforzativo*) not even.
nebbia ['nebbja] *sf* fog; (*foschia*) haze, mist. **nebbioso** *agg* foggy.
necessario [netʃes'sarjo] *agg* necessary, needed (for). *sm* necessary. **lo stretto necessario** the bare necessities *pl*.
necessità [netʃessi'ta] *sf* necessity, need. **di prima necessità** essential. **in caso di necessità** if necessary. **trovarsi nella necessità di** to be obliged to.
negare [ne'gare] *v* deny. **negato** *agg* denied; (*senza disposizione*) hopeless (at). **negazione** *sf* denial, negation.
negativa [nega'tiva] *sf* negative. **negativo** *agg* negative.
negli ['neʎi] *prep* + *art* **in gli**.
negligente [negli'dʒɛnte] *agg* negligent. **negligenza** *sf* negligence.
negoziare [nego'tsjare] *v* negotiate.
negozio [ne'gɔtsjo] *sm* shop; (*affare*) deal. **negoziante** *s(m+f)* shopkeeper; dealer; (*all'ingrosso*) wholesaler; (*al minuto*) retailer.
negro ['negro], **-a** *agg* Negro, black. *sm*, *sf* Negro, black person. **negriere** *sm* slaver; (*fig*) slave-driver.
nei ['nei] *prep* + *art* **in i**.
nel [nel] *prep* + *art* **in il**.
nell' [nell] *prep* + *art* **in l'**.
nella ['nella] *prep* + *art* **in la**.
nelle ['nelle] *prep* + *art* **in le**.
nello ['nello] *prep* + *art* **in lo**.
nemico [ne'miko], **-a** *agg* enemy, hostile; (*dannoso*) bad. *sm*, *sf* enemy.
nemmeno [nem'meno] *V* **neanche**.
neo ['nɛo] *sm* mole; (*posticcio*) beauty-spot.
neon ['nɛon] *sm* neon.
neonato [neo'nato], **-a** *agg* new-born. *sm*, *sf* new-born baby.
neozelandese [neodzelan'deze] *agg* New Zealand. *sm*, *sf* New Zealander.
nepotismo [nepo'tizmo] *sm* nepotism.
neppure [nep'pure] *V* **neanche**.

nerbo ['nɛrbo] *sm* whip; (*fig*) force.
nero ['nero] *agg*, *sm* black. **bestia nera** *sf* bugbear. **borsa nera** *sf* black market. **nerastro** *agg* blackish.
nervo ['nɛrvo] *sm* nerve; (*bot*) rib, vein; (*corda*) string. **avere i nervi** be on edge, be irritable. **dare ai** *or* **sui nervi a qualcuno** get on somebody's nerves. **nervoso** *agg* nervous; irritable; (*eccitabile*) highly strung. **esaurimento nervoso** *sm* nervous breakdown.
nesso ['nɛsso] *sm* connection.
nessuno [nes'suno] *agg* no. *pron* (*persone*) nobody, no-one; (*cose*) none; (*qualcuno*) anybody.
nettare [net'tare] *sm* nectar.
netto ['netto] *agg* clean; (*fig*) clear, sharp; (*peso*, *comm*) net. **nettezza** *sf* cleanliness; (*precisione*) clarity. **nettezza urbana** *sf* street-cleaning; refuse collection.
neutrale [neu'trale] *s(m+f)*, *agg* neutral. **neutralità** *sf* neutrality. **neutralizzare** *v* neutralize; (*fig*) counteract.
neutro ['neutro] *sm*, *agg* neutral; (*gramm*, *sesso*) neuter. **neutrone** *sm* neutron.
neve ['neve] *sf* snow. **cumulo di neve** *sm* snowdrift. **pupazzo di neve** *sm* snowman. **nevato** *or* **nevoso** *agg* snowy.
nevicare [nevi'kare] *v* snow. **nevicata** *sf* snowfall.
nevischio [ne'viskjo] *sm* sleet.
nevralgia [nevral'dʒia] *sf* neuralgia.
nevrosi [ne'vrɔzi] *sf* neurosis. **nevrotico**, **-a** *s*, *agg* neurotic.
nibbio ['nibbjo] *sm* kite.
nicchia ['nikkja] *sf* niche, recess.
nichel ['nikel] *sm* nickel. **nichelare** *v* nickel-plate. **nichelatura** *sf* nickel-plating.
nichilismo [niki'lizmo] *sm* nihilism. **nichilista** *s(m+f)* nihilist.
nicotina [niko'tina] *sf* nicotine.
nido ['nido] *sm* nest. **nido d'ape** honeycomb. **nido d'infanzia** crèche, day nursery. **nidiata** *sf* brood.
niente ['njɛnte] *pron* nothing; (*con altra negazione*) anything. *sm* nothing; (*cosa da poco*) slightest thing. **da niente** unimportant. **niente paura!** don't be afraid! **non fa niente** (*non importa*) it doesn't matter.
ninfa ['ninfa] *sf* nymph. **ninfomane** *sf*, *agg* nymphomaniac.
ninfea [nin'fea] *sf* water lily.
ninna-nanna [ninna'nanna] *sf* lullaby.

ninnolo ['ninnolo] *sm* (*balocco*) toy; (*gingillo*) knick-knack.

nipote [ni'pote] *sm* (*di nonni*) grandson; (*di zii*) nephew. *sf* (*di nonni*) granddaughter; (*di zii*) niece.

nitido ['nitido] *agg* neat; (*fig*) clear.

nitrire [ni'trire] *v* neigh. **nitrito** *sm* neigh.

no [nɔ] *avv* no. **no** no; (*rifiuto*) refusal. **come no!** of course! and how! **se no** otherwise, or else. **uno sì e uno no** every other one.

nobile ['nɔbile] *agg* noble. *sm* nobleman. *sf* noblewoman. **nobiltà** *sf* nobility.

nocca ['nɔkka] *sf* knuckle; (*del cavallo*) fetlock.

nocciola [not'tʃɔla] *sf* hazel-nut. *agg, sm invar* (*colore*) hazel. **nocciolina (americana)** *sf* peanut. **nocciolo** *sm* (*pianta*) hazel.

nocciolo [not'tʃɔlo] *sm* (*bot*) stone, kernel; (*fig*) heart, point; (*tec*) core.

noce ['notʃe] *sm* (*albero*) walnut(-tree); (*legno*) walnut. *sf* (*frutto*) walnut. **noce di burro** pat of butter. **noce di cocco** coconut. **noce moscata** nutmeg. **nocepesca** *sf* nectarine.

nocivo [no'tʃivo] *agg* harmful.

nodo ['nɔdo] *sm* knot; (*incrocio*) junction; (*trama*) plot. **avere un nodo alla gola** have a lump in one's throat. **nodo scorsoio** slip-knot. **nodoso** *agg* knotty.

noi ['noi] *pron* (*soggetto*) we; (*oggetto*) us.

noia ['nɔja] *sf* (*tedio*) boredom; (*fastidio*) nuisance; (*fam*) bore. **avere delle noie con** have trouble with. **dare noia (a)** trouble, bother. **noioso** *agg* boring; (*fastidioso*) troublesome.

noleggiare [noled'dʒare] *v* hire, rent. **noleggio** *sm* hire; (*prezzo*) rental. **nolo** *sm* freight. **dare a nolo** hire (out). **prendere a nolo** hire, rent.

nomade ['nɔmade] *agg* nomadic. *s(m+f)* nomad.

nome ['nome] *sm* name; (*gramm*) noun. **a nome di** on behalf of. **conoscere di nome** know by name. **fare il nome di** mention; (*proporre*) propose. **nome di battaglia** pseudonym. **nomignolo** *sm* nickname.

nomina ['nɔmina] *sf* appointment. **nominare** *v* mention; name; (*eleggere*) appoint.

non [non] *avv* not. **non ... affatto** not at all. **non ... mai** never. **non ... nessuno** nobody. **non ... niente** *or* **nulla** nothing. **nonché** *cong* as well as.

noncurante [nonku'rante] *agg* heedless.

nondimeno [nondi'meno] *cong* nevertheless.

nonno ['nɔnno] *sm* grandfather; (*fam*) grand-dad. **nonna** *sf* grandmother; (*fam*) grandma, granny. **nonni** *sm pl* grandparents *pl*.

nono ['nɔno] *sm, agg* ninth.

nonostante [nonos'tante] *prep* notwithstanding, in spite of. *cong* (al)though.

nontiscordardimè [nontiskordardi'me] *sm* forget-me-not.

nord [nɔrd] *sm* north. **a nord** north. **del nord** north, northern. **nord-est** *sm* north-east. **nord-ovest** *sm* north-west.

norma ['nɔrma] *sf* rule, standard; (*istruzione*) direction; regulation. **a norma di legge** according to (the) law.

normale [nor'male] *agg* normal, regular; standard. *sf* perpendicular. **normalmente** *avv* as a rule.

Norvegia [nor'vedʒa] *sf* Norway. **norvegese** *s(m+f)*, *agg* Norwegian.

nostalgia [nostal'dʒia] *sf* nostalgia; (*della casa*) homesickness. **aver nostalgia di** miss. **nostalgico** *agg* nostalgic, homesick.

nostro ['nɔstro] *agg* our. *pron* ours. **nostrano** *agg* local, home-grown.

nota ['nɔta] *sf* note; list.

notaio [no'tajo] *sm* notary.

notare [no'tare] *v* note; (*osservare*) notice. **far notare** point out.

notificare [notifi'kare] *v* notify; inform. **notificazione** *sf* notification; (*avviso*) notice.

notizia [no'titsja] *sf* news (item), information. **notiziario** *sm* news (bulletin).

noto ['nɔto] *agg* well-known, renowned. **render noto** make known.

notorio [no'tɔrjo] *agg* renowned; (*spreg*) notorious. **notorietà** *sf* renown.

notte ['nɔtte] *sf* night. **buona notte!** goodnight! **dare la buona notte** bid goodnight. **nottata** *sf* night.

notturno [not'turno] *agg* night, nocturnal. *sm* (*musica*) nocturne.

novanta [no'vanta] *sm, agg* ninety. **novantesimo** *sm, agg* ninetieth.

nove ['nove] *sm, agg* nine.

novella [no'vella] *sf* short story. **novellista** *s(m+f)* short-story writer.

novello [no'vello] *agg* new.

novembre [no'vembre] *sm* November.

novità [novi'ta] *sf* novelty; (*notizie*) news.

novizio [no'vitsjo] *sm* beginner, novice.

nozione [no'tsjone] *sf* notion, idea.

nozze ['nɔttse] *sf pl* wedding *sing*. **viaggio di nozze** honeymoon.

nube ['nube] *sf* cloud. **nubifragio** *sm* cloudburst.

nubile ['nubile] *agg* unmarried, single.

nuca ['nuka] *sf* nape of the neck.

nucleo ['nukleo] *sm* nucleus. **nucleo familiare** family. **nucleare** *agg* nuclear.

nudo ['nudo] *agg* bare, naked. *sm* nude. **a piedi nudi** barefoot. **nudismo** *sm* nudism. **nudista** *s(m+f)* nudist. **nudità** *sf* nudity, nakedness.

nulla ['nulla] *pron* nothing; (*con altra negazione*) anything. *sm* nothing; (*cosa da poco*) slightest thing. **da nulla** unimportant. **non fa nulla!** (*non importa*) it doesn't matter!

nullo ['nullo] *agg* null. **dichiarar nullo** annul. **nullaosta** *sm invar* clearance. **nullità** *sf* cipher.

numero ['numero] *sm* number; (*segno*) numeral. **numero chiuso** quota. **numero legale** quorum.

numismatica [numiz'matika] *sf* numismatics. **numismatico, -a** *sm*, *sf* numismatist.

*****nuocere** ['nwotʃere] *v* harm.

nuora ['nwɔra] *sf* daughter-in-law.

nuotare [nwo'tare] *v* swim. **nuotatore, -trice** *sm*, *sf* swimmer. **nuoto** *sm* swimming.

nuovo ['nwɔvo] *agg* new. **Nuova York** *sf* New York. **Nuova Zelanda** *sf* New Zealand.

nutrire [nu'trire] *v* feed, nourish. **nutrire affetto per** feel affection for. **nutriente** *agg* nourishing. **nutrimento** *sm* nourishment.

nuvola ['nuvola] *sf* cloud. **senza nuvole** cloudless. **nuvoloso** *agg* cloudy; (*cielo*) overcast.

nuziale [nu'tsjale] *agg* wedding.

O

o [o] *cong* or. **o ... o ...** either ... or .... **o l'uno o l'altro** either.

oasi ['ɔazi] *sf* oasis (*pl* -ses).

*****obbedire** [obbe'dire] *v* obey. **obbedienza** *sf* obedience.

obbligare *v* bind, force. **obbligarsi** *v* undertake. **obbligato** *agg* fixed, set; (*riconoscente*) obliged. **obbligatorio** *agg* compulsory. **obbligazione** *sf* (*dir*) obligation; (*comm*) bond, debenture. **obbligo** *sm*, *pl* -**ghi** duty, obligation. **essere d'obbligo** be compulsory *or* obligatory.

obbrobrio [ob'brɔbrjo] *sm* disgrace.

obeso [o'bezo] *agg* obese. **obesità** *sf* obesity.

obiettare [objet'tare] *v* object. **obiezione** *sf* objection.

obiettivo [objet'tivo] *sm* objective; (*scope*) aim; (*foto, ecc.*) lens. *agg* objective.

obitorio [obi'tɔrjo] *sm* morgue.

oblazione [obla'tsjone] *sf* offering.

oblio [o'blio] *sm* oblivion.

obliquo [o'blikwo] *agg* oblique.

oblò [o'blɔ] *sm* porthole.

oblungo [o'blungo] *agg* oblong.

oboe ['ɔboe] *sm* oboe.

oca ['ɔka] *sf* goose (*pl* geese); (*maschio*) gander.

occasionale [okkazjo'nale] *agg* (*fortuito*) chance; immediate; (*saltuario*) occasional.

occasione [okka'zjone] *sf* chance, opportunity; (*buon affare*) bargain; (*circostanza*) occasion.

occhiali [ok'kjali] *sm pl* glasses *pl*, spectacles *pl*. **occhiali da sole** sun-glasses *pl*. **occhialuto** *agg* bespectacled.

occhio ['ɔkkjo] *sm* eye; (*bot*) bud. **a occhi chiusi** blindly. **a occhio** by sight. **a occhio nudo** with the naked eye. **a quattr'occhi** in private. **costare un occhio della testa** cost the earth. **dare nell'occhio** catch the eye. **tenere d'occhio** keep an eye on.

occidente [ottʃi'dɛnte] *sm* west. **occidentale** *agg* west, western.

*****occorrere** [ok'korrere] *v* be necessary. **all'occorrenza** in case of need.

occulto [ok'kulto] *agg* occult; (*nascosto*) hidden.

occupare [okku'pare] *v* occupy; (*far lavorare*) employ; (*tempo*) spend; (*carica*) hold; (*tener occupato*) keep busy. **occuparsi di** concern oneself with. **occupato** *agg* engaged; (*indaffarato*) busy. **occupazione** *sf* occupation.

oceano [o'tʃeano] *sm* ocean.

ocra ['ɔkra] *sf* ochre.

oculare [oku'lare] *agg* **testimonio oculare** *sm* eye-witness.

oculista [oku'lista] *s(m+f)* oculist.

ode ['ɔde] *sf* ode.

odiare [o'djare] *v* hate, loathe. **odio** *sm* hatred, hate, loathing. **avere in odio** hate, detest. **odioso** *agg* hateful.

odierno [o'djɛrno] *agg* of today; modern.

odissea [odis'sɛa] *sf* odyssey.

odontoiatria [odontoja'tria] *sf* dentistry.

odorare [odo'rare] *v* smell. **odorato** *sm* sense of smell. **odore** *sm* smell, odour. **sentir un odore di** smell. **odoroso** *agg* sweet-smelling.

*offendere [of'fɛndere] *v* offend; (*ledere*) injure, hurt. **offendere la legge** break the law. **offendersi** *v* take offence. **offensiva** *sf* offensive. **offensivo** *agg* offensive. **offensore** *sm* attacker; (*dir*) offender.

offerta [of'fɛrta] *sf* offer; (*comm*) bid; (*econ*) supply. **offerente** *s(m+f)* bidder.

offesa [of'feza] *sf* offence; insult; (*danno*) harm.

officina [offi'tʃina] *sf* works, workshop. **capo officina** *sm* (works) foreman.

*offrire [of'frire] *v* offer; (*comm*) bid. **offrirsi** *v* offer; present oneself.

offuscare [offus'kare] *v* dim; (*foto, ecc.*) blur; (*fig*) obscure.

oggetto [od'dʒɛtto] *sm* object; (*argomento*) subject; (*cosa*) thing. **oggettività** *sf* objectivity. **oggettivo** *agg* objective.

oggi ['ɔddʒi] *avv*, *sm* today. **al giorno d'oggi** nowadays. **oggi a otto** a week today.

ogni ['ɔɲi] *agg* every, each. **ad** or **in ogni modo** in any case. **ogni tanto** every so often, now and then.

Ognissanti [oɲis'santi] *sm* All Saints' Day.

ognuno [o'ɲuno] *pron* everybody, everyone; (*ciascuno*) each.

ohimè [oi'mɛ] *inter* alas!

Olanda [o'landa] *sf* Holland. **olandese** *agg* Dutch. **gli olandesi** the Dutch.

oleodotto [oleo'dotto] *sm* (*oil*) pipeline.

oleoso [ole'ozo] *agg* oily.

olfatto [ol'fatto] *sm* sense of smell.

olimpiade [olim'piade] *sf* Olympic games *pl*. **olimpico** *agg* Olympian. **olimpionico** *agg* Olympic.

olio ['ɔljo] *sm* oil. **olio combustibile** (*gasolio*) fuel oil.

oliva [o'liva] *sf* olive. **oliveto** olive grove. **olivo** *sm* olive-tree.

olmo ['olmo] *sm* elm-tree.

olocausto [olo'kausto] *sm* holocaust, sacrifice.

oltraggiare [oltrad'dʒare] *v* outrage. **oltraggio** *sm* outrage. **oltraggio al pudore** indecent behaviour. **oltraggioso** *agg* outrageous.

oltranza [ol'trantsa] *sf* **ad oltranza** to the (bitter) end.

oltre ['oltre] *avv* (*luogo*) further, farther; (*tempo*) beyond. *prep* beyond; (*più di*) more than, over. **oltre a** besides, apart from.

oltremare [oltre'mare] *avv* overseas.

oltremodo [oltre'mɔdo] *avv* exceedingly.

oltrepassare [oltrepas'sare] *v* exceed; surpass.

omaggio [o'maddʒo] *sm* (*dono*) (complimentary) gift. **porgere omaggi a** pay respects to. **rendere omaggio a** pay homage to.

ombelico [ombe'liko] *sm*, *pl* **-chi** navel. **ombelicale** *agg* umbilical.

ombra ['ombra] *sf* shadow; (*opposto di luce*) shade. **ombretto** *sm* eye-shadow.

ombrello [om'brɛllo] *sm* umbrella.

omero ['ɔmero] *sm* humerus.

*omettere [o'mettere] *v* omit, leave out.

omicida [omi'tʃida] *agg* murderous. *s(m+f)* murderer, murderess. **omicidio** *sm* homicide, murder. **omicidio colposo** manslaughter.

omissione [omis'sjone] *sf* omission.

omogeneo [omo'dʒɛneo] *agg* homogeneous. **omogeneità** *sf* homogeneity.

omologare [omolo'gare] *v* ratify.

omonimo [o'mɔnimo] *agg* homonymous. *nm* namesake; (*parola*) homonym.

omosessuale [omosessu'ale] *s(m+f)*, *agg* homosexual. **omosessualità** *sf* homosexuality.

oncia ['ontʃa] *sf* ounce.

onda ['onda] *sf* wave. **a onde** wavy. **ondata** *sf* wave, surge.

onde ['onde] *avv* whence. *cong* so that.

ondeggiare [onded'dʒare] *v* wave, sway, roll; (*fig*) waver.

ondulare [ondu'lare] *v* (*capelli*) wave. **ondulato** *agg* wavy; (*lastra, cartone*) corrugated.

onere ['ɔnere] *sm* burden. **oneroso** *agg* burdensome.

onesto [o'nesto] *agg* honest; (*prezzo*) fair. **onestà** *sf* honesty, integrity.

onice ['ɔnitʃe] *sm* onyx.

onnipotente [onnipo'tɛnte] *agg* omnipotent.

onnivoro [on'nivoro] *agg* omnivorous.

onomastico [ono'mastiko] *sm* saint's day.

onorare [ono'rare] *v* honour.

onorario [ono'rarjo] *agg* honorary. *sm* fee.

onore [o'nore] *sm* honour. **a onor del vero** to tell the truth. **fare onore** a honour; do credit *or* justice to. **farsi onore** distinguish oneself. **onorevole** *agg* honourable.

onorificenza [onorifi'tʃɛntsa] *sf* honour. **onorifico** *agg* honorary.

onta ['onta] *sf* shame.

ontano [on'tano] *sm* alder.

opaco [o'pako] *agg, m pl* -**chi** opaque, dull.

opale [o'pale] *sm* opal.

opera ['ɔpera] *sf* work; (*teatro*) opera; (*azione*) deed; institution. **mettere in opera** put into practice; instal. **per opera di** thanks to. **operetta** *sf* operetta, light opera. **operoso** *agg* active.

operaio [ope'rajo], -**a** *sm, sf* worker. *agg* working.

operare [ope'rare] *v* function, work; (*med*) operate. **farsi operare** have an operation. **operatore** *sm* (*cinema*) cameraman; (*di borsa*) stockbroker. **operatorio** *agg* operating. **operazione** *sf* operation.

opinione [opi'njone] *sf* opinion.

oppio ['ɔppjo] *sm* opium.

opponente [oppo'nɛnte] *agg* opposing. *s(m+f)* adversary.

*****opporre** [op'porre] *v* oppose. **opporre resistenza** offer resistance. **opporsi** a set oneself against; object to.

opportuno [oppor'tuno] *agg* opportune. **opportunismo** *sm* opportunism. **opportunista** *s(m+f)* opportunist. **opportunità** *sf* opportunity.

opposizione [oppozi'tsjone] *sf* opposition.

opposto [op'posto] *agg, sm* opposite. **all'opposto** on the contrary.

oppressione [oppres'sjone] *sf* oppression. **oppresso** *agg* oppressed. **oppressore** *sm* oppressor.

*****opprimere** [op'primere] *v* oppress, burden.

oppure [op'pure] *cong* or, or else.

opulento [opu'lɛnto] *agg* opulent.

opuscolo [o'puskolo] *sm* pamphlet, booklet.

ora[1] ['ora] *sf* hour; (*tempo*) time. **alla**

buon'ora! at last! **all'ora** (*velocità*) per hour. **di buon'ora** early. **ora di punta** rush-hour. **ora legale** summer-time. **ora straordinaria** overtime.

ora[2] ['ora] *avv* (*adesso*) now; (*appena*) just. **d'ora in poi** from now on, henceforth. **or ora** just (now).

orale [o'rale] *agg* oral. *sm* (*esame*) viva.

orario [o'rarjo] *agg* (*all'ora*) per hour; time. **in senso orario** clockwise. **segnale orario** time-signal. **ore** (*ore*) hours *pl*; (*tabella*) timetable. **in orario** on time.

orazione [ora'tsjone] *sf* speech. **oratore** *sm* orator. **oratorio** *sm* (*chiesa*) oratory; (*musica*) oratorio.

orbene [or'bene] *avv* well (now).

orbita ['orbita] *sf* orbit. **orbitare** *v* orbit.

orchestra [or'kɛstra] *sf* orchestra. **orchestrare** *v* orchestrate. **orchestrazione** *sf* orchestration.

orchidea [orki'dɛa] *sf* orchid.

orco ['ɔrko] *sm* ogre.

orda ['ɔrda] *sf* horde.

ordigno [or'dino] *sm* device.

ordinare [ordi'nare] *v* order; (*mettere in ordine*) tidy up; (*sistemare*) arrange; (*rel*) ordain. **ordinamento** *sm* order; arrangement; system. **ordinazione** *sf* order; (*rel*) ordination.

ordinario [ordi'narjo] *agg, sm* ordinary.

ordine ['ordine] *sm* order. **ordine del giorno** agenda.

ordire [or'dire] *v* (*tessile*) warp; (*fig*) hatch. **ordito** *sm* warp; (*fig*) plot.

orecchio [o'rekkjo] *sm* ear. **a orecchio** by ear. **a portato d'orecchio** within earshot. **orecchino** *sm* ear-ring. **orecchioni** *sm pl* mumps *sing*.

orefice [o'refitʃe] *sm* goldsmith, jeweller. **oreficeria** *sf* jewellery; (*negozio*) jeweller's (shop).

orfano ['ɔrfano], -**a** *s, agg* orphan. **orfanotrofio** *sm* orphanage.

organico [or'ganiko] *agg* organic. *sm* personnel. **organismo** *sm* organism; (*fig*) body.

organizzare [organid'dzare] *v* organize, arrange. **organizzazione** *sf* organization, body. **organizzatore**, -**trice** *sm, sf* organizer.

organo ['ɔrgano] *sm* organ. **organetto** *sm* barrel-organ.

orgasmo [or'gazmo] *sm* orgasm.

orgia ['ɔrdʒa] *sf* orgy.

orgoglio [or'goʎo] sm pride. **orgoglioso** agg proud.

orientare [orjen'tare] v orient(ate); direct. **orientarsi** v find one's bearings; tend. **orientamento** sm orientation; (direzione) trend. **senso d'orientamento** sm sense of direction.

oriente [o'rjɛnte] sm East. **orientale** agg oriental, eastern, east.

orifizio [ori'fitsjo] sm orifice, opening.

origano [o'rigano] sm oregano.

originare [oridʒi'nare] v (avere origini) originate; (dare origini) give rise to.

origine [o'ridʒine] sf origin; (inizio) beginning. **originale** sm, agg original; eccentric. **originalità** sf originality; eccentricity. **originario** agg native.

origliare [oriʎ'ʎare] v eavesdrop.

orina [o'rina] sf urine. **orinare** v urinate. **orinatorio** agg urinary.

oriundo [o'rjundo] agg native.

orizzonte [orid'dzonte] sm horizon. **giro d'orizzonte** sm general survey. **orizzontale** agg horizontal. **orizzontarsi** v find one's bearings.

orlo [or'lo] sm edge; (abisso) brink; (bicchiere) rim; (tessuto) hem. **orlare** v hem; (bordare) trim.

orma [orma] sf footprint; track.

ormai [or'mai] avv by now; (passato) by then.

ormeggiare [ormed'dʒare] v moor. **ormeggio** sm mooring.

ormone [or'mone] sm hormone.

ornare [or'nare] v adorn, decorate. **ornamentale** agg ornamental. **ornamento** sm ornament, decoration.

ornitologia [ornitolo'dʒia] sf ornithology. **ornitologo, -a** sm, sf ornithologist.

oro [ɔro] sm gold. **d'oro** gold, golden.

orologio [orolɔdʒo] sm clock; (da polso o tasca) watch. **orologeria** sf clockwork; (negozio) watchmaker's (shop). **bomba ad orologeria** sf time-bomb. **orologiaio** sm watchmaker.

oroscopo [o'rɔskopo] sm horoscope.

orpello [or'pɛllo] sm tinsel.

orrendo [or'rɛndo] agg hideous, horrifying.

orribile [or'ribile] agg horrible, dreadful.

orrore [or'rore] sm horror, dread, loathing. **avere orrore di** loathe.

orso [orso] sm, **-a** sf bear. **orsacchiotto** sm bear-cub; (giocattolo) teddy-bear.

ortica [or'tika] sf nettle. **orticaria** sf nettle-rash.

orto [ɔrto] sm kitchen garden. **ortaggi** sm pl vegetables pl. **orticoltore** sm horticulturist. **orticoltura** sf horticulture. **ortolano** sm greengrocer.

ortodosso [orto'dosso] agg orthodox. **ortodossia** sf orthodoxy.

ortografia [ortogra'fia] sf spelling. **errore ortografico** sm spelling mistake.

ortopedia [ortope'dia] sf orthopaedics. **ortopedico** agg orthopaedic.

orzaiolo [ordza'jɔlo] sm stye.

orzo [ɔrdzo] sm barley.

osare [o'zare] v dare; risk.

osceno [o'ʃeno] agg obscene. **oscenità** sf obscenity.

oscillare [oʃil'lare] v swing, oscillate.

oscurare [osku'rare] v darken; (fig) obscure. **oscuramento** sm darkening; (guerra) black-out. **oscurità** sf dark; (fig) obscurity.

ospedale [ospe'dale] sm hospital. **ospedaliero** agg hospital.

ospitare [ospi'tare] v offer hospitality (to); (albergare) put up. **ospitale** agg hospitable.

ospite [ɔspite] s(m+f) (persona ospitata) guest; (oste) host, hostess.

ospizio [os'pitsjo] sm hostel.

ossatura [ossa'tura] sf (arch) framework; (anat) bone structure.

ossequio [os'sɛkwjo] sm homage. **ossequi** sm pl (saluti) regards pl. **ossequioso** agg respectful.

osservare [osser'vare] v obscure; (notare) notice. **osservanza** sf observance. **osservatore, -trice** sm, sf observer. **osservatorio** sm observatory. **osservazione** sf observation; (nota) remark. **fare un'osservazione** comment; criticize.

ossessionare [ossessjo'nare] v haunt. **ossessionante** agg haunting. **ossessione** sf obsession. **ossesso** agg possessed.

ossia [os'sia] cong or rather, in other words.

ossigeno [os'sidʒeno] sm oxygen. **ossidare** v oxidize. **ossido** sm oxide.

osso [ɔsso] sm, pl **-a** f in collective sense bone. **ossuto** agg bony.

ostacolare [ostako'lare] v hinder, obstruct. **ostacoio** sm obstacle, hindrance; (atletica) hurdle. **corsa a ostacolo** sf obstacle race; hurdling.

ostaggio [os'taddʒo] sm hostage.

oste ['ɔste] sm host, innkeeper.

ostello [os'tɛllo] sm refuge; (per la gioventù) (youth-)hostel.

ostentare [osten'tare] v show off. **ostentato** agg ostentatious.

osteria [oste'ria] sf inn.

ostetrico [os'tɛtriko] sm obstetrician. **ostetrica** sf obstetrician; (levatrice) midwife. **ostetricia** sf obstetrics; midwifery.

ostia ['ɔstja] sf (rel) host; (cialda) wafer.

ostile [os'tile] agg hostile. **ostilità** sf hostility.

ostinarsi [osti'narsi] v persist. **ostinatezza** sf obstinacy, stubbornness. **ostinato** agg obstinate, stubborn.

ostrica ['ɔstrika] sf oyster.

ostruire [ostru'ire] v obstruct, block. **ostruzione** sf obstruction.

otite [o'tite] sf otitis.

otorinolaringoiatra [otorinolaringo'jatra] s(m+f) ear, nose, and throat specialist.

ottagono [ot'tagono] sm octagon.

ottano [ot'tano] sm octane.

ottanta [ot'tanta] m, agg eighty. **ottantesimo** agg, sm eightieth.

ottava [ot'tava] sf octave. **ottavo** sm, agg eighth.

*ottenere [otte'nere] v obtain, get. **ottenibile** agg obtainable.

ottico ['ɔttiko] agg optic. sm optician. **ottica** sf (persona) optician; (scienza) optics.

ottimismo [otti'mizmo] agg optimistic.

ottimo ['ɔttimo] agg excellent, very good.

otto ['ɔtto] agg, sm eight.

ottobre [ot'tobre] sm October.

ottone [ot'tone] sm brass. **ottoni** sm pl (musica) brass pl.

otturare [ottu'rare] v plug; (dente) fill. **otturatore** sm (foto) shutter.

ottuso [ot'tuzo] agg dull; (non tagliente) blunt; (angolo) obtuse.

ovaia [o'vaja] sf ovary.

ovale [o'vale] agg, sm oval.

ovatta [o'vatta] sf wadding; (cotone idrofilo) cotton wool.

ovazione [ova'tsjone] sf ovation.

ovest ['ɔvest] sm west. **a ovest di** (to the) west of. **dell'ovest** west, western.

ovile [o'vile] sm sheepfold.

ovulo ['ɔvulo] sm ovum; (bot) ovule. **ovulazione** sf ovulation.

ovunque [o'vunkwe] avv everywhere. cong wherever.

ovvero [ov'vero] cong or (rather).

ovvio ['ɔvvjo] agg obvious.

oziare [o'tsjare] v loaf. **ozio** sm (pigrizia) idleness; (tempo libero) leisure, spare time. **ozioso** agg idle.

P

pacato [pa'kato] agg calm.

pacchia ['pakkja] sf godsend.

pacco ['pakko] sm parcel. **pacchetto** sm packet, small parcel.

pace ['patʃe] sf peace.

pacificare [patʃifi'kare] v pacify, appease; reconcile. **pacifico** agg peaceful; (ovvio) self-evident.

pacifismo [patʃi'fizmo] sm pacifism. **pacifista** s(m+f) pacifist.

padella [pa'della] sf frying pan.

padiglione [padi'ʎone] sm pavilion.

Padova ['padova] sf Padua.

padre ['padre] sm father. **padre adottivo** foster-father. **padrino** sm godfather.

padrone [pa'drone], -a sm, sf master, mistress; owner; (fam) boss. **padronale** agg private; (non di servizio) owner's. **padronanza** sf mastery. **padroneggiarsi** v control oneself.

paesaggio [pae'zaddʒo] sm landscape.

paese [pa'eze] sm country; village; (città) town. **paesano** agg rural, country.

paffuto [paf'futo] agg plump.

paga ['paga] sf pay, wages pl.

pagaia [pa'gaja] sf paddle.

pagano [pa'gano], -a s, agg pagan, heathen.

pagare [pa'gare] v pay. **pagamento** sm payment.

pagella [pa'dʒɛlla] sf school report.

paggio ['paddʒo] sm page(-boy).

pagina ['padʒina] sf page.

paglia ['paʎa] sf straw. **pagliericcio** sm palliasse. **paglietta** sf steel wool; (cappello) straw hat.

pagliaccio [pa'ʎattʃo] sm clown. **pagliacciata** sf buffoonery.

pagnotta [pa'ɲɔtta] sf loaf (of bread).

pago ['pago] agg contented (with).

pagoda [pa'gɔda] sf pagoda.

paio ['pajo] sm, pl -a f pair; (due o circa due) couple.

pala ['pala] *sf* shovel; (*di remo*) blade. **palata** *sf* shovel(ful). **soldi a palate** *sm pl* pots *or* bags of money *pl*.

palato [pa'lato] *sm* palate.

palazzo [pa'lattso] *sm* (*edificio*) building; (*appartamenti*) block of flats; (*casa di principe, ecc.*) palace. **palazzina** *sf* villa.

palco ['palko] *sm* platform, stand; (*teatro*) box. **palcoscenico** *sm* stage.

palese [pa'leze] *agg* obvious, clear. **palesare** *v* reveal.

palestra [pa'lestra] *sf* gymnasium.

paletto [pa'letto] *sm* bolt.

palio ['paljo] *sm* **mettere in palio** offer as a prize.

palla ['palla] *sf* ball. **pallacanestro** *sm* basketball. **pallanuoto** *sm* water polo.

palleggiare [palled'dʒare] *v* (*tennis*) knock up; (*calcio*) dribble. **palleggio** *sm* knock-up, dribbling.

pallido ['pallido] *agg* pale; (*fig*) faint.

pallino [pal'lino] *sm* (*bocce*) jack; (*fig*) craze. **a pallini** with polka dots.

pallone [pal'lone] *sm* ball; (*calcio*) football; (*aerostato*) balloon.

pallottola [pal'lɔttola] *sf* pellet; (*rivoltella*) bullet.

palma¹ ['palma] *sf* (*albero*) palm(-tree).

palma² ['palma] *sf* (*anat*) palm. **piede palmato** *sm* webbed foot.

palmo ['palmo] *sm* palm.

palo ['palo] *sm* pole; (*di porta*) post.

palombaro [palom'baro] *sm* diver.

palpare [pal'pare] *v* feel; (*mec*) *agg* palpable. **palpabile** *agg* palpable.

palpebra ['palpebra] *sf* eyelid. **battere le palpebre** blink.

palpitare [palpi'tare] *v* throb.

paltò [pal'tɔ] *sm invar* overcoat.

palude [pa'lude] *sf* marsh, swamp. **terreno paludoso** *sm* marshland.

panca ['panka] *sf* bench. **panchetto** *sm* (foot)stool. **panchina** *sf* bench, garden seat. **pancone** *sm* work-bench.

pancetta [pan'tʃetta] *sf* bacon.

pancia ['pantʃa] *sf* belly; (*fam*) tummy. **mal di pancia** *sm* (*fam*) tummy-ache. **panciotto** *sm* waistcoat. **panciuto** *agg* (*persona*) pot-bellied; (*cosa*) bulging.

pancreas ['pankreas] *sm invar* pancreas.

panda ['panda] *sm invar* panda.

pandemonio [pande'mɔnjo] *sm* uproar.

pane ['pane] *sm* bread; (*forma*) loaf. **buono come il pane** as good as gold.

guadagnarsi il pane earn one's living. **pan grattato** breadcrumbs *pl*. **pan tostato** toast. **panettiere** *sm* baker. **panificio** *sm* bakery.

panfilo ['panfilo] *sm* yacht.

panico [paniko] *sm* panic.

paniere [pa'njere] *sm* basket.

panino [pa'nino] *sm* roll. **panino imbottito** sandwich.

panna¹ ['panna] *sf* cream. **panna montata** whipped cream.

panna² ['panna] *sf* (*mec*) breakdown.

pannello [pan'nello] *sm* panel.

panno ['panno] *sm* cloth. **panni** *sm pl* (*vestiti*) clothes *pl*. **pannolino** *sm* nappy.

panorama [pano'rama] *sm* panorama, view.

pantaloni [panta'loni] *sm pl* trousers *pl*; (*corti*) shorts *pl*.

pantano [pan'tano] *sm* bog.

pantera [pan'tera] *sf* panther.

pantofola [pan'tɔfola] *sf* slipper.

pantomima [panto'mima] *sf* play-acting.

paonazzo [pao'nattso] *agg* purple.

papa ['papa] *sm* pope. **ogni morte di papa** once in a blue moon. **vivere come un papa** live like a lord. **papale** *agg* papal.

papà [pa'pa] *sm* (*fam*) dad(dy).

papavero [pa'pavero] *sm* poppy.

papera ['papera] *sf* slip, blunder. **prendere una papera** slip up.

papero ['papero], **-a** *sm*, *sf* gosling.

papiro [pa'piro] *sm* papyrus; (*fam*) paper.

pappa ['pappa] *sm* mush. **pappare** *v* gobble up.

pappagallo [pappa'gallo] *sm* parrot.

paprica ['paprika] *sf* paprika.

parabola [pa'rabola] *sf* (*storia*) parable; (*mat*) parabola.

parabrezza [para'brettsa] *sm invar* windshield.

paracadute [paraka'dute] *sm invar* parachute. **paracadutista** *s(m + f)* parachutist; (*mil*) paratrooper.

paradiso [para'dizo] *sm* paradise, heaven.

paradosso [para'dɔsso] *sm* paradox. **paradossale** *agg* paradoxical.

parafango [para'fango] *sm* mudguard.

paraffina [paraf'fina] *sf* paraffin.

parafrasi [pa'rafrazi] *sf* paraphrase.

parafulmine [para'fulmine] *sm* lightning conductor.

parafuoco [para'fwɔko] *sm*, *pl* **-chi** fireguard, firescreen.

paragonare [parago'nare] *v* compare. **paragonabile** *agg* comparable. **paragone** *sm* comparison. **senza paragone** without equal.

paragrafo [pa'ragrafo] *sm* paragraph.

paralisi [pa'ralizi] *sf* paralysis (*pl* -ses). **paralitico, -a** *sm, sf* cripple. **paralizzare** *v* paralyse.

parallelo [paral'lɛlo] *agg, sm* parallel. **parallela** *sf* parallel (line). **parallelogrammo** *sm* parallelogram.

paralume [para'lume] *sm* lampshade.

paranoia [para'nɔja] *sf* paranoia. **paranoico** *agg* paranoid.

parapetto [para'pɛtto] *sm* parapet.

parare [pa'rare] *v* adorn; (*evitare*) ward off; (*sport*) save.

parasole [para'sole] *sm* sunshade.

parassita [paras'sita] *agg* parasitic. *s(m + f)* parasite.

parata[1] [pa'rata] *sf* (*sfilata*) parade.

parata[2] [pa'rata] *sf* (*scherma*) parry; (*calcio, ecc.*) save.

parato [pa'rato] *sm* **carta da parati** *sf* wallpaper.

paraurti [para'urti] *sm invar* bumper.

paravento [para'vɛnto] *sm* screen.

parcheggiare [parked'dʒare] *v* park. **parcheggio** *sm* parking; (*luogo*) car park.

parchimetro [par'kimetro] *sm* parking meter.

parco[1] ['parko] *sm* park; (*industriale*) depot; (*auto*) fleet.

parco[2] ['parko] *agg* frugal, moderate.

parecchio [pa'rekkjo] *agg* quite a lot of, several. **parecchio tempo** quite a long time. *pron* quite a lot, several. *avv* quite a lot.

pareggiare [pared'dʒare] *v* equal; (*sport*) draw; (*comm*) balance. **pareggio** *sm* balance; draw.

parente [pa'rɛnte] *s(m + f)* relative, relation. **parentela** *sf* relationship; (*parenti*) relations *pl*.

parentesi [pa'rɛntezi] *sf* bracket, parenthesis (*pl* -ses). **fra parentesi** incidentally.

*****parere** [pa'rere] *v* seem, appear; (*suono*) sound; (*fatto*) feel. **faccio come mi pare** I do as I like. *sm* opinion.

parete [pa'rete] *sf* wall; (*monte*) face.

pari ['pari] *agg* equal, same; (*non dispari*) even; equivalent. **alla pari** (*in famiglia*) au pair. **essere pari** be quits; (*forze*) be equal *or* level. *s(m + f)* equal, peer.

Parigi [pa'ridʒi] *sf* Paris. **parigino, -a** *s, agg* Parisian.

parità [pari'ta] *sf* parity. **a parità di condizioni** all things being equal.

parlamento [parla'mento] *sm* parliament. **parlamentare** *agg* parliamentary.

parlare [par'lare] *v* speak, talk. **parlar chiaro** speak clearly; (*fig*) speak one's mind. *sm* talk; (*parlata*) way of speaking, dialect.

parmigiano [parmi'dʒano] *agg* Parmesan. *sm* Parmesan cheese.

parodia [paro'dia] *sf* parody.

parola [pa'rɔla] *sf* word. **parola d'ordine** password. **parole crociate** *sf pl* crossword *sing*.

parolacce [paro'lattʃe] *sf pl* bad language *sing*.

parrocchia [par'rɔkkja] *sf* parish. **parroco** *sm, pl* -**chi** parish priest.

parrucca [par'rukka] *sf* wig.

parrucchiere [parruk'kjɛre] *sm* hairdresser.

parte ['parte] *sf* part; (*porzione*) share; (*lato*) side; (*dir*) party. **a parte** apart; extra. **dall'altra parte** on the other hand. **da parte** aside. **da parte mia** from me. **da queste parti** round here. **per parte mia** as far as I am concerned.

partecipare [partetʃi'pare] *v* participate, take part; (*condividere*) share; announce. **partecipazione** *sf* sharing; announcement; presence.

partenza [par'tɛntsa] *sf* departure; (*sport*) start.

participio [parti'tʃipjo] *sm* participle.

particolare [partiko'lare] *agg* particular, special. *sm* detail.

partigiano [parti'dʒano] *-a s, agg* partisan.

partire [par'tire] *v* leave; go away; start.

partita [par'tita] *sf* game; (*incontro*) match; (*contabilità*) entry; (*merci*) lot.

partito [par'tito] *sm* party; condition; decision. **mal partito** predicament. **per partito preso** having made up one's mind.

partitura [parti'tura] *sf* score.

parto ['parto] *sm* birth; (*umano*) childbirth; (*atto*) delivery. **partorire** *v* give birth (to).

parziale [par'tsjale] *agg* partial; (*predisposto*) biased.

pascere ['paʃere] *v* feed (on). **ben pasciuto** well-fed, plump.

pascolare [pasko'lare] *v* graze. **pascolo** *sm* pasture.

Pasqua ['paskwa] *sf* Easter. **Pasqua degli ebrei** Passover.

passabile [pas'sabile] *agg* fair.

passaggio [pas'saddʒo] *sm* passage; (*traversata*) crossing. **dare un passaggio** give a lift. **diritto di passaggio** *sm* right of way. **essere di passaggio** be on the way through. **vietato il passaggio** no thoroughfare.

passaporto [passa'porto] *sm* passport.

passare [pas'sare] *v* pass; go past; (*gastr*) strain.

passatempo [passa'tɛmpo] *sm* pastime.

passato [pas'sato] *agg* past; (*scorso*) last. *sm* past.

passatoia [passa'toja] *sf* runner.

passeggero [passed'dʒɛro], **-a** *agg* passing, transient. *sm*, *sf* passenger.

passeggiare [passed'dʒare] *v* go for a walk *or* stroll. **passeggiata** *sf* walk, stroll; (*non a piedi*) ride.

passerella [passe'rɛlla] *sf* footbridge.

passero ['passero] *sm* sparrow.

passibile [pas'sibile] *agg* liable (to).

passione [pas'sjone] *sf* passion.

passivo [pas'sivo] *agg* passive; (*comm*) debit. *sm* (*gramm*) passive; (*comm*) liability.

passo ['passo] *sm* step; (*andatura*) pace; (*velocità*) rate; (*geog*) pass; (*di vite*) thread. **cedere il passo** give way. **fare due passi** go for a stroll. **sbarrare il passo** block the way. **segnare il passo** mark time.

pasta ['pasta] *sf* dough; (*minestra*) pasta; (*impasto*) paste; (*dolce*) pastry. **pasta frolla** shortcrust pastry. **pasta sfoglia** puff pastry.

pastello [pas'tɛllo] *sm* pastel.

pasticca [pas'tikka] *sf* lozenge.

pasticceria [pastittʃe'ria] *sf* (*negozio*) confectioner's (shop); (*paste*) pastries *pl*. **pasticciere** *sm* confectioner.

pasticciare [pastit'tʃare] *v* bungle, mess up. **pasticcio** *sm* mess; (*gastr*) pie.

pastiglia [pas'tiʎa] *sf* tablet.

pasto ['pasto] *sm* meal. **vino da pasto** *sm* table wine.

pastore [pas'tore] *sm* shepherd; (*prete*) minister. **cane pastore** *sm* sheepdog. **pastorale** *agg* pastoral.

pastorizzare [pastorid'dzare] *v* pasteurize. **pastorizzazione** *sf* pasteurization.

pastoso [pas'tozo] *agg* mellow.

pastrano [pas'trano] *sm* overcoat.

pastura [pas'tura] *sf* pasture.

patata [pa'tata] *sf* potato.

patella [pa'tɛlla] *sf* (*anat*) knee-cap; (*zool*) limpet.

patente¹ [pa'tɛnte] *agg* patent.

patente² [pa'tɛnte] *sf* licence.

paterno [pa'tɛrno] *agg* paternal. **paternale** *sf* lecture. **paternità** *sf* paternity.

patetico [pa'tɛtiko] *agg* pathetic, moving.

patibolo [pa'tibolo] *sm* gallows.

patina ['patina] *sf* coat.

patire [pa'tire] *v* suffer. **patimento** *sm* suffering, pain. **patito** *sm* (*fam*) fan.

patologico [pato'lɔdʒiko] *agg* pathological.

patria ['patrja] *sf* country; home.

patrigno [pa'triɲo] *sm* stepfather.

patrimonio [patri'mɔnjo] *sm* estate; fortune. **patrimonio pubblico** public heritage.

patriota [patri'ɔta] *s(m+f)* patriot. **patriottico** *agg* patriotic. **patriottismo** *sm* patriotism.

patrocinio [patro'tʃinjo] *sm* defence. **patrocinare** *v* defend.

patrono [pa'trono] *sm* patron. **patronato** *sm* patronage; institution.

pattinare [patti'nare] *v* skate. **pattinaggio** *sm* skating. **pattino** *sm* skate; (*mec*) shoe.

patto ['patto] *sm* pact, agreement; condition, term. **pattuire** *v* agree.

pattuglia [pat'tuʎa] *sf* patrol.

pattumiera [pattu'mjera] *sf* dustbin.

paura [pa'ura] *sf* fear; (*spavento*) fright. **aver paura di** be afraid of, fear. **far paura** scare. **pauroso** *agg* (*che fa paura*) frightening; (*che ha paura*) timid, afraid.

pausa ['pauza] *sf* pause, interval.

pavimento [pavi'mento] *sm* floor.

pavone [pa'vone] *sm* peacock. **pavonessa** *sf* peahen.

pavoneggiarsi [pavoned'dʒarsi] *v* show off.

paziente [pa'tsjente] *s(m+f)*, *agg* patient. **pazientare** *v* wait patiently. **pazienza** *sf* patience.

pazzo ['pattso], **-a** *agg* crazy, insane. *sm*, *sf* lunatic. **pazzesco** *agg* mad; incredible. **pazzia** *sf* madness, folly.

peccare [pek'kare] *v* sin. **pecca** *sf* fault. **peccato** *sm* sin. **che peccato!** what a pity! **peccatore**, **-trice** *sm*, *sf* sinner.

pece ['petʃe] sf pitch.

pecora ['pɛkora] sf sheep; (femmina) ewe.

peculiare [peku'ljare] agg peculiar.

pedaggio [pe'daddʒo] sm toll.

pedale [pe'dale] sm pedal. **pedalare** v pedal.

pedana [pe'dana] sf platform; (sport) springboard.

pedante [pe'dante] agg pedantic. s(m+f) pedant.

pedata [pe'data] sf kick; (orma) footprint.

pedestre [pe'dɛstre] agg pedestrian.

pediatria [pedja'tria] sf paediatrics. **pediatra** s(m+f) paediatrician. **pediatrico** agg paediatric.

pedicure [pedi'kure] sf (cura) pedicure. s(m+f) invar chiropodist.

pedina [pe'dina] sf (pezzo; (scacchi) pawn. **muovere una pedina** make a move; (fig) pull strings.

pedinare [pedi'nare] v shadow.

pedone [pe'done] s(m+f) pedestrian. **pedonale** agg pedestrian.

peggio ['peddʒo] agg (comparativo) worse; (superlativo) the worst. sm the worst. **alla peggio** if the worst comes to the worst.

peggiorare [peddʒo'rare] v (stare) get worse; (rendere) make worse. **peggioramento** sm worsening.

peggiore [ped'dʒore] agg (comparativo) worse; (superlativo) the worst. s(m+f) the worst.

pegno ['peŋo] sm pledge, pawn.

pelare [pe'lare] v peel, skin; (fig) fleece. **pelarsi** v (fam) go bald.

pelle ['pelle] sf skin; (cuoio) hide; (frutta) peel; (carnagione) complexion. **rimetterci la pelle** lose one's life.

pellegrino [pelle'grino] sm pilgrim. **pellegrinaggio** sm pilgrimage.

pellicano [pelli'kano] sm pelican.

pelliccia [pel'littʃa] sf fur; (mantello) fur coat. **pellicciaio** sm furrier.

pellicola [pel'likola] sf film; membrane.

pelo ['pelo] sm hair; (pelame) coat. **cercare il pelo nell'uovo** split hairs. **contro pelo** against the grain. **per un pelo** by a whisker.

peltro ['peltro] sm pewter.

peluria [pe'lurja] sf down.

pelvi ['pɛlvi] sf pelvis.

pena ['pena] sf (dolore) pain; (disturbo) trouble; punishment. **valere la pena** be worth it, be worthwhile.

penale [pe'nale] agg criminal, penal. sf fine.

penare [pe'nare] v find difficult, be hardly able to.

pendente [pen'dɛnte] agg hanging; (dir, comm) pending; (torre) leaning. sm pendant. **pendenza** sf slope, incline.

pendere ['pɛndere] v hang (down); incline, slope; (dir) be pending.

pendio [pen'dio] sm slope.

pendolare [pendo'lare] v swing. s(m+f) commuter. **pendolo** sm pendulum.

pene ['pene] sm penis.

penetrare [pene'trare] v penetrate, pierce. **penetrante** agg penetrating, piercing; acute. **penetrazione** sf penetration.

penicillina [penitʃil'lina] sf penicillin.

penisola [pe'nizola] sf peninsula.

penitente [peni'tɛnte] s(m+f), agg penitent. **penitenza** sf penance; (gioco) forfeit. **penitenziario** sm jail.

penna ['penna] sf feather; (da scrivere) pen. **penna a sfera** ball-point pen. **penna stilografica** fountain pen. **pennuto** agg feathered.

pennello [pen'nello] sm brush.

penombra [pe'nombra] sf twilight.

penoso [pe'nozo] agg painful.

pensare [pen'sare] v think; intend. **pensarci** v think about it. **pensarci sopra** think it over. **pensatore, -trice** sm, sf thinker.

pensiero [pen'sjero] sm thought; (mente, parere) mind. **essere in pensiero** worry. **pensieroso** agg thoughtful; pensive.

pensile ['pensile] agg hanging.

pensionare [pensjo'nare] v pension off. **pensionato** sm pensioner; (collegio) boarding-school. **pensione** sf pension. **essere in pensione** be retired. **mezza pensione** half board. **pensione completa** full board.

pentagono [pen'tagono] sm pentagon. **pentagonale** agg pentagonal.

Pentecoste [pente'kɔste] sf Whitsun.

pentirsi [pen'tirsi] v regret, be sorry for; (rel) repent. **pentimento** sm regret; repentance.

pentola ['pentola] sf pot.

penultimo [pe'nultimo] agg penultimate.

penzolare [pendzo'lare] v dangle. **penzoloni** avv dangling.

pepe ['pepe] sm pepper. **pepare** v pepper. **pepato** agg peppery, hot. **peperone** sm

capsicum; (*frutto*) pepper; (*peperoncino*) chili.

pepita [pe'pita] *sf* nugget.

per ['per] *prep* for; (*attraverso*) through; (*mat, entro, tramite*) by. **per caso** by chance. **per cento** per cent. **per di più** in addition. **per lo meno** at least. **per ora** for the present. **per terra** on the floor. **per volta** at a time. **stare per** be about to, be on the point of.

pera ['pera] *sf* pear. **pero** *sm* pear-tree.

perbacco [per'bakko] *inter* by Jove!

perbene [per'bene] *agg invar* respectable, nice. *avv* well, nicely.

percentuale [pertʃentu'ale] *agg* per cent. *sf* percentage.

percepire [pertʃe'pire] *v* notice, be aware (of); (*riscuotere*) receive. **percepibile** *agg* noticeable; (*comm*) due. **percettibile** *agg* perceptible. **percezione** *sf* perception.

perché [per'ke] *avv* why. *cong* because, as; (*affinché*) so that. *sm* reason.

perciò [per'tʃo] *cong* so, therefore.

*****percorrere** [per'korrere] *v* cover.

percorso [per'korso] *sm* trip, run.

percossa [per'kɔssa] *sf* blow, impact.

*****percuotere** [per'kwotere] *v* strike, hit. **percussione** [perkus'sjone] *sf* percussion.

*****perdere** [perdere] *v* lose; (*colare*) leak; (*sprecare*) waste. **lascia perdere!** skip it! **perdere di vista** lose sight of. **perdersi** *v* get lost. **perdita** *sf* loss; leak; waste.

perdonare [perdo'nare] *v* forgive. **perdono** *sm* forgiveness, pardon.

perenne [pe'renne] *agg* perpetual.

perfetto [per'fetto] *agg* perfect.

perfezionare [perfetsjo'nare] *v* (*migliorare*) improve; make perfect. **perfezionarsi** *v* specialize. **perfezionamento** *sm* specialization. **perfezione** *sf* perfection. **perfezionista** *s(m+f)* perfectionist.

perfidia [per'fidja] *sf* treachery, wickedness. **perfido** *agg* treacherous, wicked.

perfino [per'fino] *avv* even.

perforare [perfo'rare] *v* pierce, perforate.

pergamena [perga'mena] *sf* parchment.

pericolo [pe'nikolo] *sm* danger; risk. **pericolante** *agg* unsafe. **pericoloso** *agg* dangerous; risky.

periferia [perife'ria] *sf* periphery; (*città*) suburbs *pl.* **periferico** *agg* suburban; peripheral.

perimetro [pe'rimetro] *sm* perimeter.

periodico [peri'ɔdiko] *agg* periodic. *sm* periodical.

periodo [pe'riodo] *sm* period.

peripezia [peripe'tsia] *sf* vicissitude.

perire [pe'rire] *v* perish, die.

periscopio [peri'skɔpjo] *sm* periscope.

perito [pe'rito], **-a** s, *agg* expert. **perizia** *sf* (*bravura*) skill, expertise; (*pratica*) experience; (*valutazione*) examination, expert opinion.

perla ['perla] *sf* pearl.

perlomeno [perlo'meno] *avv* at least.

perlustrare [perlus'trare] *v* patrol; (*mil*) reconnoitre. **perlustrazione** *sf* patrol; reconnaissance.

permaloso [perma'lozo] *agg* touchy.

permanente [perma'nɛnte] *agg* permanent, lasting. *sf* (*fam*) perm. **permanenza** *sf* (*soggiorno*) stay. **in permanenza** permanently. **permanere** *v* remain.

permeare [perme'are] *v* permeate. **permeabile** *agg* permeable.

permesso [per'messo] *sm* permission; licence; (*congedo*) leave, pass. (**con**) **permesso?** may I? (*inter*) allow me!

*****permettere** [per'mettere] *v* allow, permit.

pernice [per'nitʃe] *sf* partridge.

perno ['perno] *sm* pivot, pin. **far perno su** hinge on.

pernottare [pernot'tare] *v* spend the night.

pero ['pero] *sm* pear-tree. **pera** *sf* pear.

però [pe'ro] *cong* but; (*tuttavia*) still, yet, however.

perossido [per'rossido] *sm* peroxide.

perpendicolare [perpendiko'lare] *agg, sf* perpendicular.

perpetuo [per'petuo] *agg* perpetual.

perplesso [per'plesso] *agg* puzzled; (*incerto*) undecided. **perplessità** *sf* perplexity; indecision.

perquisire [perkwi'zire] *v* search. **perquisizione** *sf* search.

perseguire [perse'gwire] *v* pursue. **perseguimento** *sm* pursuit.

perseguitare [persegwi'tare] *v* persecute. **persecuzione** *sf* persecution.

perseverare [perseve'rare] *v* persevere. **perseveranza** *sf* perseverance.

persiana [per'sjana] *sf* shutter, blind.

persiano [per'sjano] *agg* Persian.

persico ['persiko] *agg* Persian. (**pesce**) **persico** *sm* perch.

persino [per'sino] *avv* even.

*persistere [per'sistere] v persist. **persistenza** sf persistence.

perso ['pɛrso] agg lost. **a tempo perso** in one's spare time.

persona [per'sona] sf person; (qualcuno) somebody. **di** or **in persona** in person, personally; (personificato) personified. **persona di servizio** domestic (help).

personaggio [perso'nadd3o] sm (teatro, ecc.) character; celebrity.

personale [perso'nale] agg personal. sm (aspetto) figure; (dipendenti) staff. sf (mostra) one-man show. **personale di direzione** management. **personale qualificato** skilled workers pl.

personalità [personali'ta] sf personality.

personificare [personifi'kare] v personify. **personificazione** sf personification.

perspicace [perspi'katʃe] agg keen, shrewd.

*persuadere [persua'dere] v persuade; convince. **persuasione** sf persuasion; conviction. **persuasivo** agg convincing. **persuaso** agg convinced.

pertanto [per'tanto] cong thus, therefore, so.

pertica ['pertika] sf pole.

pertinace [perti'natʃe] agg stubborn; (deciso) determined.

pertinente [perti'nɛnte] agg pertaining (to); (domanda) relevant.

pertosse [per'tɔsse] sf whooping cough.

*pervadere [per'vadere] v pervade.

*pervenire [perve'nire] v arrive (at).

pervertire [perver'tire] v corrupt, pervert. **perverso** agg perverse. **pervertito**, **-a** sm, sf pervert.

pesare [pe'zare] v weigh. 'pesa sf (pesatura) weighing; (basculla) weighbridge. **pesante** agg heavy; (aria) stuffy; (duro) rough. **peso** sm weight; (onere) burden.

pesca[1] ['peska] sf (bot) peach. **pesco** sm peach-tree.

pesca[2] ['peska] sf fishing; (industria) fishery; (quantità) catch. **pescare** v fish; (trovare) pick up, get hold of; (acciuffare) catch. **pescatore** sm fisherman; (con lenza) angler.

pesce ['peʃe] sm fish. **buttarsi a pesce su** make a dive for. **pesce d'aprile** April fool. **sano come un pesce** fit as a fiddle. **pescivendolo**, **-a** sm, sf fishmonger.

pessimismo [pessi'mizmo] sm pessimism.

pessimista s(m+f) pessimist. **pessimistico** agg pessimistic.

pessimo ['pɛssimo] agg very bad; (scadente, incapace) very poor.

pestare [pes'tare] v crush; (fam: picchiare) give a (good) hiding. **pestare i piedi a qualcuno** tread on someone's toes. **pestello** sm pestle.

peste ['pɛste] sf plague; (fig) pest, curse.

pesto ['pesto] agg crushed. **essere buio pesto** be pitch dark.

petalo ['pɛtalo] sm petal.

petizione [peti'tsjone] sf petition.

petrolifero [petro'lifero] agg oil.

petrolio [pe'trɔljo] sm oil. **lampada a petrolio** sf paraffin lamp. **petroliera** sf (oil-)tanker.

pettegolo [pet'tegolo], **-a** sm, sf gossip. agg gossipy. **pettegolezzo** sm gossip.

pettinare [petti'nare] v comb. **pettinarsi** v comb one's hair. **pettinato** sm (tessuto) worsted. **pettinatura** sf combing; (acconciatura) hair-style. **pettine** sm comb.

petto ['pɛtto] sm breast; (torace) chest. **a doppio/un petto** double-/single-breasted.

petulante [petu'lante] agg pert.

pezza ['pɛttsa] sf rag; (toppa) patch; (pannolino) napkin. **pezza da piedi** doormat. **pezza di tessuto** roll of cloth. **pezzato** agg spotted. **pezzente** s(m+f) beggar.

pezzo ['pɛttso] sm piece; (tempo) period; (giornale) article. **pezzo di ricambio** spare part. **pezzo di terreno** plot of land. **pezzo grosso** (fam) VIP, big shot.

*piacere [pja'tʃere] v please. **mi piace ...** I like .... sm pleasure; favour. **a piacere** ad lib, freely. **far piacere a** please. **per piacere** please, if you please. **piacevole** agg pleasant.

piaga ['pjaga] sf sore; (fig) wound.

piagnucolare [pjanuko'lare] v whine, whimper. **piagnucolio** sm whining, whimpering. **piagnucolone**, **-a** sm, sf (fam) cry-baby.

pialla ['pjalla] sf plane. **piallare** v plane.

pianella [pja'nɛlla] sf (mattonella) tile; (pantofola) mule, slipper.

pianerottolo [pjane'rottolo] sm landing.

pianeta [pja'neta] sm planet.

*piangere [pjand3ere] v weep, cry. **far piangere** v move to tears; (ironico) be pathetic.

pianificare [pjanifi'kare] v plan. **pianificatore**, **-trice** sm, sf planner. **pianificazione** sf planning.

pianista [pja'nista] s(m+f) pianist.

piano[1] ['pjano] agg flat, level; (chiaro) clear. avv (adagio) slow, slowly; (con cautela) carefully; (a voce bassa) softly. **pian piano** very slowly, very softly; (poco alla volta) little by little.

piano[2] ['pjano] sm plane, level; (casa) floor, storey; (autobus) deck. **primo piano** foreground. **secondo piano** background.

piano[3] ['pjano] sm (progetto) plan. **piano di studi** syllabus. **piano regolatore** town plan.

pianoforte [pjano'forte] sm pianoforte; (fam) piano. **pianoforte a coda** grand piano.

pianta ['pjanta] sf (bot) plant; (disegno) plan; (carta di città) map. **di sana pianta** from scratch. **in pianta stabile** on the permanent staff. **pianta del piede** sole.

piantagione [pjanta'dʒone] sf plantation.

piantare [pjan'tare] v plant; (conficcare) drive; (tenda) pitch; (abbandonare) quit. **piantare grave** (fam) make trouble. **piantare in asso** leave in the lurch.

pianterreno [pjanter'reno] sm ground floor.

pianto ['pjanto] sm crying; tears pl.

pianura [pja'nura] sf plain.

piastra ['pjastra] sf plate. **piastrella** sf tile. **piastrellare** v tile.

piattaforma [pjatta'forma] sf platform. **piattaforma di lancio** launching pad. **piattaforma girevole** turntable.

piatto ['pjatto] agg flat. sm plate; (portata) dish, course; (bilancia) pan. **lavare i piatti** wash up.

piazza ['pjattsa] sf square; (comm) market; (posto) place; (fam: calvizie) bald patch. **a due piazze** (letto, ecc.) double. **a una piazza single. far piazza pulita** make a clean sweep. **scendere in piazza** demonstrate. **piazzaforte** sf stronghold. **piazzale** sm square. **piazzare** v place. **piazzista** sm salesman, commercial traveller.

picca ['pikka] sf pike. **picche** sf pl (carte) spades pl. **rispondere picche** turn down flat.

piccante [pik'kante] agg sharp, spicy; (arguto) spirited; (licenzioso) racy.

picchiare [pik'kjare] v hit, strike; (colpire) beat; (bussare) knock. **picchiata** sf (aereo) (nose-)dive.

picchio ['pikkjo] sm woodpecker.

piccino [pit'tʃino] agg tiny. sm child (pl -ren).

piccione [pit'tʃone] sm pigeon, dove. **piccionaia** sf dovecot; (fam: teatro) (the) gods.

picco ['pikko] sm peak. **a picco** sheer. **colare** or **mandare a picco** sink.

piccolo ['pikkolo], -a agg small, little. sm, sf little one, child (pl -ren). **da piccolo** as a child. **fin da piccolo** since childhood. **in piccolo** on a small scale. **piccolezza** sf (inezia) trifle.

piccone ['pikkone] sm pick-axe.

pidocchio [pi'dokkjo] sm louse (pl lice). **pidocchioso** agg lousy; (fig) mean.

piede ['pjede] sm foot (pl feet). **a piedi** on foot. **a piedi nudi** barefoot. **essere tra i piedi** be in the way. **fatto con i piedi** (fam) slipshod. **in piedi** standing. **togliersi dai piedi** get out of the way. **piedistallo** sm pedestal.

piega ['pjega] sf fold; crease; (ornamento) pleat. **messa in piega** sf set. **mettere in piega** v set. **prendere una brutta piega** take a turn for the worse.

piegare [pje'gare] v bend; (foglio, tessuto) fold.

pieghettare [pjeget'tare] v pleat.

pieghevole [pje'gevole] agg folding; flexible.

piena ['pjena] sf flood, spate; (folla) crowd.

pieno ['pjeno] agg full. **in pieno** completely; exactly. **(nel mezzo)** in the middle of. **pieno zeppo** full up, chock full. **fare il pieno** (auto) fill up.

pietà [pje'ta] sf pity, compassion; (devozione) piety. **fare pietà** arouse pity. **pietoso** agg pitiful.

pietanza [pje'tantsa] sf dish, course.

pietra ['pjetra] sf stone. **pietra dura** semi-precious stone. **pietra di paragone** touch-stone. **pietrina** sf flint.

piffero ['piffero] sm pipe; (sonatore) piper.

pigiama [pi'dʒama] sm pyjamas pl.

pigiare [pi'dʒare] v press, squeeze. **pigiatura** sf pressing.

pigione [pi'dʒone] sf rent.

pigliare [pi'ʎare] (fam) V **prendere**.

pigmento [pig'mento] sm pigment. **pigmentazione** sf pigmentation.

pigmeo [pig'meo] sm pygmy.

pigna ['piɲa] sf pine-cone.

pignatta [pi'ɲatta] sf pot.

pignolo [pi'ɲɔlo], **-a** agg fussy, pedantic. sm, sf pedant.

pigolare [pigo'lare] v peep, chirp. **pigolìo** sm peeping, chirping.

pigro ['pigro], **-a** agg idle, lazy. sm, sf lazy person, loafer. **pigrizia** sf laziness, idleness.

pila ['pila] sf pile; (elett) battery.

pilastro [pi'lastro] sm pillar, column.

pillola ['pillola] sf pill.

pilone [pi'lone] sm pillar; (ponte) pier; (elett) pylon.

pilotare [pilo'tare] v pilot; (auto) drive. **pilota** sm pilot.

pinacoteca [pinako'tɛka] sf picture gallery.

pineta [pi'neta] sf pine forest.

pingue ['pingwe] agg fat.

pinguino [pin'gwino] sm penguin.

pinna ['pinna] sf fin.

pinnacolo [pin'nakolo] sm pinnacle.

pino ['pino] sm pine (tree). **pinolo** sm pine-seed.

pinza ['pintsa] sf pliers pl; (zool) pincer. **pinzetta** sf tweezers pl.

pio ['pio] agg pious.

pioggia ['pjɔddʒa] sf rain. **pioggerella** sf also **pioggia fine** drizzle.

piolo [pi'ɔlo] sm peg; (scala) rung.

piombare[1] [pjom'bare] v hurtle, plunge; (avventarsi) pounce.

piombare[2] [pjom'bare] v (otturare) fill; (sigillare) seal (with lead). **piombo** sm lead; (piombino) plummet.

pioniere [pjo'njɛre] sm, sf pioneer.

pioppo ['pjoppo] sm poplar.

*****piovere** ['pjovere] v rain; (fig) pour (in). **piovere a catinelle** rain cats and dogs. **piovigginare** v drizzle. **piovoso** agg rainy.

piovra ['pjovra] sf (giant) squid; (persona) blood-sucker.

pipa ['pipa] sf pipe.

pipistrello [pipi'strɛllo] sm bat.

pira ['pira] sf pyre.

piramide [pi'ramide] sf pyramid.

pirata [pi'rata] sm pirate. **pirata della strada** hit-and-run driver. **pirateria** sf piracy.

piroscafo [pi'rɔskafo] sm steamer; (da carico) freighter; (di linea) liner.

piscia ['piʃa] sf (volg) piss. **pisciare** v piss.

piscina [pi'ʃina] sf swimming pool.

pisello [pi'zɛllo] sm pea. **pisello odoroso** sweet pea.

pisolino [pizo'lino] sm **fare** or **schiacciare un pisolino** take a nap.

pista ['pista] sf track; (aero) runway.

pistola [pis'tɔla] sf pistol. **pistola a spruzzo** spray-gun. **pistolettata** sf pistol-shot.

pistone [pis'tone] sm piston.

pitocco [pi'tɔkko], **-a** sm, sf beggar; (avaro) miser.

pitone [pi'tone] sm python.

pittore [pit'tore] sm painter.

pittoresco [pitto'resko] agg picturesque.

pittura [pit'tura] sf painting; (descrizione) picture; (vernice) paint. **pitturare** v paint.

più [pju] avv (comparativo) more; (superlativo) most. **al più presto** as soon as possible. **il più** the majority. **il più possibile** as much as possible. **più volte** several times. **sempre più . . .** more and more . . . . **tanto più** especially. **tutt'al più** at most.

piuma ['pjuma] sf feather. **piumino** sm down; (per cipria) powder-puff; (letto) eiderdown, duvet.

piuttosto [pjut'tosto] avv rather.

piviere [pi'vjɛre] sm plover.

pizzicare [pittsi'kare] v pinch; (pungere) sting; (musica) pluck. **pizzico** sm, pl **-chi** pinch, dash. **pizzicore** sm itch. **pizzicotto** sm pinch.

pizzo ['pittso] sm (merletto) lace; (barba) goatee.

placare [pla'kare] v calm down, placate.

placca [plakka] sf plate; (ornamento) plaque; (med) patch.

placenta [pla'tʃɛnta] sf placenta.

placido [platʃido] agg placid.

plagiare [pla'dʒare] v plagiarize. **plagiario**, **-a** sm, sf plagiarist.

planare [pla'nare] v glide. **planata** sf glide.

plasmare [plaz'mare] v mould. **plasma** sm plasma.

plastica ['plastika] sf (arte) modelling; (med) plastic surgery; (materia) plastic. **plasticare** v model. **plastico** agg plastic.

platano ['platano] sm plane-tree.

platea [pla'tɛa] sf stalls pl.

platino ['platino] sm platinum.

platonico [pla'tɔniko] agg platonic.

plausibile [plau'zibile] agg plausible.

plebe ['plɛbe] sf plebs pl; (plebaglia) mob, riff-raff. **plebeo** agg plebeian; common.

plebiscito [plebi'ʃito] sm plebiscite.

pleurite [pleu'rite] sf pleurisy.

plico ['pliko] sm parcel.

plotone [plo'tone] *sm* platoon.

plumbeo ['plumbeo] *agg* leaden.

plurale [plu'rale] *agg, sm* plural.

plutocratico [pluto'kratiko] *agg* plutocratic. **plutocrate** *sm* plutocrat. **plutocrazia** *sf* plutocracy.

pneumatico [pneu'matiko] *sm* tyre. *agg* (*mec*) pneumatic; (*gonfiabile*) inflatable.

po' [pɔ] *V* poco.

pochino [po'kino] *agg* not much *or* many. *avv, pron* very little *or* few. *sm* bit.

poco ['pɔko] *agg* little; (*tempo*) short. *avv* little, not very. *pron* little, not much. **a poco a poco** little by little. **da poco** unimportant. **fra poco** soon. **pochi** *pron, agg* few *pl*. **poco dopo** not long after. **poco fa** a short while ago. **poco male!** never mind! **un poco** *or* **po'** a little.

podere ['pɔdere] *sm* estate.

podestà [podes'ta] *sm* mayor.

podio ['pɔdjo] *sm* platform.

podismo [po'dizmo] *sm* track events *pl*; (*corsa*) running. **podista** *s(m+f)* track athlete; runner.

poema [po'ɛma] *sm* poem.

poi ['pɔi] *avv* then; (*più tardi*) later. *sm* future. **da . . . in poi** from . . . onwards. **il senno di poi** hindsight.

poiché [poi'ke] *cong* as, since.

polacco [po'lakko] *-a agg* Polish. *sm, sf* Pole. *sm* (*lingua*) Polish.

polarizzare [polarid'dzare] *v* polarize. **polare** *agg* polar. **stella polare** *sf* pole star.

polca ['pɔlka] *sf* polka.

polemica [po'lɛmika] *sf* polemic; controversy. **polemico** *agg* contentious, polemical.

polenta [po'lɛnta] *sf* (*gastr*) maize porridge; (*fam: persona lenta*) slow-coach.

policlinico [poli'kliniko] *sm* hospital.

poligamo [po'ligamo] *-a agg* polygamous. *sm, sf* polygamist. **poligamia** *sf* polygamy.

poligono [po'ligono] *sm* polygon.

polimero [po'limero] *sm* polymer.

polistirolo [polisti'rɔlo] *sm* polystyrene.

politecnico [poli'tɛkniko] *sm* polytechnic.

politene [poli'tene] *sm* polythene.

politico [po'litiko] *agg* political. *sm* politician. **politica** *sf* politics; (*linea di condotta*) policy.

polizia [polit'tsia] *sf* police. **poliziesco** *agg* police. **romanzo** *or* **film poliziesco** *sm* thriller. **poliziotto** *sm* policeman.

polizza ['polittsa] *sf* policy; (*ricevuta*) voucher.

pollame [pol'lame] *sm* poultry. **pollaio** *sm* chicken coop. **pollastra** *sf* pullet; (*fam*) lass, chick. **pollastro** cockerel; (*fam*) gullible person, mug.

pollice ['pollitʃe] *sm* thumb; (*del piede*) big toe.

polline ['polline] *sm* pollen.

pollo ['pollo] *sm* chicken. **far ridere i polli** be ridiculous.

polmone [pol'mone] *sm* lung. **polmonare** *agg* pulmonary. **polmonite** *sf* pneumonia.

polo ['pɔlo] *sm* pole. **essere ai poli opposti** be poles apart.

Polonia [po'lɔnja] *sf* Poland.

polpa ['pɔlpa] *sf* flesh; (*carne*) meat; (*fig*) substance. **polpetta** *sf* meatball. **polposo** *agg* fleshy.

polpaccio [pol'pattʃo] *sm* (*anat*) calf.

polso ['pɔlso] *sm* wrist; (*med*) pulse; (*polsino*) cuff.

poltiglia [pol'tiʎa] *sf* mush; mixture.

poltrona [pol'trona] *sf* easy chair, armchair; (*teatro*) stall.

poltrone [pol'trone] *-a sm, sf* idler, loafer.

polvere ['pɔlvere] *sf* dust; powder. **polveriera** *sf* powder-keg. **polverizzare** *v* pulverize. **polveroso** *agg* dusty.

pomata [po'mata] *sf* ointment.

pomeriggio [pome'riddʒo] *sm* afternoon. **pomeridiano** *agg* afternoon.

pomice ['pomitʃe] *sf* pumice-stone.

pomo ['pomo] *sm* (*frutto*) apple; (*albero*) apple-tree.

pomodoro [pomo'dɔro] *sm* tomato.

pompa¹ ['pompa] *sf* pump. **pompa antincendio** fire-engine. **pompare** *v* pump (up).

pompa² ['pompa] *sf* pomp. **far pompa di** show off. **impresario di pompe funebri** *sm* undertaker. **pomposo** *agg* pompous.

pompelmo [pom'pelmo] *sm* grapefruit.

pompiere [pom'pjɛre] *sm* fireman.

ponderare [ponde'rare] *v* consider. **ponderato** *agg* careful. **ponderoso** *agg* ponderous.

ponente [po'nɛnte] *sm* west.

ponte ['ponte] *sm* bridge; (*impalcatura*) scaffolding. **ponte aereo** air-lift. **ponte radio** radio link. **ponte sospeso** suspension bridge.

pontefice [pon'tefitʃe] *sm* pontiff. **pontificare** *v* pontificate. **pontificio** *agg* papal.

pontile [pon'tile] *sm* pier; (*da sbarco*) landing stage.

popolare [popo'lare] *agg* popular; working-class; (*tradizionale*) folk. **casa popolare** *sf* council house. *v* populate. **popolarità** *sf* popularity. **popolarizzare** *v* popularize.

popolo ['popolo] *sm* people; common people. **popolazione** *sf* population.

popone [po'pone] *sm* melon.

poppa¹ ['poppa] *sf* (*mar*) stern. **avere il vento in poppa** sail before the wind.

poppa² ['poppa] *sf* (*anat*) breast. **poppare** *v* suck.

porcellana [portʃel'lana] *sf* porcelain, china.

porco ['porko] *sm*, *pl* **-ci** pig. *agg* (*volg*) bloody. **porcaio** *sm* pig-sty. **porcellino d'India** *sm* guinea-pig. **porcheria** *sf* muck, filth; (*cibo*) disgusting stuff; (*cosa malfatta*) rubbish. **porcospino** *sm* porcupine.

*****porgere** ['pordʒere] *v* give, hand. **porgere aiuto** offer help.

pornografia [pornogra'fia] *sf* pornography. **pornografico** *agg* pornographic.

poro ['poro] *sm* pore. **poroso** *agg* porous.

porpora ['porpora] *agg invar*, *sf* purple.

*****porre** ['porre] *v* put; set, place. **porre in dubbio** question. **porre in evidenza** stress. **porre rimedio** set right.

porro ['porro] *sm* leek.

porta ['porta] *sf* door. **a porte chiuse** behind closed doors; (*dir*) in camera. **mettere alla porta** (*fig*) throw out. **porta di sicurezza** emergency exit.

portabagagli [portaba'gaʎi] *sm invar* luggage-rack; (*facchino*) porter.

portabile [por'tabile] *agg* portable.

portacenere [porta'tʃenere] *sm invar* ashtray.

portachiavi [porta'kjavi] *sm invar* key-ring.

portaerei [porta'erei] *sf* aircraft-carrier.

portafinestra [portafi'nestra] *sf*, *pl* **portefinestre** French window.

portafoglio [porta'fɔʎʎo] *sm* wallet; (*borsa*) briefcase; (*pol*) portfolio.

portalettere [porta'lettere] *sm invar* postman.

portamonete [portamo'nete] *sm invar* purse.

portare [por'tare] *v* bring; (*prendere*)

take; (*trasportare*) carry; (*indossare*) wear; (*addurre*) put forward. **essere portato** have a gift (for). **portatore** *sm* carrier; (*comm*) bearer.

portasapone [portasa'pone] *sm invar* soap-dish.

portasigarette [portasiga'rette] *sm invar* cigarette-case.

portaspilli [porta'spilli] *sm invar* pin-cushion.

portauovo [portauovo] *sm invar* egg-cup.

portavoce [porta'votʃe] *sm invar* spokesman, mouthpiece.

portento [por'tento] *sm* portent; (*persona*) prodigy.

portico ['portiko] *sm* arcade; (*di casa*) porch.

portinaio [porti'najo], **-a** *sm*, *sf* doorkeeper; caretaker. **portineria** *sf* caretaker's lodge.

porto¹ ['porto] *sm* port, harbour.

porto² ['porto] *sm* (*comm*) carriage. **porto d'armi** gun licence.

porto³ ['porto] *sm* (*vino*) port.

Portogallo [porto'gallo] *sm* Portugal. **portoghese** *agg*, *s(m + f)* Portuguese; *sm* (*lingua*) Portuguese. **fare il portoghese** gate-crash.

portone [por'tone] *sm* front door.

porzione [por'tsjone] *sf* portion, share.

posa ['poza] *sf* (*atteggiamento*) pose; (*foto*) exposure.

posare [po'zare] *v* put *or* lay down; rest; (*ritratto*) pose.

poscritto [pos'kritto] *sm* postscript.

positivo [pozi'tivo] *agg* positive; affirmative; practical. **positiva** *sf* (*foto*) positive.

posizione [pozi'tsjone] *sf* position.

*****posporre** [pos'porre] *v* postpone; (*mettere dopo*) place after. **posposizione** *sf* postponement.

*****possedere** [posse'dere] *v* possess, own. **possedimento** *sm also* possesso possession. **possessore** *sm* owner.

possibile [pos'sibile] *agg* possible. **fare il possibile** do one's best. **possibilità** *sf* possibility; (*capacità*) means. **possibilmente** *avv* if possible.

posta¹ ['posta] *sf* post, mail; (*ufficio*) post office. **a giro di posta** by return of post. **mettersi alla posta (di)** be on the look-out (for). **posta aerea** air mail. **postale** *agg* postal.

posta² ['posta] *sf* (*gioco*) bet, stake.

post-bellico [post'belliko] *agg* post-war.

posteggiare [posted'dʒare] *v* park. **posteggio** *sm* parking; (*spazio*) parking space.

posteriore [poste'rjore] *agg* back, rear; (*tempo*) later.

posterità [posteri'ta] *sf* posterity.

posticcio [pos'tittʃo] *agg* artificial. *sm* hairpiece.

posticipare [postitʃi'pare] *v* defer.

postino [pos'tino] *sm* postman.

posto ['posto] *sm* (*luogo*) place; (*spazio*) room; (*impiego*) position; (*da sedere*) seat. **essere a posto** be in order; (*star bene*) be well, be content. **mettere a posto** tidy up; repair. **sul posto** on the spot.

postumo ['postumo] *agg* posthumous.

potabile [po'tabile] *agg* (*spreg*) drinkable. **acqua potabile** drinking water.

potare [po'tare] *v* prune.

potassio [po'tassjo] *sm* potassium. **potassa** *sf* potash.

potente [po'tɛnte] *agg* powerful; (*efficace*) potent; (*valido*) forceful. **potenza** *sf* power; (*forza*) strength; (*efficacia*) potency.

potenziale [poten'tsjale] *agg*, *sm* potential. **potenzialità** *sf* capacity.

potenziare [poten'tsjare] *v* strengthen, expand. **potenziamento** *sm* strengthening, expansion.

***potere¹** [po'tere] *v* can, be able; (*possibilità, permesso*) may. **non poterne più** (*essere sfinito*) be exhausted; (*essere al limite della sopportazione*) be unable to stand it any longer. **può darsi** maybe.

potere² [po'tere] *sm* power.

povero ['povero], **-a** *agg* poor. *sm*, *sf* poor person. **povero di** lacking in. **povertà** *sf* poverty; (*scarsità*) want, lack.

pozza ['pottsa] *sf* pool. **pozzanghera** *sf* puddle.

pozzo ['pottso] *sm* well; (*cavità*) shaft. **pozzo nero** cesspool.

pranzare [pran'tsare] *v* have dinner; (*a mezzogiorno*) have lunch. **pranzo** *sm* dinner; lunch. **dopo pranzo** (*nel pomeriggio*) in the afternoon. **sala da pranzo** *sf* dining room.

pratica ['pratika] *sf* practice; experience; (*incartamento*) file. **praticante** *s(m+f)* apprentice; (*rel*) churchgoer. **praticare** *v* practise; (*fare*) make; frequent; associate (with).

pratico ['pratiko] *agg* practical; (*esperto*) skilled; (*funzionale*) useful, handy.

all'atto pratico in practice. **essere pratico di** be familiar with.

prato ['prato] *sm* meadow; (*giardino*) lawn. **pratolina** *sf* daisy.

preavvisare [preavvi'zare] *v also* **preavvertire** inform in advance; (*ammonire*) warn. **preavviso** *sm* (*advance*) notice; warning.

pre-bellico [pre'belliko] *agg* pre-war.

precario [pre'karjo] *agg* precarious.

precauzione [prekau'tsjone] *sf* (*cautela*) caution, care; (*provvedimento*) precaution. **precauzionale** *agg* precautionary.

precedente [pretʃe'dɛnte] *agg* previous, preceding, former. *sm* (*dir*) precedent. **precedenti** (*penali*) *sm pl* (criminal) record *sing*. **precedentemente** *avv* before. **precedenza** *sf* priority. **in precedenza** previously.

precedere [pre'tʃedere] *v* precede.

precipitare [pretʃipi'tare] *v* hurl (down); (*affrettare*) hasten; (*chim*) precipitate; (*cadere*) crash; (*piombare*) plunge. **precipitoso** *agg* hurried; (*fig*) rash.

precipizio [pretʃi'pitsjo] *sm* precipice.

precisare [pretʃi'zare] *v* specify; (*fam*) spell out. **precisazione** *sf* clarification. **precisione** *sf* precision. **preciso** *agg* precise, exact; identical.

precoce [pre'kɔtʃe] *agg* precocious; premature, untimely.

preconcetto [prekon'tʃetto] *sm* preconceived idea, prejudice.

precursore [prekur'sore] *sm* forerunner.

preda ['prɛda] *sf* prey; (*bottino*) booty. **essere in preda a** be struck by. **in preda alle fiamme** in flames. **predare** *v* plunder.

predecessore [predetʃes'sore] *sm* predecessor.

predestinare [predesti'nare] *v* preordain.

predetto [pre'detto] *agg* aforesaid.

predica ['predika] *sf* sermon; (*ramanzina*) telling-off. **predicare** *v* preach.

prediletto [predi'letto], **-a** *s*, *agg* favourite.

***predire** [pre'dire] *v* predict, foretell.

***predisporre** [predis'porre] *v* arrange (in advance); predispose.

predominare [predomi'nare] *v* prevail. **predominio** *sm* sway.

prefabbricato [prefabbri'kato] *agg* prefabricated.

prefazione [prefa'tsjone] *sf* preface, foreword.

preferire [prefe'rire] *v* prefer. **preferenza** *sf* preference. **preferibile** *agg* preferable.

prefetto [pre'fɛtto] *sm* prefect. **prefettura** *sf* prefecture.

*****prefiggere** [pre'fiddʒere] *v* fix (in advance); *(gramm)* prefix. **prefiggersi** *v* resolve.

prefisso [pre'fisso] *sm* (*gramm*) prefix; *(telefono)* (area) code.

pregare [pre'gare] *v* pray. **prego** *inter* (*per favore*) please! (*risposta*) don't mention it!

pregevole [pre'dʒevole] *agg* valuable.

preghiera [pre'gjɛra] *sf* prayer; (*domanda*) request.

pregiato [pre'dʒato] *agg* valued. **pregio** *sm* regard; merit. **di nessun pregio** worthless.

pregiudicare [predʒudi'kare] *v* prejudice; (*danneggiare*) harm. **pregiudicato** *sm* ex-convict.

pregiudizio [predʒu'ditsjo] *sm* prejudice, bias.

pregustare [pregus'tare] *v* look forward to.

preistorico [preis'tɔriko] *agg* prehistoric.

prelato [pre'lato] *sm* prelate.

prelevare [prele'vare] *v* withdraw.

prelibato [preli'bato] *agg* exquisite.

preliminare [prelimi'nare] *agg* preliminary. *sm* element.

preludio [pre'ludjo] *sm* prelude.

prematuro [prema'turo] *agg* premature.

premeditato [premedi'tato] *agg* premeditated.

premere ['prɛmere] *v* press. **mi preme (di) sapere** I am anxious to know.

premiare [pre'mjare] *v* award a prize to; (*ricompensare*) reward. **premio** *sm* prize; reward; (*comm*) premium.

preminente [premi'nente] *agg* pre-eminent.

premura [pre'mura] *sf* (*fretta*) haste; (*riguardo*) solicitude, attention. **fare premura** a hurry up. **farsi premura** take care. **premuroso** *agg* thoughtful, solicitous.

*****prendere** ['prɛndere] *v* take; (*cogliere, subire, catturare*) catch; (*ricevere*) receive; (*ritirare*) pick up; (*occupare*) take up; (*assumere*) take on; (*ottenere*) get. **andare a prendere** fetch. **prendere alla lettera** take literally. **prendere per il naso** mock. **prendere qualcuno per il bavero** pull someone's leg. **prendere un**

granchio (*fig*) make a blunder. **prendersela** *v* take it amiss; (*con qualcuno*) get angry with; (*a cuore*) take it to heart.

prenotare [preno'tare] *v* book, reserve. **prenotazione** *sf* booking, reservation.

preoccupare [preokku'pare] *v* worry. **preoccupazione** *sf* worry.

preparare [prepa'rare] *v* prepare; (*tavola*) lay; (*letto*) make. **preparare la strada** pave the way. **preparativo** *sm* arrangement. **preparazione** *sf* preparation.

preposizione [preposi'tsjone] *sf* preposition.

prepotente [prepo'tente] *agg* overbearing. *s(m+f)* (*fam*) bully.

prerogativa [preroga'tiva] *sf* privilege.

presa ['preza] *sf* hold; (*stretta*) grasp; (*elett*) socket; (*carte*) trick; (*cattura*) capture. **cane da presa** retriever. **essere alle prese con** wrestle with. **far presa** set. **macchina da presa** *sf* cine-camera. **presa di posizione** taking sides. **presa in giro** leg-pull. **venire alle prese** come to grips.

presbite ['prɛzbite] *agg* long-sighted.

prescindere [pre'ʃindere] *v* **a prescindere da** apart from.

*****prescrivere** [pre'skrivere] *v* prescribe. **prescrizione** *sf* ordinance. **prescrizione medica** doctor's orders *pl*; (*ricetta*) prescription.

presentare [prezen'tare] *v* present; (*far conoscere*) introduce; (*mostrare*) show; offer. **presentatore, -trice** *sm, sf* compere, question-master.

presente [pre'zɛnte] *agg* present; in the presence of; (*questo*) this. *sm* present. **i presenti** those present *pl*. **tener presente** keep in mind.

presentimento [presenti'mento] *sm* presentiment, foreboding.

presenza [pre'zentsa] *sf* presence; appearance. **di presenza** personally. **fare atto di presenza** put in an appearance. **presenziare (a)** *v* attend.

preservare [prezer'vare] *v* preserve; protect. **preservativo** *agg* preservative; (*guaina profilattica*) condom. **preservazione** *sf* preservation.

preside ['prɛzide] *sm* headmaster; (*di facoltà*) dean. *sf* headmistress.

presidente [prezi'dɛnte] *sm* president; (*di assemblea*) chairman. **presidente della camera** (*pol*) speaker. **presidente del Consiglio** (*pol*) Prime Minister. **presidenza**

(*pol*) presidency; chairmanship. **assumere la presidenza** take the chair.

presidio [pre'zidjo] *sm* garrison; (*fig*) protection. **presidiare** *v* garrison; protect.

*presiedere [pre'sjedere] *v* be in charge (of).

pressa ['prɛssa] *sf* press. **pressare** *v* press.

pressappoco [pressap'poko] *avv* about, roughly.

pressione [pres'sjone] *sf* pressure.

presso ['prɛsso] *prep* near; (*insieme a, fra*) with; (*accanto a*) by; (*indirizzo*) care of, c/o. *avv* nearby. **pressoché** *avv* almost.

prestabilire [prestabi'lire] *v* prearrange.

prestare [pres'tare] *v* lend. **prestare aiuto** help. **prestar fede** believe. **prestar giuramento** take an oath. **prestazione** (*rendimento*) performance. **prestazioni** *sf pl* services *pl*.

prestigio [pres'tidʒo] *sm* prestige. **gioco di prestigio** *sm* conjuring trick. **prestigiatore, -trice** *sm, sf* conjurer. **prestigioso** *agg* prestigious.

prestito ['prɛstito] *sm* loan. **dare in prestito** lend. **prendere in prestito** borrow.

presto ['prɛsto] *avv* (*tra poco*) soon; (*in fretta*) quickly; (*di buon'ora*) early. **si fa presto** (*facilmente*) it's easy.

*presumere [pre'zumere] *v* imagine. **presunto** *agg* presumed; (*erede*) presumptive. **presuntuoso** *agg* presumptuous. **presunzione** *sf* presumption.

*presupporre [presup'porre] *v* presuppose, assume; (*richiedere*) require. **presupposizione** *sf* assumption.

prete ['prɛte] *sm* priest.

*pretendere [pre'tɛndere] *v* (*esigere, presumere*) expect; (*sostenere*) claim. **pretensioso** *agg* pretentious.

pretesa [pre'teza] *sf* claim; (*presunzione*) pretention. **aver poche/molte pretese** be easy/difficult to please.

pretesto [pre'tɛsto] *sm* pretext; (*occasione*) opportunity.

prettamente [pretta'mente] *avv* typically.

*prevalere [preva'lere] *v* prevail.

*prevedere [preve'dere] *v* foresee; (*considerare*) provide for. **prevedibile** *agg* foreseeable.

*prevenire [preve'nire] *v* (*precedere*) arrive before; (*fig*) anticipate; (*evitare*) avert; (*avvertire*) warn. **prevenuto** *agg* (*maldisposto*) biased.

preventivo [preven'tivo] *agg* precautionary; (*dir*) preventive. *sm* estimate. **preventivare** *v* estimate. **prevenzione** *sf* (*ostilità*) bias; (*provvedimento*) prevention.

previdente [previ'dɛnte] *agg* far-sighted, provident. **previdenza** *sf* foresight. **previdenza sociale** social security.

previo ['prɛvjo] *agg* prior.

previsione [previ'zjone] *sf* forecast; (*aspettativa*) anticipation; (*comm*) estimate. **previsto** *agg* foreseen; (*dir*) provided for. **meno/più del previsto** less/more than anticipated.

prezioso [pre'tsjozo] *agg* precious, valuable.

prezzemolo [pret'tsemolo] *sm* parsley.

prezzo ['prɛttso] *sm* price; (*tariffa*) rate; (*trasporto pubblico*) fare. **a buon prezzo** cheaply.

prigione [pri'dʒone] *sf* prison, jail. **prigionia** *sf* captivity. **prigioniero, -a** *sm, sf* prisoner.

prima ['prima] *avv* (*in anticipo*) first, in advance; (*precedentemente*) before; (*più presto*) earlier; (*una volta*) once; (*in primo luogo*) first. *sf* (*teatro*) première; (*auto*) first gear; (*treno*) first class.

primario [pri'marjo] *agg* primary. *sm* (*med*) consultant.

primato [pri'mato] *sm* supremacy; record.

primavera [prima'vera] *sf* spring. **primaverile** *agg* spring.

primitivo [primi'tivo] *agg* primitive; original.

primizia [pri'mitsja] *sf* early produce; (*notizia*) latest news.

primo ['primo] *agg* first; (*precedente*) former; (*principale*) main. **per primo** first.

primula ['primula] *sf* primrose.

principale [printʃi'pale] *agg* principal, main. *sm* principal; (*fam*) boss.

principe ['printʃipe] *sm* prince. **principato** *sm* principality. **principesco** *agg* princely. **principessa** *sf* princess.

principio [prin'tʃipjo] *sm* beginning; (*fondamento*) principle; origin. **da** or **in principio** at first. **per principio** on principle.

priorità [priori'ta] *sf* priority.

prisma ['prizma] *sm* prism.

privare [pri'vare] *v* deprive.

privato [pri'vato], **-a** *agg* private; personal. *sm, sf* private citizen. **privatista** *s(m+f)* (*scolaro*) private school pupil;

(*candidato*) external student. **privativa** *sf*
monopoly. **privazione** *sf* privation, loss.
privilegio [privi'ledʒo] *sm* privilege.
privilegiato *agg* privileged.
privo ['privo] *agg* devoid (of), without.
privo di denaro penniless. **privo di sensi**
(*svenuto*) unconscious.
probabile [pro'babile] *agg* probable, likely. **poco probabile** unlikely. **probabilità** *sf*
probability, likelihood; (*possibilità*)
chance.
problema ['problema] *sm* problem.
problematico *agg* problematic; doubtful.
proboscide [pro'boʃide] *sf* trunk.
procedere [pro'tʃɛdere] *v* proceed; (*comportarsi*) behave. **procedimento** *sm*
(*svolgimento*) course; (*tec*) process; (*dir*)
proceedings *pl.*
processione [protʃes'sjone] *sf* procession.
processo [pro'tʃɛsso] *sm* process; (*dir*) trial, lawsuit. **essere sotto processo** be on
trial. **processo verbale** minutes *pl.*
procinto [pro'tʃinto] *sm* **essere in procinto
di** be on the point of, be about to.
proclamare [prokla'mare] *v* proclaim.
proclamazione *sf* proclamation.
proclive [pro'klive] *agg* prone (to).
procreare [prokre'are] *v* procreate.
procreazione *sf* procreation.
procurare [proku'rare] *v* get; (*dare,
causare*) give. **procura** *sf* power of attorney. **per procura** by proxy. **procuratore**
sm proxy; (*magistrato*) attorney; (*comm*)
agent.
proda ['prɔda] *sf* bank.
prode ['prɔde] *agg* valiant.
prodigare [prodi'gare] *v* lavish. **prodigo**
agg, m pl **-ghi** prodigal, lavish.
prodigio [pro'didʒo] *sm* prodigy. **prodigioso** *agg* wonderful, marvellous.
prodotto [pro'dotto] *sm* product; (*alimentare*) foodstuff; (*chimico*) chemical.
*****produrre** [pro'durre] *v* produce; cause;
(*mostrare*) show; (*fare*) make. **produrre
un testimonio** call a witness. **produttivo**
agg productive. **produttività** *sf* productivity. **produttore** *sm* producer. **produzione**
sf production; (*fabbricazione*) manufacture; (*quantità*) output.
profanare [profa'nare] *v* desecrate; (*contaminare*) debase. **profano** *agg* profane;
(*empio*) sacrilegious; (*inesperto*) ignorant.
*****proferire** [profe'rire] *v* utter, pronounce.
professare [profes'sare] *v* profess. **professionale** *agg* professional; vocational;

(*connesso alla professione*) occupational.
professione *sf* profession; (*mestiere*)
trade. **di professione** by profession.
professionista *s(m+f)* professional (person).
professore [profes'sore], **-essa** *sm, sf*
teacher. **professore titolare/incaricato**
university professor/lecturer.
profeta [pro'fɛta] *sm* prophet. **profetico**
agg prophetic. **profezia** *sf* prophecy.
proficuo [pro'fikuo] *agg* useful.
profilo [pro'filo] *sm* profile; (*contorno*)
outline. **profilare** *v* outline; (*mec*) profile.
profilato *sm* (*mec*) section.
profittare [profit'tare] *v* profit; (*approfittare*) take advantage; (*progredire*) make
progress. **profittatore** *sm* profiteer. **profitto** *sm* profit; advantage. **trarre profitto**
benefit.
profondo [pro'fondo] *agg* deep; (*radicato*)
deep-rooted. *sm* depth. **profondare** *v*
sink. **profondità** *sf* depth.
profugo ['prɔfugo], **-a** *sm, pl* **-ghi**, *sf* refugee.
profumare [profu'mare] *v* perfume. **profumato** *agg* perfumed; fragrant. **profumeria**
sf perfumery. **profumo** *sm* fragrance,
scent.
profusione [profu'zjone] *sf* profusion.
progettare [prodʒet'tare] *v* plan; (*tec*)
design. **progettazione** *sf* planning. **progetto** *sm* project, plan. **progetto di legge** bill.
progetto di massima preliminary plan.
prognosi ['prɔɲozi] *sf* prognosis.
programma [pro'gramma] *sm* program-
gramme; prospectus; (*scuola*) syllabus.
programmare *v* programme. **program-
matore**, **-trice** *sm, sf* programmer.
programmazione *sf* programming.
progredire [progre'dire] *v* make progress,
get on. **progressione** *sf* progression.
progressivo *agg* progressive. **progresso**
sm progress. **fare progressi** improve,
make progress.
proibire [proi'bire] *v* forbid, prohibit.
proibito *agg* forbidden. **proibizionismo**
sm prohibition.
proiettare [projet'tare] *v* project; (*gettar
fuori*) eject; (*cine*) screen. **proiettile** *sm*
projectile; (*mil*) shell. **a prova di proiettile** bullet-proof. **proiettore** *sm* projector.
prole ['prɔle] *sf* offspring.
proletario [prole'tarjo], **-a** *s, agg* proletarian. **proletariato** *sm* proletariat.

prolifico [pro'lifiko] *agg* prolific.

prolisso [pro'lisso] *agg* long-winded.

prologo [pro'lɔgo] *sm, pl* **-ghi** prologue.

prolungare [prolun'gare] *v* extend; (*tempo*) prolong; (*spazio*) lengthen. **prolungarsi** *v* (*dilungarsi*) dwell (on). **prolunga** *sf* extension. **prolungamento** *sm* extension.

promemoria [prome'mɔrja] *sm invar* memorandum.

***promettere** [pro'mettere] *v* promise. **promessa** *sf* promise. **promesso** *agg* promised. **promettente** *agg* promising.

prominente [promi'nente] *agg* prominent, jutting (out). **prominenza** *sf* prominence, projection.

promiscuo [pro'miskuo] *agg* mixed; (*scuola*) co-educational; (*relazioni*) promiscuous.

promontorio [promon'tɔrjo] *sm* headland.

promozione [promo'tsjone] *sf* promotion.

***promuovere** [pro'mwɔvere] *v* promote; provoke.

pronome [pro'nome] *sm* pronoun.

pronosticare [pronosti'kare] *v* forecast. **pronostico** *sm* forecast.

pronto ['pronto] *agg* ready; (*rapido*) prompt; (*vivace*) lively. *inter* (*telefono*) hello!

prontuario [prontu'arjo] *sm* handbook.

pronunciare [pronun'tʃare] *v* pronounce. **pronunciarsi a favore di** declare oneself in favour of. **pronuncia** *sf* pronunciation.

propaganda [propa'ganda] *sf* propaganda. **propagandista** *s(m+f)* propagandist.

propagare [propa'gare] *v* propagate.

propenso [pro'penso] *agg* inclined; favourable.

propizio [pro'pitsjo] *agg* propitious; favourable.

proponimento [proponi'mento] *sm* resolution.

***proporre** [pro'porre] *v* propose; intend; suggest.

proporzione [propor'tsjone] *sf* proportion; (*mat*) ratio. **in proporzione a** compared with. **proporzionale** *agg* proportional.

proposito [pro'pɔzito] *sm* purpose; intention; (*scopo*) aim; (*progetto*) plan. **a proposito** (*opportunamente*) at the right time; (*inter*) by the way; (*opportuno*) to the point. **a proposito di** with regard to. **cambiare proposito** change one's mind.

proposizione [propozi'tsjone] *sf* proposition; clause.

proposta [pro'posta] *sf* proposal.

proprietà [proprje'ta] *sf* property; (*precisione, decoro*) propriety; (*possesso*) ownership. **essere di proprietà di** belong to. **proprietà letteraria** copyright.

proprio ['prɔprjo] *agg* one's (own); (*mat, gramm*) proper, characteristic. *avv* exactly, just; (*veramente*) really.

propulsione [propul'sjone] *sf* propulsion.

prora ['prɔra] *sf* prow.

prorogare [proro'gare] *v* (*rinviare*) put off, adjourn; (*prolungare*) extend. **proroga** *sf* adjournment; extension.

***prorompere** [pro'rompere] *v* burst out.

prosa ['prɔza] *sf* prose; theatre. **prosaico** *agg* prosaic.

prosciugare [proʃu'gare] *v* drain.

prosciutto [pro'ʃutto] *sm* ham.

***proscrivere** [pro'skrivere] *v* proscribe.

proseguire [prose'gwire] *v* continue, go on. **proseguimento** *sm* continuation.

prosperare [prospe'rare] *v* prosper, thrive. **prosperità** *sf* prosperity. **prospero** *agg* prosperous, thriving.

prospettiva [prospet'tiva] *sf* (*tec*) perspective; (*previsione*) prospect, outlook. **prospettare** *v* (*esporre*) show; (*guardare*) look out (on). **prospettarsi** *v* (*essere in vista*) be in sight.

prospetto [pros'petto] *sm* (*tabella*) list; (*pubblicità*) prospectus.

prossimo ['prɔssimo] *agg* near; (*seguente*) next; (*vicino nel passato, stretto*) close. **passato/trapassato prossimo** *sm* (*gramm*) present/past perfect. *sm* neighbour. **prossimità** *sf* proximity.

prostituire [prostitu'ire] *v* prostitute. **prostituta** *sf* prostitute. **prostituzione** *sf* prostitution.

protagonista [protago'nista] *s(m+f)* protagonist, chief character.

***proteggere** [pro'teddʒere] *v* protect, shelter; favour.

proteina [prote'ina] *sf* protein.

protesi ['prɔtezi] *sf* prosthesis.

protesta [pro'tɛsta] *sf* protest. **protestare** *v* protest; (*dichiarare*) declare. **protesto** *sm* protest.

protestante [protes'tante] *s(m+f)*, *agg* Protestant.

protetto [pro'tɛtto], **-a** *agg* protected; favourite. *sm, sf* protégé; favourite. **protettorato** *sm* protectorate. **protettore** *sm* protector, defender. **santo protettore** patron saint.

protezione [prote'tsjone] *sf* protection; *(mecenatismo)* patronage. **protezione antincendio** fireproofing.

protocollo [proto'kɔllo] *sm* protocol; register. **carta protocollo** *sf* foolscap (paper).

protone [pro'tone] *sm* proton.

prototipo [pro'tɔtipo] *sm* prototype.

*****protrarre** [pro'trarre] *v* protract; *(prorogare)* put off.

prova ['prɔva] *sf* proof; evidence; *(esame, testimonianza)* test; *(cimento)* trial; *(tentativo)* try; *(sarto)* fitting; *(teatro)* rehearsal. **a prova di acqua** waterproof. **a prova di fuoco** fireproof. **dar buona prova di sé** give a good account of oneself. **reggere alla prova** stand the test.

provare [pro'vare] *v* try (out); *(collaudare)* test; *(spettacolo)* rehearse; *(assaggiare)* taste; *(dimostrare)* prove; *(mettere alla prova)* put to the test; *(abito, ecc.)* try on.

*****provenire** [prove'nire] *v* come (from); *(fig)* spring (from), be caused (by). **provenienza** *sf* origin, source.

proverbio [pro'vɛrbjo] *sm* proverb, saying. **proverbiale** *agg* proverbial.

provetta [pro'vetta] *sf* test-tube.

provincia [pro'vintʃa] *sf* province. **di provincia** provincial.

provocare [provo'kare] *v* provoke, cause. **provocatorio** *agg* provocative. **provocazione** *sf* provocation.

*****provvedere** [provve'dere] *v* make provision for, provide for; *(prendere provvedimenti)* take steps; *(badare a)* see to; *(procurare)* provide. **provvedimento** *sm* step, measure. **provveditore** *sm* administrator; *(agli studi)* education officer.

provvidenza [provvi'dentsa] *sf* providence; *(fam)* godsend. **provvidenziale** *agg* providential.

provvigione [provvi'dʒone] *sf* commission.

provvisorio [provvi'zɔrjo] *agg* provisional.

provvista [prov'vista] *sf* provisions *pl*, stock. **provvisto** *agg* supplied, provided.

prua ['prua] *sf* prow.

prudente [pru'dɛnte] *agg* prudent, careful, cautious. **prudenza** *sf* care, caution.

*****prudere** ['prudere] *v* itch. **prurito** *sm* itch.

prugna ['pruɲa] *sf* plum; *(secca)* prune. **prugno** *sm* plum-tree.

pseudonimo [pseu'dɔnimo] *sm* pseudonym.

psicanalisi [psika'nalizi] *sf* psycho-analysis. **psicanalista** *s(m+f)* psycho-analyst. **psicanalitico** *agg* psycho-analytical.

psichiatra [psi'kjatra] *s(m+f)* psychiatrist. **psichiatria** *sf* psychiatry.

psichico ['psikiko] *agg* psychic.

psicologo [psi'kɔlogo], -a *sm, sf* psychologist. **psicologia** *sf* psychology. **psicologico** *agg* psychological.

psicopatico [psiko'patiko], -a *agg* psychopathic. *sm, sf* psychopath.

psicosi [psi'kɔzi] *sf* psychosis. **psicotico, -a** *s, agg* psychotic.

psicosomatico [psikoso'matiko] *agg* psychosomatic.

psicoterapia [psikotera'pia] *sf* psychotherapy. **psicoterapista** *s(m+f)* psychotherapist.

pubblicare [pubbli'kare] *v* publish. **pubblicazione** *sf* publication, issue. **pubblicista** *s(m+f)* (freelance) journalist.

pubblicità [pubblitʃi'ta] *sf* publicity; advertising. **fare pubblicità** advertise. **piccola pubblicità** classified advertisements *pl*. **pubblicitario** *agg* advertising, publicity.

pubblico ['pubbliko] *agg* public. *sm* public; *(teatro)* audience.

pubertà [puber'ta] *sf* puberty.

pudico [pu'diko] *agg, m pl* **-chi** modest; *(vergognoso)* bashful.

pudore [pu'dore] *sm* modesty; *(vergogna)* shame. **oltraggio al pudore** *sm* indecent behaviour. **senza pudore** shameless.

puerile [pue'rile] *agg* puerile.

pugilato [pudʒi'lato] *sm* boxing. **fare del pugilato** box. **pugile** *sm* boxer. **pugilistico** *agg* boxing.

pugnalare [puɲa'lare] *v* stab. **pugnalata** *sf* stab. **pugnale** *sm* dagger.

pugno ['puɲo] *sm* fist; *(colpo)* punch; *(piccola quantità)* fistful. **essere un pugno in un occhio** be an eyesore. **fare a pugni** fight; *(fig)* clash. **prendere a pugni** punch. **tenere in pugno** clutch; *(fig)* control.

pulce ['pultʃe] *sf* flea. **gioco della pulce** *sm* tiddly-winks.

pulcino [pul'tʃino] *sm* chick. **bagnato come un pulcino** wet through.

puledro [pu'ledro] *sm* colt. **puledra** *sf* filly.

puleggia [pu'leddʒa] *sf* pulley.

pulire [pu'lire] *v* clean; *(lavando)* wash; *(con strofinaccio, ecc.)* wipe (clean); *(con* spazzola) brush; (sfregando) scour; (lucidare) polish. **pulirsi il naso** blow one's nose. **pulito** agg clean.

pulizia [puli'tsia] sf (il pulire) cleaning; (l'essere pulito) cleanliness. **far le pulizie** do the cleaning. **far pulizia** clean; (sgombrare) clear out.

pullman ['pullman] sm invar coach.

pullover [pul'lɔver] sm invar pullover.

pullulare [pullu'lare] v swarm.

pulpito ['pulpito] sm pulpit. **montare in pulpito** preach.

pulsare [pul'sare] v throb, beat. **pulsante** sm button; (campanello) buzzer.

*****pungere** ['pundʒere] v sting; (morsicare) bite; (con spillo) prick. **pungente** agg pungent; (fig) sharp; (ispido) prickly. **pungiglione** sm sting. **pungolo** sm goad.

punire [pu'nire] v punish. **punibile** agg punishable. **punitivo** agg punitive. **punizione** sf punishment; (sport) penalty.

punta ['punta] sf point; (estremità) tip. **ora di punta** sf rush hour. **prendere di punta** clash (with).

puntare [pun'tare] v point, direct; (scommettere) bet.

puntata [pun'tata] sf (scritto) instalment, part.

punteggiare [punted'dʒare] v punctuate. **punteggiatura** sf punctuation.

punteggio [pun'teddʒo] sm score.

puntellare [puntel'lare] v prop up. **puntello** sm prop; (fig) support.

puntiglioso [puntiʎ'ʎozo] agg stubborn. **puntiglio** sm stubbornness.

puntina [pun'tina] sf (da disegno) drawing pin; (grammofono) stylus.

punto ['punto] sm point; (segno) d t; (med, ricamo, maglia) stitch. avv (affatto) at all. **di punto in bianco** point-blank. **due punti** colon. **in punto** (tempo) on the dot, sharp. **mettere a punto** put right; (auto) tune; (fig) clarify. **punto esclamativo/interrogativo** exclamation/question mark. **punto e virgola** semicolon. **punto fermo** full stop.

puntuale [puntu'ale] agg punctual, on time.

puntualizzare [puntualid'dzare] v define, precisely.

puntura [pun'tura] sf sting, bite; (di spillo, ecc.) prick; (med) injection, puncture; (dolore) stitch.

punzecchiare [pundzek'kjare] v sting, bite, prick; (stuzzicare) tease.

punzonare [puntso'nare] v punch. **punzonatrice** sf punch. **punzone** sm punch, die.

pupa ['pupa] sf (fam) baby; (bambola) doll. **pupattola** sf doll. **pupazzo** sm puppet. **pupo** ['pupo] (fam) baby, little boy.

pupilla [pu'pilla] sf pupil.

purché [pur'ke] cong provided that, as long as.

pure ['pure] avv also, too. cong even (though); (tuttavia) yet.

purè [pu're] sm invar purée. **purè di patate** mashed potatoes pl.

purgare [pur'gare] v purge; purify. **purga** sf purge; (il purgare) purging, cleansing; (purgante) laxative; (gastr) soaking.

purgatorio [purga'tɔrjo] sm purgatory.

purificare [purifi'kare] v purify.

puritano [puri'tano] -a s, agg puritan.

puro ['puro] agg pure. **purezza** sf purity. **purosangue** agg, sm invar throughbred.

purpureo [pur'pureo] agg purple.

purtroppo [pur'trɔppo] avv unfortunately.

pus [pus] sm invar pus.

*****putrefare** [putre'fare] v putrefy, rot. **putrefatto** or **putrido** agg putrid, rotten.

puttana [put'tana] sf whore; (fam) tart.

puzzare [put'tsare] v stink, smell. **puzzo** sm stench, smell. **puzzolente** agg stinking.

Q

qua [kwa] avv here. (**di**) **di qua di** on this side of. **di qua** (stato in luogo) here; (moto a luogo) over here; (da qui) from here. **fin qua** (spazio) up to here; (tempo) so far. **per di qua** this way. **qua sopra/sotto/vicino** up/down/near here.

quacchero ['kwakkero], -a sm, sf Quaker.

quaderno [kwa'derno] sm exercise-book.

quadrante [kwa'drante] sm (mat, astron) quadrant; (orologio) dial; (solare) sundial.

quadrato [kwa'drato] agg square; (sensibile) level-headed. sm square. **quadrare** v square; (far senso) make sense; (garbare) please.

quadretto [kwa'dretto] sm small square; (fig) scene. **a quadretti** check(ed), chequered.

quadrifoglio [kwadri'fɔʎʎo] *sm* four-leafed clover; *(autostrada)* clover-leaf.

quadro¹ ['kwadro] *agg* square.

quadro² ['kwadro] *sm (dipinto)* picture; *(ambito)* scope; *(tabella)* table. **quadri** *sm pl (carte)* diamonds *pl*. **a quadri** check(ed), chequered.

quadrupede [kwa'drupede] *agg, sm* quadruped.

quaggiù [kwad'dʒu] *avv* down here.

quaglia ['kwaʎa] *sf* quail.

qualche ['kwalke] *agg* some, any; *(alcuni)* a few. **in qualche luogo** somewhere. **in qualche modo** somehow. **qualcosa** *pron also* **qualche cosa** something, anything. **qualcuno** *pron* somebody, anybody.

quale ['kwale] *agg, pron* what; *(fra numero limitato)* which; *(come)* as. **tale e quale** just like. *inter* what! *avv* as.

qualificare [kwalifi'kare] *v* qualify. **qualifica** *sf* title; position; *(doti professionali)* qualification; *(giudizio)* report. **qualificativo** *agg* qualifying. **qualificato** *agg* skilled.

qualità [kwali'ta] *sf* quality; *(specie)* sort, kind. **qualitativo** *agg* qualitative.

qualora [kwa'lora] *cong* in case.

qualunque [kwa'lunkwe] *agg invar also* **qualsiasi** any; *(ogni)* every; *(non importa quale)* whatever, whichever. **l'uomo qualunque** the man in the street.

quando ['kwando] *avv* when. *cong* when; *(ogniqualvolta)* whenever; *(mentre)* whereas; *(giacché)* since. **da quando** *(dacché)* (ever) since; *(da quanto tempo)* since when. **di quando in quando** from time to time. **fino a quando** until; *(interrogativo)* until when; *(per quanto tempo)* how long.

quantità [kwanti'ta] *sf* quantity. **quantitativo** *sm* amount.

quanto ['kwanto] *agg* how much *or* many; *(esclamativo)* what (a lot of); *(relativo)* as much *or* many ... as. *pron* how much *or* many; as much *or* many; *(quello che)* what. *avv* how (much *or* many); *(tempo)* how long; *(distanza)* how far; *(come)* as; *(nella misura che)* as much as. **da quanto** *(tempo)* how long; *(per ciò che)* as far as. **per quanto** however; *(per ciò che)* as far as. **quanto a** as for. **quanto fa?** how much is it? **quanto mai** very much indeed. **quanto prima** soon. **quanto tempo** how long.

quaranta [kwa'ranta] *agg, sm* forty.

quarantena *sf* quarantine. **quarantesimo** *sm, agg* fortieth.

quaresima [kwa'rezima] *sf* Lent.

quarta ['kwarta] *sf (auto)* fourth *or* top gear; *(musica)* fourth. **partire in quarta** *(fam)* be off like a shot.

quartetto [kwar'tetto] *sm* quartet.

quartiere [kwar'tjere] *sm* district, quarter. **quartieri bassi** slums *pl*.

quarto ['kwarto] *agg* fourth. *sm* quarter. **sono le due e/meno un quarto** it is a quarter past/to two.

quarzo ['kwartso] *sm* quartz.

quasi ['kwazi] *avv* nearly, almost; *(con valore negativo)* hardly. *cong (come se)* as if.

quassù [kwas'su] *avv* up here.

quatto quatto ['kwatto 'kwatto] *avv* quickly.

quattordici [kwat'torditʃi] *agg, sm* fourteen. **quattordicesimo** *agg, sm* fourteenth.

quattrini [kwat'trini] *sm pl* money *sing*; *(fam)* cash *sing*. **quattrini a palate** loads of money *sing*. **senza quattrini** penniless.

quattro ['kwattro] *sm, agg* four. **dirne quattro a qualcuno** give someone a piece of one's mind. **far quattro passi** go for a stroll. **farsi in quattro** go out of one's way.

quegli [kwe'ʎi] *V* **quello**.

quei ['kwei] *V* **quello**.

quel [kwel] *V* **quello**.

quello ['kwello] *agg* that *(pl* those). *pron* that (one) *(pl* those); *(lo stesso)* **che** the same. **di quello che** than. **quello che** the one who *(pl* those who); *(ciò che)* what.

quercia ['kwertʃa] *sf* oak.

querela [kwe'rela] *sf* lawsuit, action. **presentare** *or* **sporgere querela** bring an action. **querelante** *s(m+f)* plaintiff.

questionario [kwestjo'narjo] *sm* questionnaire.

questione [kwes'tjone] *sf* question; *(affare)* matter; problem; *(disputa)* argument. **fare una questione** make an issue. **mettere in questione** question.

questo ['kwesto] *agg* this *(pl* these). *pron* this (one) *(pl* these). **con questo** *(con queste parole)* with these words; *(ciònonostante)* in spite of this.

questura [kwes'tura] *sf* police station. **questore** *sm* police inspector.

qui ['kwi] *avv* here. **di qui** from here; *(moto a luogo)* here; *(tempo)* from now (on). **fin qui** up to here; (*tempo*) up to now.

quietanza [kwje'tantsa] *sf* receipt.

quietare [kwje'tare] *v* calm. **quiete** *sf* calm; (*assenza di moto*) rest.

quindi ['kwindi] *cong* so. *avv* afterwards.

quindici ['kwinditʃi] *agg, sm* fifteen. **quindici giorni** a fortnight. **quindicesimo** *agg, sm* fifteenth. **quindicinale** *sm* fortnightly.

quinta ['kwinta] *sf* (*teatro*) wing. **dietro le quinte** behind the scenes.

quintessenza [kwintes'sɛntsa] *sf* quintessence.

quintetto [kwin'tetto] *sm* quintet.

quinto ['kwinto] *sm, agg* fifth.

quota ['kwɔta] *sf* (*porzione*) share; (*altitudine*) height; (*livello*) level; (*econ*) quota. **quota zero** square one. **quotare** *v* appreciate; (*borsa*) quote. **quotazione** *sf* quotation.

quotidiano [kwoti'djano] *agg, sm* daily.

quoziente [kwo'tsjɛnte] *sm* quotient.

R

rabarbaro [ra'barbaro] *sm* rhubarb.

rabberciare [rabber'tʃare] *v* patch, mend; (*scritto*) re-hash.

rabbia ['rabbja] *sf* fury, rage; (*idrofobia*) rabies. **che rabbia!** how infuriating! **fare rabbia a** make angry. **rabbioso** *agg* furious; (*idrofobo*) rabid.

rabbino [rab'bino] *sm* rabbi. **rabbinico** *agg* rabbinical.

rabbonire [rabbo'nire] *v* calm down, soothe.

rabbrividire [rabbrivi'dire] *v* shiver; (*fig*) shudder.

rabbuffare [rabbuf'fare] *v* (*scompigliare*) ruffle; (*sgridare*) scold. **rabbuffo** *sm* telling-off, scolding.

rabbuiarsi [rabbu'jarsi] *v* darken.

raccapezzare [rakkapet'tsare] *v* scrape together. **raccapezzarsi** *v* make out.

raccapricciare [rakkaprit'tʃare] *v* be horrified. **raccapricciante** *agg* horrifying.

raccattare [rakkat'tare] *v* pick up, collect.

racchetta [rak'ketta] *sf* racket; (*ping-pong*) bat.

***raccogliere** [rak'kɔʎere] *v* pick; (*riprendere da terra*) pick up; (*riunire*)

collect; (*fare il raccolto*) gather, harvest. **raccoglimento** *sm* attention. **raccoglitore** *sm* (*cartella*) binder.

raccolta [rak'kɔlta] *sf* collecting; collection; (*agric*) harvesting. **fare la raccolta (di)** collect.

raccolto [rak'kɔlto] *agg* (*concentrato nei pensieri*) deep in thought; (*rannicchiato*) crouching. *sm* harvest, crop.

raccomandare [rakkoman'dare] *v* recommend; (*esortare*) urge. **mi raccomando!** please do! **raccomandarsi a** rely on. (*lettera*) **raccomandata** *sf* registered letter. **raccomandato, -a** *sm, sf* protégé. **raccomandazione** *sf* recommendation.

raccomodare [rakkomo'dare] *v* also **racconciare** repair, mend.

raccontare [rakkon'tare] *v* tell. **racconto** *sm* story, tale; (*resoconto*) account.

raccorciare [rakkor'tʃare] *v* shorten.

raccordare [rakkor'dare] *v* connect. **raccordo** *sm* connection; (*strada, ecc.*) junction.

racimolare [ratʃimo'lare] *v* scrape together.

radar ['radar] *sm invar* radar.

raddolcire [raddol'tʃire] *v* sweeten; (*acqua*) soften.

raddoppiare [raddop'pjare] *v* double; (*fig*) redouble.

raddrizzare [raddrit'tsare] *v* straighten; (*elett*) rectify. **raddrizzatore** *sm* rectifier.

***radere** ['radere] *v* (*sbarbare*) shave; (*sfiorare*) graze. **radere al suolo** raze to the ground.

radiale [ra'djale] *agg* radial.

radiare [ra'djare] *v* expel; (*mil*) cashier; cancel. **radiare dall'albo** strike off the register.

radiatore [radja'tore] *sm* radiator.

radiazione¹ [radja'tsjone] *sf* (*fis*) radiation.

radiazione² [radja'tsjone] *sf* expulsion; cancellation.

radica ['radika] *sf* briar.

radicale [radi'kale] *agg* radical. *sm* (*chim*) radical; (*mat*) root.

radicare [radi'kare] *v* (take) root. **radicato** *agg* deep-rooted.

radicchio [ra'dikkjo] *sm* chicory.

radice [ra'ditʃe] *sf* root. **mettere radici** take root. **radice quadrata/cubica** square/cube root.

radio¹ ['radjo] *sm invar* radium.

radio² ['radjo] *sf invar* radio. **giornale radio** *sm* news (broadcast). **segnale radio** *sm* time signal.

radioattivo [radjoat'tivo] *agg* radioactive. **radioattività** *sf* radioactivity.

radiocontrollato [radjokontrol'lato] *agg* radio-controlled.

radiodiffusione [radjodiffu'zjone] *sf also* **radiotrasmissione** broadcast. **radiodiffuso** *agg* broadcast.

radiografare [radjogra'fare] *v* X-ray. **radiografia** *sf* (*immagine*) X-ray; (*procedimento*) radiography.

radiologo [ra'djɔlogo], **-a** *sm*, *pl* **-ghi**, *sf* radiologist.

rado ['rado] *agg* sparse. **di rado** rarely. **radura** *sf* clearing.

radunare [radu'nare] *v* gather. **radunarsi** *v* assemble. **radunata** *sf* assembly, meeting. **raduno** *sm* meeting.

rafano ['rafano] *sm* radish.

raffica ['raffika] *sf* (*vento*) gust; (*colpi*) volley.

raffigurare [raffigu'rare] *v* represent.

raffinare [raffi'nare] *v* refine. **raffinatezza** *sf* refinement. **raffinazione** *sf* refining. **raffineria** *sf* refinery.

rafforzare [raffor'tsare] *v* reinforce.

raffreddare [raffred'dare] *v* cool. **raffreddarsi** *v* (*diventar freddo*) cool down; (*fam: prendersi un raffreddore*) catch a cold. **raffreddamento** *sm* cooling (down or off). **raffreddore** *sm* cold.

raffrenare [raffre'nare] *v* restrain.

raffrontare [raffron'tare] *v* compare. **raffronto** *sm* comparison.

rafia ['rafja] *sf* raffia.

raganella [raga'nɛlla] *sf* rattle.

ragazza [ra'gattsa] *sf* girl; (*innamorata*) girl-friend. **da ragazza** as a girl. **nome da ragazza** *sm* maiden name. **ragazza madre** unmarried mother.

ragazzo [ra'gattso] *sm* boy, lad; (*fam*) fellow, chap; (*innamorato*) boy-friend. **da ragazzo** as a boy. **fin da ragazzo** since childhood.

raggiare [rad'dʒare] *v* radiate.

raggio ['raddʒo] *sm* ray; (*geom*) radius; (*ambito*) range; (*ruota*) spoke. **raggio d'azione** range; (*fig*) scope. **fare i raggi** X-ray.

raggirare [raddʒi'rare] *v* trick. **raggiro** *sm* trick.

*raggiungere [rad'dʒundʒere] *v* reach; (*riunirsi*) join; (*allinearsi*) catch up

(with); (*conseguire*) attain. **raggiungibile** *agg* within reach; attainable.

raggiustare [raddʒus'tare] *v* mend; (*fig*) set right.

raggomitolare [raggomito'lare] *v* roll up. **raggomitolarsi** *v* curl up.

raggrinzare [raggrin'tsare] *v also* **raggrinzire** wrinkle, crease.

raggrumare [raggru'mare] *v* clot.

raggruppare [raggrup'pare] *v* group (together). **raggrupparsi** *v* assemble. **raggruppamento** *sm* grouping; (*gruppo*) group; (*mil*) unit.

ragguagliare [raggwa'Aare] *v* level; (*paragonare*) compare; inform; (*mat*) convert. **ragguaglio** *sm* comparison; information; (*resoconto*) report; conversion.

ragia [ra'dʒa] *sf* **acqua ragia** *sf* turpentine.

ragionare [radʒo'nare] *v* reason; discuss. **ragionamento** *sm* reasoning; discussion.

ragione [ra'dʒone] *sf* reason; (*diritto*) right; (*rapporto*) rate; (*spiegazione*) account; (*mat*) ratio. **a ragione** rightly. **ragion veduta** after due consideration. **aver ragione** be right. **dar ragione a qualcuno** admit that someone is right. **rendersi ragione (di)** account (for).

ragioneria [radʒone'ria] *sf* accountancy. **ragioniere**, **-a** *sm*, *sf* accountant.

ragionevole [radʒo'nevole] *agg* reasonable.

ragliare [ra'Aare] *v* bray. **raglio** *sm* bray.

ragno [ra'ɲo] *sm* spider. **ragnatela** *sf* cobweb.

ragù [ra'gu] *sm* meat sauce.

raid ['reid] *sm invar* (*mil*) raid; (*sport*) rally.

raion ['rajon] *sm invar* rayon.

rallegrare [rallegˈgrare] *v* cheer up. **rallegrarsi** *v* be delighted; congratulate. **rallegramenti** *sm pl* congratulations *pl*.

rallentare [rallen'tare] *v* slacken, slow down. **rallentamento** *sm* slackening, slowing down.

rame ['rame] *sm* copper. **ramaiolo** *sm* ladle.

ramengo [ra'mengo] *sm* **andare a ramengo** (*fam*) go to the dogs.

ramificare [ramifi'kare] *v* ramify. **ramificazione** *sf* ramification.

ramino [ra'mino] *sm* rummy.

rammaricarsi [rammari'karsi] *v* regret; (*lamentarsi*) complain. **rammarico** *sm*, *pl* **-chi** regret.

rammendare [rammen'dare] *v* darn. **rammendo** *sm* (*atto*) darning; (*parte rammendata*) darn.

rammentare [rammen'tare] *v* (*ricordare*) recall; (*richiamare alla memoria*) call to mind.

rammollire [rammol'lire] *v* soften. **rammollito** *agg* soft; (*rimbambito*) doddering.

ramo ['ramo] *sm* branch. **ramoscello** *sm* twig.

rampa ['rampa] *sf* ramp; (*scala*) flight. **rampante** *agg* rampant.

rampicante [rampi'kante] *agg* climbing. *sm* (*pianta*) creeper.

rampino [ram'pino] *sm* hook.

rampollo [ram'pollo] *sm* offspring; (*pianta*) shoot; (*acqua*) spring.

rampone [ram'pone] *sm* (*pesca*) harpoon; (*alpinismo*) crampon.

rana ['rana] *sf* frog; (*nuoto a rana*) breaststroke. **uomo rana** *sm* frogman.

rancido ['rantʃido] *agg* rancid.

rancio ['rantʃo] *sm* meal.

rancore [ran'kore] *sm* grudge.

randagio [ran'dadʒo] *agg* stray.

randello [ran'dɛllo] *sm* club.

rango ['rango] *sm* rank; (*posizione sociale*) standing.

rannicchiarsi [rannik'kjarsi] *v* crouch, huddle.

rannuvolarsi [rannuvo'larsi] *v* cloud over; (*fig*) darken.

ranocchio [ra'nokkjo] *sm* frog.

rantolare [ranto'lare] *v* wheeze.

ranuncolo [ra'nunkolo] *sm* buttercup.

rapa ['rapa] *sf* turnip.

rapace [ra'patʃe] *agg* rapacious. **uccello rapace** *sm* bird of prey.

rapare [ra'pare] *v* crop.

rapido ['rapido] *agg* quick, rapid. *sm* express (train).

rapina [ra'pina] *sf* robbery. **rapinare** *v* rob.

rapire [ra'pire] *v* (*rapinare*) rob; (*persone*) kidnap, abduct; (*estasiare*) enrapture. **rapimento** *sm* kidnapping; (*estasi*) rapture.

rappezzare [rappet'tsare] *v* patch.

***rapprendersi** [rap'prendersi] *v* coagulate; (*latte*) curdle.

rappresaglia [rappre'zaʎa] *sf* reprisal.

rappresentare [rappresen'tare] *v* represent; (*significare*) mean; (*teatro*) show. **rappresentante** *s*(*m*+*f*) representative, agent. **rappresentanza** *sf* agency. **rappresentativo** *agg* representative. **rappresentazione** *sf* representation; description; (*teatro, cine*) performance.

raro ['raro] *agg* rare; exceptional. **rarità** *sf* rarity.

rasare [ra'zare] *v* shave; (*erba, ecc.*) cut. **rasoio** *sm* razor.

raschiare [ras'kjare] *v* scrape; (*cancellare*) scratch out. **raschiatura** *sf* scratching; scratch. **raschietto** *sm* scraper.

rasentare [razen'tare] *v* go close to; (*fig*) come close to.

raso ['razo] *agg* (*liscio*) smooth; (*sbarbato*) shaved. *sm* (*tessuto*) satin.

raspa ['raspa] *sf* rasp. **raspare** *v* rasp.

rassegnare [rasse'ɲare] *v* **rassegnare le dimissioni** resign. **rassegnarsi** *v* resign oneself. **rassegna** *sf* review; inspection; (*resoconto*) survey.

rasserenarsi [rassere'narsi] *v* clear up; (*fig*) cheer up.

rassettare [rasset'tare] *v* tidy up; (*accomodare*) repair.

rassicurare [rassiku'rare] *v* reassure.

rassomigliare [rassomi'ʎare] *v* resemble. **rassomigliarsi** *v* look alike.

rastrello [ras'trɛllo] *sm* rake. **rastrellamento** *sm* (*polizia*) round-up. **rastrellare** *v* rake; (*fig*) comb. **rastrelliera** *sf* rack.

rata ['rata] *sf* instalment.

ratificare [ratifi'kare] *v* ratify. **ratifica** *sf* ratification.

ratto[1] ['ratto] *sm* (*zool*) rat.

ratto[2] ['ratto] *sm* (*rapimento*) rape.

rattoppare [rattop'pare] *v* patch. **rattoppo** *sm* (*toppa*) patch.

rattrappire [rattrap'pire] *v* make numb.

rattristare [rattris'tare] *v* sadden. **rattristarsi** *v* become sad, grieve.

rauco ['rauko] *agg* hoarse.

ravanello [rava'nello] *sm* radish.

***ravvedersi** [ravve'dersi] *v* mend one's ways.

ravviare [ravvi'are] *v* tidy (up).

ravvicinare [ravvitʃi'nare] *v* bring near; reconcile. **ravvicinamento** *sm* (*pol*) rapprochement.

ravvisare [ravvi'zare] *v* recognize.

ravvivare [ravvi'vare] *v* revive.

***ravvolgere** [rav'voldʒere] *v* wrap (up).

raziocinio [ratsjo'tʃinjo] *sm* reason; common sense.

razionale [ratsjo'nale] *agg* rational. **razionalizzare** *v* rationalize. **razionalizzazione** *sf* rationalization.

razionare [ratsjo'nare] *v* ration. **razionamento** *sm* rationing. **razione** *sf* ration.

razza¹ ['rattsa] *sf* race; (*specie*) kind; (*stirpe*) descent; (*animali*) breed. **di ogni razza** of all sorts. **di razza incrociata** crossbred. **di razza (pura)** (*animali*) pedigree, thoroughbred. **razziale** *agg* racial. **razzismo** *sm* racialism, racism. **razzista** *agg, s(m+f)* racist, racialist.

razza² ['rattsa] *sf* (*pesce*) ray, skate.

razzia [rat'tsia] *sf* raid.

razzo ['rattso] *sm* rocket.

re [re] *sm* king.

reagire [rea'dʒire] *v* react. **reagente** *sm* reagent.

reale¹ [re'ale] *agg* real. **realismo** *sm* realism. **realista** *s(m+f)* realist. **realistico** *agg* realistic. **realtà** *sf* reality. **in realtà** in (actual) fact.

reale² [re'ale] *agg* (*regale*) royal. **realista** *agg, s(m+f)* royalist.

realizzare [realid'dzare] *v* realize; (*effettuare*) put into effect; (*sport*) score. **realizzabile** *agg* feasible. **realizzazione** *sf* realization; (*teatro, ecc.*) production. **prezzo di realizzo** cost price.

reato [re'ato] *sm* offence; (*grave*) crime.

reattivo [reat'tivo] *agg* reactive. *sm* (*chim*) reagent; (*psic*) test.

reattore [reat'tore] *sm* reactor; (*aereo*) jet.

reazione [reat'tsjone] *sf* reaction. **motore a reazione** jet engine. **reazionario, -a** *s, agg* reactionary.

rebbio ['rebbjo] *sm* prong.

recapito [re'kapito] *sm* (*indirizzo*) address; (*consegna*) delivery. **recapitare** *v* deliver.

recare [re'kare] *v* (*portare*) bear; (*arrecare*) cause.

recensire [retʃen'sire] *v* review. **recensione** *sf* review. **recensore, -a** *sm, sf* reviewer.

recente [re'tʃɛnte] *agg* recent. **recentissime** *sf pl* latest news *sing*.

recessione [retʃes'sjone] *sf* recession.

recinto [re'tʃinto] *sm* enclosure; (*per animali*) pen. **recintare** *v* enclose.

recipiente [retʃi'pjɛnte] *sm* container.

reciproco [re'tʃiproko] *agg* reciprocal, mutual. **reciprocare** *v* reciprocate. **ciprocità** *sf* reciprocity.

recitare [retʃi'tare] *v* (*versi, ecc.*) recite; (*una parte*) play; (*sostenere un ruolo*) act; (*fingere*) put on an act. **recita** *sf* performance. **recital** *sm invar* recital. **recitazione** *sf* recitation.

reclamare [rekla'mare] *v* complain; (*richiedere*) demand; protest. **reclamo** *sm* complaint.

reclame [re'klam] *sf invar* advertisement. **fare (della) reclame** advertise.

reclusione [reklu'zjone] *sf* confinement; imprisonment.

reclutare [reklu'tare] *v* recruit. **recluta** *sf* recruit.

record ['rekord] *sm invar* record.

recriminare [rekrimi'nare] *v* recriminate.

redarguire [redargu'ire] *v* rebuke.

redattore [redat'tore], **-trice** *sm, sf* editor. **redazione** *sf* editorial staff; (*ufficio*) editor's office; (*atto del redigere*) editing, compiling.

reddito ['reddito] *sm* income; (*statale*) revenue; (*utile*) return. **imposta sul reddito** of income tax. **reddito imponibile** taxable income.

redentore [reden'tore] *agg* redeeming. *sm* redeemer.

*****redigere** [re'didʒere] *v* (*compilare*) draw up; (*scrivere*) write; (*giornale*) edit.

*****redimere** [re'dimere] *v* redeem. **redimibile** *agg* redeemable.

redini ['redini] *sf pl* reins *pl*.

redivivo [redi'vivo] *agg* (*fig*) another.

reduce ['redutʃe] *agg* returning. *sm* (*mil*) veteran; (*superstite*) survivor.

refe ['refe] *sm* thread.

referendum [refe'rɛndum] *sm invar* referendum.

referenza [refe'rɛntsa] *sf* reference.

refettorio [refet'tɔrjo] *sm* refectory.

refrattario [refrat'tarjo] *agg* refractory; (*fig*) unmoved (by).

refrigerare [refridʒe'rare] *v* refresh, cool.

regalare [rega'lare] *v* give (away). **regalo** *sm* gift, present.

regale [re'gale] *agg* regal.

regata [re'gata] *sf* regatta.

reggente [red'dʒɛnte] *sm* ruler. *agg* ruling.

*****reggere** ['reddʒere] *v* (*sostenere*) hold; support; (*resistere*) stand; (*dirigere*) run; (*gramm*) govern; (*durare*) last. **reggere al confronto con** bear comparison with. **reggere alla prova** stand the test. **reggersi** *v* stand.

reggia ['rɛddʒa] sf royal palace.

reggimento [reddʒi'mento] sm regiment.

reggipetto [reddʒi'pɛtto] sm bra.

regia [re'dʒia] sf (cinema) direction; (teatro) production.

regime [re'dʒime] sm regime. **essere a regime** be on a diet. **regime di vita** way of life.

regina [re'dʒina] sf queen.

regio ['rɛdʒo] agg royal.

regione [re'dʒone] sf region. **regionale** agg regional.

regista [re'dʒista] sf (cine) director; (teatro, TV) producer.

registrare [redʒis'trare] v record; (in registro) register; (mettere a punto) adjust. **registratore** sm recorder; register. **registrazione** sf record; registration; adjustment; (radio, TV) recording. **registro** sm register. **cambiar registro** (fam) change one's tune.

regnare [re'nare] v rule, reign. **regno** sm (territorio) kingdom, realm; (periodo, potere) reign.

regola ['rɛgola] sm rule; norm. **di regola** normally. **in regola** in order. **per vostra regola** for your information. **regolamentare** agg prescribed. **regolamento** sm (il regolare) regulation; (norme) rules pl; (comm) settlement.

regolare [rego'lare] v regulate; (mettere a punto) adjust; (comm) settle. **regolarsi** v act; control oneself. agg regular. **regolarità** sf regularity. **regolarizzare** v regularize.

regolo ['rɛgolo] sm ruler; (calcolatore) slide-rule.

reincarnazione [reinkarna'tsjone] sf reincarnation.

reintegrare [reinte'grare] v reinstate. **reintegrazione** sf reinstatement.

relativo [rela'tivo] agg relative; concerning; (corrispondente) relevant. **relativamente** a regarding. **relatività** sf relativity.

relazione [rela'tsjone] sf relation(ship), connection; (resoconto) report. **essere in buone relazioni** be on good terms. **in relazione a** as regards. **mettere in relazione** relate.

relegare [rele'gare] v relegate.

religione [reli'dʒone] sf religion. **religiosa** sf nun. **religioso** agg religious.

reliquia [re'likwja] sf relic. **reliquiario** sf reliquary.

relitto [re'litto] sm wreck; (rottame) wreckage.

remare [re'mare] v row. **remata** sf stroke. **fare una remata** go for a row.

reminiscenza [remini'ʃentsa] sf recollection.

remissivo [remis'sivo] agg meek.

remoto [re'mɔto] agg remote.

*****rendere** ['rɛndere] v return; (fruttare) bring in; (far diventare) make; be efficient. **render conto di** account for. **render l'idea** make oneself clear. **rendere omaggio** pay homage. **rendersi conto** (spiegare) explain; (capire) realize. **rendere un servizio** do a favour.

rendimento [rendi'mento] sm (utile) yield; (resa) output; (fis, mec) efficiency.

rendita ['rendita] sf income; (econ) revenue; (reddito) yield.

rene ['rɛne] sm kidney. **reni** sf pl (fam) back sing.

renna ['rɛnna] sf reindeer.

reparto [re'parto] sm department; (mil) unit. **capo reparto** departmental head; (maestranza) foreman; (negozio) supervisor.

repellente [repel'lɛnte] agg repellent; (ripugnante) repulsive.

repentaglio [repen'taʎo] sm **mettere a repentaglio** jeopardize.

reperibile [repe'ribile] agg to be found; (disponibile) available.

repertorio [reper'tɔrjo] sm repertoire; (elenco) list.

replica ['replika] sf repetition; (risposta) reply; (teatro) performance; objection; copy. **replicare** v repeat; reply; perform again; object.

repressione [repres'sjone] sf repression. **represso** agg repressed.

*****reprimere** [re'primere] v repress, control.

*****repubblica** [re'pubblika] sf republic. **repubblicano** agg republican.

reputare [repu'tare] v consider. **reputazione** sf reputation.

requisire [rekwi'zire] v requisition. **requisito** sm requirement. **requisitoria** sf (dir) indictment; (rimprovero) reproof.

resa ['reza] sf (l'arrendersi) surrender; (restituzione) return; (rendimento) yield. **resa dei conti** statement (of accounts); (fig) reckoning.

*****rescindere** [re'ʃindere] v rescind.

residente [rezi'dɛnte] s(m+f), agg resident. **residenza** sf residence; (permanenza) stay.

residuo [re'ziduo] agg residual. sm residue; (fig) trace. **residuato** sm surplus.

resina ['rezina] sf resin.

resistere [re'zistere] v resist; (sopportare) bear; (non essere danneggiato) be resistant (to). **resistente** agg resistant, proof (against). **resistenza** sf resistance; (capacità di resistere) endurance.

resoconto [rezo'konto] sm report.

*respingere [res'pindʒere] v push back, repel; (rifiutare) reject; (bocciare) fail. **respingente** sm buffer.

respirare [respi'rare] v breathe. **respiratore** sm respirator. **respiratorio** agg respiratory. **respirazione** sf respiration. **respiro** sm breath; (fig) breathing space. **sentirsi mancare il respiro** feel breathless.

responsabile [respon'sabile] agg responsible. s(m+f) person responsible. **responsabilità** sf responsibility. **prendersi la responsabilità** take the responsibility.

ressa ['rɛssa] sf crowd.

restare [res'tare] v remain; (avanzare) be left (over). **restarci male** (delusi) be disappointed; (offesi) be offended. **restare d'accordo** agree. **restante** sm remainder.

restaurare [restau'rare] v restore. **restauro** sm restoration; (riparazione) repair.

restio [res'tio] agg restive; (bambini) fractious.

restituire [restitu'ire] v return; (fig) restore. **restituzione** sf return.

resto ['rɛsto] sm remainder; (di denaro) change. **del resto** (d'altronde) on the other hand; (inoltre) besides.

*restringere [res'trindʒere] v (limitare) restrict; (ridurre di larghezza) narrow; (vestiario) take in; (tessuto) shrink. **restringimento** sm shrinkage, narrowing. **restrizione** sf restriction.

rete ['rete] sf net; (sistema, tec) network; (calcio) goal; (inganno) trap. **rete metallica** wire netting.

reticente [reti'tʃɛnte] agg reticent.

reticolato [retiko'lato] sm (disegno) grid; (graticcio) grating. **reticolo** sm lattice, grating.

retina ['rɛtina] sf retina.

retorica [re'tɔrika] sf rhetoric. **retorico** agg rhetorical.

retribuire [retribu'ire] v reward. **retribuzione** sf reward; (paga) payment.

retro ['rɛtro] sm back.

retroattivo [retroat'tivo] agg retrospective.

*retrocedere [retro'tʃɛdere] v recede; (ritirarsi) retreat; (mil) demote; (sport) move down.

retrodatare [retroda'tare] v back-date.

retrogrado [re'trɔgrado] agg retrograde; (fig) backward, reactionary.

retroguardia [retro'gwardja] sf rearguard.

retromarcia [retro'martʃa] sf reverse.

retroscena [retro'ʃɛna] sm invar backstage; (fig) background.

retrospettivo [retrospet'tivo] agg retrospective.

retrovisore [retrovi'zore] sm rear-view mirror.

retta[1] ['rɛtta] sf (geom) straight line.

retta[2] ['rɛtta] sf **dar retta a** listen to, pay attention to.

retta[3] ['rɛtta] sf fee for board and lodging.

rettangolo [ret'tangolo] sm rectangle. **rettangolare** agg right-angled, rectangular.

rettificare [rettifi'kare] v rectify, correct; (mec) grind. **rettifica** sf rectification, correction; grinding.

rettile ['rɛttile] sm reptile.

rettilineo [retti'lineo] agg straight.

retto ['rɛtto] agg straight; (leale) upright, straightforward; correct; (geom) right.

rettore [ret'tore] sm rector.

reumatismo [reuma'tizmo] sm rheumatism. **reumatico** agg rheumatic.

reverendo [reve'rɛndo] agg reverend. sm (fam) priest.

reversibile [rever'sibile] agg reversible.

revisione [revi'zjone] sf revision; (tec) overhaul; (dei conti) audit; (dir) review. **revisore** sm auditor; (di bozze) proofreader.

revocare [revo'kare] v revoke.

riabbassare [riabbas'sare] v lower again.

riabbottonare [riabbotto'nare] v button up.

riabbracciare [riabbrat'tʃare] v embrace again.

riabilitare [riabili'tare] v rehabilitate. **riabilitazione** sf rehabilitation.

riaccompagnare [riakkompa'nare] v take back.

riacquistare [riakkwis'tare] v (ricomprare) buy back; (recuperare) recover.

riaddormentarsi [riaddormen'tarsi] v fall asleep again.

riaffermare [riaffer'mare] v reaffirm.

riallacciare [riallat't∫are] v re-tie; (fig) renew.

rialto [ri'alto] sm rise.

rialzare [rial'tsare] v raise (again). **rialzo** sm rise.

***riammettere** [riam'mettere] v re-admit. **riammissione** sf re-admission.

riammogliarsi [riammo'ʌarsi] v remarry.

rianimare [riani'mare] v revive; (fig) cheer (up).

***riapparire** [riappa'rire] v reappear.

***riaprire** [riap'rire] v reopen; (riprendere) resume. **riapertura** sf reopening; resumption.

riarmare [riar'mare] v rearm; (nave) refit; (edificio) reinforce. **riarmamento** sm rearmament.

riassestare [riasses'tare] v rearrange.

riassettare [riasset'tare] v tidy up.

riassicurare [riassiku'rare] v reassure; (dir) reinsure. **riassicurazione** sf reassurance; reinsurance.

***riassumere** [rias'sumere] v take on again; (compendiare) sum up; (condensare) summarize. **riassunto** sm summary. **riassunzione** sf re-employment; (dir) resumption.

riattaccare [riattak'kare] v (con filo) sew on again; (con colla) stick on again; (riprendere) resume.

riattivare [riatti'vare] v reactivate; pu' back into service; (strada) reopen.

***riavere** [ria'vere] v have again; (ricuperare) recover.

riavvicinare [riavvit∫i'nare] v approach again; (fig) reconcile. **riavvicinamento** sm (pol) rapprochement.

ribadire [riba'dire] v rivet; (fig) confirm.

ribaldo [ri'baldo] sm rogue.

ribaltare [ribal'tare] v turn over; (mandar sottosopra) overturn. **ribalta** sf (asse) flap; (teatro) proscenium; (fig) limelight. **tornare alla ribalta** (questione) come up again. **venire alla ribalta** come on to the scene. **ribaltabile** agg folding; (tavolo) drop-leaf; (camion) tip-up.

ribassare [ribas'sare] v reduce. **ribasso** sm reduction. **essere in ribasso** drop.

ribattere [ri'battere] v hit back; (chiodo) rivet; (sport) return; (confutare) refute; (replicare) answer back.

ribelle [ri'bɛlle] agg rebellious. s(m+f)

rebel. **ribellarsi** v revolt. **ribellione** sf rebellion.

ribes ['ribes] sm (red)currant. **ribes nero** blackcurrant.

riboccare [ribok'kare] v overflow.

ribollire [ribol'lire] v boil (again); ferment; (fig) seethe.

ribrezzo [ri'brettso] sm disgust. **far ribrezzo** disgust. **provar ribrezzo** be disgusted (by).

ributtare [ribut'tare] v throw again; (buttar fuori) throw out; vomit; (rifiutare) reject.

ricacciare [rikat't∫are] v turn out (again); (rimettere) push back.

***ricadere** [rika'dere] v fall (back); (pendere) hang (down). **ricaduta** sf relapse.

ricalcare [rikal'kare] v (disegno) trace; (fig) follow faithfully. **ricalco** sm tracing.

ricamare [rika'mare] v embroider. **ricamo** sm embroidery.

ricambiare [rikam'bjare] v (sostituire) change; (scambiare) exchange; (di nuovo) change again. **di ricambio** spare.

ricapitolare [rikapito'lare] v sum up.

ricaricare [rikari'kare] v recharge; (armi) reload; (orologio) wind up again; (pipa) refill.

ricattare [rikat'tare] v blackmail. **ricattatore, -trice** sm, sf blackmailer. **ricatto** sm blackmail.

ricavare [rika'vare] v obtain, get; (dedurre) deduce. **ricavato** or **ricavo** sm proceeds pl.

ricchezza [rik'kettsa] sf wealth.

riccio¹ ['rit∫o] agg curly. sm curl; (voluta) scroll. **riccioluto** or **ricciuto** agg curly.

riccio² ['rit∫o] sm (zool) hedgehog; (castagna) (chestnut) husk. **riccio di mare** sea-urchin.

ricco ['rikko], **-a** agg rich. sm, sf rich person.

ricerca [ri't∫erka] sf search; (scientifica) research; (indagine) investigation. **ricercare** v search (for); investigate. **ricercato** agg (much-)wanted; in (great) demand; (affettato) precious; (raffinato) refined. **ricercatezza** sf affectation; refinement. **ricercatore, -trice** sm, sf (persona) research worker; (apparecchio) detector.

ricetta [ri't∫etta] sf recipe.

ricettare [rit∫et'tare] v receive. **ricettatore** sm receiver (of stolen goods).

ricettivo [ritʃet'tivo] *agg* receptive. **ricettività** *sf* receptivity.

****ricevere** [ri'ʃevere] *v* receive; *(accogliere)* welcome. **ricevimento** *sm* reception; *(ricevuta)* receipt. **ricevitore** *sm* receiver; *(impiegato)* collector. **ricevuta** *sf* receipt. **ricezione** *sf* reception.

richiamare [rikja'mare] *v* call back; *(far tornare, ricordare)* recall; *(rimproverare)* rebuke. **richiamare in vita** revive. **richiamo** *sm* call; recall; rebuke. **far da richiamo** act as a decoy.

****richiedere** [ri'kjedere] *v* *(aver bisogno)* require; *(per sapere)* ask; *(per ottenere)* ask for. **richiesta** *sf* request; *(econ)* demand; *(burocratica)* application. **richiesto** *agg* in (great) demand; necessary.

ricino [ri'tʃino] *sm* **olio di ricino** *sm* castor-oil.

ricominciare [rikomin'tʃare] *v* start again.

ricompensa [rikom'pensa] *sf* reward. **ricompensare** *v* *(contraccambiare)* repay; *(premiare)* reward.

riconciliare [rikontʃi'ljare] *v* reconcile; *(procurare di nuovo)* win back. **riconciliarsi** *v* make it up.

ricondurre [rikon'durre] *v* take back; *(di nuovo)* take again.

****riconoscere** [riko'noʃere] *v* recognize; *(ammettere)* admit. **riconoscente** *agg* grateful. **riconoscenza** *sf* gratitude. **riconoscibile** *agg* recognizable. **riconoscimento** *sm* recognition; admission; identification.

riconquistare [rikonkwis'tare] *v* win back.

ricopiare [riko'pjare] *v* copy.

****ricoprire** [riko'prire] *v* cover (again); *(occupare)* hold; *(rivestire)* coat; *(colmare)* smother.

****ricordare** [rikor'dare] *v* remember; *(richiamare alla memoria)* recall; *(far ricordare)* remind. **ricordo** *sm* recollection; *(oggetto)* souvenir. **ricordo di famiglia** heirloom. **ricordo d'infanzia** childhood memory. **ricordi** *sm pl* *(libro)* memoirs *pl*.

****ricorrere** [ri'korrere] *v* resort; *(dir)* appeal; *(ripetersi)* recur. **ricorso** *sm* resort, recourse; *(dir)* appeal.

ricostituente [rikostitu'ente] *sm* tonic. **ricostituire** *v* reconstitute.

****ricostruire** [rikostru'ire] *v* rebuild; *(fig)* reconstruct. **ricostruzione** *sf* reconstruction.

ricotta [ri'kɔtta] *sf* cottage cheese.

ricoverare [rikove'rare] *v* take in; *(all'ospedale)* send to hospital. **ricoverato, -a** *sm*, *sf* *(ospedale)* patient; *(ospizio)* inmate. **ricovero** *sm* shelter; *(ospizio)* home; *(in ospedale)* admission to hospital.

ricrearsi [rikre'arsi] *v* amuse oneself. **ricreazione** *sf* recreation; *(scuola)* playtime; *(pausa)* break.

ricredersi [ri'kredersi] *v* change one's mind.

ricuperare [rikupe'rare] *v* recover; *(mar)* salvage. **ricupero** *sm* recovery; salvage.

ricurvo [ri'kurvo] *agg* bent.

ricusare [riku'zare] *v* decline.

****ridare** [ri'dare] *v* *(dare nuovamente)* give again; *(restituire)* give back.

****ridere** ['ridere] *v* laugh. **(cosa) da ridere** *(divertente)* funny; *(inezia)* of no importance. **far ridere** be funny; be ridiculous. *sm* laughter.

ridicolo [ri'dikolo] *agg* ridiculous. *sm* absurdity; *(derisione)* ridicule.

ridimensionare [ridimensjo'nare] *v* reorganize; *(ridurre)* cut down; *(fig)* reappraise.

****ridire** [ri'dire] *v* *(riferire)* tell; *(criticare)* find fault with; *(dire di nuovo)* repeat.

ridosso [ri'dɔsso] *sm* **a ridosso di** close to; *(dietro)* behind.

****ridurre** [ri'durre] *v* reduce; *(trasformare)* turn. **riduzione** *sf* reduction; cut; adaptation.

rielaborare [rielabo'rare] *v* work out again; modify.

****riempire** [riem'pire] *v* fill; *(compilare)* fill in; *(gastr)* stuff. **riempitivo** *sm* filler; *(fig)* stopgap.

rientrare [rien'trare] *v* *(tornare)* return; *(rincasare)* come *or* go home; *(far parte)* come within, form part of; *(entrare nuovamente)* re-enter. **rientro** *sm* return; re-entry; *(rientranza)* recess.

riepilogare [riepilo'gare] *v* summarize. **riepilogo** *sm*, *pl* -**ghi** recapitulation.

riesumare [riezu'mare] *v* exhume; *(fig)* unearth.

rievocare [rievo'kare] *v* recall; commemorate.

****rifare** [ri'fare] *v* make *or* do again; *(ricostruire)* rebuild; imitate.

riferire [infe'rire] *v* relate; report. **riferimento** *sm* reference. **punto di riferimento** *sm* landmark.

rifilare [rifi'lare] (*fam*) v palm off; (*dire d'un fiato*) reel off.

rifinire [rifi'nire] v (*dare l'ultima mano*) give the finishing touch; (*ritoccare*) touch up. **rifinitura** sf finishing touches pl; (*guarnizione*) fittings pl.

rifiutare [rifju'tare] v refuse; decline. **rifiuto** sm refusal; (*scarto*) refuse, rubbish.

riflessione [rifles'sjone] sf reflection; (*osservazione*) remark.

riflessivo [rifles'sivo] agg thoughtful; (*gramm*) relexive.

riflesso [ri'flesso] sm reflection; (*med*) reflex. **di riflesso** indirectly.

*__riflettere__ [ri'flettere] v reflect; (*pensarci su*) think (over *or* about). **riflettersi** su (*ripercuotersi*) affect. **riflettore** sm reflector; (*cinema, ecc.*) floodlight.

*__rifondere__ [ri'fondere] v recast; (*ricomporre*) recompose; (*risarcire*) refund.

riformare [rifor'mare] v reform; (*formare di nuovo*) re-form. **riforma** sf reform.

rifornire [rifor'nire] v supply (with). **rifornirsi di benzina** (*auto*) fill up. **rifornimento** sm supply.

rifuggire [rifud'dʒire] v escape (again); (*fig*) shrink (from).

rifugiarsi [rifu'dʒarsi] v (take) shelter. **rifugiato, -a** sm, sf refugee.

rifugio [ri'fudʒo] sm shelter. **rifugio antiaereo** air-raid shelter. **rifugio fiscale** tax-haven.

*__rifulgere__ [ri'fuldʒere] v glow.

riga ['riga] sf line; (*fila*) row; (*righello*) ruler. **a righe** striped. **riga a T** T-square.

rigare v rule; (*tracciar strisce*) stripe; (*scalfire*) score.

rigaglie [ri'gaʎe] sf pl giblets pl.

rigettare [ridʒet'tare] v (*buttar fuori*) throw out; (*fig*) reject; vomit; (*gettare indietro*) throw back.

rigido [ri'dʒido] agg rigid, stiff; (*freddo*) severe. **rigidezza** *or* **rigidità** sf rigidity; (*fig*) rigour, severity.

rigirare [ridʒi'rare] v turn round; (*fig*) twist round. Please **rigiro** sm twist. **giri e rigiri** sm pl twists and turns pl.

rigo ['rigo] sm line; (*musica*) stave.

rigoglioso [rigoʎ'ʎozo] agg blooming.

rigonfio [ri'gonfjo] agg swollen.

rigore [ri'gore] sm rigour; (*calcio*) penalty (kick). **a rigor di logica** strictly speaking. **a rigore** in point of fact. **di rigore** compulsory. **rigoroso** agg rigorous.

rigovernare [rigover'nare] v (*i piatti*) wash up; (*animali*) tend.

riguardare [rigwar'dare] v regard. **riguardo** sm regard; (*cautela*) care; consideration. **di riguardo** of consequence. **riguardo a** regarding. **riguardo a me** as for me. **senza riguardo** inconsiderate. **riguardoso** agg thoughtful, respectful.

rilanciare [rilan'tʃare] v launch; (*asta, carte*) raise.

rilasciare [rila'ʃare] v (*liberare*) release; (*consegnare*) issue.

rilassare [rilas'sare] v relax; (*allentare*) slacken. **rilassamento** sm relaxation.

rilegare [rile'gare] v bind; (*incastonare*) set. **rilegatura** sf binding.

*__rileggere__ [ri'leddʒere] v re-read.

rilevare [rile'vare] v (*notare*) notice; (*comm*) take over; (*topografia*) survey.

rilievo [ri'ljevo] sm relief; importance; (*osservazione*) remark; survey. **mettere in rilievo** stress, emphasize.

riluttante [rilut'tante] agg reluctant.

rima ['rima] sf rhyme.

rimandare [riman'dare] v send back; (*posporre*) defer.

*__rimanere__ [rima'nere] v remain; (*essere*) be. **rimanere d'accordo** agree. **rimanere in dubbio** be left in doubt. **rimaner male** be put out; (*deluso*) be disappointed; (*offeso*) be hurt.

rimasugli [rima'zuʎi] sm pl left-overs pl.

rimbalzare [rimbal'tsare] v bounce; (*proiettile*) ricochet.

rimbambire [rimbam'bire] v become childish. **rimbambito** agg (*fam*) gaga.

rimbeccare [rimbek'kare] v retort. **di rimbecco** sharply.

rimboccare [rimbok'kare] v turn down. **rimboccarsi le maniche** roll up one's sleeves.

rimbombare [rimbom'bare] v resound.

rimborsare [rimbor'sare] v reimburse. **rimborso** sm refund.

rimediare [rime'djare] v remedy; (*fam: racimolare*) scrape together; (*accomodare*) patch; (*provvedere*) take care. **rimedio** sm remedy.

rimescolare [rimesko'lare] v stir; (*carte*) shuffle.

rimessa [ri'messa] sf (*deposito*) depot; garage; (*trasferimento*) remittance; (*perdita*) loss. **rimessa in gioco** (*calcio*) throw-in.

*__rimettere__ [ri'mettere] v put back; (*indossare*) put back on; (*spedire*) send; (*denaro*) remit. __rimetterci__ v lose. __rimettersi__ v (*riaversi*) recover; (*affidarsi*) trust.

__rimodernare__ [rimoder'nare] v modernize.

__rimontare__ [rimon'tare] v (*mettere insieme*) reassemble; (*sport*) catch up; (*risalire*) go up; (*a cavallo*) remount; (*auto*) get back in.

__rimorchiare__ [rimor'kjare] v (have in) tow. __rimorchio__ sm trailer. __cavo da rimorchio__ sm tow-rope.

__rimorso__ [ri'morso] sm remorse. __rimorso di coscienza__ pangs of conscience pl.

__rimostrare__ [rimos'trare] v remonstrate.

__rimpasto__ [rim'pasto] sm (*fig*) reshuffle.

__rimpatriare__ [rimpa'trjare] v repatriate. __rimpatrio__ sm repatriation.

*__rimpiangere__ [rim'pjandʒere] v regret. __rimpianto__ sm regret.

__rimpiattino__ [rimpjat'tino] sm hide-and-seek.

__rimpiazzare__ [rimpjat'tsare] v replace.

__rimpiccolire__ [rimpikko'lire] v make smaller.

__rimpinzarsi__ [rimpin'tsarsi] v stuff oneself, gorge.

__rimproverare__ [rimprove'rare] v reproach; (*sgridare*) scold; (*fam*) tell off; (*biasimare*) blame. __rimprovero__ sm reproach; blame.

*__rimuovere__ [ri'mwovere] v remove; (*distogliere*) dissuade.

__Rinascimento__ [rinaʃi'mento] sm Renaissance.

__rinascita__ [ri'naʃita] sf rebirth; (*fig*) revival.

__rincagnato__ [rinka'ɲato] agg __naso rincagnato__ sm pug nose, snub nose.

__rincalzare__ [rinkal'tsare] v (*sorreggere*) prop up; (*lenzuola*) tuck in.

__rincarare__ [rinka'rare] v (*rendere più caro*) raise (the price of); (*essere più caro*) rise, become more expensive.

__rincasare__ [rinka'zare] v return home.

*__rinchiudere__ [rin'kjudere] v shut in. __rinchiuso__ [rin'kjuzo] agg shut in; (*aria*) stale, fusty. sm enclosure. __saper di rinchiuso__ smell fusty or musty.

*__rincorrere__ [rin'korrere] v run after, chase. __rincorsa__ sf run-up.

*__rincrescere__ [rin'kreʃere] v cause regret or sorrow. __mi rincresce di . . .__ I'm sorry to . . . . __ti rincresce . . . ?__ do you mind . . . ? __rincrescimento__ sm regret.

__rinculare__ [rinku'lare] v recoil.

__rinforzare__ [rinfor'tsare] v reinforce, strengthen. __rinforzo__ sm reinforcement.

__rinfrescare__ [rinfres'kare] v cool; (*pulire*) freshen up; (*memoria*) refresh; (*ravvivare*) brush up. __rinfrescata__ sf cooling. __darsi una rinfrescata__ freshen up. __rinfreschi__ sm pl refreshments pl. __rinfresco__ sm (*ricevimento*) party.

__rinfusa__ [rin'fuza] sf __alla rinfusa__ higgledy-piggledy.

__ringhiare__ [rin'gjare] v growl, snarl.

__ringhiera__ [rin'gjera] sf railing; (*delle scale*) banister.

__ringiovanire__ [rindʒova'nire] v rejuvenate; (*nell'aspetto*) make look younger.

__ringraziare__ [ringra'tsjare] v thank. __ringraziamento__ sm thanks pl. __lettera di ringraziamento__ sf thank-you letter.

__rinnegare__ [rinne'gare] v deny. __rinnegato, -a__ s, agg renegade.

__rinnovare__ [rinno'vare] v renew. __rinnovamento__ sm renewal; (*rimodernamento*) renovation. __rinnovazione__ sf renewal; renovation.

__rinoceronte__ [rinotʃe'ronte] sm rhinoceros.

__rinomato__ [rino'mato] agg renowned. __rinomanza__ sf renown.

__rinsaldare__ [rinsal'dare] v consolidate; (*inamidare*) starch.

__rintoccare__ [rintok'kare] v (*campana*) toll; (*orologio*) strike. __rintocco__ sm toll; stroke.

__rintracciare__ [rintrat'tʃare] v trace; track down.

__rintronare__ [rintro'nare] v thunder; (*assordare*) deafen.

__rintuzzare__ [rintut'tsare] v (*rendere ottuso*) blunt; (*respingere*) repel; (*ribattere*) refute; (*frenare*) check.

__rinunciare__ [rinun'tʃare] v give up; (*fare a meno*) forgo; (*dir*) renounce; (*non voler fare*) refrain (from). __rinunce__ sf pl (*privazioni*) hardship sing. __rinuncia__ sf abandonment; renunciation.

*__rinvenire__[1] [rinve'nire] v (*ritrovare*) recover.

*__rinvenire__[2] [rinve'nire] v (*ritornare in sè*) come to; (*riprendere freschezza*) revive.

__rinviare__ [rinvi'are] v (*mandare indietro*) send back; (*posporre*) put off; (*dir*) adjourn; (*indirizzare*) refer. __rinvio__ sm postponement; adjournment; (*testo*) (cross-)reference.

invigorire [rinvigo'rire] v invigorate; (ritornar vigoroso) regain strength.

ione [ri'one] sm district. **rionale** agg local.

riordinare [riordi'nare] v rearrange; (comm) reorder.

riorganizzare [riorganid'dzare] v reorganize. **riorganizzazione** sf reorganization.

ripagare [ripa'gare] v pay back.

riparare [ripa'rare] v (aggiustare) repair; (porre rimedio) make up (for), redress; protect; (esame) repeat. **ripararsi** v take shelter. **riparazione** sf repair; redress.

riparo [ri'paro] sm shelter; (protezione) cover; (mec) guard. **mettersi al riparo (da)** shelter (from).

ripartire¹ [ripar'tire] v (partire di nuovo) leave or start (up) again.

ripartire² [ripar'tire] v (dividere) split up; distribute.

ripassare [ripas'sare] v (tornare) pass again; (visitare) call back; (attraversare) cross again; (rivedere) review; (mec) overhaul. **ripassata** sf (pittura) fresh coat of paint; revision, overhaul; (stirata) press.

ripensare [ripen'sare] v think (over); (mutare pensiero) reconsider. **ripensare a** (tornare col pensiero) recall.

ripentirsi [ripen'tirsi] v repent; (cambiar pensiero) have second thoughts.

ripercuotersi [riper'kwotersi] v (suono) reverberate; (fig) have an effect. **ripercussione** [riperkus'sjone] sf repercussion.

ripetere [ri'petere] v repeat. **ripetizione** sf repetition; (studio) coaching.

ripiano [ri'pjano] sm terrace; (scomparto) shelf.

ripido [ripido] agg steep.

ripiegare [ripje'gare] v fold again; (fig) make do. **di ripiego** makeshift.

ripieno [ri'pjeno] agg filled, stuffed. sm filling, stuffing.

riporre [ri'porre] v put (back).

riportare [ripor'tare] v (portare indietro) bring back; (ricondurre) take again; (riferire) report; (ricevere) get; (mat) carry. **riporto** sm carrying forward; amount carried forward.

riposare [ripo'zare] v rest. **riposarsi** v take a rest. **riposo** sm rest. **andare a riposo** retire. **mettere a riposo** pension off. **senza riposo** without interruption.

ripostiglio [ripos'tiʎo] sm cubby-hole.

***riprendere** [ri'prɛndere] v take again; (recuperare) recover; (ricominciare) resume. **riprendersi (da)** get over.

ripresa [ri'preza] sf resumption; (innovamento) renewal; (calcio) second half; (boxe) round; (auto) acceleration; (cine) shot.

ripristinare [ripristi'nare] v restore. **ripristino** sm restoration.

***riprodurre** [ripro'durre] v reproduce. **riproduzione** sf reproduction.

riprova [ri'prɔva] sf fresh proof; confirmation. **riprovare** v blame; (esame) fail.

ripudiare [ripu'djare] v repudiate.

ripugnante [ripu'ɲante] agg repugnant. **ripugnare** v disgust.

ripulsione [ripul'sjone] sf repulsion.

risaia [ri'zaja] sf rice-field.

risalire [risa'lire] v (andar su) go up (again); (nel tempo) go back.

risaltare [risal'tare] v (distinguersi) stand out; (sporgere) project. **far risaltare** bring out. **risalto** sm emphasis; projection.

risanare [risa'nare] v heal; (fig) improve; (bonificare) reclaim.

risaputo [risa'puto] agg well-known.

risarcire [rizart'fire] v compensate. **risarcimento** sm compensation.

risata [ri'zata] sf laugh. **fare** or **farsi una bella risata** have a good laugh. **scoppiare in una risata** burst out laughing.

riscaldare [riskal'dare] v heat, warm up. **riscaldamento** sm heating; (impianto) heating system.

riscatto [ris'katto] sm ransom; (econ) redemption. **riscattare** v ransom; redeem.

rischiarare [riskja'rare] v illuminate.

rischiare [ris'kjare] v risk. **rischiare di** run the risk of. **rischio** sm risk. **rischioso** agg risky.

risciacquare [riʃa'kware] v rinse. **risciacquatura** sf (atto) rinsing; (acqua) dishwater. **risciacquo** sm mouthwash.

riscontrare [riskon'trare] v (rilevare) find; (confrontare) compare; (controllare) check. **riscontro** sm finding; comparison; check; (lettera) reply.

riscossa [ris'kɔssa] sf (riconquista) recovery; (insurrezione) revolt.

***riscuotere** [ris'kwotere] v (ritirare denaro) draw; (riportare) win, earn; (scuotere) shake.

risentire [risen'tire] v (provare) feel; (mostrare) show; (udire di nuovo) hear again; (soffrire) feel the effects of. **risentirsi** v resent. **risentimento** *sm* resentment; consequence.

riserbo [ri'serbo] *sm* reserve.

riserva [ri'serva] *sf* (*provvista*) supply; (*scorta, sport*) reserve; (*dubbio*) reservation. **riservare** *v* reserve, keep; (*prenotare*) book; (*dimostrare*) show. **riservatezza** *sf* discretion; (*segretezza*) confidential nature; (*carattere*) reserve. **riservato** *agg* reserved; confidential.

risibile [ri'zibile] *agg* laughable.

risiedere [ri'sjɛdere] *v* reside.

risma ['rizma] *sf* (*carta*) ream; (*spreg*) kind.

riso¹ ['rizo] *sm* (*bot*) rice.

riso² ['rizo] *sm, pl* **-a** *f* laughter; (*risata*) laugh; ridicule.

risoluto [riso'luto] *agg* resolute. **risolutezza** *sf* decisiveness.

risoluzione [risolu'tsjone] *sf* resolution; (*mat*) solution; (*dir*) cancellation.

*****risolvere** [ri'solvere] *v* resolve; (*mat, indovinello*) solve; (*dir*) cancel; (*scomporre*) break down. **risolversi** *v* (*fig*) turn out; decide.

risonare [riso'n. ɛ] *v also* **risuonare** ring; (*echeggiare*) resound.

*****risorgere** [ri'sordʒere] *v* rise again. **far risorgere** revive. **risorgimento** *sm* revival.

risorsa [ri'sorsa] *sf* resource.

risparmiare [rispar'mjare] *v* spare; (*economizzare, mettere da parte*) save. **risparmiatore, -trice** *sm, sf* saver. **risparmio** *sm* saving; (*denaro*) savings *pl*. **fare risparmio (di)** save.

rispecchiare [rispek'kjare] *v* reflect.

rispettare [rispet'tare] *v* respect; (*mantenere*) keep.

rispettivo [rispet'tivo] *agg* respective.

rispetto [ris'petto] *sm* respect. **rispetto a** (*in relazione a*) with respect to, as to; (*in confronto*) compared to. **rispettoso** *agg* respectful.

risplendere [ris'plɛndere] *v* shine.

*****rispondere** [ris'pondere] *v* answer; (*rimbeccare*) answer back; (*obbedire*) respond; (*carte*) follow suit. **rispondere di no/sì** say no/yes. **rispondere male** give a wrong answer; (*sgarbatamente*) answer back. **rispondere picche** give a flat refusal.

risposta [ris'posta] *sf* answer, reply. **botta e risposta** tit for tat. **per tutta risposta** merely. **senza risposta** unanswered.

rissa ['rissa] *sf* brawl.

ristabilire [ristabi'lire] *v* restore.

ristagnare [rista'nare] *v* stagnate; (*fig*) come to a standstill; (*comm*) be slack. **ristagno** *sm* stagnation; (*econ*) slump.

ristampare [ristam'pare] *v* reprint. **ristampa** *sf* reprint.

ristorante [risto'rante] *sm* restaurant. **vagone ristorante** *sm* dining car.

ristorare [risto'rare] *v* restore. **ristorarsi** *v* refresh oneself. **ristoro** *sm* refreshment.

ristretto [ris'tretto] *agg* (*limitato*) restricted; (*angusto*) narrow; (*caffè*) very strong. **brodo ristretto** *sm* consommé.

risultare [rizul'tare] *v* appear; gather; (*conseguire*) ensue. **mi risulta che ...** I gather that ....

risultato [rizul'tato] *sm* result.

risuonare [riswo'nare] *V* **risonare**.

risurrezione [risurre'tsjone] *sf* resurrection.

risuscitare [risuʃi'tare] *v* revive; (*rel*) resurrect.

risvegliare [rizve'ʎare] *v* wake (up); (*fig*) awaken, revive.

ritaglio [ri'taʎo] *sm* cutting.

ritardare [ritar'dare] *v* be late; (*orologio*) be slow; (*differire*) delay. **ritardatario, -a** *sm, sf* latecomer. **ritardo** *sm* delay. **in ritardo** late.

ritegno [ri'teɲo] *sm* reserve; (*freno*) restraint.

*****ritenere** [rite'nere] *v* think; consider; (*trattenere*) hold.

ritirare [riti'rare] *v* withdraw; (*ottenere in consegna*) collect. **ritirarsi** *v* withdraw; (*interrompere un'attività*) retire. **ritirata** *sf* retreat. **ritiro** *sm* withdrawal; (*prendere*) collection; (*luogo appartato*) retreat.

ritmo ['ritmo] *sm* rhythm. **ritmico** *agg* rhythmic(al).

rito ['rito] *sm* rite; (*usanza*) custom. **di rito** customary.

ritoccare [ritok'kare] *v* touch up.

ritornare [ritor'nare] *v* return; (*andare indietro*) go back. **biglietto di andata e ritorno** return ticket. **di ritorno** back. **viaggio di andata e ritorno** round trip. **ritornello** *sm* refrain.

*****ritrarre** [ri'trarre] *v* (*tirare indietro*) draw back; (*rappresentare*) portray.

ritratto [ri'tratto] *sm* portrait. **ritrattista** *s(m+f)* portrait-painter.

ritroso [ri'trozo] *agg* (*scontroso*) contrary; (*restio*) unwilling. **a ritroso** (*indietro*) backwards; (*controcorrente*) against the stream.

ritrovare [ritro'vare] *v* find (again); (*recuperare*) recover; (*incontrare*) meet again. **ritrovarsi** *v* meet (again); (*orientarsi*) get one's bearings; (*essere a proprio agio*) feel at ease. **ritrovato** *sm* invention; expedient. **ritrovo** *sm* meeting-place; club.

itto ['ritto] *agg* upright.

ituale [ritu'ale] *agg, sm* ritual.

iunire [riu'nire] *v* gather; (*ricongiungere*) reunite; (*convocare*) call. **riunione** *sf* meeting.

'riuscire [riu'ʃire] *v* succeed; (*andare a finire*) turn out; (*aver capacità*) be good (at). **mi riesce antipatico/simpatico** I dislike/like him. **riuscita** *sf* result; success.

iva ['riva] *sf* shore; (*fiume*) bank.

ivale [ri'vale] *s(m+f)*, *agg* rival. **rivalità** *sf* rivalry.

ivalutare [rivalu'tare] *v* (*econ*) revalue; (*fig*) reappraise. **rivalutazione** *sf* revaluation; reappraisal.

ivedere [rive'dere] *v* see again; (*incontrare*) meet again; (*ripassare*) go over. **rivedere i conti** audit (the accounts).

ivelare [rive'lare] *v* reveal. **rivelatore** *sm* (*tec*) detector. **rivelazione** *sf* revelation.

ivendere [ri'vendere] *v* resell; (*al dettaglio*) retail. **rivendita** *sf* resale; (*negozio*) shop.

ivendicare [rivendi'kare] *v* claim.

iverberare [riverbe'rare] *v* reverberate.

iverire [rive'rire] *v* revere; respect; (*salutare*) pay one's respects (to). **riverenza** *sf* reverence; respect; (*inchino*) bow; (*di dama*) curtsy.

ivestire [rives'tire] *v* cover; (*vernice*) coat; (*fodera*) line. **rivestire una carica** hold an office; (*conferirla*) confer an office. **rivestirsi** *v* dress again, change (clothes). **rivestimento** *sm* covering, coating; lining.

ivetto [ri'vetto] *sm* rivet.

iviera [ri'vjera] *sf* coastal region. **Riviera** *sf* Riviera.

vincita [ri'vintʃita] *sf* return match. **prendersi la rivincita** take one's revenge.

rivista [ri'vista] *sf* review; (*periodico*) magazine; (*teatro*) revue.

rivolgere [ri'voldʒere] *v* turn. **rivolgersi** *v* (*indirizzare*) address; (*ricorrere*) turn to; (*per domandare, ecc.*) apply.

rivolta [ri'volta] *sf* revolt; (*mar, mil*) mutiny.

rivoltare [rivol'tare] *v* turn; (*ripugnare*) revolt; (*insalata*) toss. **rivoltarsi** *v* (*ribellarsi*) revolt.

rivoltella [rivol'tella] *sf* revolver. **rivoltellata** *sf* shot.

rivoluzione [rivolu'tsjone] *sf* revolution. **rivoluzionario, -a** *s, agg* revolutionary.

rivulsione [rivul'sjone] *sf* revulsion.

rizzare [rit'tsare] *v* raise; erect. **far rizzare i capelli** make one's hair stand on end. **rizzare le orecchie** prick up one's ears.

roba ['roba] *sf* stuff, things *pl*. **bella roba!** that's a fine thing! **robaccia** *sf* rubbish.

robusto [ro'busto] *agg* sturdy; solid. **robustezza** *sf* sturdiness; (*fig*) vigour.

rocca¹ ['rokka] *sf* fortress. **cristallo di rocca** *sm* rock-crystal.

rocca² ['rokka] *sf* (*conocchia*) distaff; (*bobina*) reel. **rocchetto** *sm* reel; (*elett*) coil.

roccia ['rottʃa] *sf* rock; (*sport*) rock-climbing. **roccioso** *agg* rocky.

rodaggio [ro'daddʒo] *sm* running-in.

*rodere ['rodere] *v* gnaw. **rodersi il fegato** (*fig*) be eaten up. **roditore** *sm* rodent.

rododendro [rodo'dendro] *sm* rhododendron.

rogna ['roɲa] *sf* (*animali*) mange; (*agric*) scab; (*fam*) pain in the neck. **rognoso** *agg* mangy; (*noioso*) boring.

rognone [ro'ɲone] *sm* kidney.

rogo ['rogo] *sm* stake; (*incendio*) fire.

Roma ['roma] *sf* Rome. **romano, -a** *s, agg* Roman. **fare alla romana** go Dutch.

Romania [roma'nia] *sf* Romania. **romeno, -a** *s, agg* Romanian.

romanico [ro'maniko] *agg* Romanesque.

romantico [ro'mantiko] *agg* romantic. **romanticismo** *sm* romanticism; sentimentalism.

romanza [ro'mandza] *sf* romance.

romanzo¹ [ro'mandzo] *sm* novel; (*storia inventata*) fiction. **romanzo a fumetti** comic strip. **romanzo d'appendice** serial story. **romanzo fiume** saga. **romanzesco** *agg* romantic; fantastic.

romanzo² [ro'mandzo] *agg* (*lingua*) Romance.

rombo¹ ['rombo] *sm* (*geom*) rhombus; (*pesce*) turbot.

rombo² ['rombo] sm roar. rombare v roar.

*rompere ['rompere] v break; (spezzare) break off. rompere l'anima (volg) pester. rompicapo sm (fam) headache; (indovinello) puzzle. a rompicollo at breakneck speed. rompiscatole s(m+f) (fam) pain in the neck.

ronda ['ronda] sf fare la ronda (mil) be on watch; (polizia) be on the beat.

rondella [ron'dɛlla] sf washer.

rondine ['rondine] sf swallow.

rondo¹ [ron'do] sm (musica) rondo.

rondò² [ron'do] sm (incrocio) roundabout.

rondone [ron'done] sm swift.

ronfare [ron'fare] v (fam) snore.

ronzare [ron'dzare] v buzz. ronzio sm buzz(ing).

ronzino [ron'dzino] sm nag.

rosa ['rɔza] sf rose. all'acqua di rose (fam) watered-down. agg invar pink. veder tutto rosa see everything through rose-coloured spectacles. rosato agg (vino) rosé. roseo agg rosy. rosetta sf (coccarda) rosette; (mec) washer.

rosario [ro'zarjo] sm rosary.

rosbif [rɔz'bif] sm roast beef.

rosicare [rozi'kare] v also rosicchiare nibble; (rodere) gnaw.

rosmarino [rozma'rino] sm rosemary.

rosolare [rozo'lare] v brown.

rosolia [rozo'lia] sf German measles.

rospo ['rɔspo] sm toad.

rossetto [ros'setto] sm lipstick; (belletto) rouge.

rosso ['rosso] agg red. sm red; (l'essere rosso) redness. rosso d'uovo egg-yolk. rossastro or rossiccio agg reddish. rossore sm blush.

rosticceria [rostittʃe'ria] sf rotisserie.

rostro ['rɔstro] sm rostrum.

rotaia [ro'taja] sf rail.

rotare [ro'tare] v rotate. rotatorio agg rotatory. rotazione sf rotation.

roteare [rote'are] v wheel; (occhi) roll.

rotella [ro'tɛlla] sf small wheel; (mobili) castor; (ginocchio) knee-cap. gli manca una rotella (fam) he has a screw loose. pattino a rotelle sm roller-skate.

rotolare [roto'lare] v roll. rotolo sm roll. andare a rotoli or rotoloni go to rack and ruin. rotoloni avv rolling (over and over).

rotondo [ro'tondo] agg round.

rotta¹ ['rotta] sf route. cambiar rotta change course.

rotta² ['rotta] sf (disfatta) rout; (breccia)

breach. a rotta di collo at breakneck speed. mettere in rotta (put to) rout.

rotto ['rotto] agg broken. per il rotto della cuffia by the skin of one's teeth. rottame sm fragment. rottami sm pl scrap sing. rottura sf break; (violazione) breach; (interruzione) breakdown.

rovente [ro'vɛnte] agg red-hot.

rovere ['rovere] sm oak.

rovesciare [roveʃ'ʃare] v upset; (abbattere) overthrow; (gettare) throw (back). rovesciarsi v overturn; (barca, ecc.) capsize; (affluire) pour. rovescio sm shower; (retro) back; (danno) setback; (sport) backhand. andare a rovescio go wrong. rovescio the wrong way round; (capovolto) upside-down; (col denti fuori) inside out.

rovinare [rovi'nare] v ruin. rovina sf ruin. andare in rovina collapse. mandare in rovina ruin. rovinoso agg ruinous.

rovistare [rovis'tare] v ransack.

rovo ['rovo] sm bramble.

rozzo ['roddzo] agg rough; (fig) coarse.

ruba ['ruba] sf andare a ruba sell like hot cakes.

rubacchiare [rubak'kjare] v pilfer.

rubare [ru'bare] v steal. rubacuori s(m+ charmer. rubare il tempo a qualcuno take up someone's time. ruberia sf theft.

rubinetto [rubi'netto] sm tap. rubinetto chiusura stopcock.

rubino [ru'bino] sm ruby.

rubrica [ru'brika] sf (indirizzi) address book; (telefonica) directory; (quaderno index-book; (giornale) feature.

rude ['rude] agg rough.

rudere ['rudere] sm ruin; (persona) wreck ruffiano [ruf'fjano] sm pimp; (adulatore bootlicker.

ruga ['ruga] sf wrinkle. rugoso agg wrinkled.

ruggine ['ruddʒine] sf rust; (astio) ill-feeling. rugginoso agg rusty.

ruggire [rud'dʒire] v roar. ruggito sm roar.

rugiada [ru'dʒada] sf dew. goccia di rugiada sf dewdrop.

rullare [rul'lare] v roll; (aereo) taxi. rullio sm rolling. rullo sm roll; (tec) roller.

rum [rum] sm rum.

ruminare [rumi'nare] v ruminate.

rumore [ru'more] sm noise; (diceria) rumour; sensation. rumoreggiare v make a noise; rumble. rumoroso agg noisy.

ruolo ['rwɔlo] *sm* roll; (*teatro, funzione*) role. **insegnante non di ruolo** supply teacher. **personale di ruolo** permanent staff.

ruota ['rwɔta] *sf* wheel. **andare a ruota libera** free-wheel. **a ruota** circular. **far la ruota** (*pavoneggiarsi*) show off. **seguire a ruota** follow close behind.

rupe ['rupe] *sf* cliff.

rupia [ru'pia] *sf* rupee.

rurale [ru'rale] *agg* rural.

ruscello [ru'fɛllo] *sm* stream.

ruspa ['ruspa] *sf* bulldozer. **(pollo) ruspante** *sm* free-range chicken.

russare [rus'sare] *v* snore.

Russia ['russja] *sf* Russia. **russo, -a** *s, agg* Russian.

rustico ['rustiko] *agg* rustic; (*contadino*) rural; (*rozzo*) rough.

ruttare [rut'tare] *v* belch. **rutto** *sm* belch.

ruvido ['ruvido] *agg* rough. **ruvidezza** *sf* roughness.

ruzzare [rut'tsare] *v* romp.

ruzzolare [ruttso'lare] *v* tumble; (*rotolare*) roll (down). **ruzzolone** *sm* tumble. **fare un ruzzolone** (*fam*) come a cropper.

S

sabato ['sabato] *sm* Saturday. **il** *or* **di sabato** on Saturdays.

sabbia ['sabbja] *sf* sand. **sabbie mobili** quicksand *sing*. **sabbiare** *v* sand-blast. **sabbioso** *agg* sandy.

sabotaggio [sabo'taddʒo] *sm* sabotage. **sabotare** *v* sabotage. **sabotatore, -trice** *sm, sf* saboteur.

sacca ['sakka] *sf* bag; (*fig*) pocket.

saccarina [sakka'rina] *sf* saccharine.

saccente [sat'tʃɛnte] *s(m+f)*, *agg* know-all.

saccheggiare [sakked'dʒare] *v* sack, loot. **saccheggiatore** *sm* plunderer, looter. **saccheggio** *sm* sacking, looting.

sacco ['sakko] *sm* sack. **cogliere con le mani nel sacco** catch red-handed. **sacco a pelo** sleeping-bag. **sacco da montagna** rucksack. **sacco postale** mail-bag. **un sacco di** lots of.

sacerdote [satʃer'dɔte] *sm* priest. **sacerdozio** *sm* priesthood.

sacramento [sakra'mento] *sm* sacrament.

sacrificare [sakrifi'kare] *v* sacrifice; (*rinunciare*) give up; (*non valorizzare*) waste. **sacrificio** *sm* sacrifice; (*di sè*) self-sacrifice.

sacrilegio [sakri'ledʒo] *sm* sacrilege; (*fig*) crime. **sacrilego** *agg, m pl* **-ghi** sacrilegious; criminal.

sacro ['sakro] *agg* sacred. *sm* (*osso*) sacrum. **sacrosanto** *agg* sacrosanct.

sadico ['sadiko], **-a** *agg* sadistic. *sm, sf* sadist. **sadismo** *sm* sadism.

saetta [sa'etta] *sf* flash (of lightning); (*mec*) bit; (*freccia*) arrow.

sagace [sa'gatʃe] *agg* sagacious. **sagacia** *sf* sagacity.

saggio[1] ['saddʒo], **-a** *agg* wise; (*sapiente*) sage. *sm, sf* sage. **saggezza** *sf* wisdom.

saggio[2] ['saddʒo] *sm* trial; (*metalli preziosi*) assay; (*prova*) proof; (*dimostrazione pubblica*) display; (*scritto critico*) essay. **saggiare** *v* test; assay. **saggiatura** *sf* assay; (*segno*) hallmark. **saggista** *s(m+f)* essayist.

Sagittario [sadʒit'tarjo] *sm* Sagittarius.

sagoma ['sagoma] *sf* outline; (*forma, modello*) pattern. **sagomare** *v* shape.

sagra ['sagra] *sf* feast.

sagrestano [sagres'tano] *sm* sacristan. **sagrestia** *sf* vestry.

sala ['sala] *sf* room, hall. **sala da pranzo** dining-room. **sala d'aspetto** waiting-room. **sala di lettura/macchine** reading-/engine-room. **sala operatoria** operating theatre.

salace [sa'latʃe] *agg* salacious.

salamandra [sala'mandra] *sf* salamander.

salame [sa'lame] *sm* salami; (*fig*) fool.

salamoia [sala'mɔja] *sf* brine. **mettere in salamoia** pickle.

salare [sa'lare] *v* salt. **salato** *agg* salty; (*conservato*) salted; (*caro*) dear.

salario [sa'larjo] *sm* pay; (*settimanale*) wages *pl*; (*mensile*) salary. **salariale** *agg* pay.

salassare [salas'sare] *v* bleed.

salda ['salda] *sf* size, sizing. **dare la salda a** size; (*inamidare*) starch.

saldare [sal'dare] *v* (*tec*) solder; (*autogeno*) weld; (*econ*) settle, pay. **saldatore** *sm* (*operaio*) solderer, welder; (*utensile*) soldering iron. **saldatrice** *sf* welder. **saldatura** *sf* welding; soldering.

saldo[1] ['saldo] *agg* solid; firm. **saldezza** *sf* solidity; firmness.

saldo² ['saldo] *sm* settlement; (*somma da pagare*) balance. **saldi** *sm pl* (*merce*) remnants *pl*.

sale ['sale] *sm* salt. **non aver sale in zucca** be stupid. **restar di sale** be dumbfounded. **salgemma** *sm* rock-salt. **salino** *agg* saline.

salice ['salitʃe] *sm* willow(-tree). **salice piangente** weeping willow.

saliente [sa'ljɛnte] *agg, sm* salient.

*salire [sa'lire] *v* climb, go up; (*autobus, treno*) board, get on; (*auto*) get in; (*alzarsi, crescere*) rise. **far salire** send up.

saliscendi *sm invar* (*chiusura*) latch; (*fig*) ups and downs *pl*. **salita** *sf* climb; entrance; (*tratto che sale*) slope. **in salita** uphill; (*che aumenta*) rising.

saliva [sa'liva] *sf* saliva. **salivale** *agg* salivary. **salivare** *v* salivate.

salma ['salma] *sf* corpse.

salmo ['salmo] *sm* psalm.

salmone [sal'mone] *sm* salmon.

salone [sa'lone] *sm* living-room; (*esposizione*) show; (*parrucchiere*) salon.

salotto [sa'lɔtto] *sm* drawing-room, lounge.

salpare [sal'pare] *v* weigh anchor.

salsa ['salsa] *sf* sauce; (*a base di carne*) gravy. **in tutte le salse** in all kinds of ways. **salsiera** *sf* sauce-boat; gravy-boat.

salsiccia [sal'sittʃa] *sf* sausage.

salso ['salso] *agg* salt(y). **salsedine** *sf* saltiness.

saltare [sal'tare] *v* jump; (*balzare*) leap; (*tralasciare*) skip; (*bottone, etc.*) come off; (*gastr*) sauté. **far saltare** destroy, blow up; (*serratura*) force; (*governo*) bring down. **saltare di palo in frasca** switch from one subject to another. **saltare (in aria)** (*esplodere*) blow up. **saltare in bestia** fly into a rage. **saltare in mente** cross one's mind, get into one's head.

saltellare [saltel'lare] *v also* **salterellare** skip *or* hop about.

saltimbanco [saltim'banko] *sm* acrobat; (*spreg*) charlatan.

salto ['salto] *sm* jump, leap; (*omissione*) gap. **in un salto** in a jiffy. **salto con l'asta** pole-vault. **salto in alto/lungo** high-/long-jump. **saltuario** *agg* intermittent, occasional.

salubre ['salubre] *agg* healthy.

salumeria [salume'ria] *sf* delicatessen.

salumi *sm pl* cold meats *pl*. **salumiere, -a** *sm, sf* pork-butcher; grocer.

salutare [salu'tare] *v* greet; (*mil*) salute. **salutami tuo fratello** remember me to your brother. **saluto** *sm* greeting; salute. **cordiali/distinti saluti** yours sincerely/faithfully.

salute [sa'lute] *sf* health; (*benessere*) welfare. *inter* (*a chi starnutisce*) bless you! (*nei brindisi*) cheers!

salvare [sal'vare] *v* save; (*trarre in salvo*) rescue; protect. **salvacondotto** *sm* pass. **salvadanaio** *sm* money-box. **salvagente** *sm* (*ciambella*) lifebelt; (*giacca*) life-jacket; (*strada*) traffic island. **salvaguardare** *v* safeguard. **salvaguardia** *sf* safeguard. **salvataggio** *sm* rescue.

salve ['salve] *inter* hello! (*salute*) bless you!

salvia ['salvja] *sf* sage.

salvietta [sal'vjetta] *sf* (*tovagliolo*) napkin; (*asciugamano*) towel.

salvo ['salvo] *agg* safe. **mettere in salvo** save, put aside. *prep* except (for), bar(ring). **salvo che** except that; (*a meno che*) unless. **salvezza** *sf* salvation; (*sicurezza*) safety.

sambuco [sam'buko] *sm, pl* **-chi** elder.

sanare [sa'nare] *v* heal; (*porre rimedio*) rectify; (*bonificare*) reclaim. **sanatorio** *sm* sanatorium.

sancire [san'tʃire] *v* sanction; ratify.

sandalo¹ ['sandalo] *sm* sandal.

sandalo² ['sandalo] *sm* (*legno*) sandalwood.

sangue ['sangwe] *sm* blood. **al sangue** (*gastr*) rare. **a sangue caldo/freddo** warm-/cold-blooded. **farsi cattivo sangue** get worked up. **puro sangue** thoroughbred. **sangue freddo** sang-froid, composure. **sanguemisto** *sm* half-breed.

sanguigno [san'gwiɲo] *agg* blood; (*colore*) blood-red; (*costituzione*) sanguine.

sanguinare [sangwi'nare] *v* bleed. **sanguinario** *agg* bloodthirsty. **sanguinolento** *agg* bleeding; (*insanguinato*) bloody. **sanguinoso** *agg* bloody.

sanguisuga [sangwi'suga] *sf* leech.

sanità [sani'ta] *sf* health; (*salubrità*) wholesomeness. **sanità mentale** sanity. **sanitario** *agg* sanitary; (*di medicina*) medical.

sano ['sano] *agg* healthy; (*integro*) sound; (*salubre*) wholesome; (*di mente*) sane;

intact. **sano come un pesce** sound as a bell. **sano e salvo** safe and sound.

santo ['santo], **-a** *agg* holy; (*seguito da nome*) Saint; pious; sacred; (*rafforzativo*) blessed. *sm*, *sf* saint. **santerello**, **-a** *sm*, *sf* (*fam*) goody-goody. **santificare** *v* sanctify; (*venerare*) hallow; canonize. **santità** *sf* holiness; (*fig*) sanctity. **santuario** *sm* sanctuary.

sanzione [san'tsjone] *sf* sanction. **sanzionare** *v* sanction.

***sapere** [sa'pere] *v* know; (*essere capace, aver imparato*) can, know how (to); (*aver odore*) smell (of); (*aver sapore*) taste (of). **buono a sapersi** worth knowing. **far sapere a** let know, inform. **non ne voglio sapere** I don't want to have anything to do with it. **non si sa mai** you never can tell. **per quanto ne sappia** as far as I know. **saperla lunga** know a thing or two. **venire a sapere** learn, gather. *sm* knowledge, learning.

sapienza [sa'pjɛntsa] *sf* wisdom; learning. **sapiente** *agg* wise; learned. **sapientone**, **-a** *sm*, *sf* (*fam*) know-all.

sapone [sa'pone] *sm* soap. **sapone in polvere** soap-powder. **saponetta** *sf* bar of soap. **saponiera** *sf* soap-dish. **saponoso** *agg* soapy.

sapore [sa'pore] *sm* taste, flavour. **saporito** *agg* tasty; (*salato*) rather salty; (*arguto*) witty.

saracinesca [saratʃi'neska] *sf* roller-blind; (*di chiusa*) floodgate.

sarcasmo [sar'kazmo] *sm* sarcasm. **sarcastico** *agg* sarcastic.

sarchio ['sarkjo] *sm* hoe. **sarchiare** *v* hoe.

sarda ['sarda] *sf also* **sardina** pilchard, sardine.

Sardegna [sar'deɲa] *sf* Sardinia. **sardo**, **-a** *s, agg* Sardinian.

sardonico [sar'dɔniko] *agg* sardonic.

sarta ['sarta] *sf* dressmaker. **sarto** *sm* tailor. **sartoria** *sf* (*laboratorio*) dressmaker's *or* tailor's workshop; (*tecnica*) dressmaking, tailoring.

sasso ['sasso] *sm* stone; (*ciottolo*) pebble; (*roccia*) rock. **prendere a sassate** pelt with stones, stone. **sassoso** *agg* stony.

sassofono [sas'sɔfono] *sm* saxophone. **sassofonista** *s*(*m+f*) saxophonist.

Satana ['satana] *sm* Satan. **satanico** *agg* satanic.

satellite [sa'tɛllite] *agg*, *sm* satellite.

satirico [sa'tiriko] *agg* satirical. **satira** *sf*

satire. **satireggiare** *v also* **mettere in satira** satirize.

satiro ['satiro] *sm* satyr.

satollo [sa'tollo] *agg* full up.

saturare [satu'rare] *v* saturate; (*fig*) cram. **saturazione** *sf* saturation. **saturo** *agg* saturated; crammed, full.

savio ['savjo] *agg* wise; prudent.

saziare [sa'tsjare] *v* satisfy; (*riempire presto*) be filling. **saziarsi** *v* have one's fill; (*stancarsi*) tire. **sazietà** *sf* surfeit. **a sazietà** more than enough. **mangiare a sazietà** eat *or* have one's fill. **sazio** *agg* satisfied; (*fam*) full up; (*stanco*) tired.

sbadato [zba'dato] *agg* careless, thoughtless. **sbadataggine** *sf* carelessness, thoughtlessness.

sbadigliare [zbadi'ʎare] *v* yawn. **sbadiglio** *sm* yawn.

sbafare [zba'fare] *v* (*scroccare*) scrounge; (*mangiare avidamente*) gobble up. **mangiare/vivere a sbafo** scrounge a meal/living.

sbagliare [zba'ʎare] *v* make a mistake; (*scambiare*) mistake. **sbagliare i calcoli** miscalculate; (*fig*) make a (big) mistake. **sbagliar il passo** stumble; (*mil*) be out of step. **sbagliar numero** get the wrong number. **sbagliar ortografia** spell incorrectly. **sbagliarsi sul conto di** be wrong about. **sbagliato** *agg* wrong, mistaken. **calcolo sbagliato** *sm* miscalculation. **pronuncia sbagliata** *sf* mispronunciation. **sbaglio** *sm* mistake.

sbalestrato [zbales'trato] *agg* unsettled; (*smarrito*) lost.

sballare [zbal'lare] *v* (*merce*) unpack. **sballato** *agg* wild.

sballottare [zballot'tare] *v* toss about. **sballottamento** *sm* tossing.

sbalordire [zbalor'dire] *v* astonish; (*turbare*) bewilder, shock. **sbalordimento** *sm* astonishment; shock, bewilderment. **sbalorditivo** *agg* amazing; (*incredibile*) staggering.

sbalzare[1] [zbal'tsare] *v* throw, fling. **sbalzo** *sm* jerk, jolt; (*fig*) jump. **a sbalzi** jerkily; (*fig*) by fits and starts.

sbalzare[2] [zbal'tsare] *v* (*metallo*) emboss. **lavoro a sbalzo** *sm* embossing.

sbandare [zban'dare] *v* (*auto*) skid; (*mar*) list; (*aero*) bank; (*disperdere*) break *or* split up. **sbandata** *sf* skid. **prendere una sbandata per** have a crush on. **sbandato** *agg* scattered; (*fig*) bewildered.

sbaragliare [zbara'ʎare] v (put to) rout. **andare** or **buttarsi allo sbaraglio** risk everything. **mettere allo sbaraglio** jeopardize.

sbarazzarsi [zbarat'tsarsi] v get rid of.

sbarbare [zbar'bare] v shave. **sbarbatello** sm novice.

sbarcare [zbar'kare] v land; (merce) unload. **sbarco** sm landing; unloading.

sbarra ['zbarra] sf bar, barrier; (segno grafico) stroke. **sbarramento** sm barrage; block(age). **sbarrare** v bar, block; (porta) bolt; (assegno) cross; (occhi) open wide.

sbatacchiare [zbatak'kjare] v slam; (ali) flap.

sbattere ['zbattere] v (scaraventare) fling; (chiudere violentemente) slam; (urtare) bash; (ali) flap; (gastr) whip, beat. **non saper dove sbattere la testa** not know which way to turn. **sbatter fuori** (fam) chuck out.

sbavare [zba'vare] v (emettere bava) dribble; (colore, ecc.) smudge. **sbavatura** sf dribble; smudge.

sberla [zberla] sf slap.

sbiadire [zbja'dire] v fade. **sbiadito** agg faded; (fig) dull.

sbiancare [zbjan'kare] v whiten.

sbianchire [zbjan'kire] v whiten; (gastr) blanch.

sbieco ['zbjɛko] agg crooked. **guardar di sbieco** look askance at. **tagliar di sbieco** cut on the bias.

sbigottire [zbigot'tire] v astonish; (turbare) dismay. **sbigottimento** sm astonishment; dismay.

sbilancio [zbi'lantʃo] sm (squilibrio) lack of equilibrium; (econ) deficit. **sbilanciare** v unbalance.

sbilenco [zbi'lenko] agg crooked.

sbloccare [zblok'kare] v free, release; (prezzi) unfreeze.

sboccare [zbok'kare] v come out; (condurre) lead; (fiume) flow (into). **sbocco** sm outlet.

sbocciare [zbot'tʃare] v bloom, blossom.

sbollentare [zbollen'tare] v blanch.

sbornia [zbornja] sf postumi di una **sbornia** sm pl hangover sing. **prendere una sbornia** get drunk.

sborsare [zbor'sare] v pay out, disburse. **sborso** sm disbursement.

sbottare [zbot'tare] v burst out.

sbottonare [zbotto'nare] v unbutton.

sbozzare [zbot'tsare] v sketch; (fig) outline.

sbracciarsi [zbrat'tʃarsi] v gesticulate; (rimboccarsi le maniche) roll up one's sleeves; (fig) do one's utmost. **sbracciato** agg (abito) sleeveless.

sbraitare [zbrai'tare] v yell; protest.

sbranare [zbra'nare] v tear to pieces.

sbrattare [zbrat'tare] v tidy up. **stanza di sbratto** sf lumber-room.

sbriciolare [zbritʃo'lare] v crumble.

sbrigare [zbri'gare] v get done, finish (off); (risolvere) settle. **sbrigarsi** v (far presto) hurry up; (liberarsi) get rid (of). **sbrigativo** agg quick; (superficiale) hasty.

sbrigliare [zbri'ʎare] v unbridle, give free rein (to). **sbrigliatezza** sf unruliness. **sbrigliato** agg unruly, wild.

sbrindellare [zbrindel'lare] v tear to shreds. **sbrindellato** agg in rags or tatters.

sbrodolare [zbrodo'lare] v (insudiciare) soil; (fig) spin out; (fam) waffle.

sbrogliare [zbro'ʎare] v disentangle. **sbrogliarsi** v extricate oneself.

sbronzo ['zbrondzo] agg drunk. **prendersi una sbronza** get drunk.

sbruffare [zbruf'fare] v spurt; (fig) brag.

sbucare [zbu'kare] v come out, emerge; (fig) spring up.

sbucciare [zbut'tʃare] v peel; (escoriare) scrape. **sbucciapatate** sm invar potato-peeler. **sbucciatura** sf scrape, graze.

sbudellare [zbudel'lare] v disembowel; (gastr) gut. **sbudellarsi dal ridere** split one's sides laughing.

sbuffare [zbuf'fare] v puff, pant; (rabbia) snort.

scabbia ['skabbja] sf scabies. **scabbiosa** sf (bot) scabious.

scabroso [ska'brozo] agg also **scabro** rough; (problema) thorny, knotty.

scacciare [skat'tʃare] v drive out or away; (fig) dispel; expel.

scacco ['skakko] sm (quadretto) check; (figurina del gioco) chessman. **scacchi** sm pl (gioco) chess sing. **scacco matto** checkmate. **subire uno scacco** suffer a setback. **scacchiera** sf chess-board; (per dama) draught-board.

*****scadere** [ska'dere] v expire; (perdere valore) decline; (econ) fall due. **scadente** agg poor. **scadenza** sf expiry; (effetti) maturity. **a breve/lunga scadenza** short-/long-term. **scadimento** sm decline.

scafandro [ska'fandro] *sm* diving-suit; (*astronauta*) space-suit.

scaffale [skaf'fale] *sm* shelf. **scaffalatura** *sf* shelving.

scafo [skafo] *sm* hull.

scagionare [skadʒo'nare] *v* exonerate.

scaglia ['skaʎa] *sf* scale; (*sapone*) flake. **scagliare** *v* flake.

scagliare [ska'ʎare] *v* (*lanciare*) fling, hurl.

scaglione [ska'ʎone] *sm* group; (*mil*) echelon. **scaglionare** *v* stagger; (*mil*) range. **scaglionamento** *sm* staggering.

scala ['skala] *sf* stairs *pl*, staircase; (*piano*) level; (*misura, rapporto*) scale; (*apparecchio*) ladder. **far le scale** climb the stairs; (*musica*) practise scales. **scala a chiocciola** spiral staircase. **scala di corda** rope-ladder. **scala portatile** steps *pl*, step-ladder. **scalinata** *sf* flight of stairs.

scalare [ska'lare] *v* scale. *agg* graduated; (*fis*) scalar. **scalata** *sf* climb. **scalatore, -trice** *sm, sf* climber.

scalcagnato [skalka'nato] *agg* shabby.

scaldare [skal'dare] *v* warm (up); (*a temperatura più elevata*) heat (up). **scaldabagno** *sm* water-heater.

scalfire [skal'fire] *v* scratch.

scalmanato [skalma'nato] *agg* flustered. *sm, sf* hothead. **scalmana** *sf* chill; (*fig*) craze.

scalo ['skalo] *sm* (*banchina*) pier; (*porto d'approdo*) port of call; (*aero*) stopover. **far scalo** (*mar*) call; (*aero*) land, stop. **scalo merci** (*mar*) wharf; (*ferr*) goods yard. **senza scalo** non-stop.

scalogna [ska'loɲa] *sf* bad luck. **scalognato** *agg* unlucky.

scaloppa [ska'lɔppa] *sf* cutlet. **scaloppina** *sf* escalope.

scalpello [skal'pello] *sm* chisel; (*chirurgia*) scalpel. **scalpellare** *v* chisel; cut away.

scalpore [skal'pore] *sm* sensation.

scaltro ['skaltro] *agg* shrewd.

scalzo ['skaltso] *agg* barefoot.

scambiare [skam'bjare] *v* (*dare in cambio*) exchange; (*confondere*) mistake, mix up. **scambievole** *agg* mutual. **scambio** *sm* exchange; (*ferr*) points *pl*. **libero scambio** free trade.

scamosciato [skamo'ʃato] *agg* suede.

scampagnata [skampa'ɲata] *sf* outing.

scampanato [skampa'nato] *agg* flared.

scampare [skam'pare] *v* escape; (*evitare*) avoid. **Dio ce ne scampi!** God forbid!

scamparla bella have a narrow escape. **scampato, -a** *sm, sf* (*superstite*) survivor. **scampo** *sm* way out.

scampo [skampo] *sm* prawn.

scampolo ['skampolo] *sm* remnant.

scanalare [skana'lare] *v* groove; (*colonna*) flute. **scanalatura** *sf* groove; flute.

scandagliare [skanda'ʎare] *v* sound (out). **scandaglio** *sm* sounding.

scandalizzare [skandalid'dzare] *v* shock; (*dar scandalo*) scandalize. **scandalo** *sm* scandal. **scandaloso** *agg* scandalous.

scandire [skan'dire] *v* (*pronunciare*) articulate; (*versi*) scan.

scanno ['skanno] *sm* stall.

scansare [skan'sare] *v* dodge, shirk; (*spostare*) shift. **scansarsi** *v* get out of the way. **scansafatiche** *s(m+f)* *invar* loafer.

scapaccione [skapat'tʃone] *sm* slap.

scapestrato [skapes'trato], **-a** *agg* wild, unruly. *sm, sf* madcap, daredevil.

scapigliato [skapi'ʎato] *agg* dishevelled; (*fig*) reckless.

scapitare [skapi'tare] *sm* loss; (*danno*) injury. **a scapito di** to the detriment of.

scapola ['skapola] *sf* shoulder-blade.

scapolo ['skapolo] *agg* single. *sm* bachelor.

scappamento [skappa'mento] *sm* (*auto*) exhaust.

scappare [skap'pare] *v* run away; escape, flee. **devo scappare** (*ho fretta*) I must rush. **lasciarsi scappar di bocca** blurt out. **scappare di mente** slip one's mind. **scappatella** *sf* escapade. **scappatoia** *sf* way out; (*fig*) loophole.

scappellotto [skapel'lɔtto] *sm* smack. **passare a scappellotti** (*fam*) scrape through.

scarabocchio [skara'bokkjo] *sm* (*macchia*) blot; (*sgorbio*) scrawl; (*disegno*) doodle. **scarabocchiare** *v* scrawl; doodle.

scarafaggio [skara'faddʒo] *sm* cockroach.

scaramanzia [skaraman'tsia] *sf* spell. **per scaramanzia** for luck.

scaramuccia [skara'muttʃa] *sf* skirmish.

scaraventare [skaraven'tare] *v* hurl, fling.

scarcerare [skartʃe'rare] *v* release (from prison). **scarcerazione** *sf* release.

scardinare [skardi'nare] *v* unhinge.

scaricare [skari'kare] *v* discharge; (*deporre un carico*) unload; (*sfogare*) vent; (*liquido*) empty; (*gas*) let out. **scaricare la colpa** shift the blame. **scarica** *sf* discharge; (*raffica*) volley. **scaricalasino** *sm* *invar* piggy-bank.

scarico ['skariko] *sm, pl* **-chi** discharge; unloading; (*di rifiuti*) dumping; (*i rifiuti stessi*) rubbish; (*deposito di rifiuti*) dump; (*auto*) exhaust. **a mio scarico** in my defence. **a scarico di coscienza** to clear one's conscience. *agg* (*vuoto*) empty; (*batteria*) flat.

scarlattina [skarlat'tina] *sf* scarlet fever.

scarlatto [skar'latto] *agg, sm* scarlet.

scarno ['skarno] *agg* skinny; (*spoglio*) bare; (*povero*) scanty.

scarpa ['skarpa] *sf* shoe. **scarpe da ginnastica** *or* **tennis** plimsolls *pl*. **scarpone** *sm* boot. **scarponi da calciatore/sci** football-/ski-boots *pl*.

scarso ['skarso] *agg* poor; (*manchevole*) lacking (in); (*insufficiente*) short. **un chilo scarso** just under a kilo. **scarseggiare** *v* be scarce; be short (of); (*fig*) lack (in). **scarsezza** *or* **scarsità** *sf* shortage; lack.

scartabellare [skartabel'lare] *v* skim *or* flip through.

scartare¹ [skar'tare] *v* (*togliere dalla carta*) unwrap; (*respingere*) discard, reject. **scarto** *sm* (*cosa scartata*) reject; (*alle carte*) discard. **merci di scarto** *sf pl* inferior goods *pl*, rejects *pl*.

scartare² [skar'tare] *v* (*spostarsi lateralmente*) swerve. **scarto** *sm* swerve, skid; difference.

scassare [skas'sare] *v* (*fam: guastare*) smash, bust; (*il terreno*) break up. **furto con scasso** *sm* burglary.

scassinare [skassi'nare] *v* force (open). **scassinatore, -trice** *sm, sf* burglar; (*di banche*) bank-robber.

scatenare [skate'nare] *v* unleash; cause. **scatenarsi** *v* break out.

scatola ['skatola] *sf* box; carton; (*di latta*) can. **averne piene le scatole** (*fam*) be fed up to the back teeth (with). **cibo in scatola** *sm* tinned food. **rompere le scatole** (*fam*) be a nuisance. **scatolame** *sm* tinned goods *pl*.

scattare [skat'tare] *v* spring; (*rilasciarsi*) spring up; (*armi*) go off; (*aprirsi*) spring open; (*chiudersi*) snap shut. **far scattare** release. **scattare a vuoto** misfire. **scatto** *sm* release; (*rumore*) click; (*sport*) spurt; (*accesso*) outburst. **a scatti** jerkily. **di scatto** suddenly.

scaturire [skatu'rire] *v* gush; (*fig*) arise.

scavalcare [skaval'kare] *v* step *or* climb over; (*saltando*) jump over; (*sbalzare di sella*) throw; (*superare*) overtake.

scavare [ska'vare] *v* dig; mine; (*pozzo*) sink; (*trovare*) dig up; (*sartoria*) widen. **scavatore** *sm* digger. **scavatura** *sf* excavation. **scavo** *sm* excavation.

*•**scegliere** ['ʃeʎere] *v* choose. **c'è (molto) da scegliere** there is plenty to choose from. **c'è poco da scegliere** there is little choice.

scellerato [ʃelle'rato], **-a** *agg* wicked. *sm, sf* wicked person. **scelleratezza** *sf* wickedness; (*atto*) misdeed.

scelta ['ʃelta] *sf* choice, selection; quality. **a scelta** according to preference. **non aver possibilità di scelta** have no choice. **scelto** *agg* chosen, picked; (*eccellente*) choice.

scemare [ʃe'mare] *v* diminish.

scemo ['ʃemo], **-a** *agg* stupid, idiotic; (*sciocco*) foolish. *sm, sf* fool, idiot. **scemenza** *sf* (*azione*) idiocy, foolishness; (*parole*) nonsense.

scena ['ʃena] *sf* scene; (*palcoscenico*) stage. **mettere in scena** stage, produce. **scenario** *sm* (*teatro*) set; (*cinema*) scenario, script; (*fig*) setting. **scenata** *sf* scene, row. **sceneggiare** *v* adapt, dramatize. **sceneggiatura** *sf* script. **scenico** *agg* scenic.

*•**scendere** ['ʃendere] *v* (*andar giù*) go down; (*venir giù*) come down; (*autobus, treno*) get off; (*auto*) get out; (*calare*) drop; (*sostare*) stop. **scendere a un accordo** reach an agreement. **scendere dal letto** get up. **scendiletto** *sm invar* (*tappetino*) bedside rug; (*vestaglia*) dressing-gown.

sceriffo [ʃe'riffo] *sm* sheriff.

scervellarsi [ʃervel'larsi] *v* rack one's brains. **scervellato** *agg* hare-brained.

scettico ['ʃettiko], **-a** *agg* sceptical. *sm, sf* sceptic. **scetticismo** *sm* scepticism.

scettro ['ʃettro] *sm* sceptre.

scheda ['skeda] *sf* card; (*di schedario*) index-card; (*elettorale*) ballot(-paper). **schedare** *v* catalogue; (*polizia*) record. **schedario** *sm* file; (*mobile*) filing cabinet; (*elenco*) list. **schedina** *sf* coupon.

scheggia ['skeddʒa] *sf* splinter. **scheggiare** *v* splinter, chip.

scheletro ['skeletro] *sm* skeleton; (*tec*) framework. **scheletrico** *agg* skeletal; (*fig*) bare.

schema ['skema] *sm* scheme; (*abbozzo*) outline; (*modello*) pattern. **schema di legge** bill. **schematico** *agg* schematic.

scherma ['skerma] *sf* fencing. **tirare di scherma** fence. **schermaglia** *sf* skirmish. **schermitore, -trice** *sm, sf* fencer.

schermo ['skermo] *sm* screen; (*difesa*) shield. **schermare** *v* screen, shield. **schermire** *v* protect.

schernire [sker'nire] *v* scorn, mock. **schernitore, -trice** *agg* scornful, mocking. **scherno** *sm* mockery, derision; (*oggetto di scherno*) laughing-stock.

scherzare [sker'tsare] *v* joke; (*prendere alla leggera*) trifle (with); (*giocare*) play. **c'è poco da scherzare** it is not a laughing matter. **scherzi!** *inter* you must be joking! **scherzo** *sm* joke; (*tiro*) trick; (*musica*) scherzo. **per scherzo** for fun, as a joke. **scherzoso** *agg* playful; (*giocoso*) jocular.

schettinare [sketti'nare] *v* roller-skate. **schettinaggio** *sm* roller-skating. **schettino** *sm* roller-skate.

schiacciare [skjat't∫are] *v* (*spiacciare*) squash; (*frantumare*) crush; (*noci*) crack. **schiacciare un pisolino** have a nap. **schiacciante** *agg* crushing. **schiaccianoci** *sm* nutcrackers *pl.* **schiacciasassi** *sm* steam-roller.

schiaffare [skjaf'fare] *v* (*fam*) chuck.

schiaffo ['skjaffo] *sm* slap. **schiaffeggiare** *v* slap.

schiamazzare [skjamat'tsare] *v* cackle; (*far baccano*) make a row. **schiamazzo** *sm* cackle; row.

schiantare [skjan'tare] *v* shatter, burst. **schianto** *sm* crash.

schiappa ['skjappa] *sf* (*fam*) washout.

schiarire [skja'rire] *v* clear (up). **schiarimento** *sm* clearing up; (*spiegazione*) explanation; information.

schiavo ['skjavo], **-a** *s, agg* slave. **schiavitù** *sf* slavery.

schiena ['skjɛna] *sf* back. **colpire alla schiena** stab in the back. **mal di schiena** *sm* backache. **schienale** *sm* back.

schiera ['skjɛra] *sf* band; (*moltitudine*) mass, crowd. **schieramento** *sm* formation; line-up. **schierare** *v* line up; (*mil*) deploy. **schierarsi contro** take sides against. **schierarsi dalla parte di** side with.

schietto ['skjetto] *agg* sincere; genuine; frank. **a dirla schietta** (to speak) frankly. **schiettezza** *sf* genuineness; frankness.

schifo ['skifo] *sm* disgust. **avere a schifo** loathe. **far schifo** *v* (*essere disgustoso*) be disgusting; (*disgustare*) (fill with) disgust. **schifare** *v* disgust. **schifezza** *sf* rubbish, muck. **schifiltoso** *agg* fussy; (*esigente*) fastidious. **schifoso** *agg* disgusting.

schioccare [skjok'kare] *v* crack; (*dita*) snap.

schioppo ['skjɔppo] *sm* gun; (*da caccia*) shotgun. **schioppettata** *sf* (gun)shot.

*schiudersi ['skjudersi] *v* open (up).

schiuma ['skjuma] *sf* foam; (*birra*) froth; (*sapone*) lather; (*feccia*) scum. **aver la schiuma alla bocca** foam at the mouth. **schiumare** *v* skim. **schiumoso** *agg* foamy; frothy; lathery.

schivare [ski'vare] *v* avoid; (*fam*) dodge; (*boxe*) duck.

schizofrenia [skitsofre'nia] *sf* schizophrenia. **schizofrenico, -a** *s, agg* schizophrenic.

schizzare [skit'tsare] *v* (*zampillare*) spurt; (*spruzzare*) squirt; (*sporcare*) splash; (*disegnare*) sketch. **schizzar via** dash off. **schizzetto** *sm* spray; syringe; (*giocattolo*) water-pistol. **schizzo** *sm* spurt; squirt; splash; sketch.

schizzinoso [skittsi'nozo] *agg* fastidious; squeamish.

sci [∫i] *sm* (*attrezzo*) ski; (*attività*) skiing. **fare dello sci** ski, go skiing. **sci nautico** water-ski; water-skiing. **sciare** *v* ski. **sciatore, -trice** *sm, sf* skier.

scia ['∫ia] *sf* wake; (*traccia*) trail. **seguire la scia di** follow in the footsteps of.

sciabola ['∫abola] *sf* sabre.

sciacallo [∫a'kallo] *sm* jackal.

sciacquare [∫ak'kware] *v* rinse (out). **sciacquata** *sf* rinse. **sciacquatura** *sf* (*azione*) rinsing; (*acqua*) dishwater. **sciacquo** *sm* rinsing; (*liquido*) mouthwash.

sciagura [∫a'gura] *sf* disaster; (*incidente*) accident, crash. **sciagurato** *agg* (*sfortunato*) unlucky, wretched; (*malvagio*) wicked.

scialacquare [∫alak'kware] *v* squander. **scialacquatore, -trice** *sm, sf* spendthrift.

scialbo ['∫albo] *agg* pale; faint; (*fig*) dull.

scialle ['∫alle] *sm* shawl.

scialo ['∫alo] *sm* waste.

sciame ['∫ame] *sm* swarm. **sciamare** *v* swarm.

sciancato [∫an'kato] *agg* lame; (*sedia, ecc.*) shaky, rickety.

sciarada [∫a'rada] *sf* charade.

sciarpa ['ʃarpa] sf scarf.

sciatica ['ʃatika] sf sciatica. sciatico agg sciatic.

sciatto ['ʃatto] agg slovenly; (fam) sloppy.

scientifico [ʃen'tifiko] agg scientific.

scienza ['ʃɛntsa] sf science. scienziato, -a sm, sf scientist; (studioso) scholar.

scimmia ['ʃimmja] sf monkey; (senza coda) ape. brutto come una scimmia as ugly as sin. scimmiottare v also fare la scimmia a ape.

scimpanzè [ʃimpan'tse] sm chimpanzee.

scimunito [ʃimu'nito], -a agg foolish. sm, sf fool.

*scindere ['ʃindere] v separate; divide.

scintilla [ʃin'tilla] sf spark. dare or emettere scintille spark. scintillare v sparkle; (lampeggiare) flash.

sciocco ['ʃɔkko], -a agg foolish. sm, sf fool. sciocchezza sf foolish thing; (cosa da niente) trifle; (l'essere sciocco) foolishness. dire sciocchezze talk nonsense.

*sciogliere ['ʃɔʎere] v (fondere) melt; dissolve; (porre fine) break up; (disfare) undo; (allentare) loosen; (slegare) untie; (società) wind up. scioglimento sm dissolution; breaking up; melting.

sciolto ['ʃɔlto] agg loose; (agile) nimble. aver la lingua sciolta have the gift of the gab. versi sciolti sm pl blank verse sing. scioltezza sf nimbleness; (fig) fluency.

scioperare [ʃope'rare] v (go on) strike. scioperante s(m+f) striker. scioperato agg lazy. sciopero sm strike. entrare in sciopero go on strike. far sciopero strike. sciopero bianco/lampo sit-down/wildcat strike.

sciorinare [ʃori'nare] v (bucato) hang out; (fig) show off; (spreg) dash off. sciorinare bugie tell a string of lies.

sciovinismo [ʃovi'nizmo] sm chauvinism. sciovinista s(m+f) chauvinist.

scipito [ʃi'pito] agg insipid.

scippare [ʃip'pare] v snatch. scippatore, -trice sm, sf bag-snatcher.

scirocco [ʃi'rokko] sm sirocco.

sciroppo [ʃi'roppo] sm syrup. sciroppato agg in syrup. sciropposo agg syrupy.

scisma ['ʃizma] sm schism. scismatico agg schismatic.

scissione [ʃis'sjone] sf split. scisso agg split.

sciupare [ʃu'pare] v (rovinare) ruin, spoil; (perdere) waste. sciuparsi v (salute) ruin one's health; (sgualcirsi) get creased. sciupato agg ruined; wasted; (di aspetto) haggard. sciupio sm waste. sciupone, -a sm, sf wastrel.

scivolare [ʃivo'lare] v slide; (sfuggire, sdrucciolare) slip; (aero) glide. scivolata sf slide; glide. scivolo sm chute; (mar) slipway. scivolone sm slip; (caduta) tumble. scivoloso agg slippery.

sclerosi [skle'rɔzi] sf sclerosis. sclerotico agg sclerotic.

scoccare [skok'kare] v (orologio) strike; (scagliare) fling.

scocciare [skot'tʃare] v bother. scocciarsi v get bored. scocciatore, -trice sm, sf bore; (fam) pest. scocciatura sf bore.

scodella [sko'della] sf bowl. scodellare v serve; (minestra) ladle out; (fig) come out with.

scoglio ['skɔʎo] sm rock; (fig) stumbling block. scogliera sf cliff; (a fior d'acqua) reef. scoglioso agg rocky.

scoiattolo [sko'jattolo] sm squirrel.

scolare [sko'lare] v drain; (gastr) strain. scolapiatti sm invar draining-board. scolo sm drainage; (condotto) drain.

scolaro [sco'laro], -a sm, sf pupil; disciple. scolastica agg (della scuola) school; (spreg) bookish; (filosofia) scholastic.

scollato [skol'lato] agg low-necked.

scolorire [skolo'rire] v also scolorare discolour, fade. scolorito agg faded.

scolpire [skol'pire] v sculpt; (incidere) carve; (fig) impress.

scombinare [skombi'nare] v upset. scombinato agg (mal combinato) badly arranged; confused.

scombro ['skombro] sm also sgombro mackerel.

scombussolare [skombusso'lare] v upset; (stordire) stun.

*scommettere [skom'mettere] v bet. scommessa sf bet. scommettitore, -trice sm, sf punter.

scomodare [skomo'dare] v trouble, inconvenience. scomodità sf discomfort; (disagio) inconvenience. scomodo agg (non comodo) uncomfortable; inconvenient.

scompaginare [skompadʒi'nare] v throw into disarray; (fig) upset.

*scomparire [skompa'rire] v disappear; (fig) look insignificant.

scomparso [skom'parso], -a agg vanished. sm, sf deceased. sf disappearance.

scompartimento [skomparti'mento] *sm* compartment. **scomparto** *sm* compartment; (*parete*) partition.

scompigliare [skompi'ʎare] *v* upset; confuse; (*capelli*) ruffle. **scompiglio** *sm* confusion.

***scomporre** [skom'porre] *v* take apart; resolve; decompose; (*turbare*) perturb. **senza scomporsi** unperturbed. **scomposto** *agg* broken down; (*in disordine*) untidy; (*indecoroso*) unseemly.

scomunicare [skomuni'kare] *v* excommunicate. **scomunica** *sf* excommunication.

sconcertare [skont∫er'tare] *v* baffle. **sconcertato** *agg* bewildered.

sconcio ['skont∫o] *agg* indecent; obscene. *sm* disgrace. **sconcezza** *sf* obscenity. **dire sconcezze** use foul language. **sconciare** *v* spoil.

sconfessare [skonfes'sare] *v* repudiate.

***sconfiggere** [skon'fiddʒere] *v* defeat. **sconfitta** *sf* defeat. **sconfitto** *agg* defeated, beaten. **dichiararsi sconfitto** acknowledge defeat.

sconfortante [skonfor'tante] *agg* disheartening. **sconforto** *sm* discouragement; depression.

scongelare [skondʒe'lare] *v* defrost.

scongiurare [skondʒu'rare] *v* beseech; (*evitare*) avoid; (*rel*) exorcise. **scongiuro** *sm* exorcism.

sconnettere [skon'nettere] *v* disconnect. **sconnesso** *agg* (*fig*) disjointed.

sconosciuto [skono'∫uto], **-a** *agg* unknown. *sm, sf* stranger.

sconquassare [skonkwas'sare] *v* smash; shake (up). **sconquassato** *agg* shattered.

sconsiderato [skonside'rato] *agg* thoughtless. **sconsideratezza** *sf* thoughtlessness.

sconsigliare [skonsi'ʎare] *v* advise against; dissuade.

sconsolato [skonso'lato] *agg* disconsolate.

scontare [skon'tare] *v* (*detrarre*) deduct; (*econ*) discount; (*debito*) pay off. **sconto** *sm* discount.

scontentare [skonten'tare] *v* dissatisfy; (*lasciare scontento*) disappoint. **scontentezza** *sf* dissatisfaction; disappointment. **scontento** *agg* displeased; disappointed.

scontrarsi [skon'trarsi] *v* meet; (*veicoli*) crash. **scontro** *sm* encounter; (*discussione*) argument; (*violento*) clash; crash.

scontrino [skon'trino] *sm* check.

scontroso [skon'troso] *agg* surly. **scontrosità** *sf* surliness.

***sconvenire** [skonve'nire] *v* be unsuitable; (*non essere decoroso*) be unbecoming. **sconveniente** *agg* unfavourable; unbecoming.

***sconvolgere** [skon'vɔldʒere] *v* upset. **sconvolgimento** *sm* upset; confusion. **sconvolto** *agg* upset.

scopa ['skopa] *sf* broom. **scopare** *v* sweep; (*volg*) screw.

scoperchiare [skoper'kjare] *v* take the lid off.

scoperto [sko'perto] *agg* uncovered; (*aperto*) open; (*nudo*) bare. *sm* open; (*conto*) overdraft. **allo scoperto** outdoors, in the open (air). **scoperta** *sf* discovery.

scopo ['skɔpo] *sm* purpose. **a** *or* **allo scopo di** in order to. **senza scopo** pointless.

scoppiare [skop'pjare] *v* burst; explode; (*manifestarsi*) break out. **scoppiettare** *v* crackle. **scoppio** *sm* explosion; outbreak; (*rumore*) bang.

***scoprire** [sko'prire] *v* (*fatti, cose nuove*) discover; (*togliere copertura*) uncover, bare; (*esporre*) expose; (*manifestare*) show. **scoprire le (proprie) carte** lay one's cards on the table.

scoraggiare [skorad'dʒare] *v* discourage, dishearten.

scorbuto [skor'buto] *sm* scurvy. **scorbutico** *agg* (*fig*) cantankerous.

scorciare [skor'∫are] *v* shorten. **scorciatoia** *sf* short cut.

scordare [skor'dare] *v* *also* **scordarsi** forget.

scordato [skor'dato] *agg* (*musica*) out of tune.

scoreggia [sko'reddʒa] (*volg*) *sf* fart. **scoreggiare** *v* fart.

***scorgere** [skɔrdʒere] *v* notice.

scoria ['skɔrja] *sf* slag; (*fig*) dross.

scorno ['skorno] *sm* humiliation.

scorpione [skor'pjone] *sm* scorpion. **Scorpione** *sm* Scorpio.

scorrazzare [skorrat'tsare] *v* run about. **scorrazzata** *sf* trip.

***scorrere** ['skorrere] *v* (*liquido*) run, flow; (*tempo*) pass (by); (*scivolare*) glide; (*leggere in fretta*) run through. **scorrevole** *agg* flowing. **scorrevolezza** *sf* fluidity; (*fig*) fluency.

scorretto [skor'retto] *agg* incorrect; (*sgarbato*) impolite; (*non leale*) unfair.

scorrettezza *sf* incorrectness, lack of manners; unfairness.

scorsa ['skɔrsa] *sf* glance.

scorso ['skɔrso] *agg* last. **l'anno scorso** last year.

scorsolo [skor'sɔjo] *agg* **nodo scorsolo** *sm* slip-knot.

scorta ['skɔrta] *sf* escort; (*provvista*) stock, supply; reserve. **di scorta** spare. **fare la scorta a** escort. **fare una scorta (di)** stock up (on). **sotto la scorta di** under the guidance of. **sulla scorta di** on the basis of. **scortare** *v* escort.

scortese [skor'teze] *agg* rude. **scortesia** *sf* rudeness.

scorticare [skorti'kare] *v* skin; (*escoriare*) graze.

scorza ['skɔrtsa] *sf* skin; (*corteccia*) bark.

scosceso [skoʃ'ezo] *agg* steep.

scossa ['skɔssa] *sf* shock; (*scatto, sbalzo*) jerk; (*tremore*) shake. **a scosse** jerkily. **scosso** *agg* shaken.

scostare [skos'tare] *v* shift. **scostarsi** *v* move aside; (*deviare*) stray. **scostamento** *sm* shifting; (*mat*) deviation. **scostante** *agg* unpleasant.

scostumato [skostu'mato] *agg* dissolute, licentious. **scostumatezza** *sf* licentiousness.

scotennare [skoten'nare] *v* skin; (*di cuoio capelluto*) scalp.

scottare [skot'tare] *v* burn; (*con liquido bollente*) scald; (*causare bruciatura*) scorch; (*essere caldo*) be hot. **scottatura** *sf* burning; scalding; scorching; (*ustione*) burn, scald.

scovare [sko'vare] *v* (*stanare*) flush out; (*rintracciare*) track down; (*trovare*) find.

Scozia ['skɔtsja] *sf* Scotland. **scozzese** *agg* Scottish, Scotch; *s(m+f)* Scot.

screanzato [skrean'tsato] *agg* rude.

screditare [skredi'tare] *v* discredit.

scremare [skre'mare] *v* skim.

screpolare [skrepo'lare] *v* crack. **screpolatura** *sf* crack.

screziato [skre'tsjato] *agg* variegated.

scribacchiare [skribak'kjare] *v* scribble.

scricchiolare [skrikkjo'lare] *v* creak. **scricchiolio** *sm* creaking noise.

scricciolo [skritt'ʃolo] *sm* wren.

scrigno ['skriɲo] *sm* casket.

scriminatura [skrimina'tura] *sf* parting.

scritta ['skritta] *sf* inscription; (*dir*) document.

scritto ['skritto] *agg* written. *sm* writing; letter; document. **scrittoio** *sm* (writing-)desk. **scrittore, -trice** *sm, sf* writer.

scrittura [skrit'tura] *sf* writing; (*contratto*) engagement; (*calligrafia*) handwriting. (**Sacra**) **Scrittura** (Holy) Scripture. **scritturare** *v* engage.

scrivania [skriva'nia] *sf* (writing-)desk.

***scrivere** ['skrivere] *v* write; (*compitando*) spell. **scrivere bene/male** (*calligrafia*) have a good/bad handwriting; (*stile*) write well/badly; (*compitare*) spell correctly/incorrectly.

scroccare [skrok'kare] *v* scrounge. **vivere a scrocco** scrounge a living. **scroccone, -a** *sm, sf* scrounger.

scrocco ['skrɔkko] *sm* **coltello a scrocco** *sm* clasp-knife. **serratura a scrocco** *sf* spring-lock, latch.

scrofa ['skrɔfa] *sf* sow.

scrollare [skrol'lare] *v* shake; (*spalle*) shrug.

scrosciare [skroʃ'are] *v* thunder; (*pioggia*) pelt down. **scroscio** *sm* (*pioggia*) downpour. **scroscio di applausi** thunderous applause. **scroscio di risa** roar of laughter.

scrostare [skros'tare] *v* scrape (off).

scroto ['skrɔto] *sm* scrotum.

scrupolo ['skrupolo] *sm* scruple, qualm. **avere o farsi scrupoli (di)** have qualms (about). **essere onesto fino allo scrupolo** be scrupulously honest. **senza scrupoli** unscrupulous. **scrupoloso** *agg* scrupulous, meticulous.

scrutare [skru'tare] *v* scan; (*indagare*) delve into. **scrutatore, -trice** *sm, sf* scrutineer. **scrutinare** *v* scrutinize. **scrutinio** *sm* scrutiny; (*elezioni*) poll.

scucire [sku'tʃire] *v* unstitch. **scucitura** *sf* rip.

scudo ['skudo] *sm* shield. **farsi scudo** shield oneself. **scuderia** *sf* (*ricovero*) stable; (*allevamento*) stud; (*auto*) racing team. **scudetto** *sm* (*calcio*) league championship.

scugnizzo [sku'ɲittso] *sm* urchin.

sculacciare [skulat'tʃare] *v* spank. **sculacciata** *sf* spanking.

scultore [skul'tore] *sm* sculptor. **scultrice** *sf* sculptress. **scultura** *sf* sculpture.

scuola ['skwɔla] *sf* school. **scuola dell'obbligo** compulsory schooling. **scuola guida** driving school. **scuola materna** nursery school. **scuola pubblica** state school.

*scuotere ['skwɔtere] v shake; (le spalle) shrug. **scuotersi di dosso** shrug off.

scure ['skure] sf axe.

scuro ['skuro] agg dark. sm dark, darkness. **scuretto** sm (window-)shutter.

scurire v darken.

scusa ['skuza] sf excuse; apology. **chiedere scusa a qualcuno** beg someone's pardon. **scusabile** agg excusable; justifiable. **scusante** sf excuse; justification. **scusare** v excuse; pardon. **scusarsi** v apologize; justify oneself. **mi scusi!** (I'm) sorry! I beg your pardon!

sdegnare [zde'ɲare] v (disprezzare) scorn; irritate. **sdegnato** agg indignant; irritated. **sdegno** sm indignation. **sdegnoso** agg disdainful.

sdoppiare [zdop'pjare] v split (in two). **sdoppiamento** sm split. **sdoppiamento della personalità** split personality.

sdraiarsi [zdra'jarsi] v (stendersi) stretch out; (mettersi a giacere) lie down. **sdraia** sf also **sedia a sdraio** deck-chair.

sdrucciolare [zdruttʃo'lare] v slip. **sdrucciolevole** agg slippery. **sdrucciolone** sm slip.

sdrucire [zdru'tʃire] v rip.

se¹ [se] cong if; whether; (se solo) if only. **come se** as though. **se non altro** if nothing else, at least.

se² [se] V **si**.

sè [se] pron one(self); (lui) him(self); (lei) her(self); (cosa, animale) it(self); (loro) them(selves). **da sè** on one's own. **di per sè** in itself. **fra sè e sè** to oneself. **va da sè** it goes without saying.

sebbene [seb'bene] cong (al)though.

seccare [sek'kare] v dry (up); (importunare) bother. **seccarsi** v (diventar secco) dry up; (annoiarsi) get bored; (infastidirsi) get annoyed. **secca** sf shallow; (fig) fix. **seccante** boring; annoying. **seccato** agg annoyed; (fam) fed up. **seccatore, -trice** sm, sf nuisance. **seccatura** sf nuisance. **secco** agg dry; (essicato) dried; (fig) sharp. **lavare a secco** dry-clean. **rimanere in secco** be left high and dry.

secchia ['sekkja] sf bucket. **secchio** sm pail; (per carbone) coal-scuttle. **secchione** sm (fam: sgobbone) swot.

*secernere [se'tʃɛrnere] v secrete.

secessione [setʃes'sjone] sf secession.

secolo ['sɛkolo] sm century; (periodo) age. **al secolo** alias. **secolare** agg centuries old; (laico) secular.

secondino [sekon'dino] sm warder.

secondo¹ [se'kondo] sm, agg second. **in un secondo tempo** on a later occasion. **secondo fine** sm ulterior motive.

secondo² [se'kondo] prep according to; depending on. **inter** it depends!

secrezione [sekre'tsjone] sf secretion.

sedano ['sɛdano] sm celery. **sedano rapa** celeriac.

sedare [se'dare] v calm; (reprimere) quell. **sedativo** agg, sm sedative.

sede ['sɛde] sf seat; (comm) office; residence; (seduta) sitting. **in altra sede** (luogo) elsewhere; (tempo) some other time. **Santa Sede** Holy See. **sede centrale** headquarters. **sede legale** registered office.

*sedere [se'dere] v sit (down). **dar da sedere** offer a seat. **sedersi** v sit down, take a seat. **tirarsi su a sedere** sit up. sm (deretano) bottom. **sedentario** agg sedentary.

sedia ['sɛdja] sf chair.

sedicente [sedi'tʃɛnte] agg so-called, would-be.

sedici ['sɛditʃi] agg, sm sixteen. **sedicesimo** sm, agg sixteenth.

sedile [se'dile] sm seat.

sedimento [sedi'mento] sm sediment. **sedimentazione** sf sedimentation.

sedizione [sedi'tsjone] sf sedition; rebellion. **sedizioso** agg seditious.

*sedurre [se'durre] v seduce; (attrarre) entice. **seducente** agg alluring, tempting. **seduttore, -trice** agg seductive. **seduzione** sf seduction; temptation.

seduta [se'duta] sf session; (pasto, posa) sitting; (riunione) meeting. **seduta spiritica** seance. **seduta stante** forthwith.

sega ['sega] sf saw. **a sega** saw-toothed. **sega a catena** chain-saw. **sega da traforo** fretsaw. **segare** v saw. **segatrice** sf saw. **segatura** sf (azione) sawing; (frammenti) sawdust.

segale ['segale] sf rye.

seggio ['sɛddʒo] sm seat; (carica) chair. **seggiola** sf chair. **seggiolino** sm seat. **seggiolone** sm armchair; (per bambini) high chair.

seggiovia [seddʒo'via] sf chair-lift.

seghettare [seget'tare] v serrate.

segmento [seg'mento] sm segment. **segmentare** v divide up. **segmentazione** sf segmentation; (fig) breaking up.

segnalare [seɲaˈlare] v signal; (*indicare*) point out; (*render noto*) report. **segnalato** agg announced, reported; (*straordinario*) outstanding. **segnalatore** sm (*persona*) signaller; indicator; alarm. **segnalazione** sf signalling; report; notification; (*nota informativa*) notice. **segnalazione stradale** road sign. **segnale** sm signal; (*cartello*) sign; (*telefono*) tone. **segnaletica** sf road signs pl.

segnalibro [seɲaˈlibro] sm bookmark.

segnapunti [seɲaˈpunti] sm invar (*tabellone*) score-board; (*libretto*) score-book.

segnare [seˈɲare] v mark; (*marchiare*) brand. **segnare i punti** keep the score. **segnare le ore** tell the time.

segno [ˈseɲo] sm sign; (*traccia*) mark. **come** or **in segno di** as a sign of, in token of. **essere segno che** mean. **tiro a segno** sm target practice.

sego [ˈsego] sm fallow.

segregare [segreˈgare] v segregate, set apart. **segregazione** sf segregation; isolation. **segregazione cellulare** solitary confinement.

segretario [segreˈtarjo], **-a** sm, sf secretary; (*chi redige verbali, ecc.*) clerk. **segretariato** sm secretariat. **segreteria** sf secretary's office; (*enti pubblici*) secretariat.

segreto [seˈgreto] agg secret. sm secret; (*intimità*) depth; (*segretezza*) secrecy. **in segreto** in secret; (*riservatamente*) confidentially. **nel segreto più assoluto** in utmost secrecy. **segreti del mestiere** tricks of the trade pl. **segreto di Pulcinella** open secret. **segreta** sf dungeon. **segretezza** sf secrecy.

seguace [seˈgwatʃe] s(m+f) follower; disciple.

seguente [seˈgwɛnte] agg following; (*futuro*) next.

segugio [seˈgudʒo] sm bloodhound; (*fig*) sleuth.

seguire [seˈgwire] v follow; (*frequentare*) attend. **segue a tergo** continued overleaf, PTO. **seguitare** v continue. **seguito** sm following; succession; favour; continuation; consequence. **di seguito** on end, non-stop. **in seguito** later (on). **in seguito a** as a result of, because of.

sei [ˈsɛi] agg, sm six.

selce [ˈseltʃe] sf of flint; (*strada*) paving-stone. **selciato** sm paving.

selettivo [seletˈtivo] agg selective. **selettività** sf selectivity. **selettore**, **-trice** sm, sf selector.

selezionare [seletsjoˈnare] v select; grade. **selezionamento** sm selection. **selezione** sf selection; (*scelta*) choice. **selezione automatica** (*telefono*) automatic dialling, STD.

sella [ˈsɛlla] sf saddle. **sellare** v saddle.

seltz [ˈsɛlts] sm invar soda-water.

selva [ˈselva] sf forest. **selvoso** agg wooded.

selvaggio [selˈvaddʒo], **-a** agg wild; (*incivile*) savage. sm, sf savage. **selvaggina** sf game. **selvatico** agg wild; (*scontroso*) uncouth.

semaforo [seˈmaforo] sm traffic lights pl.

semantica [seˈmantika] sf semantics. **semantico** agg semantic.

sembrare [semˈbrare] v seem. **cosa te ne sembra?** what do you think of it?

seme [ˈseme] sm seed; (*di mele, pere, ecc.*) pip; (*carte da gioco*) suit. **sementa** sf (*operazione*) sowing; (*semente*) seed. **semente** sf seed. **semenza** sf seed; (*perle*) seed-pearls pl.

semestre [seˈmɛstre] sm half-year. **semestrale** agg half-yearly.

semibreve [semiˈbrɛve] sf semibreve.

semicerchio [semiˈtʃerkjo] sm semicircle. **semicircolare** [semitʃirkoˈlare] agg semicircular.

semicroma [semiˈkrɔma] sf semiquaver.

semidio [semiˈdio] sm demi-god.

semifinale [semifiˈnale] sf semifinal. **semifinalista** s(m+f) semifinalist.

semiminima [semiˈminima] sf crotchet.

seminare [semiˈnare] v sow; (*fig*) scatter, strew. **semina** sf sowing. **seminale** agg seminal. **uscire dal seminato** digress.

seminario [semiˈnarjo] sm (*rel*) seminary; (*università*) seminar. **seminarista** sm seminarist.

seminterrato [seminterˈrato] sm basement.

seminudo [semiˈnudo] agg half-naked.

semita [seˈmita] s(m+f) Semite. agg also **semitico** Semitic.

semitono [semiˈtɔno] sm semitone.

semivivo [semiˈvivo] agg half-dead.

semola [ˈsemola] sf (*crusca*) bran. **semolino** sm semolina.

semovente [semoˈvɛnte] agg self-propelled.

semplice ['semplitʃe] *agg* simple; *(di un solo elemento)* single; *(senza affettazione)* plain. **semplicemente** *avv* simply; *(soltanto)* only. **semplicione** *sm* simpleton. **semplicità** *sf* simplicity. **semplificare** *v* simplify; facilitate. **semplificazione** *sf* simplification.

sempre ['sempre] *avv* always; *(ancora)* still. **da sempre** from the beginning. **per sempre** for ever. **sempre che** *(purché)* as long as, provided that; *(ammesso che)* supposing that. **sempre più** more and more. **sempreverde** *s(m+f)*, *agg* evergreen. **una volta per sempre** once and for all.

senape ['snape] *sf* mustard.

senato [se'nato] *sm* senate. **senatore** *sm* senator.

senile [se'nile] *agg* senile. **senilità** *sf* senility.

senno ['senno] *sm* wits *pl*; *(sensatezza)* (common) sense. **con senno** sensibly. **senno di poi** hindsight. **uscir di senno** go out of one's mind.

seno ['seno] *sm* bosom, breast; *(grembo)* womb; *(anat)* sinus; *(mat)* sine; *(geog)* inlet. **allattare al seno** breast-feed. **in seno a** *(nel mezzo di)* within; *(tra le braccia)* in the arms of.

sensale [sen'sale] *sm* broker.

sensato [sen'sato] *agg* sensible. **sensatezza** *sf* good sense.

sensazione [sensa'tsjone] *sf* feeling, sensation. **sensazionale** *agg* sensational.

sensibile [sen'sibile] *agg* *(che sente)* sensitive; *(notevole)* appreciable; perceptible; susceptible. **sensibilità** *sf* sensitivity. **sensibilizzare** *v* sensitize.

sensitivo [sensi'tivo] *agg* *(funzione)* sensory; *(sensibile)* sensitive. **sensitività** *sf* sensitivity.

senso ['senso] *sm* sense; *(significato)* meaning; *(direzione, modo)* way. **a senso** in one's own words; *(tradurre)* freely. **far senso** *(ripugnare)* disgust. **in senso antiorario** anticlockwise. **in senso orario** clockwise. **non aver senso** not make sense; be pointless. **senso proibito** no entry. **senso unico** one-way. **sensorio** *agg* sensory. **sensuale** *agg* sensual; sensuous. **sensualità** *sf* sensuality; sensuousness.

sentenza [sen'tentsa] *sf* sentence, judgment; *(massima)* saying. **sputare sentenze** be sententious. **sentenziare** *v*

pass judgment *or* sentence; rule; decree.

sentenzioso *agg* sententious.

sentiero [sen'tjero] *sm* path.

sentimento [senti'mento] *sm* feeling; *(concetto)* sense. **sentimenti** *sm pl (modo di sentire)* sentiments *pl*.

sentinella [senti'nella] *sf* sentry.

sentire [sen'tire] *v* feel; *(col gusto)* taste; *(con l'udito)* hear; *(con l'olfatto)* smell; *(dare ascolto)* listen to; *(aver notizia)* gather. **al mio modo di sentire** to my way of thinking. **sentirsela** *v* feel like. **sentirsi** *v* feel.

sentito [sen'tito] *agg* *(udito)* heard; sincere. **per sentito dire** by hearsay.

sentore [sen'tore] *sm* inkling.

senza ['sentsa] *prep* without. **rimanere senza** run out of. **senza contare** apart from; over and above. **senza dire** not to mention. **senza fallo** certainly. **senz'altro** definitely. **senza soldi** penniless. **senzatetto** *s(m+f)* *invar* homeless person.

separare [sepa'rare] *v* separate, divide. **separarsi** *v* part; *(coniugi)* separate. **separazione** *sf* separation, division; parting.

sepolcro [se'polkro] *sm* tomb. **sepolcrale** *agg* sepulchral.

sepolto [se'polto] *agg* buried. **sepoltura** *sf* burial.

*seppellire [seppel'lire] *v* bury.

seppia ['seppja] *sf* *(zool)* cuttlefish. *agg*, *sm invar* (colore) sepia.

seppure [sep'pure] *cong* even though, even if.

sequela [se'kwela] *sf* succession.

sequestrare [sekwes'trare] *v* seize, confiscate; *(persona)* imprison unlawfully; *(rapire)* kidnap. **sequestro** *sm* seizure, confiscation; kidnapping; illegal confinement.

sera ['sera] *sf* evening, night. **buona sera!** *(di pomeriggio)* good afternoon! *(di sera)* good evening! **si fa sera** it is getting dark. **serale** *agg* evening, night. **serata** *sf* evening, night; *(ricevimento)* party; *(teatro)* performance.

serbare [ser'bare] *v* *(mantenere)* keep; *(metter da parte)* put aside. **serbare gratitudine** verso be grateful to. **serbatoio** *sm* tank; *(penna)* barrel; *(fucile, ecc.)* magazine.

serbo ['serbo] *sm* **dare in serbo** put into

custody. **mettere in serbo** put by or aside. **tenere in serbo** keep in store.

serenata [sere'nata] sf serenade.

serenella [sere'nɛlla] sf lilac.

sereno [se'reno] agg calm, serene; (cielo) clear; (senza preoccupazioni) carefree; objective. sm clear sky; (aperto) open air. **serenità** sf serenity; objectivity.

sergente [serd'ʒɛnte] sm sergeant.

serico ['sɛriko] agg silk.

serie ['sɛrje] sf invar series; (assortimento) set; (sport) division. **fuori serie** (auto) custom-built. **modello di serie** sm production model. **prodotto in serie** massproduced. **produzione in serie** sf massproduction.

serio ['sɛrjo] agg serious; (degno di fiducia) trustworthy; (comm) reputable. sm seriousness. **sul serio** (seriamente) seriously; (davvero) really. **serietà** sf seriousness; (fidatezza) reliability.

sermone [ser'mone] sm sermon; (rimprovero) lecture.

serpeggiare [serped'dʒare] v wind.

serpente [ser'pɛnte] sm snake, serpent. **serpente a sonagli** rattlesnake. **serpentino** agg snake-like.

serra ['sɛrra] sf greenhouse, hothouse.

serraglio [ser'raʎo] sm menagerie.

serrare [ser'rare] v close; (a chiave) lock; (stringere) tighten; (denti, pugni) clench. **serrare al cuore** embrace. **serramento** sm (di finestra) window-frame; (di porta) door-frame. **serrata** sf lock-out. **serrato** agg closed; (fila) serried; (fig) to the point.

serratura [serra'tura] sf lock. **buco della serratura** sm keyhole. **serratura a cilindro** Yale lock ®. **serratura a lucchetto** padlock. **serratura a scatto** latch.

servire [ser'vire] v serve; (fam: occorrere) be useful; (carte da gioco) deal. **a cosa serve?** what is the use? **cosa ti serve?** what do you need? **posso servirti?** can I help you? **servirsi** v use; make use; (di cibo) help oneself. **servile** agg servile; (fig) slavish. **servitore** sm servant. **servitù** sf (schiavitù) slavery; (personale di servizio) servants pl. **ridurre in servitù** enslave.

servizio [ser'vitsjo] sm service; (lavoro) work; favour; (giornale) report; (turno) duty. **a mezzo servizio** part-time. **donna di servizio** sf maid. **fare servizio** (trasporto) run; (negozio) be open. **fuori servizio** off duty; (che non funziona) out of order. **in servizio** on duty. **servizievole** agg obliging.

servo ['sɛrvo], **-a** sm, sf servant.

sesamo ['sɛzamo] sm sesame.

sessanta [ses'santa] agg, sm sixty. **sessantesimo** agg, sm sixtieth.

sessione [ses'sjone] sf session.

sesso ['sɛsso] sm sex. **sessuale** agg sexual. **sessualità** sf sexuality.

sestetto [ses'tetto] sm sextet.

sesto[1] ['sɛsto] sm, agg sixth.

sesto[2] ['sɛsto] sm order; (di arco) curve. **mettere in sesto** tidy up. **rimettersi in sesto** get back on one's feet again.

seta ['seta] sf silk.

setaccio [se'tattʃo] sm sieve. **setacciare** v also passare al setaccio sift, sieve.

sete ['sete] sf thirst. **aver sete** be thirsty. **mettere la seta** make thirsty.

setola [setola] sf bristle.

setta ['sɛtta] sf sect. agg sm sectarian.

settanta [set'tanta] agg, sm seventy. **settantesimo** agg, sm seventieth.

sette ['sɛtte] agg, sm seven. **settimo** agg, sm seventh.

settembre [set'tɛmbre] sm September.

settentrione [setten'trjone] sm north. **settentrionale** agg northern, north.

settico ['sɛttiko] agg septic. **setticemia** sf blood-poisoning.

settimana [setti'mana] sf week; (paga) week's wages. **a metà settimana** midweek. **a settimane** by the week; (una sì e una no) every other week. **fine settimana** sf week-end. **settimanale** agg, sm weekly.

settore [set'tore] sm sector; (campo) field.

severo [se'vero] agg severe, strict; (grave) serious. **severità** sf severity.

seviziare [sevi'tsjare] v torture; (violentare) rape. **sevizie** sf pl torture sing.

sezione [se'tsjone] sf section; (tribunale) division; (sezionamento) dissection. **sezionare** v dissect; (dividere in sezioni) section.

sfaccendato [sfattʃen'dato], **-a** agg idle. sm, sf loafer.

sfaccettare [sfattʃet'tare] v cut.

sfacchinare [sfakki'nare] v slave. **sfacchinata** sf heavy work.

sfacciato [sfat'tʃato], **-a** agg impudent; (svergognato) shameless; (vistoso) gaudy. sm, sf impudent or shameless person.

sfacciataggine sf impudence; shamelessness.

sfacelo [sfa'tʃɛlo] sm ruin; (disfacimento) decay. andare in sfacelo break up; (fam) go to rack and ruin.

sfaldarsi [sfal'darsi] v flake; (sbriciolarsi) crumble. sfaldatura sf flaking; crumbling.

sfalsare [sfal'sare] v stagger.

sfamare [sfa'mare] v feed. sfamarsi v satisfy one's hunger.

sfarfallare [sfarfal'lare] v (svolazzare) flutter; (esser volubile) flit; (auto) wobble.

sfarzo [sfartso] sm magnificence, pomp. senza sfarzo simply. sfarzosità sf sumptuousness; ostentation. sfarzoso agg sumptuous; ostentatious.

sfasciare [sfa'ʃare] v (rompere) smash.

sfatare [sfa'tare] v refute.

sfavillante [sfavil'lante] agg glittering, sparkling.

sfavore [sfa'vore] sm disfavour, discredit. andare a sfavore di go against. sfavorevole agg unfavourable; (contrario) adverse.

sfegatato [sfega'tato] agg passionate.

sfera ['sfɛra] sf sphere; (ambiente) circle; (campo) field. cuscinetto a sfere sm ball-bearing. penna a sfera sf ball-point pen. sferico agg spherical.

sferrare [sfer'rare] v (attacco) launch; (pugno) deal. sferrare un calcio kick.

sferza ['sfɛrtsa] sf whip. sferzare v whip; lash.

sfiatato [sfja'tato] agg breathless; (strumento musicale) cracked; (fam) hoarse.

sfibrare [sfi'brare] v (indebolire) weaken. sfibrante agg enervating. sfibrato agg exhausted.

sfida ['sfida] sf challenge. sfidare v challenge; (invitare) defy; (fig) brave.

sfiducia [sfi'dutʃa] sf distrust. avere sfiducia di distrust; lack confidence in. sfiduciarsi v lose confidence. sfiduciato agg distrustful; (di sè stesso) diffident; (scoraggiato) disheartened.

sfigurare [sfigu'rare] v disfigure; make a bad impression.

sfilacciare [sfilat'tʃare] v fray.

sfilare [sfi'lare] v (togliere di dosso) take off; (ago) unthread.

sfilare² [sfi'lare] v parade. sfilata sf parade; (lunga fila) long row.

sfilza [sfiltsa] sf string.

sfinge [sfindʒe] sf sphinx.

sfinire [sfi'nire] v wear out. sfinimento sm exhaustion.

sfiorare [sfjo'rare] v skim (over); (toccando) graze, barely touch; (successo, ecc.) be on the verge of.

sfiorito [sfjo'rito] agg withered.

sfitto ['sfitto] agg vacant.

sfocato [sfo'kato] agg (foto) out of focus; (fig) hazy.

sfociare [sfo'tʃare] v flow (into); (fig) result. sfocio sm outlet.

sfogare [sfo'gare] v let out; (fig) give vent to. sfogarsi v (sfogar l'ira) give vent to one's anger; (confidarsi) pour out one's heart; (bambino) run wild. sfogo sm outlet; (sollievo) relief.

sfoggiare [sfod'dʒare] v show off. sfoggio sm display; ostentation.

sfogliare¹ [sfo'ʎare] v also dare una sfogliata a (pagine) leaf or skim through.

sfogliare² [sfo'ʎare] v (levar le foglie) strip (of leaves). sfoglia sf leaf; (gastr) puff pastry.

sfolgorare [sfolgo'rare] v blaze; (occhi) shine.

sfollare [sfol'lare] v disperse; evacuate. sfollamento sm evacuation. sfollato, -a sm, sf evacuee.

sfondare [sfon'dare] v break through; (schiantare) smash; (logorare) wear out. sfondato agg (senza fondo) bottomless; (logoro) worn out. ricco sfondato rolling in money. sfondo sm background, setting.

sformare [sfor'mare] v pull out of shape; (estrarre dalla forma) turn out. sformato sm (gastr) pie.

sfornito [sfor'nito] agg sfornito di lacking in, without.

sfortuna [sfor'tuna] sf bad luck; (contrattempo) misfortune. sfortunato agg unlucky; (senza successo) unfortunate.

sforzare [sfor'tsare] v force, strain. sforzarsi di try hard to. sforzo sm effort.

sfottere ['sfottere] v (fam) take the mickey (out of). sfottimento sm teasing, ridicule.

sfracellare [sfratʃel'lare] v shatter.

sfrangiato [sfran'dʒato] agg fringed.

sfrattare [sfrat'tare] v turn out, evict. sfratto sm eviction.

sfregare [sfre'gare] v rub; (lucidando) polish; (lavando) scrub. sfregamento sm rubbing; polishing; scrubbing.

sfrenare [sfre'nare] v let loose. sfrenatezza sf lack of restraint; wild behaviour. sfrenato agg unbridled; (senza ritegno) immoderate.

*sfriggere ['sfriddʒere] v also sfrigolare sizzle.

sfrondare [sfron'dare] v prune.

sfrontato [sfron'tato] agg impudent, brazen; (fam) cheeky. sfrontatezza sf effrontery; (fam) cheek.

sfruttare [sfrut'tare] v exploit. sfruttamento sm exploitation; utilization. sfruttatore, -trice sm, sf exploiter.

sfuggire [sfud'dʒire] v shun; (scappare) escape from. lasciarsi sfuggire let slip; (occasione) let go by. sfuggire di mano slip out of one's hand. sfuggire di mente slip one's mind. sfuggente agg (mento, fronte) receding. di sfuggita fleetingly.

sfumare [sfu'mare] v (svanire) disappear; (colori, suoni) fade away, tone down. sfumato agg (pittura) shaded; (fig) vague. sfumatura sf nuance.

sfuriata [sfu'rjata] sf outburst; (tempesta) storm; (rabbuffo) telling-off.

sfuso ['sfuzo] agg (sciolto) loose; (liquefatto) melted.

sgabello [zga'bɛllo] sm stool.

sgabuzzino [zgabut'tsino] sm cubby-hole.

sgambettare [zgambet'tare] v (camminare a piccoli passi) toddle (along); (fare lo sgambetto) trip up.

sganciare [zgan'tʃare] v unhook; (bombe) release; (fam: sborsare) fork out.

sgangherato [zgange'rato] agg (sfasciato) rickety; (sconnesso) incoherent; (esagerato) boisterous.

sgarbato [zgar'bato] agg rude, discourteous. sgarbatezza sf rudeness, discourtesy.

sgarbugliare [zgarbu'ʎare] v disentangle.

sgargiante [zgar'dʒante] agg showy.

sgarrare [zgar'rare] v be or go wrong.

sgelare [zdʒe'lare] v thaw out; (surgelati) defrost.

sghembo ['zgembo] agg crooked. di sghembo askew.

sgherro ['zgɛrro] sm thug.

sghignazzare [zgiɲat'tsare] v laugh sarcastically, sneer; (sguaiatamente) guffaw. sghignazzata sf sarcastic laughter; guffaw.

sghiribizzo [zgiri'bittso] sm whim.

sgobbare [zgob'bare] (fam) v slave. sgobbata sf grind. sgobbone, -a sm, sf slogger; (studente) swot.

sgocciolare [zgottʃo'lare] v drip; (vuotare) drain. sgocciolatura sf dripping; (macchie) drips pl. essere agli sgoccioli be or have nearly finished.

sgolarsi [zgo'larsi] v shout oneself hoarse.

sgombrare [zgom'brare] v also sgomberare clear; (vuotare) empty; (portar via) clear away; evacuate; (lasciar libero) vacate.

sgombro¹ ['zgombro] sm also sgombero (trasloco) move; clearing (away); evacuation. agg clear; empty.

sgombro² ['zgombro] V scombro.

sgomentare [zgomen'tare] v dismay. sgomento sm dismay.

sgonfiare [zgon'fjare] v deflate; (fam) annoy. sgonfiarsi v go down; (pneumatico) go flat; (fig) be deflated. sgonfio agg deflated, flat.

sgorbia ['zgɔrbja] sf gouge.

sgorbio ['zgɔrbjo] sm (macchia) blot; (scarabocchio) scrawl.

sgorgare [zgor'gare] v gush out); (uscire) spring.

sgradevole [zgra'devole] agg disagreeable, unpleasant. sgradito agg disagreeable; (non gradito) unwelcome.

sgrammaticato [zgrammati'kato] agg ungrammatical.

sgranare [zgra'nare] v shell; (occhi) open wide.

sgranchire [zgran'kire] v stretch.

sgravare [zgra'vare] v relieve; (partorire) give birth.

sgraziato [zgra'tsjato] agg ungainly, awkward.

sgretolare [zgreto'lare] v break up. sgretolarsi v crumble. sgretolato agg crumbling.

sgridare [zgri'dare] v scold; (fam) tell off. sgridata sf scolding; (fam) telling-off.

sguaiato [zgwa'jato] agg unseemly; vulgar; (grossolano) coarse. sguaiataggine sf vulgarity; coarseness.

sgualcire [zgwal'tʃire] v crease, crumple.

sgualdrina [zgwal'drina] sf (spreg) tart.

sguardo ['zgwardo] sm look; (occhiata) glance; (fisso) stare; (prolungato) gaze. al primo sguardo at first sight. fissare lo sguardo su stare at. gettare uno sguardo su glance at.

sguarnire [zgwar'nire] v strip.

sguattero ['zgwattero], -a sm, sf skivvy.

simpatia

sguazzare [zgwat'tsare] v splash about; (fig) wallow.

sguinzagliare [zgwintsa'ʎare] v let loose.

sgusciare¹ [zgu'ʃare] v (scivolare) slip.

sgusciare² [zgu'ʃare] v shell; (uova, noci) crack.

shampoo [ʃam'pu] sm invar shampoo.

si [si] pron (lui) himself; (lei) herself; (cosa, animale) itself; (loro) themselves; (reciproco) each other; (riflessivo) one-self; (indefinito) one.

sì [si] avv yes. **credo di sì** I think so. **dire di sì** say yes. **far cenno di sì** nod. **spero di sì** I hope so. **un giorno sì e uno no** every other day.

sia ['sia] cong **sia ... sia ...** whether ... or ... ; (entrambi) both.

siamese [sia'meze] agg, s(m+f) Siamese.

sibilare [sibi'lare] v hiss. **sibilo** sm hiss.

sicario [si'karjo] sm hired assassin.

sicché [sik'ke] cong (di modo che) and so; (e perciò) so that.

siccità [sittʃi'ta] sf drought.

siccome [sik'kome] cong as, since.

Sicilia [si'tʃilja] sf Sicily. **siciliano, -a** s, agg Sicilian.

sicomoro [siko'moro] sm sycamore.

sicura [si'kura] sf safety catch.

sicurezza [siku'rettsa] sf safety; certainty; (garanzia) security; (confidenza) self-assurance. **di sicurezza** safety. **per maggior sicurezza** to be on the safe side. **pubblica sicurezza** police. **sicurezza sociale** social security; welfare.

sicuro [si'kuro] agg safe; (tranquillo) secure; certain, sure; (fidato) reliable; (saldo) steady. sm safety; safe place. **andar sul sicuro** take no chances. **dare per sicuro** be certain about. **di sicuro** certainly. **star sicuro** not worry.

sidro ['sidro] sm cider.

siepe ['sjɛpe] sf hedge.

siero ['sjɛro] sm serum.

siesta ['sjɛsta] sf siesta; (fam) nap. **fare la siesta** take a nap.

sifilide [si'filide] sf syphilis.

sifone [si'fone] sm siphon.

sigaretta [siga'retta] sf cigarette. **sigaro** sm cigar.

sigillare [sidʒil'lare] v seal. **sigillatura** sf sealing, seal. **sigillo** sm seal. **anello con sigillo** sm signet-ring.

sigla ['sigla] sf initials pl; (auto) registration number. **sigla musicale** signature tune. **siglare** v initial.

significare [siɲifi'kare] v mean; (simboleggiare) stand for. **significativo** agg meaningful, significant; important. **significato** sm meaning; importance.

signora [si'ɲora] sf lady; (donna) woman (pl women); (cortesia) madam; (seguito dal cognome) Mrs; (padrona) mistress; (moglie) wife. **fare la signora** live like a lady.

signore [si'ɲore] sm gentleman; (uomo) man (pl men); (cortesia) sir; (seguito dal cognome) Mr; (padrone) master.

signoreggiare [siɲored'dʒare] v rule.

signoria [siɲo'ria] sf domination.

signorile [siɲo'rile] agg elegant, high-class; (uomo) gentlemanly; (donna) lady-like. **signorilità** sf elegance; refinement.

signorina [siɲo'rina] sf young lady or woman; (cortesia) madam; (seguito dal cognome) Miss; (non sposata) unmarried woman. **nome da signorina** sm maiden name.

silenzio [si'lɛntsjo] sm silence. **far silenzio** be quiet. **silenziare** v muffle. **silenziatore** sm silencer. **silenzioso** agg silent, quiet.

silicio [si'litʃo] sm silicon. **silice** sf silica. **silicone** sm silicone. **silicosi** sf silicosis.

sillaba ['sillaba] sf syllable. **sillabare** v (gramm) syllabify; (fig) spell out. **sillabario** sm spelling book.

silo ['silo] sm silo.

silofono [si'lɔfono] sm xylophone.

silurare [silu'rare] v torpedo; (far fallire) wreck; (destituire) dismiss. **siluramento** sm torpedoing; wrecking; dismissal. **siluro** sm torpedo.

silvestre [sil'vɛstre] agg woody; (selvaggio) wild.

silvia ['silvja] sf (bot) wood anemone; (zool) warbler.

simbolo ['simbolo] sm symbol; (rel) creed. **simboleggiare** v symbolize. **simbolico** agg symbolic.

simile ['simile] agg like, similar; (predicato) alike; (tale) such. **similitudine** sf simile.

simmetria [simme'tria] sf symmetry. **simmetrico** agg symmetrical.

simpatia [simpa'tia] sf (sentimento di attrazione) liking; (qualità) likeableness; (affinità) sympathy. **avere** or **provare simpatia per** like, take to. **simpatico** agg nice, likeable; (piacevole) agreeable; (anat) sympathetic. **simpatizzare** v sympathize.

simposio [sim'pozjo] *sm* symposium.

simulare [simu'lare] *v* feign; (*imitare*) simulate. **simulacro** *sm* image; (*fig*) semblance. **simulazione** *sf* simulation.

simultaneo [simul'taneo] *agg* simultaneous. **simultaneità** *sf* simultaneity.

sinagoga [sina'gɔga] *sf* synagogue.

sincero [sin'tʃero] *agg* sincere, true; (*non artefatto*) genuine. **sincerità** *sf* sincerity.

sincopare [sinko'pare] *v* syncopate. **sincope** *sf* syncope; (*musica*) syncopation.

sincronizzare [sinkronid'dzare] *v* synchronize. **sincronizzatore** *sm* synchronizer. **sincronizzazione** *sf* synchronization.

sindacale [sinda'kale] *agg* (*di sindacato*) (trade) union. **sindacalismo** *sm* trade unionism. **sindacalista** *s(m+f)* trade unionist.

sindacare [sinda'kare] *v* check; (*contabilità*) audit; (*fig*) criticize.

sindacato [sinda'kato] *sm* (*operaio*) trade union; (*padronale*, *d'impresa*) consortium; (*finanziario*) syndicate.

sindaco ['sindako] *sm* mayor; (*comm*) auditor.

sindrome ['sindrome] *sf* syndrome.

sinfonia [sinfo'nia] *sf* symphony. **sinfonico** *agg* symphonic. **orchestra sinfonica** *sf* symphony orchestra.

singhiozzare [singjot'tsare] *v* (*avere il singhiozzo*) hiccup; (*piangere*) sob. **singhiozzo** *sm* sob; hiccup. **a singhiozzi** by fits and starts.

singolare [singo'lare] *agg* singular; (*strano*) strange. *sm* singular. **singolarità** *sf* singularity; strangeness.

singolo ['singolo] *agg* single, individual. *sm* (*persona*) individual; (*telefono*) private line; (*tennis*) singles; (*canottaggio*) skiff.

sinistra [si'nistra] *sf* left(-hand side); (*mano*) left hand. **a sinistra** on *or* to the left. **tenere la sinistra** keep to the left. **uomo di sinistra** *sm* left-winger.

sinistrare [sinis'trare] *v* damage. **sinistrato, -a** *sm*, *sf* victim. **zona sinistrata** *sf* disaster area.

sinistro [si'nistro] *agg* left; (*lato*) left-hand; (*fig*) sinister. *sm* accident; (*pugilato*) left.

sino ['sino] *cong* **sino a** (*tempo*) until; (*luogo*) as far as. *avv* (*persino*) even. **sinora** *avv* (*per ora*) so far; (*fino ad ora*) up to now.

sinossi [si'nɔssi] *sf* synopsis (*pl* -ses). **sinottico** *agg* synoptic.

sintassi [sin'tassi] *sf* syntax. **sintattico** *agg* syntactic(al).

sintesi ['sintezi] *sf* synthesis (*pl* -ses). **in sintesi** (*in poche parole*) in short; (*sommariamente*) summing up. **sintetico** *agg* synthetic; (*fig*) concise. **sintetizzare** *v* synthesize; (*riassumere*) summarize.

sintomo ['sintomo] *sm* symptom. **sintomatico** *agg* symptomatic.

sintonizzare [sintonid'dzare] *v* tune in.

sinuoso [sinu'ozo] *agg* sinuous, winding.

sinusite [sinu'zite] *sf* sinusitis.

sipario [si'parjo] *sm* curtain.

sirena [si'rena] *sf* siren; (*creatura*) mermaid.

siringa [si'ringa] *sf* syringe; (*bot*) lilac; catheter. **siringare** *v* syringe; catheterize.

sismico ['sizmiko] *agg* seismic. **sismografo** *sm* seismograph.

sistema [sis'tɛma] *sm* system; (*modo di fare*) way; method. **sistemare** *v* (*mettere a posto*) arrange; (*put in*) order; (*risolvere*) settle; organize; (*collocare*) place; install. **sistemarsi** *v* settle (down); (*lavoro*) get a job. **sistematico** *agg* systematic; methodical. **sistemazione** *sf* arrangement; (*composizione*) settlement; (*alloggio*) accommodation; (*lavoro*) job.

situare [situ'are] *v* place; (*collocare*) locate. **situazione** *sf* situation. **situazione di fatto** state of affairs.

slabbrare [zlab'brare] *v* (*vasellame*) chip; (*tessuto*) tear.

slacciare [zlat'tʃare] *v* undo, untie.

slanciare [zlan'tʃare] *v* hurl. **slanciato** *agg* slender, slim. **slancio** *sm* swing; (*di passione, ecc.*) burst. **di slancio** in a rush; (*fig*) on impulse.

slattare [zlat'tare] *v* wean.

slavato [zla'vato] *agg* washed out; (*fig*) dull.

sleale [zle'ale] *agg* disloyal; (*fatto senza lealtà*) unfair. **gioco sleale** *sm* foul play. **slealtà** *sf* disloyalty; unfairness.

slegare [zle'gare] *v* untie. **slegato** *agg* untied; (*non rilegato*) unbound; (*fig*) disjointed.

slip [zlip] *sm invar* (*mutande*) briefs *pl*; (*da bagno*) swimming trunks *pl*.

slitta ['zlitta] *sf* sleigh, sledge; (*tec*) slide. **slittare** *v* slip; (*ruote*) skid; (*scivolare*) slide.

slogan ['zlɔgan] *sm invar* slogan.
slogare [zlo'gare] *v* dislocate. **slogatura** *sf* dislocation.
sloggiare [zlod'dʒare] *v* dislodge.
smacchiare [zmak'kjare] *v* clean. **smacchiatore** *sm* stain-remover. **smacchiatura** *sf* cleaning.
smacco ['zmakko] *sm* defeat.
smagliante [zma'ʎante] *agg* dazzling.
smagliarsi [zma'ʎarsi] *v* (*calze*) ladder; (*pelle*) stretch.
smagrire [zma'grire] *v* slim.
smaltare [zmal'tare] *v* enamel; (*unghie*) paint; (*ceramica*) glaze. **smalto** *sm* enamel; (*per le unghie*) nail-varnish.
smaltire [zmal'tire] *v* digest; (*fig*) swallow; (*comm*) dispose of.
smanceroso [zmantʃe'rozo] *agg* affected; (*smorfioso*) mawkish. **smanceria** *sf* affectation.
smania ['zmanja] *sf* craving; (*agitazione*) frenzy. **aver la smania addosso** fidget. **smaniare** *v* (*essere agitato*) fret; (*essere furioso*) rave; (*desiderare*) crave (for).
smantellare [zmantel'lare] *v* dismantle; (*fig*) pull to pieces.
smargiassata [zmardʒas'sata] *sf* brag; bravado. **smargiasso, -a** *sm, sf* braggart. **fare lo smargiasso** brag.
smarrire [zmar'rire] *v* lose; (*non riuscire a trovare*) mislay. **smarrirsi** *v* (*persone*) lose one's way; (*cose*) be mislaid, go astray. **smarrimento** *sm* loss; (*svenimento*) fainting-fit; (*turbamento*) bewilderment.
smascherare [zmaske'rare] *v* unmask, reveal. **smascheramento** *sm* unmasking.
smembrare [zmem'brare] *v* dismember.
smemorato [zmemo'rato], **-a** *agg* forgetful; (*distratto*) absent-minded. *sm, sf* forgetful *or* absent-minded person. **smemorataggine** *sf* forgetfulness; (*dimenticanza*) lapse of memory. **smemoratezza** *sf* forgetfulness; absent-mindedness.
smentire [zmen'tire] *v* deny; (*ritrattare*) retract; (*dimostrare la falsità*) belie. **smentita** *sf* denial.
smeraldo [zme'raldo] *sm* emerald. *agg invar* (*colore*) emerald-green.
smerciare [zmer'tʃare] *v* sell. **smercio** *sf* sale.
smerigliare [zmeri'ʎare] *v* (*mec*) grind; (*vetro*) frost. **carta smerigliata** *sf* (*grossa*) emery paper; (*fine*) sandpaper. **vetro smerigliato** *sm* frosted glass. **smeriglio** *sm* emery.

smerlare [zmer'lare] *v* scallop. **smerlo** *sm* scallop.
*smettere ['zmettere] *v* stop.
smidollato [zmidol'lato] *agg* spineless.
smilitarizzare [zmilitarid'dzare] *v* demilitarize. **smilitarizzazione** *sf* demilitarization.
smilzo ['zmiltso] *agg* lean.
sminuire [zminu'ire] *v* diminish; (*fig*) belittle.
sminuzzare [zminut'tsare] *v* break into small pieces; (*sbriciolare*) crumble.
smistare [zmis'tare] *v* sort (out); (*ferr*) shunt.
smisurato [zmizu'rato] *agg* boundless; enormous.
smobilitare [zmobili'tare] *v* demobilize. **smobilitazione** *sf* demobilization.
smoderato [zmode'rato] *agg also* **smodato** immoderate. **smoderatezza** *sf* lack of moderation; excess.
smoking ['zmɔkiŋ] *sm invar* dinner-jacket.
smontare [zmon'tare] *v* (*scomporre*) dismantle, take apart; (*totalmente*) strip; (*da veicoli*) get out *or* off. **smontaggio** *sm* dismantling; stripping.
smorfia ['zmɔrfja] *sf* wry face. **fare una smorfia** pull a face; (*di dolore*) wince with pain. **smorfioso** *agg* simpering.
smorto ['zmɔrto] *agg* pale, wan; (*fig*) colourless.
smorzare [zmor'tsare] *v* (*colori*) tone down; (*suoni*) muffle; (*luce*) dim; (*fig*) dampen. **smorzata** *sf* (*tennis*) drop-shot.
smunto ['zmunto] *agg* emaciated.
*smuovere ['zmwɔvere] *v* shift; (*commuovere*) touch; dissuade.
smussare [zmus'sare] *v* smooth; (*angolo*) round off; (*fig*) soften. **smussarsi** *v* become blunt.
snaturare [znatu'rare] *v* distort. **snaturato** *agg* unnatural; degenerate.
snazionalizzare [znatsjonalid'dzare] *v* denationalize. **snazionalizzazione** *sf* denationalization.
snellire [znel'lire] *v* slim (down); simplify; speed up. **snellezza** *sf* slimness. **snello** *agg* slim; (*agile*) nimble; simple, easy.
snervare [zner'vare] *v* exhaust.
snidare [zni'dare] *v* drive out.
snob [znɔb] *agg*, *s(m+f)* *invar* snob. **snobbare** *v* snub. **snobismo** *sm* snobbery.
snocciolare [znottʃo'lare] *v* stone; (*fam: spendere*) shell out; (*fam: spiattellare*) rattle off.

snodare [zno'dare] v unknot; (articolare meglio) loosen (up); (piegare) bend. snodabile agg (tec) articulated. snodato agg flexible, loose.

soave [so'ave] agg delicate, sweet. soavità sf sweetness, delicacy.

sobbalzare [sobbal'tsare] v jolt; (trasalire) jump. di sobbalzo with a start.

sobbarcarsi [sobbar'karsi] v undertake.

sobbollire [sobbol'lire] v simmer.

sobborgo [sob'borgo] sm suburb.

sobillare [sobil'lare] v incite, stir up. sobillatore, -trice sm, sf trouble-maker.

sobrio ['sɔbrjo] agg sober. sobrietà sf sobriety.

*socchiudere [sok'kjudere] v half-close. socchiuso agg half-closed; (porta) ajar.

soccombere [sok'kombere] v succumb.

*soccorrere [sok'korrere] v assist; come to the aid of; (salvare) rescue.

soccorritore [sokkorri'tore], -trice agg helping. sm, sf helper.

soccorso [sok'korso] sm help, assistance; rescue. pronto soccorso first aid; (all'ospedale) casualty ward. soccorsi sm pl (rinforzi) reinforcements pl; (rifornimenti) supplies pl.

socialdemocratico [sotʃaldemo'kratiko], -a sm, sf social democrat. socialdemocrazia sf social democracy.

sociale [so'tʃale] agg social; (benessere) welfare; (comm) relating to a firm, company. assistente sociale s(m+f) welfare officer, social worker. assistenza sociale sf welfare. tessera sociale sf membership card.

socialismo [sotʃa'lizmo] sm socialism. socialista agg, s(m+f) socialist.

società [sotʃe'ta] sf society; (comm) company, partnership; association. gioco di società sm parlour game. mettersi in società go into partnership. società anonima limited company. società dei consumi consumer society. società per azioni limited company.

socievole [so'tʃevole] agg social; (persona) sociable. socievolezza sf sociability.

socio ['sɔtʃo], -a sm, sf partner; member.

sociologia [sotʃolo'dʒia] sf sociology. sociologico agg sociological. sociologo, -a sm, sf sociologist.

soda ['sɔda] sf soda.

sodalizio [soda'litsjo] sm brotherhood; (amicizia) fellowship.

*soddisfare [soddis'fare] v satisfy; (appagare) gratify; (riparare) make amends for. soddisfacente agg satisfactory; satisfying. soddisfatto agg satisfied; (contento) pleased. soddisfazione sf satisfaction. bella satisfazione! big deal!

sodio ['sɔdjo] sm sodium.

sodo ['sɔdo] agg firm; (fig) sound. uovo sodo sm hard-boiled egg. avv hard; (profondamente) soundly.

sofà [so'fa] sm sofa, settee.

sofferente [soffe'rɛnte] agg suffering. sofferenza sf suffering.

soffermarsi [soffer'marsi] v linger (over).

soffiare [sof'fjare] v blow; (sbuffare) puff; (dama, scacchi) huff. soffiare di rabbia fume (with rage). soffio sm puff; (med) murmur. in un soffio in a flash. per un soffio by a whisker.

soffice ['soffitʃe] agg soft.

soffietto [sof'fjetto] sm bellows pl; (fam: articoletto) plug. a soffietto folding. lavorar di soffietto (fam) tell tales.

soffitta [sof'fitta] sf attic.

soffitto [sof'fitto] sm ceiling.

soffocare [soffo'kare] v suffocate, choke; (reprimere) suppress, stifle. soffocamento sm suffocation.

*soffriggere [sof'friddʒere] v brown.

*soffrire [sof'frire] v suffer (from); (sopportare) bear, stand; (consentire) allow. soffrire la fame go hungry. soffrir di (mal di) cuore have heart trouble.

sofisma [so'fizma] sm sophistry. sofisticare v (sottilizzare) quibble; (fam) split hairs; (adulterare) doctor.

soggetto [sod'dʒetto] sm subject; (argomento) topic; person. recitare a soggetto improvise. agg subject, liable; (sottomesso) subjected; (predisposto) prone. soggettivo agg subjective. soggezione sf subjection; embarrassment; (timore) awe. aver soggezione di (sentirsi imbarazzato) feel uneasy in the presence of; (averne timore) be overawed by. ispirare soggezione a make uneasy; overawe.

sogghignare [soggi'nare] v sneer.

*soggiacere [soddʒa'tʃere] v be subjected; succumb.

soggiorno [sod'dʒorno] sm stay; (luogo) resort; (stanza) living room. permesso di soggiorno sm residence permit. soggiornare v stay.

*soggiungere [sod'dʒundʒere] v add.

soglia ['sɔʎa] sf threshold.

sogliola ['sɔʎola] sf sole.

sognare [so'nare] v dream; (ad occhi aperti) daydream. **sognatore, -trice** sm, sf dreamer. **sogno** sm dream. **fare un sogno** have a dream. **neanche per sogno!** not likely!

soia ['sɔja] sf soya (bean).

solaio [so'lajo] sm (soffitta) loft; (piano di edificio) floor.

solare [so'lare] agg solar. **luce solare** sf sunlight.

solco ['sɔlko] sm (agric) furrow; (traccia) track; (lampo) streak; (disco) groove.

soldato [sol'dato] sm soldier. **andare soldato** join up. **fare il soldato** be in the army.

soldo ['sɔldo] sm penny. **soldi** sm pl (denaro) money sing. **essere al soldo di** be in the pay of. **essere senza soldi** be penniless.

sole ['sole] sm sun. **al sole** in the sun. **chiaro come il sole** clear as daylight. **fare un bagno di sole** sunbathe. **occhiali da sole** sm pl sun-glasses pl. **soleggiato** agg sunny.

solenne [so'lɛnne] agg solemn; (fig) tremendous. **solennità** sf solemnity; (festa) holiday. **solennizzare** v solemnize.

*solere [so'lere] v be in the habit of.

soletta [so'letta] sf sole; (suola interna) insole.

solfato [sol'fato] sm sulphate. **solforico** agg sulphuric. **solfuro** sm sulphide.

solidale [soli'dale] agg (tec) integral; (d'accordo) in agreement (with); (dir) joint. **solidarietà** sf solidarity.

solidificare [solidifi'kare] v harden. **solidificarsi** v set. **solidificazione** sf hardening; setting.

solido ['sɔlido] agg solid; stable; (robusto, valido) sound; (colori) fast. sm solid. **solidità** sf solidity; stability; soundness; fastness.

soliloquio [soli'lɔkwjo] sm soliloquy.

solista [so'lista] s(m+f) soloist.

solitario [soli'tarjo], **-a** agg solitary. sm, sf loner. sm (brillante, gioco) solitaire.

solito ['sɔlito], **-a** agg usual. pron same. sm (abitudine) habit; (cosa) usual. **come al solito** as usual. **di solito** usually, as a rule. **essere solito a fare** be used to doing.

solitudine [soli'tudine] sf solitude.

sollazzare [sollat'tsare] v amuse.

sollecitare [solletʃi'tare] v press for; (affrettare) speed up; (mec) stress; (chiedere con insistenza) solicit. **sollecitazione** sf solicitation, entreaty; (mec) stress. **lettera di sollecitazione** sf reminder.

sollecito [sol'letʃito] agg (fatto con premura) prompt; (premuroso) solicitous. **sollecitudine** sm (prontezza) dispatch; (preoccupazione) solicitude.

solleticare [solleti'kare] v tickle; (fig) arouse. **solletico** sm tickle. **fare il solletico** tickle. **sentire or soffrire il solletico** be ticklish.

sollevare [solle'vare] v raise; (tirar su) lift (up). **sollevarsi** v rise; (riprendersi) recover.

sollievo [sol'ljɛvo] sm relief.

solo ['solo] agg alone; by oneself; (unico) only, sole; (semplice) mere; (musica) unaccompanied. avv (soltanto) only; (ma) but. **da solo** alone, by oneself. **solo che** only. **solo soletto** quite alone. **una sola volta** once only. **un solo** just one, only one.

solstizio [sol'stitsjo] sm solstice.

soltanto [sol'tanto] avv only.

solubile [so'lubile] agg soluble. **solubilità** sf solubility. **soluzione** sf solution.

solvente [sol'vɛnte] agg, sm solvent. **solvibile** agg (comm) solvent. **solvibilità** sm (comm) solvency.

soma ['soma] sf burden.

somaro [so'maro] sm donkey.

somigliare [somi'ʎare] v resemble, be like. **somigliante** agg similar. **somiglianza** sf resemblance.

somma ['somma] sf sum. **fare la somma** add up. **tirare le somme** sum up. **sommare** v add or sum up. **tutto sommato** all things considered.

sommario [som'marjo] agg brief; (dir) summary. sm summary, outline.

*sommergere [som'mɛrdʒere] v submerge. **sommergibile** sm submarine.

sommesso [som'messo] agg meek.

somministrare [somminis'trare] v administer.

sommità [sommi'ta] sf peak, summit.

sommo ['sommo] agg highest; (fig) supreme. sm peak.

sommossa [som'mɔssa] sf riot.

sommozzatore [sommottsa'tore] sm skindiver; (mil) frogman.

sonaglio [so'naʎo] *sm* bell. **serpente a sonagli** *sm* rattlesnake.

sonare [so'nare] *v also* **suonare** sound; (*campanello*) ring; (*musica*) play; (*orologio*) strike; (*fam: imbrogliare*) cheat.

sonata *sf* (*musica*) sonata; (*fam: bastonatura*) caning; (*fam: fregatura*) swindle. **prendersi una sonata** be taken in.

sonato *agg* (*compiuto*) past; (*rimbambito*) gaga.

sonda ['sonda] *sf* probe. **sondaggio** *sm* probing, sounding; (*indagine*) poll. **sondare** *v* sound, probe.

sonnambulo [son'nambulo], **-a** *sm, sf* sleep-walker.

sonnecchiare [sonnek'kjare] *v* doze.

sonnifero [son'nifero] *agg* soporific. *sm* sleeping pill.

sonno ['sonno] *sm* sleep; (*senso di torpore*) drowsiness. **aver sonno** be sleepy. **fare un bel sonno** have a good sleep. **sonnolento** *agg* sleepy, drowsy. **sonnolenza** *sf* drowsiness.

sonoro [so'nɔro] *agg* sound; (*che risona*) resonant; (*consonanti*) voiced. **sonorità** *sf* resonance; (*fis*) acoustics *pl*.

sontuoso [sontu'ozo] *agg* sumptuous. **sontuosità** *sf* sumptuousness.

soporifero [sopo'rifero] *agg, sm* soporific.

sopperire [soppe'rire] *v* provide for.

soppesare [soppe'zare] *v* weigh up.

soppiantare [soppjan'tare] *v* supplant.

soppiatto [sop'pjatto] *agg* **di soppiatto** stealthily. **entrare/uscire di soppiatto** steal in/away.

sopportare [soppor'tare] *v* (*reggere*) support; (*fig*) bear, stand. **sopportabile** *agg* bearable. **sopportazione** *sf* endurance.

****sopprimere** [sop'primere] *v* suppress; abolish. **soppressione** *sf* suppression; abolition.

sopra ['sopra] *prep* on, upon; (*senza contatto diretto*) over, above. **al di sopra di** above; (*oltre*) beyond. *avv* on; (*più in su*) above; (*al piano superiore*) upstairs. **come/vedi sopra** (*nei rinvii*) as/see above.

soprabito [so'prabito] *sm* overcoat.

sopracciglio [soprat'tʃiʎo] *sm* eyebrow.

sopraccitato [soprattʃi'tato] *agg* above-mentioned.

sopraccoperta [soprakko'perta] *sf* (*letto*) counterpane; (*libro*) dust-jacket.

****sopraffare** [sopraf'fare] *v* overcome; dominate.

sopraffino [sopraf'fino] *agg* excellent; highly refined.

sopraggiungere [soprad'dʒundʒere] *v* turn up; (*accadere improvvisamente*) happen, arise.

sopralluogo [sopral'lwɔgo] *sm, pl* **-ghi** (*on the spot*) inspection; (*statistica*) poll.

sopralzo [so'praltso] *sm* extension.

soprammobile [sopram'mɔbile] *sm* knick-knack.

soprannaturale [soprannatu'rale] *agg, sm* supernatural.

soprannome [sopran'nome] *sm* nickname. **soprannominare** *v* call.

soprannumero [sopran'numero] *sm* excess.

soprano [so'prano], **-a** *sm, sf* soprano.

soprappensiero [soprappen'sjero] *avv* lost in thought.

soprappiù [soprap'pju] *sm* surplus; (*aggiunta*) addition. **di o per soprappiù** in addition, besides.

soprapprezzo [soprap'prettso] *sm* (*econ*) premium; (*maggiorazione*) increase in price.

soprassalto [sopras'salto] *sm* sudden start. **di soprassalto** suddenly.

soprassedere [soprasse'dere] *v* put off.

soprattassa [soprat'tassa] *sf* additional charge.

soprattutto [soprat'tutto] *avv* above all; (*per la maggior parte*) mainly.

sopravanzare [sopravan'tsare] *v* be left over.

sopravvalutare [sopravvalu'tare] *v* overrate. **sopravvalutazione** *sf* overestimate.

sopravvenire [sopravve'nire] *v* turn up; (*accadere all'improvviso*) happen, arise.

sopravvento [soprav'vɛnto] *agg, avv* windward. *sm* (*fig*) upper hand.

****sopravvivere** [soprav'vivere] *v* survive. **sopravvissuto**, **-a** *sm, sf* survivor. **sopravvivenza** *sf* survival.

soprelevare [soprele'vare] *v* raise.

****soprintendere** [soprin'tendere] *v* supervise; be in charge of. **soprintendente** *s(m + f)* superintendent. **soprintendenza** *sf* (*atto*) supervision; (*ufficio*) superintendence.

sopruso [so'pruzo] *sm* outrage.

soqquadro [sok'kwadro] *sm* **mettere a soqquadro** turn upside down.

sorbetto [sor'betto] *sm* sorbet, water ice.

sorbire [sor'bire] *v* sip. **sorbirsi** *v* (*sopportare*) put up with.

sorcio [sortʃo] *sm* mouse (*pl* mice).

sordido ['sordido] *agg* sordid. **sordidezza** *sf* sordidness.

sordina [sor'dina] *sf* (*musica*) mute. **in sordina** (*fig*) on the quiet.

sordo ['sordo], **-a** *agg* deaf; (*smorzato*) dull; (*fig*) hidden. **sordo come una campana** deaf as a post. *sm, sf* deaf person. **fare il sordo** feign deafness. **sordità** *sf* deafness.

sordomuto [sordo'muto], **-a** *agg* deaf and dumb. *sm, sf* deaf-mute.

sorella [so'rella] *sf* sister. **sorellastra** *sf* step-sister, half-sister.

*sorgere [sor'dʒere] *v* rise; (*aver origine*) arise. **sorgente** *sf* source. **acqua sorgiva** *sf* spring water.

soriano [so'rjano] *sm, agg* tabby.

sormontare [sormon'tare] *v* surmount; (*stoffa*) overlap.

sornione [sor'njone] *agg* sly.

sorpassare [sorpas'sare] *v* (*oltrepassare*) overtake; (*eccedere*) exceed. **sorpassare in altezza/lunghezza** be higher/longer. **sorpassato** *agg* (*non più attuale*) out of date. **sorpasso** *sm* overtaking. **divieto di sorpasso** *sm* no overtaking.

*sorprendere [sor'prɛndere] *v* surprise; (*cogliere all'improvviso*) catch. **sorprendente** *agg* surprising. **sorpresa** *sf* surprise.

*sorreggere [sor'rɛddʒere] *v* hold up; sustain. **sorreggersi** *v* stand upright.

*sorridere [sor'ridere] *v* smile; (*destar piacere*) appeal. **sorridente** *agg* smiling. **sorriso** *sm* smile.

sorso ['sorso] *sm* (*sorsata*) sip; (*d'un fiato*) gulp; (*piccola quantità*) drop. **sorseggiare** *v* also **bere a piccoli sorsi** sip.

sorta ['sorta] *sf* kind, sort. **di sorta** (*di nessun tipo*) whatever.

sorte ['sorte] *sf* fate; fortune; (*condizione propria*) lot. **sorteggiare** *v* also **tirare a sorte** draw lots. **sorteggio** *sm* draw.

sortilegio [sorti'ledʒo] *sm* spell.

sorvegliare [sorve'ʎare] *v* watch; (*sovrintendere*) oversee; (*vigilare*) keep an eye on. **sorvegliante** *s(m+f)* overseer; (*custode*) caretaker; (*guardiano*) watchman. **sorveglianza** *sf* surveillance, watch.

sorvolare [sorvo'lare] *v* fly over; (*fig*) skip.

sosia ['sɔzja] *sm invar* double.

*sospendere [sos'pɛndere] *v* suspend; (*attaccare in alto*) hang; interrupt; (*seduta*) adjourn; defer. **sospendere il lavoro** stop work. **sospensione** *sf* suspension; interruption; (*cessazione*) stoppage. **sospeso** *agg* hanging; (*non definito*) outstanding. **col fiato sospeso** with bated breath. **in sospeso** in suspense; (*non risolto*) pending.

sospettare [sospet'tare] *v* suspect; (*diffidare*) distrust, be suspicious (of). **sospetto** [sos'pɛtto] *agg* suspect, suspicious. **persona sospetta** *sf* suspect. *sm* suspicion. **sospettoso** *agg* distrustful.

*sospingere [sos'pindʒere] *v* push; (*fig*) drive. **a ogni piè sospinto** at every step.

sospirare [sospi'rare] *v* sigh; (*aspettare con ansia*) long *or* yearn for. **sospiro** *sm* sigh.

sosta ['sɔsta] *sf* stop; pause; (*riposo*) rest; (*aspettare*) wait. **divieto di sosta** no waiting. **senza sosta** ceaselessly; without stopping. **sostare** *v* stop; pause; wait; rest.

sostantivo [sostan'tivo] *agg* substantive. *sm* noun.

sostanza [sos'tantsa] *sf* matter; (*parte utile*) substance; (*parte nutritiva*) nourishment; (*patrimonio*) property. **cibo di sostanza** nourishing food. **in sostanza** essentially. **sostanza alimentare** foodstuff. **sostanziale** *agg* substantial; essential. **sostanzioso** *agg* nourishing.

sostegno [sos'teɲo] *sm* support.

*sostenere [soste'nere] *v* support; (*asserire*) maintain; (*tenere alto*) keep up; (*tollerare*) stand. **sostenere una carica** hold an office. **sostenere una parte** act a part. **sostenersi** *v* (*star su*) hold oneself up, stand up; (*fig*) hold water. **sostenibile** *agg* tenable.

sostenitore [sosteni'tore], **-trice** *agg* supporting. *sm, sf* supporter.

*sostentare [sosten'tare] *v* support; maintain. **sostentamento** *sm* support; maintenance.

sostenuto [soste'nuto] *agg* (*contegnoso*) reserved; (*musica*) sostenuto. **sostenutezza** *sf* reserve.

sostituire [sostitu'ire] *v* substitute; (*rimpiazzare*) replace. **sostituto**, **-a** *sm, sf* deputy, substitute. **sostituzione** *sf* substitution; replacement.

sottaceto [sotta'tʃeto] avv **mettere sottaceto** pickle. **sottaceti** sm pl pickles pl.

sottalimentazione [sottalimenta'tsjone] sf undernourishment.

sottana [sot'tana] sf skirt; (sottoveste) slip, underskirt; (rel) cassock.

sottecchi [sot'tekki] avv **di sottecchi** stealthily.

sottentrare [sotten'trare] v replace.

sotterfugio [sotter'fudʒo] sm subterfuge.

sotterraneo [sotter'raneo] agg underground. sm basement. **sotterranea** sf underground (railway); (fam) tube.

sotterrare [sotter'rare] v bury. **sotterra** avv underground.

sottile [sot'tile] agg thin; fine; (acuto) sharp. **sottigliezza** sf thinness; sharpness; (sofisticheria) nicety.

sottinsù [sottin'su] avv **di sottinsù** from below.

*__sottintendere__ [sottin'tɛndere] v imply, infer; (non esprimere) leave out. **sottinteso** agg implied; (chiaro da sè) understood. sm allusion. **senza sottintesi** plainly.

sotto ['sotto] prep under; (al di sotto di) below, beneath; (in cambio di) on. avv underneath, below; (al piano di sotto) downstairs. **andar sotto le armi** join up. **metter sotto** (investire) run down. **mettersi sotto** get down to. **sotto la pioggia** in the rain. **sotto questo punto di vista** from this point of view. **sotto questo riguardo** in this respect. **sotto sotto** deep down.

sottobanco [sotto'banko] avv under the counter.

sottobicchiere [sottobik'kjɛre] sm mat, coaster.

sottobraccio [sotto'brattʃo] avv arm-in-arm. **prendere sottobraccio qualcuno** take someone's arm.

sottocchio [sot'tɔkkjo] avv **tenere sottocchio** keep an eye on.

sottocommissione [sottokommis'sjone] sf subcommittee; subcommission.

sottocoppa [sotto'kɔppa] sm invar mat; (piattino) saucer.

*__sottoesporre__ [sottoes'porre] v underexpose.

sottofondo [sotto'fondo] sm foundation; (suono) background noise. **musica in sottofondo** sf background music.

sottolineare [sottoline'are] v underline; (fig) stress.

sottomano [sotto'mano] avv (a portata di mano) within (easy) reach, on hand; (di nascosto) on the quiet; (sport) underhand.

*__sottomettere__ [sotto'mettere] v (assoggettare) subject; (costringere a sottostare) subdue; subordinate. **sottomettersi** v submit. **sottomesso** agg subdued; (obbediente) submissive.

sottopassaggio [sottopas'saddʒo] sm underpass.

*__sottoporre__ [sotto'porre] v (presentare) submit; (costringere) subject, expose. **sottoporsi a un'operazione** undergo an operation. **sottoposto, -a** agg, sf subordinate.

sottoprodotto [sottopro'dotto] sm byproduct.

sottordine [sot'tordine] sm suborder. **in sottordine** of minor importance.

*__sottoscrivere__ [sottos'krivere] v sign; (fig) support; (econ) underwrite, subscribe. **sottoscritto, -a** sm, sf undersigned; (fam) yours truly. **sottoscrizione** sf subscription.

sottosopra [sotto'sopra] avv upside down.

*__sottostare__ [sottos'tare] v be under; (sottomettersi) give in. **sottostante** agg (down) below.

sottosuolo [sotto'swɔlo] sm subsoil.

sottoterra [sotto'tɛrra] avv underground.

sottotitolo [sotto'titolo] sm subtitle.

sottovalutare [sottovalu'tare] v underestimate.

sottoveste [sotto'vɛste] sf slip.

sottovoce [sotto'votʃe] avv in a low voice, softly.

*__sottrarre__ [sot'trarre] v remove; (mat) subtract; (salvare) save (from). **sottrarsi a** escape; (evitare) avoid. **sottrazione** sf subtraction; removal.

sottufficiale [sottuffi'tʃale] sm non-commissioned officer; (mar) petty officer.

sovente [so'vɛnte] avv also **di sovente** frequently.

soverchio [so'verkjo] agg excessive. **soverchieria** sf bullying; (sopruso) outrage.

sovietico [so'vjɛtiko], **-a** s, agg Soviet.

sovrabbondante [sovrabbon'dante] agg plentiful; excessive. **sovrabbondanza** sf plenty; excess.

sovraccaricare [sovrakkari'kare] v overburden; (tec) overload. **sovraccarica** sf overcharge. **sovraccarico** agg, m pl **-chi** overloaded.

*sovr(a)esporre [sovr(a)es'porre] *v* over-expose. **sovresposizione** *sf* over-exposure.

sovraffollato [sovraffol'lato] *agg* over-crowded.

sovrano [so'vrano], **-a** *agg* sovereign, supreme. *sm, sf* sovereign. **sovranità** *sf* sovereignty; (*fig*) supremacy.

sovrappopolato [sovrappopo'lato] *agg* overpopulated.

*sovrapporre [sovrap'porre] *v* superimpose; (*fig*) set over; (*accavallare*) overlap.

sovrastante [sovra'stante] *agg* towering; (*imminente*) impending.

sovreccitare [sovrettʃi'tare] *v* over-excite. **sovreccitarsi** *v* become over-excited. **sovreccitazione** *sf* over-excitement.

sovrumano [sovru'mano] *agg* superhuman.

sovvenzione [sovven'tsjone] *sf* subsidy. **sovvenzionare** *v* subsidize.

sovversione [sovver'sjone] *sf* subversion. **sovversivo, -a** *s, agg* subversive. **sovvertire** *v* subvert.

sozzo ['sottso] *agg* filthy; (*fig*) loathsome. **sozzura** *sf* filth; loathsomeness.

spaccare [spak'kare] *v* (*fendere*) split; (*rompere*) break; (*legna*) chop. **spaccarsi** *v* split (open); break (up). **spaccare il minuto** be dead on time. **fare la spaccata** do the splits. **spacco** *sm* split; (*strappo*) tear; (*giacca*) vent.

spacciare [spatt'fare] *v* (*vendere*) sell off; (*mettere in circolazione*) peddle; (*dichiarar inguaribile*) give up. **spacciato** *agg* (*fam: rovinato*) done for. **spacciatore, -trice** *sm, sf* pedlar; (*di droghe*) pusher; (*di notizie false*) rumour-monger. **spaccio** *sm* sale; (*negozio*) shop; (*mil, fabbrica*) canteen.

spaccone [spak'kone] *sm* braggart. **fare lo spaccone** brag.

spada ['spada] *sf* sword; (*sport*) épée. **a spada tratta** vigorously. **pesce spada** *sm* sword-fish. **tirar di spada** fence. **spadaccino** *sm* swordsman. **spadista** *s(m+f)* fencer.

spadroneggiare [spadroned'dʒare] *v* be bossy.

spaesato [spae'zato] *agg* lost.

Spagna ['spaɲa] *sf* Spain. **spagnolo, -a** *agg, sm* Spanish; *sm, sf* (*abitante*) Spaniard.

spago ['spago] *sm* string, twine.

spalancare [spalan'kare] *v* open wide.

spalancare gli orecchi prick up one's ears. **spalancato** *agg* wide open.

spalare [spa'lare] *v* shovel.

spalla ['spalla] *sf* shoulder; (*dorso*) back. **alle spalle di** (*stato*) behind; (*moto*) from behind. **aver le spalle grosse** be broad-shouldered. **aver sulle spalle** (*fig*) be responsible for. **alzar le spalle** shrug one's shoulders. **ridere alle spalle di qualcuno** laugh behind someone's back. **vivere alle spalle di** live off. **spallata** *sf* (*spinta*) push with the shoulder; (*alzata di spalle*) shrug. **spalletta** *sf* parapet.

spalmare [spal'mare] *v* spread.

spanare [spa'nare] *v* strip.

spanciare [span'tʃare] *v* bulge. **spanciarsi dalle risa** split one's sides laughing.

*spandere [spandere] *v* (*versare*) shed; (*involontariamente*) spill; (*stendere, divulgare*) spread.

spanna ['spanna] *sf* span.

spappolare [spappo'lare] *v* crush.

sparare [spa'rare] *v* fire; (*tirare*) shoot. **spararle grosse** (*fam*) shoot a line; tell tall stories. **sparata** *sf* volley. **sparo** *sm* shot.

sparecchiare [sparek'kjare] *v* clear (away).

spareggio [spa'reddʒo] *sm* (*sport*) decider.

*spargere [spardʒere] *v* scatter; (*versare*) shed; (*involontariamente*) spill; (*sale, pepe, ecc.*) sprinkle; (*diffondere*) spread.

*sparire [spa'rire] *v* disappear. **far sparire** (*nascondere*) hide; (*fam: rubare*) pinch.

sparlare [spar'lare] *v* speak ill (of).

sparo ['sparo] *sm* shot.

sparpagliare [sparpaʎ'ʎare] *v* scatter.

spartire [spar'tire] *v* divide; (*in parti*) share out; (*musica*) score. **spartiacque** *sm invar* watershed. **spartineve** *sm invar* snow-plough. **spartitraffico** *sm* traffic island. **spartito** *sm* score.

sparuto [spa'ruto] *agg* gaunt; (*esiguo*) scanty.

sparviere [spar'vjere] *sm* sparrow-hawk.

spasimare [spazi'mare] *v* suffer agonies; (*fig*) crave, long (for). **spasimo** *sm* pang; (*med*) spasm. **spasmodico** *agg* spasmodic.

spassarsela [spas'sarsela] *v* enjoy oneself.

spassionato [spassjo'nato] *agg* dispassionate.

spasso ['spasso] *sm* fun. **andare a spasso** go for a walk. **mandare a spasso** (*fam: licenziare*) sack; (*fam: liberarsene*) get rid of. **portare a spasso** take for a walk. **quel**

ragazzo è uno spasso! that boy is a scream! spasso agg amusing.
spastico ['spastiko], -a s, agg spastic. spasticità sf spasticity.
spatola ['spatola] sf spatula; (di pittore) palette-knife; (zool) spoonbill.
spatriare [spatri'are] v expatriate.
spaurire [spau'rire] v scare. spauracchio sm scarecrow.
spavaldo [spa'valdo] agg defiant; (baldanzoso) bold; (arrogante) cocky. spavalderia sf defiance; boldness; cockiness.
spaventare [spaven'tare] v frighten, scare. spaventarsi v get frightened, get scared. spaventapasseri sm scarecrow. spaventevole agg terrifying. spavento sm fright. fare spavento frighten, scare. prendersi uno spavento have a fright. spaventoso agg frightful; (terribile) dreadful; (enorme) tremendous.
spazientirsi [spatsjen'tirsi] v lose one's patience.
spazio ['spatsjo] sm space; (estensione limitata) room; distance. spaziale agg space, spatial. spaziare v space; (fig) range. spazioso agg roomy.
spazzare [spat'tsare] v sweep; (spazzar via) sweep away. spazzacamino sm chimney-sweep. spazzaneve sm invar snow-plough. spazzatura sf cleaning; sweeping; (rifiuti) rubbish. spazzaturaio sm dustman. spazzino sm road sweeper.
spazzola [spat'tsola] sf brush. capelli a spazzola crew-cut. spazzola per capelli hairbrush. spazzolare v brush. spazzolino da denti/unghie sm tooth-/naii-brush. spazzolone (per lavare) scrubbing brush.
specchio ['spɛkkjo] sm mirror; model; (prospetto) table; summary. specchio d'acqua sheet of water. specchio retrovisore driving mirror. specchiarsi v (guardarsi) look at oneself in the mirror; (riflettersi) be reflected. specchiato agg (fig) exemplary. specchiera sf large mirror; (toeletta) dressing-table. specchietto sm small mirror; (tavola) table, summary.
speciale [spe'tʃale] agg special; particular; (fuori del solito) peculiar. specialista s(m + f) specialist. specialità sf speciality; (prodotto speciale) specialty; (farmaceutica) proprietary medicine. specializzarsi v specialize. specializzato agg specialized;

(operaio) skilled; (medico) specialist. specializzazione sf specialization.
specie ['spetʃe] sf invar kind, sort; (bot, zool) species; surprise. mi fa specie it surprises me. sotto specie di in the form of.
specificare [spetʃifi'kare] v specify. specifica sf detailed list. specificazione sf specification. specifico agg specific.
speculare [speku'lare] v speculate. speculativo agg speculative. speculatore, -trice sm, sf speculator; (di borsa) stockbroker. speculazione sf speculation.
spedalità [spedali'ta] sf hospitalization.
spedire [spe'dire] v send; post; (inoltrare) forward. spedire all'altro mondo (fam) bump off. spedito agg (veloce) quick; (corrente) fluent. speditore, -trice sm, sf sender; (comm) shipper. spedizione sf dispatch; (trasporto) shipment; (cosa spedita) consignment. casa di spedizione forwarding or shipping agents pl. fare una spedizione send a consignment. spedizioniere sm shipping or forwarding agent.
*spegnere ['spɛɲere] v extinguish, put out; (con interruttore) switch or turn off; (sete) quench. spegnersi v go out; (motore) stall.
spelacchiato [spelak'kjato] agg (con pochi peli) mangy; (logoro) threadbare.
spellare [spel'lare] v skin; (escoriare) graze. spellarsi v peel. spellatura sf skinning; grazing; peeling.
spelonca [spe'lonka] sf hovel.
*spendere ['spɛndere] v spend. senza spender fatica effortlessly. spendere bene/male use one's money wisely/unwisely. spendereccio agg extravagant.
spennacchiare [spennak'kjare] v also spennare pluck; (fig) fleece.
spensierato [spensje'rato] agg carefree. spensierataggine sf thoughtlessness; irresponsibility. spensieratezza sf lightheartedness.
spento ['spento] agg out, off; (fig) dull.
spenzolare [spendzo'lare] v dangle.
speranza [spe'rantsa] sf hope. avere buone speranze have high hopes. avere una speranza have a chance. filo di speranza sm glimmer of hope. senza speranza hopeless.
sperare [spe'rare] v hope; (aspettarsi) expect. sperare (in) bene hope for the

best. **sperare in Dio** trust in God. **spero di no/sì** I hope not/so.

sperdersi [sper'dersi] v get lost. **sperduto** agg lost; (*fuori mano*) out-of-the-way; (*solo*) lonely.

spergiurare [sperdʒu'rare] v commit perjury, perjure oneself. **spergiuro** sm perjury; (*persona*) perjurer.

spericolato [speriko'lato] agg reckless.

sperimentare [sperimen'tare] v experiment (with); (*mettere alla prova*) try out, test; (*farne esperienza*) experience. **sperimentale** agg experimental.

sperma ['sperma] sm sperm.

sperone [spe'rone] sm spur; (*mar*) ram. **sperone di cavaliere** larkspur. **speronare** v ram.

sperperare [sperpe'rare] v squander. **sperpero** sm waste.

sperticato [sperti'kato] agg (*fig*) excessive.

spesa ['speza] sf expenditure; (*costo*) expense; (*acquisto*) purchase; (*compra*) shopping. **a spese di** at the expense of. **con poca spesa** cheaply; (*fig*) easily. **conto spese** sm expense account. **far la spesa** go shopping. **non badare a spese** spare no expense. **senza spesa free.** **spese** sf pl cost sing, charges pl. **spese generali** overheads pl. **essere spesato** have one's expenses paid.

spesso ['spesso] agg thick. avv often, frequently. **spesse volte** very often, frequently. **spessore** sm thickness.

spettacolo [spet'takolo] sm show; (*rappresentazione*) performance; (*vista*) sight. **dare spettacolo di sè** make an exhibition of oneself. **spettacolo pomeridiano** matinée. **spettacoloso** agg spectacular.

spettare [spet'tare] v (*competere per dovere*) be up (to); (*appartenere per diritto*) be due (to); (*essere di pertinenza*) be the concern of.

spettatore [spetta'tore], **-trice** sm, sf spectator; (*testimone*) witness. **spettatori** sm pl audience sing.

spettinare [spetti'nare] v ruffle the hair of. **spettinato** agg unkempt, dishevelled.

spettro ['spettro] sm ghost; (*fig*) spectrum.

spezie ['spetsje] sf pl spices pl.

spezzare [spet'tsare] v break; (*staccando*) break off; (*fare a pezzi*) break up; (*gastr*) cut up. **spezzatino** sm stew. **spezzettare** v chop (up). **spezzone incendiario** sm incendiary bomb.

spia ['spia] sf spy, informer; (*indizio*) sign; (*apertura*) spy-hole; (*tec*) warning light. **fare la spia** be a spy; (*polizia*) inform; (*riportare*) tell tales.

spiaccicare [spjattʃi'kare] v squash.

spiacere [spja'tʃere] v displease. **mi spiace ...** I dislike .... **mi spiace di ...** (*rammarico*) I'm sorry .... **se non ti spiace** if you don't mind. **spiacevole** agg unpleasant, disagreeable; (*increscioso*) regrettable.

spiaggia [spja'ddʒa] sf (sea-)shore, beach.

spianare [spja'nare] v level; (*render liscio*) smooth; (*radere al suolo*) flatten, raze (to the ground); (*fig*) iron out. **spianato** agg smooth. **spianatoia** sf pastry board. **spianatoio** sm rolling-pin. **a tutto spiano** flat out.

spiantare [spjan'tare] v uproot; (*rovinare*) ruin.

spiare [spi'are] v spy (on); (*aspettare*) look out for; explore.

spiazzo [spi'attso] sm open space; (*radura*) clearing.

spiccare [spik'kare] v pick; (*pronunciare distintamente*) spell out; (*dir*) issue; (*comm*) draw; (*risaltare*) stand out. **spiccare il volo** take off. **spiccato** agg distinct, marked; (*notevole*) striking. **spicco** sm prominence. **far spicco** catch the eye.

spicchio ['spikkjo] sm segment; (*aglio*) clove.

spicciare [spit'tʃare] v dispatch. **spicciarsi** v hurry up. **spicciativo** agg quick; (*brusco*) abrupt. **spiccio** agg swift. **alla spicciolata** in ,dribs and drabs. **spiccioli** sm pl (small) change sing. **spicciolo** agg small.

spiedo ['spjedo] sm spit. **spiedino** sm skewer.

spiegare [spje'gare] v (*distendere*) unfold; (*ali*) spread; (*vele*) unfurl; (*render chiaro*) explain. **spiegarsi** v (*capire*) understand; (*diventar comprensibile*) explain oneself, make oneself understood. **spieghiamoci!** let's get it straight! **spiegabile** agg explicable.

spiegazione [spjega'tsjone] sf explanation; (*ragione*) reason.

spiegazzare [spjegat'tsare] v crumple (up), crease.

spietato [spje'tato] agg (*senza pietà*) pitiless; (*accanito*) relentless.

spifferare [spiffe'rare] v blab, blurt out. **spiffero** sm (*fam*) draught.

spiga ['spiga] *sf* ear. **disegno a spiga** *sm* herringbone pattern.

spigliato [spi'ʎato] *agg* (free and) easy; (*padrone di sè*) self-possessed. **spigliatezza** *sf* ease.

spigola ['spigola] *sf* bass.

spigolare [spigo'lare] *v* glean. **spigolature** *sf pl* tit-bits *pl*.

spigolo ['spigolo] *sm* corner; edge.

spilla ['spilla] *sf* brooch. **spilla da cravatta** tie-pin.

spillare [spil'lare] *v* tap; (*attingere*) draw.

spillo ['spillo] *sm* pin. **spillo di sicurezza** safety-pin.

spilluzzicare [spilluttsi'kare] *v* nibble.

spilorcio [spi'lortʃo], **-a** *agg* stingy. *sm, sf* miser. **spilorceria** *sf* meanness.

spina ['spina] *sf* (*bot*) thorn; (*aculeo*) sting; (*riccio*) quill; (*elett*) plug. **birra alla spina** *sf* draught beer. **spina di pesce** fishbone. **spina dorsale** backbone. **star sulle spine** on tenterhooks. **spinare** *v* bone. **spinato** *agg* (*pesce*) filleted; (*filo*) barbed.

spinacio [spi'natʃo] *sm* (*bot*) spinach. **spinaci** *sm pl* (*gastr*) spinach *sing*.

*****spingere** ['spindʒere] *v* push, drive; (*stimolare*) urge; (*premere*) press.

spino ['spino] *sm* (*bot*) blackthorn, bramble. **spineto** *sm* bramble bush. **spinoso** *agg* prickly, thorny.

spinta ['spinta] *sf* push; pressure; (*aiuto*) (helping) hand; (*stimolo*) boost; (*fis*) thrust. **spinto** *agg* pushed; disposed; (*fam*) extremist. **spintone** *sm* hard push, shove; (*raccomandazione*) good word.

spionaggio [spio'naddʒo] *sm* espionage. **spione** *sm* (*fam*) tell-tale.

spiovente [spjo'vɛnte] *agg* (*baffi*) drooping; (*spalle*) stooping; (*tetto*) sloping.

spira ['spira] *sf* coil. **spirale** *agg, sf* spiral.

spiraglio [spi'raʎo] *sm* chink; (*di luce, speranza*) glimmer; (*aria*) breath (of air).

spirare¹ [spi'rare] *v* (*soffiare*) blow; (*emettere*) give off or out; (*emanare*) be given off or out.

spirare² [spi'rare] *v* (*morire*) expire.

spirito ['spirito] *sm* spirit; (*animo*) mind; sense of humour. **bello spirito** wit. **condizioni di spirito** *sm pl* mood *sing*. **con spirito** wittily. **pieno di spirito** (*vivace*) lively; (*arguto*) witty.

spiritosaggine [spirito'zaddʒine] *sf* witticism.

spiritoso [spiri'tozo], **-a** *agg* witty. *sm, sf* funny person.

spirituale [spiritu'ale] *agg* spiritual. **spiritualismo** *sm* spiritualism. **spiritualista** *s(m+f)* spiritualist.

spiumare [spju'mare] *v* pluck.

spizzicare [spittsi'kare] *v* nibble. **a spizzico** *or* **spizzichi** in dribs and drabs.

*****splendere** ['splɛndere] *v* shine. **splendido** *agg* brilliant; (*meraviglioso*) splendid. **splendore** *sm* brilliance; splendour.

spodestare [spodes'tare] *v* (*cacciare*) oust; (*privare di beni*) dispossess.

spogliare [spoʎ'ʎare] *v* strip; (*svestire*) undress; (*esaminare*) go through; sort out. **spogliarsi** *v* undress. **spogliarello** *sm* strip-tease. **spogliatoio** *sm* changing-room. **spoglie** *sf pl* (*bottino*) spoils *pl*; (*mortali*) (mortal) remains *pl*. **spoglio** *agg* (*nudo*) bare; (*privo*) devoid (of); (*libero*) free (from). **fare lo spoglio** (*corrispondenza*) sort out; (*dati*) extract; (*voti*) scrutinize.

spola ['spola] *sf* shuttle; (*macchina da cucire*) spool, bobbin. **far la spola** shuttle, ply. **spoletta** *sf* bobbin; (*tec, mil*) fuse.

spolmonarsi [spolmo'narsi] *v* shout oneself hoarse.

spolverare [spolve'rare] *v* dust. **spolverat(ur)a** *sf* dusting.

sponda ['sponda] *sf* (*mare, lago*) shore; (*fiume*) bank; (*bordo*) edge; (*biliardo*) cushion.

spontaneo [spon'taneo] *agg* spontaneous. **di mia spontanea volontà** of my own free will. **spontaneità** *sf* spontaneity.

spopolare [spopo'lare] *v* depopulate; (*vuotare*) empty; (*aver successo*) be a hit.

spora ['spora] *sf* spore.

sporadico [spo'radiko] *agg* sporadic.

sporco ['sporko] *agg* dirty; dishonest. **aver la coscienza sporca** have a guilty conscience. **sporcizia** *sf* dirt, filth; (*fam*) muck.

*****sporgere** ['spordʒere] *v* stick out, project, protrude. **sporgersi** *v* lean out. **sporgere querela contro sue. sporgente** *agg* jutting out; (*dente*) protruding; (*occhio*) bulging. **sporgenza** *sf* projection.

sport [sport] *sm invar* sport. **fare per sport** do for fun.

sporta ['sporta] *sf* (*sacca*) shopping-bag; (*quantità*) bagful. **una sporta di legnate** a good hiding. **un sacco e una sporta** a lot.

sportello [spor'tɛllo] *sm* counter; (*per biglietti*) ticket office; (*porta*) door.

sportivo [spor'tivo] *agg* sports; (*interessato*) sporty, sporting; (*leale*) sportsmanlike, sporting. *sm* sportsman. **sportiva** *sf* sportswoman.

sposa ['spɔza] *sf* bride. **sposalizio** *sm* wedding. **sposare** *v* marry; (*fig*) wed. **sposarsi** *v* get married. **sposata** *sf* married woman. **sposato** *sm* married man. **sposino, -a** *sm, sf* newly-wed. **sposo** *sm* bridegroom.

spossare [spos'sare] *v* exhaust. **spossatezza** *sf* exhaustion; (*stanchezza*) weariness. **spossato** *agg* worn out, weary.

spossessare [sposses'sare] *v* dispossess.

spostare [spos'tare] *v* shift; (*rimuovere*) displace; (*turbare*) upset; transfer. **spostamento** *sm* shift; displacement; transfer. **spostato** [spos'tato], **-a** *agg* (*fuori posto*) out of place; (*fig*) unsettled. *sm, sf* misfit.

spranga ['spranga] *sf* crossbar; (*chiavistello*) bolt. **sprangare** *v* bolt.

sprazzo ['sprattso] *sm* flash.

sprecare [spre'kare] *v* waste. **è tempo/fiato sprecato** it is a waste of breath/time. **spreco** *sm* waste. **sprecone, -a** *sm, sf* spendthrift.

spregevole [spre'dʒevole] *agg* despicable.

spregiare *v* despise, spurn. **spregiativo** *agg* disparaging; (*gramm*) pejorative.

spregiudicato [spredʒudi'kato], **-a** *agg* (*senza pregiudizi*) open-minded; (*senza scrupoli*) unscrupulous. *sm, sf* unscrupulous person. **spregiudicatezza** *sf* open-mindedness; unscrupulousness.

spremere ['spremere] *v* squeeze. **spremersi il cervello** rack one's brains. **spremilimoni** *sm* lemon squeezer. **spremuta** *sf* (*bevanda*) juice.

sprezzare [spret'tsare] *v* despise. **sprezzante** *agg* contemptuous. **sprezzo** *sm* scorn.

sprigionare [spridʒo'nare] *v* give off.

sprint [sprint] *sm invar* (*sport*) sprint; (*auto*) pick-up. *sf* sports car.

sprizzare [sprit'tsare] *v* (*acqua*) squirt; (*sangue*) spurt; (*fig*) burst with.

sprofondare [sprofon'dare] *v* collapse; (*affondare*) sink; (*lasciarsi sopraffare*) be overwhelmed (by). **sprofondarsi** *v* sink; (*fig*) immerse oneself. **sprofondamento** *sm* collapse. **sprofondato** *agg* (*fig*) immersed, engrossed.

spronare [spro'nare] *v* spur (on). **spronata** *sf* spur. **sprone** *sm* spur.

sproporzionato [sproportsjo'nato] *agg*

out of proportion; disproportionate. **sproporzione** *sf* lack of proportion.

sproposito [spro'pozito] *sm* blunder; (*strafalcione*) howler. **a sproposito** (*inopportunamente*) at the wrong time; (*fuori luogo*) in the wrong place. **commettere uno sproposito** do something silly. **costare uno sproposito** cost the earth. **spropositato** *agg* excessive.

sprovvisto [sprov'visto] *agg also* **sprovveduto** short (of); (*privo*) lacking (in). **alla sprovvista** unawares.

spruzzare [sprut'tsare] *v* spray; (*senza intenderlo*) splash. **spruzzata** *sf* sprinkling. **spruzzatore** *sm* sprinkler; (*profumi*) atomizer. **spruzzo** *sm* spray; (*schizzo*) spurt; splash.

spudorato [spudo'rato] *agg* shameless. **spudoratezza** *sf* shamelessness.

spugna ['spuɲa] *sf* sponge; (*tessuto*) towelling; (*fam*) boozer. **bere come una spugna** drink like a fish. **spugnatura** *sf* sponging down. **spugnoso** *agg* spongy.

spuma ['spuma] *sf* froth. **spumante** *sm* sparkling wine. **spumare** *v* (*bevande gassate*) fizz; (*vino*) sparkle. **spumare dalla rabbia** (*fam*) foam at the mouth. **spumeggiare** *v* froth. **spumoso** *agg* frothy.

spuntare [spun'tare] *v* (*germogliare*) sprout; (*apparire improvvisamente*) emerge; (*sorgere*) rise; (*fig*) overcome; (*capelli, ecc.*) trim. **spuntato** *agg* (*matita*) blunt; (*vino*) sour.

spuntino [spun'tino] *sm* snack.

spunto ['spunto] *sm* cue; idea; (*sport*) spurt. **prendere lo spunto da** start (off) from.

spuntone [spun'tone] *sm* spike.

spurgare [spur'gare] *v* clear out. **spurgarsi** *v* clear one's throat.

spurio ['spurjo] *agg* spurious.

sputacchiare [sputak'kjare] *v* splutter. **sputacchiera** *sf* spitoon.

sputare [spu'tare] *v* spit. **sputa fuori!** spit it out! **sputar sentenze** lecture. **sputar veleno** speak spitefully. **sputo** *sm* spit(tle), saliva; (*espettorato*) sputum.

squadernare [skwader'nare] *v* leaf through.

squadra¹ ['skwadra] *sf* (*strumento*) square. **a squadra** at right angles. **fuori squadra** crooked; (*fuori posto*) out of place; (*disordinato*) disorderly. **squadrare** *v* square; (*fig*) eye.

squadra² ['skwadra] *sf* (*mil*) section, squad; (*aero*) squadron; (*gruppo*) gang; (*sport*) team. **squadra mobile** flying squad. **squadriglia** *sf* band; (*mar*, *aero*) squadron.

squadro ['skwadro] *sm* angel-fish.

squagliarsi [skwa'ʎarsi] *v* melt. **squagliarsela** *v* sneak off.

squalificare [skwalifi'kare] *v* disqualify. **squalifica** *sf* disqualification.

squallido [skwallido] *agg* dismal; (*fig*) squalid. **squallore** *sm* dreariness, squalor.

squalo ['skwalo] *sm* dog-fish; (*pescecane*) shark.

squama ['skwama] *sf* scale. **squamare** *v* scale. **squamoso** *agg* scaly.

squarciare [skwar'tʃare] *v* tear (to pieces), rend. **a squarciagola** at the top of one's voice. **squarcio** *sm* (*stoffa*) tear; (*ferita*) gash; (*fig*) passage.

squartare [skwar'tare] *v* quarter. **squartatoio** *sm* cleaver.

squassare [skwas'sare] *v* shake violently.

squattrinato [skwattri'nato] *agg* penniless.

squilibrare [skwili'brare] *v* unbalance. **squilibrarsi** *v* lose one's balance. **squilibrato** *agg* (mentally) unbalanced. **squilibrio** *sm* lack of equilibrium; (*econ*) imbalance; disproportion; (*mentale*) derangement.

squillare [skwil'lare] *v* ring; (*tromba*) sound; (*voce*) be shrill. **squillo** *sm* ring; (*suono*) squeal; (*tromba*) sound. **ragazza squillo** *sf* call-girl.

squinternare [skwinter'nare] *v* take to pieces; (*fig*) upset.

squisito [skwi'zito] *agg* excellent; delicious; (*raffinato*) exquisite. **squisitezza** *sf* deliciousness; delicacy.

squittire [skwit'tire] *v* (*uccelli*) chirp; (*topi*) squeak.

sradicare [sradi'kare] *v* (*divellere*) uproot; (*fig*) root out, eradicate.

sregolato [srego'lato] *agg* (*smodato*) immoderate; (*scapestrato*) wild.

stabbio ['stabbjo] *sm* pen; (*porcile*) pigsty; (*letame*) dung.

stabile ['stabile] *agg* stable; (*che non oscilla*) steady; permanent; (*durevole*) lasting. **stabilimento** [stabili'mento] *sm* establishment; (*fabbrica*) factory, works; (*edificio*) building.

stabilire [stabi'lire] *v* establish; decide. **stabilirsi** *sm* settle. **stabilità** *sf* stability.

stabilito *agg* (*istituito*) established; (*fissato*) fixed; (*convenuto*) agreed. **stabilizzare** *v* stabilize. **stabilizzarsi** *v* settle. **stabilizzazione** *sf* stabilization.

staccare [stak'kare] *v* (*togliere*) take off; (*separare*) detach; (*tagliando*) cut off; (*strappando*) pluck; (*sganciare*) unhook; (*risaltare*) stand out. **staccare il lavoro** (*fam*) knock off work. **staccarsi** *v* move away; (*venir via*) come off; separate. **staccato** *agg* detached; separate; (*musica*) staccato.

stadio ['stadjo] *sm* (*sport*) stadium; (*tec*, *fase*) stage.

staffa ['staffa] *sf* stirrup; (*mec*) bracket; (*calza*) heel. **perdere le staffe** (*fig*) lose one's temper. **staffetta** *sf* courier; (*sport*) relay(-race).

staffilare [staffi'lare] *v* lash; (*fig*) lash out (at). **staffilata** *sf* lash; (*fig*) lashing criticism. **staffile** *sm* stirrup-strap; (*sferza*) lash.

stagione [sta'dʒone] *sf* season; (*condizioni atmosferiche*) weather. **fuori stagione** out of season; (*fig*) untimely. **stagionale** *agg* seasonal. **stagionare** *v* season; (*invecchiare*) age; mature. **stagionatura** *sf* ageing; maturing; seasoning.

stagno¹ ['stano] *sm* (*metallo*) tin. **stagnare** *v* tin; (*saldare*) solder; (*chiudere*) seal. **stagnola** *sf* tin foil.

stagno² ['stano] *sm* (*bacino d'acqua*) pool. *agg* (*a tenuta d'acqua*) watertight. **stagnare** *v* stagnate; (*sangue*) stanch; (*fermare*) stop.

stalagmite [stalag'mite] *sf* stalagmite.

stalattite [stalat'tite] *sf* stalactite.

stalla ['stalla] *sf* stable; (*bovini*) cow-shed; (*fig*) pigsty. **stallaggio** *sm* stabling. **stallone** *sm* stallion.

stallo ['stallo] *sm* seat; (*scacchi*) stalemate. **andare in stallo** (*aero*) stall.

stamattina [stamat'tina] *avv also* **stamani** this morning.

stamberga [stam'berga] *sf* hovel.

stambugio [stam'budʒo] *sm* cubby-hole.

stame ['stame] *sm* (*bot*) stamen; (*tessile*) fine yarn.

stamigna [sta'mina] *sf* bunting.

stampa ['stampa] *sf* printing; (*giornali*) press; (*immagine*, *foto*) print. **errore di stampa** *sm* misprint. **stampe** *sf pl* (*posta*) printed matter *sing*. **stampaggio** (*foto*) printing; (*metallo*) forging; (*plastici*) moulding. **stampare** *v* print; publish;

(con pressa) press; forge; mould. **stampatello** sm block letters pl. **stampato** sm printed matter; (modulo) form; (disegno) print. **stampatore, -trice** sm, sf printer.

stampella [stam'pɛlla] sf crutch.

stampiglia [stam'piʎa] sf stamp. **stampigliare** v stamp.

stampino [stam'pino] sm stencil; (punzone) punch.

stampo ['stampo] sm mould; (matrice) die; (fig) kind, sort.

stanare [sta'nare] v drive out.

stancare [stan'kare] v tire; (annoiare) bore. **stancarsi** v get tired, tire. **stanchezza** sf tiredness; (fiacchezza) fatigue. **stanco** agg tired; bored.

standard ['standard] sm invar standard. **standardizzare** v standardize. **standardizzazione** sf standardization.

stanga ['stanga] sf bar. **stangare** v (colpire) thrash; (bocciare) fail; (scuola) give a bad mark; (far pagare troppo) rob. **stangata** sf blow.

stanotte [sta'nɔtte] avv tonight.

stante ['stante] agg a sè stante apart. **seduta stante** straight away. prep (a causa di) on account of.

stantio [stan'tio] agg stale.

stantuffo [stan'tuffo] sm piston; (di pressa idraulica) plunger.

stanza ['stantsa] sf room; (poesia) stanza. **stanza da bagno** bathroom. **stanza da pranzo** dining-room.

stanziare [stan'tsjare] v allocate; deliberate.

stappare [stap'pare] v uncork.

*****stare** ['stare] v stay, remain; (abitare) live; (essere) be; (vestiario) suit; (spettare) be up to. **come stai?** how are you? **lasciar stare** leave alone. **non poter stare senza** be unable to do without. **stare a dieta** be on a diet. **stare in guardia** be on one's guard. **stare per** be about to. **sto bene** I am well. **sto male** I am not well.

starna ['starna] sf partridge.

starnutire [starnu'tire] v sneeze. **starnuto** sm sneeze.

stasera [sta'sera] avv this evening.

stasi ['stazi] sf standstill.

statale [sta'tale] agg state. **strada statale** sf trunk road. s(m+f) sf civil servant.

statica ['statika] sf statics. **statico** agg static; (senza movimento) motionless.

statista [sta'tista] sm statesman.

statistica [sta'tistika] sf statistics. **statistico** agg statistical.

stato ['stato] sm state; condition; (posizione sociale) status. **colpo di stato** sm coup d'état. **Stati Uniti** sm pl United States pl. **stato d'animo** mood. **ufficio di stato civile** sm register office. **statunitense** s(m+f), agg American.

statua ['statua] sf statue. **statuario** agg statuary.

statura [sta'tura] sf (altezza) height; (fig) stature.

statuto [sta'tuto] sm statute; constitution. **statutario** agg statutory.

stavolta [sta'vɔlta] avv this time.

stazione [sta'tsjone] sf station; (località di soggiorno) resort. **stazionamento** sm parking. **stazionare** v stop; park. **stazionario** agg stationary.

stecca ['stekka] sf small stick; (biliardo) cue; (persiane) slat; (sigarette) carton; (hockey) stick. **steccare** v fence (in); (sonare) play a wrong note. **steccato** sm fence. **a stecchetto** (senza soldi) hard up; (senza cibo) on short rations. **stecchito** agg (rinsecchito) dried up; (magrissimo) skinny. **morto stecchito** stone dead. **stecco** sm dry twig. **stecone** sm post.

stella ['stella] sf star. **alle stelle** (prezzi) sky-high. **stella alpina** edelweiss. **stella cadente** or **filante** shooting star; (di carta) streamer. **stella di mare** starfish. **stellare** agg (astron) stellar; (forma) star-shaped; (bot) stellate. **stellato** agg starry; (fig) studded. **stelletta** (mil) star; (fam) pip.

stelo ['stɛlo] sm stem; (fiore) stalk; (gambo di utensile) shank.

stemma ['stɛmma] sm coat of arms.

stemp(e)rare [stemp(e)'rare] v dissolve.

stendardo [sten'dardo] sm standard.

*****stendere** ['stɛndere] v (allungare) stretch (out); (distendere) spread (out); (bucato) hang out; (contratto) draw up. **stendersi** v stretch out.

stenodattilografia [stenodattilogra'fia] sf shorthand typing. **stenodattilografo, -a** sm, sf shorthand typist. **stenografare** v take down in shorthand. **stenografia** sf shorthand. **stenografo, -a** sm, sf stenographer.

stentare [sten'tare] v find it hard, have difficulty. **stentatezza** sf difficulty. **stentato** agg laboured; (di crescita arrestata) stunted; (pieno di stenti) hard.

stento *sm* hardship; difficulty. **a stento** barely.

steppa ['steppa] *sf* steppe.

sterco ['sterko] *sm* excrement; (*letame*) dung.

stereo ['stereo] *agg*, *sm* stereo.

stereofonico [stereo'fɔniko] *agg* stereophonic; (*fam*) stereo.

stereotipato [stereoti'pato] *agg* stereotyped; (*fisso*) frozen. **concezione stereotipata** *sf* stereotype.

sterile ['sterile] *agg* sterile; (*fig*) vain. **sterilire** *v* sterilize. **sterilità** *sf* sterility; (*fig*) uselessness. **sterilizzare** *v* sterilize. **sterilizzatore** *sm* sterilizer. **sterilizzazione** *sf* sterilization.

sterlina [ster'lina] *sf* pound (sterling).

sterminare [stermi'nare] *v* exterminate. **sterminato** *agg* boundless. **sterminio** *sm* extermination.

sterna ['sterna] *sf* tern.

sterno ['sterno] *sm* breastbone.

sterzo ['stertso] *sm* (*auto*) steering; (*bicicletta*) handlebars *pl*. **sterzare** *v* (*auto*) steer; (*fig*) swerve. **sterzata** *sf* steering; swerve. **fare una sterzata** make a sharp turn.

stesso ['stesso] *agg* same; (*proprio*) very; (*personificato*) itself; (*in persona*) personally; (*rafforzativo*, *riflessivo*) myself, yourself, etc.

stesura [ste'zura] *sf* drafting; draft.

stetoscopio [stetos'kɔpjo] *sm* stethoscope.

stia ['stia] *sf* chicken coop. **essere (pigiati) come in una stia** be cooped up.

stigma ['stigma] *sm* stigma. **stigmatizzare** *v* stigmatize.

stilare [sti'lare] *v* draw up.

stile ['stile] *sm* style; (*eleganza*) stylishness. **di stile** stylish. **in grande stile** in style. **stilista** *s(m+f)* stylist. **stilistico** *agg* stylistic. **stilizzare** *v* stylize.

stilla ['stilla] *sf* drop. **a stilla a stilla** drop by drop. **stillare** *v* (*trasudare*) ooze, exude; (*gocciolare*) drip. **stillarsi il cervello** rack one's brains. **stillicidio** *sm* constant trickle.

stilo ['stilo] *sm* (*per scrivere*) stylus; (*stadera*) beam. **stilografica** *sf* fountain-pen.

stima ['stima] *sf* (*buona opinione*) esteem, regard; (*giudizio*) estimation; (*valutazione*) estimate. **a mia stima** in my estimation. **aver stima di** hold in high esteem. **con (la massima) stima** (*in lettere*) yours faithfully.

stimare [sti'mare] *v* estimate; (*apprezzare*) value, esteem; consider. **stimatore, -trice** *sm*, *sf* (*perito*) valuer; (*ammiratore*) admirer.

stimolare [stimo'lare] *v* stimulate; (*fig*) arouse; (*appetito*) whet. **stimolante** *sm* stimulant. **stimolatore cardiaco** *sm* pacemaker. **stimolazione** *sf* (*med*) stimulation; (*fig*) arousal. **stimolo** *sm* stimulus (*pl* -li).

stinco ['stinko] *sm* shin. **stincata** *sf* blow on the shin.

*****stingere** ['stindʒere] *v* (*macchiare*) run; (*sbiadire*) fade.

stipare [sti'pare] *v* pack, cram.

stipendio [sti'pendjo] *sm* salary. **stipendio arretrato** back pay.

stipite [stipite] *sm* doorpost.

stipulare [stipu'lare] *v* stipulate. **stipulazione** *sf* stipulation.

stiracchiare [stirak'kjare] *v* stretch; (*lesinare*) skimp. **stiracchiare sul prezzo** haggle. **stiracchiamento** *sm* stretching; haggling. **stiracchiatura** *sf* distortion.

stirare [sti'rare] *v* (*col ferro*) iron, press. **stirarsi** *v* stretch. **stiro** *sm* ironing; pressing. **ferro da stiro** *sm* iron. **tavolo da stiro** *sm* ironing-board.

stirpe ['stirpe] *sf* (*origine*) descent, extraction; (*razza*) race; family; (*discendenti*) offspring.

stitico ['stitiko] *agg* constipated; (*fig*) stingy. **stitichezza** *sf* constipation.

stiva ['stiva] *sf* hold. **stivaggio** *sm* stowage.

stivale [sti'vale] *sm* boot. **lustrar gli stivali a** (*fig*) lick the boots of. **rompere gli stivali a** (*fig*) pester.

stivaletto [stiva'letto] *sm* bootee.

stizza ['stittsa] *sf* anger. **avere** *or* **provare stizza per** be angry about. **stizzire** *v* anger. **stizzirsi** *v* get angry. **stizzito** *agg* angry. **stizzoso** *agg* irritable.

stoccafisso [stokka'fisso] *sm* dried cod.

stoccata [stok'kata] *sf* stab; (*scherma*) thrust; (*battuta*) gibe. **stocco** *sm* rapier.

Stoccolma [stok'kolma] *sf* Stockholm.

stoffa ['stɔffa] *sf* fabric, material; (*dote*) makings *pl*. **ha della stoffa** he has what it takes.

stoico ['stɔiko] *agg* stoical. *sm*, *sf* stoic.

stoino [sto'ino] *sm* doormat.

stola ['stɔla] *sf* stole.

stolto ['stolto], **-a** *agg* foolish. *sm, sf* fool. **stoltezza** *sf* foolishness; (*azione*) foolish action; (*parole*) nonsense.

stomaco ['stɔmako] *sm* stomach; (*fam*) tummy; (*fam: coraggio*) guts. **mal di stomaco** *sm* stomach-ache. ... **mi sta** *or* **rimane sullo stomaco** I cannot stomach .... **stomacare** *v* nauseate. **stomachevole** *agg* revolting.

stonare [sto'nare] *v* (*cantare*) sing out of tune; (*sonare*) play out of tune; (*contrastare*) clash. **stonata** *sf* wrong note. **stonato** *agg* out of tune; clashing; (*turbato*) upset.

stoppa ['stoppa] *sf* tow. **stoppare** *v* (*otturare*) block; (*sport*) stop. **stoppaccio** *sm* wad. **stoppie** *sf pl* stubble *sing*. **stoppino** *sm* wick.

*storcere ['stortʃere] *v* stun; (*piegare*) bend. **storcersi il naso** turn up one's nose. **storcersi la bocca** make a wry face. **storcersi per il dolore** writhe in pain. **storcimento** *sm* twisting; wrench.

stordire [stor'dire] *v* stun; (*rumore*) deafen. **stordimento** *sm* (*stato d'animo*) bewilderment. **stordito** *agg* stunned; bewildered; (*distratto*) scatter-brained.

storia ['stɔrja] *sf* history; (*racconto*) story, tale; (*frottola*) fib, lie; (*faccenda*) business. **la solita storia** the same old story. **libro di storia** history book. **storie** *sf pl* (*trambusto*) fuss *sing*. **storiella** *sf* little story; (*barzelletta*) joke; (*fandonia*) fib.

storico ['stɔriko], **-a** *agg* (*della storia*) historical; (*famoso*) historic. *sm, sf* historian.

storione [sto'rjone] *sm* sturgeon.

stormo ['stormo] *sm* (*uccelli*) flock; (*cani*) pack; (*persone*) crowd; (*fig*) mass. **sonare a stormo** sound the alarm.

stornare [stor'nare] *v* (*allontanare*) avert; dissuade; transfer; annul. **storno** *sm* transfer.

stornello [stor'nello] *sm* also **storno** (*uccello*) starling.

storno ['storno] *agg* dapple-grey.

storpio ['stɔrpjo], **-a** *agg* crippled. *sm, sf* cripple. **storpiare** *v* cripple; mispronounce.

storto ['stɔrto] *agg* crooked; (*sbagliato*) wrong. **aver gli occhi storti** squint. **aver le gambe storte** bandy-legged. **storta** *sf* twist, sprain; (*recipiente*) retort. **prendersi una storta alla caviglia** twist one's ankle.

stoviglie [sto'viʎe] *sf pl* crockery *sing*. **lavar le stoviglie** wash the dishes, wash up.

strabico ['strabiko] *agg* cross-eyed. **strabismo** *sm* squint. **essere affetto da strabismo** have a squint.

strabiliante [strabi'ʎante] *agg* amazing.

straboccare [strabok'kare] *v* overflow. **strabocchevole** *agg* excessive.

stracarico [stra'kariko] *agg, m pl* **-chi** overloaded; (*fig*) overburdened.

stracciare [strat'tʃare] *v* tear; (*facendo a pezzi*) tear up.

straccio ['strattʃo] *sm* rag. *agg* waste. **straccione, -a** *sm, sf* ragamuffin; beggar.

stracco ['strakko] (*fam*) *agg* worn out, done in. **stracco morto** dead beat.

stracotto [stra'kɔtto] *agg* overcooked. **cotto e stracotto** overdone. *sm* (*gastr*) stew, casserole.

strada ['strada] *sf* road, street; (*percorso*) way; (*itinerario*) route; (*cammino*) journey; (*varco*) path. **a mezza strada** halfway. **che strada fai?** which way are you going? **far strada a qualcuno** show someone the way. **farsi strada** (*aprirsi un passaggio*) clear a way for oneself; (*ottener successo*) do well for oneself. **fuori strada** off the road; (*fig*) on the wrong track. **lungo** *or* **per la strada** on the way. **strada facendo** on the way. **stradale** *agg* road. **codice stradale** *sm* highway code. **lavori stradali** *sm pl* roadworks *pl*.

strafalcione [strafal'tʃone] *sm* blunder.

*strafare [stra'fare] *v* overdo it.

straforo [stra'fɔro] *sm* **di straforo** indirectly; (*di nascosto*) on the quiet; (*di sfuggita*) in passing.

strage ['stradʒe] *sf* slaughter; (*distruzione*) havoc; (*fam*) mass.

stragrande [stra'grande] *agg* huge. **stragrande maggioranza** *sf* great majority.

stralciare [stral'tʃare] *v* take out; (*dedurre*) deduct; (*mettere in liquidazione*) wind up. **stralcio** *sm* removal; extract; liquidation. **vendere a stralcio** sell off.

stralunare [stralu'nare] *v* roll one's eyes. **stralunato** *agg* (*fig*) distraught.

stramazzare [stramat'tsare] *v* fall to the ground.

strambo ['strambo] *agg* odd; eccentric. **stramberia** *sf* oddity; eccentricity.

strampalato [strampa'lato] *agg* weird.

strangolare [strango'lare] *v* strangle. **strangolarsi** *v* choke. **strangolamento** *sm* strangulation.

straniero [stra'njɛro], **-a** *agg* foreign. *sm, sf* foreigner; (*termine burocratico*) alien.

strano ['strano] *agg* strange, odd. **strano** *or* odd thing. **strano a dirsi** oddly enough. **stranezza** *sf* peculiarity; (*atteggiamento*) odd behaviour.

straordinario [straordi'narjo] *agg* extraordinary; (*insolito*) unusual; special. **lavoro straordinario** *sm* overtime. *sm* unusual thing; overtime.

strapagare [strapa'gare] *v* (*fam*) pay through the nose.

strapazzare [strapat'tsare] *v* wear out; (*trattar male*) ill-treat. **uova strapazzate** *sf pl* scrambled eggs *pl*. **strapazzata** *sf* (*sgridata*) dressing-down; (*faticata*) strain. **strapazzo** *sm* strain; ill-treatment. **vestiti da strapazzo** *sm pl* working clothes *pl*.

strapieno [stra'pjɛno] *agg* full up.

strapiombare [strapjom'bare] *v* overhang, jut out. **a strapiombo** sheer, overhanging.

strappare [strap'pare] *v* snatch; (*portar via*) pull off *or* out; (*rompendo*) tear (off *or* out); (*in più pezzi*) tear up. **strappata** *sf* tug. **strappo** *sm* pull, tug; (*strattone*) jerk; tear. **strappo muscolare** pulled *or* torn muscle.

straripare [strari'pare] *v* overflow. **straripamento** *sm* overflowing.

strascicare [straʃi'kare] *v* trail; (*con fatica*) drag; (*fig*) drag out; (*pronuncia*) drawl. **strascico** *sm*, *pl* **-chi** (*fig*) after-effect; (*vestito*) train.

strascinare [straʃi'nare] *v* drag along.

stratagemma [strata'dʒɛmma] *sm* stragem; (*fig*) trick.

strategia [strate'dʒia] *sf* strategy. **strategico** *agg* strategic. **stratego**, **-a** *sm, sf* strategist.

strato ['strato] *sm* layer; (*vernice*) coat; (*geol, classe*) stratum (*pl* -a). **stratificato** *agg* stratified.

strattone [strat'tone] *sm* pull, jerk. **a strattoni** jerkily.

stravagante [strava'gante] *agg* extravagant. **stravaganza** *sf* extravagance.

stravecchio [stra'vɛkkjo] *agg* very old.

*stravincere [stra'vintʃere] *v* win hands down; (*battere*) beat hollow.

straviziare [stravi'tsjare] *v* over-indulge. **stravizio** *sm* over-indulgence.

*stravolgere [stra'vɔldʒere] *v* twist; (*fig*) affect deeply. **stravolgere gli occhi** roll one's eyes. **stravolgimento** *sm* twisting; contortion. **stravolto** *agg* twisted; (*fig*) deeply upset.

straziare [stra'tsjare] *v* torture, torment. **straziare il cuore a qualcuno** break someone's heart. **cuore straziato** *sm* broken heart. **strazio** *sm* torment, agony. **far strazio di** (*fig*) play havoc with.

strega ['strega] *sf* witch. **stregare** *v* bewitch. **stregone** *sm* wizard; (*mago*) sorcerer; (*popoli primitivi*) witch-doctor. **stregoneria** *sf* witchcraft; sorcery. **fare stregonerie** cast spells.

stregua ['stregwa] *sf* **alla stregua di** in the same way as. **a questa stregua** at this rate.

stremato [stre'mato] *agg* exhausted. **stremo** ['strɛmo] *sm* limit.

strenna ['strɛnna] *sf* gift.

strenuo ['strɛnuo] *agg* valiant; (*fig*) untiring.

strepitare [strepi'tare] *v* make a din; (*gridando*) shout. **strepito** *sm* clamour, uproar. **fare strepito** cause a stir. **strepitoso** *agg* noisy; (*fragoroso*) resounding; (*fig*) tremendous.

streptococco [strepto'kɔkko] *sm* streptococcus. **streptomicina** *sf* streptomycin.

stretta ['stretta] *sf* hold; (*abbraccio*) embrace; (*presa*) grip; critical point; (*situazione difficile*) predicament. **essere** *or* **trovarsi alle strette** be in a tight corner. **stretta alla gola** lump in the throat. **stretta di mano** handshake.

stretto ['stretto] *agg* narrow; (*vestiario*) tight; (*rigoroso*) strict; (*denti, pugni*) clenched. *sm* strait. **strettoia** *sf* (*strada*) narrowing of the road; (*fig*) tight spot.

striato [stri'ato] *agg* striped.

stricnina [strik'nina] *sf* strychnine.

stridere ['stridere] *v* (*stirllare*) shriek, screech; (*insetti*) chirp; (*cigolare*) squeak; (*fig*) clash. **stridente** *agg* strident; clashing. **strido** *sm*, *pl* **-a** *f* shriek, screech; squeak; chirp.

strigliata [stri'ʎata] *sf* dressing-down.

strillare [stril'lare] *v* scream; (*parlare ad alta voce*) shout. **strillo** *sm* scream. **strillone** *sm* news-verdfdor.

striminzito [strimin'tsito] *agg* skimpy; (*magro*) skinny.

strimpellare [strimpel'lare] v strum.

strinare [stri'nare] v scorch.

stringa ['stringa] sf lace. **stringare** v lace (up); (fig) condense.

***stringere** ['strindʒere] v (avvicinare) squeeze or press (together); (serrare) clasp, clutch; (vestiario) pinch; (concludere) make; (denti, pugni) clench. **il tempo stringe** time is getting short. **stringere i tempi** speed things up; (musica) quicken the tempo. **stringere la cinghia** (fig) tighten one's belt. **stringere la mano** a shake hands with. **stringere un'amicizia** strike up a friendship. **stringi stringi** when all is said and done.

striscia ['striʃa] sf strip; (riga larga) stripe; (traccia) streak. **a strisce** striped. **strisce pedonali** sf pl zebra crossing sing. **strisciare** v creep, crawl; (sfiorando) slide; (sfiorare) graze. **strisciare i piedi** drag one's feet. **colpire di striscio** graze. **striscione** sm banner.

stritolare [strito'lare] v crush.

strizzare [strit'tsare] v wring out; (spremere) squeeze. **strizzar l'occhio** wink. **strizzata** sf squeeze; wink.

strofinare [strofi'nare] v rub. **strofinaccio** sm rag. **strofinata** sf quick rub. **strofinio** sm prolonged rubbing.

strombazzare [strombat'tsare] v shout from the roof-tops. **strombazzare i propri meriti** blow one's own trumpet.

strombettare [strombet'tare] v blare; (auto) blow the horn.

stroncare [stron'kare] v break off; (tagliando) cut off; (fig) cut short; (criticare) slate. **stroncatura** sf slating.

stronzo ['strontso] sm (volg) turd; (fig) idiot.

stropicciare [stropit'tʃare] v rub. **stropicciarsene** v (fam) not care a damn.

strozzare [strot'tsare] v strangle, choke; (med) strangulate. **strozzatura** sf narrowing; (occlusione) bottle-neck; strangling. **strozzino, -a** sm, sf usurer.

***struggere** ['struddʒere] v melt; (fig) eat up. **struggersi** v be consumed.

strumento [stru'mento] sm instrument; (arnese) tool. **strumento ad arco** stringed instrument. **strumento a fiato** woodwind instrument. **strumentale** agg instrumental. **strumentare** v orchestrate.

strusciare [struʃare] v scrape.

strutto ['strutto] sm lard.

struttura [strut'tura] sf structure. **strutturale** agg structural. **strutturare** v structure. **strutturazione** sf organization.

struzzo ['struttso] sm ostrich. **fare lo struzzo** bury one's head in the sand.

stuccare¹ [stuk'kare] v plaster; (decorare) stucco. **stuccatore** sm plasterer; stuccoworker. **stucco** sm plaster; (per finestre) putty; (arte) stucco. **rimaner di stucco** be dumbfounded.

stuccare² [stuk'kare] v (nauseare) make sick; (annoiare) bore. **stucchevole** agg sickly; boring. **stucco** agg sick (of).

studente [stu'dente], **-essa** sm, sf student. **studentesco** agg (di scuola) school; university.

studiare [stu'djare] v study; (cercar di trovare) try and find. **studiare a memoria** learn by heart. **studiato** agg studied; affected.

studio ['studjo] sm study; (progetto) plan; (di avvocato) office; (di medico) surgery; (di artista, fotografo, ecc.) studio. **allo studio** under consideration. **fare gli studi** study.

studioso [stu'djozo], **-a** agg studious. sm, sf scholar.

stufa ['stufa] sf stove, heater. **stufare** v (gastr) stew; (fam: annoiare) bore. **stufarsi di** get sick and tired of. **stufato** sm stew. **stufo** agg fed up (with).

stuoia ['stwɔja] sf mat. **stuoino** sm doormat.

stuolo ['stwolo] sm crowd.

***stupefare** [stupe'fare] v astound. **stupefacente** sm drug, narcotic. **stupefatto** agg astonished, amazed.

stupendo [stu'pendo] agg stupendous.

stupido ['stupido] agg stupid; (sciocco) foolish. **stupidaggine** sf stupidity; (atto) foolish thing; (parole) nonsense; (inezia) trifle. **dir stupidaggini** talk nonsense. **stupidità** sf stupidity.

stupire [stu'pire] v amaze, astonish. **stupirsi** v be amazed or astonished (at). **stupore** sm astonishment, amazement; (med) stupor.

stuprare [stu'prare] v rape. **stupro** sm rape.

sturare [stu'rare] v uncork. **sturabottiglie** sm invar corkscrew. **sturalavandini** sm invar plunger.

stuzzicare [stuttsi'kare] v prod; (*molestare*) annoy; (*punzecchiare*) tease; (*stimolare*) excite. **stuzzicadenti** sm invar toothpick. **stuzzicar l'appetito** whet the appetite. **stuzzicante** agg exciting; appetizing.

su [su] prep on; (*senza contatto*) over; (*più in alto di*) above; (*vicino*) by; (*verso*) towards; (*intorno a, circa*) about; (*oltre*) after. **dare su** look out over. **novanta volte su cento** (fig) nine times out of ten. **avv** (*in alto*) up; (*indosso*) on; (*al piano superiore*) upstairs. **avercela su con** (fam) be cross with. **in su** up; (*età, numero*) upwards. **su per giù** roughly. inter come on!

subacqueo [su'bakkweo] agg underwater.

subaffittare [subaffit'tare] v sublet. **dare in subaffitto** sublet.

subalterno [subal'terno], -a s, agg subordinate.

subappaltare [subappal'tare] v subcontract. **subappalto** sm subcontract.

subbia ['subbja] sf chisel.

subbio ['subbjo] sm beam.

subbuglio [sub'buʎo] sm turmoil; confusion.

subconscio [sub'kɔnʃo] sm, agg subconscious.

subdolo ['subdolo] agg underhand.

subentrare [suben'trare] v take the place of; succeed.

subire [su'bire] v suffer; (*sottoporsi a*) undergo.

subissare [subis'sare] v (fig) overwhelm. **subisso** sm (fam) load; (*rovina*) ruin.

subito ['subito] avv at once, immediately. **subito prima** just before. **subitaneità** sf suddenness. **subitaneo** agg sudden.

sublimare [subli'mare] v sublimate. **sublimato** sm sublimate. **sublimazione** sf sublimation.

sublime [sub'lime] agg, sm sublime.

subnormale [subnor'male] agg, sm subnormal.

subodorare [subodo'rare] v subodorare un inganno smell a rat.

subordinare [subordi'nare] v subordinate. **subordinato**, -a agg, s subordinate. **subordinazione** sf subordination.

subornare [subor'nare] v suborn. **subornazione** sf subornation.

suburbano [subur'bano] agg suburban.

*succedere [sut'tʃedere] v follow; suc‐ ceed; (*capitare*) happen. **cosa sta suc‐ cedendo?** what is happening? **cosa ti suc‐ cede?** what is the matter with you? **son cose che succedono** these things wil happen.

successione [suttʃes'sjone] sf succession **successione delle colture** crop rotation **tasse di successione** sf pl death duties p **successivamente** avv subsequently. **suc‐ cessivo** agg (*seguente*) following; (*un dopo l'altro*) consecutive. **successore** sr successor.

successo [sut'tʃɛsso] sm success. **aver cat tivo successo** be unsuccessful. **aver suc cesso** be successful.

succhiare [suk'kjare] v suck. **succhietto** o **succhiotto** sm dummy. **succhione** sr sucker.

succhiello [suk'kjɛllo] sm gimlet.

succinto [sut'tʃinto] agg scanty; (fig) suc cinct.

succitato [suttʃi'tato] agg above-men tioned.

succo ['sukko] sm juice; (fig) essence, gist **succoso** agg juicy; (fig) meaty. **suc culento** agg succulent, juicy; (*pasto* tasty.

succube ['sukkube] s(m+f) slave.

succursale [sukkur'sale] sf branch.

sud [sud] sm south. **abitante del su** s(m+f) southerner. **al sud** (*stato*) in th south; (*moto*) to the south. **dei sud** south southern. **Sudafrica** sf South Africa **sudafricano**, -a s, agg South African **Sudamerica** sf South America. **sudameri cano**, -a s, agg South American.

sudare [su'dare] v sweat, perspire (*lavorar molto*) toil. **sudar freddo** be in cold sweat. **sudata** sf sweat. **sudaticci** agg sweaty.

suddetto [sud'detto] agg above-men tioned.

suddito ['suddito], -a sm, sf subject.

*suddividere [suddi'videre] v subdivide divide. **suddivisione** sf division, subdivi sion.

sud-est [sud'ɛst] sm south-east. **del sud** est south-east(ern).

sudicio ['suditʃo] agg dirty; (*molto sporce* filthy. sm invar filth. **sudiciume** sm filth

sudore [su'dore] sm sweat, perspiration.

sud-ovest [sud'ɔvest] sm south-west. **de sud-ovest** south-west(ern).

sufficiente [suffi'tʃɛnte] agg enough

(*adeguato*) sufficient; presumptuous. **sufficiente a se stesso** self-sufficient. *sm* enough. **avere il sufficiente per vivere** have enough to live on. **sufficienza** *sf* sufficiency. **a sufficienza** more than enough.

suffisso [suf'fisso] *sm* suffix.

suffragio [suf'fradʒo] *sm* suffrage. **suffragetta** *sf* suffragette.

suffumicare [suffumi'kare] *v* fumigate. **suffumicazione** *sf* fumigation.

suga ['suga] *agg* **carta suga** *or* **sugante** *sf* blotting paper.

suggello [sud'dʒɛllo] *sm* seal. **suggellare** *v* seal.

suggerire [suddʒe'rire] *v* suggest; (*consigliare*) advise; (*richiamare*) bring to mind; (*teatro*) prompt. **suggerimento** *sm* suggestion; piece of advice. **suggeritore, -trice** *sm, sf* prompter.

suggestione [suddʒes'tjone] *sf* suggestion; impression; (*fascino*) charm. **suggestionabile** *agg* easily influenced, impressionable. **suggestionabilità** *sf* suggestibility. **suggestionare** *v* influence; (*persuadere*) induce. **suggestivo** *agg* suggestive; evocative. **domanda suggestiva** *sf* leading question.

sughero ['sugero] *sm* cork.

sugli ['suʎi] *prep* + *art* **su gli**.

sugna ['suɲa] *sf* pork fat.

sugo ['sugo] *sm* (*succo*) juice; (*salsa*) sauce; (*fig*) (main) point. **senza sugo** (*fig*) pointless. **sugoso** *agg* juicy; (*fig*) meaty.

sui ['sui] *prep* + *art* **su i**.

suicida [sui'tʃida] *agg* suicidal. *s(m + f)* suicide. **suicidarsi** *v* commit suicide. **suicidio** *sm* suicide.

suino [su'ino] *sm* pig, swine. *agg* pig. **carne suina** *sf* pork.

sul [sul] *prep* + *art* **su il**.

sulfureo [sul'fureo] *agg* sulphurous.

sull' [sull] *prep* + *art* **su l'**.

sulla ['sulla] *prep* + *art* **su la**.

sulle ['sulle] *prep* + *art* **su le**.

sullo ['sullo] *prep* + *art* **su lo**.

sultano [sul'tano] *sm* sultan. (**uva**) **sultanina** *sf* sultana.

sunto ['sunto] *sm* summary. **sunteggiare** *v* *also* **fare il sunto** sum up, summarize.

suo ['suo], *m pl* **suoi** *agg* (*uomo*) his; (*donna*) her; (*cosa, animale*) its; (*riflessivo*) one's. *pron* his; hers. **a ciascuno il suo** to each his own.

suocera ['swɔtʃera] *sf* mother-in-law;

(*spreg*) battle-axe. **suocero** *sm* father-in-law.

suola ['swɔla] *sf* sole. **suolare** *v* (*mettere la suola*) sole.

suolo ['swɔlo] *sm* ground; (*terreno*) soil.

suonare [swo'nare] *V* **sonare**.

suono ['swɔno] *sm* sound; tone. **suono falso** discord; (*fig*) false ring.

suora ['swɔra] *sf* nun, sister.

super ['super] *agg* (*benzina*) four-star.

superare [supe'rare] *v* (*dimensione, quantità*) exceed; (*oltrepassare*) go beyond, surpass; (*di passaggio*) pass, overtake; (*sostenere*) get over or through. **superato** *agg* (*antiquato*) old-fashioned; (*non più valido*) obsolete.

superbo [su'perbo] *agg* haughty; (*fiero*) proud; (*fig*) magnificent, superb. **superbia** *sf* haughtiness. **senza superbia** modestly.

supercongelato [superkondʒe'lato] *agg* deep-frozen.

superficie [super'fitʃe] *sf* surface; area. **alla superficie** on the surface. **superficiale** *agg* superficial; (*geom*) plane. **tensione superficiale** *sf* surface tension.

superfluo [su'perfluo] *agg* (*eccessivo*) superfluous; (*inutile*) unnecessary. *sm* surplus.

superiore [supe'rjore] *agg* (*più in alto*) upper; (*maggiore*) higher; (*fig*) superior; (*di grado*) senior; advanced. **superiore alla media** above average. **superiorità** *sf* superiority.

superlativo [superla'tivo] *sm, agg* superlative.

supermercato [supermer'kato] *sm* supermarket.

supero ['supero] *sm* surplus.

supersonico [super'sɔniko] *agg* supersonic.

superstite [su'pɛrstite] *agg* surviving. *s(m + f)* survivor.

superstizione [superstit'tsjone] *sf* superstition. **superstizioso** *agg* superstitious.

superuomo [supe'rwɔmo] *sm* superman.

supervisione [supervi'zjone] *sf* supervision. **supervisore** *sm* supervisor.

supino [su'pino] *agg* supine. **giacere supino** lie on one's back.

suppellettili [suppel'lettili] *sf pl* furnishings *pl*; (*di casa*) household goods *pl*.

suppergiù [supper'dʒu] *avv* roughly, more or less.

supplemento [supple'mento] *sm* supplement; (*prezzo*) additional charge; (*biglietto*) excess fare. **supplementare** *agg* additional, extra; (*econ, mat*) supplementary.

supplicare [suppli'kare] *v* implore. **supplica** *sf* plea. **in atto di supplica** imploringly. **supplicante** *s(m+f)* supplicant. **supplichevole** *agg* imploring.

supplire [sup'plire] *v* make up for; (*fare le veci*) stand in for. **supplente** *s(m+f)* supply teacher.

supplizio [sup'plitsjo] *sm* torture; (*pena di morte*) capital punishment. **suppliziare** *v* torture.

*supporre [sup'porre] *v* suppose; imagine. **supposizione** *sf* supposition. **supposto che** assuming that, supposing.

supporto [sup'porto] *sm* support; (*mec*) bearing; (*sostegno*) stand.

supposta [sup'posta] *sf* suppository.

suppurare [suppu'rare] *v* fester. **suppurazione** *sf* festering.

supremo [su'prɛmo] *agg* supreme; (*massimo*) highest. **supremazia** *sf* supremacy.

surgelare [surdʒe'lare] *v* freeze. **surgelato** *sm* frozen food.

surreale [surre'ale] *agg* unreal. **surrealismo** *sm* surrealism. **surrealista** *s(m+f)*, *agg* surrealist.

surriscaldare [surriskal'dare] *v* overheat. **surriscaldamento** *sm* overheating.

surrogare [surro'gare] *v* substitute. **surrogato** *sm*, *agg* substitute. **surrogazione** *sf* surrogation.

suscettibile [suʃet'tibile] *agg* capable (of), susceptible; (*facile a risentirsi*) touchy. **suscettibilità** *sf* susceptibility. **offendere la suscettibilità di qualcuno** hurt someone's feelings.

suscitare [suʃi'tare] *v* provoke, give rise to.

susina [su'zina] *sf* plum, damson. **susino** *sm* plum-tree, damson-tree.

susseguirsi [susse'gwirsi] *v* follow (each other). **susseguente** *agg* following, subsequent.

sussidiare [sussi'djare] *v* subsidize. **sussidiario** *agg* subsidiary. **sussidio** *sm* aid; (*di denaro*) subsidy.

sussistere [sus'sistere] *v* exist; (*esser fondato*) subsist. **sussistenza** *sf* subsistence; (*mil*) catering.

sussultare [sussul'tare] *v* (give a) start. **far sussultare** startle. **sussulto** *sm* start.

sussurrare [sussur'rare] *v* murmur; (*dire a bassa voce*) whisper. **sussurro** *sm* murmur; whisper.

sutura [su'tura] *sf* suture. **suturare** *v* suture.

suvvia [suv'via] *inter* come on!

svago ['zvago] *sm* diversion; (*divertimento*) amusement. **svagare** *v* distract. **svagarsi** *v* amuse oneself. **svagatezza** *sf* absent-mindedness. **svagato** *agg* absent-minded.

svaligiare [zvali'dʒare] *v* ransack. **svaligiatore**, **-trice** *sm*, *sf* burglar.

svalutare [zvalu'tare] *v* devalue. **svalutazione** *sf* devaluation.

svanire [zva'nire] *v* vanish; (*fig*) fade away; (*esaurirsi*) lose strength. **svanito** *agg* (*odore*) evaporated; (*mente*) feeble-minded.

svantaggio [zvan'taddʒo] *sm* disadvantage; (*pregiudizio*) drawback; (*danno*) detriment. **svantaggiato** *agg* handicapped. **svantaggioso** *agg* disadvantageous; detrimental.

svariare [zva'rjare] *v* vary; diversify. **svariato** *agg* various.

svasato [zva'zato] *v* flared. **svasatura** *sf* flare.

svastica ['zvastika] *sf* swastika.

svecchiare [zvek'kjare] *v* renew.

svedese [zve'deze] *agg* Swedish. *sm* (*lingua*) Swedish; (*fiammifero*) safety match. *s(m+f)* (*persona*) Swede.

svegliare [zve'ʎare] *v* wake up; (*fig*) arouse. **svegliarsi** *v* wake up. **sveglia** *sf* call; (*mil*) reveille; (*orologio*) alarm-clock. **sveglio** *agg* awake; (*fig*) quick (-witted).

svelare [zve'lare] *v* reveal.

svelto [zvɛlto] *agg* quick; intelligent (*slanciato*) slim. **svelto di mano** light fingered. **sveltezza** *sf* quickness; (*rapidità*) speed; slimness. **sveltire** *v* quicken (*render disinvolto*) smarten *or* liven up make (*more*) slender.

svendere ['zvendere] *v* sell off. **svendita** *sf* sale.

*svenire [zve'nire] *v* faint. **svenevole** *agg* mawkish. **svenimento** *sm* fainting fit.

sventare [zven'tare] *v* foil. **sventatezza** *sf* thoughtlessness. **sventato** *agg* thoughtless.

sventola ['zvɛntola] *sf* fan; (*pugilato*) hook; (*schiaffo*) slap. **sventolare** *v* flutter (*arieggiare*) air.

sventrare [zven'trare] v rip open; (animale) disembowel; (fig) demolish. **sventramento** sm demolition.

sventura [zven'tura] sf misfortune; (mala sorte) bad luck. **per colmo di sventura** to crown it all. **per mia sventura** unluckily for me. **sventurato** agg unlucky.

svergognare [zvergo'ɲare] v (put to) shame. **svergognatezza** sf impudence. **svergognato, -a** sm, sf shameless or impudent person.

svernare [zver'nare] v winter.

sverza ['zvɛrtsa] sf splinter. **sverzare** v splinter.

svestire [zves'tire] v undress.

Svezia ['zvɛtsja] sf Sweden.

svezzare [zvet'tsare] v wean. **svezzamento** sm weaning.

sviare [zvi'are] v divert; (fig) lead astray. **sviare il discorso** change the subject. **sviamento** sm diversion. **sviato** agg misguided.

svignarsela [zviɲ'narsela] v sneak away.

svigorire [zvigo'rire] v weaken.

sviluppo [zvi'luppo] sm development; (crescita) growth. **età dello sviluppo** of puberty. **sviluppare** v develop; (produrre) generate; (estendersi) grow.

svincolare [zvinko'lare] v release; (riscattare) redeem. **svincolarsi** v free oneself (from). **svincolo** sm release; (comm) clearance; (autostrada) exit.

svisare [zvi'zare] v twist.

sviscerare [zviʃe'rare] v disembowel; (fig) exhaust. **sviscerarsi per** dote on. **sviscerato** agg passionate; (spreg) obsequious.

svista ['zvista] sf oversight.

svitare [zvi'tare] v unscrew. **svitato, -a** sm, sf (fam) nut.

Svizzera ['zvittsera] sf Switzerland. **svizzero, -a** s, agg Swiss.

svogliato [zvoʎ'ʎato] agg listless; unenthusiastic; (indolente) slack. **svogliatezza** sf listlessness.

svolazzare [zvolat'tsare] v flutter. **svolazzo** sm flourish.

*__svolgere__ ['zvɔldʒere] v develop. **svolgersi** v proceed, go; (distendersi) unfold; (voltarsi) turn. **svolgimento** sm development. **svolta** sf turning; (fig) turning point; curve.

svuotare [zvwo'tare] v empty.

T

tabacco [ta'bakko] sm tobacco. **tabaccaio, -a** sm, sf tobacconist. **tabaccheria** sf tobacconist's (shop).

tabella [ta'bella] sf table; list. **tabellone** sm notice-board; (per affissioni murali) hoarding; (sport) score-board.

tabù [ta'bu] agg, sm taboo.

tabulatore [tabula'tore], **-trice** sm, sf tabulator.

tacca ['takka] sf nick; (macchia) blotch; (qualità) kind; (difetto) fault.

taccagno [tak'kaɲo] agg stingy. **taccagneria** sf stinginess.

taccheggiatore [takkeddʒa'tore], **-trice** sm, sf shop-lifter. **taccheggio** sm shoplifting.

tacchino [tak'kino] sm turkey.

taccia ['tattʃa] sf (bad) reputation. **tacciare** v accuse.

tacco ['takko] sm heel. **battere i tacchi** click one's heels.

taccuino [takku'ino] sm note-book.

*__tacere__ [ta'tʃere] v be or keep quiet; (fam) shut up; (non dir nulla) say nothing. **far tacere** hush.

tachimetro [ta'kimetro] sm speedometer.

tacito ['tatʃito] agg tacit; (silenzioso) silent. **taciturno** agg taciturn.

tafano ['tafano] sm horsefly.

tafferuglio [taffe'ruʎo] sm brawl.

taglia ['taʎa] sf (premio) reward; (statura) size.

tagliando [ta'ʎando] sm coupon; (scontrino) voucher.

tagliare [ta'ʎare] v cut; (staccare, interrompere) cut off; (trinciare) carve; (in più parti) cut up; (vino) blend. **tagliaboschi** sm invar woodcutter. **tagliacarte** sm invar paper-knife. **tagliapietre** sm invar stonemason. **tagliare la testa al toro** settle a matter once and for all.

tagliente [ta'ʎɛnte] agg cutting.

tagliere [ta'ʎere] sm chopping board.

taglio ['taʎo] sm cut; (parte staccata) piece; (parte tagliente) (cutting) edge; (importo) denomination.

tagliola [ta'ʎɔla] sf trap.

tagliuzzare [taʎut'tsare] v chop up; (a strisce) cut to shreds.

tailleur [ta'jœr] sm suit.

talco ['talko] sm talc.

tale ['tale] agg such; certain. **tal dei tali** so-and-so. **tale quale** exactly like. **tale ... tale ...** like ... like ... **un (certo) tale** a certain person.

talento [ta'lento] sm talent.

talismano [taliz'mano] sm talisman, charm.

tallomcino [tallon't∫ino] sm counterfoil.

tallone [tal'lone] sm heel. **tallonare** v shadow; (sport) mark.

talora [ta'lora] avv at times.

talpa ['talpa] sf mole.

taluni [ta'luni] pron, agg some.

talvolta [tal'vɔlta] avv sometimes.

tamburo [tam'buro] sm drum; (sonatore) drummer; (mec) barrel, drum. **tamburellare** v drum. **tamburello** sm tambourine.

Tamigi [ta'midʒi] sm Thames.

tamponare [tampo'nare] v plug; (auto) bump into. **tamponare una falla** stop a leak. **tampone** sm plug; tampon.

tana ['tana] sf den.

tanfo ['tanfo] sm musty smell.

tangente [tan'dʒɛnte] sf tangent. **tangenziale** sf (strada) ring road.

tangibile [tan'dʒibile] agg tangible.

tango ['tango] sm tango.

tanto ['tanto] agg (so) much or many; (altrettanto) as much or many; (molto) a lot (of). **tanto ... quanto ...** as much ... as .... pron a lot; much or many. **tanti** pron (persone) so many (people). **tanto per** so much for. avv so (much); (soltanto) just. **da tanto** (tempo) for such a long time. **di tanto in tanto** from time to time. **ogni tanto** from time to time. **tanti auguri!** best wishes! congratulations! **tanto meglio** so much the better. **tanto più che** especially as.

tappa ['tappa] sf stage; (sosta) stop.

tappare [tap'pare] v shut; (con tappo) bung (up). **tapparsi il naso** hold one's nose. **tapparsi le orecchie** close one's ears.

tapparella [tappa'rella] sf blind.

tappeto [tap'peto] sm carpet; (piccolo) rug; (sport, tec) mat. **mettere al tappeto** knock down.

tappezzare [tappet'tsare] v (di carta) paper; (di legno) panel; (di stoffa) cover, upholster. **tappezzeria** sf (carta) wallpaper; (stoffa) tapestry; (legno) panelling; (mobili) upholstery. **tappezziere** sm decorator; upholsterer.

tappo ['tappo] sm stopper, plug; (sughero) cork; (a vite) screw-cap.

tara ['tara] sf tare; defect. **tarato** agg (tec) calibrated; (difettoso) tainted.

tarantola [ta'rantola] sf tarantula.

tarchiato [tar'kjato] agg sturdy.

tardare [tar'dare] v be late. **tardi** avv late. **tardivo** agg late; retarded. **tardo** agg (lento) slow; (tempo) late; (età) ripe old.

targa ['targa] sf plate; (auto) number-plate. **targare** v (auto) register.

tariffa [ta'riffa] sf rate; (trasporto pubblico) fare; (dogana) tariff.

tarlo ['tarlo] sm woodworm. **tarlo del dubbio** gnawing doubt. **tarlato** agg wormeaten.

tarma ['tarma] sf moth.

tarpare [tar'pare] v **tarpare le ali a** clip the wings of.

tartagliare [tarta'ʎʎare] v stammer.

tartaro [tar'taro] sm tartar.

tartaruga [tarta'ruga] sf tortoise.

tartassare [tartas'sare] v ill-treat.

tartina [tar'tina] sf canapé.

tartufo [tar'tufo] sm truffle.

tasca ['taska] sf pocket. **avere le tasche piene (di)** (fam) be sick and tired (of). **conoscere come le proprie tasche** know like the back of one's hand. **tascabile** agg pocket.

tassa ['tassa] sf tax; (imposta) duty; (giudiziaria, scolastica) fee. **tassametro** sm meter.

tassare [tas'sare] v tax. **tassare troppo** (fig) overtax. **tassabile** agg taxable; subject to duty. **tassativo** agg express; definite.

tassello [tas'sɛllo] sm dowel; (prelievo) wedge; (indumento) gusset.

tassì [tas'si] sm taxi. **tassista** sm taxi-driver.

tasso¹ ['tasso] sm (zool) badger.

tasso² ['tasso] sm (bot) yew(-tree).

tasso³ ['tasso] sm (rapporto) rate.

tastare [tas'tare] v feel. **tastare il terreno** (fig) see how the land lies. **tastiera** sf keyboard. **tasto** sm key; (argomento) subject; (tatto) touch. **a tastoni** feeling one's way.

tattica ['tattika] sf tactics pl. **tattico** agg tactical.

tatto ['tatto] sm touch; (fig) tact. **con tatto** tactfully. **mancare di tatto** be tactless. **senza tatto** tactlessly.

tatuaggio [tatu'add30] *sm* tattoo. **tatuare** *v* tattoo.

tautologia [tautolo'd3ia] *sf* tautology. **tautologico** *agg* tautological.

taverna [ta'vɛrna] *sf* inn, pub.

tavola ['tavola] *sf* table; (*asse*) board. **tavola calda** snack-bar. **tavola da disegno/stiro** drawing/ironing board. **tavola di comando** console. **tavola nera** blackboard. **tavola reale** (*gioco*) backgammon.

tavolato [tavo'lato] *sm* (*pavimento*) flooring; (*assito*) partition; (*geog*) plateau.

tavolo ['tavolo] *sm* table; (*ufficio, studio*) desk.

tavolozza [tavo'lɔttsa] *sf* palette.

tazza ['tattsa] *sf* cup; (*gabinetto*) lavatory basin; (*fontana*) basin.

te [te] *pron* you. *V* ti.

tè [te] *sm* tea.

teatro [te'atro] *sm* theatre; (*attività professionale*) stage; (*complesso di opere*) plays *pl.* **teatro lirico** (*edificio*) opera house; (*genere*) opera. **teatrale** *agg* theatrical.

tecnica ['tɛknika] *sf* technique; technology.

tecnico ['tɛkniko], **-a** *agg* technical. *sm, sf* technician, engineer; expert. **tecnicismo** *sm* technicality.

tecnologia [teknolo'd3ia] *sf* technology. **tecnologico** *agg* technological.

tedesco [te'desko], **-a** *s, agg* German.

tedio ['tɛdjo] *sm* tediousness. **tedioso** *agg* tedious.

tegame [te'game] *sm* (frying-)pan. **uova al tegame** *sf pl* fried eggs *pl.*

teglia ['teʎa] *sf* baking tin.

tegola ['tegola] *sf* (roofing-)tile. **coprire di tegole** tile. **tetto di tegole** *sm* tiled roof.

tela ['tela] *sf* cloth; (*pittura*) canvas; (*teatro*) curtain. **tela cerata** oilcloth. **tela da lenzuola** sheeting. **tela di lino** linen.

telaio [te'lajo] *sm* loom; (*auto*) chassis; (*tec*) frame.

telecabina [teleka'bina] *sf* cable-car.

telecomando [teleko'mando] *sm* remote control. **telecomandare** *v* operate by remote control.

telecronaca [tele'krɔnaka] *sf* news bulletin. **telecronista** *s(m+f)* television commentator.

telefonare [telefo'nare] *v* telephone; (*fam*) phone. **telefonata** *sf* telephone call. **telefonata urbana/interurbana/con preavviso** local/trunk/personal call. **telefonico**

agg telephone. **telefonista** *s(m+f)* telephonist. **telefono** *sm* telephone.

telegiornale [teled3or'nale] *sm* television news.

telegrafare [telegra'fare] *v* telegraph. **telegrafico** *agg* telegraph; (*conciso*) telegraphic. **telegrafista** *s(m+f)* telegraph operator.

telegramma [tele'gramma] *sm* telegram.

telepatia [telepa'tia] *sf* telepathy. **telepatico** *agg* telepathic.

teleschermo [tele'skɛrmo] *sm* television screen.

telescopio [tele'skɔpjo] *sm* telescope.

telespettatore [telespetta'tore], **-trice** *sm, sf* viewer.

teletrasmissione [teletrazmis'sjone] *sf* television programme.

televisione [televi'zjone] *sf* televison; (*fam*) TV. **televisore** *sm* television set.

telone [te'lone] *sm* tarpaulin.

tema ['tɛma] *sm* theme, subject; (*scolastico*) essay. **fuori tema** off the point.

temerario [teme'rarjo] *agg* reckless; (*avventato*) rash. **temerità** *sf* temerity.

temere [te'mere] *v* fear, be afraid. **non temere!** don't worry!

temperamento [tempera'mento] *sm* temperament.

temperare [tempe'rare] *v* temper; (*matita*) sharpen. **temperato** *agg* temperate. **temperino** *sm* pen-knife.

temperatura [tempera'tura] *sf* temperature.

tempesta [tem'pɛsta] *sf* storm. **tempestare** *v* storm; (*ornare*) stud; (*importunare*) bombard. **tempestoso** *agg* stormy.

tempestivo [tempes'tivo] *agg* timely. **tempestività** *sf* timeliness.

tempia ['tɛmpja] *sf* temple.

tempio ['tɛmpjo] *sm* temple.

tempista [tem'pista] *s(m+f)* opportunist.

tempo ['tɛmpo] *sm* time; (*atmosferico*) weather; (*gramm*) tense; (*musica*) tempo, movement. **a suo tempo** (*passato*) originally; (*futuro*) in due course; (*al momento giusto*) at the right time. **a tempo debito** in due course. **a tempo perso** in one's spare time. **da tempo** for some time. **in un primo tempo** at first. **tempo da cani** foul weather.

temporale[1] [tempo'rale] *agg* temporal.

temporale[2] [tempo'rale] *sm* (thunder)storm. **temporalesco** *agg* stormy.

temporaneo [tempo'raneo] *sm* temporary.

temporeggiare [tempored'dʒare] *v* mark time, temporize.

temprare [tem'prare] *v* temper. **tempra** *sf* (*tec*) tempering, temper; (*fig*) fibre; (*voce*) timbre.

tenace [te'natʃe] *agg* firm; (*fig*) tenacious. **tenacia** *sf* tenacity. **tenacità** *sf* tenacity, firmness.

tenaglie [te'naʎe] *sf pl* pincers *pl*; (*pinze*) pliers *pl*; (*molle*) tongs *pl*.

tenda ['tɛnda] *sf* (*drappo*) curtain; (*da campo*) tent; (*tendone da sole*) awning. **tenda alla veneziana** Venetian blind. **tendina** *sf* net curtain.

tendenza [ten'dɛntsa] *sf* tendency; (*attitudine*) bent; (*orientamento*, *econ*) trend. **tendenziale** *agg* potential. **tendenzioso** *agg* tendentious.

°tendere ['tɛndere] *v* (*mettere in tensione*) stretch; (*porgere*) hold out; (*reti*) cast. **tendere a** (*mirare*) aim at; be inclined to; (*volgersi verso*) tend towards. **tendere un tranello** set a trap.

tendine ['tɛndine] *sm* tendon.

tenebre ['tɛnebre] *sf pl* darkness *sing*. **tenebroso** *agg* dark; (*fig*) mysterious.

tenente [te'nɛnte] *sm* lieutenant.

°tenere [te'nere] *v* hold; (*mantenere*, *trattenere*) keep; (*seguire una direzione*) keep to. **tenerci a** attach great importance to. **tenere a** (*volere*) want. **tener d'occhio** keep an eye on. **tener presente** bear in mind.

tenero ['tɛnero] *agg* tender. **tenerezza** *sf* tenderness.

tenia ['tɛnja] *sf* tapeworm.

tennis ['tɛnnis] *sm* tennis. **tennista** *s(m+f)* tennis player.

tenore [te'nore] *sm* tenor; content. **a tenore di** in accordance with. **tenore di vita** living standard.

tensione [ten'sjone] *sf* tension.

tentacolo [ten'takolo] *sm* tentacle.

tentare [ten'tare] *v* (*cercare*) try; (*sperimentare*) try out; (*cercare di fare*) attempt; (*invogliare*) tempt. **tentativo** *sm* attempt. **tentatore** *sm* tempter. **tentatrice** *sf* temptress. **tentazione** *sf* temptation. **aver la tentazione (di)** be tempted (to).

tentennare [tenten'nare] *v* wobble; hesitate.

tentoni [ten'toni] *avv* **a tentoni** groping one's way.

tenue ['tɛnue] *agg* slender; (*debole*) faint; (*fig*) slight.

tenuta [te'nuta] *sf* (*divisa*) uniform; (*possedimento fondiario*) estate; capacity; (*auto*) road-holding; (*tec*) seal. **a tenuta d'acqua** water-tight. **a tenuta d'aria** air-tight.

teologia [teolo'dʒia] *sf* theology. **teologico** theological. **teologo, -a** *sm*, *sf* theologist.

teorema [teo'rɛma] *sm* theorem.

teoria [teo'ria] *sf* theory. **in teoria** theoretically.

teorico [te'ɔriko], **-a** *agg* theoretical. *sm*, *sf* theorist.

tepore [te'pore] *sm* warmth.

teppa ['tɛppa] *sf also* **teppaglia** rabble. **teppismo** *sm* hooliganism. **teppista** *s(m+f)* hooligan.

terapia [tera'pia] *sf* therapy. **terapeutico** *agg* therapeutic. **terapista** *s(m+f)* therapist.

tergicristallo [terdʒikris'tallo] *sm* windshield-wiper.

tergiversare [terdʒiver'sare] *v* prevaricate.

tergo ['tɛrgo] *sm* **a tergo di** (*di dietro*) behind. **vedi a tergo** (*nei rinvii*) please turn over, PTO.

terme ['tɛrme] *sf pl* (thermal) baths *pl*. **termale** *or* **termico** *agg* thermal.

terminare [termi'nare] *v* end. **terminazione** *sf* ending. **termine** *sm* term; limit; (*punto estremo*) end; (*comm*) expiry (date). **a breve/lungo termine** short-/long-term. **ai termini di legge** by law. **a rigor di termini** strictly speaking. **terminologia** *sf* terminology.

termodinamica [termodi'namika] *sf* thermodynamics.

termometro [ter'mɔmetro] *sm* thermometer.

termonucleare [termonukle'are] *agg* thermonuclear.

termos *V* **thermos**.

termosifone [termosi'fone] *sm* radiator.

termostato [ter'mɔstato] *sm* thermostat. **termostatico** *agg* thermostatic.

terra ['tɛrra] *sf* earth; (*estensione di terreno, paese*) land; (*suolo*) soil. **a terra** (*senza soldi*) broke; (*depresso*) in low spirits; (*gomma*) flat. **collegare** *or* **mettere a terra** (*elett*) earth. **raso terra** close to the ground.

terraglia [ter'raʎa] *sf* earthenware. **terraglie** *sf pl* (*vasellame*) crockery *sing*.

terrapieno [terra'pjɛno] *sm* embankment.

terrazza [ter'rattsa] *sf* terrace. **terrazzo** *sm* terrace; (*alpinismo*) ledge.

terremoto [terre'mɔto] *sm* earthquake. **terremotato, -a** *sm, sf* earthquake victim.

terreno[1] [ter'reno] *agg* earthly, worldly. **piano terreno** ground floor.

terreno[2] [ter'reno] *sm* land; (*suolo*) ground; (*podere*) plot (of land); (*fig*) field.

terreo ['tɛrreo] *agg* earthy; (*colorito*) deathly pale.

terrestre [ter'rɛstre] *agg* terrestrial.

terribile [ter'ribile] *agg* terrible.

territorio [terri'tɔrjo] *sm* territory. **territoriale** *agg* territorial.

terrore [ter'rore] *sm* terror. **aver terrore (di)** be terrified (of). **terrorismo** *sm* terrorism. **terrorista** *s(m+f)* terrorist. **terroristico** *agg* terrorist. **terrorizzare** *v* terrorize.

terzo ['tɛrtso] *agg, sm* third. **terzi** *sm pl* (*comm, dir*) third party *sing*. **terzina** *sf* triplet.

tesa ['teza] *sf* (*cappello*) brim; (*reti*) spreading.

teschio ['tɛskjo] *sm* skull.

tesi ['tɛzi] *sf* thesis (*pl* -ses).

teso ['tezo] *agg* taut; (*nervoso*) tense. **stare con le orecchie tese** prick up one's ears.

tesoro [te'zɔro] *sm* treasure; (*tesoreria, pol*) treasury. **far tesoro (di)** treasure. **tesoriere** *sm* treasurer.

tessera ['tɛssera] *sf* card; (*lasciapassare*) pass; (*ferr*) season-ticket. **tesseramento** *sm* rationing. **tesserare** *v* give a membership card; ration.

tessere ['tɛssere] *v* weave. **tessitura** *sf* weaving; (*stabilimento*) (weaving) mill; (*trama*) plot. **tessuto** *sm* fabric; (*bot, zool, fig*) tissue.

tessile ['tɛssile] *agg* textile. *sm* textile; (*operaio*) textile worker.

testa ['tɛsta] *sf* head. **a testa** (*ciascuno*) each, per head. **colpo di testa** *sm* (*sport*) header; (*fig*) whim. **essere in testa** be in the lead. **fare a testa e croce** toss up. **passare in testa** take the lead. **rompersi la testa** rack one's brains.

testamento [testa'mento] *sm* will; (*bibbia*) testament.

testardo [tes'tardo] *agg* stubborn. **testardaggine** *sf* stubbornness.

testata [tes'tata] *sf* (*intestazione*) heading;

(*colpo di testa*) butt; (*auto*) cylinder head; (*parte anteriore*) head.

testicolo [tes'tikolo] *sm* testicle.

testimone [testi'mone] *s(m+f)* witness. **testimoniale** *sm* evidence. **testimonianza** *sf* testimony; (*prova*) evidence. **testimoniare** *v* testify; (*deporre in giudizio*) (bear) witness.

testo ['tɛsto] *sm* text; (*libro*) text-book. **far testo** be an authority. **testuale** *agg* exact.

testone [tes'tone] *sm* (*stupido*) blockhead; (*testardo*) pig-headed person.

testuggine [tes'tuddʒine] *sf* tortoise; (*di mare*) turtle.

tetano ['tɛtano] *sm* tetanus.

tetro ['tetro] *agg* gloomy.

tetta ['tɛtta] *sf* (*fam*) breast. **tettarella** *sf* dummy.

tetto ['tɛtto] *sm* roof (*pl* -s). **essere senza tetto** be homeless. **tettoia** *sf* roofing, canopy.

Tevere ['tevere] *sm* Tiber.

thermos ® or **termos** ['tɛrmos] *sm invar* thermos (flask) ®.

ti [ti], **te** *pron* (to) you; (*riflessivo*) yourself.

tiara ['tjara] *sf* tiara.

tic [tik] *sm invar* tic.

ticchettare [tikket'tare] *v* click; (*pioggia*) patter; (*orologio*) tick.

ticchio ['tikkjo] *sm* whim.

tictac [tik'tak] *sm* tick.

tiepido ['tjɛpido] *agg* lukewarm.

tifo ['tifo] *sm* (*med*) typhus; (*fam: sport*) fanaticism. **fare il tifo per** be a fan of. (*febbre*) **tifoide** *sf* typhoid (fever).

tifone [ti'fone] *sm* typhoon.

tifoso [ti'fozo], **-a** *sm, sf* fan.

tiglio ['tiʎo] *sm* lime(-tree); (*fibra*) bast.

tigna ['tiɲa] *sf* ringworm.

tignola [ti'ɲola] *sf* moth.

tigre ['tigre] *sf* tiger.

timbrare [tim'brare] *v* stamp; (*posta*) postmark. **timbro** *sm* stamp; postmark; (*suono*) timbre.

timido ['timido] *agg* shy; (*timoroso*) timid.

timo ['timo] *sm* (*bot*) thyme.

timone [ti'mone] *sm* rudder; (*fig*) helm. **timoniere** *sm* helmsman; (*canottaggio*) cox.

timore [ti'more] *sm* fear. **senza timore** fearless. **timoroso** *agg* fearful; (*preoccupato*) anxious.

timpano ['timpano] *sm* (*anat*) ear-drum;

(*musica*) kettle-drum. **timpani** *sm pl* timpani *pl*.

tinca ['tinka] *sf* tench.

***tingere** ['tindʒere] *v* dye; (*macchiare*) spot.

tino ['tino] *sm* tub, vat.

tinta ['tinta] *sf* colour; (*sfumatura*) shade. **tintarella** *sf* tan. **tinto** *agg* dyed; (*macchiato*) tinged. **tintore** *sm* dyer. **tintoria** *sf* cleaners. **tintura** *sf* dyeing; (*med*) tincture.

tipo ['tipo] *sm* type; (*genere*) sort, kind. **tipico** *agg* typical.

tipografia [tipogra'fia] *sf* typography; (*stamperia*) press. **tipografico** *agg* typographical. **tipografo, -a** *sm, sf* printer.

tiranneggiare [tiranned'dʒare] *v* tyrannize. **tirannia** *sf* tyranny. **tirannico** *agg* tyrannical. **tiranno** *sm* tyrant.

tirante [ti'rante] *sm* (*connecting*) rod; brace.

tirapiedi [tira'pjɛdi] *sm invar* hanger-on.

tirare [ti'rare] *v* pull, draw; (*lanciare*) throw; (*sparare*) shoot. **tirare avanti** keep going. **tirar fuori** pull out; (*estrarre*) take out. **tirare in lungo** draw out. **tirarsi indietro** draw back. **tirarsi su** draw oneself up; (*fam*) get back on one's feet. **tirata** *sf* pull; (*discorso*) tirade. **tiratura** *sf* printing; (*numero*) run.

tirchio ['tirkjo] *agg* stingy.

tiritera [tiri'tɛra] *sf* rigmarole.

tiro ['tiro] *sm* (*lancio*) throw; (*arma*) shot. **fuori tiro** out of range.

tirocinio [tiro'tʃinjo] *sm* apprenticeship.

tiroide [ti'rɔide] *sf* thyroid.

titolare [tito'lare] *agg* titular, regular. *s(m+f)* proprietor.

titolo ['titolo] *sm* title; (*comm*) share; (*obbligazione*) bond; (*filato*) count. **a titolo di** out of.

titubare [titu'bare] *v* hesitate.

tizio ['titsjo] *sm* fellow. **Tizio, Caio, e Sempronio** Tom, Dick, and Harry.

tizzo ['tittso] *sm* ember.

toboga [to'bɔga] *sm invar* toboggan.

toccare [tok'kare] *v* touch; (*riguardare*) concern. **tocca a me** it is my turn; (*spettare di diritto*) I am entitled; (*spettare di dovere*) it is up to me. **toccasana** *sm invar* panacea.

tocco¹ ['tokko] *sm* touch; (*campana*) stroke; (*l'una*) one o'clock.

tocco² ['tokko] *sm* (*pezzo*) hunk.

toga ['tɔga] *sf* toga.

***togliere** ['tɔʎere] *v* take away; (*indumenti*) take off. **ciò non toglie che** it does not alter the fact that. **togliere di mezzo** get out of the way. **togliersi** *v* (*levarsi*) take off; (*soddisfare*) satisfy.

toletta [to'letta] *sf also* **toilette** toilet; (*mobile*) dressing table; (*acconciatura*) toilette; (*abito*) outfit.

tollerare [tolle'rare] *v* tolerate, stand; (*permettere*) allow. **tollerabile** *agg* bearable. **tollerante** *agg* tolerant. **tolleranza** *sf* tolerance.

tomaia [to'maja] *sf* upper.

tomba ['tomba] *sf* tomb.

tombola¹ ['tombola] *sf* (*gioco*) tombola; bingo.

tombola² ['tombola] *sf* (*caduta*) fall.

tomo ['tɔmo] *sm* tome; (*tipo strano*) odd type.

tonaca ['tɔnaka] *sf* (*frati, monache*) habit; (*preti*) cassock.

tonalità [tonali'ta] *sf* tonality; (*colore*) shade.

tonare [to'nare] *v* thunder.

tonchio ['tonkjo] *sm* weevil.

tondo ['tondo] *agg* round. *sm* round plate; (*forma*) circle. **parlar chiaro e tondo** speak bluntly.

tonfo ['tonfo] *sm* thud; (*nell'acqua*) splash.

tonico ['tɔniko] *agg* tonic. **tonica** *sf* (*musica*) tonic.

tonnellata [tonnel'lata] *sf* ton. **tonnellaggio** *sm* tonnage.

tonno ['tonno] *sm* tuna, tunny.

tono ['tɔno] *sm* tone. **cambiar tono** change (one's) tune. **fuori tono** out of tune. **giù di tono** out of sorts. **in tono** in tune; (*fisicamente*) fit.

tonsilla [ton'silla] *sf* tonsil. **tonsillite** *sf* tonsillitis.

tonto ['tonto], **-a** *agg* silly. *sm, sf* fool.

topazio [to'patsjo] *sm* topaz.

topico ['tɔpiko] *agg* local; (*fig*) topical.

topo ['tɔpo] *sm* mouse (*pl* mice); (*campagnolo*) fieldmouse. **topo di biblioteca** bookworm.

topografia [topogra'fia] *sf* topography. **topografico** *agg* topographical.

toporagno [topo'raɲo] *sm* shrew.

toppa ['tɔppa] *sf* patch; (*serratura*) keyhole.

torace [to'ratʃe] *sm* chest.

torba ['torba] *sf* peat.

torbido ['torbido] *agg* turbid, muddy. **c'è del torbido** there's something fishy going on.

***torcere** ['tortʃere] *v* twist; (*strizzare*) wring out. **torcere il collo a qualcuno** wring someone's neck. **torcere il naso** turn up one's nose. **torcersi il collo** crane one's neck. **torcicollo** *sm* crick in the neck.

torchio ['torkjo] *sm* press. **torchiare** *v* press.

torcia ['tortʃa] *sf* torch.

tordo ['tordo] *sm* thrush.

Torino [to'rino] *sf* Turin.

torma ['torma] *sf* herd; (*persone*) throng.

tormentare [tormen'tare] *v* torment. **tormento** *sm* torment; (*infastidire*) plague.

tornaconto [torna'konto] *sm* advantage.

tornante [tor'nante] *sm* hairpin bend.

tornare [tor'nare] *v* return; (*andare di nuovo*) go back; (*venire di nuovo*) come back; (*ricominciare*) start again. **ben tornato!** welcome back! **qualcosa non torna** something is not quite right.

torneo [tor'nɛo] *sm* tournament.

tornio ['tornjo] *sm* lathe. **tornire** *v* turn. **tornitore** *sm* (*tec*) lathe operator; (*di legno*) wood turner.

toro ['tɔro] *sm* bull. **Toro** *sm* Taurus.

torpedine [tor'pedine] *sf* torpedo.

torpedone [torpe'done] *sm* coach.

torpido ['tɔrpido] *agg* sluggish. **torpore** *sm* sluggishness.

torre ['torre] *sf* tower; (*scacchi*) rook, castle. **torretta** *sf* turret.

torrefare [torre'fare] *v* roast. **torrefazione** *sf* roasting.

torrente [tor'rɛnte] *sm* torrent. **torrenziale** *agg* torrential.

torrido ['torrido] *agg* torrid.

torrone [tor'rone] *sm* nougat.

torso ['torso] *sm* stalk; (*frutta*) core; (*anat*) torso. **a torso nudo** bare-chested.

torsolo ['torsolo] *sm* stalk; (*frutta*) core.

torta ['torta] *sf* cake; (*di frutta*) tart; (*pasticcio*) pie.

tortiglione [torti'ʎone] *sm* spiral. **a tortiglione** spiral.

torto¹ ['torto] *sm* wrong; (*colpa*) fault. **a torto** wrongfully. **aver torto** be wrong. **dar torto a** prove wrong.

torto² ['torto] *agg* twisted.

tortora ['tortora] *sf* turtle-dove.

tortuoso [tortu'ozo] *agg* tortuous.

torturare [tortu'rare] *v* torture. **tortura** *sf* torture.

torvo ['torvo] *agg* surly.

tosare [to'zare] *v* shear; (*cani*) clip; (*fig*) fleece. **tosatrice** *sf* (*capelli*) hair-clippers *pl*; (*erba*) lawn-mower. **tosatura** *sf* shearing; clipping.

Toscana [tos'kana] *sf* Tuscany. **toscano, -a** *s, agg* Tuscan.

tosse ['tosse] *sf* cough. **tossire** *v* cough.

tossico ['tossiko] *agg* poisonous. *sm* poison. **tossicità** *sf* toxicity. **tossicomane** *s(m+f)* drug addict. **tossicomania** *sf* drug addiction. **tossina** *sf* toxin.

tostare [tos'tare] *v* roast; (*pane*) toast. **tostapane** *sm invar* toaster.

tosto ['tosto] *agg* **faccia tosta** *sf* (*fam*) cheek.

totale [to'tale] *agg, sm* total. **totalità** *sf* entirety.

totalitario [totali'tarjo] *agg* (*pol*) totalitarian.

totano ['totano] *sm* squid.

totocalcio [toto'kaltʃo] *sm* football pools *pl*.

tovaglia [to'vaʎa] *sf* table-cloth. **tovagliolo** *sm* napkin, serviette.

tozzo¹ [tottso] *agg* squat; (*persone*) stocky.

tozzo² ['tottso] *sm* piece.

tra [tra] *prep* among(st); (*tra due*) between; (*nel mezzo*) in the midst of; (*tempo*) in. **tra breve** *or* **poco soon. tra l'altro** among other things; (*inoltre*) besides.

traballare [trabal'lare] *v* wobble; (*persone, fig*) totter.

traboccare [trabok'kare] *v* overflow. **trabocchetto** *sm* trap.

tracannare [trakan'nare] *v* gulp down.

traccia ['trattʃa] *sf* track, trail; (*orma*) footprint; (*indizio*) trace. **tracciare** *v* trace; (*abbozzare*) sketch (out); (*a grandi linee*) outline. **tracciato** *sm* layout.

trachea [tra'kɛa] *sf* windpipe.

tracolla [tra'kolla] *sf* shoulder-strap. **a tracolla** over one's shoulder. **borsetta a tracolla** *sf* shoulder-bag.

tradire [tra'dire] *v* betray; (*coniugi*) be unfaithful (to). **tradimento** *sm* treachery; (*dir*) treason. **a tradimento** by surprise. **traditore** *sm* traitor. **traditrice** *sf* traitress.

tradizione [tradi'tsjone] *sf* tradition. **tradizionale** *agg* traditional.

*tradurre [tra'durre] v translate; (condurre) convey. traduttore, -trice sm, sf translator. traduzione sf translation.

trafelato [trafe'lato] agg out of breath.

trafficare [traffi'kare] v (commerciare) trade, deal; (spreg) traffic; (darsi da fare) busy oneself. traffico sm traffic.

*trafiggere [tra'fiddʒere] v pierce.

trafila [tra'fila] sf (operazione) (lengthy) procedure. trafilare v draw. trafiletto sm paragraph.

traforare [trafo'rare] v bore, drill; (legno) cut with a fretsaw. traforatrice sf drill; (sega) fretsaw. traforo sm tunnel; fretsaw.

tragedia [tra'dʒɛdja] sf tragedy.

traghetto [tra'getto] sm ferry. traghettare v ferry (across).

tragico ['tradʒiko] agg tragic. sm tragedy; (autore) tragedian; (attore) tragic actor. prendere sul tragico dramatize.

tragitto [tra'dʒitto] sm journey; (traversata) crossing.

traguardo [tra'gwardo] sm finish; (sport) winning-post; (fig) goal.

traiettoria [trajet'tɔrja] sf trajectory; (di volo) flight-path.

trainare [trai'nare] v pull or haul along; (rimorchiare) tow. traino sm haulage; (rimorchio) trailer; (con pattini) sledge.

tralasciare [trala'ʃare] v leave out; interrupt; (trascurare) neglect.

tralcio ['traltʃo] sm shoot.

traliccio [tra'littʃo] sm (tessuto) ticking; (struttura) truss; (graticcio) trellis.

tram [tram] sm invar tram.

trama ['trama] sf (tessile) weft; (fig) plot. tramare v plot.

tramandare [traman'dare] v hand down.

trambusto [tram'busto] sm turmoil.

tramezzare [tramed'dzare] v interpose; (dividere un locale) partition (off). tramezzo sm partition.

tramite ['tramite] sm means pl; intermediary. prep (per mezzo di) through.

tramontana [tramon'tana] sf (nord) north; (vento) north wind.

tramontare [tramon'tare] v set; (aver fine) come to an end; (dileguarsi) wane. tramonto sm sunset; (fig) decline.

tramortire [tramor'tire] v stun.

trampolino [trampo'lino] sm springboard; (piscina) diving-board; (palestra) trampoline; (sci) ski-jump.

trampolo ['trampolo] sm stilt.

tramutare [tramu'tare] v transform.

trancia ['trantʃa] sf (taglierina) cutter; (gastr) slice.

tranello [tra'nello] sm trap; (fig) catch.

trangugiare [trangu'dʒare] v gulp down; (fig) swallow.

tranne ['tranne] prep except or but (for).

tranquillo [tran'kwillo] agg quiet, calm. stare tranquillo keep quiet or calm; (non turbarsi) not worry. tranquillità sf calm. tranquillante sm tranquillizer.

transatlantico [transat'lantiko] agg transatlantic. sm ocean liner.

transazione [transat'sjone] sf (comm) transaction; (dir) settlement.

transistor [tran'sistor] sm invar transistor.

transitivo [transi'tivo] agg transitive.

transito [tran'sito] sm transit. transito interrotto road closed. transitabile agg practicable. transitorio agg transitory; (fis) transient.

transizione [transit'sjone] sf transition.

tranvai [tran'vaj] sm tram. tranvia sf tramway.

trapanare [trapa'nare] v drill. trapanatrice sf drill. trapanatura sf drilling. trapano sm drill.

trapassare [trapas'sare] v run through; pass. trapassato sm past perfect. trapasso sm passing; transition; (dir) transfer.

trapelare [trape'lare] v leak out.

trapezio [tra'pɛtsjo] sm (geom) trapezium; (sport) trapeze. trapezista s(m+f) trapeze artist.

trapiantare [trapjan'tare] v transplant. trapianto sm transplant; (agric) transplantation.

trappola ['trappola] sf trap, snare.

trapuntare [trapun'tare] v quilt; (ricamare) embroider. trapunta sf quilt.

*trarre [trarre] v draw. trarre in inganno deceive. trarre in tentazione lead into temptation.

trasalire [trasa'lire] v jump.

trasandato [trazan'dato] agg untidy.

*trascendere [tra'ʃɛndere] v transcend.

trascinare [traʃi'nare] v drag; (fig) carry away.

*trascorrere [tras'korrere] v spend; (tempo) pass.

*trascrivere [tras'krivere] v transcribe. trascrizione sf transcription.

trascurare [trasku'rare] v neglect; (omettere) fail. trascurato agg neglected; (noncurante) careless; (sciatto) slovenly.

trasferire [trasfe'rire] *v* transfer. **trasferirsi** *v* (*traslocare*) move. **trasferibile** *agg* transferable. **trasferimento** *sm* transfer. **trasferta** *sf* (*sport*) away match; (*viaggio*) business trip; (*indennità*) travelling expenses *pl*.

trasformare [trasfor'mare] *v* transform; (*cambiare*) change. **trasformare** in turn into. **trasformatore** *sm* transformer. **trasformazione** *sf* transformation.

trasfusione [trasfu'zjone] *sf* (*med*) transfusion.

trasgredire [trazgre'dire] *v* disobey; (*legge*) infringe. **trasgressione** *sf* infringement.

traslocare [trazlo'kare] *v* move; (*impiegato*) transfer. **trasloco** *sm*, *pl* -**chi** move; transfer.

*****trasmettere** [traz'mettere] *v* transmit; (*communicare*, *dir*) convey; (*radio*) broadcast. **trasmettitore** *sm* transmitter; (*malattia*) carrier. **trasmissione** *sf* transmission; broadcast. **trasmittente** *sf* transmitter.

trasmodato [trazmo'dato] *agg* excessive.

trasognato [traso'nato] *agg* dreamy.

trasparente [traspa'rente] *agg* transparent. *sm* transparency. **trasparenza** *sf* transparency.

trasparire [traspa'rire] *v* show through; (*alla luce*) shine through; (*palesarsi*) appear.

traspirare [traspi'rare] *v* transpire.

trasportare [traspor'tare] *v* carry; (*trascinare*) transport, carry away. **trasportatore** *sm* carrier; (*tec*) conveyor. **trasporto** *sm* transport; (*comm*) carriage; (*inoltro*) forwarding; (*per nave*) shipping.

trastullare [trastul'lare] *v* amuse. **trastullo** *sm* amusement; (*fig*) plaything.

trasudare [trasu'dare] *v* ooze.

trasversale [trazver'sale] *agg* transverse.

trasvolare [trazvo'lare] *v* fly across; (*fig*) barely touch.

tratta ['tratta] *sf* (*comm*) draft; (*traffico illecito*) trade.

trattare [trat'tare] *v* treat, deal with, handle. **si tratta di . . .** it is about . . . , it is a question of . . . . **trattabile** *agg* negotiable; (*persona*) tractable. **trattamento** *sm* treatment. **trattativa** *:f* negotiation. **trattato** *sm* (*opera*) treatise; (*dir*) treaty.

tratteggiare [tratted'dʒare] *v* hatch; (*abbozzare*) outline.

*****trattenere** [tratte'nere] *v* (*far rimanere*)

keep (back); (*frenare*) restrain, hold back; (*detrarre*) withhold. **trattenersi** *v* (*restare*) stay; restrain oneself. **trattenimento** *sm* reception; (*spettacolo*) show.

tratto ['tratto] *agg* drawn. *sm* stroke; (*elemento caratteristico*) feature; (*frazione*) stretch; (*brano*) passage. **a tratti** at times. **di tratto in tratto** every now and then. **d'un tratto** all of a sudden.

trattore [trat'tore] *sm* tractor.

trattoria [tratto'ria] *sf* restaurant.

traudire [trau'dire] *v* mishear.

trauma ['trauma] *sm* trauma. **traumatico** *agg* traumatic.

travagliare [trava'ʎare] *v* torment. **travaglio** *sm* torment; (*angoscia*) distress. **travaglio di parto** labour.

travasare [trava'zare] *v* decant.

trave ['trave] *sf* beam; (*di tetto*) rafter; (*di soffitto*) joist. **fare una trave di ogni fuscello** make a mountain out of a molehill.

traversare [traver'sare] *v* cross; (*da parte a parte*) go through. **traversata** *sf* crossing. **traversina** *sf* sleeper.

traverso [tra'verso] *agg* cross, transverse. *sm* breadth, width. **andare di traverso** (*cibo*) go down the wrong way. **a traverso** sideways on. **guardare di traverso** look askance at. **prendere di traverso** take the wrong way.

travestire [traves'tire] *v* disguise. **travestito, -a** *sm*, *sf* (*psic*) transvestite.

traviare [travi'are] *v* lead astray. **traviamento** *sm* straying; corruption.

travisare [travi'zare] *v* distort. **travisamento** *sm* distortion.

*****travolgere** [tra'voldʒere] *v* sweep away; (*investire*) knock down; (*fig*) overwhelm. **travolgente** *agg* sweeping: overwhelming.

trazione [tra'tsjone] *sf* traction; (*auto*) drive.

tre [tre] *agg*, *sm* three.

trebbiare [treb'bjare] *v* thresh. **trebbia** *or* **trebbiatrice** *sf* threshing machine. **trebbiatura** *sf* threshing.

treccia ['trettʃa] *sf* braid, plait. **farsi le trecce** plait one's hair.

tredici ['treditʃi] *agg*, *sm* thirteen. **tredicesimo** *sm*, *agg* thirteenth.

tregua ['tregwa] *sf* truce; (*riposo*) rest. **senza tregua** unremitting; without respite; (*senza sosta*) non-stop.

tremare [tre'mare] *v* tremble; (*di freddo*) shiver; (*per emozioni*) shudder. **la tremarella** *sf* (*fam*) the shivers *pl*.

tremendo [tre'mɛndo] *agg* terrible, dreadful.

trementina [tremen'tina] *sf* turpentine.

tremito ['tremito] *sm* shaking, shudder(ing).

tremolare [tremo'lare] *v* quiver; (*stelle*) twinkle; (*luce*) flicker.

tremore [tre'more] *sm* tremor; (*agitazione*) trembling.

treno ['trɛno] *sm* train. **treno accelerato/diretto/direttissimo/rapido** slow/fast/through/express train. **treno di gomme/ruote** set of tyres/wheels.

trenta ['trenta] *sm, agg* thirty. **trentesimo** *sm, agg* thirtieth.

trepidare [trepi'dare] *v* be anxious.

trespolo ['trespolo] *sm* trestle; (*sgabello*) stool.

triangolo [tri'angolo] *sm* triangle. **triangolare** *agg* triangular.

tribolare [tribo'lare] *v* suffer; (*far soffrire*) torment. **vita tribolata** *sf* hard life.

tribordo [tri'bordo] *sm* starboard.

tribù [tri'bu] *sf* tribe. **membro di tribù** *sm* tribesman.

tribuna [tri'buna] *sf* platform; (*palco riservato*) gallery; (*campo sportivo*) stand; (*coperta*) grandstand.

tribunale [tribu'nale] *sm* court.

tributo [tri'buto] *sm* tribute. **tributare** *v* render. **tributario** *agg* (*tributi*) tax; (*fiume*) tributary.

tricheco [tri'kɛko] *sm* walrus.

triciclo [tri'tʃiklo] *sm* tricycle.

tricolore [triko'lore] *sm, agg* tricolour.

tric-trac ['tric'trac] *sm invar* backgammon.

tridimensionale [tridimensjo'nale] *agg* three-dimensional.

trifoglio [tri'fɔʎʎo] *sm* clover.

triglia ['triʎa] *sf* red mullet. **far l'occhio di triglia** (*fam*) make sheep's eyes.

trigonometria [trigonome'tria] *sf* trigonometry.

trillare [tril'lare] *v* trill. **trillo** *sm* trill.

trilogia [trilo'dʒia] *sf* trilogy.

trimestre [tri'mɛstre] *sm* quarter; (*scolastico*) term. **trimestrale** *agg* quarterly.

trina ['trina] *sf* lace.

trincare [trin'kare] *v* drink.

trincea [trin'tʃεa] *sf* (*mil*) trench; (*ferr*) cutting. **trincerare** *v* entrench. **trinceramento** *sm* entrenchment.

trinciare [trin'tʃare] *v* cut up; (*pollo, ecc.*)

carve; (*in strisce sottili*) shred. **trinciato** *sm* (*tabacco*) shag.

trinità [trini'ta] *sf* trinity.

trio ['trio] *sm* trio.

trionfare [trion'fare] *v* triumph. **trionfale** *agg* triumphal. **trionfante** *agg* triumphant. **trionfo** *sm* triumph; success.

triplice [triplitʃe] *agg* threefold. **in triplice copia** in triplicate. **triplo** *agg* treble, triple; (*di tre parti*) threefold. **il triplo** *sm* three times as much.

tripode ['tripode] *sm* tripod.

trippa ['trippa] *sf* tripe.

tripudiare [tripu'djare] *v* rejoice. **tripudio** *sm* jubilation.

triste ['triste] *agg* sad. **tristezza** *sf* sadness.

tristo ['tristo] *agg* (*malvagio*) wicked; (*meschino*) mean.

tritare [tri'tare] *v* grind; (*carne*) mince. **carne tritata** *sf* mince. **tritacarne** *sm invar* mincer. **trito** *agg* chopped, ground, minced; (*fig*) trite.

trittico [trittiko] *sm* triptych.

trivellare [trivel'lare] *v* drill, bore. **trivella** *sf* auger; (*succhiello*) gimlet; (*miniera*) drill. **trivellazione** *sf* drilling, boring.

triviale [tri'vjale] *agg* vulgar; (*banale*) trivial. **trivialità** *sf* vulgarity; triviality.

trofeo [tro'fɛo] *sm* trophy.

trogolo ['trɔgolo] *sm* trough.

troia ['trɔja] *sf* (*volg*) *sf* (*scrofa*) sow; (*prostituta*) whore. **troiaio** *sm* pigsty. **troiata** *sf* (*lavoro mal fatto*) awful mess; (*azione sudicia*) dirty trick.

tromba ['tromba] *sf* trumpet; (*mil*) bugle; (*auto*) horn; (*ascensore, scale*) well; (*anat*) tube. **tromba d'aria** tornado. **trombetta** *sm* trumpeter; (*trombettiere*) bugler. **trombone** *sm* trombone. **trombonista** *s*(*m*+*f*) trombonist.

trombosi [trom'bɔzi] *sf* thrombosis.

troncare [tron'kare] *v* cut off; (*spezzare, fig*) break off.

tronco[1] ['tronko] *agg* cut off, broken off; (*mat, parole*) truncated.

tronco[2] ['tronko] *sm* trunk; (*tratto*) section; (*arch*) shaft.

tronfio [tronfjo] *agg* puffed up, pompous.

trono ['trono] *sm* throne.

tropico ['trɔpiko] *sm* tropic. **tropicale** *agg* tropical.

troppo ['troppo] *agg* too much; (*pl*) too many. *avv* too much; (*con agg e avv*) too.

trota ['trɔta] *sf* trout.

trottare [trot'tare] v trot. **trotto** sm trot; (andatura svelta) brisk pace. **andare al piccolo trotto** jog-trot. **rompere il trotto** break into a gallop. **trotterellare** v jog (along); (bambini) toddle (along).

trottola ['trottola] sf (spinning) top.

trovare [tro'vare] v find. **andare a trovare** go to see, call on. **trovare in fallo** catch red-handed. **trovarsi** v (essere) be; (per caso) happen to be; (sentirsi) get on; (incontrarsi) meet; (pensare) think. **trovata** sf good idea; expedient. **trovata pubblicitaria** publicity stunt. **trovatello, -a** sm, sf foundling.

truccare [truk'kare] v make up; (falsificare) doctor; (auto) soup up; (sport) fix. **truccarsi** v disguise oneself; (imbellettarsi) put make-up on. **truccatore, -trice** sm, sf make-up artist. **truccatura** sf (teatro) making-up; (belletto, ecc.) make-up. **trucco** sm make-up; (inganno) trick.

truce ['trutʃe] agg grim.

trucciolo ['trutʃolo] sm (wood) chip, shaving.

truffare [truf'fare] v cheat, swindle; (dir) defraud. **truffa** sf swindle; (dir) fraud. **truffatore, -trice** sm, sf swindler, cheat.

truppa ['truppa] sf troop; (fig) horde.

tu [tu] pron you. **a tu per tu** face to face.

tuba ['tuba] sf (musica) tuba; (cappello) top-hat; (anat) tube.

tubare [tu'bare] v coo.

tubercolosi [tuberko'lɔzi] sf tuberculosis.

tubo ['tubo] sm pipe, tube; (flessibile) hose(-pipe); (anat) canal. **tubazione** sf piping. **tubetto** sm tube. **tubolare** agg tubular.

tuffare [tuf'fare] v plunge, dip. **tuffarsi** v plunge; (fare un tuffo) dive. **tuffo** sm dive.

tulipano [tuli'pano] sm tulip.

tumefatto [tume'fatto] agg swollen.

tumore [tu'more] sm tumour.

tumulto [tu'multo] sm uproar; (sommossa) riot. **tumultuoso** agg tumultuous; (chiassoso) rowdy.

tunica ['tunika] sf tunic.

tuo ['tuo], m pl **tuoi** agg your. pron yours.

tuono ['twono] sm thunder. **tuonare** v thunder.

tuorlo ['tworlo] sm yolk.

turare [tu'rare] v plug; (con sughero) cork. **turarsi il naso** hold one's nose. **turacciolo**

sm stopper; (di sughero) cork; (botte) bung.

turba ['turba] sf mob.

turbante [tur'bante] sm turban.

turbare [tur'bare] v trouble; disturb; (sconvolgere) upset. **turbarsi** v get upset. **turbamento** sm disturbance, anxiety.

turbina [tur'bina] sf turbine.

turbine ['turbine] sm whirl; (neve, sabbia) storm; (fig) seething horde. **turbine di vento** whirlwind. **turbolento** agg turbulent; (inquieto) unruly.

turchese [tur'keze] s(m+f), agg turquoise.

Turchia [tur'kia] sf Turkey. **turco, -a** sm, agg Turkish; sm, sf (persona) Turk. **bestemmiare come un turco** swear like a trooper. **fumare come un turco** smoke like a chimney. **parlare (in) turco** (fam) talk double Dutch.

turchino [tur'kino] agg, sm deep blue.

turismo [tu'rizmo] sm tourism; (culturale) sight-seeing. **fare del turismo** tour, travel. **turista** s(m+f) tourist; sightseer.

turlupinare [turlupi'nare] v swindle; (fam) take in.

turno ['turno] sm (volta) turn; (lavoro) shift; (mil) guard. **essere di turno** be on duty. **fare a turno** take turns. **lavoro a turni** sm shift-work.

turpe ['turpe] agg foul. **turpiloquio** sm foul language.

tuta ['tuta] sf overalls pl; (sport) track-suit.

tutela [tu'tela] sf defence; (dir) guardianship, protection. **tutelare** v protect; (salvaguardare) safeguard.

tuttavia [tutta'via] cong nevertheless.

tutto ['tutto] agg all; (intero) the whole (of); (pl) every. pron everything; (pl) everybody sing. avv everybody. **a tutta velocità** at full speed. **il tutto** the whole (thing), everything. **innanzi tutto** first of all. **in tutti i modi** anyhow. **noi tutti** all of us. **tutt'ad un tratto** all of a sudden. **tutt'altro** anything but. **tutti e due** both (of them). **tutti i giorni** every day. **una volta per tutte** once and for all.

tuttora [tut'tora] avv still.

U

ubbia [ub'bia] *sf* silly idea; prejudice.

ubbidire [ubbi'dire] *v* obey; (*essere ubbidiente*) be obedient; (*dar retta*) listen (to). **ubbidiente** *agg* obedient. **ubbidienza** *sf* obedience.

ubriacare [ubria'kare] *v* make drunk, intoxicate. **ubriacarsi** *v* get drunk. **ubriachezza** *sf* drunkenness. **ubriaco, -a** *s, agg, m pl* **-chi** drunk. **ubriaco fradicio** dead drunk.

uccello [ut'tʃello] *sm* bird.

*****uccidere** [ut'tʃidere] *v* kill; (*assassinare*) murder. **uccisione** *sf* killing; murder. **ucciso** *agg* killed; murdered. **uccisore** *sm* killer; murderer.

*****udire** [u'dire] *v* hear. **udibile** *agg* audible. **udienza** *sf* hearing; (*formale*) audience. **uditivo** *agg* (*fis*) audible; (*med*) auditory. **udito** *sm* hearing. **uditore, -trice** *sm, sf* listener. **uditorio** *sm* audience.

uffa ['uffa] *inter* uffa, **che noia!** what a bore!

ufficiale [uffi'tʃale] *agg* official. *sm* officer. **ufficiale di stato civile** registrar.

ufficio [uf'fitʃo] *sm* office; (*dovere, compito*) duty. **d'ufficio** official; (*ufficialmente*) officially; (*in veste ufficiale*) ex officio. **ufficio di collocamento** employment exchange. **ufficioso** *agg* unofficial.

ufo ['ufo] *avv* a ufo for nothing. **mangiare a ufo** scrounge a meal.

uggia ['uddʒa] *sf* boredom. **avere in uggia** dislike. **prendere in uggia** take a dislike to. **uggioso** *agg* boring.

uggiolare [uddʒo'lare] *v* whine.

ugola ['ugola] *sf* (*anat*) uvula; (*fig*) voice.

uguagliare [ugwa'ʎare] *v* (*essere uguale*) equal; (*rendere uguale*) equalize, even out; (*livellare*) level. **uguaglianza** *sf* equality.

uguale [u'gwale] *agg also* **eguale** the same; uniform; (*mat*) equal. *sm* equal. **ugualmente** *avv* equally; uniformly; (*tuttavia*) just or all the same.

ulcera [ul'tʃera] *sf* ulcer.

uliva [u'liva] *V* oliva.

ulteriore [ulte'rjore] *agg* further. **ulteriormente** *avv* further; (*più avanti*) farther on; (*in seguito*) subsequently.

ultimo [ul'timo] *-a agg* last; (*più recente*) latest; (*fondamentale*) ultimate. *sm, sf* last. **all'ultimo** at the end; (*in fine*) finally. **fino all'ultimo** to the very end. **ultimamente** *avv also* **negli ultimi tempi** lately.

ultimare *v* finish. **ultimatum** *sm invar* ultimatum. **ultimazione** *sf* completion.

ultrasensibile [ultrasen'sibile] *agg* hypersensitive.

ultrasonico [ultra'sɔniko] *agg* supersonic.

ultravioletto [ultravio'letto] *agg* ultraviolet.

ululare [ulu'lare] *v* howl. **ululato** *sm* howling; (*urlo*) howl.

umanesimo [uma'nezimo] *sm* humanism. **umanista** *s(m+f)* humanist. **umanistico** *agg* humanist.

umano [u'mano] *agg* human; (*compassionevole*) humane; (*comprensivo*) understanding. **umanità** *sf* humanity. **umanitario** *agg* humanitarian.

umettare [umet'tare] *v* moisten.

umido [u'mido] *agg* damp; (*clima*) humid. *sm* dampness; humidity; (*gastr*) stew. **cucire in umido** stew. **umidità** *sf* dampness; humidity.

umile ['umile] *agg* humble. **umiltà** *sf* (*virtù, sentimento*) humility; (*qualità*) humbleness.

umiliare [umi'ljare] *v* humiliate, humble. **umiliazione** *sf* humiliation.

umore [u'more] *sm* (*disposizione*) mood; (*indole*) temperament; (*liquido*) humour. **essere di buon/cattivo umore** be in a good/bad mood; (*abitualmente*) be good-/bad-tempered. **umorismo** *sm* humour. **umorista** *s(m+f)* humorist. **umoristico** *agg* humorous; (*spiritoso*) witty.

un [un] *V* uno.

unanime [u'nanime] *agg* unanimous. **unanimità** *sf* unanimity. **all'unanimità** unanimously.

uncino [un'tʃino] *sm* hook. **uncinare** *v* hook. **croce uncinata** *sf* swastika. **uncinetto** *sm* crochet-hook. **lavorare all'uncinetto** crochet.

undici ['unditʃi] *agg, sm* eleven. **undicesimo** *sm, agg* eleventh.

*****ungere** [un'dʒere] *v* grease; (*rel*) anoint.

Ungheria [unge'ria] *sf* Hungary. **ungherese** *s(m+f)*, *agg* Hungarian.

unghia ['ungja] *sf* nail; (*artiglio*) claw; (*minima distanza*) hair's breadth. **unghie** *sf pl* (*fig*) clutches *pl*. **unghiata** *sf* scratch; (*temperino*) indentation.

unguento [un'gwɛnto] *sm* ointment.

unico [u'niko] *agg* only; (*esclusivo*) sole; (*senza pari*) unique; (*enfatico*) one and only. **unicamente** *avv* only.

unicorno [uni'kɔrno] *sm* unicorn.

unificare [unifi'kare] *v* unify; (*fondere*) merge; standardize. **unificazione** *sf* union; merger; standardization.

uniforme [uni'fɔrme] *sf*, *agg* uniform. **uniformare** *v* (*adattare*) bring into line (with); (*render piano*) level out; standardize. **uniformarsi** *v* comply (with); adapt (to). **uniformità** *sf* uniformity; (*di superficie*) evenness; (*accordo*) agreement.

unione [u'njone] *sf* union; (*concordia*) unity.

unire [u'nire] *v* join; (*fig*) unite. **unirsi** *v* join; (*insieme con altri*) join up with.

unità [uni'ta] *sf* unity; (*misura*, *mil*) unit. **unità di misura** measure.

unito [u'nito] *agg* united; (*tinta*) plain. **unitamente a** together with.

università [universi'ta] *sf* university. **universitario**, **-a** *sm*, *sf* university student.

universo [uni'vɛrso] *sm* universe. **universale** *agg* universal.

uno ['uno] *agg* one, a. *art* a, an. *pron* one; (*qualcuno*) someone. **fare un po' per uno** share equally. **nè l'uno nè l'altro** neither. **non me ne va bene una!** I can't get one thing right! **tutt'uno** the same thing. **uno a uno** one by one.

unto ['unto] *agg* (*cosparso di grasso*) greasy, oily; (*spalmato*) greased, oiled; (*sporco*) dirty. *sm* grease; (*gastr*) fat. **untuoso** *agg* greasy; (*fig*) unctuous.

uomo ['wɔmo] *sm*, *pl* **uomini** man (*pl* men). **l'uomo qualunque** the man in the street. **uomo d'affari** businessman. **uomo di fiducia** right-hand man. **uomo di spirito** wit.

uopo ['wɔpo] *sm* **all'uopo** (*a tale scopo*) for this purpose; (*al momento opportuno*) at the right moment. **essere d'uopo** be necessary.

uovo ['wɔvo] *sm*, *pl* **-a f** egg. **uovo al burro** or **tegame** fried egg. **uovo alla coque** boiled egg. **uovo in camicia** poached egg. **uovo sodo/strapazzato** hardboiled/ scrambled egg.

uragano [ura'gano] *sm* hurricane; (*tempesta*) storm.

uranio [u'ranjo] *sm* uranium.

urbano [ur'bano] *agg* (*di città*) town, urban; (*cortese*) polite. **nettezza urbana** refuse collection. **urbanistica** *sf* town-planning. **urbanista** *s(m+f)* town-planner.

urgente [ur'dʒɛnte] *agg* urgent. **urgenza** *sf* urgency. **aver urgenza di** need urgently. **chiamata d'urgenza** *sf* emergency call.

urgere ['urdʒere] *v* (*sollecitare*) urge; (*abbisognare*) be required urgently.

urina [u'rina] *sf* urine. **urinare** *v* urinate. **urinario** *agg* urinary.

urlare [ur'lare] *v* scream; (*animali*) howl; (*dire ad alta voce*) shout. **urlo** *sm*, *pl* **-a f** shout; howl; scream.

urna ['urna] *sf* urn. **andare alle urne** go to the polls.

urrà [ur'ra] *inter* hurrah!

urtare [ur'tare] *v* knock *or* bump (into); (*dare uno spintone*) jostle; (*fig*) annoy. **urtarsi** *v* (*scontrarsi*) clash; (*auto*) collide; (*fig*) get irritated. **urto** *sm* (*spinta*) push; (*scontro*) clash, collision.

usare [u'zare] *v* use; (*essere solito a*) be accustomed to; (*essere di moda*) be fashionable; (*servirsi di*) make use of; (*fig*) exercise. **usanza** *sf* custom; habit.

uscio ['uʃo] *sm* door. **mettere fuori dell'uscio** turn out (of the house). **uscio di casa** front door.

*****uscire** [u'ʃire] *v* leave; (*andar fuori*) go out; (*venir fuori*) come out; (*scendere*) get off; (*sboccare*) lead. **uscir di mente** slip one's mind. **uscir di strada** go off the road. **uscire in macchina** go for a drive. **uscita** *sf* (*passaggio*) exit, way out; (*sbocco*) outlet; (*motto di spirito*) witty remark; (*spesa*) outlay; (*a carte*) lead. **essere in linea uscita** be off duty. **giorno di libera uscita** *sm* day off. **uscita di sicurezza** emergency exit.

usignolo [uzi'ɲɔlo] *sm* nightingale.

uso ['uzo] *sm* use; (*usanza*) custom; (*voga*) fashion. **c'è l'uso** it is customary. **uso e consumo** wear and tear. **usuale** *agg* usual; customary; common.

ustionare [ustjo'nare] *v* scald. **ustione** *sf* scald.

usufruire [uzufru'ire] *v* benefit (from).

usura[1] [u'zura] *sf* usury. **a usura** with interest. **usuraio**, **-a** *sm*, *sf* usurer.

usura[2] *sf* (*tec*) wear. **resistente all'usura** hard-wearing.

usurpare [uzur'pare] *v* usurp. **usurpatore**, **-trice** *sm*, *sf* usurper.

utensile [u'tɛnsile] *sm* tool, utensil. **macchina utensile** *sf* machine tool.

utente [u'tɛnte] *s(m+f)* user.

utero ['utero] *sm* womb.

utile ['utile] *agg* useful; *(persona di aiuto)* helpful. **in tempo utile** in good time. **tornar utile** come in handy. *sm* profit. **utili** *sm pl (reddito)* income *sing.* **utilità** *sf* usefulness, use; profit. **utilizzare** *v* utilize. **utilizzazione** *sf* utilization.

utopia [uto'pia] *sf* utopia.

uva ['uva] *sf* grapes *pl.* **acino d'uva** *sm* grape. **uva secca** *or* **passa** raisins *pl.* **uva spina** gooseberry.

V

vacanza [va'kantsa] *sf* holiday; *(l'essere vacante)* vacancy. **vacante** *agg* vacant.

vacca ['vakka] *sf* cow. **vaccata** *sf (volg)* rubbish. **vacchetta** *sf (cuoio)* cowhide.

vaccinare [vattʃi'nare] *v* vaccinate. **vaccinazione** *sf* vaccination. **vaccino** *sm* vaccine.

vacillare [vatʃil'lare] *v* totter; *(essere incerto)* waver.

vagabondo [vaga'bondo] **-a** *agg* roving. *sm, sf* vagrant; *(spreg)* loafer. **vagabondare** *v* wander (about).

vagare [va'gare] *v* stray.

vagina [va'dʒina] *sf* vagina.

vagire [va'dʒire] *v* wail. **vagito** *sm* wail(ing).

vaglia¹ ['vaʎa] *sm invar* money order. **vaglia postale** postal order.

vaglia² ['vaʎa] *sf* **di vaglia** of note.

vagliare [va'ʎare] *v* sift; *(argomenti, ecc.)* weigh (up). **vagliatura** *sf* sifting; *(esame attento)* careful consideration. **vaglio** *sm* sieve; close examination.

vago ['vago] *agg* vague. **vaghezza** *sf* vagueness.

vagone [va'gone] *sm (per passeggeri)* carriage; *(per merci)* wagon. **vagone letto/ristorante** sleeping-/dining-car.

vaiolo [va'jɔlo] *sm* smallpox.

valanga [va'langa] *sf* avalanche; *(fig)* shower.

valente [va'lɛnte] *agg* skilled, clever.

***valere** [va'lere] *v (aver valore)* be worth; *(aver merito)* be good; *(aver forza legale)* apply; *(esser regolare)* be valid; *(contare)* count; *(essere utile)* be of use; *(importare)* matter. **far valere** assert. **farsi valere** demand respect; *(imporsi)* assert

oneself. **vale a dire** that is to say. **tanto vale** one might as well. **valere la pena** be worth it. **valere un occhio della testa** be worth a fortune.

valevole [va'levole] *agg* valid.

valicare [vali'kare] *v* cross. **valico** *sm, pl* **-chi** pass; crossing.

valido ['valido] *agg* valid; *(efficace)* effective; *(forte)* strong. **validità** *sf* validity.

valigia [va'lidʒa] *sf* suitcase. **far le valigie** pack. **valigeria** *sf (merce)* travel goods *pl.*

valle ['valle] *sf also* **vallata** valley. **a valle di** below. **scendere a valle** go downhill. **vallone** *sm* deep valley; *(depressione)* gorge.

valletto [val'letto] *sm* page; assistant.

valore [va'lore] *sm* value; *(pregio)* worth; validity; *(significato)* meaning; *(coraggio)* valour. **aver valore di** amount to. **carte valori** *pl* securities *pl.* **di valore** of value, valuable; *(professionista)* leading. **imposta di valore aggiunto (IVA)** valued added tax (VAT). **privo di valore** worthless; of no value. **valori** *sm pl* valuables *pl.*

valorizzare [valorid'dzare] *v* exploit; *(mettere in evidenza)* make the most of. **valorizzazione** *sf* exploitation.

valuta [va'luta] *sf* currency.

valutare [valu'tare] *v* value; *(calcolare)* estimate; *(tenere in considerazione)* rate; *(vagliare)* weigh. **valutazione** *sf* evaluation; estimation; *(calcolo approssimativo)* estimate.

valvola ['valvola] *sf* valve; *(elett)* fuse. **valvola di sicurezza** safety-valve.

valzer ['valtser] *sm invar* waltz.

vampa ['vampa] *sf* blaze; *(arrossamento)* flush. **vampata** *sf* blaze; *(fig)* burst; flush; *(al viso)* blush.

vampiro [vam'piro] *sm* vampire.

vandalo ['vandalo] *sm* vandal. **vandalismo** *sm* vandalism.

vaneggiare [vaned'dʒare] *v* rave.

vanesio [va'nɛzjo] *agg* fatuous, vain.

vangare [van'gare] *v* dig (over). **vanga** *sf* spade.

vangelo [van'dʒɛlo] *sm* gospel.

vaniglia [va'niʎa] *sf* vanilla.

vanità [vani'ta] *sf* vanity. **vanitoso** *agg* vain.

vano ['vano] *agg* vain. *sm (locale)* room; *(spazio)* space. **rendere vano** make useless. **riuscir vano** be unsuccessful.

vantaggio [van'taddʒo] *sm* advantage; (*sport*) lead, handicap; profit. **vantaggiare** *v* favour. **vantaggioso** *agg* advantageous.

vantare [van'tare] *v* boast (of). **vantarsi** *v* boast, brag. **vantatore**, **-trice** *sm*, *sf* boaster, braggart. **vanteria** *sf* boasting, bragging. **vanto** *sm* (*vanteria*) boasting, bragging; (*atto*) boast.

vanvera ['vanvera] *sf* **a vanvera** (*senza riflettere*) without thinking; (*a casaccio*) at random.

vapore [va'pore] *sm* steam; (*nave*) steamer. **a tutto vapore** full steam ahead. **vaporizzare** *v* vaporize. **vaporizzatore** *sm* vaporizer; (*profumi*) atomizer.

varare [va'rare] *v* launch. **varo** *sm* launch(ing).

varcare [var'kare] *v* cross; (*eccedere*) go beyond. **varco** *sm* opening. **aspettare al varco** lie in wait (for).

variare [va'rjare] *v* change; (*esser diverso*) vary. (**tanto**) **per variare** (just) for a change. **variare d'aspetto** look different. **variabile** *sf*, *agg* variable. **variabilità** *sf* variability. **variante** *sf* variant. **variato** *agg* varied. **variazione** *sf* variation.

varicella [vari't∫ɛlla] *sf* chicken-pox. **varicoso** [vari'kozo] *agg* varicose.

varietà [varje'ta] *sf* variety. *sm* (*teatro*) variety.

vario ['varjo] *agg* (*variato*) varied; (*diverso*) various, different; (*non regolare*) variable. **variopinto** *agg* multicoloured. **vari** *pron pl* various people *pl*, several people *pl*.

vasca ['vaska] *sf* basin; (*da bagno*) bathtub; (*tino*) vat; (*piscina*) (swimming-)pool. **fare una vasca** (*sport*) swim a length.

vascello [va'∫ɛllo] *sm* vessel, warship. **ufficiale di vascello** *sm* naval officer.

vasellame [vazel'lame] *sm* crockery; (*di metallo prezioso*) plate; (*di porcellana*) china; (*di vetro*) glassware.

vaso ['vazo] *sm* pot; (*per fiori recisi*) vase; (*anat*) vessel. **vaso da fiori** flower-pot. **vaso da notte** chamber-pot. **vasaio**, **-a** *sm*, *sf* potter.

vassoio [vas'sojo] *sm* tray; (*del muratore*) mortar-board.

vasto ['vasto] *agg* wide, vast. **vastità** *sf* vastness.

Vaticano [vati'kano] *sm* Vatican. **città del Vaticano** *sf* Vatican City.

vaticinio [vati't∫injo] *sm* prediction. **vaticinare** *v* predict.

ve [ve] *V* **vi**.

vecchio ['vekkjo] *agg* old. *sm* old man. **vecchia** *sf* old woman. **vecchiaia** *sf* old age. **vecchiotto** *agg* oldish, fairly old; (*fuori moda*) out-of-date.

vece [vet∫e] *sf* **fare le veci di** take the place of. **in mia vece** in my place.

*vedere [ve'dere] *v* see. **avere a che vedere con** have to do with. **dare a vedere** let it be understood. **far vedere** show. **non vederci più** (*fam*) be furious. **non veder l'ora di** look forward to. **stare a vedere** (*attendere*) see; (*guardare*) watch; (*scommettere*) bet. **vedere di buon occhio** approve (of). **vediamo un po'** let's see *sm*. **a mio vedere** in my opinion.

vedetta [ve'detta] *sf* look-out.

vedova ['vedova] *sf* widow. **vedovo** *sm* widower. **rimaner vedova** *or* **vedovo** be widowed. **vedovanza** *sf* widowhood.

veemente [vee'mɛnte] *agg* vehement.

vegetale [vedʒe'tale] *agg*, *sm* vegetable. **vegetariano**, **-a** *s*, *agg* vegetarian. **vegetativo** *agg* vegetative. **vegetazione** *sf* vegetation.

vegetare [vedʒe'tare] *v* vegetate. **vegeto** *agg* flourishing. **vivo e vegeto** alive and kicking.

vegliare [ve'ʎare] *v* (*vigilare*) watch; (*fare la veglia*) keep watch; (*star sveglio*) stay up. **veglia** *sf* watch, vigil; (*lo star desto*) wakefulness; (*festa*) party; (*funebre*) wake. **veglione** *sm* ball, party.

veicolo [ve'ikolo] *sm* vehicle; (*malattia*) carrier.

vela ['vela] *sf* sail; (*sport*) sailing. **a gonfie vele** booming. **barca a vela** *sf* sailing-boat. **volo a vela** *sm* gliding. **veleggiare** *v* sail; (*velivolo*) glide. **veliero** *sm* sailing-ship.

velare [ve'lare] *v* veil; cover; (*offuscare*) cloud, dim; (*suono*) muffle.

veleno [ve'leno] *sm* poison. **avere il veleno in corpo** (*fam*) have a chip on one's shoulder. **sputare veleno** (*fig*) vent one's spleen. **velenoso** *agg* poisonous; (*fig*) venomous.

velino [ve'lino] *agg* **carta velina** *sf* flimsy (paper). **velina** *sf* (*copia*) carbon copy.

velivolo [ve'livolo] *sm* aircraft; (*aliante*) glider.

velleità [vellei'ta] *sf* vain ambition.

vellicare [velli'kare] v titillate.

vello ['vɛllo] sm fleece.

velluto [vel'luto] sm velvet. **di velluto** velvet. **vellutato** agg velvety.

veloce [ve'lotʃe] agg quick, fast. **velocista** s(m+f) sprinter. **velocità** sf speed; (fis) velocity. **eccedere la velocità** (auto) speed.

velodromo [ve'lɔdromo] sm cycle-track.

veltro ['veltro] sm greyhound.

vena ['vena] sf vein; (fig) talent; inspiration. **essere in vena** be in the mood.

venale [ve'nale] agg saleable; (spreg) mercenary.

vendemmiare [vendem'mjare] v harvest (grapes). **vendemmia** sf grape harvest.

vendere ['vendere] v sell. **aver ... da vendere** have ... to spare; have plenty of .... **vendere a contanti** sell for cash. **vendere al dettaglio** or **minuto** retail. **vendere all'asta** auction. **vendere all'ingrosso** sell wholesale. **vendere fumo** bluff. **vendibile** agg saleable; (messo in vendita) for sale.

vendetta [ven'detta] sf revenge; (castigo meritato) vengeance.

vendicare [vendi'kare] v avenge. **vendicarsi** take revenge. **vendicativo** agg vindictive.

vendita ['vendita] sf sale. **vendita a rate** hire-purchase. **venditore**, **-trice** sm, sf vendor; (negoziante) shopkeeper.

venerare [vene'rare] v revere; (rel) worship. **venerabile** agg venerable. **venerazione** sf veneration.

venerdì [vener'di] sm Friday. **Venerdì Santo** Good Friday.

venereo [ve'nɛreo] agg venereal.

Venezia [ve'nɛtsja] sf Venice. **veneziana** sf Venetian blind. **veneziano**, **-a** s, agg Venetian.

veniale [ve'njale] agg venial.

•**venire** [ve'nire] v come; (riuscire) come out; (essere) be. **far venire** (mandare a chiamare) call, send for. **mi viene da ...** I feel like .... **venire alle mani** come to blows. **venire incontro** come towards; (incontrare) meet; (fig) meet halfway. **venir meno** (mancare) be lacking; (svenire) pass out.

ventaglio [ven'taʎo] sm fan.

venti ['venti] agg, sm twenty. **ventesimo** agg, sm twentieth.

ventilare [venti'lare] v air; (agric) winnow. **ventilato** agg airy, ventilated. **ventilazione** sf ventilation.

vento ['vɛnto] sm wind.

ventosa [ven'toza] sf sucker.

ventre ['vɛntre] sm stomach; abdomen; (forma) belly; (grembo materno) womb. **ventrale** agg ventral.

ventricolo [ven'trikolo] sm ventricle.

ventriloquo [ven'trilokwo], **-a** sm, sf ventriloquist.

ventura [ven'tura] sf fortune. **alla ventura** at random. **andare** or **mettersi alla ventura** trust to luck; take a chance. **soldato di ventura** mercenary.

venturo [ven'turo] agg next.

vera ['vera] sf wedding ring.

verace [ve'ratʃe] agg (veritiero) truthful; (vero) true, real. **veracità** sf truthfulness.

veranda [ve'randa] sf veranda.

verbale [ver'bale] sm record, minutes pl. **mettere a verbale** put on record. agg verbal.

verbo ['vɛrbo] sm verb; (parola) word. **verboso** agg verbose, long-winded.

verde ['verde] agg green. sm green; (natura) greenery; (zona) green belt. **essere** or **trovarsi al verde** be broke. **verdastro** agg greenish. **verdeggiare** v be verdant; (diventar verde) turn green.

verdetto [ver'detto] sm verdict.

verdura [ver'dura] sf greens pl, vegetables pl.

verga ['verga] sf rod. **verga magica** magic wand. **vergare** v line; (scrivere) write.

vergine ['verdʒine] sf, agg virgin. **Vergine** sf Virgo. **verginale** agg virginal. **verginità** sf virginity.

vergogna [ver'gona] sf shame; (disonore) disgrace. **fare vergogna** shame. inter shame on you! **vergognarsi** v be or feel ashamed (of); (non osare) be too shy (to). **vergognoso** agg shameful; shy.

verificare [verifi'kare] v check. **verificarsi** v (avvenire) occur; (avverarsi) come true. **verifica** sf control; verification; (dei conti) audit. **verificabile** agg verifiable. **verificazione** sf verification, check; audit.

verità [veri'ta] sf truth; (giustezza) truthfulness. **veritiero** agg truthful.

verme ['verme] sm worm; (larva di insetto) maggot.

vermiglio [ver'miʎo] agg, sm vermilion.

vermut ['vermut] sm invar vermouth.

verniciare [verni'tʃare] v paint; (con vernice trasparente) varnish; (a smalto) enamel. **vernice** sf varnish, lacquer; (apparenza) veneer; (strato sottile) film. **verniciata** sf coat of paint. **verniciatura** sf painting; varnishing.

vero ['vero] agg true; real. sm truth. **a onor del vero** to tell the truth. **di vero cuore** from the bottom of one's heart. **vero e proprio** out and out.

verosimile [vero'simile] agg likely. **aver del verosimile** be likely.

verricello [verri'tʃello] sm winch.

verro ['vɛrro] sm boar.

verruca [ver'ruka] sf wart.

versare [ver'sare] v pour (out); (rovesciare) spill; (spargere) shed; (pagare) pay; (trovarsi) find oneself. **versamento** sm payment, deposit. **versante** sm side. **versato** agg paid (up); (pratico) skilled.

versatile [ver'satile] agg versatile. **versatilità** sf versatility.

versione [ver'sjone] sf version; (traduzione) translation.

verso¹ ['vɛrso] prep towards; (circa) about. **verso il basso** down(wards). **verso l'alto** up(wards).

verso² ['vɛrso] sm (metrica) verse; (suono particolare) sound; gesture; direction; (modo) means. **in verso antiorario** anti-clockwise. **in verso orario** clockwise. **per un verso o per un altro** in one way or another.

vertebra ['vertebra] sf vertebra (pl -brae). **vertebrato** agg, sm vertebrate.

vertenza [ver'tɛntsa] sf dispute; (dir) lawsuit.

verticale [verti'kale] agg, sf vertical.

vertice ['vɛrtitʃe] sm summit; (mat) vertex.

vertigini [ver'tidʒini] sf pl dizziness sing; (attacco) dizzy spell sing; (med) vertigo sing. **aver le vertigini** feel dizzy or giddy. **vertiginoso** agg dizzy.

vescica [ve'ʃika] sf bladder; (bolla cutanea) blister.

vescovo ['veskovo] sm bishop. **vescovado** sm (dignità) bishopric; (territorio) diocese; (palazzo) bishop's palace. **vescovile** agg episcopal.

vespa ['vɛspa] sf wasp. **vespaio** sm wasps' nest.

vestaglia [ves'taʎa] sf dressing-gown; (vestaglietta) housecoat.

veste ['vɛste] sf dress; (rel) vestment; (fig) capacity. **in veste di amico** as a friend. **in veste ufficiale** in an official capacity. **vestiario** sm wardrobe; (indumenti) clothes pl. **capo di vestiario** sm item of clothing.

vestibolo [ves'tibolo] sm vestibule, lobby.

vestire [ves'tire] v dress; (indossare) wear; (detto di abiti) fit. **vestirsi** v dress. **vestito** sm dress.

veterano [vete'rano], -a s, agg veteran.

veterinario [veteri'narjo] agg veterinary. sm veterinary surgeon, vet. **veterinaria** sf veterinary science.

veto ['veto] sm invar veto.

vetro ['vetro] sm glass; (di finestra) pane. **vetro smerigliato** frosted glass. **vetraio** sm glazier. **vetrata** sf (porta) glass door; (finestra) stained-glass window.

vetta ['vetta] sf top.

vettore [vet'tore] sm vector; (comm) carrier.

vettovaglie [vetto'vaʎe] sf pl provisions pl.

vettura [vet'tura] sf carriage; (auto) car. **biglietto di vettura** sm (comm) bill of lading.

vezzeggiare [veddzed'dʒare] v fondle.

vi [vi], **ve** pron (to) you; (riflessivo) yourselves; (reciproco) each other. avv (qui) here; (lì) there.

via¹ ['via] sf way; (strada) street; (sentiero) path. **in via di costruzione** under construction. **in via eccezionale** exceptionally. **per via aerea** by air. **per via di** (a causa di) because of. **via mare/terra** by sea/land.

via² ['via] avv away; (suvvia) come on. sm invar starting signal. **e così via** and so on. **va via!** go on! **via le mani!** hands off! **via via** gradually; (a mano a mano) as.

viabilità [viabili'ta] sf road conditions pl.

viadotto [via'dotto] sm viaduct.

viaggiare [viad'dʒare] v travel; (veicoli) run; (essere trasportato) be carried. **viaggiatore, -trice** sm, sf traveller; passenger. **piccione viaggiatore** sm carrier pigeon.

viaggio [vi'addʒo] sm journey, trip. **mettersi in viaggio** set out or off. **viaggio d'andata/di ritorno** outward/return journey. **viaggio d'andata e ritorno** round trip. **viaggio di nozze** honeymoon.

viale [vi'ale] sm avenue.

viandante [vian'dante] s(m+f) wayfarer.

viavai [via'vaj] sm coming and going.

vibrare [vib'rare] v vibrate; (fig) quiver; (assestare) hurl. **vibrare un colpo** deal a blow. **vibrazione** sf vibration; (fremito) quiver.

vicario [vi'karjo] sm vicar.

viceconsole [vitʃe'kɔnsole] s(m+f) vice-consul.

vicedirettore [vitʃediret'tore], **-trice** sm, sf assistant manager; (scuola) deputy head.

vicenda [vi'tʃenda] sf event; succession. **vicendevolmente** avv also **a vicenda** (a turno) in turns; (scambievolmente) each other, one another.

vicepresidente [vitʃeprezi'dɛnte], **-essa** sm, sf vice-president, vice-chairman.

viceversa [vitʃe'vɛrsa] avv vice versa; (invece) but.

vicinanza [vitʃi'nantsa] sf vicinity.

vicinato [vitʃi'nato] sm neighbourhood.

vicino [vi'tʃino], **-a** agg near; (accanto) next; (confinante) neighbouring; (fig) close. avv close (by); near (by); (accanto a) beside, by. **da vicino** at close quarters. sm, sf neighbour. **vicino di casa** next-door neighbour.

vicolo ['vikolo] sm alley.

video ['video] sm invar (television) screen.

vidimare [vidi'mare] v certify. **vidimazione** sf certification.

vietare [vje'tare] v prohibit; (impedire) prevent. **vietato** agg forbidden. **ingresso vietato** no admission. **sosta vietata** no parking.

vigente [vi'dʒɛnte] agg current; (dir) in force.

vigilare [vidʒi'lare] v watch (over); keep a watch (on). **vigilante** agg watchful. **vigilanza** sf vigilance; (controllo) supervision; (urbana) police.

vigile ['vidʒile] agg watchful. sm policeman. **vigile del fuoco** fireman.

vigilia [vi'dʒilja] sf eve; (rel) vigil. **vigilia di Natale/Capodanno** Christmas/New Year's Eve.

vigliacco [vi'ʎakko] agg cowardly. sm, sf coward. **vigliaccheria** sf cowardice; cowardly action.

vigna ['viɲa] sf vineyard.

vignetta [vi'ɲetta] sf sketch; (umoristica) cartoon.

vigore [vi'gore] sm force; (forza vitale) vigour. **entrare in vigore** (dir) come into force. **vigoria** sf energy.

vile ['vile] agg (vigliacco) cowardly; (basso) base, low. s(m+f) coward. **vilipendio** sm contempt.

villa ['villa] sf villa. **villa di campagna** country house.

villaggio [vil'laddʒo] sm village.

villano [vil'lano], **-a** agg rude; (rozzo) uncouth; offensive. sm, sf lout, boor. **villania** sf rudeness.

villeggiare [villed'dʒare] v spend a holiday. **villeggiatura** sf holidays pl.

viltà [vil'ta] sf cowardice; cowardly action.

viluppo [vi'luppo] sm tangle.

vimini ['vimini] sm pl wicker sing. **di vimini** wicker. **lavoro in vimini** sm wickerwork.

vincere ['vintʃere] v win; (battere) beat; (sopraffare) overcome; (sconfiggere) defeat. **lasciarsi vincere (da)** yield (to). **vincita** sf win.

vincitore [vintʃi'tore], **-trice** sm, sf winner; (di battaglia) victor. agg winning, victorious.

vincolare [vinko'lare] v bind; (comm) tie up. **vincolo** sm tie.

vino ['vino] sm wine. **vino di mele** cider. **vinicolo** agg wine.

viola¹ ['viɔla] sf (bot) violet. agg, sm invar (colore) violet. **viola del pensiero** pansy. **violacciocca** sf stock; (gialla) wallflower. **violaceo** agg violet.

viola² ['viɔla] sf (musica) viola.

violare [vio'lare] v violate; (una donna) rape; (domicilio) break into. **violare l'ordine pubblico** cause a breach of the peace. **violazione** sf violation. **violazione carnale** rape. **violazione della pace** breach of the peace. **violazione di domicilio** house-breaking.

violentare [violen'tare] v force; (una donna) rape. **violentatore** sm rapist. **violento** agg violent. **violenza** sf violence.

violetta [vio'letta] sf violet. **violetto** agg, sm invar violet.

violino [vio'lino] sm violin. **violinista** s(m+f) violinist.

violoncello [violon'tʃello] sm (violon)cello. **violoncellista** s(m+f) (violon)cellist.

viottolo [vi'ɔttolo] sm path.

vipera ['vipera] sf viper.

virale [vi'rale] agg viral.

virare [vi'rare] v (alare) haul (in); (mutar

direzione) veer, change course; (*aero*) turn.

virgola ['virgola] *sf* comma; (*mat*) point. **tra virgolette** in inverted commas.

virile [vi'rile] *agg* virile; masculine; (*fig*) manly. **virilità** *sf* virility.

virtù [vir'tu] *sf* virtue; faculty. **in virtù di** by virtue of, in accordance with. **virtuale** *agg* virtual.

virtuoso [virtu'ozo], **-a** *agg* virtuous. *sm*, *sf* virtuoso.

virulento [viru'lɛnto] *agg* virulent.

virus ['vɪrus] *sm invar* virus.

viscere [viʃere] *sm* internal organ. *sf pl* intestines *pl*; (*di animali*) entrails *pl*. **le viscere della terra** the bowels of the earth *pl*.

vischio ['viskjo] *sm* mistletoe; (*estratto*) bird-lime; (*fig*) snare. **viscido** *agg* slimy.

visconte [vis'konte] *sm* viscount.

viscoso [vis'kozo] *agg* viscous. **viscosa** *sf* viscose. **viscosità** *sf* viscosity.

visibile [vi'zibile] *agg* visible. **andare/mandare in visibilio** go/send into raptures. **visibilità** *sf* visibility.

visiera [vi'zjera] *sf* visor; (*berretto*) peak; (*scherma*) mask.

visione [vi'zjone] *sf* sight; (*apparizione*) vision; idea; (*cinema*) showing. **prendere in visione** inspect. **ricevere in visione** receive on approval. **visionario**, **-a** *sm*, *sf* visionary.

visita ['vizita] *sf* visit; (*persona*) visitor; (*esame*) examination. **visita domiciliare** domiciliary visit; (*perquisizione*) house search. **visitare** *v* visit; (*andare a trovare*) call on; (*med*) examine. **visitatore**, **-trice** *sm*, *sf* visitor.

visivo [vi'zivo] *agg* visual. **campo visivo** *sm* field of vision.

viso [vi'zo] *sm* face. **a viso aperto** openly. **far buon viso a cattiva sorte** make the best of it. **fare il viso lungo** sulk.

visone [vi'zone] *sm* mink.

vispo [vi'spo] *agg* lively; (*svelto*) brisk.

vista ['vista] *sf* sight; (*spettacolo*) view. **avere in vista** have in mind. **a vista** on sight. **a vista d'occhio** before one's very eyes. **conoscere di vista** know by sight. **perdere di vista** lose sight (of).

visto ['visto] *sm* visa. **visto di soggiorno** tourist visa.

vistoso [vis'tozo] *agg* showy; (*notevole*) considerable.

visuale [vizu'ale] *agg* visual. *sf* view; line of vision. **visualizzare** *v* visualize.

vita¹ ['vita] *sf* life; (*durata*) lifetime. **a vita** for life. **condanna a vita** *sf* life sentence. **essere in fin di vita** be at death's door. **guadagnarsi la vita** earn one's living.

vita² ['vita] *sf* (*corpo*) waist.

vitale [vi'tale] *agg* vital. **vitalità** *sf* vitality.

vitalizio [vita'litsjo] *agg* life(long). *sm* (*rendita*) annuity.

vitamina [vita'mina] *sf* vitamin.

vite¹ ['vite] *sf* (*bot*) vine. **viticcio** *sm* tendril. **viticoltura** *sf* viticulture.

vite² ['vite] *sf* (*mec*) screw. **cadere in vite** (*aero*) go into a spin.

vitello [vi'tɛllo] *sm* calf; (*gastr*) veal. **vitellone** *sm* bullock; (*fig*) loafer.

vitreo ['vitreo] *agg* glassy, vitreous.

vittima ['vittima] *sf* victim; (*chi subisce danni*) casualty. **essere vittima di un incidente** be involved in an accident. **fare la vittima** (*fig*) be a martyr.

vitto ['vitto] *sm* food; (*nutrimento giornaliero*) board. **vitto e alloggio** board and lodging.

vittoria [vit'tɔrja] *sf* victory; (*sport*) win. **vittorioso** *agg* victorious.

vituperare [vitupe'rare] *v* berate. **vituperio** *sm* insult; (*causa*) disgrace.

viva ['viva] *inter* hurrah! **viva ... !** long live ... !

vivacchiare [vivak'kjare] *v* manage.

vivace [vi'vatʒe] *agg* lively; (*intenso*) bright. **vivacità** *sf* liveliness; brightness.

vivaio [vi'vajo] *sm* nursery; (*pesci*) fish-pond.

vivanda [vi'vanda] *sf* food; (*piatto*) dish.

*vivere ['vivere] *v* live; (*trascorrere*) spend. **avere di che vivere** have enough to live on. **lasciar vivere** leave in peace. **vivere alla giornata** live from hand to mouth. *sm* life; (*modo di vivere*) living.

viveri ['viveri] *sm pl* provisions *pl*.

vivido ['vivido] *agg* vivid.

vivisezione [vivise'tsjone] *sf* vivisection.

vivo ['vivo] *agg* living; (*vivace*) lively; (*intenso*) bright. **a viva forza** by force. **farsi vivo** show up; (*mettersi in contatto*) get in touch. **la viva** living person; (*fig*) heart. **ferire nel vivo** wound to the quick.

viziare [vi'tsjare] *v* spoil; (*dir*) vitiate.

vizio ['vitsjo] *sm* vice; bad habit; defect; (*peccato*) sin. **vizio parziale** (**di mente**) diminished responsibility. **vizioso** *agg* depraved.

vizzo ['vittso] agg withered.

vocabolo [vo'kabolo] sm word. **vocabolario** sm vocabulary; dictionary.

vocale [vo'kale] agg vocal. sf vowel.

vocazione [voka'tsjone] sf vocation; (inclinazione naturale) leaning. **vocazionale** agg vocational.

voce ['votʃe] sf voice; expression; (elemento di elenco) heading; opinion. **a bassa voce** softly. **ad alta voce** out loud. **aver voce in capitolo** have a say in the matter. **corre voce** rumour has it. **dire a (viva) voce** tell personally. **sotto voce** in an undertone.

vociare [vo'tʃare] v bawl.

vociferare [votʃife'rare] v talk at the top of one's voice; (fig) rumour.

vodka ['vɔdka] sf vodka.

vogare [vo'gare] v row. **vogatore** sm oarsman.

voglia ['vɔʎa] sf wish; (disposizione) will; (capriccio) fancy; (med) birthmark. **avere una gran voglia di** be dying to. **aver voglia di** (fare) feel like (doing), want to (do). **di buona voglia** willingly. **di cattiva or mala voglia** unwillingly.

voi ['voi] pron you.

volano [vo'lano] sm (mec) flywheel; (sport) shuttlecock.

volare [vo'lare] v fly. **volar giù** hurtle down. **volata** sf (sport) sprint; (corsa rapida) dash. **di volata** in a rush. **fare una volata** make a dash.

volatile [vo'latile] agg volatile.

volentieri [volen'tjɛri] avv willingly; with pleasure. **fare volentieri** like doing.

*****volere** [vo'lere] v want; (desiderare) wish; (comando) will; (intendere) mean; (cortesia) like. **l'hai voluto tu!** you've asked for it! **neanche a volere** not even if you try. **non vuol dire** (non ha importanza) it doesn't matter. **se Dio vuole** God willing. **senza volere** without meaning to. **volerci** v take. **voler bene a** (aver affetto) be fond of; (amare) love. **voler dire** mean.

volgare [vol'gare] agg vulgar; common. sm (lingua) vernacular. **volgarità** sf vulgarity. **volgarizzare** v popularize.

*****volgere** ['vɔldʒere] v turn. **col volgere degli anni** with the passing of time. **volgere alla fine** near the end. **volgere la parola a** address.

volgo ['vɔlgo] sm common people pl.

volo ['volo] sm flight. **cogliere al volo** seize. **volo a vela** gliding. **volo in picchiata** nose-dive.

volontà [volon'ta] sf will. **di mia spontanea** or **propria volontà** of my own free will.

volontario [volon'tarjo], -a voluntary. sm, sf volunteer. **volontario del sangue** blood donor. **volontariato** sm voluntary service.

volonteroso [volonte'rozo] agg willing.

volpe ['volpe] sf fox; (femmina) vixen.

volta[1] ['vɔlta] sf time; turn. **alla volta** at a time. **alla volta di** towards. **a volte** sometimes. **spesse volte** often. **una buona volta** once and for all. **una volta** once; (nelle fiabe) once upon a time.

volta[2] ['vɔlta] sf (arch) vault.

voltare [vol'tare] v turn. **voltagabbana** s(m + f) invar fickle person.

volto ['vɔlto] sm fate.

volubile [vo'lubile] agg fickle.

volume [vo'lume] sm volume; (mole) size. **voluminoso** agg voluminous; (ingombrante) bulky.

voluta [vo'luta] sf scroll.

voluttuoso [voluttu'ozo] agg voluptuous. **voluttà** sf voluptuousness.

vomitare [vomi'tare] v vomit, be sick. **aver voglia di vomitare** feel sick. **vomito** sm (atto) vomiting; (materia) vomit. **mi viene il vomito** I feel sick.

vongola ['vongola] sf clam.

vorace [vo'ratʃe] agg greedy.

voragine [vo'radʒine] sf chasm, gulf.

vortice ['vɔrtitʃe] sm vortex; (gorgo) whirlpool; (fig) whirl.

vostro ['vɔstro] agg your. pron yours.

votare [vo'tare] v vote; (approvare) pass; put to the vote; (dedicare) devote. **votazione** sf voting; (scrutinio) ballot; (scuola) marks pl. **voto** sm vote; (promessa) vow; (scuola) mark. **a pieni voti** with full marks. **pronunciare i voti** take one's vows.

vulcano [vul'kano] sm volcano. **vulcanico** agg volcanic; (fig) brilliant.

vulnerabile [vulne'rabile] agg vulnerable. **vulnerabilità** sf vulnerability.

vuotare [vwo'tare] v empty. **vuotare il sacco** (fig) spill the beans.

vuoto ['vwɔto] agg empty. sm void; (fis) vacuum; (fig) emptiness, gap. **andare a vuoto** fail. **a vuoto** in vain. **girare a vuoto** (mec) idle.

X

xenofobo [kseˈnɔfobo], **-a** agg xenophobic. sm, sf xenophobe. **xenofobia** sf xenophobia.

xerocopiare [kserokoˈpjare] v Xerox ®.

xilofono [ksiˈlɔfono] sm xylophone.

Y

yoga [ˈjɔɡa] sm invar yoga.

yoghurt [ˈjɔɡurt] sm invar yoghurt.

Z

zacchera [ˈdzakkera] sf splash (of mud).

zaffata [dzafˈfata] sf whiff; (getto di liquido) splash.

zafferano [dzaffeˈrano] sm saffron.

zaffiro [dzafˈfiro] sm sapphire.

zaino [ˈdzajno] sm kit-bag; (alpinisti) rucksack.

zampa [ˈdzampa] sf leg; (con unghie) paw; (maiale) trotter. **a quattro zampe** on all fours. **zampe di gallina** sf pl (rughe) crow's-feet pl; (scrittura) scrawl sing.

zampare v paw (the ground). **aver lo zampino in** have a hand in. **mettere lo zampino** interfere.

zampillare [dzampilˈlare] v spurt, gush. **zampillo** sm spurt.

zampogna [dzamˈpoɲa] sf bagpipes pl.

zangola [ˈdzaŋɡola] sf churn. **zangolare** v churn.

zanna [ˈdzanna] sf fang; (di elefante, cinghiale) tusk.

zanzara [dzanˈdzara] sf mosquito. **zanzariera** sf mosquito-net.

zappare [dzapˈpare] v hoe. **zappa** sf hoe.

zattera [ˈdzattera] sf raft.

zazzera [ˈdzaddzera] sf mop of hair.

zebra [ˈdzebra] sf zebra. **zebre** sf pl (passaggio) zebra crossing sing. **zebrato** agg striped.

zecca¹ [ˈdzekka] sf mint. **nuovo di zecca** brand-new. **zecchino** sm gold coin.

zecca² [ˈdzekka] sf (zool) tick.

zelo [ˈdzelo] sm zeal. **zelante** agg keen, zealous.

zenzero [ˈdzendzero] sm ginger.

zeppa [ˈdzeppa] sf wedge. **zeppare** v

wedge.

zeppo [ˈdzeppo] agg (pieno) zeppo packed, cram-full.

zerbino [dzerˈbino] sm (door-)mat.

zero [ˈdzɛro] sm nought; (fig, mat) zero; (sport) nil; (tennis) love.

zia [ˈdzia] sf aunt.

zibellino [dzibelˈlino] sm sable.

zibetto [dziˈbetto] sm civet.

zigzag [dzigˈdzag] sm zigzag. **andare a zigzag** zigzag.

zimbello [dzimˈbɛllo] sm decoy; (oggetto di scherno) laughing-stock. **zimbellare** v lure.

zinco [ˈdzinko] sm zinc.

zingaro [ˈdzingaro], **-a** s, agg gipsy.

zio [ˈdzio] sm uncle.

zirlare [dzirˈlare] v chirp.

zitella [dziˈtɛlla] sf spinster. **vecchia zitella** (spreg) old maid.

zittire [dzitˈtire] v (far tacere) hush; (disapprovazione) hiss.

zitto [ˈdzitto] agg quiet. **star zitto** keep quiet; (fam) shut up.

zoccolo [ˈdzɔkkolo] sm clog; (zool) hoof; base; (parete) skirting-board.

zodiaco [dzoˈdiako] sm zodiac.

zolfo [ˈdzolfo] sm sulphur.

zolla [ˈdzɔlla] sf clod.

zona [ˈdzɔna] sf zone; area. **zona pedonale** pedestrian precinct. **zona verde** (periferica) green belt.

zonzo [ˈdzonzo] avv **andare a zonzo** wander about.

zoo [dzo] sm invar zoo.

zoologia [dzooloˈdʒia] sf zoology. **zoologico** agg zoological. **zoologo**, **-a** sm, sf zoologist.

zoppicare [dzoppiˈkare] v limp; (tavolo, ecc.) be rickety; (fig) be shaky. **zoppo** agg lame; rickety; shaky.

zotico [ˈdzɔtiko], **-a** agg boorish. sm, sf boor.

zucca [ˈdzukka] sf pumpkin; (fam: testa) nut. **zuccone** sm (fam) blockhead.

zucchero [ˈdzukkero] sm sugar. **zucchero a velo** icing sugar. **zucchero semolato** castor sugar. **zuccherare** v sweeten.

zucchino [dzukˈkino], **-a** sm, sf courgette.

zuffa [ˈdzuffa] sf scuffle, brawl.

zuppa [ˈdzuppa] sf soup. **zuppa inglese** trifle. **zuppiera** sf tureen. **zuppo** agg drenched.